Contemporary Authors®

A Bio-Bibliographical Guide to
Current Writers in Fiction, General Nonfiction,
Poetry, Journalism, Drama, Motion Pictures,
Television, and Other Fields

SUSAN M. TROSKY
Editor

NEW REVISION SERIES
volume 40

Gale Research Inc. • *DETROIT* • *WASHINGTON, D.C.* • *LONDON*

STAFF

Susan Trosky, *Editor, New Revision Series*

Bruce Ching, Elizabeth A. Des Chenes, Susan M. Reicha, Kenneth R. Shepherd,
Deborah A. Stanley, and Thomas Wiloch, *Associate Editors*

Pamela S. Dear, Jeff Hill, Margaret Mazurkiewicz, Thomas F. McMahon,
Cornelia A. Pernik, Terrie M. Rooney, and Pamela L. Shelton, *Assistant Editors*

Marilyn K. Basel, Joan Goldsworthy, Anne Janette Johnson, and Michaela Swart Wilson, *Contributing Editors*

James G. Lesniak, *Senior Editor, Contemporary Authors*

Victoria B. Cariappa, *Research Manager*

Mary Rose Bonk, *Research Supervisor*

Reginald A. Carlton, Clare Collins, Andrew Guy Malonis, and Norma Sawaya, *Editorial Associates*

Patricia Bowen, Rachel A. Dixon, Eva Marie Felts, Shirley Gates,
Sharon McGilvray, and Devra M. Sladics, *Editorial Assistants*

This book is printed on acid-free paper that meets the minimum requirements
of American National Standard for Information Sciences—
Permanence Paper for Printed Library Materials, ANSI Z39.48-1984.

Library of Congress Catalog Card Number 81-640179
ISBN 0-8103-1994-2
ISSN 0275-7176

Printed in the United States of America.

Published simultaneously in the United Kingdom
by Gale Research International Limited
(An affiliated company of Gale Research Inc.)

I(T)P™

The trademark ITP is used under license.
10 9 8 7 6 5 4 3 2 1

Contents

Indexing note: All *Contemporary Authors New Revision Series* entries are indexed in the *Contemporary Authors* cumulative index, which is published separately and distributed with even-numbered *Contemporary Authors* original volumes and odd-numbered *Contemporary Authors New Revision Series* volumes.

As always, the most recent *Contemporary Authors* cumulative index continues to be the user's guide to the location of an individual author's listing.

Preface

The *Contemporary Authors New Revision Series* (*CANR*) provides completely updated information on authors listed in earlier volumes of *Contemporary Authors* (*CA*). Entries for individual authors from *any* volume of *CA* may be included in a volume of the *New Revision Series*. *CANR* updates only those sketches requiring significant change.

Authors are included on the basis of specific criteria that indicate the need for significant revision. These criteria include bibliographical additions, changes in addresses or career, major awards, and personal information such as name changes or death dates. All listings in this volume have been revised or augmented in various ways. Some sketches have been extensively rewritten, and many include informative new sidelights. As always, a *CANR* listing entails no charge or obligation.

How to Get the Most out of *CA* and *CANR:* Use the Index

The key to locating an author's most recent listing is the *CA* cumulative index, which is published separately and distributed with even-numbered original volumes and odd-numbered revision volumes. It provides access to *all* entries in *CA* and *CANR*. Always consult the latest index to find an author's most recent entry.

For the convenience of users, the *CA* cumulative index also includes references to all entries in these related Gale literary series: *Authors and Artists for Young Adults, Authors in the News, Bestsellers, Black Literature Criticism, Black Writers, Children's Literature Review, Concise Dictionary of American Literary Biography, Concise Dictionary of British Literary Biography, Contemporary Authors Autobiography Series, Contemporary Authors Bibliographical Series, Contemporary Literary Criticism, Dictionary of Literary Biography, Drama Criticism, Hispanic Writers, Major Authors and Artists for Children and Young Adults, Major 20th Century Writers, Poetry Criticism, Short Story Criticism, Something about the Author, Something about the Author Autobiography Series, Twentieth-Century Literary Criticism, World Literature Criticism,* and *Yesterday's Authors of Books for Children.*

A Sample Index Entry:

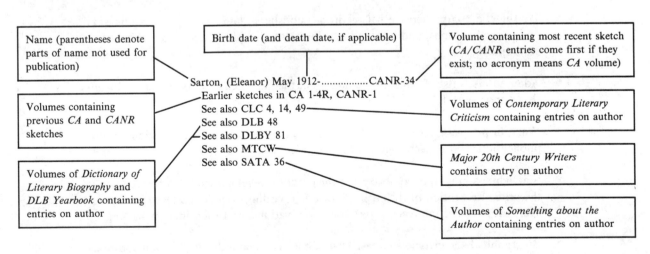

For the most recent *CA* information on Sarton, users should refer to Volume 34 of the *New Revision Series,* as designated by "CANR-34"; if that volume is unavailable, refer to CANR-1. And if CANR-1 is unavailable, refer to CA 1-4R, published in 1967, for Sarton's First Revision entry.

How Are Entries Compiled?

The editors make every effort to secure new information directly from the authors. Copies of all sketches in selected *CA* and *CANR* volumes published several years ago are routinely sent to listees at their last-known addresses, and returns from these authors are then assessed. For deceased writers, or those who fail to reply to requests for data, we consult other reliable biographical sources, such as those indexed in Gale's *Biography and Genealogy Master Index,* and bibliographical sources, such as *National Union Catalog, LC Marc,* and *British National Bibliography.* Further details come from published interviews, feature stories, and book reviews, and often the authors' publishers supply material. *Indicates that a listing has been compiled from secondary sources believed to be reliable but has not been personally verified for this edition by the author sketched.

What Kinds of Information Does an Entry Provide?

Sketches in *CANR* contain the following biographical and bibliographical information:

- **Entry heading:** the most complete form of author's name, plus any pseudonyms or name variations used for writing

- **Personal information:** author's date and place of birth, family data, educational background, political and religious affiliations, and hobbies and leisure interests

- **Addresses:** author's home, office, or agent's addresses as available

- **Career summary:** name of employer, position, and dates held for each career post; résumé of other vocational achievements; military service

- **Awards and honors:** military and civic citations, major prizes and nominations, fellowships, grants, and honorary degrees

- **Membership information:** professional, civic, and other association memberships and any official posts held

- **Writings:** a comprehensive list of titles, publishers, dates of original publication and revised editions, and production information for plays, television scripts, and screenplays

- **Adaptations:** a list of films, plays, and other media which have been adapted from the author's work

- **Work in progress:** current or planned projects, with dates of completion and/or publication, and expected publisher, when known

- **Sidelights:** a biographical portrait of the author's development; information about the critical reception of the author's works; revealing comments, often by the author, on personal interests, aspirations, motivations, and thoughts on writing

- **Biographical and critical sources:** a list of books and periodicals in which additional information on an author's life and/or writings appears

Related Titles in the *CA* Series

Contemporary Authors Autobiography Series complements *CA* original and revised volumes with specially commissioned autobiographical essays by important current authors, illustrated with personal photographs they provide. Common topics include their motivations for writing, the people and experiences that shaped their careers, the rewards they derive from their work, and their impressions of the current literary scene.

Contemporary Authors Bibliographical Series surveys writings by and about important American authors since World War II. Each volume concentrates on a specific genre and features approximately ten writers; entries list works written by and about the author and contain a bibliographical essay discussing the merits and deficiencies of major critical and scholarly studies in detail.

Suggestions Are Welcome

The editors welcome comments and suggestions from users on any aspects of the *CA* series. If readers would like to suggest authors whose entries should appear in future volumes of the series, they are cordially invited to write: The Editors, *Contemporary Authors,* 835 Penobscot Bldg., Detroit, MI 48226-4094; call toll-free at 1-800-347-GALE; or fax to 1-313-961-6599.

CA Numbering System and Volume Update Chart

Occasionally questions arise about the *CA* numbering system and which volumes, if any, can be discarded. Despite numbers like "29-32R," "97-100" and "139," the entire *CA* series consists of only 106 physical volumes with the publication of *CA New Revision Series* Volume 40. The following chart notes changes in the numbering system and cover design, and indicates which volumes are essential for the most complete, up-to-date coverage.

CA First Revision
- 1-4R through 41-44R (11 books)
  Cover: Brown with black and gold trim.
  There will be no further First Revision volumes because revised entries are now being handled exclusively through the more efficient *New Revision Series* mentioned below.

CA Original Volumes
- 45-48 through 97-100 (14 books)
  Cover: Brown with black and gold trim.
- 101 through 139 (39 books)
  Cover: Blue and black with orange bands.
  The same as previous *CA* original volumes but with a new, simplified numbering system and new cover design.

CA Permanent Series
- *CAP*-1 and *CAP*-2 (2 books)
  Cover: Brown with red and gold trim.
  There will be no further *Permanent Series* volumes because revised entries are now being handled exclusively through the more efficient *New Revision Series* mentioned below.

CA New Revision Series
- *CANR*-1 through *CANR*-40 (40 books)
  Cover: Blue and black with green bands.
  Includes only sketches requiring extensive changes; **sketches are taken from any previously published *CA, CAP,* or *CANR* volume.**

If You Have:	You May Discard:
CA First Revision Volumes 1-4R through 41-44R **and** *CA Permanent Series* Volumes 1 and 2	*CA* Original Volumes 1, 2, 3, 4 Volumes 5-6 through 23-24 Volumes 25-28 through 41-44
CA Original Volumes 45-48 through 97–100 and 101 through 139	NONE: These volumes will not be superseded by corresponding revised volumes. Individual entries from these and all other volumes appearing in the left column of this chart will be revised and included in the various volumes of the *New Revision Series*.
CA New Revision Series Volumes *CANR*-1 through *CANR*-40	NONE: The *New Revision Series* does not replace any single volume of *CA*. Instead, volumes of *CANR* include entries from many previous *CA* series volumes. All *New Revision Series* volumes must be retained for full coverage.

A Sampling of Authors and Media People
Featured in This Volume

Andre Breton
Breton, credited as the founder of the Surrealist movement in France, wrote the popular novel *Nadja*.

Robert A. Caro
Pulitzer Prize winner Caro presents powerful political figures in his biographies *The Power Broker* and *The Years of Lyndon Johnson*.

Jean Cocteau
Although he worked in many media, Cocteau is renowned for his visionary films, which include *La Belle et la bete* and *Les Enfants terribles*.

Francis Ford Coppola
Best known for his *Godfather* trilogy, Coppola also wrote and directed the Vietnam War epic *Apocalypse Now*.

Michael Crichton
Pioneer of the "techno-thriller," Crichton's bestselling novels include *The Andromeda Strain* and *Jurassic Park*.

Fannie Flagg
Flagg evokes the South of the past through the strong female characters in her novel, and subsequent screenplay, *Fried Green Tomatoes at the Whistle Stop Cafe*.

James Herriot
English veterinarian Herriot writes of his career in *All Creatures Great and Small, All Things Bright and Beautiful,* and *Every Living Thing*.

Tracy Kidder
Kidder, who makes the super-mini computer accessible to laymen in his Pulitzer-winning *The Soul of a New Machine*, also examines the modern classroom in the popular *Among Schoolchildren*.

John Knowles
Knowles explores the effects of rivalry and suppressed emotions in his critically acclaimed novel *A Separate Peace*.

Fritz Leiber
An award-winning and prolific science fiction and fantasy author, Leiber is best known for his "Fafhrd and the Gray Mouser" series.

Robert K. Massie
Massie's portrait of the architect of modern Russia, *Peter the Great,* garnered him a Pulitzer Prize for biography.

W. Somerset Maugham
Described as the consummate storyteller of the twentieth century, Maugham is best known for his short stories and his popular novel *Of Human Bondage*.

Tim O'Brien
Drawing on personal experience, O'Brien provides vivid portrayals of the Vietnam conflict in *Going after Cacciato* and *The Things They Carried*.

Ezra Pound
Pound, whose revolutionary poetry includes *Hugh Selwyn Mauberley* and the *Cantos,* was a major contributor to the Imagist movement, as well as an influential critic.

John Saul
Saul's prolific outpouring of bestselling horror novels includes *Suffer the Children* and *Shadows*.

Neil Sheehan
A foreign correspondent during the Vietnam War, Sheehan presents the conflict in his Pulitzer Prize-winning work, *A Bright and Shining Lie*.

Susan Sheehan
The case studies contained in Sheehan's *A Prison and a Prisoner* and Pulitzer-winning *Is There No Place on Earth for Me?* were originally written for the *New Yorker*.

Aleksandr Solzhenitsyn
Nobel laureate Solzhenitsyn achieved fame with *One Day in the Life of Ivan Denisovich,* the first Soviet work to portray the concentration camps present under Stalin's rule.

I. F. Stone
An independent journalist, Stone debunked the claims of establishment politics in his *I. F. Stone's Weekly*.

Scott Turow
Turow used his inside knowledge as a lawyer to create such suspenseful bestsellers as *Presumed Innocent* and *The Burden of Proof*.

Elie Wiesel
A survivor of Auschwitz, Wiesel depicts the Holocaust in his widely acclaimed works *Night, Dawn,* and *The Accident*.

Thornton Wilder
A three-time Pulitzer winner, Wilder is best known for his novels and the play *Our Town*.

Contemporary Authors®

NEW REVISION SERIES

*Indicates that a listing has been compiled from secondary sources believed to be reliable
but has not been personally verified for this edition by the author sketched.

ADLER, C(arole) S(chwerdtfeger) 1932-

PERSONAL: Born February 23, 1932, in Rockaway Beach, Long Island, NY; daughter of Oscar Edward (an automobile mechanic and chief petty officer in the Naval Reserve) and Clarice (an office manager; maiden name, Landsberg) Schwerdtfeger; married Arnold R. Adler (an engineer), June, 1952; children: Steven, Clifford (twins), Kenneth. *Education:* Hunter College (now of the City University of New York), B.A. (cum laude), 1953; Russell Sage College, M.S., 1964.

ADDRESSES: Home—1350 Ruffner Rd., Schenectady, NY 12309.

CAREER: Worthington Corp., Harrison, NJ, advertising assistant, 1952-54; Niskayuna Middle Schools, Niskayuna, NY, English teacher, 1967-77; writer, 1977—.

MEMBER: Authors Guild, Authors League of America, Society of Children's Book Writers, Phi Beta Kappa.

AWARDS, HONORS: "Children's Choice" citation from International Reading Association and Children's Book Council, 1979, for *The Magic of the Glits*, 1987, for *Split Sisters*, and 1991, for *One Sister Too Many* and *Ghost Brother;* Golden Kite Award from Society of Children's Book Writers, and "Book of the Year" citation from Child Study Association, both 1979, and William Allen White Children's Book Award, 1982, all for *The Magic of the Glits;* "Best Young Adult Book of the Year" citation, American Library Association, 1983, for *The Shell Lady's Daughter;* Children's Book Award from Child Study Children's Book Committee, Bank St. College of Education, 1985, for *With Westie and the Tin Man; Eddie's Blue-Winged Dragon* and *Always and Forever Friends* were included in the International Reading Association and Children's Book Council list of "99 Favorite Paperbacks 1991"; many of Bunting's books have been featured on an-

nual state lists, including the Mark Twain Award list, the Sunshine State list, and the Volunteer State list.

WRITINGS:

The Magic of the Glits (illustrated by Ati Forberg), Macmillan, 1979.
The Silver Coach (Junior Literary Guild selection), Coward, 1979.
In Our House Scott Is My Brother, Macmillan, 1980.
Shelter on Blue Barns Road, Macmillan, 1981.
The Cat That Was Left Behind (Junior Literary Guild selection), Clarion Books, 1981.
Down by the River, Coward, 1981.
Footsteps on the Stairs, Delacorte, 1982.
Some Other Summer (sequel to *The Magic of the Glits*), Macmillan, 1982.
The Evidence That Wasn't There, Clarion Books, 1982.
The Once in a While Hero, Coward, 1982.
Binding Ties, Delacorte, 1983.
Get Lost, Little Brother, Clarion Books, 1983.
Roadside Valentine, Macmillan, 1983.
The Shell Lady's Daughter, Coward, 1983.
Fly Free, Coward, 1984.
Good-bye, Pink Pig, Putnam, 1985.
Shadows on Little Reef Bay, Clarion Books, 1985.
With Westie and the Tin Man (Junior Literary Guild selection), Macmillan, 1985.
Split Sisters (illustrated by Mike Wimmer), Macmillan, 1986.
Kiss the Clown, Clarion Books, 1986.
If You Need Me (Junior Literary Guild selection), Macmillan, 1987.
Carly's Buck (Junior Literary Guild selection), Clarion Books, 1987.
Eddie's Blue-Winged Dragon, Putnam, 1988.
Always and Forever Friends, Clarion Books, 1988.

One Sister Too Many: A Sequel to Split Sisters, Macmillan, 1989.

The Lump in the Middle, Clarion Books, 1989.

Ghost Brother, Clarion Books, 1990.

Help, Pink Pig! (sequel to *Good-Bye, Pink Pig*), Putnam, 1990.

Mismatched Summer, Putnam, 1991.

A Tribe for Lexi, Macmillan, 1991.

Tuna Fish Thanksgiving, Clarion Books, 1992.

Contributor of articles and stories to periodicals, including *American Girl, Co-Ed,* and *Ingenue.*

ADAPTATIONS: Get Lost, Little Brother (cassette), Talking Books, 1983.

SIDELIGHTS: Since selling her first novel in 1979, C. S. Adler has been the prolific author of over thirty books for children and young adults. Adler's works—which include romances, mysteries, and young adult novels—often feature adolescents facing family problems or difficulties with other people they care about. Reviewers have praised Adler for her insightful and compassionate treatment of her protagonists, and for her realistic depictions of their situations. She has received several honors for her writings, including the Golden Kite Award and William Allen White Award for *The Magic of the Glits,* a "Best Young Adult Book of the Year" citation from the American Library Association for *The Shell Lady's Daughter,* and a Child Study Book Award from Bank Street College for *With Westie and the Tin Man.*

Adler was born on Long Island in New York, and grew up in various sections of New York City. "I had a restless father, so we moved every couple of years; I saw all the boroughs. . . .," she explained in an interview for *Authors and Artists for Young Adults (AAYA).* "Moving around so much was probably good experience for becoming a children's author. . . . That experience made me sympathetic to that particular aspect of a child's problems." As a young girl, Adler enjoyed exploring New York's many museums and parks, but was most fond of reading, and spent much of her time visiting libraries and poring through both children's and adult books. "The writing came almost immediately after I'd learned to read," she told *AAYA.* "By age seven, I'd begun writing stories for myself. . . . I'd write little stories and put them together with cardboard covers and rubber bands to make them into a book. Every once in awhile, I would con a friend into listening to one. I never showed them to teachers. It was just something I liked to do for fun." She sent her first story to a magazine when she was thirteen, but it was turned down—the first in her "proverbial drawer full of rejection slips."

Adler's father left her family when she was twelve, and she was then raised by her mother, aunt, and grandmother.

The experience of her family's breakup was one which would later make Adler, as she told *AAYA,* "comfortable writing about divorce and separation." Adler became very close to her mother, who worked as an office manager, and who instilled in her values that would become especially important in her writing about other people. "She was understanding, liberal, and tolerant of all people," Adler told *AAYA.* "She taught me to treat everybody as an individual, evaluating a person on his character rather than anything else." Adler's home environment was a very supportive one, and her books for children especially emphasize the importance of family support for young people. "My mother and aunt encouraged me to think well of myself. . . . Having someone who thinks that is just what you need when you're a child."

As a teenager, Adler settled in Manhattan with her family, and she attended Hunter High School. She went on to study at Hunter College and finished in three years, so she could marry her husband Arnold, an engineer. "In the fifties," she wrote in *Six Biographies of Juvenile Authors,* "getting married was the most essential part of life for most women." Adler was married in 1952, and the next year received her degree with honors from Hunter. During the next few years, Adler moved numerous times as a result of her husband's job, and she also became a mother with children to raise. She wrote stories and novels, yet she continued to receive rejection letters. When she finally sold her first short story, a romance, at the age of thirty-one to *American Girl,* Adler was doubtful that writing would become a successful career for her. "The seventeen teenage love stories I sold thereafter didn't make me feel like a professional writer," she commented in *Sixth Book of Junior Authors.*

By the early 1960s, Adler had settled with her family in Schenectady, New York, and she decided she would try to earn a living as a teacher. She obtained her master's degree in education at Russell Sage College in Troy, New York, and began teaching English to middle school and junior high school students. Adler worked for nearly ten years as a teacher, but, as she once commented, her true inspiration and desire was always to become an author: "I *never* gave up the idea of myself as a writer, and only became a teacher as a source of income since I couldn't seem to earn anything from the writing." She continued in *AAYA:* "The experiences I had teaching were what made me a writer, and that's the age I write about. I was fascinated by my students; I thought they were the most interesting people around. Teenagers are up front with their problems and emotions. . . . Watching them, I empathized and got into emotional relationships with them, all very useful in my writing as it turned out. Many of the kids I taught appear in my books, not their particular problems or lives—I don't do that—but their personalities."

Adler left teaching in 1977, to devote herself to full-time writing. Her first novel, *The Magic of the Glits,* was published in 1979, and told the story of a young boy who helps a little girl overcome the trauma of her mother's death. The novel received several awards and critical recognition, and Adler went on to write a number of books for both children and young adults. Adler has written romances and mysteries for children, in addition to young adult novels which have dealt with problems such as relationships, separation, mental illness, and abuse. "My interests are basically personal: emotional problems and family relationships," Adler told *AAYA.* "Those things fascinate me most. I'm not a very political or cause-minded person. When I look at the newspaper, I'm not worrying about nuclear war; I'm looking for things about child abuse or latch-key children. Those issues would stick in my mind and probably become the theme of another story."

Adler's books are noted for presenting characters and situations in a mature, sensitive, and insightful manner. Regarding the young adult romantic relationship in *Down by the River,* Hildagarde Gray in *Best Sellers* calls the "story's resolution . . . an unusual one, emphasizing maturity as a question of emotional, not physiological, growth." In *The Shell Lady's Daughter,* which deals with a fourteen-year-old girl's understanding of her mother's mental breakdown, Adler offers, according to Zena Sutherland in *Bulletin of the Center for Children's Books,* a "trenchant and touching . . . book written with insight and compassion; the story has a natural flow and tight structure, and the few characters are sharply-etched and psychologically intricate and believable." And regarding *Fly Free,* which focuses on a thirteen-year-old girl's breaking free from her physically and verbally abusive mother, Karen K. Radtke notes in *School Library Journal* that the novel's "solid, realistic incidents remove the topic of physical and emotional abuse from the realm of the sensational and into the sadly commonplace."

Throughout her fiction, Adler strives to impart positive values to her young readers as a means to cope with the pressures of growing up. She told *AAYA:* "I note from my fan mail that children find bits and pieces of their own problems and themselves in my books. . . . Maybe they'll also see ways of dealing with life that they hadn't thought of before." Adler added in *Sixth Book of Junior Authors:* "In this world, it's important for children to know that things can work out well sometimes, and even if they don't, that you can survive and hope for better."

BIOGRAPHICAL/CRITICAL SOURCES:

BOOKS

Authors and Artists for Young Adults, Volume 4, Gale, 1990, pp. 11-18.

Contemporary Literary Criticism, Volume 35, Gale, 1985.
Sixth Book of Junior Authors, Wilson, 1989, pp. 5-6.

PERIODICALS

Best Sellers, January, 1982, pp. 400-1.
Booklist, April 15, 1982, p. 1091; December 1, 1982, p. 495; January 15, 1983, p. 672; June 1, 1984, p. 1395; August, 1984, p. 1622.
Books and Bookmen, July, 1982, pp. 33-34.
Bulletin of the Center for Children's Books, January, 1983, p. 81; June, 1983, p. 181; January, 1984, p. 81; June, 1984, p. 179; April, 1988; May, 1988.
Children's Book Review Service, July, 1984, p. 139.
Horn Book, April, 1979; December, 1983, p. 714; August, 1984, p. 471.
Junior Literary Guild, April-September, 1988.
Kirkus Reviews, April 1, 1983, p. 379.
New York Times Book Review, October 10, 1982.
School Librarian, September, 1982, p. 249.
School Library Journal, December, 1981, pp. 69-70; May, 1982, p. 83; December, 1982, p. 80; September, 1983, pp. 129-130; May, 1984, p. 103; October, 1984, p. 153.
Voice of Youth Advocates, February, 1982, p. 28; April, 1983, p. 35; August, 1983, p. 144; June, 1984, p. 94.

*   *   *

AJAYI, J(acob) F(estus) Ade(niyi)   1929-

PERSONAL: Born May 26, 1929, in Ikole-Ekiti, Nigeria; son of Ezekiel Adeniji (a retired customary court judge) and Comfort Bolajoko (Omoleye) Ajayi; married Christie Aduke Martins, October 23, 1956; children: Yetunde, Adeniyi, Olufunmilayo, Titilola, Bisola. *Education:* Attended Higher College, Lagos, 1947; University of Ibadan, B.A., 1951; University of Leicescer, D.R. (history), 1955; King's College, London, Ph.D., 1958.

ADDRESSES: Home—1, Ojobadan Ave., Bodija, Ibadan, Nigeria. *Office*—P.O. Box 14617, University of Ibadan, Ibadan.

CAREER: University of Ibadan, Ibadan, Nigeria, lecturer, 1958-62, senior lecturer, 1962-63, professor, 1963-89, Emeritus 1989-; University of Lagos, Lagos, Nigeria, vice-chancellor, 1972-78. Member, Committee on National Archives, 1961-72, Public Service Commission, Western State, Nigeria, 1966, and National Antiquities Commission, 1971-75; fellow of the Center for Advanced Study in Behavioral Sciences, 1970-71; member of executive board, Association of African Universities, 1974-80; United Nations University Council, member, 1974-80, chairman, 1976-77; chairman of executive commmittee, International African Institute, 1975-87.

MEMBER: International Congress of African Studies (president, 1978-85), International Association of Universities (member of executive board, 1980-1990), Historical Society of Nigeria (president, 1972-81; Foundation Yellow, 1980), Ghana Historical Association (fellow), Royal Historical Society (corresponding fellow).

AWARDS, HONORS: LL.D., University of Leicester, 1975; D.Litt., University of Birmingham, 1984, Nigerian National Merit Award, 1986; Hon. D.Litt, Ondo State University, Ado-Ekiti.

WRITINGS:

Milestones in Nigerian History, Ibadan University College, 1962, new edition, Longman, 1980.

Western Nigeria: Commission of Inquiry into the Rise in Fees Charged by Public Secondary Grammar Schools and Teacher Training Colleges, [Ibadan], 1962.

(Director of compilation) *Population Census of Nigeria, 1963: Lists of Historical Events for Determination of Individual Ages,* [Ibadan], 1962, 3rd edition (compiled with Adonola A. Igun), 1975.

(With Robert Smith) *Yoruba Warfare in the Nineteenth Century,* Cambridge University Press, 1961, 2nd edition, 1971.

(Editor with Ian Espie) *A Thousand Years of West African History,* Nelson, 1965, revised edition, Ibadan University Press, 1969.

Christian Missions in Nigeria, 1841-1891: The Making of a New Elite, Northwestern University Press, 1965.

(Editor with Michael Crowder) *History of West Africa,* two volumes, Longman, 1971, Columbia University Press, 1972, 2nd edition, Columbia University Press, 1976.

(Editor with T. N. Tamuno) *University of Ibadan, 1948-73: A History of the First Twenty-Five Years,* Ibadan University Press, 1973.

(Editor with Crowder) *A Historical Atlas of Africa,* Longman, 1985.

(Editor with B. A. Ikara) *Evolution of Political Culture in Nigeria,* Universities Press [Ibadan], 1985.

(Editor) *Africa in the Nineteenth Century until the 1880s* (*Unesco General History of Africa,* vol.vi), Heinemann, 1989.

(With Peter Pugh) *Cementinq a Partnership: The Story of WAPCO, 1960-1990,* Business Publishing Co., 1990.

History and the Nation and Other Addresses, Spectrum Books [Ibadan], 1990.

A Patriot to the Core: Samuel Ajayi Crowther, Hiswill Information Resources [Ibadan], 1992.

Also contributor to David L. Sills, editor, *International Encyclopaedia of the Social Sciences,* Volume 6, 1968; *Emerging Themes of African History: Proceedings of the International Congress of African Historians,* ERPH, Nai-

robi, 1968; Gann and Duignan, editors, *Colonialism in Africa,* Volume 1, Cambridge, 1969; Sidney W. Mintz, editor, *Slavery, Colonialism and Racism: Essays,* Norton, 1974; *Encyclopaedia Brittanica,* Volume 29, 1990 edition; Abiola Irele and Hans Zell, editors, *African Education and Identity: Proceedings of the 5th Session of the International Congress of African Studies, Ibadan 1985,* Spectrum Books, 1992. Contributor to *Daedalus.*

*   *   *

ALTICK, Richard Daniel 1915-

PERSONAL: Born September 19, 1915, in Lancaster, PA; son of Edward Charles and Laura (Reinhold) Altick; married Helen W. Keller, August 15, 1942; children: Anne, Elizabeth. *Education:* Franklin and Marshall College, A.B., 1936; University of Pennsylvania, Ph.D., 1941.

ADDRESSES: Home—276 West Southington Ave., Worthington, OH 43085. *Office*—Department of English, Ohio State University, Columbus, OH 43210.

CAREER: Franklin and Marshall College, Lancaster, PA, instructor in English, 1941-45; Ohio State University, Columbus, assistant professor, 1945-47, associate professor, 1947-50, professor, 1950-68, Regents' professor of English, 1968-82, Regents' professor emeritus, 1982—. Visiting professor at New York University, 1950, and Stanford University, 1956.

MEMBER: Phi Beta Kappa.

AWARDS, HONORS: Newberry Library fellow; American Council of Learned Societies fellow; Guggenheim fellow; Litt.D., Franklin and Marshall College, 1964; Ohio State University distinguished research award, 1979; George Freedley Memorial Book Award, 1980, for *The Shows of London;* Ohio State University distinguished service award, 1983; Christian Gauss award, 1991, for *The Presence of the Present: Topics of the Day in the Victorian Novel.*

WRITINGS:

Preface to Critical Reading, Holt, 1946, 6th edition (with Andrea A. Lunsford), 1984.

The Cowden Clarkes, Oxford University Press, 1948, reprinted, Greenwood Press, 1973.

The Scholar Adventurers, Macmillan, 1950, 6th edition, 1979.

The English Common Reader, University of Chicago Press, 1957, reprinted, Midway, 1983.

(With William R. Matthews) *Guide to Dissertations in Victorian Literature,* University of Illinois Press, 1960.

(With Andrew Wright) *Selective Bibliography for the Study of English and American Literature,* Macmillan, 1960, 6th edition, 1979.

The Art of Literary Research, Norton, 1963, 4th edition (with John J. Fenstermaker), 1992.

Lives and Letters, Knopf, 1965, reprinted, Greenwood Press, 1979.

(Editor) Thomas Carlyle, *Past and Present,* Houghton, 1965.

(With James F. Loucks II) *Browning's Roman Murder Story: A Reading of "The Ring and the Book,"* University of Chicago Press, 1968.

To Be in England, Norton, 1969.

Victorian Studies in Scarlet, Norton, 1970.

(Editor) Robert Browning, *The Ring and the Book,* Penguin, 1971.

Victorian People and Ideas, Norton, 1973.

The Shows of London: A Panoramic History, 1600-1862, Harvard University Press, 1978.

Paintings from Books: Art and Literature in Britain, 1760-1900, Ohio State University Press, 1986.

Deadly Encounters: Two Victorian Sensations, University of Pennsylvania Press, 1986.

Writers, Readers, and Occasions: Selected Essays on Victorian Life and Literature, Ohio State University Press, 1989.

Of a Place and a Time: Remembering Lancaster, Archon, 1991.

The Presence of the Present: Topics of the Day in the Victorian Novel, Ohio State University Press, 1991.

OTHER

Contributor of more than 150 scholarly articles and reviews to numerous journals.

*   *   *

ATHELING, William
   See POUND, Ezra (Weston Loomis)

B

BABYLAS
See GHELDERODE, Michel de

* * *

BAGNOLD, Enid 1889-1981
(A Lady of Quality)

PERSONAL: Born October 27, 1889, in Rochester, England; died March 31, 1981, in London, England; daughter of Arthur Henry (a colonel with the Royal Engineers) and Ethel (Alger) Bagnold; married Sir Roderick Jones (chairman of Reuter's News Agency), July 8, 1920 (died, 1962); children: Laurienne (Countess Pierre D'Harcourt), Timothy, Richard, Dominick. *Education:* Attended Priors Field in Godalming, England, and schools in France, Switzerland, and Germany; studied drawing and painting with Walter Sickert.

CAREER: Writer. Worked as a journalist for *Hearth and Home* and *Modern Society* magazines, 1912-14. During World War I served in English hospital for two years, then as a driver attached to French Army.

AWARDS, HONORS: Arts Theatre Prize, 1951, for *Poor Judas;* Award of Merit Medal from American Academy of Arts and Letters, 1956, for play *The Chalk Garden;* named Commander of the British Empire, 1976.

WRITINGS:

BOOKS FOR CHILDREN

Alice and Thomas and Jane (illustrated by daughter, Laurienne Jones), Heinemann, 1930, Knopf, 1931.
National Velvet (illustrated by L. Jones), Morrow, 1935, reprinted with illustrations by Paul Brown, 1967, reprinted with illustrations by Ted Lewin, 1985.

BOOKS FOR ADULTS

A Diary without Dates, Heinemann, 1918, reprinted, with new introduction by Monica Dickens, Virago, 1978.
Sailing Ships (poems), Heinemann, 1918.
The Happy Foreigner, Century, 1920.
(Under pseudonym A Lady of Quality) *Serena Blandish: Or, the Difficulty of Getting Married* (novel), Heinemann, 1924, reprinted, Curtis Books, 1972.
The Door of Life (novel), Morrow, 1938, published in England as *The Squire* (also see below), Heinemann, 1940.
The Loved and Envied (novel), Doubleday, 1951, reprinted, Greenwood Press, 1970.
The Girl's Journey (contains *The Happy Foreigner* and *The Squire*), Doubleday, 1954.
Enid Bagnold's Autobiography: From 1889, Heinemann, 1969, Little, Brown, 1970.
Poems of Enid Bagnold, Whittington Press, 1979.
Letters to Frank Harris and Other Friends, edited by R. P. Lister, Whittington Press/Heinemann, 1980.
Early Poems of Enid Bagnold, Whittington Press, 1987.

PLAYS

Lottie Dundass (first produced in Santa Barbara, CA, 1942; first produced in London at the Vaudeville Theatre, July 21, 1943; also see below), Heinemann, 1941.
National Velvet (three-act; adapted from her novel of same title; first produced in London at the Embassy Theatre, April 23, 1946), Dramatists Play Service, 1961, large print edition, Lythway Press, 1978.
Poor Judas (also see below), first produced in London at the Arts Theatre, July 18, 1951.
Two Plays (contains *Lottie Dundass* and *Poor Judas*), Doubleday, 1951.
Gertie (comedy), first produced in New York at the Plymouth Theatre, January 30, 1952; first produced in

London, under title *Little Idiot,* at the Q Theatre, November 10, 1953.

The Chalk Garden (first produced on Broadway at the Ethel Barrymore Theatre, October 26, 1955; first produced in London at the Haymarket Theatre, April 11, 1956; also see below), Random House, 1956, Samuel French, 1981.

The Last Joke (also see below), first produced in London at the Phoenix Theatre, September 28, 1960.

The Chinese Prime Minister (three-act comedy; first produced in New York at the Royal Theatre, January 2, 1964; first produced in London at the Globe Theatre, May 20, 1965; also see below), Random House, 1964.

Call Me Jacky (also see below), first produced in Oxford at the Oxford Playhouse, February 27, 1968; revised version, under title *A Matter of Gravity* (three-act comedy), first produced in Washington, DC, 1975, and in New York at the Broadhurst Theatre, February 3, 1976.

Four Plays (contains *The Chalk Garden, The Last Joke, The Chinese Prime Minister,* and *Call Me Jacky*), Heinemann, 1970, Little, Brown, 1971.

TRANSLATOR

Princess Marthe Bibesco, *Alexander of Asia,* Heinemann, 1935.

ADAPTATIONS: National Velvet was filmed in 1944 by Metro-Goldwyn-Mayer, starring Elizabeth Taylor, was adapted as a radio play by the Theatre Guild on the Air, 1950, and was adapted as a television series by NBC-TV, 1960-62; *The Chalk Garden* was filmed in 1964 by Universal Studios, starring Deborah Kerr and Hayley Mills; *International Velvet,* based on *National Velvet,* was filmed in 1978 by Universal Artists, starring Tatum O'Neal; *Serena Blandish* was adapted as a play by S. H. Behrmann, first produced on Broadway at Morosco Theatre, January 23, 1929, and published in *Three Plays* by Farrar, Straus, 1934; *Alice and Thomas and Jane* was adapted as a two-act play for children by Vera Beringer and published by Samuel French, 1934; *Lottie Dundass* was adapted as a radio play by the Theatre Guild on the Air, 1950.

SIDELIGHTS: The late Enid Bagnold was best known as a playwright and a novelist for adults, but she also wrote an enduring children's classic, *National Velvet.* The story of horse-crazy Velvet Brown and her victory in England's Grand National race has been immortalized in book, play, and film; *Saturday Review of Literature* critic Christopher Morley called the work "a masterpiece" and a "lovely escapade."

Bagnold was born in Rochester, England, in 1889. Her well-to-do father was a colonel with the Royal Engineers. According to the author in her work *Enid Bagnold's Autobiography,* Arthur Henry Bagnold "was severe. I didn't get to know him. He wouldn't have minded that. He wanted obedience." Enid Bagnold seemed destined for a traditional British upbringing until fate intervened—her father was given an appointment in Jamaica in 1898.

"The day we neared Jamaica an inner life began," Bagnold recalled in her autobiography. "It must have, for I never remember anything earlier—of ecstasy, of admiration for nature. Beauty never hit me until I was nine. But when we landed, the lack of mist, flowers higher than I was, emerald leaves of black leather, the shine of black people, their thrush's eyes, the zigzagging quiver of air hit by heat, the tropic leap into the spangled night—this was the first page of my life as someone who can 'see.' It was like a man idly staring at a field suddenly finding he had Picasso's eyes. In the most startling way I never felt young again. I remember myself then just as I feel now."

Bagnold began writing short stories and poems in Jamaica as a nine-year-old. She continued writing—sometimes late at night in bed—after the family returned to England. Her father insisted that she receive a solid education, so she was sent to Prior's Field School in Godalming, England, a school run by the mother of Aldous and Julian Huxley. Of her school years Bagnold wrote: "I was rough and difficult to snub, and gay. I was clever enough but of that I took no notice. Clever enough not to show up as a 'show-off-er' but I managed very well as a card. Being fat (the result of Jamaica) I was cut out for clowning. To make them laugh one had to spend oneself without counting the esteem-cost. That was not a bad lesson. Often I got it wrong and looked a fool. But that I had to bear, and soon I got the timing."

Bagnold continued her education on the continent, spending time in Germany, Paris, and Switzerland before returning to England to make her debut at the age of eighteen. *Dictionary of Literary Biography* contributor Richard B. Gidez noted that as a young woman Bagnold "lived a bohemian existence in London as suffragette, artist's model, and artist." She also continued to write and supplemented the income her parents sent her by working for magazines such as *Hearth and Home* and *Modern Society.*

During World War I Bagnold served in British hospital stations as a nurse and driver. She was appalled by the conditions at the Royal Herbert Hospital and wrote a book, *A Diary without Dates,* based on her experiences there. When the book was published in 1918 she was discharged from her duties at the hospital. Undaunted, she became an ambulance driver in France, staying there until the end of the war.

In 1920 Bagnold married Sir Roderick Jones, owner and director of Reuter's News Agency. The marriage lasted until his death in 1962 and produced four children. Throughout her married life Bagnold filled many roles—as socialite, mother, and writer—somehow managing to find three hours every morning to devote to her creative work. Her career as an author spanned some sixty years, during which time she produced novels, poems, award-winning plays such as *The Chalk Garden,* and two children's books.

National Velvet first appeared in 1935, with illustrations by Bagnold's daughter Laurienne. The tale unfolds amidst a humble butcher's family. Velvet Brown, the butcher's daughter, has a passion for horses and quietly becomes an expert on their training and care. To her great joy, she wins a horse of her own, Piebald, in a raffle. Against all the odds, she works with Piebald until he qualifies for the prestigious Grand National, then she disguises herself as a man so she can ride her own horse in the race.

"*National Velvet* is no wistful story of a child's world," wrote Harriet Colby in a *New York Herald Tribune Books* piece. "There is in it no false tenderness, no maudlin 'understanding.' Its realism is sustained, uncompromising and completely adult. Unforeseen in subject and manner, it is full of small, quick surprises—in the uneven rhythm of its prose, in the crystal, tonic freshness of its language, in its unique and irrepressible humor. Sudden and lovely, it breathes and lives in the unexpected."

American readers flocked to the book version of *National Velvet* after it was filmed by Metro-Goldwyn-Mayer in 1944. The film treatment of *National Velvet* was the first starring vehicle for child actress Elizabeth Taylor; it also featured Mickey Rooney as a groom who helps Velvet take the title. In her autobiography, Bagnold concluded: "I started *National Velvet* as a study in a girl's relationship with her pony. But it turned immediately and by itself into a story. All our [family's] gay life and its details, dogs, canaries, emotions of children, everything jumped into my hands. I had only to snatch and type on and all our full life was on the page. All the fantastic joy and fun."

Bagnold died at her home in London in 1981. Right up until the end of her life she continued to write, mostly books and plays with mature themes. In her autobiography she said: "How many years have I been writing . . . the hours so happy as the pages come together. To me it's an ascent of hard and grinding joy till I reach the peak and come out into the open."

BIOGRAPHICAL/CRITICAL SOURCES:

BOOKS

Bagnold, Enid, *Enid Bagnold's Autobiography,* Little, Brown, 1969.
Contemporary Literary Criticism, Volume 25, Gale, 1983.
Dictionary of Literary Biography, Volume 13: *British Dramatists since World War II,* Gale, 1982.

Hobson, Harold, *The Theatre Now,* Longmans, Green, 1953, pp. 99-100.
Sebba, Anne, *Enid Bagnold: The Authorized Biography,* Weidenfeld & Nicolson, 1986, Taplinger, 1987.
Tynan, Kenneth, *Curtains: Selections from the Drama Criticism and Related Writings,* Atheneum, 1961, pp. 127-128.

PERIODICALS

Atlantic Monthly, October, 1952.
Books, May 17, 1931; April 28, 1935.
Drama Review, December, 1958, pp. 42-50.
Drama: Theatre Quarterly Review, winter, 1979.
New Republic, February 1, 1964, p. 28.
New Statesman and Nation, April 6, 1935, p. 489; February 10, 1951, pp. 165-166.
New Yorker, January 27, 1951, p. 86.
New York Herald Tribune, October 27, 1955; January 20, 1964, pp. 395-396.
New York Herald Tribune Books, April 28, 1935, p. 5; October 2, 1938, p. 4.
New York Magazine, February 16, 1976, p. 71.
New York Post, October 27, 1955; February 4, 1976.
New York Times, October 27, 1955; January 3, 1964; February 4, 1976.
New York Times Book Review, May 5, 1935, p. 6; November 24, 1935, p. 11; December 31, 1950, p. 5; August 30, 1970, p. 4.
Punch, July 10, 1978.
Saturday Review, November 12, 1955, p. 24; January 18, 1964, p. 22.
Saturday Review of Literature, May 4, 1935, p. 6; October 1, 1938, p. 7.
Theatre Arts, January, 1964.
Times Literary Supplement, December 4, 1969; February 1, 1979.

OBITUARIES:

PERIODICALS

Chicago Tribune, April 1, 1981.
Newsweek, April 13, 1981.
New York Times, April 1, 1981.
Publishers Weekly, April 24, 1981.
School Library Journal, May, 1981.
Time, April 13, 1981.
Times (London), April 1, 1981.
Washington Post, April 3, 1981.

*   *   *

BALACHANDRAN, M(adhavarao) 1938-

PERSONAL: Born March 25, 1938, in Madras, India; came to the United States in 1968, naturalized citizen,

1977; son of Seshagiri (a teacher) and Sadhana (Bail) Madhavarao; married Sarojini Anathakrishnaiyer (a librarian and writer), May 30, 1969. *Education:* University of Madras, B.A., 1957, M.A., 1959; University of Bombay, LL.B., 1967; University of Illinois, J.D., 1971, M.S.L.S., 1972. *Politics:* Independent. *Religion:* Hindu. *Avocational interests:* Outdoor activities (especially jogging and swimming), travel.

ADDRESSES: Home—2113 South Burlison Dr., Urbana, IL 61801. *Office*—Commerce Library, University of Illinois at Urbana-Champaign, 1408 West Gregory, Urbana, IL 61801.

CAREER: Indian Express Newspapers Ltd., Madurai, India, assistant editor, 1959-61; Life Insurance Corp. of India, Bombay, administrative office, 1962-68; University of Illinois at Urbana-Champaign, Urbana, commerce reference librarian, 1972-74, assistant commerce librarian, 1974-81, commerce librarian, 1982—, instructor, 1972-74, assistant professor, 1974-77, associate professor, 1977-81, professor of library administration, 1982—, assistant director for Departmental Library Services, 1985—.

MEMBER: American Library Association, American Bar Association, Illinois Bar Association, Beta Phi Mu.

WRITINGS:

EDITOR

A Guide to Trade and Securities Statistics, Pierian, 1977.
(With wife, Sarojini Balachandran) *Reference Book Review Index, 1973-1975,* Pierian, 1979.
(With S. Balachandran) *Subject Guide to Reference Books, 1970-1975,* Pierian, 1979.
Regional Statistics: A Guide to Information Sources, Gale, 1980.
A Guide to Statistical Sources in Money, Banking, and Finance, Oryx Press, 1987.
State and Local Statistics Sources, Gale, 1990.
Encyclopedia of European Business Information Sources, Gale, 1993.

OTHER

Co-editor of series, "Reference Sources," Pierian, 1979—. Contributor of articles and reviews to library journals.

SIDELIGHTS: M. Balachandran once told *CA:* "I strongly believe that as an academic reference librarian it is my job not only to help other scholars with their research, but also to keep myself abreast of new developments in my subject area, which is business and economics. This enables me to perform my job with utmost efficiency. Now one of the best ways a reference librarian can achieve this efficiency is to get involved in one's own research activities. This is the reason why I spend a considerable amount of my time surveying the needs of the li-

brary users in my area and trying to come up with helpful guidebooks, directories, and indexes that facilitate faster retrieval of needed information. I also believe that research and publication activities are a necessary concomitant of the faculty status bestowed upon most academic librarians in this country."

*　　　*　　　*

BALACHANDRAN, Sarojini　1934-

PERSONAL: Born May 12, 1934, in Madras, India; came to the United States in 1968, naturalized citizen, 1977; daughter of K. V. A. Iyer (a civil engineer) and Madhurambal Anathakrishnaiyer; married Madhavarao Balachandran (a librarian, professor, and writer), May 30, 1969. *Education:* University of Madras, B.Sc., 1954, M.A., 1958; Indiana State University, M.S., 1970; University of Illinois, M.S.L.S., 1972. *Politics:* Independent. *Religion:* Hindu. *Avocational interests:* Swimming, jogging, flying small aircraft, travel, professional football and baseball.

ADDRESSES: Office—RBD Library, Auburn University, Auburn, AL 36849-5606.

CAREER: Bhabha Atomic Research Centre, Bombay, India, scientific officer, 1959-68; University of Illinois at Urbana-Champaign, Urbana, cataloger and instructor of library administration, 1972-76, cataloger and assistant professor of library administration, 1976-78, assistant engineering librarian and associate professor of library administration, 1978-82; California State Polytechnic University, Pomona, CA, engineering and physical sciences reference specialist, 1982-84; Washington University, St. Louis, MO, head of science and engineering services, 1984-88; Auburn University, Auburn, AL, head of department of science and technology, 1988—. U.S.A.I.D. consultant on agriculture and fisheries libraries in Southeast Asia, 1990.

MEMBER: American Library Association.

WRITINGS:

EDITOR

Employee Communication: A Bibliography, American Business Communication Association, 1976.
Airport Planning, 1965-1975, Council of Planning Librarians, 1976.
Energy Statistics: A Guide to Sources, Council of Planning Librarians, 1976.
A Selected Bibliography in Home Economics Education, 1966 to 1976, Department of Vocational and Technical Education, Division of Home Economics Education, University of Illinois, 1977.

Technical Writing, American Business Communication Association, 1977.

(With husband, Madhavarao Balachandran) *Reference Book Review Index, 1973-1975,* Pierian, 1979.

(With M. Balachandran) *Subject Guide to Reference Books, 1970-75,* Pierian, 1979.

New Product Planning: A Guide to Information Sources, Gale, 1980.

Energy Statistics: A Guide to Information Sources, Gale, 1980.

Directory of Publishing Sources, Wiley Interscience, 1982.

Decision Making: A Guide , Oryx Press, 1984.

State and Local Statistics, Gale, 1990.

Encyclopedia of Environmental Information Sources, Gale, 1992.

Co-editor of series, "Reference Sources," for Pierian, 1979—.

OTHER

Contributor of articles and reviews to scientific and library journals.

WORK IN PROGRESS: Revision of the first edition of *State and Local Statistics,* for Gale.

SIDELIGHTS: Sarojini Balachandran told *CA* that, as an information professional, she has been influenced in her writing "by acute awareness of the needs of academic library users. I think the most important job of any library and information science professional is providing easy access to library materials. It is for this reason I have devoted considerable amounts of time to the preparation of indexes, guidebooks, and literature surveys. The response from my users convinces me of the utility of this type of activity."

*   *   *

BALDWIN, Alex
See BUTTERWORTH, W(illiam) E(dmund III)

*   *   *

BALIAN, Lorna   1929-

PERSONAL: Surname rhymes with "stallion"; born December 14, 1929, in Milwaukee, WI; daughter of Henry W. (a telephone company employee) and Molly (Pope) Kohl; married John J. Balian (an artist), March 4, 1950; children: Heather, Japheth, Ivy, Aram, Lecia, Poppy. *Education:* Attended Layton School of Art, 1948-49. *Avocational interests:* Gardening, cooking, sewing, painting.

ADDRESSES: Home and office—6698 Highway E., Hartford, WI 53027.

CAREER: American Lace Co., Milwaukee, WI, artist, 1949-51; free-lance artist, 1948—. Teacher of crafts in adult vocational school.

MEMBER: Society of Children's Book Writers, Children's Cooperative Book Center, Children's Reading Round Table.

AWARDS, HONORS: Wisconsin Little Archer Award; Colorado Children's Book Award; Georgia Children's Book Award.

WRITINGS:

SELF-ILLUSTRATED; FOR CHILDREN

Humbug Witch, Abingdon, 1965.
I Love You, Mary Jane, Abingdon, 1967.
The Aminal, Abingdon, 1972.
Sometimes It's Turkey—Sometimes It's Feathers, Abingdon, 1973.
Where in the World Is Henry?, Bradbury, 1973.
Humbug Rabbit, Abingdon, 1974.
The Sweet Touch, Abingdon, 1976.
Bah! Humbug?, Abingdon, 1977.
A Sweetheart for Valentine, Abingdon, 1979.
Leprechauns Never Lie, Abingdon, 1980.
Mother's Mother's Day, Abingdon, 1982.
Humbug Potion: An AB Cipher, Abingdon, 1984.
A Garden for a Groundhog, Abingdon, 1985.
Amelia's Nine Lives, Abingdon, 1986.
The Socksnatchers, Abingdon, 1988.
Wilbur's Space Machine, Holiday House, 1990.

SIDELIGHTS: Lorna Balian told *CA:* "Writing and illustrating books for children is something I love to do. My hope is that my books will help persuade children that reading is something they love to do. To free children's imagination, and to compete with television, their books must be appealing and give pleasure.

"My story ideas are often inspired by my childhood. I am a grandmother now, but I have clear recall of my earliest years. I have observed—with six children and fourteen grandchildren—that feelings and interests of young children are universal and do not change. No matter how sophisticated or complex life may become later, the basic needs of the very young remain the same through the generations. . . . I have spent my whole life in the midwest, most of it in rural settings. That has provided me with a simple and tranquil perspective. I enjoy sharing my insights and feelings with children in amusing ways, through my stories and illustrations.

"I truly believe that one of the most important things we can do for children is to instill in them the love of books. They will benefit from this enrichment all of their lives."

BIOGRAPHICAL/CRITICAL SOURCES:

PERIODICALS

Chicago Tribune Book World, August 1, 1982.

*   *   *

BARCUS, Nancy B(idwell) 1937-

PERSONAL: Born November 9, 1937, in Cleveland, OH; daughter of Paul (an engineer) and Doris (a radio commentator; maiden name, Garvin) Bidwell; married James Edgar Barcus, Jr. (an English teacher and department chairman), 1961; children: Heidi Anne, Jeffrey Thomas Villaverde (adopted nephew), James Hans. *Education:* Attended University of Rochester, 1955-58; University of Kentucky, A.B. (magna cum laude), 1961; attended Temple University, 1961-62; State University of New York at Geneseo, M.A. (with distinction), 1970; received training as writing consultant from Chicago Writing Institute, National College of Education. *Politics:* Democrat. *Religion:* "Protestant, ecumenical."

ADDRESSES: Home—8317 Gatecrest Drive, Waco, TX 76712. *Office*—J. H. Hines School, Waco I. S. D., 1102 Paul Quinn Street, Waco, TX 76704.

CAREER: Audubon public schools, Audubon, NJ, high school English teacher, 1962-64; Houghton College, Houghton, NY, assistant professor of English, creative writing, and journalism, 1964-80; Baylor University, Waco, TX, publications feature writer and assistant director for public relations, 1980-86; J.H. Hines Elementary Magnet School, Waco, teacher of creative writing and violin, 1987—. Workshop leader, speaker, presenter, and lecturer at writing conferences and workshops; co-director, Central Texas Writing Project, 1989—; consulting editor, *Discover Waco* (magazine), 1991—. Co-chairman, Allegany County Council of Adopted Parents, 1974-79; vice-president and member of board of directors, Downtown Waco, Inc., 1983-86. Instructor in Suzuki violin method, 1975-80; violinist, Waco Symphony Orchestra, 1987—.

MEMBER: National Council of Teachers of English, National Writing Project, American Suzuki Association, Phi Beta Kappa.

AWARDS, HONORS: Danforth associate, 1966; Outstanding Educator of America citation, 1973; first place award for fiction, National Evangelical Press Association, 1974, for "Waking Up Christian"; first place honors for university newsletter editing, 1984-85, for Baylor University *Insight.*

WRITINGS:

Developing a Christian Mind, Inter-Varsity Press, 1977.

Help Me, God, I'm a Working Mother!, Judson Press, 1982.
The Family Takes a Child, Judson Press, 1983.
(Co-author) *A String of Pearls,* Word, Inc., 1985.
(With Robert Gilbert) *No Excuses Accepted,* Broodman, 1986.
Where Are You, God, from Nine to Five?, Revell, 1986.
Write to Discover: A Writing Program for Urban and At-Risk Students (monograph), Waco I. S. D., 1990.

Contributor of more than one hundred articles to magazines, including *Baylor University Report, Discover Waco,* and *Second Opinion.* Author of numerous monographs, brochures, promotional pieces, and multimedia scripts in the public relations field.

WORK IN PROGRESS: Making School Work; Our Last Best Hope, a book about teaching at-risk children.

SIDELIGHTS: Nancy B. Barcus once told *CA:* "I am very interested in people in their infinite variety and in families, children, minorities, social concerns, and the arts. As a teacher, I want to raise people to their highest potential. As a Christian, I am concerned about issues of faith at work in the world. I want to see ethnic groups understand one another more fully, and to that end I have joined the faculty of a predominantly black inner-city school, learning to know people 'where they live,' instead of from a distance. In that setting, I am developing a talent education program, using my background in music, literature, and the creative arts.

"My first book, *Developing a Christian Mind,* was prompted by my concern that Christian students did not have an adequate 'apologia' for their faith as they were confronted with contemporary ideas. I wanted to offer positive approaches to current ideas in order to counteract the negativism that often accompanies modern-day defenses of basic Christianity. I was teaching college classes at the time.

"My second and third books came out of family experiences. Working women often must counteract the guilt they are asked to feel for their pursuit of professional goals. I wanted to give a positive approach to the dilemma of the 'working family,' stressing appreciation for all those in the network of humanity who help to make families work: teachers, babysitters, neighbors, churches, willing husbands, and the children themselves.

"*The Family Takes a Child* chronicles our experiences in adopting our nephew, who came to us at age eleven. I had long been interested in adoption of an older child and we learned firsthand the grief and growing pains to all concerned when a family takes on this enterprise. I discovered that very little had been written on this subject and I hoped the book would help to fill that gap. We were pretty much on our own to negotiate the precarious ups and downs of those first two years.

"*No Excuses Accepted* is the spiritual biography of the Reverend Robert Gilbert, pastor of a black Baptist church in Waco. He invited me to write his biography and to 'walk in the shoes' of people I had only known at a distance. Gilbert was severely crippled with arthritis and in constant pain, yet he persevered as pastor of his church and as a community leader seeking opportunities for Waco minorities. The several months I spent with him taught me to 'see through different eyes' and to appreciate the contributions of the black community to our culture as a whole. This association let me to seek professional employment among his people, and I am now teaching at a school in his neighborhood."

Making School Work; Our Last Best Hope is Barcus's account of her experiences interacting with minority children. Her time spent teaching at an inner-city school in Waco has given her insight into learning to teach at-risk young people in a manner that enables her to "elicit their creative potential."

*   *   *

BARR, Densil Neve
  See BUTTREY, Douglas N(orton)

*   *   *

BAUR, Susan   1940-
  (Susan Schlee)

PERSONAL: Original name, Susan Whiting Baur; born January 22, 1940, in New York, NY; daughter of John I. H. (the director of the Whitney Museum of American Art) and Louise Chase (a teacher) Baur; married John Schlee (a marine geologist), December, 1969 (divorced, 1984); children: Scott Hubbard, Louisa Schlee. *Education:* Vassar College, A.B., 1961; attended Florida Atlantic University, 1967, and Duke University, 1968; Harvard University, A.L.M., 1987; Boston College, Ph.D., 1990. *Politics:* Democrat. *Religion:* None. *Avocational interests:* Running, art.

ADDRESSES: Home—P.O. Box 1620, North Falmouth, MA 02556. *Office*—Thorne Clinic, P.O. Box 989, Pocasset, MA 02559. *Agent*—Miriam Altshuler, Russell & Volkening, 50 West 29th St., New York, NY 10001.

CAREER: Thorne Clinic, Pocasset, MA, psychologist, 1989—; writer. Worked variously as a computer programmer, reporter, editor, instructor in marine literature, and investigator at a biological laboratory.

MEMBER: American Psychological Association.

AWARDS, HONORS: Mark Ethridge fellow, Duke University, 1968; Pfizer Award for best book in the history of science, 1974, for *The Edge of an Unfamiliar World;* Thomas Small Prize for academic excellence, Harvard University, 1987.

WRITINGS:

Hypochondria: Woeful Imaginings, University of California Press, 1988.
The Dinosaur Man: Tales of Madness and Enchantment from the Back Ward, HarperCollins, 1991.

UNDER NAME SUSAN SCHLEE

The Edge of an Unfamiliar World: A History of Oceanography, Dutton, 1973.
On Almost Any Wind: The Saga of the Oceanographic Research Vessel Atlantis, Cornell University Press, 1978.

OTHER

Contributor to periodicals, including *Natural History, Wilson Quarterly,* and *Smithsonian.* Baur's works have been translated into Spanish and German.

WORK IN PROGRESS: Riding the Glass Rollercoaster: Stories and Storytelling in the Hillsdale Clinic.

SIDELIGHTS: In *Hypochondria: Woeful Imaginings* Susan Baur discusses the condition in which healthy people believe they are suffering from physical ailments. Although reasons for the development of hypochondria vary, the author suggests that one of its primary causes lies in society's tendency to offer sympathy to people who are physically ill over those who might be suffering emotionally or mentally. For example, a person involved in a detrimental marriage might feel safer complaining about arthritis to gain consolation rather than risk revealing the truth about his or her dissatisfaction with the relationship. In Baur's opinion many children are conditioned to become hypochondriacs because they are exposed to habitual complainers and learn that they can receive love and attention for feigning illness. Although some reviewers complained that the book fails to explore the biological reasons for hypochondria to the fullest extent, several critics acknowledged that Baur adeptly explores a number of psychological and sociological issues surrounding the condition.

Throughout her book Baur investigates medical history, providing information about some of the most extreme hypochondriacs and offering anecdotes about figures such as biologist Charles Darwin and singer Enrico Caruso who regularly feared physical illness. Several reviewers felt that *Hypochondria* benefits from the inclusion of quotes from primary-source materials such as the journals of biographer James Boswell, who was obsessed with death and dying. Some commentators, however, felt that Baur's work was not comprehensive. Alex Raksin, writing in the *Los Angeles Times Book Review,* remarked, "Viewed as an incomplete survey of hypochondria . . . this book is singular, intelligent and entertaining." Commenting on Baur's content and style, Mike Oppenheim of the *New York Times Book Review* remarked that "despite its impressive scholarship, the book is gracefully written and accessible."

In *The Dinosaur Man: Tales of Madness and Enchantment from the Back Ward* Baur continues her exploration of psychological phenomena, deriving material from her experiences working with schizophrenic patients. The author focuses on delusions—irrational beliefs held by individuals, usually about themselves and their past experiences. In the author's view, delusions provide mentally unstable people with a sense of identity and a way to cope with their fragmented lives. In this respect they serve a similar function to memories for sane individuals who use episodes from the past to define themselves. At the center of the book is the story of the "Dinosaur Man," who convinces himself that he was once a powerful "Nicodemosauras." Baur also includes encounters with a person who thinks that his mother was once transformed into a bee with huge eyes and a patient who cries when he believes he hears his children telling him to behave. Terri Apter of the *New York Times Book Review* remarked that despite Baur's professional status "what comes through most clearly is not the voice of the psychologist but the many voices of the lovable, comic, tormented patients, who relentlessly try to construct a self out of a mind that continually sabotages itself."

Baur told *CA:* "The more I study storytelling, both from a writer's and a psychologist's point of view, the more convinced I become that the continual trading and refining of tales—from the common conversation to the heroic presentation—is the root metaphor for knowing. We think by talking. As [twentieth-century philosopher and author] Hannah Arendt maintained, individuals mature by talking to each other, and groups of people become communities in the same way. As I see it, the goal is to become inclusive. The richest stories, like the richest lives and richest communities, incorporate the most diverse and unexpected viewpoints. Much of my writing tries to capture the hidden gifts of the profoundly mentally ill and sneak them back into the community for the benefit of *all.*"

BIOGRAPHICAL/CRITICAL SOURCES:

PERIODICALS

Los Angeles Times Book Review, March 27, 1988, p. 4.
New York Times, April 26, 1988.
New York Times Book Review, March 27, 1988, p. 39; September 1, 1991, p. 7.

People, August 29, 1988, p. 81.
Times Literary Supplement, November 18, 1988, p. 1273.

*   *   *

BAXTER, Charles   1947-

PERSONAL: Born May 13, 1947, in Minneapolis, MN; son of John T. and Mary (Eaton) Baxter; married Martha Hauser (a teacher); children: Daniel. *Education:* Macalester College, B.A., 1969; State University of New York at Buffalo, Ph.D., 1974.

ADDRESSES: Home—1585 Woodland Dr., Ann Arbor, MI 48103. *Office*—7611 Haven Hall, Ann Arbor, MI 48109-1045.

CAREER: High school teacher in Pinconning, MI, 1969-70; Wayne State University, Detroit, MI, assistant professor, 1974-79, associate professor, 1979-85, professor of English, 1985-89; University of Michigan, Ann Arbor, MI, professor of English, 1989—. Warren Wilson College, faculty member, 1986—; University of Michigan, visiting faculty member, 1987.

AWARDS, HONORS: Faculty Research Fellowship, Wayne State University, 1980-81; Lawrence Foundation Award, 1982, and Associated Writing Programs Award Series in Short Fiction, 1984, both for *Harmony of the World;* National Endowment for the Arts fellowship, 1983, Michigan Council for the Arts fellowship, 1984; Faculty Recognition Award, Wayne State University, 1985 and 1987; Guggenheim fellowship, 1985-86; Michigan Council of the Arts grant, 1986; Arts Foundation of Michigan Award, 1991; Lawrence Foundation Award, 1991; Reader's Digest Foundation fellowship, 1992.

WRITINGS:

Chameleon (poetry), illustrated by Mary E. Miner, New Rivers Press, 1970.
The South Dakota Guidebook, New Rivers Press, 1974.
Harmony of the World (short stories), University of Missouri Press, 1984.
Through the Safety Net (short stories), Viking, 1985.
First Light (novel), Viking, 1987.
Imaginary Paintings and Other Poems, Paris Review Editions, 1990.
A Relative Stranger (short stories), Norton, 1990.
Shadow Play (novel), Norton, 1993.

Poems have been featured in numerous anthologies, including *The Fifth Annual Best Science Fiction,* edited by Harry Harrison and Brian Aldiss, Putnam, 1972; *Toward Winter,* edited by Robert Bonazzi, New Rivers Press, 1972; *The Pushcart Prize Anthology XVI,* Pushcart Press, 1991; and *Best American Short Stories,* 1982, 1986, 1987,

1989 and 1991. Contributor to periodicals, including *Minnesota Review, Kayak, Prairie Schooner, Antioch Review, Michigan Quarterly Review, Georgia Review, New England Review, Centennial Review, New York Times,* and *Journal of Modern Literature.* Associate editor of *Minnesota Review,* 1967-69; editor of *Audit/Poetry,* 1973-74; associate editor of *Criticism.*

Baxter's works have been translated into Japanese, Swedish, German, Russian, and Romanian.

SIDELIGHTS: Charles Baxter initially caught critics' attention with his poetry and criticism, but it was the graceful prose and human understanding of his short stories and novels that secured his place as one of the foremost contemporary American writers. In the *Nation,* critic Theodore Solotaroff asserted: "Baxter . . . has the special gift of capturing the shadow of genuine significance as it flits across the face of the ordinary." Baxter's sharply drawn, unique characters—one of his hallmarks—elicited praise from Jonathan Yardley in the *Washington Post Book World:* "Unlike so many other young American writers . . . Baxter cares about his people, recognizes the validity and dignity of their lives, grants them humor and individuality."

Baxter's first prose volume, *Harmony of the World,* includes the award-winning title story as well as several others. "Harmony of the World," originally published in the *Michigan Quarterly Review,* is about a young pianist who decides to become a newspaper critic after one of his performances elicits a particularly scathing review from a music teacher. His affair with a somewhat untalented singer and the events that bring both of their lives to a crisis are the means through which Baxter explores "the ache of yearning for perfection, in love and art, a perfection human beings can never attain however close they come to apprehending it," observed *Michigan Quarterly Review* editor Laurence Goldstein in the *Ann Arbor News.* Goldstein praised Baxter for the "imaginative sympathy and marvelous craft" of his short stories, a view shared by Peter Ross of the *Detroit News:* "There are no weak spots in *Harmony of the World,* no falterings of craft or insight. Baxter's influences are many and subtle, but his voice is his own and firmly in control. . . . *Harmony of the World* is a serious collection by a serious writer; it deserves as much attention, study and praise as anything being written today."

Baxter's second collection of short stories, *Through the Safety Net,* was published just one year after *Harmony of the World* and was received with great enthusiasm by critics. "It's a nice surprise that a second collection is so speedily upon us and that it improves on the first," wrote Ron Hansen in the *New York Times Book Review.* *Through the Safety Net* is an exploration of the inevitable perils of everyday life. Baxter's characters—among them,

an unsuccessful graduate student, a five-year-old boy trying to understand his grandmother's death, and a spurned lover who becomes obsessed with the object of his desire— spend their energies trying to escape pain and loss, but inevitably fail. In the title story, Diana visits a psychic only to be told that she is headed for a great calamity. "What kind? The Book of Job kind," the psychic tells her. "I saw your whole life, your house, car, that swimming pool you put in last summer, the career, your child, and the whole future just start to radiate with this ugly black flame from the inside, poof, and then I saw you falling, like at the circus, down from the trapeze. Whoops, and down, and then down through the safety net. Through the ground." In another narrative, a psychopath, lamenting his lack of fame, remarks: "If you are not famous in America, you are considered a mistake. They suspend you in negative air and give you bad jobs working in basements pushing mops from eight at night until four in the morning."

Yardley characterized the people in Baxter's stories as individuals without purpose, "amiably retreating from life's challenges. . . . though the forms of their retreats and the motives for them vary." A *Publishers Weekly* reviewer found the stories "flawed by a fondness for excessive detail, implausible turns and mere trickiness," but conceded that they contained "bright flashes of unmistakable talent." Baxter's careful attention to detail was praised by a *New York Times* critic: "An extraordinarily limber writer, Mr. Baxter makes his characters' fears palpable to the reader by slowly drawing us into their day-to-day routine and making us see things through their eyes." The stories in *Through the Safety Net,* concludes Hansen, are "intelligent, original, gracefully written, always moving, frequently funny and—that rarest of compliments—wise."

When Baxter's first novel, *First Light,* was published in 1987, it immediately garnered praise for its unique structure. Prefaced by a quote from Danish philosopher Kierkegaard—"Life can only be understood backwards, but it must be lived forwards"—the novel presents events in *reverse* chronological order. Thus, each chapter is a step further back into the past of the characters. At the outset of *First Light,* Hugh Welch and his sister Dorsey are uneasy adults reunited for a Fourth of July celebration. Their strained, distant relationship is clearly a source of anguish to them both. As the novel progresses, Hugh and Dorsey become younger and younger, and the many layers of their life-long bond are slowly uncovered. "We see their youth and childhoods revealed, like rapidly turning pages in a snapshot album," observed Michiko Kakutani in the *New York Times.* By the time the novel ends, Hugh is a young child being introduced to his newborn baby sister. "In reading of these events," Kakutani wrote, "we see why Dorsey and Hugh each made the choices they did, how their childhood dreams were translated into adult decisions." The combination of Baxter's unique narrative structure and fine characterization results in "a remarkably supple novel that gleams with the smoky chiaroscuro of familial love recalled through time," concludes Kakutani.

Although *First Light* was Baxter's first published novel, it was not his first attempt at the novel form. His first three novels, he remarked in the *New York Times,* are "apprentice" efforts he would never consider publishing. "I did take a brief episode out of one of them but, for the most part, I can't stand to look at them now so I wouldn't want anyone else to." Describing the structure of *First Light,* he commented: "The technique resembles those little Russian dolls that fit into each other—you open them up and they keep getting smaller and smaller. What I am trying to say is that grownups don't stop being the people they were many years before, in childhood."

Baxter's 1990 collection of short stories, *A Relative Stranger,* features characters who "are constantly having odd encounters with strangers that disrupt their quiet, humdrum lives and send them skidding in unexpected new directions," Kakutani stated in a *New York Times* review. In one story, a man's attempt to help an insane, homeless man sparks the jealousy of his wife and son. In another, a woman who secretly is in love with her husband's best friend develops an irrational fear of burglars. Describing the couple's suburban home as one of many "little rectangular temples of light," the friend scoffs at the wife's fear. "Nothing here but families and fireplaces and Duraflame logs and children of God," he tells the husband. "Not the sort of place," he continues, "where a married woman ought to be worried about prowlers."

Recommending *A Relative Stranger* in the *Nation,* Ted Solotaroff opined: "Baxter is well on his way to becoming the next master of the short story." *A Relative Stranger* was also praised by Kakutani: "All the stories in this collection attest to Mr. Baxter's ability to orchestrate the details of mundane day-to-day reality into surprising patterns of grace and revelation, his gentle but persuasive knack for finding and describing the fleeting moments that indelibly define a life. . . . we finish the book with the satisfaction of having been immersed in a beautifully rendered and fully imagined world."

Baxter's 1993 novel, *Shadow Play,* revolves around Wyatt Palmer, a man whose chaotic childhood has left him unable to deal with emotions. Instead, he focuses on maintaining a neatly ordered life with his understanding wife and two children. Wyatt's job as an assistant city manager leads him to cross paths with a former high school classmate interested in starting a chemical company in their economically depressed hometown. The former classmate, Jerry Schwartzwalder, asks Wyatt to bend the rules in order to help him launch his new company. In exchange for his cooperation, Jerry offers Wyatt's unstable foster brother, Cyril, a job at the plant. When Cyril shows signs of a fatal disease caused by exposure to toxins, Wyatt becomes enraged and vows to take revenge. The story of how Wyatt deals with his emotional handicaps is told in "language so carefully honed it sings," observed a *Publishers Weekly* critic. Baxter's "metaphors and apercus are striking and luminous, and several scenes—notably Wyatt and Cyril's final bonding—are unforgettable," the critic continued. While some readers may find it frustrating that the novel avoids a neat, conventional conclusion, the critic concludes that the "lyrical, witty, dramatic and moving story has the clarity of sunshine, the haunting suggestion of shadow play."

While reviewers hailed *Shadow Play* as the book that would thrust Baxter into the national literary limelight, Baxter himself refused to set such high expectations for the novel. "When *First Light* came out, I was full of the American Dream," he recalled in the *Detroit News.* "I thought the birds of money were going to land in a huge flock on the roof, and I'd be proclaimed from housetop to housetop. It was foolish, and that's what young writers are. . . . I'm trying not to get my hopes up. I worked on [*Shadow Play*] so long, I just want it to do well. I just want people to like it and to find it interesting and find it has some meaning to their lives."

In both his short stories and novels, Baxter's exploration of his characters' inner desires and outward realities has touched a chord within critics and readers alike. "If there is a consistent theme in Baxter's work, it is the difficulty people have in accommodating themselves to a world that is complex, mysterious, and demanding, that offers rewards that glitter all the more brightly because so few attain them," Yardley summarized in the *Washington Post Book World.* "Whether he's writing about an overly self-conscious intellectual or an inarticulate street person," concluded Kakutani, "Mr. Baxter is able to map out their emotions persuasively and delineate the shape of their spiritual confusion."

Praising the fluid beauty of the author's style, John Saari wrote in the *Antioch Review:* "Many writers today feel no depth of compassion for their characters. Baxter, in contrast, is adept at portraying his characters as human beings, even when some of them are not the best examples."

BIOGRAPHICAL/CRITICAL SOURCES:

BOOKS

Baxter, Charles, *Through the Safety Net,* Viking, 1985.
Baxter, C., *A Relative Stranger,* Norton, 1990.
Contemporary Literary Criticism, Volume 45, Gale, 1987.

PERIODICALS

Ann Arbor News, May 16, 1982.
Antioch Review, fall, 1985, p. 498.
Detroit Free Press, December 23, 1992.
Detroit News, May 20, 1984; December 28, 1992, p. 1D.
Los Angeles Times Book Review, July 6, 1986, p. 10; December 6, 1987, p. 3; September 29, 1991.
Nation, December 30, 1991, p. 862.
New York Times, June 26, 1985; August 24, 1987; September 7, 1987; September 4, 1990; September 29, 1991.
New York Times Book Review, August 25, 1985, p. 1; October 23, 1988, p. 60.
Publishers Weekly, May 24, 1985; October 19, 1992.
Time, September 14, 1987.
Washington Post Book World, July 10, 1985.

Sketch by Cornelia A. Pernik

*　　　*　　　*

BEAVER, Paul (Eli) 1953-

PERSONAL: Born April 3, 1953, in Winchester, United Kingdom; son of Norman Kenneth (an engineer) and Olive Mary (a horticulturist) Beaver. *Education:* Attended Farnborough College of Technology, 1971-72, Sheffield City Polytechnic, 1973-77, and Henley Management College, 1988-89. *Religion:* Church of England.

ADDRESSES: Home—Poppy Cottage, Barfields, Bletchingley, Surrey RH1 4RD, United Kingdom.

CAREER: Free-lance writer, broadcaster (in Europe, North America, and Japan), and photographer, 1973—. *Jane's Defence Weekly,* Horley, United Kingdom (UK), naval editor, 1987-88, publisher, 1989—; Jane's Information Group, London, UK, managing editor, 1988-89; defence correspondent, SKY-TV News, 1990—. Nelson Birthday Lecturer, Portsmouth, UK, 1988. General editor for Trilion Television, London, 1986-87; partner in United Writers Group, Basingstoke, UK, 1986-87. *Military service:* Territorial Army (Army Air Corps), 1987—; captain.

MEMBER: Royal Institute of Chartered Surveyors, Fleet Air Army Officers Association, Airborne Law Enforcement Association, Army Aviation Association of America, Helicopter Club of Great Britain.

AWARDS, HONORS: Nominated Editor of the Year, 1984.

WRITINGS:

"Ark Royal": A Pictorial History of the Royal Navy's Last Conventional Aircraft Carrier, Patrick Stephens, 1979.
U-Boats in the Atlantic, Patrick Stephens, 1979.

German Capital Ships, Patrick Stephens, 1980.
E-Boats and Coastal Craft, Patrick Stephens, 1980.
German Destroyers and Escorts, Patrick Stephens, 1981.
The British Aircraft Carrier, Patrick Stephens, 1982, 3rd edition, 1987.
(Editor) *Encyclopaedia of the Modern Royal Navy, Including the Fleet Air Arm and Royal Marines,* Patrick Stephens, 1982, Naval Institute Press, 1983, 3rd edition, Patrick Stephens, 1987.
Carrier Air Operations since 1945, Arms & Armour Press, 1983.
"Invincible Class," Ian Allan, 1984.
Fleet Command, Ian Allan, 1984.
Missile Systems, Ian Allan, 1985.
British Naval Air Power, Arms & Armour Press, 1985.
The Royal Navy of the 1980s, Arms & Armour Press, 1985.
NATO Navies of the 1980s, Arms & Armour Press, 1985.
Nuclear-Powered Submarines, Patrick Stephens, 1986.
Modern British Missiles, Patrick Stephens, 1986.
Encyclopedia of Aviation, Octopus, 1986.
Modern Royal Naval Warships, Patrick Stephens, 1987.
Attack Helicopters, Arms & Armour Press, 1987.
Modern Military Helicopters, Patrick Stephens, 1987.
Encyclopaedia of the Fleet Air Arm since 1945, Patrick Stephens, 1987.
Today's Army Air Corps, Patrick Stephens, 1987.
The Modern Royal Navy, Patrick Stephens, 1988.
Today's Royal Marines, Patrick Stephens, 1988.
World Naval Aviation, Jane's Publishing, 1989.

Also author of *China's Military,* Jane's Publishing. Writer and technical adviser for Scottish television series *Rescue,* 1989. Contributor to periodicals, including the *Guardian,* London, UK, and *Nikkei Business,* Tokyo, Japan. Editor, *Helicopter World* and *Defence Helicopter World,* both 1982-86.

SIDELIGHTS: Paul Beaver once told *CA,* "Those who wish to become specialist writers should know their subject and not worry about reading for degrees or diplomas in journalism." He added that he believes in "factual, accurate, and timely writing."

*　　　*　　　*

BEECH, Webb
See BUTTERWORTH, W(illiam) E(dmund III)

*　　　*　　　*

BEGIEBING, Robert J(ohn) 1946-

PERSONAL: Surname is pronounced "be-*gee*-bing"; born November 18, 1946, in Adams, MA; son of Robert H. (an engineer and musician) and Patricia (a bank administrator; maiden name, Verow) Begiebing; married Linda Adams (in office administration), June 5, 1968; children: Brie A., Kate A. *Education:* Norwich University, B.A. (with high honors), 1968; Boston College, A.M., 1970; University of New Hampshire, Ph.D., 1977.

ADDRESSES: Home—Box 19, Main St., Newfields, NH 03856. *Office*—Department of English, New Hampshire College, 2500 North River Rd., Manchester, NH 03124. *Agent*—Jane Otte, 9 Goden St., Belmont, MA 02178.

CAREER: New Hampshire College, Manchester, assistant professor, 1977-80, associate professor, 1980-82, professor of English, 1982—. Evaluation consultant for New Hampshire Council on the Humanities. *Military service:* U.S. Army, 1970-71; became first lieutenant.

MEMBER: Modern Language Association of America, American Studies Association, New England Modern Language Association, Thoreau Lyceum.

AWARDS, HONORS: Research fellowships from University of New Hampshire, 1976-77, and New Hampshire College, 1982 and 1983.

WRITINGS:

Acts of Regeneration: Allegory and Archetype in the Works of Norman Mailer, University of Missouri Press, 1981.
(Editor with Owen Grumbling) *The Literature of Nature: The British and American Traditions* (anthology), Plexus, 1990.
Toward a New Synthesis: John Fowles, John Gardner, and Norman Mailer, University of Rochester Press, 1990.
The Strange Death of Mistress Coffin (novel), Algonquin Books, 1991.

Poetry represented in anthology *Cracks in the Ark.* Contributor of poetry to journals, including *Country Journal, Connecticut Quarterly, Loon Feather,* and *Xanadu.* Contributor of articles to numerous periodicals, including *Harvard Magazine, USA Today, New Hampshire Times, New Hampshire Spotlight, American Imago, Essays in Literature,* and *Gypsy Scholar.* Editor, *New Hampshire College Journal,* 1983-86.

SIDELIGHTS: In a review for the *Times Literary Supplement* Rupert Christiansen described the thesis of Robert J. Begiebing's literary study *Acts of Regeneration: Allegory and Archetype in the Works of Norman Mailer:* "For the author of this monograph . . . Mailer is neither novelist nor reporter, but visionary allegorist, writing texts 'in which the material world is given transcendental meaning.' " Deeming the position "generally fruitful," the critic observed that Begiebing's analysis of Mailer novels from the eras of U.S. president John F. Kennedy and the Viet-

nam War, in particular, "is greatly enhanced by [this allegorical] perspective."

Begiebing told *CA:* "Finding in Mailer what I admire most in American writers, living or dead—courage, the willingness to take huge risks, the rebellious artist, the renegade, and the prophet—inspired *Acts of Regeneration.* In it I try to assess Mailer's artistic successes and failures as well as the allegorical and archetypal nature of his work. The book was widely reviewed here and abroad, with the usual divisions of opinion over its greater or lesser value, but I was most happy to get from the horse's mouth, so to speak, Mailer's judgment of my book on him. He said that it, 'unlike most . . . has a close idea of what I'm up to. I was much impressed with it; . . . it's a damned good job.' Meeting Mailer for my piece on him for *Harvard Magazine* and corresponding a bit with him since has confirmed my own ideas about the need for a writer to courageously live his own life and follow his own convictions.

"*The Literature of Nature,* a critical/historical anthology of nature writings from Britain and America since the eighteenth century, grew out of my—and my co-editor's—feeling for nature and writers who use the stunning details of natural creatures and systems in their work. It also stems from our belief that, in our time, the crucial issue before humanity is its relationship with the natural world."

"As a free-lance writer and poet I have found the response to my work more immediate and satisfying—the broadest audience (within reason) is the best and most satisfying audience. For one who started—and continues—as an academic, this comes as a revelation. (When I speak of a broad audience for a poet, I speak of readings, workshops, visits to schools, and so forth.) Poets whose world I admire, among others, and who have helped me personally are Donald Hall and Wesley McNair. May they both prosper."

Expressing his thoughts on writing his first novel at the age of forty-four, Begiebing told an interviewer for the *New Hampshire Seacoast:* "I wanted to make a change, to find a more creative area for growth in my life. I was dissatisfied with writing literary criticism—I had gotten tired of it—and I was starting to get dissatisfied with teaching. So I went back to something I'd had in mind for years, something I really wanted to do: write fiction."

BIOGRAPHICAL/CRITICAL SOURCES:

PERIODICALS

Boston Globe, April 2, 1983.
Harvard Magazine, April-May, 1983.
New Hampshire Seacoast, April 14, 1991, pp. 13-14.
Times Literary Supplement, September 18, 1981, p. 1077.

BELLAK, Leopold 1916-

PERSONAL: Born June 22, 1916, in Vienna, Austria; immigrated to the United States, 1938, naturalized citizen, 1942; son of Siegfried and Marie (Weiler) Bellak; married Sonya Sorel (a sculptor), December 20, 1950 (divorced, 1979); children: Karola, Katrina. *Education:* Attended University of Vienna, 1935-38; Boston University, M.A., 1939; Harvard University, M.A., 1942; New York University, M.D., 1944. *Avocational interests:* Writing detective stories, karate and aikido (black belt), judo (brown belt).

ADDRESSES: Home—Larchmont, NY. *Office*—22 Rockwood Dr., Larchmont, NY 10538. *Agent*—Maria Pelikan, 5500 Fieldston Rd., Riverdale, NY.

CAREER: St. Elizabeth's Hospital, Washington, DC, 1944-46, began as intern, became resident; private practice in psychiatry, Larchmont, NY, 1946—; City Hospital, New York City, director and psychiatrist, 1958-64; New York University, New York City, clinical professor of psychology, 1965—; Albert Einstein College of Medicine, New York City, clinical professor of psychiatry, 1971-87, emeritus professor of psychiatry, 1987—. Visiting professor or lecturer at New School of Social Research, 1947-55, City College of New York (now City College of the City University of New York), 1948-54, Columbia University, 1965-69, and George Washington University, 1970-76. Principal investigator and project director for the National Institute of Mental Health grants, 1951—. Established Trouble Shooting Clinic in New York City, 1958. Member of board of advisers of New Rochelle Guidance Center, 1960—. Consultant to Jewish Board of Guardians, 1947-57, U.S. Military Academy, 1966—, and RAND Corp., 1969—. *Military service:* U.S. Army Medical Corps, 1942-46.

MEMBER: American Psychoanalytic Association (life fellow), American Psychological Association (life fellow), American Psychiatric Association (life fellow), American Orthopsychiatric Association (fellow), Royal Society of Medicine (fellow), Society for Projective Techniques and Rorschach Institute (fellow; president, 1952-56, 1957-58), Westchester Psychoanalytic Society (president, 1962-63), Sigma Xi.

AWARDS, HONORS: Annual merit award from New York Society of Clinical Psychologists, 1964; award for contribution to the theory and practice of community psychiatry from Psychiatric Outpatient Centers of America, 1976; Frieda Fromm-Reichmann Award from American Academy of Psychoanalysis, 1981, for contributions towards better understanding of schizophrenia; Bruno Klopfer Award from Society for Personality Assessment, 1991.

WRITINGS:

Dementia Praecox: The Past Decade's Work and Present Status; A Review and Evaluation, Grune, 1948.

(Editor with Lawrence E. Abt, and contributor) *Projective Psychology: Clinical Approaches to the Total Personality,* Knopf, 1950.

Manic-Depressive Psychosis and Allied Disorders, Grune, 1952.

(Editor and contributor) *The Psychology of Physical Illness: Psychiatry Applied to Medicine, Surgery, and the Specialties,* Grune, 1952.

The Thematic Apperception Test and the Children's Apperception Test in Clinical Use, Grune, 1954, 3rd edition published as *The Thematic Apperception Test, the Children's Apperception Test, and the Senior Apperception Technique in Clinical Use,* 1975, 5th edition, Allyn & Bacon, 1992.

(Editor with P. K. Benedict, and contributor) *Schizophrenia: A Review of the Syndrome,* Logos Press, 1958.

(Editor and contributor) *Conceptual and Methodological Problems in Psychoanalysis,* New York Academy of Sciences, 1959.

(Co-editor) Emilio Mira y Lopez, *Myokinetic Psychodiagnosis,* Logos Press, 1960.

(Editor) *Contemporary European Psychiatry,* Grove, 1961.

(Editor and contributor) *A Handbook of Community Psychiatry and Community Mental Health,* Grune, 1964.

(With Leonard Small) *Emergency Psychotherapy and Brief Psychotherapy,* Grune, 1965, 2nd edition, 1978.

The Broad Scope of Psychoanalysis: Selected Papers of Leopold Bellak, edited by Donald P. Spence, Grune, 1967.

(Editor with Laurence Loeb) *The Schizophrenic Syndrome,* Grune, 1969.

(Editor with Harvey H. Barten, and contributor) *Progress in Community Mental Health,* Grune, Volume 1, 1969, Volume 2, 1972, Volume 3, Brunner, 1975.

The Porcupine Dilemma, Citadel, 1970.

(With Marvin Hurvich and Helen Gediman) *Ego Functions in Schizophrenics, Neurotics, and Normals,* Wiley, 1973.

(Editor and contributor) *A Concise Handbook of Community Psychiatry and Community Mental Health,* Grune, 1974.

The Best Years of Your Life: A Guide to the Art and Science of Aging, Atheneum, 1975.

Overload: The New Human Condition, Behavioral Publications, 1975.

(Editor with Toksoz B. Karasu, and contributor) *Geriatric Psychiatry: A Handbook for Psychiatrists and Primary Care Physicians,* Grune, 1976.

(Editor with Leonard Small) *Emergency Psychotherapy and Brief Psychotherapy,* Grune, 1978.

(Editor and contributor) *Disorders of the Schizophrenic Syndrome,* Basic Books, 1979.

(Editor and contributor) *Psychiatric Aspects of Minimal Brain Dysfunction in Adults,* Grune, 1979.

(With Peri Faithorn) *Crises and Special Problems in Psychoanalysis and Psychotherapy,* Brunner, 1980.

(Editor and contributor with Karasu) *Specialized Techniques in Individual Psychotherapy,* Brunner, 1980.

(With Samm Baker) *Reading Faces,* Holt, 1981.

(With Helen Siegel) *Handbook of Intensive Brief and Emergency Psychotherapy,* C.P.S., 1984, 2nd edition, 1991.

(Editor with Lisa Goldsmith) *The Broad Scope of Ego Function Assessment,* Wiley Interscience, 1984.

Manual for Intensive Brief and Emergency Psychotherapy and B.E.P. Recording Blank, C.P.S., 1987.

Ego Function Assessment, C.P.S., 1989.

Psychoanalysis As a Science: A Textbook for Skeptics, Allyn & Bacon, 1992.

Contributor to numerous books, including *Progress in Neurology and Psychiatry,* edited by E. A. Spiegel, Volumes 4-10, Grune, 1949-55; *Projective Techniques with Children,* edited by Albert I. Rabin and Mary R. Haworth, Grune, 1960; *The Schizophrenic Reactions,* edited by R. Cancro, Brunner, 1970; *Aspects of Community Psychiatry: Review and Preview,* edited by J. M. Divic and M. Dinoff, University of Alabama Press, 1978; *Attention Deficit Disorder: Diagnostic, Cognitive, and Therapeutic Understanding,* edited by Lewis Bloomingdale, SP Medican and Scientific Books, 1984; and *Contemporary Approaches to Psychological Assessment,* edited by Wetzler and Katz, Brunner, 1989.

Contributor to *International Encyclopedia of Social Sciences,* 1968. Also contributor of many articles and book reviews to professional journals, magazines, and newspapers, including *American Journal of Psychology, International Journal of Group Psychotherapy, New England Journal of Medicine,* and *New York Post.*

*   *   *

BENNETT, Hal Zina 1936-
(Harold Zina Bennett)

PERSONAL: Born September 29, 1936, in Detroit, MI; son of Merle F. (a furniture manufacturer) and Martha (a housewife; maiden name, Evenson) Bennett; married Susan J. Sparrow (a health practitioner), September 15, 1985; children: Nathan. *Education:* San Francisco State College (now University), B.A., 1964; Columbia Pacific University, M.S., Ph.D.

ADDRESSES: Home—1075 Spacepark Way, Suite 352, Mountain View, CA 94306.

CAREER: Writer. Self-employed as consulting psychologist in Mountain View, CA, 1989—. Publishing consultant in Mountain View. Has taught workshops and classes in numerous locations, including California and New York.

WRITINGS:

Behind the Scenes (juvenile novel) Century Communications, 1967.

The Vanishing Pirate (juvenile novel), Leswing Communications, 1967.

Battle of Wits (juvenile novel), Lewsing Communications, 1968.

Brave the Dragon (juvenile novel), Century Communications, 1969.

No More Public School, Random House, 1972.

(With Michael Samuels) *The Well Body Book,* Random House, 1972.

(With Samuels) *Spirit Guides: Access to Secret Worlds,* Random House, 1973.

(With Samuels) *Be Well,* Random House, 1973.

Cold Comfort: Colds and Flu—Everybody's Guide to Self-Treatment, Clarkson Potter, 1977.

The Doctor Within, Clarkson Potter, 1978.

Sewing for the Outdoors, Outdoors Life Book Club, 1979.

(With John Marino) *John Marino's Bicycling Book,* J. P. Tarcher, 1980.

The Complete Bicycle Commuter, Sierra Books, 1982.

(With Samuels) *Well Body, Well Earth,* Sierra Books/Random House, 1984.

(With Charles Garfield) *Peak Performance: Mental Training Techniques of the World's Greatest Athletes,* J. P. Tarcher/Warner Books, 1984.

Mind Jogger: A Problem-Solving Companion, Celestial Arts/Ten Speed Press, 1986.

Inner Guides, Visions and Dreams, Celestial Arts/Ten Speed Press, 1987.

The Lens of Perception, Celestial Arts/Ten Speed Press, 1987.

(With Michael Larsen) *How to Write with a Collaborator,* Writers Digest, 1988.

(With wife, Susan J. Sparrow) *Follow Your Bliss: Let the Power of What You Love Guide You to Personal Fulfillment in Your Work and Relationships,* Avon, 1990.

(With Stanislav Grof) *The Holotropic Mind: Three Levels of Human Consciousness and How They Shape Our Lives,* Harper, 1992.

The Zuni Fetish, Harper, 1993.

Collaborator on a number of books, including *Living Your Dying,* with Stanley Keleman, Random House, 1974; *The Tooth Trip,* with Thomas McGuire, Random House, 1974; *The Well Body Student Health Manual,* University of California, 1980; *The Marriage Fantasy: Directions for a New Intimacy,* with Daniel Beaver, Harper, 1983; *Inner*

Bridges: A Guide to Energy Movement and Body Structure, with Fritz Smith, Humanics Press, 1986; *Out of Darkness, into the Light,* with Gerald G. Jampolsky, Bantam, 1989; *One Person Can Make a Difference,* with Jampolsky, Bantam, 1990; *Don't Go Away Mad: Making Peace with Your Partner,* with James L. Creighton, Doubleday/Bantam, 1990; *Recovery Plus: Freedom from Co-Dependency,* with Joe Alexander, Health Communications, 1990; *The Art and Practice of Loving,* with Frank Andrews, Tarchev Books, 1991; *Losing a Parent: Passage to a New Way of Living,* with Alexander Kennedy, Harper, 1991; *Love Is the Answer: Creating Loving Relationships,* with Jampolsky and Diane Cirincione, Bantam, 1991; and *Healing with Love: The Principles and Practice of Holoenergetic Healing,* with Leonard Laskow, Harper, 1992. Editor of *Soul Return: Transpersonal Integration,* by Aminah Raheem, 1986. Contributor to *The Peoples' Almanac.* Contributor to *Funk & Wagnall's Encyclopedia.* Contributor to periodicals, including *Logos Review, Well Being Journal, Medical Self-Care Magazine,* and *Shaman's Drum Magazine.*

SIDELIGHTS: Hal Zina Bennett told *CA:* "While my own interest is intuitive psychology and Native American spirituality, I deeply enjoy collaborating with other professionals. About two-thirds of my books are collaborations, the other one-third being books I do on my own."

*   *   *

BENNETT, Harold Zina
See BENNETT, Hal Zina

*   *   *

BEST, Gary Dean 1936-

PERSONAL: Born September 18, 1936, in Estherville, IA; son of Frederick William and Maxine Avis (Bassett) Best; married second wife, Lani Brooks, December 7, 1984. *Education:* University of Hawaii at Manoa, B.A., 1968, M.A., 1969, Ph.D., 1973.

ADDRESSES: Home—471 Hilinai St., Hilo, HI 96720. *Office*—Department of History, University of Hawaii at Hilo, Hilo, HI 96720.

CAREER: Sophia University, Tokyo, Japan, assistant professor of history, 1973-74; University of Hawaii at Hilo, assistant professor, 1975-78, associate professor, 1979-82, professor of history, 1982—. Visiting scholar, Hoover Institution on War, Revolution, and Peace, 1983; visiting professor, University of Nebraska at Omaha, 1990-91. *Military service:* U.S. Navy, 1954-59.

MEMBER: Organization of American Historians, American Association of University Professors.

AWARDS, HONORS: American-East Asian relations fellow, American Historical Association, 1973-74; Fulbright scholar in Japan, 1974-75; National Endowment for the Humanities grant, 1976, fellow, 1982-83.

WRITINGS:

The Politics of American Individualism: Herbert Hoover in Transition, 1918-1921, Greenwood Press, 1975.
To Free a People: American Jewish Leaders and the Jewish Problem in Eastern Europe, 1890-1914, Greenwood Press, 1982.
Herbert Hoover: The Post-Presidential Years, 1933-1964, two volumes, Hoover Institution, 1983.
Pride, Prejudice, and Politics: Roosevelt versus Recovery, 1933-1938, Praeger, 1991.
FDR and the Bonus Marchers, 1933-1935, Praeger, 1992.
The Critical Press and the New Deal: The Press versus Presidential Power, 1933-1938, Praeger, 1993.

Contributor to history journals.

WORK IN PROGRESS: A critical study of the "liberalism" of FDR and the New Deal.

BIOGRAPHICAL/CRITICAL SOURCES:

PERIODICALS

American Historical Review, October, 1976.

*   *   *

BETTS, Richard K(evin) 1947-

PERSONAL: Born August 15, 1947, in Easton, PA; son of John Rickards (a professor of history) and Cecelia (Fitzpatrick) Betts; married Adela M. Bolet, July 25, 1987; children: Elena Christine, Michael Francis, Diego Fitzpatrick. *Education:* Harvard University, B.A. (magna cum laude), 1969, M.A., 1971, Ph.D., 1975. *Politics:* Democrat.

ADDRESSES: Home—1199 The Strand, Teaneck, NJ 07666. *Office*—Institute of War and Peace Studies, Columbia University, 420 West 118th St., New York, NY 10027.

CAREER: Harvard University, Cambridge, MA, lecturer in government, 1975-76; Brookings Institution, Washington, DC, research associate in foreign policy, 1976-81, senior fellow, 1981-90; Columbia University, New York, NY, professor of political science and member of Institute of War and Peace, 1990—. Professorial lecturer at Johns Hopkins University, 1978-85, 1988-90; lecturer at Columbia University, 1979-85. Visiting professor of government, Harvard University, 1985-88. Staff member, U.S. Senate Select Committee to Study Governmental Operations with Respect to Intelligence Activities, 1975-76; consultant to National Security Council, 1977, National Intelligence Council, and Central Intelligence Agency, 1980-91. Foreign policy adviser for the 1984 Mondale-Ferraro democratic presidential campaign. Has testified before committees of the U.S. Congress on foreign policy matters. Occasional lecturer at the National War College, Foreign Service Institute, U.S. Military Academy, and other service schools and government educational programs. *Military service:* U.S. Army Reserve, Military Intelligence, 1969-71; became second lieutenant.

MEMBER: International Institute for Strategic Studies, International Studies Association, Society for Historians of American Foreign Relations, American Political Science Association, Academy of Political Science, Arms Control Association, Council on Foreign Relations, Inter-University Seminar on Armed Forces and Society, Consortium for the Study of Intelligence, Association for Retarded Citizens.

AWARDS, HONORS: National Intelligence Study Center Award, for best scholarly articles on intelligence, 1979 and 1981; Harold D. Laswell Award, Inter-University Seminar on Armed Forces and Society, 1979, for *Soldiers, Statesmen, and Cold War Crises;* Woodrow Wilson Award, American Political Science Association, 1980, for *The Irony of Vietnam.*

WRITINGS:

Soldiers, Statesmen, and Cold War Crises, Harvard University Press, 1977, 2nd edition, Columbia University Press, 1991.
(With Leslie H. Gelb) *The Irony of Vietnam: The System Worked,* Brookings Institution, 1979.
(With Joseph Yager and others) *Nonproliferation and U.S. Foreign Policy,* Brookings Institution, 1980.
(Editor and contributor) *Cruise Missiles: Technology, Strategy, Politics,* Brookings Institution, 1981, revised and abridged edition published as *Cruise Missiles and U.S. Policy* (monograph), 1982.
Surprise Attack: Lessons for Defense Planning, Brookings Institution, 1982.
Conventional Strategy, Unconventional Criticism, and Conventional Wisdom, Magnes Press, 1984.
NATO Deferrence Doctrine: No Way Out, Center for International and Strategic Affairs, University of California, Los Angeles, 1985.
Nuclear Blackmail and Nuclear Balance, Brookings Institution, 1987.
The Military Readiness Tangle, Brookings Institution, in press.

Author of monographs. Contributor to numerous books, including *World in Transition: Challenges to Human Rights, Development and World Order,* University Press of America, 1979; *The Strategic Imperative: New Policies for American Security,* edited by Samuel P. Huntington, Ballinger, 1982; *Preventing Nuclear War,* edited by Barry Blechman, Indiana University Press, 1985; *Security Interdependence in the Asia Pacific Region,* D. C. Heath, 1986; *America in the World, 1962-1987,* St. Martin's, 1987; and *The Strategic Defense Initiative: Shield or Snare?,* Harold Brown, 1987.

Contributor to proceedings and political science journals. Member of editorial board of *Orbis, Journal of Strategic Studies* (London), *Atlantic Quarterly* (London), and of the Democratic Party.

SIDELIGHTS: Richard K. Betts told *CA:* "A professor of mine once said that the only issues in international affairs worth studying are ones that involve large amounts of blood or treasure. Since I've never been able to grasp the subtleties of economics, that choice left me with war— and peace, which is only the other side of the coin.

"Within the general field of security and conflict I've written on a number of subjects: nuclear strategy, civil-military relations, arms trade, nuclear proliferation, strategic intelligence, the history of decision-making in the Vietnam War, conventional deterrence, NATO, Japanese defense policy, and others. My writing is primarily academic and theortical, but heavily tinged with practical analysis of current policies. As a result, my work may smack a wee bit too much of the ivory tower to people in government, and it may seem a bit too caught up with nuts and bolts to my colleagues in universities. But in not going completely in either direction, my writing strikes most people in both camps as fairly reasonable. Perhaps that's the best of both worlds.

"In any case, it has been the mixture of my academic training and a little experience in unique government jobs that has given my research its cutting edge."

*   *   *

BIRD, Wendell R(aleigh)

PERSONAL: Born in Atlanta, GA; son of Raleigh M. and R. Jean (Edwards) Bird; married Celia Ann Reed, December 22, 1978; children: Courtenay Asheton. *Education:* Vanderbilt University, B.A. (summa cum laude), 1975; Yale University Law School, J.D., 1978.

ADDRESSES: Home—Atlanta, GA. *Office*—Bird & Associates, 1150 Monarch Plaza, 3414 Peachtree Rd. N.E., Atlanta, GA 30326.

CAREER: U.S. Court of Appeals, Fourth Circuit, Durham, NC, law clerk to Judge J. Dickson Phillips, 1978-79; U.S. Court of Appeals, Fifth Circuit, Birmingham, AL, law clerk to Judge Robert S. Vance, 1979-80; attorney in private law practice, San Diego, CA, 1980-82; Parker, Johnson, Cook & Dunlevie, Atlanta, GA, attorney, 1982-86; Bird & Associates, Atlanta, attorney, 1986—. Member of Bars of U.S. Supreme Court, U.S. Courts of Appeals for the Second, Third, Fourth, Fifth, Sixth, Seventh, Eighth, Ninth, Tenth, and Eleventh Circuits, various U.S. District Courts, and the States of Georgia, California, Alabama, and Florida. Washington Non-Profit Tax Conference, lecturer, 1982—; Emory University Law School, adjunct professor, 1986—. Council for National Policy, member of board of governors. Has spoken at conferences.

MEMBER: American Law Institute, American Bar Association (past chairman, Subcommittee on Religious Organizations; chairman, Task Force of State and Local Taxes; member, Committee on Exempt Organizations and Committee on Charitable Contributions, Section of Taxation and Section of Litigation), Association of Trial Lawyers of America, Phi Beta Kappa.

AWARDS, HONORS: Egger Prize, Yale University Law School.

WRITINGS:

Home Education and Constitutional Liberties, Crossway, 1984.
The Origin of Species Revisited, 2 volumes, Philosophical Library, 1987.

Contributor to periodicals, including *Harvard Journal of Law and Public Policy, Practical Tax Lawyer,* and *Religious Freedom Reporter.* Member of editorial board, *Yale Law Journal,* 1977-78.

SIDELIGHTS: Wendell R. Bird concentrates on general corporate law, litigation, and exempt organization law. He won one of the twenty largest judgments nationally in history ($129,000,000) and argued *Edwards v. Aguillard* before the U.S. Supreme Court (which he told *CA* was "treated as the most important 1986 decision").

*   *   *

BIXBY, Ray Z.
  See TRALINS, S(andor) Robert

*   *   *

BLACKBURN, Simon 1944-

PERSONAL: Born December 7, 1944; son of Cuthbert Walter and Edna (Walton) Blackburn; married Angela Margaret Bowles (an editor); children: Gwendolen,

James. *Education:* Trinity College, Cambridge, B.A., 1963; Churchill College, Cambridge, Ph.D., 1969. *Politics:* "Middle." *Religion:* None.

ADDRESSES: Home—219 Morrell Ave., Oxford, England. *Office*—Pembroke College, Oxford University, Oxford, England.

CAREER: Oxford University, Pembroke College, Oxford, England, fellow and tutor in philosophy, 1969—.

WRITINGS:

Reason and Prediction, Cambridge University Press, 1973.
(Editor) *Meaning, Reference, and Necessity,* Cambridge University Press, 1975.
Spreading the Word: Groundings in the Philosophy of Language, Oxford University Press, 1984.
Knowledge, Truth, and Reliability, Longwood, 1986.

WORK IN PROGRESS: Research in philosophical logic, the theory of meaning, and epistemology.

*   *   *

BLAKE, Walker E.
  See BUTTERWORTH, W(illiam) E(dmund III)

*   *   *

BLUE CLOUD, Peter (Aroniawenrate) 1933-

PERSONAL: Born June 10, 1933, in Kahnawake, Quebec, Canada; son of Ahriron and Wahriah Williams; children: Meyokeeskow, Ariron, Kaherine. *Education:* Attended grammar school in Kahnawake, Quebec, Canada, and Buffalo, NY. *Religion:* Native American Indian.

ADDRESSES: Home—P.O. Box 666, Kahnawake, Quebec, Canada J0L 1B0.

CAREER: Writer. Worked earlier as ironworker, logger, carpenter, and woodcutter; previously associated with newspapers *Akwesasne Notes* and *Indian Time.*

AWARDS, HONORS: American Book Award, Before Columbus Foundation, 1981.

WRITINGS:

(Editor) *Alcatraz Is Not an Island* (nonfiction), Wingbow Press, 1972.
Coyote and Friends, Blackberry Press, 1976.
Turtle, Bear, and Wolf (poetry), Akwesasne Press, 1976.
Back Then Tomorrow (poetry/prose), Blackberry Press, 1978.
White Corn Sister (poetry/play), Strawberry Press, 1979.
Elderberry Flute Song (poetry/prose), Crossing Press, 1982.

(Editor with James Koller, Gogisgi Carroll Arnett, and Steve Nemirow) *Coyote's Journal* (poetry/prose), Bookpeople, 1983.

Sketches of Winter with Crows (poetry), Strawberry Press, 1984.

The Other Side of Nowhere (poetry/prose), White Pine, 1990.

Clans of Many Nations: Selected Poems, 1969-1992, White Pine, 1993.

WORK IN PROGRESS: Searching for Eagles: New Poems; short stories; a novel.

*   *   *

BLY, Janet (Chester) 1945-

PERSONAL: Born February 23, 1945, in Visalia, CA; daughter of Raymond Thomas Chester (a contractor) and Betty Hart (a homemaker; maiden name, Carpenter); married Stephen A. Bly (a pastor and writer), June 14, 1963; children: Russell, Michael, Aaron. *Education:* College of the Sequoias, A.A., 1977; Lewis-Clark State College, B.A., 1991. *Avocational interests:* Music, literature, camping, auctions.

ADDRESSES: Home—P.O. Box 157, Winchester, ID 83555.

CAREER: Moore's Miniature Roses, Visalia, CA, secretary, 1962-74; free-lance writer, 1976—. Active in churches, including positions as choir director and Bible study leader. Lecturer at conference and workshops. Has appeared on numerous regional and national radio and television programs. Co-founder of "Welcome to the Family," a seminar ministry.

MEMBER: Christian Women's Club (chairman, 1962), Junior Women's Club.

AWARDS, HONORS: Writer of the Year Award (with husband, Stephen), Mount Hermon (California) Christian Writer's Conference, 1982.

WRITINGS:

(With husband, Stephen A. Bly) *Devotions with a Difference* (young adult), Moody, 1982.

(With S. Bly) *Questions I'd Like to Ask* (juvenile), Moody, 1982.

(With S. Bly) *The Crystal Series,* 6 volumes, David Cook, 1984 and 1986.

Hawaiian Computer Mystery (juvenile), David Cook, 1985.

(With S. Bly) *How to Be a Good Mom,* Moody, 1988.

(With S. Bly) *Be Your Mate's Best Friend,* Moody, 1989.

(With S. Bly) *How to Be a Good Grandparent,* Moody, 1990.

Friends Forever: The Art of Lifetime Relationships, Aglow Publications, 1991.

If My Kids Drive Me Crazy, Am I a Bad Mom?, Navpress, 1991.

When Your Marriage Disappoints You, Navpress, 1991.

Managing Your Restless Search: Finding Your Place of Service in God's Plan, Victor Books, 1992.

Also author of other books. Contributor to *A Moment a Day,* Regal Books, 1988. Contributor of numerous articles, stories, devotions, and poems to religion periodicals. *Friends Forever: The Art of Lifetime Relationships* has been published in German.

WORK IN PROGRESS: A book examining the phenomenon of woman runaways; a mystery fiction series.

SIDELIGHTS: Janet Bly once told *CA:* "I find satisfaction in both editing and writing. I'm on the growing edge of creative tension through team writing efforts with my writer husband. Clear, fresh, imaginative craftsmanship that glorifies God continues to be my consuming goal.

"My husband and I both believe we are better writers together than we would have been alone. We prod and poke one another in our weak areas. He's brimming with creative ideas. I picture the developed product on the page and work through the nitty gritty of depth of treatment. Sometimes we clash, but we know enough to know we've got a long way to go. Out best work is yet to come. All that's been written before is our practice. Even so, we trust it's still beneficial and entertaining for our readers.

"Since my first writing attempts and sales in 1976 after the burst of inspiration from a writer's conference, we together have published over four hundred fifty articles, stories, and poems, and soon will see our thirtieth book in print. We have other book projects at various stages and numerous other article and story ideas waiting their turn.

"We began writing together because I could see writing potential through my husband's sermons and other speaking, and pestered him until he allowed me to edit his work and submit it to publishers. When he realized they bought everything I sent to them, he decided to join me as a serious partner.

"Most all our books center either on radical discipleship to Jesus Christ, or the best of the moral traditions of the Old West. Most our writings reflect our spiritual commitments and our expertise in the founding of the West, 1840-1910. One reason our success rate in published works is fairly high for today's market is due to the fact we scout around to find out editors' needs. Then, we look into our lifestyle or experiences to see how we can match that need. That's how *Questions I'd Like to Ask* and *Devotions with a Difference* were created. We worked with youth and had teenage sons, and an editor mentioned at a writer's conference, 'We haven't had a devotional for kids or teens in over fifteen years.'

"Many of our other books came about because an editor, familiar with our work through consistent contacts, asked us to do a particular project. Religious books are selling today because people don't buy the idea that God is dead. There's too much occult activity in the world around and in the media. They know it's real and can't be laughed away. If they can find their way to God, maybe they'll find the answers to the deep questions to the apparent meaninglessness of their own existence. Even kids sense the despair of our times and are asking unsettling questions. We're just one of many pilgrims who're digging deep, to the best of our talents and integrity, to help them find the way."

*   *   *

BLY, Robert W(ayne) 1957-

PERSONAL: Born July 21, 1957, in Paterson, NJ; son of Fabian W. (an insurance agent) and Mildred (an insurance agent; maiden name, Langer) Bly; married Amy Sprecher (a public relations account executive), May 29, 1983. *Education:* University of Rochester, B.S., 1979. *Religion:* Jewish.

ADDRESSES: Home—174 Holland Ave., New Milford, NJ 07646. *Office*—22 East Quackenbush Ave., Dumont, NJ 07628. *Agent*—Dominick Abel, 146 West 82nd St., New York, NY 10024.

CAREER: Westinghouse Electric Corp., Baltimore, MD, staff writer, 1979-80; Koch Engineering, New York City, advertising manager, 1980-82; free-lance copywriter and consultant specializing in industrial and high-tech advertising, 1982. Lecturer at New York University, 1989. Gives lectures and seminars on business topics.

MEMBER: American Institute of Chemical Engineers, Business/Professional Advertising Association, Society for Technical Communication, American Society for Training and Development, Sales and Marketing Executive Club.

WRITINGS:

NONFICTION

(With Gary Blake) *Technical Writing: Structure, Standards, and Style,* McGraw, 1982.
(With Blake) *How to Promote Your Own Business,* New American Library, 1983.
The Personal Computer in Advertising, Banbury, 1983.
(With Blake) *Dream Jobs: A Guide to Tomorrow's Top Careers,* Wiley, 1983.

(With Blake) *Creative Careers: Real Jobs in Glamour Fields,* Wiley, 1985.
The Copywriter's Handbook: A Step-by-Step Guide to Writing Copy That Sells, Dodd, 1985, new edition, Henry Holt, 1990.
Creating Successful Sales Literature, Wiley, 1985.
Selling Your Secrets, Henry Holt, 1990.
Secrets of a Freelance Writer, Henry Holt, 1990.
(With Blake) *The Elements of Business Writing,* Macmillan, 1991.
The Advertising Manager's Handbook, Prentice-Hall, 1992.
Business-to-Business Direct Marketing, NTC, 1992.
Keeping Clients Satisfied, Prentice-Hall, 1992.
Targeted Public Relations, Henry Holt, 1993.
(With wife, Amy Bly) *How to Sell Your House, Co-op, or Condo,* Consumer Reports Books, 1993.
(With Blake) *The Elements of Technical Writing,* Macmillan, 1993.

JUVENILES

A Dictionary of Computer Words, Banbury, 1983.
Ronald's Dumb Computer, Standish, 1983.
Computers: Pascal, Pac-Man, and Pong, Banbury, 1984.
Computers: Cookies, Marbles, and Games, Banbury, 1984.

OTHER

Contributor to periodicals, including *Amtrak Express, Business Marketing, Writer's Digest, Chemical Engineering, Communicator's Journal, Cosmopolitan,* and *Direct Marketing.*

SIDELIGHTS: Robert W. Bly told *CA:* "I am primarily a writer of advertising copy, not of books or articles. I produce sales letters, brochures, catalogs, direct mail material, press releases, and print advertisements for clients in computers, software, electronics, telecommunications, and other high-tech and industrial areas. I've also written books, many on such topics as advertising, communication, sales, computers, and careers. My writing tends to be of the 'how-to' variety—it gives specific advice and information to a select audience, such as job-hunters, computer hobbyists, or entrepreneurs."

He added: "Approximately twenty percent of my time is spent giving training sessions, lectures, and seminars on the business topics covered in my books to corporations and associations. Most of these requests to speak are generated as a direct result of someone reading one of my books."

BIOGRAPHICAL/CRITICAL SOURCES:

BOOKS

Bly, Robert W., *Secrets of a Freelance Writer,* Henry Holt, 1990.

BLY, Stephen A(rthur) 1944-

PERSONAL: Born August 17, 1944, in Visalia, CA; son of Arthur Worthington (a farmer) and Alice Pearl (a homemaker; maiden name, Wilson) Bly; married Janet Chester (a free-lance writer), June 14, 1963; children: Russell, Michael, Aaron. *Education:* Fresno State College (now California State University, Fresno), B.A. (summa cum laude), 1971; Fuller Theological Seminary, M.Div., 1974.

ADDRESSES: Home—P.O. Box 157, Winchester, ID 83555.

CAREER: Ordained Presbyterian minister, 1974; Bly Farms, Ivanhoe, CA, ranch foreman, 1965-71; youth pastor in Los Angeles, CA, 1971-72; First Presbyterian Church, Woodlake, CA, pastor, 1974-78; First Presbyterian Church, Fillmore, CA, pastor, 1978-81; Winchester Community Church, Winchester, ID, youth pastor, 1981-82; Fillmore Bible Church, Fillmore, senior pastor, 1982-88; free-lance writer. Youth pastor in Orosi, CA, 1969-70. Lecturer at Moody Bible Institute's Family Living Conference, 1982—; member of teaching staff at Mount Hermon (CA) Christian Writer's Conference, 1986-89; speaker on marriage and family issues.

AWARDS, HONORS: Writer of the Year Award (with wife, Janet Bly), Mount Hermon (CA) Christian Writer's Conference, 1982.

WRITINGS:

Radical Discipleship, Moody, 1981.
God's Angry Side, Moody, 1982.
(With wife, Janet Bly) *Devotions with a Difference* (young adult), Moody, 1982.
(With J. Bly) *Questions I'd Like to Ask* (juvenile), Moody, 1982.
The President's Stuck in the Mud and Other Wild West Escapades (juvenile), David Cook, 1982.
Quality Living in a Complicated Age, Here's Life, 1984.
(With J. Bly) *The Crystal Series,* 6 volumes, David Cook, 1984 and 1986.
Trouble in Quartz Mountain Tunnel (juvenile), David Cook, 1985.
How to Be a Good Dad, Moody, 1986.
The Land Tamers (novel), Tyndale, 1987.
(With J. Bly) *How to Be a Good Mom,* Moody, 1988.
(With J. Bly) *Be Your Mate's Best Friend,* Moody, 1989.
(With J. Bly) *How to Be a Good Grandparent,* Moody, 1990.
Hard Winter at Broken Arrow Crossing (novel), Crossway, 1991.
Rivers in Arizona (juvenile), three volumes, Back to the Bible Broadcast, 1991-93.

The Dog Who Would Not Smile (juvenile), Crossway, 1992.
False Claims at the Little Stephen Mine (novel), Crossway, 1992.
Last Hanging at Paradise Meadow (novel), Crossway, 1992.
Coyote True (juvenile), Crossway, 1992.
You Can Always Trust a Spotted Horse (juvenile), Crossway, 1993.
Standoff at Sunrise Creek (novel), Crossway, 1993.
The Empty Nest? Parenting Adult Children, Focus on the Family, 1993.

Contributor of more that 400 articles, short stories, and radio scripts to numerous Christian publishers.

WORK IN PROGRESS: Two adult western novels, for Crossway; three juvenile novels, for Crossway.

SIDELIGHTS: Stephen A. Bly once told *CA:* "My writing career is indebted to the inspiration and guidance of seminars taught at various writers' conferences. Much of my writing relates directly to Christian readers. I also have an interest in nineteenth-century western historical writings.

"In all of my writing, I feel the necessity to aim for some kind of spiritual purpose, whatever the genre or topic. My world view, filtered through the eyes and mind of Jesus Christ, recognizes that all history and human endeavor evolves from God's eternal plans. To center my life's energies on anything less would be fruitless. So I continue to strive for increasing excellence, in order to be a better spokesman for God. I seek God's wisdom and direction at every phase of my writing, so I can communicate better to hurting, aimless readers. That is why I feel that writing for publication, as a Christian, makes me part of the 'big leagues,' although much of my writing produces smaller remuneration and recognition than it would if I wrote for big-name, secular houses. A word I write may change a heart or will for eternity. That means I am playing for the highest stakes there are."

*　　　*　　　*

BODECKER, N(iels) M(ogens) 1922-1988

PERSONAL: Born January 13, 1922, in Copenhagen, Denmark; immigrated to the United States, 1952; died of cancer of the colon, February 1, 1988, in Hancock, NH; married Mary Ann Weld, 1952 (marriage dissolved, 1959); children: three sons. *Education:* Attended Technical Society's Schools (Copenhagen), School of Architecture, 1939-41, School of Applied Arts, 1941-44, and Copenhagen School of Commerce, 1942-44.

ADDRESSES: Home—Hancock, NH 03449.

CAREER: Free-lance writer and illustrator. *Military service:* Royal Danish Artillery, 1945-47.

AWARDS, HONORS: Spring Book Festival honor awards, 1954, for *Half Magic,* and 1959, for *Magic or Not?;* Ohioana Book Award, Ohioana Library Association, 1957, for *Knight's Castle,* and 1963, for *Seven-Day Magic;* Society of Illustrators citation, 1965, for *David Copperfield; Miss Jaster's Garden* was named among the year's ten best illustrated books, *New York Times,* 1972; American Library Association notable book citation, best books of the year citation, School Library Association, best children's books of the year citation, National Book League of the United Kingdom, all 1973, Christopher Award, 1974, and Biennial of Illustration selection, American Institute of Graphic Artists, 1976, all for *It's Raining Said John Twaining: Danish Nursery Rhymes; The Mushroom Center Disaster* was named a Children's Book Showcase title, 1975; Christopher Award, 1977, for *Hurry, Hurry, Mary Dear! and Other Nonsense Poems; A Little at a Time* was named a Children's Book Showcase title, 1977.

WRITINGS:

POETRY

Digtervandring (title means "Poets Ramble"), Forum, 1943.
Graa Fugle (title means "Grey Birds"), Prior, 1946.

JUVENILES

The Mushroom Center Disaster, illustrated by Erik Blegvad, Atheneum, 1974.
Quimble Wood, illustrated by Branka Starr, Atheneum, 1981.
Carrot Holes and Frisbee Trees, illustrated by Nina Winters, Atheneum, 1983.
Water Pennies and Other Poems, illustrated by Blegvad, Macmillan, 1991.

SELF-ILLUSTRATED JUVENILES

Miss Jaster's Garden, Golden Press, 1972.
(Translator and editor) *It's Raining Said John Twaining: Danish Nursery Rhymes,* Atheneum, 1973.
Let's Marry Said the Cherry, and Other Nonsense Poems, Atheneum, 1974.
Hurry, Hurry, Mary Dear! And Other Nonsense Poems, Atheneum, 1976.
A Person from Britain Whose Head Was the Shape of a Mitten, and Other Limericks, Atheneum, 1980.
The Lost String Quartet, Atheneum, 1981.
Pigeon Cubes and Other Verse, Atheneum, 1982.
Snowman Sniffles and Other Verse, Atheneum, 1983.

ILLUSTRATOR

Sigfred Pedersen, *Spillebog for Hus, Hjem og Kro* (title means "Book of Games for House, Home and Inn"), Erichsen (Copenhagen), 1948.
Patric Dennis, *Oh! What a Wonderful Wedding,* Crowell, 1953.
Roger Eddy, *The Bulls and the Bees,* Crowell, 1956.
Russell Lynes, *Cadwallader: A Diversion,* Harper, 1959.
Mark Caine, *The S-Man,* Houghton, 1960.
Agnes DeMille, *The Book of the Dance,* Golden Press, 1963.
Charles Dickens, *David Copperfield,* Macmillan, 1966.

ILLUSTRATOR OF JUVENILES

Edward Eager, *Half Magic,* Harcourt, 1954.
Evan Commager, *Cousins,* Harper, 1956.
Eager, *Knight's Castle,* Harcourt, 1956.
Anne Barrett, *Songberd's Grove,* Bobbs-Merrill, 1956.
Eager, *Magic by the Lake,* Harcourt, 1957, revised edition, 1985.
Commager, *Beaux,* Harper, 1958.
Eager, *The Time Garden,* Harcourt, 1958.
Eager, *Magic or Not?,* Harcourt, 1959.
Eager, *The Well-Wishers,* Harcourt, 1960.
Adelaide Holl, *Sylvester, the Mouse with the Musical Ear,* Golden Press, 1961.
Eager, *Seven-Day Magic,* Harcourt, 1962.
Miriam Schlein, *The Snake in the Carpool,* Abelard, 1963.
Doris Adelberg, *Lizzie's Twins,* Dial, 1964.
Josephine Gibson, *Is There a Mouse in the House?,* Macmillan, 1965.
Mary Francis Shura, *Shoe Full of Shamrock,* Atheneum, 1965.
Robert Kraus, *Good Night, Little One,* Springfellow Books, 1972.
Kraus, *Good Night, Richard Rabbit,* Springfellow Books, 1972.
Kraus, *Good Night, Little A.B.C.,* Springfellow Books, 1972.
Michael Jennings, *Mattie Fritts and the Flying Mushroom,* Windmill Books, 1973.
Kraus, *The Night-Lite Calendar 1974,* Windmill Books, 1973.
Kraus, *The Night-Lite Calendar 1975,* Windmill Books, 1974.
Kraus, *The Night-Lite Storybook,* Windmill Books, 1975.
David A. Adler, *A Little at a Time,* Random House, 1976.

OTHER

Poetry represented in the anthology *Ung Dansk Lyrik* (title means "Young Danish Poetry"), edited by Niels Kaas Johansen, Hirschsprung (Copenhagen), 1949. Contributor of illustrations to books, including *Helen Gould Was My Mother-in-Law,* by Celeste Andrews Seton and

Clark Andrews, Crowell, 1953; *Confessions of a Dilettante,* by Russell Lynes, Harper, 1966; *Fun and Laughter: A Treasure House of Humor,* Reader's Digest, 1967; *English Drama in Transition,* edited by Henry F. Salerno, Pegasus, 1968; *The English Short Story in Transition,* edited by Helmut E. Gerber, Pegasus, 1968; and *English Poetry in Transition,* edited by John M. Munro, Pegasus, 1968. Also contributor of illustrations to magazines, including *Holiday, McCall's, Saturday Evening Post, Esquire,* and *Ladies' Home Journal.* Bodecker's books have been published in Canada, England, France, Sweden, Denmark, Italy, Germany, Holland, and Spain.

SIDELIGHTS: N. M. Bodecker was an author and illustrator of children's books whose first love was poetry. After publishing two books of verse in Danish, he began illustrating, predominately children's books, and eventually began to write and illustrate his own books for young readers. He was perhaps best known as translator, editor, and illustrator of *It's Raining Said John Twaining: Danish Nursery Rhymes,* a collection that was named one of 1973's notable books by the School Library Association, the American Library Association, and the National Book League of the United Kingdom. Bodecker enjoyed writing books for children, and once remarked, "I have retained strong emotional ties to the childhood condition and need to share my imaginings with a sympathetic audience." By the time of his death, Bodecker had illustrated or contributed illustrations to over forty books and received many awards both for his writing and illustrations.

Bodecker was born in Copenhagen, Denmark, on January 13, 1922. He received an extensive education in Copenhagen that included several years each at the School of Architecture, the School of Applied Arts, and the Copenhagen School of Commerce, and then two years with the Royal Danish Artillery. His first book of poetry, *Digtervandring,* was published while he was still in school in 1943. After the military, he did some work as an illustrator in Denmark before coming to the United States at the age of thirty, where he married Mary Ann Weld. They eventually had three sons, but the marriage ended a few years afterwards. Bodecker then lived for a while in New York City and Westport, Connecticut, finally settling in Hancock, New Hampshire. He worked for twenty years as an illustrator while he was learning to write poetry in English, ultimately beginning to write and illustrate his own books for children. "Writing for children took me by surprise," he commented in *Twentieth-Century Children's Writers.* "I hadn't planned it, it just happened."

Bodecker's sons became the inspiration for one of his own attempts at a children's book—*It's Raining Said John Twaining: Danish Nursery Rhymes.* A collection of Danish nursery rhymes he had translated for his sons, edited, and then illustrated, the volume was well-received by critics.

Full of nonsense verse, "the poems have a tongue-twisting rhythm and logical illogic which cry to be read aloud," as Margaret F. Maxwell explained in *Twentieth-Century Children's Writers.* The collection includes such tales as the one about guinea pigs who go to see the King, and a woman who takes her mice with her on trips across ice. A reviewer in the *New York Times Book Review* praised Bodecker's work, claiming the rhymes were "nimbly translated." Jean Mercier in *Publishers Weekly* commented that the illustrations were perfectly suited to the tales and called the collection "fresh and funny."

Bodecker's talent for whimsy was shown in books like *The Lost String Quartet,* in which the members of the Daffodil String Quartet, on their way to a concert, end up giving a performance of the "Spring Quartet in E Minor" using string beans, an alpenhorn, a tirelin (once a violin), and a viola constrictor. After a wrong turn takes them into one disaster after another, including the almost total destruction of their instruments (a boa swallows one of the instruments, so they rent the boa and play a viola constrictor, for example), the quartet finally arrive for their performance and find an enthusiastic audience. Both written and illustrated by Bodecker, the book received mixed reviews. The text was often criticized as uneven, or as Holly Sanhuber in the *School Library Journal* claimed, "choppy." A reviewer in the *Bulletin for the Center of Children's Books* declared that the "abrupt end" was disappointing and distracting. Critics generally praised the drawings, however, with Mercier calling them "magnetically wild." And a reviewer in the *Bulletin for the Center of Children's Books* commented that the illustrations closely reflect the "lunatic quality of the text."

Bodecker illustrated many of his other works, including *Pigeon Cubes and Other Verse.* A look at the comic realities of life, the collection wryly discusses such topics as a tulip blooming in a garbage dump, piles of loose photos that multiply before they can be put into an album, and the fate of the early worm at the mercy of the early bird. Mercier commented that Bodecker expresses feelings "in sharp but not cruel satire and just as often in sensitive contemplation." Ethel R. Twichell in *Horn Book* noted the "sly humor and . . . skillful manipulation of rhyme," and remarked that Bodecker's drawings add a "touch of whimsical humor." "Text and illustration are inseparable," concluded Peter Neumeyer in the *School Library Journal.*

In *Carrot Holes and Frisbee Trees,* Bodecker turns from poetry and rhyme to straight story-telling, presenting the tale of William and Pippin Plumtree. A happily married couple, the Plumtrees grow the best and largest vegetables in the neighborhood within their garden, and are very content—until their carrots grow to the size of a third grade child. Problems mount as the Plumtrees try to utilize the surplus, first canning, then eventually starting a post hole business (capitalizing on the size of the holes left when the growing carrots are removed from the ground). But each solution has its own problems, such as frisbee-sized carrot seeds. In the end, the lumber industry has a promising use for the gigantic carrots. Marge Loch-Wouters, writing in the *School Library Journal,* called *Carrot Holes and Frisbee Trees* "an unusual tale that sparkles with humor and absurd situations." Mercier praised Bodecker's "bone-dry" presentation, which "increases the fun in the fantasy." Mary B. Burns, writing in *Horn Book,* asserted that the line drawings by Nina Winters complement the "original and engaging" text, and concluded: "A fresh, funny story, ideal for reading aloud."

Bodecker's last and posthumously published work, *Water Pennies and Other Poems,* is a collection of short poems about the small wonders of nature to be found around a pond. From butterflies and moths, to grasshoppers and slugs, Bodecker uses his imagination as he reveals the tiny creatures for young readers. The delicate line drawings were done by Erik Blegvad, a fellow Dane who had previously illustrated *The Mushroom Center Disaster,* and complemented the world Bodecker created with his words. Ann Stell, writing in the *School Library Journal,* commented on the "whimsical reinvention" of the pond creatures, but noted that the collection often lacked the clever wording for which Bodecker was known. Nancy Vasilakis in *Horn Book,* on the other hand, lauded the "strong, insistent rhythms," and called the book a "beautiful little volume" that conveyed the "buzz and busyness" of the world of the pond. A reviewer in the *New York Times Book Review* had a similar view, and declared that *Water Pennies* was "full of small delights." Today, Bodecker's name remains most often associated with his nonsense verse for children.

BIOGRAPHICAL/CRITICAL SOURCES:

BOOKS

Twentieth-Century Children's Writers, edited by Tracy Chevalier, 3rd edition, St. James Press, 1989.

PERIODICALS

Bulletin of the Center for Children's Books, February, 1973, p. 86; October, 1974, p. 24; March, 1975, p. 106; September, 1981, p. 6.
Horn Book, April, 1977, p. 181; October, 1980, pp. 532-33; February, 1983, pp. 56-57; June, 1983, p. 318; February, 1984, p. 49; January/February, 1992, p. 85.
New York Times Book Review, November 13, 1977, p. 40; June 21, 1981, p. 37; February 2, 1992, p. 30.
Publishers Weekly, December 3, 1973, p. 40; November 18, 1974, p. 53; November 22, 1976, p. 52; April 23, 1979, p. 80; May 29, 1981, p. 43; September 10, 1982,

p. 75; March 4, 1983, p. 100; September 9, 1983, p. 64; August 10, 1984, p. 83.
School Library Journal, November, 1978, p. 30; September, 1980, p. 66; August, 1981, p. 63; November, 1982, p. 77; May, 1983, pp. 56, 58; January, 1984, p. 72; January, 1992, pp. 101-02.

OBITUARIES:

PERIODICALS

New York Times, February 3, 1988.
Publishers Weekly, February 26, 1988.
School Library Journal, March, 1988.*

—*Sketch by Terrie M. Rooney*

*　　*　　*

BONANNO, Margaret Wander 1950-
(Rick North)

PERSONAL: Born February 7, 1950, in Brooklyn, NY; daughter of William H. (an accountant) and Patricia M. (Gosse) Wander; married Russell E. Bonanno (a teacher and actor), April 3, 1971; children: Danielle, Michaelangelo. *Education:* St. Joseph's College, Brooklyn, NY, B.A., 1971. *Politics:* "Independent, with a slight tilt to the left." *Religion:* "Ex-Catholic."

ADDRESSES: Home—Staten Island, NY. *Agent*—Scott Meredith Literary Agency, Inc., 845 Third Ave., New York, NY 10022.

CAREER: New York City Board of Education, New York City, teacher of English and remedial reading, 1971-72; free-lance writer for a local newspaper, 1972-73. Acting member of Adelphian Players, 1969-81.

MEMBER: Science Fiction and Fantasy Writers of America.

WRITINGS:

A Certain Slant of Light (novel), Seaview Books, 1979.
Ember Days, Seaview Books, 1980.
Callbacks, Seaview Books, 1981.
Dwellers in the Crucible ("Star Trek" novel), Pocket Books, 1985.
Angela Lansbury: A Biography, St. Martin's, 1987.
Strangers from the Sky ("Star Trek" novel), Pocket Books, 1987.
Risks, St. Martin's, 1989.
The Others: A Science Fiction Novel, St. Martin's, 1990.
(Under pseudonym Rick North) *Young Astronauts #4: Destination Mars,* Zebra Books, 1991.
(Under pseudonym Rick North) *Young Astronauts #6: Citizens of Mars,* Zebra Books, 1991.
OtherWhere (sequel to *The Others*), St. Martin's, 1991.
OtherWise (sequel to *OtherWhere*), St. Martin's, 1993.

SIDELIGHTS: Margaret Wander Bonanno writes, "In an ideal world there would be no need for a separate 'women's fiction' or for the glass ceiling which separates 'science fiction' from 'mainstream fiction' but, in the very real world we live in, it is for some reason deemed necessary to make these distinctions. While it was not my stated goal to challenge by some personal crusade these little Procrustean boxes that writers are stuffed into, it would nevertheless seem to be the result of the twists and turns my career has taken. Someday I hope to figure out whatever *je ne sais quoi* I lack (the right degree from the right school? the proper ethnic mix?) that precludes me from the ranks of those who write 'literary fiction.' In the meantime, say that I write serious fiction; that should be sufficient. Say also that I have been blessed with the freedom to do what I do best and to earn my livelihood from it. In an ideal world, all humans would be so fortunate."

BIOGRAPHICAL/CRITICAL SOURCES:

PERIODICALS

New York Times, February 26, 1992.
Washington Post, April 19, 1979.

*   *   *

BRACHER, Karl Dietrich 1922-

PERSONAL: Born March 13, 1922, in Stuttgart, Germany; son of Theodor (an educator) and Gertrud (Zimmermann) Bracher; married Dorothee Schleicher, May 13, 1951; children: Christian, Susanne. *Education:* University of Tuebingen, Ph.D., 1948; Harvard University, postdoctoral study, 1949-50. *Religion:* Protestant. *Avocational interests:* Playing the piano, mountain hiking.

ADDRESSES: Home—Stationsweg 17, Bonn, Germany. *Office*—University of Bonn, Am Hofgarten 15, Bonn, Germany.

CAREER: Free University, Berlin, Germany, assistant, 1950-53, lecturer, 1954-55, professor of modern history and political science, 1955-58; University of Bonn, Bonn, West Germany, professor of political science and contemporary history, 1959—. Guest professor, Sweden, 1962, Athens, Greece, 1966, 1978, London, England, 1967, Oxford University, 1971, Tel Aviv University, 1974, Jerusalem, Israel, 1974, Japan, 1975, Florence, Italy, 1976, Madrid, Spain, 1976, Rome, Italy, 1979, and Seattle, WA, 1984. Fellow, Center for Advanced Study in the Behavioral Sciences, 1963-64; member, Institute for Advanced Study, 1967-68, 1974-75, and Wilson Center, Washington, DC. Consultant to and member of science and government committees of the Federal Republic of Germany.

MEMBER: German Association of Political Science (chairman, 1965-67), Association of German Scientists, German Association of Foreign Policy, Historical Association, Commission of History of Parliamentarism and Political Parties (chairman of board), German P.E.N. Center, German Academy of Language and Poetry, Austrian Academy of Sciences (corresponding fellow), British Academy (corresponding fellow), American Philosophical Society, American Academy of Arts and Sciences (honorary member), Academy of Sciences (Duesseldorf).

AWARDS, HONORS: D.H.L. from Florida State University; honorary doctor of law from University of Graz; Dr. rer. pol. from Free University; Premio Acqui Storia, 1973, for *The German Dictatorship: The Origins, Structure, and Effects of National Socialism;* Prix Adolphe Bentinck, 1981, for *Europa in der Krise: Innengeschichte und Weltpolitik seit 1917.*

WRITINGS:

(Compiler with Annedore Leber and Willy Brandt) *Das Gewissen steht auf: Vierundsechzig Lebensbilder aus dem deutschen Widerstand, 1933-1945,* Mosaik Verlag, 1954, translation by Rosemary O'Neill published as *Conscience in Revolt: Sixty-four Stories of Resistance in Germany, 1933-45,* Associated Booksellers, 1957.

Die Aufloesung der Weimarer Republik: Eine Studie zum Problem des Machtverfalls in der Demokratie (title means "The Dissolution of the Weimarer Republic"), Ring-Verlag, 1955, 6th edition, 1978.

Nationalsozialistische Machtergreifung und Reichskonkordat (title means "Nazi Seizure of Power and the Concordat"), C. Ritter, 1956.

(Editor with Ernst Fraenkel) *Staat und Politik* (title means "State and Politics"), Fischer Buecherei, 1957.

(Compiler with Leber and Brandt) *Das Gewissen entscheidet: Bereiche des deutschen Widerstandes von 1933-45 in Lebensbildern* (sequel to *Das Gewissen steht auf;* title means "Conscience Decides"), Mosaik Verlag, 1957.

Die Nationalsozialistische Machtergreifung (title means "The National Socialist Seizure of Power"), Westdeutscher Verlag, 1960, 3rd edition, 1974.

Ueber das Verhaeltnis von Politik und Geschichte (title means "On the Relation of Politics and History"), Peter Hanstein, 1961.

Die Entstehung der Weimarer Verfassung (title means "The Genesis of the Weimar Constitution"), [Hannover], 1963.

Adolf Hilter, Scherz Verlag, 1964.

Deutschland zwischen Demokratie und Diktatur (title means "Germany between Democracy and Dictatorship"), Scherz, 1964.

Theodor Heuss und die Wiederbegruendung der Demokratie in Deutschland (title means "Theodor Heuss and the Refounding of Democracy in Germany"), R. Wunderlich Verlag, 1965.

(Editor with others) *Modern Constitutionalism and Democracy,* two volumes, J. C. B. Mohr (Tuebinger), 1966.

(Editor with Fraenkel) *Internationale Beziehungen,* Fischer-Buecherei, 1969.

Die deutsche Diktatur: Entstehung, Struktur, Folgen des Nationalsozialismus, Koeln, Kiepenheuer & Witsch, 1969, 6th edition, 1979, translation by Jean Steinberg published as *The German Dictatorship: The Origins, Structure, and Effects of National Socialism,* Praeger, 1970.

(Editor) *Nach fuendundzwanzig Jahren* (title means "After Twenty-five Years"), Kindler, 1970.

(Editor with others) *Bibliographie zur Politik,* Droste, 1970.

Das deutsche Dilemma: Leidenswege der politischen Emanzipation, R. Piper, 1971, translation published as *The German Dilemma: The Throes of Political Emancipation,* Weidenfeld & Nicolson, 1974.

Zeitgeschichtliche Kontroversen (title means "Controversies in Contemporary History"), Piper, 1976, 5th edition, 1984.

Die Krise Europas, 1917-1975 (title means "The Crisis of Europe, 1917-1975"), Propylaen, 1976, new edition published as *Europa in der Krise: Innengeschichte und Weltpolitik seit 1917,* 1979.

Schluesselworter in der Geschichte (title means "Key Words in History"), Droste, 1978.

Geschichte und Gewalt (title means "History and Violence"), Severin & Siedler, 1981.

Zeit der Ideologien: Eine Geschichte politischen Denkens im zwanzig Jahrhundert, Deutsche Verlags Anstalt, 1982, translation by Ewald Osers published as *The Age of Ideologies,* Weidenfeld & Nicolson, 1984.

(Editor with others) *Nationalsotialistishe Diktatur,* Droste, 1984, 6th edition, 1987.

Fortschrift und Verfall im Den Ken des foruehen roemischen Kaiserzeit, Boehlav, 1987.

Die totalitaere Erfahrung, Piper, 1987.

Die Weimarer Republik, 1918-1933, Droste, 1988.

Deutschland zwischen Krieg und Frieden, Droste, 1991.

Contributor to books, including *On the Track of Tyranny,* edited by Max Beloff, Valentine, Mitchell, 1960; *A New Europe?,* edited by Stephen R. Graubard, Houghton, 1964; *Fascism: A Reader's Guide,* edited by Walter Laqueur, University of California Press, 1976; *Germany in the Age of Total War,* Barnes & Noble, 1981; and *The Challenge of the Third Reich,* Clarendon Press, 1986.

Contributor to *International Encyclopedia of the Social Sciences* and *Dictionary of the History of Ideas.* Editor, *Vierteljahrshefte fuer Zeitgeschichte;* member of editorial

boards, *Politische Vierteljahresschrift, Neue Politische Literatur, Bonner Historische Forschungen, Journal of Contemporary History, Government and Opposition, Societas, History of the Twentieth Century,* and *Bonner Schriften zur Politik und Zeitgeschichte.*

*   *   *

BRAGANTI, Nancy (Sue) 1941-

PERSONAL: Born May 24, 1941, in Boston, MA; daughter of Jacob (a chemist) and Mildred (a housewife; maiden name, Goldberg) Lichman; married Fausto Braganti (in airline management), March 21, 1970; children: Tanya R. *Education:* Brandeis University, B.A., 1963. *Religion:* Jewish. *Avocational interests:* Playing guitar and piano, international folk dancing, travel, volunteer mediation.

ADDRESSES: Home—Marblehead, MA.

CAREER: Teacher of French at schools in Marblehead, MA, Tel-Aviv, Israel, London, England, and Waltham, MA, 1963-80; Comprehensive Employment Training Act (CETA) Program, Salem, MA, teacher of English as a second language, 1978; American Institute for Foreign Studies, Marblehead, teacher of English as a second language, 1980; travel agent, Odina Travel, 1980-81; Abbot Public Library, Marblehead, library assistant, 1982—. Coordinator of drawing committee, Marblehead Arts Festival, 1980-81.

MEMBER: Massachusetts Foreign Language Association.

WRITINGS:

WITH ELIZABETH DEVINE

The Travelers' Guide to European Customs and Manners, Meadowbrook Press, 1984, revised and expanded edition published as *European Customs and Manners,* 1992.

The Travelers' Guide to Asian Customs and Manners, St. Martin's, 1986.

The Travelers' Guide to Latin American Customs and Manners, St. Martin's, 1988.

The Travelers' Guide to Middle Eastern and North African Customs and Manners, St. Martin's, 1991.

The Travelers' Guide to Asian Customs and Manners has been published in Dutch.

WORK IN PROGRESS: The Travelers' Guide to African Customs and Manners.

SIDELIGHTS: Nancy Braganti once told *CA:* "After teaching and traveling in Europe for several years I realized the need for a guidebook on various European cultures. Such a book would enable travelers to better understand the people and customs of other countries and to avoid embarrassing and awkward situations. Elizabeth Devine and I decided to collaborate on a book that would help tourists to feel more comfortable in foreign settings by providing them with information on such subjects as table manners, greetings, appropriate conversation topics, dress, tipping, business conduct, public transportation, visiting private homes, gifts, driving, and legal and safety matters. We interviewed approximately seventy people, including Europeans from each country and Americans who had lived abroad. Because we received such an enthusiastic response to our book, we decided to expand our scope of research to include other countries."

BIOGRAPHICAL/CRITICAL SOURCES:

PERIODICALS

Boston Sunday Globe, March 25, 1984.
Chicago Tribune, March 18, 1984.
USA Today, April 5, 1984.

*   *   *

BRANCH, William (Blackwell) 1927-

PERSONAL: Born September 11, 1927, in New Haven, CT; son of James Matthew (a minister) and Iola (Douglas) Branch; divorced; children: Rochelle Ellen. *Education:* Northwestern University, B.S., 1949; Columbia University, M.F.A., 1958, graduate study, 1958-60; Yale University, graduate study, 1965-66.

ADDRESSES: Home and office—53 Cortlandt Ave., New Rochelle, NY 10801.

CAREER: Ebony, field representative, 1949-60; free-lance producer, writer, and director of plays, films, and news documentaries, 1950—; director of *The Jackie Robinson Show,* National Broadcasting Co. (NBC-Radio), 1959-60; staff producer, contributing writer, and director of documentary films for "The City" series, Educational Broadcasting Corp., 1962-64; writer and director of "The Alma John Show" (syndicated radio program), 1963-65; screenwriter, Universal Studios, 1968-69; writer and producer of television news specials for NBC, 1972-73; William Branch Associates (development, production, and consulting firm), New Rochelle, NY, president, 1973—; executive producer, "Black Perspectives on the News," Public Broadcasting Service, 1978-79; Cornell University, Ithaca, NY, professor of theater, dramatic literature, and communications, 1985—.

Visiting professor at University of Ghana, 1963, and University of Maryland Baltimore County, 1979-82; associate in film, Columbia University, 1968-69; visiting playwright

at Smith College, summer, 1970, and North Carolina Central University, spring-summer, 1971; visiting Luce Fellow, Williams College, 1983; lecturer at numerous colleges and universities, including Harvard University, Fisk University, and University of California, Los Angeles. Member of board of directors, American Society of African Culture, 1963-70, National Citizens Committee for Broadcasting, 1969-71; member of national advisory board, Center for the Book, Library of Congress, 1979-83; member of advisory board, W. E. B. DuBois Foundation, 1987—. *Military service:* U.S. Army, 1950-53; served as educational instructor in Germany.

AWARDS, HONORS: Robert E. Sherwood Television Award and National Conference of Christians and Jews citations, 1958, both for television drama *Light in the Southern Sky;* Hannah del Vecchio Award, Columbia University, 1958; Guggenheim fellowship in creative writing in drama, 1959-60; Yale University/American Broadcasting Company fellowship for creative writing in television drama, 1965-66; Emmy Award nomination and American Film Festival blue ribbon, 1969, both for television documentary *Still a Brother: Inside the Negro Middle Class;* National Conference of Christians and Jews citation, 1988, for television drama, "A Letter from Booker T"; American Book Award, 1992, for *Black Thunder: An Anthology of Contemporary African American Drama.*

WRITINGS:

(Editor and contributor) *Black Thunder: An Anthology of Contemporary African American Drama,* Mentor, 1992.
(Editor and contributor) *Crosswinds: An Anthology of Black Dramatists in the Diaspora,* Indiana University Press, in press.

PLAYS

A Medal for Willie, first produced in New York City at Club Baron, 1951.
In Splendid Error (three-act), first produced in New York City at Greenwich Mews Theatre, 1954.
Experiment in Black, first produced in New York, 1955.
Light in the Southern Sky (also see below), first produced in New York at Waldorf Astoria, 1958.
Fifty Steps toward Freedom, first produced in New York at New York Coliseum, 1959.
A Wreath for Udomo (based on a novel by Peter Abrahams), first produced in Cleveland at Karamu Theatre, 1960.
The Man on Meeting Street, first produced at Waldorf Astoria, 1960.
To Follow the Phoenix, first produced in Chicago at Civic Opera House, 1960.
Baccalaureate, first produced in Hamilton, Bermuda, at City Hall Theatre, 1975.

SCREENPLAYS

(Story outline) *Benefit Performance,* Universal, 1969.
(Scenario) *Judgement!,* Belafonte Enterprises, 1969.
Together for Days, Olas, 1971.

TELEVISION DOCUMENTARIES AND DRAMAS

The Better Lot, American Broadcasting Co., 1955.
What Is Conscience?, Columbia Broadcasting System, 1955.
Let's Find Out (syndicated series), National Council of Churches, 1956.
Light in the Southern Sky, National Broadcasting Co. (NBC-TV), 1958.
Legacy of a Prophet, Educational Broadcasting Corp., 1959.
"The Explorer's Club," *The City,* Educational Broadcasting Corp., 1963.
"Fair Game," *The City,* Educational Broadcasting Corp., 1964.
"Gypsy in My Soul," *The City,* Educational Broadcasting Corp., 1964.
Still a Brother: Inside the Negro Middle Class, National Educational Television, 1968.
The Case of the Non-Working Workers, NBC-TV, 1972.
The 20 Billion Dollar Rip-Off, NBC-TV, 1972.
No Room to Run, No Place to Hide, NBC-TV, 1972.
Build, Baby Build, NBC-TV, 1972.
The Black Church in New York, NBC-TV, 1973.
Afro-American Perspectives, Maryland Center for Public Broadcasting, 1973-74.
Black Perspectives on the News (series), Public Broadcasting Service (PBS), 1978-79.
"A Letter from Booker T," *Ossie & Ruby,* PBS, 1987.

OTHER

Also author of filmstrips and radio scripts; contributor to anthologies, including *Black Scenes,* edited by Alice Childress, Doubleday, 1971; *Black Theater: A Twentieth Century Collection of the Work of Its Best Playwrights,* edited by Lindsay Patterson, Dodd, 1971; *Black Drama Anthology,* edited by Woodie King, Jr., and Ron Milner, Columbia University Press, 1972; *Black Theatre U.S.A.,* edited by James V. Hatch and Ted Shine, Free Press, 1974; *Standing Room Only,* edited by Daigon and Bernier, Prentice-Hall, 1977; *Meeting Challenges,* edited by J. Nelson, American Book, 1980; and *Black Heroes: Seven Plays,* edited by Errol Hill, Applause, 1989. Contributor to *The American Negro Writer and His Roots,* edited by John A. Davis, American Society of African Culture, 1960, and *Dictionary of Literary Biography Yearbook: 1984,* edited by Jean W. Ross, Gale, 1985; coauthor with Jackie Robinson of syndicated newspaper column, 1959-61. Author of narration for film, *Decision in Hong Kong,* Broadcast and Film Commission of the National Council of Churches,

1955. Contributor to periodicals, including *Black Scholar, New York Times,* and *Television Quarterly.*

WORK IN PROGRESS: A play and a screenplay.

SIDELIGHTS: Playwright, producer, director, and lecturer William Branch "is best noted for his moralistic stage productions that have won acclaim from audiences in the United States and parts of Europe, Africa, and the Far East," Clara Robie Williams wrote in the *Dictionary of Literary Biography.* "During the 1950s Branch was one of the leading black playwrights in America along with Alice Childress, Langston Hughes, Loften Mitchell, and Louis Peterson." Branch's first play, *A Medal for Willie,* depicts a family bitter at officials' hypocrisy over the loss of their son, a soldier, and a hero only after his death. "*A Medal for Willie* succinctly shows that the families, especially the black American women, who have lost their loved ones in war cannot be expected to hail their country or give total allegiance to it when racial oppression and suffering are ever prevalent," Williams noted. "Black families deserve to have a better legacy than a mere medal in the name of democracy; they deserve democracy itself."

The low level of support for black theater in the 1950s and early 1960s prompted Branch to venture into radio, television, and motion picture writing and producing. Williams related Branch's feeling that during those years, in the field of educational theater, theater departments were uninterested in plays featuring black characters; white colleges preferred plays about white people, and black colleges were interested only in keeping pace with white colleges by performing Broadway hits. Branch once told *CA:* "Though considerable progress, relatively, seems to have been made in the recent past in mainstream utilization of Black Americans as subject matter in the arts and the media, and of Black American writers and other creative professionals in these fields, my concern continues to be focused upon how much further there is yet to go before racism no longer constitutes the unspoken barrier which must almost constantly be overcome before we can then move on to more basic and realistic *curriculum vitae* such as talent, craft, and creative vision."

BIOGRAPHICAL/CRITICAL SOURCES:

BOOKS

Abramson, Doris E., *Negro Playwrights in the American Theatre, 1925-1959,* Columbia University Press, 1969, pp. 171-188, 255-258.
Aptheker, Herbert, *Toward Negro Freedom,* New Century, 1956, pp. 68-72.
Berry, Mary Frances, and John W. Blassingame, *Long Memory,* Oxford University Press, 1982.
Dictionary of Literary Biography, Volume 76: *Afro-American Writers, 1940-1955,* Gale, 1988, pp. 8-10.

Emanuel, James, and Theodore Gross, editors, *Dark Symphony,* Free Press, 1968.

Low, W. Augustus, and Virgil A. Clift, editors, *Encyclopedia of Black America,* McGraw, 1981.

Mitchell, Loften, *Black Drama: The Story of the American Negro in the Theatre,* Hawthorne, 1967.

Molette, Carlton W., and Barbara J. Molette, *Black Theatre: Premise and Presentation,* Wyndham Hall Press, 1986, pp. 122-123.

Spradling, Mary, *In Black and White,* Gale, 1980, p. 108.

PERIODICALS

Black World, February, 1971, pp. 41-45.
Crisis, April, 1965, pp. 219-223.
Freedomways, summer, 1963.
Negro Digest, January, 1968, p. 30.
New York Times, October 16, 1951; October 27, 1954; July 14, 1968; December 20, 1978; November 5, 1989; October 24, 1990.

*   *   *

BRETON, Andre   1896-1966

PERSONAL: Born February 19, 1896, in Tinchebray (Orne), France; died of a heart attack, September 28, 1966; son of Louis (an accountant) and Marguerite (Le Gongues) Breton; married Simone Kahn, September, 1921 (divorced); married Jacqueline Lamba, August, 1934 (divorced); married Elisa Bindhoff, August 20, 1945; children: (second marriage) Aube (Mrs. Yves Elesnet). *Education:* Attended College Chaptal, Paris, 1906-12, Faculte de Medicine, Paris, 1913-15.

CAREER: Major participant in Dada arts movement, 1919-21; founder and editor, with Louis Aragon and Philippe Soupault, of the journal *Litterature,* 1919, sole editor, 1922-24; secured interview with Freud after having utilized his methods of psychoanalysis and recorded monologues of patients, 1921; founder of Bureau of Surrealist Research, 1924; editor of *La Revolution Surrealiste,* 1925-29; editor of *Le Surrealisme au Service de la Revolution,* 1930-33; principal director of the literary and art review, *Minotaure,* 1933-39; lecturer on surrealism in Brussels, Prague, and the Canary Islands, 1935; founder, with others, of the Commission of Inquiry into the Moscow Trials, 1936; in Mexico, with Leon Trotsky and Diego Rivera, he established the *Federation Internationale de l'Art Revolutionnaire Independant,* 1938; guest of the Committee of American Aid to Intellectuals in Marseilles, 1940-41; following censorship of some of his works and interrogation by the Vichy government, Breton went to Martinique where he was arrested and confined in a concentration camp; succeeded in coming to the United States, 1941; in New York City, he was founder and editor, with Marcel Duchamp, Max Ernst, and David Hare of the magazine *VVV,* 1942-44; speaker for the "Voice of America," 1942-45; delivered address at Yale University, 1942; studied occultism in the rites of Indian tribes in Arizona, New Mexico, and the West Indies; gave a series of lectures on surrealism in Haiti which precipitated an insurrection there, 1945; returned to France, 1946; adhered to the *Front Humain* movement which became the *Citoyens du Monde,* 1948-49; member of the Committee for the Defence of Garry Davis, 1949; director of the Galerie a l'Etoile Scellee, 1952-54; editor of *Le Surrealisme, Meme,* 1956-57; editor of the surrealist review *La Breche,* 1961-66; organized several exhibitions of surrealism, in London, 1936, Paris, 1938 (fourteen countries represented), 1947, 1958, and 1965, Prague, 1948, New York, 1942 and 1960, and Milan, 1961. *Wartime service:* Medical assistant in army psychiatric centers, 1915-19; medical director of the Ecole de Pilotage at Poitiers, 1939-40.

WRITINGS:

PROSE

Manifeste du surrealisme [et] Poisson-soluble, Editions du Sagittaire, 1924, revised edition augmented with *Lettre aux voyantes,* Simon Kra, 1929.

Les Pas Perdus: Essais, N.R.F., 1924, revised edition, Gallimard, 1969.

Legitime defense, Editions Surrealistes, 1926.

Introduction au discours sur le peu de realite, N.R.F. 1927.

Nadja, Gallimard, 1928, revised edition, 1963, translation by Richard Howard, Grove, 1960.

Le Surrealisme et la peinture, Gallimard, 1928, revised edition, 1965, translation by Simon W. Taylor published as *Surrealism and Painting,* Macdonald & Co., 1972.

Second manifeste du surrealisme, Editions Kra, 1930.

Misere de la poesie: "L'Affaire Aragon" devant l'opinion publique, Editions Surrealistes, 1932.

Les Vases Communicants, Editions des Cahiers Libres, 1932, reprinted, Gallimard, 1970, translation by Mary Ann Caws and Geoffrey Harris published as *Communicating Vessels,* University of Nebraska Press, 1990.

Point du jour, Gallimard, 1934, revised edition, 1970.

Qu'est-ce que le Surrealisme? (text of lecture given in Brussels), R. Henriquez, 1934, translation by David Gascoyne published as *What is Surrealism?,* Faber, 1936.

Du temps que les surrealistes avaient raison, Editions Surrealistes, 1935.

Position politique du surrealisme (collection of Breton's lectures, speeches, and interviews), Editions du Sagittaire, 1935, reprinted, J. J. Pauvert, 1971.

Au lavoir noir, Editions G.L.M., 1936.

L'Amour fou, Gallimard, 1937, reprinted, 1966, translation by Mary Ann Caws published as *Mad Love,* Nebraska University Press, 1988.

Limites non frontiers du surrealisme, N.R.F., 1937.

(Editor and contributor) *Trajectoire du reve,* Editions G.L.M., 1938. (Editor) *Anthologie de l'humour noire,* Editions du Sagittaire, 1940, definitive edition, 1966.

Arcane 17, Brentano's, 1944.

Situation du surrealisme entre les deux guerres (text of lecture given at Yale), Editions de la Revue Fontaine, 1945.

Yves Tanguy (bilingual edition with translation by Bravig Imbs), Pierre Matisse Editions (New York), 1946.

Arcane 17, ente d'Ajours, Editions du Sagittaire, 1947, revised edition augmented with *Andre Breton ou la transparence,* by Michael Beaujour, Plon, 1965.

Les Manifestes du Surrealisme, [suivis de] Prolegomenes a un troisieme manifeste du surrealisme ou non, Editions du Sagittaire, 1947, revised edition augmented with *Du surrealisme en ses oeuvres vives et d'Ephemerides surrealistes,* 1955.

La Lampe dans l'horloge, Robert Marin, 1948.

Flagrant delit: Rimbaud devant la conjuration de l'imposture et du truquage, Thesee, 1949.

(Editor) *Judas, ou Le Vampire surrealiste,* by Ernest de Gengenbach, Les Editions Premieres, 1949.

(Editor with Benjamin Peret) *Almanach surrealiste du demi-siecle,* Editions du Sagittaire, 1950.

Entretiens, 1913-1952 (text of radio interviews with Breton), Gallimard, 1952, revised edition, 1969.

La Cle des champs, Editions du Sagittaire, 1953.

Adieu ne plaise (text of speech at the funeral of Francis Picabia, December 4, 1953), Editions P.A.B., 1954.

(Author of text) *Gardenas,* Feigen Gallery, 1961.

(Author of text) *Les Inpires et leurs demeurs* (photographs by Gilles Ehrmann), Editions du Temps, 1962.

(Author of text) *Un Art a l'etat brut: Peintures et sculptures des aborigenes d'Australie,* by Karc Kupka, La Guilde du Livre (Lausanne), 1962.

Manifestes du Surrealisme, definitive edition, J. J. Pauvert, 1962, complete edition, 1972, translation by Richard Seaver and Helen R. Lane published as *Manifestoes of Surrealism,* University of Michigan Press, 1969.

(Author of text) *Pierre Moiliner* (film by Raymond Borde), Le Terrain Vague, 1964.

(Author of text) *L'Ecart absolu,* L'Oeil galerie d'art, 1965.

(Editor) *Le Surrealisme au service de la revolution* (contains all six issues of the magazine), Arno Press, 1968.

Perspective cavaliere, edited by Marguerite Bonnet, Gallimard, 1970.

L'Un dans l'autre, E. Losfeld, 1970.

Communication de Andre-Yves Breton sur l'activite de la 6e Commission depuis 1965, City of Paris, 1971.

(With Paul Eluard) *Sculptures d'Afrique [and]* (with Guillaume Apollinaire) *Sculptures Negres,* Hacker Art Books, 1975.

What Is Surrealism?: Selected Writings, edited by Franklin Rosemont, Anchor Foundation, 1978.

Also author of *Le Roman francais au XVIIIe siecle,* published by Boivin & Cie.

POETRY AND PROSE POETRY

Mont de piete, Au Sans Pareil, 1919.

(With Philippe Soupault) *Les Champs magnetiques,* Sans Pareil, 1920, reprinted, Gallimard, 1971, translation by David Gascoyne published as *The Magnetic Fields,* Atlas Press, 1985.

Claire de terre, Collection Litterature, 1923, reprinted, Gallimard, 1966, translation by Bill Zavatsy and Zack Rogow published as *Earthlight,* Sun and Moon (California), 1990.

(With Rene Char and Paul Eluard) *Ralentir travaux,* Editions Surrealistes, 1930, reprinted, J. Corti, 1968.

(Published anonymously) *L'Union libre,* privately printed, 1931.

Le Revolver a cheveux blancs, Editions des Cahiers Libres, 1932.

(With others) *Violette Nozieres,* Nicolas Flamel (Brussels), 1933.

L'Air de l'eau, Editions Cahiers d'Art, 1934.

Le Chateau Etoile, Editions du Minotaure, 1937.

Fata Morgana, Editions des Lettres Francaises (Buenos Aires), 1942, translation by Clark Mills published under same title, Black Swan Press, 1969.

Pleine marge, Editions Karl Nierendorf (New York), 1943.

Young Cherry Trees Secured Against Hares: Jeunes cerisiers garantis contreles lievres, bilingual edition with translation by Edouard Roditi, View (New York), 1946, reprinted, University of Michigan Press, 1969.

Ode a Charles Fourier, Editions de la Revue Fontaine, 1947, revised edition with an introduction and notes by Jean Gaulmier, Librairie Klincksieck, 1961, bilingual edition, with translation by Kenneth White, published as *Ode to Charles Fourier,* Cape Goliard Press, 1969.

(With Andre Masson) *Martinique, charmeuse de serpents,* Editions du Sagittaire, 1948, new edition, J. J. Pauvert, 1972.

Poemes, Gallimard, 1948.

Au regard des divinites, Editions Messages, 1949.

Constellations (prose poems), with 22 illustrations by Joan Miro, Pierre Matisse (New York), 1959.

Le la, Editions P.A.B., 1961.

Signe ascendant, suivi de Fata Morgana, les Etats generaux, Des Epingles tremblantes, Xenophiles, Ode a

Charles Fourier, Constellations, Le la, Gallimard, 1968.

Selected Poems, translated by Kenneth White, J. Cape, 1969.

Poems of Andre Breton: A Bilingual Anthology, University of Texas Press, 1982.

CO-AUTHOR

(With Louis Aragon) *Permettez,* [Paris], 1927.

(With Paul Eluard) *L'Immaculee conception,* Editions Surrealistes, 1930, reprinted, Seghers, 1968, translation by J. Graham published as *Immaculate Conception,* Atlas Press, 1990.

(With Paul Eluard) *Notes sur la poesie,* Editions G.L.M., 1936.

(With Louis Aragon and Paul Eluard) *Lautremont envers et contre tout,* [Paris], 1937.

(With Jindrich Heisler and Benjamin Peret) *Toyen,* Sokolova (Paris), 1953.

(With Gerard Legrand) *L'Art magique,* Club Francais du Livre, 1957.

(With others) *Antonin Artaud, ou, La Sante des poetes,* La tour de feu, 1959.

(With Antoine Adam and R. Etiemble) *L'Affaire Rimbaud,* J. J. Pauvert, 1962.

(With Marcel Duchamp) *Surrealist Intrusion in the Enchanteurs Domain,* Libraire Fischbacker, 1965.

(With others) *Le Groupe, la rupture,* Editions du Seuil, 1970.

CONTRIBUTOR

Herbert Read, editor, *Surrealism,* Faber, 1936, Praeger, 1971.

Ubu enchaine et l'objet aime, Imprimerie de Rocroy, 1937.

La Terre n'est pas une vallee des larmes, Editions "La Boetie," 1945.

Maurice Nadeau, editor, *Documents Surrealistes,* Editions du Seuil, 1948.

Donati, W. N. Dennis, 1949.

Farouche a quatre feuilles, Grasset, 1954.

Robert Lebel, *Sur Marcel Duchamp,* Editions Trianon, 1959, translation by George Heard pub]ished as *Marcel Duchamp,* Grove, 1959.

La Poesie dans ses meubles, Officina Undici (Rome), 1964.

Michael Benedikt and George E. Wellwarth, editors and translators, *Modern French Theatre,* Dutton, 1964.

AUTHOR OF INTRODUCTION OR PREFACE

Jean Genbach (Ernst de Gengenbach), *Satan a Paris,* H. Meslin, 1927.

Max Ernst, *La Femme, 100 tetes* (collage novel), Editions Carrefour, 1929.

Man Ray: La Photographie n'est pas l'art, Editions G.L.M., 1937.

M. Guggenheim, editor, *Art of This Century,* Art Aid Corporation, 1942.

Benjamin Peret, *La Parole est a Peret,* Editions Surrealistes, 1943.

Francis Picabia, *Choix de poemes,* Editions G.L.M., 1947.

Aime Cesaire, *Cahier d'un retour au pays natal,* Bordas, 1947.

Jacques Vache, *Les Lettres de guerre de Jacques Vache, suivies d'une nouvelle,* K Editeur, 1949.

Maurice Fourre, *A La Nuit du Rose-hotel,* Gallimard, 1950.

Xavier Forneret, *Oeuvres,* Arcanes, 1952.

Achim Arnim, *Contes bizarres,* Arcanes, 1953.

Jean Ferry, *Une Etude sur Raymond Roussel,* Arcanes, 1953.

J. Ferry, *Le 81 Mecanicien,* Gallimard, 1953.

Georges Darien, *Le Voleur,* Union general d'editions, 1955.

Oscar Panizza, *Concile d'amour,* J. J. Pauvert, 1960.

Pietre Mabille, *Le Miroir de merveilleux,* Editions de Minuit, 1962.

Jean-Pierre Duprey, *Derriere son double,* Le Soleil Noir, 1964.

Konrad Klapheck, [Paris], 1965.

Charles Maturin, *Melmouth, ou l'homme errant,* Editions G. P., 1965.

AUTHOR OF INTRODUCTION TO EXHIBITION CATALOGS

La Peinture surrealiste, Galerie Pierre, 1925.

Crise de l'objet, Charles Ratton, 1936.

(With Pau Eluard) *Dictionnaire abrege du surrealisme,* Galerie Beaux-Arts, 1938.

Mexique, Renou et Colle, 1939.

First Papers of Surrealism: "Hanging" by Andre Breton/ His Twine Marcel Duchamp, Coordinating Council of French Relief Societies, 1947.

Exposition Baya: Derriere le miroir, Galerie Maeght, 1947.

Exposition Toyen, Galerie Denise Rene, 1947.

Jacques Herold, Cahiers d'Art, 1947.

Preliminaires sur matta: Surrealisme et la peinture, Galerie Rene Drouin, 1947.

Seconde Arche, Fontaine, 1947.

Le Surrealisme en 1947, Galerie Maeght, 1947.

Le Cadavre exquis, Galerie Nina Dousset, 1948.

Oceanie, Andree Olive, 1948.

(With Michel Tapie) *Les Statues magiques de Maria,* Galerie Rene Drouin, 1948.

491, Jumelles pour yeux bandes, Galerie Rene Drouin, 1949.

Yves Laloy, La Cour d'Ingres, 1958.

(With Jose Pierre) *Enseignes sournoises,* Galerie Mona Lisa, 1964.

Magritte: Le Sens propre, Galerie Alexandre Iolas, 1964.

OTHER

(With Soupault) *S'il vous plait* (play), first produced in Paris at the Theatre de l'Oeuvre, March 27, 1920. *Oeuvres completes,* Gallimard, 1988.

Also author of *Les Malformations congenitales du Poumon,* 1957.

Contributor to many anthologies, including *Petite anthologie poetique du surrealisme,* edited by Georges Hugnet, Editions Jeanne Bucher, 1934; *New Directions in Prose and Poetry: 1940,* New Directions, 1940; *Anthologie du poeme en prose,* edited by Maurice Chapelan, Julliard, 1947; *The Dada Painters and Poets,* edited by Robert Motherwell, Wittenborn, Schultz, 1951; *Mid-Century Anthology of Modern French Poetry from Baudelaire to the Present Day,* edited by C. A. Hackett, Macmillan, 1956; *Le Poeme en prose,* edited by Suzanne Bernard, Libraire Nizet, 1959; *La Poesie surrealiste,* edited by Jean-Louis Bedouin, Editions Seghers, 1964; *Twentieth-Century French Literature to World War II,* edited by Harry T. Moore, Teffer & Simons, 1966.

Contributor to numerous art, literary, political, history, and other journals worldwide.

SIDELIGHTS: In a statement for *CA,* Andre Breton summarized the scope and purpose of his literary career. "My principle objective," he stated, "has been to promote in art pure psychic automatism 'removed from all control exercised by the reason and disengaged from all esthetic or moral preoccupations' [*Manifeste du surrealisme,* 1924]. My entire life has been devoted to exalting the values of *poetry, love,* and *liberty.* I flatter myself in being one of the very first writers to have denounced the 'Moscow trials.' I have not deviated from that to which I committed myself at the beginning of my career. I have striven, with others, to pursue the struggle that leads to a *recasting of human understanding.* To that end, surrealism was proposed as a means to transform, first and foremost, man's sensibilities. In my opinion, it has not fallen far short of this goal."

Called "one of the most influential personalities of modern French literature" by Robert Atwan in the *Los Angeles Times Book Review,* Breton was both a writer of poetry and manifestoes and the founder of the surrealist movement in France. Surrealism was an outgrowth of the defeatism of post-World War I France as well as a reaction against the nihilism of Dada, an earlier art movement with which Breton and other surrealists had been associated. Dada had called for a complete nihilistic rejection of all systematic thought, particularly logic. To the Dadaists, logic had led mankind into World War I, the most destructive war in human history. Logic, therefore, needed to be overcome. The Dadaists created art and literature created by chance, according to random factors, or in imitation of primitive or child-like art.

After several years association with Dada, Breton and several associates turned against the movement. They believed that Dada's basic insights were correct but that the movement offered no constructive alternatives. In contrast to the negativism of Dada, Breton called for an artistic search beyond logic, a revolution in man's consciousness, a state of "surreality," the objective of which was "the total liberation of the mind." Writing in *Surrealism: The Road to the Absolute,* Anna Balakian explained: "It dawned on these young writers and artists that perhaps it was not man's mind that was wanting, or even the world of realities that was absurd, but the limited utilization of the mind and of the objects of its experience." Roger Cardinal and Robert Stuart Short, writing in *Surrealism: Permanent Revelation,* defined surrealism as "an impatient interrogation of reality, an endeavour to 'change life' by disputing all received ideas about the world, by discrediting the so-called 'reality' structured by an incomplete consciousness." In the first manifesto of surrealism, published in 1924, Breton called for an emancipation from logic, which limited mankind's potential, and the discovery of "something more resourceful than logic," as Balakian explained. Breton soon became the budding surrealist group's "ranking writer, ringleader, and chief propagandist, the one person with the power to embrace other writers or excommunicate them from the group," according to Leonard Schwartz in the *American Book Review.*

To expand the mind's potential, the surrealists under Breton turned to modern psychology, the occult, and the primitive. Psychologists of the 1920s had been experimenting with automatic writing, hypnosis, and dream analysis as means of tapping the unconscious mind. As a medical student, Breton read of this research and sought to apply the techniques to the larger realm of the arts. Freud's theories of the unconscious were of particular interest to him. (Breton dedicated his book *Les Vases Communicants* to Freud.) But while Freud examined the unconscious for the roots of psychological illness, Breton wanted to reconcile the unconscious with the conscious mind to form a higher synthesis. "I believe," Breton wrote, "that in the future these two so apparently contradictory states of dream and reality will be resolved into a sort of absolute reality, of surreality." Breton and his colleagues, who included, among others, Philippe Soupault, Paul Eluard, Robert Desnos, and Rene Crevel, experimented daily with writing "automatic texts" (written without conscious control of the language), recounting dreams while in hypnotic trance, deliberately inducing hallucinations and aberrant mental states, and holding seances.

With the surrealist movement's first manifesto of beliefs, Breton set forth the guiding principles of the group's artistic concerns and the means by which they had been exploring them. By 1930, when the surrealists' second manifesto appeared, again written by Breton, there came a change of direction. Breton announced that the surrealist group and its revolution in human consciousness had joined the larger communist revolution. The group's concerns had shifted from such things as automatic writing to what Breton called "automatic life," taking the surrealist revolution to include a liberation from all the restrictive conditions of life. En masse, the surrealists joined the French Communist Party, but the relationship between the individualistic artists and the doctrinaire communists did not last long. By 1935, disgusted with Soviet dictator Joseph Stalin's bloody purge trials, Breton and the other surrealists left the communist party. Along with other disaffected leftists, Breton was a founder of the Commission of Inquiry into the Moscow Trials in 1936. Although he was to remain a political leftist for the remainder of his life, and was a friend and supporter of communist revolutionary Leon Trotsky, Breton refused to support the Soviet Union.

Throughout the 1930s, the surrealist group conducted research, published books and magazines, and organized art exhibitions, theatrical performances, and poetry readings. But many of the experiments first initiated in the 1920s were abandoned at this time. There was a danger in some of these experiments, Jean-Pierre Cauvin reported in his introduction to *Poems of Andre Breton: A Bilingual Anthology.* "Collective sessions devoted to dream narration and automatic writing" took an alarming turn, Cauvin stated. "The spectre of violent and self-destructive behavior on the part of the participants led Breton to terminate these sessions." Cardinal and Short reported that "after one session of hypnotic sleeps Breton barely managed to stop Rene Crevel and a number of others from hanging themselves from the chandeliers."

Perhaps the most intense episode from this period was the writing session experienced by Breton and Philippe Soupault in 1919. During an eight-day session of self-hypnotic trance, the two poets wrote a series of hallucinatory prose poems later published as *Les Champs magnetiques.* The trance state, Cauvin explained, "enormously [enhanced] their receptivity to the subliminal messages dictated by their inner voices. In the process, they in effect became the passive scribes of their unconscious. The hallucinogenic impact of such sessions, while literarily fruitful, nonetheless gave Breton pause. . . . Breton acknowledged that he had felt at times possessed by the mental images that had emerged from such hypnotic trances, and that madness or even suicide lurked just around the corner."

With the advent of the Second World War and the Nazi invasion of France, the surrealist group broke up. Breton fled to Vichy France, a Nazi puppet state in the southern part of the nation, where he was subjected to interrogation over his activities. To escape the harassment, he moved to the French colony of Martinique in the West Indies. Eventually arrested and imprisoned, Breton managed to leave Martinique in 1941 and come to the United States to join such other exiled surrealists as Max Ernst and Marcel Duchamp. The exiles spent the war years in America, publishing the magazine *VVV* and conducting research into American Indian arts and customs.

After the Second World War Breton returned to Paris to resurrect the surrealist group, although many of the original members were now living overseas. By this time surrealism was an influence on the international art world. Individual surrealists, like Salvador Dali, Max Ernst, and Rene Magritte, had achieved recognition for their work, while the group's theoretical ideas, primarily composed by Breton, were known worldwide. His creative writings had also become known.

Breton was among this century's most influential writers on modern art, introducing and publicizing a number of important painters, art styles, and ideas. "Not only was he the first to recognize a multitude of individual talents," Short noted in *Studio International,* "he also established the order of expectations with which we still approach their work. It was Breton who first understood the significance of Marcel Duchamp's itinerary and of his ultimate silence, whose interpretation of Chirico remains the most suggestive. With prodigious style, Breton established the metaphysic of the object, drew attention from African to Oceanic art, anticipated Abstract Expressionism in the United States, and offered the most profound analysis of the processes of mediumistic inspiration in art. Andre Breton was more than an initiate in the temple of painting, he was high priest."

As a poet, Breton ranked "somewhere between the polar influences of, on the one hand, Benjamin Peret, the exponent of an integral automatism tending towards sheer nonsense, and on the other, Paul Eluard, the foremost lyricist of Surrealism and arguably its most aesthetically appealing poet," according to Roger Cardinal in *Queen's Quarterly.* As Atwan explained, when writing poetry, Breton "was less interested in exploring the unconscious than in transcribing the interaction between conscious and unconscious thought. That dialectic, Breton felt, yielded a new, disorienting form of consciousness that he considered the prime condition of Surrealism." Writing in the *Dictionary of Literary Biography,* Balakian explained that Breton's poetry has "been of seminal importance to Latin American writers. He has also had an impact on black writers such as West Indian poet Aime Cesaire and African poet and statesman Leopold Senghor, who have been guided to explore the forces of native geography and folklore and the inherent compulsion for liberation as fundamental elements of a universal surrealism."

Among Breton's most successful works was *Nadja* (1928). This novel, one of the few written by the surrealists, is a "free series of encounters between the author and a woman (apparently surrealist in life style)," as Nahma Sandrow wrote in *Surrealism: Theater, Arts, Ideas*. Bethany Ladimer noted in *Feminist Studies* that "Breton's account is a somewhat fictionalized, though ostensibly completely faithful diary, of their unsuccessful love affair." Nadja's life is magically permeated with sublime and startling coincidences, repeated chance encounters, and spontaneous, poetic reactions to life. "It is an adventure for Breton to share the perceptions in high gear that make Nadja see a blue wind in the trees and a hand in flame in the Seine river," Balakian wrote in the *Dictionary of Literary Biography*. Though their relationship lasts for only one week before Nadja is committed to a mental institution, Breton learns from her the importance of creative freedom.

Several critics see *Nadja* as a depiction of a psychic evolution, with Breton as narrator gaining surrealist revelations from his association with Nadja. She is, according to Michael Sheringham in the *Times Literary Supplement*, "an incarnation of the spirit of surrealism: another surface on which Breton can catch reflections of his ghostly countenance." Laurence M. Porter, writing in *L'Esprit Createur*, saw a correlation between the story of *Nadja* and the psychological theories of Carl Jung. "Breton's ideas reveal striking affinities with Jung's," Porter wrote. "Woman, as object of his passionate and at times almost mystical adoration, suggests a projected Anima. In *Nadja*, she guides the poet to and through the domain of meaningful coincidence which Breton calls 'objective chance.' This domain, which resembles closely that of 'synchronicity, an acausal connecting principle,' in Jungian thought, seems to hold the promise of knowledge which may lead to individuation. Obviously Breton is engaged in an intense effort at psychic development." Sheringham concluded that "*Nadja's* coherence derives from its seismographic sensitivity to Breton's *imaginaire*. As such it is consistent with the way, in Breton, surrealism was not a matter of slogans, or literary terrorism, but an existential project, enacted in remarkably innovatory literary forms."

Breton's primary project, Sheringham explained, was "to try and make poetic revelation a force to change human existence." Though the surrealist movement he founded failed to bring about such a change, a task probably too ambitious for any art movement, most observers credit surrealism with many positive accomplishments. Cardinal and Short pointed out that "Surrealism is best seen as an

exemplary search in which the expectant journey itself, as in the quest for the Holy Grail, is somehow more significant than its destination. . . . The way of feeling which is Surrealism remains alive and is still communicated through its creations. Its proud refusal to resign itself to 'the derisory conditions of existence down here,' its belief in revolt as the first stage of man's transcendence over his present limitations, its infectious confidence in his creative powers, in his real, though hidden, potential to re-create the world in harmony with his desires: the evidence of all these is available to us."

"As a writer," Leonard Schwartz stated in the *American Book Review*, "Breton was a master at catching up the tiniest prereflective rays of hope, at illuminating those instants of expectation which in and of themselves can pass over into joy. For Breton, poetry was, in effect, a strategy for affirmation, and surrealism, a complex strategy by which poetry might endure. It is to this optimism, I think, that we are instinctively drawn, and it is by the failure to make this optimism plausible often enough that we are disappointed."

BIOGRAPHICAL/CRITICAL SOURCES:

BOOKS

Alquie, Ferdinand, *Philosophie du Surrealism,* Flammarion, 1955, translation by Bernard Waldrop published as *The Philosophy of Surrealism,* University of Michigan Press, 1965.

Balakian, A. E., *Andre Breton: Magus of Surrealism,* Oxford University Press, 1971.

Balakian, Anna, *The Literary Origins of Surrealism: A New Mysticism in French Poetry,* New York University Press, 1947.

Balakian, Anna, *Surrealism: The Road to the Absolute,* Noonday, 1959, revised edition, Dutton, 1970.

Balakian, Anna, and Rudolf E. Kuenzli, editors, *Andre Breton Today,* Willis, Locker & Owens, 1989.

Bonnet, Marguerite, *Andre Breton: Naissance de l'aventure surrealiste,* Jose Corti, 1975.

Bonnet, Marguerite, and Jacqueline Chenieux-Gendron, *Revues Surrealistes Francaises Autour d'Andre Breton, 1948-1972,* Kraus International, 1982.

Breton, Andre, *Poesie et Autre,* edited by Gerard Legrand, Club du Meilleur Livre, 1960.

Breton, Andre, *Poems of Andre Breton: A Bilingual Anthology,* University of Texas Press, 1982.

Browder, Clifford, *Andre Breton: Arbiter of Surrealism,* Librairie Droz (Geneva), 1967.

Cardinal, Roger and Robert Stuart Short, *Surrealism: Permanent Revelation,* Studio Vista, 1970.

Caws, Mary Ann, *Surrealism and the Literary Imagination,* Humanities, 1966.

Caws, Mary Ann, *Andre Breton,* Twayne, 1971.

Contemporary Literary Criticism, Gale, Volume 2, 1974, Volume 9, 1978, Volume 15, 1980, Volume 54, 1989.

Crastre, Victor, *Andre Breton,* Arcanes, 1952.

Dictionary of Literary Biography, Volume 65: *French Novelists, 1900-1930,* Gale, 1988.

Fowlie, Wallace, *Age of Surrealism,* Indiana University Press, 1960.

Gascoyne, David, *A Short Survey of Surrealism,* Cogden-Sanderson, 1936.

Homage to Andre Breton, Wittenbom, 1967.

Gershman, Herbert S., *The Surrealist Revolution in France,* University of Michigan Press, 1973.

Gracq, Julien, *Andre Breton: Quelques Aspects de l'Ecrivain,* Jose Corti, 1948.

Hugnet, Georges, *L'Aventure Dada,* Editions Seghers, 1971.

Josephson, Matthew, *Life Among the Surrealists: A Memoir,* Holt, 1962.

Lemaitre, Georges, *From Cubism to Surrealism in French Literature,* Harvard University Press, 1941.

Matthews, J. H., *An Introduction to Surrealism,* Pennsylvania State University Press, 1965.

Matthews, J. H., *Andre Breton,* Columbia University Press, 1967.

Matthews, J. H., *Andre Breton: Sketch for an Early Portrait,* John Benjamins, 1986.

Mauriac, Claude, *Andre Breton,* Editions de Flore, 1949.

Nadeau, Maurice, *Histoire du Surrealisme,* Editions du Seuil, 1946, translation by Richard Howard published as *The History of Surrealism,* Macmillan, 1965.

Picon, Gaeton, and Skira-Rizzoli, *Surrealists and Surrealism,* Rissoli International, 1983.

Raymond, Marcel, *De Baudelaire au Surrealisme,* R. A. Correa, 1933, translation by G.M. published as *From Baudelaire to Surrealism,* Wittenborn, Schultz, 1950.

Richter, Hans, *Dada: Art and Anti-Art,* McGraw, 19??.

Rubin, William S., *Dada, Surrealism, and Their Heritage,* Museum of Modern Art, 1968.

Sandrow, Nahma, *Surrealism: Theater, Arts, Ideas,* Harper, 1972.

Sheringham, Michael, *Andre Breton: A Bibliography,* Grant & Cutler, 1972.

PERIODICALS

American Book Review, September-October, 1988.
L'Esprit Createur, summer, 1982.
Feminist Studies, spring, 1980.
Le Figaro Litteraire, October 5, 1946; October 6, 1966.
Los Angeles Times Book Review, January 23, 1983.
Le Monde, September 29, 1966.
New York Review of Books, January 29, 1970.
New York Times, October 9, 1966.
New York Times Book Review, July 20, 1969; July 26, 1987.

Nouvelles Litteraires, October 6, 1966.
Queen's Quarterly, winter, 1984.
Saturday Review, March 12, 1966; October 29, 1966.
Spectator, December 16, 1972.
Studio International, November, 1972.
Times Literary Supplement, October 7-13, 1988.
Twentieth Century Literature, February, 1975.
Yale French Studies, Number 31, 1964.

OBITUARIES:

PERIODICALS

New York Times, September 29, 1966.
Time, October 7, 1966.

*   *   *

BRIDGECROSS, Peter
See CARDINAL, Roger (Thomas)

*   *   *

BRITTON, Peter Ewart   1936-
(Peter Lemesurier)

PERSONAL: Born December 8, 1936, in Brighton, England; son of William Ewart (a police officer) and Evelyn Agnes (Baldock) Britton. *Education:* St. John's College, Cambridge, B.A., 1961, M.A., 1965.

ADDRESSES: Home—Pembroke, Wales. *Office*—c/o Element Books, Longmead, Shaftesbury, Dorset SP7 8PL, England.

CAREER: Teacher of French and German in Newhaven, England, 1962-77, head of department of modern languages, 1968-77; writer, 1977—. Church organist, 1952-70; associate of the Royal College of Organists, 1960. *Military service:* Royal Air Force, pilot, 1956-58; became flying officer.

MEMBER: Society of Authors, Translators Association.

WRITINGS:

UNDER PSEUDONYM PETER LEMESURIER

The Endless Tale, Compton Russell Element, 1975.
The Great Pyramid Decoded, St. Martin's, 1977.
Gospel of the Stars: A Celebration of the Mystery of the Zodiac, Compton Russell Element, 1977, St Martin's, 1979, revised edition published as *Gospel of the Stars: The Mystery of the Cycle of the Ages,* Element Books, 1990.
The Armageddon Script, St. Martin's, 1981.
The Cosmic Eye, Findhorn, 1982.
Beyond All Belief, Element Books, 1983.

The Great Pyramid: Your Personal Guide, Element Books, 1987.

The Healing of the God, Element Books, 1988.

This New Age Business, Findhorn, 1990.

TRANSLATOR

P. M. Hamel, *Through Music to the Self,* Compton Russell Element, 1978.

Horst Hammitzsch, *Zen in the Art of the Tea Ceremony,* Element Books, 1979.

Thorwald Dethlefsen, *The Healing Power of Illness,* Element Books, 1990.

Ingrid and Wulfing von Rohr, *Harmony is the Healer,* Element Books, 1992.

WORK IN PROGRESS: "*The Gods Within,* a life-to-death exploration of inner mythology; *The New Age Lexicon,* a satirical A-Z of New Ageism in all its forms; *The Many Ways of Knowing,* an examination of the many routes to self-knowledge conducted in terms of the Greek gods; *The Shakespeare Enigma,* a 'whodunit' exploration of the true authorship of the plays and poems, and probably the first to explore the whole field of candidates relatively impartially."

SIDELIGHTS: Peter Ewart Britton once told *CA:* "I spent half a lifetime as a member of the Church of England, followed by a period of agnosticism/atheism, and a pilgrimage through Buddhism and Hinduism, which eventually led me back to the inner teachings of Jesus of Nazareth. Here, thanks partly to contact with the Findhorn Foundation in Scotland, new insights resulted in a deep, though by no means uncritical, commitment to what is loosely termed the 'New Age Movement,' and in a quest for the total transformation of human consciousness, which is needed if man is to survive into the twenty-first century and beyond." He later added, "Paradoxically, that quest seems to be best served by dropping all quests whatever and learning to realize that the world is absolutely perfect as it is."

BIOGRAPHICAL/CRITICAL SOURCES:

PERIODICALS

Booklist, June 1, 1977.

Raleigh News and Observer, March 1, 1978.

Science of Thought Review, February, 1978.

Times (London), March 17, 1977.

*   *   *

BROOKE, Christopher N(ugent) L(awrence) 1927-

PERSONAL: Born June 23, 1927, in Cambridge, England; son of Zachary Nugent (a university professor) and Rosa G. (Stanton) Brooke; married Rosalind B. Clark (a historian and author), August 18, 1951; children: Francis C., Philip D. B., Patrick L. H. *Education:* Attended Winchester College, 1940-45; Gonville and Caius College, Cambridge, B.A., 1948, M.A., 1952. *Religion:* Anglican.

ADDRESSES: Office—Gonville and Caius College, Cambridge University, Cambridge CB2 15A, England.

CAREER: Cambridge University, Cambridge, England, history fellow of Gonville and Caius College, 1949-56, assistant lecturer and lecturer, 1953-56; University of Liverpool, Liverpool, England, professor of medieval history, 1956-67; University of London, Westfield College, London, England, professor of history, 1967-77; Cambridge University, Dixie Professor of Ecclesiastical History and fellow of Gonville and Caius College, 1977—. *Military service:* British Army, 1948-50; became temporary captain.

MEMBER: Royal Historical Society (fellow), British Academy (fellow), Monumenta Germaniae Historica (corresponding member), Medieval Academy of America (corresponding fellow), Society of Antiquaries of London (fellow).

AWARDS, HONORS: Honorary Dr. Univ., University of York.

WRITINGS:

(With W. T. Mellows and P. I. King) *The Book of William Morton,* Northamptonshire Record Society, 1954.

(With W. J. Millor and H. E. Butler) *The Letters of John of Salisbury,* Nelson, 1955.

The Dullness of the Past, Liverpool University Press, 1957.

(With others) *Studies in the Early British Church,* Cambridge University Press, 1958.

(With M. Postan) *Carte Nativorum: A Peterborough Abbey Cartulary of the Fourteenth Century,* Northamptonshire Record Society, 1960.

From Alfred to Henry III, Nelson, 1961.

The Saxon and Norman Kings, Batsford, 1963.

(With others) *Celt and Saxon,* Cambridge University Press, 1963.

Europe in the Central Middle Ages, Longmans, Green, 1964.

(With Adrian Morey) *Gilbert Foliot and His Letters,* Cambridge University Press, 1965.

(With Morey) *The Letters and Charters of Gilbert Foliot, Bishop of Hereford and London, 1148-1187,* Cambridge University Press, 1967.

The Twelfth-Century Renaissance, Harcourt, 1971.

(With D. Knowles and V. C. M. London) *Heads of Religious Houses in England and Wales, 940-1216,* Cambridge University Press, 1972.

(With Wim Swaan) *The Monastic World,* Elek, 1974.

(With G. Keir) *London, 800-1216: The Shaping of a City,* Secker & Warburg, 1975.

Marriage in Christian History, Cambridge University Press, 1978.

(With D. Whitelock and M. Brett) *Councils and Synods with Other Documents Relating to the English Church, 871-1204,* Oxford University Press, 1981.

(With wife, Rosalind Brooke) *Popular Religion in the Middle Ages: Western Europe, 1000-1300,* Thames & Hudson, 1984.

A History of Gonville and Caius College, Boydell & Brewer, 1985.

The Church and the Welsh Border in the Central Middle Ages, Boydell & Brewer, 1986.

(With Roger Highfield and Swann) *Oxford and Cambridge,* Cambridge University Press, 1988.

The Medieval Idea of Marriage, Oxford University Press, 1989.

(With others) *David Knowles Remembered,* Cambridge University Press, 1991.

A History of the University of Cambridge, 1870-1990, Cambridge University Press, 1992.

Contributor to journals.

BIOGRAPHICAL/CRITICAL SOURCES:

PERIODICALS

Times Literary Supplement, April 6, 1984.

*   *   *

BROWN, Diana   1928-

PERSONAL: Born August 8, 1928, in Twickenham, Middlesex, England; came to the United States in 1949, naturalized citizen, 1957; daughter of Antranik and Muriel (Maynard) Magarian; married Ralph Herman Brown, December 31, 1964 (deceased, June 2, 1988); children: Pamela Hope, Clarissa Faith. *Education:* Attended Sacramento City College, 1972-73; San Jose City College, A.A., 1974; San Jose State University, B.A., 1976, M.A. (librarianship) 1976, M.A. (instructional technology), 1977. *Religion:* Church of England. *Avocational interests:* Walking, observing, friendship, and books.

ADDRESSES: Home—1612 Knollwood Ave., San Jose, CA 95125.

CAREER: British Embassy, Washington, DC, secretary to telecommunications attache, 1951-53; Pakistan Consulate General, San Francisco, CA, librarian, 1953-57; U.S. Army, civilian secretary for intelligence agency in Japan and for medical section in Korea, both 1957-59, for European Military Communications Coordinating Committee and North Atlantic Treaty Organization (NATO) in

France, 1960-62, and for Armed Forces Network in Korea, 1965-66; television production assistant in San Francisco, 1962-65; U.S. Navy Electronics Laboratory, San Diego, CA, film editor, 1967-68; Signetics Corp., Sunnyvale, CA, librarian, 1978-79; National Aeronautics and Space Administration (NASA), Ames Research Center, Moffett Field, CA, librarian, 1979-80. Held various positions in the fields of public relations and librarianship in the U.S., Far East, and Europe since 1980.

MEMBER: Jane Austen Society, Phi Kappa Phi.

AWARDS, HONORS: Fellowship from Virginia Center for the Creative Arts at Sweet Briar, 1982; Adult Editors' Choice Award for outstanding adult novel, *Booklist,* 1984, for *The Hand of a Woman.*

WRITINGS:

The Emerald Necklace, St. Martin's, 1980, condensed edition published as *Edge of Heaven* in *Good Housekeeping,* April, 1980.
Come Be My Love, St. Martin's, 1981.
A Debt of Honour, Signet Books, 1981.
St. Martin's Summer, Signet Books, 1981.
The Sandalwood Fan, St. Martin's, 1983.
The Hand of a Woman, St. Martin's, 1984.
The Blue Dragon, St. Martin's, 1988.

Contributor to *How to Get Happily Published.* Contributor to periodicals, including *The Writer.* Author's works have been translated into Spanish and Greek.

WORK IN PROGRESS: A multi-generational novel of a Welsh family in New England.

SIDELIGHTS: Diane Brown is the author of several popular novels that place young women into historical settings that involve them in romance and intrigue. *The Blue Dragon,* her most recent book, takes place in nineteenth-century Korea and finds Brown's heroine, an unwilling missionary to that country, embroiled in the machinations of Queen Min. Meanwhile, she repeatedly encounters an American adventurer with whom she becomes romantically involved. Commenting on *The Blue Dragon,* John Espey of the *Los Angeles Times Book Review* praises the novel's "splendid pace and action . . . with its mixture of accurate history, risky intrigue, and titillating romance."

Brown once told *CA:* "*The Hand of a Woman* marked my first step away from a familiar background—that of early nineteenth-century England—that had attracted me since girlhood. Having lived in America for so many years, I had wanted to work with a background of U.S. history but feared I did not have an American voice. Still, when the story of the disastrous yellow fever epidemic in Memphis in the 1870's and the gallant work of Episcopal nuns there caught my imagination, I had no choice but to try my hand—or pen."

Brown later commented on the process of writing, telling *CA:* "Writing becomes more difficult and yet more exciting. The possibilities are endless, though to move from idea to written word requires fortitude and an infinite belief in my own ability to adequately convey to the reader the world I see in my head. I write of women in times past because, in looking back, I gain understanding of their position vis-a-vis our own today."

"Because writing is a lonely occupation, I believe the writer needs constant infusion from others, particularly other writers. In discussions, ideas generate other ideas, the yeast works, the loaf forms."

BIOGRAPHICAL/CRITICAL SOURCES:

PERIODICALS

Booklist, September, 1984; March 15, 1988.
Library Journal, February 1, 1980; March 15, 1988.
Los Angeles Herald Examiner, July 13, 1980.
Los Angeles Times Book Review, April 3, 1988.
San Francisco Examiner & Chronicle, July 27, 1980; February 28, 1988.
Spokane Daily Chronicle, September 5, 1980.

*   *   *

BROWN, E(ugene) Richard 1942-

PERSONAL: Born February 17, 1942, in Plainfield, NJ; married Marianne Parker (a health educator), June 19, 1966; children: Delia Mara, Adrienne Elana. *Education:* University of California, Berkeley, A.B., 1963, Ph..D., 1975.

ADDRESSES: Office—School of Public Health, University of California, Los Angeles, CA 90024-1772.

CAREER: University of California, School of Public Health, Berkeley, coordinator and associate of health care program, 1972-76; consultant in Berkeley, CA, 1976-77; Alameda County Health Care Agency, Data Management and Analysis Bureau, Oakland, CA, health planner, 1977-78; University of California, School of Public Health, Los Angeles, assistant professor, 1979-84, associate professor, 1984-90, professor of public health, 1990—. Visiting assistant professor at Antioch College, 1972. Founder and co-director of field studies program at Wright Institute, 1969-70. Principal investigator of a series of studies on health insurance coverage for the State of California. Member, Task Force for Health Care Access in Los Angeles County. Health policy advisor to Senator Bob Kerrey.

MEMBER: International Group for Advanced Study of Political Economy of Health, National Association for Public Health Policy, American Public Health Association, Society for Public Health Education, Delta Omega.

WRITINGS:

(Contributor) John Ehrenreich, editor, *The Cultural Crisis of Modern Medicine,* Monthly Review Press, 1978.
Rockefeller Medicine Men: Medicine and Capitalism in America, University of California Press, 1979.
(Contributor) Susan Reverby and David Rosner, editors, *Health Care in America: Essays in Social History,* Temple University Press, 1979.
(Contributor) Robert F. Arnove, editor, *Philanthropy and Cultural Imperialism: The Foundations at Home and Abroad,* G. K. Hall, 1980.
Public Medicine in Crisis: Public Hospitals in California, Institute for Governmental Studies, University of California, 1981.
(Contributor) Meredith Minkler and Carroll L. Estes, editors, *Readings in Political Economy of Aging,* Baywood, 1984.
(Contributor) Victor Sidel and Ruth Sidel, editors, *Reforming Medicine: Lessons of the Last Quarter Century,* Pantheon, 1984.
(With others) *Californians without Health Insurance: A Report to the California Legislature,* University of California, 1987.
(With others) *Changes in Health Insurance Coverage of Californians, 1979-1986,* University of California, 1988.
(With others) *Capitation and the Use of Preventive Services: A Comparison of HMOs with Fee-for-Service in the United States,* Science Center Berlin for Social Research, 1991.
(With others) *Health Insurance Coverage of Californians in 1989,* University of California, 1991.

Also contributor to books, including *Securing Access to Health Care: The Ethical Implications of Differences in the Availability of Health Services,* President's Commission for the Study of Ethical Problems in Medicine and Biomedical and Behavioral Research, 1983; *Individual and Societal Actions for Health Promotion: Strategies and Indicators,* edited by S. B. Kar, Springer, 1989; and *Changing U.S. Health Care: A Study of Four Metropolitan Areas,* edited by E. Ginzberg, H. S. Berliner, and M. Ostow, Westview, in press.

Author of numerous research reports; contributor to proceedings. Contributor of articles to periodicals, including *American Journal of Public Health, International Journal of Health Services, Health Education Quarterly,* and *Journal of Health Politics, Policy and Law.*

SIDELIGHTS: E. Richard Brown told *CA:* "I've studied and written about a broad range of health policies, programs, and institutions, but all my work, at bottom, concerns issues that affect access to health care for all persons, but especially low-income people. I try to make my research and writing relevant to the public policy process, in part by bringing it directly to public officials and organized groups of concerned people. In this context, I've presented invited testimony to numerous committees of the California legislature and the United States Congress, and have provided consultation to many private, state, federal, and international agencies.

"My most recent work has focused on the lack of health insurance, including research on the uninsured. I have been extensively involved in the development of public policies to solve this problem."

*   *   *

BROWN, Fern G.   1918-

PERSONAL: Born December 23, 1918, in Chicago, IL; daughter of Samuel M. (in business) and Miriam (Portnoy) Goldberg; married Leonard J. Brown (a plumbing contractor), November 21, 1940; children: Hal Murray, Marilyn Bette Brown Barnett. *Education:* Chicago Teachers College, B.A., 1940; Northwestern University, M.A., 1956. *Politics:* Independent. *Religion:* Jewish. *Avocational interests:* Reading, horse riding, playing golf, swimming, bowling, playing the piano, all kinds of music, ballet and modern dance, travel (Mexico, Dominican Republic, Puerto Rico, Virgin Islands, Jamaica).

ADDRESSES: Home and office—2929 Orange Brace Rd., Riverwoods, Deerfield, IL 60015.

CAREER: Teacher (third-eighth grades) in Chicago, IL, 1940-49; free-lance writer/photographer, 1958—. Lecturer at University of Illinois—Chicago campus and at Roosevelt University. Conducts creative writing workshops; participates in writers' and authors' conferences; public speaker in the Chicago area.

MEMBER: Society of Children's Book Writers, Children's Reading Round Table, Midwest Writers, Society of Midland Authors, Off Campus Writer's Workshop (chairman, 1960-61).

AWARDS, HONORS: Carl Sandburg Award for best children's book of 1981-82, Chicago Public Library Friends, for *Behind the Scenes at the Horse Hospital;* recommended book for the "reluctant young adult reader," Young Adult Services Division of American Library Association, 1989, and selection as a young adult honor book, New York City Library, 1990, both for *Teen Guide to Childbirth;* non-

fiction juvenile finalist award, Midland Authors, 1992, for *Owls.*

WRITINGS:

JUVENILES

(With Andree V. Grabe) *When Grandpa Wore Knickers* (nonfiction), Albert Whitman, 1966.
Hard Luck Horse (fiction), Albert Whitman, 1975.
Racing against the Odds: Jockey Robyn Smith (biography), Raintree, 1976.
Scooby Doo and the Headless Horseman (picture book), Rand McNally, 1976.
Scooby Doo and the Counterfeit Money (picture book), Rand McNally, 1976.
Scooby Doo and the Santa Claus Mystery (picture book), Rand McNally, 1977.
Clue Club and the Case of the Missing Race Horse (picture book), Rand McNally, 1977.
Dynomutt and the Pie in the Sky Caper (picture book), Rand McNally, 1977.
Bugs Bunny, Pioneer (picture book), Western Publishing, 1977.
You're Somebody Special on a Horse (fiction), Albert Whitman, 1977.
Jockey, or Else! (fiction), Albert Whitman, 1978.
The Great Money Machine (nonfiction), Messner, 1981.
Behind the Scenes at the Horse Hospital (nonfiction), Albert Whitman, 1981.
Valentine's Day (nonfiction), F. Watts, 1983.
Etiquette (nonfiction), F. Watts, 1985.
Amelia Earhart Takes Off (biography), Albert Whitman, 1985.
Horses and Foals (nonfiction), F. Watts, 1985.
Our Love (fiction), Fawcett, 1986.
Hereditary Diseases (nonfiction), F. Watts, 1987.
Rodeo Love (fiction), Fawcett, 1988.
Baby Sitter on Horseback (fiction), Fawcett, 1988.
Teen Guide to Childbirth (nonfiction), F. Watts, 1989.
Franklin Pierce, 14th President (biography), Garrett Educational Publishing, 1989.
Teen Guide to Caring for Your Unborn Baby (nonfiction), F. Watts, 1989.
James Garfield, 20th President (biography), Garrett Educational Publishing, 1990.
Owls (nonfiction), F. Watts, 1991.
Special Olympics (nonfiction), F. Watts, 1992.
Girl Scouting with Daisy (biography of Juliette Low), Albert Whitman, 1993.

OTHER

Also author of coloring books. Contributor of more than fifty articles and stories to periodicals, including *American Girl, Outdoor World, Midwest, Modern Maturity, Discovery, Modern Veterinary Practice,* and *Teen Time.* Contributing editor of *American Horseman,* 1977. *Our Love* and *Rodeo Love* have been published in German.

WORK IN PROGRESS: News at the Zoo, for World Book; *Linda Craig and the Stagecoach Robbery,* for Mega Books.

SIDELIGHTS: Fern G. Brown told *CA:* "I am interested in children and in getting them to read because I think reading is very important for each child's future. My slogan is *Read, Baby, Read.*" Brown recently added: "I am also working on encouraging children to write. I now have two slogans. *Write, Baby, Write* is the newest."

BIOGRAPHICAL/CRITICAL SOURCES:

PERIODICALS

Chicago, winter, 1969.
Highland Park News, December 11, 1975.
Highland Park Star, December, 1964.
North Shore, April-May, 1978.
Wheeling Herald, December 27, 1974.

*   *   *

BRYER, Jackson R(obert) 1937-

PERSONAL: Born September 11, 1937, in New York, NY; son of Joseph Jerome (a lawyer) and Muriel (Jackson) Bryer; married Deborah Churchill Chase, August 27, 1960 (divorced April, 1972); married Mary Claire Hartig, April 27, 1988; children: Kathryn Chase, Jeffrey Russell, Elizabeth Jackson, Margaret Anne Hartig. *Education:* Friends Seminary, New York, NY, diploma, 1955; Amherst College, B.A., 1959; Columbia University, M.A., 1960; University of Wisconsin, Ph.D., 1965.

ADDRESSES: Home—4205 Glenridge St., Kensington, MD 20895. *Office*—Department of English, University of Maryland, College Park, MD 20742.

CAREER: University of Maryland, College Park, assistant professor, 1965-68, associate professor, 1968-72, professor in English department, 1972—.

MEMBER: Modern Language Association of America, South Atlantic Modern Language Association, Northeast Modern Language Association, F. Scott Fitzgerald Society, Eugene O'Neill Society, Ernest Hemingway Society.

WRITINGS:

(With Samuel French Morse and Joseph N. Riddel) *Wallace Stevens Checklist and Bibliography of Stevens Criticism,* Alan Swallow, 1963.
(With Robert A. Rees) *A Checklist of Emerson Criticism, 1951-1961,* Transcendental, 1964.

The Critical Reputation of F. Scott Fitzgerald: A Bibliographical Study, Shoe String, 1967, first supplement, Archon Books, 1984.
(Contributor) Irving Malin, editor, *Critical Views of Isaac Bashevis Singer,* New York University Press, 1969.
Fifteen Modern American Authors: A Survey of Research and Criticism, Duke University Press, 1969, revised edition published as *Sixteen Modern American Authors: A Survey of Research and Criticism,* Norton, 1973, Volume 2 published as *A Survey of Research and Criticism since 1972,* Duke University Press, 1990.
(Editor with Matthew J. Bruccoli) *F. Scott Fitzgerald in His Own Time: A Miscellany,* Kent State University Press, 1971.
(Editor with John Kuehl) *Dear Scott—Dear Max: The Fitzgerald-Perkins Correspondence,* Scribner, 1971.
(With Eugene Harding) *Hamlin Garland and the Critics: An Annotated Bibliography,* Whitston Publishing, 1973.
Louis Auchincloss and His Critics: A Bibliographical Record, G. K. Hall, 1977.
William Styron: A Reference Guide, G. K. Hall, 1978.
F. Scott Fitzgerald: The Critical Reception, B. Franklin, 1978.
(With M. Thomas Inge and Maurice Duke) *Black American Writers: Bibliographical Essays,* St. Martin's, 1978.
(With Adrian M. Shapiro and Kathleen Field) *Carson McCullers: A Descriptive Listing and Annotated Bibliography of Criticism,* Garland Publishing, 1980.
(Editor with Travis Bogard) *"The Theatre We Worked For": The Letters of Eugene O'Neill to Kenneth Macgowan,* Yale University Press, 1982.
The Short Stories of F. Scott Fitzgerald: New Approaches in Criticism, University of Wisconsin Press, 1982.
(Editor with Inge and Duke) *American Women Writers: Bibliographical Essays,* Greenwood Press, 1983.
Conversations with Lillian Hellman, University Press of Mississippi, 1987.
(Editor with Bogard) *Selected Letters of Eugene O'Neill,* Yale University Press, 1988.
Conversations with Thornton Wilder, University Press of Mississippi, 1992.

Contributor to periodicals, including *Texas Studies, Modern Drama, Modern Fiction Studies, Books Abroad, Bulletin of Bibliography,* and *New Mexico Quarterly.*

WORK IN PROGRESS: A history of *The Little Review;* an edition of the correspondence between Thomas Wolfe and his Scribner's editors.

BIOGRAPHICAL/CRITICAL SOURCES:

PERIODICALS

Washington Post Book World, March 28, 1982.

*   *   *

BUKOWSKI, Charles 1920-

PERSONAL: Born August 16, 1920, in Andernach, Germany; brought to the United States, 1922; married Barbara Fry, October, 1955 (divorced); married Linda Lee Beighle; children: Marina Louise. *Education:* Attended Los Angeles City College, 1939-41. *Politics:* None. *Religion:* None. *Avocational interests:* Playing the horses, symphony music.

ADDRESSES: Office—c/o Black Sparrow Press, 24 10th St., Santa Rosa, CA 95401.

CAREER: Worked as an unskilled laborer, beginning 1941, in various positions, including dishwasher, truck driver and loader, mailman, guard, gas station attendant, stock boy, warehouseman, shipping clerk, post office clerk, parking lot attendant, Red Cross orderly, and elevator operator; has also worked in dog biscuit factory, slaughterhouse, cake and cookie factory, and has hung posters in New York subways. Former editor of *Harlequin,* and *Laugh Literary and Man the Humping Guns;* columnist ("Notes of a Dirty Old Man"), *Open City* and *L.A. Free Press.* Currently "surviving as a professional writer."

AWARDS, HONORS: National Endowment for the Arts grant, 1974; Loujon Press Award; Silver Reel Award, San Francisco Festival of the Arts, for documentary film.

WRITINGS:

POETRY

Flower, Fist, and Bestial Wail, Hearse Press, 1959.
Longshot Pomes for Broke Players, 7 Poets Press, 1961.
Run with the Hunted, Midwest Poetry Chapbooks, 1962.
Poems and Drawings, EPOS, 1962.
It Catches My Heart in Its Hands: New and Selected Poems, 1955-1963, Loujon Press, 1963.
Grip the Walls, Wormwood Review Press, 1964.
Cold Dogs in the Courtyard, Literary Times, 1965.
Crucifix in a Deathhand: New Poems, 1963-1965, Loujon Press, 1965.
The Genius of the Crowd, 7 Flowers Press, 1966.
True Story, Black Sparrow Press, 1966.
On Going out to Get the Mail, Black Sparrow Press, 1966.
To Kiss the Worms Goodnight, Black Sparrow Press, 1966.
The Girls, Black Sparrow Press, 1966.
The Flower Lover, Black Sparrow Press, 1966.
Night's Work, Wormwood Review Press, 1966.

2 by Bukowski, Black Sparrow Press, 1967.
The Curtains Are Waving, Black Sparrow Press, 1967.
At Terror Street and Agony Way, Black Sparrow Press, 1968.
Poems Written before Jumping out of an 8-Story Window, Litmus, 1968.
If We Take . . . , Black Sparrow Press, 1969.
The Days Run Away Like Wild Horses over the Hills, Black Sparrow Press, 1969.
Another Academy, Black Sparrow Press, 1970.
Fire Station, Capricorn Press, 1970.
Mockingbird, Wish Me Luck, Black Sparrow Press, 1972.
Me and Your Sometimes Love Poems, Kisskill Press, 1972.
While the Music Played, Black Sparrow Press, 1973.
Love Poems to Marina, Black Sparrow Press, 1973.
Burning in Water, Drowning in Flame: Selected Poems, 1955-1973, Black Sparrow Press, 1974.
Chilled Green, Alternative Press, 1975.
Africa, Paris, Greece, Black Sparrow Press, 1975.
Weather Report, Pomegranate Press, 1975.
Winter, No Mountain, 1975.
Tough Company, bound with *The Last Poem* by Diane Wakoski, Black Sparrow Press, 1975.
Scarlet, Black Sparrow Press, 1976.
Maybe Tomorrow, Black Sparrow Press, 1977.
Love Is a Dog from Hell: Poems, 1974-1977, Black Sparrow Press, 1977.
Legs, Hips, and Behind, Wormwood Review Press, 1979.
Play the Piano Drunk Like a Percussion Instrument until the Fingers Begin to Bleed a Bit, Black Sparrow Press, 1979.
A Love Poem, Black Sparrow Press, 1979.
Dangling in the Tournefortia, Black Sparrow Press, 1981.
The Last Generation, Black Sparrow Press, 1982.
Sparks, Black Sparrow Press, 1983.
War All the Time: Poems 1981-1984, Black Sparrow Press, 1984.
The Roominghouse Madrigals: Early Selected Poems, 1946-1966, Black Sparrow Press, 1988.
The Last Night of the Earth Poems, Black Sparrow Press, 1992.

NOVELS

Post Office, Black Sparrow Press, 1971.
Factotum, Black Sparrow Press, 1975.
Women, Black Sparrow Press, 1978.
Ham on Rye, Black Sparrow Press, 1982.
Horsemeat, Black Sparrow Press, 1982.
Hollywood, Black Sparrow Press, 1989.

SHORT STORIES

Notes of a Dirty Old Man, Essex House, 1969, 2nd edition, 1973.

Erections, Ejaculations, Exhibitions, and General Tales of Ordinary Madness, City Lights, 1972, abridged edition published as *Life and Death in the Charity Ward,* London Magazine Editions, 1974; selections, edited by Gail Ghiarello, published as *Tales of Ordinary Madness* and *The Most Beautiful Woman in Town, and Other Stories,* two volumes, City Lights, 1983.

South of No North: Stories of the Buried Life, Black Sparrow Press, 1973.

Bring Me Your Love, illustrated by R. Crumb, Black Sparrow Press, 1983.

Hot Water Music, Black Sparrow Press, 1983.

There's No Business, Black Sparrow Press, 1984.

OTHER

Confessions of a Man Insane Enough to Live with Beasts, Mimeo Press, 1966.

All the Assholes in the World and Mine, Open Skull Press, 1966.

A Bukowski Sampler, edited by Douglas Blazek, Quixote Press, 1969.

(Compiler with Neeli Cherry and Paul Vangelisti) *Anthology of L.A. Poets,* Laugh Literary, 1972.

Art, Black Sparrow Press, 1977.

What They Want, Neville, 1977.

We'll Take Them, Black Sparrow Press, 1978.

You Kissed Lilly, Black Sparrow Press, 1978.

Shakespeare Never Did This, City Lights, 1979.

(With Al Purdy) *The Bukowski/Purdy Letters: A Decade of Dialogue, 1964-1974,* edited by Seamus Cooney, Paget Press (Ontario), 1983.

You Get So Alone at Times That It Just Makes Sense, Black Sparrow Press, 1986.

Barfly (screenplay based on Bukowski's life), Cannon Group, 1987, published as *The Movie "Barfly,"* Black Sparrow Press, 1987.

A Visitor Complains of My Disenfranchise, limited edition, Illuminati, 1987.

Bukowski at Bellevue (video cassette of poetry reading; broadcast on EZTV, West Hollywood, CA, 1988), Black Sparrow Press, 1988.

Septuagenarian Stew: Stories and Poems, Black Sparrow Press, 1990.

Also author of the short story "The Copulating Mermaids of Venice, California." Work represented in anthologies, including *Penguin Modern Poets 13,* 1969, *Six Poets,* 1979, and *Notes from the Underground,* edited by John Bryan. Also author of a one-hour documentary film, produced by KCET public television Los Angeles. A collection of Bukowski's papers is housed at the University of California, Santa Barbara.

ADAPTATIONS: Stories from *Erections, Ejaculations, Exhibitions and General Tales of Ordinary Madness* were adapted by Marco Ferreri, Sergio Amidei, and Anthony Foutz into the film *Tales of Ordinary Madness,* Fred Baker, 1983; a film adaptation of *Love Is a Dog from Hell* was produced in 1988; *The Works of Charles Bukowski,* based upon more than thirty of his works published by Black Sparrow Press, was staged by California State University in Los Angeles, 1988; *Crazy Love,* based on "The Copulating Mermaids of Venice, California," was filmed in 1989.

SIDELIGHTS: Charles Bukowski is a prolific underground writer who depicts the depraved metropolitan environments of the down-trodden members of American society in his poetry and prose. A cult hero, Bukowski relies on experience, emotion, and imagination in his works, often using direct language and violent and sexual imagery. While some critics find his style offensive, others claim that Bukowski is satirizing the machismo attitude through his routine use of sex, alcohol abuse, and violence. "Without trying to make himself look good, much less heroic, Bukowski writes with a nothing-to-lose truthfulness which sets him apart from most other 'autobiographical' novelists and poets," points out Stephen Kessler in the *San Francisco Review of Books,* adding: "Firmly in the American tradition of the maverick, Bukowski writes with no apologies from the frayed edge of society, beyond or beneath respectability, revealing nasty and alarming underviews." Michael Lally, writing in *Village Voice,* maintains that "Bukowski is . . . a phenomenon. He has established himself as a writer with a consistent and insistent style based on what he projects as his 'personality,' the result of hard, intense living."

Bukowski has "a sandblasted face, warts on his eyelids and a dominating nose that looks as if it were assembled in a junkyard from Studebaker hoods and Buick fenders," describes Paul Ciotti in the *Los Angeles Times Magazine.* "Yet his voice is so soft and bemused that it's hard to take him seriously when he says: 'I don't like people. I don't even like myself. There must be something wrong with me.'" Born in Germany, Bukowski was brought to the United States at the age of two. His father believed in firm discipline and often beat Bukowski for the smallest offenses. A slight child, Bukowski was also bullied by boys his own age, and was frequently rejected by girls because of his bad complexion. "When Bukowski was 13," writes Ciotti, "one of [his friends] invited him to his father's wine cellar and served him his first drink of alcohol. 'It was magic,' Bukowski would later write. 'Why hadn't someone told me?'"

In 1939, Bukowski began attending Los Angeles City College, dropping out at the beginning of World War II and moving to New York to become a writer. The next few years were spent writing and traveling and collecting a pile of rejection slips. By 1946 Bukowski had decided to give up his writing aspirations, and what followed was a binge that took him all over the world and lasted for approximately ten years. Ending up near death, Bukowski's life changed and he started writing again. "If a writer must sample life at its most elemental, then surely Bukowski qualifies as a laureate of poetic preparedness," observes Bob Graalman in the *Dictionary of Literary Biography;* Bukowski's many jobs over the years have included stock boy, dishwasher, postal clerk, and factory worker. He did not begin his professional writing career until the age of thirty-five, and like other contemporaries, Bukowski began by publishing in underground newspapers, especially his local papers *Open City* and the *L.A. Free Press.* "It is tempting to make correlations between [Bukowski's] emergence in Los Angeles literary circles and the arrival of the 1960s, when poets were still shaking hands with Allen Ginsberg and other poets of his generation while younger activist poets tapped on their shoulders, begging for an introduction," explains Graalman. "Bukowski cultivated his obvious link to both eras—the blackness and despair of the 1950s with the rebellious cry of the 1960s for freedom."

"Published by small, underground presses and ephemeral mimeographed little magazines," describes Jay Dougherty in *Contemporary Novelists,* "Bukowski has gained popularity, in a sense, through word of mouth." Many of his fans regard him as one of the best of the Meat School poets, who are known for their tough and direct masculine writing. "The main character in his poems and short stories, which are largely autobiographical, is usually a down-and-out writer [Henry Chinaski] who spends his time working at marginal jobs (and getting fired from them), getting drunk and making love with a succession of bimbos and floozies," relates Ciotti. "Otherwise, he hangs out with fellow losers—whores, pimps, alcoholics, drifters, the people who lose their rent money at the race track, leave notes of goodby on dressers and have flat tires on the freeway at 3 a.m."

Since his first book of poetry was published in 1959, Bukowski has written over forty others. Ciotti maintains: "Right from the beginning, Bukowski knew that if a poet wants to be read, he has to be noticed first. 'So,' he once said, 'I got my act up. I wrote vile (but interesting) stuff that made people hate me, that made them curious about this Bukowski. I threw bodies off my porch into the night. I sneered at hippies. I was in and out of drunk tanks. A lady accused me of rape.' "

Flower, Fist and Bestial Wail, Bukowski's first book of poetry, covers the major interests and themes that occupy many of his works, the most important being "the sense of a desolate, abandoned world," as R. R. Cuscaden points out in the *Outsider.* In addition to this sense of desolation, Bukowski also fills his free verse with all the absurdities

of life, especially in relation to death. "Bukowski's world, scored and grooved by the impersonal instruments of civilized industrial society, by 20th-century knowledge and experience, remains essentially a world in which meditation and analysis have little part," asserts John William Corrington in *Northwest Review.* Among the subjects used to present this bleak world are drinking, sex, gambling, and music. The actual style of these numerous poems, however, has its virtues, including "a crisp, hard voice; an excellent ear and eye for measuring out the lengths of lines; and an avoidance of metaphor where a lively anecdote will do the same dramatic work," maintains Ken Tucker in *Village Voice.*

It Catches My Heart in Its Hands, published in 1963, collects poetry written by Bukowski between the years of 1955 and 1963. "Individual poems merge to form together a body of work unrivalled in kind and very nearly unequalled in quality by Bukowski's contemporaries," states Corrington. The poems touch on topics that are familiar to Bukowski, such as rerolling cigarette butts, the horse that came in, a hundred-dollar call girl, and a rumpled hitchhiker on his way to nowhere. *It Catches My Heart in Its Hands* contains poems which "are energetic, tough, and unnerving," relates Dabney Stuart in *Poetry.* And Kenneth Rexroth asserts in the *New York Times Book Review* that Bukowski "belongs in the small company of poets of real, not literary, alienation."

Bukowski's more recent poetry, such as *Dangling in the Tournefortia,* published in 1982, continues along the same vein as his first collection. "Low-life bard of Los Angeles, Mr. Bukowski has nothing new for us here," observes Peter Schjeldahl in the *New York Times Book Review,* "simply more and still more accounts in free verse of his follies with alcohol and women and of fellow losers hitting bottom and somehow discovering new ways to continue falling." Despite the subject matter, though, Schjeldahl finds himself enjoying the poems in *Dangling in the Tournefortia.* "Bukowski writes well," he continues, "with ear-pleasing cadences, wit and perfect clarity, which are all the more beguiling for issuing from a stumblebum persona. His grace with words gives a comic gleam to even his meanest revelations." William Logan, writing in the *Times Literary Supplement,* concludes: "Life here has almost entirely mastered art."

Similar to his poetry in subject matter, Bukowski's short stories also deal with sex, violence, and the absurdities of life. In his first collection of short stories, *Erections, Ejaculations, Exhibitions, and General Tales of Ordinary Madness,* later abridged and published as *Life and Death in the Charity Ward,* Bukowski "writes as an unregenerate lowbrow contemptuous of our claims to superior being," describes Thomas R. Edwards in the *New York Review of Books.* On the other hand, Peter Ackroyd maintains in the

Spectator, "A dull character finally emerges, and it is a dullness which spreads through these stories like a stain." Thomas, however, concludes that "in some of these sad and funny stories [Bukowski's] status as a relic isn't wholly without its sanctity."

The protagonists in the stories in *Hot Water Music,* published in 1983, live in cheap hotels and are often struggling underground writers, similar to Bukowski himself. Bukowski's main autobiographical figure is Henry Chinaski, who appears in a few of these stories and in many of his novels. Among the semi-autobiographical stories in this collection are two which deal with events following the funeral of Bukowski's father. The other stories deal with numerous violent acts, including a jealous wife shooting her husband over an old infidelity, a drunk bank manager molesting young children, a former stripper mutilating the man she is seducing, and a young man who gets over his impotence by raping a neighbor in his apartment elevator. "Lives of quiet desperation explode in apparently random and unmotivated acts of bizarre violence," describes Michael F. Harper in the *Los Angeles Times Book Review,* adding: "There is certainly a raw power in these stories, but Bukowski's hard-boiled fatalism seems to me the flip side of the humanism he denies and therefore just as false as the sentimentality he ridicules." Erling Friis-Baastad, writing in the Toronto *Globe and Mail,* concludes, "In his best work, Bukowski comes close to making us comprehend, if not the sense of it all, then at least its intensity. He cannot forget, and he will not let us forget, that every morning at 3 a.m. broken people lie 'in their beds, trying in vain to sleep, and deserving that rest, if they could find it.' "

Bukowski continues his examination of "broken people" in such novels as *Post Office* and *Ham on Rye.* In *Post Office,* Henry Chinaski is very similar to ex-postman Bukowski; he is a remorseless drunk and womanizer who spends a lot of time at the race track. Chinaski also has to deal with his monotonous and strenuous job, as well as a number of harassing supervisors. Eventually marrying a rich nymphomaniac from Texas, Chinaski is inevitably dumped for another man and finds himself back at the post office. "Bukowski's loser's string of anecdotes, convulsively funny and also sad, is unflagging entertainment but in the end doesn't add up to more than the sum of its parts, somehow missing the novelist's alchemy," asserts a *Times Literary Supplement* contributor. But Valentine Cunningham, also writing in the *Times Literary Supplement,* sees the novel as a success: "Pressed in by Post Office bureaucrats, their mean-minded regulations and their heaps of paperwork, the misfit [Chinaski] looks frequently like an angel of light. His refusal to play respectability ball with the cajoling, abusive, never-take-no-for-an-answer loops who own the mailboxes he attends . . . can make

even this ribald mess of a wretch seem a shining haven of sanity in the prevailing Los Angeles grimnesses."

Ham on Rye, published in 1982, also features Henry Chinaski as its protagonist. Bukowski travels into new territory with this novel, describing his/Chinaski's childhood and adolescent years. The first part of the book is dominated by Chinaski's brutal and domineering father, focusing more on Henry as he moves into his lonely and isolated adolescent years. Following high school, Chinaski holds a job and attends college for a short period of time before beginning his "real" life of cheap hotels, sleazy bars, and the track. It is also at this time that Henry starts to send stories to magazines and accumulate a number of rejection slips. "Particularly striking is Bukowski's uncharacteristic restraint: the prose is hard and exact, the writer's impulse towards egocentricity repressed," comments David Montrose in the *Times Literary Supplement.* Ben Reuven, writing in the *Los Angeles Times Book Review,* describes the "first-person reminiscences" in *Ham on Rye* as being "taut, vivid, intense, sometimes poignant, [and] often hilarious," concluding that Bukowski's "prose has never been more vigorous or more powerful."

Continuing the examination of his younger years, Bukowski wrote the screenplay for the movie *Barfly,* which was released in 1987, starring Mickey Rourke. The movie focuses on three days in the life of Bukowski at the age of twenty-four. As the lead character, Henry Chinaski, Rourke spends most of these three days in a seedy bar, where he meets the first real love of his life, Wanda, played by Faye Dunaway. While this new romance is developing, a beautiful literary editor takes an interest in Chinaski's writings, and tries to seduce him with success. Chinaski must then choose between the two women. "At first *Barfly* seems merely a slice of particularly wretched life," observes David Ansen in *Newsweek.* "But under its seedy surface emerges a cunning comedy—and a touching love story." Vincent Canby, writing in the *New York Times,* sees the film as dealing "in the continuing revelation of character in a succession of horrifying, buoyant, crazy confrontations of barflies, bartenders, police and other representatives of the world of the sober." And Michael Wilmington concludes in the *Los Angeles Times:* "Whatever its flaws, [*Barfly*] does something more films should do: It opens up territory, opens up a human being. The worst of it has the edge of coughed-up whimsy and barroom bragging. But the best has the shock of truth and the harsh sweet kiss of dreams."

Bukowski's experiences with the making of *Barfly* became the basis of his 1989 novel *Hollywood.* Chinaski is now an old man, married to Sarah, a shrewd woman apt to interrupt him during his many repetitive stories. The couple is off hard liquor, but are faithful drinkers of good red wine, and their life is a peaceful one until a filmmaker asks

Chinaski to write a screenplay based upon his previous lifestyle; he agrees, figuring that this new venture will leave him enough time to spend at the track. Entering the world of show business, Chinaski finds himself mingling with famous stars, but must also deal with a number of other things, including a tax man (who advises him to spend his advance money before the government can get it). As the project progresses, its funding becomes shaky, the producer threatens to dismember parts of his body if the movie is not made, there are many rewrites, and Chinaski is hit with a terrible sadness. The movie is about what he used to be—a poetic barfly—and covers a time in his life when he feels he did his best writing. An old man now, Chinaski can watch his life being acted out at the movies, but he cannot jump back into it; he is now a successful man leading a respectable life. "The words often jar and Bukowski is better when he lets his dialogue do his griping for him. But this is still a superb snapshot of what filmmaking at the fag-end of the Hollywood dream is all about," relates Toby Moore in the *Times Literary Supplement.* Gary Dretzka, writing in the *Chicago Tribune,* asserts that "Bukowski offers an often insightful and continually outrageous view of how some movies get made." Dretzka goes on to advise: "Have some fun: Read this book, then go out and rent the *Barfly* video. Grab a beer and offer a toast to Charles Bukowski—survivor."

Like Dretzka, Kessler also believes in Bukowski's survival abilities, concluding that he "is a soulful poet whose art is an ongoing testimony to perseverance. It's not the drinking and f---ing and gambling and fighting and shitting that make his books valuable, but the meticulous attention to the most mundane experience, the crusty compassion for his fellow losers, the implicit conviction that by frankly telling the unglamorous facts of hopelessness some stamina and courage can be cultivated."

BIOGRAPHICAL/CRITICAL SOURCES:

BOOKS

Contemporary Literary Criticism, Gale, Volume 2, 1974, Volume 5, 1976, Volume 9, 1978, Volume 41, 1987.
Contemporary Novelists, 4th edition, edited by D. L. Kirkpatrick, St. James Press, 1986.
Dictionary of Literary Biography, Volume 5: *American Poets since World War II,* Gale, 1980.
Dorbin, Sanford, *A Bibliography of Charles Bukowski,* Black Sparrow Press, 1969.
Fox, Hugh, *Charles Bukowski: A Critical and Bibliographical Study,* Abyss Publications, 1969.
Sherman, Jory, *Bukowski: Friendship, Fame, and Bestial Myth,* Blue Horse Press, 1982.
Weinberg, Jeffrey, editor, *A Charles Bukowski Checklist,* Water Row Press, 1987.

PERIODICALS

Chicago Tribune, July 18, 1989.
Globe and Mail (Toronto), January 21, 1984.
Los Angeles Times, March 17, 1983; November 3, 1987; November 5, 1987; September 23, 1988.
Los Angeles Times Book Review, October 3, 1982, p. 6; August 28, 1983, p. 6; December 11, 1983, p. 2; March 17, 1985, p. 4; November 3, 1987; June 4, 1989, p. 4.
Los Angeles Times Magazine, March 22, 1987, pp. 12-14, 17-19, 23.
Newsweek, October 26, 1987, p. 86.
New York Review of Books, October 5, 1972, pp. 21-23.
New York Times, September 30, 1987.
New York Times Book Review, July 5, 1964, p. 5; January 17, 1982, pp. 13, 16; June 11, 1989, p. 11; November 25, 1990, p. 19.
Northwest Review, fall, 1963, pp. 123-29.
Outsider, spring, 1963, pp. 62-65.
People, November 16, 1987, pp. 79-80.
Poetry, July, 1964, pp. 258-64.
Review of Contemporary Fiction, fall, 1985, pp. 56-59.
San Francisco Review of Books, January-February, 1983, p. 11.
Spectator, November 30, 1974.
Times (London), March 3, 1988; July 8, 1989.
Times Literary Supplement, April 5, 1974, p. 375; June 20, 1980, p. 706; September 4, 1981, p. 1000; November 12, 1982, p. 1251; December 3, 1982, p. 1344; May 4, 1984, p. 486; August 11, 1989, p. 877; September 7, 1990, p. 956.
Village Voice, March 26, 1964, pp. 11-12; February 20, 1978, pp. 89-90; March 23, 1982, pp. 42-43.
Washington Post, November 20, 1987.

—*Sketch by Susan M. Reicha*

*   *   *

BULLA, Clyde Robert   1914-

PERSONAL: Born January 9, 1914, in King City, MO; son of Julian and Sarah (Henson) Bulla. *Education:* "Largely self-educated." *Avocational interests:* Music, painting in oils and water colors, travel.

ADDRESSES: Home—1230 Las Flores Dr., Los Angeles, CA 90041.

CAREER: Children's writer and composer. Linotype operator and columnist, *Tri-County News,* King City, MO, 1943-49.

MEMBER: Authors League of America, Authors Guild, Society of Children's Book Writers.

AWARDS, HONORS: Boys' Clubs of America Gold Medal, 1955, for *Squanto, Friend of the White Men;* Authors Club of Los Angeles award for outstanding juvenile book by Southern California author, 1961, for *Benito;* Southern California Council on Children's Literature award, 1962, for distinguished contribution to field of children's literature, and 1975, for *Shoeshine Girl;* George F. Stone Center for Children's Books award, 1968, for *White Bird;* Commonwealth Club of California silver medal, 1970, for *Jonah and the Great Fish;* Christopher Award, 1971, for *Pocahontas and the Strangers; Noah and the Rainbow: An Ancient Story* was selected as a Children's Book Showcase title, 1973; Charlie May Simon Award, 1978, Sequoyah Children's Book Award, 1978, and South Carolina School Children award, 1980, all for *Shoeshine Girl; A Lion to Guard Us* was selected as a Notable Children's Trade Book in Social Studies, 1982.

WRITINGS:

These Bright Young Dreams, Penn, 1941.
The Donkey Cart, Crowell, 1946.
Riding the Pony Express, Crowell, 1948.
The Secret Valley, Crowell, 1949.
Surprise for a Cowboy, Crowell, 1950.
A Ranch for Danny, Crowell, 1951.
Song of St. Francis, Crowell, 1952.
Johnny Hong of Chinatown, Crowell, 1952.
Eagle Feather, Crowell, 1953.
Star of Wild Horse Canyon, Crowell, 1953.
Down the Mississippi, Crowell, 1954.
Squanto, Friend of the White Men, Crowell, 1954, published as *Squanto: Friend of the Pilgrims,* Scholastic Inc., 1971.
A Dog Named Penny, Ginn, 1955.
White Sails to China, Crowell, 1955.
The Poppy Seeds, Crowell, 1955.
John Billington: Friend of Squanto, Crowell, 1956.
The Sword in the Tree, Crowell, 1956.
Old Charlie, Crowell, 1957.
Ghost Town Treasure, Crowell, 1957.
Pirate's Promise, Crowell, 1958.
The Valentine Cat, Crowell, 1959.
Stories of Favorite Operas, Crowell, 1959.
Three-Dollar Mule, Crowell, 1960.
A Tree Is a Plant, Crowell, 1960.
The Sugar Pear Tree, Crowell, 1960.
Benito, Crowell, 1961.
The Ring and the Fire: Stories from Wagner's Niebelung Operas, Crowell, 1962.
What Makes a Shadow?, Crowell, 1962.
Viking Adventure, Crowell, 1963.
Indian Hill, Crowell, 1963.
St. Valentine's Day, Crowell, 1965.
More Stories of Favorite Operas, Crowell, 1965.
Lincoln's Birthday, Crowell, 1966.
White Bird, Crowell, 1966.

Washington's Birthday, Crowell, 1967.
Flowerpot Gardens, Crowell, 1967.
The Ghost of Windy Hill, Crowell, 1968.
Mika's Apple Tree: A Story of Finland, Crowell, 1968.
Stories of Gilbert & Sullivan Operas, Crowell, 1968.
New Boy in Dublin: A Story of Ireland, Crowell, 1969.
The Moon Singer, Crowell, 1969.
Jonah and the Great Fish, Crowell, 1970.
Pocahontas and the Strangers, Crowell, 1971.
Joseph the Dreamer, Crowell, 1971.
Open the Door and See All the People, Crowell, 1972.
Noah and the Rainbow (adapted from a story by Max Bollinger), Crowell, 1972.
Dexter, Crowell, 1973.
The Wish at the Top, Crowell, 1974.
Shoeshine Girl, Crowell, 1975.
Marco Moonlight, Crowell, 1976.
The Beast of Lor, Crowell, 1977.
(With Michael Syson) *Conquista!,* Crowell, 1978.
Keep Running, Allen!, Crowell, 1978.
Last Look, Crowell, 1979.
Daniel's Duck, Harper, 1979.
The Stubborn Old Woman, Crowell, 1980.
My Friend, the Monster, Crowell, 1980.
Almost a Hero, Dutton, 1981.
A Lion to Guard Us, Crowell, 1981.
Dandelion Hill, Dutton, 1982.
Poor Boy, Rich Boy, Harper, 1982.
Charlie's House, Crowell, 1983.
The Cardboard Crown, Crowell, 1984.
A Grain of Wheat: A Writer Begins, David Godine, 1985.
The Chalk Box Kid, Random House, 1987.
Singing Sam, Random House, 1989.
The Christmas Coat, Knopf, 1990.

COMPOSER OF MUSIC FOR SONG BOOKS; LYRICS BY LOIS LENSKI

Cotton in My Sack, Lippincott, 1949.
I Like Winter, Walck, 1950.
Prairie School, Lippincott, 1951.
We Are Thy Children, Crowell, 1952.
Mamma Hattie's Girl, Lippincott, 1953.
On a Summer Day, Walck, 1953.
Corn-Farm Boy, Lippincott, 1954.
Songs of Mr. Small, Oxford University Press, 1954.
A Dog Came to School, Oxford University Press, 1955.
Songs of the City, Edward B. Marks Music Corp., 1956.
Up to Six: Book I, Hansen Music, 1956.
Flood Friday, Lippincott, 1956.
Davy and Dog, Walck, 1957.
I Went for a Walk, Walck, 1958.
At Our House, Walck, 1959.
When I Grow Up, Walck, 1960.

Also composer of incidental music for plays *The Bean Pickers, A Change of Heart,* and *Strangers in a Strange Land,* all written by Lois Lenski, all published by the National Council of Churches, 1952; composer of librettos for two unproduced operas.

ADAPTATIONS: The Moon Singer was adapted into an orchestration, with music by William Winstead, first performed at the Academy of Music, by the Philadelphia Orchestra, 1972; *Shoeshine Girl* was adapted into a film produced by Learning Corporation of America, 1980.

SIDELIGHTS: Clyde Robert Bulla once told *CA:* "When young writers ask me for advice, I tell them: 'Read a lot. Write a lot. Keep looking, listening, and wondering.' "

BIOGRAPHICAL/CRITICAL SOURCES:

BOOKS

American Bicentennial Reading, Children's Book Council, 1975.
Arbuthnot, May Hill, *Children and Books,* 3rd edition, Scott, Foresman, 1964.
Books for Children, 1960-1965, American Library Association, 1966.
Bulla, Clyde Robert, *A Grain of Wheat: A Writer Begins,* Godine, 1985.
Bulla, essay in *Something about the Author Autobiography Series,* Volume 6, Gale, 1988.
The Children's Bookshelf, Child Study Association of America, 1965.
Hopkins, Lee Bennett, *Books Are by People,* Citation Press, 1969.
Huck and Young, *Children's Literature in the Elementary School,* Holt, 1961.
Larrick, Nancy, *A Teacher's Guide to Children's Books,* Merrill, 1966.

PERIODICALS

Cricket, November, 1980.
Elementary English, November, 1971.
Writer, December, 1948; December, 1954.

*   *   *

BURNLEY, (John) David 1941-

PERSONAL: Born October 22, 1941, in Wakefield, England; son of Jack (a civil servant) and Barbara (Hall) Burnley; married Helen Dowell (a teacher), September 3, 1965; children: Emma, Richard. *Education:* University of Durham, B.A., 1964, M.A., 1967, Ph.D., 1973; University of Exeter, P.G.C.E., 1965.

ADDRESSES: Home—69 Whirlowdale Road, Sheffield S7 2NF, England. *Office*—Department of English Language, University of Sheffield, Sheffield 510 2TN, England.

CAREER: University of Lancaster, Bailrigg, England, lecturer in English, 1969-73; University of Sheffield, Sheffield, England, lecturer, 1973-83, senior lecturer, 1983-1990, reader in English language and linguistics, 1990—.

MEMBER: International Courtly Literature Society, Early English Text Society, New Chaucer Society, Medieval Academy of America, Henry Sweet Society.

WRITINGS:

Chaucer's Language and the Philosophers' Tradition, Rowman & Littlefield, 1979.
A Guide to Chaucer's Language, University of Oklahoma Press, 1983, reissued as *The Language of Chaucer,* 1989.
The History of the English Language: A Sourcebook, Longman, 1992.
(With M. Tajima) *Annotated Bibliography of the Language of Middle English Literature,* D. S. Brewer, 1993.

WORK IN PROGRESS: A book on courtliness in medieval England.

SIDELIGHTS: British educator David Burnley is the author of several books that focus upon the works of Geoffrey Chaucer, whose *Canterbury Tales* is one of the cornerstones in any study of English literature. In a review of *A Guide to Chaucer's Language,* published in 1983, Chris Pasles notes in the *Los Angeles Times Book Review* that author Burnley "traces with intellectual delight the warp and woof of one of England's great 14th-century poets."

Divided into two sections, *A Guide to Chaucer's Language* includes a survey of the grammatical conventions of Middle English, and incorporates into its second part a lengthy discussion of both the context and meaning of the language of Chaucer's epoch. *Times Literary Supplement* reviewer Bernard O'Donoughue deemed Burnley's book to be valuable as a guide "through the places where the reader might go wrong by analogy with modern English."

Burnley once told *CA:* "In my book *Chaucer's Language and the Philosophers' Tradition,* I sought to investigate through their language and usage some of the conceptual structures in moral psychology which conditioned the ways in which Chaucer and his contemporaries viewed both history and fictional story. This book had a literary and conceptual orientation, but was founded upon linguistic analysis.

"*A Guide to Chaucer's Language,* on the other hand, is a description of certain aspects of language that might prove especially deserving of the critic's attention when seeking to interpret Chaucer as literature. I have tried both to proffer information and suggest lines for individual enquiry. Both books are animated by the conviction that the center of interest in a literary author should be his text, and that the text is best interpreted by detailed knowledge of his language in its historical context."

Burnley described his 1992 work, *The History of the English Language: A Sourcebook,* as a volume that "makes available to students and teachers of the history of English an extensive collection of illustrative texts that have been chosen to represent important general developments. Also included are many less familiar texts in a variety of discourse types, which facilitate tracing the development of particular genres and themes."

BIOGRAPHICAL/CRITICAL SOURCES:

PERIODICALS

Los Angeles Times Book Review, April 8, 1984.
Times Literary Supplement, May 18, 1984.

*   *   *

BURNS, Tex
    See L'AMOUR, Louis (Dearborn)

*   *   *

BUTTERWORTH, W(illiam) E(dmund III)
1929-
    (Alex Baldwin, Webb Beech, Walker E. Blake, James McM. Douglas, Jack Dugan, W. E. B. Griffin, Eden Hughes, Allison Mitchell, Edmund O. Scholefield, Patrick J. Williams)

PERSONAL: Born November 10, 1929, in Newark, NJ; son of William E. Butterworth and Gladys (Schnable) Butterworth Cottrell; married Emma Josefa Macalik (a writer), July 12, 1950; children: Patricia Olga, William Edmund IV, John Scholefield II. *Avocational interests:* Military firearms.

ADDRESSES: Office—309 North Creek Dr., Fairhope, AL 36532. *Agent*—Jane Cushman, JCA Literary Agency, Inc., 27 West 20th St., Suite 1103, New York, NY 10011.

CAREER: Writer. *Military service:* U.S. Army, 1946-47, 1951-53; served as combat correspondent in Korea; received Expert Combat Infantryman's Badge.

AWARDS, HONORS: Cited as "Most Prolific Alabama Author of All Time," Alabama Writers Conclave, Samford University, 1971; *LeRoy and the Old Man* was named to the American Library Association's "Best Books for

Young Adults" list, 1980; inducted into Alabama Academy of Distinguished Authors, 1982; awarded honorary membership in U.S. Army Otter & Caribou Association, 1985, in U.S. Marine Raider Association, 1988, and in U.S. Marine Corps Combat Correspondents Association, 1991; honorary Doctor of Literature, Norwich University, 1989; Denig Award, U.S. Marine Corps Combat Correspondents Association, 1991.

WRITINGS:

Comfort Me with Love, New American Library, 1961.
Hot Seat, New American Library, 1961.
Where We Go from Here, New American Library, 1962.
The Court-Martial, New American Library, 1962.
The Love-Go-Round, Berkley Publishing, 1962.
Hell on Wheels, Berkley Publishing, 1962.
The Girl in the Black Bikini, Berkley Publishing, 1962.
Le Falot, Gallimard (Paris), 1963.
The Wonders of Rockets and Missiles, Putnam, 1964.
The Wonders of Astronomy, Putnam, 1964.
Fast Green Car, Norton, 1965.
Stock Car Racer, Norton, 1966.
Soldiers on Horseback: The Story of the United States Cavalry, Norton, 1966.
Helicopter Pilot, Norton, 1967.
Road Racer, Norton, 1967.
The Image Makers, Scripts Publishing (Melbourne), 1967.
Air Evac, Norton, 1967.
Orders to Vietnam, Little, Brown, 1968.
Redline 7100, Norton, 1968.
Stop and Search, Little, Brown, 1969.
Wheel of a Fast Car, Norton, 1969.
Grand Prix Driver, Norton, 1969.
Steve Bellamy, Little, Brown, 1970.
Marty and the Micro Midgets, Norton, 1970.
Fast and Smart, Norton, 1970.
Susan and Her Classic Convertible, Four Winds, 1970.
Moving West on 122, Little, Brown, 1970.
Crazy to Race, Grosset, 1971.
My Father's Quite a Guy, Little, Brown, 1971.
Return to Racing, Grosset, 1971.
Flying Army: The Modern Air Arm of the U.S. Army, Doubleday, 1971.
Wheels and Pistons: The Story of the Automobile, Four Winds, 1971.
Team Racer, Grosset, 1972.
The High Wind: The Story of NASCAR Racing, Grosset, 1972.
The Race Driver, Action, 1972.
The Narc, Four Winds, 1972.
Dateline: Talladega, Grosset, 1972.
Skyjacked!, Scholastic, Inc., 1972.
Race Car Team, Grosset, 1973.
Yankee Driver, Grosset, 1973.

Flying Army, Doubleday, 1973.

Dave White and the Electric Wonder Car, Four Winds, 1974.

Stop Thief!, Four Winds, 1974.

Return to Daytona, Grosset, 1974.

Tires and Other Things: Some Heroes of Automotive Evolution, Doubleday, 1974.

The Roper Brothers and Their Magnificent Steam Automobile, Four Winds, 1976.

Mighty Minicycles, Harvey House, 1976.

Black Gold: The Story of Oil, Four Winds, 1975.

Careers in the Services, F. Watts, 1976.

An Album of Automobile Racing, F. Watts, 1977.

Christina's Passion, Playboy Paperbacks, 1977.

Hi-Fi: From Edison's Phonograph to Quadraphonic Sound, Four Winds, 1977.

Next Stop Earth, Walker, 1978.

Tank Driver, Four Winds, 1978.

The Air Freight Mystery, Four Winds, 1978.

Under the Influence, Four Winds, 1979.

LeRoy and the Old Man, Four Winds, 1980.

"M*A*S*H" SERIES; WITH RICHARD HOOKER

M*A*S*H Goes to Paris, Pocket Books, 1974.

. . . New Orleans, Pocket Books, 1975.

. . . Morocco, Pocket Books, 1975.

. . . London, Pocket Books, 1976.

. . . Las Vegas, Pocket Books, 1976.

. . . Hollywood, Pocket Books, 1976.

. . . Vienna, Pocket Books, 1976.

. . . Miami, Pocket Books, 1976.

. . . San Francisco, Pocket Books, 1976.

. . . Texas, Pocket Books, 1977.

. . . Montreal, Pocket Books, 1977.

. . . Moscow, Pocket Books, 1978.

UNDER PSEUDONYM ALEX BALDWIN; "MEN AT WAR" SERIES

The Last Heroes, Pocket Books, 1985.

The Secret Warriors, Pocket Books, 1986.

The Soldier Spies, Pocket Books, 1987.

The Fighting Agents, Pocket Books, 1988.

UNDER PSEUDONYM WEBB BEECH

No French Leave, Gold Medal, 1960.

Article 92: Murder-Rape, Fawcett, 1965.

Warrior's Way, Fawcett, 1965.

Make War in Madness, Fawcett, 1966.

UNDER PSEUDONYM WALKER E. BLAKE

The Loved and the Lost, Monarch, 1962.

Heartbreak Ridge, Monarch, 1962.

Once More with Passion, Monarch, 1964.

Doing What Comes Naturally, Monarch, 1965.

UNDER PSEUDONYM JAMES McM. DOUGLAS

Hunger for Racing, Putnam, 1967.

Racing to Glory, Putnam, 1969.

The Twelve-Cylinder Screamer, Putnam, 1970.

Drag Race Driver, Putnam, 1971.

A Long Ride on a Cycle, Putnam, 1972.

UNDER PSEUDONYM JACK DUGAN

The Deep Kill, Charter Books, 1984.

UNDER PSEUDONYM W. E. B. GRIFFIN; "BROTHERHOOD OF WAR" SERIES

The Lieutenants, Jove, 1983.

The Captains, Jove, 1983.

The Majors, Jove, 1984.

The Colonels, Jove, 1985.

The Berets, Jove, 1985.

The Generals, Jove, 1986.

"CORPS" SERIES

Semper Fi, Jove, 1986.

Call to Arms, Jove, 1987.

Counterattack, Putnam, 1990.

Battleground, Putnam, 1991.

Line of Fire, Putnam, 1992.

Close Combat, Putnam, 1992.

"BADGE OF HONOR" SERIES

Men in Blue, Jove, 1988.

Special Operations, Jove, 1989.

The Victim, Jove, 1991.

The Witness, Jove, 1992.

The Assassin, Jove, 1992.

UNDER PSEUDONYM EDEN HUGHES

The Wiltons, New American Library, 1981.

The Selkirks, New American Library, 1983.

UNDER PSEUDONYM ALLISON MITCHELL

Wild Harvest, New American Library, 1984.

Wild Heritage, New American Library, 1985.

UNDER PSEUDONYM EDMUND O. SCHOLEFIELD

Tiger Rookie, World Publishing, 1966.

L'il Wildcat, World Publishing, 1967.

Bryan's Dog, World Publishing, 1967.

Maverick on the Mound, World Publishing, 1968.

Yankee Boy, World Publishing, 1971.

UNDER PSEUDONYM PATRICK J. WILLIAMS

Fastest Funny Car, Four Winds, 1967.

Grand Prix Racing, Four Winds, 1968.

Up to the Quarterdeck, Four Winds, 1969.

The Green Ghost, Scholastic, Inc., 1969.

Racing Mechanic, Scholastic, Inc., 1969.

WORK IN PROGRESS: Additional books in the "Corps" and "Badge of Honor" series; a novel about Argentina's military.

SIDELIGHTS: W. E. Butterworth told *CA* that as of September 1992, he has had sixteen consecutive books on the *New York Times* Best Seller lists.

*   *   *

BUTTREY, Douglas N(orton) (Densil Neve Barr)

PERSONAL: Born in Harrogate, England. *Education:* Received M.Sc. from University of London.

ADDRESSES: Home—15 Churchfields, Broxbourne, Hertfordshire, England.

CAREER: Scientific/technical consultant with BX Plastics, United Kingdom, Catalin Corp., United Kingdom and United States, and Imperial Chemical Industries, United Kingdom, through 1977; writer, 1977—.

MEMBER: International P.E.N., Player-Playwrights.

WRITINGS:

NOVELS; UNDER PSEUDONYM DENSIL NEVE BARR

The Man with Only One Head (novel), Rich & Cowan, 1955.
Death of Four Presidents, Elite, 1991.

RADIO PLAYS

The Clapham Lamp-Post Saga, broadcast by Radio Telefis Eireann (RTE), 1967.
Gladys on the Wardrobe, broadcast by New Zealand Broadcasting Co. (NZBC), 1970.
But Petrovsky Goes on Forever, broadcast by RTE, 1971.
The Last Tramp, broadcast by British Broadcasting Corp. (BBC), 1972.
The Square at Bastogne, broadcast by RTE, 1973.
The Battle of Brighton Beach, broadcast by BBC, 1975.
With Puffins for Pawns, broadcast by Radio New Zealand (RNZ), 1978.
Anatomy of an Alibi, broadcast by RNZ, 1978.
The Speech, broadcast by South African Broadcasting Corp. (SABC), 1979.
Two Gaps in the Curtain, broadcast by Radio Stortford, 1979.
Klemp's Diary, broadcast by SABC, 1980.
Who Was Karl Raeder?, broadcast by SABC, 1980.
The Boy in the Cellar, broadcast by SABC, 1981.
The Glory Hallelujah Microchip, broadcast by SABC, 1981.
The Dog that Was Only a Prophet, broadcast by RNZ, 1982.

St. Paul Transferred, broadcast by SABC, 1983.
The Mythical Isles, broadcast by SABC, 1983.

OTHER

Author of three technical books; also author of several short stories under the pseudonym, Densil Neve Barr. Editor of a book on plastics. Contributor of over one hundred articles to international journals.

WORK IN PROGRESS: Two novels; radio and stage plays.

SIDELIGHTS: Douglas N. Buttrey told *CA:* "After a satisfying technical career involving many facets of research, development, consultancy, lecturing, and travel, I decided to write full time in 1977 using my pseudonym Densil Neve Barr for fiction. Although my novel and short stories were successful and achieved international recognition, I became attracted to play writing as an approach towards greater reality than in narrative fiction.

"I like writing radio plays particularly because of the freedom of imagination they allow to both the writer and the listener, and the technical challenge they provide. I write intensively for the period of time necessary to write the play, with relaxing periods in between. I do not write methodically each day all the year round because I find I have to absorb myself completely in the work in progress until it is completed, then I need a mind-clearing period to mull over new ideas. I am attracted to fantasy or the theater of the absurd as a means of conveying reality through ideas rather than realistic sermonizing.

"A wide traveling experience in my earlier career has developed a more international rather than national outlook towards man and politics, and this reflects in my writing, making my plays more acceptable in various parts of the world. I translate my own material into other forms. For example, I have used my novel and a number of my earlier short stories as a basis for plays. I do not search for ideas but wait until some idea or theme has persistently gone round in my mind for long enough to convince me it has to be written about, and I reject ideas which are not insistent in their demand to be written up.

"Playwrights that have most impressed me, and probably influenced me, have been Pirandello, Brecht, and Beckett, each in his own way using myth or unreality to pinpoint the real. My plays tend to reflect a concern for the individual in an ordered world and a basic belief in the preservation of individuality. There is also a strong sense of the ridiculousness of institutionalism in many facets of life, irrespective of politics. Finally, I write only what I want to write; and while presenting it in a form I hope most acceptable for publication in its broadest sense, I do not 'formula' write merely for the market.

"I continue to be intrigued because my plays, which I regard as liberal in approach, find acceptance in countries of differing political persuasions. I like to think that I am helping to promote a general humanitarian outlook which overrides the immediate political scene.

"More recently I have returned to the novel. Other than a paperback reissue of my earlier novel, a new thriller novel was published in 1991 and two further novels are in course of publication. I find that playwriting has done much to improve tightness, fluidity, and impact in dialogue. As in my plays, I enjoy pushing credibility to its limits."

C

CAHILL, Kevin Michael 1936-

PERSONAL: Born May 6, 1936, in New York, NY; son of John D. and Genevieve (Campion) Cahill; married Kathryn McGinity, March 4, 1961; children: Kevin Michael, Sean C., Christopher P., Brendan H., Denis D. *Education:* Fordham University, A.B. (cum laude), 1957; Cornell University, M.D., 1961; University of London, diploma in tropical medicine and hygiene, 1963.

ADDRESSES: Office—850 Fifth Ave., New York, NY 10021.

CAREER: St. Vincent's Hospital, New York City, intern, 1961-62; U.S. Naval Medical Research Unit, Cairo, Egypt, director of tropical medicine, 1963-65; private practice of tropical medicine in New York City, 1965—. Diplomate of American Board of Preventive Medicine and American Board of Microbiology. Lecturer at University of Cairo and University of Alexandria, 1963-65; associate professor at New York Medical College, 1965-66, director of its Tropical Disease Center, 1966—; professor and director of tropical medicine at Royal College of Surgeons, Dublin, Ireland, 1969—; professor at New Jersey College of Medicine, 1974—. Member of attending staff at Lenox Hill Hospital and Flower Fifth Avenue Hospital; member of scientific advisory board of American Foundation for Tropical Medicine, 1966—; chairman of New York State Health Planning Commission and Health Research Council, 1975-80; president of Center for International Health and Cooperation; consultant to U.S. Public Health Service. *Military service:* U.S. Naval Reserve, active duty, 1963-65.

MEMBER: American College of Chest Physicians (fellow), American College of Preventive Medicine (fellow), American Public Health Association, American Society of Tropical Medicine and Hygiene, American Irish Historical Society, Royal Society of Tropical Medicine and Hygiene, New York Society of Tropical Medicine (president), Knights of Malta.

WRITINGS:

Tropical Diseases in Temperate Climates, Lippincott, 1964.

Health on the Horn of Africa: A Study of the Major Diseases of Somalia, Spottiswoode, Ballantyne, 1969.

Medical Advice for the Traveler, Holt, 1970.

(Editor) *Symposia in Clinical Tropical Medicine,* Tropical Disease Center, New York Medical College, 1970.

The Untapped Resource: Medicine and Diplomacy, Orbis, 1971.

Clinical Tropical Medicine, Volume 1: *Schistomiasis, Hepatitis: American Contributions to Tropical Medicine,* Volume 2: *Malaria, Amebiasis, Cholera,* University Park Press, 1972.

Teaching Tropical Medicine, University Park Press, 1973.

(Editor) *Health and Development,* Orbis, 1976.

Tropical Diseases: A Handbook for Practitioners, Technomic, 1976.

Health in New York State: A Progress Report, Health Education Services, 1977.

Irish Essays, John Jay Press, 1980.

Somalia: A Perspective, State University of New York Press, 1980.

Threads for a Tapestry, New York Medical Press, 1981.

(Editor) *Famine,* Orbis, 1982.

(Editor) *The AIDS Epidemic,* St. Martin's, 1983.

(Editor) *The American Irish Revival,* Associated Faculty Press, 1984.

Pets and Your Health, Heinemann, 1987.

A Bridge to Peace, Haymarket Doyma (New York), 1988.

Tropical Medicine: A Clinical Text, Heinemann, 1990.

(Editor) *Imminent Peril: Public Health in a Declining Economy,* Twentieth Century Fund, 1991.

Contributor of over two hundred research articles to medical journals.

SIDELIGHTS: The AIDS Epidemic is a transcript of papers presented at a conference held in 1983 to discuss Acquired Immune Deficiency Syndrome (AIDS). It has been translated into several languages, including Japanese, Portuguese, Spanish, French, and Arabic.

BIOGRAPHICAL/CRITICAL SOURCES:

PERIODICALS

New York, July 24, 1978.
Publishers Weekly, April 29, 1983.

* * *

CAMPA, Arthur L(eon) 1905-

PERSONAL: Born February 20, 1905, in Guaymas, Mexico; naturalized U.S. citizen; son of Daniel and Delfina (Lopez) Campa; married Lucille Cushing, April 23, 1943; children: Mary Del (Mrs. Larry Price), Danielle Lucille (Mrs. Michael M. Kiley), Arthur Leon, Jr., Celia Nita (Mrs. Rick Hamm), David Louis. *Education:* University of New Mexico, B.A., 1928, M.A., 1930; Columbia University, Ph.D., 1940. *Politics:* Republican. *Religion:* Protestant.

ADDRESSES: Home—2031 South Madison, Denver, CO 80210. *Office*—Department of Modern Languages, University of Denver, Denver, CO 80210.

CAREER: Albuquerque High School, Albuquerque, NM, chairman of department of modern languages, 1928; Columbia University, New York, NY, instructor in Spanish, 1930-31; University of New Mexico, Albuquerque, instructor, 1932-33, assistant professor, 1935-37, associate professor, 1937-41, professor of modern languages, 1942-46; University of Denver, Denver, CO, 1946—, began as professor of modern languages, chairman of department, and director of Center for Latin American Studies, became professor emeritus, chairman of Division of languages and Literature, 1946-50. Lecturer in Spain, U.S. Department of State, 1953-54; cultural attache, U.S. Embassy, Lima Peru, 1955-57; training project director and Denver University liaison officer, Peace Corps. President, National Folk Festival Association, Inc., Washington, DC. *Military service:* U.S. Army Air Forces, 1942-45; served in European theater; became major; received Bronze Star Medal and ten campaign stars.

MEMBER: American Association of Teachers of Spanish and Portuguese, Modern Language Association of America, American Anthropological Association, National Folklore Festival Association (president), American Folk-

lore Society (councillor), Westerners (Denver Posse), American Dialect Society, Rocky Mountain Modern Language Association, Colorado Authors League, Colorado Folklore Society (president, 1953), Pan American Club of Denver (president, 1948, 1952).

AWARDS, HONORS: Spanish Arts Foundation fellow, 1932; Rockefeller research grant, 1933-34; Guggenheim fellowship, 1952; Top Hand Award of Colorado Authors League for nonfiction article, 1955 and 1964, and for nonfiction book, 1963.

WRITINGS:

Acquiring Spanish, Macmillan, 1944.
Spanish Folk-Poetry in New Mexico, University of New Mexico Press, 1946.
Treasure of the Sangre de Cristos: Tales and Traditions of the Spanish Southwest, University of Oklahoma Press, 1963.
Hispanic Folklore Studies of Arthur Campa: An Original Anthology, edited by Carlos Coates, Arno, 1976.
Hispanic Culture in the Southwest, University of Oklahoma Press, 1979.
Sayings and Riddles in New Mexico, Borgo Press, 1982.
Spanish Religious Folktheatre in the Southwest, Borgo Press, 1982.

Also author of more than seventy monographs, bulletins, and articles for folklore and other professional journals. Editor, *Westerners Roundup* (monthly magazine).*

* * *

CAPLAN, Gerald 1917-

PERSONAL: Born March 6, 1917, in Liverpool, England; son of David and Sophia (Zassman) Caplan; married Ann Siebenberg, March 29, 1942; children: Ruth. *Education:* University of Manchester, B.Sc., 1937, M.B. and Ch.B., 1940, M.D., 1945; Royal College of Physicians and Surgeons, D.P.M., 1942; Royal College of Psychiatry, F.R.C.Psych., 1974.

ADDRESSES: Home—30 King David St., Jerusalem, Israel 94-101. *Office*—Jerusalem Institute for the Study of Psychological Stress, 46 Jabotinsky St., Jerusalem, Israel 92182.

CAREER: House physician, Derbyshire Royal Infirmary, 1940; assistant psychiatrist, Birmingham Psychological Clinics, 1940-43; Birmingham Mental Hospital, Birmingham, England, assistant medical officer, 1941-43; psychiatrist, Merthyr General Hospital, 1943-45; Swansea Mental Hospital, Swansea, Wales, deputy medical superintendent, 1943-45; Tavistock Clinic, London, England, psychiatrist, 1945-48; clinical assistant, London Clinic of Psychoanalysis, 1947-48; Ministry of Health, Jerusalem, Israel, adviser in psychiatry, 1948-49; Lasker Mental Hygiene and Child Guidance Center, Hadassah, Jerusalem, founder and director, 1949-52; Harvard University, Boston, MA, School of Public Health, lecturer, 1952-54, associate professor of mental health and director of Community Mental Health Unit, 1954-64, clinical professor in Medical School, 1964-70, professor of psychiatry, 1970-78, emeritus professor of psychiatry, 1978—, psychiatric director of Family Guidance Center and director of Laboratory of Community Psychiatry, 1964-78; Hebrew University of Jerusalem, professor of child psychiatry, 1978-84, professor of child psychiatry and head of Department of Child and Adolescent Psychiatry, Hadassah University Hospitals, 1978-84; scientific director, Jerusalem Institute for the Study of Psychological Stress, 1984—.

Fellow in child psychiatry, Child Guidance Council of England, 1945-46. Visiting psychiatrist, Northumberland House Mental Hospital, London, 1945-48; supervising psychiatrist, Judge Baker Guidance Center, Boston, 1952-53; associate in psychiatry, Beth Israel Hospital, Boston, 1952-54. Massachusetts General Hospital, Boston, associate psychiatrist, 1956-61, psychiatrist, 1961-77. Member of honorary staff and visiting lecturer, Tavistock Clinic, 1964-73; visiting professor of psychiatry, Hebrew University of Jerusalem, 1977-78.

Consulting psychiatrist, Wellesley Human Relations Service, 1952-64, Harvard School of Public Health Family Clinic, 1952-56, Harvard Field Training Unit, City of Boston Health Center, 1953-56, Lawrence Child Guidance Center, 1955-64, and Massachusetts Mental Health Planning Project, 1963-65. Consultant in community psychiatry to Massachusetts Department of Mental Health, 1954-78, City of Boston Health Department, 1957-78, U.S. Army Hospital, Fort Devens, 1962-70, Boston State Hospital, 1964-70, and U.S. Public Health Service. Member of board of directors of Health Council and chairman of Mental Health Committee of United Community Services of Metropolitan Boston, 1956-58; member of medical committee, Crittenton Hastings House of the Florence Crittenton League, 1967-68.

Member of National Institute of Mental Health advisory committee on special grants, 1960-64 and of committee of consultants, Acta Paedopsychiatrica, 1963—. Senior consultant to U.S. Peace Corps, 1961-72, and Office of Economic Opportunity, 1967-74; consultant, Indian Health Area Office, U.S. Public Health Service, 1966-67; chairman of Advisory Council on Mental Health and Retardation, Commonwealth of Massachusetts, 1968-72. *Military service:* Royal Air Force, 1942-43; became flying officer.

MEMBER: International Association for Child Psychiatry and Allied Professions (member of executive commit-

tee, 1946—; treasurer, 1954-70; honorary president, 1970—), International Psychoanalytic Association, British Psychoanalytic Society, Royal Society of Health (London; fellow), American Psychiatric Association (fellow), American Orthopsychiatric Association (fellow), American Public Health Association (fellow), American Association for the Advancement of Science (fellow), Group for the Advancement of Psychiatry (chairman of committee on preventive psychiatry, 1957-61), Academy of Religion and Mental Health, Society for General Systems Research, Law and Society Association (trustee, 1967—), Massachusetts Association for Public Health, Delta Omega.

AWARDS, HONORS: Honorary psychiatrist, London Jewish Hospital, 1946-48; M.A., Harvard University, 1970; Psychiatric Outpatient Centers of America annual recognition award, 1970; Kings View Foundation distinguished service award, 1974; W. I. Dublin Award, American Association of Suicidology, 1986.

WRITINGS:

Electronarcosis, Lancet, 1947.
(Editor and contributor) *Emotional Problems of Early Childhood,* Basic Books, 1955.
Mental Health Aspects of Social Work in Public Health, edited by Ruth Cooper, University of California (Berkeley), 1956.
Concepts of Mental Health and Consultation, with supplementary material by Virginia Insely, Children's Bureau, U.S. Department of Health, Education, and Welfare, 1959.
(Editor with Serge Lebovici) *Adolescence: Psychosocial Perspectives,* Basic Books, 1960.
(Editor and contributor) *Prevention of Mental Disorders in Children: Initial Explorations,* Basic Books, 1961.
An Approach to Community Mental Health, Grune, 1961.
Manual for Psychiatrists Participating in the Peace Corps Program, Peace Corps, 1962.
(With V. Cadden) *Adjusting Overseas: A Message to Each Peace Corps Trainee,* Peace Corps, 1962.
Principles of Preventive Psychiatry, foreword by Robert H. Felix, Basic Books, 1964.
(Author of foreword) Hans R. Huessy, editor, *Mental Health with Limited Resources,* Grune, 1966.
(Editor and author of introduction with Lebovici, and contributor) *Psychiatric Approaches to Adolescence,* Excerpta Medica Foundation, 1966.
(Author of introduction) Leigh Roberts, *Comprehensive Mental Health: The Challenge of Evaluation,* University of Wisconsin Press, 1968.
(With daughter, Ruth B. Caplan) *Psychiatry and the Community in Nineteenth-Century America: Recurring Concern with Environment in the Prevention and Treatment of Mental Disorder,* Basic Books, 1969.

(Author of introduction) Stuart B. Golann, *Coordinate Index Reference Guide to Community Mental Health,* Behavioral Publication, 1969.

(With L. Macht and A. Wolf) *Manual for Mental Health Professionals Participating in the Job Corps Program,* Office of Economic Opportunity, 1969.

Theory and Practice of Mental Health Consultation, Basic Books, 1970.

(With R. Caplan) *Helping the Helpers to Help: The Development and Evaluation of Mental Health Consultation to Aid Clergymen in Pastoral Work,* Seabury, 1972.

Support Systems and Community Mental Health, Behavioral Publishing, 1974.

(Editor) *The American Handbook of Psychiatry,* Volume II, Basic Books, 1974.

(Editor with Marie Killilea, and contributor) *Support Systems and Mutual Help: Multidisciplinary Explorations,* Grune, 1976.

(Author of foreword) H. Parad, H. L. P. Resnik, and L. Parad, editors, *Emergency and Disaster Management,* Charles Press, 1976.

Arab and Jew in Jerusalem: Explorations in Community Mental Health, Harvard University Press, 1980.

(Author of epilogue) H. C. Schulberg and Killilea, editors, *The Modern Practice of Community Mental Health—A Volume in Honor of Gerald Caplan, M.D.,* Jossey-Bass, 1982.

(Author of foreword) Mary Sue Infante, editor, *Crisis Theory: A Framework for Nursing Practice,* Reston, 1982.

(Author of foreword) David E. Biegel and Arthur J. Naparstek, editors, *Community Support Systems and Mental Health: Practice, Policy, and Research,* Springer Publishing, 1982.

(With H. LeBrow, M. Schiller, and D. Selinger) *Child Psychiatry and Human Development,* Wiley, 1983.

Population-Oriented Psychiatry, Human Sciences Press, 1989.

(With R. Caplan) *Mental Health Consultation and Collaboration,* Jossey-Bass, 1992.

Contributor to over twenty-five books, including *The Elements of a Community Mental Health Program,* Milbank Memorial Fund, 1956; *Child Psychiatry and Prevention,* edited by D. Arn van Krevelen, Verlag Hans Huber, 1964; *The Strength of Us: Self-Help Groups in the Modern World,* F. Watts, 1976; *The Child in His Family: Tomorrow's Parents,* Wiley, 1982; and *Consultation in Community, School, and Organizational Practice: Gerald Caplan's Contributions to Professional Psychology,* edited by William P. Erchul, Hemisphere Publishing, 1993.

Also author of pamphlet *Common Problems of Early Childhood,* for the Georgia Department of Public Health, 1961, and report *Mental Health Teaching in Schools of*

Public Health, Columbia University, 1961; author of preface to "A Chance to Grow," by Norman Paul, WGHB Radio, 1967. Contributor of numerous articles and reviews to professional journals in the United States and abroad, including *British Medical Journal, Journal of Mental Science, Mental Hygiene, Megamot,* and *Medical Social Work;* occasional contributor to popular magazines, including *McCall's, Redbook,* and *Reader's Digest.* Member of editorial advisory board of *Journal of Child Psychology and Psychiatry and Allied Disciplines,* 1964-83, *New International Journal of Social Science and Medicine,* 1964—, and *Family Process,* 1964—; editorial consultant to *Journal of the Fort Logan Mental Health Center,* 1965—, and *American Journal of Psychiatry,* 1966—.

BIOGRAPHICAL/CRITICAL SOURCES:

PERIODICALS

Times Literary Supplement, January 8, 1971.

*   *   *

CAPUTO, Philip   1941-

PERSONAL: Born June 10, 1941, in Chicago, IL; son of Joseph (a plant manager) and Marie Ylonda (Napolitan) Caputo; married Jill Esther Ongemach (a librarian), June 21, 1969 (divorced, 1982); married Marcelle Lynn Besse, October 30, 1982 (divorced, 1985); married Leslie Blanchard Ware, June 4, 1988; children: (first marriage) Geoffrey Jacob, Marc Antony. *Education:* Attended Purdue University; Loyola University, Chicago, B.A., 1964. *Politics:* Democrat. *Religion:* Roman Catholic. *Avocational interests:* Deep sea and fly fishing.

ADDRESSES: Agent—Aaron Priest Literary Agency, 122 East 42nd St., New York, NY 10168.

CAREER: Author, journalist, and screenwriter. 3-M Corp., Chicago, IL, promotional writer and member of staff of house paper, 1968-69; *Chicago Tribune,* Chicago, local correspondent, 1969-72, foreign correspondent in Rome, Beirut, Saigon, and Moscow, 1972-77; freelance writer, 1977—. Mercury-Douglas Productions, Paramount Pictures, screenwriter, 1987—. *Military service:* U.S. Marine Corps, 1964-67, served in Vietnam; became lieutenant.

MEMBER: PEN, Authors Guild, Authors League of America, National Writers Union, Writers Guild of America.

AWARDS, HONORS: Pulitzer Prize (with George Bliss), 1973, for coverage of primary election fraud; George Polk Award, 1973; also received Illinois Associated Press Award, Illinois United Press Award, Green Gavel Award from American Bar Association, Overseas Press Club award, and Sidney Hillman award.

WRITINGS:

A Rumor of War (memoir), Holt, 1977.
Horn of Africa (novel), Holt, 1980.
DelCorso's Gallery (novel), Holt, 1983.
Indian Country: A Novel, Bantam, 1987.
Means of Escape (memoir), HarperCollins, 1991.

SIDELIGHTS: Philip Caputo first appeared on the literary scene with his acclaimed Vietnam memoir *A Rumor of War.* A former Pulitzer Prize-winning reporter with the *Chicago Tribune,* Caputo has drawn from his experiences as a Marine lieutenant in Vietnam and a newspaper correspondent in Beirut and Saigon to record in direct, vivid prose horrific depictions of war and its devastating effects on the people who fought it and survived its ugliness. The ideas introduced in *Rumor*—the power of war to corrupt and dehumanize soldiers, the potential for evil that lies in all men's hearts, man's inhumanity to man, the senseless destruction of people and property—resurface in Caputo's later works and serve to unify his writings.

Hailed by *New York Times Book Review* critic Peter Andrews as "the finest memoir of men at arms in our generation," *A Rumor of War* chronicles Caputo's metamorphosis from an eager young Marine fresh from officer's training school to a callous killer, and finally, to a soldier grown disgusted with the waste and folly of the war. Arriving in Danang convinced of a quick military victory for the United States, Caputo instead found Vietnam an unsettling and unforgiving place. "Everything rotted and corroded quickly over there: bodies, boot leather, canvas, metal, morals," he writes in *A Rumor of War.* "Scorched by the sun, wracked by the wind and rain of the monsoon, fighting in alien swamps and jungles, our humanity rubbed off of us as the protective bluing rubbed off the barrels of our rifles."

Patrols were unlike those the author had experienced during training. Unprepared for the rugged terrain, thick vegetation, and oppressive heat, Caputo soon tired of futile missions spent searching for an elusive enemy. The guerrilla tactics used by the Viet Cong terrified, exhausted, and overwhelmed even the best of soldiers. Yet the most traumatic of Caputo's Vietnam experiences came not in the battlefield but when he was investigated for an atrocity committed by soldiers under his command. Following Caputo's orders to search out and capture an enemy duo operating near their company, the soldiers instead shot two innocent South Vietnamese boys. Caputo recalls his feelings about the killings in *A Rumor of War:* "It was not only the specter of a murder charge that tormented me; it was my own sense of guilt . . . Perhaps the war had awakened something evil in us, some dark, malicious

power that allowed us to kill without feeling. Well, I could drop the 'perhaps' in my own case. Something evil had been in me that night. It was true that I had ordered the patrol to capture the two men if at all possible, but it was also true that I had wanted them dead." After a five-month investigation, one of the soldiers was acquitted of murder charges, and charges were dropped against Caputo and the other soldier.

In his review of *A Rumor of War,* Christopher Lehmann-Haupt of the *New York Times* calls the book "singular and marvelous," one that "tells us, as no other book that I can think of has done, what it was actually like to be fighting in that hellish jungle." Theodore Solotaroff, writing in the *New York Times Book Review,* agrees that Caputo accurately captures the horrors of battle as felt by the foot soldier, also noting that the author places his involvement in a larger context, questioning the whole American effort in Vietnam. "For the ultimate effect of this book," Solotaroff opines, "is to make the personal and public responsibility merge into a nightmare of horror and waste experienced humanly by the Caputos and inhumanly by the politicians and generals. Out of the force of his obsession with the war and his role in it, Caputo has revealed the broken idealism and suppressed agony of America's involvement."

Caputo draws upon his experiences in other war-ravaged lands for *Means of Escape.* Described by the author as an "imaginative autobiography . . . a marriage of memory and imagination," *Means of Escape* is Caputo's account of his adventures as a *Chicago Tribune* foreign correspondent whose assignments sent him to such places as Beirut, Afghanistan, Israel, South Vietnam, and Africa's Horn.

By Caputo's own admission, *Means of Escape* mixes fact with imagination, an admission which raises questions of accuracy and authenticity. Reviewing *Means of Escape* in the Chicago *Tribune Books,* Harrison E. Salisbury argues that Caputo "has taken the liberty of rearranging facts, thoughts and episodes to suit what he calls 'creative hindsight'. . . . The reader cannot help asking himself again and again: Did this really happen, or is this what Caputo imagines might have happened?" Morley Safer, writing in the *New York Times Book Review,* observes that "there are some good yarns to be told. . . . But whose voice is it? Is it the memoirist speaking or the character he has created?" Yet even those critics who question Caputo's approach admire his style. Salisbury, for example, describes several passages as "pure Caputo, terse, rich in closely observed detail, sharply etched, ironic, tragic." And another reviewer finds *Means of Escape* powerful and affecting. "Caputo's memoir, '*Means of Escape*'," writes William Broyles, Jr., in the *Los Angeles Times Book Review,* "is far more than one man's journeys into the dark regions of our times; it is, through him, an American journey from abundance and promise, through defeat and disillusionment, to a kind of peace."

Caputo has also turned his talents to fiction, penning tales that refine and rework his notions about war. His first novel, entitled *Horn of Africa,* is a story of political and personal corruption that draws from Caputo's experiences as a reporter covering the civil war in Ethiopia. The novel follows a trio of malajusted soldiers-of-fortune as they attempt to deliver CIA-provided weapons to Moslem rebels in the desert wastelands of Africa's Horn. The team, comprised of American Vietnam veteran Charles Gage and ex-British officer Moody, and led by a brutish, obsessive, Nietszche-quoting warrior named Norstrand, meets with ruin in its efforts to carry out the ill-fated, poorly-designed plan.

Critics laud Caputo's efforts as a first-time novelist. *The New York Times Book Review*'s Peter Andrews calls *Horn of Africa* "the genuine article: a real novel stuffed with excitement and filled with sharply drawn characters." Seconding that opinion, a critic in *Publishers Weekly* remarks, "This first novel is a brutally vibrant, arresting achievement." And writing in *Library Journal,* Robert H. Donahugh judges Caputo's Nordstrand to be "one of the most fascinating characters in modern American fiction."

Continuing to examine what he sees as war's destructive yet hypnotic pull, Caputo set his second novel, *DelCorso's Gallery,* in Vietnam and Lebanon. The book recounts photojournalist Nicholas DelCorso's decision to leave his marriage and career and enter the world of modern warfare, a world he knew as a Vietnam combat soldier and "the only reality he truly understands," believes *Los Angeles Times Book Review* critic Elaine Kendall. Once returned to that reality, amid the despair of Saigon and the savagery of Beirut, DelCorso wars against his mentor and now chief rival, P. X. Dunlop. Their feud builds over opposing ideologies about war and conflicting views about their roles as war photographers. While Dunlop seeks to glorify combat through his battlefield photos, DelCorso's goal, writes Joe Klein in the *New York Times Book Review,* is to "show the public the true face of war. It has become an obsession with him . . . a crusade."

Kendall finds the portrayals of both men to be accurate and telling, but she notes that the characters and their relationships only serve as a vehicle for the book's true purpose and source of strength—its ability to ask questions about war's existence and its attempts "to answer such urgent questions." *Washington Post Book World* reviewer Howard Chapnick agrees, and adds that *DelCorso's Gallery* sheds light on "some of the philosophic questions of journalistic practice and the public's right to know." He concludes, "Philip Caputo has written a tough, painful

and provocative book that will cause introspection in the journalistic community."

Caputo focused his attention on the plight of troubled Vietnam veterans for his third novel *Indian Country.* The title has a dual meaning: on one level it refers to the book's setting, Ojibwa territory in Michigan's Upper Peninsula, and on another to what Caputo describes in the novel as "a place, condition or circumstance that is alien and dangerous." An examination of the emotional and psychological deterioration of combat veteran Christian Starkman, *Indian Country* details Starkman's lapses into states of depression, isolation, and paranoia. Familiar surroundings take on "alien and dangerous" characteristics. Haunted by guilt over the death of his boyhood friend and combat partner Bonny George, a death he caused by an error in battlefield judgement, Starkman "implodes into delayed disintegration," according to *Los Angeles Times Book Review* staffer Dick Roraback. His character retreats further and further from reality until an old Ojibwa medicine man, the grandfather of Bonny George, offers him a chance for redemption and healing.

Critics agree that the idea of healing was central to Caputo's narrative, and they praise *Indian Country* for its powerful conclusion. "Caputo . . . grabs the threads he has scattered about . . . and wraps up the whole story magnificently, concluding on a message of hope," asserts *Washington Post Book World* reviewer John Byrne Cooke. Roraback summarizes the work as "a story of forgiveness, ostensibly the forgiveness of Starkman by Bonny George's grandfather; in reality, the forgiveness that must come from within." Finally, *New York Times Book Review* contributor Frank Conroy finds that the work successfully illustrates the pain felt by many Vietnam veterans. He states: "Indian Country is a fine traditional novel that handles a difficult theme both cleverly and artfully . . . it has real strength."

Philip Caputo has returned to war again and again, in his life and in his works. Reflecting on this truth, Broyles notes that Caputo's life bears "a striking parallel to our own national experience . . . He [Caputo] goes to Vietnam as a patriot, returns disillusioned and in disgrace. An exile in his own land, he wanders the world looking for redemption, seeks in vain to find his place in the Old Country of his ancestors, is held helpless hostage, peers into other hearts darker than his own, confronts his own mortality and limits, then finally finds a kind of peace." It is this journey that has shaped Caputo's life and through which he has found the substance and the forcefulness that mark his works.

BIOGRAPHICAL/CRITICAL SOURCES:

BOOKS

Beidler, Philip D., *American Literature & The Experience of Vietnam,* University of Georgia Press, 1982.

Beidler, P. D., *Rewriting America,* University of Georgia Press, 1991.

Caputo, Philip, *A Rumor of War,* Holt, 1977.

Caputo, P., *Means of Escape: An Imagined Memoir,* HarperCollins, 1991.

Hellman, John, *American Myth & The Legacy of Vietnam,* Columbia University Press, 1986.

Meyers, Thomas, *Walking Point: American Narratives of Vietnam,* Oxford University Press, 1988.

Rowe and Berg, *The Vietnam War and American Culture,* Columbia University Press, 1991.

PERIODICALS

Los Angeles Times Book Review, October 23, 1983; June 21, 1987; October 27, 1991.

Library Journal, December 15, 1980.

New York Times, May 26, 1977; May 29, 1977.

New York Times Book Review, May 29, 1977; November 2, 1980; November 13, 1983; May 17, 1983; October 27, 1991.

Newsweek, June 6, 1977.

Publishers Weekly, August 22, 1980.

Saturday Review, June 11, 1977.

Washington Post, June 12, 1977.

Washington Post Book World, October 23, 1986; May 10, 1987.

Time, July 4, 1977.

Tribune Books (Chicago), November 3, 1991.

—*Sketch by Thomas F. McMahon*

*   *   *

CARDINAL, Roger (Thomas) 1940-
(Peter Bridgecross)

PERSONAL: Born February 27, 1940, in Bromley, England; son of Thomas (an engineer) and Ada (Melbourne) Cardinal; married Agnes Meyer, August, 1965; children: Daniel, Felix. *Education:* Cambridge University, B.A., 1962, Ph.D., 1965. *Politics:* "Anarchist-surrealist." *Religion:* None.

ADDRESSES: Home—Heath Field, Chartham Hatch, Kent CT4 7NS, England. *Office*—Keynes College, University of Kent, Canterbury, England.

CAREER: University of Manitoba, Winnipeg, assistant professor of French, 1965-67; University of Warwick, Coventry, Warwick, England, lecturer in French, 1967-68; University of Kent, Keynes College, Canterbury, Kent, England, lecturer, 1968-76, senior lecturer in French, 1976-81, reader in comparative literary studies, 1981-87, professor of literary and visual studies, 1987—. Visiting associate professor, University of Toronto, 1976-77; research fellow, Australian National University, Canberra, 1988.

WRITINGS:

(With Robert S. Short) *Surrealism: Permanent Revelation,* Dutton, 1970.

Outsider Art, Praeger, 1972.

German Romantics, Studio Vista, 1975.

(Editor) *Sensibility and Creation: Studies in Twentieth-Century French Poetry,* Barnes & Noble, 1977.

Primitive Painters, St. Martin's, 1978.

Outsiders, Arts Council of Great Britain, 1979.

Figures of Reality: A Perspective on the Poetic Imagination, Barnes & Noble, 1981.

Expressionism, Paladin, 1984.

Andre Breton: Nadja, Grant & Cutler, 1986.

The Landscape Vision of Paul Nash, Reaktion Books, 1989.

Contributor to periodicals, including *Times Literary Supplement, Raw Vision, Moment, Queen's Quarterly, Melmoth,* and *L'Art Brut;* contributor under pseudonym Peter Bridgecross to *Wheels* and *Red River Poems.*

WORK IN PROGRESS: Research into imaginative process in fields of French poetry, surrealism, expressionism, Art Brut, and psychopathological creation; a "major book on the marginal arts."

SIDELIGHTS: Roger Cardinal once told *CA:* "My intellectual awareness of so many things has been stimulated by surrealism, and it is by the light of the work of Andre Breton and of the surrealist poets and painters that I have travelled into the territories of modern European poetry, German romanticism and expressionism, French symbolism, psychotic and mediumistic drawing and writing, naive and folk art, the cinema. My interests extend into such areas as response to landscape and the sense of place, the analysis of metaphoric forms of expression, primitive thinking and tribal art, and the role of imagination in scientific research.

"My work obliges me to seek to eradicate the orthodox division between 'creative' and 'critical' writing. My aim is to illuminate the processes of the creative imagination in its handling of the inner and outer worlds and to contribute to a widening of critical perspectives on the arts in highlighting the sensibility of the individual creator and his personal imagery, whether verbal or visual. My hope as a writer is to be able to speak of poetry, painting, or any other experience in my life without the change in subject entailing any shift in style or seriousness.

"Since 1966 I have kept a journal in many volumes, containing poems, drawings, reflections, reading notes, and cuttings. This provides me with a pool of stimuli from which I constantly benefit. In my teaching I have been lucky enough to establish courses in areas corresponding to my enthusiasms; rather than being typecast as exclusively a teacher of French literature, I currently work in comparative literary studies and teach courses on European literature of the fantastic, primitivism in the visual arts, the photograph, the folktale, and anarchism.

"I hope to contribute towards a view of creativity as an impulse springing from identifiable and essential needs, both private and collective, and hence capable of elucidation in a language which will transcend traditional disciplines and help to map the amazing tracks opened up by the imagination—what Novalis once called 'that wondrous sense which supersedes all our senses.' "

Of Cardinal's book *Expressionism,* S. S. Prawer notes in the *Times Literary Supplement,* "[This] short book performs a difficult feat exceedingly well: it combines an introduction that can be read with profit by those who know little about Expressionism with an exposition from which experts will also be glad to learn." Prawer concludes that the book contains a "lucid and fresh description of an important range of Modernist styles."

BIOGRAPHICAL/CRITICAL SOURCES:

PERIODICALS

Times Literary Supplement, May 21, 1970; June 25, 1982; June 7, 1985.

*   *   *

CARLISLE, Thomas John   1913-1992

PERSONAL: Born October 11, 1913, in Plattsburgh, NY; died August 17, 1992, in Waterford, NY; son of Thomas Houston (a florist) and Ruby Grace (a florist; maiden name, Mann) Carlisle; married Dorothy Mae Davis, August 20, 1936 (died January 21, 1991); children: Thomas Dwight, Christopher Davis, David Livingstone Harold and Jonathan Tristram (twins). *Education:* Williams College, B.A. (cum laude), 1934; Union Theological Seminary, New York, NY, M.Div., 1937. *Avocational interests:* World peace and social justice, the writings of Emily Dickinson, Nova Scotia, philately.

CAREER: Ordained United Presbyterian minister, 1937; pastor of Tupper Lake Presbyterian Church, Tupper Lake, NY, 1937-42, and Second Presbyterian Church, Delhi, NY, 1942-49; Stone Street Presbyterian Church, Watertown, NY, pastor, 1949-78, pastor emeritus, 1978-92. Gave poetry readings; poet-in-residence and vis-

iting scholar at colleges and universities. Tutor at State University of New York Empire State College; member of continuing education and seminar faculty at Princeton Theological Seminary, 1977-84, and Princeton Institute of Theology, 1985. Instructor at Cape Cod Writers Conference, 1984, and St. David's Christian Writers Conference, 1985; teacher of poetry at Finger Lakes Conference, 1988, 1989. Founding member and past member of board of directors of area Family Counseling Service and Mental Health Association and Clinic. Co-founder of Watertown Urban Mission.

MEMBER: New York Poetry Forum, Poetry Society of Georgia, Poetry Society of Virginia, Phi Beta Kappa, Delta Sigma Rho, Watertown Rotary Club (president, 1960-61).

AWARDS, HONORS: Phillips-Rice Award from Jefferson County Association for Mental Health, 1960; Paul Harris Award from Watertown Rotary Club, 1977; outstanding North Country citizen citation from St. Lawrence University, 1985.

WRITINGS:

POETRY

My Names Are Different, American Weave Press, 1957.
I Need a Century, Richard R. Smith Co., 1963.
You! Jonah!, Eerdmans, 1968.
Celebration!, Eerdmans, 1970.
Mistaken Identity, Eerdmans, 1973.
Journey with Job, Eerdmans, 1976.
Eve and After: Old Testament Women in Portrait, Eerdmans, 1984.
Journey with Jonah, Forward Movement Publications, 1984.
Tales of Hopkins Forest, Williams College, 1984.
Beginning with Mary: Gospel Women in Portrait, Eerdmans, 1986.
Invisible Harvest, Eerdmans, 1987.

OTHER

Also author of lyrics for "Rise Up, My Love, My Fair One." Contributor of more than 1500 articles and poems to newspapers, religious and literary publications, and magazines, including *Saturday Review, Poetry Now, Alive Now!, Presbyterian Survey, Berkshire Review, Ladies' Home Journal,* and *Christian Century.* Past member of editorial board of *Sketch.*

WORK IN PROGRESS: Looking for Jesus, over 200 poems providing a commentary on the acts and words of Jesus, from Eerdmans; *Love among the Rhubarb Leaves,* a new book of love poems.

SIDELIGHTS: Thomas John Carlisle once wrote CA: "I am fascinated by the way words can be brought into unique, resonant, and evocative combinations. I have been involved in my poetry in providing a modern and dynamic equivalent to the memorable stories in both the Old and New Testaments. I have also been concerned to demonstrate the spiritual in what we too commonly term *secular.*

"In addition to my concentration on my own poetry, I have devoted myself to helping people find the joy of reading poetry for themselves, how they can discover the poetry that will enrich and enable their lives. There is a vast untapped audience.

"Of special encouragement to me are the many letters I receive from people who have found insights of liberation and renewal from reading my poems.

"I myself am continually finding areas I have overlooked—most recently, the attraction and power of the black poetic heritage."

[Sketch reviewed by son, Reverend Jonathan T. Carlisle]

*   *   *

CARO, Robert A. 1935-

PERSONAL: Born October 30, 1935, in New York, NY; son of Benjamin (a businessman) and Cele; married, wife's name Ina Joan Sloshberg; children: Chase. *Education:* Princeton University, B.A., 1957.

ADDRESSES: Home—91 Central Park West, New York, NY 10023. *Office*—250 West 57th St., New York, NY 10019. *Agent*—Lynn Nesbit, Janklow and Nesbit Associates, 598 Madison Ave., New York, NY 10022.

CAREER: Writer. *New Brunswick Home News,* New Brunswick, NJ, reporter, 1957-59; *Newsday,* Garden City, NY, investigative reporter, 1959-66.

MEMBER: Authors Guild (former president), PEN (former vice president).

AWARDS, HONORS: Society of Silurians award for public service writing, 1965; Nieman fellow at Harvard University, 1965-66; Carnegie Foundation fellow, 1967; Pulitzer Prize for biography, Francis Parkman Prize, Society of American Historians, and *Washington Monthly* Political Book Award, all 1975, all for *The Power Broker;* National Book Critics Circle Award for best nonfiction book, Texas Institute of Letters Award for best nonfiction book, *Washington Monthly* Political Book Award, and H. L. Mencken Prize, all 1983, and English-Speaking Union Books-Across-the-Sea Ambassador of Honor Book Award, 1985, all for *The Path to Power;* American Academy and Institute of Arts and Letters award in literature, 1986; National Book Critics Circle Award for best biogra-

phy, and *Washington Monthly* Political Book Award, both 1991, both for *Means of Ascent.*

WRITINGS:

The Power Broker: Robert Moses and the Fall of New York, Knopf, 1974.
The Years of Lyndon Johnson: The Path to Power (Book-of-the-Month Club main selection), Knopf, 1982.
The Years of Lyndon Johnson: Means of Ascent, (Book-of-the-Month Club main selection), Knopf, 1990.

SIDELIGHTS: A Pulitzer Prize-winning biographer, Robert A. Caro specializes in writing about powerful political figures. His *The Power Broker: Robert Moses and the Fall of New York* chronicles the career of New York state's long-time public works commissioner. In *Path to Power* and *Means of Ascent,* the first two volumes of a projected four-volume life of U. S. President Lyndon Baines Johnson, Caro examines Johnson's career, presenting the contrasting light and dark sides of his nature and achievement. "The basic concern of all my books," Caro told *Time,* "is how political power works in America."

The Power Broker is an epic biography of the man who controlled public works developments in New York for more than forty years. In his unelected capacity as president of the Long Island State Park Commission and superintendent of New York City construction, as well as ten other quasi-public posts, Moses was the undisputed czar of public construction who built almost all of the parks, highways, public housing and bridges in the New York City area. Caro details in 1,200 pages the building projects Moses planned, organized and completed during his career. He also examines the enormous power that public authority commissions—which are funded by their own taxes and run by unelected bureaucrats—have in the nation's big cities. Moses used his power to dominate local politicians and force building projects on reluctant communities. Without public discussion or the approval of elected officials, he was able to restructure New York city's waterfront according to his own tastes. Over seven years of writing, Caro interviewed over 500 persons and searched numerous public documents and blueprints to unearth the truth about Moses' career.

In examining the empire Moses created, Caro, writes Richard C. Wade in the *New York Times Book Review,* "questions almost everything about Moses—his strategy and tactics, his methods and ends, his vision and ideology, his honesty and integrity, his character and decency. Everything but his intelligence and self-discipline. These qualities Moses had in lavish amounts, and more than anything else they account for his spectacular success. Yet, Caro sees this genius applied to destructive purposes, warped to undermine democratic process and turned unfairly, even viciously, on his adversaries."

Speaking to Philip Herrera of *Time,* Caro recalls the seven interviews he was allowed with Moses. "They weren't interviews," he explains. "They were monologues. He was absolutely charming. The world's greatest storyteller, a fantastic memory for names and facts. But when I started asking questions about some of those facts that I knew were disproved, Moses pounded the table." The interviews were subsequently ended.

Atlantic Monthly's Benjamin DeMott finds *The Power Broker* to be "a source book about political power, its creation and nurture. . . . Caro's examination of the methods by which Robert Moses simultaneously accumulated enormous political power and built an array of parks, bridges, and highways without historical precedent . . . teaches a shrewd course in 'public sector' relationships of money, power, and imagination." Awarded a Pulitzer Prize in 1974, *The Power Broker* has become a standard text in over one hundred colleges.

After the seven years spent on chronicling Moses' career, Caro decided to tackle a more enjoyable figure, Lyndon Baines Johnson. "I thought I would find a man who was shrewd, but whose driving motivation was to help the people he grew up with," Caro explained to Fred Bernstein in *People.* After beginning his research, however, Caro found that his new subject "was very depressing." He soon discovered that many of the flattering stories found in previous Johnson biographies were simply falsehoods invented by Johnson himself. Worse, Johnson's rise to political power had been accomplished with the use of deception, financial chicanery and a ruthless willingness to do and say whatever was necessary. "Early on," Caro tells Alan L. Miller of the *Detroit News,* "I realized that the truth about Lyndon Johnson had never been told. The reason is that this talented, yet devious, man devoted a great deal of energy to guaranteeing that none of it would ever be known."

In *The Path to Power,* the first of a proposed four-volume biography of Johnson, Caro deals with the politician's career until the outbreak of World War II. To present this story, Caro spent three years sifting through some 34 million documents in the Johnson Library and conducted over one thousand interviews with people who knew the politician. In addition, the Caros moved to Johnson's home county, where they lived for three years. The flattering stories they heard about Johnson when they first arrived as Eastern outsiders were in time recanted and replaced with other, less flattering tales of Johnson's early life as the Caros were accepted as neighbors and friends.

Among the less flattering stories presented in *The Path to Power* are those surrounding Johnson's college years. During this time, as Richard Eder describes it in the *Los Angeles Times Book Review,* Johnson won "the favor of the college president, using this favor to influence the apportionment of student jobs—crucial in hard times—and pyramiding this embryonic patronage, along with high-pressure tactics, vote-stealing and some mild blackmail, into a political machine." Known as "Bull" in college (short for "bullshit"), Johnson even arranged to cut the unsavory nickname from hundreds of already-published college yearbooks.

Once in politics, Johnson bought a congressional seat with the assistance of several corrupt officials in rural Texas who, for a price, could arrange appropriate vote totals in their areas. As a congressman, Johnson worked closely to guide profitable New Deal building projects like dams and military bases to his friend Texas construction man Herman Brown. In return, Brown donated large amounts to Johnson's campaign coffers. (In his unsuccessful 1941 race for the Senate, Johnson raised a half a million dollars—in a time when an $80,000 campaign was considered extravagent.) Later, Brown would donate money for other Democratic congressional candidates as well, allowing Johnson to distribute the gifts where they would buy the most influence.

Caro's insights into the hidden side of Johnson's career were appreciated by the critics. "The details that Mr. Caro has dug up," Christopher Lehman-Haupt writes in the *New York Times,* "are astonishing, and he has pieced them together to tell a monumental political saga." Miller calls *The Path to Power* "a magnificent mix of narrative history and investigative reporting." *The Path to Power* was awarded a National Book Critics Circle Award for best nonfiction book, the Texas Institute of Letters Award for best nonfiction book, the *Washington Monthly* Political Book Award, and the H. L. Mencken Prize.

In the second book of his ongoing biography of Lyndon Johnson, *Means of Ascent,* Caro traces the politician's career from World War II until his election to the U.S. Senate in 1948. Again, scandalous details of Johnson's career are revealed. In particular, Johnson's service record during World War II and his Senate victory of 1948, which he won by a contested 87 votes, are examined in detail.

During World War II, Congressman Johnson served as an inspector of training programs in naval shipyards on the West Coast. When it seemed advisable for political reasons to at least visit a battlefield, Johnson pulled strings to have President Franklin Roosevelt send him on a fact-gathering mission to the Southwest Pacific Theatre. While there, Johnson flew as an observer during a routine bombing run against a Japanese airbase in New Guinea. His plane was fired upon but returned to base safely. Despite being a mere passenger on the bomber, Johnson was awarded a Silver Star by General Douglas MacArthur.

Although the medal was meant to flatter a congressman who could expedite military appropriations back home, Johnson was soon telling the tale of his combat heroics to stateside audiences. As the years went by, his tale became more and more embroidered: He flew many missions, shot down many Japanese fighter planes himself, and knew the pain and suffering of combat. Even as president, Johnson still enjoyed regaling guests with his exaggerated claims. Caro's investigation of the actual record was the first time the matter had been publicly revealed.

The Senate race of 1948 could have ended Johnson's political career had he lost. Because of the importance of the election, Johnson spent more money campaigning than he ever had before. He became the first candidate in the nation to travel by helicopter from town to town, something so unusual as to bring out crowds just to see the craft. More importantly, Johnson cut deals with county bosses in south Texas to stuff the ballot box on election day. When the results were in, Johnson's opponent was ahead by 854 votes. But after several days of recounting, the lead was cut to just over 150 votes. That's when a ballot box was discovered in Alice, Texas, containing 200 votes for Johnson. Out of nearly one million votes cast, Johnson won the election by 87 votes.

Subsequent investigation revealed that Johnson's 200 additional votes in Alice, Texas, were written in a different colored ink than the other votes, were written in the same handwriting, and were in alphabetical order. Some of the people listed told authorities they had not voted. Nonetheless, Johnson's people were able to have their candidate certified as the winner and squelch a federal investigation of the election.

Although the information Caro presents in his ongoing biography of Johnson is backed by documents and interviews, some critics of his books find his approach to his subject to be biased. As Charles Trueheart asks in the *Washington Post,* "Does Caro's relentlessly ugly portrait of Johnson make his history suspect?" Even the *American Spectator*'s Victor Gold, who worked in Barry Goldwater's presidential campaign against Johnson in 1964, sees Caro as "a biographer in a hurry to have at Lyndon Johnson." Responding to such criticism, Caro explains to Richard Sandomir of the *Los Angeles Times:* "Everything in this book is true and documented beyond the possibility of any doubt. That's just the way it is."

Speaking of Caro's research techniques, which are derived from his days as an investigative newspaper reporter, Peter S. Prescott of *Newsweek* explains: "This is the way Caro goes about ferreting out the hidden evidence: he asks questions, hears a lot of lies, returns to rummage among the documents, then he goes back to the same people and challenges their stories." Caro has conducted over 1,000

interviews for his Johnson biography, even tracking down every living member of Johnson's grammar school class. He also has a knack for getting interviews with people who do not normally give interviews. Former Texas governor John Connally gave Caro his first interview ever about his old friend and boss, while Johnson's brother Sam Houston Johnson admitted to Caro for the first time that many of the childhood tales told about the president were fabrications.

Writing in *Telling the Untold Story: How Investigative Reporters Are Changing the Craft of Biography,* Steve Weinberg argues that Caro's approach to political biography has changed the nature of the genre entirely. With *The Power Broker,* Weinberg notes, Caro "deeply influenced the modern-day craft of biography. Biographers had a new model: the nearly thirteen-hundred-page book was much longer than the average biography; artfully written, sometimes using techniques from the realm of fiction, while still adhering to the chronology of Moses's life as he lived it; daring in its analysis of Moses's motives; unusual in the depth of its portrayal of Moses's times, as well as his life; heavily dependent on previously secret documents; quintessentially muckraking; and done by an investigative journalist, not a historian or urban planning professor. Caro's success opened the gates for other journalists to write biographies of controversial, contemporary subjects." As Weinberg summarizes, "a few biographers and theorists could be said to have influenced the practice of the craft—but none in quite the combination of ways that Caro did. . . . The combination of his research skills, his way with words, his boldness in attributing motives, and his gutsiness in writing about powerful contemporary figures make his work topic A during any informed discussion of biography over the last quarter of the twentieth century."

BIOGRAPHICAL/CRITICAL SOURCES:

BOOKS

Keeler, Robert F., *Newsday: A Candid History,* Arbor House/Morrow, 1990.

Weinberg, Steve, *Telling the Untold Story: How Investigative Reporters Are Changing the Craft of Biography,* University of Missouri Press, 1992.

Zinsser, William, editor, *Extraordinary Lives: The Art and Craft of American Biography,* American Heritage Press, 1986.

PERIODICALS

America, September 21, 1974, p. 135.

American Scholar, spring, 1975, p. 306.

American Spectator, December, 1986, p. 26; December, 1987, p. 42; December, 1989, p. 32; July, 1990, p. 37.

Atlantic Monthly, December, 1974, p. 106.

Books and Bookmen, February, 1983, p. 9.
Business Week, March 26, 1990, p. 18.
Chicago Tribune Book World, November 28, 1982, p. 1; November 27, 1983, p. 27.
Christian Century, August 22, 1990, p. 766.
Christian Science Monitor, September 18, 1974, p. 13; December 3, 1982, p. 81.
Commentary, December, 1974, p. 74.
Commonweal, December 6, 1974, p. 238; April 22, 1983, p. 247.
Detroit News, January 26, 1983.
Economist, February 12, 1983, p. 87; April 28, 1990, p. 95.
Esquire, December, 1975, p. 60.
Historian, spring, 1991, p. 581.
Human Events, October 23, 1982, p. 9.
Journal of American History, December, 1975, p. 751; September, 1983, p. 457.
Listener, June 16, 1983, p. 24; November 8, 1990, p. 26.
London Review of Books, June 2, 1983, p. 6.
Los Angeles Times, March 13, 1990.
Los Angeles Times Book Review, December 5, 1982, p. 1; March 18, 1990, p. 1; March 24, 1991, p. 10.
Maclean's, December 27, 1982, p. 44.
Nation, September 28, 1974, p. 277; December 25, 1982, p. 693; December 27, 1986, p. 738; October 8, 1990, p. 389.
National Review, December 6, 1974, p. 1419; April 15, 1983, p. 445; April 30, 1990, p. 46.
New Leader, December 13, 1982, p. 11; April 16, 1990, p. 18.
New Republic, September 7, 1974, p. 18; February 7, 1983; June 4, 1990, p. 29.
Newsday, October 25, 1974; November 21, 1982.
Newsweek, September 16, 1974, p. 80; November 29, 1982, p. 100; March 19, 1990, p. 66.
New York, March 5, 1990, p. 100.
New York Review of Books, October 17, 1974, p. 3; February 17, 1982, p. 25; April 26, 1990, p. 7.
New York Times, August 21, 1974; November 18, 1982, p. 23.
New York Times Book Review, September 15, 1974, p. 1; November 21, 1982, p. 1; March 11, 1990, p. 1; March 24, 1991, p. 34.
Observer, February 6, 1983, p. 33; November 11, 1990, p. 68.
People, January 17, 1983, pp. 31-32.
Political Science Quarterly, fall, 1975, p. 521; fall, 1984, p. 558; summer, 1991, p. 349.
Progressive, April, 1983, p. 56; June, 1990, p. 38.
Psychology Today, February, 1983, p. 12.
Publishers Weekly, November 25, 1983, pp. 37-41.
Saturday Review, March, 1983, p. 61.
Southern Humanities Review, summer, 1984, p. 245.
Spectator, February 5, 1983, p. 20.
Texas Monthly, April, 1990.
Time, September 16, 1974, p. 100; November 29, 1982, p. 94; November 13, 1989, pp. 98-99; March 5, 1990, p. 67.
Times Educational Supplement, October 12, 1990, p. R1.
Times Literary Supplement, January 17, 1975, p. 57; March 25, 1983, p. 287; September 28, 1990, p. 1024.
Tribune Books (Chicago), March 18, 1990, p. 1; December 2, 1990, p. 7.
Vanity Fair, April, 1990.
Village Voice, November 30, 1982, p. 55.
Voice Literary Supplement, April, 1990, p. 20.
Wall Street Journal, September 9, 1974, p. 12; November 30, 1982, p. 30.
Washington Monthly, March, 1983, p. 28.
Washington Post, March 21, 1990.
Washington Post Book World, November 21, 1982, p. 1; March 4, 1990, p. 1.

—*Sketch by Thomas Wiloch*

*   *   *

CASTLEMAN, (Esther) Riva 1930-

PERSONAL: Born August 15, 1930, in Chicago, IL; daughter of William and Ann (Steinberg) Castleman. *Education:* University of Iowa, B.A. (with honors), 1951; graduate study at New York University, Institute of Fine Arts, 1951.

ADDRESSES: Office—Museum of Modern Art, 11 West 53rd St., New York, NY 10019.

CAREER: Art Institute, Chicago, IL, assistant to curator of department of decorative arts, 1951-55; California Historical Society, San Francisco, assistant editor and curator, 1956-57; John Fleming Rare Books, New York City, assistant, 1958-63; Museum of Modern Art, New York City, cataloger, 1963-64, curatorial assistant, 1965-66, assistant curator, 1967-69, associate curator, 1970-71, curator of prints and illustrated books, 1971-75, director of prints and illustrated books, 1976-86, deputy director for curatorial affairs, 1986—. Judge of San Juan Biennial of Latin American Prints, 1970 and 1972, Ljubljana Biennial of Prints, 1971 and 1973, Krakow Biennial, 1972 and 1974, Bradford Biennial, 1974, and Tokyo Biennial, 1977. Lecturer.

MEMBER: Cintas Foundation (director), Print Council of America, Grolier Club, Phi Beta Kappa.

AWARDS, HONORS: Corning Museum of Glass, fellow, 1954; grant for Tamarind Lithography Workshop, 1965.

WRITINGS:

Technics and Creativity: Gemini G.E.L., Museum of Modern Art, 1972.

Contemporary Prints, Viking, 1973.

Modern Prints since 1942, Barrie & Jenkins, 1973.

Modern Art in Prints, Museum of Modern Art, 1973.

Latin American Prints from The Museum of Modern Art, Center for Inter-American Relations, 1974.

American Prints 1913-1963 (introduction), Bibliotheque royale Albert 1er, 1976.

Prints of the Twentieth Century: A History, Museum of Modern Art, 1976, revised edition, Thames and Hudson, 1988.

Matisse in the Collection of The Museum of Modern Art, Museum of Modern Art, 1978.

Printed Art: A View of Two Decades, Museum of Modern Art, 1980.

Modern Artists as Illustrators, Museum of Modern Art, 1981.

Prints from Blocks, Museum of Modern Art, 1983.

American Impressions: Prints Since Pollock, Knopf, 1985.

Jasper Johns: A Print Retrospective, Museum of Modern Art, 1986.

Prints of Andy Warhol, Museum of Modern Art, 1990.

Art of the Forties, Museum of Modern Art, 1991.

Seven Master Printmakers: Innovations in the Eighties, Museum of Modern Art, 1991.

Also author of exhibition catalogues. Contributor to scholarly journals and periodicals, including *Art international* and *Print Review.* Member of editorial board, *Curator.*

Castleman's work has been translated into German, French, Spanish, Japanese, and Portugese.

BIOGRAPHICAL/CRITICAL SOURCES:

PERIODICALS

Art News, October, 1979; April, 1982.
New York Times Book Review, January 12, 1986.
Times Literary Supplement, September 24, 1976.
Washington Post Book World, December 8, 1985.

*   *   *

CHALON, Jean 1935-

PERSONAL: Born March 8, 1935, in Carpentras, France; son of Marcel (a tradesman) and Marie-Therese (Comtat) Chalon. *Education:* Attended University of Aix-en-Provence, 1956-60. *Religion:* Roman Catholic.

ADDRESSES: Home—48 Rue Lemercier, Paris 75017, France. *Office*—*Le Figaro Litteraire,* 37 Rue du Louvre, Paris 75017, France. *Agent*—Helmet Meyer, 330 East 79th St., New York, NY 10021.

CAREER: Le Figaro Litteraire, Paris, France, literary journalist, 1961—.

MEMBER: French Association of Friends of Anais Nin and Louise de Vilmorin.

AWARDS, HONORS: Prix Cazes from Lipp Brasserie, and Prix Sevigne, both 1976, both for *Portrait d'une seductrice.*

WRITINGS:

Les Plaisirs infinis (novel; title means "Infinite Pleasures"), Editions du Seuil, 1961.

L'Honneur de plaire (novel; title means "To Seduce Is an Honor"), Editions du Seuil, 1962.

Les Amours imaginaires (novel; title means "Fancy Love"), Gallimard, 1964.

Les Couples involontaires (novel; title means "Different Couples"), Flammarion, 1966.

Les Bonheurs defendus (novel; title means "Forbidden Happiness"), Flammarion, 1969.

(Editor) Louise Tourzel, *Memories de Madame la duchesse de Tourzel,* Mercure de France, 1969.

Un Eternel Amour de trois semaines (title means "An Eternal Love of Three Weeks"), Fayard, 1971.

Une Jeune Femme de soixante ans (title means "A Young Lady of Sixty"), Fayard, 1973.

Zizou, artichaut, coquelicot, oiseau (juvenile; title means "Zizou, Artichoke, Corn-Poppy, Bird"), Grasset, 1974.

Ouvrir une maison de rendezvous (title means "How to Open a Whorehouse"), Julliard, 1974.

Les Paradis provisoires (novel; title means "Temporary Paradise"), Fayard, 1975.

Portrait d'une seductrice (biography), Stock, 1976, translation by Carol Barko published as *Portrait of a Seductress,* Crown, 1978.

L'Ecole des arbres, Mercure de France, 1980.

Un Amour d'arbre, Plon, 1983.

Le Lumineux Destin d'Alexandra David-Neel (biography), Perrin, 1985.

Chere Marie-Antoinette, Perrin, 1988.

Chere George Sand, Flammarion, 1991.

Also author of *Le Mauvais Genre* (title means "The Wrong Behavior").

WORK IN PROGRESS: A biography of Liane de Pougy.

SIDELIGHTS: Jean Chalon's *Portrait of a Seductress* is a biography of Natalie Barney, the famed lesbian temptress. The daughter of a wealthy Ohio industrialist and his wife, a portrait painter, Barney left the United States in the early 1900s and settled in Paris, where she became renowned for her numerous affairs with such prominent women as Colette, Liane de Pougy, Djuna Barnes, and Romaine Brooks. Oblivious to world events and serious about nothing, including her own writing, Barney devoted her life purely to giving and receiving pleasure. Chalon became Barney's confidant when the woman was eighty-seven years old, and during ten years of weekly visits with her he learned details of her many liasons.

Le Lumineux Destine d'Alexandra David-Neel is Chalon's biography of the first European woman to journey to the "Forbidden City," Lhasa, the inaccessible seat of the Dalai Lama in the Tibetan highlands. David-Neel, who based her book *Voyage d'une Parisienne a Lhassa* on her experience, has received the Prix Mumm Kleber Haedens.

BIOGRAPHICAL/CRITICAL SOURCES:

PERIODICALS

New York Times Book Review, July 8, 1979, p. 15.
Washington Post Book World, November 4, 1979.

*   *   *

CHAPLIN, L(inda) Tarin 1941-

PERSONAL: Born December 4, 1941, in Brooklyn, NY; daughter of Sidney and Flora (a secretary; maiden name, Feldman) Kurland; married Anton Chaplin, January 31, 1960 (divorced October, 1976); children: Scott, Tamara, Daniel. *Education:* Moorpark Junior College, A.A., 1970; Pennsylvania State University, B.A. (summa cum laude), 1973; University of California, Los Angeles, M.A., 1976; attended Middlebury College, 1981, Yad Vashem: International Center for Holocaust Studies, 1984, and King Edward College, 1989-90. *Religion:* Jewish.

ADDRESSES: Home—Route 1, Box 4340, Montpelier, VT 05602.

CAREER: University of California, Los Angeles, CA, dance department, teaching associate, 1974-76; Goddard College, Plainfield, VT, director of dance, 1976-81; Johnson State College, Johnson, VT, visiting assistant professor of dance, 1979-81; Middlebury College, Middlebury, VT, assistant professor of dance and head of dance program, 1981-85; Hebrew University, Jerusalem Rubin Academy of Music and Dance, Israel, artist-in-residence, 1985-86; Pennsylvania State University, University Park, PA, artist-in-residence, 1986-87; University of London, Laban Centre for Movement & Dance, London, England, visiting faculty member, 1987-88; Simon Fraser University, School for Contemporary Arts, Canada, visiting faculty member, 1989-90; University of Montana, Department of Drama/Dance, visiting artist, 1990-91; Lesley College, MA, adjunct faculty member, 1991—; free-lance dance work, 1991—. Resthaven Hospital, Los Angeles, CA, movement therapist for the deaf, summer, 1975; Bucknell University, Lewisburg, PA, movement therapist for the blind, summer, 1977; Pennsylvania Governor's School for the Arts, faculty member, summer, 1977; Lyn-

don State College, Governor's Institute on the Arts, dance faculty member, summer, 1983; Burlington College, Dance Therapy Program, faculty member, summer, 1986; guest artist at Duke University, California Institute of the Arts, University of California, Santa Cruz, and Pennsylvania State University. Vermont International Performance Project, director and co-producer, 1987—; Dance Council of Ireland, National Youth Dance Company, artistic director, summer season, and National Choreography Course, director, 1988—; The Carlisle Project, artistic staff member and workshop leader, 1988—. Artistic director and founder of tarin chaplin & co., Dance/Image/Gallery, and student touring company, Dancetroupe; member of Dance Notation Bureau, Vermont Alliance for Arts in Education, and Vermont Council on the Arts; member of board of directors of Vermont Dance Alliance; consultant to several groups, including Green Mountain Consortium, New England Touring Program, Vermont Council on the Arts, and Dance Forum Ireland. Guest at a number of institutions, including Hong Kong City Contemporary Dance Co., Vermont Touring Artists Program, DanceArt Boston, and American College Dance Festivals. Choreographer of *Song of the Shoes,* a Holocaust memorial.

MEMBER: American College Dance Festival Association, American Dance Guild, Laban Institute for Movement Studies, Phi Beta Kappa, Phi Kappa Phi.

AWARDS, HONORS: Vermont Council on the Arts fellowships, 1977, 1980, 1981, 1985, 1988, 1989; National Endowment for the Humanities fellowship, 1980; scholar at International Symposium on Teaching Holocaust Studies, 1980; winner of Vermont Dance Festival choreographic competition, 1982, 1983; Middlebury College grants, 1982, 1983, 1985, 1986; Marion and Jasper Whiting Foundation grant, 1984; National Endowment for the Arts fellowship, 1985; grants from Israeli-American Cultural Foundation, 1986, the Laban Centre, 1987, and Asian Cultural Council, 1990.

WRITINGS:

(With Lynne Blom) *The Intimate Act of Choreography,* University of Pittsburgh Press, 1982.
Song of the Shoes (theatre script), Library of Congress, 1988.
(With Blom) *The Moment of Movement: Dance Improvisation,* University of Pittsburgh Press, 1989.

Contributor to magazines and periodicals, including *Journal of AAHPER, Quest, Teaching Theatre, Dance Teacher Now, Montana Journal,* and *Connector.*

WORK IN PROGRESS: The Embodied Actor; A New Attitude: Choreographing for the Ballet; Dancing beyond Technique; Digging Deeper; and *Story of a Story.*

SIDELIGHTS: L. Tarin Chaplin once wrote: "Certainly dance is about the body, but it is much more than that. It is about the entire self in the process of being. Dance as an art form is symbolic and communicative, not merely an activity of the physical cells. It is also a creative process (the very crux of man's advancement through the ages), an intellectual process (with a body of knowledge), and an experiential process (a way of knowing ourselves).

"We must recognize the range that an educated definition of dance includes—performance itself (involving technique, choreography, and production), its evolution and aesthetics as an art form, how it functions cross-culturally, movement analysis with its therapeutic and creative aspects, the sciences upon which it is based (kinesiology, anatomy, physiology), and its major kinetic role in perception and learning.

"Dance in the fullest sense of the word is thus a part of life—an essential, neither a frill nor an isolated entity, but part of the whole. Art is not separate from science, nor literature from physical education. Can I show the connection between dance and a line from e. e. cummings, or a concept of Nietzsche's? That is my challenge as teacher.

"Students are not empty vessels waiting to be filled. In order for learning to take place, they must digest, integrate, and synthesize what they receive in light of their own backgrounds. I believe the student who is free to respond, create, question, and actively participate, who is motivated and involved with teachers and peers, is the one who will learn and grow. But to try and mold a passive body—no, thank you, that is not for me.

"The thrill that comes from sparking a student's response and that which comes from creating, performing, and producing new works are, although different, nonetheless integral to my sense of professional satisfaction and success. And so to complete the cycle of teacher, I must continue to develop myself as a dancer. My own choreography and work with my company is of the utmost importance to me. I need and thrive on the objective critiques, the on-the-line demands, the practical headaches, and the striving for artistic excellence that comes with being a performing artist.

"Dance need not be esoteric because its medium, movement, is universal to the human species and basic to every individual's growth and development. My goal is to use its potential as an element common to us all and as a vehicle for heightening people's perception of themselves and their world through greater kinesthetic/aesthetic awareness."

BIOGRAPHICAL/CRITICAL SOURCES:

PERIODICALS

Dance Teacher Now, September/October, 1980.

CHARLESWORTH, Maxwell John 1925-

PERSONAL: Born December 30, 1925, in Numurkah, Victoria, Australia; son of William Arthur and Mabel (Ferrari) Charlesworth; married Stephanie Armstrong, 1950; children: Sara, Hilary, Stephen, Lucy, Bruno, Anna, Esther. *Education:* University of Melbourne, M.A., 1949; University of Louvain, Ph.D., 1955.

ADDRESSES: Home—86 Lang St., North Carlton, Victoria, Australia.

CAREER: University of Melbourne, Melbourne, Victoria, Australia, tutor, 1949-50; University of Auckland, Auckland, New Zealand, lecturer, 1956-58; University of Melbourne, lecturer, 1959-62, senior lecturer, 1962-67, reader in philosophy, 1968-74; Deakin University, Geelong, Victoria, Australia, dean of humanities and professor of philosophy, 1974-90, emeritus professor, 1991—.

WRITINGS:

Aristotle on Art and Nature, Auckland University Press, 1957.
Philosophy and Linguistic Analysis, Duquesne University Press, 1959.
(Editor and translator) St. Anselm, *Proslogion,* Clarendon Press, 1965.
(Translator and author of introduction) Thomas Aquinas, *The World Order,* McGraw, 1970.
Philosophy of Religion: The Historic Approaches, Herder & Herder, 1972.
Church, State and Conscience, University of Queensland Press, 1973.
The Problem of Religious Language, Prentice-Hall, 1974.
The Existentialists and Jean-Paul Sartre, University of Queensland Press, 1975.
The Golden Bough and After, University of Tasmania Press, 1977.
The Responsibility of Intellectuals, La Trobe University Press, 1978.
Science, Non-Science and Pseudo-Science, Deakin University Press, 1982.
The Aboriginal Land Rights Movement, Deakin University Press, 1984.
(Editor) *Religion in Aboriginal Australia,* University of Queensland Press, 1984.
Life among the Scientists: An Anthropological Study of an Australian Scientific Community, Oxford University Press, 1989.
Life, Death, Genes and Ethics, ABC Press (Sydney), 1989.
Religious Worlds, Penguin Books, 1989.
Ancestor Spirits: Aspects of Australian Aboriginal Life and Spirituality, Deakin University Press, 1990.

Sophia: A Journal for Discussion in Philosophical Theology, founder, 1962, editor, 1962-90.

WORK IN PROGRESS: Bioethics in a Liberal Society.

*   *   *

CHARNEY, Maurice (Myron) 1929-

PERSONAL: Born January 18, 1929, in New York, NY; son of A. Benjamin (a business executive) and Sadie A. (Stang) Charney; married Hanna Kurz (a professor of French), June 20, 1954; children: Leopold Joseph, Paul Robert. *Education:* Harvard University, A.B. (magna cum laude), 1949; Princeton University, M.A., 1951, Ph.D., 1952.

ADDRESSES: Home—168 West 86th St., New York, NY 10024. *Office*—English Department, Rutgers University, CN 5054, New Brunswick, NJ 08903.

CAREER: Hunter College (now Hunter College of the City University of New York), New York City, instructor in English, 1953-54; Rutgers University, New Brunswick, NJ, instructor, 1956-59, assistant professor, 1959-62, associate professor, 1962-67, professor, 1967-75, distinguished professor of English, 1975—. Fulbright exchange professor at University of Bordeaux and University of Nancy, 1960-61; visiting summer professor at Hunter College of the City University of New York, 1963, Harvard University, 1965, Shakespeare Institute of Canada, 1969, Shakespeare Institute of America, 1970, 1971, and 1975, Concordia University, 1981, McMaster University, 1983; visiting professor at Folger Institute, 1985. Co-chairman, American Civilization Seminar, Columbia University, 1977-79. Member of central executive committee, Folger Institute, 1978-80; member of national board of directors, Shakespeare Globe Center, 1988—. Literary adviser, Methuen & Co., 1980-84. *Military service:* U.S. Army, 1954-56.

MEMBER: Academy of Literary Studies (charter member; president, 1985-87), Modern Language Association of America (chairman of Shakespeare Division, 1973, 1976), Shakespeare Association of America (president, 1987-88), Malone Society, Renaissance Society of America, American Association of University Professors, American Society for Theatre Research, Marlowe Society, Friends of Vic and Sade, Phi Beta Kappa.

AWARDS, HONORS: Medal of the City of Tours, 1989.

WRITINGS:

Shakespeare's Roman Plays, Harvard University Press, 1961.
(Editor and author of introduction) *Discussions of Shakespeare's Roman Plays,* Heath, 1964.
(Editor) William Shakespeare, *Timon of Athens,* Signet, 1965.

(Editor) *The Tragedy of "Julius Caesar,"* Bobbs-Merrill, 1969.
Style in "Hamlet," Princeton University Press, 1969.
How to Read Shakespeare, McGraw, 1971.
Comedy High and Low, Oxford University Press, 1978.
(Editor) *Comedy: New Perspectives,* New York Literary Forum, 1978.
(Editor) *Shakespearean Comedy,* New York Literary Forum, 1980.
Sexual Fiction, Methuen, 1981.
Joe Orton, Macmillan, 1984.
(Editor with Joseph Reppen) *The Psychoanalytic Study of Literature,* Analytic Press, 1985.
(Editor) *Classic Comedies,* New American Library, 1985.
(Editor with Reppen) *Psychoanalytic Approaches to Literature and Film,* Fairleigh Dickinson University Press, 1987.
Hamlet's Fictions, Routledge & Kegan Paul, 1988.
(Editor) *"Bad" Shakespeare,* Fairleigh Dickinson University Press, 1988.
Titus Andronicus, Harvester Press-Wheatsheaf Books, 1990.
All of Shakespeare, Columbia University Press, 1993.

Contributor of articles and reviews to over fifty periodicals. Member of editorial board, *Shakespeare Quarterly, Review of Psychoanalytic Books, Pirandellian Studies, Assaph,* and *New York Literary Forum.*

SIDELIGHTS: Maurice Charney once told *CA:* "I have always been much impressed by Anthony's words for the dead Caesar: 'You all did love him once, not without cause.' That would make a perfect epitaph for a writer, who imagines his career as a form of flirtation and seduction of an unknown public. The writer hopes that his works will enlist him in the magic circle of humanity, what Hawthorne called 'catching hold of the magnetic chain' of humanity. This is a strange, remote, and audacious attempt to sign on to the human race. Its mental and oneiric quality endows it with special properties set apart from daily life. The writer as thaumaturge can transcend his other roles as father, husband, teacher, and ritual clown that characterize his daily life."

BIOGRAPHICAL/CRITICAL SOURCES:

PERIODICALS

Times Literary Supplement, December 11, 1981; August 30, 1985.

*   *   *

CLIFFORD, J(ohn) Garry 1942-

PERSONAL: Born March 22, 1942, in Haverhill, MA; son of John G. (a businessman) and Doris M. (a hair stylist; maiden name, Champagne) Clifford; married Dale Lothrop, December 22, 1969 (divorced December 22, 1972); married Carol Keltner Davidge (a writer), June 13, 1976. *Education:* Williams College, B.A., 1964; Indiana University, M.A., 1965, Ph.D., 1969. *Politics:* Democrat.

ADDRESSES: Home—Box 27, Old Colony Rd., Eastford, CT 06242. *Office*—Department of Political Science, U-24 University of Connecticut, Storrs, CT 06268.

CAREER: University of Tennessee, Knoxville, instructor in history, 1968-69; University of Connecticut, Storrs, assistant professor, 1969-72, associate professor, 1973-84, professor of political science, 1984—. Dartmouth College, visiting associate professor, 1972-73.

MEMBER: Society for Historians of American Foreign Relations, American Association of University Professors, Phi Beta Kappa.

AWARDS, HONORS: Frederick Jackson Turner Award, Organization of American Historians, 1971, for *The Citizen Soldiers: The Plattesburg Training Camp Movement, 1913-1920.*

WRITINGS:

The Citizen Soldiers: The Plattesburg Training Camp Movement, 1913-1920, University Press of Kentucky, 1972.
(Editor with Norman Cousins) *Grenville Clark: Memoirs of a Man,* Norton, 1975.
(With Thomas Paterson and Kenneth Hagan) *American Foreign Policy: A History,* Heath, 1977, 3rd edition, two volumes, 1987, 3rd revised edition, 1990.
(With Samuel R. Spencer) *The First Peacetime Draft,* University Press of Kansas, 1986.

Associate editor, "Modern War" series, University Press of Kansas, 1988—. Member of editorial board, *Diplomatic History,* 1992-95.

WORK IN PROGRESS: A book-length study of President Roosevelt and the coming of World War II.

*   *   *

CLINE, Edward 1946-

PERSONAL: Born October 22, 1946, in Pittsburgh, PA. *Education:* Attended South Texas Junior College, 1966-67. *Politics:* "Radical for Capitalism." *Religion:* Atheist.

ADDRESSES: Home—275 Hawthorne Ave., No. 125, Palo Alto, CA 94301. *Agent:*Bleecker Street Associates, New York, NY.

CAREER: Writer, 1972—. Also worked in factories, construction, airline communications, computer operations,

inventing management, banking, and insurance business, and worked as a bank teller, book editor, and computer screen designer. *Military service:* U.S. Air Force, Air Police, 1964-65.

MEMBER: Mystery Writers of America, American Crime Writers League.

WRITINGS:

A Layman's Guide to Understanding OPEC and the Fuel Crisis, Lion Enterprises, 1979.
First Prize (detective novel), Mysterious Press, 1988.
(Author of introduction) Victor Hugo, *The Man Who Laughs,* Atlantean Press, 1991.
Whisper the Guns (suspense novel), Atlantean Press, 1992.

Author of monograph *The Wizards of Disambiguation: A Critique of Detective Genre Literary Criticism,* 1991. Author of "Over There," a column in *Gryphon.* Contributor of articles and short stories to numerous periodicals, including *Ego, Institute Scholar, Wall Street Journal,* and *Reason,* and of reviews to various periodicals, including *Library Journal, Armchair Detective, Mystery Readers Journal, Intellectual Activist,* and *Reason.* Book, movie, and television reviewer, *On Principle.*

WORK IN PROGRESS: The Head of Athena and *China Basin,* both detective novels.

SIDELIGHTS: Edward Cline once told *CA:* "I regard myself as primarily a novelist, of the school Ayn Rand has defined as 'Romantic Realism.' My interest in drama and conflict was aroused when I saw *The Time Machine* in 1960. While not strictly a romantic film, it presented value conflicts and imagination as I'd never seen them before, but its chief value to me was its scope and presentation of a comprehensive view of man and history. *North by Northwest,* which I saw the same year, is a film I enjoyed enormously and still enjoy almost without qualification. A little romanticism will go a long way."

Cline recently wrote *CA:* "I've always had confidence in the value and marketability of my novels, but it has been hard to communicate that confidence to modern editors and publishers, who not only seem to resent such confidence but seem determined to deny that a market for Romantic Realism exists. There are economic as well as cultural reasons for the sorry state of modern literature and art. Ayn Rand discussed them best in her essay, 'Moral Inflation.' We live today in an esthetic desert created by the salinity of subjectivism and the fungus of naturalism, in which television programming and films have become vehicles for propaganda, and in which novels, non-fiction, plays, and artwork are not only produced with government subsidies but win cultural recognition. The writer or artist who offers man- and reason-affirming values is today a pariah, to be shunned, ignored, or mocked lest his work expose the fraud of modern literature and art. Still, it is possible for such a writer or artist to succeed, and, barring overt censorship by the government, I believe one should strive to reach the esthetic and literary markets which our bankrupt literati and esthetic middlemen protest too volubly do not exist. 'When reason and philosophy are reborn,' wrote Rand in 1969, 'literature will be the first phoenix to rise out of today's ashes.' It is not an easy thing to try to be a phoenix—one may often question the glory in it—but the knowledge that it *is* possible, in one's own work, and in that of others, ought to be fuel enough for a lifetime of effort."

*   *   *

COCTEAU, Jean (Maurice Eugene Clement) 1889-1963

PERSONAL: Born July 5, 1889, in Maisons-Lafitte, Yvelines, France; died October 11, 1963; buried at Milly-la-Foret, Essone, France, in the garden of the chapel Saint-Blaise-des Simples, which he designed himself; son of Georges (a lawyer) and Eugenie (Lecomte) Cocteau. *Education:* Studied at Lycee Condorcet, Paris; attended private classes.

CAREER: Poet, playwright, novelist, essayist, painter, and director. Founder, with Blaise Cendrars, of Editions de la Sirene, 1918. *Military service:* During World War I, Cocteau went to Rheims as a civilian ambulance driver, and then to Belgium, where he joined a group of marine-riflemen, until it was discovered that his presence was unauthorized; also served for a time with an auxiliary corps in Paris.

MEMBER: Academie Francaise, Academie Royale de Belgique, Academie Mallarme, American Academy, German Academy (Berlin), Academie de Jazz (president), Academie du Disque, Association France-Hongrie, National Institute of Arts and Letters (New York; honorary member).

AWARDS, HONORS: Prix Louions-Delluc, 1946; Grand Prix de la Critique Internationale, 1950; Grand Prix du Film Avant-garde, 1950, for *Orphee;* D.Litt., Oxford University, 1956; Commandeur de la Legion d'Honneur, 1961.

WRITINGS:

POETRY

La Lampe d'Aladin, Societe d'Editions, 1909.
Le Prince frivole, Mercure de France, 1910.
La Danse de Sophocle, Mercure de France, 1912.
Le Cap de Bonne-Esperance, Editions de la Sirene, 1919.
L'Ode a Picasso, Francois Bernouard, 1919.
(With Andre Lhote) *Escales,* Editions de la Sirene, 1920.

Poesies: 1917-20, Editions de la Sirene, 1920.
Vocabulaire, Editions de la Sirene, 1922.
Plain-Chant, Stock, 1923.
Poesie, 1916-23, Gallimard, 1924.
La Rose de Francois, Francois Bernouard, 1924.
Cri ecrit, Imprimerie de Montane (Montpellier), 1925.
Pierre Mutilee, Editions des Cahiers Libres, 1925.
L'Ange heurtebise, Stock, 1925.
Opera: Oeuvres poetiques 1925-27, Stock, 1927, revised edition, 1959, published as *Oeuvres poetiques: 1925-27,* Dutilleul, 1959.
Morceaux choisis, Gallimard, 1932, published as *Poemes,* H. Kaeser (Lausanne), 1945.
Mythologie (poems written on lithographic stones; contains 10 original lithographs by Giorgio di Chirico), Editions de Quatre-Chemins, 1934.
Allegories, Gallimard, 1941.
Leone, Nouvelle Revue Francaise, 1945, translation by Alan Neame published as *Leoun,* [London], 1960.
La Crucifixion, Morihien, 1946.
Le Chiffre sept, Seghers, 1952.
Appogiatures (with a portrait of Cocteau by Modigliani), Editions du Rocher (Monaco), 1953.
Dentelle d'eternite, Seghers, 1953.
Clair-Obscur, Editions du Rocher, 1954.
Poemes: 1916-55, Gallimard, 1956.
(Contributor) Paul Eluard, *Corps memorabiles,* Seghers, 1958.
De la Brouille, Editions Dynamo (Liege), 1960.
Ceremonial espagnol du Phoenix [suivi de] *La Partie d'echecs,* Gallimard, 1961.
Le Requiem, Gallimard, 1962.
Faire-Part (ninety-one previously unpublished poems), foreword by Jean Marais and Claude-Michel Cluny, Librairie Saint-Germain des Pres, 1968.
Vocabulaire, Plain-Chant et autre poemes, Gallimard, 1983.
Poemes (contains *Appogiatures, Clair-Obscur,* and *Paraprosodies*), Editions du Rocher, 1984.

NOVELS

Le Potomak, Societe Litteraire de France, 1919, definitive edition, Stock, 1924.
(Self-illustrated) *Le Grand Ecart,* Stock, 1923, reprinted, 1970, translation by Lewis Galantiere published as *The Grand Ecart,* Putnam, 1925, translation by Dorothy Williams published as *The Miscreant,* P. Owen, 1958.
Thomas l'imposteur, Nouvelle Revue Francaise, 1923, revised edition, edited by Bernard Garniez, Macmillan, 1964, translation and introduction by Galantiere published as *Thomas the Impostor,* Appleton, 1925, translation by Williams published as *The Impostor,* Noonday Press, 1957.

Les Enfants terribles (also see below), Grasset, 1929, re-printed, 1963, revised edition, edited by Jacques Hardre, Blaisdell, 1969, translation by Samuel Putnam published as *Enfants Terribles,* Harcourt, 1930, translation by Rosamund Lehmann published in England as *The Children of the Game,* Harvill, 1955, same translation published as *The Holy Terrors* (not the same as translation of *Les Monstres sacres,* below), New Directions, 1957.

La Fin du Potomak, Gallimard, 1940.

Deux travestis (contains lithographs by Cocteau), Fournier, 1947.

PLAYS

(With Frederic de Madrazo) *Le Dieu bleu* (ballet), first produced in Paris at the Theatre du Chatelet, June, 1912.

(With Pablo Picasso, Erik Satie, Leonide Massine, and Sergei Pavlovich Diaghilev) *Parade* (ballet), first produced in Paris at the Theatre du Chatelet, May 18, 1917.

(Author of scenario) *Le Boeuf sur le toit ou, The Do Nothing Bar,* with music by Darius Milhaud, first produced in Paris at the Comedie des Champs-Elysees, February 21, 1920.

Les Maries de la tour Eiffel (ballet; first produced in Paris at the Theatre des Champs-Elysses, June 18, 1921), Nouvelle Revue Francaise, 1924, translation by Dudley Fitts published as *The Eiffel Tower Wedding Party,* in *The Infernal Machine, and Other Plays,* New Directions, 1963, translation by Michael Benedikt published as *The Wedding on the Eiffel Tower,* in *Modern French Plays,* Faber, 1964.

Antigone (based on the play by Sophocles, with music by Arthur Honegger; first produced in Paris at the Theatre de l'Atelier, December 20, 1922), Nouvelle Revue Francaise, 1928, translation by Wildman published in *Four Plays,* MacGibbon & Kee, 1961.

Romeo et Juliette (five-acts and twenty-three tableaux), first produced in Paris at the Theatre de la Cigale, June 2, 1924.

Orphee (one-act tragedy; first produced in Paris at the Theatre des Arts, June 15, 1926), Stock, 1927, translation by Carl Wildman published as *Orphee: A Tragedy in One Act* (first produced in New York at the Living Theatre as *Orpheus,* September 30, 1954), Oxford University Press, 1933, translation by John Savacool published as *Orphee,* New Directions, 1963.

La Voix humaine (one-act; first produced in Paris at the Comedie-Francaise, February 17, 1930; also see below), Stock, 1930, translation by Wildman published as *The Human Voice,* Vision Press, 1951 (produced in New York, 1980).

La Machine infernale (four-act tragedy; first produced in Paris at the Theatre Louis Jouvet, April 10, 1934), Grasset, 1934, reprinted, Livre de Poche, 1974, published in England in French, under the original title, with an introduction and notes by W. M. Landers, Harrap, 1957, translation and introduction by Wildman published as *The Infernal Machine,* Oxford University Press, 1936, translation by Albert Bermel published as *The Infernal Machine,* New Directions, 1963.

Oedipe-Roi (based on the play by Sophocles), first produced in 1937.

Les Chevaliers de la table ronde (four-act; first produced in Paris at the Theatre de l'Oeuvre, October 14, 1937), Gallimard, 1937, reprinted, 1966, translation by W. H. Auden published as *The Knights of the Round Table,* New Directions, 1963.

Les Parents terribles (three-act; first produced in Paris at the Theatre des Ambassadeurs, November 14, 1938; also see below), Gallimard, 1938, reprinted, 1972, revised edition, edited by R. K. Totton, Methuen, 1972, translation by Charles Frank published as *Intimate Relations,* MacGibbon & Kee, 1962.

Les Monstres sacres (three-act; first produced in Paris at the Theatre Michel, February 17, 1940), Gallimard, 1940, translation by Edward O. Marsh published as *The Holy Terrors,* MacGibbon & Kee, 1962.

La Machine a ecrire (three-act; first produced in Paris at the Theatre Hebertot, April 29, 1941), Gallimard, 1941, translation by Ronald Duncan published as *The Typewriter,* Dobson, 1957.

Renaud et Armide (three-act tragedy; first produced in Paris at the Comedie-Francaise, April 13, 1943), Gallimard, 1943.

L'Aigle a deux tetes (three-act; first produced in Paris at the Theatre Hebertot, November, 1946; also see below), Gallimard, 1946, reprinted, 1973, translation by Duncan published as *The Eagle Has Two Heads,* Funk, 1948, translation by Wildman published as *The Eagle with Two Heads,* MacGibbon & Kee, 1962.

(Adaptor) Tennessee Williams, *Un Tramway nomme desir* (first produced in Paris at the Theatre Edouard VII, October 17, 1949), Bordas, 1949.

Bacchus (three-act; first produced in Paris at the Theatre Marigny, December 20, 1951), Gallimard, 1952, translation by Mary C. Hoeck published as *Bacchus: A Play,* New Directions, 1963.

(Translator and adaptor) Jerome Kilty, *Cher menteur* (first produced in Paris at Theatre de l'Athenee, October 4, 1960), Paris-Theatre, 1960.

L'Impromptu du Palais-Royal (first produced in Tokyo, May 1, 1962), Gallimard, 1962.

OPERA

Oedipus rex: Opera-oratorio en deux actes d'apres Sophocle, Boosey & Hawkes, 1949.

FILMS

(And director) *Le Sang d'un Poete* (produced, 1932), Editions du Rocher, 1948, augmented edition, 1957, translation by Lily Pons published as *The Blood of a Poet,* Bodley Press, 1949.

La Comedie du bonheur, produced, 1940.

Le Baron fantome (appeared also as actor), produced, 1942.

L'Eternel retour (produced, 1944), Nouvelles Editions Francaises, 1948.

Les Dames du Bois du Boulogne, produced, 1944.

(And director) *La Belle et la bete* (based on a fairy tale by Mme. Leprince de Beaumont; produced, 1945), Editions du Rocher, 1958, bilingual edition, New York University Press, 1970.

Ruy Blas (adaptation of the play by Victor Hugo; produced, 1947), Editions du Rocher, 1947.

La Voix humaine (adaptation of the play), produced, 1947.

(And director) *L'Aigle a deux tetes* (adaptation of the play), produced, 1947.

Noces de sable, produced 1948.

(And director) *Les Parents terribles* (adaptation of the play; produced, 1948), Le Monde Illustre, 1949, translation and adaptation by Charles Frank produced under title *Intimate Relations* (also known as *Disobedient*), 1952.

Les Enfants terribles (adaptation of the novel), produced, 1948.

(And director) *Orphee* (Cocteau speaks a few lines as "author"; produced, 1949), Andre Bonne, 1951.

(And director) *Santo Sospiro* (short film), produced, 1951.

Ce Siecle a cinquante ans (short film), produced, 1952.

La Coronna nagra, produced, 1952.

(And director) *Le Rouge est mis* (short film), produced, 1952.

(And director) *Le Testament d'Orphee* (produced, 1959), Editions du Rocher, 1959.

NONFICTION

Le Coq et l'arlequin (with a portrait of Cocteau by Picasso), Editions de la Sirene, 1918, translation by Rollo H. Myers published as *Cock and Harlequin: Notes Concerning Music,* Egoist Press (London), 1921.

Dans le ciel de la patrie, Societe Spad, 1918.

Le Secret professionnel, Stock, 1922.

Dessins, Stock, 1923, translation published as *Drawings,* Dover, 1972.

Picasso, Stock, 1923.

Lettre a Jacques Maritain, Stock, 1926, published as *Lettre a Maritain: Reponse a Jean Cocteau* (including response by Maritain), Stock, 1964.

Le Rappel a l'ordre, Stock, 1926, translation by Myers published as *A Call to Order,* Faber & Gwyer, 1926, reprinted, Haskell House, 1974.

Romeo et Juliette: Pretexte a mise en scene d'apres le drame de William Shakespeare, Se Vend au Sans Pareil, 1926.

Le Mystere laic (an essay on indirect study), Editions de Quatre Chemins, 1928, published as *Essai de critique indirecte: Le mystere laic-Des beaux arts consideres comme un assassinat,* introduction by Bernard Grasset, Grasset, 1932.

(Published anonymously) *Le Livre blanc,* Les Quatre Chemins (Paris), 1928, reprinted, B. Laville, 1970, translation published as *The White Paper,* Olympia Press (Paris), 1957, Macaulay, 1958, translation with an introduction by Crosland, containing woodcuts by Cocteau, published as *Le Livre blanc,* P. Owen, 1969, revised edition published as *Le Livre blanc suivi de quatorze textes erotiques inedits; illustre de dix-huit dessins,* Persona (Paris), 1981.

(Self-illustrated) *Opium: Journal d'une desintoxication,* Stock, 1930, reprinted, 1972, translation by Ernest Boyd published as *Opium: The Diary of an Addict* (contains twenty-seven illustrations by Cocteau), Longmans, Green, 1932, translation by Margaret Crosland and Sinclair Road published as *Opium: The Diary of a Cure,* P. Owen, 1957, revised edition, 1968, Grove, 1958.

(Self-illustrated) *Portraits-Souvenir, 1900-1914,* Grasset, 1935, translation by Crosland published as *Paris Album, 1900-1914,* W. H. Allen, 1956.

(Contributor) Gea Augsbourg, *La Vie de Darius Milhaud,* Correa, 1935.

60 dessins pour "Les Enfants terribles", Grasset, 1935.

Mon premier voyage: Tour du monde en 80 jours, Gallimard, 1936, translation by Stuart Gilbert published as *Round the World Again in Eighty Days,* G. Routledge, 1937, translation by W. J. Strachan published as *My Journey Round the World,* P. Owen, 1958.

Dessins en marge du texte des "Chevaliers de la table ronde," Gallimard, 1941.

Le Greco, Le Divan, 1943.

Portrait de Mounet-Sully (contains sixteen drawings by Cocteau), F. Bernouard (Paris), 1945.

La Belle et la bete: Journal d'un film, Janin, 1946, translation by Ronald Duncan published as *Diary of a Film,* Roy, 1950, revised edition published as *Beauty and the Beast: Diary of a Film,* Dover, 1972.

Poesie critique (poetry criticism), edited by Henri Parisot, Editions des Quatre Vents, 1946, published in two volumes, Gallimard, 1959.

(With Paul Claudel, Paul Eluard, and Stephane Mallarme) *De la musique encore et toujours!,* preface by Paul Valery, Editions du Tambourinaire, 1946.

La Difficulte d'etre, P. Morihien, 1947, translation by Elizabeth Sprigge published as *The Difficulty of Being,* introduction by Ned Rorem, P. Owen, 1966, Coward, 1967.

Le Foyer des artistes, Plon, 1947.

L'Eternel retour, Nouvelles Editions Francaises, 1947.

Art and Faith: Letters between Jacques Maritain and Jean Cocteau, Philosophical Library, 1948.

(Self-illustrated) *Drole de menage,* P. Morihien, 1948.

Lettre aux Americains, Grasset, 1949.

(Editor) *Almanach du theatre et du cinema,* Editions de Flore, 1949.

Maalesh: Journal d'une tournee de theatre, Gallimard, 1949, translation by Mary C. Hoeck published as *Maalesh: Theatrical Tour in the Middle East,* P. Owen, 1956.

(Editor) *Choix de lettres de Max Jacob a Jean Cocteau: 1919-1944,* P. Morihien, 1949.

Dufy, Flammarion, 1950.

(With Andre Bazin) *Orson Welles,* Chavane, 1950.

Modigliani, F. Hazin (Paris), 1950.

(With others) *Portrait de famille,* Fini, 1950.

Jean Marais, Calmann-Levy, 1951, reprinted, 1975.

Entretiens autour de cinematographe, recueillis par Andre Fraigneau, A. Bonne, 1951, translation by Vera Traill published as *Cocteau on Film: A Conversation Recorded by Andre Fraigneau,* Roy, 1954, reprinted, Dover, 1972.

Journal d'un inconnu, Grasset, 1952, translation by Alec Brown published as *The Hand of a Stranger,* Elek Books (London), 1956, Horizon, 1959, translation by Jese Browner published as *Diary of an Unknown,* Paragon House, 1988.

Reines de la France, Grasset, 1952.

(With Julien Green) *Gide vivant* (includes commentary by Cocteau and excerpts from the diary of Green), Amiot-Dumont, 1952.

Carte blanche (prose sketches with drawings, watercolors and photographs by Cocteau), Mermod (Lausanne), 1953.

(With others) *Prestige de la danse,* Clamart, 1953.

Discours de reception de M. Jean Cocteau a l'Academie francaise et reponse de M. Andre Maurois, Gallimard, 1955.

Look to the Glory of Your Firm and the Excellence of Your Merchandise, for If You Deem These Good, Your Welfare Becomes the Welfare of All, translated by Lewis Galantiere, Draeger (Montrouge), c.1955.

Aux confins de la Chine, Edition Caracteres, 1955.

Colette: Discours de reception a l'Academie Royale de Belgique, Grasset, 1955 (extracts in English published in *My Contemporaries,* 1967; also see below).

Lettre sur la poesie, Dutilleul, 1955.

Le Dragon des mers, Georges Guillot, 1955.

(Contributor) *Marbre et decoration,* Federation Marbriere de France, c.1955.

Journals (contains sixteen drawings by Cocteau), edited and translated with an introduction by Wallace Fowlie, Criterion Books, 1956.

Adieu a Mistinguett, Editions Dynamo, 1956.

Art et sport, Savonnet (Limoges), 1956.

Impression: Arts de la rue, Editions Dynamo, 1956.

(Author of introduction and notes) Jean Dauven, compiler, *Jean Cocteau chez les sirens: Une experience de linguistic sur le discours de reception a l'Academie francaise de M. Jean Cocteau* (illustrations by Picasso), Editions du Rocher, 1956.

Temoignage (with portrait and engraving by Picasso), P. Bertrand, 1956.

Le Discours de Strasbourg, Societe Messine d'Editions et d'Impressions (Metz), 1956.

Le Discours d'Oxford, Gallimard, 1956, translation by Jean Stewart published as *Poetry and Invisibility,* in *London Magazine,* January, 1957.

(With Louis Aragon) *Entretiens sur le Musee de Dresde,* Cercle d'Art, 1957, translation published as *Conversations on the Dresden Gallery,* Holmes, 1983.

Erik Satie, Editions Dynamo, 1957.

La Chapelle Saint Pierre, Villefranche sur Mer, Editions du Rocher, 1957.

La Corrida du premier mai, Grasset, 1957.

Comme un miel noir (in French and English), L'Ecole Estienne, 1958.

(With Roloff Beny and others) *Merveilles de la Mediterranee,* Arthaud, 1958.

Paraprosodies precedees de 7 dialogues, Editions Du Rocher, 1958.

(Contributor) G. Coanet, *De bas en haut,* La Societe Messine d'Editions et d'Impressions (Metz), 1958.

La Salle des mariages, Hotel de ville de Menton, Editions du Rocher, 1958.

La Canne blanche, Editions Estienne, 1959.

Gondole des morts, All'Insegne del Pesce d'Oro (Milan), 1959.

Guide a l'usage des visiteurs de la Chapelle Saint Blaise des Simples, Editions du Rocher, 1960, reprinted, 1975.

De la brouille, Editions Dynamo, 1960.

Notes sur "Le Testament d'Orphee," Editions Dynamo, 1960.

(Editor) *Amedeo Modigilani: Quinze dessins,* Leda, 1960.

Decentralisation, [Paris], 1961.

(With others) *Insania pingens,* Ciba (Basle), 1961, published as *Petits maitres de la folies,* Clairfontaines (Lausanne), 1961.

Le Cordon ombilical, Plon, 1962.

Picasso: 1916-1961 (with twenty-four original lithographs by Picasso), Editions du Rocher, 1962.

Discours a l'Academie royale de langue et de litterature francaises, Editions Dynamo, 1962.

Hommage, Editions Dynamo, 1962.

Interview par Jean Breton (preceded by two poems by Cocteau, *Malediction au laurier,* and *Hommage a Igor Stravinsky*), [Paris], 1963.

Adieu d'Antonio Ordonez, Editions Forces Vives, 1963.

(Contributor) *La Comtesse de Noailles,* Librairie Academique Perrin, 1963.

(Contributor) *Exposition les peintres temoins de leur temps* (catalog), Musee Galliera (Paris), 1963.

(Contributor) *Toros muertos,* Editions Forces Vives, 1963.

La Mesangere, De Tartas, 1963.

Jean Cocteau: Entretien avec Roger Stephane (interview), J. Tallandier, 1964.

(Contributor) *Exposition Lucien Clergue* (catalog), Le Musee (Luneville), 1964.

Entretien avec Andre Fraigneau (interview), preface by Pierre de Boisdeffre, Union Generale d'Editions, 1965.

Pegase, Nouveau Cercle Parisien du Livre, 1965.

My Contemporaries, translated, edited, and introduced by Crosland, P. Owen, 1967, Chilton, 1968.

Entre Radiguet et Picasso, Editions Hermann, 1967.

Professional Secrets: The Autobiography of Jean Cocteau (not related to 1922 book), translated by Richard Howard, edited by Robert Phelps, Farrar, Straus, 1970.

Lettres a Andre Gide avec quelques reponses d'Andre Gide, La Table Ronde, 1970.

(With Raymond Radiguet) *Paul et Virginie,* Edition Speciale, 1973.

Lettres a Milorad, 1955-1963, Editions Saint-Germain-des-Pres, 1975.

Correspondence avec Jean-Marie Magnan, Belfond, 1981.

Le Passe defini I, 1951-1952, journal, edited by Pierre Chanel, Gallimard, 1983, translation by Richard Howard published as *Past Tense: The Diaries of Jean Cocteau,* Volume 1, Harcourt, 1986.

Lettres a Jacques Maritain, Stock, 1984.

Le Passe defini II, 1953, journal, edited by Chanel, Gallimard, 1985.

OMNIBUS VOLUMES

Call to Order (contains *Cock and Harlequin, Professional Secrets,* and other critical essays), translated by Rollo H. Myers, Holt, 1923, reprinted, Haskell House, 1974.

Oedipe Roi [and] *Romeo et Julliette,* Plon, 1928.

Jean Cocteau (contains a study of Roger Lannes, poems, and a bibliography), Seghers, 1945, revised edition, 1969.

Oeuvres completes, 11 volumes, Marguerat, 1947-51.

Theatre, 2 volumes, Gallimard, 1948, augmented edition, 2 volumes, Grasset, 1957.

Poemes (contains *Leone, Allegories, La Crucifixion,* and *Neige*), Gallimard, 1948.

Theatre de Poche, P. Morihien, 1949, published as *Nouveau theatre de poche,* Editions du Rocher, 1960.

Anthologie poetique de Jean Cocteau, Le Club Francais du Livre, 1951.

Venise images par Ferruccio Leiss [and] *L'Autre face de Venise par Jean Cocteau,* D. Guarnati (Milan), 1953.

Le Grand ecart [and] *La Voix humaine,* Club des Editeurs, 1957.

Impression [with] *Arts de la rue* [and] *Eloge de l'imprimerie,* Editions Dynamo, 1957.

Cocteau par Lui-meme, edited by Andre Fraigneau, Editions du Seuil, 1957.

Ceremonial espagnal du phenix [with] *La Partie d'eches,* Gallimard, 1961.

Five Plays (contains *Orphee, Antigone, Intimate Relations, The Holy Terrors,* and *The Eagle with Two Heads*), Hill & Wang, 1961.

Orpheus, Oedipus Rex, [and] *The Infernal Machine,* translated with a foreword and introductory essay by Wildman, Oxford University Press, 1962.

Four Plays (contains *Antigone, Intimate Relations, The Holy Terrors,* and *The Eagle with Two Heads*), Mac-Gibbon Kee, 1962.

Les Enfants terribles [and] *Les Parents terribles,* Club des Librairies de France, 1962.

Special Cocteau: Les Maries de la Tour Eiffel [and] *Les Chevaliers de la table ronde,* [Paris], 1966.

Opera [with] *Le Discours du grand sommeil,* preface by Jacques Brosse, Gallimard, 1967.

The Infernal Machine, and Other Plays, New Directions, 1967.

Opera [with] *Plain-Chant,* Livre de Poche, 1967.

Le Cap de Bonne Esperance [with] *Discours du grand sommeil,* Gallimard, 1967.

Pages choisies, edited by Robert Prat, Hachette, 1967.

Opera [with] *Des mots, De mon style,* Tchou, 1967.

Two Screenplays: The Blood of a Poet [and] *The Testament of Orpheus,* translated by Carol Martin-Sperry, Orion Press, 1968.

Screenplays and Other Writings on the Cinema (contains *The Blood of a Poet, Beauty and the Beast,* and *Testament of Orpheus*), Orion Press, 1968.

White Paper [with] *The Naked Beast at Heaven's Gate,* the latter by P. Angelique, Greenleaf Classics, 1968.

Three Screenplays: L'Eternal retour, Orphee, La Belle et la bete, translated by Carol Martin-Sperry, Orion Press, 1968.

Cocteau's World: An Anthology of Writings by Jean Cocteau, translated and edited by Margaret Crosland, P. Owen, 1971, Dodd, 1973.

Du cinematographie (collected works), edited by Andre Bernard and Claude Gauteur, P. Belfond, 1973.

Entretiens sur le cinematographie, edited by Bernard and Gauteur, P. Belfond, 1973.

Mon Premier voyage, Des beaux-arts consideres comme un assassinat, Lettre a Maritan, Vialetay, 1973.

Orphee: Extraits de la tragedie d'Orphee ainsi que des films Orphee et Le Testament d'Orphee, Bordas, 1973.

Poesie de journalism, 1935-1938, P. Belfond, 1973.

Also author of *Sept dialogues avec le Seigneur qui est en nous,* Editions du Rocher.

OTHER

Contributor on the arts to *Paris-Midi,* March to August, 1919; wrote a regular series for *Ce Soir,* 1937-38; founder, with Maurice Rostand and others, of the review *Scheherazade.*

Some of Cocteau's manuscripts are housed at the Archives Jean Cocteau, Milly-la-Foret, Essonne, France.

ADAPTATIONS: There are several recordings of Cocteau's works in French; *Opium: Journal of a Cure* has been dramatized by Roc Brynner and produced in Dublin and London, 1969, and in New York, 1970.

SIDELIGHTS: Jean Cocteau had a wide-ranging career as a poet, dramatist, screenwriter, and novelist. "Cocteau's willingness and ability to turn his hand to the most disparate creative ventures," James P. Mc Nab wrote in the *Dictionary of Literary Biography,* "do not fit the stereotypical image of the priestlike—or Proust-like—writer single-mindedly sacrificing his life on the altar of an all-consuming art. But the best of his efforts, in each of the genres that he took up, enriched that genre." Among Cocteau's most influential works are *Parade,* a seminal work of the modern ballet, *La Machine infernale,* a play that is still performed some sixty years after it was written, such films as *La Belle et le bete* and *La Sang d'un Poete (The Blood of a Poet),* and his novel *Les Enfants terrible,* a study of adolescent alienation. A *National Observer* writer suggested that, "of the artistic generation whose daring gave birth to Twentieth Century Art, Cocteau came closest to being a Renaissance man." Cocteau, according to Annette Insdorf in the *New York Times,* "left behind a body of work unequalled for its variety of artistic expression."

Thrown out of school as a boy, Cocteau was the problem child of a well-to-do Parisian family. After his father com-

mitted suicide when Cocteau was ten, the boy grew closer to his mother, who appears as the dominant female character in much of his later work. As a child Cocteau also formed a lifelong passion for the theatre, which he described many times as being "the fever of crimson and gold." Wallace Fowlie reported: "The atmosphere of the theatre became a world for him. . . . Every detail of a theatre production fascinated him, from the luminously painted backdrop to the women selling caramels in the intermission." Neal Oxenhandler, writing in his book *Scandal and Parade: The Theater of Jean Cocteau,* saw a definite relationship between Cocteau's love for his mother and his love for the theater. Oxenhandler stated: "Cocteau's first experience of the glamor and prestige of the theater was the smell of his mother's perfume and the shimmering beauty of her dresses as she prepared to go out for an evening at the Comedie-Francaise or the Opera. She *was* the theater."

When Cocteau was eighteen years old, his poems were publicly read in Paris by the actor Edouard de Max and several of his theatre friends. Enamored with the young poet's work, the actors presented a reading at a theatre on the Champs-Elysees. Following this introduction, Cocteau became an active participant in the Paris arts scene. In the period before World War I, he was associated with the avant-garde Cubists, Fauvists and Futurists. Cocteau met and worked with such artists as Pablo Picasso and Erik Satie, published several volumes of poems, began writing plays and ballets, and established himself as a leading member of the French avant-garde. Always a poet first and foremost, Cocteau emphasized from the beginning of his career that, whatever the genre in which he worked, all of his creations were essentially poetry.

Cocteau's first early success was the ballet *Parade,* written with composer Erik Satie, painter Pablo Picasso, choreographer Leonide Massine, and Sergei Pavlovich Diaghilev of the Russian Ballet. Telling of a group of mysterious promoters trying unsuccessfully to entice spectators into a circus tent where an undefined spectacle is taking place, *Parade* is generally considered to be the first of the modern ballets. It was also Cocteau's "first public attempt," Alan G. Artner explained in the *Chicago Tribune,* "to express the mysterious and eternal in the everyday." Jacques Guicharnaud and June Beckelman wrote in *Modern French Theatre from Giraudoux to Beckett* that *Parade* "has a theme that might serve as a symbol for the whole of Cocteau's works: Cocteau keeps his public outside. The true spectacle of the inner circus remains forbidden, despite the poet's innumerable invitations to enter. And perhaps that inner circus is no more than an absolute vacuum."

A casual remark made by Diaghilev was Cocteau's inspiration for the ballet. As the two men were walking down a street, Cocteau wondered why it was that Diaghilev was so reserved in his critical judgements of Cocteau's work. The Russian adjusted his monocle and said: "Astonish me." *Parade* was written to do just that. The Futurist-inspired sets and costumes by Picasso and the satirical music of Satie, both of which caused an uproar with the Parisian audience, were complemented by Cocteau's wild scenario involving acrobats, a juggler, and a girl riding a bicycle. "Whatever else *Parade* may have been," Oxenhandler commented, "it was above all a series of visual surprises." *Parade* is still in the repertories of the Joffrey Ballet and the Metropolitan Opera Ballet.

Another early success was 1921's *Les Maries de la Tour Eiffel* (*The Wedding on the Eiffel Tower*). Written for Les Ballets Suedois, a Swedish ballet troupe working in Paris, the ballet consists of a series of unrelated nonsense scenes set during a wedding reception at the Eiffel Tower. Wild events take place: a camera gives birth to an ostrich; a lion eats several cast members. "The poetry of *Les Maries de la Tour Eiffel*," Guicharnaud and Beckelman wrote, "consists in replacing traditional coherence by an inner chance that is quite contrary to the logic of everyday reality. 'The scenes fit together like the words of a poem,' says Cocteau in his preface [to the ballet]. Here the poem would be a surrealist *divertissement* or, to be more explicit, a collage. Its interest lies both in its amusing absurdity and its challenge to accepted forms of poetry and painting." Cocteau claimed that the work was meant to introduce a "classicism of shock" to ballet. Whatever its intentions, *The Wedding on the Eiffel Tower* was denounced by the avant-garde Dadaists of the day as well as by the Parisian middle-class audience.

Cocteau's involvement with the ballet and theatre brought him in the early 1920s into contact with a group of six young composers. Acting as their spokesman, Cocteau brought "Les Six," as they became known, into prominence throughout Europe. Fowlie remarked: "The group of *Les Six*—Honegger, Poulenc, Milhaud, Taillefer, Auric and Durey—owes [Cocteau] its name and the early support it received in Paris." In addition, Fowlie related, Cocteau served as an "impresario and interpreter" for such other artists as Satie, Braque, Picasso and Stravinsky, all of whom "owe some of their glory to Cocteau."

During this time Cocteau also began a homosexual relationship with Raymond Radiguet, the young author of several novels. When Radiguet died of typhoid in 1923, Cocteau was distraught. He turned to opium, then a brief reconciliation with the Catholic Church, and finally to a series of young lovers. One of these lovers, Jean Desbordes, inspired a novella entitled *Le Livre blanc*. Published anonymously because Cocteau wished to avoid embarrassing his mother, the book is a frank, first-person account of a homosexual's life in 1920s France, ending with the narrator leaving the country to seek freedom and love.

"Although the aesthetic interest of *Le Livre blanc* is quite slim," Mc Nab admitted, "it is as rich a compendium of Cocteau's obsessions as any single work he ever wrote."

Opium: The Diary of an Addict recounted the facts of Cocteau's opium addiction, for which he twice required hospitalization before being cured. The book is based on Cocteau's notes of a three-month hospital stay in late 1928 and early 1929. It is, as Mc Nab described it, "a fascinating account of the stages of withdrawal." Cocteau also wrote several poems, collected in *Opera,* in which the opium experience figured prominently. These poems, according to Bettina Liebowitz Knapp in her study *Jean Cocteau,* "are chiseled in incisive strokes. The feelings of lightness and giddiness are conveyed in harmonious tonalities, a blend of sharp consonants and free-flowing vowels, very nearly concretizing his drug-induced euphoria. During these periods he seemed to attain a kind of second sight that enabled him to discern the invisible from the visible, the inhuman from the human, and to express these visions in dramatic and poignant terms."

During the 1920s Cocteau also devoted his time to writing several novels, a new genre for him. These novels are usually concerned with protagonists who cannot leave their childhoods behind them. In *Le Grand Ecart,* for example, Jacques Forestier finds that beauty always brings him pain, a pattern established when he was a child. As a young man, the pattern continues when he loses his first love to another man, leading Jacques to attempt suicide. Germaine Bree and Margaret Guiton note in *The French Novel from Gide to Camus* that Jacques is "the most directly autobiographical of Cocteau's fictional characters." In addition, as Mc Nab pointed out, the novel anticipates Cocteau's later obsession with childhood.

In *Thomas l'Imposteur,* a novel released only days after *Le Grand Ecart,* Cocteau tells the story of a young boy of sixteen who finds stability and purpose in his life only by joining the French Army during World War I. To enlist in the army, Guillaume Thomas has lied about his age and borrowed a friend's uniform. Soon he is even posing as the nephew of a military hero. "Cocteau hastens to add, however, that this is not an ordinary imposture, a vulgar means of 'getting ahead,' " as Bree and Guiton explained. "Guillaume, floating on the edges of a dream, is more at home, more himself, in a fictional than in a real existence." As Mc Nab noted, for Guillaume, "the enemy soldiers are merely a kind of catalyst, allowing his game to go on."

Les Enfants Terribles (*The Children of the Game*) was begun while Cocteau was in the clinic recovering from his opium addiction. It was first published in 1929. The novel focuses on the doomed relationship between a brother and sister whose isolated existence is threatened and eventually destroyed by the outside world. To escape the loss of their isolation, the two siblings commit a double suicide. "On the one hand," wrote Leon S. Roudiez in *MOSAIC,* "the text extols the impossible values of a lost paradise of childhood; on the other hand, it condemns the contemporary world on account of its ugliness and evil. But Elizabeth and Paul demonstrate that the lost paradise is a myth. . . . The choice between total rejection, which can only be achieved in death, and total compromise, which means corruption of the individual, represents the truth that the text proclaims." Speaking of the book's structure, Bree and Guiton wrote: "*Les Enfants terribles* . . . has the rigorous economy of means, the geometrical construction, the almost claustrophobic *unite de lieu* of a classical tragedy. . . . This most ordered of Cocteau's novels also has the strongest poetic impact."

Les Enfants terribles has won lasting critical acclaim for its haunting evocation of childhood. Knapp praised "the manner in which Cocteau catches and describes with such accuracy the protagonists' innermost thoughts and sensations. . . . The frequent omissions of rational plot sequences, the starkly drawn portraits of the children, the flavor of mystery and excitement which comes with the introduction of the unknown . . . , and the march of Fate . . . lend an enduring haunting quality to the book." Tom Bishop, writing in *Saturday Review,* described *Les Enfants terribles* as "a haunting novel of youth, classic in form yet highly original in its portrayal of a brother and sister living in a bizarre world of their own." "During the past thirty years," Fowlie stated in *French Literature: Its History and Its Meaning,* "this book has become a classic, both as a novel belonging to the central tradition of the short French novel and as a document of historical-psychological significance." Knapp claimed that *Les Enfants terribles* was "Cocteau's great work: a novel possessing the force, the tension, poetry, and religious flavor of an authentic Greek tragedy." After publishing *Les Enfants terribles,* Cocteau essentially gave up long fiction.

During the 1930s Cocteau devoted his time to the theatre, writing two of his most accomplished dramatic works at this time: *La Machine infernale* and *Les Parents terribles.* *La Machine infernale* is an update of the Oedipus legend from ancient Greece. But Cocteau transforms the story into a kind of "Parisian drawing-room comedy," as Joseph Chiari wrote in *The Contemporary French Theatre: The Flight from Naturalism.* This was accomplished by having the characters live in ancient Greece and modern France at the same time, a "time simultaneity," according to Knapp. She explained: Cocteau "succeeded in bringing about such a feat by scenic manipulation. . . . The characters, who lived in the contemporary world, performed on a brightly lit daislike structure placed in the center of the stage; the rest of the area, symbolizing the ancient

mythological, inexorable aspect of existence, was clothed in darkness." Characters speak in contemporary slang, jazz music can be heard in the background, and talk of war and revolution is common. All of these factors successfully mingle the present and the past. "This realism," Knapp believed, "makes disturbingly actual the plight of the entire family—a whole society—which is at the mercy of an inescapable fate." In addition, the blending of present and past was specifically designed to appeal to the Parisian audience. Speaking of the play in *Literary Criticism—Idea and Act: The English Institute, Selected Essays, 1939-1972,* Francis Fergusson found that Cocteau "presents a very ancient myth, the myth of Oedipus, not as a joke, but as a perennial source of insight into human destiny. Yet at the same time the play is addressed to the most advanced, cynical, and even *fashionable* mind of contemporary Paris. It is at one and the same time chic and timeless." Oxenhandler, writing in *Jean Cocteau and the French Scene,* declared that *La Machine infernale* "has always been considered Cocteau's greatest work for the theater."

With *Les Parents terribles* Cocteau adopted a Naturalist approach to the theatre. "The characters," Guicharnaud and Beckelman explained, "constantly remind us that they are acting out a play—vaudeville, drama, or tragedy, depending on the moment and situation." The plot revolves around a troubled marriage and a mother's obsessive love for her son. When the son falls in love with a young girl, his mother is distraught. Unknown to both of them, however, is that the girl is also the mistress to the boy's father. The play ends with the mother's suicide. As Oxenhandler noted in his *Scandal and Parade: The Theater of Jean Cocteau,* the play "possesses the chief virtues of good naturalistic theater: psychological depth and insight coupled with a generally liberal and humanitarian view. . . . It is one of the peaks of Cocteau's achievement. . . . But in renouncing the world of myth and poetry where he situates his earlier works [Cocteau] has diminished himself."

The play was first produced at the Theatre des Ambassadeurs in Paris in 1938, where it ran for 200 performances. When the Municipal Council of Paris protested that a play about incest was being performed in a city-owned theatre, however, *Les Parents terribles* moved to the Bouffes Parisiens, where it ran for another 200 performances. In 1941, when a revival of the play was staged in occupied Paris, fascist opponents organized nightly disruptions until the police were forced to close the play. A later attempt to produce the play in Vichy France ended when the Nazi occupiers forbade it.

Cocteau's cinematic work began in 1932 with *Le Sang d'un Poete* (*The Blood of a Poet*), a film that C. G. Wallis in the *Kenyon Review* called "one of the authentic classics of the cinema, in the small group that includes *Caligari, Ten Days That Shook the World,* some Rene Clair, and some Chaplin." Divided into four parts, the film follows the poet through a series of hallucinatory experiences which transform him from a naive young man into a "depersonalized poet," as Wallis noted. Cocteau described the film as "a realistic documentary of unreal events."

The protagonist of *Le Sang d'un Poete* speaks to a living statue, steps through a mirror into another realm, gambles for his fate, and—twice—commits suicide. The film ends with the living statue, a woman, rising into an immortal realm accompanied by a bull. "The woman is transformed into an emblematic abstraction, the work of art as posterity sees it, distant, precise, finally made clear if not understandable," Oxenhandler explained. "Looking at *Le Sang d'un Poete* superficially," Wallis wrote, "it is obvious that its aesthetic power resides in its special combination of simplicity of elements, enigma of intention, and a pervading sense of an underlying rationality." Insdorf found that the film can "be appreciated as a voyage through the poet's internal landscape, and as a celebration of film's unique powers." Cocteau, Oxenhandler noted, "repeatedly refused to explain *Le Sang d'un Poete.*"

Cocteau's visionary approach to film is also evident in his *La Belle et la bete,* an adaptation of the beauty and the beast legend. Bosley Crowther of the *New York Times* found the film to be "an eminent model of cinema achievement in the realm of poetic fantasy," while Oxenhandler, writing in *Yale French Studies,* claimed that "the camerawork in this beautiful film situates it in that area of imagination where we half believe the impossible, where metaphor is normal speech and miracle is a deeper truth than nature."

La Belle et la bete tells the story of a beautiful maiden who falls in love with a monstrous-looking man. Cocteau's version of the story tells a psychological drama with autobiographical overtones. When the beast discovers that he is loved, he is no longer an outsider, he gains self-knowledge. The film ends with the beast becoming beautiful. "This fable suggest to us . . . ," wrote Oxenhandler, "the yearning of a man who has always secretly felt himself an exile from society and dramatizes his triumphant acceptance by society." Crowther believed that "Freudian or metaphysician, you can take from [the film] what you will." He praised it as "a priceless fabric of subtle images. . . . A fabric of gorgeous visual metaphors, of undulating movements and rhythmic pace, of hypnotic sounds and music, of casually congealing ideas."

Cocteau also filmed his plays *Les Parents terribles* and *Les Enfants terribles,* as well as *Orphee* and *Le Testament d'Orphee,* both adaptations of ancient Greek myths. The best of his films, Alan G. Artner wrote in the *Chicago Tri-bune,* "are masterpieces that equal if not surpass his work in poetry and the theater. Their visions have haunted spectators the world over." "Cocteau," Insdorf stated, "was a boldly personal, stylistically innovative and internationally influential filmmaker. His legacy of elegantly crafted fantasy and dark poetry can be felt in such diverse films as those of Vincent Minnelli and Jacques Demy, as well as David Lynch's 'Elephant Man.' "

In all of his work, Cocteau held true to certain principles of artistic creation. One of these principles was the invocation of mystery. He once explained that "the less a work of art is understood, the less quickly it will open its petals and the less quickly it will wither." Similarly, he believed that "the secret of poetry is to take things from the places in which habit has set them and reveal them from a different angle as though we see them for the first time."

Some of the mystery that Cocteau sought in his art is also found in the enduring public image he created for himself. As he wrote in his *Journal d'un Inconnu,* translated as *Diary of an Unknown,* "Man seeks to escape himself in myth, and does so by any means at his disposal. Drugs, alcohol, or lies. Unable to withdraw into himself, he disguises himself. . . . He invents. He transfigures. He mythifies. He creates. He fancies himself an artist."

Evaluations of Cocteau's career note the variety of his work and his prolific creation. Bishop wrote: "Cocteau's output is staggering in quantity and diversity, encompassing novels, plays, poems, films, essays, autobiographical writings, journalism, painting, and a voluminous correspondence. Much of this *oeuvre* is minor and some is frankly bad, but enough of it is outstanding, either intrinsically or as pure invention. . . . His failures do not diminish his major accomplishments." "One overlooks a lot in the case of Cocteau," Artner stated, "from narcissism and opium addiction to some less than sterling behavior during the Occupation. One overlooks it because he worked so very hard at becoming a poet and achieved it so irresistibly in film and in the ballet theater." Bree, writing in *Contemporary Literature,* called Cocteau "one of the most versatile and talented personalities France has produced in our own time, a poet, essayist, novelist, playwright, film-maker, draftsman, and animator whose accomplishments have yet to be assessed."

BIOGRAPHICAL/CRITICAL SOURCES:

BOOKS

Anderson, Alexandra and Carol Saltus, editors, *Jean Cocteau and the French Scene,* Abbeville Press, 1984.

Bernard, Andre and Claude Gauteur, *Entretiens sur le cinematographe,* Belfond, 1973.

Bree, Germaine and Margaret Guiton, *The French Novel from Gide to Camus,* Harcourt, 1962.

Brown, Frederick, *An Impersonation of Angels: A Biography of Jean Cocteau,* Viking, 1968.

Chanel, Pierre, *Album Cocteau,* Tchou (Paris), 1970.

Chiari, Joseph, *The Contemporary French Theatre: The Flight from Naturalism,* Rockliff, 1958, reprinted, Gordian Press, 1970.

Cocteau, Jean, *Journal d'un inconnu,* Grasset, 1952, translation by Alec Brown published as *The Hand of a Stranger,* Elek Books (London), 1956, Horizon, 1959, translation by Jese Browner published as *Diary of an Unknown,* Paragon House, 1988.

Cocteau, Jean, *Professional Secrets: The Autobiography of Jean Cocteau,* translated by Richard Howard, edited by Robert Phelps, Farrar, Straus, 1970.

Contemporary Literary Criticism, Gale, Volume 1, 1973, Volume 8, 1978, Volume 15, 1980, Volume 16, 1981, Volume 43, 1987.

Crosland, Margaret, *Jean Cocteau,* Knopf, 1956.

Crowson, Lydia, *The Esthetic of Jean Cocteau,* University Press of New England, 1978.

Dictionary of Literary Biography, Volume 65: *French Novelists, 1900-1930,* Gale, 1988.

Dubourg, Pierre, *La Dramaturgie de Jean Cocteau,* Bernard Grasset, 1954.

Evans, Arthur B., *Jean Cocteau and His Films of Orphic Identity,* Art Alliance, 1975.

Fifield, William, *Jean Cocteau,* Columbia University Press, 1974.

Fowlie, Wallace, editor and translator, *The Journals of Jean Cocteau,* Criterion, 1956.

Fowlie, *Jean Cocteau: The History of a Poet's Age,* Indiana University Press, 1966.

Fowlie, *French Literature: Its History and Its Meaning,* Prentice-Hall, 1973, pp. 244-246.

Fraigneau, Andre, *Jean Cocteau: Entretiens autour du cinematographe,* Andre Bonne, 1951, translation by Vera Traill published as *Cocteau on the Film: A Conversation Recorded by Andre Fraigneau,* Dobson, 1954.

Fraigneau, *Cocteau par lui-meme,* Editions du Seuil, 1957, translation by Donald Lehmkuhl published as *Cocteau,* Grove, 1961.

Fraigneau, *Jean Cocteau: Entretiens avec Andre Fraigneau,* preface by Pierre de Boisdeffre, Union Generale d'Editions, 1965.

Gilson, Rene, *Jean Cocteau,* Seghers, 1964, Crown, 1969.

Guicharnaud, Jacques and June Beckelman, *Modern French Theatre from Giraudoux to Beckett,* Yale University Press, 1961, pp. 48-68.

Kihm, Jean-Jacques and Elizabeth Sprigge, *Jean Cocteau: The Man and the Mirror,* Coward-McCann, 1968.

Knapp, Bettina Liebowitz, *Jean Cocteau,* Twayne, 1970.

Lannes, Roger and Henri Parisot, *Jean Cocteau,* Seghers, 1945.

Magnan, Jean-Marie, *Cocteau,* Desclee de Brouwer (Paris), 1968.

Mauriac, Claude, *Jean Cocteau ou la verite du mensonge,* Odette Lieutier, 1945.

Millecam, Jean-Pierre, *L'Etoile de Jean Cocteau,* Editions du Rocher, 1952.

Mourgue, Gerard, *Jean Cocteau,* Editions Universitaires, 1965.

Oxenhandler, Neal, *Scandal and Parade: The Theatre of Jean Cocteau,* Rutgers University Press, 1957.

Peters, Arthur King, *Jean Cocteau and Andre Gide: An Abrasive Friendship,* Rutgers University Press, 1973.

Sprigge, Elizabeth and Jean-Jacques Kihm, *Jean Cocteau: The Man and the Mirror,* Gollancz, 1968.

Steegmuller, Francis, *Cocteau: A Biography,* Little, Brown, 1970.

Styan, J. L., *Modern Drama in Theory and Practice: Symbolism, Surrealism and the Absurd,* Volume 2, Cambridge University Press, 1981, pp. 51-60.

West, Paul, *The Modern Novel, Volume I,* Hutchinson University Library, 1963.

Wimsatt, W. K., editor, *Literary Criticism—Idea and Act: The English Institute, Selected Essays, 1939-1972,* University of California Press, 1974, pp. 590-601.

PERIODICALS

Adam, Number 300, 1965.

American Imago, summer, 1976.

Cahiers Jean Cocteau, Numbers 1-10, 1969-1985.

Chicago Tribune, May 17, 1988; July 2, 1989.

Choice, November, 1973.

Commentary, April, 1971.

Commonweal, November 17, 1967.

Contemporary Literature, Volume 9, number 2, 1968, p. 251.

Dance Scope, fall-winter, 1976-77, pp. 52-67.

Empreintes (Brussels), May, 1950; June, 1950; July, 1950.

Films and Filming, July, 1960, p. 21.

French Review, spring, 1974, pp. 162-170.

Kenyon Review, winter, 1944, pp. 24-42.

London Magazine, March, 1967.

Los Angeles Times, February 12, 1989.

Modern Drama, March, 1976, pp. 79-87.

MOSAIC, spring, 1972, pp. 159-166.

Nation, October 19, 1970, p. 379.

National Observer, June 12, 1967.

New Yorker, September 27, 1969.

New York Times, December 24, 1947, p. 12; May 13, 1984; April 17, 1988; September 22, 1989.

New York Times Book Review, December 25, 1966.

Paris Review, summer-fall, 1964, pp. 13-37.

Paris-Theatre, February, 1954.

Romanfilm, 1946.

Saturday Review, September 19, 1970.

La Table Ronde, October, 1955.
Time, September 28, 1970, p. 77.
Times (London), November 28, 1984; April 4, 1985; April 2, 1987.
Times Literary Supplement, October 6-12, 1989.
Yale French Studies, Number 5, 1950; Number 17, 1956, pp. 14-20.
Yale Romantic Studies, April, 1961.*

* * *

COHEN, Anthea 1913-

PERSONAL: Born August 26, 1913, in Guildford, England. *Education:* Educated in England. *Politics:* Liberal. *Religion:* Society of Friends (Quakers). *Avocational interests:* Visiting discotheques.

ADDRESSES: Home and office—3 Camden Court, Dover St., Ryde, Isle of Wight, England. *Agent*—Vanessa Holt, 59 Crescent Road, Leigh-on-Sea, Essex, England.

CAREER: Writer. Worked variously as an antiques buyer, shoe salesperson, and nurse.

WRITINGS:

Be Patient: Your Life in Their Hands, Butterworth & Co., 1967.
Popular Hospital Misconceptions, International Publishing Corp., 1969.

NOVELS

Angel of Vengeance, Quartet, 1982, Doubleday, 1984.
Angel without Mercy, Quartet, 1982, Doubleday, 1984.
Angel of Death, Quartet, 1984, Doubleday, 1985.
Fallen Angel, Quartet, 1984.
Dangerous Love (young adult), Pan Books, 1984.
Guardian Angel, Doubleday, 1985.
Hell's Angel, Quartet, 1986.
Substance & Shadow, Severn House, 1986.
Ministering Angel, Quartet, 1987.
Destroying Angel, Quartet, 1988.
Angel Dust, Quartet, 1989.
Recording Angel, Constable, 1991.
Angel in Action, Constable, 1992.

OTHER

Author of several short stories; also author of columns in *Nursing Mirror,* 1970-73, and "Green Girl" in *Scholastic,* 1978. Columnist for *World Medicine.* Contributor to trade journals and women's magazines. Many of Cohen's works have been translated into German.

WORK IN PROGRESS: Another "Angel" novel.

COHEN, Matt 1942-

PERSONAL: Born December 30, 1942, in Kingston, Ontario, Canada; son of Morris (a chemist) and Beatrice (Sohn) Cohen. *Education:* University of Toronto, B.A., 1964, M.A., 1965.

ADDRESSES: Home—P.O. Box 401, Verona, Ontario K0H 2W0, Canada.

CAREER: Writer, 1968—. McMaster University, Hamilton, Ontario, Canada, lecturer in religion, 1967-68; University of Alberta, Edmonton, Canada, writer-in-residence, 1975-76; University of Western Ontario, London, writer-in-residence, 1980-81. Visiting assistant professor of creative writing, University of Victoria, 1979; visiting professor, University of Bologna, 1984.

MEMBER: Writers Union of Canada (chairman, 1985-86).

AWARDS, HONORS: Senior Canadian Council Arts Award, 1977, 1984, and 1991; Canadian Fiction Award for best short story, 1982; Annual Contributor's Prize, *Canadian Fiction,* 1983, for "The Sins of Tomas Benares"; John Glasso Translation Prize, 1991.

WRITINGS:

ADULT FICTION

Korsoniloff (novella), House of Anansi, 1969.
Johnny Crackle Sings (novella), McClelland & Stewart, 1971.
Too Bad Galahad (short stories), illustrated by Margaret Hathaway, Coach House, 1972.
Columbus and the Fat Lady and Other Stories, House of Anansi, 1972.
The Disinherited (novel), McClelland & Stewart, 1974.
Wooden Hunters (novel), McClelland & Stewart, 1975.
The Colours of War (novel), McClelland & Stewart, 1977, Methuen, 1978.
Night Flights: Stories New and Selected, Doubleday, 1978.
The Sweet Second Summer of Kitty Malone (novel), McClelland & Stewart, 1979.
Flowers of Darkness (novel), McClelland & Stewart, 1981.
The Expatriate: Collected Short Stories, General Publishing, 1982, Beaufort Books, 1983.
Cafe Le Dog (short stories), McClelland & Stewart, 1983, published as *Life on This Planet and Other Stories,* Beaufort Books, 1985.
The Spanish Doctor (novel), McClelland & Stewart, 1984, Beaufort Books, 1985.
Nadine (novel), Viking, 1986, Crown, 1987.
Living on Water (short stories), Viking, 1988.
Emotional Arithmetic (novel), Lester & Orpen Dennys, 1990.
Freud: The Paris Notebooks (stories), Quarry Press, 1991.

(Editor) *The Story So Far/2,* Coach House, 1973.
Peach Melba (poetry), Coach House, 1974.
The Leaves of Louise (children's book), illustrated by Rikki, McClelland & Stewart, 1978.
(Editor) *The Dream Class Anthology: Writings from Toronto High Schools,* Coach House, 1983.
(Editor with Wayne Grady) *Intimate Strangers: New Stories from Quebec* (translated from the French), Penguin, 1986.
In Search of Leonardo (poetry), illustrated by Tony Urquhart, Coach House, 1986.

Contributor of criticism and short stories to periodicals, including *Canadian Literature* and *Canadian Fiction.* Author's work has been translated into many languages, including Croatian, French, German, Italian, Portuguese, Russian, Dutch, Hungarian, and Spanish.

WORK IN PROGRESS: A novel.

SIDELIGHTS: Canadian author Matt Cohen has gained a reputation as a prolific writer of experimental prose. Concerning himself with man's continuing quest for understanding and purpose in life, Cohen uses a variety of literary forms—short story, poetry, song, novella, and full-length novel—to illustrate his underlying theme: that summoning the energy needed to gain possession of oneself, to truly "get to be alive," creates the seeds of one's own destruction. "All values are violently subverted by the energy with which they are pursued," Jon Kertzer explains in *Essays on Canadian Writers.* "This central paradox explains the ferocity that prevails in Cohen's writing. The intense energy of life, which is the motive of passion, ambition, love, and conflict, is so powerful that it becomes destructive: life burns itself up."

Comprising what critics have hailed as some of his best work, Cohen's short story collections—including *Columbus and the Fat Lady, Too Bad Galahad, Night Flights, Cafe Le Dog,* and *Life on this Planet*—contain vignettes encapsulating his thematic search for self knowledge. *Night Flights,* published in 1978, received critical praise both for its perceptive insights into character and for the dreamlike quality of its prose. However, Cohen's initial story collections did not achieve a consensus of opinion among reviewers. Describing the array of protagonists in Cohen's early short works as "flat characters inhabiting vague landscapes and often involved in superficial relationships," J. M. Zezulka expresses criticism of Cohen's approach in *Dictionary of Literary Biography,* commenting that it is "as if the whole notion of personality stripped of accidentals were under scrutiny." By contrast, Zezulka notes, such later works as 1983's *Cafe Le Dog* manifest a shift by the author towards a more "joyful" style. And, commending Cohen for his ability to "catch the small mo-

ments, to notice the phrase or gesture or incident that lights up a major shift in the emotional alignment of the world," reviewer Douglas Hill goes on to praise Cohen for the understated humor and vivid narrative voice he employs throughout *Cafe Le Dog.* The shift away from the experimentation of Cohen's early writing towards a more traditional style is exemplified not only in his short stories but also in the author's longer fictional works.

In 1974 Cohen published the first of what would be a series of four novels taking as their setting the mythical Canadian town of Salem, Ontario. *The Disinherited,* a saga of the Thompsons, a farming family whose members have been wedded to the ancestral land for many years, is described by critic Eric Thompson as "an ambitious attempt to trace the disintegration of Ontario's myth of idyllic rural life over a span of four generations" in *Canadian Forum.* The three books that followed—*The Colours of War, The Sweet Summer of Kitty Malone,* and *Flowers of Darkness*—focus upon specific characters and situations in an examination of people's inner conflicts and outward responsibilities. Praising *Flowers of Darkness,* the last of Cohen's "Salem" novels, for its well-drawn characters and vivid portrayal of small-town life, Paul Stuewe comments in *Quill & Quire:* "There's a fine line between [telling] us more than we want to know and insufficient realism, which makes it difficult for us to feel a part of fictional creation, and I think that here Cohen has hit it just about right." The reviewer adds that Cohen "leaves no doubt . . . about the reality of Salem and its citizens, but we're also encouraged to use our imaginations in filling in some of the ambiguities which the author wisely refuses to resolve."

Distinguished from his later works by its relatively disjointed prose style, Cohen's early writing is full of "a lively sense of confusion and perversity . . . [shifting] deviously in time, tone, and point of view," according to Kertzer. The author's ability to shift from surrealism to realism within a single work has been compared by other critics to magic realist painting. In some instances, however, such shifts of time have generated confusion: "Lucid and descriptive moments are diluted by confusing transitions from . . . present to [past]," notes a reviewer in *West Coast Review of Books.* "Cohen's prose is crisp; his images, vivid; his characters believable; but his outlook is always guarded," adds Alan Cooper in *Library Journal.* And Linda Leith comments in *Essays on Canadian Writers* that Cohen's prose moves too deeply into the realm of experimentation. "He can write well when he relaxes and just writes," Leith states. "When he eschews the precious concern with technique and irritating cleverness that mar too many of his stories he achieves the very success that so eludes him when he strives for it."

Cohen's protagonists reflect his preoccupation with experimentation—his characters are typically social misfits: dropouts, nihilists, people discontented with their lives and with society. Many of the people that inhabit his fiction are burdened by life inside a physical shell that has been abused by alcohol or drugs, are infirm, or are in the process of physiological ageing. Others are engaged in a ceaseless internal dialogue with their pasts in an effort to distill a purpose through which to create a meaningful future. Still others border on the perverse: "Cohen leans toward a sort of Ontario Gothic—in which the physical deformities and impoverished lives of the inhabitants almost become too grotesque to be real," writes Michael Smith in *Books in Canada.* In his first novel, *Korsoniloff,* Cohen writes of the title character that he "cannot survive the consequences of his own existence." A schizophrenic assistant professor of philosophy, Andre Korsoniloff is engaged in a battle between, as Zezulka notes, "the roles he is expected to play, which will ensure some measure of acceptance, and his private urges, which alone can provide him with the sense of integrity and freedom he seeks." In the 1971 novella *Johnny Crackle Sings* the protagonist is a victim, not only of the drug-induced state into which he retreats, but also of the passage of time which results in a future that is "a sideways mirror to the unforgotten past." Theodore Beam, a displaced and hesitant young man, is pulled in two directions on the time continuum when he embarks on a transcontinental train journey home to confront his alcoholic father in *The Colours of War;* in facing his father Beam himself is faced by both his past and his mortality. At the same juncture, Beam is drawn into another possible future when he becomes superficially involved with political insurrectionist activities aboard the train. Zezulka notes that though Cohen portrays his flawed characters in a sympathetic manner, hidden beneath this are "betrayals, raw sexuality, violence, and intrigue; against these forces his characters struggle to affirm whatever measure of human dignity they can manage."

Beyond Cohen's central theme of self-actualization, there are other elements unifying Cohen's prolific career as a writer. Throughout his works he juxtaposes the elements of Time and the concept of Family—the passing of one generation into the next in a continuum. Kertzer discusses the relationship integrating time and the family: "Cohen's characters find their struggle to unite the fragments of their lives both sustained and subverted by their families: sustained because the family confers identity, subverted because it obscures the individual within his lineage. On one hand, the family provides a continuity of kinship that triumphs over the dislocations of time. On the other, the family denies importance or uniqueness to the individual by subsuming his brief span of years within a larger process of regeneration and degeneration." Cohen's four

"Salem" novels illustrate these themes through their concentration upon such subjects as inheritance, the diaries of ancestors that are read by an individual a map for his own future, the power that the "family land" has to dominate the individual. As Kertzer writes in a review for *Canadian Forum:* "[*Kitty Malone*] is suffused with time and morality. Image after image—clocks, lengthening shadows, family photos, heirlooms, layers of paint—signals the passing of time, reminding characters how they have forfeited their youth before they savoured it; how they are turning into copies of their parents; and worst of all, how they are losing hold of their very selves."

Cohen weaves a fiction that defines his native country as a Canada where, as Peter Gunn notes in the *Times Literary Supplement,* "vastness . . . is an illusion of the map." Cohen's protagonists age as he himself ages. 1969's *Korsoniloff* depicted a young man searching for meaning in his past in an effort to gain control over a future that stretched before him; twenty years later, in *Living on Water,* Gunn sees in Cohen's work a prescription for the predicament of the middle-aged: "a series of maintenance instructions for living in a place of confinement." Cohen's fictional characters view the rugged natural landscape of Canada from a distance, they are no longer participants in the struggle for autonomy, in the struggle to "get to be alive." "What is left, muffled by money and the urban clemencies for which Canadian cities are so justly renown, is the daily round," Gunn writes. Within his prolific outpouring of novels and short stories Cohen has outlined for his reader what he sees as life's central paradox: the struggle for self-possession without self-annihilation. As Nancy Wigston writes in the *Globe & Mail,* "he can balance the pathos and dark comedy of his reluctant hero's story, and let it speak for all the incongruities in our lives, the mysteries that make us what we are."

BIOGRAPHICAL/CRITICAL SOURCES:

BOOKS

Cohen, Matt, *Korsoniloff,* Anansi Press, 1969.

Cohen, Matt, *Johnny Crackle Sings,* McClelland & Stewart, 1971.

Contemporary Literary Criticism, Volume 19, Gale, 1981, pp. 111-116.

Gibson, Graeme, *Eleven Canadian Novelists,* Anansi Press, 1972, pp. 55-85.

Moss, John, *Sex and Violence in the Canadian Novel: The Ancestral Past,* McClelland & Stewart, 1977.

Twigg, Alan, *For Openers: Conversations with Twenty-Four Canadian Writers,* Harbour, 1981, pp. 175-184.

Woodcock, George, *The World of Canadian Writing: Critiques and Recollections,* University of Washington Press, 1980.

Zezulka, J. M., "Matt Cohen," *Dictionary of Literary Biography,* Volume 53: *Canadian Writers Since 1960,* Gale, 1986, pp. 135-141.

PERIODICALS

Books in Canada, April, 1979, p. 5.
Canadian Children's Literature, Volume 21, 1987, pp. 80-82.
Canadian Forum, March, 1975, p. 39; December, 1977, p. 41; May, 1979.
Canadian Literature, autumn, 1980, pp. 122-123.
Essays on Canadian Writers, fall, 1978, pp. 56-59; spring, 1980, pp. 93-101.
Globe & Mail (Toronto), April 15, 1984; March 30, 1985; September 27, 1986; October 8, 1988; October 27, 1990.
Library Journal, April 15, 1978, p. 896.
Los Angeles Times Book Review, April 28, 1985, p. 4.
Maclean's, March 12, 1979, pp. 54, 175-184.
New York Times Book Review, September 12, 1985, p. 18; February 16, 1986, p. 10; August 9, 1987, p. 20; May 1, 1988, p. 22.
Publishers Weekly, February 6, 1978, p. 90; February 13, 1978, p. 123.
Quill & Quire, February, 1981, p. 45.
Saturday Night, November, 1969, pp. 61-63; September, 1977, pp. 73-75; March, 1981, pp. 50-51.
Times Literary Supplement, December 1, 1989, p. 1338.
Washington Post, April 21, 1987.
West Coast Review of Books, September, 1977, p. 34.

*   *   *

COMDEN, Betty 1919-

PERSONAL: Born May 3, 1919, in Brooklyn, NY; daughter of Leo (a lawyer) and Rebecca (a school teacher; maiden name, Sadvoransky) Comden; married Steven Kyle (a designer and businessman), January 4, 1942; children: Susanna, Alan. *Education:* New York University, B.S., 1938.

ADDRESSES: Home—New York, NY. *Office*—c/o The Dramatists Guild, 234 West 44th St., New York, NY 10036. *Agent*—Ronald S. Konecky, 1 Dag Hammarskjold Plaza, New York, NY 10017.

CAREER: Author of musical comedies and screenplays, collaborating with Adolph Green, 1939—. Actress, performing in night club act "The Revuers," in Broadway musicals *On the Town,* 1944, *A Party with Betty Comden and Adolph Green,* 1958 and 1977, and *Isn't It Romantic,* 1983, and in films *The Band Wagon,* 1953, and *Garbo Talks,* 1985.

MEMBER: Writers Guild of America (East and West), American Federation of Television and Radio Artists, Screenwriters Guild, American Guild of Variety Artists, American Society of Composers, Authors, and Publishers, Dramatists Guild (member of council, 1948—), Authors League of America.

AWARDS, HONORS: Screenwriters Guild of America Award, 1949, for *On the Town,* 1952, for *Singin' in the Rain,* and 1955, for *It's Always Fair Weather;* Donaldson Award for lyrics, 1953, for *Wonderful Town;* Antoinette Perry (Tony) Award for lyrics, 1953, for *Wonderful Town,* for best score, 1968, for *Hallelujah, Baby,* for best book for musical, 1970, for *Applause,* for best book and lyrics, 1978, for *On the Twentieth Century,* and for best book and lyrics, 1982, for *A Doll's Life; Village Voice* Off-Broadway (Obie) Award, 1959, for *A Party with Betty Comden and Adolph Green;* Woman of Achievement Award, New York University Alumnae Association, 1978; New York City Mayor's Award for Art and Culture, 1978; named to Songwriters Hall of Fame, 1980.

WRITINGS:

MUSICALS; WITH ADOLPH GREEN

(Book and lyrics) *On the Town,* music by Leonard Bernstein, first produced on Broadway, 1944.
(Book and lyrics) *Billion Dollar Baby,* music by Morton Gould, first produced on Broadway, 1945.
(Book and lyrics) *Bonanza Bound,* music by Saul Chaplin, first produced in Philadelphia at Shubert Theatre, 1947.
(Sketches and lyrics) *Two on the Aisle,* music by Jule Styne, first produced on Broadway, 1951.
(Lyrics) *Wonderful Town,* music by Bernstein, first produced on Broadway, 1953.
(Additional lyrics) *Peter Pan,* music by Styne, first produced on Broadway, 1954.
(Book and lyrics) *Bells Are Ringing* (first produced on Broadway, 1956), music by Styne, Random House, 1957.
Say, Darling, music by Styne, first produced on Broadway, 1958.
A Party (revue based on collection of their previously written songs and sketches), first produced Off-Broadway, 1958, expanded version produced on Broadway as *A Party with Betty Comden and Adolph Green,* 1958, new version produced on Broadway, 1977.
(Lyrics) *Do Re Mi,* music by Styne, first produced on Broadway, 1960.
(Book and lyrics) *Fade Out—Fade In* (first produced on Broadway, 1964), music by Styne, Random House, 1965.

(Lyrics) *Hallelujah, Baby,* music by Styne, first produced on Broadway, 1967.

(Book) *Applause* (based on film *All About Eve,* original story by Mary Orr; first produced on Broadway, 1970), lyrics by Lee Adams, music by Charles Strouse, Random House, 1971.

Lorelei, first produced on Broadway, 1974.

(Book and lyrics) *On the Twentieth Century,* (based on plays by Ben Hecht, Charles MacArthur, and Bruce Millholland; first produced on Broadway, 1978), music by Cy Coleman, Samuel French, 1980.

(Book and lyrics) *A Doll's Life,* (based on play *A Doll's House,* by Henrik Ibsen; first produced on Broadway, 1982), music by Larry Grossman, Samuel French, 1983.

SCREENPLAYS; WITH ADOLPH GREEN

Good News, Metro-Goldwyn-Mayer, 1947.

The Barkleys of Broadway, Metro-Goldwyn-Mayer, 1949.

(And lyrics) *On the Town,* Metro-Goldwyn-Mayer, 1949.

(And lyrics) *Singin' in the Rain,* Metro-Goldwyn-Mayer, 1952, Viking, 1972; adapted for theater with first stage production on Broadway, 1985.

(And lyrics) *The Band Wagon,* Metro-Goldwyn-Mayer, 1953.

(And lyrics) *It's Always Fair Weather,* Metro-Goldwyn-Mayer, 1955.

Auntie Mame, Warner Bros., 1958.

(And lyrics) *Bells Are Ringing,* Metro-Goldwyn-Mayer, 1960.

(And lyrics) *What a Way to Go,* Twentieth Century-Fox, 1964.

OTHER

Also author, with Green, of music, book, and lyrics for night club act, "The Revuers," 1939-43; lyrics for film, *Take Me Out to the Ballgame,* Metro-Goldwyn-Mayer, 1949; musical television comedy specials for the American Broadcasting Company; and of book, *Comden and Green on Broadway.* Contributor to magazines, including *Esquire* and *Vogue.*

SIDELIGHTS: Together with her collaborator, Adolph Green, Betty Comden has written the lyrics, and often the librettos, for some of the most memorable musicals of all time. Cited by the *New Yorker*'s Brendan Gill as being "among the most gifted people on Broadway," Comden's and Green's successes through the years have included *On the Town, Singin' in the Rain, Applause, On the Twentieth Century,* and *Hallelujah, Baby.*

Singin' in the Rain, which starred Gene Kelly as the man so in love with life that he danced down a rainy street, was described by *New York Times* reviewer Frank Rich as "the happiest movie musical ever made." *Chicago Tribune* re-

viewer Howard Reich said: "Ask any film buff to name the greatest movie musical of all time, and odds are he will cite *Singin' in the Rain* or *The Band Wagon,* both of which Comden and Green wrote." Of the 1985 Broadway stage version, however, Rich declared: "It says much about the stage version of the film that it doesn't send us home with the image of a joyous man singing and dancing. What is most likely to be remembered about this *Singin' in the Rain* is the rain." Rich attributed the play's shortcomings to a fundamental difference in genre which director Twyla Tharp was unable to overcome. "*Singin' in the Rain* was a fantasy movie about the dream factory of the movies," Rich said. "Once transposed to the stage in realistic terms, the fantasy evaporates even as the rain pours down. No matter how much Miss Tharp recreates specific gestures from the film, they play differently in the theater. Watching her Don Lockwood splash about, we aren't carried away into never-never Hollywoodland. . . . We're still in the humdrum everyday world, wondering how stage technicians achieve the effect and watching an actor get very, very wet."

One of Comden's and Green's biggest hits was not a conventional Broadway show. *A Party with Betty Comden and Adolph Green,* originally produced in 1958 and revived in 1977, presents an overview of the pair's best material, performed by the authors themselves. Some portions of the show date back to their nightclub revue days of the late 1930s; although much of the satire contained in the skits was topical when first produced, audiences and reviewers found it no less entertaining the second time around. Said Gill in the *New Yorker,* "Comden and Green's acute, affectionately bantering view of human frailty covers a period of four decades and manages to end up looking little worse for the wear. And no more do they; in their eager determination to win all hearts, they might be charming young folk at the very beginning of their careers. . . . [They] have never lost their freshness, and it is plainly their intention, growing older, never to grow old. I salute them with respect and envy."

Nation's Harold Clurman praised Comden's and Green's singing, noting that while they are not professional singers, "they deliver [their lyrics] with gusto in unaffected good humor. . . . Their intelligent and spirited joshing is infectious. They strike one as part of our family, a family of citizens aware of the absurdities and peccadilloes we enjoy poking fun at. There is something 'clean' and fresh about them (Betty Comden possesses a natural dignity) and, without being in the least condescending about it, one can honestly call their 'party' nice home revelry."

A *Time* critic agreed with these assessments, concluding that "a party, according to Webster's, is a social gathering for pleasure, and by the definition—or any other—an evening with Betty Comden and Adolph Green is an invitation into high society. . . . Rarely has so much wit and fun been packed into two hours. To cop a line from another songwriter, Cole Porter, what a swellegant, elegant party this is."

Despite numerous Tony awards and household-name shows, Comden and Green are best known for their longevity as a team. Said the *Chicago Tribune*'s Reich in 1990, "No one . . . has written more hit songs over the decades than Comden and Green, who, after fifty triumphant and oft-tumultuous years together, remain unchallenged as the longest-running act on Broadway." Citing standard tunes such as "New York, New York (It's a Hell of a Town)," "Make Someone Happy," and "Never Never Land," Reich described Comden and Green as "the wordsmiths who have helped define—and energize—the great American musical."

BIOGRAPHICAL/CRITICAL SOURCES:

PERIODICALS

America, March 11, 1978.
Chicago Tribune, August 10, 1990.
Insight, June 5, 1989.
Life, April 3, 1970.
Nation, April 20, 1970; May 7, 1977; March 11, 1978; October 16, 1982, pp. 378-379.
New Leader, March 27, 1978.
New Republic, May 23, 1970; March 18, 1978.
Newsweek, April 13, 1970; February 21, 1977; March 6, 1978.
New York, October 4, 1982, pp. 91-92.
New Yorker, April 11, 1970; May 12, 1975; February 21, 1977; March 6, 1978; October 4, 1982, p. 122.
New York Times, July 27, 1971; November 1, 1971; November 7, 1971; September 24, 1982; November 4, 1984; June 9, 1985, pp. 1, 24; August 3, 1985.
Saturday Review, April 18, 1970; April 22, 1972; April 15, 1978.
Stereo Review, April, 1973.
Time, April 13, 1970; February 21, 1977; March 6, 1978.*

*   *   *

CONLIN, Joseph Robert 1940-

PERSONAL: Born January 7, 1940, in Philadelphia, PA; son of Joseph R. (a shipper) and Lenore (Harbidge) Conlin; married first wife, Mary A., September 2, 1962 (divorced, 1973); married second wife, Deborah M., 1976; children: Eamonn J., Anna L. *Education:* Villanova University, A.B., 1961; University of Wisconsin, M.A., Ph.D., 1964.

ADDRESSES: Home—1406 Bidwell Ave., Chico, CA 95926. *Office*—Department of History, California State University, Chico, CA 95926.

CAREER: Teacher at various colleges in the East and the Midwest, 1964-67; California State University, Chico, professor of history, 1967—. Professor at University of Warwick, 1971, University of California, Davis, 1972-73, and Centro di Studi Americani, Rome, 1979.

MEMBER: American Historical Association, Organization of American Historians, Labour Historians (England), Pacific Northwest Labor History Society.

WRITINGS:

American Anti-War Movements, Glencoe Press, 1968.
Big Bill Haywood and the Radical Union Movement, Syracuse University Press, 1969.
Bread and Roses, Too: Studies of the Wobblies, edited by Stanley I. Kutler, Greenwood Press, 1970.
(Editor and author of introduction) *The American Radical Press, 1880-1960,* two volumes, Greenwood Press, 1974.
(Editor) *At the Point of Production: The Local History of the I.W.W.,* Greenwood Press, 1981.
The Troubles: A Jaundiced Glance Back at the Movement of the Sixties, F. Watts, 1982.
The American Past: A Survey of American History (one volume; contains *Part One: A Survey of American History to 1877* and *Part 2: A Survey of American History since 1865*), Harcourt, 1984, 3rd edition, 1990.
The Morrow Book of Quotations in American History, Morrow, 1984.
Our Land, Our Time: A History of the United States, Coronado, 1985.
An American Harvest: Readings in American History, Harcourt, 1986, Volume 1: (With C. H. Peterson) *A Survey of American History to 1877,* Volume 2: *A Survey of American History since 1865,* 2nd edition, 1987.
Bacon, Beans and Galantines: Food and Foodways on the Western Mining Frontier, University of Nevada Press, 1986.

Contributor to *Pacific Northwest Quarterly, Wisconsin Magazine of History, Virginia Cavalcade,* and other newspapers and journals.*

*   *   *

COOPER, B(rian) Lee 1942-

PERSONAL: Born October 4, 1942, in Hammond, IN; son of Charles Albert and Kathleen Marie (a nurse; maiden name, Kunde) Cooper; married Jill Elizabeth

Cunningham (a pre-school director), June 13, 1964; children: Michael Lee, Laura Ellen, Julie Allison. *Education:* Bowling Green State University, B.S., 1964; Michigan State University, M.A., 1965; Ohio State University, Ph.D., 1971; post-doctoral study at Harvard University, 1980. *Politics:* Democrat. *Religion:* United Methodist.

ADDRESSES: Home—9375 Pineview Dr., Olivet, MI 49076. *Office*—Olivet College, Olivet, MI 49076.

CAREER: Urbana College, Urbana, OH, associate professor, 1968-73, professor of history, 1974-76, dean of student affairs, 1973-74, dean of college, 1974-76; Newberry College, Newberry, SC, professor of history and vice-president for academic affairs, 1976-85; Olivet College, Olivet, MI, professor of history and academic vice-president, 1986—. Guest lecturer at University of Kentucky, Kansas Newman College, and Clemson University. Family development consultant. United Methodist Church, marshall, 1972-74, member of governing board, 1987-89.

MEMBER: American Association of Higher Education, American Historical Association, National Council for the Social Studies, American Culture Association (vice-president, 1988-90; member of governing board, 1991-95), Popular Culture Association, Association for Recorded Sound Collections, Midwest Popular Culture Association, Michigan Academy of Science, Arts, and Letters, Council of South Carolina Academic Deans (vice-president, 1981), Sonneck Society for American Music.

AWARDS, HONORS: Deems Taylor Award from American Society of Composers, Authors, and Publishers, 1983, for *Images of American Society in Popular Music: Essays on Reflective Teaching.*

WRITINGS:

Images of American Society in Popular Music: Essays on Reflective Teaching, Nelson-Hall, 1982.
The Popular Music Handbook: A Resources Guide, Libraries Unlimited, 1984.
A Resource Guide to Themes in Contemporary Song Lyrics, 1950-1985, Greenwood Press, 1986.
(Compiler with Frank W. Hoffman) *The Literature Rock II,* Scarecrow, 1990.
(With Wayne S. Haney) *Response Recordings: An Answer Song Discography,* Scarecrow, 1990.
(With Haney) *Rockabilly: A Bibliographic Resource Guide,* Scarecrow, 1990.
Popular Music Perspectives: Ideas, Themes, and Patterns in Contemporary Lyrics, Bowling Green State University Press, 1991.

Work represented in anthologies, including *Twentieth-Century Popular Culture in Museums and Libraries,* edited by Fred. E. H. Schroeder, Bowling Green University

Popular Press, 1981, and *Nonprint in the Secondary Curriculum: Readings for Reference,* edited by James L. Thomas, Libraries Unlimited, 1982.

Contributor to library, history, music, and popular culture journals and periodicals, including *Popular Music and Society, Rockingchair,* and *Fireball Mail.* Member of editorial advisory board, *Popular Music and Society,* 1990—.

WORK IN PROGRESS: Focusing on the Familiar, for Haworth Press; *Literature of Rock III,* for Scarecrow; *Baseball in American Culture,* for McFarland.

SIDELIGHTS: B. Lee Cooper told *CA:* "My teenage years were divided geographically between Chicago and Cleveland during the 1950s. The music which flooded my domestic environment and which was enjoyed and sanctioned by my parents featured Frank Sinatra, Perry Como, the Four Aces, Guy Lombardo, Vaughn Monroe, Patti Page, Jo Stafford, and Kay Starr. My post-10:00 p.m. radio listening, however, introduced me to a new universe of revolutionary sounds: rhythm 'n' blues and rock 'n' roll. The heroes of this late-night musical world were Fats Domino, Chuck Berry, the Dell-Vikings, Frankie Lymon and the Teenagers, Elvis Presley, and Bill Haley and the Comets. I was particularly enamored with raucous renderings of Little Richard, whose rockin' version of 'Long Tall Sally' exploded late at night while Pat Boone's bland vocal duplication of the same song was being aired on daytime radio."

Cooper added: "I'm a history teacher, by professional training and personal inclination. I happen to be an academic vice-president at the moment, but I frequently re-enter the classroom with my lyric sheets and stereo cassette tape player. I am also a propagandist for the use of popular music as an instructional tool and oral history resource. Whenever I use popular music in an instructional setting, I organize it into thematic patterns that can be readily related to a key social or political questions. Philosophically and psychologically, my learning theory roots are directly connected to Socrates' 'know thyself' position.

"I don't want to be accused of using the hackneyed term 'relevance' to sell the idea of utilizing popular music. What I am saying, though, is that basic student enthusiasm should be tapped by using elements of popular culture which are familiar to them. The learners themselves will readily branch out from the known (recordings) into the unknown (newspapers, magazines, films, and other types of materials). The students will also be more willing to participate in a learning design if they think that their teacher is also a 'learner.' In the field of popular music, I can't imagine any individual who knows the lyrics of country, jazz, bluegrass, folk, and rock songs well enough to say, 'Yea, I know *everything* about that!' When facing classes of twenty-five to forty students, teachers will be pleasantly surprised to discover that young people know quite a bit about music—and it's sometimes particularly intriguing to point out to the students which specific music styles they know *most* about. When I taught in southwestern Ohio, for instance, I was frequently amazed at the lack of knowledge of black music among my white, rural, middle-class students. My students rarely mentioned songs by Stevie Wonder, Wilson Pickett, Otis Redding, Aretha Franklin, or Ray Charles—yet they knew the most obscure tunes of country singers ranging from Tanya Tucker to Merle Haggard.

"You might wonder what kinds of problems I've encountered in propagandizing about teaching *with* music. I deliberately emphasized the *'with'* in the previous sentence. I am not a musician. I teach with recorded music, primarily through lyric review. I do not pretend to conduct content analysis with my students because I think that this formal research approach is too systematic and too restrictive to introduce in a survey-level classroom environment. What I attempt to generate is a reflective environment which opens student minds to philosophic inquiry. I am more interested in what the music means to each learner than in what lyric configurations say statistically or even in what the recording artist may have originally intended to say through his or her song. The 'receiver' is the persona I am concerned about and, as one of several receivers in the classroom, I feel free to introduce my own position just as I expect my students to communicate their positions to me. In essence, the thesis that I have tested while teaching with and writing about popular music is that the pluralistic belief pattern of American society is illustrated by the music.

"Specifically, what are the problems confronting an individual who is teaching with popular music? Let me cite four typical responses. I am not presenting them in any particular order, and I don't want to imply that one is more of a problem than another. I do want to depict these responses in a kind of psychological framework, though, because I feel that they represent fairly distinctive syndromes of colleague behavior. The first one I call the 'Pandering to Student Whims' syndrome. Proponents of this position argue that popular music can't possibly be a valuable teaching resources because students like it. This goes back to a fairly fundamental learning theory position— that all *real* education is misery, and the best thing that can be said about a particular course is that it makes students 'miserable.' The next best thing that you can say to a faculty member—apparently—is that he or she is miserable and boring.

"The second belittling faculty response is the 'You Must Be Ignoring the Really Significant Material' syndrome. I hear this comment frequently from my fellow historians.

My colleagues contend, 'We can barely cover all of the necessary material in our classes now, so how can you expect us to introduce that music junk and still get through the Louisiana Purchase and Teapot Dome Scandal?'

"The third response is the 'Let Him Alone . . . He'll Get Over It' syndrome. The idea being expressed in this response is that creative people will sometimes go off the deep end with a particular educational experiment, but they'll eventually drift back to academic reality.

"The fourth commentary falls into the 'I'd Love to Try It, But I've Got a Tin Ear' syndrome. Here the unspoken assumption is that one must be musically talented to employ music in the classroom, 'I don't play the piano, so I can't use music.' It takes quite a bit of explanation on my part to convince a skeptical colleague that I don't sing or play either."

*   *   *

COPPOLA, Francis Ford 1939-

PERSONAL: Surname is pronounced *Cope*-o-la; born April 7, 1939, in Detroit, MI; son of Carmine (a musician and composer) and Italia (Pennino) Coppola; married Eleanor Neil (an artist); children: Sofia, Gian-Carlo (died, 1986), Roman. *Education:* Hofstra University, B.A., 1959; University of California, Los Angeles, M.F.A., 1967.

ADDRESSES: Office—American Zoetrope, 916 Kearny St., San Francisco, CA 94133.

CAREER: Director, producer, and screenwriter, 1962—. Founder, Zoetrope Studios (film production company), 1969, and American Zoetrope, 1979-83. Publisher of *City* magazine, 1975-76. Director of films, including *Dementia 13,* Filmgroup Inc., 1963; *You're a Big Boy Now,* Seven Arts, 1967; *Finian's Rainbow,* Warner Brothers/Seven Arts, 1968; *The Rain People,* Warner Brothers, 1969; *The Godfather,* Paramount, 1972; *The Conversation,* Paramount, 1974; *The Godfather Part II,* Paramount, 1974; *Apocalypse Now,* United Artists (UA), 1979; *One from the Heart,* Columbia, 1982; *The Outsiders,* Warner Brothers, 1983; *Rumble Fish,* Universal, 1983; *The Cotton Club,* Orion, 1984; *Peggy Sue Got Married,* Tri-Star, 1986; *Gardens of Stone,* Tri-Star, 1987; *Tucker: The Man and His Dream,* Paramount, 1988; *New York Stories* ("Life without Zoe"), Touchstone, 1989; *The Godfather Part III,* Paramount, 1990; and *Bram Stoker's Dracula,* Columbia, 1992. Executive producer of films, including *THX 1138,* Warner Brothers, 1971; *American Graffiti,* Universal, 1973; *The Black Stallion,* UA, 1979; *Kagemusha,* Twentieth Century-Fox, 1980; *Hammett,* Warner Brothers, 1982; *The Black Stallion Returns,* UA, 1983; *The Escape Artist,* Warner Brothers, 1983; *Mishima: A Life in Four*

Chapters, Filmlink International/Lucasfilm, 1985; *Tough Guys Don't Dance,* Cannon Films, 1987; and *Wind,* Tri-Star, 1992.

MEMBER: Directors' Guild of America, Academy of Motion Picture Arts and Sciences.

AWARDS, HONORS: Samuel Goldwyn Award, 1962; San Sebastian International Cinema Festival award, 1970, for *The Rain People;* Academy Award for best screenplay (co-recipient), Academy of Motion Picture Arts and Sciences, 1970, for *Patton;* Academy Award nomination for best director, Academy Award for best picture and for best screenplay based on material from another medium (co-recipient), all 1972, all for *The Godfather;* Directors' Guild of America best director citation, 1972; Golden Palm Award, Cannes Film Festival, and Academy Award nominations for best screenplay and best picture, all 1974, all for *The Conversation;* Academy Award for best picture, best director, and best screenplay based on material from another medium (co-recipient), all 1974, all for *The Godfather Part II;* named best director by Directors' Guild of America, 1974; honorary degree, Hofstra University, 1977; Golden Palm Award and FIPRESCI Prize, Cannes Film Festival, 1979, Academy Award nominations for best picture, best director, and best screenplay, and British Academy Award nomination for best picture, all 1980, all for *Apocalypse Now;* Academy Award nominations for best picture, best director, and best screenplay, all 1991, all for *The Godfather Part III.*

WRITINGS:

SCREENPLAYS

(And director) *Dementia 13,* American International, 1963.
(With Gore Vidal, Jean Aurenche, Pierre Bost, and Claude Brule) *Is Paris Burning?,* Paramount, 1965.
(With Fred Coe and Edith Sommer) *This Property Is Condemned,* Paramount, 1965.
(And director) *You're a Big Boy Now,* Seven Arts, 1966.
(And director) *The Rain People,* Warner Brothers, 1969.
(With Edmund H. North) *Patton,* Twentieth Century-Fox, 1970.
(With Mario Puzo; and director) *The Godfather,* Paramount, 1972.
(And director) *The Conversation,* Paramount, 1974.
(With Puzo; and director) *The Godfather Part II,* Paramount, 1974.
The Great Gatsby, Paramount, 1974.
(With John Milius; and director) *Apocalypse Now,* United Artists, 1979.
(With Armyan Bernstein; and director) *One from the Heart,* Columbia, 1982.
(With S. E. Hinton; and director) *Rumble Fish,* Universal, 1983.

(With William Kennedy; and director) *The Cotton Club,* Orion, 1984.
(With Sofia Coppola; and director) "Life without Zoe," *New York Stories,* Touchstone, 1989.
(With Puzo; and director) *The Godfather Part III,* Paramount, 1990.

ADAPTATIONS: Hearts of Darkness: A Filmmaker's Apocalypse, a documentary about the filming of *Apocalypse Now,* was produced for the Showtime cable television network in 1991.

SIDELIGHTS: Francis Ford Coppola rests in an elite company of American film directors who often write their own screenplays and even from time to time produce their own movies. He has won five Academy Awards and is the first director ever to win the Golden Palm Award at the Cannes Film Festival twice. Best known for his *Godfather* trilogy of films about organized crime and his Vietnam War epic *Apocalypse Now,* Coppola has forged a career from his fascination with the themes of family love, violence, the seductions of power, and the moral bankruptcy of modern life. *Village Voice* correspondent Andrew Sarris calls Coppola "a major American director, whose work is mandatory viewing for every serious cineaste."

"Few film directors have left a greater mark than Coppola on the American motion picture industry [since 1970]," writes Robert Lindsey in the *New York Times Magazine.* "The first in a generation of celebrity directors whose talents were nurtured not on Hollywood's sound stages but in film schools, he co-authored 'Patton,' which in 1970 brought him the first of his five Oscars. Also in the early 1970's, he directed two of the most honored and profitable movies of all time, 'The Godfather' and 'The Godfather Part II' . . . . Coppola's early blockbusters made him a force to be reckoned with in the motion picture business, and he used them to assert his independence from the seven Hollywood studios that finance and distribute most movies." Lindsey adds that Coppola's influence "swept through the movie business at a critical time. . . . Coppola helped make American movie-making a director's medium. . . . Often swimming upstream against convention and established power, Coppola seemed to be reinventing the rules."

Almost from the start, Coppola was viewed as a maverick, an artist who believed in experimentation, who put daily worries secondary to the process of creation and the evolution of his medium. "If Francis Ford Coppola had not existed, Hollywood would never have bothered to invent him," notes Joseph Morgenstern in *Newsweek.* "He would have gotten in the way. . . . He comes from a long, honorable line of rule breakers and system buckers—the family name is Artist." *Rolling Stone* contributor David Ehrenstein maintains that the path Coppola has blazed across the decades with his films has met "with a mixture of awe, sympathy and distrust" from critics and audiences alike.

Representing the distrustful element amongst American critics is *Film Comment* essayist Richard T. Jameson, who calls Coppola "a totem of pseudo-style who plunders the inspiration of better artists, and confuses art with state-of-the-art." Others, such as *Partisan Review* correspondent David Denby, cite Coppola for his realistic depictions of bizarre American contradictions and moral ambiguity. "Coppola appears to be a uniquely central and powerful American talent," Denby contends. "His feeling for American surfaces—the glancing intimations of social status in gesture, tone of voice, decor, clothes—is as precise as any director's in American film history." The critic concludes: "Coppola's unusual curiosity about such things as fatherhood, marriage, power, spiritual anguish, etc., sets him apart from the run of Hollywood directors as a central interpreter of American experience, a man taking the big risks, working outside the limits of traditional genres."

Coppola was born in Detroit, Michigan, in 1939, the second of three children of professional flutist and composer Carmine Coppola and his wife Italia. The director's middle name honors the famous automobile maker Henry Ford, who sponsored a radio show for the Detroit Symphony, and thereby helped to feed the Coppola family. When Coppola was still a baby, his family moved to New York City, where his father took the position of first flutist in Arturo Toscanini's NBC Symphony Orchestra. Needless to say, the Coppola parents were artists who were dedicated to the pursuit of excellence. Although Coppola has calculated that his family moved thirty times and he attended 24 schools before college, he learned an appreciation of the arts from his parents and siblings. "I think that a lot of what I'm like is from the fact that I was the audience of the most remarkable family," Coppola told *Film Comment.* "And I took it all as magic—I believed everything."

Older brother August was a particularly strong influence on young Coppola. The brothers attended movies together, shared books, and served as critics of one another's work. Coppola told *Film Comment* of his brother: "He was a very advanced kid. He was a great older brother to me and always looked out for me, but in addition, he did very well in school and received many awards for writing and other things, and he was like the star of the family and I did most of what I did to imitate him." The director admitted that his brother's proficiency as a writer stimulated him to follow that profession. "I . . . took his short stories and handed them in under my name when I went to the writing class in high school myself," Coppola said. "My whole beginning in writing started in copying him, think-

ing that if I did those things, then I could be like he was. . . . At any rate, this relationship with him during those years was a powerful part of my life."

The three siblings were especially close—Coppola's sister is actress Talia Shire—because illness isolated Coppola for part of his childhood. At ten he contracted polio and was partially paralyzed and bedridden for nearly a year. During that time he was not allowed to see other children except his brother and sister, who helped to entertain him and who served as the audience for the projects he created from his bed.

The forced inactivity was made easier by Coppola's interest in gadgets such as radios, record players, and tape recorders. He used the technology at hand to create elaborate puppet shows that he staged for his family. Coppola told the *New York Times Magazine:* "When you had polio then, nobody brought their friends around; I was kept in a room by myself, and I used to read and occupy myself with puppets and mechanical things. . . . I became interested in the concept of remote control, I think because I had polio. I'm good with gadgets, and I became a tinkerer." The process of learning to tinker was one step toward a career in the film industry. Daydreaming about movies and entertaining people was another. Coppola told the *New Yorker* that during his illness he "was always hungry to be with other children." He added: "When I put on my shows alone in my room, I dreamed about the day when I would put on shows with others and people would come to see them. I was dreaming, I'm sure, about having a place like my [Zoetrope] studio, where we could learn, and teach what we learned to others."

As a teen Coppola earned a music scholarship for tuba to the New York Military Academy on the Hudson River. He was intensely unhappy there, however, and far from certain that he wanted to pursue music seriously. After spending a summer with his brother in Los Angeles, he returned to New York City and finished high school at Great Neck High School in Queens. Coppola began writing plays and doing theatre work at sixteen, and he carried the interest with him to Hofstra University, where he majored in theatre arts.

Coppola's years at Hofstra, from 1956 to 1960, were significant for two reasons: first, he balked at the restrictive environment of the theatre department and tried to organize his own student-led drama company; and second, he bought a 16-millimeter movie camera and switched his chief focus from theatre to film. He was particularly drawn to the innovative cinema work of Russian filmmaker Sergei Eisenstein. After earning his bachelor's degree in 1960, Coppola was accepted in the film school at the University of California, Los Angeles.

Right away Coppola augmented his studies with work on commercial films. He took a job as production assistant with the well-known B-movie director Roger Corman and was soon learning the intricacies of filmmaking by performing all sorts of tasks for Corman. Early in 1962, he submitted a screenplay called *Pilma, Pilma* and won the Samuel Goldwyn Award for young writers. Coppola admitted in *Rolling Stone* that he was uncertain about his ability as a writer and was over-impressed by contemporaries who seemed to be having more success. "The issue of talent was an important thing," he said, "but then I realized that you don't have to have talent, you just have to have a lot of enthusiasm."

That enthusiasm was not lost on Roger Corman, who allowed Coppola to direct the film *Dementia 13* in 1963. A horror movie about a series of axe murders shot on location in Ireland, *Dementia 13* is not particularly remarkable. *Dictionary of Literary Biography* contributor Randall Clark notes, however, that as a 23-year-old's first commercial movie, the work "did demonstrate that Coppola had passed his apprenticeship."

Soon after finishing *Dementia 13,* Coppola signed a writing contract with Seven Arts. Between 1963 and 1967 he wrote or collaborated on more than a dozen screenplays, including big-budget productions such as *This Property Is Condemned,* starring Natalie Wood, and *Is Paris Burning?* Once again his enthusiasm helped him to advance. In 1966, Seven Arts allowed him to direct a film he had written called *You're a Big Boy Now.* The work is a character study of a sensitive young man coming of age in New York City. *Saturday Review* essayist Hollis Alpert observes that the film "has not at all the look of a standard Hollywood product, as it skips along, pausing to examine some of the odder and colorfully seamy aspects of New York. It has an improvisatory air, and touches of modish mockery, particularly popular with the very young and certain film critics." In *Newsweek,* Morgenstern contends that *You're a Big Boy Now* "will wow the Presley crowd at rural drive-ins, charm the eyes off those snakes on foreign film-festival juries, pack them in at cosmopolitan art houses, make it acceptable and even fashionable for stars to play small character roles, open the way for other young directors to break into the commercial film world. . . . For kids it will be a national anthem." Such praise helped Coppola secure backing for another feature film, *The Rain People,* a small-budget art movie about a disenchanted housewife and her aimless wanderings across the country.

While shooting *The Rain People* in 1969, Coppola decided to open his own independent film studio. With a $400,000 advance from Warner Brothers, he rented a warehouse in San Francisco and founded American Zoetrope (later known as Zoetrope) Studios. At the age of thirty, Coppola had become disenchanted with Hollywood's corporate at-mosphere. He wanted to put films back into the hands of their creators, and he attracted a staff of would-be movie-makers that included director/screenwriter George Lucas, Carroll Ballard, and Walter Murch, among others. In order to finance his independence, Coppola continued to take work from the standard Hollywood hierarchy. In 1970 he scored a major career coup with *Patton.*

Several other writers had already tried to craft a screenplay about the controversial World War II general George Patton when Coppola was hired by Twentieth Century-Fox. His script was finally filmed as *Patton* in 1970. The movie, starring George C. Scott, was one of the year's most successful, both commercially and with the critics. It won Coppola his first Academy Award, helped him to bankroll his fledgling studio, and put him on the short list for other big-budget screenplay work.

In 1971, faced with his studio's first financial setback, Coppola contracted with Paramount to co-write and direct a movie adaptation of Mario Puzo's bestseller *The Godfather.* His fee for the job was $75,000 and a six percent profit share. A London *Times* reporter notes: "Coppola perceived in *The Godfather* a journeyman assignment that might yet transcend the conventions of the gangster genre. With hindsight, *The Godfather* can be seen as the tide in Coppola's affairs which, taken at the flood, led on to fortune."

As director of *The Godfather,* Coppola insisted on including several well-known actors—including James Caan, Al Pacino, and Marlon Brando—in the cast. His sister, Talia Shire, also received a role. Since its release in 1972, *The Godfather* has reaped near record-setting earnings. Its theme of an Italian family forging a fortune from organized crime managed to convey Mafia activities without ethnic stereotype or glamorization. In the *Journal of Popular Film,* Jonathan P. Latimer contends that watching the film "is like watching the Viet Nam War from the Pentagon; it is all a simple bookkeeping operation. . . . What we recognize, what appeals, is the fact that the film creates a kind of metaphor for life in the United States today. And, what sets it apart from other films is the fact that it not only depicts, but it also offers explanations for what have seemed to be such irrational acts in the last few years. It provides a backdrop of necessity for almost any act of mayhem, so long as you are true to your own."

The Godfather won Academy Awards for best picture of the year, best actor (Marlon Brando), and best screenplay. Coppola shared the latter honor with co-writer Mario Puzo. *Chicago Tribune* reviewer Dave Kehr maintains that the movie "remains one of the most solid and enduring pieces of American popular culture, an exceedingly well-told film that celebrated the protective insularity of the family against the hostility of a vast and impersonal outside world." *New Yorker* critic Pauline Kael calls the work "the greatest gangster picture ever made," citing Coppola for his "wide, startlingly vivid view of a Mafia dynasty." In *American Film Now: The People, the Power, the Money, the Movies,* James Monaco writes: "If Francis Coppola never made another film save *The Godfather,* his place in the history of American film would be assured."

Receipts from *The Godfather* helped Coppola to keep Zoetrope Studio afloat, and the company produced its own blockbusters in *The Black Stallion* and *American Graffiti.* Coppola's reputation as a screenwriter and director were enhanced by his 1974 film *The Conversation,* a timely work about electronic surveillance. *The Conversation* won Coppola a Golden Palm award at the Cannes Film Festival and was nominated for Academy Awards for best picture and best original screenplay.

The concept of a sequel to a popular movie had not gained prominence in Hollywood by 1974, when Coppola teamed with Puzo to create *The Godfather Part II.* The screenwriters decided to craft a film that showed, through flashback, the rise of the Corleone dynasty, interspersed with the continuing story of the family's changing relationships in the second generation. Once again a major cast, including Robert DeNiro and Al Pacino, was assembled, and once again the picture was a success, winning six Academy Awards, including best screenplay and best director for Coppola.

In the *Journal of Popular Film,* John Yates claims that, taken together, *The Godfather* and *The Godfather Part II* "are at their deepest level a brilliant revelation of the family, how it worked through the generations, and how it now falls apart." *New York Times* correspondent Larry Rohter suggests that the works "are still regarded as two of the finest films in the history of American cinema and the undisputed pinnacle of Mr. Coppola's turbulent career."

"Turbulent" is an apt word to describe the years following the success of *The Godfather Part II.* Coppola himself told the *New York Times Magazine* that all the notoriety and awards "went to my head like a rush of perfume. I thought I couldn't do anything wrong." The director set to work on an epic Vietnam War movie from a script by John Milius. Elaborate sets were constructed in the Philippines for a sixteen-week location shoot. Unfortunately, the film that would become *Apocalypse Now* was beset by problems, from typhoons to casting changes to script rewrites. Leading player Martin Sheen suffered a heart attack, and Coppola nearly collapsed as the filming dragged on for over a year and the costs of the project skyrocketed from $12 million to $32 million.

Apocalypse Now opened to mixed reviews in 1979, but it eventually earned several Academy Award nominations and made a large profit at the box office. Coppola, who had invested $16 million of his own money in the project, recouped his investment as the movie went on to gross over $140 million. *Apocalypse Now* is a modern interpretation of Joseph Conrad's novel *Heart of Darkness.* In the film, a military hit-man named Willard (played by Martin Sheen) is dispatched into Cambodia to "terminate" a rogue soldier (played by Marlon Brando). Although *New York Times* reviewer Vincent Canby called the finished work a "profoundly anticlimactic intellectual muddle," most critics praised the film for its graphic depiction of the insanities of war. *Washington Post* correspondent Rita Kempley concludes, for instance, that ever since *Apocalypse Now* made its debut, "the chop of helicopter blades has symbolized the hell of Vietnam."

Soon after the completion of *Apocalypse Now,* Coppola engineered the purchase of the former Hollywood General Studios in Los Angeles. He invested his own money and borrowed from others in order to buy state-of-the-art equipment and renovations for the dilapidated property. Re-named Zoetrope Studios, the studio was intended to be "a paradise for creative film makers independent of the Hollywood establishment," according to Lindsey. Coppola described American Zoetrope as an experiment in fusing the latest in cinematic technology with the old-fashioned concept of contract players and directors.

Financial disaster hit soon after the release of Coppola's first film from American Zoetrope, *One from the Heart.* A musical set in Las Vegas but filmed entirely on elaborate sets, *One from the Heart* ran $11 million over budget and "was greeted vitriolically by most critics," according to Aljean Harmetz in the *New York Times.* The movie cost $27 million to make and earned less than $2 million at the box office, and Coppola, who had sunk most of his personal fortune into the studio, was faced with payments on a debt approaching $50 million. The studio was put up for auction on February 14, 1983, having released only three motion pictures. In 1987, Coppola told the *Washington Post:* "I was just so enthusiastic about movies and having an old-fashioned studio and a wacky project . . . I just wasn't careful and didn't watch exactly what was happening around me. Now, I've sort of been punished. . . . I never had my mind on money. Just the fun of it and the good company of other people . . . a group of people connected in friendship. . . . Today we don't have that anymore. It's corporate America."

His image tarnished by the management of *Apocalypse Now* and *One from the Heart,* Coppola returned to work immediately on smaller, more intimate projects that he hoped would keep his creditors at bay. He became, to quote Lindsey, "a cinematic hired gun, directing, at the rate of one a year, other people's movies for about $2.5 million apiece, plus ten percent of the profits." Two such films were *The Outsiders* and *Rumble Fish,* both based on novels by S. E. Hinton. Coppola filmed *The Outsiders* from a screenplay written by others, calling the movie "a way for me to soothe my heartache over the terrible rejection" of *One from the Heart.* After completing that work he moved to *Rumble Fish,* directing from a script he co-wrote. *Rumble Fish,* the story of two disenchanted brothers and their alcoholic father, met a skeptical reception when it was released in 1983. As Kempley notes, however, the movie "has recently attracted cult audiences."

In 1984, Coppola was called in to rewrite the screenplay and direct *The Cotton Club,* yet another major picture that ran over budget and took months and months to shoot. This time Coppola did not sustain the damage to his own finances or to his reputation. The project was in trouble when he joined it, and he worked for a salary and a percentage of the profits. The director told the *Washington Post:* "I was frightened that I owed so much money that if I took any time off, I didn't know if I would always be in the position to command the kind of money that would be necessary to pay off the debt. . . . I didn't care that my position in the film industry might erode. I just wanted to . . . get that debt paid off. Because as long as that debt existed it meant that I couldn't go on to the next level . . . so I very definitely took one job after another so that I'd be free."

Coppola could still choose his projects with care, and he turned out at least one box-office hit, *Peggy Sue Got Married,* starring Kathleen Turner as a time-traveling homecoming queen. Other films more reflective of the writer-director's philosophies were *Tucker: The Man and His Dream,* about an overzealous automobile designer, and *Gardens of Stone,* about officers charged with burying dead soldiers in Arlington Cemetery. During the early shooting for *Gardens of Stone,* Coppola's oldest son and colleague, Gian-Carlo, was killed in a boating accident on the Chesapeake Bay.

Personal grief was compounded by the slow box office business for projects like *Tucker* and *Gardens of Stone.* Coppola had rejected several offers to write yet another *Godfather* sequel, but his waning reputation—and a lawsuit that threatened further debt—convinced him to undertake the project in 1990. Coppola and Puzo wrote another script and convinced most of the *Godfather* cast to return for another outing. The director told the *New York Times:* "I'm hoping a good reception for 'Godfather' will allow me to change my life. Most important, it'll give me a chance to think for a second, to stop worrying about my extinction and try to find something fun and enjoyable to me."

The Godfather Part III was not quite as successful as *Part I,* but more than *Part II,* and the advent of home video has given the series a whole new life. In 1992 Coppola re-edited all three films into a new format which was boxed and sold for more than $200. A less expensive boxed set of the films as they were shot also sold well on the video market. In the meantime, Coppola turned to another big-budget project, *Bram Stoker's Dracula,* a rendering of the popular Dracula story faithful to the original novel.

Lindsey writes: "Mr. Coppola remains among a handful of directors—Woody Allen, Steven Spielberg, George Lucas, perhaps a few others—whose track records and names alone are likely to induce a studio to finance a new movie." His flamboyant personality and open disdain for Hollywood's corporate structures notwithstanding, Coppola has been able to command seven-figure salaries and hefty profit shares on the films to which he has lent his name. According to Gene Siskel in the *Chicago Tribune,* Coppola's fans perceive that he "simply has bigger dreams than most other filmmakers, that he wants to do more than make movies, that his goal is nothing less than revolutionizing the film business, artistically and financially."

In 1990, Coppola told the *New York Times:* "I'm very embarrassed about my career over the last 10 years. You know, an Italian family puts a lot of stock in not losing face, not making what we call *una brutta figura,* or bad showing. When you have people writing about you in a mocking way and making fun of your ideas and calling you a crackpot, that's a real *brutta figura.* I want to be considered a vital American film maker and have the country be proud of me."

Coppola insists that his best work lies ahead, that he will not go down in history as the creator of "the greatest gangster picture ever made." He told the *New Yorker:* "It's so silly in life not to pursue the highest possible thing you can imagine, even if you run the risk of losing it all, because if you don't pursue it you've lost it anyway. You can't be an artist and be safe." He concluded: "I don't know why some of the reaction to what I do is so cynical. I know that I'm for intelligence, creativity, and friendliness, as opposed to greed, power, and hostility. Whether you're the director or the producer or the owner of a movie, as soon as you form an organization to make a picture you're a businessman. The problem is to be all that and still to be free."

BIOGRAPHICAL/CRITICAL SOURCES:

BOOKS

Contemporary Literary Criticism, Volume 16, Gale, 1981.
Cowie, Peter, *Coppola: A Biography,* Scribner, 1990.
Dictionary of Literary Biography, Volume 44: *American Screenwriters, Second Series,* Gale, 1986.
Johnson, Robert K., *Francis Ford Coppola,* Twayne, 1977.
Kael, Pauline, *Deeper into Movies,* Little, Brown, 1973.

Monaco, James, *American Film Now: The People, the Power, the Money, the Movies,* New American Library, 1979.

Pechter, William S., *Movies Plus One,* Horizon, 1981.

PERIODICALS

American Film, April, 1983.

Atlantic, August, 1976.

Chicago Tribune, January 18, 1982; February 11, 1982; October 5, 1986; March 3, 1989; December 15, 1990.

Commentary, July, 1972; July, 1974.

Film Comment, October, 1983; April, 1985.

Film Quarterly, spring, 1986.

Journal of Popular Film, Volume 2, number 2, 1973; Volume 4, number 2, 1975.

Los Angeles Times, December 19, 1988; January 26, 1990; December 30, 1990.

Nation, April 3, 1972.

Newsday, December 22, 1974.

Newsweek, February 20, 1967; November 25, 1974; December 23, 1974; June 13, 1977; January 31, 1983; October 14, 1991.

New Yorker, March 18, 1972; April 15, 1974; December 23, 1974; November 8, 1982.

New York Times, August 12, 1979; August 15, 1979; March 18, 1980; March 21, 1980; November 23, 1980; February 11, 1982; April 16, 1982; May 3, 1987; March 1, 1989; March 12, 1989; December 23, 1990; December 25, 1990.

New York Times Magazine, August 5, 1979; July 24, 1988.

Partisan Review, Volume 43, number 1, 1976.

Playboy, July, 1975.

Rolling Stone, March 19, 1981; March 18, 1982.

Saturday Review, February 4, 1967; May 4, 1974.

Sight and Sound, autumn, 1972; summer, 1974.

Time, December 16, 1974; January 18, 1982; December 17, 1984.

Times (London), January 21, 1988; November 14, 1988; February 11, 1989.

Vanity Fair, June, 1990.

Village Voice, May 28, 1979; August 27, 1979; April 21, 1980; April 5, 1983.

Washington Post, February 4, 1970; December 16, 1984; May 8, 1987; August 7, 1988; March 3, 1989; December 25, 1990.

—*Sketch by Anne Janette Johnson*

*　　*　　*

COSTENOBLE, Philostene
See GHELDERODE, Michel de

COURLANDER, Harold 1908-

PERSONAL: Born September 18, 1908, in Indianapolis, IN; son of David (a primitive painter) and Tillie (Oppenheim) Courlander; married Emma Meltzer, June 18, 1949; children: Erika, Michael, Susan. *Education:* University of Michigan, B.A., 1931.

ADDRESSES: Home and office—5512 Brite Dr., Bethesda, MD 20817.

CAREER: Farmer in Romeo, MI, 1933-38; Douglas Aircraft Co., Eritrea (now in Ethiopia), historian, 1942-43; U.S. Office of War Information, New York City, and Bombay, India, editor, 1943-45; U.S. Information Agency, Voice of America, New York City, editor, 1945-54, Washington, DC, senior political analyst, 1960-74. United Nations, New York City, press officer for U.S. Mission, 1954, writer and editor, *United Nations Review,* 1956-59.

AWARDS, HONORS: Avery Hopwood Awards, 1931, 1932; Franz Boas Fund research grant for folklore study in Dominican Republic, 1939; American Council of Learned Societies grants for research in Haiti, 1939, 1940; American Philosophical Society grants for studies in New World Negro cultures, 1946, 1954, 1955; Wenner-Gren Foundation grants for work in United States and West Indian Negro folk music, 1946, 1954, 1955, 1956, 1962; Guggenheim fellowships for studies in African and Afro-American cultures, 1948, 1955; Laura Ingalls Wilder Award nomination, 1980; University of Michigan outstanding achievement award, 1984.

WRITINGS:

Swamp Mud, Blue Ox Press, 1936.

Home to Langford County, Blue Ox Press, 1938.

Haiti Singing, University of North Carolina Press, 1939, Cooper Square, 1973.

The Caballero, Farrar & Rinehart, 1940.

The Drum and the Hoe: Life and Lore of the Haitian People, University of California Press, 1960, new edition, 1985.

Shaping Our Times: What the United Nations Is and Does, Oceana, 1960, revised edition, 1962.

On Recognizing the Human Species, One Nation Library, 1960.

Negro Songs from Alabama, Wenner-Gren Foundation for Anthropological Research, 1960, Oak, 1963.

The Big Old World of Richard Creeks, Chilton, 1962.

Negro Folk Music U.S.A., Columbia University Press, 1963, new edition, Dover, 1992.

(With Remy Bastien) *Religion and Politics in Haiti,* Institute for Cross-Cultural Research, 1966.

The African, Crown, 1967.

The Fourth World of the Hopis, Crown, 1971.

Tales of Yoruba Gods and Heroes, Crown, 1973.

The Son of the Leopard, Crown, 1974.

A Treasury of African Folklore, Crown, 1975.

A Treasury of Afro-American Folklore, Crown, 1976.

The Mesa of Flowers, Crown, 1977.

(With Albert Yava) *Big Falling Snow,* Crown, 1978.

Hopi Voices: Recollections, Traditions, and Narratives of the Hopi Indians, University of New Mexico Press, 1982.

The Heart of the Ngoni, Crown, 1982.

The Master of the Forge: A West African Odyssey (novel), Crown, 1985.

The Bordeaux Narrative, University of New Mexico Press, 1990.

FOLK TALE COLLECTIONS

Uncle Bouqui of Haiti, Morrow, 1942.

(With George Herzog) *The Cow-Tail Switch, and Other West African Stories,* Holt, 1947.

Kantchil's Lime Pit, and Other Stories from Indonesia, Harcourt, 1950.

(With Wolf Leslau) *The Fire on the Mountain, and Other Ethiopian Stories,* Holt, 1950.

Ride with the Sun, Whittlesey House, 1955.

Terrapin's Pot of Sense, Holt, 1957.

(With Albert K. Prempeh) *The Hat Shaking Dance, and Other Ashanti Tales from Ghana,* Harcourt, 1957.

The Tiger's Whisker, and Other Tales and Legends from Asia and the Pacific, Harcourt, 1959.

The King's Drum, and Other African Folk Tales, Harcourt, 1962.

The Piece of Fire, and Other Haitian Tales, Harcourt, 1964.

(With Ezekiel A. Eshugbayi) *Olode the Hunter, and Other Tales from Nigeria,* Harcourt, 1968, published in England as *Ijapa the Tortoise, and Other Nigerian Tales,* Bodley Head, 1969.

People of the Short Blue Corn: Tales and Legends of the Hopi Indians, Harcourt, 1970.

The Crest and the Hide and Other African Stories, Coward McCann, 1982.

COMPILER AND EDITOR OF RECORD ALBUMS; FROM OWN FIELD RECORDINGS

Cult Music of Cuba, Ethnic Folkways Library, 1949.

Negro Folk Music of Alabama, Volumes 1-6, Ethnic Folkways Library, 1950-56.

Meringues, Folkways Records, 1950.

Drums of Haiti, Ethnic Folkways Library, 1950.

Folk Music of Haiti, Ethnic Folkways Library, 1950.

Folk Music of Ethiopia, Ethnic Folkways Library, 1951.

Songs and Dances of Haiti, Ethnic Folkways Library, 1952.

Haitian Piano, Folkways Records, 1952.

Also compiler and editor of other collections for Ethnic Folkways Library, including *Caribbean Folk Music, Folk Music, U.S.A., African and Afro-American Drums,* and *Afro-American Folk Music.*

OTHER

Contributor to books, including *Miscelanea de estudios dedicados a Fernando Ortiz,* [Havana], 1955. Also contributor of articles to *Saturday Review, Musical Quarterly, New Republic, Journal of Negro History, Opportunity, African Arts, Chicago Sun-Times, Village Voice, Resound, Michigan Alumnus, Bulletin du Bureau National d' Ethnologie, Phylon, American Scholar, Quarterly Magazine of the Historical Society of Michigan,* and *Negro History Bulletin.*

SIDELIGHTS: Harold Courlander once told *CA:* "Although my work has been both fiction and nonfiction (often scholarly), I think of myself primarily as a narrator. I have always had a special interest in using fiction and nonfiction narration to bridge communications between other cultures and our own. While a number of my publications seem to be mere 'folklore,' I consider them to be fragments of a large body of oral literature. Folk tales as such have no special meaning for me unless they convey human values, philosophical outlook, cultural heritage and, hopefully, literary essence.

"Frequently I have taken a culture with which I have become very familiar and used it as the setting for a fictional work. In retrospect I see that I have written novels and novelle about 18th century Sudanic Africa, rural Alabama and Mississippi, the Dominican Republic of the Trujillo era, the middle passage and slavery days in the Old South, and the Hopi Indian Southwest before the arrival of the white man."

With forty years of folklore research and authorship behind him, Courlander wrote his novel *The African.* While in itself a relatively successful book, it has the added distinction of being the subject of a successful copyright infringement suit against *Roots* author Alex Haley. Haley's book, the result of twelve years of family research, was first published ten years after Courlander's. In the settlement of the suit, Haley acknowledged that portions of *Roots* had been taken from *The African.* At the time the suit was settled, Courlander's book had sold 28,000 copies in hard cover and 150,000 soft cover copies, while Haley had earned $2.6 million from hardcover sales alone. Subsequently *The African* was widely published in foreign languages. Courlander told *CA* that press reports on the amount of the settlement ranged from $500,000 to $650,000, and while he expressed willingness to make the exact figure public, Haley was not willing to do so.

BIOGRAPHICAL/CRITICAL SOURCES:

PERIODICALS

Book World, May 5, 1968.
National Observer, September 22, 1968.
New York Times Book Review, April 28, 1968.
Times Literary Supplement, October 16, 1969.
Washington Post, December 16, 1978; November 5, 1985.
Washington Post Book World, May 9, 1982.

*   *   *

COURTNEY, Dayle
See GOLDSMITH, Howard

*   *   *

CRAIG, Alisa
See MacLEOD, Charlotte

*   *   *

CRAIGE, Betty Jean   1946-

PERSONAL: Born May 20, 1946, in Chicago, IL; daughter of Branch, Jr. (a physician) and Jean (a homemaker; maiden name, McCracken) Craige. *Education:* Pomona College, B.A., 1968; University of Washington, Seattle, M.A., 1970, Ph.D., 1974.

ADDRESSES: Home—215 Snapfinger Dr., Athens, GA 30605. *Office*—Department of Comparative Literature, Park Hall, University of Georgia, Athens, GA 30602.

CAREER: University of Georgia, Athens, instructor, 1973-75, assistant professor, 1975-79, associate professor, 1979-83, professor of comparative literature, 1983—. Member of board of directors, Georgia Endowment for the Humanities, 1984-87. Member of editorial board, University of Georgia Press, 1982-86, 1989-92. Member, Frederic W. Ness Book Award Committee, 1990—.

MEMBER: International Comparative Literature Association, Modern Language Association of America (Commission on the Status of Women in the Profession, member, 1985-88, co-chair, 1987-88; delegate assembly, member, 1988-91, member of steering committee, 1989), American Comparative Literature Association, Teachers for a Democratic Culture, South Atlantic Modern Language Association (member of book prize committee, 1984-88, 1990—).

AWARDS, HONORS: Frederic W. Ness Book Award for contributing to the "understanding and improvement of liberal education," Association of American Colleges, 1989, for *Reconnection: Dualism to Holism in Literary Study;* summer stipend, National Endowment for the Humanities, 1978; Committee for the Humanities in Georgia grant, 1981, for symposium.

WRITINGS:

Lorca's "Poet in New York": The Fall into Consciousness, University Press of Kentucky, 1977.
(Translator and author of introduction) *Selected Poems of Antonio Machado,* Louisiana State University Press, 1978.
Literary Relativity: An Essay on Twentieth-Century Narrative, Bucknell University Press, 1982.
(Editor) *Relativism in the Arts,* University of Georgia Press, 1983.
(Translator and author of introduction) *The Poetry of Gabriel Celaya,* Bucknell University Press, 1984.
(Translator and author of introduction) Manuel Mantero, *Manuel Mantero: New Songs for the Ruins of Spain,* Bucknell University Press, 1986.
Reconnection: Dualism to Holism in Literary Study, University of Georgia Press, 1988.
(Editor) *Literature, Language, and Politics,* University of Georgia Press, 1988.
Laying the Ladder Down: The Emergence of Cultural Holism, University of Massachusetts Press, 1992.

Editorial consultant for "Cultura Ludens" series, John Benjamins. Contributor to periodicals, including *PMLA, Women's Review of Books, Atlanta Constitution, Pomona College Today, Chronicle of Higher Education,* and *National Forum.*

SIDELIGHTS: Betty Jean Craige told *CA:* "I have spent the last ten years trying to explain, in one way or another, what I perceive to be a transformation in the West's conceptualization of reality from a dualistic, atomistic, hierarchical model to a holistic model. The holistic model, which we see perhaps most clearly in the scientific discipline of ecology, is manifesting itself culturally in the various civil rights movements, the push for a multiculturalist curriculum, the environmentalist movement, and the international peace movement.

"I use the term 'cultural holism' to describe a vision of human society as an evolving system of interacting cultures and individuals that develop in relation to each other and to their non-human environment. Cultural holism is incompatible with absolutism of any sort. Whereas absolutism signifies an intolerance of differences, holism signifies an appreciation of differences, of diversity; whereas absolutism implies a resistance to change, holism implies a willing acceptance of change, an understanding of reality as continuous flux.

"We are witnessing in the United States a resistance to cultural holism in the efforts made by the political right to uphold traditional social and economic hierarchies. My book, *Laying the Ladder Down: The Emergence of Cultural Holism,* is an attempt to explain some of the controversies of our times in terms of the clash of models."

*   *   *

CRICHTON, (John) Michael 1942-
(Jeffrey Hudson, John Lange; Michael Douglas, a joint pseudonym)

PERSONAL: Surname is pronounced "*Cry*-ton"; born October 23, 1942, in Chicago, IL; son of John Henderson (a corporate president) and Zula (Miller) Crichton; married Joan Radam, January 1, 1965 (divorced, 1970); married Kathleen St. Johns, 1978 (divorced, 1980); married Suzanne Childs (marriage ended); married Anne-Marie Martin, 1987; children: (fourth marriage) Taylor (a daughter). *Education:* Harvard University, A.B. (summa cum laude), 1964, M.D., 1969.

CAREER: Salk Institute for Biological Studies, La Jolla, CA, post-doctoral fellow, 1969-70; full-time writer of books and films; director of films and teleplays, including *Pursuit* (based on his novel *Binary*), American Broadcasting Companies, Inc. (ABC-TV), 1972, *Westworld,* Metro-Goldwyn-Mayer, 1973, *Coma,* United Artists (UA), 1978, *The Great Train Robbery,* UA, 1979, *Looker,* Warner Brothers, 1981, and *Runaway,* Tri-Star Pictures, 1984.

MEMBER: Mystery Writers Guild of America (West), Authors Guild, Authors League of America, Academy of Motion Picture Arts and Sciences, Directors Guild of America, PEN, Aesculaepian Society, Phi Beta Kappa.

AWARDS, HONORS: Edgar Award, Mystery Writers of America, 1968, for *A Case of Need,* and 1979, for *The Great Train Robbery;* writer of the year award, Association of American Medical Writers, 1970, for *Five Patients: The Hospital Explained.*

WRITINGS:

NOVELS

The Andromeda Strain (Literary Guild selection), Knopf, 1969.
(With brother Douglas Crichton, under joint pseudonym Michael Douglas) *Dealing: Or, The Berkeley-to-Boston Forty-Brick Lost-Bag Blues,* Knopf, 1971.
The Terminal Man, Knopf, 1972.
Westworld (also see below), Bantam, 1974.
The Great Train Robbery (also see below), Knopf, 1975.
Eaters of the Dead: The Manuscript of Ibn Fadlan, Relating His Experiences with the Northmen in A.D. 922, Knopf, 1976.

Congo, Knopf, 1980.
Sphere, Knopf, 1987.
Jurassic Park, Knopf, 1990.
Rising Sun, Knopf, 1992.

NONFICTION

Five Patients: The Hospital Explained, Knopf, 1970.
Jasper Johns, Abrams, 1977.
Electronic Life: How to Think about Computers, Knopf, 1983.
Travels (autobiography), Knopf, 1988.

SCREENPLAYS

Extreme Close-up, National General, 1973.
Westworld (based on novel of same title), Metro-Goldwyn-Mayer, 1973.
Coma (based on a novel of same title by Robin Cook), United Artists, 1977.
The Great Train Robbery (based on novel of same title), United Artists, 1978.
Looker, Warner Brothers, 1981.
Runaway, Tri-Star Pictures, 1984.

UNDER PSEUDONYM JOHN LANGE

Odds On, New American Library, 1966.
Scratch One, New American Library, 1967.
Easy Go, New American Library, 1968, published as *The Last Tomb,* Bantam, 1974.
Zero Cool, New American Library, 1969.
The Venom Business, New American Library, 1969.
Drug of Choice, New American Library, 1970.
Grave Descend, New American Library, 1970.
Binary, Knopf, 1971.

UNDER PSEUDONYM JEFFREY HUDSON

A Case of Need, New American Library, 1968.

ADAPTATIONS: The Andromeda Strain was filmed by Universal, 1971; *A Case of Need* was filmed by Metro-Goldwyn-Mayer, 1972; *Binary* was filmed as *Pursuit,* ABC-TV, 1972; *The Terminal Man* was filmed by Warner Brothers, 1974.

WORK IN PROGRESS: Screenplay for Steven Speilberg's film adaptation of *Jurassic Park.*

SIDELIGHTS: Michael Crichton has had a number of successful careers—physician, teacher, film director, screenwriter—but he is perhaps best known for pioneering the "techno-thriller" with novels such as *The Andromeda Strain, Sphere,* and *Jurassic Park.* Whether writing about a deadly microorganism, brain surgery gone awry, or adventures in the Congo, Crichton's ability to blend the tight plot and suspense of the thriller with the technical emphasis of science fiction has made him a favorite with readers of all ages. Crichton's fame is not limited to literary endeavors; he has also directed a number of popular films with subjects ranging from body organ piracy (*Coma*) to advertising manipulation and murder (*Looker*). Summing up Crichton's appeal in the *Dictionary of Literary Biography Yearbook,* Robert L. Sims writes: "His importance lies in his capacity to tell stories related to that frontier where science and fiction meet. . . . Crichton's best novels demonstrate that, for the immediate future at least, technological innovations offer the same possibilities and limitations as their human creators."

Crichton's first brush with literary success occurred after he entered medical school. To help pay for tuition and living expenses, he began writing paperback thrillers on the weekends and during vacations. One of these books, *A Case of Need,* became an unexpected hit. Written under a pseudonym, the novel revolves around a Chinese-American obstetrician who is unjustly accused of performing an illegal abortion on the daughter of a prominent Boston surgeon. Critical reaction to the book was very positive. "Read *A Case of Need* now," urges Fred Rotondaro in *Best Sellers,* "it will entertain you; get you angry—it will make you think." Allen J. Hubin, writing in the *New York Times Book Review,* concurs, noting that "this breezy, fast-paced, up-to-date first novel . . . demonstrates again the ability of detective fiction to treat contemporary social problems in a meaningful fashion."

Also published while the author was still in medical school, *The Andromeda Strain* made Crichton a minor celebrity on campus (especially when the film rights were sold to Universal Studios). Part historical journal, the novel uses data such as computer printouts, bibliographic references, and fictional government documents to lend credence to the story of a deadly microorganism that arrives on Earth aboard a NASA space probe. The virus quickly kills most of the residents of Piedmont, Arizona. Two survivors—an old man and a baby—are taken to a secret government compound for study by Project Wildfire. The Wildfire team—Stone, a bacteriologist, Leavitt, a clinical microbiologist, Burton, a pathologist, and Hall, a practicing surgeon—must race against the clock to isolate the organism and find a cure before it can spread into the general population.

Andromeda's mix of science and suspense causes problems for some reviewers. While admitting that he stayed up all night to finish the book, Christopher Lehmann-Haupt of the *New York Times* feels cheated by the conclusion: "I figured it was all building to something special—a lovely irony, a chilling insight, a stunning twisteroo. . . . The whole business had to be resolved before I could sleep. . . . It wasn't worth it, because . . . Mr. Crichton resolves his story with a series of phony climaxes precipitated by extraneous plot developments." Richard Schickel, writing in *Harper's,* is more concerned with a short-

age of character development. "The lack of interest in this matter is . . . amazing. Perhaps so much creative energy went into his basic situation that none was left for people," he writes. Not all critics are as harsh in their evaluation of the novel, however. "The pace is fast and absorbing," claims Alexander Cook in *Commonweal,* "the writing is spare and its quality is generally high; and the characters, if not memorable, are at any rate sufficiently sketched in and have been given little personal touches of their own."

Crichton also uses the world of science and medicine as a backdrop for *The Terminal Man.* The title refers to computer scientist Harry Benson who, as the result of an automobile accident, suffers severe epileptic seizures. As the seizures grow in intensity, Benson has blackouts during which he commits violent acts. At the urging of his doctors, Benson decides to undergo a radical procedure in which an electrode is inserted into his brain. Hooked up to a packet in the patient's shoulder, the electrode is wired to locate the source of the seizures and deliver a shock to the brain every time an episode is about to occur. Unfortunately, something goes wrong, and Benson's brain is overloaded; as the shocks increase, Benson becomes more irrational, dangerous, and eventually, murderous.

John R. Coyne of the *National Review* finds *The Terminal Man* "one of the season's best." He adds: "Crichton proves himself capable of making the most esoteric material completely comprehensible to the layman. . . . Even more important, he can create and sustain that sort of suspense that forces us to suspend disbelief." And, in an *Atlantic Monthly* review of the novel, Edward Weeks opines that Crichton has "now written a novel quite terrifying in its suspense and implication."

In *The Great Train Robbery,* Crichton moves out of the realm of science and into the world of Victorian England. Loosely based on an actual event, the book explores master criminal Edward Pierce's attempt to steal a trainload of army payroll on its way to the Crimea. "*The Great Train Robbery* combines the pleasures, guilt, and delight of a novel of gripping entertainment with healthy slices of instruction and information interlarded," declares Doris Grumbach in the *New Republic.* Lehmann-Haupt enthuses that he found himself "not only captivated because it is Mr. Crichton's best thriller to date . . . but also charmed most of all by the story's Victorian style and content." And Weeks, writing in the *Atlantic Monthly,* calls the novel "an exciting and very clever piece of fiction."

Congo marks Crichton's return to the field of science and technology. In the novel, three adventurers travel through the dense rain forests of the Congo in search of a cache of diamonds with the power to revolutionize computer technology. The trio is accompanied by an intelligent, linguistically-trained gorilla named Amy, the designated intermediary between the scientists and a band of killer apes who guard the gems. The small band's search is hampered by cannibals, volcanos, and mutant primates; it is also marked by a sense of desperation, as the team fights to beat a Euro-Japanese rival company to the prize. In a review of *Congo* for *Best Sellers,* Justin Blewitt terms the novel "an exciting, fast-paced adventure. It rang very true and at the same time was a terrific page-turner. That's a rare combination. . . . [*Congo* is] really a lot of fun."

A scientific—and monetary—search is also the emphasis in *Sphere.* An American ship laying cable in the Pacific hits a snag; the snag turns out to be a huge spaceship, estimated to be at least three centuries old. An undersea research team is ordered to investigate the strange craft from the relative safety of an underwater habitat. Among the civilian and military crew is psychologist Norman Johnson, whose apprehension about the entire project is validated by a number of increasingly bizarre and deadly events: a bad storm cuts the habitat off from the surface, strange messages begin appearing on computer screens, and an unseen—but apparently huge—squid attacks the crew's quarters.

"Michael Crichton's new novel . . . kept me happy for two hours sitting in a grounded plane," writes Robin McKinley in the *New York Times Book Review,* adding that "no one can ask for more of a thriller. . . . Take this one along with you on your next plane ride." While noting that he had some problems with *Sphere*—including stilted dialogue and broad characterizations—James M. Kahn muses that Crichton "keeps us guessing at every turn. . . . [He is] a storyteller and a damned good one." And Michael Collins of the *Washington Post* notes that "the pages turn quickly." He urges readers to "suspend your disbelief and put yourself 1,000 feet down."

Huge creatures—in this case, dinosaurs—are also integral to the plot of Crichton's next thriller, *Jurassic Park. Jurassic Park* chronicles the attempts of self-made billionaire John Hammond to build an amusement park on a remote island off the coast of Costa Rica. Instead of roller coasters and sideshows, the park features actual life-sized dinosaurs bred through the wonders of biotechnology and recombinant DNA. There are some problems before the park opens, however: workmen begin to die in mysterious accidents and local children are attacked by strange lizards. Fearful that the project's opening is in jeopardy, Hammond calls together a team of scientists and technicians to look things over. Led by a paleontologist named Grant, the group is initially amazed by Hammond's creation. Their amazement quickly turns to horror when the park's electronic security system is put out of commission and the dinosaurs are freed to roam at will. What ensues is a deadly battle between the vastly underarmed human contingent and a group of smarter-than-anticipated tyrannosaurs, pterodactyls, stegosaurs, and velociraptors.

John Skow of *Time* considers *Jurassic Park* the author's "best [techno-thriller] by far since *The Andromeda Strain.*" He adds that "Crichton's sci-fi is convincingly detailed." In a review of the book for the *Los Angeles Times Book Review,* Andrew Ferguson demurs, remarking that "having read Crichton's fat new novel . . . I have a word of advice for anyone owning real estate within 10 miles of the La Brea tar pits: Sell." Ferguson ultimately finds that *Jurassic Park*'s "only real virtue" lies in "its genuinely interesting discussion of dinosaurs, DNA research, paleontology, and chaos theory." Gary Jennings of the *New York Times Book Review* is less harsh, arguing that the book has "some good bits. . . . All in all, *Jurassic Park* is a great place to visit."

Crichton leaves the world of science in *Rising Sun.* The novel's plot involves the murder of a young American woman during a party for a huge Japanese corporation. The case is given to detective Peter J. Smith, who finds himself up against an oriental syndicate with great political and economic power. As Smith gets closer to the truth, the Japanese corporation uses all it's influence to thwart his investigation, influence that includes corruption and violence. John Schwartz of *Newsweek* recognizes that "Crichton has done his homework," but still feels that *Rising Sun* is too full of "randy propaganda instead of a more balanced view" to be effective.

Although Crichton is best known for his works of fiction, he has also written a number of nonfiction books that reflect his varied interests. *Five Patients: The Hospital Examined* explores how a modern hospital functions using five case studies as examples. The topics Crichton discusses in *Five Patients* include the rising cost of health care, advancing technology, and the relationships between doctors and their patients. According to Sims, "*Five Patients* is written by a doctor who prefers writing about medicine to practicing it." Some of the issues raised in *Five Patients* are also touched on in Crichton's autobiographical *Travels.* In *Travels,* the author talks with candor about both his personal and professional life, a life that includes journeys to mysterious lands. "I was ultimately swept away, not just by [Crichton's] richly informed mind, but his driving curiosity," remarks Patricia Bosworth in the *New York Times Book Review.*

Crichton's ability to mesh science, technology, and suspense is not limited to novels. Many of the films that the author has directed, such as *Westworld* and *Runaway,* feature a struggle between humans and technology. Despite the often grim outlook of both his films and novels, Crichton reveals in an interview with Ned Smith of *American Way* that his primary intention in making movies and writing books is to "entertain people." He notes that one of the rewards he gets from filmmaking and writing lies in "telling stories. It's fun to manipulate people's feelings and to be manipulated. To take a movie, or get a book and get very involved in it—don't look at my watch, forget about other things." As for critical reaction to his work, Crichton tells Smith: "Every critic assumes he's a code-breaker; the writer makes a code and the critic breaks it. And it doesn't work that way at all. As a mode of working, you need to become very uncritical."

BIOGRAPHICAL/CRITICAL SOURCES:

BOOKS

Contemporary Literary Criticism, Gale, Volume 2, 1974, Volume 6, 1976, Volume 54, 1989.
Crichton, Michael, *Travels,* Knopf, 1988.
Dictionary of Literary Biography Yearbook: 1981, Gale, 1982, pp. 189-194.

PERIODICALS

American Way, September, 1975, pp. 66-69.
Atlantic Monthly, May, 1972, pp. 108-110.
Best Sellers, August 15, 1968, pp. 207-208; February, 1981, p. 388.
Commonweal, August 9, 1969, pp. 493-94.
Harper's, August, 1969, p. 97.
Los Angeles Times Book Review, July 12, 1987, pp. 1, 13; November 11, 1990, p. 4.
National Review, June 23, 1972, pp. 700-701.
New Republic, June 7, 1975, pp. 30-31.
Newsweek, February 17, 1992, p. 64.
New York Times, May 30, 1969, p. 25; June 10, 1975.
New York Times Book Review, August 18, 1968, p. 20; July 12, 1987, p. 18; June 26, 1988, p. 30; November 1, 1990, pp. 14-15.
Time, November 12, 1990, p. 97.
Washington Post Book World, June 14, 1987, pp. 1, 14.*

*   *   *

CRITCHFIELD, Richard (Patrick) 1931-

PERSONAL: Born March 23, 1931, in Minneapolis, MN; son of Ralph James (a doctor) and Ann Louise (Williams) Critchfield. *Education:* University of Washington, Seattle, B.A., 1953; Columbia University, M.S., 1957; graduate study at University of Innsbruck and University of Vienna, 1958-59, and Northwestern University, 1960. *Politics:* Independent. *Religion:* Protestant.

ADDRESSES: Home—1304 Henry St., Berkeley, CA 94709. *Office*—c/o Peggy Trimble, 4532 Airlie Way, Annandale, VA 22003. *Agent*—Stuart Krichevsky, Sterling

Lord Literistic, Inc., 1 Madison Ave., New York, NY 10010.

CAREER: Journalist and author. Assistant farm editor of *Cedar Rapids Gazette,* Cedar Rapids, IA; Washington correspondent, *Deseret News,* Salt Lake City, Utah, 1957-58; free-lance writer in Asia, 1959, 1962-63; *Washington Star,* Washington, DC, reporter, 1963-72. Lecturer, University of Nagpur, 1960-62. Correspondent covering Washington, DC, 1957-58, 1968, 1971-72, the China-India conflict, 1962, Vietnam war, 1964-68, Indo-Pakistan war, 1965, and the White House, 1968-69. First American foreign correspondent to specialize wholly in reporting on the lives of ordinary people from villages in Asia, Africa, and Latin America, 1969-71, 1972—. Consultant to Agency for International Development, 1979, 1981. Visiting fellow, Overseas Development Council, 1985-92. *Military service:* U.S. Army, Engineers, 1953-55; became sergeant; served in Korea.

MEMBER: Overseas Press Club, Explorers Club (New York), Cosmos Club (Washington), Commonwealth Club of California (San Francisco).

AWARDS, HONORS: Overseas Press Club award, 1965, for "The Marines in Vietnam" and "The Battle for Five Mountains," as best daily newspaper or wire service from abroad; Alicia Patterson Fund award, 1970; Ford Foundation grants, 1972-75, 1976-79, 1986-87, 1990-92; Rockefeller Foundation Humanities fellowship to study cultural change in rural Asia, Africa, and Latin America, 1978; Rockefeller Foundation grants, 1980-81, 1990-92; MacArthur Foundation Prize fellowship, 1981-86; honorary Doctorate of Humanities, North Dakota State University, 1986; visitor, Wadham College, Oxford University, 1986.

WRITINGS:

(Editor and illustrator) Kesar Lall, *Lore and Legend of Nepal,* Jagat Lall (Kathmandu), 1961.
The Indian Reporter's Guide, Vakil, Feffer & Simons, 1962.
The Long Charade: Political Subversion in the Vietnam War, Harcourt, 1968.
The Golden Bowl Be Broken: Peasant Life in Four Cultures, Indiana University Press, 1974.
Shahhat: An Egyptian, Syracuse University Press, 1978.
Villages, Doubleday, 1981.
Those Days: An American Album, Doubleday, 1986.
An American Looks at Britain, Doubleday, 1990, revised edition, 1991, published in England as *Among the British,* Hamish Hamilton, 1990.
Trees, Why Do You Wait? America's Changing Rural Culture, Island Press, 1992.

Also author of twenty-two reports, including *Look to Suffering, Look to Joy,* and *The Peasant and the West,* published by American Universities Field Staff, 1978. Critchfield's experimental writings on the lives of ordinary people have included series on "The Lonely War," 1964, "The Marines in Vietnam" and "The Battle for Five Mountains," 1965, "People at War," 1966-67, "How We Live" (ten-part series about lifestyles in Washington, DC), 1972, and others. Special correspondent on rural development, *Economist* (London). Contributor to periodicals, including *Foreign Affairs, New Republic, Nation, New York Times, Observer* (London), *International Herald-Tribune,* and *Washington Post.*

Critchfield's notes, including 450 Vietnam notebooks, are kept at the Mass Communications Library of the State Historical Society of Wisconsin.

SIDELIGHTS: Richard Critchfield has traveled in sixty countries and has lived in India, Vietnam, Indonesia, Egypt, Korea, Nepal, Sudan, Philippines, Iran, Morocco, Austria, and Poland; he speaks French, German, Portuguese, Hindustani, Arabic, Urdu, and some Russian.

Critchfield told *CA:* "Since 1969, except for one year in Washington doing similar sketches of Americans, I have been exploring ways to make cultural responses to science and technology more comprehensible to American readers. From 1969 to 1981, I lived for periods of three to eighteen months in villages and a few urban slums in a score of countries in Asia, Africa, and Latin America. The results were reported in newspaper and magazine articles, scholarly reports, and books. The subjects were chosen to represent some aspect of cultural change brought by science and technology to the world's peasant peoples. These included an Arab Bedouin shepherd on the Iran-Iraq border, Mauritian octopus divers, Sikh Punjabis in northwest India who prospered from the green revolution in wheat, a Javanese rice peasant who seasonally migrated to Jakarta to pedal a rickshaw, a Moroccan ex-villager who became a gangster on the Casablancan waterfront, then went to Paris and ended up with a fifteen-year jail sentence, Brazilian frontiersmen during carnival in Bahia, Filipinos caught up in a Muslim insurgency in Mindanao, an African witch doctor among Sudan's Nuba tribe, Egypt's fellahin in the Nile Delta and on the Upper Nile, and villagers in Kenya, Sri Lanka, Bangladesh, Pakistan, Nepal, Bali, Thailand, and elsewhere.

"My central finding, that the spread of Western medicine, agriculture, and communications were bringing about a great change in the general human condition, was reported in the *Economist* on March 9, 1979. This article was expanded in 'Science and the Villager: The Last Sleeper Wakes,' written for the 60th anniversary edition of *Foreign Affairs.*" Critchfield then expanded his explora-

tion of rural cultures' responses to changes in science and technology and applied it to the study of America, with *Those Days: An American Album,* set in Iowa and North Dakota from 1880 to 1940, and *Trees, Why Do You Wait? America's Changing Rural Culture,* which considered the contemporary rural crisis in the same region and presented the thesis that "no substitute has been invented for the rural basis of urban culture."

"This in turn led to applying the same approach to a whole contemporary society, in this case Britain," Critchfield continued. "*An American Looks at Britain* was highly controversial in Britain itself; it was excerpted in the *Guardian* and received over fifty reviews, both pro and con. The updated version went as far as John Major's premiership and the Gulf War.

"A fourth village book is in progress with research, partly funded by the Ford and Rockefeller foundations, involving two round-the-world trips over two years to villages in Poland, Russia, Egypt, India's Punjab, Thailand, Java, Hong Kong, Korea, and the Philippines, as well as earlier trips to Kenya, the African Sahel, and Mexico. This work, to be called *The Sleeper Wakes: Science and the Villager,* will comprise both long, illustrative stories using devices of narrative fiction, and essays, partly drawing on the ideas of Arnold Toynbee and anthropologist Robert Redfield with the help of historian William H. McNeill, Toynbee's early disciple and Redfield's student, and Norman E. Borlaug, the Iowa plant geneticist who received the 1970 Nobel Peace Prize for his work in dwarf wheat. This new work, a progression of all my books, deals with five basic contemporary themes, each illustrated with a village story. Parts of the book have already appeared in the *Economist, International Herald Tribune,* and *World Monitor.* As with all my village books, it will be illustrated with photographs."

BIOGRAPHICAL/CRITICAL SOURCES:

PERIODICALS

New York Times Book Review, January 14, 1979; June 14, 1981.
Washington Post Book World, June 28, 1981.

*   *   *

CUMMINGS, Monette 1914-

PERSONAL: Born June 30, 1914, in Kansas City, MO; daughter of Everett Monroe and Anna (Bayer) Cummings. *Education:* Attended high school in North Kansas City, MO. *Politics:* Republican. *Religion:* Protestant.

ADDRESSES: Home—2424 Melrose Ln., No. D209, Lawrence, KS 66047.

CAREER: Inter-Collegiate Press, Kansas City, MO, accounts payable clerk, 1946-48; Colyear Motor Sales Co., Los Angeles, CA, file clerk and bookkeeper, 1948-61; *Exhaust* (magazine), Los Angeles, 1961-67, began as assistant editor, became editor; Griffin Printing Co., Glendale, CA, magazine advertising liaison with customers, 1967-72; TrophyCraft Co., Los Angeles, bookkeeper in general office, 1973-76; writer.

MEMBER: Romance Writers of America.

AWARDS, HONORS: Romance Writers of America, finalist for Golden Medallion, 1984, for *See No Love,* Silver Medallion, 1985, for *Lady Sheila's Groom,* and Golden Medallion, 1986, for best Regency of 1985, for *The Beauty's Daughter.*

WRITINGS:

Exile and Other Tales of Fantasy, Caravelle, 1968.

ROMANCE/REGENCY NOVELS

Guardian Devil, Nordon, 1981.
Don't Wager on Love, Nordon, 1981.
The Scandalous Widow, Nordon, 1982.
See No Love, Walker & Co., 1983.
Lady Sheila's Groom, Walker & Co., 1984.
The Beauty's Daughter, Walker & Co., 1985.
Royal Conspiracy, Pageant Books, 1988.
A Husband for Holly, Charter/Diamond, 1990.
Scarlet Lady, Charter/Diamond, 1991.
A Kiss for Caroline, Charter/Diamond, 1991.
A Heart in Disguise, Charter/Diamond, 1991.
The Wicked Stepdaughter, Charter/Diamond, 1992.

OTHER

Contributor to anthologies, including *A Regency Holiday,* Jove, 1991; *New Poets Two; Inkling Anthology;* and *Shadows of the Mind.* Contributor to periodicals, including *Cappers Weekly.*

WORK IN PROGRESS: Three Regency romances: *Second Season, To Tame a Rake,* and *Crossed Hearts;* a historical romance, *Bright River Gold.*

SIDELIGHTS: "Like any writer," Monette Cummings once told *CA,* "I can't *not* write. I enjoy books of almost all types: history, travel, romance, adventure, and mystery. I have done little traveling, aside from two weeks in the British Isles some years ago, and would like to travel more. I have strong views on a great many things, from disarmament (but *never* unilaterally) to the proper care of pets.

"I have been scribbling as far back as I can remember: short stories, bits of verse (most of which, fortunately, remained unpublished). I had completed my second (still unpublished) biographical historical when a friend, knowing what an admirer I had always been of Georgette Heyer's work, suggested that I try my hand at romances.

"Although I try to be historically accurate, my books are intended primarily to entertain. The novels are light romances, set in early nineteenth-century England. The only resemblance between myself and any of my characters is that I am near-sighted—although my myopia is not nearly so severe as that of my heroine in *See No Love.* Nor would I intentionally model any of my characters (except for known historical personages) upon anyone I know."

*　　　*　　　*

CUOMO, Mario Matthew 1932-

PERSONAL: Born June 15, 1932, in Queens County, NY; son of Andrea and Immaculata (Giordano) Cuomo; married Matilda N. Raffia, 1954; children: Margaret I., Andrew M., Maria C., Madeline C., Christopher C. *Education:* St. John's College, B.A. (summa cum laude), 1953; St. John's University, Jamaica, NY, LL.B. (cum laude), 1956. *Politics:* Democrat. *Religion:* Roman Catholic.

ADDRESSES: Home—Executive Mansion, Eagle St., Albany, NY 12210. *Office*—Office of the Governor, State Capitol, Albany, NY 12224.

CAREER: Admitted to New York Bar, 1956, and U.S. Supreme Court Bar, 1960; confidential legal assistant for New York State Court of Appeals, 1956-58; Corner, Weisbrod, Froeb & Charles, Brooklyn, NY, associate, 1958-63, partner, 1963-75; State of New York, Albany, secretary of state, 1975-79, lieutenant governor, 1979-83, governor, 1983—. Owned a real estate practice in New York City. Member of faculty at St. John's University, Jamaica, NY, 1963-75. Counsel to Corona Homeowners, 1966-72. Charter member of First Ecumenical Commission of Christians and Jews for Brooklyn and Queens.

MEMBER: American Bar Association, American Judicature Society, Federation of Italian-American Democratic Organizations, New York State Bar Association, Nassau County Bar Association, Queens County Bar Association, Catholic Lawyers Guild of Queens County (president, 1966-67), Association of the Bar of the City of New York, Brooklyn Bar Association, Columbian Lawyers Association, St. John's University Alumni Federation (chair of board of directors, 1970-72), Big Brothers of America (member of regional board of directors), Skull and Circle, Pi Alpha Sigma, Delta Theta Pi.

AWARDS, HONORS: Pietas Medal, St. John's University, 1972; named man of the year by Glendal chapter of Universal Cooperatives, 1974; humanitarian award, Long Beach lodge of B'nai B'rith, 1975; Rapallo Award, Columbia Lawyers Association, 1976; Dante Medal in Government, American Association of Teachers of Italian, 1976; silver medallion, Columbia Coalition, 1976; outstanding public administration award, C. W. Post College of Long Island University, 1977.

WRITINGS:

The New York City Secondary School System, Thomas More Institute, 1966.

Forest Hills Diary: The Crisis of Low-Income Housing, Random House, 1974.

Diaries of Mario M. Cuomo: The Campaign for Governor, Random House, 1984.

Message to the Legislature, Albany, New York, January 7, 1987, State of New York, 1987.

Public Papers of Governor Mario M. Cuomo, 1983, State of New York, 1987.

Message to the Legislature, Albany, New York, January 6, 1988, State of New York, 1988.

Message to the Legislature, Albany, New York, January 4, 1989, State of New York, 1989.

Public Papers of Governor Mario M. Cuomo, 1984, State of New York, 1989.

Public Papers of Governor Mario M. Cuomo, 1985, State of New York, 1989.

(Editor and author of introduction with Harold Holzer) *Lincoln on Democracy,* HarperCollins, 1990.

Public Papers of Governor Mario M. Cuomo, 1986, State of New York, 1990.

Contributor to law journals.

SIDELIGHTS: Mario Matthew Cuomo is perhaps best known as governor of the state of New York. A Catholic lawyer respected for his moral integrity and public oration, Cuomo turned to politics in the 1970s with his appointment to Secretary of State of New York in 1975. Within ten years, he was elected to the state's highest office. Cuomo recorded his experiences in the political arena in journals, several of which he has edited and published, including *Forest Hills Diary: The Crisis of Low-Income Housing* and *Diaries of Mario Cuomo: The Campaign for Governor.* He also co-edited and wrote the introduction to *Lincoln on Democracy,* a volume compiling many of former President Lincoln's words, works, and sentiments. A man of many talents, Cuomo was once described by Mary McGrory in the *Washington Post* as "an orator of the first rank, a leader who had brought majesty to awful moral issues, an intellectual with the common touch and a wicked wit."

Public interests and publishing coincided early in Cuomo's political career. While a lawyer and real estate practitioner in New York City, Cuomo was appointed in 1972 by Mayor John Lindsay to devise a compromise between the New York Housing Authority and community groups in Forest Hills, New York. Contention centered on a proposed low-income housing project—massive, tower structures not in keeping with the generally middle-class neighborhood homes. Cuomo suggested decreasing the project by half, thereby creating a better continuity with the surrounding buildings. *Forest Hills Diary: The Crisis of Low-Income Housing* is Cuomo's chronicle of his involvement with this compromise. In diary format, he records his personal reactions to events as they unfold and the people involved, from the administrators and politicians to demonstrators and local housewives. *New York Times* contributor Steven R. Weisman judged *Forest Hills Diary* "woefully incomplete" as a history because of the narrow perspective (only Cuomo is represented), but then lauded the book as a "fascinating and remarkably candid account of [Cuomo's] manner of operation as he paddled his way through the treacherous waters of community and city politics to achieve his compromise." Critic Murray Kempton expressed similar views in the *New York Review of Books,* writing that "This is . . . an especially useful study of crisis management because its author reveals himself . . . as someone concerned not merely with getting the crisis past him but with its origins, its development, and what is permanent in its effects, whatever the temporary resolution." And Sam Bass Warner, Jr., writing in the *New Republic,* praised *Forest Hills Diary* as a "fascinating book" and noted that "There is a wonderful you-are-there quality in the lawyer's record and speculations that will challenge the reader's values and emotions."

Cuomo continued with both his public service and the recording of his thoughts in journals. In 1982, he was elected to the post of Governor of the state of New York, and two years later *Diaries of Mario M. Cuomo: The Campaign for Governor* was edited and published. Covering the dates November 5, 1980 to January 8, 1983, the book details Cuomo's hard-fought campaign, beginning with his indecision about running and concluding with the final glory of winning and being installed in office. Cuomo also includes, at the very end, a collection of his most successful speeches—such as those outlining his positions on the death penalty and on race relations. Most critics noted the intensity of the author, and his integrity in writing of his personal struggles. "On all accounts, the Cuomo diaries are rewarding, but in none so much as in what they tell us about the inner man," remarked Harry M. Rosenfeld in the *Washington Post Book World.* "Philosophical and intensely introspective," wrote Michael Oreskes in the *New York Times.* One critic, Doug Ireland, knew Cuomo on a personal level and was familiar with some of the events depicted. Contributing to the *Nation,* Ireland reported a few minor inconsistencies in the book, mainly events that happened before the gubernatorial race began, such as Cuomo's downplaying of his relationship with one of the Democratic bosses in New York, Meade Esposito.

However, in his conclusion, Ireland wrote that Cuomo's "diaries are, in large measure, an appealing book from an appealing man." William Kennedy, writing in the *New York Times Book Review,* concluded that Cuomo "has put together a suspenseful, inciteful, thoughtful, funny and frequently elegant book about contemporary politics."

An intellectual politician with an interest in history, Governor Cuomo was once asked to name an American writer who best voiced the spirit and meaning of democracy. His response was Abraham Lincoln. *Lincoln on Democracy* is the result of that answer and of a promise made by Cuomo to a group of attentive, visiting Polish educators to attempt to make Lincoln's words available in translation (after learning that none of Lincoln's works had been available in Poland for many years). Edited by Cuomo and Harold Holzer, the volume is compiled from speeches, letters, and other written fragments, all focused on Lincoln's ideas about democracy. It also contains essays by many Lincoln scholars that serve to connect the sections and offer biographical information. "This isn't simply another Lincoln book," declared *Chicago Tribune* reporter Patrick T. Reardon as he praised the "interesting and illuminating essays" and the text containing "the man's words in all their elegance and clarity—and, at times, tartness." Herbert Mitgang, writing in the *New York Times,* concluded: "*Lincoln on Democracy* should be a helpful guide in Poland. It might even be educational for this plain-English edition to be read in Washington, too."

BIOGRAPHICAL/CRITICAL SOURCES:

PERIODICALS

Chicago Tribune, December 21, 1987; January 7, 1988; November 19, 1990.
Library Journal, June 15, 1974.
Los Angeles Times, April 10, 1988.
Los Angeles Times Book Review, September 23, 1984, p. 9.
Nation, May 26, 1984, pp. 647-50.
New Republic, October 19, 1974, pp. 29-30.
New York Review of Books, September 19, 1974, pp. 42-44; July 19, 1984, pp. 3-5.
New York Times, July 16, 1974, p. 33; April 15, 1984; April 26, 1984; December 18, 1987; March 18, 1988; April 5, 1988; April 10, 1988; April 11, 1988; April 22, 1988; October 31, 1990.
New York Times Book Review, May 13, 1984, p. 13.
Washington Post, November 24, 1987; December 22, 1987; February 25, 1988; March 19, 1988; April 24, 1988.
Washington Post Book World, May 27, 1984, pp. 15, 17.

—Sketch by Terrie M. Rooney

CURTIS, Anthony 1926-

PERSONAL: Born in 1926 in London, England; son of Emanuel and Eileen Curtis; married Sarah Myers (a journalist), October 3, 1960; children: Job, Charles, Quentin. *Education:* Merton College, Oxford, B.A., 1950, M.A., 1984.

ADDRESSES: Home—9 Essex Villas, London W.8, England. *Office*—*Financial Times,* Bracken House, London EC4P 4BY, England.

CAREER: British Institute of the Sorbonne, Paris, France, lecturer, 1951; *Times Literary Supplement,* London, England, staff member, 1955; *Sunday Telegraph,* London, literary editor, 1961-69; *Financial Times,* London, literary editor and radio and theatre reviewer, 1970-90, chief book reviewer and literary correspondent, 1990—. Writer for British Broadcasting Corp. (BBC)-Radio. Committee member and treasurer, Royal Literary Fund; jury member, Booker McConnell Prize for fiction, 1984. *Military service:* Royal Air Force, 1944-48.

MEMBER: International PEN, Society of Authors, Critics' Circle, Garrick Club, Travellers' Club, Beefsteak Club, Hurlingham Club.

AWARDS, HONORS: Chancellor's Essay Prize, Oxford University, 1949; Harkness fellowship for study at Yale University and Huntington Library, 1959-60.

WRITINGS:

New Developments in the French Theatre: Sartre, Camus, de Beauvoir, and Anouilh, Curtain Press, 1949.
The Pattern of Maugham: A Critical Portrait, Taplinger, 1974.
(Editor and contributor) *The Rise and Fall of the Matinee Idol,* St. Martin's Press, 1974.
Somerset Maugham, Macmillan, 1977.
(Editor and author of introductions) *Rattigan Plays,* Methuen, Volume 1, 1981, Volume 2, 1985.
Spillington and the Whitewash Clowns (juvenile), Pepper Press, 1981.
Somerset Maugham (monograph), Scribner, 1982.
(Editor and author of introduction) Henry James, *"The Aspern Papers" and "The Turn of the Screw,"* Penguin Books, 1984.
(Editor with John Whitehead) *W. Somerset Maugham: The Critical Heritage,* Routledge & Kegan Paul, 1987.
(Editor) Somerset Maugham *The Razor's Edge,* Penguin Books, 1992.

Contributor to *The Nonesuch Storytellers,* Nonesuch Library, 1990. Also contributor to periodicals, including *Critics' Forum, Kaleidoscope, Drama,* and *Plays and Players.*

SIDELIGHTS: Anthony Curtis told *CA:* "My main job for many years was that of literary editor and book critic on a newspaper. I stood down as literary editor in 1990 only to be signed up as weekly reviewer. With (theoretically) more free time I have plans for longer critical projects in book-form. My output between stiff covers reveals how difficult in practice I find it to do this double act and where my priorities lie."

He once told *CA:* "For relaxation I enjoy playing chess by correspondence but I am not a strong player and still have difficulty in beating my chess computer. Chess has similarities to the old-style, well-made play, something that interests me professionally. Pinero, Maugham, Rattigan, Ayckbourn, and the rest are like chess grandmasters creating maximum tension in a minimum number of moves. One day the possibilities of chess may be exhausted, and of this type of theatre, but there is no sign of that yet."

BIOGRAPHICAL/CRITICAL SOURCES:

PERIODICALS

New York Times Book Review, January 22, 1978.

*   *   *

CUTLER, Winnifred B(erg) 1944-

PERSONAL: Born October 13, 1944, in Philadelphia, PA; married, 1962; children: two. *Education:* Ursinus College, B.S., 1973; University of Pennsylvania, Ph.D., 1979. *Politics:* Republican. *Religion:* Presbyterian.

ADDRESSES: Office—Athena Institute for Women's Wellness, Inc., 30 Coppertown Rd., Haverford, PA 19041.

CAREER: Stanford University, Stanford, CA, research fellow in physiology to develop Stanford Menopause Study, 1979-80; University of Pennsylvania, Philadelphia, research associate in obstetrics and gynecology, 1980-86, affiliated scientist at Monell Chemical Senses Center,

1982-86, research director of Women's Wellness Program at university hospital, 1984-86; Athena Institute for Women's Wellness, Inc., Haverford, PA, founder, 1986—. Assistant professor at Beaver College, 1981-82.

MEMBER: International Academy of Sex Research, International Society of Psychoneuroendocrinology, International Society for the Study of Time, American Fertility Society, Human Biology Council, Sigma Xi.

AWARDS, HONORS: National Science Foundation fellow, 1982-83; named business woman of the year, National Association of Women Business Owners, 1992.

WRITINGS:

(With C. R. Garcia and D. E. Edwards) *Menopause: A Guide for Women and the Men Who Love Them,* Norton, 1983, revised edition, 1992.
(With Garcia) *The Medical Management of the Menopause and Premenopause: Their Endocrinologic Basis,* Lippincott, 1984.
Hysterectomy: Before and After, Harper, 1988.
Love Cycles: The Science of Intimacy, Villard, 1991.
Searching for Courtship: The Smart Woman's Guide for Finding a Good Husband, Villard, 1993.

Author of over thirty scientific papers. Contributor to medical and scientific journals.

WORK IN PROGRESS: "Preparation of special reports describing the latest knowledge in simple language on specific health issues for patients and health care providers."

SIDELIGHTS: Winnifred B. Cutler told *CA:* "It is my personal goal to work toward those activities that can help to improve the quality of health care for women. To that end, I've devoted the last ten years to studying the psychology, endocrinology, psychoneuroendocrinology, and medical research relating to women's biology, focusing on hormonal therapies and hysterectomy aftereffects. It is these different studies that suggest new research questions."

D

DAVIDSON, Frank P(aul) 1918-

PERSONAL: Born May 20, 1918, in New York, NY; son of Maurice Philip (an attorney and public official) and Blanche (a housewife) Davidson; married Izaline Marguerite Doll (a housewife), May 19, 1951; children: Roger Conrad, Nicholas Henry, Charles Geoffrey. *Education:* Harvard University, B.S. (magna cum laude), 1939, J.D., 1948. *Politics:* Democrat.

ADDRESSES: Home—140 Walden St., Concord, MA 01742. *Office*—System Dynamics Steering Committee, E40-294, Massachusetts Institute of Technology, Cambridge, MA 02139.

CAREER: Houston Chamber of Commerce, Houston, TX, assistant to general manager, 1948-50; American Embassy, Paris, France, contract analyst, 1950-53; private practice of law in New York City, 1953-70; Massachusetts Institute of Technology, Cambridge, lecturer in engineering and chairman of system dynamics steering committee, 1971—, lecturer for and program coordinator of macro-engineering research group. President of Technical Services, Inc. Lecturer in Japan, 1981; Lewis Mumford Fellows Lecturer at Rensselaerville Institute, 1984.

Former vice-chairman of Institute for Educational Services; senior adviser to Institute on Man and Science, Rensselaerville, NY; former member of board of trustees of Fund for Boston Public Schools. Member of renewable services group of National Academy of Sciences, 1981; member of high speed ground transportation advisory committee of U.S. Department of Transportation, 1964-68; member of venture capital panel of U.S. Department of Commerce, 1969-70; past member of Massachusetts Transportation Task Force and Connecticut Committee on Nuclear Power Plant Location; founder of Isthmian Canal Study Group. *Military service:* Canadian Army, squadron commander, 1941-46; received Bronze Star.

MEMBER: American Association for the Advancement of Science, American Society for Macro-Engineering (vice-chancellor), American Bar Association, Association of the Bar of the City of New York, Phi Beta Kappa, Knickerbocker Club, Harvard Club (New York City), St. Botolph's Club, Signet Club.

WRITINGS:

(With John Stuart Cox) *Macro: A Clear Vision of How Science and Technology Will Shape Our Future,* Morrow, 1983, new edition published as *Macro: Big Is Beautiful,* Anthony Blond, 1986.

EDITOR

Before America Decides: Foresight in Foreign Affairs, Harvard University Press, 1938.
American Youth: An Enforced Reconnaissance, Harvard University Press, 1940.
(With others) *Macro-Engineering and the Infra-Structure of Tomorrow,* Westview, 1978.
(With C. Lawrence Meader and Robert Salkeld) *How Big and Still Beautiful?: Macro-Engineering Revisited,* Westview, 1980.
Macro-Engineering and the Future: A Management Perspective, Westview, 1982.
Tunneling and Underground Transport, Elsevier Science, 1987.
(With Meader) *Macro-Engineering: Global Infrastructure Solutions,* Simon & Schuster, 1992.

OTHER

Also editor of *Macro-Engineering: The Rich Potential,* 1982. Member of editorial advisory board of *Technology in Society, Interdisciplinary Science Reviews,* and *Project Appraisal.*

WORK IN PROGRESS: Research on the possibility of developing an interstate bikeway system.

SIDELIGHTS: Frank P. Davidson once told *CA:* "My interest is less in innovation than in the imaginative use of present (or past) technological knowledge. For instance, the purpose of a . . . conference at Massachusetts Institute of Technology was to attempt to demonstrate a miniaturized working model of a supersonic subway that would make Boston-to-San Francisco trips possible in less than one hour.

"The American public is slowly waking up to the fact that in order to make the best use—for both environmental and economic reasons—of our technological abilities, there must be genuine as opposed to merely formal cooperation between the public and private sectors. Modern engineering systems are often more useful if applied on a large scale. A 'small is beautiful' approach will not solve the drastic water shortages of the Sahel region in Africa; what is needed is *a lot of water,* not a little. And the supersonic subway would only make sense if employed over very long distances—coast-to-coast or on a trans-Atlantic basis.

"While engineering alone cannot provide complete answers to social problems, it is inaccurate to say that 'there is no such thing as a *technological fix*': roofs *do* keep off the rain, and refugees would be better off on reclaimed land of their own (on the Dutch precedent) than in hopeless refugee camps! Probably the United Nations ought to have an advisory group on macroengineering to select and design engineering programs that could help people and relieve international tensions.

"This country has been too fascinated by innovation and novelty. Probably we should envisage a Graduate School of Engineer Management where our most able students would be prepared, on an interdisciplinary basis, to help select and design those large-scale engineering systems that could best provide an environment for personal and community growth and amenity."

Davidson is conducting research on the prospects for an interstate bikeway system, modeled in part on the existing Appalachian Trail system. Previously, his company, Technical Studies, Inc., was involved in planning for the English Channel Tunnel.

BIOGRAPHICAL/CRITICAL SOURCES:

BOOKS

Preiss, Jack, *Camp William James,* Argo Books, 1978.

DAVIS, John H.   1929-

PERSONAL: Born June 14, 1929, in New York, NY; son of John Ethelbert (a stockbroker) and Maude (Bouvier) Davis; married Nancy B. Whicker, December 23, 1959 (divorced). *Education:* Princeton University, A.B. (cum laude), 1951; Columbia University, independent study, 1953-54; Benedetto Croce Institute, Naples, Italy, Libera Docenza, 1956. *Politics:* Independent.

ADDRESSES: Home—20 East 10th St., New York, NY 10003. *Agent*—Marianne Strong, 65 East 96th St., New York, NY 10028.

CAREER: American Studies Center, Naples, director, 1956-59; Tufts University, Intercollegiate Center of Italian Studies, Naples, director of center and lecturer in Italian civilization, 1962-66; University of Maryland, Overseas Extension Program, Italy, lecturer in Italian history, 1965-66; writer. Has appeared on radio and television shows, including *The Today Show* and *CBS Evening News. Military service:* U.S. Navy, 1951-53; became lieutenant junior grade.

AWARDS, HONORS: Fulbright scholar in Italy, 1954-56; notable book citation, American Library Association, 1978, for *The Guggenheims: An American Epic;* Guggenheim grant for *Mafia Kingfish: Carlos Marcello and the Assassination of John F. Kennedy.*

WRITINGS:

The Bouviers: Portrait of an American Family, Farrar, Straus, 1969.
Venice, Newsweek, 1973.
The Guggenheims: An American Epic, Morrow, 1978, revised edition, Shapolsky, 1989.
The Kennedys: Dynasty and Disaster, 1848-1983, McGraw, 1984, revised edition published as *The Kennedys: Dynasty and Disaster, 1848-1984,* 1985, second revised edition, S. P. I. Books, 1992.
Mafia Kingfish: Carlos Marcello and the Assassination of John F. Kennedy, McGraw, 1988.
Mafia Dynasty—The Rise and Fall of the Gambino Crime Family, HarperCollins, in press.

Davis's works have been published in German and Japanese.

SIDELIGHTS: John H. Davis wrote *The Bouviers: Portrait of an American Family* from an insider's point of view: the author is himself a Bouvier on his mother's side and a first cousin of the clan's most famous member, Jacqueline Bouvier Kennedy Onassis. "Since the summer of 1815, when 23-year-old Michel Bouvier (1792-1874) left his home in southern France to emigrate to America," writes Christopher Lehmann-Haupt in a *New York Times* review, "the Bouviers have had a remarkable history.

DAVIS

CONTEMPORARY AUTHORS • New Revision Series, Volume 40

Through six generations they have swum in the mainstream of American social and financial history."

In a *Saturday Review* article, Phyllis L. Mears faults *The Bouviers* for being "frequently flat and repetitive." Mears comments that the book "is agonizingly replete with generations of begats, birthday verses of elderly Bouviers, amounts of family bequests and taxes (including the cents), snippets from girlish diaries, and descriptions of the orange blossoms and tulle veils at the weddings of couples no one but the Bouviers and their intimates ever have heard of." However, a *New Republic* reviewer takes a different view: "I must admit that I opened the book with foreboding, expecting to plow through 400 pages at least five degrees duller than the *Statistical Abstract of the United States.* [*The Bouviers*] proved to be, instead, a narrative full of candor, humor and grace, only once or twice plunging into thickets of genealogy wherein the reader loses his way."

Davis's next family biography, *The Guggenheims: An American Epic,* is the story of Meyer Guggenheim, his five sons, and their various descendents, a mining dynasty that once "exploited people as ruthlessly as they did minerals," *Time* critic Gerald Clarke comments. "Yet they could also be uncommonly generous, and before they exhausted their funds and energies, they set new standards for imaginative philanthropy." The author is "an avid, although discriminating, admirer of [the family], but he is first of all a biographer and he will not tarnish his reputation by whitewashing the warts off his sometimes bespotted cast of characters," notes C. David Heymann. "The result is a well-documented but eminently readable overview of a family that has helped direct the course of contemporary American society," Heymann concludes in his *New Republic* article.

To *New York Times Book Review* critic Frederic Morton, Davis's book lacks "a consistent moral framework vis-a-vis a subject that urgently demands it." For example, the reviewer explains, "[Peggy Guggenheim's] daughter Pegeen, one of the most talented and appealing of all Guggenheims, killed herself on the fifth try; she was practically destitute at the time. Mother Peggy, of course, had and has many millions. Mr. Davis says: '[She] continued to keep both son and daughter begging. Not that she did this intentionally; it was just that she was so immersed in her role as Grand Patroness of modern art.' And the book goes right on admiring her grandness." Morton, however, does admire the "great painstaking length" Davis has gone to "in documenting the eminence and sometimes even the ambivalence of Guggenheim success. [The author] leads us along a wonderfully gaudy frieze."

Perhaps no other American family has caught the country's attention in the twentieth century as much as the sub-jects of Davis's next book, *The Kennedys: Dynasty and Disaster, 1848-1983* (revised in 1985 as *The Kennedys: Dynasty and Disaster, 1848-1984).* In this study, Davis assesses the clan, indicating that "the ancient Greeks had a word to describe a trait that destroyed the Kennedy brothers. It was *hubris,* which to the Greeks meant 'excessive pride and arrogance that offends the gods.'" Elaborates Forrest McDonald in the *National Review:* "Consider young Joe, killing himself (and incidentally his copilot) in a desperate attempt to outshine the PT-boat heroics of his younger brother [John], which in fact turn out to have been bogus." McDonald finds the tone of *The Kennedys* "somewhat supercilious, gossipy, and even catty. [Davis] has, however, done a thorough job of research, and, except for the occasional repetitiveness, has told the tale well. The result is an absorbing book and probably as accurate a one as can be pieced together from currently available sources."

In his 1988 work *Mafia Kingfish: Carlos Marcello and the Assassination of John F. Kennedy,* Davis offers his theory that underworld figure Carlos Marcello was responsible for plotting the death of President Kennedy. A reviewer for *New York Times Book Review* states "Davis has brought together many data bearing on [the] thesis that Carlos Marcello arranged Kennedy's murder [and] J. Edgar Hoover covered up the conspiracy. . . ." And a *Publishers Weekly* reviewer calls the book "an engrossing, startlingly detailed biography of a Mafia don. Marcello's rise from a street thug to undisputed boss of the oldest Mafia family in the country is superbly narrated . . . Davis presents a well organized summary of the large body of circumstantial evidence pointing to Marcello as mastermind of the assassination of John F. Kennedy."

BIOGRAPHICAL/CRITICAL SOURCES:

BOOKS

Davis, John H., *The Guggenheims: An American Epic,* Morrow, 1978.
Davis, J. H., *The Kennedys: Dynasty and Disaster, 1848-1983,* McGraw, 1984.

PERIODICALS

National Review, November 2, 1984.
New Republic, April 12, 1969; March 4, 1978.
New York Times, April 9, 1969.
New York Times Book Review, April 20, 1969; February 26, 1978.
Saturday Review, April 12, 1969.
Time, April 10, 1978.

DAY, Beth (Feagles) 1924-
(Elizabeth Feagles, Beth Day Romulo)

PERSONAL: Born May 25, 1924, in Fort Wayne, IN; daughter of Ralph L. (an engineer) and Mary A. (West) Feagles; married Donald Day, 1945 (divorced, 1960); married Harry Padva, June 15, 1962 (deceased); married Carlos P. Romulo (former foreign minister of the Philippines), 1978 (died, 1985). *Education:* University of Oklahoma, B.A., 1945.

ADDRESSES: Home—2411 Bougainvilla St., Dashmarinas Village, Makati, Philippines. *Office*—35 East 38th St., New York, NY 10016. *Agent*—Paul R. Reynolds, Inc., 12 East 41st St., New York, NY 10017.

CAREER: Member of staff of magazine of Douglas Aircraft; editorial assistant, *Southwest Review,* Dallas, TX; free-lance writer and speaker on international affairs.

MEMBER: American Society of Journalists and Authors, Authors League of America, Society of Women Geographers, Chaine des Rotisseurs.

AWARDS, HONORS: Honorary doctorate, Philippine Women's University, 1975; citation for "furthering Philippine-American understanding," University of Pangasinan.

WRITINGS:

Little Professor of Piney Woods: The Story of Professor Laurence Jones, Messner, 1955.
Grizzlies in Their Back Yard (also see below), Messner, 1956.
Glacier Pilot: The Story of Bob Reeve and the Flyers Who Pushed Back Alaska's Air Frontiers, Holt, 1957.
No Hiding Place (also see below), Holt, 1957.
A Shirttail to Hang To: The Story of Cal Farley and His Boys Ranch, with preface by J. Edgar Hoover, Holt, 1959.
This Was Hollywood: An Affectionate History of Filmland's Golden Years, Doubleday, 1960.
Passage Perilous, Putnam, 1962.
(With Helen Klaben) *Hey, I'm Alive,* McGraw, 1964.
(With Tom Pyle) *Pocantico: Fifty Years on the Rockefeller Domain,* Duell, Sloan & Pearce, 1964.
(With Frank Wilson) *Special Agent,* Holt, 1965.
(With Helen Margaret Liley) *Modern Motherhood: Pregnancy, Childbirth and the Newborn Baby,* Random House, 1967, revised edition, 1969.
(With Louanne Ferris) *I'm Done Crying,* M. Evans, 1969.
My Name Is Dr. Rantzau, Fayard, 1970.
(With Jacqui Schiff) *All My Children,* M. Evans, 1971.
Sexual Life between Blacks and Whites: The Roots of Racism, with introduction by Margaret Mead, World Publishing, 1972.

The Philippines: Shattered Showcase of Democracy in Asia, with introduction by husband, Carlos P. Romulo, M. Evans, 1974.
The Manila Hotel, National Media, 1979.

UNDER NAME BETH DAY ROMULO

Perspective of a Diplomat's Wife, Foreign Service Institute, 1981.
Aspects of Cultural Reporting, Foreign Service Institute, 1982.
(With husband, Carols P. Romulo) *40 Years: A Third World Soldier at the U.N.,* Freedom House, 1986.
Inside the Palace, Putnam, 1987.
(With Romulo) *The Philippine Presidents,* New Day Press, 1988.

JUVENILES

(With husband, Donald Day) *Will Rogers, the Boy Roper,* Houghton, 1950.
(With Jessie Joyce) *Joshua Slocum, Sailor,* Houghton, 1953.
Gene Rhodes, Cowboy, Messner, 1954.
America's First Cowgirl, Lucille Mulhall, with introduction by Charles Mulhall, Messner, 1955.
(Under name Elizabeth Feagles) *Talk Like a Cowboy: A Dictionary of Real Western Lingo for Young Cowboys and Cowgirls,* Naylor, 1955.
(With Liley) *The Secret World of the Baby,* Random House, 1969.
The World of the Grizzlies (based on her adult nonfiction book *Grizzlies in Their Backyard*), Doubleday, 1969.
Life on a Lost Continent: A Natural History of New Zealand, Doubleday, 1971.

OTHER

Also author of television plays *The Man Nobody Wanted* and *No Hiding Place,* the latter based on her book of the same title. Contributor of articles to periodicals, including *Ladies' Home Journal, McCall's, Reader's Digest, Catholic Digest, Parents, Redbook,* and *New York Times Magazine.* Assistant editor and columnist, *Manila Bulletin;* contributing editor, *Asia Inc.* Day's books have been translated into French, Italian, and German.

ADAPTATIONS: Hey, I'm Alive has been adapted for television.

WORK IN PROGRESS: Articles on Southeast Asia.

SIDELIGHTS: Beth Day's work covers a variety of subject matter, including sociology, history, biography, medicine, and current socio-political events. Day once told *CA:* "I have always viewed my work as serving as a sort of translator or bridge between my readers and either specialized information or unique knowledge of an interesting personality." Day added that for the past few years her work has focused on promoting "new understanding between the Philippines and Southeast Asia and the American public," and that she employs a dual approach to the subject by "explaining Asian things to Americans and American custom and thinking to Asians."

BIOGRAPHICAL/CRITICAL SOURCES:

PERIODICALS

New York Times Book Review, April 21, 1968; November 3, 1968.
Saturday Review, February 22, 1969.
Writer's Digest, March, 1971.

*   *   *

DEBO, Angie   1890-1988

PERSONAL: Born January 30, 1890, in Beattie, KN; died February 21, 1988, in Enid, OK; daughter of Edward Peter (a farmer) and Lina Elbertha (Cooper) Debo. *Education:* University of Oklahoma, A.B., 1918, Ph.D., 1933; University of Chicago, A.M., 1924. *Politics:* Democrat. *Religion:* United Church of Christ.

CAREER: Rural school teacher near Marshall, OK, 1907-09, 1913-15; principal of village school, Enid, OK, 1918-19; Enid High School, history teacher, 1919-23; West Texas State Teachers College (now West Texas State University), Canyon, assistant professor of history, 1924-33; Panhandle-Plains Historical Museum, Canyon, TX, curator, 1933-34; free-lance writer, 1934-88. Member of faculty at Stephen F. Austin State Teachers College, summer, 1935; Oklahoma State University, Stillwater, member of history faculty, summers, 1945-46, 1957-58, curator of maps and member of library staff, 1947-55. State director of Federal Writers Program for Oklahoma, 1940-41.

MEMBER: Association on American Indian Affairs (member of board of directors, 1956-66), American Civil Liberties Union (Oklahoma; member of board of directors, 1956-66, 1973-76), Oklahoma Historical Society (honorary life member), Oklahoma Writers Federation (honorary life member), Stillwater Writers (honorary life member), Marshall Woman's Club, Rebekah Lodge.

AWARDS, HONORS: John H. Dunning Prize, American Historical Association, 1935, for *The Rise and Fall of the Choctaw Republic;* Alfred A. Knopf History Fellowship, 1942; University of Oklahoma fellow, 1946; inducted into Oklahoma Hall of Fame, 1950; extraordinary service award, Navajo Community College, 1972; Henry G. Bennett Distinguished Service Award, Oklahoma State University, 1976; Southwest Book Award, Border Regional Library Association, 1977, Western Heritage Wrangler

Award for non-fiction, Western Heritage and Cowboy Hall of Fame, 1978, and Biennial Book Award, Southwestern Library Association, 1978, all for *Geronimo: The Man, His Time, His Place;* Award of Merit, American Association for State and Local History, 1979; Distinguished Service Citation, University of Oklahoma, 1983; portrait added to Oklahoma State Capitol, 1985; Governor's Award for Scholarly Distinction, American Historical Association, 1987.

WRITINGS:

(With Fred J. Rippy) *The Historical Background of the American Policy of Isolation,* Smith College, 1924.
The Rise and Fall of the Choctaw Republic, University of Oklahoma Press, 1934, 2nd edition, 1984.
And Still the Waters Run: The Betrayal of the Five Civilized Tribes, Princeton University Press, 1940.
The Road to Disappearance: A History of the Creek Indians, University of Oklahoma Press, 1941.
(Editor with John M. Oskison) *Oklahoma: A Guide to the Sooner State,* University of Oklahoma Press, 1941.
Tulsa: From Creek Town to Oil Capital, University of Oklahoma Press, 1943.
Prairie City: The Story of an American Community, Knopf, 1944.
Oklahoma: Foot-Loose and Fancy-Free, University of Oklahoma Press, 1949.
The Five Civilized Tribes of Oklahoma: A Report on Social and Economic Conditions, Indian Rights Association, 1951.
(Editor) *The Cowman's Southwest: Being the Reminiscences of Oliver Nelson,* Arthur Clark, 1953.
(Editor) H. B. Cushman, *History of the Choctaw, Chickasaw, and Natchez Indians,* Redlands Press, 1962.
A History of the Indians of the United States, University of Oklahoma Press, 1970.
Geronimo: The Man, His Time, His Place, University of Oklahoma Press, 1976.
(Editor with Harold H. Leake) Dell O'Hara, *With Five Reservations,* Creekside Publications, 1986.

Also author of "This Week in Oklahoma History" column in *Oklahoma City Times,* 1952-54. Contributor to *Encyclopedia Americana.* Contributor of articles and reviews to magazines and newspapers.

SIDELIGHTS: American historian Angie Debo, known as the "first lady of Oklahoma," devoted her life to the study of that state and of the history and culture of Native Americans. Debo once wrote: "In 1899 my father bought a farm near Marshall, Oklahoma Territory, and brought his family there in a covered wagon. I have a distinct memory of the warm, sunny day, the lively little new town, and the greening wheat fields we passed as we lumbered slowly down the road to our new home. I attended rural one-room schools in Kansas and Oklahoma. There was no library, no magazines, and only the one book our parents managed to buy for each of us children as a Christmas present."

Of her writing, she said, "I have only one goal: to discover truth and publish it. My research is objective, but when I find all the truth on one side, as has sometimes happened in my study of Indian history, I have the same obligation to become involved as any other citizen."

Debo's books on the struggle and ultimate defeat of American Indians by white settlers have succeeded in drawing attention to a shameful chapter in U.S. history. *A History of the Indians of the United States,* regarded by several reviewers as the best available source on Native American history upon its publication in 1970, is characterized by disturbing facts presented with criticism but not condemnation. Arthur H. Derosier, Jr., writing in the *Annals of the American Academy of Political and Social Science,* described the book as "a labor of love, a synthesis of the Indians as a factor in United States history. . . . It is 'the master' capping an outstanding career with a work that will be studied and discussed as long as persons remain interested in American Indians."

BIOGRAPHICAL/CRITICAL SOURCES:

BOOKS

Contemporary Issues Criticism, Volume 1, Gale, 1982, pp. 140-144.

PERIODICALS

Annals of the American Academy of Political and Social Science, September, 1971, pp. 176-178.

OBITUARIES:

PERIODICALS

Chicago Tribune, February 24, 1988.
Los Angeles Times, February 27, 1988.
New York Times, February 23, 1988.*

*　　　*　　　*

De SANTO, Charles P(asquale)　1923-

PERSONAL: Born September 25, 1923, in Philadelphia, PA; son of Michael (a builder) and Jennie (a homemaker; maiden name, Corrado) De Santo; married Norma A. Michener (an elementary school teacher); children: Stephen, Deborah, Susan, Timothy. *Education:* Temple University, B.S., 1949; Louisville Presbyterian Theological Seminary, M.Div., 1952; Duke University, Ph.D., 1957; Ball State University, M.A., 1968.

ADDRESSES: Home—7118 Bohnke Dr., Fort Wayne, IN 46815.

CAREER: Ordained Presbyterian minister, 1952; Springwood Presbyterian Church, Whitsett, NC, pastor, 1952-56; Blacknall Memorial Presbyterian Church, Durham, NC, pastor, 1956-58; Leavenworth Community Presbyterian Church, Leavenworth, IN, pastor, 1958-60; Maryville College, Maryville, TN, assistant professor of religion, 1960-62; Sterling College, Sterling, KS, associate professor of religion, 1963-66; Huntington College, Huntington, IN, associate professor of sociology, 1966-69; Lock Haven University, Lock Haven, PA, professor of sociology, 1969-90, professor emeritus, 1990—; member of faculty at Taylor University, 1990-91. Adjunct professor at Indiana Wesleyan University, Huntington College, and Purdue University; exchange professor at Trent Polytechnic, 1972-73, 1978-79. Marriage and family counselor. Member of National Yokefellow Prison Ministry and Whitewater Valley Presbytery. *Military service:* U.S. Navy, 1943-46.

WRITINGS:

The Book of Revelation, Baker Book, 1967.
Love and Sex Are Not Enough, Herald Press, 1977.
A Reader in Sociology: Christian Perspectives, Herald Press, 1980.
Dear Tim, Herald Press, 1982.
Social Problems: Christian Perspectives, Hunter Textbooks, 1985.
Putting Love to Work in Marriage, Hunter Textbooks, 1989.
A Christian Perspective on Social Problems, Wesley Press, 1992.

WORK IN PROGRESS: A book on juvenile delinquency, with John Myers.

SIDELIGHTS: Charles P. De Santo once told *CA:* "I am interested in relating the Christian faith to social problems and issues. My area of special interest is courtship, marriage, and the family.

"My interest in the family arose out of my growing conviction that the family is *the* most influential social institution in society—the basic one, the foundation of all others. It is within the family that one learns values and beliefs and behaviors. Not only are statuses ascribed to us by our family, but our achieved statuses are largely the result of the socialization we received in the home. While it may sound trite, it is true that as goes the family, so goes the nation. Teaching sociology enables me to deal with the family as a social institution, exploring with students those variables that are functional, as well as those that are dysfunctional, to societal well-being.

"*Love and Sex Are Not Enough* emphasizes that those factors that make for marital happiness are not 'romantic love' and 'sex,' per se. Similarity of social background (such as socio-economic class, religion, ethnicity/race, and values) plays an important part. Personality, temperament, and personal values also are very important factors in a happy marriage. Unless two people share common life goals and values, romance and desire for sexual intimacy with a spouse with whom one cannot communicate will vanish.

"*Dear Tim* is a book of essays in the form of letters to my youngest son, Tim, who was then nineteen years of age, dealing with the Christian faith. I share with Tim basic Christian beliefs about God, persons, Christ, being a Christian, and the church. In addition, I examine why faith is relevant for today. The concluding chapters deal with elements of a Christian lifestyle for young people."

De Santo adds: "*Putting Love to Work in Marriage* was published in 1989. It contains practical suggestions for improving marriage. Unique chapters deal with 'Expectations and Reality' and 'Push and Pull' factors—things that lead to marital unhappiness.

"My work in progress is a book on juvenile delinquency. It includes ten case studies showing the common variables as they relate to theory. The book emphasizes the crucial role of the family and early socialization."

*   *   *

DIXON, Stephen 1936-

PERSONAL: Born June 6, 1936, in New York, NY; son of Abraham Mayer and Florence (Leder) Ditchik; married Anne Frydman (a translator and lecturer), January 17, 1983; children: Sophia Cara, Antonia. *Education:* City College of New York (now City College of the City University of New York), B.A., 1958. *Avocational interests:* Reading, writing, listening to serious music, reading the *New York Times* over several cups of black coffee.

ADDRESSES: Home—2103 Sulgrave Ave., Baltimore, MD 21209. *Office*—The Writing Seminars, Johns Hopkins University, Baltimore, MD 21218.

CAREER: Writer. Worked as fiction consultant, junior high school teacher, tour leader, school bus driver, department store salesclerk, artist model, waiter, bartender, reporter for a radio news service, magazine editor, and assistant producer of a television show, *In Person,* for the Columbia Broadcasting System; New York University, School of Continuing Education, New York City, instructor, 1979; Johns Hopkins University, Baltimore, MD, as-

sistant professor, 1980-85, associate professor, 1985-89, professor of fiction, 1989—.

AWARDS, HONORS: Stegner fellow, Stanford University, 1964-65; National Endowment for the Arts grant for fiction, 1974-75, 1990-91; O. Henry Award, 1977, for "Mac in Love," and 1982, for "Layaways"; Pushcart Prize, 1977, for "Milk Is Very Good for You"; American Academy-Institute of Arts and Letters prize for literature, 1983; Guggenheim Fellowship for fiction, 1984-85; John Train Humor Prize, *Paris Review,* 1986; National Book Awards finalist in fiction, 1991, and PEN/Faulkner finalist in fiction, 1992, both for *Frog.*

WRITINGS:

SHORT STORY COLLECTIONS

No Relief, Street Fiction Press, 1976.
Quite Contrary, Harper, 1979.
14 Stories, Johns Hopkins University Press, 1980.
Movies, North Point Press, 1983.
Time to Go, Johns Hopkins University Press, 1984.
The Play and Other Stories, Coffee House, 1989.
Love and Will, British American Publishing, 1989.
All Gone, Johns Hopkins University Press, 1990.
Friends: More Will & Magna Stories, Asylum Arts, 1990.
Moon, British American Publishing, 1993.

NOVELS

Work, Street Fiction Press, 1977.
Too Late, Harper, 1978.
Fall & Rise, North Point Press, 1985.
Garbage, Cane Hill Press, 1988.
Frog, British American Publishing, 1991.

OTHER

Contributor to anthologies, including *Making a Break,* Latitudes Press, 1975. Also contributor of more than 350 short stories to periodicals, including *Harper's, Glimmer Train, Western Humanities Review, Viva, Playboy, Paris Review, American Review, Atlantic, Pequod, Esquire, Yale Review, South Carolina Review, Triquarterly,* and *Chicago Review.*

WORK IN PROGRESS: Interstate.

SIDELIGHTS: "One of the short story's most accomplished if quirky practitioners," according to Patricia Blake in *Time,* Stephen Dixon has published over three hundred pieces of short fiction and several novels over the course of his career. His work has appeared in a wide variety of magazines, as Blake notes, "from the venerable *North American Review* to the ephemeral *Nitty-Gritty,*" and some critics have seen the success of his published short story collections as an indication of a "boomlet" of interest in that genre. Dixon, who worked odd jobs for years while trying to sell his fiction, admits in a *Baltimore Sun* article that he didn't really start publishing books until he was forty. "By being published late, I learned I could endure and survive and still write. If I lost my job [as professor of creative writing at Johns Hopkins University], . . . I would get a job as a waiter or a bartender and go on writing."

A pervasive theme in Dixon's work is the plight of "ordinary people, usually in urban settings," says John T. Irwin in the *Baltimore Sun*. A native New Yorker, Dixon often sets his fiction's action in that city. Paul Skenazy notes in the *San Francisco Chronicle* that Dixon "writes about people who live in rundown apartments, . . . he gives a reader the irritating, wearing feel of city life. He captures that rubbing of noise and excitement against the grain of one's inertia, that constant intrusion of human traffic. But at its best the tone is less tough than worn-at-the-cuffs, frayed and slightly frantic from observing people who let their pride escape while they were watching TV or doing the laundry." "Dixon's imagination sticks close to home," writes John Domini in the *New York Times Book Review*. "His principal subject is the clash of the mundane and aberrant, those unsettling run-ins with wackos or former lovers all too familiar to anyone who's ever lived in a city." In a story in *Movies,* for example, a young man grossly disfigured by several accidents is harassed by his neighbors and even rejected by a freak show. A plastic surgeon tells him, "Wear a ski mask, they're very chic nowadays." Skenazy feels that Dixon's urban stories "frequently have a powerful impact that, while distasteful, is bracing; and there is something of the feel of that part of life too often ignored by fiction." "His stories are deceptively low-key," Irwin suggests. "They remind you of a combination of a Frank Capra comedy and a Kafka short story in their ability to be extremely funny then suddenly become terrifying and bizarre."

Much of Dixon's work also chronicles the pitfalls and problems of male-female relationships, painting "a harrowing portrait of therapeutic man and therapeutic woman trying to experience love," according to Anatole Broyard in the *New York Times*. A *Kirkus Reviews* critic writes: "Dixon's theme becomes clear: love affairs are like fiction—stories that are added to, rubbed out, obsessively changed, matters of chosen order and nuance and correction." "His male protagonists are generally so yearning and irritably hungry for sex and/or intimacy that they either don't look before they leap, or if they do look, leap anyway no matter what they see ahead," claims David Aitken in the *Baltimore Sun*. "As a result, their lives are almost always in uncontrollable comic disarray."

This theme is apparent in Dixon's novel *Fall & Rise,* in which the leading character tries, through a long New York night, to woo a woman he met at a party earlier in the evening. It is also the controlling idea behind Dixon's O. Henry Award-winning short story "Mac in Love," in which a repulsed suitor yells wistful nonsense at his date's balcony until the beleaguered woman calls the police. The final effect in many of Dixon's male-female imbroglios is, in Aitken's opinion, "vaguely Woody Allenish. Dixon's comedy is stronger than Allen's though, in being less stylized and drawn with a fresher eye for the particulars of life."

Some critics find fault with aspects of Dixon's work. In his review of *Time to Go,* Aitken comments: "One wishes Dixon didn't republish so many of his weaker stories. It dilutes the impression his best work makes." Domini similarly finds that in *Time to Go,* "all Mr. Dixon's encounters lack any but the most general physicality. . . . The repression of rhetoric and an emphasis on the trivial are hallmarks of many contemporary short stories. But Mr. Dixon is so unrelenting in both regards that he ends up compounding a lack of imagination with a near absence of passion." James Lasdun writes in the *Times Literary Supplement:* "One has the feeling that Dixon begins most of his stories with little more in mind than a vague idea, a couple of characters, or a briefly observed scene, relying on his ready wit to transform it into a convincing piece of fiction. This is fine when it works, but occasionally the initial impulse is too flimsy and the story fails to take off."

In general, however, Dixon's literary output has elicited considerable critical approval. Lasdun notes: "The best of these stories have a certain manic quality about them, caused largely by Dixon's delight in speeding life up and compressing it, to the point where it begins to verge on the surreal." In the *Chicago Tribune Book World,* George Cohen concludes: "Dixon's best is superb, tragic, funny, cynical. He's telling us all the bizarre things we already know about ourselves, and he's right on the mark." "Every overworked adjective of praise in the lit[erary] crit[icism] business applies to Dixon's writing, beginning with 'versatile,' " comments a reviewer in the *Baltimore Sun*. And Richard Burgin, in an article for the *St. Petersburg Times,* calls Dixon "a prolific and versatile writer whose strong vision balances anxiety and darkness with humor and compassion. . . . It is high time that the larger American literary community recognized that he is one of our finest writers of short fiction."

The same unique style Dixon employs in his short stories can also be found in his novels. A reviewer for the *Virginia Quarterly Review* elaborates, explaining that "Dixon writes rapid-fire fiction; the action is fast and unceasing." Ken Kalfus states in the *Philadelphia Inquirer:* "Dixon's trademark is a peculiar run-on sentence that closely emulates the way people speak and think," hastening the pace of the story. "One doesn't exactly read a story by Stephen Dixon, one submits to it," claims Alan H. Friedman in the

New York Times Book Review. "An unstoppable prose expands the arteries while an edgy, casual nervousness overpowers the will."

In one of his more recent pieces, a novel titled *Garbage,* this quick paced delivery intensifies the action of the plot, helping to create a dark and hopeless mood. An average bar owner, Shaney Fleet, has two choices when a garbage collection service tries to extort money—pay or fight. Fleet decides to fight, and in the process his apartment is burned down, he goes to jail where he is so badly beaten that he ends up in the hospital, at which point his neighbors help themselves to whatever he has left. The police are remote and unable to help. In the end, Fleet loses his bar, but retains his fighting spirit. "In 'Garbage,' the good guys don't triumph over the bad guys. What triumphs is simply the human spirit," declares Margo Hammond in the *Baltimore Sun.* Albert E. Wilhelm in the *Library Journal* calls *Garbage* a "well-wrought parable of modern urban life." *The Plain Dealer*'s Michael Heaton concludes: "More than an entertainment, Dixon's novel is an achievement. He is a writer's writer whose mastery of the mundane elevates the common life experience to high art. Put simply, *Garbage* is glorious."

In *Frog,* a National Book Award finalist, Dixon brings together a collection of short stories, novellas, letters, essays, poems and two novels surrounding the life of one protagonist—Howard Tetch, a teacher and family man—and forms a single novel. The stories, or chapters, are arranged without regard to chronology, so Tetch's marriage, childhood, anecdotes of his children's lives, and aging and death intermix, creating a conglomeration of his fantasies and memories. Episodes overlap, variations on the same story are presented, and the reader is often left to decipher the "truth." Within the space of two chapters, for example, Tetch's daughter Olivia is lost forever at the beach, only to show up as a member of the family at his funeral, without the separation indicated. "Events rotate in a kaleidoscope, the bright fragments fall, and the author's eye focuses on his protagonist's self-absorption, through chains of immense paragraphs, each a story in itself," describes Friedman. Sybil Steinberg in *Publishers Weekly* advises: "Readers attuned to the author's run-on style may warm to a cunning, sexy, audacious performance; others will find this an arty bore." Jim Dwyer in the *Library Journal* praises *Frog* for its "labyrinthine structure, rapid-fire wordplay, vivid descriptions, and raw emotional power." And *Washington Post Book World* contributor Steven Moore concludes, "For readers who can see through such 'bad writing' and relish the immediacy it offers, its vitality, its feel of catching life on the wing as Dixon's characters endlessly try to explain themselves to others or to themselves, *Frog* will be a memorable experience."

"My writing comes first in my work," Dixon recently told *CA.* "But to get to my writing, I first must finish all my school work. And I have lots of school work to do, but I never feel free to write, and I have to feel free and unburdened of looming work of other kinds, so I do all my school work before I do my writing. That sometimes means I'll stay up to 3:00 a.m. finishing student papers; I'll go to bed tired but I wake up liberated, and ready to write. I must teach in order to pay the bills. I like teaching, but I'd prefer just to read and write. I've a lot to write and I write every single day. New ideas always come when I'm writing, so the process of writing is very important for me. I'm not a writer who sits around thinking a great deal about his work and penciling in designs of what he's going to write. I go right to it, on a manual, unelectrified typewriter, and the writing always bursts open on the page. Later, away from the typewriter, I reflect on what I've written, even if I didn't intend to reflect, and do some of the revising that way. I work on a page till it's finished. Then I go on to the next. That page might take twenty if not forty revisions. By the time I'm finished with a page, I've memorized it. It all has to sound right, look right, feel right, read perfectly, to me. I do, though, first write a quick draft of a short story, if it's a story I'm writing, or a chapter, if it's a chapter of a novel I'm writing, or a scene, if it's a scene of a novel I'm writing. That first draft, of about ten to twenty pages, can take an hour or two to write. But the finished draft will take fifteen to thirty days, if not more. I only write one thing at a time. I start a story and finish it. I don't let anything else—any other writing—interfere with the completion of that work. Then, the following day, I write the first draft of another story, or a chapter, scene, whatever. That's how I work. It's all quite aimed, directed; I've been writing this way for thirty years. I found early on that if I'm writing several stories at once, I won't complete one of those stories; that they tend to dilute one another. But if I write one thing till it's finished, everything in me gets into that single story, and the work is stronger by it. My novel *Frog* was written with the same kind of unswerving direction. It took me close to six years to write. I started with the first story in the novel, 'Frog in Prague,' and ended with the last chapter in the novel, the title novella, 'Frog,' and everything in the table of contents is in the order the chapters were written. I didn't reshuffle the collection once it was finished. I wrote every single day except the days I was traveling for a day, and I spent an additional four months copyediting and proofreading the book, and even still, there are about 150 typos and errors in the novel. I can't pretend to have remembered most of the errors, but I think I have half of them in my head; they stick and hurt.

"My biggest problem after finishing *Frog,* which to me did it all for the being, was what to do after it? I hate repeating myself; if I redo a story—meaning tell a story that's like another story I've told—it's always done in a different way with new illumination. But with *Frog,* I told the story of that character with all the multiple possibilities and alternative narrations I could think of. So I wrote several of what I call story-plays, then the new collection, *Moon,* which has characters and styles I've never touched before, and am now well into a new novel called *Interstate.* It'll be like nothing I've done, in styles I've never used before. Whatever it'll mean to anyone else, I write only for myself, my writing has to excite me or it's worthless, boring, and I then have to try something else; and I must always do something new. If I ever find myself going over familiar ground in a familiar way, meaning my familiar or other writers', I'd give up writing—that wouldn't be so hard; I've written plenty, more than anyone would ever want to read—and try something else, or just read, walk, think, and keep my manual typewriter polished and clean for possible future writing days."

BIOGRAPHICAL/CRITICAL SOURCES:

BOOKS

Contemporary Literary Criticism, Volume 52, Gale, 1989.
Dixon, Stephen, *Movies,* North Point Press, 1983.
Klinkowitz, Jerome, *Self-Apparent Word,* University of Southern Illinois Press, 1988.

PERIODICALS

Baltimore Sun, January 22, 1984; July 22, 1984; October 19, 1988; April 30, 1989.
Chicago Sun-Times, June 4, 1978.
Chicago Tribune Book World, July 15, 1979; January 4, 1981.
Kansas City Star, August 12, 1984.
Kirkus Reviews, May 1, 1979.
Library Journal, August, 1988, p. 173; December, 1989; January, 1992, p. 172.
Los Angeles Times Book Review, December 3, 1989.
New York Times, June 9, 1979.
New York Times Book Review, July 31, 1977; May 7, 1978; October 14, 1984; July 7, 1985; June 4, 1989; December 17, 1989, p. 23; November 17, 1991, p. 14.
Philadelphia Inquirer, Volume 8, 1988.
Plain Dealer (Cleveland), January 22, 1988.
Publishers Weekly, September, 29, 1989; November 8, 1991, p. 48.
St. Petersburg Times, August 26, 1984.
San Francisco Chronicle, January 29, 1984.
Small Press, May/June, 1985.
Soho Weekly News, December 2, 1976.
South Carolina Review, November, 1978.
Time, August 13, 1984.
Times Literary Supplement, May 29, 1981.
Virginia Quarterly Review, autumn, 1988.

Washington Post Book World, February 22, 1981; August 5, 1984; July 20, 1985; January 19, 1992, pp. 6-7.

*   *   *

DOUGLAS, James McM.
    See BUTTERWORTH, W(illiam) E(dmund III)

*   *   *

DOUGLAS, Michael
    See CRICHTON, (John) Michael

*   *   *

DRAKE, (Bryant) Stillman   1910-

PERSONAL: Born December 24, 1910, in Berkeley, CA; son of Bryant Stillman (a chemist) and Flora (Frickstad) Drake; married Eda Salzmann, November 14, 1937 (divorced, 1950); married Lucille Daneri, February 23, 1951 (divorced, 1961); married Florence Selvin, April 1, 1967; children: (first marriage) Mark, Daniel Lee. *Education:* University of California, Berkeley, A.B., 1932.

ADDRESSES: Home—#3309, 44 Charles St. W., Toronto, Canada M4Y 1R8.

CAREER: Heller, Bruce & Co., San Francisco, CA, bond analyst, 1946-56; Government Development Bank, San Juan, Puerto Rico, assistant vice-president, 1956-58; Blyth & Co., Inc., San Francisco, CA, financial consultant, 1958-67; University of Toronto, Toronto, Ontario, professor of history of science, 1967-78, acting director, Centre for Renaissance Studies, 1972-73.

MEMBER: International Academy of History of Science, American Academy of Arts and Sciences, Royal Society of Canada.

AWARDS, HONORS: LL.D., University of California, Berkeley, 1968, and University of Toronto, 1979; Guggenheim Foundation fellow, 1971-72, and 1976-77; Vincitore del Premio Internationale Galileo Galilei dei Rotary Italiani, 1984; Sarton Medal, History of Science Society, 1988.

WRITINGS:

(Translator and author of introduction and notes) Galileo Galilei, *Dialogue Concerning the Two Chief World Systems,* foreword by Albert Einstein, University of California Press, 1953, 3rd edition, 1967.
(Editor, translator, and author of introduction and notes) *Discoveries and Opinions of Galileo,* Doubleday, 1957.
(Translator with C. D. O'Malley, and author of introduction and notes) Galilei, *Controversy on the Comets of 1618,* University of Pennsylvania Press, 1960.

(With I. E. Drabkin, translator, and author of introduction and notes) *Galileo on Motion* (Drake translated *Le Meccaniche* [Mechanics] for this edition, and Drabkin translated *De Motu* [Motion]), University of Wisconsin Press, 1960.

(Author of introduction and notes) Galilei, *Discourse on Bodies in Water,* translation by Thomas Salusbury, University of Illinois Press, 1960.

(Translator and author of notes) Ludovico Geymonat, *Galileo Galilei,* McGraw, 1965.

(With Drabkin, translator and author of introduction and notes) *Mechanics in Sixteenth-Century Italy: Selections from Tartaglia, Benedetti, Guido Ubaldo, and Galileo,* University of Wisconsin Press, 1969.

(Author of new introduction) A. B. Johnson, *The Meaning of Words,* reprint of 1854 edition, Greenwood Press, 1969.

Galileo Studies, Personality, Tradition and Revolution, University of Michigan Press, 1970.

(Translator and author of introduction and notes) Galilei, *Two New Sciences,* University of Wisconsin Press, 1974.

Galileo against the Philosophers, Zeitlin Ver Brugge, 1976.

Galileo at Work: His Scientific Biography, University of Chicago Press, 1978.

Cause, Experiment, and Science: A Galilean Dialogue Incorporating a New English Translation of Galileo's "Bodies That Stay atop Water or Move in It," University of Chicago Press, 1981.

Telescopes, Tides, and Tactic: A Galilean Dialogue about the "Starry Messenger" and Systems of the World, University of Chicago Press, 1983.

History of Free Fall, Wall & Thompson, 1989.

Galileo: Pioneer Scientist, University of Toronto Press, 1989.

Contributor to numerous books, including *Men and Moments in the History of Science,* edited by H. M. Evans, University of Washington Press, 1959; *Art, Science and History in the Renaissance,* Johns Hopkins University Press, 1967; and *On Pre-Modern Technology and Science,* Center for Medieval and Renaissance Studies, University of California, 1976.

Writer of series of more than twenty "Galileo Gleanings," published in *Isis, Osiris, Physis,* and other journals. Contributor to *Dictionary of Scientific Biography,* Scribner, 1970.

SIDELIGHTS: In a review of Stillman Drake's *Galileo at Work: His Scientific Biography* for the *Washington Post,* David Dickson wrote: "The scholarship involved in [Drake's] task is daunting. . . .Drake has painstakingly reconstructed the exact sequence of Galileo's published and unpublished notes . . . to demonstrate how certain ideas emerged and evolved over periods that ranged from days to years."

BIOGRAPHICAL/CRITICAL SOURCES:

PERIODICALS

Washington Post, February 23, 1979.

*   *   *

DUBANEVICH, Arlene   1950-

PERSONAL: Born December 6, 1950, in Springfield, VT; daughter of Frank J. and Sophie (Hayna) Dubanevich; married J. Seeley (a professor of fine arts and a photographer). *Education:* Rhode Island School of Design, B.F.A., 1972.

ADDRESSES: Home—59 South Rd., Portland, CT 06480.

CAREER: Free-lance illustrator, 1971—; childrens' picture book author, 1983—.

MEMBER: Authors League of America, Authors Guild.

AWARDS, HONORS: Certificate of Excellence from American Institute of Graphic Arts, Parent's Choice Award for Illustration, both 1983, and selection as a best book of 1983 by *School Library Journal,* all for *Pigs in Hiding.*

WRITINGS:

(Illustrator) Carl Sesar, translator, *Selected Poems of Catullus,* Mason Lipscomb, 1974.
Pig William, Bradbury, 1984.
(Illustrator) Louis Phillips, *Way Out!,* Viking, 1989.
(Illustrator) Dayle Ann Dodds, *Do Bunnies Talk?,* HarperCollins, 1992.

SELF-ILLUSTRATED

(With Thomas R. Nassisi) *Hearts* (humor), Macmillan, 1981.
Pigs in Hiding (Junior Literary Guild selection), Four Winds, 1983.
Pigs at Christmas (Book-of-the-Month Club selection), Bradbury, 1986.
The Piggest Show on Earth, Orchard Books, 1989.
Tom's Tail, Viking, 1990.
Calico Cows, Viking, 1993.

SIDELIGHTS: Arlene Dubanevich told *CA:* "I thought my writing life would be more relaxed by now. I thought I would be more prolific. So few words yet each book takes me forever. I hoped it would become easier. Balancing the visual and the verbal elements in a picture book becomes more fascinating with each project. In time, if possible, it will be clear when a project needs work, when it doesn't, when there is hope, when to give up.

"Occasionally, I meet with friends who are in the same profession. We share our experiences, moan, groan, complain, laugh. I really enjoy this because I spend so much time working alone.

"In my first books, all text was enclosed within speech balloons. Now I use the balloons as a bridge between illustration and formal text. This style is comfortable for me, and a child being read to can participate by reading a few speech balloons here and there without feeling the pressure of the larger block of text. I'm still more secure when illustrating, but am enjoying writing more and more as I gain experience and confidence."

BIOGRAPHICAL/CRITICAL SOURCES:

PERIODICALS

Hartford Courant, September 8, 1989; November 19, 1991.
Middletown Press, December 17, 1983; December 30, 1991.
Northeast Magazine, October 21, 1990.
Regional Standard, February 10, 1990.

*   *   *

DUBROVIN, Vivian 1931-

PERSONAL: Born March 24, 1931, in Chicago, IL; daughter of Ross (a school superintendent) and Emilie (a teacher; maiden name, Robert) Herr; married Kenneth P. Dubrovin (a director of agricultural research), September 5, 1954; children: Kenneth R., Darryl, Diana, Laura, Barbara. *Education:* University of Illinois, B.S., 1953. *Religion:* Episcopalian.

ADDRESSES: Home—1901 Arapahoe Dr., Longmont, CO 80501.

CAREER: Cuneo Press, Chicago, IL, editor of "Cuneo Topics," 1953; U.S. Savings and Loan League, Chicago, staff writer for *News,* 1954; University of Wisconsin Press, Madison, editor, 1955-56; free-lance writer, 1971—. Director of numerous writing conferences. Consultant, lecturer, and participant in writing programs and workshops.

MEMBER: National League of American Penwomen (president, Central Colorado branch, 1978-80), American Association of University Women (member of executive board and chapter editor, 1978-79), Society of Children's Book Writers (Rocky Mountain chapter, vice-president, 1978-79, president, 1979-80), Western Women in the Arts (honorary life member).

WRITINGS:

Write Your Own Story, F. Watts, 1984.
Running a School Newspaper, F. Watts, 1985.
Creative Word Processing, F. Watts, 1987.
A Guide to Alternative Education and Training, F. Watts, 1988.
The ABC's of the New Print Shop, Sybex, 1990.

"SUMMER FUN/WINTER FUN" SERIES

Baseball Just for Fun, EMC Corp., 1974.
The Magic Bowling Ball, EMC Corp., 1974.
The Track Trophy, EMC Corp., 1974.
Rescue on Skis, EMC Corp., 1974.

"SADDLE UP" SERIES

A Better Bit and Bridle, EMC Corp., 1975.
A Chance to Win, EMC Corp., 1975.
Trailering Troubles, EMC Corp., 1975.
Open the Gate, EMC Corp., 1975.

OTHER

Contributor of stories and articles to *Highlights for Children, Jack and Jill, Humpty Dumpty, Curriculum Review, Focus, Instructor,* and other publications.

SIDELIGHTS: Vivian Dubrovin told *CA:* "I've been writing for as long as I can remember. In elementary school, I wrote plays and pageants that my classmates performed on the school stage. In high school I worked on the school yearbook and newspaper.

"I can't remember ever deciding that I wanted to be a writer. My teachers, relatives, and friends all just assumed I would be. Perhaps that was because I was always writing.

"My father insisted that if I wanted to make writing my career, I'd need a degree in journalism. So, I graduated from the University of Illinois with a degree in journalism. I worked for several years as an editor and staff writer for trade publications and a publishing company while my husband earned his Ph.D. in Soil Chemistry at the University of Wisconsin.

"While raising our two boys and three girls, I became interested in children's literature. I began writing short stories for children's magazines. Our family was very active. I was a Camp Fire leader, a Cub Scout den mother, and a Sunday School teacher. The short stories and fiction books were based on our experiences.

"After the fiction books were published, I began to visit classrooms to tell boys and girls how I wrote the stories. One day, a young boy raised his hand and asked, 'Can you tell us how *we* can write stories, too?' I began working with teachers as a consultant. Since there was no book written for children on how to write short stories, I wrote *Write Your Own Story*. But boys and girls like to write many things and in some of the classrooms where I spoke, the children were trying to create classroom newspapers. So, I put my journalism training and experience into *Running a School Newspaper*. The newspaper book was created on a computer with word processing software. I enjoyed using word processing so much that I wanted boys and girls to enjoy it, too. *Creative Word Processing* tells boys and girls about projects they can do with word processing.

"In the summer of 1986, using the writing books as textbooks, I began teaching teachers in university workshops. Each year I stressed more strongly how easy it was for teachers to publish their students' writing. In 1989, I included desktop publishing in the workshops and began collecting and creating the material for a new book telling children how much fun it was to use desktop publishing."

BIOGRAPHICAL/CRITICAL SOURCES:

PERIODICALS

Boulder Town and Country, December 25, 1974.
Longmont Times-Call, October 31, 1974.
Loveland Reporter-Herald, April 19, 1975.

*   *   *

DUGAN, Jack
    See BUTTERWORTH, W(illiam) E(dmund III)

*   *   *

DUNCAN, Alastair   1942-

PERSONAL: Born May 11, 1942, in Cape Town, South Africa; immigrated to United States, 1976; naturalized citizen, 1980; son of Angus and Francis V. Duncan; married Alice Levi (an art expert), November 24, 1977; children: Caroline, Nicholas. *Education:* University of Miami, Coral Gables, FL, B.A., 1972; University of California, Berkeley, M.B.A., 1973.

ADDRESSES: Office—1435 Lexington Ave., New York, NY 10128.

CAREER: Rank Xerox, London, England, market analyst, 1973-76; Christie, Manson & Woods International, Inc. (art auction house), New York, NY, in charge of nineteenth- and twentieth-century decorative arts, 1977-82, art consultant, 1983-86. Member of advisory council of National Art Deco Trust and Foundation. Lecturer at museums and for cultural organizations, including the Smithsonian Institution Adult Resident Program,

Corning Museum of Glass, Baltimore Museum of Art, and Walters Museum of Art.

MEMBER: British Society of Master Glass Painters (fellow), Appraisers Association of America, Decorative Arts Society of the Royal Pavilion in Brighton, New York Art Deco Society (member of advisory council).

WRITINGS:

The Technique of Leaded Glass, Watson-Guptill, 1975.
Art Nouveau Sculpture, Academy Editions, 1978.
Art Nouveau and Art Deco Lighting, Simon & Schuster, 1978.
Tiffany Windows, Simon & Schuster, 1980.
Tiffany at Auction, Rizzoli International, 1981.
Art Nouveau Furniture, Crown, 1982.
The Lamps of Tiffany Studios, Thames & Hudson, 1982.
Glass by Galle, Holt, 1984.
American Art Deco, Thames & Hudson, 1986.
The Encyclopedia of Art Deco, Headline, 1988.
Treasures of the American Arts and Crafts Movement, Thames & Hudson, 1988.
Art Deco, Thames & Hudson, 1988.
(With Georges de Bartha) *Art Nouveau and Art Deco Bookbindings,* Abrams, 1989.
Fin-de-Siecle Masterpieces from the Silverman Collection, Abbeville, 1989.
Fantasy Furniture, Rizzoli, 1989.
Masterworks of Louis Comfort Tiffany, Abrams, 1989.
Louis Majorelle: Master of Art Nouveau Design, Abrams, 1991.
Louis Comfort Tiffany, Abrams, 1992.

Contributor to magazines, including *Vogue, Journal of Decorative and Propaganda Arts, House and Garden, Elle Decor, Connoisseur,* and *Connaissance des Arts.*

SIDELIGHTS: Alastair Duncan was with Christie's auction house since the firm opened its galleries in New York City in 1977, until 1990. During that time he has organized and cataloged scores of sales devoted to art nouveau, art deco, and nineteenth-century decorative arts. He established a world auction record for twentieth-century decorative arts when he sold a rare Spider Web lamp for $396,000 in 1980, a figure that was surpassed in 1984, with the price of $528,000 for a Tiffany Magnolia floor lamp.

Duncan has traveled widely throughout the United States, Europe, South America, and the Far East to examine collections of nineteenth- and twentieth-century decorative arts.

DUPUY, T(revor) N(evitt) 1916-

PERSONAL: Born May 3, 1916, in New York, NY; son of R. Ernest (an Army officer and writer) and Laura (Nevitt) Dupuy; married Christine Geissbuhler, 1957; married Jonna Slok Bjerggaard (a researcher), October 16, 1968; children: (previous marriage) Trevor, Ernest, George, Laura, Charles, Mirande, Arnold, Fielding; (current marriage) Signe (daughter). *Education:* Attended St. Peter's College, 1933-34; U.S. Military Academy, B.S., 1938; Harvard University, graduate study in public administration, 1953-55.

ADDRESSES: Home—6730 North 26th St., Arlington, VA 22213. *Office*—8316 Arlington Blvd., No. 400, Fairfax, VA 22031.

CAREER: U.S. Army, Artillery, career officer, 1938-58, began as second lieutenant, became colonel; during World War II commanded an American artillery battalion, a Chinese artillery group, and the artillery of the British 36th Division in Burma; later served in Washington, in Operations Division, War Department General Staff; after war attended British Joint Services Staff College, 1948-49, commanded 5th Field Artillery Battalion in Germany, served as operations and planning officer on Supreme Headquarters, Allied Powers Europe (SHAPE) staff in Paris, as professor of military science and tactics at Harvard University, 1952-56, and as director of military history courses at Ohio State University, 1956-57; involved in writing, teaching, and research, 1958-; president, T. N. Dupuy Associates, 1967-83. Visiting professor in International Relations Program, Rangoon University, 1959-60; member of International Studies Division, Institute for Defense Analyses, 1960-62. President, executive director, and member of board of directors, Historical Evaluation and Research Organization, 1962—; president and chairman of board of directors, Data Memory Systems, Inc., 1983—.

MEMBER: American Military Institute (president, 1958-59), Association of the U.S. Army, Institute for Strategic Studies (London), United States Naval Institute, United States Strategic Institute, Army-Navy Club (Washington), Cosmos Club (Washington).

AWARDS, HONORS: Military—Legion of Merit, Bronze Star Medal, Air Medal, British Distinguished Service Order, Chinese Cloud and Banner, Honorary Colonel of U.S. 7th Field Artillery Regiment. Civilian: Co-winner of Fletcher Pratt Memorial Award, Civil War Round Table of New York, 1961, for *Compact History of the Civil War* as best Civil War book of 1960.

WRITINGS:

(With father, R. Ernest Dupuy) *To the Colors,* Row, Peterson, 1942.

Faithful and True (privately printed history of 5th Field Artillery Battalion), Schwabisch-Hall, 1949.

(With R. E. Dupuy) *Military Heritage of America,* McGraw, 1956, 2nd revised edition, Kendall/Hunt, 1992.

Campaigns of the French Revolution and of Napoleon, Department of Military Science and Tactics, Harvard University, 1956.

(With R. E. Dupuy) *Brave Men and Great Captains,* Harper, 1959.

(With R. E. Dupuy) *Compact History of the Civil War,* Hawthorn, 1960.

First Book of Civil War Land Battles (for teenagers), F. Watts, 1961.

First Book of Civil War Naval Actions (for teenagers), F. Watts, 1961.

Military History of World War II, nineteen volumes, F. Watts, 1962-65.

(With R. E. Dupuy) *Compact History of the Revolutionary War,* Hawthorn, 1963.

(Editor) *Holidays: Days of Significance for All Americans,* F. Watts, 1965.

Military History of World War I, twelve volumes, F. Watts, 1967.

The Battle of Austerlitz, Macmillan, 1968.

Modern Libraries for Modern Colleges: Research Strategies for Design and Development, Communications Service Corp., 1968.

Ferment in College Libraries: The Impact of Information Technology, Communications Service Corp., 1968.

The Military History of the Chinese Civil War, F. Watts, 1969.

(With R. E. Dupuy) *Encyclopedia of Military History,* Harper, 1970, 4th edition, 1993.

(With Gay M. Hammerman) *The Military History of Revolutionary War Land Battles,* F. Watts, 1970.

(With Grace P. Hayes) *The Military History of Revolutionary War Naval Battles,* F. Watts, 1970.

(Editor and co-author) *Almanac of World Military Power,* T. N. Dupuy Associates, 1970, 4th edition, 1978.

(With Hammerman) *Documentary History of Arms Control and Disarmament,* Bowker, 1973.

(With Hammerman) *People and Events of the American Revolution,* Bowker, 1974.

(With R. E. Dupuy) *Outline History of the American Revolution,* Harper, 1975.

A Genius for War: The German Army and General Staff, Prentice-Hall, 1977.

Elusive Victory: The Arab-Israeli Wars, 1947-1974, Harper, 1978.

Numbers Prediction and War, Bobbs-Merrill, 1979.

The Evolution of Weapons and Warfare, Bobbs-Merrill, 1979.

(With Paul Martell) *Great Battles on the Eastern Front,* Bobbs-Merrill, 1982.

Options of Command, Hippocrene, 1984.

(With Martell) *Flawed Victory: The Arab-Israeli Conflict and the 1982 War in Lebanon,* HERO Books, 1986.

(With Hayes and Curt Johnson) *Dictionary of Military Terms,* H. W. Wilson, 1986.

Understanding War: History and Theory of Combat, Paragon, 1987.

Understanding Defeat, Paragon, 1990.

Attrition: Forecasting Battle Casualties and Equipment Losses in Modern War, HERO Books, 1990.

(With Johnson, David Baugard and Arnold Dupuy) *How to Defeat Sadam Hussein,* Warner Books, 1991.

(With Johnson and Baugard) *Encyclopedia of Military Biography,* HarperCollins, 1992.

Future Wars, Sidgwick & Jackson, 1992.

"MILITARY LIVES" SERIES; PUBLISHED BY F. WATTS, 1969-70

Alexander the Great of Macedon.
Hannibal: Father of Strategy.
Julius Caesar: Imperator.
Genghis: Khan of Khans.
Gustavus Adolphus: Father of Modern War.
Frederick the Great of Prussia.
George Washington: American Soldier.
Napoleon: Emperor of the French.
Abraham Lincoln: Commander-in-Chief.
Hindenburg and Ludendorff of Imperial Germany.
Adolph Hitler: Fuehrer of Germany.
Winston Churchill of Britain.

OTHER

Contributor to *Encyclopaedia Britannica* and *Grolier Encyclopedia.* Contributor to military publications and to periodicals and newspapers, including *U.S. News & World Report, American Heritage, Boston Globe,* and *New York Herald Tribune* (Paris edition).

*   *   *

DURRELL, Lawrence (George) 1912-1990
(Charles Norden, Gaffer Peeslake)

PERSONAL: Name pronounced *Dur*-el; born February 27, 1912, in Jullundur, India; died of emphysema, November 7, 1990, in Sommieres, France; son of Lawrence Samuel (a British civil engineer) and Louise Florence (Dixie) Durrell; married Nancy Isobel Myers (an artist), 1935 (divorced, 1947); married Yvette Cohen, February 26, 1947 (divorced); married Claude-Marie Vincendon (a novelist), March 27, 1961 (died, 1967); married Ghyslaine de Boissons, 1973 (divorced, 1979) children: (first marriage) Pe-

nelope Berengaria; (second marriage) Sappho-Jane. *Education:* Attended College of St. Joseph, Darjiling, India, and St. Edmund's School, Canterbury, England. *Religion:* "Of course I believe in God; but every kind of God. But I rather dread the word 'religion' because I have a notion that the reality of it dissolves the minute it is uttered as a concept."

ADDRESSES: Home—Provence, France. *Agent*—c/o National and Grindlay's Bank, Parliament St., Whitehall SW1, England.

CAREER: Worked variously as an automobile racer, jazz pianist and composer, and real estate agent; ran a photographic studio with first wife. *The Booster,* Paris, France, editor with Henry Miller and Alfred Perles, 1937-39; British Institute, Kalamata, Greece, teacher, 1940; *Egyptian Gazette,* Cairo, columnist, 1941; British Information Office, Cairo, foreign press service officer, 1941-44; *Personal Landscape,* Cairo, co-editor, 1942-45; Alexandria, Egypt, press attache, 1944-45; Dodecanese Island, Greece, public relations director, 1946-47; British Institute, Cordoba, Argentina, director, 1947-48; British legation, Belgrade, Yugoslavia, press attache, 1949-52; teacher, 1951; British government, Cyprus, director of public relations, c. 1953; *The Economist,* special correspondent in Cyprus, 1953-55; *Cyprus Review,* Nicosia, editor, 1954-55; full-time writer, 1957—. Andrew Mellon visiting professor of Humanities, California Institute of Technology, 1974.

MEMBER: Royal Society of Literature (fellow, 1954).

AWARDS, HONORS: Duff Cooper Memorial Prize, 1957, for *Bitter Lemons;* Prix du Meilleur Livre Etranger, 1959, for *Justine* and *Balthazar;* James Tait Black Memorial Prize, 1975, for *Monsieur; or, The Prince of Darkness;* first prize in international competition, Union of Hellenic Authors and Journalists of Tourism, 1979, for *The Greek Islands; Constance; or, Solitary Practices* was shortlisted for the Booker McConnell Prize, 1981; Cholmondeley Award for Poetry, British Society of Authors, 1986.

WRITINGS:

NOVELS

Pied Piper of Lovers, Cassell, 1935.

(Under pseudonym Charles Norden) *Panic Spring* (thriller), Covici-Friede, 1937.

The Black Book; An Agon, Obelisk Press, 1938, Dutton, 1960.

Cefalu: A Novel (social satire), Editions Poetry, 1947, published as *The Dark Labyrinth,* Ace Books, 1958, Dutton, 1962.

White Eagles over Serbia (adventure), Criterion, 1957.

Justine: A Novel (also see below), Dutton, 1957, published with illustrations by David Palladini, Franklin Library, 1980.

Balthazar: A Novel (also see below), Dutton, 1958.
Mountolive: A Novel (also see below), Dutton, 1958.
Clea: A Novel (also see below), Dutton, 1960.
The Alexandria Quartet: Justine, Balthazar, Mountolive, Clea, Dutton, 1961.
Tunc: A Novel (also see below), Dutton, 1968.
Nunquam: A Novel (also see below), Dutton. 1970.
The Revolt of Aphrodite (includes *Tunc* and *Nunquam*), Faber, 1974.
Monsieur; or, The Prince of Darkness (first part of "Avignon Quinicux"), Faber, 1974, Viking, 1975.
Livia; or, Buried Alive (second part of "Avignon Quinicux"), Faber, 1978, Viking, 1979.
Constance, or Solitary Practices (third part of "Avignon Quinicux"), Viking, 1982.
Sebastian, or, Ruling Passions (fourth part of "Avignon Quinicux"), Viking, 1983.
Quinx, or The Ripper's Tale (final part of "Avignon Quinicux"), Viking, 1985.

POETRY

Quaint Fragment: Poems Written between the Ages of Sixteen and Nineteen, Cecil Press, 1931.
A Ballade of Slow Decay, [Bournemouth], 1931.
Ten Poems, Caduceus Press, 1932.
(Under pseudonym Gaffer Peeslake) *Bromo Bombastes: A Fragment from a Laconic Drama by Gaffer Peeslake, When Same Being a Brief Extract from His Compendium of Lisson Devices*, Caduceus Press, 1933.
Transitions: Poems, Caduceus Press, 1934.
Mass for the Old Year, [Bournemouth], 1935.
(With others) *Proems: An Anthology of Poems*, Fortune Press, 1938.
A Private Country, Faber, 1943.
The Parthenon: For T. S. Eliot, [London], c. 1945.
Cities, Plains, and People, Faber, 1946.
On Seeming to Presume, Faber, 1948.
A Landmark Gone, Reuben Pearson, 1949.
Deus Loci: A Poem, Di Mato Vito, 1950.
Nemea, [London], 1950.
Private Drafts, Proodos Press, 1955.
The Tree of Idleness and Other Poems, Faber, 1955.
Selected Poems, Grove, 1956.
Collected Poems, Faber, 1960, Dutton, 1968.
Poetry, Dutton, 1962.
Beccafico Le Becfigue, with French translation by F. J. Temple, La Licorne, 1963.
A Persian Lady, Tragara Press, 1963.
La Descente du Styx, with French translation by Temple, La Murene, 1964, published as *Down the Styx*, Capricorn Press, 1971.
Selected Poems 1935-63, Faber, 1964.
The Ikons and Other Poems, Faber, 1966, Dutton, 1967.
In Arcadia (also see below), Turret Books, 1968.

Faustus: A Poem, [London], 1970.
The Red Limbo Lingo: A Poetry Notebook for 1968-1970, Dutton, 1971.
On the Suchness of the Old Boy, illustrated by daughter, Sappho Durrell, Turret Books, 1972.
Vega and Other Poems, Overlook Press, 1973.
The Plant-Magic Man, Capra Press, 1973.
Lifelines: Four Poems, Tragara Press, 1974.
Selected Poems, edited and with an introduction by Alan Ross, Faber, 1977.
Collected Poems, 1931-1974, edited by James A. Brigham, Viking, 1980.

SHORT STORIES

Esprit de Corps: Sketches from Diplomatic Life (humor), illustrated by V. H. Drummond, Faber, 1957, published with illustrations by Vasiliu, Dutton, 1968.
Stiff Upper Lip: Life among the Diplomats (humor), Faber, 1958, Dutton, 1961.
Sauve qui peut, illustrated by Nicholas Bentley, Faber, 1966, Dutton, 1967.
The Best of Antrobus, illustrated by Bentley, Faber, 1974.
Antrobus Complete, Faber, 1985.

PLAYS

Sappho; A Play in Verse (broadcast on BBC-Radio, 1957, produced in Hamburg, Germany, 1959), Faber, 1950, Dutton, 1958.
An Irish Faustus: A Morality in Nine Scenes (produced in Sommerhausen, Germany, 1966), Faber, 1963, Dutton, 1964.
Acte: A Play (produced in Hamburg, Germany, 1961), Faber, 1964, Dutton, 1965.
Ulysses Come Back: Outline/Sketch of a Musical Based upon the Last Three Love Affairs of Ulysses the Greek Adventurer of Mythology, Adapted Rather Light-Heartedly from Homer (with recording), Turret Books, 1970.

OTHER

(Editor, with others) *Personal Landscape: An Anthology of Exile*, Editions Poetry, 1945.
Prospero's Cell: A Guide to the Landscape and Manners of the Island of Corcyra (travelogue), Faber, 1945, published with *Reflections on a Marine Venus* (also see below), Dutton, 1960, revised edition published with *Lear's Corfu* (also see below), Faber, 1975, Penguin, 1978.
(Translator) *Six Poems from the Greek of Sekilianos and Seferis*, [Rhodes], 1946.
Zero and Asylum in the Snow: Two Excursions into Reality, [Rhodes], published as *Two Excursions into Reality*, Circle Editions, 1947.

(Translator with Bernard Spenser and Nanos Valaoritis) Georges Seferis, *The King of Asine, and Other Poems,* John Lehmann, 1948.

(Translator) Emmanuel Royidis, *The Curious History of Pope Joan,* Rodney, Phillips, & Green, 1948, published as *Pope Joan: A Personal Biography,* Deutsch, 1960, Dutton, 1961.

A Key to Modern Poetry, Peter Nevill, 1952, published as *A Key to Modern British Poetry,* University of Oklahoma Press, 1952.

Reflections on a Marine Venus: A Companion to the Landscape of Rhodes, Faber, 1953, revised edition, Dutton, 1960.

Bitter Lemons (on Cyprus), Faber, 1957, Dutton, 1958.

Art and Outrage: A Correspondence about Henry Miller between Alfred Perles and Lawrence Durrell, with an Intermission by Henry Miller, Putnam, 1959, Dutton, 1961.

(Editor) *A Henry Miller Reader,* New Directions, 1959, published as *The Best of Henry Miller,* Heinemann, 1960.

Groddeck (biography), translated by Grete Weill, Limes-Verlag, 1961.

(Editor, with Elizabeth Jennings and R. S. Thomas) *Penguin Modern Poets I,* Penguin, 1962.

(Coauthor) *Cleopatra* (screenplay), Twentieth Century-Fox, 1963.

Lawrence Durrell and Henry Miller: A Private Correspondence, edited by George Wickes, Dutton, 1963.

(Editor) *New Poems 1963: A PEN Anthology of Contemporary Poetry,* Hutchinson, 1963.

(Editor) *Lear's Corfu: An Anthology Drawn from the Painter's Letters,* Corfu Travel, 1965.

Spirit of Place: Letters and Essays on Travel, edited by Alan G. Thomas, Dutton, 1969.

Le Grand suppositoire: Ententiens avec Marc Alyn, illustrated with paintings by Durrell, Editions Pierre Belfond, 1972, translation by Francine Barker published as *The Big Supposer: A Dialogue with Marc Alyn,* Abelard Schuman, 1973, Grove, 1974.

The Happy Rock (on Henry Miller), Village Press, 1973.

(Editor) *Wordsworth,* Penguin, 1973.

Blue Thirst, Capra Press, 1975.

Sicilian Carousel, Viking, 1977.

The Greek Island, illustrated with maps, Viking, 1978.

A Smile in the Mind's Eye, Wildwood House, 1980, Universe, 1982.

(Translator) *Three Poems of Cavalry,* Tragara Press, 1980.

Literary Lifelines: The Richard Aldinton—Lawrence Durrell Correspondence, edited by Ian S. MacNiven and Harry T. Moore, Viking, 1981.

The Durrell—Miller Letters, 1935-1980, edited by MacNiven, New Directions, 1988.

Lawrence Durrell: Letters to Jean Fanchette, 1958-1963, Two Cities, 1988.

Caesar's Vast Ghost: A Portrait of Provence, Arcade, 1990.

Also author of numerous prefaces and other contributions to books and periodicals, including *Holiday;* author of television script, *The Lonely Road,* 1971. Author of story used as basis of screenplay by John Michael Hayes for *Judith,* Paramount, 1965. Author's manuscript included in collections at the University of California-Los Angeles and University of Illinois, Urbana. Author's work has been translated into other languages, including Danish, French, German, Italian, Spanish, Swedish, and Turkish.

ADAPTATIONS: Nothing is Lost, Sweet Self (poem), set to music by Wallace Southam, published by Turret Books, 1967; *In Arcadia* (poem), with music by Southam, Trigram Press, 1968.

SIDELIGHTS: "Anyone caring for the language and the future of the novel will have to come to grips with this singular work," wrote George Steiner in the *Yale Review,* in praise of the *Alexandria Quartet.* And of Lawrence Durrell, its author, Steiner added: "No one else writing in English today has a comparable command of the light and music of language." In the *Philadelphia Inquirer,* reviewer Bruce Cook spoke of Durrell as "something of a literary legend," and a writer "widely considered to be the greatest prose stylist of our age." Even with such praise, the vast body of Durrell's work has elicited a mixed response from critics—some have gone so far as to refer to the author as "a pompous charlatan." Alan Warren Friedman, in his introduction to *Critical Essays on Lawrence Durrell,* concluded that responses to any single Durrell novel are often so extreme that they seem to be inspired by different books. But although critics have attacked as well as praised his work, Durrell's reputation rests on no narrow base, certainly not on the *Quartet* alone. "Prolific and various" in his genius, as Suzanne Henig characterized him in the *Virginia Woolf Quarterly,* he published—in addition to his novels—poetry, drama, "island books," humor, criticism, translations (Durrell was fluent in English, French, and Greek), a "young person's story," several volumes of essays and letters, and numerous articles and introductions.

The son of British citizens, Durrell was born in Jullundur, India, where his father, a British civil engineer, had gone to assist in the construction of India's first railway. The author's early years were spent in that country, but after receiving some education at Darjiling's College of St. Joseph, Durrell moved to England to study at St. Edmund's School in Canterbury. Refused admission to Cambridge University, Durrell left England when he was twenty-three, and spent his twenties and thirties predominantly in Greece or, during World War II, in Egypt. In 1957, he took up residence in France where he remained until his death in 1990 at the age of seventy-eight. In "From the Elephant's Back," a lecture he delivered at the Centre Pompidou, Paris, in 1981, Durrell said to his audience, "I would prefer to present my case in terms of biography, for my thinking is coloured by the fact that I am a colonial, an Anglo-Indian, born into that strange world of which the only great poem is the novel *Kim* by [Rudyard] Kipling. I was brought up in its shadow, and like its author I was sent to England to be educated. The juxtaposition of the two types of consciousness was extraordinary and created, I think, an ambivalence of vision that was to both help and hinder me as a writer." Feeling both Indian and English, he was further affected by the Irish heritage of his mother. Feeling alienated upon his arrival in England as a boy of twelve and hating the stifling conformism of the British school system, Durrell developed a dislike of the complacency characteristic of English daily life, but also acquired an abiding love of its language and literature.

Durrell's work never enjoyed as distinguished a reputation in Great Britain as it gained elsewhere. Although the author served in the British Diplomatic Corps and taught abroad through the English service, he was never intrinsically "English" but belonged instead to the multinational fellowship of such writers as Vladimir Nabokov, V. S. Naipaul, and Samuel Beckett. Reed Way Dasenbrock declared in an essay collected in *On Miracle Ground II*, "I simply do not see Durrell as an exile, with the exile's ambivalent attitude towards home. I see him rather as a man without a home to be ambivalent about." Dasenbrock's insight seems confirmed by a 1945 letter from Durrell to novelist Henry Miller: "When shall we be meeting again? Soon I hope, in Greece or Paris, Tibet or Damascus. It's all one. I belong equally everywhere now. Am happy."

Durrell's early writing sprang out of his love of words, his wide reading, and his enjoyment of life. "Words I carry in my pocket, where they breed like white mice," he wrote Miller. In a letter to Alan G. Thomas included in *Spirit of Place* he explained, "I'm starting at Vol. I of the *Encyclopaedia Brit.* and reading through all the big subjects." And later, in an interview with Marc Alyn, published in 1973 as *The Big Supposer,* Durrell identified his favorite poets as William Shakespeare, John Donne, and Ovid. "Always merry and bright!" commented Miller in an essay included in *The World of Lawrence Durrell,* "Always coming toward you with countenance a-gleam, the *heraldic* (his favorite word then) gleam of the blazoned escutcheon. The golden boy." Gerald Durrell characterized his brother in *My Family and Other Animals:* "Larry was designed by Providence to go through life like a small, blond firework, exploding ideas in other people's minds, and then curling up with cat-like unctuousness and refusing to take any blame for the consequences."

Regarding his earliest book, the novel *Pied Piper of Lovers* which was published in 1935, as the work of an apprentice, Durrell showed no interest in reissuing either it or *Panic Spring,* which followed two years later. *Pied Piper of Lovers* is linear in design and obviously a first novel, but *Panic Spring* is more interesting, for in his second novel Durrell was already experimenting with form and technique. "I've tried, just for an exercise in writing, to create characters on two continuous planes of life—the present—meaning the island [the Greek setting of the book] and their [the characters'] various pasts," he wrote Thomas. "It does not progress as an ordinary novel progresses. The tentacles push out sideways while the main body is almost static." The young author added: "I am beginning to feel that my pencil is almost sharpened. Soon I'll be ready to begin on a BOOK."

James A. Brigham viewed *Pied Pipers of Lovers* and *Panic Spring* as the first parts of an "unacknowledged trilogy" in his article in *Collected Essays on Lawrence Durrell.* Brigham contended that the culmination of the trilogy, the "BOOK" Durrell referred to, was *The Black Book.* Published in 1938, *The Black Book* proved to be Durrell's first foray into literary notoriety, and a giant step forward in his literary career. Brigham noted that Durrell himself always thought in terms of sets of novels. In a letter to Miller he had described a projected trilogy: "I have planned AN AGON, A PATHOS, AN ANAGNORISIS. If I write them they should be The Black Book, The Book of Miracles, The Book of the Dead." "The Book of the Dead" was his original title for *The Alexandria Quartet,* but its accomplishment lay twenty years in the future. In 1960, after the fame of the *Quartet* finally persuaded U.S. publishers to make *The Black Book* available to American readers, Durrell prefaced the new edition with his own judgment of its merit: "This novel . . . may yet leave its mark upon the reader who can recognize it for what it is: a two-fisted attack on literature by an angry young man of the thirties. . . . With all its imperfections lying heavy on its head, I can't help being attached to it because in the writing of it I first heard the sound of my own voice, lame and halting perhaps, but nevertheless my very own."

The Black Book is structured around the narrator, Lawrence Lucifer, who in composing his autobiography on a Greek island, recalls the "English Death" of a waste-land London and encloses within his life story parts of a fictional diary attributed to one "Death" Gregory. The book concerns itself with sickness, sex, prostitution, death, and decay—the stifling, destructive existence of the impoverished artist. In corrosive language the writer attacks England's smugness and sterility within his "scenario of despair," prompting G. S. Fraser to suggest in *Lawrence Durrell* that in *The Black Book* Durrell "explored Hell" and "just got out."

One of the most significant influences on Durrell during his search for his own voice as a writer was Henry Miller's *Tropic of Cancer.* Miller's 1934 novel, which opened whole new areas of frankness in subject matter and expression, was published in France, banned in England, and immediately joined James Joyce's *Ulysses* (1922) and D. H. Lawrence's *Lady Chatterley's Lover* (1928) as major books that were widely read "underground." Durrell was influenced by the innovations of all three writers: He admired Miller's openness, Joyce's formal experimentations, and Lawrence's erotic honesty and spirit of revolt. T. S. Eliot's *The Waste Land,* published in 1922, its surface of kaleidoscopic vignettes of modern London overlying layers of meaning below, also helped to inspire in Durrell a new fictional method. In *The Black Book* he had deliberately tried to create a plot that would move in memory but remain static in linear time, radiating instead out into space. He referred to this principle—which he would go on to refine in *The Alexandria Quartet*—as "heraldic." "I chose the word 'heraldic,' " he wrote Miller, "for a double reason. First, because in the relation of the work to the artist it seemed to me that it expressed the exact quality I wanted. Also because in heraldry I seem to find that quality of magic and spatial existence which I want to tack on to art." Durrell later told Alyn: "The heraldic structure, preservation in essence, exists just as much in a sculpture as in a poem. I wanted to bring it out in the novel." Durrell assumed that Faber & Faber decline to publish *The Black Book.* However, T. S. Eliot, employed as an editor of the English publishing house, was impressed with the novel and convinced Faber & Faber to issue it in an expurgated edition. Durrell was tempted by the offer, but Miller argued for "artistic integrity" and *The Black Book* was finally published uncut in France. The importance of this novel—written when its author was only twenty-four years old—to Durrell's career cannot be overestimated. Eliot, in a statement that would appear on the dust jacket of *The Black Book,* called it "the first piece of work by a new English writer to give me any hope for the future of prose fiction."

In 1939 Durrell returned to Greece from his stay in Paris and London; when World War II began soon after, he fled ahead of the German troops into Egypt where he became a British foreign press officer, first in Cairo and then in Alexandria. After the war he filled diplomatic and teaching positions in such diverse locations as Rhodes, Argentina, Yugoslavia, and Cyprus, until he finally settled in Provence, France. Through the 1940s and 1950s Durrell continued to write, gaining serious recognition in two different genres—"island books" and poetry. It is for these two bodies of writing that his reputation is greatest among English readers.

Durrell's "island" or landscape books are drawn from the Greek world, but they are far more than travelogues, or catalogues of places to visit. Like the travel literature of Norman Douglas and D. H. Lawrence, they recreate the ambience of places loved, the characters of people known, and the history and mythology of each unique island world. The first three landscape books, *Prospero's Cell* (1945), *Reflections on a Marine Venus* (1953), and *Bitter Lemons* (1957), form a kind of trilogy mounting in intensity and power. *Prospero's Cell* is considered by critics to be the most beautiful of the three, evoking the Corfu of the young Durrell, his Greek friends, and the history of the island, and resonating with myths from Homer to Shakespeare and beyond. *Reflections on a Marine Venus* is, by comparison, a harsher, less romantic look at the life of the people of Rhodes immediately after the war. In *Reflections* Durrell classified his love of islands as "Islomania": "This book is by intention a sort of anatomy of islomania, with all its formal defects of inconsequence and shapelessness." *Bitter Lemons* is critically seen to be the finest of Durrell's island studies and among the most outstanding of his works. Published in 1957, the book was written immediately after he returned to England from Cyprus, where his romance with Greece had been tragically strained by the island's nationalistic uprisings. He felt helpless, caught between England's wavering paternalistic position and the intense desire for "Enosis"—union with Greece—developing among the island people he loved. The author's helplessness is expressed forcefully and vividly in *Bitter Lemons.* In the *New York Times Book Review,* Freya Stark praised its "integrity of purpose, . . . careful brilliant depth of language and . . . the feeling of destiny which pervades it," declaring that the book elevated Durrell to the first rank of writers.

Durrell wrote two other island books later in his career. *Sicilian Carousel* (1977) is the record of a guided tour through Sicily, highlighting its classical and romantic spots. *The Greek Islands* (1978) revisits the Greek world in all its variety, island by island, with superb illustrations. Both are more clearly travel books, however, than the beautiful and often profound "trilogy."

Durrell drew upon his fascination with islands in *Cefalu,* a satiric novel written in 1947. Published under the title *The Dark Labyrinth* in the United States, the story follows a group of English tourists into a Cretan cave—perhaps the site of the ancient labyrinth—where a landslide prevents their exit. Forced into their inner selves in search of their destinies, one couple makes their way into a sort of mythic world beyond time. Describing it to Miller, Durrell referred to *Cefalu* "a queer cosmological tale." With mythic depths, philosophic quest, and breakthrough into the Heraldic Universe, it presages on a minor scale his work to come.

Asked by Alyn which of his work was closest to his heart, Durrell answered: "My poetry, naturally. The poetic form expresses what is most intimate, most profound in man as he relates to the world. It's also the most terrifying form; you have to compress into, say, three lines the most unbelievably complex experience." Durrell's verse revealed, in a condensed form, the emotions and thoughts that existed throughout the whole of his writings: As he told Alyn, "For me, as I have said, poetry is a way of breathing." In *Spirit of Place* he wistfully viewed the art of poetry as "A tragic game, in a sense. I would so much like to be a poet. . . . One can be a very good poet without necessarily being a great poet."

Indeed, Durrell was critically considered a very good poet. In the 1930s and early 1940s, his was a beautifully modulated "new voice in a new time," as Fraser noted in *Lawrence Durrell.* Urbane, compassionate, often infused with loneliness yet filled with a sense of wry fun, his poems draw deeply on two traditions: the first of ancient Greece and its rebirth in the works of such modern Greek poets as Constantine Cavafy and George Seferis, and the second of the Renaissance, of Shakespeare and Donne as reinvented by the twentieth-century "metaphysicals" Eliot and W. H. Auden. Although Durrell journeyed with the moderns across a waste land, his poetry is suffused with Greek light. Hayden Carruth wrote in *The World of Lawrence Durrell,* "the poet of the historic consciousness who is recording the end of a civilization is intimately aware of the beginning, and the figure of Homer, the blind brother in the mists of ancientness, overlooks these poems, overlooks the *Quartet* too, I think." Many of his lyrics, such as "Nemea," "Lesbos," and "Mneiae," recall the ancient Greek Anthology put together from many sources in the Byzantine period, while his character poems, with their interplay of art and idea, are closer to Cavafy. In this latter category can be placed "Petron, the Desert Father" and "A Portrait of Theodora," the second of which reflects not only the modern Greek woman but, through her, the Byzantine empress as a girl. The character poems, especially "Fangbrand: A Biography," display "a kind of golden fullness of expression," Derek Stanford declared in his essay collected in *The World of Lawrence Durrell.*

In his best poems, as in *The Alexandria Quartet,* a profound understanding both of the past and of mythology underlies Durrell's quick and lively awareness of the present, with its attendant humor and many sorrows. Among these poems is "Deus Loci," a kind of classical hymn to the "small sunburnt" god—a charming and elegant personification of the spirit of place. Friedman wrote in *Lawrence Durrell and The Alexandria Quartet* that "Deus Loci" "offers an archetypal treatment of place—that pervading, ever-recurring motif—that may serve as a paradigm not only for the bulk of Durrell's poetry but also for

such works as *Sappho,* the island books, and the *Quartet.*" Another of his best-known poems, "Alexandria," evokes the atmosphere of the city and the poet's own loneliness, "the artist at his papers/ Up there alone, upon the alps of night".

Durrell's poetry has been seen as moving from early lyrics to the classically-based and metaphysically strong poems of his middle years. His later poetry, more conversational in tone, becomes even stronger in its anguished concern with "the three big words of Durrell's poetic vocabulary . . . art, love, and death," according to Ian S. MacNiven in *Critical Essays.* One of the most moving of these poems is the elegy, "Seferis." Poems like "A Patch of Dust" and "Last Heard Of" evince a remarkable sureness and power. In reflecting a maturing style, Durrell's poetic works form a kind of *Ars poetica,* a portrait of the developing artist. In his early "Soliloquy of Hamlet" he wrote, "Walk upon dreams, and pass behind the book." In his middle period he added, "I now move/ Through many negatives to what I am." In his later poetry he concluded, "The major darkness comes and art beckons/ With its quiet seething of the writer's mind." To Alyn's description of Durrell's poetry as "a tight network of ideas and feelings," the poet responded: "And of sensuality and intellectual acuity. . . . at the same time strong and fragile, hermetic and luminous. The shell knitted to the body," adding later: "There is a point where sunlight and inner light meet."

Inspired by authors Eliot, Christopher Fry, and probably Jean-Paul Sartre and Jean Anouilh, Durrell tried his hand at three "verse dramas": *Sappho* in 1950, *Acte* and *An Irish Faustus* in the 1960s. He also worked on the screenplay for the 1963 film *Cleopatra* and wrote a draft of *Judith* for the screen. Although Durrell was enthusiastic about his plays, they never met with great popular or critical success. Like the closet verse plays of the nineteenth-century English Romantics, they respond more to reading than to performing although each has been accorded major theatrical productions.

Sappho, the earliest and most lyrical of the plays, creates, as Fraser noted in *Critical Essays on Lawrence Durrell,* "an atmosphere of a lost civilization at once primitive and lucid." But, although its plot covers much time and ground, the play contains more talk than action. The writing in *Acte,* a Corneillelike tragedy set in Nero's Rome, is terser and more theatrically oriented than *Sappho,* but *Acte* also fails to achieve great power as drama. Here Durrell seems more interested in Petronius as the play's creative artist than in the play's central love story. *An Irish Faustus* is the most intriguing of the three dramas. Basing his philosopher-magician on the character portrayed in the works of both Christopher Marlowe and Johann Wolfgang von Goethe, Durrell portrays Faustus' need to understand both black and white magic before he can find peace. *An Irish Faustus* cleverly reverses Marlowe's *Dr. Faustus;* the concluding act finds Faustus high on a mountain top playing cards with Matthew the Hermit, Martin the Pardoner, and Mephisto, the primary devil in the Faust legend. Upon gaining the knowledge that "when nothing begins to happen . . . the dance of the pure forms begins," Faustus is allowed entrance to Durrell's Heraldic Universe. Both Jungian psychology and Eastern thought are woven into the play, expanding the medieval German legend through time and space. Although possibly his best play, Friedman perceived it as "nearly sterile." In contrast, Fraser praised the work in *Collected Essays on Lawrence Durrell,* deeming *An Irish Faustus* "a small masterpiece."

Durrell's satires of diplomatic life were much more popular among English readers than his verse dramas. These slight but hilarious pieces, revolving around the bumbling diplomat Antrobus, have a delightfully Wodehousian flavor. In a *Paris Review* interview collected in George Plimpton's *Writers at Work,* Durrell acknowledged his debt to the great British humourist by saying that "even when I'm writing this Antrobus nonsense, I'm writing it with a reverence to P. G. Wodehouse." Between 1957 and 1966 he turned out three volumes—*Esprit de Corps, Stiff Upper Lip,* and *Sauve Qui Peu.* A selection of twenty sketches was published in 1974 as *The Best of Antrobus* and all were included in *Antrobus Complete,* issued in 1985. Although these are his only official books of humor, a high—and low—sense of the comic runs through all his work, including his many letters and recorded conversations.

With the publication of *Justine* in 1957, Durrell achieved worldwide fame. The first volume of his "Alexandria Quartet," *Justine* was followed by *Balthazar* and *Mountolive* in 1958, and *Clea* in 1960. In *Spirit of Place* Thomas explained that "when a book comes to fruition in [Durrell's] mind, he writes with exceptional speed, often for long hours at a stretch." This speed is deceptive, however, for long periods of gestation were needed for most ambitious books. As early as 1937 he wrote Miller that he was planning "The Book of the Dead," and in 1945 he wrote Eliot—in letters reprinted in *Twentieth Century Literature*—that he planned his major works to be "The Black Book," "The Book of the Dead," and "The Book of Time." These working titles seemed almost to foretell the three major fictional works: *The Black Book, The Alexandria Quartet,* and *The Avignon Quintet.* Durrell told Eliot, tongue-in-cheek: "But I cannot do them all at once—they must grow on me like frogs' eggs and meanwhile I must write for practice for fun for money and for my girl friends—no?"

Originally Durrell planned to locate "The Book of the Dead" in Athens, but his years in Egypt provided him with a setting for even more diversity. In the summer of 1956, he wrote Miller from Cyprus: "I have just finished a book about Alexandria called *Justine*—the first *serious* book since *The Black Book,* much clearer and better organized, I think. . . . It's a sort of prose poem to one of the great capitals of the heart, the Capital of Memory." In discussing the novel with Alyn he explained its genesis: "It took me years to evolve *Justine,* because I was having to work on so many levels at once; history, landscape (which had to be fairly *strange* to symbolize our civilization), the weft of occultism and finally the novel about the actual process of writing. What I was trying to achieve was a canvas that was both historic and ordinary; to get that I made use of every modern technique." Durrell wanted *Justine,* in its conception, "to turn, for example, to Einstein, or to go back to the origins: *The Book of the Dead,* Plato, to the occult traditions which are still alive in the East."

The Alexandria Quartet was an experiment in form. The outer plot, a story of love, mystery, and spies, is narrated by a young writer who takes an archetypal journey to find love, self-knowledge, and his artistic voice. He writes a first novel—*Justine*—about a love affair in Alexandria, follows with another—*Balthazar*—that, in quoting other people, contradicts the first. Finally, after the interjection of a third omniscient volume revealing the "facts"—*Mountolive*—the narrator adds a last novel—*Clea*—that moves forward in time toward his attainment of maturity and wisdom. George P. Elliott, discussing Durrell's fictional strategies in *Critical Essays,* found that the "shifting of the point of view from volume to volume is the most spectacular of these, its effect being the expansion, alteration, deepening of our knowledge of what has happened."

The form of the *Quartet* is intrinsic to the work; Durrell had been concerned for many years with how the new physics of space-time might apply to fiction. Deeply read in Sigmund Freud and Carl Jung and in Sir James Frazer's mythic theory, he saw modern thought returning full circle to Far Eastern and Indian philosophy, and he wanted to weave all these concepts into the tapestry of the novel. He explained in *Paris Review* that "Eastern and Western metaphysics are coming to a point of confluence in the most interesting way. It seems unlikely in a way, but nevertheless the two main architects of this breakthrough have been Einstein and Freud. . . . Well, this novel is a four-dimensional dance, a relativity poem." Durrell's concept of space-time has been greatly debated by critics of his work. Anthony Burgess contended in *The Novel Now,* that "To learn more and more as we go on is what we expect from any good novel, and we need no benefit of 'relativity.' " John Unterecker voiced the opposing point of view in *Lawrence Durrell:* "the relativity theory involves a reorientation for the modern writer not only toward the materials of his art but also toward himself, his audience, his world." In no sense a pretentious or superfluous theory imposed on the *Quartet,* space-time is, in many ways, the central structure of the work. Indeed, Durrell had presaged its use five years before *Justine.* In his *Key to Modern British Poetry* he discussed how modern writers were beginning to think in terms both of Einsteinian space-time and of Freudian and Jungian psychology.

The portrait of the city of Alexandria itself is both sensually and intellectually painted, and the characters in it are multi-faceted. Durrell told the *Paris Review* that "Freud torpedoed the idea of the stable ego so that personality began to diffuse." "And if human personality is an illusion? And if as biology tells us, every single cell in our bodies is replaced every seven years by another?," he asks in *Clea.* "At the most I hold in my arms something like a fountain of flesh, continuously playing, and in my mind a rainbow of dust." In *Justine* he says more simply, "To every one we turn a different face of the prism." This "sort of prism-sightedness," then, is another central characteristic of the *Quartet* as Durrell attempts to come closer to the real personalities of people psychologically perceived.

Finally, *The Alexandria Quartet* is a prose poem—a novel that only a poet could write—to the city of Alexandria itself. The novel's middle-eastern atmosphere especially annoyed English critics who agreed with Burgess: "It is conceivable that the tetralogy might have seemed more original if it had been set in a British middle-class environment." Durrell, however, had spent nearly his whole adult life in the Mediterranean world; it is the English setting that would have been foreign to him. Also, by setting the *Quartet* in the ancient center of both the Western and Mid-Eastern worlds, he was able to come closer to creating a microcosm of the whole twentieth-century world: as Richard Aldington wrote in *The World of Lawrence Durrell,* "Durrell is a writer of 'the outer world,' beyond the stale and swarming capitals of the West." To critic D. J. Enright's indignant attack in the *International Literary Annual*—"Alexandria *is* a rather melodramatic city. . . . Why, then, did Durrell feel obliged to paint the lily and throw an extra stench on the putrescence?"—Hilary Corke responded in *Encounter:* "The correspondences of Durrell's Alexandria with what I knew of the sister city [Cairo] are extraordinarily exact. . . . I do not mean just the outward scene but the emotional landscapes, the fetid politics, the sexual patterns." Beyond modern Alexandria, Robert Scholes in *Fabulation and Metafiction* found the *Quartet* "completely faithful to the ancient spirit of the place"; and the French critic, Victor Brombert, in *The World of Lawrence Durrell* saw the city as the expression of a myth. The *Quartet's* symbolism is rich with allusions to the past—historical, legendary, and mythical—and levels of meaning beneath the narrative present suggest those ancient worlds. In fact

the whole *Quartet* is what Durrell in *The Big Supposer* called a "sort of palimpsest." The tetralogy is designed to move through the city's history, as Carol Peirce showed in her essay in *Twentieth Century Literature:* it "is imbued with the spirit of the city founded by Alexander, ruled by Cleopatra, idealized by Plotinus," and "it includes the city as philosophic center of Neo-Platonism, Gnosticism, Hermeticism, and the conflicting orders of early Christianity." At the same time it symbolically follows the initiate's journey toward the Grail implicit in the Tarot cards, as the hero-narrator of the *Quartet* progresses toward the final achievement of his own Grail quest and heraldic vision.

Durrell's symbol of the Heraldic Universe is closely linked both to medieval vision and to Eastern thought. His use of the Heraldic symbol and the quest is not far, either, from Eliot's definition, in a review of *Ulysses* reprinted in *Selected Prose of T. S. Eliot,* of the mythical method that he and Joyce were using, "a way of controlling, of ordering, of giving a shape and a significance to the immense panorama of futility and anarchy which is contemporary history." Durrell too sought more than social realism, concluding in *Clea:* "A novel should be an act of divination by entrails, not a careful record of a game of pat-ball on some vicarage lawn!" John Weigel concluded in *Lawrence Durrell:* "The *Quartet* is *about* the city, *about* love, *about* death, and *about* truth. It is a trick done with words—and mirrors. It is as esoteric and complex as a Tarot deck. If you like, it is work to divine by."

In spite of charges of esoteric setting, improbable characters, and over-luxuriant prose, *The Alexandria Quartet* seems an enduring achievement. As reviewer Curtis Cate wrote in the *Atlantic Monthly:* "Yet, with all its failings, the *Alexandria Quartet* is the work of an extraordinarily gifted prose poet." Jane Pinchin, in *Alexandria Still,* called it "a masterpiece of size." And Friedman concluded: "the *Quartet* is simultaneously promise and fulfillment, culmination and prophecy, a vast all-inclusive multiple genre bearing all the signs of an enduring and proliferating achievement."

After the *Quartet* Durrell was constantly asked what he planned to write next. He usually replied that it would be a comic novel of some kind. But in the *Paris Review* he went further: "I want to stay nearer Rabelais; I want to be coarse and vulgarly funny. . . . I don't know whether that's permissible, whether it would come off, or whether the results might be in appalling bad taste with no redeeming feature." *Tunc* (1968) and *Nunquam* (1970), together forming *The Revolt of Aphrodite,* were the result; and critics faulted him—to some extent with *Tunc* but substantially with *Nunquam*—for exactly the reasons he foresaw. Gerald Sykes in the *New York Times Book Review* called *Tunc* a failure replete with "School boyish indecencies."

Christopher Ricks ridiculed *Nunquam* in the *New York Review of Books,* tongue in cheek, as a feminist effusion by a "fragile relic" of a poetess and not Durrell's work at all. This critical reception has prevailed, although later reviewers have begun to take the two novels more seriously.

The Revolt of Aphrodite is set in a futuristic world of big business and computers and deals with a company called "The Firm" that totally controls the lives of those under it. The "Aphrodite" of the title is a female robot created in the image of a dead movie star. The theme of the work is the need for freedom in an increasingly mechanized world. At the end of *Nunquam* Durrell adds a note: "It's a sort of novel-libretto based on the preface to [Oswald Spengler's] *The Decline of the West.*" He is again concerned with Freud, as he explained in an interview for *Ralits,* "In *Tunc* and *Nunquam* I play with the castration complex—much more terrifying than the Oedipus complex." In the *Paris Review* Durrell explained, "whatever I do will depend upon trying to crack forms." At least two critics have seen this experimentation with forms as a clue to the misunderstanding of *The Revolt of Aphrodite.* In *Lawrence Durrell* Fraser interpreted the work as a serious philosophic romance embodying both the popular and the intellectual, like William Godwin's *Caleb Williams* or Mary Shelley's *Frankenstein.* Dasenbrock in *Twentieth Century Literature* maintained that whereas *The Alexandria Quartet* is modern, using the modes of modernism, *Tunc* and *Nunquam* are postmodern and "deliberately confront, mock, and subvert" these modes. They are ironic, unorthodox novels, "a fierce if funny, savage if entertaining attack on our complacencies," Dasenbrock declared. He saw *Revolt* as Durrell's "most powerful, and ultimately most satisfying work of art."

The Avignon Quintet, Durrell's next major work, was, perhaps, his most ambitious undertaking; a set of five novels designed partly after the medieval quincunx garden unit of five trees—one in the middle, the others four-square. The plot involves a search during and after World War II for the lost golden treasure of the Knights Templar, which becomes also a quest for understanding and wisdom. The work is informed by gnosticism, the philosophy that holds the things of this world evil but seeks, somewhere beyond, for a universal spirit of light. And the *Quintet* carries from the *Quartet*—while making other links to it—the belief in the disappearance of the discrete ego.

The first volume, *Monsieur,* published in 1974, is presented as a novel written by one of the characters of the *Quintet.* Exploring and illustrating methods of characterization, Durrell has the "created" novelist create characters who show up in other volumes alongside characters *not* created by the fictional novelist. Durrell makes clear, however, that even these characters are creations, adding an Old Testament Envoi to *Monsieur* beginning "So D./

begat . . ." that proclaims himself the god behind the machine. Through this device Durrell shows his continued self-consciousness about his art and his delight in the mirror play of illusion and reality.

The other four volumes of the *Quintet* develop plot somewhat differently from the method used in the *Quartet.* Durrell told interviewer James Carley in the *Malahat Review* that perhaps the novels are like a *gigogne* or set of nested boxes. As always, form was most important to him, but the pattern of the *Quintet* depended on one further layer of understanding: it is ultimately an "Eastern" novel. Durrell explained in an interview quoted from *La Stampa* in the *World Press Review:* "In India the ego does not exist. The human condition is composed of five 'compartments,' and for me they represent the conscience. Each one corresponds to a volume of the *Quintet.* The effect should be like a tapestry, like forms that intersect." Contrasting positive Eastern values, Durrell posited five negative Western "M's," of which MacNiven wrote in *The Modernists,* "Misused, monotheism, messianism, monogamy, and materialism lead to destruction, and *merde* represents a symbolic inversion of all values." In his "Elephant's Back" lecture Durrell explained further that he was attempting "a small group of novels, interlaced and interdependent, based on the five-power system of the Buddhist psychology." He added, "In this book I proposed to return to India—to move from the four dimensions to the five skandas [elements of consciousness]. The old stable ego had already gone, reality has realized itself there, so to speak. In a sense all my new people are aspects of one great person, age, culture. I would like to make a metaphor for the human condition as we are living it now."

Durrell was an experimentalist, always attempting new forms, new ways of presenting his fictions of and to the twentieth century. Yet each new experiment initially puzzled and challenged critics. As is typical in reviews of Durrell's work, critics have differed sharply over the "Avignon Quintet." Anne Tyler commented on *Constance* in *Critical Essays,* "Is this to say that the novel fails? No, not completely; for it's hard to imagine any work of Durrell's that is not ringingly evocative, full of character and possibility." Nicholas Shrimpton, in a *London Sunday Times* review of 1983's *Sebastian,* found that Durrell was "four-fifths of the way through one of the great novels of our time". However, in reviewing *Quinx* two years later, Shrimpton commented that the final novel of the *Avignon* series "leaves me with a feeling of high ambition not quite achieved." Critic Barbara Williamson, discussing *Quinx* in the *New York Times Book Review,* reached the opposite conclusion: "Reading the theories in any one volume alone, one is tempted to think Mr. Durrell is silly. Reading them all, one is convinced he is wise." Thus *The Avignon*

Quintet, more subtle than the *Quartet,* more experimental than *The Revolt of Aphrodite,* strange and admirable in itself, can be seen as growing toward something unique and different. Yet it is closely united to Durrell's other work as well. In his "Elephant's Back" lecture, he connected the *Quartet* and the *Quintet:* "I am not of course sure that my idea will work, but if it does I will have two floating structures, poems of celebration drawn from the East and the West. Imagine two Calder-mobiles. After that I shall be happy to retire."

Durrell's major works are sometimes considered to regress in quality from the high point of *The Alexandria Quartet,* to *The Revolt of Aphrodite,* down to the *Avignon Quintet.* But it may be more accurate to say that their progression parallels the movement of the century from modern to postmodern consciousness and techniques. Durrell did not stand still in his writing. When the *Quartet* first appeared, its affiliations were generally seen to lie with Marcel Proust and Joyce. Cecily Mackworth stated in *The World of Lawrence Durrell:* "He starts where Proust left off, but starts afresh." In the same volume, Lionel Trilling wrote of *Justine* and *Balthazar* that Durrell's prose was "helping to save the language of the novel from Joyce." To a public enthralled with the *Quartet,* the later fiction came as a shock. But Durrell continually fulfilled his intention to experiment and to move forward with each new generation, explaining in the *Paris Review* interview, "what we as artists are trying to do is to sum up in a sort of metaphor the cosmology of a particular moment in which we are living. When an artist does that completely and satisfactorily he creates a crises in the form. The artists immediately following him become dissatisfied with the existing forms and try to invent or grope around for new forms." In *Clea,* Pursewarden, Durrell's fictional novelist, concludes, "But tackled in this way you would not, like most of your contemporaries, be drowsily cutting along a dotted line!" Thus, beginning with *Quartet* and moving into his later work, Durrell can be considered more closely affiliated with Nabokov, Thomas Pynchon, and Gabriel Garcia Marquez than with the moderns. He was, as Scholes demonstrated, a fabulator and a postmodernist. East new work conquered new, previously unexplored territory.

Although critics have differed widely in their assessments of Durrell's carom, they have never questioned the quality of the "Island" books or the fine, restrained elegance of his poetry. But from the *Quartet* onward, contention swirled around his experiments with form, with characterization, with layering of ideas, and with language itself. Steiner insisted that Durrell's style was at the center of the controversy, that style being "the inward sanctuary of Durrell's meaning." Durrell himself said in a *Ralits* interview in 1969 that critics were "disconcerted by my changes of tone, by the mixture of poetry, meditation, humour, and *grand guignol* in my novels." Yet his work, viewed as a whole, finally takes on, as Unterecker said in *On Contemporary Literature,* a "marble constancy" all its own; it "fuses together into something that begins to feel like an organic whole." With an expanding but unified vision, Durrell experimented in almost all of the literary forms of his century and wrote seriously over a span of more than half that century. His place in literature is secured as that of both consummate artist and an international man of letters.

BIOGRAPHICAL/CRITICAL SOURCES:

BOOKS

Burgess, Anthony, *Ninety-Nine Novels: The Best in English since 1939,* Allison & Bushy, 1984.

Cartwright, Michael, editor, *Proceedings of the First National Lawrence Durrell Conference,* The Lawrence Durrell Society, 1982.

Closter, Susan Vander, *Joyce Cary and Lawrence Durrell: A Reference Guide,* G. K. Hall, 1985.

Contemporary Literary Criticism, Gale, Volume 1, 1973, Volume 4, 1975, Volume 6, 1976, Volume 8, 1978, Volume 13, 1980, Volume 27, 1984, Volume 41, 1987.

Dictionary of Literary Biography, Gale, Volume 15: *British Novelists, 1930-1959,* 1983, Volume 27: *Poets of Great Britain and Ireland, 1945-1960,* 1984.

Durrell, George, *My Family and Other Animals,* Rupert Hart-Davis, 1956.

Durrell, Lawrence, *The Big Supposer: A Dialogue with Marc Alyn,* Grove Press, 1975.

Durrell, Lawrence, *The Durrell-Miller Letters, 1935-1980,* edited by Ian S. MacNiven, New Directions, 1988.

Durrell, Lawrence, *Lawrence Durrell and Henry Miller: A Private Correspondence,* edited by George Wickes, Dutton, 1963.

Durrell, Lawrence, *Literary Lifelines: The Richard Aldinton—Lawrence Durrell Correspondence,* edited by MacNiven and Harry T. Moore, Viking, 1981.

Durrell, Lawrence, *Spirit of Place: Letters and Essays on Travel,* edited by Alan G. Thomas, Dutton 1969.

Eliot, T. S., *Selected Prose,* edited by Frank Kermode, Harcourt, 1975.

Fedden, Robin, *Personal Landscape,* Turret Books, 1966.

Fraser, George Sutherland, *Lawrence Durrell,* Longman, 1970.

Fraser, George Sutherland, *Lawrence Durrell: A Critical Study* (includes biography by Alan G. Thomas), Dutton, 1968.

Fraser, George Sutherland, "Lawrence Durrell," *Contemporary Poets,* St. James Press, 1980, pp. 407-410.

Friedman, Alan Warren, *Critical Essays on Lawrence Durrell,* G. K. Hall, 1987.

Friedman, Alan Warren, *Lawrence Durrell and the Alexandria Quartet: Art for Love's Sake,* University of Oklahoma Press, 1970.

Friedman, Alan Warren, *The Turn of the Novel,* Oxford University Press, 1966.

Gamache, Lawrence, and Ian S. MacNiven, editors, *The Modernists: Studies in a Literary Phenomenon,* Farleigh Dickinson University Press, 1987.

Glicksberg, Charles I., *The Self in Modern Literature,* Pennsylvania State University Press, 1963.

Karl, Frederick R., *A Reader's Guide to the Contemporary English Novel,* Farrar, Strauss, 1972.

Kellman, Steven G., *The Self-Begetting Novel,* Columbia University Press, 1980.

Kostelanetz, Richard, editor, *On Contemporary Literature,* Avon, 1964.

Lemon, Lee, *Portraits of the Artist in Contemporary Fiction,* University of Nebraska Press, 1985.

Markert, Lawrence W., and Carol Peirce, editors, *On Miracle Ground II: Second International Lawrence Durrell Conference Proceedings,* University of Baltimore Monograph Series, 1984.

Moore, Harry T., editor, *The World of Lawrence Durrell,* Souther Illinois University Press, 1962.

Perles, Alfred, *My Friend, Lawrence Durrell,* Scorpion Press, 1961.

Pinchin, Jane Lagoudis, *Alexandria Still: Forster, Durrell, and Cavafy,* Princeton University Press, 1977.

Plimpton, George, editor, *Writers at Work: The Paris Review Interviews,* Secker & Warburg, 1963.

Potter, Robert A., and Brooke Whiting, *Lawrence Durrell: A Checklist,* University of California Library, 1961.

Scholes, Robert, *Fabulation and Metafiction,* University of Illinois Press, 1979.

Shapiro, Karl, editor, *Contemporary British Novelists,* Southern Illinois University Press, 1965.

Stade, George, editor, *Six Contemporary British Novelists,* Columbia University Press, 1976.

Sutherland, William O., Jr., editor, *Six Contemporary Novels: Six Introductory Essays in Modern Fiction,* University of Texas, 1962.

Thomas, Alan G., and James A. Brigham, *Lawrence Durrell: An Illustrated Checklist,* Southern Illinois University Press, 1983.

Unterecker, John, *Lawrence Durrell* (essay with bibliography), Columbia University Press, 1964.

Weigel, John A., *Lawrence Durrell,* Twayne, 1966.

PERIODICALS

Books and Bookmen, February, 1960.

Chicago Tribune, April 15, 1979, p. 7-3; October 29, 1978, p. 7-3.

Chicago Tribune Book World, November 14, 1982, pp. 1, 2; February 22, 1981, p. 4.

Detroit News, August 29, 1982, p. 1E; October 13, 1985.

Encounter, December, 1959, pp. 61-68.

Globe & Mail (Toronto), March 31, 1984.

Los Angeles Times, October 20, 1980.

Los Angeles Times Book Review, September 9, 1979, p. 13; June 13, 1982, p. 6; June 18, 1982, p. 9; November 14, 1982, p. 3; July 15, 1984, p. 2; October 27, 1985, p. 3; February 2, 1986.

Manchester Guardian, May 6, 1961.

Modern Fiction Studies, summer, 1971.

New Republic, May 9, 1960, pp. 20-22.

New York Times Book Review, March 2, 1958, p. 6; November 6, 1960, p. 7; April 3, 1960, pp. 1, 28; April 14, 1969, pp. 4, 14; April 10, 1979, p. C13; April 22, 1979, p. 14; August 1, 1982, p. 27; December 2, 1982; April 1, 1984, p. 22; September 15, 1985, p. 16.

New York Review of Books, July 23, 1971, p. 8.

Paris Review, autumn-winter, 1959.

Saturday Review, March 21, 1964; April 2, 1960, p. 15.

Shenandoah, winter, 1971.

Sunday Times (London), November 6, 1983, p. 41; June 2, 1985, p. 44.

Times (London), July 5, 1980; October 14, 1982; October 27, 1983; May 30, 1985; October 24, 1985.

Times Literary Supplement, May 22, 1969; October 15, 1982, p. 1122; October 28, 1983, p. 1184; May 31, 1985, p. 597; December 20, 1985, p. 1453; November 27, 1987, p. 1397.

Virginia Quarterly Review, summer, 1967.

Washington Post, May 29, 1986, pp. B1, 4.

Washington Post Book World, June 19, 1979, p. B1; April 15, 1984, p. 4; October 14, 1984, p. 12; September 1, 1985, p. 9.

OBITUARIES:

PERIODICALS

New York Times, November 9, 1990, p. B7.*

—*Sketch by Carol Peirce*

E

EBEJER, Francis 1925-

PERSONAL: Surname is pronounced Eb-*ey*-er; born August 28, 1925, in Malta; son of Joseph (a teacher) and Josephine (Cutajar) Ebejer; married Jane Cauchi-Gera, September 5, 1948 (separated, 1958); children: Francis Joseph (deceased), Mary Jane, Damian. *Education:* Attended Royal University of Malta, 1942-43, St. Mary's College, Twickenham, England, 1948-50, and University of Utah, 1961. *Religion:* Roman Catholic.

ADDRESSES: Home—Apt. 3, Nivea Ct., Swieqi Valley, St. Andrews, Malta.

CAREER: British Military administration, Eighth Army, Tripoli, Libya, English-Italian interpreter, 1943-44; principal and educationist in drama and creative writing in Malta; novelist, playwright, and poet. Producer of amateur and professional theatre in Malta; member of drama group, Manoel Theatre (national theater of Malta); drama adviser, Malta Television and Broadcasting. Honorary president, Movement for the Promotion of Literature in Malta.

MEMBER: International PEN (fellow, English Center), Malta Academy of Letters, French Academy of Vancluse.

AWARDS, HONORS: Fulbright travel grant in United States, 1961-62; special mention for third place, Golden Harp Award International TV Festival in Dublin, Ireland, 1969, for "An Eye to Reckon With"; Malta's Best Publication of the Year Awards, 1971, 1976, and 1983; Phoenica Trophy Award for Culture, 1982; medal of honour, city of Avignon, 1986; Citta di Valletta Award, 1989; Manoel Award and Cheyney Award for play; other first prizes for stage and radio plays.

WRITINGS:

NOVELS

A Wreath for the Innocents, MacGibbon & Kee, 1958 (published in Malta as *A Wreath of Maltese Innocents,* 1981).
Evil of the King Cockroach, MacGibbon & Kee, 1960 (published in Malta as *Wild Spell of Summer,* 1968).
In the Eye of the Sun, Macdonald & Co., 1969.
Come Again in Spring, Union Press, 1973.
Requiem for a Malta Fascist, A. C. Aquilina & Co. (Malta), 1980.
Leap of Malta Dolphins, Vantage, 1982.
Storja: il-Harsa ta' Ruzann, Klabb Kotba Maltin (Malta), 1984.

Also author of *The Maltese Baron . . . and I Lucian.*

PLAYS IN ENGLISH

Menz, produced in Tokyo, Japan, 1971.
Hefen Plus Zero, first produced on Third Programme, Spanish National Radio, 1974, produced on stage at Warwick University Drama Department, 1980.
Summer Holidays, A. C. Aquilina & Co., 1980.
Golden Tut, produced in London at Pentamenters Lunchtime Theatre, 1981.
The Cliffhangers, produced in Erlangen, Germany, 1991.

Also author of *Mark of the Zebra, Cleopatra Slept (Badly) Here, Bloody in Bolivia, Boulevard, Hour of the Sun,* and *Saluting Battery.*

PLAYS IN MALTESE

Also author of plays *Iz-Zjara, Bwani, Ix-Xorti ta'Mamzell, Is-Sejha ta'Sarid, Il-Hadd fuq il-Bejt, L-Imnarja Zmien il-Qtil, Meta Morna tal-Mellieha, L-Imwarrbin, Vum-Barala-Zungare, Karnival, Hitan, Morru Sejhu lill-Werrieta, Majjistral, Dawra Durella, Il-*

Karba ta' l-Art, Izfen, Ors, Izfen, L-Ghassiesa ta' l-Alpi, Il-Bidu Jintemm, Wara Hajt, Id-Dar tas-Soru, Persuna Quieghda Tigi Nvestigata Dwar. . ., Mixtieq il-Kenn, and *Hemm Barra.*

OTHER

Also author of television script "An Eye to Reckon With."

Contributor of short stories to *P.E.N. Broadsheet, For Rozina: A Husband and Fifteen Other Malta Stories,* and *Short Story International.*

ADAPTATIONS: Requiem for a Malta Fascist has been adapted for film and television by Film Rights Ltd. (London); Polish translation of *Hour of the Run* broadcast on Polish TV, 1992.

SIDELIGHTS: Francis Ebejer told *CA:* "I'm obsessed with continuity, preferably in so far as it indicated valid progression. Consequently my novels and a number of my plays, deal with emancipation: the emancipation of Malta, an island, from a colonial status to one of independence for the first time in its chequered history. Concurrently with this source run the rivulets, ever widening, of personal and sex emancipation in a universal context, extending from that of specific society.

"My first two novels, in fact, *A Wreath of Maltese Innocents* and *Wild Spell of Summer,* deal with women protagonists in the fifties and sixties—Lucija and Rosie seeking identity by trying to find a way out of the social, psychological, religious, and political cage inside which the majority of Maltese women have been more or less imprisoned for centuries. I wish to think that the modern emancipated Maltese woman is what Lucija and Rosie tried to be in my books.

"With *Requiem for a Malta Fascist,* I let the main character, Lorenz, start as a child in the twenties, when there were as yet only faint rumblings of the fascist phenomenon that was later to sweep over the Mediterranean, and then on to the fascist thirties and the Second World War, when the Maltese Islands received a savage bashing from the Axis powers. All this to provide a perspective of years to a better understanding and appreciation of independence when ultimately this was achieved. Its subtitle in *The Interrogation*—the whole novel is one, questioning motives and motivations on a wider scale than just country.

"In *Leap of Malta Dolphins,* the Maltese are presented as being finally masters in their own house, and, this time, the emancipation sought for is of the land itself; hence the novel's environmental and ecological theme, echoing global concern.

"As I said, *continuity* . . . even if only at the rate of two small steps forward to one backward."

BIOGRAPHICAL/CRITICAL SOURCES:

PERIODICALS

Canadian Theatre Review, summer, 1975.
Dagens Nyheter (Sweden), January 14, 1974.
Times Literary Supplement, December, 1958; October, 1960; October 16, 1969; February 29, 1980.
World Literary Today, summer, 1980; winter, 1981; spring, 1982; summer, 1983.

*　　*　　*

EIDSMOE, John 1945-

PERSONAL: Surname is pronounced *Ides*-mo, with a long "i"; born October 18, 1945, in Yankton, SD; son of Russell M. (a professor) and Beulah A. (a homemaker; maiden name, Hoffert) Eidsmoe; married S. Marlene Van Dyke (a homemaker), August 8, 1970; children: David Christopher, Kirsten Heather, Justin Luther. *Education:* St. Olaf College, B.A., 1967; University of Iowa, J.D., 1970; Lutheran Brethren Seminary, M.Div., 1980; Dallas Theological Seminary, M.A., 1980; Oral Roberts University, D.Min., 1985. *Politics:* Conservative Republican. *Religion:* Lutheran Brethren.

ADDRESSES: Home—2648 Pine Acres, Pike Road, AL 36064. *Office*—Thomas Goode Jones School of Law, Faulkner University, 5345 Atlanta Highway, Montgomery, AL 36193-4601.

CAREER: Ordained minister, 1983; County of Woodbury, Sioux City, IA, assistant county attorney, 1970-71; Juvenile Court, Grand Forks, ND, referee, 1976-77; Rufer, Hefte, Pemberton, Schulze, Sorlie & Sefkow, Fergus Falls, MN, attorney, 1977-81; Oral Roberts University, Tulsa, OK, visiting professor of law, beginning 1981; currently professor of law at Thomas Goode Jones School of Law, Faulkner University, Montgomery, AL. Lutheran Brethren Seminary, Fergus Falls, MN, and Tulsa Seminary of Biblical Languages, adjunct professor of theology, both beginning 1981; United States Air Force Academy, Department of Law, adjunct lecturer. Republican precinct chairman in Tulsa County, beginning 1983; Republican State committeeman, parliamentarian, and platform chairman, 1989-91; member of National Right to Life Committee and Center for Law and Religious Freedom. *Military service:* U.S. Air Force, judge advocate, 1971-76; became captain. U.S. Air Force Reserve, judge advocate, 1976—; present rank, lieutenant colonel.

MEMBER: American Conservative Union, Christian Legal Society, Officers' Christian Fellowship, Air Force Association, Reserve Officers Association, Rutherford Institute.

AWARDS, HONORS: Bishop's Medal, Roman Catholic diocese of Sioux City, IA, 1971; outstanding professor award, Oral Roberts University, 1984, 1986; George Washington Honor Medal, Freedoms Foundation at Valley Forge, 1988.

WRITINGS:

God and Caesar: Christian Faith and Political Action, Crossway, 1984.

The Christian Legal Advisor, Mott Media, 1984.

(With Arnold Burron and Dean Turner) *Classrooms in Crisis: Parents Rights and the Public School,* Accent, 1985.

(With Burron) *Christ in the Classroom: The Christian Teacher and the Public School,* Accent, 1987.

Christianity and the Constitution, Baker Book, 1987.

Basic Principles of New Age Thought, New Leaf, 1991.

Columbus and Cortez: Conquerors for Christ, New Leaf, 1992.

Also author of *Can Dispensationalists and Reconstructionists Work Together? Yes, If They Read Luther!,* privately printed. Contributor to books, including *Death Decision,* edited by Leonard J. Nelson III, Servant Publications, 1984; and *Proceedings of the Second International Conference on Creationism,* Creation Science Fellowship, 1990. Contributor to *Journal of Christian Jurisprudence* and *Valparaiso University Law Review.*

SIDELIGHTS: "I am committed to the belief that the Bible is God's inspired and inerrant word," John Eidsmoe once commented, "that the Bible is relevant to the issues of today, and that one of today's greatest needs is for the articulation of a comprehensive biblical view of current issues and a comprehensive biblical view of law. I am further committed to the belief that America's constitutional heritage is based on solid biblical principles and that an understanding of this constitutional heritage is essential to the preservation of American freedom. *Christianity and the Constitution* . . . [is] a detailed study of the religious beliefs of the founders of this nation and the role the United States of America plays in the plan of God. I urge writers in every field of academic discipline to think through their positions carefully, in the light of God's word, the Bible."

*   *   *

ELLIS, Albert   1913-

PERSONAL: Born September 27, 1913, in Pittsburgh, PA; son of Henry (an insurance broker) and Hettie (Hanigbaum) Ellis; married Karyl Corper (divorced, 1938); married Rhoda Winter (divorced, 1958). *Education:* City College (now City College of the City University of New York), B.B.A., 1934; Columbia University, M.A., 1943, Ph.D., 1947.

ADDRESSES: Home and office—45 East 65th St., New York, NY 10021.

CAREER: Modern Age Books, Inc., New York City, reader, 1937; Distinctive Creations, Inc., New York City, personnel manager, 1938-48; private practice in psychotherapy and marriage counseling, New York City, 1943-58; Northern New Jersey Mental Hygiene Clinic, Greystone Park, clinical psychologist, 1948-49; Rutgers University, New Brunswick, NJ, instructor, 1948-49; New York University, New York City, instructor, 1949; New Jersey Diagnostic Center, Menlo Park, chief psychologist, 1949-50; New Jersey Department of Institutions and Agencies, Trenton, chief psychologist, 1950-52; Institute for Rational Emotive Therapy, New York City, president, 1959—. Adjunct professor, Rutgers University, 1972—, United States International University, San Diego, 1974—, Pittsburgh State University, and Kansas State University. Has conducted workshops and lectured extensively in the United States and abroad. Consultant in clinical psychology, Veterans Administration, 1961-67.

MEMBER: American Psychological Association (president, division of consulting psychology, 1962; member, council of representatives, 1964), Authors League of America, National Council on Family Relations (chairman of marriage counseling section, 1954-55), American Sociological Association (fellow), American Association for the Advancement of Science (fellow), American Academy of Psychotherapists (member of executive committee, 1956-62; vice-president, 1962-64), Association for Applied Anthropology (fellow), American Association of Marital and Family Therapists (member of executive committee, 1958-60), Society for the Scientific Study of Sex (president, 1960-62), American Anthropological Association, Association for the Advancement of Psychotherapy, Eastern Psychological Association, New York State Psychological Association, New York Society of Clinical Psychologists (member of executive committee, 1951-53), Mensa.

AWARDS, HONORS: Humanist of the Year award, American Humanist Association, 1971; Distinguished Sex Researcher award, Society for the Scientific Study of Sex, 1972; Distinguished Professional Psychologist award, Division of Psychotherapy, American Psychological Association, 1974; Distinguished Sex Educator and Therapist award, American Association of Sex Educators, Counselors, and Therapists, 1976; Distinguished Psychologist award, Academy of Psychologists in Marital and Family Therapy, 1982; National Academy of Practice award, 1983; Distinguished Professional Contributions to

Knowledge award, American Psychological Association, 1985.

WRITINGS:

An Introduction to the Principles of Scientific Psychoanalysis, Journal Press, 1950.

Folklore of Sex, Grove, 1951, revised edition, 1961.

(With A. P. Pillay) *Sex, Society, and the Individual,* International Journal of Sexology Press, 1953.

The American Sexual Tragedy, Lyle Stuart, 1954, revised edition, 1962.

Sex Life of the American Woman and the Kinsey Report, Greenberg, 1954.

New Approaches to Psychotherapy Techniques, Journal of Clinical Psychology Press, 1955.

(With Ralph Brancale) *The Psychology of Sex Offenders,* C. C. Thomas, 1956.

How to Live with a Neurotic: At Work or at Home, Crown, 1957, revised edition, 1974.

Sex without Guilt, Lyle Stuart, 1958, revised edition, 1966.

What Is Psychotherapy, American Academy of Psychotherapists, 1959.

The Place of Values in the Practice of Psychotherapy, American Academy of Psychotherapists, 1959.

Art and Science of Love, Lyle Stuart, 1960, revised edition, Dell, 1965.

Encyclopedia of Sexual Behavior, Hawthorn, 1961.

(With Robert A. Harper) *Creative Marriage,* Lyle Stuart, 1961, revised edition, Tower, 1966.

(With Harper) *A Guide to Rational Living,* Prentice-Hall, 1961.

Reason and Emotion in Psychotherapy, Lyle Stuart, 1962.

If This Be Sexual Heresy, Lyle Stuart, 1963.

Sex and the Single Man, Lyle Stuart, 1963.

The Intelligent Woman's Guide to Manhunting, Lyle Stuart, 1963.

The Origins and the Development of the Incest Taboo, Lyle Stuart, 1963.

(With Edward Sagarin) *Nymphomania: A Study of the Oversexed Woman,* Gilbert Press, 1964.

The Case for Sexual Liberty, Seymour Press, 1965.

Homosexuality: Its Causes and Cure, Lyle Stuart, 1965.

Suppressed: Seven Key Essays Publishers Dared Not Print, New Classics House, 1965.

The Search for Sexual Enjoyment, Macfadden, 1966.

How to Prevent Your Child from Becoming a Neurotic Adult, Crown, 1966, published as *How to Raise an Emotionally Healthy, Happy Child,* Wilshire Book Co., 1973.

(With Roger O. Conway) *The Art of Erotic Seduction,* Lyle Stuart, 1968.

Is Objectivism a Religion?, Lyle Stuart, 1968.

Growth through Reason, Science and Behavior Books, 1971.

Executive Leadership: A Rational Approach, Citadel, 1972.

(With Flora Setuya and Susan Losher) *Sex and Sex Education: A Bibliography,* Bowker, 1972.

(With John Gullo) *Murder and Assassination,* Lyle Stuart, 1972.

How to Master Your Fear of Flying, Peter H. Wyden, 1972.

The Civilized Couple's Guide to Extramarital Adventure, Peter H. Wyden, 1972.

The Sensuous Person: Critique and Corrections, Lyle Stuart, 1972.

Humanistic Psychotherapy: The Rational-Emotive Approach, Julian Press, 1973.

(With Harper) *A New Guide to Rational Living,* Prentice-Hall, 1975.

Sex and the Liberated Man, Lyle Stuart, 1976.

How to Live with and without Anger, Reader's Digest Press, 1977.

(With William Knaus) *Overcoming Procrastination; or, How to Think and Act Rationally in Spite of Life's Inevitable Hassles,* Institute for Rational Living, 1977.

(With Russell Grieger) *Handbook of Rational-Emotive Therapy,* Springer Publishing, Volume 1, 1977, Volume 2, 1985.

A Garland of Rational Songs, Institute for Rational Living, 1977.

Speculative Leadership, Institute for Rational Living, 1978.

(With Eliot Abrahms) *Brief Psychotherapy in Medical and Health Practice,* Springer Publishing, 1978.

The Intelligent Woman's Guide to Marriage and Dating, Lyle Stuart, 1979.

(With John M. Whiteley) *Theoretical and Empirical Foundations of Rational-Emotive Therapy,* Brooks/Cole, 1979.

(With Irving Becker) *A Guide to Personal Happiness,* Wilshire, 1982.

(With Michael Bernard) *Rational-Emotive Approaches to the Problems of Childhood,* Plenum, 1983.

Overcoming Resistance: Rational-Emotive Therapy with Difficult Clients, Springer Publishing, 1985.

(With Bernard) *Clinical Applications of Rational-Emotive Therapy,* Plenum, 1985.

The Case against Religion: A Psychotherapist's View and the Case against Religiosity, Citadel Press, 1985.

(With Windy Dryden) *The Practice of Rational-Emotive Therapy,* Springer Publishing, 1987.

Inside Rational-Emotive Therapy, Academic Press, 1988.

How to Stubbornly Refuse to Make Yourself Miserable about Anything—Yes, Anything!, Lyle Stuart, 1988.

(With V. McInerney, R. Di Giuseppe and Raymond Yeager) *Rational-Emotive Therapy with Alcoholics and Substance Abusers,* Pergamon, 1988.

(With J. Sichel, D. Di Mattia, Yeager, and Di Giuseppe) *Rational-Emotive Couples Therapy,* Pergamon, 1989.

(With Yeager) *Why Some Therapies Don't Work: The Dangers of Transpersonal Psychology,* Prometheus Books, 1989.

(With Dryden) *The Essential Albert Ellis,* Springer Publishing, 1990.

(With Dryden) *Dialogue with Albert Ellis: Against Dogma,* Open University, 1991.

(With Emmet Velten) *When AA Doesn't Work for You,* Barricade Books, 1992.

Also author of *Guide to Successful Marriage,* Wilshire. Contributor of more than one hundred chapters to psychology and sociology books and anthologies. Columnist for *Independent* and *Realist;* contributor of more than six hundred articles to professional journals and of more than one hundred articles to popular periodicals, including *Pageant, This Week, Cosmopolitan, Playboy, Penthouse, Saturday Review,* and *Mademoiselle.*

WORK IN PROGRESS: Rational Eating; How to Stop People from Pushing Your Buttons.

SIDELIGHTS: Albert Ellis is the developer of Rational-Emotive Psychotherapy, which rejects Freudian theories and advocates the belief that emotions come from conscious thought "as well as internalized ideas of which the individual may be unaware." Ellis once told *CA* that he works "with psychotherapy and marriage counseling clients from 9:30 A.M. to 11:00 P.M., including the holding of sessions with eight different psychotherapy groups every week. Do most writing on Sundays, if I am not on the road somewhere here or abroad, giving workshops on RET or sex therapy."

A *Newsweek* reporter writes: "In the 1950s, Dr. Albert Ellis . . . began publishing the first widely read books that broke firmly with the tradition of marital romance and sexual piety. Ellis exhorted his readers to fearless sensuality, assuming that some form of premarital experience is not only likely but in fact beneficial. In plain, hard-headed language, he offered the inexperienced specific and pragmatic advice on everything from the first good-night kiss to some of the farther reaches of sexual experimentation—most of which he heartily endorsed. At first, Ellis was labeled a sensationalist and sexual radical by many of his colleagues. But . . . other sex manuals have appeared that either lash out or laugh at traditional guilts. . . . Ellis's 'do-it' books have turned out to be the heralds of a new era in positive sex instruction."

BIOGRAPHICAL/CRITICAL SOURCES:

PERIODICALS

Newsweek, August 24, 1970.

EULERT, Don(ald Dean) 1935-

PERSONAL: Surname is pronounced *You*-lert; born September 12, 1935, in Russell County, KS; son of Otto C. (a rancher) and Elsie (Reich) Eulert; married Karen Hawthorne (a family psychologist and art therapist), 1990; children (previous marriage): Melissa D., J. Colby, Bret Alexander J. *Education:* Fort Hays Kansas State College, (now Fort Hays State University), B.A., 1957, M.A., 1960; additional study at University of Kansas, 1960-61; University of New Mexico, Ph.D., 1968; postdoctoral study at C. G. Jung Institute (Zurich, Switzerland), 1978-79.

ADDRESSES: Home—18898 Old Julian Trail, Santa Ysabel, CA 92070. *Office*—California School of Professional Psychology, 6212 Ferris Square, San Diego, CA 92121.

CAREER: High school teacher of English and journalism in Colby, KS, 1957-60; University of Kansas, Lawrence, assistant instructor in English, 1960-61; Wisconsin State University-Platteville (now University of Wisconsin-Platteville), assistant professor of English, 1961-64; Sandia Laboratories, Albuquerque, NM, technical writer, 1964-68; United States International University, San Diego, CA, associate professor of English, 1968-71, professor of intercultural and international studies, 1973-82; California School of Professional Psychology—San Diego, professor of cultural and behavioral studies and director for humanities, 1976—.

Senior computer programmer for Educational Researc Associates, 1965-66; coordinator and member of steering committee for Bethesda Conference on Medical Uses of Technology, 1968-69; director of San Diego Council for Poetry, 1970-71; director of seminars on psychology, literature, and writing in the United States and abroad. Fulbright lecturer at University of Iasi, Romania, 1971-72, 1972-73; State Department lecturer, 1972, 1973, 1974, 1976, 1978; lecturer at International University—Europe, 1978.

Has given poetry readings from his own work; has appeared on radio and television programs for WSWW Radio (Platteville), WHA-FM Radio (Madison), KHFM Radio, KPBS-FM Radio (San Diego), KSDS-FM Radio, Bucharest Radio, Iasi Radio, KNME-TV (New Mexico), and KCET-TV (Los Angeles). Orgaizing director for writing congerences and education forums with audio-visual publication.Consultant to General Resources Corp. 1968—; writing consultant to Technar, Inc., 1968-70; educational consultant to San Diego County Curriculum Services, 1969-71.

MEMBER: Institute for Noetic Sciences, American Psychological Association, Elmwood Institute, National Council for Independent Political Action, Association for

Moral Education, Co-op America, Southern Poverty Law Center, Association of American Indian Affairs.

AWARDS, HONORS: Kansas Quill Award, 1961; William Carruth Memorial Poetry Award, 1961; Carolina Quarterly poetry award, 1962; short story and poetry awards from Wisconsin Regional Writers, 1973; senior Fulbright fellow, 1971-73; International Research Exchange grant, 1974; National Endowment for the Humanities grant, 1981-82.

WRITINGS:

(Editor) *The Rolamite Conference* (monograph), University of New Mexico Press, 1969.
Haiku and Senryu, Minerva Press, 1973.
(Editor, and translator with Stefan Avadanei) *Anthology of Modern Romanian Poetry,* Junimea Press, 1973.
(Editor and translator) *Selected Poems of Lucian Blaga,* Minerva Press, 1975.
(With Max Lerner) *U.S. Ideas and Ideals* (textbook), U.S. International University, 1978, revised edition, 1981.
Outposts: Letters and Poems of Buffalo Bill Cody and Annie Oakley, Wild Mustard Press, 1979.
(Translator) *Some Poems of Mihia Ursachi,* Junimea Press, 1980.
Animal, Plant, Mineral, Good Morning Press, 1986.

OTHER

Contributor to anthologies, including August Derleth, editor, *A Wisconsin Harvest,* Hawk Press, 1966; J. R. Le Master, editor, *Poets of the Midwest,* Young Publications, 1967; A. D. Winans, editor, *California Bicentennial Poets Anthology,* Second Coming Press, 1976; *San Diego Poets,* Solo Press, 1981; *Coast Highway,* Wild Mustard Press, 1982; Fred Moramarco and Al Zolymas, editors, *Men of Our Times,* University of Georgia Press, 1992. Work is also anthologized *in Crawl out Your Window, In Miss Virginia's Basement,* and *Cafe Solo.*

Contributor of articles, short stories, poems, and reviews to literary journals, including *American Transcendental Quarterly, New England Review, East-West Review, American Haiku, Prairie Schooner, Midwest Quarterly, id Coyote Journal, Pacific Review, Colorado Quarterly,* and *Shaman's Drum.* Editor of *Western Poet,* 1960-62, and of *Signals,* 1986-90; founder and editor of *American Haiku,* 1962-64; member of editorial staff of *Abstracts of English Studies,* 1962-71, and *Lemming Review,* 1969-71.

WORK IN PROGRESS: *The Lunacy Poems,* a cycle of moon poems; *Outpost II,* poems and letters; *Field,* a haiku cycle; *Pizarro's Undiscovered Isthmus; The Apocalyptic in American Culture,* a collection of essays; *Strategies of Plants,* essays and poems; *Divining,* a novel; *Marijuana Army,* a political diatribe.

SIDELIGHTS: Don Eulert is especially interested in ritual, folk customs, and the primacy of mythic sources for experience and literature. He has traveled and lectured in Africa, the Balkans, Central and Western Europe, and Scandinavia. He lives on an old mining claim patent in the mountains east of San Diego, CA, in a house he is building with periodic help from friends, using mostly hand tools.

He notes the gratification of work in a learning community "to make public" without authorship. Since 1976 he has directed a program in which clinical psychology graduates include ethics, humanities and the arts in their training.

Commenting on his interest in psychology and poetry, Eulert wrote to *CA:* "In its oldest and highest tradition, poetry aims at healing balance in the world and mind. Psychotherapy and poetry are both talking cures, but poetry has the additional advantage of singing and dancing."

F

FABRIZIUS, Peter
See KNIGHT, Max

*   *   *

FALK, Gerhard   1931-

PERSONAL: Born August 22, 1931, in Hamburg, Germany; son of Leonhard and Hedwig (Cibulski) Falk; married Ursula Adler, January 8, 1950; children: Cynthia, Daniel, Clifford. *Education:* Western Reserve University (now Case Western Reserve University), B.A., 1953, M.A., 1955; State University of New York at Buffalo, Ed.D., 1969.

ADDRESSES: Home—109 Louvaine Dr., Buffalo, NY 14223. *Office*—Department of Sociology, State University of New York College at Buffalo, 1300 Elmwood Ave., Buffalo, NY 14222.

CAREER: State University of New York College at Buffalo, assistant professor, 1957-62, associate professor, 1962-70, professor of sociology, 1970—.

MEMBER: Western New York Sociological Association (past president), Western New York Group Psychotherapy Association (past president), Alpha Tau Kappa.

WRITINGS:

(With wife, Ursula Falk) *The Nursing Home Dilemma,* R & E Research Associates, 1976.
(With U. Falk and George Tomashevich) *Aging in America and Other Cultures,* R & E Research Associates, 1981.
Murder: An Analysis of Its Forms, Conditions and Causes, McFarland & Co., 1990.
The Life of the Academic Professional in America, Edwin Mellen, 1990.
The Jew in Christian Theology, McFarland & Co., 1992.

Contributor to books, including *Interdisciplinary Problems in Criminology,* edited by Walter Reckless, Ohio State University, 1966; *Marital Counseling,* edited by Hirsch L. Silverman, C. C Thomas, 1967; *An American Historian,* edited by Milton Plesur, State University of New York College at Buffalo, 1980; and *S & M: Studies in Sado-Masochism,* edited by Thomas S. Weinberg and G. W. Levi Kamel, Prometheus Books, 1983. Also contributor of articles to a wide variety of scholarly journals, including *International Behavioral Scientist, Journal of Reform Judaism, Deviant Behavior, Nursing Outlook, Journal of Pastoral Counseling,* and *Improving College and University Teaching.*

WORK IN PROGRESS: An American Century: Life in the United States, 1901-2000.

SIDELIGHTS: Gerhard Falk wrote *CA:* "On becoming an assistant professor I recognized that progress in achieving promotion and salary increases depends on publication of scholarly articles and monographs. Therefore I worked on such publications diligently and succeeded in producing forty-five journal articles and chapters in books. Then, in 1988 I happened to see the archives of a defunct newspaper in the library. This led me to look for material on murder because I teach a course in criminology. I found news clippings going back over forty years concerning murder. This led me to write a whole book on that subject including such matters as the place of the murder, whether inside or outside, the room in the house where the murder took place, the weapon used, the day of the week, the hour of the day, the relationship of the killer to the victim and many other details.

"Having published that book I recognized that writing books is much more enjoyable than writing articles, not only because books are more visible, but also because books permit the author much more leeway in expressing his views and intentions. In short, books are not as confining as articles. Thereupon I decided to write on anything that interests me. Hence I next wrote a book concerning my profession and called *The Life of the Academic Professional.* Then I wrote *The Jew in Christian Theology* because I had come across the Holocaust murders while writing the previous book. Now I am working on *An American Century* because I seek to show how we lived these one hundred years. The book deals with daily life. It is not a history book but a sociology of the century.

"My principal purpose in writing these books is to bring these topics to the attention of readers and to 'put my two cents in.' I write on topics not well exposed and sometimes not researched at all. I want these topics to be available in libraries. Until I did so, there was no book on how to become and be a professor. While the relationship of Christianity to the Holocaust is mentioned in various publications, it was never before fully exposed, particularly since I translated, as part of my book, an 85-page work by Martin Luther which has never been translated before."

*   *   *

FARIA, A(nthony) J(ohn)   1944-

PERSONAL: Born December 29, 1944, in Highland Park, MI; son of Anthony (an electrician) and Barbara (Hemeli) Faria; married Marilyn Ann Gaylord, June 9, 1968 (divorced July, 1980); married Barbara Elaine Oakes; children: (first marriage) Lara Marie, Robert Gordon. *Education:* Wayne State University, B.S., 1967, M.B.A., 1969; Michigan State University, Ph.D., 1974. *Politics:* Republican. *Religion:* Roman Catholic.

ADDRESSES: Home—2635 Vine Ct., Windsor, Ontario, Canada N8T 2X4. *Office*—Department of Marketing, University of Windsor, Windsor, Ontario, Canada N9B 3P4.

CAREER: Chrysler Corp., Centerline, MI, buyer, 1969; Georgia Southern College (now University), Statesboro, assistant professor of marketing, 1973-75; University of Windsor, Windsor, Ontario, chairman of marketing department, 1975—. President of Marcon Marketing Consultants, 1978—.

MEMBER: International Simulation and Gaming Association, North American Simulation and Gaming Association, Canadian Association for Administrative Studies, American Marketing Association, Association for Business Simulation and Experiential Learning, National Gaming Council, Academy of Marketing Sciences, American Institute for the Decision Sciences, Windsor Advertising and Sales Club.

WRITINGS:

Creative Selling, South-Western Publishing, 1966, 5th edition, 1993.
Compete: A Dynamic Marketing Simulation, Irwin, 1974, 4th edition, 1993.
How to Use the Business Library, South-Western Publishing, 1985, 6th edition, 1993.
LAPTOP: An Introductory Marketing Simulation, Irwin, 1987.
The Sales Management Simulation, South-Western Publishing, 1993.
The Retail Management Game, South-Western Publishing, 1993.

Contributor to marketing, management, and business journals.

SIDELIGHTS: A. J. Faria told *CA:* "I teach in the marketing strategy and marketing planning areas, continue to consult in these areas for 12-15 major corporations, and continue to write in the marketing strategy, survey response, and simulation areas.

"I was invited to put on two weeks of seminars for Russian university professors on the topic of simulation gaming in St. Petersburg and Moscow during the summer of 1992."

*   *   *

FEAGLES, Elizabeth
See DAY, Beth (Feagles)

*   *   *

FECHER, Constance
See HEAVEN, Constance

*   *   *

FERGUSON, Trevor   1947-

PERSONAL: Born November 11, 1947, in Seaforth, Ontario, Canada; son of Percy Alexander (a clergyman) and M. V. Joyce (a teacher; maiden name, Sanderson) Ferguson; married Lynne Hill (an academic advisor), December 16, 1983. *Education:* Attended high school in Montreal, Quebec, Canada. *Religion:* Presbyterian.

ADDRESSES: Home—3463 Walkley Ave., Montreal, Quebec H4B 2K2, Canada.

CAREER: Construction worker in Alberta and British Columbia, 1964-70; taxicab driver and bartender in Montreal, Quebec, 1970-76; writer in Montreal, 1977—. Writer-in-residence, University of Alberta, Edmonton, 1992-93.

MEMBER: Writers' Union of Canada (chairman, 1990-91).

WRITINGS:

NOVELS

High Water Chants, Macmillan, 1977.
Onyx John, McClelland & Stewart, 1985.
The Kinkajou, Macmillan, 1989.
The True Life Adventures of Sparrow Drinkwater, Harper-Collins, 1992.

WORK IN PROGRESS: "*Santa's Summer,* in which Santa Claus, by means of a summer sojourn through the world, must achieve a new understanding of his place in the cosmos, is a comic, metaphysical fiction for adults."

SIDELIGHTS: Trevor Ferguson's 1985 novel, *Onyx John,* recounts the eventful life of Onyx John Cameron and his quest for meaning in a mad world. Like his father, an alchemist in search of the philosopher's stone, Onyx John struggles to transcend the banality of ordinary life and thus attain self-knowledge. But Onyx John's odyssey, which takes him to a grotesque realm of crime, sex, sin, and passion, unravels, as Toronto *Star*'s Ken Adachi explains, "a tangled family and personal epic of incest, near-madness, and violence." Adachi, who describes Ferguson's novel as a "book that reads at once as a family saga, a thriller and as a comic portrait of North American life," praises the imaginative power of *Onyx John,* noting that "it is the sheer linguistic fun of Ferguson's prose style, the occasional incandescence of vision and a certain lovable nuttiness which is sustained throughout the book that seduce the reader and keep him turning the pages." The critic concludes that Ferguson's work "is a vigorous, delightfully idiosyncratic novel, full of verve and intelligence." Ferguson's narrative skill and stylistic achievement impressed Montreal *Gazette* reviewer Michael Carin, who remarks that Ferguson writes "as a gymnast leaps: with total abandon rescued by cunning precision." Carin describes *Onyx John,* which develops "the themes of exile and flight" and explores "the tension between faith and reason," as a "rollicking binge of a book" that "never stops humming as fervent fiction."

Ferguson once told *CA:* "My first novel, *High Water Chants,* was set off the northern coast of British Columbia on an island inhabited by native and white populations. The tensions between the two groups, under the stress of sudden economic development, ignites a wild, rambunctious chase through the rain forest wilderness, and into the lives and histories of the characters. I was particularly concerned in that book with the power and force that historical, and even ancient, events exert on the present."

He adds: "*Onyx John* is a novel about coming of age through the fifties, sixties, and seventies. It also compares contemporary values to those of a mythical, visionary past. It is this examination of the relationship between God (and perceptions of God) and man that is central to my work. *The Kinkajou* explored that relationship through a 'God is Dead' scenario. *The True Life Adventures of Sparrow Drinkwater,* ostensibly a novel about money and madness, is also about the search for spiritual identity out of a ruptured, and even criminal, past.

"Interviewers are prone to asking me why I do it. Success has come my way, but only after two decades of difficult times. When I was younger, and my dreams were bright, I would have answered that I seemed to see the world through a personal perspective and that I found the usual expressions of the world unsatisfactory. That remains true, though what continues to fuel my drive now is not my dreams so much as that covenant I made with my younger self: to explore this planet and the human psyche as deeply as it is possible to plunge, to continue to express wonder in a materialistic world, and to use the imagination as a means, perhaps our best means, of conversing with the infinite. To ever stop would seriously violate that pact with myself."

*   *   *

FIRMIN, Peter   1928-

PERSONAL: Born December 11, 1928, in Harwich, England; son of Lewis Charles (a railway telegrapher) and Lila Isobel (a homemaker; maiden name, Burnett) Firmin; married Joan Ruth Clapham (a bookbinder), July 29, 1952; children: Charlotte, Hannah, Josephine, Katherine, Lucy, Emily. *Education:* Colchester Art School, diploma, 1947; Central School of Art, diploma, 1952. *Politics:* Socialist. *Religion:* Methodist. *Avocational interests:* Walking, sailing, birds, books.

ADDRESSES: Home—Hillside Farm, 36 Blean Hill, Blean, Canterbury, Kent CT2 9EF, England.

CAREER: Free-lance book illustrator, writer, puppet maker, and cartoon film artist, 1952—. Worked variously as a teacher, stained-glass designer, and publicity studio staff artist. *Military service:* Royal Navy, 1947-49.

AWARDS, HONORS: Children's Book of the Year designation, Child Study Association of America, 1976, for *Basil Brush at the Beach;* PYE Award, 1984, for services to children's television; honorary M.A., University of Kent, 1987.

WRITINGS:

SELF-ILLUSTRATED CHILDREN'S BOOKS

The Winter Diary of a Country Rat, Kaye & Ward, 1982.
Chicken Stew, Pelham, 1983.
Tricks and Tales, Kaye & Ward, 1983.
The Midsummer Notebook of a Country Rat, Kaye & Ward, 1984.
Nina's Machines, A. & C. Black, 1988.
My Dog Sandy, Deutsch, 1988.
Making Faces, Collins, 1988.
Happy Miss Rat, Delacorte, 1989.
Hungry Mr. Fox, Delacorte, 1989.
Foolish Miss Crow, Delacorte, 1989.
Boastful Mr. Bear, Delacorte, 1989.
Magic Mash, A. & C. Black, 1989.
Story Castle (press-out and build book), Walker Books, 1991.
Theatre of Varieties, Walker Books, 1991.
Paper Tricks and Moving Pictures, Collins, 1991.

SELF-ILLUSTRATED CHILDREN'S BOOKS; "BASIL BRUSH" SERIES

Basil Brush Goes Flying, Kaye & Ward, 1969, Prentice-Hall, 1977.
Basil Brush Goes Boating, Kaye & Ward, 1969, Prentice-Hall, 1976.
Basil Brush in the Jungle, Kaye & Ward, 1970, Prentice-Hall, 1979.
Basil Brush at the Seaside, Kaye & Ward, 1970, published as *Basil Brush at the Beach,* Prentice-Hall, 1976.
Basil Brush and the Dragon, Kaye & Ward, 1971, published as *Basil Brush and a Dragon,* Prentice-Hall, 1978.
Basil Brush Finds Treasure, Kaye & Ward, 1971, Prentice-Hall, 1979.
Basil Brush Build a House, Kaye & Ward, 1973, Prentice-Hall, 1977.
Basil Brush Gets a Medal, Kaye & Ward, 1973, Prentice-Hall, 1978.
Basil Brush and the Windmills, Kaye & Ward, 1979, Prentice-Hall, 1980.
Basil Brush on the Trail, Kaye & Ward, 1979, Prentice-Hall, 1981.
Three Tales of Basil Brush (two volumes), Kaye & Ward, 1979.
Two Tales of Basil Brush, Fontana, 1982.
Basil Brush Takes Off, Kaye & Ward, 1983.

SELF-ILLUSTRATED CHILDREN'S BOOKS; "MAKE IT WORK" SERIES

Mills and Big Wheels, A. & C. Black, 1993.
Ships and Cranes, A. & C. Black, 1993.
Racing Cars and Cycles, A. & C. Black, 1993.
Flying Machines, A. & C. Black, 1993.

SELF-ILLUSTRATED CHILDREN'S BOOKS; "PINNY" SERIES

Pinny Finds a House, Deutsch, 1985, Viking, 1986.
Pinny in the Snow, Deutsch, 1985, Viking, 1986.
Pinny and the Bird, Deutsch, 1985, Viking, 1986.
Pinny's Party, Deutsch, 1987.
Pinny and the Floppy Frog, Deutsch, 1987.

ILLUSTRATOR; CHILDREN'S BOOKS BY OLIVER POSTGATE; "SAGA OF NOGGIN" SERIES

Ice Dragon, Kaye & Ward, 1968.
King of the Nogs, Kaye & Ward, 1968.
Flying Machine, Kaye & Ward, 1968.
The Omruds, Kaye & Ward, 1968.
The Firecake, Kaye & Ward, 1969.
The Island, Kaye & Ward, 1969, published as *Noggin and the Island,* Fontana, 1980.
The Flowers, Kaye & Ward, 1971, published as *Noggin and the Flowers,* Fontana, 1980.
The Pie, Kaye & Ward, 1971.
The Game, Kaye & Ward, 1972.
The Monster, Kaye & Ward, 1972.
The Blackwash, Kaye & Ward, 1975.
Nogmania, Kaye & Ward, 1977.
Noggin the Nog, Armada, 1980.
Four Stories: The Saga of Noggin the Nog, HarperCollins, 1992.

ILLUSTRATOR; CHILDREN'S BOOKS BY OLIVER POSTGATE; "STARTING TO READ" SERIES

Noggin and the Whale, Kaye & Ward, 1965.
Noggin the King, Kaye & Ward, 1965.
Noggin and the Moon Mouse, Kaye & Ward, 1967.
Noggin and the Dragon, Kaye & Ward, 1972.
Nogbad Comes Back, Kaye & Ward, 1972.
Nogbad and the Elephant, Kaye & Ward, 1972.
Noggin and the Money, Kaye & Ward, 1973.
Noggin and the Snorks, Kaye & Ward, 1973.
Three Tales of Noggin, two volumes, Kaye & Ward, 1981.

ILLUSTRATOR; CHILDREN'S BOOKS BY OLIVER POSTGATE; "IVOR THE ENGINE" SERIES

Ivor the Engine: The First Story, Fontana, 1977.
Ivor the Engine: The Snowdrifts, Fontana, 1977.
Ivor the Engine: The Dragon, Collins, 1979.
Ivor the Engine: The Elephant, Collins, 1979.
Ivor the Engine: The Foxes, Armada, 1982.
Ivor's Birthday, Collins, 1984.

ILLUSTRATOR; CHILDREN'S BOOKS BY OLIVER POSTGATE

Bagpuss in the Sun, Collins, 1974.
Bagpuss on a Rainy Day, Collins, 1974.
Mr. Rumbletum's Gumboot, Carousel Books, 1977.
Silly Old Uncle Feedle, Carousel Books, 1977.
The Song of the Pongo, Carousel Books, 1977.

ILLUSTRATOR; CHILDREN'S BOOKS, EXCEPT AS INDICATED

Biddy Baxter, *The "Blue Peter" Book of Limericks,* Pan Books, 1976.

Baxter, *The "Blue Peter" Book of Odd Odes,* BBC Publications, 1976.

Peter Meteyard, *Stanley: The Tale of the Lizard,* Deutsch, 1979.

Edith Nesbit, *The Last of the Dragons,* Macdonald & Jane's, 1980.

Nesbit, *Melisande,* Macdonald & Co., 1982.

Heather Amory, *Day and Night,* EDC, 1986.

Amory, *Summer and Winter,* EDC, 1986.

Amory, *Then and Now,* EDC, 1986.

Dick King-Smith, *The Jenius,* Gollancz, 1988.

Chris Powling, *Ziggy and the Ice Ogre,* Heinemann, 1988.

Pat Thomson, *Best Pest,* Gollancz, 1989.

Vita Sackville-West, *The Land and the Garden* (adult), Webb & Bower, 1989.

Gillian Cross, *The Monster from Underground,* Heinemann, 1990.

Rosamond Richardson, *Swanbrooke Down* (adult), Scribners, 1990.

ANIMATOR; TELEVISION SERIES

With Postgate, *Alexander the Mouse* (six-episodes; live/animated format), Rediffusion-TV, 1958.

Robert Bolt, *The Miller and the Magic Trees,* Rediffusion-TV, 1958.

Rolf Harris and Wally Whyton, *Musical Box* (fifteen-minute live, weekly episodes), Rediffusion-TV, 1960-68.

Postgate, *Ivor the Engine* (forty five-minute color cartoons), Smallfilms, Rediffusion-TV, 1960-68, BBC-TV, 1975, 1977.

(With Postgate) *Noggin,* BBC-TV, 1960-70, 1981.

(With Postgate) *Dogwatch,* Rediffusion-TV, 1961.

PUPPET-MAKER; TELEVISION SERIES

Basil Brush, Rediffusion-TV, 1962-68, BBC-TV, 1969-88.

Olly and Fred, Rediffusion-TV, 1962.

Blue Peter, BBC-TV, 1964.

(With Postgate) *Pogle's Wood,* BBC-TV, 1964.

Postgate, *The Clangers* (26 ten-minute episodes broadcast on *Watch with Mother* series), BBC-TV, 1969-72.

Postgate, *Bagpuss* (thirteen fifteen-minute films; broadcast on *Watch with Mother* series), BBC-TV, 1972.

(With Postgate) Rumer Godden, *Tottie and the Doll's House,* BBC-TV, 1983.

WRITER AND ILLUSTRATOR; TELEVISION SERIES

Pinny's House (thirteen five-minute films), BBC-TV, 1984—.

Most films resulting from the partnership of Firmin and Postgate have been distributed in Australia, New Zealand, Sweden, and Germany and are rebroadcast on British television.

ADAPTATIONS:

Basil Brush in the Jungle (record), Scholastic Book Services, 1976.

Beebtots (includes "Bagpuss," "Ivor," "Clangers," and "Noggin" stories), BBC-Video, 1981.

BBC Children's Favorites (includes "Bagpuss," "Ivor," and "Clangers"), BBC-Video, 1982.

Ivor the Engine and the Dragons, BBC-Video, 1984.

Ivor the Engine and the Elephants, BBC-Video, 1985.

Ivor the Engine (record), BBC-Records & Tapes, 1985.

Clangers, BBC-Video, 1990.

Noggin the Nog: Tales of the Northlands, BBC-Video, 1990.

Clangers 2, BBC-Video, 1991.

Noggin the Nog: The Omruds and The Firecake, BBC-Video, 1991.

Ivor the Engine: The First Story, BBC-Video, 1991.

Pogle's Wood, BBC-Video, 1991.

SIDELIGHTS: Peter Firmin is a multi-talented artist who has adapted the puppet and cartoon characters he has created for numerous British television productions into picture-book characters. As well as illustrating the books of other authors and illustrating books, designing puppets, and creating film sets for collaborator Oliver Postgate, Firmin has written almost forty books featuring characters such as Basil Brush, Pinny and Victor, and Branwell the Country Rat, beloved by young people in both his native England and abroad.

Firmin demonstrated artistic talent even as a young boy growing up in the coastal town of Harwich in Essex. "Coming from a fairly unsophisticated background, most of the fiction I came across was either in Christmas books or comics," Firmin once commented. "I tried to make my own comics, drawing strips once or twice. We didn't have any examples of great artists such as Arthur Rackham, but our set of *Charles Dickens*—most families owned a standard set—with illustrations by George Cruikshank and Phiz was very powerful. We had plenty of stimulus from pictures in *Picture Post* and *John Bull,* but no pictures on our walls. No art with a capital 'A.'"

Firmin became a student at the Colchester School of Art at the age of fifteen. He remained there for three years, during which time he studied such subjects as life drawing, costume designing, perspective, measured drawing, and art history, ending his education by passing the Intermediate Examination in Arts and Crafts. After spending several years in the British Navy, Firmin became eligible for a grant to continue his art training and travelled to London to study graphics at the Central School of Art. "I was in the illustration department taught by such luminary painters as Laurence Scarfe, Keith Vaughan, and engraver Gertrude Hermes," Firmin recalled.

In 1958, Firmin met his future collaborator, Oliver Postgate. He noted: "I was teaching at Central School of Art when Oliver came looking for someone to illustrate a television story—someone who was hard up and would do a lot of drawing for very little money. Things clicked between us straight away because he was quite inventive, had lots of ideas and push, and I didn't mind working hard." Firmin was now married and, with the prospect of a growing family, he jumped at the opportunity that working with Postgate provided him. The partnership between the two men went on to inspire numerous successful film series for British television.

Their first collaboration was *Alexander the Mouse,* about a mouse who becomes king. It was a series of TV programs using 'Visimotion,' a live-animation process using magnets to move the figures. The three TV cameras looked through mirrors at pictures animated by three animators. Postgate both wrote and narrated the stories while Firmin designed and painted backgrounds and made paper figures. The two men considered 'Visimotion' a primitive and unreliable technique, so Postgate adapted a 16mm. cine-camera to create 'stop-frame' cartoon films. The first film made in this manner was *Ivor the Engine* which was eventually adapted into a BBC-TV series. Firmin and Postgate have gone on to include "The Saga of Noggin the Nog," featuring a Viking cartoon character based upon some ivory chessmen in the British Museum, "Bagpuss," a fat furry cat, and "The Clangers," a race of pink creatures living in outer space.

All Firmin and Postgate's series became picture books, with the text written by Postgate and the illustrations by Firmin. When a new character was needed to follow the "Noggin" series of first-readers, Firmin started writing his own stories. His first illustrated book for children, *Basil Brush Goes Flying,* was based on the most popular puppet he had ever made, the joke-telling fox, Basil Brush. He then went on to write books with other original characters, such as Pinny, an inch-high wooden doll, and Branwell, the country rat who keeps a nature diary. He has also written books encouraging children to make their own models and puppets.

More recently, Firmin has taken a break from the writing and illustrating of children's books: "I'd been doing some lino-cuts for pleasure and always wanted to illustrate a whole book either with engravings or lino-cuts," he noted. "My wife suggested that I illustrate an edition of Vita Sackville-West's *The Land,* a long philosophical poem about England and its countryside. The original publication was out of print and I found out that someone was interested in reissuing it. I did one or two specimen prints and eventually Webb & Bower . . . backed the project."

Firmin's own family has grown almost as quickly as the family of puppets that he has created over the years. He told *CA:* "I always think of the children who will read the books [I write and illustrate]. As I have five grandsons and three granddaughters, from 3 years to 9 years in age, I have plenty of opportunities to try out my books on them. The series I am working on now, making simple working models from junk, has been helped by working with the kids."

BIOGRAPHICAL/CRITICAL SOURCES:

BOOKS

Books for Keeps (pamphlet), July, 1980.
Firmin and Postgate Present . . . "Pinny's House" and *"Tottie"* (pamphlet), September, 1986.
Peppin, Brigid, and Lucy Micklethwait, *Book Illustrators of the Twentieth Century,* Arco, 1984.

*   *   *

FISCHER, Joel 1939-

PERSONAL: Born April 22, 1939, in Chicago, IL; son of Sam and Ruth Fischer; married Ursula R. (a tennis professional), June 14, 1964 (marriage ended); married Renee H. Furuyama (a social worker), October 31, 1992; children: (first marriage) Lisa, Nicole. *Education:* University of Illinois, B.A., 1961, M.S.W., 1964; University of California, Berkeley, D.S.W., 1970.

ADDRESSES: Home—1371-4 Hunekai, Honolulu, HI 96816. *Office*—School of Social Work, University of Hawaii, Honolulu, HI 96822.

CAREER: University of Hawaii, Honolulu, professor of social work, 1970—. Visiting professor at Washington University, St. Louis, MO, 1977, University of Wisconsin, 1978-79, and University of Hong Kong, 1986.

MEMBER: National Association of Social Workers, Academy of Certified Social Workers, American Association of University Professors, Council on Social Work Education, Hawaii Committee on Africa, Unity Organizing Committee, Bertha Reynolds Society.

WRITINGS:

Interpersonal Helping: Emerging Approaches for Social Work Practice, Charles C. Thomas, 1973.

Planned Behavior Change: Application of Behavior Modification to Social Work Practice, Free Press, 1975.

The Effectiveness of Social Casework, Charles C. Thomas, 1976.

Effective Casework Practice: An Eclectic Approach, McGraw, 1978.

Handbook of Behavior Therapy with Sexual Problems, two volumes, Pergamon, 1978.

Treat Yourself to a Better Sex Life, Prentice-Hall, 1980.

Fundamentals of Social Work Practice, Wadsworth, 1981.

Evaluating Practice, Prentice-Hall, 1982, 2nd edition, 1993.

Helping the Sexually Oppressed, Prentice-Hall, 1987.

Measures for Clinical Practice, Free Press, 1987, 2nd edition, two volumes, 1993.

Visions for the Future, University of Hawaii, 1988.

East-West Directions, University of Hawaii, 1992.

Contributor of more than 120 articles to professional journals.

*   *   *

FLACHMANN, Michael   1942-

PERSONAL: Born November 3, 1942, in St. Louis, MO; son of Charles R. (an insurance executive) and Charlotte (Widen) Flachmann; married Kim Marschel (a college professor), August 31, 1969; children: Christopher M., Laura M. *Education:* University of the South, B.A. (magna cum laude), 1964; University of Virginia, M.A., 1965; University of Chicago, Ph.D., 1972. *Avocational interests:* Tennis, judo (fourth degree black belt).

ADDRESSES: Home—1236 Fairway Dr., Bakersfield, CA 93309. *Office*—Department of English and Communications, California State University, 9001 Stockdale Hwy., Bakersfield, CA 93311.

CAREER: Southern Illinois University, Edwardsville, instructor in English, 1965-68; University of Chicago, Chicago, IL, director of pre-freshman summer program, 1971-72; Triton College, Chicago, IL, assistant professor, 1971-72; California State University, Bakersfield, assistant professor, 1972-76, associate professor, 1976-81, professor of English, 1981—, director of English graduate studies, 1985-90, and university honors program, 1986—, chair of program, 1988—; California Institute of the Arts, Critical Studies, and Theatre Divisions, Valencia, visiting professor, 1987-88 and 1989-90. Director of educational programs at California Shakespearean Festival, 1979-81, and La Jolla Playhouse, 1983-85; dramaturg and director

at Utah Shakespearean Festival, 1986—; founder and director of Camp Shakespeare, 1988—, and Shakespeare for Teachers, 1988—. Member of Western Region Advisory Council of the Shakespeare Globe Center, 1983—, and International Committee for the Bibliography for *Shakespeare Quarterly,* 1985—.

MEMBER: Modern Language Association of America, Shakespeare Association of America, Bibliographical Society, Early English Text Society, Renaissance Society of America, Association for Theatre in Higher Education, Southern California Educational Theatre Association, Phi Beta Kappa.

AWARDS, HONORS: Dupont fellow, University of Virginia, 1965; Exeter College summer fellow, 1967; William Raney Harper fellow, University of Chicago, 1969-71; Distinguished Professor Award, California State College (now University), 1973; Meritorious Performance and Professional Promise Awards, California State University, 1985, 1987, 1989, 1991; Outstanding Professor Award, California State University, 1992.

WRITINGS:

(With Libby Appel) *Shakespeare's Lovers: A Text for Performance and Analysis,* Southern Illinois University Press, 1982.

(With Appel) *Shakespeare's Women: A Playscript for Performance and Analysis,* Southern Illinois University Press, 1986.

(With wife, Kim Flachmann) *The Prose Reader: Essays for College Writers,* Prentice Hall, 1986, 2nd edition published as *The Prose Reader: Essays for Thinking, Reading, and Writing,* 1989, 3rd edition, 1992; *The Annotated Instructor's Edition,* 3rd edition, 1992; *Quiz Book,* 3rd edition, 1992; *The Instructor's Resource Manual,* 3rd edition, 1992.

(Editor with William A. Ringler, Jr.) *Beware the Cat: The First English Novel,* Huntington Library Press, 1988.

Contributor of numerous articles and reviews to literary and theatrical journals, including *Studies in Philology, Shakespeare Quarterly, Studies in English Literature, Medieval and Renaissance Drama in England, Theatre Journal,* and *On-Stage Studies;* also contributor of articles to Shakespeare festival programs.

WORK IN PROGRESS: The Wonderful News of the Death of Paul III; The Play's the Thing: Strategies for Teaching Dramatic Literature in the English Classroom.

SIDELIGHTS: Michael Flachmann once told *CA:* "I feel strongly that Shakespeare's plays should be approached in the college English classroom as both literary documents and 'scripts for performance.' Libby Appel and I have therefore constructed our first two books as playscripts that invite literary as well as theatrical consideration.

These two scripts are collections of scenes from Shakespeare which are woven into unified dramatic narratives. Presented on stage, they allow audience members the opportunity to investigate certain Shakespearean themes (e.g., love, women) drawn from many different plays.

"In addition to performing my scholarly chores, I continue to serve whenever possible as dramaturg for professional productions of Shakespeare's plays. Having worked at the California Shakespearean Festival, the La Jolla Playhouse, the Utah Shakespeare Festival, and the Oregon Shakespeare Festival, I find I am happiest when bridging the gap between Shakespeare as 'dramatic literature' and Shakespeare as 'theatrical production.' The worlds of literature and theatre have much to learn from each other, and I am glad to be involved in the exchange of information.

"I have also greatly enjoyed my excursions into the area of early English prose fiction," Flachmann recently commented. "Particularly my editions of *Beware the Cat* and *The Image of Idleness,* and into the teaching of composition, which has generated so far three editions of a very successful college English textbook (co-edited with my wife, Kim Flachmann) entitled *The Prose Reader.* All of my books, in fact, are extensions of my work in the university and in professional theatre; as such, they are attempts to expand my audience past classroom walls and engage in a dialogue about topics that concern me deeply."

*   *   *

FLAGG, Fannie 1941-

PERSONAL: Original name, Patricia Neal; born September 21, 1941, in Birmingham, AL; daughter of William H. (a small business owner and projectionist) and Marion Leona (LeGore) Neal. *Education:* Attended the University of Alabama, the Pittsburgh Playhouse, and the Town and Gown Theatre.

ADDRESSES: Home—Santa Barbara, CA; and New York, NY.

CAREER: Actress, comedienne, producer, and writer. Producer of *Morning Show* (WBRC-TV), Birmingham, AL, 1964-65. Appeared at the Upstairs at the Downstairs (nightclub), New York City. Appeared in television series, including *Candid Camera,* Columbia Broadcasting System, Inc. (CBS-TV), 1966-67, syndicated, 1974-80; *The New Dick Van Dyke Show,* CBS-TV, 1971-73; and *Harper Valley,* National Broadcasting Company, Inc. (NBC-TV), 1981-82. Appeared in television pilots, including *Comedy News,* American Broadcasting Companies, Inc. (ABC-TV), 1972; *Comedy News II,* ABC-TV, 1973; *Home Cookin',* ABC-TV, 1975; and *Harper Valley PTA,*

NBC-TV, 1981. Appeared in television movies, including *The New, Original Wonder Woman,* ABC-TV, 1975; and *Sex and the Married Woman,* NBC-TV, 1977. Appeared as a guest on television shows, including *The Bobbie Gentry Special,* syndicated, 1971, *The David Frost Show, The Mike Douglas Show, The Jackie Gleason Show, The Match Game, Love Boat, The Tonight Show,* and *The Merv Griffin Show.* Appeared in motion pictures, including *Five Easy Pieces,* Columbia, 1970; *Some of My Best Friends Are . . . ,* American International, 1971; *Stay Hungry,* United Artists, 1976; *Grease,* Paramount, 1978; and *Rabbit Test,* Avco Embassy, 1978. Appeared in plays, including *Cat on a Hot Tin Roof,* Town and Gown Theatre, Birmingham, AL; *Just for Openers,* Upstairs at the Downstairs, 1966; *Patio/Porch,* New York, 1977; *Come Back to the Five and Dime, Jimmy Dean, Jimmy Dean,* on Broadway, 1979; and *The Best Little Whorehouse in Texas,* on Broadway, 1980. Major tours include *Private Lives, Annie, Mary Mary, Finishing Touches,* and *Once More with Feeling,* all U.S. cities. Speaker on the Equal Rights Amendment.

MEMBER: American Federation of Television and Radio Artists, Screen Actors Guild, Actors' Equity Association, American Guild of Variety Artists, American Women in Radio and Television.

AWARDS, HONORS: Pittsburgh and Pasadena playhouses scholarships, both 1962; Fashion Award, Ad Club, 1965; named outstanding woman of America, Who's Who in American Women in Radio and Television, 1966; two first place awards in fiction, Santa Barbara Writers Conference.

WRITINGS:

Rally 'round the Flagg (recording), RCA Victor, 1967.
My Husband Doesn't Know I'm Making This Phone Call (recording), Sunflower, 1971.
Coming Attractions: A Wonderful Novel (Book-of-the-Month Club alternate selection), Morrow, 1981, published as *Daisy Fay and the Miracle Man,* Warner Books, 1992.
Fried Green Tomatoes at the Whistle Stop Cafe, Random House, 1987.
(Adaptor with Jon Avnet) *Fried Green Tomatoes at the Whistle Stop Cafe* (screenplay), Universal, 1991.

Also author of comedy routines and scripts for television series, including *Candid Camera,* CBS-TV, 1956-66. Author of four comedy albums. Contributor of articles to magazines and newspapers.

WORK IN PROGRESS: The Maude Noel Secret Society of Great Dames, a play.

SIDELIGHTS: Originally a movie and television personality associated with such shows as *Candid Camera* and

Harper Valley, Fannie Flagg has since made a name for herself as a novelist and screenwriter. Her novels *Coming Attractions* (also published as *Daisy Fay and the Miracle Man*) and *Fried Green Tomatoes at the Whistle Stop Cafe* bring back the South of the past through casts of primarily strong female characters and splashes of humor. The two tales are of the homespun variety, portraying the hardships and delights of small-town life through the eyes of their female residents. In addition to her novels, Flagg, in collaboration with Jon Avnet, also brought the modest town of Whistle Stop to life in the popular 1991 film adaption of *Fried Green Tomatoes,* starring Kathy Bates, Jessica Tandy, Mary Stuart Masterson, and Mary-Louise Parker.

The success of both the book and movie versions of *Fried Green Tomatoes* created a renewed interest in Flagg's first novel, which she published under a new title in 1992. *Coming Attractions* begins when eleven-year-old Daisy Fay Harper decides to start keeping a diary on April 1, 1952. She then spends the next six years writing down the zany and troublesome aspects of her life. The daughter of an alcoholic projectionist always in search of a get-rich-quick scheme and a ladylike and mannerly mother, Daisy seems to be a magnet for mishaps as she comes of age in the pages of her diary. Typical of Daisy's many entries is the following: "I am a second-year Brownie. I got a first-aid badge that really comes in handy. One time after school, Jimmy Lee got hit by a car and was bleeding all over the place. I remembered what to do. I sat down and put my head between my knees to keep from fainting." Flagg "has put together a rollicking, funny, bubbling novel," asserts Barbara A. Bannon in her *Publishers Weekly* review of *Coming Attractions.* And Laura Cunningham, writing in the *New York Times Book Review,* concludes: "A lot of people are going to enjoy Daisy Fay Harper 'cause she's just as sweet as her favorite movie-munchin' candy, Bit-O-Honey."

Flagg's second novel, *Fried Green Tomatoes at the Whistle Stop Cafe,* takes place in both the past and the present. The present tale is that of the growing friendship between Ninny Threadgoode, an Alabama nursing home resident, and Evelyn Couch, a middle-aged woman unsure of what to do with the rest of her life. The tale of the past is told through a variety of sources, including Ninny's reminiscences and excerpts from the *Weems Weekly* (a local journal published during the 1920s and 1930s), and focuses on the town of Whistle Stop, Alabama, and two young women who run a cafe there. Idgie Threadgoode, a tomboy who drinks, smokes, and defends blacks, rescues her friend Ruth Jamison from an abusive husband and brings her back to Whistle Stop, where they eventually open the cafe. The two women build a life together with Ruth's son until her husband shows up and tries to take him back. A

murder follows and Idgie is accused and acquitted, but Ninny reveals who really committed the crime during her conversations with Evelyn. "The core of the story is the unusual love affair between Idgie and Ruth, rendered with exactitude and delicacy, and with just the balance of clarity and reticence that would have made it acceptable in that time and place," observes Jack Butler in the *New York Times Book Review.* Butler also praises Flagg's portrayal of the time period, pointing out that she "evokes, in fine detail, Hoovervilles, the Klan, a 'hunting camp' that is more nearly a juke joint, a hot jazz spot in the black section of Birmingham and many other settings." And a *Publishers Weekly* contributor concludes that "the book's best character, perhaps, is the town of Whistle Stop itself. Too bad the trains don't stop there anymore."

Trains, and a number of interesting characters, were able to stop at Whistle Stop one more time in the 1991 movie version of *Fried Green Tomatoes at the Whistle Stop Cafe.* The characters of Ninny (played by Jessica Tandy) and Evelyn (played by Kathy Bates) meet when Evelyn goes to the nursing home to visit her mother-in-law. A timid middle-aged compulsive over-eater, Evelyn shares her food with Ninny as she sits in the lounge listening to the story of Idgie (played by Mary Stuart Masterson) and Ruth (played by Mary-Louise Parker). The tale of these two strong women eventually inspires Evelyn, and she starts to lose weight, begins a new job, and stops doing *everything* for her husband. "I think it's time that women *have* to stand up and say we do not want to be seen in a demeaning manner," explains Flagg in an interview with Bruce Bibby for *Premiere.* Bibby sees this happening in the movie, asserting that "Flagg's women are as tart as the title dish." A *New York Times* contributor concludes that the movie version of *Fried Green Tomatoes* is a "compelling adaptation of . . . Flagg's novel about the sustaining powers of friendship . . . in a small Alabama town."

BIOGRAPHICAL/CRITICAL SOURCES:

BOOKS

Flagg, Fannie, *Coming Attractions,* Morrow, 1981, published as *Daisy Fay and the Miracle Man,* Warner Books, 1992.

PERIODICALS

New Republic, February 3, 1992, p. 28.
New York Times, August 20, 1992, p. C26.
New York Times Book Review, August 2, 1981, p. 15; October 18, 1987, p. 14.
Premiere, February, 1992, pp. 33-34.
Publishers Weekly, April 10, 1981, p. 58; August 28, 1987, pp. 64-65.
School Library Journal, October, 1981, p. 160.
Voice of Youth Advocates, October, 1981, p. 32.*

FLECK, Richard Francis 1937-

PERSONAL: Born August 24, 1937, in Philadelphia, PA; son of J. Keene (a librarian) and Anne M. (a legal secretary; maiden name, DeLeon) Fleck; married Maura McMahon, 1963; children: Richard Sean, Michelle Marie, Ann Maureen. *Education:* Rutgers University, B.A., 1959; Colorado State University, M.A., 1962; University of New Mexico, Ph.D., 1970. *Politics:* Democrat. *Religion:* Roman Catholic.

ADDRESSES: Home—845 South York St., Denver, CO 80209. *Office*—Humanities Division, Teikyo Loretto Heights University, 3001 South Federal Blvd., Denver, CO 80236.

CAREER: Princeton University, Princeton, NJ, bibliographical assistant at library, 1962-63; North Adams State College, North Adams, MA, instructor in French and English, 1963-65; University of Wyoming, Laramie, instructor, 1965-70, assistant professor, 1970-75, associate professor, 1975-80, professor of English, 1980-90; Teikyo Loretto Heights University, Denver, CO, director of humanities division, 1990—. Exchange professor at Osaka University, Japan, 1981-82. *Military service:* U.S. Navy, 1961-63.

MEMBER: Thoreau Society, Sierra Club, Rocky Mountain Modern Languages Association.

AWARDS, HONORS: Summer research grants from University of Wyoming, 1967, 1971; grant from Wyoming State Historical Society, 1973; grants from Wyoming Council for the Humanities, 1978, 1979; award from University of Wyoming Alumni Association, 1983.

WRITINGS:

Palms, Peaks, and Prairies (poetry), Golden Quill, 1967.
The Indians of Thoreau, Hummingbird Press, 1974.
Cottonwood Moon (poetry), Jelm Mountain, 1979.
Clearing of the Mist (novel), Dustbooks, 1979.
(Author of preface) John Muir, *Our National Parks,* University of Wisconsin Press, 1981.
Bamboo in the Sun (poetry), S.U. Press, 1983.
(Editor) Muir, *Mountaineering Essays,* Peregrine Smith, 1984.
Henry Thoreau and John Muir among the Indians, Archon Books, 1985.
(Contributor) Dave Marsh and Don Henley, editors, *Heaven Is under Our Feet,* Longmeadow Press, 1991.
(Editor) *Critical Perspectives on Native American Fiction,* Three Continents, 1992.

Contributor to scholarly journals. Editor of *Thoreau Quarterly Journal,* 1975-77; member of editorial board of *Paintbrush.*

WORK IN PROGRESS: Where Land Is Mostly Sky.

SIDELIGHTS: Richard F. Fleck once told *CA:* "The most significant events in my life were my marriage to my Irish wife, Maura, and our frequent visits to and six-month residence in Ireland. My experience in Ireland has linked together with my knowledge of American Indians to inspire two novels connecting Irish and Indian struggles for cultural liberation. My interest in Muir and Thoreau has led to scholarly investigations of their sources of inspiration which are similar to my own. Their sense of place has been particularly important to me. N. Scott Momaday and Leslie Silko are two Native American writers who have inspired me with a sense of place.

"As a Thoreau specialist, I was given the opportunity (along with my family) of living and teaching in Japan for one year. 'Sense of place' in Japan has inspired me greatly in my climbs of Mount Fuji and Miyajimayama, in my wanderings about the cities of Osaka and Tokyo, in my visits to the temples of Kyoto and Nara. During my stay in Japan I published poems in *Mainichi Daily News,* one of Japan's leading English-language newspapers, and in *Poetry Nippon.* Two island nations, Ireland and Japan, then have crystallized my artistic impulse."

BIOGRAPHICAL/CRITICAL SOURCES:

BOOKS

Boswell, Jeanetta, *Henry David Thoreau and the Critics,* Scarecrow, 1981.
Harding, Walter, *A New Thoreau Handbook,* New York University Press, 1980.

*   *   *

FLEW, Antony G(arrard) N(ewton) 1923-

PERSONAL: Born February 11, 1923, in London, England; son of Robert Newton (a minister) and Alice Winifred (Garrard) Flew; married Annis Ruth Harty Donnison (a school teacher); children: Harriet Rebecca, Joanna Naomi. *Education:* St. John's College, Oxford, M.A. (with first class honors), 1948. *Politics:* Conservative. *Avocational interests:* Travel, walking, house maintenance.

ADDRESSES: Home—26 Alexandra Rd., Reading RG1 5PD, England.

CAREER: Oxford University, Christ Church, Oxford, England, lecturer in philosophy, 1949-50; University of Aberdeen, Scotland, lecturer in moral philosophy, 1950-54; University of Keele, Keele, England, professor of philosophy, 1954-71; University of Calgary, Calgary, Alberta, professor of philosophy, 1972-73; University of Reading, Reading, England, professor of philosophy, 1973-82, professor emeritus, 1982—. Visiting professor at New York University, 1958, Swarthmore College, 1961,

University of Pittsburgh, 1965, University of Malawi, 1967, University of Maryland, 1970, State University of New York at Buffalo, 1971, and University of California, San Diego, 1978-79; Gavin David Young Lecturer, University of Adelaide, 1963. Distinguished research fellow, Social Philosophy and Policy Center, Bowling Green State University, part-time, 1983-91. Has participated in talks and discussions on radio and television in England, Zambia, Australia, Canada, and United States. *Military service:* Royal Air Force, Intelligence, 1943-45.

MEMBER: Mind Association, Aristotelian Society, Rationalist Press Association (vice-president, 1972-88), Freedom Association (member of council), Voluntary Euthanasia Society (chairman of executive committee, 1976-79).

AWARDS, HONORS: John Locke Prize, Oxford University, 1948; D.Litt., University of Keele, 1974; Laureate of the Academy of Humanism, 1983; In Praise of Reason Award, 1985.

WRITINGS:

A New Approach to Psychical Research, C. A. Watts, 1953.
Hume's Philosophy of Belief, Humanities, 1961.
God and Philosophy, Hutchinson, 1966, Harcourt, 1967, revised edition published as *God: A Philosophical Critique,* Open Court, 1984.
Evolutionary Ethics, St. Martin's, 1967.
An Introduction to Western Philosophy, Bobbs-Merrill, 1971.
Crime or Disease?, Barnes & Noble, 1973.
Thinking about Thinking, Collins, 1975, published as *Thinking Straight,* Prometheus Books, 1977.
The Presumption of Atheism (philosophical essays), Barnes & Nobel, 1976, published as *God, Freedom and Immortality,* Prometheus Books, 1984.
Sociology, Equality and Education (philosophical essays), Barnes & Noble, 1976.
(With T. B. Warren) *The Warren-Flew Debate,* National Christian Press, 1977.
A Rational Animal (philosophical essays), Clarendon Press, 1978.
Philosophy: An Introduction, Hodder & Stoughton, 1979.
The Politics of Procrustes (philosophical essays), Temple Smith, 1981.
Darwinian Evolution, Granada Paladin, 1985.
David Hume: Philosopher of Moral Science, Basil Blackwell, 1986.
(With Godfrey Vesey) *Agency and Necessity,* Basil Blackwell, 1987.
The Logic of Mortality, Basil Blackwell, 1987.
Power to the Parents: Reversing Educational Decline, Sherwood, 1987.
Equality in Liberty and Justice, Routledge, 1989.
(With Terry Miethe) *Does God Exist?,* Harper, 1991.

Thinking about Social Thinking, Harper, 1992.

EDITOR

(And author of introduction) *Logic and Language,* Humanities, Volume 1, 1951, Volume 2, 1953.
(With A. C. MacIntyre) *New Essays in Philosophical Theology,* Macmillan, 1955.
Essays in Conceptual Analysis, Macmillan (London), 1956.
(And author of introduction) *Hume on Human Nature and Understanding,* Collier, 1962.
(And author of introduction) *Body, Mind and Death,* Macmillan, 1964.
(And author of introduction) *Malthus: An Essay on the Principle of Population,* Penguin, 1971.
(And contributor) *A Dictionary of Philosophy,* Macmillan, 1979.
Philosophical Problems of Parapsychology, Prometheus Books, 1987.
(And author of introduction) *Hume's Inquiry Concerning Human Understanding,* Open Court, 1988.
(And author of introduction) *Hume's Writings on Religion,* Open Court, in press.

OTHER

Contributor to numerous books, including *Religious Belief and Philosophical Thought,* edited by W. P. Alston, Harcourt, 1963; *Philosophy and Parapsychology,* edited by J. K. Ludwig, Prometheus Books, 1977; *Sidney Hook: Philosopher of Democracy and Humanism,* edited by P. Kurtz, Prometheus Books, 1983; *Philosophy in the United Kingdom Today,* edited by S. Shanker, Croom Helm, 1986; and *Reincarnation: Fact or Fable,* edited by A. Berger and J. Berger, Harper-Collins, 1991.

Contributor to encyclopedias, including *Encyclopaedia of Philosophy, Encyclopaedia Britannica,* and *Collier's Encyclopaedia.* Also contributor to professional journals in England, Germany, Australia, and the United States. Member of editorial board, *Sociological Review,* 1954-71; member of editorial advisory board, *Question,* 1958—; consulting editor, *Humanist,* 1972—, *Journal of Critical Analysis,* 1974—, *Hume Studies,* 1976—, and *Journal of Libertarian Studies,* 1976—.

SIDELIGHTS: Various books and articles by Antony G. N. Flew have been translated into German, Italian, Spanish, Thai, Portuguese, Welsh, Danish, Japanese, and Hebrew.

*　　　*　　　*

FLORES, Angel 1900-1992

PERSONAL: Born October 2, 1900, in Barceloneta, PR; died January 3, 1992, in Guadalajara, Mexico; son of

Nepomuceno (in business) and Paula (a teacher; maiden name, Rodriguez) Flores; married Kate Mann Berger (a writer), 1936; children: Ralph, Juan, Barbara Flores Dederick. *Education:* New York University, A.B., 1923; Lafayette College, A.M., 1925; Cornell University, Ph.D., 1947.

ADDRESSES: Home—63 Malden Ave., Palenville, NY 12463.

CAREER: Union College, Schenectady, NY, instructor in Spanish, 1924-25; Rutgers University, New Brunswick, NJ, instructor in Spanish language and literature, 1925-29; editor of *Alhambra,* 1929-30; Cornell University, Ithaca, NY, instructor in Spanish, 1930-33; editor of *Literary World,* 1934-45; Queens College of the City University of New York, Flushing, NY, assistant professor, 1945-47, associate professor, 1948-52, professor of romance languages and comparative literature, 1952-70, professor emeritus, 1970-92. Visiting professor at University of Wisconsin (now University of Wisconsin—Madison), 1953-54; professor at Graduate Center of the City University of New York, 1968-70. Editor of Dragon Press, 1931-33. Member of Pan American Union's Division of Intellectual Cooperation, 1941-45.

MEMBER: Instituto Internacional de Literatura Iberoamericana.

WRITINGS:

IN ENGLISH

Spanish Literature in English Translation, H. W. Wilson, 1926.
Lope de Vega: Monster of Nature, Brentano's, 1930, reprinted, Kennikat, 1969.
(With M. J. Benardete) *Cervantes across the Centuries,* Dryden, 1947, reprinted, Gordian, 1969.
Masterpieces of the Spanish Golden Age, Rinehart, 1957.
The Medieval Age, Dell, 1963.
The Literature of Spanish America, five volumes, Las Americas, 1966-69.
Ibsen: Four Essays, Haskell Booksellers, 1970.
(With Helene M. Anderson) *Masterpieces of Spanish American Literature,* two volumes, Macmillan, 1972.
A Bibliography of Spanish-American Writers, 1609-1974, Gordian, 1975.
A Kajka Bibliography, 1908-1976, Gordian, 1976.
The Problem of "The Judgment": Eleven Approaches to Kafka's Story, Gordian, 1977.

EDITOR; IN ENGLISH

(With Benardete) *The Anatomy of Don Quixote,* Dragon Press, 1932.
(With Dudley Poore) *Fiesta in November: Stories from Latin America,* Houghton, 1942.

The Kafka Problem: An Anthology of Criticism about Franz Kafka, New Directions, 1946, revised edition, Gordian, 1975.
Spanish Writers in Exile, Bern Porter, 1947, reprinted, 1977.
Great Spanish Stories, Modern Library, 1956.
An Anthology of French Poetry from Nerval to Valery, Doubleday, 1958.
(With Homer Swander) *Franz Kafka Today,* University of Wisconsin Press, 1958, revised edition, Gordian, 1977.
Nineteenth Century German Tales, Doubleday, 1959.
An Anthology of German Poetry from Hoelderlin to Rilke, Doubleday, 1960.
An Anthology of Spanish Poetry from Garcilaso to Garcia Lorca, Doubleday, 1961.
Great Spanish Short Stories, Dell, 1962.
Spanish Drama, Bantam, 1962.
Anthology of Medieval Lyrics, Modern Library, 1962.
Leopardi: Poems and Prose, Indiana University Press, 1966.
The Kafka Debate: New Perspectives for Our Times, Gordian, 1977.
ExpIain to Me: Some Stories of Kafka, Gordian, 1983.
(With wife, Kate Flores) *The Defiant Muse: Hispanic Feminist Poems from the Middle Ages to the Present,* Feminist Press, 1986.
Great Spanish Plays in English Translation, Dover, 1991.
Spanish American Authors: The Twentieth Century, H. W. Wilson, 1992.

TRANSLATOR TO ENGLISH

Jose E. Rodo, *The Motives of Proteus,* Brentano's, 1928.
Ramon Gomez de la Serna, *Movieland,* Macaulay, 1930.
Miguel de Unamuno, *Three Exemplary Novels,* Boni, 1930, reprinted, Grove Press, 1956.
Miguel A. Menendez, *Nayar,* Farrar & Rinehart, 1942.
German Arciniegas, *Germans in the Conquest of America,* Macmillan, 1943.
Benjamin Subercaseaux, *Chile: A Geographic Extravaganza,* Macmillan, 1943, reprinted, Haffner, 1971.
Pablo Neruda, *Residence on Earth,* New Directions, 1946.
Neruda, *Three Material Songs,* East River Editions, 1948.
Jaime Sabartes, *Picasso: An Intimate Portrait,* Prentice-Hall, 1948.
Humberto Diaz Casanueva, *Requiem,* Grupo Fuego, 1958.
(With Esther S. Dillon) Baldomero Lillo, *The Devil's Pit,* UNESCO Collection of Representative Works, 1959.
Esteban Echeverria, *The Slaughter House,* Las Americas, 1959.
Neruda, *Nocturnal Collection: A Poem,* [Madison, WI], 1966.

IN SPANISH

(Translator) T. S. Eliot, *Tierra baldia* ("The Waste Land"), Editorial Cervantes, 1930, reprinted, Ocnos, 1973.

(With Alberto Vasquez) *Paisaje y hombres de America,* Dryden, 1947.

Historiay antologia del cuento y la novela en Hispanoamerica, Las Americas, 1959.

First Spanish Reader, Bantam, 1964.

La literatura de Espana, Las Americas, 1970.

Aproximaciones a Cesar Vallejo (title means "Approaches to Cesar Vallejo"), two volumes, Las Americas, 1971.

Aproximaciones a Octavio Paz (title means "Approaches to Octavio Paz"), Mortiz, 1974.

Aproximaciones a Pablo Neruda (title means "Approaches to Pablo Neruda"), Ocnos, 1974.

Origenes del cuento hispanoamericana (title means "Origins of the Spanish-American Short Story"), Premia, 1979.

Selecciones espanolas (title means "Spanish Selections"), Macmillan, 1979.

Realismo magico (title means "Magical Realism"), Premia, 1981.

Cesar Vallejo (biography), Premia, 1981.

Narrativa hispanoamericana: Historia y antologia (title means "Spanish-American Fiction: History and Anthology"), Siglo XXI, 1981.

Expliquemonos a Kafka, Siglo XXI, 1983.

El realismo magico en el cuento hispanoamericano, Premi, 1985.

Nuevas aproximaciones a Pablo Neruda, Fondo de Cultura Economica, 1987.

OTHER

(Editor) *Spanish Stories* (in Spanish and English), Bantam, 1960, 8th edition, 1979.

Also author of volumes devoted to Jorge Luis Borges and other Hispanic writers.*

[Sketch reviewed by children, Barbara Flores Dederick and Juan Flores]

*   *   *

FOSTER, Edward Halsey 1942-

PERSONAL: Born December 17, 1942, in Williamsburg, MA; son of Edward Clark (a teacher and geologist) and Edith (a school principal and teacher; maiden name, Derosia) Foster; married Elaine Dunphy (a teacher), June 22, 1968; children: Katherine Hearn, John Clark. *Education:* Columbia University, B.A., 1965, M.A., 1966, Ph.D., 1970. *Politics:* Democrat. *Religion:* Protestant.

ADDRESSES: Home—212 Bloomfield St., Hoboken, NJ 07030; and Nash Rd., Cummington, MA 01026. *Office*—Stevens Institute of Technology, Hoboken, NJ 07030.

CAREER: Stevens Institute of Technology, Hoboken, NJ, assistant professor, 1970-75, associate professor, 1975-85, professor of American studies, 1985—. Visiting professor of American studies, Hacettepe University, Ankara, Turkey, 1978-79, and University of Istanbul, 1985-86; visiting professor of English, Drew University Graduate School, 1991 and 1992; Fulbright lecturer, 1978-79 and 1985-86. Member of advisory committee for the Middle East, Council for International Exchange of Scholars, 1986-89.

MEMBER: Modern Language Association of America (member of American literature section).

AWARDS, HONORS: New Jersey Historical Commission research grant, 1974; National Endowment for the Humanities planning grant, 1976, grant, 1985, 1990; New Jersey State Council on the Arts grant, 1981, 1982, 1983, 1984; National Endowment for the Arts grant, 1984; United States Information Agency grant, 1989, 1992; honorary M.Eng., Stevens Institute of Technology, 1990.

WRITINGS:

Catharine Maria Sedgwick, Twayne, 1974.

The Civilized Wilderness, Macmillan, 1975.

(With Geoffrey W. Clark) *Hoboken,* Irvington Books, 1976.

Josiah Gregg and Lewis H. Garrard, Boise State University, 1977.

Susan and Anna Warner, Twayne, 1978.

Cummington Poems, Bryant, 1982.

Richard Brautigan, Twayne, 1983.

William Saroyan, Western Writers Series, 1984.

Jack Spicer, Western Writers Series, 1991.

William Saroyan: A Study of the Short Fiction, Twayne, 1991.

Understanding the Beats, University of South Carolina Press, 1992.

Between the Clock and Her Bed, Talisman, 1992.

The Talisman Interviews, Talisman, 1993.

Contributor to periodicals. Editor-in-chief, *Talisman: A Journal of Contemporary Poetry and Poetics,* 1988—; poetry editor, *MultiCultural Review,* 1991—.

WORK IN PROGRESS: The San Francisco Renaissance; The Black Mountain School.

SIDELIGHTS: Edward Halsey Foster once told *CA:* "I know of no life more to be envied than the life of a writer. It is when the words fit in perfect order that we are most alive."

FOURNIER, Pierre 1916-
(Pierre Gascar)

PERSONAL: Born March 13, 1916, in Paris, France; son of Jean and Rachel (Bernardin) Fournier; married Jacqueline Salmon, July, 1946 (marriage ended); married Alice Simon, February 10, 1958; children: (first marriage) Jean-Pierre, Jacques. *Education:* Educated in France.

ADDRESSES: Home—13 boulevard du Montparnasse, 75006 Paris, France. *Agent*—Georges Borchardt, 136 East 57th St., New York, NY 10022.

CAREER: France-Soir (newspaper), Paris, France, 1945-58, began as reporter, became literary critic; writer. Served as information officer for World Health Organization, 1956-57. Lecturer in several countries, 1958-65; visiting professor at University of Texas at Austin, 1969. *Military service:* French Army, 1937-45.

AWARDS, HONORS: Prix des Critiques, 1953, for *Les Betes;* Prix Goncourt, 1953, for *Les Betes* [and] *Le Temps des morts;* grand prix de litterature, Academie francaise, 1969; Prix litterature du Prince Pierre de Monaco, 1978; Grand Prix Litteraire de la Societe des gens de lettres, 1991; chevalier de la Legion d'honneur.

WRITINGS:

IN ENGLISH TRANSLATION; UNDER PSEUDONYM PIERRE GASCAR

Les Betes [and] *Le Temps des morts* (also see below), Gallimard, 1953, translation by Jean Stewart published as *Beasts and Men,* Little, Brown, 1956.
La Graine (novel), Gallimard, 1955, translation by Merloyed published as *The Seed* (also see below), Little, Brown, 1956.
La Barre de corail, Gallimard, 1959, translation by Lawrence published as *The Coral Barrier,* Little, Brown, 1961.
Beasts and Men [and] *The Seed,* Meridan Books, 1960.
Le Fugitif, Gallimard, 1961, translation by Lawrence published as *The Fugitive,* Little, Brown, 1964.
Chambord, photographs by Andre Martin, Delpire, 1962, translation by Richard Howard published under same title, Macmillan, 1964.
Les Moutons de feu, Gallimard, 1963, translation by Lawrence published as *Lambs of Fire,* Braziller, c. 1965.
Le Meilleur de la vie, Gallimard, 1964, translation by Lawrence published as *The Best Years,* Braziller, 1967.
Women and the Sun (contains translations of stories originally published in *Les Femmes* and *Soleils* [also see below]: "The Cistern," "The Blind Men of St. Xavier," "Marble," "The Forest Fire," "The Asylum," "The Little Square," "Ethiopian Hunt," "The Watershed," and "The Women"), Little, Brown, c. 1964.

IN FRENCH

Les Meubles (novel), Gallimard, 1949.
Le Visage clos (novel), Gallimard, 1951.
Les Betes (short stories; contains "Les Chevaux," "La Vie eclarlate," "Les Betes," "Gaston," "Le Chat," and "Entre chiens et loups"), Gallimard, 1953.
Le Temps des morts, Gallimard, 1955.
Les Femmes (contains "Les Femmes," "L'Incendie," "L'Asile," and "La Mere"), Gallimard, 1955.
Aujourd'hui la Chine, Clairefontaine, 1955.
Chine ouverte, photographs by Erby Landau, Gallimard, 1955.
L'Herbe des rue (novel), Gallimard, 1956.
La Barre de corail [and] *Les Aveugles de Saint-Xavier,* Gallimard, 1958.
Voyage chez les vivants, Gallimard, 1958.
Le Pas perdus (also see below), Gallimard, 1958.
Soleils (contains "La Citerne," "Marbre," "Les Chasses d'Ethiope," and "La Petite Place"), Gallimard, 1960.
Normandie, Arthaud, 1962.
Vertiges du present, ce difficile accord avec le monde, Arthaud, 1962.
L'Expression des sentiments chez animaux, Hachette, 1964.
Saint-Marc (title means "San Marco"), photographs by Andre Martin, Delpire, 1964.
Les Charmes (novel), Gallimard, 1965.
Histoire de la captivite de Francais en Allemagne, Gallimard, 1967.
Auto, Gallimard, 1967.
L'Or, Delpire, 1968.
Les Chimeres, Gallimard, 1969.
L'Arche, Gallimard, 1971.
Rimbaud et la commune, Gallimard, 1971.
La Chine et les chinois, photographs by Claude Arthaud and F. Herbert-Stevens, Arthaud, 1971.
Le Presage, Gallimard, 1972.
Quartier latin, Tableronde, 1973.
L'Homme et l'animal, A. Michel, 1974.
Les Sources, Gallimard, c. 1975.
Dans la foret humaine, Laffont, 1976.
Le Bal des ardents, Gallimard, 1977.
Sur les routes de France, Arthaud, 1978.
L'Ombre de Robespierre, Gallimard, 1979.
Un jardin de cure, Stock, 1979.
Les Secrets de Mattre Bernard, Gallimard, 1980.
Le Regne vegetal, Gallimard, 1981.
Gerard de Nerval et son temps, Gallimard, 1982.
Buffon, Gallimard, 1983.
Le Fortin, Gallimard, 1983.
Le diablo a Paris, Gallimard, 1984.
Humboldt l'explorateur, Gallimard, 1985.
Du cote de chez M. Pasteur, Odile Jacob, 1986.
L'Ange gardieu, Plon, 1987.

Pour le dire avec des fleurs, Gallimard, 1988.
Montesquieu, Flammarion, 1989.
Portraits et souvenirs, Gallimard, 1991.

PLAYS

Le Pas perdus (based on the author's book of the same title), first produced in Paris at Theatre Fontaine, 1957.
Les Murs (teleplay), first broadcast on 1st Station, ORTF-TV, Paris, 1964.
La Nuit parle (teleplay), first broadcast on 2nd Station, ORTF-TV, 1969.

OTHER

Contributor to periodicals, including *Atlantic, Evergreen, Harper's, Le Figaro,* and *Mademoiselle.*

SIDELIGHTS: Pierre Fournier, known primarily by his *nom de plume* Pierre Gascar, was taken prisoner by the Nazis during World War II. Twice he escaped, but was recaptured and transported to a concentration camp in the Ukraine. The profound effect that this experience had on Gascar prompted him to express his feelings in writing.

In *Beasts and Men,* a collection of six short stories and one novelette, Gascar symbolizes man's inhumanity to man by exploring the relationship between man and animals. The book won Gascar the Prix Goncourt in France and also met with favorable reviews in the United States. A *New Yorker* critic noted, "Pierre Gascar's short stories in this collection, which all touch on accepted but extremely sinister relationships between men and animals, are exceptionally fine, both in their writing and in their observation. But it is the short novel, 'The Season of the Dead,' that marks him as a writer of the first rank."

As in "The Season of the Dead," the prisoner of war theme is present in *The Fugitive.* The protagonist Paul, like the author, has escaped from a German camp after having been captured during World War II. After the war he travels throughout Germany, in search of himself and a reason for being. Reviewers' opinions on the book conflicted. "The novel has moments of real visual power," observed a *Times Literary Supplement* critic, "but it is not well sustained and proves again that Pierre Gascar is much better when he sticks to shorter forms." Taking another stance, *Saturday Review* contributor H. F. Peters expressed his view that Gascar's "evocative style," which "illuminates every page, transforms the most commonplace events, and produces an almost Rembrandtesque effect of chiaroscuro—haunting half-tones, somber and sonorous, the twilight of a soul in travail."

Not all of Gascar's works deal with the same theme. *The Seed,* for instance, considered autobiographical by some critics, is written from the point of view of a small boy.

The sensitive, unloved ten-year-old, living with an aunt and uncle in southern France, finds he must display cunning in order to survive. To help support himself he searches through garbage heaps for discarded peach seeds, begs, and builds a dam to trap fish, filching needed materials. The chance of rescue from such a stark existence arrives in the form of a scholarship. Anthony West, writing in the *New Yorker,* comments that it "is beyond question one of those imaginative and truthful novels that are destined to survive and be recognized as literature of value for a long time to come."

Gascar once told *CA* that he considers himself a literary *touche-a-tout,* or jack-of-all-trades. He has not only penned fictional works, but has also covered such diverse topics as politics, sociology, botany, ecology, animal psychology, history, and art in his writings. He groups himself with the romantic-age writers who, considering themselves educators, were well-versed in a variety of subjects. Voltaire could speak as well of the history of religion as of Newton's theories or the nature of fire, Gascar pointed out. And Jean Jacques Rousseau was able to write on botany, music, and the education of children. Gascar concluded that, as long as he can view each new topic with wonder, there is still a place for the jack-of-all-trades writer.

BIOGRAPHICAL/CRITICAL SOURCES:

BOOKS

Contemporary Literary Criticism, Volume 11, Gale, 1979.

PERIODICALS

Books Abroad, spring, 1965.
Book Week, March 12, 1967.
Christian Science Monitor, April 8, 1965.
New Yorker, June 30, 1956; July 18, 1959.
New York Times, May 31, 1959.
New York Times Book Review, April 9, 1961; February 19, 1967.
Saturday Review, April 11, 1964; March 13, 1965.
Times Literary Supplement, February 20, 1964; November 23, 1979; October 16, 1981.

*   *   *

FOX, Robert J. 1927-

PERSONAL: Born December 24, 1927, in Watertown, SD; son of Aloysius John (a farmer) and Susie Emma (Lorentz) Fox. *Education:* Attended St. John's University, 1947-50; St. Paul Seminary, B.A., 1955.

ADDRESSES: *Home*—Box 158, Alexandria, SD 57311; (summers) Fatima, Portugal.

CAREER: Ordained Roman Catholic priest, 1955; pastor of churches in South Dakota, 1961-72; St. Bernard's Church, Redfield, SD, pastor, beginning 1972; St. Mary's Church, Alexandria, SD, pastor, 1985—. Fatima Family Apostolate and Youth for Fatima Pilgrimages, national spiritual director, 1976—.

WRITINGS:

Religious Education: Its Effects, Its Challenges Today, Daughters of St. Paul, 1972.
The Catholic Prayerbook, Our Sunday Visitor, 1974.
Renewal for All God's People, Our Sunday Visitor, 1975.
Charity, Morality, Sex and Young People, Our Sunday Visitor, 1975.
The Marian Catechism, Our Sunday Visitor, 1976.
Saints and Heroes Speak, Our Sunday Visitor, 1977.
A Prayer Book for Young Catholics, Our Sunday Visitor, 1977.
Catholic Truth for Youth, Ave Maria Press, 1978.
A World at Prayer, Our Sunday Visitor, 1979.
A Catechism of the Catholic Church: Two Thousand Years of Faith and Tradition, Franciscan Herald, 1980.
Rediscovering Fatima, Our Sunday Visitor, 1982.
The Call of Heaven: Life of Stigmatist of San Vittorino, Father Gino, Christendom Publications, 1982.
Fatima Today, Christendom Publications, 1983.
The Catholic Faith, Our Sunday Visitor, 1983.
The Work of the Holy Angels, AMI International, 1984.
Immaculate Heart of Mary: True Devotion, Our Sunday Visitor, 1986.
Guidance for Future Priests, Fatima Family Apostolate, 1988.
St. Joseph Promise, Fatima Family Apostolate, 1989.
Marian Manual, Fatima Family Apostolate, 1989.
To Russia with Love, Fatima Family Apostolate, 1989.
Mary's White League for Children, Fatima Family Apostolate, 1990.
Illustrated Rosary Meditations for Children, Fatima Family Apostolate, 1990.
Protestant Fundamentalism and Born Again Catholic, Fatima Family Apostolate, 1990.
Mary Book: Mother of Evangelism, Fatima Family Apostolate, 1991.
Catechism of Church History, Fatima Family Apostolate, 1991.
The World and Work of the Holy Angels, Fatima Family Apostolate, 1991.

Also author of *The Gift of Sexuality: Guidance for Young People,* Our Sunday Visitor; also author of numerous pamphlets, booklets, and cassette recordings, including a cassette album of 24 lessons, *Instructions in the Catholic Faith,* produced by Fatima Family Apostolate, 1986, and *Sharing the Faith,* also produced by Fatima Family Apostolate, available as a 26 1/2-hour television program on VHS videocassette. Contributor to periodicals, including *Our Sunday Visitor, Homiletic and Pastoral Review, Soul, Twin Circle,* and *Priest.* Editor, *Fatima Family Messenger;* contributing editor, *National Catholic Register.*

SIDELIGHTS: Robert J. Fox told *CA:* "I started writing for Catholic periodicals about 1962. Two pastors under whom I had worked as a young priest, being associate pastor to them, had suggested I had writing ability, and one said, 'You have ink in your blood,' [or something] to that effect. I did not believe it. But once when I wrote a long letter to a Catholic editor, and he rather published it as an article, I shortly thereafter began to believe perhaps the two pastors were wiser than I. It seemed everything I turned in to editors was accepted. Soon my parish became my pen and extended throughout the U.S.A. and beyond. For some years now when my parish phone rings it is more often a long-distance call than a local parish call. I've chosen to be pastor of a small rural parish for 'my parish the pen' has become too large.

"In my parish of St. Mary of Mercy in Alexandria, South Dakota, we have mid-America's Fatima Family Shrine. People stop here at the Shrine from throughout the U.S.A. Each June a National Marian Congress is held at the Shrine drawing many participants, who often outnumber the population of the town. In 1992 I conducted my 32nd 'Youth for Fatima' pilgrimage. When the newly appointed Archbishop of Moscow (Latin Rite) led the first pilgrimage of a religious nature to leave Russia since the revolution of 1917, I was asked to come to Fatima to show and explain to the Archbishop and his small pilgrimage group everything about Fatima, Portugal. To the small town of Alexandria, South Dakota, where I built mid-America's Fatima Family Shrine, there have come participants to our annual National Congress from Europe, including the Vatican. Edouard Cardinal Gagnon, Prefect of the Pontifical Council for the Family, came in 1989 to dedicate an extension of the Shrine and to endorse the Fatima Family Apostolate. In 1987 Bishop Albert Amaral of Leiria-Fatima came to dedicate the shrine and preside over the National Congress in the small town when thousands showed up in a rural community of hardly six hundred people."

*   *   *

FREED, Ray 1939-

PERSONAL: Born February 1, 1939, in Los Angeles, CA; son of Matthew James (a film producer) and Viola Beth (a homemaker; maiden name, Atwood) Freed; married twice; divorced; children: (second marriage) Phillip, Christopher. *Education:* Attended University of Hawaii.

ADDRESSES: Home—P.O. Box 2883, Kailua-Kona, HI 96745.

CAREER: Writer and editor, 1965—.

WRITINGS:

POETRY

Morgan's Choice, privately printed, 1968, 2nd edition, Dr. Generosity Press, 1969.
(Editor) *Dr. Generosity's Almanac: Seventeen Poets,* Dr. Generosity Press, 1970.
Sea Animal on Land, Dr. Generosity Press, 1970.
Necessary Lies, Street Press, 1975.
Shinnecock Bay, Street Press, 1977.
MOOM, Street Press, 1979.
Lilacs, Tamarack Editions, 1980.
(Editor with Jim Tyack) *On Good Ground: Poems and Photographs of Eastern Long Island* (anthology), Street Press, 1981.
(Editor) *Turtle Dance,* Oceanic Publishing, 1984.
Much Cry Little Wool: 71 Selected Poems, Street Press, 1990.
Hualalai, Street Press, 1992.

OTHER

(With Tyack) *spam* (dada collage), Blackhole School of Poethnics, 1981.

SIDELIGHTS: Ray Freed told *CA:* "I feel poetry is a precious undertaking, its audience small and diminishing. Its value to me is in the act of writing—a cleansing, a making by hand and mouth. I write because I enjoy it. Like a sculptor I chisel, pound, and knock in a delirium of destruction, discarding the irrelevant and hoping that what remains will be the poem, existing where it had not been before. The power is in the poem, not in the poet."

*　　*　　*

FRENCH, Fiona 1944-

PERSONAL: Born June 27, 1944, in Bath, Somerset, England; daughter of Robert Douglas (an engineer) and Mary G. (Black) French. *Education:* Croydon College of Art, Surrey, N.D.D., 1966. *Avocational interests:* Collecting "blue and white" china and old editions of children's books.

ADDRESSES: Home—50, The Street, Sustead, Norfolk NR11 8RX, England. *Agent*—Pat White, Rogers, Coleridge and White, 20 Powis Mews, London W11 1JN, England.

CAREER: Long Grove Psychiatric Hospital, Epsom, England, children's art therapy teacher, 1967-69; Wimble-

don School of Art, Wimbledon, England, design teacher, 1970-71; free-lance illustrator, 1974—. Assistant to the painter Bridget Riley, 1967-72; Leicester and Brighton polytechnics, design teacher, 1973-74.

AWARDS, HONORS: Children's Book Showcase award, 1973, for *Blue Bird;* Kate Greenaway commended book, Library Association, 1973, for *King Tree;* Kate Greenaway Medal, 1987, for *Snow White in New York.*

WRITINGS:

SELF-ILLUSTRATED

Jack of Hearts, Harcourt, 1970.
Huni, Oxford University Press, 1971.
The Blue Bird, Walck, 1972.
King Tree, Walck, 1973.
City of Gold, Walck, 1974.
Aio the Rainmaker, Oxford University Press (London), 1975, (New York), 1978.
Matteo, Oxford University Press (London), 1976, (New York), 1978.
Hunt the Thimble, Oxford University Press, 1978.
The Princess and the Musician, Evans, 1981.
(Reteller) *John Barleycorn,* Abelard-Schuman, 1982.
Future Story, Oxford University Press, 1983, Peter Bedrick, 1984.
Maid of the Wood, Oxford University Press, 1985.
Snow White in New York, Oxford University Press (Oxford), 1986, (New York), 1987.
The Song of the Nightingale, Blackie, 1987.
(Reteller) *Cinderella,* Oxford University Press (Oxford), 1987, (New York), 1988.
Rise & Shine, Little, Brown, 1989, published in England as *Rise, Shine!,* Methuen, 1989.
The Magic Vase, Oxford University Press, 1991.
Anancy and Mr. Dry-Bone, Little, Brown, 1991.
King of Another Country, Oxford University Press, 1992.

ILLUSTRATOR

Margaret Mayo, *The Book of Magical Birds,* Kaye & Ward, 1977.
(With Joanna Troughton) Richard Blythe, *Fabulous Beasts,* Macdonald Educational, 1977.
(With Kim Blundell and George Thompson) Carol Crowther, *Clowns and Clowning,* Macdonald Educational, 1978.
Oscar Wilde, *The Star Child* (abridged by Jennifer Westwood), Evans Brothers, 1979.
Josephine Karavasil, *Hidden Animals: Investigator's Notebook,* Dinosaur, 1982.
Jennifer Westwood, *Fat Cat,* Abelard-Schuman, 1984.
Westwood, *Going to Squintum's: A Foxy Folktale,* Blackie, 1985.

OTHER

Un-Fairy Tales, privately printed, 1966.

SIDELIGHTS: Fiona French is best-known for her ability to fuse mythical themes with colorful characters and settings. Many of her works, such as *City of Gold* and *The Blue Bird,* highlight various artistic periods; other French titles, like *Snow White in New York,* present classic tales in updated settings. Of her work, French once commented: "I am very influenced by outside material, I treat each book as a new venture, during which I discover information I never knew before. I do not start a book knowing what is on each page, from cover to cover, but keep other books around me so that I can . . . look into them and be informed about details."

BIOGRAPHICAL/CRITICAL SOURCES:

BOOKS

Twentieth–Century Children's Writers, 3rd edition, edited by Tracy Chevalier, St. James Press, 1989.

PERIODICALS

New York Times Book Review, October 22, 1989, p. 55.
Publishers Weekly, March 24, 1989, p. 67; November 30, 1990, p. 71.
School Library Journal, July, 1989, p. 64; March, 1990, p. 153.
Times Educational Supplement, June 9, 1989, p. B10; November 7, 1990, p. R4.

*　　*　　*

FUCHS, Daniel　1909-

PERSONAL: Born June 25, 1909, in New York, NY; son of Jacob (a newsstand owner) and Sara (Cohen) Fuchs; married Susan Chessen, 1932; children: Jacob, Thomas. *Education:* City College (now City College of the City University of New York), B.A., 1930.

ADDRESSES: Home—430 South Fuller Ave., Apt. 9-C, Los Angeles, CA 90036. *Agent*—Irving Paul Lazar Agency, 211 South Beverly Dr., Beverly Hills, CA 90212.

CAREER: Elementary teacher at public schools in New York City, 1930-37; scriptwriter in Hollywood, CA, 1937—. *Military service:* U.S. Navy.

AWARDS, HONORS: Academy Award for best original story, Academy of Motion Picture Arts and Sciences, 1956, for *Love Me or Leave Me,* and 1962; National Institute of Arts and Letters grant, 1962; National Jewish Book Award, 1980.

WRITINGS:

FICTION

Summer in Williamsburg (first in trilogy; also see below), Vanguard, 1934.
Homage to Blenholt (second in trilogy; also see below), Vanguard, 1936; republished as part of "Proletarian Literature Series," Omnigraphics, 1991.
Low Company (third in trilogy; also see below), Vanguard, 1937, published in England as *Neptune Beach,* Constable, 1937.
(With others) *Stories,* Farrar, Straus, 1956, published in England as *A Book of Stories,* Gollancz, 1957.
Three Novels: Summer in Williamsburg, Homage to Blenholt, and Low Company, Basic Books, 1961, published as *The Williamsburg Trilogy,* Avon, 1972.
West of the Rockies, Knopf, 1971.
The Apathetic Bookie Joint (short stories), Methuen, 1979.

SCREENPLAYS

(With Bertram Millhauser and Abem Finkel) *The Big Shot,* Warner Bros., 1942.
(With Peter Viertel) *The Hard Way,* Warner Bros., 1942.
Between Two Worlds, Warner Bros., 1944.
The Gangster, Allied Artists, 1947.
Hollow Triumph, Eagle Lion, 1948.
Criss Cross, Universal, 1949.
Panic in the Streets, Twentieth Century-Fox, 1950.
(With Richard Brooks) *Storm Warning,* Warner Bros., 1951.
(With D. M. Marshman) *Taxi,* Twentieth Century-Fox, 1952.
(With Willian Sackheim) *The Human Jungle,* Allied Artists, 1954.
(With Isobel Lennart) *Love Me or Leave Me,* Metro-Goldwyn-Mayer, 1955.
(With Franklin Coen) *Interlude,* Universal, 1957.
(With Sonya Levien and John Fante) *Jeanne Eagles,* Columbia, 1957.

Also author of *The Day the Bookies Wept,* with Bert Granet and George Jeske, 1939.

OTHER

Contributor of short stories to anthologies. Contributor of short stories and articles to magazines, including *Sports Illustrated, New Yorker, Esquire, Cinema Arts, Collier's, Redbook, Cosmopolitan, Commentary, Saturday Evening Post,* and *New Republic.*

SIDELIGHTS: Daniel Fuchs based his stories about the lives of Jewish immigrants on his own upbringing in Brooklyn. His first three novels are set in a Jewish slum, the Williamsburg section of Brooklyn, at the foot of the Williamsburg Bridge. "The Williamsburg of Fuchs's youth was ethnically mixed; later there would be a more substantial Jewish migration, but in 1914, the area was true melting-pot New York," Gabriel Miller wrote in *Dictionary of Literary Biography*. "Fuchs's own block was Jewish, but the neighborhood was parceled into sections, each with its own ethnic group. The children formed gangs, both for adventure and for protection." The author described his neighborhood in "Where Al Capone Grew Up," published in *New Republic* in 1931: "The district as I knew it in my boyhood was still comparatively free of serious crime. . . . At this stage rough-house was mainly semi-pastime in nature, providing a kind of sporting *gradus honorum* for all red-blooded youths. But boy gangsters grew up into men, the East Side influence was strong, and hooliganism became in one generation a business colorlessly operated by many of the very individuals for whom it had been a boyish sport."

In *Summer in Williamsburg*, Fuchs's first chronicle of the experiences of his youth, Philip Hayman "sets out at the suggestion of a neighbor to make 'a laboratory out of Williamsburg' and thus to discover clues to the meaning he seeks," Miller noted, adding that the book "is Fuchs's most ambitious novel, crowded with people and events, an endeavor to present life as he knew it in its entirety. If the book suffers from some of a first novel's excesses and an occasional loss of control, it is nonetheless remarkable for what it does accomplish." *Homage to Blenholt* follows Max Balkan through a series of get-rich-quick schemes and his admiration of Blenholt, the commissioner of sewers, whom he considers "a hero in this flat age." In the final work of the trilogy, *Low Company*, obsessive gambler Moe Karty finds himself involved with the city's seamiest characters in an ongoing attempt to borrow money. "Read in sequence, [Fuchs's] three Williamsburg novels are a testament of a writer's quest, a struggle for a design, a knowing, and, finally, a sad acknowledgment that the only answer to be found was in acceptance of the ironic dimensions, both comic and tragic, of human nature," Miller observed.

Although Fuchs was held in high esteem by many critics, his three novels on Jewish ghetto life were at first a commercial failure. Discouraged, Fuchs switched to screenwriting in the late 1930s. It was not until *Summer in Williamsburg*, *Homage to Blenholt*, and *Low Company* were reissued in a single volume in 1961 that Fuchs received widespread critical and commercial recognition. Reading the novels for a second time, Hollis Alpert observed in *Saturday Review*, "I was fearful that they might not hold up, but time has neither dimmed nor darkened them, and I suspect they are more readable and compelling today, if only because the problems are different now, and we can meet all of the author's wonderful people simply as people and not as representatives of a condition. They are fixed

now, the nice ones, the evil ones, the old, the young, as a wonderful tapestry of 'low life' captured with unsentimental warmth."

Fuchs found success as a screenwriter in Hollywood, earning an Academy Award for his original story for the 1955 film *Love Me or Leave Me*. Among his other projects was the adaptation of his *Low Company*, which was released as *The Gangster* in 1947. Fuchs also continued to write short stories and essays, many of which were published in the *New Yorker* and other periodicals. His experiences in California led to numerous short stories, including "Dream City or the Drugged Lake," written in 1937, and "A Hollywood Diary" in 1938, and later to longer works. Fuchs returned to writing novels in 1971 with *West of the Rockies*, in which a movie star's mental breakdown reunites her with a former lover. Set in Palm Springs and peopled with wealthy Hollywood types, the novel nonetheless bears some resemblance to Fuchs's early trilogy. "The people are still 'low company,' their lives morally bankrupt; they scurry about to avoid facing their inner emptiness and the wasteland around them," Miller remarked. That feeling appears again in the novella "Triplicate," in *The Apathetic Bookie Joint*. Miller found that "Triplicate" "captures the sense of liveliness and exuberance of the Hollywood social whirlwind, exhibiting the egoism of its people and also their eloquence and drive. More compelling, however, is the portrait of the loneliness behind the facade, the deep feeling of isolation suffered among individuals crowded together at a Hollywood party, talking but not communicating and unable to escape the solitude of their own beings."

"Fuchs' career has often been given as an example of the lack of appreciation and support a gifted writer gets in America," Robert Kirsch wrote in a *Los Angeles Times* review of *The Apathetic Bookie Joint*. While some reviewers have criticized Fuchs for his switch from novels to movies, "All the talk about Fuchs as a neglected writer, as one warped or ruined by Hollywood, is insupportable," Kirsch asserted. "He never does less than his best."

BIOGRAPHICAL/CRITICAL SOURCES:

BOOKS

Contemporary Authors Autobiography Series, Volume 5, Gale, 1987.
Contemporary Literary Criticism, Gale, Volume 8, 1978, Volume 22, 1982.
Dictionary of Literary Biography, Gale, Volume 9: *American Novelists, 1910-1945*, 1981, pp. 35-38, Volume 26: *American Screenwriters*, 1984, pp. 109-114, Volume 28: *Twentieth-Century American-Jewish Fiction Writers*, 1984, pp. 74-83.
Howe, Irving, *World of Our Fathers*, Harcourt, 1976, pp. 585, 590-593.

Miller, Gabriel, *Daniel Fuchs,* Twayne, 1979.
Updike, John, *Picked-Up Pieces,* Knopf, 1975.

PERIODICALS

Commentary, July 6, 1978, pp. 29-34.
Harper's, July, 1971.
Los Angeles Times, January 9, 1980.
Nation, February 27, 1937.
New Republic, September 9, 1931; April 1, 1936; February 24, 1937; May 15, 1971.
New Yorker, October 23, 1971.
New York Herald Tribune, February 14, 1937.
New York Review of Books, December 6, 1979, p. 10.
New York Times, November 18, 1934; September 10, 1961.
New York Times Book Review, June 13, 1971; July 18, 1971.
Partisan Review, number 1, 1974.
Saturday Review, September 23, 1961, pp. 17-18.
Times Literary Supplement, October 15, 1971; May 17, 1991, p. 7.

—*Sketch by Deborah A. Stanley*

*   *   *

FURBANK, P(hilip) N(icholas) 1920-

PERSONAL: Born May 23, 1920, in Cranleigh, Surrey, England; son of William Percival and Grace (Turner) Furbank. *Education:* Emmanuel College, Cambridge, M.A., 1947. *Politics:* Labour.

ADDRESSES: Home—12 Leverton St., London NW5 2PJ, England. *Agent*—Curtis Brown Ltd., 162-168 Regent St., London W1R 5TB, England.

CAREER: Cambridge University, Emmanuel College, Cambridge, England, fellow, 1947-53; Macmillan & Co. Ltd., London, England, editor, 1964-70; Cambridge University, King's College, fellow, 1970-72; Open University, Milton Keynes, England, lecturer, 1972-77, reader, beginning 1977, now professor emeritus.

WRITINGS:

Samuel Butler: 1835-1902, Cambridge University Press, 1948.
Italo Svevo: The Man and the Writer, Secker & Warburg, 1966, University of California Press, 1967.
Reflections of the Word "Image," Secker & Warburg, 1970.
E. M. Forster: A Life, two volumes, Secker & Warburg, 1977-78, Harcourt, 1978.
(Editor with Mary Lago) *Selected Letters of E. M. Forster,* two volumes, Harvard University Press, 1984-85.
Unholy Pleasure: The Idea of Social Class, Oxford University Press, 1985.

(Author of introduction) *The Notebooks of Samuel Butler,* Hogarth, 1985.
(With W. R. Owens) *The Canonisation of Daniel Defoe,* Yale University Press, 1988.
(Translator) Denis Diderot, *"This Is Not a Story," and Other Stories,* University of Missouri Press, 1991.
Diderot: A Critical Biography, Secker & Warburg, 1992.

Contributor to periodicals, including *Listener, Guardian, Observer,* and *Encounter.*

SIDELIGHTS: P. N. Furbank's biographies of literary figures have earned praise from many reviewers. In a *New York Times Book Review* critique of *Italo Svevo: The Man and the Writer,* John Simon notes both the inherent difficulties in the genre and Furbank's skill in overcoming them: "A critical biography is rarely a complete success: the author is usually more of a biographer or more of a critic, and leans heavily to one or the other side of the fence. P. N. Furbank's 'Italo Svevo: The Man and the Writer' is, however, very nearly perfect; its only failing, if failing it be, is that it strives so resolutely for brevity as to leave us, especially on the critical side, hungry for more."

Furbank's work on British novelist E. M. Forster—a two-volume biography, dedicated to Forster, and two volumes of his correspondence—presented special difficulties. Forster had led a sheltered life, one that provided seemingly scant material for biographers. He spent the last half of his life in residence at Cambridge University, where he met Furbank. The two enjoyed a twenty-three year friendship. Near the end of his life, the novelist asked Furbank to be his official biographer. In this capacity, Furbank had access to Forster's unpublished writings, private papers, and correspondence. "Much of the material concerned Forster's homosexuality, and his whole story could not have been told without it," reports Paul Gray in *Time* magazine. "He was one of the great English novelists of this century, but the foundations of his art have rested on a buried life."

"Forster's life doesn't offer a heartening display of weaknesses overcome, fears mastered or inhibitions shed. It is a history of outward tameness, sexual debility and hampered creativity," states Walter Clemons in *Newsweek;* he adds, "Facing these obstacles, P.N. Furbank has written one of the best biographies of a writer I've ever read." Michiko Kakutani also describes *E. M. Forster: A Life* as "a superb model of biographical art. Written in lovely, casual prose that Forster himself would have admired, the book [depicts] the author and his world with candor and affection." A *New Yorker* writer summarizes the book as "*the* life of Edward Morgan Forster."

BIOGRAPHICAL/CRITICAL SOURCES:

PERIODICALS

Antioch Review, spring, 1979.
Chicago Tribune Book World, November 12, 1978.
Globe and Mail (Toronto), January 14, 1984.
Nation, November 11, 1978; May 29, 1979.
Newsweek, October 30, 1978.
New Yorker, December 25, 1978.
New York Review of Books, May 4, 1967; October 12, 1978.
New York Times, December 22, 1978.
New York Times Book Review, April 9, 1967; January 8, 1984; May 5, 1985.
Spectator, August 6, 1977; March 25, 1978.
Time, November 6, 1978.
Times (London), December 29, 1983.
Times Literary Supplement, August 11, 1966; July 29, 1977; March 24, 1978; November 18, 1983; May 24, 1985; September 13, 1985.
Washington Post Book World, December 17, 1978; January 1, 1984; May 26, 1985.
World Literature Today, spring, 1979.

*　　*　　*

FURST, Lilian Renee 1931-

PERSONAL: Born June 30, 1931, in Vienna, Austria; came to the United States in 1971, naturalized citizen, 1976; daughter of Desider (a physician and dental surgeon) and Sarah (a physician and dental surgeon; maiden name, Neufeld) Furst. *Education:* Victoria University of Manchester, B.A., 1952; Cambridge University, Ph.D., 1957.

ADDRESSES: Home—106 Arbutus Pl., Chapel Hill, NC 27514. *Office*—Department of Comparative Literature, 342 Dey Hall, University of North Carolina, Chapel Hill, NC 27599-3150.

CAREER: Queen's University of Belfast, Belfast, Northern Ireland, assistant professor, 1955-59, associate professor of German, 1959-66; Victoria University of Manchester, Manchester, England, associate professor of comparative literature and head of department, 1966-71; Dartmouth College, Hanover, NH, visiting professor of comparative literature and German, 1971-72; University of Oregon, Eugene, professor of comparative literature and Romance languages and director of graduate program, 1972-75; University of Texas at Dallas, Richardson, professor of comparative literature, 1975-86; University of North Carolina, Chapel Hill, professor of comparative literature, 1986—. Research associate at Harvard University, 1974-75; Mather Visiting Professor of English and

Foreign Languages at Case Western Reserve University, 1978-79; visiting professor of German, Stanford University, 1981-82; visiting professor of comparative literature, Harvard University, 1983-84; Kenan Distinguished Professor in the Humanities, College of William and Mary, 1985-88.

MEMBER: International Comparative Literature Association, American Comparative Literature Association, Modern Language Association of America, Modern Humanities Research Association.

AWARDS, HONORS: American Council of Learned Societies fellow, 1974-75; Guggenheim fellow, 1982-83; Marta Sutton Weeks fellow, Stanford Humanities Center, 1982-83; National Humanities Center fellow, 1988-89.

WRITINGS:

Romanticism in Perspective, Humanities, 1969, 2nd edition, 1979.
Romanticism, Barnes & Noble, 1969, 2nd edition, 1976.
(With Peter N. Skrine) *Naturalism,* Barnes & Noble, 1971.
(Contributor) Ulrich E. Finke, editor, *French Nineteenth-Century Painting and Literature,* Manchester University Press, 1972.
(Editor with J. D. Wilson) *The Anti-Hero,* Georgia State University, 1976.
Counterparts: The Dynamics of Franco-German Literary Relationships, 1770-1895, Wayne State University Press, 1977.
The Contours of European Romanticism, Macmillan (England), 1979, University of Nebraska Press, 1980.
European Romanticism: Self-Definition, Methuen, 1980.
Fictions of Romantic Irony, Harvard University Press, 1984 (published in England as *Fictions of Romantic Irony in European Narrative, 1760-1857,* Macmillan, 1984).
"L'Assommoir": A Working Woman's Life, Twayne, 1990.
Through the Lens of the Reader, SUNY Press, 1992.
Disorderly Eaters: Texts in Self-Empowerment, Pennsylvania State University Press, 1992.
Realism, Longman, 1992.

WORK IN PROGRESS: "In literature and medicine."

SIDELIGHTS: Lilian Renee Furst once wrote: "I was born in Vienna of a Hungarian father and a Polish mother, grew up in England, and have chosen to work in the United States. I am bilingual in English and German and have a thorough knowledge of French, some Italian, and a little Hebrew. I am naturally committed to the comparative study of literature.

"I regard the study of European romanticism as a vital base for the understanding of modern literature and art. The romantic movement marks a decisive turning point in the history of Western civilization. The concepts elaborated by the romantics on the role of the artist, on the creative process, on the function of art, on freedom to experiment—all these are still of central relevance to our thinking and our experience today. The tragic-comic figure of the anti-hero, for instance, is a descendant of the romantic hero at odds with the world and ambivalent about himself."

Furst's *Fictions of Romantic Irony* sets the term "romantic irony" in its historical context, using such eighteenth- and nineteenth-century classics as *Pride and Prejudice, Tristram Shandy, Madame Bovary,* and Byron's poem *Don Juan* as examples. According to *Times Literary Supplement* reviewer Rosemary Ashton, Furst's study, "by juxtaposing very different works and exposing them to a not too rigidly held 'theory' of irony, yields refreshing insights into the individual works she deals with and . . . into the shifty phenomenon, irony itself."

BIOGRAPHICAL/CRITICAL SOURCES:

PERIODICALS

Times Literary Supplement, July 5, 1985.

G

GALE, Robert L(ee) 1919-

PERSONAL: Born December 27, 1919, in Des Moines, IA; son of Erie Lee (a sales manager) and Miriam (Fisher) Gale; married Maureen Dowd, November 18, 1944; children: John, James, Christine. *Education:* Dartmouth College, B.A., 1942; Columbia University, M.A., 1947, Ph.D., 1952.

ADDRESSES: Home—131 Techview Ter., Pittsburgh, PA 15213.

CAREER: University of Delaware, Newark, instructor, 1949-52; University of Mississippi, University, assistant professor, 1952-56, associate professor, 1956-59; University of Pittsburgh, Pittsburgh, PA, assistant professor of English, 1959-60, associate professor, 1960-65, professor of American literature, 1965-87. Fulbright professor at Oriental Institute, Naples, Italy, 1956-58, and University of Helsinki, 1975. *Military service:* U.S. Army, Counter Intelligence Corps, 1942-46; became second lieutenant.

MEMBER: Modern Language Association of America, Western Writers of America, Phi Beta Kappa.

WRITINGS:

The Caught Image: Figurative Language in the Fiction of Henry James, University of North Carolina Press, 1964.

Thomas Crawford, American Sculptor, University of Pittsburgh Press, 1964.

Barron's Simplified Approach to Thoreau's "Walden," Barron's, 1965.

Plots and Characters in the Fiction of Henry James, Archon, 1965.

Barron's Simplified Approach to Ralph Waldo Emerson and Transcendentalism, Barron's, 1966.

Barron's Simplified Approach to Crane's "The Red Badge of Courage," Barron's, 1966.

Barron's Simplified Approach to "The Grapes of Wrath" by John Steinbeck, Barron's, 1966.

A Critical Study Guide to James' "The American," Littlefield, 1966.

A Critical Study Guide to James' "The Ambassadors," Littlefield, 1967, published as *Pennant Key-Indexed Study Guide to Henry James' "The Ambassadors,"* Educational Research Associates and Bantam, 1967.

A Critical Study Guide to James' "The Turn of the Screw," Littlefield, 1968.

A Critical Study Guide to Dreiser's "Sister Carrie," Littlefield, 1968.

Plots and Characters in the Fiction and Sketches of Nathaniel Hawthorne, Archon, 1968.

Barron's Simplified Approach to Edgar Allan Poe, Barron's, 1969.

Plots and Characters in the Fiction and Narrative Poetry of Herman Melville, Archon, 1969.

Richard Henry Dana, Jr., Twayne, 1969.

Barron's Simplified Approach to Edith Wharton's "Ethan Frome," Barron's, 1969.

Plots and Characters in the Fiction and Poetry of Edgar Allan Poe, Archon, 1970.

Francis Parkman, Twayne, 1973.

Plots and Characters in the Works of Mark Twain, two volumes, Archon, 1973.

Charles Warren Stoddard, Boise State University, 1977.

John Hay, G. K. Hall, 1978.

Charles Marion Russell, Boise State University, 1979.

Luke Short, G. K. Hall, 1981.

Will Henry/Clay Fisher, Boise State University, 1982.

Will Henry/Clay Fisher (Henry W. Allen), G. K. Hall, 1984.

Louis L'Amour, G. K. Hall, 1985, revised edition, 1992.

A Henry James Encyclopedia, Greenwood Press, 1989.

Matt Braun, Boise State University, 1990.

A Nathaniel Hawthorne Encyclopedia, Greenwood Press, 1991.

The Gay Nineties: A Cultural Dictionary of the 1890s in the United States, Greenwood Press, 1992.

Editor of "Plots and Characters" series, Archon, 1976-81. Contributor to books, including *Eight American Authors,* edited by James Woodress, Norton, 1971; *Academic American Encyclopedia,* twenty volumes, Arete, 1980; and *Fifty Western Writers,* by Richard W. Etulain and Fred Erisman, Greenwood Press, 1982. Also contributor to *American Literary Scholarship: An Annual,* Duke University Press, 1970, 1977-85.

WORK IN PROGRESS: A Cultural Dictionary of the American 1850s.

SIDELIGHTS: Robert L. Gale told *CA:* "Given the current proliferation of recherche and—let us hope—ephemeral literary criticism, I believe that more basic and informative writing such as I conscientiously attempt will continue to be welcomed by mainstream readers."

*   *   *

GASCAR, Pierre
See FOURNIER, Pierre

*   *   *

GAY, Volney P(atrick) 1948-

PERSONAL: Born July 17, 1948, in Portland, OR; son of John (in sales) and Phyllis (in personnel; maiden name, Ormandy) Gay; married Barbara Bushnell, April 20, 1974; children: Elizabeth, Laura. *Education:* Reed College, B.A., 1970; University of Chicago, M.A., 1973, Ph.D., 1976; St. Louis Psychoanalytic Institute, postdoctoral study, 1983-90.

ADDRESSES: Office—Department of Religious Studies, Vanderbilt University, Nashville, TN 37235.

CAREER: Center for Religion and Psychotherapy, Chicago, IL, clinical coordinator and intake worker, 1973-75; McMaster University, Hamilton, Ontario, assistant professor of religious studies, 1975-79; Vanderbilt University, Nashville, TN, assistant professor, 1979-82, associate professor of religious studies, 1982-89, professor of religion and professor of psychiatry, 1989, professor of anthropology, 1990—; psychoanalyst in private practice.

MEMBER: International Psychoanalytic Association, American Academy of Religion, American Association of University Professors, American Psychological Association, American Psychoanalytic Association, Society for the Scientific Study of Religion, Tennessee Psychological Association, St. Louis Psychoanalytic Society.

AWARDS, HONORS: Woodrow Wilson fellow, 1971-72.

WRITINGS:

Freud on Ritual: Reconstruction and Critique, Scholars Press (Decatur, GA), 1979.

Reading Freud: Psychology, Neurosis, and Religion, Scholars Press, 1983.

Reading Jung: Science, Psychology, and Religion, Scholars Press, 1984.

Understanding the Occult: Fragmentation and Repair of the Self, Fortress, 1989.

Freud on Sublimation: Reconsiderations, State University of New York Press, 1992.

Contributor to periodicals, including *American Imago, Journal of the American Academy of Religion, Journal for the Scientific Study of Religion, Psychoanalytic Review, Studies in Religion,* and *Zygon.*

WORK IN PROGRESS: Two books, *The Personal Myth in Psychoanalysis* and *Atrocity Fantasy and Atrocity Allegations.*

SIDELIGHTS: Volney P. Gay told *CA:* "In the two books in progress I seek to extend the use of contemporary psychoanalytic discoveries, made in the clinical realm, to the analysis of cultural institutions, the first being mythology, the second being atrocity allegations used in war-time situations. In *The Personal Myth* book I show how interpretative methods used to dissect public myths can help us dissect the personal myth or personal narrative. In my study of atrocity fantasy I show that a sequence of atrocity fantasy, fear, allegation, and projection often prefigures the outbreak of actual atrocities.

"As a psychoanalyst I seek ways to help my patients increase their capacity to live with more freedom from primitive fears and their childhood monsters. As an author I try to write from this clinical perspective, a perspective made possible by my patients' courage. I find that Freud was essentially correct when he said that personal neuroses were 'like' cultural institutions, that religion, for example, often is a public form of obsessional neurosis. However, I do not share Freud's disdain for religion anymore than I disdain my patients' attempt to stay alive using neurotic mechanisms."

*   *   *

GHELDERODE, Michel de 1898-1962
(Babylas, Philostene Costenoble)

PERSONAL: Birth-given name, Ademar-Adolphe-Louis-Michel Martens; name legally changed in 1929; born

April 3, 1898, in Brussels, Belgium; died April 1, 1962, in Brussels, Belgium; son of Henri-Adolphe (a clerk at the general archives in Brussels) and Jeanne-Marie (Rans) Martens; married Jeanne-Francoise Gerard, 1924. *Education:* Attended Institut St-Louis in Belgium, 1910-14. *Religion:* Roman Catholic.

CAREER: Playwright, poet, and journalist. Teacher at the Institut Dupuich, 1921; Communal House of Schaerbeek, Brussels, Belgium, archives editor, 1923-39; principal playwright with Het Vlaamsche Volkstoneel ("Flemish Peoples' Theatre"), 1925-30; member of Renaissance de l'Occident (literary group), during 1920s; co-editor, *La Flandre Litteraire,* Ostend, Belgium, during 1920s; writer and narrator of *Choses et gens de chez nous* ("Our Own Things and People"), a folklore talk series on German radio during the Second World War; charged with collaboration at war's end; received pardon and revocation of charge in 1949; writer for *Journal de Bruges,* 1946-53. *Military service:* Served in the Belgian military, 1919.

AWARDS, HONORS: Belgian Society of Authors prize, 1945; Malpertuis Prize for drama, Belgian Royal Academy of French Language and Literature, 1951; twice awarded the Prix Triennial de Litterature; Prix Picard for Dramatic Literature; Prix Rubens; Prix de Concours aux Jeunes Compagnies Parisiennes; a commemorative plaque has been placed on the house in Brussels, Belgium, where Ghelderode was born.

WRITINGS:

PLAYS

La mort regarde a la fenetre, first produced, 1918.
Le repas des fauves, first produced, 1919.
Les vieillards (one-act), published in 1924.
Le mystere de la passion de Notre Seigneur Jesus-Christ, published in 1925; first produced in Brussels at the Theatre des Marionnettes de Toone, March 30, 1934.
La farce de la Mort qui faillit trepasser, first produced in Brussels at the Het Vlaamsche Volkstoneel, November 19, 1925; published in 1952.
Oude Piet, first produced in Antwerp at the Ouvriers de la Renaissance, 1925; published in 1925.
La mort du Docteur Faust (three-act), published in 1926; first produced in Paris at the Theatre Art et Action, January 27, 1928.
Venus (one-act), published in 1927.
Images de la vie de St. Francois d'Assise, first produced in Brussels at the Het Vlaamsche Volkstoneel, February 2, 1927; published in 1928.
Le miracle dans le fauborg (one-act), first produced in Brussels, 1928.
Barabbas (three-act), first produced in Brussels at the Het Vlaamsche Volkstoneel, March 21, 1928; published in 1932.

Escurial (one-act), published in 1928; first produced in Brussels at the Theatre Flamond, January 12, 1929.
Don Juan, ou Les amants chimeriques (three-act), published in 1928.
La transfiguration dans le cirque, published in 1928.
Christophe Colomb (dramatic fairy tale in three scenes), first produced in Paris at the Theatre Art et Action, October 25, 1929.
Un soir de pitie (one-act), published in 1929.
Le massacre des innocents, published in 1929.
La tentation de St. Antoine, published in 1929.
Fastes d'enfer (one-act), published in 1929; first produced in Paris at the Theatre de l'Atelier, July 11, 1949.
Pantagleize (three-act farce), first produced in Brussels at the Het Vlaamsche Volkstoneel, April 24, 1930; published in 1934.
Noyade des songes (plastic poem), published in 1930.
Duvelor, ou La farce de diable vieux, published in 1931.
De Zeren Hoofdzonden, published in 1931; first produced under title *Le sommeil de la Raison* in Oudenaarde, December 23, 1934; published under title *Le sommeil de la Raison* in 1967.
Piet Bouteille (one-act), first produced in Brussels at the Theatre Royal du Parc, April 2, 1931.
Trois acteurs, un drame (one-act), first produced in Brussels at the Theatre Royal du Parc, April 2, 1931.
De sterrendief, published in 1931; first produced in Brussels at the Het Vlaamse Volkstoneel, April 7, 1932.
La grande tentation de Saint Antoine (burlesque cantata), published in 1932; first produced in 1957.
Godelieve (mystery; 3 tableaux, a prologue, and an epilogue), first produced in Ostend, Belgium, 1932.
Le Chagrin d'Hamlet, published in 1933.
Arc-en-ciel (fairy tale), published in 1933.
Les femmes au tombeau (one-act), published in 1934.
Magie rouge (three-act), first produced in Brussels at the Estaminet Barcelone, April 30, 1934; published in 1935.
Masques ostendais (one-act pantomime), published in 1935.
Le menage de Caroline (one-act), published in 1935; first produced in Brussels at the Theatre de l'Exposition, October 26, 1935.
Adrian et Jusemina (one-act), published in 1935; first produced in Brussels at the Theatre Residence, January 19, 1952.
La balade du grand macabre; La grande kermesse (three-act farce), published in 1935; first produced in Paris at the Studio des Champs-Elysees, October 30, 1953.
Le vieux Soudard (cantata), first produced in 1935.
Les aveugles (one-act), published in 1936; first produced in Paris at the Theatre de Poche, July 5, 1956.
Le cavalier bizarre (one-act sketch), published in 1938.
Hop, Signor! (one-act drama), published in 1938.

La pie sur le gibet (one-act farce), published in 1938.

Sire Halewyn (drama in fourteen scenes), first produced in Brussels at the Theatre Communal, January 21, 1938; published in 1943.

Sortie de l'acteur (three-act), published in 1942.

Mademoiselle Jaire (mystery in four scenes), published in 1942.

La farce des tenebreux (three-act farce), published in 1942.

L'ecole des bouffons, published in 1942, French & European Publications, 1953.

D'un diable qui precha merveilles (three-act mystery for marionettes), published in 1942.

Le soleil se couche (drama in nine scenes), published in 1942; first produced in Brussels at the Theatre Royal Flamand, January 23, 1951.

Le club des menteurs (one-act), published in 1943.

Mes statues, Editions du Carrefour, 1943, reprinted, L. Musin, 1978.

Theatre, six volumes, Gallimard, 1950-82.

Le singulier trepas de Messire Ullenspigel, published in 1951.

La folie d'Hugo van der Goes, published in 1951.

Le perroquet de Charles-Quint, published in 1951.

Marie la miserable, first produced in Brussels before the Woluew-St.-Lambert Church, June 14, 1952.

La vie publique de Pantagleize (one-act), published in 1954.

Ghelderode: Seven Plays, Volume 1 (contains *Chronicles of Hell, Barabbas, The Women at the Tomb, Pantagleize, The Blind Men, Three Actors and Their Drama,* and *Lord Halewyn*), Hill & Wang, 1960.

The Blind Men: In the Country of the Blind, the One-Eyed Man Is King, translation by Samuel Draper, Apiary Press, 1961.

Ghelderode: Seven Plays, Volume 2, Boulevard, 1966.

The Strange Rider and Seven Other Plays, translation by S. Draper, [New York], 1967.

Ghelderode: The Siege of Ostend, The Actor Makes His Exit, [and] *Transfiguration in the Circus,* Host Publications, 1991.

Plays have also been translated into English and published in anthologies.

UNPUBLISHED AND UNPRODUCED PLAYS

Tetes de bois (title means "Blockheads").

(With Jean Barleig) *La petite fille aux mains de bois* (three-act fairy tale).

Celui qui vendait de la corde de pendu (three-act farce).

Atlantique (one-act melodrama).

La Couronne de fer-blanc (two-act farce with three tableaux).

La ronde de nuit (pseudodrama for marionettes).

La nuit de mai (drama for marionettes).

Piece anatomique (short play).

Le marchand de reliques (pseudodrama).

Casimir de l'Academie . . . (pseudodrama).

Paradis presque perdu (mystery).

Genealogie (pseudodrama).

Le siege d'Ostende (military farce).

RADIO PLAYS

Le cavalier bizarre, 1932.

Le coeur Revelateur, 1932.

Annibal, speaker futur, 1933.

Bureau ouvert de neuf a midi, 1933.

Plaisir d'amour, 1933.

La ronde des prisonniers, 1933.

Cinq mai 1835, 1934.

Payuel dans le beffroi, 1934.

Payuel champion, 1934.

Payuel laureat, 1934.

Payuel au paradis, 1934.

Payuel reporter, 1934.

L'Oiseau chocolat, 1937.

Comment l'empereur Charles devint voleur des chiens, 1939.

D'un fou qui se croyait empereur, 1939.

Scenes de la vie d'un boheme: Franz Schubert, 1941.

Il Fiammingo, 1942.

OTHER

La halte catholique, [Brussels], 1922, published as *Contes et dicts hors du temps,* [Brussels], 1975.

L'Histoire comique de keizer Karel telle que la perpetuerent jusqu'a nos jours les gens de Brabent et de Flandre, [Louvain], 1922.

L'Homme sous l'uniforme, [Brussels], 1923, reprinted, 1978.

La corne d'abondance (poetry), [Brussels], 1925.

Kwiebe-Kwiebus, [Brussels], 1926.

(Under pseudonym Philostene Costenoble) *Ixelles, mes amours* (poetry), [Ostend], 1928.

Chronique de Noel, [Bruges], 1934.

Sortileges, [Paris and Brussels], 1941, French & European Publications, 1966.

Choses et gens de chez nous, [Liege and Paris], 1943.

L'Hotel de ruescas, [Antwerp], 1943.

Mes statues, [Brussels], 1943, reprinted, 1978.

La Flandre est un songe, [Brussels], 1953.

Ultimes boutades (nonfiction), [Liege], 1965.

(With Jean Jacques Gailliard) *Jean-Jacques Gailliard dessine Bruxelles,* Duculot, 1978.

Also contributor of reviews to periodicals, sometimes under the pseudonym Babylas.

SIDELIGHTS: "I have an angel on my shoulder and a devil in my pocket," Michel de Ghelderode once commented. The dichotomies between good and evil, life and death, were a constant concern with the playwright. Raised by a mother with a fervent belief in both God and the Devil, (whom she claimed to have personally seen), Ghelderode heard supernatural tales from an early age. When he began to read, stories of the macabre and fantastic were his favorites. His plays present a grotesque, absurdist world where mankind lives in torment and confusion. This "carnival of vices" is the result of a world that has lost its faith. "Obsessed by a universe of dark forces in endless ferment," Aureliu Weiss explained in the *Tulane Drama Review,* "[Ghelderode] saw evil and damnation everywhere." His plays blend elements from marionette theatre, the Medieval festival, and religious mystery plays into a personal statement unlike any other in modern drama. "The theatre," Ghelderode once stated, "is an act of instinct and not reason." Critics often compare his work to that of such other Belgians as the painters Hieronymous Bosch and Peter Breughel and the playwright Maurice Maeterlinck.

Ghelderode began writing while a young man; his first efforts were short stories and poems. Because of chronic asthma, he left school early and for the rest of his life lived as an invalid. In 1916 he developed an interest in the marionette theatres of old Brussels, searching their records for lost or forgotten plays. Some of Ghelderode's plays are reportedly based on or inspired by old marionette dramas of the sixteenth century. In 1918 he was approached by a representative from a local group of avant-garde writers and artists who invited him to give a lecture. Ghelderode accepted, but stated that his lecture would have to deal with Edgar Allan Poe's work. To accompany the lecture, the arts group asked Ghelderode if he had an appropriate short play they could perform. Although he had never written a play before, Ghelderode said that, yes, he had a suitable play. He then quickly wrote one.

The resulting work was *Death Looks through the Window.* Years later, speaking to Samuel Draper in the *Tulane Drama Review,* Ghelderode admitted that the play was "lugubrious beyond belief. . . . The stage was plunged in darkness. Three candles were the only light. It was a frightening play in which all the characters were physically or morally defective, filled with blemishes. . . . The drama unfolded in a storm during which the church bells pealed forth, and wolves howled. Everything ended in hell and damnation. It was frightful, incoherent, macabre, and flamboyant. It was a smash hit, a howling success. . . . I had, without knowing it, applied all the theatrical ingredients."

By 1923, Ghelderode was working as the archives editor in Schaerbeek, a suburb of Brussels. His lifelong interest in old manuscripts was fostered by this position. During the 1920s Ghelderode also continued his theatrical efforts, writing puppet plays based on biblical stories. The plays

La mort du Docteur Faust and *Don Juan; ou, Les Amants chimeriques* followed. When audience reaction to these French language works was not enthusiastic, he turned to the Het Vlaamsche Volkstoneel ("Flemish People's Theatre"). The theatre was strongly nationalist and Ghelderode, too, expressed support for Flemish nationalism. (Some observers attributed the playwright's pronouncements to sheer opportunism. Whenever the producers lagged in bringing his work to the stage, Ghelderode's enthusiasm for Flemish nationalism noticeably waned. In later years, the playwright was to abruptly change his political stance on several occasions.) In 1925 Ghelderode became the principal playwright for the Het Vlaamsche Volkstoneel and the theatre produced a number of his early plays. During the 1920s he was also a member of the Renaissance de l'Occident, a literary group which published his plays either in their magazine or in separate booklets. Some plays written or published at this time were not produced until many years later. By the late 1920s Ghelderode's plays were also being produced in Paris and Rome.

1930 saw the production of Ghelderode's *La vie publique de Pantagleize.* Robert W. Corrigan, writing in his *The Theatre in Search of a Fix,* claimed that *Pantagleize* is "a play that transcends both history and nationality; it is of all times and places and hence will always strike audiences with its disturbing modernity." In this play, the fashion critic Pantagleize unwittingly sets off a revolution by uttering the code phrase "What a lovely day." The revolutionary turmoil, an eclipse of the sun, and Pantagleize's accidental takeover of the national treasury combine to cause a day of confusion and violence. At day's end, Pantagleize is put on trial for his part in the revolution. His jury, composed of mannequins, finds him guilty.

In a program note to the play, Ghelderode described Pantagleize as "unfit for anything except love, friendship, and ardor—a failure, therefore, in our utilitarian age, which pushes out onto the fringe everything that is unproductive, that does not pay dividends!" Corrigan sees Pantagleize as an Everyman character, one who wants to "avoid making . . . choices; he much prefers to live quietly and peacefully, the friend of all men, the enemy of none. And yet life as it is lived denies the possibility of such neutrality. Flesh-and-blood men are always partisan; living is the taking of sides. And the great insight of Ghelderode's play is that neutrality is, in fact, the taking of sides by default."

Pantagleize also presents Ghelderode's essentially religious vision, which sees the world, by its very nature, as hopelessly corrupt. Speaking of Ghelderode's world view, George E. Wellwarth explained in the *Tulane Drama Review:* "To Ghelderode life was the vehicle of sin—and sin, in the simple, straightforward (and therefore dramatic) popular thought of the Middle Ages, warped the body of the sinner. Almost all of Ghelderode's characters have some physical quirk to reflect the moral turmoil of their minds. Many of them appear to be in the grip of actual demonic possession. . . . The world is seen as a place where the Devil is in control and moral perversity reigns." Paul M. Levitt, writing in the *French Review,* saw Ghelderode's life-long interest in puppet theatre as another manifestation of this religious vision. "A devout Pauline Catholic," Levitt wrote, "Ghelderode sees man as the puppet and God as the puppet master. By employing the world-as-stage metaphor, Ghelderode is able vividly and dramatically to place man in the religious scheme of things: namely, at the end of a string drawn by the hand of God."

During the initial production of *Pantagleize* the actor playing the lead character grew ill and died, suffering a delirium in his final days in which he argued with characters he had played in several of Ghelderode's productions. The bizarre hallucinations of the dying man inspired Ghelderode to write *Sortie de l'acteur* ("Actor's Exit"), in which an actor grows ill and dies because of the morbid plays he has been performing.

This openness to the fantastic is often present in Ghelderode's plays. In *Le menage de Caroline* ("Caroline's Household"), for example, a group of mannequins used for target practice in a shooting gallery escape to seek revenge on those who have harmed them. In *Les aveugles* ("The Blind Men"), inspired by a Brueghel painting, three blind pilgrims refuse to believe a one-eyed man who tells them they are headed in the wrong direction. They end up falling into quicksand. *Mademoiselle Jaire* tells of a dead girl brought back to life by a sorcerer who is later crucified. The reanimated girl remains alive only until spring and the arrival of Lazarus who, covered with clumps of earth and mildew, bursts into flowers. Other Ghelderode plays feature the Devil, living corpses, masked revelers at carnival time, misers, lechers, angels, historical figures, and midgets.

Wellwarth quotes a stage direction from the play *Marie la Miserable* ("Marie the Miserable") to illustrate the essentially grotesque atmosphere of Ghelderode's theatre: "Enter an extraordinary procession to the sound of cacophonous music which is at the same time arhythmic and infinitely nostalgic—the music of some other, barbaric world, played upon baroque instruments. . . . This musical dragon (actually a camouflaged automobile with its headlights on containing a jazz band whose instruments have been altered to appear as if they did not belong to any particular period and whose Negro players have been disguised to look unreal) . . . pulls a ship, a sort of fourteenth century vessel—the Ship of Fools of the medieval moralists. . . . Several scrawny and spastic couples are dancing together in front of the ship with signs of mutual disgust, as if they were fighting a merciless combat: a sav-

age frolic, with the women's hair hanging down to their waists and flying round their rigid, sallow faces and the young men dressed in shrouds, their jaws bound shut with strips of cloth, dancing like robots to the hypnotic music. Their faces express disgust and dread, their dance shows the battle of the sexes. The middle of the ship is occupied by people wearing devil masks, pigs' snouts, animal muzzles, elephant trunks, asses' ears—a swarming menagerie, clucking, bellowing, whistling. . . ."

"The surface characteristics of Ghelderode's universe are dazzling," Jacques and June Guicharnaud wrote in *Modern French Theatre.* "In many of his plays masqueraders, grotesque figures, living corpses, gluttonous and lustful men and women frantically move about in a decor of purple shadows, full of strong smells, and throw violent, foul, or mysterious phrases at each other in highly colored language filled with Belgian idioms, archaisms, and shrieks. Even in the plays where the language is closest to modern French, the dialogue and long speeches are profuse and frenetic. There is no rest in Ghelderode's theatre; the shock is permanent. Everything is pushed toward a paroxysm of language and spectacle—a flamboyant theatre, based on Flemish culture, its legends, its humor, its puppets, and its painters, from Brueghel the elder to James Ensor. But in overstressing Ghelderode's Flemish background, so obvious in itself, one is in danger of losing sight of his works' deeper value and of seeing them only as an overwhelming display of folklore. A joyful or macabre kermis, his theatre uses the village fair, the mountebank's stage, overcrowded cabarets, and the swarming streets of the red-light districts as an image of man's condition. Thus the picturesque quality of this tumultuous world becomes more than just a curiosity: rather than set up a barrier of exoticism, it heightens the colors of man's everyday world."

The carnival atmosphere of Ghelderode's plays is derived from traditional Flemish street carnivals, masquerades, and the peasant revelries found in the paintings of Brueghel (Ghelderode sets several plays in what he termed "Brueghellande"). He also credited the Elizabethans and such Spanish playwrights as Lope de Vega and Calderon as sources of inspiration. Another powerful influence was the Medieval world and its exuberant festivals, omnipresent Church, brutality, and sensuality. "Among modern dramatists," Wellwarth noted in his *The Theater of Protest and Paradox: Developments in the Avant-Garde Drama,* "Michel de Ghelderode stands by himself. If we must have a classification for him, then he can most nearly be compared to that group of novelists who have concentrated on the creation of a fictional world of their own, a microcosm in which to reflect their view of human behavior in the world as a whole. . . . Ghelderode has created an enclosed world that reflects and comments upon the larger world outside. Ghelderode's world is medieval Flanders, and his view of the world can best be described as savagely grotesque."

"Darkness hovers over the stage in Michel de Ghelderode's theatre," wrote Bettina L. Knapp in *An Anthology of Modern Belgian Theatre: Maurice Maeterlinck, Fernand Crommelynck and Michel de Ghelderode.* "There is no cleansing process; no purification of the soul. [His plays] are permeated by a sinister and fetid climate. Few, if any, of Ghelderode's characters are endowed with vision; fewer still have the strength to battle for their ideas and to pave the way for inner evolution. Their feeble natures, unhealthy psyches, and the insalubrious conditions surrounding them, impede normal growth. Their world is black, but not the rich blackness which offers a full range of harmoniously blended nutrients. Ghelderode's mixtures breed ghouls and gnomes; they are monsters endowed with distorted souls. . . . Ghelderode's theatre is like so many tooled forms in a Goya engraving: his monsters turn and churn, disrupt and disorient, but never resolve the chaos in their hearts. Instead, each brings further deterioration, greater ruin and despair."

In a letter sent to George Hauger in 1960 and published in the *Tulane Drama Review,* Ghelderode claimed: "I am a free writer who is nowhere committed—no more to a religion or a philosophy than to a political or social party. I am an anarchist-aristocrat, if this paradox can have any meaning! A Christian, yes indeed." Despite his later disavowal of politics, Ghelderode welcomed the Nazi invasion of Belgium in 1940, hoping that the Nazis would appreciate his work. Anti-Semitic and hostile to democratic government, Ghelderode took the Nazis to be German comrades of the Flemish nationalists. During the occupation, he went on German radio to broadcast a series of talks on folklore subjects under the title *Choses et gens de chez nous* ("Our Own Things and People"). Charged with collaborating with the enemy at war's end, Ghelderode lost his job and citizenship. A series of judicial appeals finally won him a pardon and a revocation of the charges against him. In 1949, he was awarded a government pension and retired from play writing.

Ironically, the year he retired saw Ghelderode earn his first international acclaim. A Paris production of his play *Fastes d'enfer* ("Chronicles of Hell"), first written in 1929, caused such a scandal that the curtain was brought down on the show after four performances. The resulting publicity launched a series of other productions in Paris, Rome, Madrid, Copenhagen, Oslo, Krakow, Cairo, and throughout Eastern Europe. By the late 1950s, Ghelderode's plays were being produced in the United States as well.

What little is known of Ghelderode's life comes primarily from a series of radio interviews he did in 1951. These were published in 1956 as *Michel de Ghelderode: Les Entretiens d'Ostende.* In these interviews Ghelderode spoke of his early life, his career as a writer, and the ideas that had shaped his work. Having suffered from illness for much of his life, Ghelderode was by nature a solitary and somewhat reclusive man. In these interviews, however, he promoted himself as a hermit-like figure. Publicity photos taken at this time showed Ghelderode in a dark, macabre study decorated with mannequins and skulls. The study, set up in a photographer's studio, was specially rigged to give the impression that Ghelderode was eccentric and perhaps a little dangerous. Rumors soon spread in France that the playwright was a defrocked priest who practiced lycanthropy.

"The masks Ghelderode wore for the world," Samuel Draper wrote in the *Tulane Drama Review,* "were in many ways unfortunate because they alienated him from his contemporaries. His weird poses frightened many admirers away, denying them the happiness of knowing Ghelderode personally. That Ghelderode's art has a secure place in modern dramatic literature is almost universally agreed. That he was an affectionate, exemplary friend, a lovable man, that he possessed a droll sense of humor, incarnated hard work and literary discipline a la Voltaire and Balzac without being spoiled by worldly success, and that he was a pauper most of his life—all this is known only to a small group of friends."

Speaking of Ghelderode's international success in the late 1940s and early 1950s, Draper noted: "Many writers would have been tempted to come before their public playing a glamorous role, responding ceremoniously to the honors which had come so late. But Ghelderode only withdrew further into his own small universe, locking his huge sixteen-foot door to celebrity seekers, journalists, and the curious, refusing to appear on television or attend the theatre, fabricating those thousand stories which have emblazoned his all-too-infernal legend. He invented tales that he was the terror of his publishers, that he was a Don Juan who changed his women as often as he wrote a story, that he was rich but hoarded his money like Hieronymous in *Red Magic,* and most ironically of all, that he was indolent and wrote only occasionally when inspiration flashed across his brain." In reality, the playwright was on good terms with his publisher, had been faithful to his wife for some forty years, had a modest income, and wrote on a daily basis. Draper remembered a meeting with Ghelderode in which the playwright spoke of what he wanted in life. "I ask only some measure of understanding from my friends," Ghelderode told Draper. "They can give me the one thing any human being can offer another: understanding. To the remark, 'That is not much,' I reply, 'It is everything.' "

BIOGRAPHICAL/CRITICAL SOURCES:

BOOKS

An Anthology of Modern Belgian Theatre: Maurice Mae-terlinck, Fernand Crommelynck and Michel de Ghelderode, translated by Alba Amoia, Bettina L. Knapp, and Nadine Dormoy-Savage, Whitston, 1982.
Contemporary Literary Criticism, Gale, Volume 6, 1976, Volume 11, 1979.
Corrigan, Robert W., editor, *The Theatre in Search of a Fix,* Delacorte, 1973.
Francis, J., *Michel de Ghelderode: Dramaturge des pays de par-deca,* [Brussels], 1949.
Ganne, Gilbert, *Interviews impubliables,* A. Bonne (Paris), 1952, p. 255.
Grossvogel, David I., *The Self-Conscious Stage in Modern French Drama,* [New York], 1958.
Guicharnaud, Jacques and June Guicharnaud, *Modern French Theatre,* Yale University Press, 1967.
Iglesis, R. and A. Trutat, *Michel de Ghelderode: Les En-tretiens d'Ostende,* L'Arche (Paris), 1956.
Lepage, Albert, *Michel de Ghelderode,* Dutilleul (Paris), 1960.
Wellworth, George, *The Theatre of Protest and Paradox: Developments in the Avant-Garde Drama,* New York University Press, 1964.

PERIODICALS

Arts, October 26, 1951.
Atlantic, April, 1954, pp. 162-163.
Boston Globe, November 10, 1961.
Christian Science Monitor, November 10, 1961; March 25, 1963.
Commonweal, December 4, 1959, pp. 279-282; October 28, 1960, pp. 113-115; June 1, 1962, pp. 259-260.
Critic, February-March, 1961, p. 66.
Drama Critique, winter, 1965.
French Review, May, 1975, pp. 973-980.
Modern Drama, September, 1961, pp. 217-218.
New Statesman, November 16, 1957, p. 648.
New Yorker, May 19, 1962.
New York Herald Tribune, May 8, 1962.
New York Post, December 23, 1963.
New York Times, July 23, 1960; May 8, 1962.
New York Times Book Review, April 22, 1962.
Revue d'histoire du theatre, April-June, 1962, pp. 118-156.
Second Coming Magazine, January-February, 1961.
Les soirees d'Anvers, Number 4, 1962.
Theatre Arts, February, 1951, pp. 34-35; April, 1953, p. 83; August, 1962, pp. 28-56.
Tulane Drama Review, spring, 1959, pp. 19-30; fall, 1963, pp. 11-71.
Village Voice, December 5, 1963, p. 12.
Yale French Studies, Number 29, 1962, pp. 92-101.

OBITUARIES:

PERIODICALS

New York Herald Tribune, April 2, 1962.
New York Times, April 2, 1962.
Time, April 13, 1962, p. 92.*

*   *   *

GIFFORD, Barry (Colby) 1946-

PERSONAL: Born October 18, 1946, in Chicago, IL. *Education:* Attended University of Missouri, 1964-65; attended Cambridge University, 1966.

ADDRESSES: Office—c/o Curtis Brown Ltd., 10 Astor Place, New York, NY 10003.

CAREER: Poet, novelist, screenwriter, memoirist, essayist, biographer. Worked variously as a merchant seaman, musician, journalist, editor, and truck driver. *Military service:* Air Force Reserves, 1964-65.

AWARDS, HONORS: American Library Association Notable Book Award, 1978 and 1988; National Endowment for the Arts Fellowship for fiction, 1982; Maxwell Perkins Award, PEN, 1983; PEN Syndicated Fiction Award, 1985.

WRITINGS:

The Blood of the Parade (poetry), Silverthorne Press, 1967.
A Boy's Novel (short stories), Christopher's Books, 1973.
Kerouac's Town (essay), photographs by Marshall Clements, Capra, 1973.
Coyote Tantras (poetry), Christopher's Books, 1973.
Persimmons: Poems for Paintings, Shaman Drum Press, 1976.
The Boy You Have Always Loved (poetry), Talon Books, 1976.
(Translator) Francis Jammes, *Selected Poems of Francis Jammes,* Utah State University Press, 1976.
A Quinzaine in Return for a Portrait of Mary Sun (poetry), Workingmans Press, 1977.
Horse Hauling Timber out of Hokkaido Forest (poetry), Christopher's Books, 1978.
(With Lawrence Lee) *Jack's Book: An Oral Biography of Jack Kerouac,* St. Martin's, 1978.
Lives of the French Impressionist Painters (poetry), Donald S. Ellis, 1978.
Landscape with Traveler: The Pillow Book of Francis Reeves (novel), Dutton, 1980.
Port Tropique (novel), Black Lizard Books, 1980.
The Neighborhood of Baseball: A Personal History of the Chicago Cubs (memoir), Dutton, 1981.

Francis Goes to the Seashore (novella and short stories), St. Martin's, 1982.

(With Lee) *Saroyan: A Biography,* Harper, 1984.

An Unfortunate Woman (novel), Creative Arts Book Co., 1984.

Giotto's Circle (poetry), St. Andrews Press, 1987.

The Devil Thumbs a Ride (essays), Grove, 1988.

A Day at the Races, Atlantic Monthly Press, 1988.

Ghosts No Horse Can Carry: Collected Poems, 1967-1987, Creative Arts Book Co., 1989.

Wild at Heart: The Story of Sailor and Lula (novel; also see below), Grove Weidenfeld, 1990.

New Mysteries of Paris (short stories), Clark City Press, 1991.

Sailor's Holiday: The Wild Life of Sailor and Lula (four novellas), Random House, 1991, published with additional novella, Vintage/Random House, 1992.

A Good Man to Know: A Semi-Documentary Fictional Memoir, Clark City Press, 1992.

Night People (four novellas), Grove, 1992.

"Tricks" and "Blackout" (teleplays), *Hotel Room,* HBO, 1993.

Author's work has been translated into fifteen languages.

WORK IN PROGRESS: Arise and Walk, a novel.

ADAPTATIONS: Gifford served as a consultant to the film-adaptation of *Wild at Heart* by David Lynch, Goldwyn, 1990.

SIDELIGHTS: Novelist, poet, screenwriter, essayist, biographer, lyricist, memoirist, and author of short stories: Barry Gifford is a prolific author who has received critical acclaim in a wide variety of genres. He began his literary career as a poet and eventually turned to biography and novels; in addition, Gifford co-founded Black Lizard Books, publishers of *noir* fiction, where he served as editor until 1989. Responding to his technique of positing colorful, quirky characters—with names like "Perdita Durango" and "Fractious Carter"—inside unconventional formats, critics have praised Gifford's ability to draw heavily on the literary technique of other authors and yet successfully achieve unique works of literary art.

Language has held a fascination for Gifford since he was a young boy. "I grew up in Chicago where my father's friends were racketeers," Gifford told *CA.* "He ran an all-night drugstore on the corner of Chicago and Rush, and I would stay up late listening to their talk and dunking doughnuts with the organ grinder's monkey. Afternoons I spent watching show girls rehearse at the Club Alabam next door." His father died when Gifford was twelve years old, which made it necessary for both he and his mother to go to work. He still found time to indulge in his love of language. "I began to read everything," Gifford recalled, citing his major literary influences: "Jack London,

Jack Kerouac, B. Traven; later Pound, Emily Dickinson, Jean Rhys, Proust, and Flaubert."

As well as serving as one of Gifford's earliest literary influences, writer Jack Kerouac became the subject of what he and coauthor Lawrence Lee have termed an "oral biography." Based upon numerous interviews with those who knew Kerouac throughout his lifetime—major literati of the Beat Generation such as Allen Ginsberg, Gregory Corso, and William S. Burroughs as well as little known friends of the late author—*Jack's Book: An Oral Biography of Jack Kerouac* was admired by reviewers for the thoroughness of its scope. "First rate," comments Bruce Cook in his review of *Jack's Book* for *Saturday Review,* praising the authors's success in "imparting sufficient detail to evoke a sense of Kerouac the man without overburdening us with the kind of day-to-day minutiae that the general reader would just as soon do without."

Gifford's first novel-length work of fiction was *Landscape with Traveler: The Pillow Book of Francis Reeves.* Organized as a blend of essay and narrative, *Landscape* is "one remarkable man's account of a life dedicated to that most difficult of propositions, the pursuit of happiness," according to Jay Tolson in his review for the *Los Angeles Times Book Review.* "Self-acceptance might well be the central mystery of this short, resonant novel, the mystery of why some do and some do not possess it, the mystery of its acquisition and its preservation," Tolson continues, adding that Gifford "wisely avoids facile or fashionable explanations." Gifford went on to write two other novels, *Port Tropique* and *An Unfortunate Woman,* before publishing *Wild at Heart: The Story of Sailor and Lula* in 1990.

Gifford's fourth novel caught the eye of director David Lynch who adapted the book into the screenplay for his highly acclaimed motion picture of the same name. *Wild at Heart* won the Palme d'Or (grand prize) at the 1990 Cannes Film Festival, propelling Gifford's novel to bestseller status. A story of the flight of newly released ex-con Sailor Ripley and his girlfriend, Lula Fortune, from the scene of one of Sailor's brushes with crime, the novel is a collage of dialogue taking place on the road. Noting Gifford's indebtedness to such writers as Thomas McGuane and Barry Hannah, a reviewer for the *New Yorker* writes: "Although it seems to be a pastiche of these earlier chroniclers of the low-rent spree, [*Wild at Heart*] is a well-made and often funny entertainment that never oversteps the limits of its mannered homage." The broad range of characters that Gifford scatters along the roadside traveled by Sailor and Lula, with their twisted personalities and diverse backgrounds, provide him with ample opportunity to demonstrate his flair for capturing the flavor of Southern dialogue.

"Among the considerable charms of *Wild at Heart* were the meandering conversations conducted in a lilting Southern drawl you could almost cut with a knife," writes Catherine Texier in the *New York Times Book Review,* "and *Sailor's Holiday* is imbued with the same voice and charm, its snapshot chapters propelling the book in bursts of manic energy." A collection of four novellas, *Sailor's Holiday* draws the reader forward ten years in the life of Lula and her lover as Sailor once again emerges from prison, only to fall into surreal surroundings when the couple's young son is kidnapped. "The main difference between the two books is one of degree," adds Richard Gehr in *Washington Post Book World.* "Gifford has darkened the horizon and upped the body count in *Sailor's Holiday* as though egged on by Lynch's more threatening perspective." Gehr voices his praise for the surrealism with which Gifford imbues his vision: "Deranged killers . . . are no less a part of this world's natural order than the pelican that casually and without causing comment smashes into the roof of Sailor and Lula's moving car."

BIOGRAPHICAL/CRITICAL SOURCES:

PERIODICALS

Chicago Tribune Book World, June 14, 1981.
Los Angeles Times Book Review, October 24, 1982.
New Yorker, June 4, 1990, p. 103.
New York Times Book Review, January 18, 1981, p. 12; May 6, 1990, p. 22; April 14, 1991, p. 11; July 14, 1991, p. 20.
Publishers Weekly, August 17, 1992.
Saturday Review, August, 1978, p. 50.
Washington Post Book World, October 22, 1978; June 29, 1980; December 26, 1980; May 2, 1982; March 29, 1991, p. B3.

*   *   *

GLUCK, Louise (Elisabeth) 1943-

PERSONAL: Surname is pronounced *Glick;* born April 22, 1943, in New York, NY; daughter of Daniel (an executive) and Beatrice (Grosby) Gluck; married Charles Hertz (divorced); married John Dranow (a writer and vice-president of the New England Culinary Institute), 1977; children: Noah Benjamin. *Education:* Attended Sarah Lawrence College, 1962, and Columbia University, 1963-66, 1967-68.

ADDRESSES: Home—Creamery Rd., Plainfield, VT 05667. *Office*—Department of English, Williams College, Williamstown, MA 01267.

CAREER: Poet. Fine Arts Work Center, Provincetown, MA, visiting teacher, 1970; Goddard College, Plainfield,

VT, artist-in-residence, 1971-72, member of faculty, 1973-74; poet in residence, University of North Carolina, Greensboro, spring, 1973, and Writer's Community, 1979; visiting professor, University of Iowa, 1976-77, Columbia University, 1979, and University of California, Davis, 1983; Goddard College, member of faculty and member of board of M.F.A. Writing Program, 1976-80; University of Cincinnati, Cincinnati, OH, Ellison Professor of Poetry, spring, 1978; Warren Wilson College, Swannanoa, NC, member of faculty and member of board of M.F.A. Program for Writers, 1980-84; University of California, Berkeley, Holloway Lecturer, 1982; Williams College, Williamstown, MA, Scott Professor of Poetry, 1983, senior lecturer in English, part time, 1984—. Phi Beta Kappa Poet, Harvard University, 1990. Poetry panelist or poetry reader at conferences and foundations, including Mrs. Giles Whiting Foundation and P.E.N. Southwest Conference; judge of numerous poetry contests, including Discovery Contest.

MEMBER: P.E.N. (member of board, 1988—).

AWARDS, HONORS: Academy of American Poets Prize, Columbia University, 1967; Rockefeller Foundation grant in poetry, 1968-69; National Endowment for the Arts creative writing fellowships, 1969-70, 1979-80, 1988-89; Eunice Tietjens Memorial Prize, *Poetry* magazine, 1971; John Simon Guggenheim Memorial Fellowship in Poetry, 1975-76, 1987-88; Vermont Council for the Arts individual artist grant, 1978-79; American Academy and Institute of Arts and Letters Award in Literature, 1981; National Book Critics Circle Award for Poetry, 1985, for *The Triumph of Achilles;* Melville Cane Award, Poetry Society of America, 1985; Sara Teasdale Memorial Prize, Wellesley College, 1986; co-recipient of Bobbitt National Prize, 1992.

WRITINGS:

POETRY

Firstborn, New American Library, 1968.
The House on Marshland, Ecco Press, 1975.
The Garden, Antaeus Editions, 1976.
Descending Figure, Ecco Press, 1980.
The Triumph of Achilles, Ecco Press, 1985.
Ararat, Ecco Press, 1990.
The Wild Iris, Ecco Press, 1992.

Work represented in numerous anthologies, including *The New Yorker Book of Poems,* Viking, 1970; *New Voices in American Poetry,* Winthrop Publishing, 1973; and *The American Poetry Anthology,* Avon, 1975. Contributor to various periodicals, including *Antaeus, New Yorker, New Republic, Poetry, Salmagundi,* and *American Poetry Review.*

SIDELIGHTS: Considered by many critics to be one of America's more gifted and talented contemporary poets, Louise Gluck creates poetry that has been described as technically precise as well as sensitive, insightful, and gripping. In her work, Gluck freely shares her most intimate thoughts on such commonly shared human experiences as love, family, relationships, and death. "Gluck demands a reader's attention and commands his respect," states R. D. Spector in the *Saturday Review.*

From her first book of poetry, *Firstborn,* to her most recent work, Gluck has become internationally recognized as a very skilled, yet perceptive author who pulls the reader into her poetry and shares the poetic experience equally with her audience. Helen Vendler comments in her *New Republic* review of Gluck's second book, *The House on Marshland,* that "Gluck's cryptic narratives invite our participation: we must, according to the case, fill out the story, substitute ourselves for the fictive personages, invent a scenario from which the speaker can utter her lines, decode the import, 'solve' the allegory. Or such is our first impulse. Later, I think, . . . we read the poem, instead, as a truth complete within its own terms, reflecting some one of the innumerable configurations into which experience falls."

For admirers of Gluck's work, the poetry in books such as *Firstborn, The House on Marshland, The Garden, Descending Figure, The Triumph of Achilles, Ararat,* and *The Wild Iris* take readers on a journey to explore their deepest and most intimate feelings. "Gluck has a gift for getting the reader to imagine with her, drawing on the power of her audience to be amazed," observes Anna Wooten in the *American Poetry Review.* "She engages a 'spectator' in a way that few other poets can do." Stephen Dobyns maintains in the *New York Times Book Review* that "no American poet writes better than Louis Gluck, perhaps none can lead us so deeply into our own nature."

One reason reviewers cite for Gluck's seemingly unfailing ability to capture her reader's attention is her expertise at creating poetry that many people can understand, relate to, and experience so intensely and completely. Gluck's poetic voice is uniquely distinctive and her language is deceptively straightforward. In her review of Gluck's *The Triumph of Achilles* Wendy Lesser notes in the *Washington Post Book World* that " 'Direct' is the operative word here: Gluck's language is staunchly straightforward, remarkably close to the diction of ordinary speech. Yet her careful selection for rhythm and repetition, and the specificity of even her idiomatically vague phrases, give her poems a weight that is far from colloquial." Lesser goes on to remark that "the strength of that voice derives in large part from its self-centeredness—literally, for the words in Gluck's poems seem to come directly from the center of herself."

Because Gluck writes so effectively about disappointment, rejection, loss, and isolation, reviewers frequently refer to her poetry as "bleak" or "dark." For example, Deno Trakas observes in the *Dictionary of Literary Biography* that "Gluck's poetry has few themes and few moods. Whether she is writing autobiographically or assuming a persona, at the center of every poem is an 'I' who is isolated from family, or bitter from rejected love, or disappointed with what life has to offer. Her world is bleak; however, it is depicted with a lyrical grace, and her poems are attractive if disturbing. . . . Gluck's poetry, despite flaws, is remarkable for its consistently high quality."

Writing on the somber nature of Gluck's recurring themes in *Nation,* Don Bogen admits that Gluck's "basic concerns—betrayal, mortality, love and the sense of loss that accompanies it—are serious. She is at heart the poet of a fallen world. . . . Gluck's work to define that mortal part shows dignity and sober compassion." Bogen elaborates further: "Fierce yet coolly intelligent, Gluck's poem disturbs not because it is idiosyncratic but because it defines something we feel yet rarely acknowledge; it strips off a veil. Gluck has never been content to stop at the surfaces of things. Among the well-mannered forms, nostalgia and blurred resolutions of today's verse, the relentless clarity of her work stand out."

Readers and reviewers have also marvelled at Gluck's custom of creating poetry with a dreamlike quality that at the same time deals with the realities of passionate and emotional subjects. Holly Prado declares in a *Los Angeles Times Book Review* piece on Gluck's fifth book, *The Triumph of Achilles,* "Gluck's poems succeed because she has an unmistakable voice that resonates and brings into our contemporary world the old notion that poetry and the visionary are intertwined." Prado continues to reflect: "The tone of her work is eerie, philosophical, questioning. Her poems aren't simply mystical ramblings. Far from it. They're sternly well-crafted pieces. But they carry the voice of a poet who sees, within herself, beyond the ordinary and is able to offer powerful insights, insights not to be quickly interpreted."

"Gluck's ear never fails her; she manages to be conversational and lyrical at the same time, a considerable achievement when so much contemporary poetry is lamentably prosaic," asserts Wooten in the *American Poetry Review.* "Her range is personal and mythical, and the particular genius of the volume rests in its fusion of both approaches, rescuing the poems from either narrow self-glorification or pedantic myopia."

Looking over Gluck's entire body of work, Dave Smith appraises her ability in a review of *Descending Figure* published in the *American Poetry Review:* "There are poets senior to Louise Gluck who have done some better work and there are poets of her generation who have done more work. But who is writing consistently better with each book? Who is writing consistently so well at her age? Perhaps it is only my own hunger that wants her to write more, that hopes for the breakthrough poems I do not think she has yet given us. She has the chance as few ever do to become a major poet and no one can talk about contemporary American poetry without speaking of Louise Gluck's accomplishment."

BIOGRAPHICAL/CRITICAL SOURCES:

BOOKS

Contemporary Literary Criticism, Gale, Volume 7, 1977, pp. 118-120, Volume 22, 1982, pp. 173-178, Volume 44, 1987, pp. 214-224.
Directory of Literary Biography, Volume 5: *American Poets since World War II,* Gale, 1980, pp. 290-295.

PERIODICALS

American Poetry Review, July/August, 1975, pp. 5-6; January/February, 1982, pp. 36-46; September/October, 1982, pp. 37-46; November/December, 1986, pp. 33-36.
Belles Lettres, November/December, 1986, pp. 6, 14; spring, 1991, p. 38.
Georgia Review, winter, 1985, pp. 849-863.
Library Journal, September 15, 1985, p. 84; July, 1990, p. 17.
Los Angeles Times Book Review, February 23, 1986, p. 10.
Nation, January 18, 1986, pp. 53-54; April 15, 1991, p. 490.
New Letters, spring, 1987, pp. 3-4.
New Republic, June 17, 1978, pp. 34-37.
New York Review of Books, October 23, 1986, p. 47.
New York Times Book Review, April 6, 1975, pp. 37-38; December 22, 1985, pp. 22-23; September 2, 1990, p. 5.
Poetry, April, 1986, pp. 42-44.
Publishers Weekly, May 11, 1992, p. 58.
Saturday Review, March 15, 1969, p. 33.
Washington Post Book World, February 2, 1986, p. 11.

—*Sketch by Margaret Mazurkiewicz*

*   *   *

GLUECK, Louise
   See GLUCK, Louise

*   *   *

GOLDBARTH, Albert   1948-

PERSONAL: Born January 31, 1948, in Chicago, IL; son of Irving (a life underwriter) and Fannie (a secretary;

maiden name, Seligman) Goldbarth. *Education:* University of Illinois, Chicago Circle, B.A., 1969; University of Iowa, M.F.A., 1971; University of Utah, graduate study, 1973-74. *Religion:* "Non-observant Jew."

ADDRESSES: Office—Department of English, University of Texas, Austin, TX 78712.

CAREER: Elgin Community College, Elgin, IL, instructor in English, 1971-72; Central YMCA Community College, instructor, 1971-73; University of Utah, Salt Lake City, instructor in creative writing, 1973-74; Cornell University, Ithaca, NY, visiting assistant professor of creative writing, 1974-76; Syracuse University, Syracuse, NY, writer-in-residence, 1976; University of Texas at Austin, Austin, professor of creative writing, 1977—. Co-director of Illinois Arts Council Traveling Writers Workshop, 1971-72; member of advisory panel to literature committee on National Endowment for the Arts.

AWARDS, HONORS: Theodore Roethke Prize, *Poetry Northwest,* 1972; first prize in poetry, *Northwest Review,* 1973; annual poetry awards, *Ark River Review,* 1973, 1975; National Endowment for the Arts creative writing fellow, 1974, 1979; creative writing award, Illinois Arts Council, 1974; National Book Award in Poetry nomination, 1975; Texas Institute of Letters Poetry Award, 1980.

WRITINGS:

POETRY

Under Cover, Best Cellar Press, 1973.
Coprolites, New Rivers Press, 1974.
Opticks: A Poem in Seven Sections, Seven Woods Press, 1974.
Jan. 31, Doubleday, 1974.
Keeping, Ithaca House, 1975.
Comings Back: A Sequence of Poems, Doubleday, 1976.
A Year of Happy, North Carolina Review Press, 1976.
Curve: Overlapping Narratives, New Rivers Press, 1976.
Different Fleshes, Hobart & William Smith Colleges Press, 1979.
(Editor) *Every Pleasure: The "Seneca Review" Long Poem Anthology,* Seneca Review Press, 1979.
Ink Blood Semen, Bits Press, 1980.
The Smuggler's Handbook, Chowder Chapbooks, 1980.
Eurekas, St. Luke's Press, 1981.
Who Gathered and Whispered behind Me, L'Epervier Press, 1981.
Original Light: New and Selected Poems 1973-1983, Ontario Review Press, 1983.
Arts and Sciences, Ontario Review Press, 1986.
Popular Culture, Ohio State University Press, 1990.
Heaven and Earth: A Cosmology, University of Georgia Press, 1991.

OTHER

Albert's Horoscope Almanac (limited edition), Bieler Press, 1986.
A Sympathy of Souls: Essays, Coffee House Press, 1990.

WORK IN PROGRESS: Several long poems.

SIDELIGHTS: Albert Goldbarth's poetry, which is acclaimed for its circuitous form and linguistic energy, covers everything from historical and scientific concerns to private and ordinary matters. His collections are often filled with long poems which range in style—some are playful and conversational, while others are serious and intellectual. Goldbarth uses this style to present a mixture of complex ideas and detailed descriptions that are woven together with verbal play and are often juxtaposed with dissimilar objects and facts. Goldbarth "has that rare gift of seeing metaphor in almost any event, of discovering a poem in the most unlikely places," describes Robert Cording in *Carolina Quarterly,* adding: "Goldbarth's poems, often dazzling in the Donne-like way they yoke disparate conceits, and almost always fearlessly playful in their approach, can mask the reasons for their being written. It's too easy to forget that for all of Goldbarth's bravura, the poems' punch lies in the way they affect us: over and over they tenderly remind us of the conditions of our humanness."

Opticks: A Poem in Seven Sections, one of Goldbarth's early works, establishes the form that many of his later poems follow. A long poem using surreal techniques and interrelated images, *Opticks* "is simply delicious as a linguistic offering," maintains *Margins* contributor Dave Oliphant. The topics and places covered in the poem range far and wide—including the Illinois tollway, World War II, and Middle Age glass makers—and are used to create an array of dramatic monologues. Dave Smith, writing in *Midwest Quarterly,* asserts that Goldbarth's "poetic blitz overwhelms us with fresh images, thought, imaginative scope, but also—as wherever mass is the product—buries us with the unfinished detritus of a mind (and an ego) whose accelerator is frozen." Oliphant, however, concludes that "*Opticks* is a banquet so heaped with juicy treats that it proves Goldbarth's truly one of the most fertile imaginations going."

The main theme of Goldbarth's 1976 *Comings Back: A Sequence of Poems* is returns. And to set the tone, the book begins with a quote from A. A. Milne in which Christopher Robin implores Pooh to never forget him. "*Comings* back—not *goings* back—suggests an interesting perspective in which everything is seen from the original place, the original time," remarks Victor Contoski in *Prairie Schooner.* "Goldbarth speaks of the poet as a maker of lists, and in effect the entire book is a list of various comings back, often in surprising contexts." *Comings Back* is

thus full of dreams and anecdotes, as well as jokes, personal letters, and quotations from a wide variety of sources. While Lorrie Goldensohn, writing in *Parnassus: Poetry in Review,* finds that "all the poems feel the same in touch and tone," Contoski contends, "The book makes its impression as a whole in which all parts are closely and unexpectedly related."

The separate parts of *Different Fleshes,* published in 1979, are also closely related, tied together by the main character who fills them, Vander Clyde. Born in Round Rock, Texas, in 1897, Clyde later travels to Paris during the 1920s, where he becomes the world-famous female impersonator Barbette. The narrative follows his progression, and eventually travels back to Texas, focusing on the present city of Austin and its contemporary gay bars. Through the character of Vander Clyde/Barbette Goldbarth presents a circular structure of metamorphoses. "*Different Fleshes* is a work partly about the distance linking the past and present, more particularly about choices made which separate one sort of future from another," comments *American Poetry Review* contributor Michael King. The book "comes closest to recounting a historical narrative," he continues, "but in each of these works [Goldbarth] takes as much pleasure in pursuing a sheer wealth of suggestive tangents and backwaters in the material, merely because they are there. He has discovered them, and he makes the reader delight also in his discoveries."

Original Light: New and Selected Poems 1973-1983 presents a wide selection of poems that are arranged thematically into three sections. Diane Wakoski, writing in the *American Book Review,* sees the main theme of the book as "what seeing really is and what really seeing is. [Goldbarth] explores light as the source of everything and like many philosophers looks for the original light, the source of everything in paradox and the paradoxes of physics." Goldbarth's "personae include adolescent lovers, masochistic slaves, aphoristic fabulists, philosophical plumbers, and semi-literate students," describes Michael Simms in *Southwest Review.* "He fashions metaphors from the deductions of historians, theologians, and physicists, integrating their arguments into poems which remain, somehow, intensely personal and concrete." Continuing on to say that "Goldbarth offers his readers many gifts," Simms concludes: "His ability to see and to see again encourages us to observe the world more closely and to take courage from the small happenings of our profoundly ordinary lives."

In two of his more recent books of poetry, *Popular Culture* and *Heaven and Earth: A Cosmology,* Goldbarth explores the elements of pop culture and the physical and chemical aspects of love. *Popular Culture* is written from the point of view of a man whose father's recent death causes him to relive certain moments from his childhood; these memories include such aspects of pop culture as comic books, television and radio shows, music, and detective fiction. In *Popular Culture,* maintains Peggy Kaganoff in *Publishers Weekly,* Goldbarth "infuses the gewgaws of pop culture—from science fiction to rock 'n' roll—with fresh energy and wit." *Heaven and Earth* "involves a scientific reading of life, one that puts into perspective the chemical and physical . . . aspects of love, spirituality and aestheticism," relates Kaganoff in her review of this work. Outlining narratives about his father and his German relatives, Goldbarth examines the many ways humans seek to communicate in spite of the numerous obstacles thrown in the way. Goldbarth's "rage for language is virtually unequaled in contemporary American poetry," concludes *Library Journal* contributor Frank Allen.

In addition to his many volumes of poetry, Goldbarth has also written one volume of essays—*A Sympathy of Souls.* The eight essays included, which were written over a ten-year period, cover subjects similar to those that can be found in Goldbarth's poetry—history, science and autobiography. In *A Sympathy of Souls,* Goldbarth makes connections between seemingly unrelated topics (such as God and Mickey Mouse) "to show how the past intertwines with the present and the mundane contains the cosmic," observes Kaganoff in her review of the collection. She goes on to add that the selections are all relevant and related, each coming across as "strengthening rites of passage."

A critically well-received author, Goldbarth remains most noted for his poetry, with John Addiego in *Northwest Review* describing him as "the fleet master-chef-poet of a generation in sensory overload, offering a transcendental soul-food of language and vision to our sterile, spiritless fare." *New York Times Book Review* contributor Phillip Lopate similarly contends that Goldbarth's "poems are so complex and omnivorous that even when they don't quite succeed, you have to admire them. In a typical performance, he will juggle many different ideas and images, not only keeping them all in the air but establishing surprising connections among them that yield a large general meaning." Simms concludes: "Goldbarth's poems are ambitious, unpredictable, profound, and funny."

BIOGRAPHICAL/CRITICAL SOURCES:

BOOKS

Contemporary Literary Criticism, Gale, Volume 5, 1976, Volume 38, 1986.

PERIODICALS

American Book Review, March-April, 1982, p. 11; May-June, 1984, p. 8.
American Poetry Review, March-April, 1980, pp. 5-6.
Carolina Quarterly, winter, 1984, pp. 91-95.

Library Journal, November 1, 1989, p. 92; June 15, 1990, p. 113; March 1, 1991, p. 94.
Margins, December, 1974, pp. 37, 58.
Midwest Quarterly, winter, 1975, pp. 221-33.
New York Times Book Review, October 2, 1983, pp. 15, 30; January 4, 1987, pp. 22, 24.
Northwest Review, Volume 20, number 1, 1982, pp. 136-40.
Parnassus: Poetry in Review, spring-summer, 1979, pp. 124-40.
Poetry, April, 1978, pp. 31-52; November, 1984, pp. 103-05.
Prairie Schooner, winter, 1977-78, pp. 419-21.
Publishers Weekly, September 19, 1986, p. 139; October 6, 1989, p. 94; May 4, 1990, p. 65; February 22, 1991, p. 216.
Southwest Review, summer, 1984, pp. 344-46.*

—*Sketch by Susan M. Reicha*

*   *   *

GOLDFARB, Ronald L. 1933-

PERSONAL: Born October 16, 1933, in Jersey City, NJ; son of Robert S. and Aida Goldfarb; married Joanne Jacobs (an architect), June 9, 1957; children: Jody, Maximilian, Nicholas. *Education:* Syracuse University, A.B., 1954, LL.B., 1956; Yale University, LL.M., 1960, J.S.D., 1962.

ADDRESSES: Home—7312 Rippon Rd., Alexandria, VA 22307. *Office*—918 16th St. N.W., Washington, DC 20006.

CAREER: Admitted to practice before Bars of District of Columbia, New York, and California, and Bar of U.S. Supreme Court. American Jewish Congress, Committee on Law and Social Action, New York City, staff counsel, 1960-61; U.S. Department of Justice, Washington, DC, special prosecutor in Organized Crime and Racketeering Section, 1961-64; Twentieth Century Fund, New York City, research director, 1964-65; Ronald Goldfarb & Associates (law firm; previously Kurzman and Goldfarb, 1966-70, and Goldfarb, Singer and Austern, beginning 1970), Washington, DC, partner. General counsel or member of group legal services program for several writers' groups and media organizations.

Chairman of the board, The Writing Co., (and general counsel) MainStreet (television production company), and several not-for-profit organizations, including Law Science Council; U.S. District Court, District of Columbia, chairman of Special Review Committee, 1975-76; member of board of trustees, Syracuse University Library Associates, 1965-70; member of governing board, Common

Cause, 1975-78, American Jewish Committee, and National Alliance for Safer Cities. President, DC Citizens' Council for Criminal Justice, Inc., 1971-72; vice-president, Washington Service Bureau, 1966-79. Member of numerous presidential task forces and national commissions. Hosted award-winning bar association discussion program, *Devil's Advocate,* and series on leading lawyers of the twentieth century, both on public television. Consultant to numerous public and private institutions and organizations, including the Ford Foundation, Brookings Institution, National College of the State Judiciary, and President's Advisory Commission on Civil Disorders. *Military service:* U.S. Air Force, staff judge advocate, 1957-60. U.S. Air Force Reserve, 1960-64; became captain.

MEMBER: American Bar Association, American Trial Lawyers Association (member of faculty), Federal Bar Association, New York State Bar Association, California State Bar Association, Yale Law School Association (Washington, DC; president, 1974), Cosmos Club (Washington, DC).

AWARDS, HONORS: Prize for best work in field of constitutional law, Federal Bar Association, 1965-66, and award from New Jersey Education Association, 1966, both for *Ransom: A Critique of the American Bail System;* Woodrow Wilson fellow, 1974-80.

WRITINGS:

The Contempt Power, Columbia University Press, 1963.
Ransom: A Critique of the American Bail System, Harper, 1965.
(With Alfred Friendly) *Crime and Publicity: The Impact of News on the Administration of Justice,* Twentieth Century Fund, 1967.
(With Linda Singer) *After Conviction: A Review of the American Correction System,* Simon & Schuster, 1973.
Jails: The Ultimate Ghetto of the Criminal Justice System, Doubleday, 1975.
Migrant Farm Workers: A Caste of Despair, Iowa State University Press, 1981.
(With James Raymond) *Clear Understanding: A Guide to Legal Writing,* Random House, 1982.
(With Gail E. Ross) *The Writer's Lawyer,* Times Books, 1989.
Frame-Up: The Ratterman Case and Robert F. Kennedy's Crusade against Organized Crime, Grove Weidenfeld, 1993.

Contributor to books, including *How to Try a Criminal Case,* American Trial Lawyers Association, 1967; and *Conspiracy: The Harrisburg Trial and the Democratic Tradition,* Harper, 1973. Contributor to numerous periodicals, including *Syracuse Law Review, Washington University Law Quarterly, New York Times, Commonweal, New Republic, Michigan Law Review,* and *Washington Post.*

* * *

GOLDSMITH, Howard 1943-
(Dayle Courtney, Ward Smith)

PERSONAL: Born August 24, 1943, in New York, NY; son of Philip (a motion picture engineer) and Sophie (Feldman) Goldsmith. *Education:* City University of New York, B.A. (with honors), 1965; University of Michigan, M.A. (with honors), 1966. *Politics:* Independent.

ADDRESSES: Home—41-07 Bowne St., Flushing, NY 11355.

CAREER: Mental Hygiene Clinic, Detroit, MI, research psychologist, 1966-70; writer and editorial consultant, 1970—. Audiovisual writer for Encyclopaedia Britannica Educational Co. and other educational publishers, 1970—; Santillana Publishing Co., senior editor, 1982-84.

MEMBER: Science Fiction Writers of America, Poets and Writers, Society of Children's Book Writers and Illustrators, Phi Beta Kappa, Phi Kappa Phi, Psi Chi, Sigma Xi.

WRITINGS:

Turvy, the Backward Horse (picture book), Xerox Education Publications, 1973.
The Whispering Sea (novel), Bobbs-Merrill, 1976.
What Makes a Grumble Smile? (picture book), Garrard, 1977.
The Shadow and Other Strange Tales, Xerox Paperback Book Clubs, 1977.
Terror by Night and Other Strange Tales, Xerox Paperback Book Clubs, 1977.
(Editor with Roger Elwood) *Spine-Chillers,* Doubleday, 1978.
(With Wallace Eyre) *Sooner round the Corner* (novel), Hodder & Stoughton, 1979.
The Plastic Age, Educational Progress, 1979.
Invasion: 2200 A.D. (novel), Doubleday, 1979.
Toto the Timid Turtle (picture book), Human Sciences Press, 1980.
The Tooth Chicken, Thomas Nelson, 1982.
Mireille l'Abeille, Harlequin, 1982.
Ninon, Miss Vison, Harlequin, 1982.
Toufou le Hibou, Harlequin, 1982.
Fortou le Kangourou, Harlequin, 1982.
Plaf le Paresseux, Harlequin, 1982.
Welcome, Makoto!, Santillana, 1983.
Treasure Hunt, Santillana, 1983.
The Contest, Santillana, 1983.
Stormy Day Together, Santillana, 1983.
The Circle, Santillana, 1983.

The Square, Santillana, 1983.
Little Dog Lost, Santillana, 1983.
Maggie the Mink, Thomas Nelson, 1984.
Sammy the Sloth, Thomas Nelson, 1984.
Helpful Julio, Santillana, 1984.
The Secret of Success, Santillana, 1984.
A Day of Fun, Santillana, 1984.
Pedro's Puzzling Birthday, Santillana, 1984.
Rosa's Prank, Santillana, 1984.
The Rectangle, Santillana, 1984.
The Twiddle Twins' Haunted House, illustrated by Jack
    Kent, Caedmon, 1985.
Ollie the Owl, Thomas Nelson, 1985.
Kelly the Kangaroo, Thomas Nelson, 1985.
(Editor) *Junior Classics,* Grosset & Dunlap, 1989.
Die Frau aus dem Meer, Cora Verlag, 1990.
The Pig and the Witch, Golden Books, 1990.
Little Quack and Baby Duckling, Golden Books, 1991.

JUVENILE NOVELS; UNDER PSEUDONYM DAYLE COURTNEY

The Ivy Plot, Standard Publishing, 1981.
Three-Ring Inferno, Standard Publishing, 1982.
The Sinister Circle, Standard Publishing, 1983.
Shadow of Fear, Standard Publishing, 1983.

OTHER

Work represented in anthologies, including *Crisis,* edited
by Roger Elwood, Thomas Nelson, 1974; *More Science
Fiction Tales,* Rand McNally, 1974; *Horror Tales,* Rand
McNally, 1974; *Starstream: Adventures in Science Fiction,*
Western Publishing, 1976; *Future Corruption,* edited by
Elwood, Warner Paperback, 1976; *Adrift in Space,* Lerner
Publications, 1976; *Distant Worlds,* William Collins, 1980;
Incubo, Mondadori, 1980; *Expressways,* Economy Com-
pany, 1981; *Frontier Worlds,* William Collins, 1983; *Top
Horror,* Heyne, 1984; *Young Ghosts,* edited by Isaac Asi-
mov, Harper, 1985; *Hitler Victorious,* edited by Gregory
Benford and Martin Greenberg, Garland Publishing,
1986; *The Further Adventures of Batman,* Bantam, 1989;
Visions of Fantasy, edited by Asimov, Doubleday, 1989;
Spooky Stories, volumes three and four, Thomas Nelson,
1990; and *Pegasus,* Kendall/Hunt, 1992.

Contributor to numerous adult and children's magazines,
including *Short Story International, London Mystery,
Scholastic, Outlook, Opinion, Child Life, Young World,
Saturday Evening Post, Highlights, Weekly Reader, Chil-
dren's Playmate, Supermag, Odyssey, Wings, World Over,
Void* (Australia), *Crux* (Australia), *Comet* (West Ger-
many), *Metagalaktika* (Hungary), *Urania* (Italy), *Quasar*
(Italy), *Horror Story* (Italy), *2 AM, Magic Window,* and
Disney Adventures.

WORK IN PROGRESS: A novel, picture books, and an
audio demonstration of short stories.

SIDELIGHTS: Howard Goldsmith told *CA:* "I have a
horror of boring the reader. We can all recall plodding
through acres of murky narrative and sunless prose. My
dread of tedium has, to a large extent, shaped my style and
guided my choice of subject matter. I write with sometimes jolting force, not to assault the reader's senses, but
to rouse him to a keener awareness. My plots emphasize
suspense and mystery that, I hope, compel attention and
intrigue the imagination. The challenge is greater in writing for young people, especially the growing numbers of
print-starved, picture-oriented non-readers and reluctant
readers.

"A controlled vocabulary is not necessary to hold a reluctant reader's attention. *High-Low Report* described my
novel *Invasion: 2200 A.D.* as a 'fast-paced adventure which
could appeal even to those adolescents who would rather
watch television space shows and movies than read a
book. . . . Although some of the vocabulary is rather sophisticated, the meaning is always clear through the context.' And a *Curriculum Review* contributor commented,
'This exciting story will serve as a good introduction to
science fiction and creative writing for middle graders.'

"A writer cannot expunge violence from the world or
from a realistic narrative, but this can be handled with
good taste. I was pleased that *Best Sellers* found that my
first mystery novel, *The Whispering Sea,* succeeded in this
respect. [Tony Siaulys of *Best Sellers* remarked:] 'This will
intrigue the younger reader. Without belaboring the grotesque and bizarre details too often found in recent offer-
ings of this type, *The Whispering Sea* has the elements of
a good scare, without gore.' "

Goldsmith continues: "On the lighter side, I sometimes indulge my bent for whimsy for the sheer pleasure of it, as
in my comic novel, *Sooner round the Corner.* It was especially gratifying to team up with the popular artist, Jack
Kent, on my picture book, *The Twiddle Twins' Haunted
House,* which was the last book the late Kent illustrated.
Jean F. Mercier of *Publishers Weekly* wrote: 'Here Kent's
droll drawings illustrate the story of a mystified hippo
family, exuberantly told by Goldsmith. . . . The denoue-
ment will come too soon for giggling readers when the
family solves the problem.'

"Nowhere is storytelling in its purest form more evident
than in literature for young people—often underrated,
deprecated, or ignored. Yet it is a craft, a discipline, and
an art form in every way as sophisticated and demanding
as adult fiction. And there is an intimacy of relationship
between reader and writer that is seldom equaled.

"I would only add that while the juvenile field is a sti-
mulating arena for the imagination, one also feels a need
to stretch and explore the full scope of a writer's experience. Hence many of my short stories have been written

for adult anthologies and magazines. A theme to which I'm often drawn (for example, in 'The Proust Syndrome') is the interpenetration of coactive strata of consciousness and time streams—the past ever present in associations refracted from childhood."

BIOGRAPHICAL/CRITICAL SOURCES:

PERIODICALS

Best Sellers, May, 1977.
Curriculum Review, September, 1980.
High-Low Report, November, 1979.
Publishers Weekly, November 22, 1985.

* * *

GOODMAN, Richard Merle   1932-1989

PERSONAL: Born July 31, 1932, in Cleveland, OH; died, 1989; son of Edwin and Florence (Grossman) Goodman; married Audrey Rosenberg, June 26, 1955; children: Jeff, Daniel, David. *Education:* University of Cincinnati, B.S., 1954; Ohio State University, M.D., 1958. *Avocational interests:* Israel archaeology, poetry.

ADDRESSES: Home—P.O. Box 1214, Ramat Hasharon, Israel.

CAREER: Cook County Hospital, Chicago, IL, intern, 1958-59, resident in medicine, 1959-61; Johns Hopkins University, Baltimore, MD, fellow in medicine, 1961-64; Ohio State University, Columbus, assistant professor of medicine and head of medical genetics, 1964-69; Tel Aviv University, Tel Aviv, Israel, professor of human genetics at Sheba Medical Center, 1970-89.

MEMBER: Israel Exploration Society.

AWARDS, HONORS: Batsheva de Rothschild Award, Rothschild Foundation, 1970; the Richard M. Goodman Fellowship in Jewish Genetic Diseases, awarded annually in his memory, was established by National Foundation for Jewish Genetic Diseases, Inc., New York City.

WRITINGS:

(With Robert J. Gorlin) *The Face in Genetic Disorders,* Mosby, 1970, 2nd edition published as *Atlas of the Face in Genetic Disorders,* 1977.
(Editor) *Genetic Disorders of Man,* Little, Brown, 1970.
Genetic Disorders among the Jewish People, Johns Hopkins University Press, 1979.
(Editor with Arnold G. Motulsky) *Genetic Disorders among Ashkenazi Jews,* Raven Press, 1979.
(With Gorlin) *The Malformed Infant and Child,* Oxford University Press, 1983.
(Editor) *Genodermatoses,* Lippincott, 1985.

Our Children along the Seashore, Maariv Book Guild, 1985.
Planning for a Healthy Baby: A Guide to Genetic and Environmental Risks, Oxford University Press, 1986.
Lines of Thought, Gefen, 1988.
Genetic Diversity among Jews, edited by Bonne-Tamir and Adam, Oxford University Press, 1992.
(With Roger E. Stevenson) *Encyclopedia of Human Malformations,* Oxford University Press, 1992.

Contributor to medicine journals. *Planning for a Healthy Baby: A Guide to Genetic and Environmental Risks* has been translated into Hebrew, Spanish, and German.

SIDELIGHTS: Richard Merle Goodman once told *CA,* "In order for man to maintain a proper perspective on man he must know what he does not know."*

[Sketch reviewed by wife, Audrey R. Goodman]

* * *

GOVIER, Katherine   1948-

PERSONAL: Surname is pronounced "Go-*vee*-ay"; born July 4, 1948, in Edmonton, Alberta, Canada; daughter of George Wheeler (an engineer) and Doris (a teacher; maiden name, Kemp) Govier; married John Honderich (a newspaper editor); children: Robin (son), Emily. *Education:* University of Alberta, B.A. (with first class honors), 1970; York University, M.A., 1972.

ADDRESSES: Agent—Lucinda Vardey Agency, 297 Seaton St., Toronto, Ontario, Canada, M5A 2T6.

CAREER: Ryerson Polytechnical Institute, Toronto, Ontario, instructor in English, 1973-75; free-lance writer, 1975—. Visiting lecturer in creative writing, York University, 1982-86; writer-in-residence, Parry Sound Public Library, 1988; writer-in-electronic-residence, 1988-91, coordinator of Writers-in-Electronic-Residence Program, Toronto, 1991—. Toronto Arts Awards literature jury, member, 1986, chair, 1991; chair of Writers' Development Trust, 1989-92; representative to board of governors of Canadian Conference of the Arts, 1989-90. Writer for Canadian Broadcasting Corp. (CBC) Radio and Television. Participated in TV-Ontario's *Academy on the Short Story;* speaks and reads work at schools, universities, and public libraries.

MEMBER: PEN International, Writers' Union of Canada (Ontario representative, 1987-88).

AWARDS, HONORS: Authors' Award, Periodical Distributors of Canada, and National Magazine Award, both 1979, for article "Radical Sheik" in *Canadian Business;* honorable mention in First Novel Competition, *Books in Canada,* 1979, and Author's Award—second place for best paperback of the year, Periodical Distributors of Canada, 1980, both for *Random Descent;* third prize, CBC Literary Contest, 1988, for short story "The Immaculate Conception Photo Gallery"; honorable mention for Talking Book of the Year, Canadian Institute for the Blind, 1991, for *Between Men;* Book Award, City of Toronto, 1992, for *Hearts of Flame.*

WRITINGS:

Random Descent (novel), Macmillan (Canada), 1979, New American Library, 1980.
Going through the Motions (novel), McClelland & Stewart, 1982, St. Martin's, 1983.
Fables of Brunswick Avenue (short stories), Penguin Books, 1985.
Between Men (novel), Viking, 1987.
Before and After (short stories), Viking, 1989.
Hearts of Flame (novel), Viking, 1991.

Also author of scripts of three stories from *Before and After* for radio dramatization for CBC *Morningside,* 1989. Contributor to *To See Ourselves,* Secretary of State (Canada), 1975. Contributor to anthologies, including *Canadian Short Stories: Fourth Series,* edited by Robert Weaver, Oxford University Press, 1985; *Celebrating Canadian Women,* edited by Greta Hofmann Nemiroff, Fitzhenry & Whiteside, 1989; and *Slow Hand,* edited by Michelle Slung, HarperCollins, 1992. Author of "Relationships," a monthly column in *Toronto Life,* 1975-77. Contributor to periodicals, including *Maclean's, Canadian Business, New Society, Canadian Forum, Cosmopolitan, Toronto Globe and Mail,* and *Quest.* Associate editor, *Weekend,* 1978.

WORK IN PROGRESS: A novel; short stories; a television script.

SIDELIGHTS: Katherine Govier told *CA:* "Each of my six books thus far has been rooted in a strongly recognizable place—whether it is Toronto's Brunswick Avenue, or, in *Between Men,* Calgary in the oil boom of the nineteen eighties with the historical murder of a Cree woman one hundred years earlier playing as a ghost-plot. But this isn't travel writing. My interest is entirely in character. The question is how the character is created and what events flow from a human personality. Now I'm writing a fictional biography; the main character has lived through most of this century and in many places."

About her position as coordinator of Toronto's writers-in-electronic-residence program, she explains that it "involves teaching students in creative writing in thirty high schools across Canada via telecommunications and modem."

BIOGRAPHICAL/CRITICAL SOURCES:

BOOKS

Contemporary Literary Criticism, Volume 51, Gale, 1989.

*   *   *

GOWANS, Alan   1923-

PERSONAL: Born November 30, 1923, in Toronto, Ontario, Canada; son of C. Allan and Ruth (Meek) Gowans; married Ruth L. Perry, 1948; children: Peter Alan, Jane Madeline, John Edward, Abigail Ruth. *Education:* University of Toronto, B.A., 1945, M.A., 1946; Princeton University, M.F.A., 1948, Ph.D., 1950. *Religion:* Episcopalian. *Avocational interests:* Photography.

ADDRESSES: Office—National Images of North American Living, 2020 F. St. N.W., #524, Washington, DC 20006-4218.

CAREER: Rutgers University, New Brunswick, NJ, 1948-53, began as instructor, became assistant professor; Middlebury College, Middlebury, VT, assistant professor, 1953-54; University of Vermont, Burlington, director of Fleming Museum, 1954-56; University of Delaware, Newark, associate professor, 1956-59, professor, 1959-66, chairman of department of art and art history, 1956-66; University of Victoria, Victoria, British Columbia, chairman of department of history in art, 1966-80, professor, 1980-88. President, Institute for the Study of Universal History, 1973-80. Visiting professor at Harvard University, 1972-73, University of Uppsala, 1978, Tufts University, 1988, and Syracuse University, 1989.

MEMBER: Society of Architectural Historians (director, 1958-61; national secretary, 1959; president, 1971-74).

WRITINGS:

Church Architecture in New France, Rutgers University Press, 1955.
Looking at Architecture in Canada, Oxford University Press, 1958, 2nd edition, revised and enlarged, 1966.
The Face of Toronto, Oxford University Press, 1960.
(Contributor) William Toye, editor, *A Book of Canada,* Collins (Glasgow), 1962.
(Contributor) R. Weaver, editor, *The First Five Years: A Selection from the Tamarack Review,* Oxford University Press (Toronto), 1962.
Images of American Living: Four Centuries of Architecture and Furniture in the United States, Lippincott, 1964.
Architecture in New Jersey, Van Nostrand, 1964.
The Restless Art: A Study of the Changing Function of Painting and Painters in Society, Lippincott, 1966.
The Unchanging Arts, Lippincott, 1970.

On Parallels in Universal History, University of Victoria, 1972.

(Contributor) *Modern Popular Arts,* Popular Press, 1981.

Prophetic Allegory: Popeye and the American Dream, American Life Foundation, 1982.

(Contributor) *Common Places: A Reader in Material Culture Studies,* University of Georgia Press, 1985.

The Comfortable House: Suburban Houses 1890-1930, MIT Press, 1986.

(Contributor) Egon Verheyen, editor, *Studies in the History of Art,* National Gallery of Art, 1986.

Styles and Types of North American Architecture: Social Function and Cultural Expression, HarperCollins, 1992.

"An Elevated State of Christian Civilization": Churches of the American Mission in Hawaii 1820-1863, Hawaii State Historic Preservation Office, 1992.

WORK IN PROGRESS: World Civilizations: A History in Architecture.

SIDELIGHTS: Alan Gowans once told *CA:* "The question is not what is art, but what is it that arts do, in and for society."

BIOGRAPHICAL/CRITICAL SOURCES:

PERIODICALS

Voice Literary Supplement, June, 1983.

* * *

GREENE, Jack P(hillip) 1931-

PERSONAL: Born August 12, 1931, in Lafayette, IN; son of Ralph B. (an agricultural engineer) and Nellie (Miller) Greene; married Sue Neuenswander, June 27, 1953; children: Megan, Granville. *Education:* University of North Carolina, A.B., 1951; Indiana University, M.A., 1952; graduate study at University of Nebraska, 1952-55, and University of Bristol, 1953-54; Duke University, Ph.D., 1956. *Politics:* Democratic. *Religion:* Protestant.

ADDRESSES: Home—Baltimore, MD. *Office*— Department of History, Johns Hopkins University, 34th and Charles Sts., Baltimore, MD 21218.

CAREER: Michigan State University, East Lansing, instructor in history, 1956-59; Western Reserve University (now Case Western Reserve University), Cleveland, OH, associate professor of history, 1959-65; University of Michigan, Ann Arbor, associate professor of history, 1965-66; Johns Hopkins University, Baltimore, professor of history, 1966-75, Andrew W. Mellon Professor of Humanities, 1975—, chairman of history department, 1970-72; University of California, Irvine, distinguished

professor, 1990-92. Visiting associate professor, Johns Hopkins University, 1964-65; Harmsworth Professor of American History, Oxford University, 1975-76; Fulbright Professor, Hebrew University of Jerusalem, 1979. Member of Institute for Advanced Study, 1970-71, and 1985-86. *Military service:* U.S. Army Reserve, Military Intelligence, 1956-63.

MEMBER: American Historical Association, Organization of American Historians, American Antiquarian Society, Royal Historical Society, Southern Historical Association, Association of Caribbean Historians, Massachusetts Historical Society, American Philosophical Society.

AWARDS, HONORS: Fellowships from Fulbright Foundation, United Kingdom, 1953-54, Guggenheim Foundation, 1964-65, Woodrow Wilson International Center for Scholars, 1974-75, and Center for Advanced Study in the Behavioral Sciences, 1979-80.

WRITINGS:

The Quest for Power: The Lower Houses of Assembly in the Southern Royal Colonies, 1689-1776, published for Institute of Early American History and Culture by University of North Carolina Press, 1963.

The Reappraisal of the American Revolution in Recent Historical Literature, Service Center for Teachers of History, 1967.

(Compiler with Edward C. Papenfuse, Jr.) *The American Colonies in the Eighteenth Century, 1689-1763,* Appleton, 1969.

The Nature of Colony Constitutions, University of South Carolina Press, 1970.

All Men Are Created Equal, Oxford University Press, 1976.

Peripheries and Center, University of Georgia Press, 1986.

Political Life in Eighteenth-Century Virginia, Colonial Williamsburg, 1986.

The Intellectual Heritage of the Constitution, Library Company of Philadelphia, 1986.

Pursuits of Happiness, University of North Carolina Press, 1988.

Imperatives, Behaviors, and Identities, University of Virginia Press, 1992.

Exceptionalism and Identity, University of North Carolina Press, 1993.

EDITOR

(And author of introduction) *The Diary of Colonel Landon Carter of Sabine Hall, 1752-1778,* two volumes, published for Virginia Historical Society by University Press of Virginia, 1965, revised introduction published separately as *Landon Carter: An Inquiry into the Personal Values and Social Imperatives of the*

Eighteenth-Century Virginia Gentry, University Press of Virginia, 1967.

Settlements to Society, 1584-1763, Norton, 1966.

Colonies to Nation, 1763-1789, Norton, 1967.

The Ambiguity of the American Revolution, Harper, 1968.

(And author of introduction) *The Reinterpretation of the American Revolution, 1763-1789,* Harper, 1968.

Great Britain and the American Colonies, 1606-1763, Harper, 1970.

(With Robert Forster, and author of introduction) *Preconditions of Revolution in Early Modern Europe,* Johns Hopkins University Press, 1970.

(With David W. Cohen) *Neither Slave nor Free: The Freedmen of African Descent in the Slave Societies of the New World,* Johns Hopkins University Press, 1972.

(And author of introduction) *The First Continental Congress: A Documentary History,* U.S. Government Printing Office, 1974.

(With Pauline Maier) *Interdisciplinary Studies of the American Revolution,* Sage Publications, 1976.

(With J. R. Pole, and author of introduction) *Colonial British America: Essays in the New History of the Early Modern Era,* Johns Hopkins University Press, 1984.

Encyclopedia of American Political History, Scribner, 1985.

(With E. Papenfuse and Charles F. Mallett, and author of introduction) *Magna Charta for America,* American Philosophical Society, 1986.

The American Revolution: Its Character and Limits, New York University Press, 1987.

(With John Cannon, R. H. C. Davis, and William Doyle) *The Blackwell Dictionary of Historians,* Basil Blackwell, 1988.

Selling a New World, University of South Carolina Press, 1989.

(With J. R. Pole) *The Blackwell Encyclopedia of the American Revolution,* Basil Blackwell, 1991.

OTHER

Also contributor of chapters to several books. Contributor to journals, including *Journal of Southern History, South Atlantic Quarterly, American Historical Review, Journal of Social History,* and *Political Science Quarterly.* Visiting editor, *William and Mary Quarterly,* 1961-62.

WORK IN PROGRESS: Paradise Defined: Studies in the Formation of Corporate Identity in Plantation America, 1650-1815; The Causal Pattern of the American Revolution.

GREGG, Charles T(hornton) 1927-

PERSONAL: Born July 27, 1927, in Billings, MT; son of Charles Thornton (a broker) and Gertrude (Hurst) Gregg; married Elizabeth Whitaker (an operating room nurse), December 20, 1957; children: Paul, Diane, Brian, Elaine. *Education:* Attended Reed College, 1948-50; Oregon State University, B.S., 1952, M.S., 1955, Ph.D., 1959. *Politics:* Liberal. *Religion:* Unitarian Universalist. *Avocational interests:* Reading, sailing, hiking, playing squash, long-distance biking.

ADDRESSES: Home—1060 Los Pueblos, Los Alamos, NM 87544. *Office*—901 Eighteenth St., Los Alamos, NM 87544.

CAREER: Oregon State University, Corvallis, instructor in agricultural chemistry, 1955-59; Johns Hopkins University, Baltimore, MD, research fellow in physiological chemistry, 1959-63; University of California, Los Alamos Scientific Laboratory, Los Alamos, NM, biochemist, 1963-85; Los Alamos Diagnostics, Los Alamos, vice president (research), 1986-1990; Innovative Surgical Technology, Los Alamos, president, 1991—. Bethco, Inc., president, 1972—; Free University of Berlin, visiting professor, 1973-74; Mesa Diagnostics, senior scientist, 1985-86. *Military service:* U.S. Navy, 1944-46; served in Pacific theater.

MEMBER: American Association for the Advancement of Science (fellow), American Society for Microbiology, Authors League of America, American Society of Biological Chemists (fellow), Authors Guild.

AWARDS, HONORS: U.S. Public Health Service fellow, 1959-63.

WRITINGS:

Plague!, Scribner, 1978.

A Virus of Love and Other Tales of Medical Detection, Scribner, 1983.

Tarawa, Stein & Day, 1984.

Contributor to books, including *Methods in Enzymology,* Volume 10: *Oxidation and Phosphorylation,* edited by Ronald W. Estabrook and Maynard E. Pullman, Academic Press, 1967; *Growth, Nutrition, and Metabolism of Cells in Culture,* Volume 1, edited by George H. Rothblat and Vincent J. Cristafalo, Academic Press, 1972; *The Biochemistry of Animal Development,* Volume 3: *Molecular Aspects of Animal Development,* edited by Rudolph Weber, Academic Press, 1975; *Physical Methods of Detecting Microorganisms,* edited by Wilfred H. Nelson, CRC Press, 1990. Contributor to *Proceedings* of the British Pharmacology Society Symposium on Stable Isotopes, 1978, and to *Proceedings* of the Third International Conference on Stable Isotopes. Contributor to scientific journals.

SIDELIGHTS: Drawing on his scientific background, Charles T. Gregg has produced numerous books and articles dealing with disease and science's ability to control it. *A Virus of Love and Other Tales of Medical Detection* concerns researchers' attempts to find the sources of various disorders, including birth defects, botulism, and Legionnaires' disease. *Los Angeles Times* book reviewer Carolyn See noted Gregg's detailed analysis of these topics and found the accounts to be "interesting reading."

Charles T. Gregg once told *CA:* "I considered myself a writer for a very long time before I had anything published. I wrote short stories, a two act play, magazine articles and queries, and half of a novel, and I accumulated a stack of rejection slips to attest to my status as a writer. I finally concluded that first I had to get a publisher's attention, and I could do that best by using my technical background to write on a subject that would be difficult for someone without my training (or the genius of Camus) to handle. It worked—hence the books *Plague!* and *A Virus of Love,* and the nonmedical book, *Tarawa.* I would sometime like to complete the novel that I turned away from some years ago when I lost control of it. Ideally, I would move back and forth between fiction and nonfiction, but it remains to be seen whether or not I can write salable fiction at all."

BIOGRAPHICAL/CRITICAL SOURCES:

PERIODICALS

Los Angeles Times, March 16, 1983.

* * *

GRIFFIN, David
　　See MAUGHAM, Robert Cecil Romer

* * *

GRIFFIN, W. E. B.
　　See BUTTERWORTH, W(illiam) E(dmund III)

* * *

GROVES, Naomi Jackson 1910-

PERSONAL: Given name is accented on first syllable; born July 21, 1910, in Montreal, Quebec, Canada; daughter of James Walton Groves (a mycologist), December 21, 1957 (died, 1970). *Education:* Attended Rannows Art School, Copenhagen, Denmark, 1928-29, and University of Heidelberg, 1932; Sir George Williams College, McGill University, B.A., 1933, M.A., 1935; additional study at University of Berlin, 1936, and University of Munich, 1937; Radcliffe College, A.M., 1938, Ph.D., 1950. *Religion:* "Anglican with Quaker leanings."

ADDRESSES: Home—2896 Highfield Crescent, Ottawa, Ontario, Canada K2B 6G5. *Office*—c/o National Gallery of Canada, 380 Sussex Dr., P.O. Box 427, Station A, Ottawa, Ontario, Canada K1N 9N4.

CAREER: McGill University, Montreal, Quebec, part-time lecturer in German, 1933-36; Wheaton College, Norton, MA, lecturer in German language and literature, 1940-42; National Gallery of Canada, Ottawa, assistant to director, 1942-43; Carleton College, Ottawa, Ontario, lecturer in German, 1943-45; relief worker in Finland and Germany for American Friends Service Committee, 1945-51; McMaster University, Hamilton, Ontario, assistant professor, 1951-56, associate professor in charge of fine arts, 1956-58; painter and writer, 1958—. Part-time lecturer at McGill University, 1951; past member of visiting committee at Harvard University. Art work exhibited in solo shows in Canada and the United States.

MEMBER: Canadian Artists Representation, Ernst Barlach Gesellschaft (member of board of directors), Phi Beta Kappa, Kappa Alpha Theta.

AWARDS, HONORS: Governor General's Gold Medal for Modern Languages, 1933; travel fellow of Canadian Federation of University Women, 1936-37; Bronze Medal from Finland's Red Cross, 1947; D.Litt. from McMaster University, 1972, and Carleton University, 1990.

WRITINGS:

The Transformation of God, Hans Christians, 1962.
A. Y. Jackson's Canada, Clarke, Irwin, 1968.
(Editor) *Ernst Barlach: Leben im Werk,* Langewiesche, 1972, translation published as *Ernst Barlach: Life in Work,* Penumbra Press, 1981.
A. Y. Jackson's Arctic Diary, Penumbra Press, 1982.
(Editor) *Young A. Y. Jackson: Lindsey A. Evans Memories, 1902-1906,* Edahl, 1982.
Greenland Caper, 1941, Penumbra Press, 1983.
(Editor) Victor Tolgesy, *Acrobatics: A Tale of Fantasy and Fact,* Edahl, 1985.
(Translator) Jens Rosing, *The Sky Hangs Low,* Penumbra Press, 1986.
One Summer in Quebec, Penumbra Press, 1988.
Art Carleton (essays), Carleton University Press, 1989.
Winter Into Summer: Lapland Diary, 1945-46, Penumbra Press, 1989.
(Editor) *Works by A. Y. Jackson from the 1930s,* Carleton University Press, 1990.
(Translator) Ernst Barlach, *A Self Told Life: Ernst Barlach,* Penumbra Press, 1990.

(Translator) Barlach, *The Flood* (play), produced at University of California, Santa Barbara, 1990.

A. Y. Jackson dessins; un ete au Quebec en 1925, Roussan Editeur, Inc., 1991.

(Translator) Barlach, *The Dead Day,* Penumbra Press, 1992.

(Translator) Rosing, *The Unicorn of the Arctic Sea,* Penumbra Press, 1993.

Contributor to periodicals, including *Geographic Quarterly, Art News,* and *Canadian Art,* and to numerous newspapers.

ADAPTATIONS: The Dead Day was adapted for stage and produced at the University of Nebraska, 1957.

WORK IN PROGRESS: Two Jacksons Abroad, 1936.

*   *   *

GUTEK, Gerald L(ee) 1935-

PERSONAL: Born July 10, 1935, in Streator, IL; son of Albert T. and Irene (Novotney) Gutek; married Patricia Ann Egan, June 12, 1965; children: Jennifer Ann, Laura Lee. *Education:* University of Illinois, B.A., 1957, M.A., 1959, Ph.D., 1964. *Religion:* Roman Catholic.

ADDRESSES: Home—437 South Edgewood Ave., LaGrange, IL 60525. *Office*—School of Education, Loyola University of Chicago, 820 North Michigan Ave., Chicago, IL 60611.

CAREER: Loyola University of Chicago, Chicago, IL, instructor, 1963-65, assistant professor, 1965-68, associate professor, 1968-72, professor of education and history, 1972—, chairman of department of foundations of education, 1969—, dean of School of Education, 1979-85, acting dean of School of Education, 1989. Visiting professor, summers, at Loyola University of Los Angeles (now Loyola Marymount University), 1965, University of Illinois, 1966, and Michigan State University, 1973; visiting professor at Loyola University in Rome, Italy, 1974-75. Grotelueschen Lecturer, Concordia College, 1979; Powell Memorial Lecturer, University of Illinois at Chicago Circle, 1982; lecturer at or participant in numerous conferences, seminars, and symposia. Member of Cook County, IL, Board of Education, 1978-81, board of trustees of Erikson Institute for Early Childhood Education, 1979-83, and Street Law Advisory Board, Chicago, 1979-83.

MEMBER: American Educational Studies Association (member of editorial review board, 1980-82; member of executive board, 1981-83), American Studies Association, American Association of Colleges for Teacher Education (Loyola University of Chicago representative, 1979-85),

National Historic Communal Societies Association, Society of Historians of the Early Republic, Comparative Education Society, History of Education Society, National Council for the Social Studies, Organization of American Historians, Philosophy of Education Society, Midwest Comparative Education Society, Midwest History of Education Society (president, 1970-71), Midwest Philosophy of Education Society, Illinois Council for the Social Studies, Phi Delta Kappa.

AWARDS, HONORS: American Philosophical Society grant, 1968, for work on an annotated edition of Joseph Neef's *Sketch of a Plan and Method of Education;* National Endowment for the Humanities grant, 1970; named Educator of the Year by Loyola University of Chicago chapter, Phi Delta Kappa, 1977; Outstanding Faculty Member of the Year, Loyola University, 1989.

WRITINGS:

Pestalozzi and Education, Random House, 1968.

The Educational Theory of George S. Counts, Ohio State University Press, 1970.

An Historical Introduction to American Education, Crowell, 1970, 2nd edition, Waveland, 1991.

A History of the Western Educational Experience, Random House, 1972, 2nd edition, Waveland, 1987.

Philosophical Alternatives in Education, C. E. Merrill, 1974.

(Contributor) Elmer L. Towns, editor, *A History of Religious Educators,* Baker Book, 1975.

(With Jasper J. Valenti) *Education and Society in India and Thailand,* University Press of America, 1977.

(Contributor) Allan C. Ornstein, editor, *An Introduction to the Foundations of Education,* Rand McNally, 1977, 5th edition, Houghton, in press.

Joseph Neef: The Americanization of Pestalozzianism, University of Alabama Press, 1978.

Basic Education: An Historical Perspective, Phi Delta Kappa Educational Foundation, 1981.

Education and Schooling: An Introduction, Prentice-Hall, 1983, 3rd edition, Allyn & Bacon, 1992.

George S. Counts and American Civilization: The Educator as Social Theorist, Mercer University Press, 1984.

(Contributor) Glenn Smith, editor, *Lives in Education: People and Ideas in the Development of Western Education,* Education Studies Press, 1984.

(With wife, Patricia Gutek) *Experiencing America's Past: A Travel Guide to Museum Villages,* Wiley, 1986.

(With P. Gutek) *Exploring the American West,* Hippocrene, 1989.

(With P. Gutek) *Exploring Mid-America: A Guide to Museum Villages,* Hippocrene, 1990.

Cultural Foundations of Education, A Biographical Introduction, Macmillan, 1991.

TAPE-RECORDED LECTURES

Pestalozzi and Education, JAB Press, 1978.
George S. Counts and a Reconstructionist Philosophy of Education, JAB Press, 1978.
The Progressive Education Movement, JAB Press, 1978.

OTHER

Contributor to *Yearbook of the American Philosophical Society,* 1969, and to proceedings; consulting editor, *Standard Education Almanac* (annual), Marquis, 1983-85. Contributor of numerous articles and reviews to periodicals, including the *History of Education Quarterly, Journal of Southern History, Social Education, Journal of American History, Educational Studies,* and *Educational Forum.*

WORK IN PROGRESS: American Education in a Global Society, for Longman.

SIDELIGHTS: Gerald L. Gutek uses the historical method to investigate educational issues and concerns, he once told *CA.* "I began my writing career as a student at Streator Township High School where I wrote essays for student publications," he recalled. "As a student in the College of Education and the Department of History at the University of Illinois, I worked to acquire the skill of writing clearly and directly without falling into jargon that besets many writers on educational topics. My interests lie in the examination of educational theory in its historical setting and in the writing of biographies of educators. I also do collaborative writing with my wife, Patricia, on historical travel guides."

* * *

GZOWSKI, Peter 1934-

PERSONAL: Surname is pronounced "*zah*-ski"; born July 13, 1934, in Toronto, Ontario, Canada; son of Harold E. and Margaret McGregor (Young) Gzowski; married wife, A. Jeanette (an interior designer), February 15, 1958; children: Peter, Allison, Maria, John, Mickey. *Education:* Attended University of Toronto.

CAREER: Journalist. Associated with *Timmins Press, Chatham Daily News, Moose Jaw Times-Herald, Toronto Telegram,* and *Toronto Star; Maclean's* (magazine), Toronto, Ontario, staff writer, 1958-64, editor, 1968; *Toronto Star Weekly,* Toronto, editor, 1966; Canadian Broadcasting Corp. (CBC), Toronto, host of daily radio program, *This Country in the Morning* (now called *Morningside*), and host of television program *90 Minutes Live;* currently free-lance writer. Director of Key Publishers and *Toronto Life* (magazine).

AWARDS, HONORS: President's Medal, 1964, for magazine writing.

WRITINGS:

NONFICTION

(With Trent Frayne) *Great Canadian Sports Stories: A Century of Competition,* Canadian Centennial Publishing Co., 1965.
(With Nancy Greene and Jack Batten) *Nancy,* Star Reader Service, 1968.
Peter Gzowski's Book about This Country in the Morning, Hurtig, 1974.
Peter Gzowski's Spring Tonic, Hurtig, 1979.
The Sacrament, McClelland & Stewart, 1980.
The New Morningside Papers, McClelland & Stewart, 1987.
The Private Voice: A Journal of Reflections, Douglas Gibson/McClelland & Stewart, 1988.
The Latest Morningside Papers, McClelland & Stewart, 1989.

Contributor to periodicals, including *Toronto Life* and *Saturday Night.*

SIDELIGHTS: Early in his career as a newsman, Peter Gzowski was known as Canada's "boy wonder of journalism." By age twenty-three he had progressed from the small *Timmins Press* to city editor of the *Chatham Daily News,* and from there to positions with *Maclean's* and Toronto's major dailies, the *Star* and *Telegram.* The articles he wrote during his years at *Maclean's* are still regarded as among the best ever published by the magazine. Gzowski stayed with *Maclean's* until 1964, when he and several other writers and editors quit over the issue of editorial freedom. During the next several years he held editing jobs at the *Star Weekly* and *Saturday Night,* wrote books and newspaper columns, and tried to launch his own magazine, *This City,* which failed. By the early seventies he had all but left newspaper and magazine writing to work in radio and television.

Gzowski's radio and television commentaries began in the late 1960s, when he also hosted a weekly radio show on Friday nights. Then he was chosen by the Canadian Broadcasting Corporation (CBC) to host a new radio program called *This Country in the Morning,* patterned largely on the talk-show format. Within a year Gzowski was nationally famous and the star of what many called "the best radio program in the world." *This Country in the Morning* became the most successful radio venture in the CBC's corporate history, and Gzowski, who was winning critical praise as an interviewer, soon found himself hosting a television show as well, called *90 Minutes Live.*

When the entertainment needs of his shows began to interfere with his professionalism as a journalist, Gzowski resigned from his broadcasting duties. He turned to writing books, instead, including a personal review of *This Coun-*

try in the Morning, an oral history, and a detailed account of a plane crash and its two survivors. In the latter book, called *The Sacrament,* Gzowski reconstructs the story of Brent Dyer and Donna Johnson, whose chartered Cessna crashed into a snow-bound Idaho mountainside on May 5, 1979, killing the pilot and Johnson's father. As their ordeal worsened they were forced to choose between starvation and cannibalism.

"It's a gripping, gruesome story touched with compassion," wrote Marty Gervais in his review for the *Windsor Star.* "[Gzowski] got into the souls of Brent Dyer and Donna Johnson." Informed by conversations with the two survivors, the author authentically recreates their emotions, ranging from the pain of hunger, the depression of imminent death, and euphoria of anticipated rescue. "The result is an exceptional account that leaves nothing unturned," Gervais continued. "It is also one that makes it quite clear that this isn't the story of cannibalism, but a story of faith, of two young people who find God."

The New Morningside Papers, a collection of transcripts of audience calls and listener letters, reveals Gzowski's ability to connect meaningfully with his audience. John Melady observed in the Toronto *Globe and Mail,* "Politicians seem to reveal more to him than anyone else. Sports stars find themselves telling him things in complete sentences. Business tycoons sound human and writers are amazed he has read their book, or at least enough to fake it. But it is the ordinary people who are never in the news who make the program what it is." Melady valued the book for extending the life of the human interest material that would otherwise no longer be available after its brief space on the air.

Bronwyn Drainie of the *Globe and Mail* commented, "These are not like letters to the editor; rather they are letters to a trusted friend. That so many people are willing to share not only their opinions but their innermost fears and joys with a national radio program is some measure of *Morningside*'s success. . . . Good for Peter Gzowski for recognizing the small treasures he had on his hands and turning it into this lively, moving and always readable collection."

BIOGRAPHICAL/CRITICAL SOURCES:

BOOKS

Gzowski, Peter, *The Private Voice: A Journal of Reflections,* Douglas Gibson/McClelland & Stewart, 1988.

PERIODICALS

Globe and Mail (Toronto), November 2, 1985; October 30, 1987; November 5, 1988; December 16, 1989.
Windsor Star, November 21, 1972.*

H

HAFEN, Brent Q(ue) 1940-

PERSONAL: Born July 17, 1940, in Salt Lake City, UT; son of Que F. and Shirley Clawson (Holm) Hafen; married Sylvia Ann Jacobson, July 23, 1959; children: Cory, Ken, Jennifer, Mark, Christy, John, Brad. *Education:* University of Utah, B.S., 1962, M.S., 1982; Southern Illinois University, Ph.D., 1969. *Religion:* Church of Jesus Christ of Latter-day Saints (Mormons).

ADDRESSES: Home—1269 North Grand Ave., Provo, UT 84602. *Office*—Department of Health Sciences, 229-E Richards Building, Brigham Young University, Provo, UT 84602.

CAREER: Hercules Powder Co., Bacchus, UT, chemical technician, 1961-63; Wyeth Laboratories, San Leandro, CA, pharmaceutical representative, 1963-65; Bemidji State College, Bemidji, MN, director of Health Center, 1965-66; Wisconsin State University, La Crosse, WI, instructor in health sciences, 1966-67; Southern Illinois University, Carbondale, instructor in health sciences, 1967-69; Brigham Young University, Provo, UT, assistant professor, 1969-72, associate professor, 1973-76, professor of health sciences, 1976—, co-director of emergency medical technician training program, 1977-82. President of Porta Pulse Corp., 1976-78; partner of Emergency Medical Services Associates. Guest lecturer at several colleges and universities, including University of Santa Clara and College of Idaho, 1974-79.

Bishop and branch president of Church of Latter-day Saints. Co-director of Institute of Human Behavior, Philadelphia, PA, 1970-73; member of board of directors of Gathering Place Drug Rehabilitation Center, 1971-74; chairman of board of trustees of Cottage International (drug and alcohol prevention program), 1977-79. Director of annual drug training programs for U.S. Department of the Interior's Youth Civilian Conservation Centers, 1968-76 and 1981-82; director of U.S. Army staff training program in suicidology and crisis intervention, Dugway Proving Grounds, 1973-74. Educational coordinator of Crisis Children's Workshop, Utah State Hospital, 1971-73. Co-director of Annual Institute of Criminal and Social Justice, 1972-74, of Annual Clinical Conference on Pre-Hospital Care and Crisis Intervention, 1977—, and of Annual Conference on Health, Wellness, and Life Crisis, 1979—. Member of advisory boards of National Center of Health Education, 1975-78, and Utah State Division of Alcoholism and Drugs, 1975-77; consultant to Spenco Medical Corp. and Vitalography Medical Instrument Co.

MEMBER: American Association of Trauma Specialists, National Association of Emergency Medical Technicians, American Public Health Association, Nutrition Today Society, American School Health Association, American Social Health Association, American Alliance for Health Education, Utah County Mental Health Association (member of board of directors, 1971-74), Eta Sigma Gamma.

AWARDS, HONORS: National Institute of Mental Health grants, 1971-73; Utah Division of Alcohol and Drugs and Provo School District grant, 1972; Brigham Young University, Utah State Hospital, and Provo School District grants, 1972-73 and 1973-74; U.S. Department of Transportation, National Alcohol Safety Action Program, Utah Department of Public Safety, and Utah Safety Action Program grants, 1973-74; faculty research fellowship, 1974-75.

WRITINGS:

Utah and Federal Drug Laws, Brigham Young University Press, 1970.
(With others) *Medicines and Drugs,* Brigham Young University Press, 1976, 3rd edition, Lea & Febiger, 1983.

Alcohol: The Crutch That Cripples, West Publishing, 1977, 2nd edition (with Molly J. Brog) published as *Alcohol,* 1983.

First Aid for Health Emergencies, West Publishing, 1977, 4th edition (with Kathryn Frandsen), 1988.

(With Brenda Peterson) *Prescriptions for Health* (with instructor's manual), Brigham Young University Press, 1977.

(With Frandsen) *Health Perspectives,* Brigham Young University Press, 1977.

(With Alton Thygerson and Ronald Rhodes) *First Aid and Emergency Care Workbook* (with instructor's manual), Morton, 1977, revised edition (with Keith Karren), 1984, 4th edition (with Karren), 1990.

Crisis Intervention for Prehospital Personnel, Creative Age Publishers, 1979.

(With Karren) *Child Abuse and Neglect,* Brigham Young University Press, 1979.

Rape and Sexual Assault, Emergency Medical Services Associates, 1979.

Surviving Health Emergencies and Disasters, Emergency Medical Services Associates, 1979.

(With Karren) *Prehospital Emergency Care and Crisis Intervention* (with workbook), Morton, 1979, 4th edition, Prentice-Hall, 1992.

(With Karren) *Health for the Elementary School Teacher,* Allyn & Bacon, 1980.

(With Karren and Rhodes) *Self-Help Health Care,* Prentice-Hall, 1980.

(With Brog and Frandsen) *The Self-Health Handbook,* Prentice-Hall, 1980.

Marijuana (monograph), Hazelden Foundation, 1980.

Drug and Alcohol Emergencies (monograph), Hazelden Foundation, 1980.

(With Karren) *The Crisis Intervention Handbook,* Creative Age Publications, 1980.

(With Frandsen) *Fetal Alcohol Syndrome,* Hazelden Foundation, 1980.

Food, Nutrition, and Weight Control, Allyn & Bacon, 1981.

(With Frandsen) *How to Live Longer,* Prentice-Hall, 1981.

(With Frandsen) *Cocaine,* Hazelden Foundation, 1981.

(With Karren) *First Aid and Emergency Care Skills Manual,* Morton, 1982.

(With Karren) *First Responder: A Skills Approach* (with workbook), Morton, 1982, revised edition, Prentice-Hall, 1992.

(With Karren) *Health Management, Promotion, and Self-Care,* Morton, 1982.

(With Frandsen) *Faces of Death: Grief, Dying, Euthanasia, Suicide,* Morton, 1983.

(With Brog) *Emotional Survival,* Prentice-Hall, 1983.

(With Brog and Frandsen) *Medical Self-Care and Assessment,* Morton, 1983.

(With Frandsen) *From Acupuncture to Yoga: Alternative Methods of Healing,* Prentice-Hall, 1983.

Psychological Emergencies and Crisis Intervention, Morton, 1985.

(With Frandsen) *Youth Suicide: Depression and Loneliness,* Cordillera Press, 1986.

(With Frandsen) *People Need People: The Importance of Relationships to Health and Wellness,* Cordillera Press, 1987.

(With Karren) *The EMT Review Manual,* Morton, 1987.

(With others) *Answers about AIDS for EMS Personnel,* Morton, 1988.

EDITOR

Readings on Drug Use and Abuse, Brigham Young University Press, 1970.

Health for the Secondary Teacher, W. C. Brown, 1971.

Man, Health, and Environment, Burgess, 1971.

(With Thygerson and Ray S. Peterson) *First Aid: Contemporary Practices and Principles,* Burgess, 1972.

(With Eugene J. Faux) *Self-Destructive Behavior: A Major Crisis,* Burgess, 1972.

(With Faux) *Drug Abuse: Psychology, Sociology, Pharmacology,* Brigham Young University Press, 1973.

Overweight and Obesity: Causes, Fallacies, Treatment, Brigham Young University Press, 1973.

(With Thygerson) *Preventative Health,* Brigham Young University Press, 1975.

(With others) *Adolescent Health for Educators and Health Personnel,* Brighton, 1978.

Addictive Behavior: Drug and Alcohol Abuse, Morton, 1985.

Also editor of *Nutrition and Health: New Concepts and Issues,* Morton.

OTHER

Co-author of *Loneliest Game in Town,* multimedia film presentation, released by U.S. Department of Transportation, 1973; co-editor of *Alcohol Media Kit,* released by U.S. Department of Transportation, 1973. Contributor to education journals and *New Woman.* Associate editor of *American Journal of Health Education,* 1976-79.

WORK IN PROGRESS: A book on health, longevity, and life-style; research projects on premenstrual syndrome (PMS).*

*   *   *

HAGUE, Harlan   1932-

PERSONAL: "Surname is pronounced like the Dutch city, The Hague"; born January 23, 1932, in Fort Worth, TX; son of Stanley W. (a bookkeeper) and Maggie (Faires)

Hague; married Carol Jackson (a teacher of English as a second language), July 16, 1960; children: Cary, Merrilee, Jennifer. *Education:* Baylor University, B.B.A., 1954; University of Texas at Austin, M.B.A., 1960; graduate study at University of California, Berkeley, 1964-65; University of the Pacific, M.A., 1968; University of Nevada at Reno, Ph.D., 1974. *Politics:* Liberal. *Religion:* "Praying agnostic." *Avocational interests:* Conservation, preservation, music of the baroque and classical periods, computers, tennis, sailing, photography, travel, fitness.

ADDRESSES: Home—2462 Sheridan Way, Stockton, CA 95207.

CAREER: Whitehouse Plastics Corp., Fort Worth, TX, controller, 1959; Pacific Telephone, San Francisco, CA, traffic manager, 1960-64; Kaiser Jeep International, Oakland, CA, market researcher, 1964; San Joaquin Delta College, Stockton, CA, instructor in U.S. history, 1964-92. Visiting associate professor at University of Oregon, 1976. *Military service:* U.S. Navy, 1954-57; later served in active reserve; became lieutenant.

MEMBER: Sierra Club, Common Cause, Wilderness Society, American Farmland Trust, Nature Conservancy, Western History Association, California Historical Society (trustee, 1990—), California Planning and Conservation League, American Society for Environmental History.

AWARDS, HONORS: National Endowment for the Humanities grants, 1975 and 1980; Huntington Library grants, 1987 and 1990; Sourisseau Academy grant, 1987; Caroline Bancroft Prize, Denver Public Library, 1990, for *Thomas O. Larkin: A Life of Patriotism and Profit in Old California.*

WRITINGS:

Road to California: The Search for a Southern Overland Route, 1540-1848, Arthur Clark, 1978.
(With David J. Langum) *Thomas O. Larkin: A Life of Patriotism and Profit in Old California,* University of California Press, 1990.

Also contributor to books, including *Pioneer Trails West: The Southern Route,* edited by Don Worcester, Caxton Printers, 1985; *American History,* edited by Robert James Maddox, Volume 1, Dushkin, 11th edition, 1991; and *Presidents and the American West,* edited by Theodore C. Hinckley, Sunflower University Press, 1992. Contributor of articles and reviews to history journals, and of travel pieces to newspapers and magazines.

WORK IN PROGRESS: A biography of Stephen Watts Kearny, for the University of Oklahoma Western Biographies series; editing a collection of unpublished letters of Thomas O. Larkin; a novel, a love story set in the American Southwest during the war between the United States and Mexico in the 1840s, and a screenplay based on the novel.

SIDELIGHTS: In *Road to California: The Search for a Southern Overland Route, 1540-1848,* Harlan Hague follows the paths of the first explorers who blazed trails through the southwestern United States. He begins with the development of the early Spanish explorers' southern route, often imprecisely called the Gila Trail, that was in use even before the arrival of French, English, and American explorers. Hague then discusses later expeditions of and routes laid by trail blazers of the Southwest, including fur trappers, traders, and military groups. In a *Journal of American History* review of Hague's book, Thomas E. Chavez described *Road to California* as "a major recent addition in its field." *Road to California* "has a story to tell and does so accurately," Chavez further remarked. "Everything about the publication is excellent."

Harlan Hague once told *CA:* "I recently retired from teaching to devote full time to writing. As a teacher, I was not so concerned that my students accumulate data. Data were easy enough to verify. I wanted them to leave my course unsatisfied, with questions rocketing around in their heads, even a little confused, but above all, *wanting* to read history. I wanted them to know the difference between history and patriotism. I wanted to introduce them to comparative history, to convince them that, in order to understand one's own history, it was useful to study it from another's viewpoint. Having impressed them of the importance of studying history, I finished by cautioning them to beware of history, since it was the creation of fallible historians."

"My latest publication, with David J. Langum, is a biography of Thomas O. Larkin," Hague recently added. "A resident of California, Larkin was the most important person in the United States acquisition of the Mexican province. As correspondent to eastern newspapers, he informed the public on California's attractions; as United States Consul and President Polk's secret agent, he influenced government policy; as confidant of California leaders, he sought to persuade them that their best interests lay not with Mexico, but with the United States. In time, he would have succeeded, but war intervened. The fault was not Larkin's, but that of impatient, ambitious adventurers and politicians.

"The protagonist in my novel, and the screenplay adapted from it, is an American soldier, a Missouri farm boy who joins the army to escape his cloistered existence, and for adventure. In Santa Fe, he finds only friends, falls in love, and decides that the Mexicans cannot be his enemies. He comes to question the morality of war and, eventually, violence."

Hague once commented that he is interested in "conservation and attitudes toward the land. I am particularly concerned about the dangers of nuclear energy (weapons and generation of electricity). I am heartened by the collapse of communism and the declining threat of nuclear holocaust. Would that peace and the end of human suffering follow. I actively support the preservation of farmland and the protection of wilderness, sources of food for the body and the spirit, and the preservation of species. I am competent, but not fluent, in the French language; I love it and study it daily. The lack of languages feeds my inferiority complex personally and constitutes for the United States a national disgrace. Traveling abroad is a consuming interest. I am fascinated with other cultures and peoples. I have lived in England and Japan, and have visited a few score countries."

BIOGRAPHICAL/CRITICAL SOURCES:

PERIODICALS

American Historical Review, October, 1979; December, 1991.
Journal of American History, December, 1979.
Pacific Historical Review, November, 1980.
Western Historical Quarterly, February, 1992.

*   *   *

HARDISON, O(sborne) B(ennett, Jr.)   1928-1990

PERSONAL: Born October 22, 1928, in San Diego, CA; died of complications from cancer, August 5, 1990, in Washington, DC; son of Osborne Bennett (a naval officer) and Ruth (Morgan) Hardison; married Marifrances Fitzgibbon, December 23, 1950; children: Charity Ruth, Sarah Frances, Laura Fitzgibbon, Agnes Margaret, Osborne Bennett, Matthew. *Education:* University of North Carolina, A.B., 1949, M.A., 1950; University of Wisconsin, Ph.D., 1956. *Politics:* Democrat.

ADDRESSES: Home—1708 21st St. NW, Washington, DC 20009. *Office*—Department of English, Georgetown University, Washington, DC 20057.

CAREER: University of Tennessee, Knoxville, instructor in English, 1954-56; Princeton University, Princeton, NJ, instructor in English, 1956-57; University of North Carolina, Chapel Hill, assistant professor, 1957-60, associate professor, 1960-63, professor of English, 1963-69; Folger Shakespeare Library, Washington, DC, director, 1969-84; Georgetown University, Washington, DC, University Professor of English, 1984-90. Co-chairman, Duke University-University of North Carolina Program in Humanities.

MEMBER: Modern Language Association of America, South Atlantic Modern Language Association, Southeast-ern Institute of Medieval and Renaissance Studies (chairman), Renaissance Society of America, Phi Beta Kappa.

AWARDS, HONORS: Fulbright Fellow, Italy, 1953-54; Folger Library Fellow, summer, 1958; Guggenheim Fellow, 1963-64; Haskins Medal, Medieval Academy of America, 1967, for *Christian Rite and Christian Drama in the Middle Ages;* Order of the British Empire, 1985; National Book Critics Circle Award nomination, 1990, for *Disappearing through the Skylight.*

WRITINGS:

Modern Continental Literary Criticism, Appleton, 1962.
The Enduring Monument, University of North Carolina Press, 1962.
Renaissance Literary Criticism, Appleton, 1963.
(With Alex Preminger and Frank Warnke) *Encyclopedia of Poetry and Poetics,* Princeton University Press, 1965.
Christian Rite and Christian Drama in the Middle Ages, Johns Hopkins University Press, 1965.
Practical Rhetoric, Appleton, 1966.
The Renaissance, P. Owen, 1968.
Toward Freedom and Dignity: The Humanities and the Idea of Humanity, Johns Hopkins University Press, 1974.
Pro Musica Antiqua (poems), Louisiana State University Press, 1978.
Entering the Maze: Identity and Change in Modern Culture (first volume in trilogy), Oxford University Press, 1982.
Disappearing through the Skylight: Culture and Technology in the Twentieth Century (second volume in trilogy), Viking, 1989.

Contributor to professional journals, to *Raleigh News and Observer,* and *Washington Times.*

WORK IN PROGRESS: The third volume of a trilogy on identity in modern culture.

SIDELIGHTS: O. B. Hardison had a long and distinguished career in the humanities. From 1969 until 1984 he served as director of the Folger Shakespeare Library in Washington, D.C., which houses the foremost collection of original Shakespeare material in America. In his 1973 book, *Toward Freedom and Dignity: The Humanities and the Idea of Humanity,* Hardison argued that answers to social problems and impetus for social change can be found in the classrooms, through a humanistic course of study.

But Hardison was also a lover of technology, a founding member of the Quark Club, an organization of scientists and humanists interested in cultural change. His last two works, *Entering the Maze* and *Disappearing through the Skylight,* form two parts of a proposed trilogy that was to examine the relationship between change and modern culture.

Hardison maintained his humanistic values in his analysis of technology and science. "My point of view," Hardison wrote in his preface to *Disappearing through the Skylight,* "is that of an involved citizen of modern culture, not that of a scientist or historian of science and technology. I . . . confess to being fascinated and dazzled by the brilliance of the achievements of modern science, and I hope my admiration is evident in what I have written. This book is not, however, an attempt to explain or popularize this or that development in science or technology. It is concerned with values rather than processes or products, and is intended for all . . . who are interested in understanding the culture we inhabit."

In *Disappearing through the Skylight,* nominated for the prestigious National Book Critics Circle Award, Hardison examines what the effect of knowing that the universe may ultimately be beyond human understanding has had on modern man. The answers we have been seeking for so long, Hardison says, have "disappeared through the skylight" even as they seemed to be coming within our reach. Drawing examples from architecture, literary movements such as Dadaism and graphic arts movements like Cubism, and sciences, including biology, physics, and mathematics, the author shows that—with the disappearance of absolute certainties—scientists, artists, poets, and architects have had to develop a new attitude toward their work or art. Instead of approaching it as a search for truth, they have had to approach it as a form of play.

The increasingly complex tools man has designed to help in his search for Truth, Hardison continued, impact his everyday existence in other ways, too. The writer claimed that the expanded use of computers, especially those that use interactive software, has made the difference between natural objects and man-made ones irrelevant. He also argued that increased use of technology promotes a global artistic consciousness that may redefine established concepts of history, art, language, and science, and that machine intelligence may one day supersede human intelligence in the universe.

"Consideration of intelligent machines," Hardison wrote in *Disappearing through the Skylight,* "suggests that the idea of humanity is changing so rapidly that it . . . can legitimately and without any exaggeration be said to be disappearing. . . . Many of the intellectual abilities of carbon man have already been modeled in [silicon], and a great deal that is important to the spirit of carbon man— his soaring imagination, his brilliance, his creativity, his capacity for vision—will probably be modeled in silicon before very long, at least as time is measured in biological

evolution. Many undesirable, self-defeating traits will be filtered out."

"This sounds less like a death than a birth of humanity," Hardison concluded. "Perhaps . . . it is a moment that realizes the age-old dream of the mystics of rising beyond the prison of the flesh to behold a light so brilliant it is a kind of darkness. William Butler Yeats wrote in his great prophetic poem 'Sailing to Byzantium': 'Consume my heart away; sick with desire/And fastened to a dying animal/It knows not what it is; and gather me/Into the artifice of eternity.' "

BIOGRAPHICAL/CRITICAL SOURCES:

BOOKS

Hardison, O. B., *Disappearing through the Skylight: Culture and Technology in the Twentieth Century,* Viking, 1989.

PERIODICALS

America, January 16, 1982.
Chicago Tribune, December 27, 1989.
Kirkus Reviews, October 15, 1989.
Library Journal, October 15, 1989.
Los Angeles Times, December 5, 1989.
New York Review of Books, April 26, 1990.
New York Times, November 28, 1989.
Publishers Weekly, October 20, 1989.
Sewanee Review, summer, 1983.
Washington Post, February 11, 1990.
Washington Post Book World, December 31, 1989.

OBITUARIES:

PERIODICALS

Chicago Tribune, August 7, 1990.
Los Angeles Times, August 7, 1990.
New York Times, August 7, 1990.
Washington Post, August 7, 1990.*

*   *   *

HARGRAVE, Rowena 1906-

PERSONAL: Born December 12, 1906, in Boonville, IN; daughter of Berry Little (a trucker) and Anna (Stephens) Hullett; married Harold Hargrave (superintendent of La Porte Community Schools), June 4, 1935; children: Ruth (Mrs. Richard Bersin). *Education:* Attended Oakland City College, 1924-25; Indiana State University, B.S., 1949; University of Chicago, M.A., 1962. *Religion:* Baptist.

ADDRESSES: Home—1808 Monroe St., La Porte, IN 46350.

CAREER: Elementary teacher in Boonville, IN, 1925-29, and La Porte, IN, 1929-39, 1942-71. Summer teacher reading clinic, University of Chicago, 1963, 1965.

MEMBER: National Retired Teachers Association, International Reading Association, American Association of University Women, Indiana State Retired Teacher's Association, Pi Lambda Theta, Delta Kappa Gamma, Civic Music Association, Woman's Literary Club, La Porte Community Hospital Auxiliary, Little Theatre Club.

WRITINGS:

"Building Reading Skills" series, six books, McCormick-Mathers, 1951, 5th revised edition, 1971.
(With daughter, Ruth Bersin) "Basic Reading Skills" series, six books, Contemporary Learning Materials, 1984.

Contributor to education journals.

SIDELIGHTS: Rowena Hargrave writes, "Children and their love of reading have been my inspiration for writing."

*   *   *

HARRIS, Trudier   1948-

PERSONAL: Born February 27, 1948, in Mantua, AL; daughter of Terrell and Unareed (Burton) Harris. *Education:* Stillman College, A.B., 1969; Ohio State University, M.A., 1972, Ph.D., 1973.

ADDRESSES: Home—121 Basswood Ct., Chapel Hill, NC 27514. *Office*—534 Greenlaw, CB# 3520, University of North Carolina, Chapel Hill, NC 27599-3520.

CAREER: College of William and Mary, Williamsburg, VA, assistant professor of English, 1973-79; University of North Carolina, Chapel Hill, associate professor, 1979-85, professor of English, 1985-88, J. Carlyle Sitterson Professor of English, 1988—, chairman of Curriculum in African and Afro-American Studies, 1990-92. University of Arkansas, Little Rock, William Grant Cooper Visiting Distinguished Professor, 1987; Ohio State University, visiting distinguished professor, 1988.

MEMBER: Modern Language Association of America, College Language Association (vice-president, 1980-81), American Folklore Society, Association of African and African American Folklorists, Langston Hughes Society, South Atlantic Modern Language Association, Southeastern Women's Studies Association, Zeta Phi Beta.

AWARDS, HONORS: National Endowment for the Humanities grant, 1977-78, 1988-89; Bunting Institute grant, 1981-82; Ford Foundation/National Research Council

grant, 1982-83; Creative Scholarship Award, College Language Association, 1987; teaching award, South Atlantic Modern Language Association, 1987; Roscoe B. Tanner Teaching Award, 1988; Center for Advanced Study in the Behavioral Sciences grant, 1989-90; University of North Carolina grant, 1990.

WRITINGS:

NONFICTION

From Mammies to Militants: Domestics in Black American Literature, Temple University Press, 1982.
(Co-editor) *Afro-American Fiction Writers after 1955,* Gale, 1984.
Exorcising Blackness: Historical and Literary Lynching and Burning Rituals, Indiana University Press, 1984.
Black Women in the Fiction of James Baldwin, University of Tennessee Press, 1985.
(Co-editor) *Afro-American Writers after 1955: Dramatists and Prose Writers,* Gale, 1985.
(Co-editor) *Afro-American Poets after 1955,* Gale, 1985.
(Editor) *Afro-American Writers before the Harlem Renaissance,* Gale, 1986.
(Editor) *Afro-American Writers from the Harlem Renaissance to 1940,* Gale, 1987.
(Editor) *Afro-American Writers from 1940 to 1955,* Gale, 1988.
(Editor) *Selected Works of Ida B. Wells-Barnett,* Oxford University Press, 1991.
Fiction and Folklore: The Novels of Toni Morrison, University of Tennessee Press, 1991.

OTHER

Contributor to books, including *Black American Literature and Humanism,* edited by R. Baxter Miller, University Press of Kentucky, 1981; *The History of Southern Literature,* edited by Louis Rubin, Jr., Blyden Jackson, and others, Louisiana State University Press, 1985; *Critical Essays on Toni Morrison,* edited by Nellie Y. McKay, G. K. Hall, 1988; and *Women's Friendships,* edited by Susan Koppelman, University of Oklahoma Press, 1991. Contributor to periodicals, including *Black American Literature Forum, MELUS, Southern Humanities Review, CLA Journal, Journal of Popular Culture,* and *Callaloo.*

WORK IN PROGRESS: Moms Mabley and American Humor; How I Got Off the Mourners Bench: Folk, Popular, and Literary Tales of Religious Conversion; The Oxford Companion to U.S. Women's Writing; The African American Tradition in Literature; The Oxford Companion to African-American Writing.

SIDELIGHTS: In *From Mammies to Militants* Trudier Harris explores the depictions of black domestics in black fiction. She discusses twenty-four works, including Toni Morrison's *The Bluest Eye* and Richard Wright's story

"Man of All Work." Reviewer Fran R. Schumer notes in the *New York Times Book Review* that "this book sheds light on a subject that has gotten far less attention than it deserves."

Harris told *CA:* "My writing continues to be motivated by a sense of commitment to treat topics in African-American literature and folklore that have not previously inspired extensive scholarly exploration. For example, one of my on-going projects is a study of the 'mourners bench' (a religious rite of passage) in African-American folk, popular, and literary traditions. While that phenomenon is certainly a known one in the culture, it is not one of those subjects that lends itself readily to scholarly treatment. I hope to show that it is indeed a rich realm of endeavor. I have similar aspirations for my biography of Jackie 'Moms' Mabley (Loretta Mary Aiken), who is recognized by many comedians as having had substantial influence upon their careers and performances, but who has not yet been accorded a significant place in American humor. Since the numbers of African-American scholars, women in particular, are not increasing substantially, I am convinced that those of us who can produce works that shed light on less-studied phenomena in the culture should be about the business of doing so."

BIOGRAPHICAL/CRITICAL SOURCES:

BOOKS

Notable Black American Women, Gale, 1992.

PERIODICALS

New York Times Book Review, March 6, 1983.

*　　*　　*

HARTE, Marjorie
　See McEVOY, Marjorie Harte

*　　*　　*

HEALEY, Joseph G(raham) 1938-

PERSONAL: Born April 29, 1938, in Detroit, MI; son of Anthony John (a horse trainer) and Virginia (a housewife; maiden name, Graham) Healey. *Education:* Attended Princeton University, 1956-59; Maryknoll Seminary (now School of Theology), B.A., 1961, M.Th., 1966; University of Missouri—Columbia, M.A., 1967; Creighton University, M.Ch.Sp., 1981. *Politics:* Democrat.

ADDRESSES: Home and office—Maryknoll Language School, P.O. Box 298, Musoma, Tanzania.

CAREER: Entered Catholic Foreign Mission Society (Maryknoll Missionaries), 1959, ordained Roman Catho-

lic priest, 1966; *Maryknoll,* Maryknoll, NY, writer, 1967-68; Catholic Bishops Conference, Nairobi, Kenya, communications secretary, 1969-74; animator of small Christian communities in Nyabihanga Village, Rulenge, Tanzania, 1976-78; Maryknoll School of Theology, Maryknoll, spiritual director and teacher, 1979-82; Iramba Parish, Musoma, Tanzania, pastor and writer, 1982-86; Maryknoll Language School, Musoma, social communications secretary and writer-in-residence, 1987—.

WRITINGS:

A Fifth Gospel: The Experience of Black Christian Values, Orbis, 1981.
What Language Does God Speak, St. Paul Publications, 1990.

IN SWAHILI

Kuishi Injili (title means "Living the Gospel"), Benedictine Publications, 1982.
(With Donald Sybertz) *Kueneza Injili Kwa Methali* (title means "Preaching the Gospel through Proverbs"), Benedictine Publications, 1984.
Kueneza Injili Kwa Methali: Kitabu Cha 2: Familia (title means "Preaching the Gospel through Proverbs: Book II: Family"), Benedictine Publications, 1993.

Co-author, with Colette Ackerman, of *Kumtafsiri Upya Theresia Wa Lizee,* 1991.

OTHER

Contributor to magazines, including *After, New People, Omnis Terra,* and *Missiology.* Editor of *AMECEA Information* and *Maryknoll Formation Journal.*

WORK IN PROGRESS: A book on African proverbs, biblical parallels, and theological reflections; a novel on Africa.

SIDELIGHTS: Joseph G. Healey once wrote: "As a Roman Catholic missionary priest who has worked in East Africa for twenty years, I am very interested in writing about the development of African Christianity, especially small Christian communities, the integration of African culture and Christian faith, missionary spirituality, missiological questions, and African proverbs. I have traveled to eighty-one countries, including thirty in Africa.

"During the years that I have spent in East Africa I have experienced again and again the African value that sharing is a way of life. As the African people share so deeply with me, I feel compelled to share my experience in Africa with people in other parts of the world. In my books and articles I have tried to let the African people and values speak for themselves, especially through small Christian communities' experiences, proverbs, sayings, riddles, and stories.

"I deeply feel that God is revealing himself today through the African people within their local situation and everyday life experiences. This I call 'Africa's Fifth Gospel.' Jesus is revealing himself in people's lives everywhere in contemporary human experience. So each person, each community, each nation, each continent has its own unique Fifth Gospel."

BIOGRAPHICAL/CRITICAL SOURCES:

PERIODICALS

Advocate, November 10, 1982.
America, May 1, 1980.
Baltimore Sun, August 20, 1969.
Catholic Review, May 1, 1975; April 15, 1981.
Faces of Africa, February, 1992.
Maryknoll, November, 1974; August, 1975; October, 1983.
Maryknoll in Touch, February, 1992.

*   *   *

HEAVEN, Constance 1911-
(Constance Fecher; Christina Merlin, a pseudonym)

PERSONAL: Born August 6, 1911, in London, England; daughter of Michael Joseph and Caroline (Rand) Fecher; married William Heaven (a theatrical director), May 11, 1939 (died, 1958). *Education:* Attended convent school in Woodford Green, England, 1920-28; London College of Music, Licentiate, 1931; King's College, London, B.A. (with honors), 1932. *Politics:* Liberal. *Religion:* Roman Catholic.

ADDRESSES: Home—Tudor Green, 37 Teddington Park Rd., Teddington TW11 8NB, Middlesex, England.

CAREER: Actress, 1938-64; began writing in early 1960s; tutor in seventeenth-century history and literature and in creative writing at City Literary Institute, London, England, 1967—. Operated a theater, with husband, William Heaven, at Henley-on-Thames, England, 1939; played with companies touring throughout England during World War II; ran a number of theatrical companies with husband after he was released from the Royal Air Force until his death in 1958; gives occasional stage recitals of verse and prose.

AWARDS, HONORS: Romantic Novelists Association major award for best romantic historical novel, 1972, for *The House of Kuragin.*

WRITINGS:

NOVELS

The House of Kuragin, Coward, 1972.

The Astrov Legacy, Coward, 1973.
Castle of Eagles, Coward, 1974.
The Place of Stones, Coward, 1975.
The Fires of Glenlochy, Coward, 1976.
The Queen and the Gypsy, Coward, 1977.
Lord of Ravensley (Literary Guild alternate selection), Coward, 1978.
Heir to Kuragin, Coward, 1979.
The Ravensley Touch, Coward, 1982.
The Wildcliffe Bird, Coward, 1983.
Daughter of Marignac, Putnam, 1984.
Castle of Doves, Putnam, 1985.
The Craven Legacy, Putnam, 1986.
The Raging Fire, Putnam, 1987.
The Fire Still Burns, Heinemann, 1989.
The Wind from the Sea, Heinemann, 1991.

NOVELS UNDER NAME CONSTANCE FECHER

Queen's Delight (first novel in trilogy), R. Hale, 1966.
Traitor's Son (second novel in trilogy), R. Hale, 1967.
King's Legacy (third novel in trilogy), R. Hale, 1967.
Player Queen, R. Hale, 1968.
Lion of Trevarrock, R. Hale, 1969.
The Night of the Wolf, R. Hale, 1971.
By the Light of the Moon, R. Hale, 1985.

NOVELS UNDER PSEUDONYM CHRISTINA MERLIN

The Spy Concerto, R. Hale, 1980.
Sword of Mithras, R. Hale, 1982.

JUVENILES UNDER NAME CONSTANCE FECHER

Venture for a Crown, Farrar, Straus, 1968.
Heir to Pendarrow, Farrar, Straus, 1969.
Bright Star (biography of Ellen Terry), Farrar, Straus, 1970.
The Link Boys, Farrar, Straus, 1971.
The Last Elizabethan: A Portrait of Sir Walter Raleigh, Farrar, Straus, 1972.
The Leopard Dagger (Junior Literary Guild selection), Farrar, Straus, 1973.

WORK IN PROGRESS: A novel concerned with social conditions in mid-nineteenth century London.

SIDELIGHTS: Constance Heaven once commented: "I write principally to please myself because I have always enjoyed 'telling a story.' I try to make the background as authentic as I can and hope that my readers get as much pleasure in reading as I find in writing." Her novels have been translated into French, German, Italian, Norwegian, Swedish, Finnish, Spanish, Turkish, and Japanese.

BIOGRAPHICAL/CRITICAL SOURCES:

PERIODICALS

Time Literary Supplement, May 1, 1981.

HEFFERNAN, Michael 1942-

PERSONAL: Born December 20, 1942, in Detroit, MI; son of Joseph W. (a refrigeration contractor) and Susan (a teacher; maiden name, Schneider) Heffernan; married Anne M. Miller, August 14, 1968 (divorced June 9, 1975); married Kathleen Spigarelli (a teacher), August 9, 1975; children: (second marriage) Joseph Rinaldo, James Brendan, Michael Eamon. *Education:* University of Detroit, A.B., 1964; University of Massachusetts, M.A., 1967, Ph.D., 1970. *Politics:* "Left-leaning Democrat." *Religion:* "A good bad-Catholic."

ADDRESSES: Home—2518 Elizabeth Ave., Fayetteville, AR 72703. *Office*—Department of English, Creative Writing Program, University of Arkansas, Fayetteville, AR 72701.

CAREER: Oakland University, Rochester, MI, 1967-69; Pittsburg State University, Pittsburg, KS, 1969-86; University of Arkansas, Fayetteville, 1986—.

MEMBER: Poetry Society of America.

AWARDS, HONORS: Woodrow Wilson fellowship, 1964; Bread Loaf Writers Conference scholarship, 1977; National Endowment for the Arts creative writing fellowship, 1978; National Endowment for the Humanities summer seminar fellowship, 1980; National Endowment for the Arts creative writing fellowship, 1987.

WRITINGS:

POETRY

Booking Passage, Bookmark, 1973.
In Front of All These People, Blue Period Books, 1977.
A Figure of Plain Force, Chowder Chapbooks, 1978.
The Cry of Oliver Hardy, University of Georgia Press, 1979.
To the Wreakers of Havoc, University of Georgia Press, 1984.
The Man at Home, University of Arkansas Press, 1988.

Also contributor to anthologies, including *Strong Measures,* edited by Philip Dacey and David Jauss, Harper, 1985; *Vital Signs,* edited by Ronald Wallace, University of Wisconsin Press, 1989; and *Western Wind* (3rd edition) by John F. Nims, McGraw Hill, 1992.

Contributor of poems and reviews to literary journals, including *American Poetry Review, Georgia Review, Gettysburg Review, Iowa Review, New England Review, Poetry, Poetry Northwest, Quarterly, Shenandoah,* and *Willow Springs.*

WORK IN PROGRESS: Love's Answer, for University of Iowa Press, 1994; a full-length book of poems.

SIDELIGHTS: Poet Michael Heffernan is "one of those writers who can juggle a dozen objects of different shapes and sizes with the grace of an angel and no help from above," according to Bonnie Costello in a *Parnassus* article. "And all the while he will seem to be talking to you about the weather." Heffernan is notable for the ordinary, everyday events he celebrates in poems that are "meditative, interior monologues, [that] define a wry personality—or several wry personalities—with a nutty sense of the world and the self," as *Georgia Review* critic Peter Stitt sees it. Stitt goes on to state that Heffernan's works are "structured on a series of transformations" and that the poet "does this sort of thing slyly, quietly, almost without our realizing what is going on. His poems are good-natured and gently humorous, though we never laugh out loud." Commenting on Heffernan's writings in the *Gettysburg Review,* Floyd Collins states that the poet "seeks grace through a disordering of the senses, through the suspension of reality induced by incantation. He lends the mundane aspects of life a numinous edge by chanting them into song. His mask is that of the Divine Fool who plays his harp with a hammer."

Heffernan told *CA:* "Having lived only briefly on either coast, I keep joyfully at a distance from mainstream fads and fashions. I also try to stay away from ideology and theory. Spending most of my life in distinctive regions like the Midwest and the South, I have worked hard to avoid the trap of regionalism. Coming from working-class Detroit, I prefer to remember how good my father looked in a suit, despite the dirt under his nails. I usually write iambic pentameter, but make no cause with the new formalists. Regardless, I labor to put on paper what the imagination knows, which is truer than what the eye knows, and far more likely to bring us to wisdom than anything taught by priests or mystics. What does it matter if I save my soul, when the whole palpable world is there for the losing? I build these realms of words for comfort's sake, but a good night's sleep, beside my love, is better."

BIOGRAPHICAL/CRITICAL SOURCES:

PERIODICALS

Carolina Quarterly, winter, 1980.
Chowder Review, summer, 1985.
Colorado Review, spring/summer, 1990.
Georgia Review, summer, 1980; summer, 1986.
Gettysburg Review, winter, 1990.
Iowa Review, Volume 19, number 3, 1989.
Parnassus, spring, 1980.
Poet & Critic, 1988.
Poet Lore, spring, 1991.
Prairie Schooner, summer, 1980.
Small Press Review, April, 1981.

HERBERT, David T(homas) 1935-

PERSONAL: Born December 24, 1935, in Rhondda, Wales; son of Trevor John (a traffic superintendent) and Megan (Pearce) Herbert; married Tonwen Maddock, December 30, 1967; children: David Aled, Nia Wyn. *Education:* University College of Swansea, University of Wales, B.A., 1959; University of Birmingham, Ph.D., 1964.

ADDRESSES: Home—36 Rhyd-y-Defaid Dr., Sketty, Swansea, Glamorgan, Wales. *Office*—Department of Geography, University College of Swansea, University of Wales, Swansea, Glamorgan, Wales.

CAREER: University of Wales, University College of Swansea, Swansea, Glamorgan, professor of geography, 1965—, faculty of economic-social studies, subdean, 1971-75, dean, 1980-84, vice-principal, 1986-89. Visiting professor at University of Toronto, 1965, University of Manitoba, 1967, University of York, 1969, University of Colorado, 1979, University of Oklahoma, 1979, University of Khartoum, 1982, and University of Warsaw, 1985; Lister Lecturer, British Association for the Advancement of Science, 1978; Killam Scholar, University of Calgary, 1989, 1992. Member of Social Science Research Council, 1976-80, Sports Council for Wales, 1984-93, and General Dental Council, 1990—.

MEMBER: Institute of British Geographers (member of council, 1979-82), British Urban Geographers (chairman, 1975-78).

WRITINGS:

Urban Geography: A Social Perspective, David & Charles, 1972, Praeger, 1973.
(With R. J. Johnston) *Spatial Perspectives on Problems,* Wiley, 1976.
(With Johnston) *Spatial Processes and Form,* Wiley, 1976.
(With Johnston) *Social Areas in Cities,* Wiley, 1978.
(With Johnston) *Geography and the Urban Environment,* Wiley, Volume 1, 1978, Volume 2, 1979, Volume 3, 1980, Volume 4, 1981, Volume 5, 1982, Volume 6, 1984.
(With David M. Smith) *Social Problems and the City,* Oxford University Press, 1979.
Geography of Urban Crime, Longman, 1982.
(With C. J. Thomas) *Urban Geography: A First Approach,* Wiley, 1982.
(With R. C. Prentice and Thomas) *Heritage Sites: Strategies for Marketing and Development,* Avebury Publishing Co., 1989.
(Editor with D. J. Evans) *The Geography of Crime,* Routledge & Kegan Paul, 1989.
(With Thomas) *Cities in Space: City as Place,* David Fulton, 1990.

(Editor with Evans and N. R. Fyfe) *Crime, Policing and Place,* Routledge & Kegan Paul, 1992.
(With W. K. D. Davies) *Communities within Cities,* Belhaven, 1993.

Contributor of about eighty articles to professional journals.

WORK IN PROGRESS: Research in intra-urban residential mobility, juvenile delinquency and urban environments, recreation and leisure studies, geography of elderly and health care; heritage tourism; geography and literature.

*   *   *

HERRIOT, James 1916-

PERSONAL: Given name, James Alfred Wight; born October 3, 1916, in Sunderland, County Tyne and Werr, England; son of James Henry (a musician) and Hannah (a professional singer; maiden name, Bell) Wight; married Joan Catherine Danbury, November 5, 1941; children: James, Rosemary. *Education:* Glasgow Veterinary College, M.R.C.V.S., 1938. *Religion:* Protestant. *Avocational interests:* Music, walking with his dog.

CAREER: General practitioner in veterinary medicine, Yorkshire, England, 1938—; writer, 1966—. *Military service:* Royal Air Force, 1943-45.

MEMBER: British Veterinary Association (honorary member), Royal College of Veterinary Surgeons (fellow).

AWARDS, HONORS: American Library Association "Best Young Adult Book" citation, 1974, for *All Things Bright and Beautiful,* and 1975, for *All Creatures Great and Small;* Order of the British Empire, 1979; D. Litt., Watt University (Scotland), 1979; honorary D.Vsc., Liverpool University, 1984; James Herriot Award established by Humane Society of America.

WRITINGS:

If Only They Could Talk (also see below), M. Joseph, 1970, large print edition, G. K. Hall, 1977.
It Shouldn't Happen to a Vet (also see below), M. Joseph, 1972.
All Creatures Great and Small (contains *If Only They Could Talk* and *It Shouldn't Happen to a Vet*), St. Martin's, 1972, large print edition, G. K. Hall, 1973.
Let Sleeping Vets Lie (also see below), M. Joseph, 1973.
Vet in Harness (also see below), M. Joseph, 1974.
All Things Bright and Beautiful (contains *Let Sleeping Vets Lie* and *Vet in Harness*), St. Martin's, 1974, large print edition, G. K. Hall, 1975.
Vets Might Fly (also see below), M. Joseph, 1976.
Vet in a Spin (also see below), M. Joseph, 1977.

All Things Wise and Wonderful (contains *Vets Might Fly* and *Vet in a Spin*), St. Martin's, 1977, large print edition, G. K. Hall, 1977.

James Herriot's Yorkshire, illustrated with photographs by Derry Brabbs, St. Martin's, 1979.

(With others) *Animals Tame and Wild,* Sterling, 1979, published as *Animal Stories: Tame and Wild,* Sterling, 1985.

The Lord God Made Them All, St. Martin's, 1981, large print edition, G. K. Hall, 1982.

The Best of James Herriot, St. Martin's, 1983.

Moses the Kitten (for children), illustrated by Peter Barrett, St. Martin's, 1984.

Only One Woof (for children), illustrated by Barrett, St. Martin's, 1985.

James Herriot's Dog Stories, illustrated by Victor G. Ambrus, St. Martin's, 1986, large print edition, G. K. Hall, 1987.

The Christmas Day Kitten, illustrated by Ruth Brown, St. Martin's, 1986.

Bonny's Big Day, illustrated by Brown, St. Martin's, 1987.

Blossom Comes Home, illustrated by Brown, St. Martin's, 1988.

The Market Square Dog, illustrated by Brown, St. Martin's, 1990.

Oscar, Cat-about-Town (picture book), illustrated by Brown, M. Joseph, 1990.

Smudge, the Little Lost Lamb, illustrated by Brown, St. Martin's, 1991.

Every Living Thing, St. Martin's, 1992.

Also author of *James Herriot's Yorkshire Calendar.*

ADAPTATIONS: All Creatures Great and Small was filmed by EMI Production, 1975, presented as a television special on NBC-TV, 1975, adapted as a television series by BBC-TV, 1978, and PBS-TV, 1979, and recorded on audio cassette by Listen for Pleasure, 1980; *All Things Bright and Beautiful* was filmed by BBC-TV, 1979, (also released as *It Shouldn't Happen to a Vet*), and recorded as an audio cassette by Listen for Pleasure, 1980; audio cassette versions were recorded by Cassette Book for *All Things Wise and Wonderful,* and by Listen for Pleasure for *The Lord God Made Them All,* 1982; Listen for Pleasure also released an audio cassette entitled *Stories from the Herriot Collection.*

SIDELIGHTS: A country veterinarian who wrote what he thought would be his only book at age fifty, the man behind the pseudonym James Herriot seeks privacy and anonymity as fervently as other authors pursue celebrity status. "It's against the ethics of the veterinary profession to advertise and when I first started writing my books, I was afraid some of my peers might think it unprofessional of me to write under my own name," Herriot explained to Arturo F. Gonzalez in *Saturday Review.* "So, I was sit-

ting in front of the TV tapping out one of my stories and there was this fellow James Herriot playing such a good game of soccer for Birmingham that I just took his name." The first book, *If Only They Could Talk,* was published in 1970; its sales of only 1,200 copies did not accurately predict the career about to unfold. "I thought it would stop at one book and nobody would ever discover the identity of the obscure veterinary surgeon who had scribbled his experiences in snatched moments of spare time," Herriot wrote in *James Herriot's Yorkshire.*

His next book, however, eliminated the possibility of the unnamed vet fading into obscurity. *It Shouldn't Happen to a Vet* was published in the United States together with *If Only They Could Talk,* under the title *All Creatures Great and Small.* The book was "an instant best seller. In fact it was almost too much of a success," Herriot related to William Foster in *Scotsman.* "I know I should be grateful when I get as many as twenty or thirty fans waiting after surgery for me to sign their books. I am, of course, but I prefer my privacy." So began Herriot's quest for the now-elusive seclusion and anonymity of a veterinarian specializing in the treatment of English countryside farm animals.

All Creatures Great and Small proved to be his most successful book, and launched a series that has included *All Things Bright and Beautiful, All Things Wise and Wonderful, The Lord God Made Them All,* and *Every Living Thing.* A film version of *All Creatures Great and Small* starring Anthony Hopkins and Simon Ward was made in 1974. Herriot, who had visited the filming location in the countryside near his home, related his feelings at watching his book being made into a movie: "People have always asked me if I felt a thrill at seeing my past life enacted then, but strangely, the thing which gave me the deepest satisfaction was to hear the words I had written spoken by those fine actors," Herriot wrote in *James Herriot's Yorkshire.* "Both of them have magnificent voices, and every word came up to me and pierced me in a way I find hard to describe. . . . I have always been puzzled by the fact that Simon Ward, who was playing me, told me later that he was absolutely petrified at the prospect of meeting me. For a man who had just made a great name for himself playing Winston Churchill, it seemed odd. An obscure country vet was surely insignificant by contrast."

Herriot decided early on what his career would be. "When I was thirteen I read in my *Meccano* magazine an article describing a vet's life and that did it," he related to Foster. "Nothing could shake my determination to train as an animal vet and I got into Glasgow Veterinary School even though they were somewhat underwhelmed, if that's the word, by my poor science record." While he pursued his degree, Herriot was sure he would become a small animal surgeon, as he wrote in *All Creatures Great and Small,* "treating people's pets in my own animal hospital where everything would be not just modern but revolutionary. The fully equipped operating theatre, laboratory and X-ray room; they had all stayed crystal clear in my mind until I had graduated M.R.C.V.S. [Member of the Royal College of Veterinary Surgeons]. How on earth, then, did I come to be sitting on a high Yorkshire moor in shirt sleeves and Wellingtons, smelling vaguely of cows?" The change came about with Herriot's first job. "I hadn't thought it possible that I could spend all my days in a high, clean-blown land where the scent of grass or trees was never far away; and where even in the driving rain of winter I could snuff the air and find the freshness of growing things hidden somewhere in the cold clasp of the wind. Anyway, it had all changed for me and my work consisted now of driving from farm to farm across the roof of England with a growing conviction that I was a privileged person." The work and the countryside would become, thirty years later, the focal points of his books.

"The life of a country vet was dirty, uncomfortable, sometimes dangerous. It was terribly hard work and I loved it. I felt vaguely that I ought to write about it and every day for twenty-five years I told my wife of something funny that had happened and said I was keeping it for the book," Herriot told Foster. "She usually said 'Yes, dear' to humour me but one day, when I was fifty, she said: 'Who are you kidding? Vets of fifty don't write first books.' Well, that did it. I stormed out and bought some paper and taught myself to type."

Writing proved difficult at first. "I started to put it all down and the story didn't work," he recalled to Foster. "All I managed to pick out on the machine was a very amateur school essay. So I spent a year or two learning my craft, as real writers say." After four years of learning to write and enduring publishers' rejections, *If Only They Could Talk* was published in England. By itself the book sold only 1,200 copies; as half of *All Creatures Great and Small,* which was also published in the United States, the story found much greater success.

Reviewers described *All Creatures Great and Small* as a welcome change of pace. "What the world needs now, and does every so often, is a warm, G-rated, down-home, and unadrenalized prize of a book that sneaks onto the bestseller lists for no apparent reason other than a certain floppy-eared puppy appeal," William R. Doerner wrote in *Time.* "However, it is only partly because warm puppies—along with cows, horses, pigs, cats and the rest of the animal kingdom—figure as his main characters that James Herriot's [*All Creatures Great and Small*] qualifies admirably." *Atlantic Monthly* reviewer Phoebe Adams noted that the book "is full of recalcitrant cows, sinister pigs, neurotic dogs, Yorkshire weather, and pleasantly demented

colleagues. It continues to be one of the funniest and most likable books around."

The popular success of *All Creatures Great and Small* prompted Herriot to continue in the same vein; *All Things Bright and Beautiful,* containing *Let Sleeping Vets Lie* and *Vet in Harness,* was published two years later. "The title is a first line from a hymn of Mrs. Cecil Alexander whose second line is the title of James Herriot's first book: *All Creatures Great and Small,*" Eugene J. Linehan noted in *Best Sellers.* "As that work was received with enthusiasm, so should this be. It's a joy." The *New York Times Book Review*'s Paul Showers described *All Things Bright and Beautiful* as "Herriot's enthusiastic endorsement of a simple, unpretentious lifestyle. No wonder the earlier book was so popular. Here is a man who actually enjoys his work without worrying about the Protestant Ethic; he finds satisfaction in testing his skill against challenges of different kinds. Beyond that, he delights in the day-to-day process of living even when things aren't going too well."

All Things Wise and Wonderful, containing *Vets Might Fly* and *Vet in a Spin,* continued Herriot's autobiographical stories. Recounting the time from his induction into the Royal Air Force during World War II to his medical discharge, Herriot "wisely interweaves flashbacks to his family and the country practice, now famous from the first two accounts," Jane Manthorne commented in the *Virginia Quarterly Review.* "Herriot's writings epitomize the process of bibliotherapy: they can be used to inspire, to nurture, to brighten and to help the reader endure," Joy K. Roy declared in the *English Journal.* "Nature, being neither kind nor unkind in this objective view, can be a balancer of thought. . . . [T]his reading can patch up the human spirit."

The Lord God Made Them All, the fourth in Herriot's original tetralogy, "begins as if the others had never ended, the same way old friends meet again and talk, at once forgetting they have been apart," Lola D. Gillebaard remarked in the *Los Angeles Times Book Review.* The book contains one of the most memorable anecdotes in all of Herriot's work: his attempt at the then-new technique of bovine artificial insemination. Having "flipped through a pamphlet on the subject," Herriot wrote, he expected that the process would be fairly simple, but he soon found himself fighting off a charging bull, wielding an eighteen-inch artificial vagina "with thrusts and lunges worthy of a fencing master." "This is Herriot at his best, the Buster Keaton of veterinary medicine, able to make us laugh, cry or nod in agreement with some snippet of universal truth," *Washington Post Book World* contributor Vic Sussman asserted.

In 1984, Herriot expanded his writing to include children's stories. *Moses the Kitten* was the first of several animal stories written for young readers. Other cat tales have included *The Christmas Day Kitten* and *Oscar, Cat-about-Town.* Dogs have received equal billing, in books including *James Herriot's Dog Stories,* many culled from his previous works, and *The Market Square Dog.* Among them is Tricky Woo, the pampered and overfed dog of *All Creatures Great and Small,* whom Herriot took into his home for several weeks of diet and exercise when the dog "had become hugely fat, like a bloated sausage with a leg at each corner." In a *Washington Post Book World* review of *James Herriot's Dog Stories,* Donald McCaig wrote, " 'I am,' James Herriot says, 'as soppy over my dogs as any old lady.' A trait which, he assures us, 'has always stood me in good stead in my dealings with clients.' But he's not 'soppy.' Not a bit." In one story, a dying woman worries that after her death she will be reunited with her loved ones, but not with her animals, because she has been told that animals have no souls. Herriot convinces her that they do, because "if having a soul means being able to feel love and loyalty and gratitude, then animals are better off than a lot of humans." "I suppose there's someone who will find this 'soppy,' " McCaig responded. "Me, I think it's true." In *The Christmas Day Kitten,* a stray cat who frequently visits Mrs. Pickering arrives ill on Christmas Day, and delivers a kitten before she dies. Mrs. Pickering adopts the kitten, naming him Buster; a year later she relates the happiness her "Christmas present" has brought to the household. "*The Christmas Day Kitten* is simply another yarn of the sort Herriot spins so effectively, a memory shared, this time, as a doctor might share it with a child on his knee. I think the average kid would be all ears," Jack Miles wrote in the *Los Angeles Times.*

Although he told Foster and others that *The Lord God Made Them All* would be his last "big" book, Herriot relented; *Every Living Thing* was published in 1992, the twentieth anniversary of the release of *All Creatures Great and Small.* Herriot told Foster in 1981, "I look at the last ten years and realise how much experience has been lost while I tapped away at a typewriter. Not enough time has been devoted to my grandchildren. I'm missing their youth and the fun of doing things with them. There's so much gardening neglected and so many walks never taken over the fells, when the air was warm and the pale sun fingering the heather." He also hoped that another experience long missing from his life—anonymity—would return. By 1985, however, his decision was no longer firm. "[I] might get what they call a rush of blood," Herriot told Monty Brower in *People.* "Besides, I'm not so good at pushing the horses and cows about as I used to be."

A *Publishers Weekly* reviewer predicted that "Herriot's many fans will not be disappointed" in *Every Living Thing,* which continues the story of the country vet's family and practice from the point where *The Lord God Made*

Them All ended. A *Kirkus Reviews* contributor declared the book a "smashingly good sequel to the beloved veterinarian's earlier memoirs, and well worth the ten-year wait since *The Lord God Made Them All.*" In a *Detroit Free Press* review Cathy Collison noted, "More than earlier volumes," *Every Living Thing* "offers more of Herriot's personal life," including his battle with a rare infection that causes him fevers, delirium, and depression. But, as is his trademark, Herriot and his family cope with this and other difficulties; he recovers and moves on. Collison concluded, "It is enough to keep the reader hoping Herriot, now retired from surgery, will turn his hand to one more volume."

BIOGRAPHICAL/CRITICAL SOURCES:

BOOKS

Contemporary Literary Criticism, Volume 12, Gale, 1980, pp. 282-284.
Herriot, James, *All Creatures Great and Small,* St. Martin's, 1972.
Herriot, *James Herriot's Yorkshire,* St. Martin's, 1979.

PERIODICALS

American Veterinary Medical Association Journal, February 1, 1974; October 15, 1975; August 1, 1979.
Atlantic Monthly, August, 1974; October, 1974.
Best Sellers, October 1, 1974, pp. 304-305.
Books and Bookmen, October, 1973.
Detroit Free Press, September 28, 1992.
English Journal, December, 1973; March, 1979, p. 57.
Kirkus Reviews, July 1, 1992, p. 827.
Life, March, 1988.
London Times, July 23, 1976.
Los Angeles Times, December 25, 1986.
Los Angeles Times Book Review, June 7, 1981, p. 4.
Maclean's (Canada), May 29, 1978.
National Observer, December 28, 1974.
New Statesman, March 10, 1972; August 20, 1976.
New York Times, December 14, 1972; September 24, 1974.
New York Times Book Review, November 3, 1974, p. 61.
Observer, February 13, 1972; May 27, 1973; August 22, 1976.
People, March 18, 1985.
Publishers Weekly, January 1, 1986; September 26, 1986; July 20, 1992, p. 238.
Radio Times, January, 1978.
Saturday Review, May/June, 1986.
Scotsman, October 16, 1981.
Smithsonian, November, 1974.
Time, February 19, 1973; June 29, 1981.
Virginia Quarterly Review, winter, 1978, p. 30.

Washington Post Book World, December 8, 1974; September 14, 1975; December 5, 1976; September 11, 1977; June 21, 1981, p. 11; May 25, 1988, p. 4.

—*Sketch by Deborah A. Stanley*

*   *   *

HILLERT, Margaret 1920-

PERSONAL: Born January 22, 1920, in Saginaw, MI; daughter of Edward Carl (a tool and die maker) and A. Ilva (Sproull) Hillert. *Education:* Bay City Junior College, A.A., 1941; University of Michigan, R.N., 1944; Wayne University (now Wayne State University), A.B., 1948.

ADDRESSES: Home—Birmingham, MI. *Office*—Children's Department, Royal Oak Public Library, 222 East Eleven Mile Rd., Royal Oak, MI 48067.

CAREER: Primary school teacher in public schools of Royal Oak, MI, beginning 1948. Poet and writer of children's books. Affiliated with Royal Oak Public Library. Lecturer at writers conferences, library seminars, and book fairs.

MEMBER: International League of Children's Poets, Society of Children's Book Writers and Illustrators, Emily Dickinson Society, Poetry Society of Michigan, Detroit Women Writers.

AWARDS, HONORS: Numerous awards for poems from Poetry Society of Michigan; Chicago Children's Reading Round Table Annual Award, 1991.

WRITINGS:

CHILDREN'S POETRY

Farther Than Far, Follett, 1969.
I Like to Live in the City, Golden Books, 1970.
Who Comes to Your House?, Golden Books, 1973.
The Sleepytime Book, Golden Press, 1975.
Come Play with Me, Follett, 1975.
What Is It?, Follett, 1978.
I'm Special . . . So Are You!, Hallmark Books, 1979.
Let's Take a Break, Continental Press, 1980.
Action Verse for the Primary Classroom, Denison, 1980.
Doing Things, Continental Press, 1980.
Fun Days, Follett, 1982.
Rabbits and Rainbows, Standard Publishing, 1985.
Dandelions and Daydreams, Standard Publishing, 1987.
Lightning Bugs and Lullabies, Standard Publishing, 1988.
Sing A Song of Christmas, Standard Publishing, 1989.

CHILDREN'S BOOKS

The Birthday Car, Follett, 1966.
The Little Runaway, Follett, 1966.
The Yellow Boat, Follett, 1966.

The Snow Baby, Follett, 1969.
Circus Fun, Follett, 1969.
A House for Little Red, Follett, 1970.
Little Puff, Follett, 1973.
Happy Birthday, Dear Dragon, Follett, 1977.
Play Ball, Follett, 1978.
The Baby Bunny, Follett, 1980.
What Am I?, Follett, 1980.
Run to the Rainbow, Follett, 1980.
I Love You, Dear Dragon, Follett, 1980.
Happy Easter, Dear Dragon, Follett, 1980.
Let's Go, Dear Dragon, Follett, 1980.
Merry Christmas, Dear Dragon, Follett, 1980.
Happy Halloween, Dear Dragon, Follett, 1980.
Away Go the Boats, Follett, 1980.
Who Goes to School?, Follett, 1981.
Big Cowboy, Little Cowboy, Follett, 1981.
City Fun, Follett, 1981.
The Witch Who Went for a Walk, Follett, 1981.
Take a Walk, Johnny, Follett, 1981.
The Purple Pussycat, Follett, 1981.
The Cow That Got Her Wish, Follett, 1981.
Let's Have a Play, Follett, 1982.
Up, Up, and Away, Follett, 1982.
I Like Things, Follett, 1982.
Why We Have Thanksgiving, Follett, 1982.
The Ball Book, Follett, 1982.
The Funny Ride, Follett, 1982.
Go to Sleep, Dear Dragon, Modern Curriculum Press, 1985.
Help for Dear Dragon, Modern Curriculum Press, 1985.
Come to School, Dear Dragon, Modern Curriculum Press, 1985.
It's Circus Time, Dear Dragon, Modern Curriculum Press, 1985.
A Friend for Dear Dragon, Modern Curriculum Press, 1985.
I Need You, Dear Dragon, Modern Curriculum Press, 1985.

CHILDREN'S STORIES RETOLD

The Funny Baby, Follett, 1963.
The Three Little Pigs, Follett, 1963.
The Three Bears, Follett, 1963.
The Three Goats, Follett, 1963.
The Magic Beans, Follett, 1966.
Cinderella at the Ball, Follett, 1970.
The Cookie House, Follett, 1978.
The Golden Goose, Follett, 1978.
Not I, Not I, Follett, 1980.
The Little Cookie, Follett, 1980.
Four Friends, Follett, 1980.
The Magic Nutcracker, Follett, 1982.
Pinocchio, Follett, 1982.

The Boy and the Goats, Follett, 1982.
Tom Thumb, Follett, 1982.
Little Red Ridinghood, Follett, 1982.

OTHER

God's Big Book, Standard Publishing, 1988.
Guess, Guess, Standard Publishing, 1988.
The Birth of Jesus, Standard Publishing, 1988.
Jesus Grows Up, Standard Publishing, 1988.

Work represented in numerous anthologies. Contributor of hundreds of poems to numerous periodicals, including *Horn Book, Christian Science Monitor, McCall's, Saturday Evening Post, Jack and Jill,* and *Western Humanities Review.* Hillert's work has been translated into Danish, Portuguese, Swedish, and German.

WORK IN PROGRESS: A collection of children's poetry and three collections of adult poetry; fifteen juveniles.

SIDELIGHTS: Although Margaret Hillert started writing poetry and stories when she was in the third grade, she submitted her first work for publication in 1961. "Nobody ever really encouraged me to try to get my stuff published," Hillert explained in the *Detroit Free Press.* "But from the time I first saw my name in print, you just couldn't keep me from submitting things."

In *Pass the Poetry, Please,* Hillert shared her thoughts on writing: "I can't give you a glib one-line definition of poetry such as many I have seen. Poetry has been an undefined but definite part of my life, and I don't think I chose to write it at all. I have been writing it ever since the first one I did when I was eight years old, which seems to indicate it has always been a part of my nature. I read widely, from the poetry stacks in the library when I was growing up—and still do to some extent. I'm not one of those people who can say, 'Today I'll write a poem.' I may go without writing anything for some time as a consequence, but once I get the grain of an idea, the thing must be worked through, sometimes for days, weeks, or months. Things don't usually come to me whole and full blown. It intrigues me to work generally, but not always, with traditional forms but in fresh ways."

To *CA,* Hillert added: "I am glad to see that much is being done to interest children in poetry, but I would like to see greater interest in reading it and listening to it instead of so much writing without sufficient background; and I cannot subscribe to the current theory that whatever a child writes can be called a poem despite any sign of imagination or creativity."

BIOGRAPHICAL/CRITICAL SOURCES:

BOOKS

Authors in the News, Volume 1, Gale, 1976, pp. 225-226.

Hopkins, Lee B., *Pass the Poetry, Please,* Citation Press, 1972.
Janeczko, Paul, *The Place My Words Are Looking For,* Bradbury, 1990.
LeMaster, J. R., *Poets of the Midwest,* Young Publications, 1966.

PERIODICALS

Detroit Free Press, May 6, 1973.

*   *   *

HINCKLEY, Ted C(harles) 1925-

PERSONAL: Born October 4, 1925, in New York, NY; son of Theodore C. and Eunice (Platt) Hinckley; married Caryl Chesmore (a teacher), June 17, 1948; children: two. *Education:* Claremont Men's College, B.A., 1950; Northwest Missouri State College, B.S., 1951; University of Kansas City, M.A., 1953; Indiana University, Ph.D., 1961. *Politics:* Independent. *Religion:* Presbyterian. *Avocational interests:* Carpentry, skiing, sailing.

ADDRESSES: Home—P.O. Box 456, Saratoga, CA 95070. *Office*—Western Washington University, 516 High St., Bellingham, WA 98225.

CAREER: Barstow School, Kansas City, MO, instructor of history 1951-53; Claremont Men's College, Claremont, CA, instructor and assistant to president, 1953-55; St. Katharine's School, Davenport, IA, headmaster, 1955-57; San Jose State University, San Jose, CA, assistant professor, 1959-63, associate professor, 1963-67, professor of history, beginning 1967, director of Sourisseau Academy, 1971-73, co-director of American Revolution Bi-Centennial Series, 1971-76; Western Washington University, Bellingham, WA, currently adjunct professor. Director of Pacific Basin History Conference, 1965, 1967; National Endowment for the Humanities lecturer, 1967, 1976; member of board of directors of American West Publishing Co., 1971—. *Military service:* U.S. Navy, 1943-46; U.S. Army Reserve, 1950-52, U.S. Navy Reserve, Air Intelligence, 1953-59; became ensign; received three air medals.

MEMBER: American Association of University Professors, Organization of American Historians, American Historical Association (Pacific Coast Branch), Presbyterian Historical Society, Western History Association.

AWARDS, HONORS: American Philosophical Society grants, 1962, 1966; Danforth associate, 1962; Distinguished Teaching Award, 1967, and Outstanding Professor Award, 1981, both from California State Colleges; American Association for State and Local History grant, 1969; Huntington Library summer fellowship, 1971.

WRITINGS:

(Editor) *Proceedings: The Westward Movement and Historical Involvement of the Americas in the Pacific Basin,* San Jose State College Press, 1965.

(Editor with Tom Wendel) *Student Manual for U.S. History, 17a,* San Jose State College Press, 1967.

The Americanization of Alaska, 1867-1897, Pacific Books, 1972.

(Editor) *Studies in Territorial History,* Sunflower University Press, 1981.

Alaskan John G. Brady: Missionary, Businessman, Judge, and Governor, 1878-1918, Ohio State University Press, 1982.

(Editor) *Business Entrepreneurs in the West,* Sunflower University Press, 1986.

(Editor) *Presidents and the American West,* Sunflower University Press, 1992.

Contributor to books, including *Alaska and Japan: Perspectives of Past and Present,* edited by Tsuguo Arai, Alaska Methodist University Press, 1972. Also contributor of about forty articles to historical journals, including *Pacific Historical Review* and *Ohio History.* Member of editorial board of *Pacific Northwest Quarterly,* 1974—.

WORK IN PROGRESS: A biography of Sheldon Jackson; a history of the assimilation of Alaska's southeastern natives into American culture.

*   *   *

HINTON, William H. 1919-

PERSONAL: Born February 2, 1919, in Chicago, IL; son of Sebastian (a lawyer) and Carmelita (Chase) Hinton; married Bertha Sneck (an English translator), June 12, 1945 (divorced July, 1954); married Joanne Raiford, November 14, 1959 (died February 2, 1986); married Katherine Chiv, August 24, 1987; children: (first marriage) Carmelita; (second marriage) Michael Howard, Alyssa Anne, Catherine Jean; stepchildren: (third marriage) May Anne Lyle, Lorin Lyle. *Education:* Attended Harvard University, 1937-39; Cornell University, B.S., 1941. *Politics:* Marxist. *Avocational interests:* Skiing, mountain climbing, hiking.

ADDRESSES: Home—R.D. 4072, Fleetwood, PA 19522. *Office*—UNICEF/Beijing, 12 Sanlitun Rd., Beijing, China 100600.

CAREER: Writer. U.S. Office of War Information, propaganda analyst in China, 1945-46; National Farmers Union, Eastern Division, organizer in Connecticut, 1946-47; tractor technician in China for United Nations Relief and Rehabilitation Administration, 1947, for North China People's Government in Shansi Province, 1947-49, and for People's Republic of China in Peking, 1949-53; truck mechanic in Philadelphia, PA, 1956-63; grain farmer in Fleetwood, PA, 1963-79. Lecturer in Oriental studies, University of Pennsylvania, 1975. Consultant, Beijing Ministry of Agriculture, 1978, 1985, United Nations Grasslands Project in Inner Mongolia, 1980-83, Food and Agriculture Organization United Nations Agricultural Mechanization Project, 1985-91, Ministry of Forestry in Mexico, 1988, and UNICEF/Beijing, 1991-92.

MEMBER: National Farmers Organization, U.S.-China People's Friendship Association (chairman, 1974-76), American Civil Liberties Union, Berks County Committee on Peace in Vietnam, Berks County Democratic Socialists, Fleetwood Grange.

WRITINGS:

Fanshen: A Documentary of Revolution in a Chinese Village (first volume of the Long Bow Trilogy; also see below), Monthly Review Press, 1967.

Iron Oxen: A Documentary of Revolution in Chinese Farming, Monthly Review Press, 1970.

Turning Point in China: An Essay on the Cultural Revolution, Monthly Review Press, 1972.

Hundred Day War: The Cultural Revolution at Tsinghua University, Monthly Review Press, 1972.

Chou En-Lai: Conversations with Americans, USCPFA, 1977.

Shenfan: The Continuing Revolution in a Chinese Village (second volume of the Long Bow Trilogy), Random House, 1983.

The Great Reversal: The Privatization of China, Monthly Review Press, 1990.

Also author of *China's Continuing Revolution,* 1970. Contributor to *New China.*

WORK IN PROGRESS: The third volume of the Long Bow Trilogy, to be entitled "Fen Shan" ("Divide the Mountain").

SIDELIGHTS: William H. Hinton provides readers with a rare glimpse into life in Communist China with such books as *Fanshen: A Documentary of Revolution in a Chinese Village* and its sequel, *Shenfan: The Continuing Revolution in a Chinese Village.*

Fanshen (the word means "to turn over") is based on notes kept by Hinton during a six-month period in which he lived in the Chinese farming village of Chang Chuang—Long Bow—in southeastern Shansi Province in 1948. The author's notes were subsequently seized by the United States Customs Service and were then acquired by the Eastland Committee on Internal Security. The resulting legal battles delayed *Fanshen*'s publication until 1967. Once released, the work garnered praise from such critics as C. T. Hu, who in *Saturday Review* calls *Fanshen* "an important book" with "a message that goes beyond the transformation of China. In this age of universal rising expectations, there still exist predominantly agrarian societies in which physical survival almost requires the abandonment of human qualities. The lesson of Long Bow village, so movingly and compassionately recorded by [Hinton], should be studied and restudied by all who have a personal concern for the future of the majority of mankind."

Acknowledging the author's Marxist leanings in his observations of life in post-revolutionary China, *New Republic* critic Harrison E. Salisbury notes that *Fanshen* "is not a study of a military commune. It does not basically deal with military life at all. It is an intimate and intensely detailed examination of how the Chinese revolution came to a village." The author "is not an objective observer," adds Salisbury, "but he is so good an observer that what he tells and what he describes becomes unequaled evidence of the sinews of the Revolution, of the raw forces of the China countryside which have been so closely woven, so mobilized through the Revolution."

In 1971, Hinton returned to Long Bow and recorded the way the rural village sustained itself in the decades following the land reform. His book *Shenfan* (the title, a literal reversal of the word "fanshen," means "to plow deeply") is described by Marilyn B. Young in *Village Voice* as a "painstaking" sequel. "No other recent account confronts so directly the most painful and disturbing aspects of the Chinese revolution in power," continues Young. "None is as complete in its mapping of the twists and turns of policy, or as relentless in its portrayal of the cancerous life cycle of factionalism. None persists so boldly in its commitment to the possibility of transformation of collectivity, or characterizes so vividly the exhilaration of communal effort and the difficult virtue of putting 'public first, self second.' "

"As in *Fanshen,* Hinton has painted a densely peopled, richly detailed panorama of a China rarely seen by foreigners," remarks *Newsweek* reviewer Jim Miller of *Shenfan.* "But the new book's canvas is far vaster—a matter of decades, not months—and its hues are much darker, perhaps because of the two central events it chronicles: the degeneration of the Chinese revolution from 'innocent idealism' into a bloody anarchy, and Hinton's own growing skepticism about the Chinese road to communism." And while *Chicago Tribune Book World* writer Ross Terrill has some criticism of *Shenfan,* saying that its political analysis "is confused, at best," *Newsweek*'s Miller concludes that, taken together, *Fanshen* and *Shenfan* "comprise a singular document of modern China in the making—an unforgettable portrait of the strange and stormy fate of a small peasant village."

BIOGRAPHICAL/CRITICAL SOURCES:

BOOKS

Hinton, William H., *Shenfan: The Continuing Revolution in a Chinese Village,* Random House, 1983.

PERIODICALS

Chicago Tribune Book World, May 22, 1983.
Los Angeles Times Book Review, September 4, 1983.
Nation, September 4, 1967.
New Republic, May 20, 1967.
Newsweek, June 6, 1983.
New York Times Book Review, March 12, 1967; January 14, 1973; July 3, 1983.
Saturday Review, March 11, 1967.
Times Literary Supplement, June 29, 1973.
Village Voice, July 19, 1983.
Washington Post Book World, June 19, 1983.

*   *   *

HOCKING, Mary (Eunice)   1921-

PERSONAL: Born April 8, 1921, in Acton, London, England; daughter of Charles (a librarian) and Eunice (Hewett) Hocking. *Education:* Educated in England.

ADDRESSES: Home—Lewes, Sussex, England. *Agent*—A. M. Heath, 79 St. Martin's Ln., London WC2N 4AA, England.

CAREER: Writer. Worked as local government officer, 1946-70. *Wartime service:* Served with meteorology branch of Fleet Air Arm during World War II.

MEMBER: Royal Society of Literature (fellow), Society of Authors.

WRITINGS:

NOVELS

The Winter City, Chatto & Windus, 1961.
Visitors to the Crescent, Chatto & Windus, 1962.
The Sparrow, Chatto & Windus, 1964.
The Young Spaniard, Chatto & Windus, 1965.
Ask No Question, Morrow, 1967.
A Time of War (also see below), Chatto & Windus, 1968.
Checkmate, Chatto & Windus, 1969.
The Hopeful Traveller (sequel to *A Time of War*), Chatto & Windus, 1970.
The Climbing Frame, Chatto & Windus, 1971.
Family Circle, Chatto & Windus, 1972.
Daniel Come to Judgement, Chatto & Windus, 1974.
The Bright Day, Chatto & Windus, 1975.
The Mind Has Mountains, Chatto & Windus, 1976.
Look, Stranger!, Chatto & Windus, 1978.
He Who Plays the King, Chatto & Windus, 1980.

March House, Chatto & Windus, 1981.

Good Daughters (first novel in trilogy), Chatto & Windus, 1984.

Indifferent Heroes (second novel in trilogy), Chatto & Windus, 1985.

Welcome Strangers (third novel in trilogy), Chatto & Windus, 1986.

An Irrelevant Woman, Chatto & Windus, 1987.

A Particular Place, Chatto & Windus, 1989.

Letters from Constance, Chatto & Windus, 1991.

SIDELIGHTS: "Mary Hocking matter-of-factly reveals the pettiness of the middle classes while sympathetically exploring her characters' personalities," *Times Literary Supplement* contributor Linda Taylor observes of *March House.* Taylor adds that Hocking has established herself as a reliable novelist because she "knows about the dreariness of everyday life" and that "she also knows how to write about it vividly." As Nick Totton notes in *Spectator,* the author "writes brilliantly on many levels at once because she knows that the everyday contains another, stranger reality: it only takes attention, an at first casual intensification of vision, to open the crack between the worlds."

Hocking once told *CA:* "I find it hard to analyze my own work, and I am grateful to perceptive critics who do the job for me. Looking back over my novels, it is a surprise to find all those people trying to struggle free of the things which hamper and prevent them in their society. So, I suppose, I am concerned with the individual searching for something that will always be beyond his grasp because there is a mystery at the center of life. I try not to be solemn about it, though, because I find I am more effective when I treat characters and events with humor.

"My advice to young writers is to write about something you believe in; take all the good criticism that comes your way, but don't let anyone try to turn you into another kind of writer because you aren't producing books that sell in vast numbers. Don't look down on your reader; write for someone as intelligent, interesting, perceptive, witty, amusing, caring, compassionate, and iconoclastic as yourself!"

BIOGRAPHICAL/CRITICAL SOURCES:

BOOKS

Contemporary Literary Criticism, Volume 13, Gale, 1980.

PERIODICALS

Listener, July 3, 1975; October 14, 1976.

New Statesman, September 17, 1971; November 3, 1972.

Observer (London), July 27, 1975; October 10, 1976; January 21, 1979; July 22, 1984.

Spectator, July 21, 1984.

Times Literary Supplement, December 8, 1972; July 4, 1975; December 17, 1976; September 11, 1981; September 14, 1984.

*   *   *

HOFFMAN, Herbert H(einz) 1928-

PERSONAL: Born January 22, 1928, in Berlin, Germany; immigrated to United States, 1954; naturalized citizen, 1960; son of Friedrich (an engineer) and Hertha (Schoenrock) Hoffman; married Rita T. Ludwig, June 7, 1952; children: Cheryl. *Education:* Los Angeles State College of Applied Arts and Sciences (now California State University, Los Angeles), B.A., 1959; University of Southern California, M.S.L.S., 1960, further graduate study, 1966-70.

ADDRESSES: Home—1700 Port Manleigh Cir., Newport Beach, CA 92706. *Office*—Rancho Santiago College Library, Santa Ana, CA 92706.

CAREER: Ford Motor Co., Newport Beach, CA, reference librarian, 1960-65; Rancho Santiago College, Santa Ana, CA, catalog librarian, 1970—; Headway Publications, Newport Beach, editor and publisher, 1976-83. *Military service:* German Air Force, 1944-45.

MEMBER: American Society for Information Science, American Society for Indexers.

WRITINGS:

Descriptive Cataloging in a New Light: Polemical Chapters for Librarians, Rayline, 1976.

What Happens in Library Filing?, Linnet Books, 1976.

Alphanumeric Filing Rules for Business Documents, Rayline, 1977.

(With Taverekere Srikantaiah) *An Introduction to Quantitative Research Methods for Librarians,* 2nd edition, Headway, 1977.

Bibliography Without Footnotes, Headway, 1977.

Simple Library Bookkeeping, Headway, 1977.

Small Library Cataloging, Headway, 1977, 2nd edition, Scarecrow, 1986.

(Compiler) *Cuento Mexicano Index,* Headway, 1978.

Paris 2: A Statement of Cataloging Principles Suggested as a Replacement for the Paris Principles of 1961, Headway, 1978.

(Compiler with wife, Rita Ludwig Hoffman) *International Index to Recorded Poetry,* H. W. Wilson, 1983.

Latin American Play Index, Scarecrow, Volume I: *1920-1962,* 1983-84, Volume II: *1962-1980,* 1983-84.

(Compiler) *Hoffman's Index to Poetry: Europe and Latin America,* Scarecrow, 1985.

International Index to Recorded Plays, American Library Association, 1985.

(Compiler) *Faces in the News: An Index to Photographic Portraits, 1987-1991,* Scarecrow, 1992.

Contributor to journals, including *Catholic Library World, Technicalities, Library Resources and Technical Services, American Libraries, Journal of Academic Librarianship, Unabashed Librarian,* and *Database.*

SIDELIGHTS: Herbert H. Hoffman told *CA:* "As a librarian I specialize in cataloging. I advocate the development of a new generation of library catalog, one that gives direct access to all the works stored on the library's shelves, including those embedded in collections and anthologies. I envision an international analytic online union catalog."

* * *

HOHENDAHL, Peter Uwe 1936-

PERSONAL: Born March 17, 1936, in Hamburg, Germany; son of Wilhelm F. (a businessman) and Emilie (Uelschen) Hohendahl; married I. Maria Zoetelief (a university lecturer), July 2, 1965; children: Deborah, Gwendolyn. *Education:* Attended the universities of Bern, Goettingen, and Hamburg, 1956-63; University of Hamburg, Ph.D., 1964. *Politics:* Independent. *Religion:* Lutheran.

ADDRESSES: Home—81 Genung Rd., Ithaca, NY 14850. *Office*—Department of German Studies, Cornell University, Ithaca, NY 14853.

CAREER: Pennsylvania State University, University Park, assistant professor of German, 1965-68; Washington University, St. Louis, MO, associate professor, 1968-69, professor of German, 1970-77, director of the German Area program, 1969-73, chairman of department, 1972-77; Cornell University, Ithaca, NY, professor of German and comparative literature, beginning 1977, became Jacob Gould Schurman Professor of German and Comparative Literature, 1985—, chairman of department, 1981-86. Visiting professor, Hamburg University, 1974; visiting research professor, Free University, Berlin, 1976, and Center for Interdisciplinary Research, 1980-81; distinguished visiting professor, Ohio State University, 1987.

MEMBER: Modern Language Association of America, American Association of Teachers of German, German Studies Association, North American Heine Society (president, 1986-90).

AWARDS, HONORS: Studienstiftung des deutschen Volkes fellow, 1960-64; Volkswagenwerk Foundation fellow, 1964-65; postdoctoral fellow at Harvard University, 1964-65; grants from Thyssen Foundation, 1975, and American Philosophical Society, 1976; fellow of the Cen-

ter for Interdisciplinary Research, University of Bielefeld, 1981, 1987; Guggenheim fellow, 1983-84; University of Paderborn, Germany, research fellow, 1990.

WRITINGS:

Das Bild der buergerlichen Welt im expressionistischen Drama, Winter, 1967.

(Editor) *Gottfried Benn—Wirkung wider Willen,* Athenaeum, 1971.

(Editor with Egon Schwartz and Herbert Lindenberger) *Essays on European Literature,* Washington University Press, 1972.

(Co-editor) *Exil und Innere Emigration II,* Athenaeum, 1973.

(Editor) *Sozialgeschichte und Wirkungsaesthetik,* Fischer-Athenaeum, 1974.

Literaturkritik und Oeffentlichkeit, Piper, 1974.

(Co-editor and contributor) *Literatur und Literaturtheorie in der D. D. R.,* Suhrkamp, 1976.

Der europaeische Roman der Empfindsamkeit, Athenaion, 1977.

(Co-editor and contributor) *Legitimationskrisen des deutschen Adels 1200-1900,* Metzler, 1979.

The Institution of Criticism, Cornell University Press, 1982.

(Co-editor and contributor) *Literatur der D. D. R. in den siebziger Jahren,* Suhrkamp, 1983.

(Editor) *Literaturkritik: Eine Textdokumentation zur Geschichte einer literarischen Gattung,* Volume 4, 1848-1870, Topos, 1984.

Literarische Kultur im Zeitalter des Liberalismus, 1830-1870, Beck, 1985.

(Editor and contributor) *Geschichte der deutschen Literaturkritik,* Metzler, 1985.

(Editor and contributor) *A History of German Literary Criticism, 1730-1980,* University of Nebraska Press, 1988.

Building a National Literature: The Case of Germany, 1830-1870, Cornell University Press, 1989.

Reappraisals: Shifting Alignments in Postwar Critical Theory, Cornell University Press, 1991.

Also contributor to books, including *Perspectives of Literary Symbolism,* edited by J. Strelka, Pennsylvania State University Press, 1968; *Popularitaet und Trivialitaet,* edited by R. Grimm and J. Hermand, Athenaeum, 1974; *Heinrich Heine: Artistik und Engagement,* edited by W. Kuttenkeuler, Metzler, 1977; *Literatur in der Bundesrepublik Deutschland seit 1965,* edited by P. M. Luetzeler and E. Schwarz, Athenaeum, 1980; *Literature and History,* edited by L. Schulze and W. Wetzels, University Press of America, 1983; *Zeitgenossenschaft: Zur deutschsprachigen Literatur im 20: Jahrhundert,* edited by P. M. Luetzeler, H. Lehnert, and G. S. Williams, Athenaeum,

1987; *Geschichte als Literatur,* edited by H. Eggert, U. Profitlich, and K. R. Scherpe, J. B. Metzler, 1990; and *Europaeische Barockrezeption,* edited by K. Garber, Otto Harrassowitz, 1991. Contributor of articles to *Orbis Litterarum, LILI, Schiller-Jahrbuch, German Quarterly, Germanisch-Romanische-Monatsschrift, Telos,* and *New German Critique.* Associate editor, *Modern International Drama,* 1967-68; member of board of editors, *Literaturwis-senschaft und Linguistik,* beginning 1971; member of advisory council, *Studies in Twentieth Century Literature,* 1976—; contributing editor, *New German Critique,* 1979; member of editorial board, *German Quarterly,* 1983-88; member of academic advisory board, *Contemporary German Studies,* 1984—; member of advisory committee, *PMLA,* 1985-87; editor of series "Probleme der Dichtung," Carl-Winter-Universitaetsverlag, 1986—; editor of series "Modern German Culture and Literature," University of Nebraska Press, 1988—.

WORK IN PROGRESS: Studies on the aesthetic theory of the Frankfurt School.

* * *

HOLMAN, Felice   1919-

PERSONAL: Born October 24, 1919, in New York, NY; daughter of Jac C. (an engineering consultant) and Celia (an artist; maiden name, Hotchner) Holman; married Herbert Valen, April 13, 1941; children: Nanine Elisabeth. *Education:* Syracuse University, B.A., 1941.

ADDRESSES: Home—Del Mar, CA. *Office*—c/o Charles Scribner's Sons, 115 Fifth Ave., New York, NY 10003.

CAREER: Poet and writer of books for children and young adults, 1960—. Worked as an advertising copywriter in New York City, 1944-50.

AWARDS, HONORS: Austrian Book Prize, Lewis Caroll Shelf Award, best book for young adults citation, and American Library Association (ALA) notable book citation, all 1978, all for *Slake's Limbo;* ALA notable book citation, 1979, for *The Murderer;* best book for young adults citation, 1985, for *The Wild Children;* Child Study Association Book Award, 1991, for *Secret City, U.S.A.*

WRITINGS:

Elisabeth, The Birdwatcher, Macmillan, 1963.
Elisabeth, The Treasure Hunter, Macmillan, 1964.
Silently, the Cat and Miss Theodosia, Macmillan, 1965.
Victoria's Castle, Norton, 1966.
Elisabeth and the Marsh Mystery, Macmillan, 1966.
Professor Diggin's Dragons, Macmillan, 1966.
The Witch on the Corner, Norton, 1966.
The Cricket Winter, Norton, 1967.

The Blackmail Machine, Macmillan, 1968.
A Year to Grow, Norton, 1968.
At the Top of My Voice: Other Poems, Norton, 1969.
The Holiday Rat and the Utmost Mouse, Grosset, 1969.
Solomon's Search, Grosset, 1970.
The Future of Hooper Toote, Scribner, 1972.
I Hear You Smiling, and Other Poems, Scribner, 1973.
The Escape of the Giant Hogstalk, Scribner, 1974.
Slake's Limbo, Scribner, 1974.
(With daughter, Nanine Valen) *The Drac: French Tales of Dragons and Demons,* Scribner, 1975.
The Murderer, Scribner, 1978.
The Wild Children, Scribner, 1983.
The Song in My Head, Scribner, 1985.
Terrible Jane, Scribner, 1987.
Secret City, U.S.A., Scribner, 1990.

ADAPTATIONS: Elisabeth and the Marsh Mystery was adapted into a film for schools and libraries; *Slake's Limbo* was adapted into the television movie *The Runaway,* broadcast by PBS, and has also been optioned for film.

SIDELIGHTS: Felice Holman told *CA:* "I have been writing books for children and young adults for a long time now, and one of the greatest delights has been the writing and publishing of poetry. It is something I have done since I was a child and it seems to come naturally to me, the way music comes to a musician, perhaps. And, in fact, it feels like singing. I am excited when anthologists ask to use my poems in their collections: Then a great many more people hear my songs.

"In recent years I have been writing what have been called 'survival stories' about children with unusual obstacles or difficult situations to cope with. The best known of these is *Slake's Limbo,* about a boy who lives for 121 days in a subway tunnel. Another is *The Wild Children,* about the wandering gangs of children in Russia. The most recent is *Secret City, U.S.A.,* which tells about homeless kids who start a new city. In each of these books, I get drawn in while I am writing. I become emotionally involved in the life of the children I am writing about and I suffer a lot of wear and tear. In the end, I feel terrific, though: I get a great deal of satisfaction from the feeling that I have 'done something.'

"Many of my books have appeared in numerous languages and I love that, even when I can't read the book. Two books have been made into films; one, *Slake's Limbo,* was adapted by PBS as a TV movie, called *The Runaway.* It was not the same story. I was very disappointed. It is also being made into a film in France and I am waiting to see what that will be like. Years ago a film for schools and libraries was done from *Elisabeth and the Marsh Mystery* and I am surprised to know it is still being distributed. It is just like the book and was, in fact, shot near my home in Connecticut.

"Now I have young grandchildren and it is very exciting for me to see their reactions to the books for younger children which I wrote long before they were born—indeed, when their mother was a child. I wonder what else I could have done, all that time ago, that would interest them as much now? . . . Their pleasure tells me that other children have pleasure from the work, too. That's the real reward."

*   *   *

HORNIG, Doug 1943-

PERSONAL: Born November 19, 1943, in New York, NY; son of Douglas C. (an engineer) and Yvonne (a nurse; maiden name, Franco) Hornig. *Education:* George Washington University, B.A., 1965.

ADDRESSES: Home—Route 3, Box 482, Afton, VA.

CAREER: Writer. Worked variously as a factory worker, journalist, taxi driver, computer programmer, delivery man, census taker, bar singer, warehouseman, bookstore clerk, food buyer, photographer, and swimming pool attendant.

AWARDS, HONORS: Edgar Allan Poe Award nomination, Mystery Writers of America, 1985, for *Foul Shot;* Best Mystery Award nomination, Private Eye Writers of America, 1986, for *Hardball;* first prize, Virginia Governor's Screenwriting Competition, 1990, for *Reunion.*

WRITINGS:

Foul Shot (mystery novel), Scribner, 1984.
Hardball (mystery novel), Scribner, 1985.
The Dark Side (mystery novel), Mysterious Press, 1986.
Waterman (political thriller), Mysterious Press, 1987.
Deep Dive (mystery novel), Mysterious Press, 1988.
(With Peter Caine) *Virus* (medical thriller), New American Library, 1989.
Stinger (political thriller), New American Library, 1990.

Also author of screenplay, *Reunion.* Work represented in anthologies, including *Today's Greatest Poems,* World of Poetry Press, 1983; *American Poetry Anthology,* Volume III, American Poetry Association, 1984; and *National Poetry Anthology,* New York Poetry Society, 1985. Also contributor of poems and stories to literary magazines, including *Fantasy and Science Fiction, Albany Review, Wooster Review, Bogg, Slipstream, Amelia, Footwork, Samisdat,* and *Ellery Queen's Mystery Magazine.*

WORK IN PROGRESS: The Old Adelphi Rolling Grist Mill, a short story cycle; *Snowbirds,* a suspense novel; *Wall Street Demystified,* a work of non-fiction.

SIDELIGHTS: Doug Hornig told *CA:* "In an era of increasing compartmentalization of authors, I prefer to be known simply as a writer. My published novels include mysteries, thrillers, and a police procedural/medical/horror hybrid. I've also published poetry, short stories (mystery, science fiction, mainstream), and magazine articles. Works presently underway include the first in a projected series of comic suspense novels to be jointly authored with a retired New York City police officer; another political thriller, and a non-fiction book on the futility of the war on drugs."

BIOGRAPHICAL/CRITICAL SOURCES:

PERIODICALS

Washington Post Book World, December 15, 1985.

*   *   *

HORTON, Louise (Walthall) 1916-

PERSONAL: Born June 23, 1916, in Granbury, TX; daughter of Moten Carl (a farmer) and Willie Belle (Bryant) Walthall; married Claude Wendell Horton, Sr. (a professor of physics and geology), November 23, 1938; children: Claude Wendell, Jr., Margaret Elaine Horton Morefield. *Education:* Rice Institute (now University), B.A., 1938. *Politics:* Republican. *Religion:* Episcopalian.

ADDRESSES: Home—Rocking H Ranch, Route 1, Box 592, Granger, TX 76530.

CAREER: Houston Chemical Commercial Laboratory, Houston, TX, chemist, 1937-38; Church of the Good Shepherd Day School, Austin, TX, teacher, 1947-48; Texas State Library, Archives Division, Austin, archivist, 1970-71.

MEMBER: Society of American Archivists, National Writers Club (professional member), American Anthropological Association, Texas State Historical Association, Kentucky Historical Society.

WRITINGS:

Samuel Bell Maxey: A Biography, University of Texas Press, 1974.
In the Hills of the Pennyroyal, White Cross Press, 1975.
Houston: A Novel, White Cross Press, 1982.
A Map for a Journey: An Epic Lyric in Terza Rima, White Cross Press, 1990.

Also author of manuscript, *The Siblings.* Contributor of poetry reviews to *Southern Humanities Review.* Also contributor to numerous poetry periodicals and journals, including *Southwestern Historical Quarterly, Bluegrass Lit-*

erary Review, Jeopardy, Pawn Review, Kentucky Register, and *Texana.*

WORK IN PROGRESS: A novel tentatively entitled, *Morgan Bird.*

SIDELIGHTS: Louise Horton once told *CA:* "I publish in the field of history because I like writing from primary source material. I began writing and publishing poetry as a child; to me writing poetry is another way of enjoying music. Serious music and nature are objective correlatives to the sensory experiences of the characters in my novels. I write moral fiction (about good and evil with symbols, myths, and images, about people in the Southwest, particularly Texas. Some of my favorite authors are Virginia Woolf, John Gardner, Flaubert, and poet Rainer Rilke (I read German and French)."

Robert E. Ford of *AP Southwest Books* called Horton's biography, *Samuel Bell Maxey,* "a scholarly and detailed biography of a man too often forgotten in Texas history." Writing in the *Journal of American History,* Robin Brooks commented: "On balance Horton has done an excellent job. In the words of the late Allan Nevins: 'We badly need more light on Confederate history, and on Congress during Reconstruction and the Grant-Garfield-Cleveland periods.' Horton has furnished some of the needed light." Alwyn Barr, who stated that Horton's book "will remain the standard biography of Maxey," further comments in the *American Historical Review* that "this volume contributes to our detailed knowledge of the Civil War in the West and of government in the Gilded Age."

BIOGRAPHICAL/CRITICAL SOURCES:

PERIODICALS

American Historical Review, December, 1976, p. 1253.
Appalachian Notes, fourth quarter, 1975.
AP Southwest Books, May 12, 1974.
Journal of American History, March, 1975, p. 1122.
Kentucky Register, October, 1976.

*   *   *

HOUSTON, W(illiam) Robert, Jr.   1928-

PERSONAL: Born June 13, 1928, in Port Arthur, TX; son of William Robert (a minister) and Bernice (Strickland) Houston; married Elizabeth Craig, July 22, 1950; children: John Robert, Elizabeth Ann, Alan Craig. *Education:* Paris Junior College, A.A., 1947; North Texas State College (now North Texas State University), B.S., 1949, M.Ed., 1952; University of Texas, Ed.D., 1961.

ADDRESSES: Home—9831 Vogue, Houston, TX 77080. *Office*—College of Education, University of Houston, 4800 Calhoun Rd., Houston, TX 77004.

CAREER: Public schools, Albuquerque, NM, teacher, 1949-51; public schools, Midland, TX, teacher, 1951-52, dean, 1952-55, elementary school principal, 1955-59; University of Texas, Main University (now University of Texas at Austin), supervisor of student teachers, 1959-60, research associate, 1960-61; Michigan State University, East Lansing, assistant professor of elementary education, 1961-63, associate professor, 1963-66, professor of education, 1967-70; University of Houston, Houston, TX; professor of education, 1970—, associate dean, 1973-92.

MEMBER: Association of Teacher Educators (president, 1985-86), National Council of Teachers of Mathematics, National Society for the Study of Education, Phi Delta Kappa.

WRITINGS:

(With M. Vere De Vault) *Sir Isaac Newton,* Steck, 1960.
(With Robert Osborn, De Vault, and Claude Boyd) *Extending Mathematics Understanding,* C. E. Merrill, 1961, revised edition, 1969.
(With De Vault and Boyd) *Television and Consultant Services as Methods of In-Service Eduction for Elementary School Teachers of Mathematics,* University of Texas Press, 1962.
(With Frank Blackington and Horton Southworth) *Professional Growth through Student Teaching,* C. E. Merrill, 1965.
Teaching in the Modern Elementary School, Macmillan, 1967.
(With William W. Joyce, W. R. Gross, and S. D. Lee) *Exploring Regions of Latin America and Canada,* Follett, 1968, revised edition published as *Exploring Our World: Latin America and Canada,* 1977.
(With Osborn, De Vault, and Boyd) *Understanding the Number System,* C. E. Merrill, 1969.
(With W. V. Hicks, R. Cheney, and R. Marquard) *The New Elementary School Curriculum,* Van Nostrand, 1970.
(Compiler with Joyce, and R. G. Oana) *Elementary Education in the Seventies,* Holt, 1970.
Strategies and Resources for Developing a Competency-Based Teacher Education Program, Multi-State Consortium on Performance-Based Education, 1972.
(With Loye Hollis) *Acquiring Competencies to Teach Mathematics in Elementary Schools,* Professional Educators Publications, 1973.
(With others) *Resources for Performance-Based Education,* Multi-State Consortium on Performance-Based Education, 1973.
(With Wilford A. Weber and James M. Cooper) *A Guide to Competency-Based Teacher Education,* Competency-Based Instructional Systems, 1973.

(With others) *Criteria for Describing and Assessing Competency-Based Programs,* Multi-State Consortium on Performance-Based Education, 1975.

(With Joyce, Gross, and Lee) *Exploring World Regions,* Follett, 1975.

(With Karl Massanari and William H. Drummond) *Emerging Professional Roles for Teacher Educators,* American Association of Colleges for Teacher Education, 1978.

(With others) *Assessing School/College/Community Needs,* Center for Urban Education, University of Nebraska at Omaha, 1978.

(With others) *Designing Short-term Instructional Programs,* Association of Teacher Educators, 1979.

(With T. E. Andrews and B. L. Bryant) *Adult Learners: A Research Study,* Association of Teacher Educators, 1981.

(With Clift, Freiberg, and Warner) *Touch the Future: Teach!,* West, 1988.

EDITOR

Improving Mathematics Education for Elementary School Teachers, Macmillan, 1967.

(With Robert B. Howsam) *Competency-Based Teacher Education: Progress, Problems, and Prospects,* Science Research Association, 1972.

Competency Assessment, Research, and Evaluation, Multi-State Consortium on Performance-Based Education, 1973.

Exploring Competency-Based Education, McCutchan, 1974.

(With L. Marshall and H. J. Freiberg) *Staff Development for Alternative Schools,* Government Printing Office, 1977.

(With Roger Pankratz) *Staff Development and Educational Change,* Association of Teacher Educators, 1980.

Mirrors of Excellence, Association of Teacher Educators, 1981.

(Editor) *Handbook of Research on Teacher Education,* Macmillan, 1990.

CONTRIBUTOR

De Vault, editor, *Improving Mathematics Programs,* C. E. Merrill, 1961.

Hugo David, editor, *Handbook for Student Teaching,* Brown, 1964.

New Directions in Mathematics, Association for Childhood Education International, 1965.

Modern Elementary Education: Teaching and Learning, Macmillan, 1976.

Focus on the Future: Implications for Education, University of Houston, 1978.

OTHER

Contributor of chapters to books on student teaching, teacher education, needs assessment, competency-based education, and mathematics education; also contributor to professional journals.

*   *   *

HUBBARD, David Allan 1928-

PERSONAL: Born April 8, 1928, in Stockton, CA; son of John King (a minister) and Helena (White) Hubbard; married Ruth Doyal, August 12, 1949; children: Mary Ruth. *Education:* Westmont College, B.A., 1949; Fuller Theological Seminary, B.D., 1952, Th.M., 1954; University of St. Andrews, Ph.D., 1957. *Avocational interests:* Travel (has been to Latin America, Europe, the Middle East, the Far East, Australia, and Africa).

ADDRESSES: Office—Fuller Theological Seminary, 135 North Oakland Ave., Pasadena, CA 91182.

CAREER: Ordained clergyman of Conservative Baptist Association, 1952, and of American Baptist Churches of the U.S.A., 1984; Westmont College, Santa Barbara, CA, assistant professor of Bible and Greek, 1957, chairman of department of biblical studies and philosophy, 1958-63; Fuller Theological Seminary, Pasadena, CA, president and chancellor, and professor of Old Testament, 1963—. Fuller Evangelistic Association, executive vice-president, 1969—, and speaker on international radio program *The Joyful Sound,* 1969-80. Interim pastor in Montecito, CA, 1960-62.

Tyndale Old Testament Lecturer in Cambridge, England, 1965; Society of Old Testament Studies lecturer in London, England, 1971; Day-Higginbotham Lecturer at Southwestern Baptist Theological Seminary, 1973; Staley Lecturer at Pacific College, 1973, and at Messiah College, 1981; Caldwell Lecturer at Louisville Presbyterian Theological Seminary, 1975; Colliver Lecturer at University of the Pacific, 1977; E. T. Earl Lecturer at Pacific School of Religion, 1978; Tipple Lecturer at Drew University, 1979. Chairman of Pasadena Urban Coalition, 1968-71; member of board of directors, National Institute of Campus Ministries, 1974-78; member of advisory board, Evangelical Book Club, 1977—; member of national advisory board, Evangelicals for Social Action, 1981—; member of California State Board of Education, 1972-75.

MEMBER: Society for Old Testament Study, Institute for Biblical Research, National Association of Professors of Hebrew, American Academy of Religion, Association of Theological Schools (member of executive committee, 1972-80; president, 1976-78), Society of Biblical Literature, Association of Governing Boards of Universities and Colleges (member of board of governors), Rotary Club.

AWARDS, HONORS: D.D., John Brown University, 1975; L.H.D., Rockford College, 1975; D.Litt., King Sejong University (Korea), 1975; D.L.H., Hope College, 1990; Ed.D., Friends University, 1990.

WRITINGS:

With Bands of Love, Eerdmans, 1968.
Is Life Really Worth Living?, Regal Books, 1969.
What's God Been Doing All This Time?, Regal Books, 1970.
What's New?, Word, Inc., 1970.
Does the Bible Really Work?, Word, Inc., 1971.
Psalms for All Seasons, Eerdmans, 1971.
Is the Family Here to Stay?, Word, Inc., 1971.
The Problem with Prayer Is . . . , Tyndale, 1972, published as *The Practice of Prayer,* Inter-Varsity Press, 1983.
How to Face Your Fears, A. J. Holman, 1972.
The Holy Spirit in Today's World, Word, Inc., 1973.
Church: Who Needs It?, Regal Books, 1974.
They Met Jesus (collection of addresses originally presented on *The Joyful Sound* radio program), A. J. Holman, 1974.
An Honest Search for a Righteous Life (collection of addresses originally presented on *The Joyful Sound* radio program), Tyndale, 1975.
More Psalms for All Seasons, Eerdmans, 1975.
Beyond Futility: Messages of Hope from the Book of Ecclesiastes (collection of addresses originally presented on *The Joyful Sound* radio program), Eerdmans, 1976.
Colossians Speaks to the Sickness of Our Times (collection of addresses originally presented on *The Joyful Sound* radio program), Word, Inc., 1976.
Happiness: You Can Find the Secret (collection of addresses originally presented on *The Joyful Sound* radio program), Tyndale, 1976.
Will We Ever Catch Up with the Bible?, Regal Books, 1977, published as *Themes from the Minor Prophets,* 1978.
Galatians: Gospel of Freedom, Word, Inc., 1977.
Strange Heroes, A. J. Holman, 1977.
Thessalonians: Life That's Radically Christian, Word, Inc., 1977.
How to Study the Bible, Word, Inc., 1978.
Why Do I Have to Die?, Regal Books, 1978.
What We Evangelicals Believe: Expositions of Christian Doctrine Based on "The Statement of Faith" of Fuller Theological Seminary, Fuller Theological Seminary, 1979.
The Book of James: Wisdom That Works, Word, Inc., 1980.

Parables Jesus Told: Pictures of the New Kingdom, Inter-Varsity Press, 1981.
Right Living in a World Gone Wrong, Inter-Varsity Press, 1981.
(With William Sanford LaSor and Frederick William Bush) *Old Testament Survey: The Message, Form, and Background of the Old Testament,* Eerdmans, 1982.
(Editor with Glenn W. Barker, John D. W. Watts, and Ralph P. Martin) *Word Biblical Commentary,* forty-four volumes, Word, Inc., 1982—.
The Second Coming, Inter-Varsity Press, 1984.
Unwrapping Your Spiritual Gifts, Word, Inc., 1985.
Proclamation 3, Pentecost 1: Aids for Interpreting the Lessons of the Church Year, Fortress, 1985.
The Holy Spirit in the World Today, Word, Inc., 1986.
Tyndale Commentary: Hosea, Inter-Varsity Press, 1989.
The Communicator's Commentary: Proverbs, Word, Inc., 1989.
Tyndale Commentary: Joel, Amos, Inter-Varsity Press, 1989.
The Communicator's Commentary: Ecclesiastes, Song of Solomon, Word, Inc., 1991.

Contributor to numerous books, including *The Wycliffe Bible Commentary,* edited by Charles F. Pfeiffer and Everett F. Harrison, Moody, 1962; *The Splendor of Easter,* edited by Floyd W. Thatcher, Word, Inc., 1972; and *Perspectives on Peacemaking: Biblical Options in the Nuclear Age,* edited by John A. Bernbaum, Regal Books, 1984. Contributor to *Baker's Dictionary of Theology,* Baker Book, 1960, revised edition, 1983. Member of editorial board, "The Ministers' Permanent Library" series, Word, Inc., 1976—. Contributor to religion periodicals, including *Christian Life, World Vision, Christianity Today, Family Life Today, Insight,* and *Christian Herald.* Has also published a recording, *Work and Wisdom: Musings on Christian Vocation in the Light of Israel's Sages,* Audio-Visual Department, Pacific School of Religion, 1978.

*   *   *

HUDSON, Jeffrey
See CRICHTON, (John) Michael

*   *   *

HUGHES, Eden
See BUTTERWORTH, W(illiam) E(dmund III)

HUGHES, Matilda
See MacLEOD, Charlotte

* * *

HUGHES, Theodore E(rmond) 1942-

PERSONAL: Born May 23, 1942, in North Conway, NH; son of Ermond D. (a newspaper writer) and Stella (a registered nurse; maiden name, Halle) Hughes; married Elizabeth A. Sabo (an attorney), August 28, 1965; children: Jennifer M., Suzanne D. *Education:* Eastern Michigan University, B.S., 1965; Detroit College of Law, J.D., 1969. *Politics:* Independent. *Religion:* Roman Catholic.

ADDRESSES: Home—2027 Lagoon Dr., Okemos, MI 48864. *Office*—Michigan Department of the Attorney General, P.O. Box 30218, 6520 Mercantile Way, Lansing, MI 48913. *Agent*—Frances Collin, Marie Rodell-Frances Collin Literary Agency, 110 West 40th St., Suite 1403, New York, NY 10018.

CAREER: Donely & Walz, Big Rapids, MI, attorney, 1969-70; Herrinton, Herrinton & Hughes, Cadillac, MI, attorney, 1970-78; Maire, Bossenbrook & Hughes, Lansing, MI, attorney, 1978-80; Michigan Department of the Attorney General, Lansing, assistant attorney general, 1980—. Teacher at Ecorse Public Schools, Ecorse, MI, 1965-66; substitute teacher at Detroit Public Schools, Detroit, MI, 1967-69; instructor at Michigan State University, 1978—; instructor at Lansing Community College, Lansing, 1979-81 and 1985-86; instructor for Michigan Department of Civil Service, Lansing, 1984-86; instructor at Thomas M. Cooley Law School, 1988—. Past member of Cadillac Housing Commission; former member of board of directors of Lansing Volunteers of America, Cadillac Industrial Development Fund, and Cadillac Salvation Army; founder and past director of Cadillac Area Big Brothers Association; member of board of directors (president 1980 and 1981) of Lansing Salvation Army; monthly commentator on estate planning and probate law for WKAR-AM public radio (Lansing).

MEMBER: Michigan Bar Association (past member of Representative Assembly), Florida Bar Association, Ingham County Bar Association (member of board of directors, 1979), Thomas M. Cooley Law School Legal Authors Society, American Society of Writers on Legal Subjects (SCRIBES), Catholic Lawyers Guild.

WRITINGS:

(With David Klein) *A Family Guide to Estate Planning, Funeral Arrangements, and Settling an Estate after Death,* Scribner, 1983, published as *The Complete Guide to Wills, Funerals, and Probate,* 1987.
(With Klein) *Ownership,* Scribner, 1984.

(With Klein) *The Parents' Financial Survival Guide,* HP Books, 1987.
Michigan Litigation Manual—Forms and Analysis, Lawyers Cooperative Publishing, 1992.

Also author of *Hughes Law School Study Aids,* 1967-73. Contributor to journals, magazines, and newspapers, including *Michigan Probate and Trust Journal, Michigan Bar Journal, Practical Lawyer, Best Years, Royal Oak Tribune, Towne Courier, Senior Beacon,* and *Capitol Times.* Consultant to *Consumer Reports* and *Money.*

SIDELIGHTS: Theodore E. Hughes once told *CA:* "My books were motivated by a desire to explain, in plain English, legal concepts of interest to the general public. Too often, important legal concepts, techniques, and transactions are shrouded in legalese and therefore cannot be clearly understood by the lay public. I intend that my past and future books demonstrate that one need not be a trained lawyer in order to understand and take advantage of basic legal principles.

"*A Family Guide to Estate Planning* is addressed to two audiences. The first part instructs the reader in how to plan his or her estate so as to retain maximum control of one's property while at the same time minimizing death taxes and making life easier for one's survivors. The second part guides the survivors as they cope with a death in the family. It explains what to do from the point of removing the body from the place of death, completing funeral arrangements at the least expense, recovering all available death benefits, arranging for the orderly transfer of assets to survivors and, if necessary, completing probate procedures so that the estate can be settled quickly and finally.

"The primary value of my 1984 book, *Ownership,* is its unique slant on personal finance which thoroughly examines sole, shared, trust, and incorporated ownership together with the limitations, advantages and disadvantages of each. *Ownership* teaches one how to manage assets so as to retain maximum control . . . so they won't be needlessly eroded by income and property taxes . . . and so they will pass swiftly into the hands of chosen survivors with minimum kickback to the probate process, to lawyers, and to death-tax collectors."

Hughes recently added: "*The Parents' Financial Guide* provides this generation's parents with the up-to-date guidance they need to deal with the material and financial aspects of raising children. This financial 'Spock' covers every aspect of child financing, from first-time planning to 'adult children.' " Hughes continued, "*Michigan Litigation Manual—Forms and Analysis* is a three volume legal reference written for attorneys engaged in civil litigation in all Michigan trial and appellate courts."

HUNTER, Alan (James Herbert) 1922-

PERSONAL: Born June 25, 1922, in Hoveton St. John, Norwich, England; son of Herbert Ernest (a poultry farmer) and Isabella (Andrew) Hunter; married Adelaide Cubitt (an antique dealer), March 6, 1944; children: Helen. *Religion:* Zen Buddhist.

ADDRESSES: Home—3 St. Laurence Ave., Brundall, Norwich NR13 5QH, England.

CAREER: Poultry farmer, Hoveton St. John, Norwich, England, 1936-40; bookseller in Norwich, 1946-57; fulltime writer, 1957—. *Military service:* Royal Air Force, 1940-46; became leading aircraftsman.

MEMBER: Society of Authors, Crime Writers Association, Norwich Writer Circle (vice-president, 1955—), Yare Valley Sailing Club (rear commodore, 1961-62; vice commodore, 1962-63; commodore, 1963—).

WRITINGS:

The Norwich Poems, 1943-44, Soman Wherry Press, 1945.
Gently Does It (also see below), Rinehart, 1955.
Gently by the Shore, Rinehart, 1956.
Gently down the Stream, Cassell, 1957, Roy, 1960.
Landed Gently, Cassell, 1957, Roy, 1960.
Gently through the Mill (also see below), Cassell, 1958.
Gently in the Sun (also see below), Cassell, 1959, Berkley Publishing, 1964.
Gently with the Painters, Cassell, 1960, Macmillan, 1976.
Gently to the Summit, Cassell, 1961, Berkley Publishing, 1965.
Gently Go Man (also see below), Cassell, 1961, Berkley Publishing, 1964.
Gently Where the Roads Go (also see below), Cassell, 1962.
Gently Floating (also see below), Cassell, 1963, Berkley Publishing, 1964.
Gently Sahib, Cassell, 1964.
Gently with the Ladies, Cassell, 1965, Macmillan, 1974.
Gently North-West, Cassell, 1967, published as *Gently in the Highlands,* Macmillan, 1975.
Gently Continental, Cassell, 1967.
Gently Coloured, Cassell, 1969.
Gently with the Innocents, Cassell, 1970, Macmillan, 1974.
Gently at a Gallop, Cassell, 1971.
Vivienne: Gently Where She Lay, Cassell, 1972.
Gently French, Cassell, 1973.
Gently in Trees, Cassell, 1974, published as *Gently through the Woods,* Macmillan, 1975.
Gently with Love, Cassell, 1975.
Gently Where the Birds Are, Cassell, 1976.
Gently Instrumental, Cassell, 1977.
Gently to a Sleep, Cassell, 1978.
The Honfleur Decision, Constable, 1980.

Gabrielle's Way, Constable, 1980, published as *The Scottish Decision,* 1981.
Fields of Heather, Constable, 1981, published as *Death on the Heath,* 1982.
Gently between Tides, Constable, 1982.
Amorous Leander, Constable, 1983, published as *Death on the Broadlands,* 1984.
The Unhung Man, Constable, 1984, published as *The Unhanged Man,* 1984.
'Once a Prostitute . . . ,' Constable, 1984.
The Chelsea Ghost, Constable, 1985.
Goodnight, Sweet Prince, Constable, 1986.
Strangling Man, Constable, 1987.
Traitor's End, Constable, 1988.
Gently with the Millions, Constable, 1989.
Gently Scandalous, Constable, 1990.
Gently to a Kill, Constable, 1992.
Gently Tragic, Constable, 1992.

OMNIBUS VOLUMES

Gently in an Omnibus: Three Complete Novels (contains *Gently Does It, Gently Through the Mill,* and *Gently in the Sun*), Cassell, 1966, St. Martin's, 1972.
Gently in Another Omnibus (contains *Gently Go Man, Gently Where the Roads Go,* and *Gently Floating*), Cassell, 1969, St. Martin's, 1972.

OTHER

Also author of several plays. Contributor of humorous short stories to BBC Publications. Contributor to periodicals.

Many of Hunter's books have been published in Germany, Sweden, Norway, France, Italy, Spain, and Yugoslavia.

ADAPTATIONS: Gently Does It was adapted for the stage and produced under the title *That Man Gently* in Harlow, England, 1961.

SIDELIGHTS: Alan Hunter once told *CA:* "I work with a pipe in my mouth, mostly at a typewriter, though I have had spells of manuscript writing. I switched to manuscript for a while to free me from being tied to a desk. Instead I drove out to some quiet spot and worked there on a clipboard—but since I write my books in the autumn and winter, the practice was limited by weather. I write comparatively slowly. For me narrative tempo/flavour is critical, and I need to get it right as I proceed; I have never been able to rough-draft a book for later redaction. My early books were all first-draft, with a few manuscript emendations, and it was not until I began writing books in manuscripts that I used a second draft. Now I continue the second draft practice, though often there is little difference between the two drafts: just here and there a minor adjustment.

"In my experience there is no effective advice that one can offer on creative writing. Those with the knack don't need advice, those without the knack can't use it. Only the latter send you the manuscript to criticise, and you will be wise to stop at praise. The former can be told nothing, except by themselves. They take their teaching from the example of others, embodying what they need and learning at length to jettison their redundancies. If I had to teach creative writing to my son I would simply point to a box of stationery.

"Every writer I have ever read has influenced me, down to copywriters for produce cartons. Simenon, Lawrence, Proust, Chandler are writers I have found unusually compatible—in their attitudes, principally: their examples of mental stance. But one learns everywhere, continuously; it may be from the next commercial. Perhaps most likely from the next commercial.

"The eye cannot see itself, the sword cannot cut itself, and I doubt if any author knows in truth why he writes. I am conscious of an audience who enjoys what I enjoy, who will find disturbing what I find disturbing, enlightening what I find enlightening, and is urgent to share these things with me. We have a direction together which I have the task of making manifest. Whence? Towards some good not possible to define. I think this is the situation of every author above the level of simple commerce. Or even below it."

About the course of his career, Hunter earlier explained: "As a child I made the illuminating discovery that it was possible to express in verse sensations and feelings too subtle to communicate in any other way, and at the same time I was seeking to imitate the dramatic stories in the current children's publications ('The Grey Streak of the Seas' was my earliest hero). During my teens I wrote verse and short stories (one published) and contributed natural history notes to the provincial evening paper. The Second World War intervened. On my release from the R.A.F. I continued writing busily—short stories, plays, verse, straight novels—until finally I found my genre in the crime novel, which I regard as perhaps the only legitimate form of tragedy current (a man stained with blood hunted by the agents of justice)."

BIOGRAPHICAL/CRITICAL SOURCES:

PERIODICALS

Books and Bookmen, April, 1970; March, 1971.
Los Angeles Times Book Review, May 24, 1981.
Punch, June 14, 1967; April 16, 1969.
Times Literary Supplement, February 5, 1982; December 31, 1982; February 21, 1986.

HUSTON, Anne Marshall

PERSONAL: Born in High Point, NC; daughter of George Fox (a real estate broker) and Anne (a clinic manager; maiden name, Clark) Marshall; married William E. Bippus (marriage ended); married James Alvin Huston (a college dean), June 5, 1983; children: (first marriage) Anne Elizabeth Irvine, William Elliott, Jr; stepchildren: Nita Diana, James Webb. *Education:* College of William and Mary, A.B., 1963, M.Ed., 1967; University of Virginia, Ed.D., 1977. *Politics:* Republican. *Religion:* Protestant Episcopal. *Avocational interests:* Travel to Europe, England, Wales, Scotland, Ireland, Algeria, Morocco, Bermuda, Virgin Islands, St. Croix, Martinique, France, Poland, Antigua, Puerto Rico, and other places.

ADDRESSES: Home—300 Langhorne Lane, Lynchburg, VA 24501. *Office*—Department of Education and Human Development, Lynchburg College, Lynchburg, VA 24501.

CAREER: Public school system of Williamsburg, VA, elementary school teacher, 1963-68, reading consultant and coordinator, 1968-70; Lynchburg College, Lynchburg, VA, assistant professor, 1970-78, associate professor, 1978-85, professor of education, 1985—, director of Reading Clinic, 1972—. Lecturer at College of William and Mary, 1968-70; visiting assistant professor at University of Virginia, summer, 1977; presents workshops for public schools.

MEMBER: International Reading Association, International Platform Association, College Reading Association, Association for Supervision and Curriculum Development, Children With Learning Disabilities, Daughters of the American Revolution (past historian), Piedmont Area Reading Association, Virginia College Reading Educators (past president), Virginia State Reading Association (past member of board of directors), Virginia Association of Children With Learning Disabilities, College of William and Mary Alumni Association (member of board of directors of Central Virginia chapter, 1981—), Phi Eta Sigma, Kappa Delta Pi, Phi Delta Kappa, St. Stephen's Episcopal Church (former vestryman).

WRITINGS:

(Coeditor) *Symposium Readings: Classical Selections on Great Issues,* ten volumes, University Press of America, 1982.
Common Sense about Dyslexia, Madison Books, 1987.
(With husband, James Huston) *Under the Double Cross,* International University Press, 1989.
Understanding Dyslexia, Madison Books, 1992.

Contributor to *Celebrating Literacy: Defending Literacy,* edited by Colin Harrison and Eric Ashworth, Basil Blackwell, 1991. Contributor to journals, including *Agora, Jour-*

nal of Instructional Psychology, and *Journal of Virginia College Educators.*

SIDELIGHTS: Anne Marshall Huston once told *CA:* "I have worked with children in regular classrooms, special clinics, and resource centers, children in all grades and of all ages from a variety of backgrounds and races; average learners, slow learners, and superior learners. I went into teacher education because of my great concern for students who have problems with school work. I believe the solution lies with well-trained, intelligent teachers who know what to do to enhance learning and what to avoid that would create barriers to learning.

"I have been working with dyslexic children for fourteen years or more. As director of a reading clinic I am responsible for the graduate reading specialist program. In addition to the regular clinical experience required of graduate students, in this program there is mandatory participation in the advanced clinic; here they gain knowledge and expertise in diagnosing and remedying dyslexia by working with children who have severe reading, spelling, and writing problems—some dyslexic, some not."

Prior to the release of *Common Sense about Dyslexia,* Huston noted, "*Common Sense about Dyslexia* has been simmering on the back burner for some time. It is being written at the request of many doctors, teachers, parents, reading specialists, and others involved with children who have special problems, and of the dyslexic children themselves. There is a need to keep our feet on the ground as far as dyslexia is concerned. We need to use our common sense and to cut through the controversies that are raging through the academic and medical circles over the correct definition of dyslexia, its cause, and whether it exists at all. The disagreement over the correct definition of dyslexia is sometimes used as an argument that dyslexia must not exist, the rationale being that if it did exist experts would be able to come up with a common definition. Yet pick up a dozen textbooks on the teaching of reading and you will find a dozen different definitions of that which is called reading. But no one says that reading does not exist!

"Dyslexia is a language communication disability. The use of the term is appropriate because in Greek the prefix 'dys' means impaired and 'lexia' refers to the use of words; dyslexia is certainly a problem with the use of words—in spelling, reading, writing, speaking, and listening.

"My main point is that, regardless of the controversies, we must take the child with dyslexia as he is now and move on. *Common Sense about Dyslexia* cuts through the accumulation of studies and reports, draws on concrete matters, and gets to the heart of the matter—dispelling myths. It is a very practical, readable, and much-needed book."

Huston described *Under the Double Cross,* written with her husband, James, as "a historical novel of adventure, romance, and intrigue set in the Ardennes in World War II, during the Battle of the Bulge. Writing this with my husband was different from anything either of us had done in the past. My husband is a military historian, and we thought it would be great fun to write a novel that would draw on both his experiences and mine. Our hero is a young captain in the Third Army under General Patton, and our heroine is a Swiss schoolteacher who, through her knowledge of dyslexia, aids in solving the mystery of fire falling on allied forces. Of course, the Third Army and General Patton were real, but our 59th Division and 759th Infantry Regiment, along with their subordinate and associate units, are purely fictional.

"We wrote the novel using our creativity and imagination, but we also did extensive research on World War II. We wanted to make sure that the book would be authentic as far as locations, distances, and strategies were concerned. So, in addition to using old maps, we followed the exact steps of our hero through France, Luxembourg, and Belgium. Friends thought we were crazy to go to these places during January, but that was the time of our novel and the weather was exactly as we described it. We had some unique—or perhaps the word is uncanny—experiences there. For example, we had described the hero walking out to a certain place and turning left to see the ruins of a castle. In our travels we took a side road to its end, and to the left we saw the ruins of a castle just as we had written it. We had several other *deja vu* experiences of this sort."

J

JOHNSON, Diane 1934-

PERSONAL: Born April 28, 1934, in Moline, IL; daughter of Dolph and Frances (Elder) Lain; married B. Lamar Johnson, Jr., July, 1953; married second husband, John Frederic Murray (a professor of medicine), May 31, 1968; children: (first marriage) Kevin, Darcy, Amanda, Simon. *Education:* Attended Stephens College, 1951-53; University of Utah, B.A., 1957; University of California, M.A., 1966, Ph.D., 1968.

ADDRESSES: Home—24 Edith Pl., San Francisco, CA 94133. *Office*—Department of English, University of California, Davis, CA 95616. *Agent*—Lynn Nesbitt, Nesbit-Janklow, New York, NY 10019.

CAREER: University of California, Davis, began in 1968 as assistant professor, then professor of English, currently holding the Harold and Mildred Strauss Living stipend from the American Academy of Arts and Letters.

MEMBER: International PEN, Modern Language Association of America.

AWARDS, HONORS: National Book Award nomination, 1973, for *Lesser Lives,* and 1979, for *Lying Low;* Guggenheim fellowship, 1977-78; Rosenthal Award, American Academy and Institute of Arts and Letters, 1979; Pulitzer Prize nomination in general nonfiction, 1983, for *Terrorists and Novelists; Los Angeles Times* book prize nomination in biography, 1984, for *Dashiell Hammett: A Life;* Pulitzer Prize nomination, 1987, for *Persian Nights.*

WRITINGS:

NOVELS

Fair Game, Harcourt, 1965.
Loving Hands at Home, Harcourt, 1968.
Burning, Harcourt, 1971.
The Shadow Knows (also see below), Knopf, 1974.
Lying Low, Knopf, 1978.
Persian Nights, Knopf, 1987.
Health and Happiness, Knopf, 1990.

BIOGRAPHY

Lesser Lives: The True History of the First Mrs. Meredith, Knopf, 1973, published in England as *The True History of the First Mrs. Meredith and Other Lesser Lives,* Heinemann, 1973.
Dashiell Hammett: A Life (also see below), Random House, 1983.

SCREENPLAYS

(With Stanley Kubrick) *The Shining* (based on the Stephen King novel of the same title), Warner Brothers, 1980.

Also author of unproduced screenplays *Grand Hotel, The Shadow Knows* (based on her novel of the same title), and *Hammett* (based on her biography *Dashiell Hammett: A Life*).

OTHER

(Author of preface) John Ruskin, *King of the Golden River* [and] Charles Dickens, *A Holiday Romance* [and] Tom Hood, *Petsetilla's Posy,* Garland Publishing, 1976.
(Author of preface) Margaret Gatty, *Parables of Nature,* Garland Publishing, 1976.
(Author of preface) George Sand, *Mauprat,* Da Capo Press, 1977.
Terrorists and Novelists (collected essays), Knopf, 1982.
(Author of preface) *Tales and Stories of E. A. Poe,* Vintage, 1991.

Also author of preface to *Frankenstein* by Mary Shelley, c. 1979, and to *Josephine Herhst: Collected Works,* 1990. Contributor of essays and book reviews to periodicals, including the *New York Times, New York Review of Books, San Francisco Chronicle,* and *Washington Post.*

WORK IN PROGRESS: A novel set in Iran.

SIDELIGHTS: In an age when writers tend to be pigeon-holed, Diane Johnson remains a difficult author to categorize. Perhaps best known as an essayist and biographer, she got her start as a novelist and continues to write successfully in this vein. She is a teacher and scholar, with expertise in nineteenth-century literature, yet she also lent a hand in writing the screenplay for *The Shining,* a popular horror film. And while her initial focus was on women and their problems in society, she has since written sympathetically of a man who faced similar difficulties in *Dashiell Hammett: A Life.* Even her early works, which have been claimed as the province of feminists, were intended to cast a wider net, as Johnson explained to Susan Groag Bell in *Women Writers of the West Coast:* "The kinds of crises, the particular troubles that I assign to my women characters, these are not necessarily meant to be feminist complaints. . . . In my mind, they may be more metaphysical or general. That sounds awfully pretentious, but I guess what I mean is that I'm not trying to write manifestos about female independence, but human lives."

Like many serious artists, Johnson sees herself as a craftsman whose work should be judged on its merits as literature, not—as is often the case with women writers—on moral or extraliterary grounds. In her highly acclaimed collection of book reviews and essays, *Terrorists and Novelists,* Johnson addresses the particular problems faced by female novelists, chiding those male critics who "have not learned to read books by women and imagine them all to be feminist polemics." She told Bell, "The writer wants to be praised for the management of formal and technical aspects of the narrative and wide-ranging perceptions about society and perhaps the quality of her sensibility, not her own character, and, mainly you want your book to be a success on its own terms."

Though all her novels and one of her biographies have California settings, Johnson was born and raised in Moline, Illinois. Her childhood was untroubled: the first child of middle-aged parents, she lived in the same house surrounded by neighboring aunts and uncles until she went away to college at seventeen. She describes herself as a "puny, bookish little child, with thick glasses," and told *Los Angeles Times* reporter Beverly Beyette that she was "the kind of whom you say, 'Let's take her to the library on Saturday.' I was typecast, but I was a type." When she was nineteen, Johnson married her first husband, then a UCLA medical student, and relocated to the West Coast where she has remained.

Despite her long residence in California, Johnson told Bell that "a certain view of life, which I very much obtained

from my Illinois childhood, does inform my work. In a couple of my books I have put a middle-western protagonist, always somebody who's displaced like I am, looking at the mess of today. This person remembers an orderly society from which subsequent events have seemed to depart." She maintains that it is the turmoil of modern society, rather than a personal preoccupation with disorder, that leads to the prevalence of violence in her books. "She is not sensational, sentimental, nor simple-minded," suggests *Critique: Studies in Modern Fiction* contributor Marjorie Ryan, who points out that Johnson writes in "the satiric-comic-realistic tradition, in a mode that may not appeal to readers nurtured on the personal, subjective, and doctrinaire."

In her early fiction, *Fair Game, Loving Hands at Home,* and *Burning,* Johnson employs "a comic tone" as well as "a central female character who is uncertain about how to conduct her life," according to Judith S. Baughman in the *Dictionary of Literary Biography Yearbook.* In each of these novels, a woman who has ventured outside the boundaries of convention "has a shocking experience which sends her back inside, but only temporarily until another experience . . . either sends her outside again or changes her whole perspective," Ryan explains.

As is often the case with a writer's first fruits, these early novels largely escaped the notice of critics—at least initially. By the time *Burning* appeared, there were flickers of interest, though it was Johnson's potential as a novelist rather than the work at hand that attracted praise. Much criticism was leveled at Johnson's choice of subject. A Southern California story of disaster, *Burning* was viewed as a genre novel that had been approached in the same fashion many times before. As R. R. Davies put it, "Group therapy and the drug-induced self-analysis of depressed citizens have been done to death as satirical material." Though *Newsweek*'s Peter Prescott finds Johnson "witty and serious," he contends that she "tries to be both at once and doesn't make it. Her book should have been either much funnier, or much grimmer or, failing that, she should have been much better." *Book World* contributor J. R. Frakes compares the crowded canvas of Johnson's apocalyptic tale to "a twelve ring circus" and welcomes its disastrous ending "almost as a relief," but then goes on to praise Johnson's style, noting that she "superintends this asylum with cool disdain and a remarkable neo-classic elegance of phrase, sentence, and chapter. It is comforting to know that someone competent is in charge."

Her competence established, Johnson began to attract more serious attention, and her fourth novel, *The Shadow Knows,* was widely reviewed. Originally set in Los Angeles, the story was relocated to Sacramento because, as the author explained to Bell, "I decided after the reception of *Burning* that Los Angeles was too loaded a place in the minds of readers." The novel takes its title from an old radio melodrama (which featured the line, "Who knows what evil lurks in the hearts of men? The Shadow knows.") and focuses on one terror-filled week in the life of a young divorcee and mother of four known simply as N. When someone slashes her tires, leaves a strangled cat on her doorstep, threatens her over the telephone, and beats up her babysitter in the basement laundry room, N. becomes convinced that she is marked for murder. But who is the assailant? Her spiteful former husband? The wife of her married lover? The psychotic black woman who used to care for her children? Her jealous friend Bess, who comes to visit with a hunting knife in her purse? Or, worst of all, is it some nameless stranger, an embodiment of evil she does not even know? N.'s attempt to identify her enemy, and her imaginary dialogue with the Famous Inspector she conjures up to help her, make up the heart of the book.

Writing in the *New Statesman,* A. S. Byatt describes the novel as a "cunning cross between the intensely articulate plaint of the under-extended intelligent woman and a conventional mystery, shading into a psychological horror-story." *Nation* contributor Sandra M. Gilbert calls it "a sort of bitter parody of a genre invented by nineteenth-century men: the detective novel." Though it masquerades as a thriller, most reviewers acknowledge that *The Shadow Knows* is really a woman's story in which N. abandons what she calls her "safe" life to follow one that is "reckless and riddled with mistakes."

"In her attempts to create a fresh, true identity unconfined by the usual social and familial influences, N. must penetrate the evils which lurk in the hearts of men, even in her own heart in order to find her 'way in the dark,' " writes Baughman. "Thus, she has not only to uncover her potential murderer but also to deal with her own considerable problems and confusions. . . . Because the pressures upon her are so great, the possibility arises that N.'s terrors are powerful projections of her own sense of guilt and confusion rather than appropriate responses to the malevolent acts of an outside aggressor." Some reviewers go so far as to suggest that N.'s problems are more imagined than real. "Understandably, N. would like to know who's doing all these bad things to her, if only to be sure that she's not making it all up," writes Thomas R. Edwards in the *New York Review of Books.* "And since we also wonder if she may not be doing that, we share her desire for knowledge."

In her interview with Bell, Johnson asserts that such disbelief stems more from readers' biases than from the way the protagonist is portrayed. "There's [a] problem that comes from having as your central character a female person," says Johnson. "The male narrative voice is still accorded more authority. The female narrative voice is al-

ways questioned—is she crazy? Are the things she's saying a delusion, or reality? The narrator in *The Shadow Knows* was intended as an exact and trustworthy reporter of what was happening to her. But many reviewers, while in general liking her, also questioned her about her hysteria, her paranoia, her untrustworthiness. Is she mad or sane? So I began to notice that female narrators, if they're of a sexual age, of a reproductive age, of an age to have affairs, aren't considered trustworthy. . . . Nonetheless, I write about women of childbearing age, because I like to fly in the face of these prejudices and hope that I can make them authoritative and trustworthy reporters."

While women still figure prominently in Johnson's next novel, *Lying Low,* the focus has shifted from psychological to political concerns and from one protagonist to several. The book, which covers four days in the lives of four characters who inhabit a boarding house in Orris, California, is a "mosaic-like juxtaposition of small paragraphs, each containing a short description, a bit of action, reflections of one of the principal characters, or a mixture of all three," according to Robert Towers in the *New York Times Book Review.* Praising its artful construction, elegant style, and delicate perceptions, Towers calls *Lying Low* "a nearly flawless performance. . . . Despite the lack of any headlong narrative rush, one's interest in the working out of the story is maintained at a high level by the skillful, unobtrusive distribution of plot fragments." *Newsweek's* Peter Prescott says it "represents a triumph of sensibility over plot" and observes that, like other feminist novels, it is "most convincing when least dramatic. Condition, not action, is [its] true concern: the problems of women confronting, or trying to ignore, their desperate lot."

Johnson's skill at rendering domestic crises makes *Saturday Review* contributor Katha Pollitt "wish Diane Johnson had kept her canvas small, a comedy or tragicomedy of manners for our decade of extreme political bewilderment. . . . When Johnson aims for a grander drama, though, she is not convincing. . . . The end [in which a bomb explodes, killing one of the main characters], seems a failure of imagination, an apocalypse produced ex machina so that we all get the point about the violence that smolders beneath the American surface." A *New Yorker* critic pronounces the conclusion "an awkward attempt to endow a cerebral narrative with the action of a thriller." And the *New Republic* likens the ending to "one of those simple-minded 1960s films in which the source of all evil is 'Amerika' " and concludes that it "seems much too jarring in a novel as full of subtleties of observation and atmosphere as this one."

In addition to novels, Johnson has written two biographies. Her portrait of the first Mrs. George Meredith, *Lesser Lives: The True History of the First Mrs. Meredith,* grew out of her doctoral dissertation. "In biographies of Meredith, there would always be this little paragraph about how he was first married to Mary Ellen Peacock who ran off and left him and then, of course, died, deserted and forlorn—like the woman in a Victorian story," Johnson told Bell. "I always thought, I bet there is her side of it too. This was when my own marriage was breaking up, and I was particularly interested in the woman's side of things."

Working from evidence she exhumed from letters and diaries, Johnson hypothesizes that the real Mary Ellen was a strong-willed, intelligent, free spirit, whose main sin was being out of step with her times. Raised by her father in the tradition of eighteenth-century individualism, she incited the wrath of her decidedly Victorian second husband, the famous novelist George Meredith, when she abandoned their loveless marriage to lead a life of her own. The portrait that survives of her as a crazed adulterer who lured a much younger man into marriage is more a reflection of George Meredith's vindictiveness than an indication of who Mary Ellen was.

Though some critics felt the biography was lacking in evidence, many praised its artful style. "Jump cutting from scene to scene, she shows what she thinks to be true, what she thinks might be true, and what, in all candor, she thinks no one can prove to be either true or false," writes Catharine R. Stimpson in *Ms.* "Like a historian, she recovers pellets of the past. Like a psychologist, she applies theory and common sense to human behavior. Like a novelist, she takes imaginative liberties and worries about the internal coherence of her work of art. . . . *Lesser Lives* has the buoyant vitality of a book in which a writer has taken risks, and won."

Even when her subject is a contemporary figure, about whom concrete facts and anecdotes are readily available, Johnson prefers an artistic to an exhaustive approach. "A biography has a responsibility which is to present the facts and get all of them straight, so that people can get the basic outlines of a person's life," Johnson explained to Miriam Berkley in *Publishers Weekly.* "And then, I think, it has to have a point of view and a shape which has to come out of the biographer as artist. I guess I am arguing for the interpretive biography, you might call it an art biography, as opposed to a compendious . . . presentation of a lot of facts."

Johnson's commitment to biography as art presented special challenges in her study of mystery writer Dashiell Hammett and the writing of *Dashiell Hammett: A Life.* The first "authorized" Hammett biographer, Johnson had access to all his personal papers and the cooperation of his family and friends. But in exchange for these privileges, Hammett's executrix and long-time companion Lillian

Hellman insisted that she be shown the final manuscript and granted the right to decide whether or not the quoted material could stand.

"She set out to be pleasant and wonderful, then, when she stopped being wonderful, I stopped going to see her," Johnson told Beverly Beyette in the *Los Angeles Times.* The problem was one of vision: "She saw him very much as her guru, this wonderfully strong, terrifically honest, fabulously intelligent dream man. I saw him as an intelligent, troubled man, an alcoholic with terrible writer's block. She didn't like to think of his life having been painful, unsuccessful." Johnson eventually obtained Hellman's permission to use Hammett's letters in her own way. "She had to agree, I guess, that it *was* the best way of presenting Hammett," Johnson told Berkley. "He was a difficult man and not entirely sympathetic, but he was certainly at his most sympathetic in his own voice."

Using a novelistic approach, Johnson intersperses excerpts from Hammett's letters with short stretches of narrative that sometimes reflect her viewpoint, sometimes that of his family and friends. *New York Times Book Review* contributor George Stade compares the technique to one Hammett perfected in his own novels, "the method of the camera eye. We see what the characters do, hear what they say, note their gestures and postures, watch them assume positions toward each other, record their suspect attempts to account for themselves and each other." But just as Hammett's readers had to decipher for themselves his protagonists' motives, so, too, must Johnson's readers "decide for themselves what made Hammett tick."

Because so much is left to the reader, some critics suggest that Johnson is withholding judgment; others conclude that she cannot reveal what she does not know. As *New York Times* reviewer Christopher Lehmann-Haupt puts it: "Silence was Hammett's weapon—silence turned against all bullies and lovers, against his readers and himself. At the bottom of that silence was an ocean of anger: that much this biography makes very clear. The mystery that remains—that will probably remain forever—is the true source of that anger." Characterizing Hammett as "a fundamentally passive individual who drifted through life with no clear motivations or deep impulses," *Washington Post Book World* critic Jonathan Yardley wonders if Johnson's inability to "penetrate through to the inner man" might just reflect the fact that there was nothing there. "Perhaps," Yardley speculates, "when you come right down to it, the 'mystery' lies within us rather than him: for expecting more of him, since he wrote good books, than was actually there, and for feeling frustrated when those expectations go unmet."

Ralph B. Sipper, on the other hand, finds Johnson's "tracking of Hammett's inner life . . . the most revealing to date" and speculates in the *Los Angeles Times Book Review* that perhaps her "most delicate accomplishment is the fine line between iffy psychologizing and creative analysis." Describing the interpretative approach to biography as one in which the writer "studies the facts and filters them through her own sensibility," Sipper concludes that "Diane Johnson has done just that with her multifaceted subject and the result is pure light."

BIOGRAPHICAL/CRITICAL SOURCES:

BOOKS

Contemporary Literary Criticism, Gale, Volume 5, 1976, Volume 13, 1983.
Dictionary of Literary Biography Yearbook: 1980, Gale, 1981.
Johnson, Diane, *Terrorists and Novelists,* Knopf, 1982.
Yalom, Marilyn, editor, *Women Writers of the West Coast: Speaking of Their Lives and Careers,* Capra, 1983.

PERIODICALS

America, March 19, 1983.
Best Sellers, September 1, 1971.
Book World, October 13, 1968; September 5, 1971.
Chicago Tribune Book World, January 9, 1983.
Critique: Studies in Modern Fiction, Volume 16, number 1, 1974.
Los Angeles Times, October 6, 1982; April 27, 1983.
Los Angeles Times Book Review, October 30, 1983; April 5, 1987, p. 1; May 22, 1988, p. 18; October 7, 1990, p. 1.
Ms., May, 1974; November, 1978.
Nation, June 14, 1975; November 11, 1978; December 17, 1983.
New Republic, November 11, 1972; November 18, 1978; April 20, 1987, p. 45.
New Statesman, November 19, 1971; June 6, 1975.
Newsweek, December 23, 1974; May 5, 1975; October 16, 1978; October 17, 1983; March 30, 1987, p. 69.
New Yorker, March 3, 1975; November 13, 1978; November 14, 1983.
New York Review of Books, November 2, 1972; February 20, 1975; November 23, 1978; April 23, 1987, p. 14; January 31, 1991, p. 18.
New York Times, November 27, 1974; May 23, 1980; October 16, 1982; October 5, 1983.
New York Times Book Review, September 5, 1971; December 31, 1972; December 22, 1974; November 19, 1978; October 31, 1982; October 16, 1983; April 5, 1987, p. 8; July 26, 1987, p. 24; May 29, 1988, p. 20; September 30, 1990, p. 18; December 15, 1991, p. 32.
Publishers Weekly, September 9, 1983.
Saturday Review, October 28, 1978.
Time, November 7, 1983; March 23, 1987, p. 83.

Times Literary Supplement, June 6, 1975; November 23, 1979; July 3, 1987, p. 714; February 15, 1991, p. 17.
Village Voice, January 8, 1979; June 30, 1987, p. 57.
Washington Post Book World, December 22, 1975; November 26, 1978; September 29, 1982; October 9, 1983; May 1, 1988, p. 12; September 30, 1990, p. 6.

*   *   *

JOHNSTON, R(onald) J(ohn) 1941-

PERSONAL: Born March 30, 1941, in Swindon, England; son of H. L. and P. J. (Liddiard) Johnston; married Rita Brennan (a researcher), April 16, 1963; children: Christopher, Lucy. *Education:* Victoria University of Manchester, B.A. (with honors), 1962, M.A., 1964; Monash University, Ph.D., 1966.

ADDRESSES: Home—Lakeside House, Wivenhoe Park, Colchester C04 35Q, England. *Office*—Vice-Chancellor, University of Essex, Wivenhoe Park, Colchester C04 35Q, England.

CAREER: University of Canterbury, Christchurch, New Zealand, lecturer, 1967-68, senior lecturer, 1969-72, reader in geography, 1973-74; University of Sheffield, Sheffield, England, professor of geography, 1974-92; University of Essex, Colchester, England, vice-chancellor, 1992—. Visiting associate professor at University of Toronto, 1972; academic visitor at School of Economics and Political Science, University of London, 1973; official overseas guest at University of the Orange Free State and visiting professor at University of the Witwatersrand, 1976.

MEMBER: Institute of British Geographers (member of council, 1977-80; honorary secretary, 1982-85; president, 1990-91), Social Science Research Council (England), New Zealand Geographical Society, Royal Geographical Society (fellow), Association of American Geographers.

AWARDS, HONORS: Erskine fellow for United States, United Kingdom, and South America, University of Canterbury, 1969; British Council fellow, 1973; Murchison Award, Royal Geographical Society, 1985, for contributions to political geography; Victoria Medal, Royal Geographical Society, 1990; Honors Award, Association of American Geographers, 1991, for distinguished contributions.

WRITINGS:

(With P. J. Rimmer) *Retailing in Melbourne,* Department of Human Geography, Australian National University, 1970.
Urban Residential Patterns: An Introductory Review, G. Bell, 1971.

Spatial Structures: An Introduction to the Study of Spatial Systems in Human Geography, Methuen, 1973.

The New Zealanders: How They Live and Work, David & Charles, 1976.

The World Trade System: Some Enquiries into Its Spatial Structure, G. Bell, 1976.

(With B. E. Coates and P. L. Knox) *Geography and Inequality,* Oxford University Press, 1977.

Multivariate Statistical Analysis in Geography: A Primer on the General Linear Model, Longman, 1978.

Political, Electoral, and Spatial Systems, Oxford University Press, 1979.

(With P. J. Taylor) *Geography of Elections,* Penguin, 1979.

Geography and Geographers: Anglo-American Human Geography since 1945, Edward Arnold, 1979, Halsted 1980, 3rd edition, 1987.

City and Society, Penguin Books, 1980.

The Geography of Federal Spending in the United States, Wiley, 1980.

The American Urban System, St. Martin's, 1981.

Geography and the State, Macmillan, 1982.

Philosophy and Human Geography, Edward Arnold, 1983, 2nd edition, 1989.

Residential Segregation: The State and Constitutional Conflict in American Urban Areas, Academic Press, 1984.

The Geography of English Politics, Croom Helm, 1985.

On Human Geography, Blackwell, 1986.

Bell Ringing: The English Art of Change Ringing, Penguin Books, 1986.

Money and Votes, Croom Helm, 1987.

(With C. J. Pattie and J. G. Allsopp) *A Nation Dividing?,* Laymen, 1988.

(With Allsopp, J. C. Baldwin, and H. Turne) *An Atlas of Bells,* Blackwell, 1989.

Question of Place, Blackwell, 1991.

EDITOR

Proceedings of the Sixth New Zealand Geography Conference, New Zealand Geographical Society, Volume 1 (with Jane M. Soons), 1971, Volume 2 (with June Chapman): *Geography and Education,* 1971.

Urbanization in New Zealand: Geographical Essays, Reed Education, 1973.

Society and Environment in New Zealand, Whitcombe & Tombs, 1974.

(With D. T. Herbert) *Social Areas in Cities,* Wiley, Volume 1: *Spatial Processes and Form,* 1976, Volume 2: *Spatial Perspectives on Problems and Policies,* 1976.

People, Places, and Votes: Essays on the Electoral Geography of Australia and New Zealand, Department of Geography, University of New England, 1977.

(With Herbert) *Geography and Urban Environment: Progress in Research and Applications,* Wiley, Volume 1,

1978, Volume 2, 1979, Volume 3, 1980, Volume 4, 1981, Volume 5, 1982, Volume 6, 1984.

(With Herbert) *Social Areas in Cities: Processes, Patterns, and Problems,* Wiley, 1978.

(With D. Gregory, P. Haggett, D. M. Smith, and D. R. Stoddart) *Dictionary of Human Geography,* Blackwell, 1981, 3rd edition, 1993.

(With J. C. Doornkamp) *The Changing Geography of the United Kingdom,* Methuen, 1982.

The Future of Geography, Methuen, 1982.

(With K. R. Cox) *Conflict: Politics and the Urban Scene,* Longman, 1982.

(With P. Claval) *Geography since the Second World War,* Croom Helm, 1984.

(With Taylor) *A World in Crisis,* Blackwell, 1986, 2nd edition, 1989.

* * *

JOSEFOWITZ, Natasha 1926-

PERSONAL: Born October 31, 1926, in Paris, France; came to the United States in 1939, naturalized U.S. citizen, 1947; daughter of Myron and Tamara (Fradkin) Chapro; married Samuel Josefowitz, April 15, 1949 (separated); children: Nina, Paul. *Education:* Scripps College, B.A., 1948; Columbia University, M.S.W., 1965; University of Lausanne, Doctorans, 1974; Sussex College, Ph.D., 1977.

ADDRESSES: Home—2235 calle Guymas, La Jolla, CA 92037. *Agent*—Ellen Levine, 15 East 26th St., New York, NY 10010.

CAREER: University of Lausanne, Lausanne, Switzerland, lecturer in social work and supervision, and therapist at Child Guidance Clinic, 1965-74; University of New Hampshire, Durham, assistant professor, 1974-78, associate professor of management, 1978-80; San Diego State University, San Diego, CA, associate professor, 1980-82, professor of management, 1982-84, adjunct professor at College of Human Services, 1984—.

MEMBER: Certified Consultants International, American Society for Training and Development, Academy of Management, Academy of Certified Social Workers, National Association of Social Workers, Organization Development Network.

AWARDS, HONORS: Named distinguished author, Women's Studies of San Diego, 1983, for contribution to literature; honored by California Women in Government, 1984, for contribution to education; Woman of the Year, Los Angeles Women in Management, 1988; Living Legacy Award, Women's International Center, 1991.

WRITINGS:

Collaborator: Effective Behavior in Organization, Irwin, 1976.

Paths to Power: A Woman's Guide from First Job to Top Executive, Addison-Wesley, 1980.

Is This Where I Was Going?, Warner Books, 1983.

You're the Boss, Warner Books, 1985.

Natasha's Words for Friends, Families, Lovers, Warner Books, 1986.

(With Herman Gadon) *Fitting In: How to Get a Good Start in Your New Job,* Addison-Wesley, 1988.

A Hundred Scoops of Ice Cream, Meadowbrook, 1989.

Columnist for *San Diego Daily Transcript, San Diego Woman,* and *Jewish Times.* Contributor to periodicals, including *Harvard Business Review, Ms., Glamour, Personnel Administrator,* and *Business Horizons.* Author of videotape *Sex and Power at Work,* released by the City of San Diego, 1982.

WORK IN PROGRESS: Love Secrets, with Harold Bloomfield.

SIDELIGHTS: Natasha Josefowitz once told *CA:* "I believe in writing both for academic audiences and for the popular press. The same week my article appeared in the *Harvard Business Review,* another appeared in *Glamour* magazine. I include my humorous verse in all my books to illustrate the points I'm making."

She further adds, "As an educator, I have noticed that by using a different medium such as verse or humor, people can be reached through the right brain where defenses haven't been built up."

BIOGRAPHICAL/CRITICAL SOURCES:

PERIODICALS

Chicago Tribune, August 19, 1985.
Los Angeles Times, November 24, 1988.

K

KAESTNER, Erich 1899-1974

PERSONAL: Born February 23, 1899, in Dresden, Saxony (now Germany); died July 29, 1974, in Munich, West Germany (now Germany); son of Emil (a harnessmaker) and Ida Amalia (Augustin) Kaestner. *Education:* Attended schools in Dresden, University of Rostock, and University of Berlin; University of Leipzig, Ph.D., 1925. *Politics:* Liberal Democrat. *Religion:* Protestant.

ADDRESSES: Home—Munich, Germany.

CAREER: Novelist, poet, playwright, essayist, editor, social critic, and author of children's books. Early jobs included bookkeeper, publicist, researcher, and journalist; *Neue Leipziger Zeitung,* Leipzig, Germany, drama critic and associate feuilleton editor, 1925-27; feuilleton editor of *Neue Zeitung,* 1945-47; founder and editor of *Pinguin* (children's magazine), 1945-49; founded two literary cabarets, "Schaubude," 1945, and "Die Kleine Freiheit," 1951. *Military service:* Imperial Army, artillery, 1917-18; became corporal.

MEMBER: International PEN (former vice-president; former president of German PEN center), Deutsche Akademie fuer Sprache und Dichtung, Akademie der Wissenschaft und Literatur (Mainz), Akademie der Schoenen Kuenste (Bavaria).

AWARDS, HONORS: Literature Prize of Munich, 1956; Buechner Prize, 1957; Hans Christian Andersen Award, 1960; Mildred L. Batchelder Award, 1968, for *Little Man.*

WRITINGS:

Fabian: Die Geschichte eines Moralisten (semi-autobiographical novel), Deutsche Verlags-Anstalt, 1931, translation by Brooks published as *Fabian: The Story of a Moralist,* Dodd, 1932.

Drei Maenner im Schnee (novel), Rascher, 1934, translation by Brooks published as *Three Men in the Snow,* J. Cape, 1935.

Die Verschwundene Miniatur; oder auch, Die Abenteuer eines empfindsamen Fleischermeisters, [Vienna], 1936, translation by Brooks published as *The Missing Miniature; or, The Adventures of a Sensitive Butcher,* J. Cape, 1936, Knopf, 1937.

Georg und die Zwischenfaelle (novel), Atrium-Verlag, 1938, translation by Brooks published as *A Salzburg Comedy,* illustrated by Trier, Ungar, 1957.

Bei Durchsicht meiner Buecher, Atrium-Verlag, 1946.

Der taegliche Kram (songs and prose), Fischer Taschenbuch, 1948.

Zeltbuch von Tumilad, Insel-Verlag, 1949.

Die kleine Freiheit: Chansons und Prosa, 1949-1952, Atrium-Verlag, 1952.

Die dreizehn Monate, C. Dressler, 1955.

Die Schule der Diktatoren: Eine Komoedie in neun Bildern (play), C. Dressler, 1956.

Eine Auswahl, C. Dressler, 1956.

(Reteller) Miguel de Cervantes, *Leben und Taten des Scharfsinnigen Ritters Don Quichotte,* Ueberreuter, 1956, translation by R. and C. Winston published as *Don Quixote,* illustrated by H. Lemke, J. Messner, 1957.

Als Ich ein kleiner Junge war, C. Dressler, 1956, translation by Isabel McHugh and Florence McHugh published as *When I Was a Little Boy,* illustrated by H. Lemke, J. Cape, 1959, F. Watts, 1961.

(With Paul Flora) *Menschen und andere Tiere,* Piper, 1957.

Rede zur Verleihung des Georg Buechner-Preises 1957, C. Dressler, 1958.

Der Gegenwart ins Gaestebuch, Buechergilde Gutenberg, 1958.

Gesammelte Schriften, seven volumes, Buechergilde, 1958.

(Editor) *Heiterkeit in Dur und Moll* (German wit and humor), Fackeltraeger-Verlag, 1958.

Ueber das Verbrennen von Buechern, C. Dressler, 1959.

Heiteres von Walter Trier, Fackeltraeger-Verlag, 1959.

(Editor) *Heiterkeit kennt keine Grenzen* (German wit and humor), Fackeltraeger-Verlag, 1960.

Notabene 45: Ein Tagebuch, C. Dressler, 1961.

Das Erich Kaestner-Buch, edited by Rolf Hochhuth, Bertelsmann/Mohn, 1961.

Wieso warum? Ausgewaehlte Gedichte, 1928-1955, Aufbau, 1962.

(Editor) *Heiterkeit braucht keine Worte* (German wit and humor), Fackeltraeger-Verlag, 1962.

Das Schwein beim Friseur und Anderes, C. Dressler, 1962.

Das Erich-Kaestner-Seemaennchen, E. Seeman, 1963.

Kurz und Buendig, Kiepenheuer & Witsch, 1965.

Der taegliche Kram: Chansons und Prosa, C. Dressler, 1965.

Warnung vor Selbstschuessen, Aufbau, 1966.

Zwei Schueler sind verschwunden, Longmans, Green, 1966.

Kaestner fuer Erwachsene, S. Fischer, 1966.

Unter der Zeitlupe, Hyperion-Verlag, 1967.

". . . Was nicht in euren Lesebuechern steht" (selections from Kaestner's works), Fischer-Buecherei, 1968.

Kaestner fuer Studenten, Harper, 1968.

Kennst du das Land, wo die Kanonen bluehn?, Atrium-Verlag, 1968.

(Editor) *Heiterkeit aus aller Welt* (German wit and humor), Fackeltraeger-Verlag, 1968.

Gesammelte Schriften fuer Erwachsene, eight volumes, Droemer, 1969.

Wer nicht hoeren will, muss lesen, Fischer Taschenbuch, 1971.

Friedrich der Grosse und die deutsche Literatur, W. Kohlhammer, 1972.

Der Zauberlehrling: Ein Roman-Fragment, Voss, 1974.

Das grosse Erich Kaestner Buch, edited by Sylvia List, foreword by Hermann Kesten, Piper, 1975.

Briefe aus dem Tessin, Arche, 1977.

Mein liebes, gutes Muttchen, du: Dein oller Junge. Briefe und Postkarten aus 30 Jahren, edited by Luise-lotte Enderle, Knaus, 1981.

Also author of *Leben in dieser Zeit* (radio and stage play), 1930.

CHILDREN'S BOOKS

Emil and the Detectives (originally published as *Emil und die Detektive,* 1928), translated by May Massee, illustrated by Walter Trier, Doubleday, Doran, 1930.

Emil und die Detektive: Ein Theaterstueck fuer Kinder, Chronos, 1930, translation by Cyrus Brooks published as *Emil and the Detectives: A Children's Play in Three Acts,* French, 1934.

Annaluise and Anton (originally published as *Puenktchen und Anton,* 1931), translated by Eric Sutton, illustrated by W. Trier, J. Cape, 1932, Dodd, 1933.

Das verhexte Telefon, Williams, 1931.

Arthur mit dem langen Arm, Williams, 1931.

The 35th of May; or, Conrad's Ride to the South Seas (originally published as *Der 35 Mai; oder, Konrad reitet in die Suedsee,* 1931), translated by Brooks, illustrated by Trier, J. Cape, 1933, Dodd, 1934.

Puenktchen und Anton: Theaterstueck (play), Chronos, 1932.

Das fliegende Klassenzimmer, F. A. Perthes, 1933, translation by Brooks published as *The Flying Classroom,* illustrated by Trier, J. Cape, 1966.

Emil und die drei Zwillinge: Die zweite Geschichte von Emil und den Detektiven, Atrium-Verlag, 1935, translation by Brooks published as *Emil and the Three Twins: Another Book about Emil and the Detectives,* J. Cape, 1935, F. Watts 1961.

Eleven Merry Pranks of Till the Jester (originally published as *Till Eulenspiegel: Zwoelf seiner Geschichten frei nacherzaehlt*), translated by Brooks, Enoch, 1939, translated by Richard Winston and Clara Winston as *Till Eulenspiegel, the Clown,* Messner, 1957.

Zu treuen Haenden: Komoedie, Chronos, 1948.

Das doppelte Lottchen, Atrium-Verlag, 1949, translation by Brooks published as *Lottie and Lisa,* illustrated by Trier, J. Cape, 1950, Little, Brown, 1951.

Die Konferenz der Tiere, Europa Verlag, 1949, translation by Zita de Schauensee published as *The Animals Conference,* illustrated by Trier, D. McKay, 1949.

(Reteller) Charles Perrault, *Der gestiefelte Kater,* C. Ueberreuter, 1950, translation by R. and C. Winston published as *Puss in Boots,* illustrated by Trier, J. Messner, 1957.

(Translator) James Matthew Barrie, *Peter Pan,* Bloch, 1951.

Des Freiherrn von Muenchhausen wunderbare Reisen und Abenteuer zu Wasser und zu Lande: Nacherzaehlt, Atrium, 1951, translation by R. and C. Winston published as *Baron Munchhausen: His Wonderful Travels and Adventures,* Messner, 1957.

Die Schildbuerger: Nacherzaehlt, Atrium, 1954, translation by R. and C. Winston published as *The Simpletons,* Messner, 1957.

Muenchhausen: Ein Drehbuch (film script), Fischer, 1960.

(Translator) Jonathan Swift, *Gulliver's Reisen* (title means "Gulliver's Travels"), C. Ueberreuter, 1961.

Der kleine Mann, C. Dressler, 1963, translation by James Kirkup published as *The Little Man,* illustrated by Rick Schreiter, Knopf, 1966.

Der kleine Mann und die kleine Miss, C. Dressler, 1967, translation by Kirkup published as *The Little Man and the Little Miss,* illustrated by Horst Lemke, J. Cape, 1969.

The Little Man and the Big Thief, translated by Kirkup, illustrated by Stanley Mack, Knopf, 1969.

(Editor) *Die lustige Geschichtenkiste,* A. Betz, 1972.

Kaestner fuer Kinder (includes many of Kaestner's children's titles), Atrium, 1985.

POETRY

Herz auf Taille, C. Weller, 1928.

Laerm im Spiegel, C. Weller, 1929.

Ein Mann gibt Auskunft, Deutsche Verlags-Anstalt, 1930.

Gesang zwischen den Stuehlen, Deutsche Verlags-Anstalt, 1932.

Doktor Erich Kaestners lyrische Hausapotheke, Atrium, 1936.

Kurz und buendig: Epigramme, Atrium-Verlag, 1950.

Let's Face It (selected poems), translated by Patrick Bridgwater and others, J. Cape, 1963.

Von Damen und anderen Weibern, Fackeltraeger-Verlag, 1963.

(Editor) *Heiterkeit in vielen Versen,* Fackeltraeger-Verlag, 1965.

Grosse Zeiten, kleine Auswahl, Fackeltraeger-Verlag, 1969.

ADAPTATIONS: The film *Paradise for Three,* starring Robert Young and Mary Astor, is based on *Three Men in the Snow,* Metro-Goldwyn-Mayer, 1938; an adaptation of *Lottie and Lisa,* entitled *The Parent Trap,* starring Hayley Mills, Maureen O'Hara, and Brian Keith, was produced by Walt Disney Productions, 1961; Walt Disney Productions also filmed *Emil and the Detectives,* starring Walter Slezak, 1964; *Baron Munchhausen: His Wonderful Travels and Adventures* was filmed as *The Adventures of Baron Munchausen,* directed by Terry Gilliam, Columbia Pictures, 1989; a German version of *Emil und die Detektive,* was released with English subtitles in the United States by the International Film Bureau.

SIDELIGHTS: Erich Kaestner was known for his writings for children as well as adults. Politically active and involved in protesting World War II, Kaestner wrote adult books that reflect his social and political beliefs, which were deeply cynical and pessimistic. Kaestner's juvenile works, however, concentrate on the values of honesty, courage, and trust, sending a more optimistic message to children. He was best known in the United States for his work *Emil and the Detectives* and *Lottie and Lisa,* which were made into the successful movies *Emil and the Detectives* and *The Parent Trap.*

Kaestner was born in Dresden, Germany, in 1899, surrounded by a large extended family. His stepfather was a harnessmaker who fell upon hard times when the industry became automated. Kaestner's mother, trained as a hairdresser, scrimped and saved so that her child would have a good education and be able to see plays and operas. Kaestner tried to repay his mother for her hard work by becoming a model student. "I dared not disappoint her," he wrote in his autobiography, *When I Was a Little Boy.* "That was why I became the best pupil in the school and the best-behaved son possible at home. I could not have borne it if she had lost her great game."

Because of the family's poverty they often took in boarders. Many of them were schoolteachers, and this influence caused Kaestner to pursue this profession. He also became a voracious reader. "I read as I breathed—as if I would suffocate if I didn't. It became an almost dangerous passion with me." In 1913, the author entered a teacher's training school where he studied for a few years. In 1917, he was drafted into the German army. Under the hands of a brutal officer, he was forced into hard labor and developed a heart condition that would last for the rest of his life. After being discharged, Kaestner realized that he did not want to be a teacher, but rather preferred to be a learner. In 1919, he entered the Koenig-Georg-Gymnasium, later attending Leipzig University where he was to complete his Ph.D. He worked briefly as a journalist before moving on to cosmopolitan Berlin.

In 1928 his first volumes of poetry were published, as well as his children's book, *Emil and the Detectives.* The children's book, an instant success, was quickly translated into several languages and adapted for stage and film. The story focuses on Emil, a poor boy whose grandmother's money is stolen by a notorious thief. Instead of taking this indignity passively, the enterprising Emil deputizes some of his buddies, and together they pursue and capture the thief. Herbert Knust wrote in the *Dictionary of Literary Biography* that "although capturing and addressing the mentality of youngsters, the short novel presents various relations between the adult world and a basically unspoiled children's world. . . . Much of the story's humor and appeal derive from the fact that the children's republic functions better than that of the grownups."

The years from 1928 to 1933 were very productive ones for Kaestner, who published new children's books annually. Kaestner found that he fell on the opposite side of the political fence from the Nazis, who censored many of his works. Nevertheless, he stayed in Germany through much of the war, refusing to ally himself with the Nazis or choose exile.

After the war was over, Kaestner founded the children's magazine *Pinguin,* which was published from 1945-49. In 1949, he wrote the novel *Lottie and Lisa,* the story of identical twin girls who meet for the first time at a camp. The sisters were separated at a young age when their parents divorced and each parent took custody of one of the twins. The story was made into a popular Disney movie entitled *The Parent Trap*, starring Brian Keith and Hayley Mills.

Kaestner continued to write children's books, but none of the works of this era "comes close to the novelty and brilliance of the works written between 1928 and 1933," Gerhard H. Weiss commented in *Writers for Children*. When Kaestner died in 1974, his work had become immensely popular, and he had won recognition and awards from several international groups.

Some of his popularity with youth may have been due to his attitude. Weiss wrote that "Kaestner writes for children without condescension. He speaks to them in a light and chatty tone, as equals. He believes that children have the same rights as adults, and he takes their world seriously. He understands a child's perspective and admonishes his readers never to forget their own childhood." Further, while Kaestner's stories usually end on a happy note, they never stoop to sappiness. The author endeavored to be honest in his children's works. "I only think that one must be honest, even if it hurts," Kaestner wrote in the preface to *The Flying Classroom*. "Honest to the core."

BIOGRAPHICAL/CRITICAL SOURCES:

BOOKS

Contemporary Literary Criticism, Volume 4, Gale, 1975.
Dictionary of Literary Biography, Volume 56: *German Fiction Writers, 1914-1945,* Gale, 1987, pp. 163-174.
Doyle, Brian, editor, *Who's Who of Children's Literature,* Schocken Books, 1968.
Kaestner, Erich, *The Flying Classroom: A Novel for Children,* translated by Cyrus Brooks, J. Cape, 1934.
Kaestner, *When I Was a Little Boy,* translated by Isabel McHugh and Florence McHugh, J. Cape, 1959.
Weiss, Gerard H., essay in *Writers for Children,* Scribner, 1988, pp. 317-322.

PERIODICALS

Lion and the Unicorn, Volume 9, 1985.*

*   *   *

KARP, Abraham J.   1921-

PERSONAL: Born April 5, 1921, in Indura, Poland; son of Aaron (a furrier) and Rachel (Short) Karp; married Deborah Burstein, June 17, 1945; children: Hillel Judah, David Jacob. *Education:* Yeshiva University, B.A. (magna cum laude), 1942; Jewish Theological Seminary of America, rabbi, 1945, M.H.L., 1949, D.D., 1971; additional study at Columbia University. *Avocational interests:* Book collecting in fields of Hebraica and early American Judaica.

ADDRESSES: Home—3333 Henry Hudson Pkwy., Bronx, NY 10463. *Office*—Jewish Theological Seminary of America, 3080 Broadway, New York, NY 10027.

CAREER: Rabbi, Temple Israel, Swampscott, MA, 1948-51, Beth Shalom, Kansas City, MO, 1951-56, and Temple Beth El, Rochester, NY, 1956-72; University of Rochester, Rochester, NY, professor of history and religious studies, beginning 1972, Philip S. Bernstein Professor of Jewish Studies, beginning 1975; Jewish Theological Seminary of America, New York, NY, professor of history, 1991—. Visiting professor, Dartmouth College, 1967, Jewish Theological Seminary of America, 1967, 1971, and Hebrew University, 1970. Corresponding member, Institute of Contemporary Jewry, Hebrew University, 1973—. Fellow, Institute of Talmudic Ethics.

MEMBER: Rabbinical Assembly of America (member of executive council, 1959-62), American Jewish Historical Society (member of executive council, beginning 1960; president, 1972-75), Jewish Publication Society of America, Jewish Academy of Arts (fellow), Phi Beta Kappa.

AWARDS, HONORS: Lee M. Friedman Medal; Valley Forge Award, for *Haven and Home.*

WRITINGS:

When Your Child Asks about God, United Synagogue, 1954.
Our December Dilemma, United Synagogue, 1958.
The Jewish Way of Life, Prentice-Hall, 1962, revised edition published as *The Jewish Way of Life and Thought,* Ktav, 1980.
A History of the United Synagogue of America, 1913-1963, United Synagogue, 1963.
(Editor and author of introduction) *The Jewish Experience in America,* America Jewish Historical Society, 1969.
(Author of introduction) *Beginnings: Early American Judaica,* Jewish Publication Society of America, 1975.
Golden Door to America: The Jewish Immigrant Experience, Viking, 1976.
To Give Life, Schocken, 1980.
American Judaism: A Pluralistic Religious Community (in Hebrew), Schocken (Israel), 1984.
Haven and Home: A History of the Jews in America, Schocken, 1985.
(Co-author) *The American Rabbinate: A Century of Continuity and Change, 1883-1983,* Ktav, 1984.
(Contributor) *American Jewish Year Book,* Jewish Publication Society of America, 1986.
Mordecai Manuel Noah: The First American Jew, Yeshiva University Museum, 1987.

From the Ends of the Earth: Judaic Treasures of the Library of Congress, Rizzoli, 1991.

SIDELIGHTS: In *Haven and Home: A History of the Jews in America,* "Abraham J. Karp shows how America, first seen as a place of refuge, became home to the largest Jewish community in the world," writes Ari L. Goldman in the *New York Times Book Review.* Karp examines Jewish history from the arrival of the first Jewish refugees to New Amsterdam (now New York) in the seventeenth century to the present. His study suggests that although they shared a religion and the immigrant experience, American Jews formed not one community, but several. Their diversity allowed them to prosper, maintains Karp. "In this useful and accessible book, Mr. Karp tells us how," concludes Goldman.

In a *Los Angeles Times Book Review* article describing *From the Ends of the Earth: Judaic Treasures of the Library of Congress,* Kenneth Turan remarks that "this beautifully produced book shows . . . more than 300 illustrations, everything from gorgeous *ketuboth* (marriage certificates) and mysterious amulets to the astronomical tables compiled by a rabbi and used by Columbus on his journeys. [Books include] the first printed Hebrew book and the first book in any language to be printed in Africa. Abraham Karp's thoughtful, informative text turns this from a guide to a collection to an intriguing gloss on all of Jewish history and culture." And on the same work, a critic for *AB Bookman's Weekly* comments, "The outstanding factor that renders the book a lasting treasure in itself is the vast scholarship of Abraham J. Karp, whose text serves to place each and every item in meaningful perspective."

BIOGRAPHICAL/CRITICAL SOURCES:

PERIODICALS

AB Bookman's Weekly, May 4, 1992.
Los Angeles Times Book Review, December 1, 1991, p. 6.
New York Times Book Review, August 4, 1985, p. 17.

*   *   *

KARR, Phyllis Ann 1944-

PERSONAL: Born July 25, 1944, in Oakland, CA; daughter of Frank Joseph (an educator) and Helena (an educator; maiden name, Beckmann) Karr; married Clifton A. Hoyt, June 2, 1990. *Education:* Colorado State University, A.B., 1966; Indiana University at Bloomington, M.L.S., 1971. *Politics:* Independent. *Religion:* "Catholic."

ADDRESSES: Home—Barnes, WI. *Agent*—Owlswick Literary Agency, 4426 Larchwood, Philadelphia, PA 19104.

CAREER: East Chicago Public Library, Roxana Branch, East Chicago, IN, branch librarian, 1967-70; Hamill & Barker Antiquarian Booksellers, Chicago, IL, shop assistant, 1971; University of Louisville Library, Louisville, KY, cataloguer, 1972-77; writer, 1977—. Volunteer reader and monitor for Recording for the Blind, Louisville; member of Communiversity Band, Rice Lake, WI, 1978-91.

MEMBER: International Wizard of Oz Club, Early English Text Society, Mystery Writers of America, Science Fiction Writers of America, Friends of the University of Michigan Gilbert and Sullivan Society, Phi Sigma Iota, Beta Phi Mu.

WRITINGS:

My Lady Quixote, Fawcett, 1980.
Frostflower and Thorn, Berkley, 1980.
Lady Susan, Everest House, 1980.
Meadow Song, Fawcett, 1981.
Perola, Fawcett, 1982.
The Elopement, Fawcett, 1982.
The Idylls of the Queen, Ace Books, 1982.
Frostflower and Windbourne, Berkley, 1982.
Wildraith's Last Battle, Ace Books, 1982.
The King Arthur Companion, Reston, 1983.
At Amberleaf Fair, Ace, 1986.

Also contributor to magazines and numerous anthologies. Author of column, "Thoughts from Oakapple Place," *GASBAG,* 1970—. Assistant editor, *Fantasy and Terror,* 1975-76.

Karr's papers have been solicited for the University of Oregon Special Collections.

WORK IN PROGRESS: Historical novel about a Spanish inquisitor.

SIDELIGHTS: Phyllis Ann Karr told *CA:* "The first goal of fiction is to entertain. True entertainment is difficult unless there is also some philosophic or other thought-provoking content, but the first duty of the fiction crafter is to tell a story on a clear, coherent level, readily comprehensible to the reader. I think fiction took a wrong turn when the 'literary' authors like James Joyce became a separate breed from the 'popular' authors of fiction. Cervantes, Dickens, and others are great because they have both a popular and a critical appeal, even though the popular may have come first and have been followed only later by the critical. The best style is the invisible style, though there are exceptions. I, personally, write because it is an inner need to maintain my balance. Fiction satisfies the need better than nonfiction and is also easier to write, as a rule.

"I can translate from non-technical French, Russian, and Middle English (from verse into verse in the latter) and hope someday to add Polish and maybe Latin. But translation seems an even harder field to break into than original composition. My biggest break to date in getting paid for my writing was the good fortune of obtaining an agent.

"From 1984 to 1989, I rented a cottage in Birchwood, Wisconsin, for a writing retreat. Through the bookmobile that serves both Birchwood and Barnes, my future husband made contact with me, seeking a fellow reader of science fiction and fantasy. A first marriage for both of us, it is turning out well worth the wait: more than ever, I rejoice that I never rushed into a relationship, but held out for the right partner."

BIOGRAPHICAL/CRITICAL SOURCES:

PERIODICALS

Washington Post Book World, October 6, 1985.

*   *   *

KARREN, Keith J(ohn) 1943-

PERSONAL: Born August 23, 1943, in Kent, England; immigrated to United States, 1969, naturalized citizen, 1981; son of Clinton H. (in Canadian Army) and Joyce Louise (in England Land Army; maiden name, Shorter) Karren; married Diane Johnson (a homemaker), January 27, 1968; children: M. Scott, Holli, James Todd, Brady John, Mandy. *Education:* Brigham Young University, B.Sc., 1969, M.S., 1970; Oregon State University, Ph.D., 1975. *Religion:* Church of Jesus Christ of Latter-day Saints (Mormon). *Avocational interests:* Jogging five miles a day, people ("especially seeing those who are given extra challenges succeed"), and raising, training, and showing Arabian horses.

ADDRESSES: Home—276 East 4960 N., Provo, UT 84604. *Office*—Department of Health Sciences, 213-RB, Brigham Young University, Provo, UT 84602.

CAREER: Mormon missionary in England and Wales, 1963-65; Ricks Junior College (now Ricks College), Rexburg, ID, professor of health science, 1970-71; Brigham Young University, Provo, UT, assistant professor of health science, 1971-72, associate professor, then professor of health science and department chair, 1975—, first aid coordinator and creator of cardiopulmonary resuscitation workshop, 1975—; Oregon State University, Corvallis, assistant professor of health science, 1973-74. Registered emergency medical technician; coordinator and instructor, Utah Emergency Medical Technician Program; instructor for American Red Cross and American Heart Association; member, Utah County Board of Health.

MEMBER: American Association for Health, Physical Education, Recreation, and Dance, American School Health Association, Emergency Medical Technician Association, Eta Sigma Gamma.

WRITINGS:

(Co-author) *Emergency First Aid Workbook,* Morton, 1977, 2nd edition, 1980.
(With Sherril A. Hundley) *God's Special Children: Helping the Handicapped Achieve,* Horizon Publishers, 1977.
(With Hundley) *Surviving Health Emergencies and Disasters,* EMS Publications, 1978.
(With Brent Q. Hafen) *Child Abuse and Neglect,* Brigham Young University Press, 1979.
(With Hafen) *Prehospital Emergency Care and Crisis Intervention* (with workbook), Morton, 1979, 4th edition, Prentice-Hall, 1992.
(With Hafen) *Health for the Elementary School Teacher,* Allyn & Bacon, 1980.
(With Hafen and Ronald Rhodes) *Self-Help Health Care,* Prentice-Hall, 1980.
(With Hafen) *The Crisis Intervention Handbook,* Creative Age Publications, 1980.
The Will to Win, Randall Publishing, 1981.
(With Hafen) *First Aid and Emergency Care Skills Manual,* Morton, 1982.
(With Hafen) *Health Management, Promotion, and Self-Care,* Morton, 1982.
(With Hafen) *First Responder: A Skills Approach* (with workbook), Morton, 1982, revised edition, Prentice-Hall, 1992.
(With Hafen) *First Aid and Emergency Care Workbook,* revised edition, Morton, 1984, 4th edition, 1990.
A Long Way Home, Bookcraft, 1985.
(With Hafen) *The EMT Review Manual,* Morton, 1987.
First Aid and Emergency Care, Prentice-Hall, 1992.
(Co-author) *The Health Effects of Emotions and Attitudes,* EMS Associates, 1992.

Contributor to books, including *First Aid: Contemporary Practices and Principles,* edited by Brent Q. Hafen, Alton L. Thygerson, and Ray A. Peterson, Burgess Publishing, 1972. Contributor to health and physical education journals.

WORK IN PROGRESS: Sexuality in Youth; a biography of Dr. Keith R. Hooker, an emergency room physician in Alaska, publication expected in 1993.

SIDELIGHTS: Keith J. Karren once told *CA:* "I was involved in ranching during my teens and early twenties; my family has a strong agricultural background and I was raised in a farming and ranching community. I have always loved the earth and the animals on it. I began rodeoing at a very young age, and bareback bronco riding became my major event. With the responsibilities of professional, family, and church life I have backed off considerably, but still enjoy raising purebred Arabian horses, which are my passion.

"My approach to prehospital emergency care is to teach the basics very well, then add depth according to my student population. I concentrate heavily on the *skills* aspect of emergency care, as is evident in my publications. My motivation in the child abuse and sexuality area is a great desire to improve the health of American youth. I am extremely concerned about well-being and the part values play in the decision-making process.

"I have two biographies in progress. One is about Keith R. Hooker, M.D., an atypical emergency room physician. He could nicely fit into the television shows 'M*A*S*H' or 'St. Elsewhere'! A strong, rugged individualist who spent years as a flying doctor to the Eskimoes of Alaska, a daring bush-pilot who has surgically operated via telephone instructions, a nature survivalist who felt somewhat invincible and continued to try to prove his manhood with daring escapades and narrow escapes while flying—this describes him. A trip to the top of Mt. McKinley in Alaska, with consequent frostbite and a close encounter with death, taught Keith he was human and fragile." Karren recently added: "The book concludes with Keith's climb of Mt. Everest in 1992, the perils and the lessons learned.

"My other biography treats Jason Buck, an Idaho farm boy, who is thwarted at every turn but never gives up. Against all odds, he becomes an All-American college football player, then a standout pro for the Cincinnati Bengals and Washington Redskins. Jason shows the character of a hero because he will not quit!"

*　　*　　*

KELDER, Diane 1934-

PERSONAL: Born May 23, 1934, in New York City; daughter of William L. (a major in the U. S. Army) and Eleanore V. (Raymond) Kelder. *Education:* Queens College (now Queens College of the City University of New York), A.B., 1955; University of Chicago, M.A., 1957; Bryn Mawr College, Ph.D., 1966.

ADDRESSES: Office—Department of Performing and Creative Arts, College of Staten Island of the City University of New York, 130 Stuyvesant Pl., Staten Island, NY 10301.

CAREER: Queens College of the City University of New York, Flushing, NY, lecturer in art history, 1959-66; Philadelphia Museum of Art, Philadelphia, PA, assistant cu-

rator of prints and drawings, 1966-67; Finch College, New York City, instructor in art history, 1967-71; College of Staten Island of the City University of New York, Staten Island, NY, professor of art history, 1971—.

MEMBER: International Art Critics Association, College Art Association of America.

AWARDS, HONORS: Fanny Workman fellowship, American Association of University Women, 1962-63; Junior Humanist fellowship, National Endowment for the Humanities, 1971; Ingram Merrill Foundation Award, 1972.

WRITINGS:

Pageant of the Renaissance, Praeger, 1969.
The French Impressionists and Their Century (juvenile; based on *Die Malher des grossen Lichtes* by Hans Platte), Praeger, 1970.
Rembrandt, McGraw, 1970.
(Author of introduction) Ferdinando Galli da Bibiena, *L'Architettura civile,* B. Blom, 1971.
(Editor) *Stuart Davis,* Praeger, 1971.
Aspects of "Official" Painting and Philosophic Art, Garland Publishing, 1975.
(Author of commentaries) *Fifty French Impressionist Masterpieces: From the National Gallery of Art, Washington, D.C.,* Crown, 1977.
Great Masterpieces by Claude Monet, Crown, 1979.
French Impressionists: From the National Gallery of Art, Washington, D.C., Abbeville Press, 1980.
The Great Book of French Impressionism, Abbeville Press, 1980.
The Great Book of Post-Impressionism, Abbeville Press, 1986.
Stuart David: Prints and Related Works, Amon Carter Museum, 1986.

Also author of numerous exhibition catalogues. Author of *Rembrandt* (slide color program of the Great Masters), McGraw, 1980. Editor of *Art Journal,* 1973-80.

*　　*　　*

KENNEDY, Dorothy M(intzlaff) 1931-

PERSONAL: Born March 8, 1931, in Milwaukee, WI; daughter of Henry Carl and Clara Anna (Lange) Mintzlaff; married Joseph Charles Kennedy (a writer under pseudonym X. J. Kennedy), January 31, 1962; children: Kathleen Anna, David Ian, Matthew Devin, Daniel Joseph, Joshua Quentin. *Education:* Milwaukee-Downer College (now Lawrence University of Wisconsin), B.A. (magna cum laude), 1953; University of Michigan, M.A.,

1956, additional graduate study, 1956-57, 1959-62. *Politics:* Independent. *Religion:* Protestant.

ADDRESSES: Home and office—4 Fern Way, Bedford, MA 01730. *Agent*—Curtis Brown Ltd., 10 Astor Pl., New York, NY 10003.

CAREER: High school teacher of English and Spanish in Milledgeville, IL, 1953-55; Ohio University, Athens, instructor in English, 1957-59; University of Michigan, Ann Arbor, teaching fellow, 1960-62; writer, 1977—.

MEMBER: National Council of Teachers of English, Phi Beta Kappa.

AWARDS, HONORS: Choice Book selection, National Council of Teachers of English, and Book of the Year selection, *School Library Journal,* both with husband, X. J. Kennedy, both 1983, both for *Knock at a Star: A Child's Introduction to Poetry.*

WRITINGS:

WITH HUSBAND, X. J. KENNEDY

Knock at a Star: A Child's Introduction to Poetry, illustrated by Karen Ann Weinhaus, Little, Brown, 1982.
The Bedford Reader, St. Martin's, 1982, 4th edition, with Jane E. Aaron, 1991.
The Bedford Guide for College Writers, St. Martin's, 1987, 2nd edition, 1990.
Talking Like the Rain: A First Book of Poems, illustrated by Jane Dyer, Little, Brown, 1992.

Co-editor, *Counter Measures,* 1972-74.

WORK IN PROGRESS: I Thought I'd Take My Rat to School: Poems for September to June, with illustrations by Abby Carter, for Little, Brown.

SIDELIGHTS: Dorothy M. Kennedy once told *CA:* "As a writer I bloomed late—maybe because I can't seem to bloom in more than one area at a time. First teaching and then childrearing took priority, and I enjoyed both. In 1977 or 1978, when our youngest child started school, I began to work on instructor's manuals, and one thing led to another—specifically to college textbooks and to children's books.

"In a way, *Knock at a Star* grew out of our work on textbooks for college freshmen. It, too, is a teaching book, though an informal one. In it we assume, contrary to general wisdom, that children will care not only about the poems collected in the book but also about how poems are written. Children delight in looking closely at animals, insects, plants, machines, mineral specimens. Why not at poetry? Couldn't rhythm and rhyme, imagery and figures of speech engage the child? We also strive to encourage our readers to write poems of their own, and we offer sug-

gestions about how to begin. Throughout the book we take a radical approach: we talk directly to the child."

About her subsequent books, Kennedy later added: "When Joe (X. J. Kennedy) and I finished working on *Knock at a Star,* we had left over both some good poems and a wonderful title that we hadn't used. These grew into the next children's anthology we did together, *Talking Like the Rain: A First Book of Poems.* As the subtitle makes clear, this book aims to acquaint the very young—those who need to be read to—with the pleasures of poetry.

"Now, at long last, I have embarked on my first solo project, tentatively titled *I Thought I'd Take My Rat to School: Poems for September to June.* If nothing else, this book will be different, I think. I don't know of another poetry anthology for school-age children that sets forth—with pictures—the pains and joys of going to school."

*   *   *

KENNEDY, Joseph Charles 1929-
(X. J. Kennedy)

PERSONAL: Born August 21, 1929, in Dover, NJ; son of Joseph Francis and Agnes (Rauter) Kennedy; married Dorothy Mintzlaff (a writer), January 31, 1962; children: Kathleen Anna, David Ian, Matthew Devin, Daniel Joseph, Joshua Quentin. *Education:* Seton Hall University, B.Sc., 1950; Columbia University, M.A., 1951; University of Paris, certificat, 1956; additional study at University of Michigan, 1956-62.

ADDRESSES: Home—4 Fern Way, Bedford, MA 01730. *Agent*—Curtis Brown, Ltd., 10 Astor Pl., New York, NY 10003.

CAREER: University of Michigan, Ann Arbor, teaching fellow, 1956-60, instructor in English, 1960-62; Woman's College of University of North Carolina (now University of North Carolina at Greensboro), lecturer in English, 1962-63; Tufts University, Medford, MA, assistant professor, 1963-67, associate professor, 1967-73, professor of English, 1973-79; free-lance writer, 1979—. Visiting lecturer at Wellesley College, 1964, and University of California, Irvine, 1966-67; Bruern fellow in American civilization at the University of Leeds, 1974-75. Judge of National Council on Arts poetry book selections, 1969, 1970. *Military service:* U.S. Navy, 1951-55.

MEMBER: Modern Language Association, National Council of Teachers of English, PEN, Authors Guild of America, John Barton Wolgamot Society, Phi Beta Kappa.

AWARDS, HONORS: Avery Hopwood Awards, University of Michigan, 1959, for poetry and essay; Bread Loaf fellowship in poetry, 1960; Bess Hokin Prize, *Poetry* magazine, 1961; Lamont Award, Academy of American Poets, 1961, for *Nude Descending a Staircase: Poems, Song, a Ballad;* National Council on the Arts grant, 1967-68; Shelley Memorial Award, 1970; Guggenheim fellowship, 1973-74; Golden Rose Trophy, New England Poetry Club, 1974; National Council of Teachers of English Teachers' Choice Book, and *School Library Journal* book of the year, both 1983, both for *Knock at a Star: A Child's Introduction to Poetry; Los Angeles Times* Book Award in poetry, 1985, for *Cross Ties: Selected Poems;* American Library Association Notable Book citation, 1986, for *The Forgetful Wishing Well: Poems for Young People;* L.H.D., Lawrence University, 1988; Michael Braude Award for Light Verse, American Academy and Institute of Arts and Letters, 1989; Sigma Tau Delta honorary member.

WRITINGS:

UNDER PSEUDONYM X. J. KENNEDY

(Editor with James E. Camp) *Mark Twain's Frontier: A Textbook of Primary Source Materials for Student Research and Writing,* Holt, 1963.

An Introduction to Poetry (textbook), Little, Brown, 1966, 8th edition (with Dana Gioia), HarperCollins, 1993.

(Editor with Camp and Keith Waldrop) *Pegasus Descending: A Book of the Best Bad Verse* (anthology), Macmillan, 1971.

(Editor) *Messages: A Thematic Anthology of Poetry,* Little, Brown, 1973.

An Introduction to Fiction (textbook with instructor's manual), Little, Brown, 1976, 6th edition (with Gioia), HarperCollins, in press.

Literature: An Introduction to Fiction, Poetry, and Drama (textbook with instructor's manual), Little, Brown, 1976, 6th edition (with Gioia), HarperCollins, in press.

(Editor) *Tygers of Wrath: Poems of Hate, Anger and Invective,* University of Georgia Press, 1981.

(With wife, Dorothy M. Kennedy) *The Bedford Reader* (textbook with instructor's manual), St. Martin's, 1982, 4th edition (with Jane E. Aaron), 1991.

The Owlstone Crown (juvenile novel), illustrated by Michele Chessare, Atheneum, 1983.

(With D. M. Kennedy) *The Bedford Guide for College Writers* (with instructor's manual), St. Martin's, 1987, 3rd edition (with Sylvia A. Holladay), 1993.

POETRY UNDER PSEUDONYM X. J. KENNEDY

Nude Descending a Staircase: Poems, Song, a Ballad, Doubleday, 1961.

Growing into Love, Doubleday, 1969.

Bulsh, Burning Deck, 1970.

Breaking and Entering, Oxford University Press, 1971.

Emily Dickinson in Southern California, Godine, 1974.

Celebrations after the Death of John Brennan, Penmaen, 1974.

(With Camp and Waldrop) *Three Tenors, One Vehicle,* Open Places, 1975.

(Translator from the French) *French Leave: Translations,* Robert L. Barth, 1983.

Missing Link, Scheidt Head, 1983.

Hangover Mass, Bits Press, 1984.

Cross Ties: Selected Poems, University of Georgia Press, 1985.

Winter Thunder, Robert L. Barth, 1990.

Dark Horses: New Poems, Johns Hopkins University Press, 1992.

CHILDREN'S POETRY UNDER PSEUDONYM X. J. KENNEDY

One Winter Night in August and Other Nonsense Jingles, illustrated by David McPhail, Atheneum, 1975.

The Phantom Ice Cream Man: More Nonsense Verse, illustrated by McPhail, Atheneum, 1979.

Did Adam Name the Vinegarroon?, illustrated by Heidi Johanna Selig, Godine, 1982.

(Compiler with D. M. Kennedy) *Knock at a Star: A Child's Introduction to Poetry,* illustrated by Karen Ann Weinhaus, Little, Brown, 1982.

The Forgetful Wishing Well: Poems for Young People, illustrated by Monica Incisa, Atheneum, 1985.

Brats, illustrated by James Watts, Atheneum, 1986.

Ghastlies, Goops and Pincushions: Nonsense Verse, illustrated by Ron Barrett, McElderry Books/Macmillan, 1989.

Fresh Brats, illustrated by Watts, McElderry Books/Macmillan, 1990.

The Kite That Braved Old Orchard Beach: Year-Round Poems for Young People, illustrated by Marian Young, McElderry Books/Macmillan, 1991.

(Compiler with D. M. Kennedy) *Talking Like the Rain: A First Book of Poems,* illustrated by Jane Dyer, Little, Brown, 1992.

The Beasts of Bethlehem, illustrated by Michael McCurdy, McElderry Books/Macmillan, 1992.

Drat These Brats!, McElderry Books/Macmillan, in press.

OTHER

Poetry editor, *Paris Review,* 1961-64; co-editor and publisher, with D. M. Kennedy, *Counter/Measures,* 1971-74.

WORK IN PROGRESS: Poems; a comic novel; another novel for children; juvenile verse.

SIDELIGHTS: Although Joseph Charles Kennedy has reached his widest audience by writing college textbooks and children's verse, publication in 1961 of his first book of poetry, *Nude Descending a Staircase: Poems, Song, a Ballad,* established his reputation as a poet for adults. Poems from the collection had already won Kennedy the

University of Michigan's Hopwood Award and *Poetry* magazine's Bess Hokin Prize, while the Academy of American Poets bestowed its Lamont Award on the volume itself. *Nude Descending a Staircase* reveals a poet who writes witty, satirical poems and—unlike the majority of his colleagues—uses traditional verse forms. This strict adherence to rhyme and measured rhythm has prevailed through all Kennedy's work, leading the poet to describe himself as "one of an endangered species."

Kennedy's thirty-year collection of poetry, *Cross Ties: Selected Poems* (winner of the *Los Angeles Times* Book Award for poetry in 1985) is praised by critics for the two factors which attracted them to his first work: humor and dexterous use of poetic construction. In a *Christian Science Monitor* review of the volume, for example, Raymond Oliver calls Kennedy "the funniest poet alive" and claims that "the secret of Kennedy's excellence is his mastery of traditional verse." *Poetry* contributor Roger Mitchell's critique of the book also highlights the same characteristics of Kennedy's work. "He is a satirist," Mitchell observes, "and few poets are funnier than he." And to those who might call Kennedy's poetry out-of-date or old-fashioned, Mitchell replies, "If [Kennedy] is driving a horse and buggy in the age of the automobile, it is an elegant, well-made buggy, and the animal is gorgeous and well-groomed." Nichols congratulates Kennedy for being different from the mass of poets: "His allegiance to traditional verse forms verifies that he is indeed a breed apart from many of his contemporaries. While not all are equally rewarding, the poems in *Cross Ties* are of a range and depth that demonstrate the viability and elasticity of a poetic voice that submits willingly to the stricture of meter and rhyme."

In his more recent collections of poetry, which are written for children, Kennedy combines his renowned rhyme with a splash of nonsense. In both *Ghastlies, Goops and Pincushions,* published in 1989, and *Fresh Brats,* published in 1990, Kennedy "turns the ordinary on its head," describes Nancy Willard in the *Washington Post Book World.* Among the characters that fill *Ghastlies, Goops and Pincushions* are an unfriendly grocer, a child who snacks on spare tires and shingles, and another youngster who manages to be swallowed by a vacuum cleaner. Kennedy's "agile verses, varied in structure, rhythm, and form, not only make the absurd seem real but also reveal the absurdity frequently found in reality," relates Mary M. Burns in *Horn Book.* In *Fresh Brats,* Kennedy almost cheerfully describes the demise of many of the mischievous children who fill this book of nonsense verse. One child drops a dead mouse in the bread his mother is baking, and another offers his ice cream cone to grizzly bears in Yellowstone, only to become their new "favorite flavor." Kennedy's "outrageous and zanily conceived goings on will be indeli-

bly imprinted on the minds of the young," concludes Ethel R. Twichell in *Horn Book.*

Aside from his nonsense verse, Kennedy has also written volumes of more serious poems for children. *The Kite That Braved Old Orchard Beach* is divided into seven sections which cover such topics as joy, growing and dreaming, friends, beasts and fish, and times of the year. "The poems in each section are celebrations of that subject, and the poetry ranges from poignant to playful in emotional content," remarks Donna L. Scanlon in the *Voice of Youth Advocates.* The poems in *The Kite That Braved Old Orchard Beach,* maintains a *Publishers Weekly* contributor, reveal Kennedy's wide variety of interests, "his experimentation with traditional forms and his sensitivity to the wonderings and experiences of young people."

Commenting on his predilection for traditional poetic forms, Kennedy once told *CA:* "As a poet, I have printed few lines that fail to rhyme and to scan metrically. Though I admire—envy!—poets who can dispense with such formalities, I find I need them. Many today dismiss the sonnet and other traditional forms as drab boxes for cramming with words. But to me the old forms are where the primitive and surprising action is. Writing in rhythm and rhyme, a poet is involved in an enormous, meaningful game, not under his ego's control. He is a mere mouse in the lion's den of the language—but with any luck, at times he can get the lion to come out."

BIOGRAPHICAL/CRITICAL SOURCES:

BOOKS

Contemporary Authors Autobiography Series, Volume 9, Gale, 1989.
Contemporary Literary Criticism, Gale, Volume 8, 1978, Volume 42, 1987.
Dictionary of Literary Biography, Volume 5: *American Poets since World War II,* Gale, 1980.

PERIODICALS

Christian Science Monitor, August 7, 1985.
Horn Book, September/October, 1989, p. 633; March/April, 1990, pp. 215-16.
National Review, July 18, 1986.
Poetry, January, 1986.
Publishers Weekly, February 15, 1991, p. 90.
School Library Journal, July, 1990, pp. 85-86; July, 1991, p. 82.
Voice of Youth Advocates, April, 1991, p. 57.
Washington Post Book World, May 14, 1989.

KENNEDY, X. J.
See KENNEDY, Joseph Charles

*   *   *

KIDDER, Tracy 1945-

PERSONAL: Born November 12, 1945, in New York, NY; son of Henry Maynard (a lawyer) and Reine (a high school teacher; maiden name, Tracy) Kidder; married Frances T. Toland, January 2, 1971; children: a boy and a girl. *Education:* Harvard University, A.B., 1967; University of Iowa, M.F.A., 1974.

ADDRESSES: Agent—Georges Borchardt, Inc., 136 East 57th St., New York, NY 10022.

CAREER: Writer, 1974—. *Military service:* U.S. Army, 1967-69, served in intelligence in Vietnam; became first lieutenant.

AWARDS, HONORS: Atlantic First Award, *Atlantic Monthly,* for short story "The Death of Major Great"; Sidney Hillman Foundation Prize, 1978, for article, "Soldiers of Misfortune"; Pulitzer Prize and American Book Award, 1982, both for *The Soul of a New Machine;* National Book Critics Circle nomination (nonfiction), 1986, for *House;* Christopher Award and National Book Critics Circle Award nomination (nonfiction), 1989, Robert F. Kennedy Award and Ambassador Book Award, 1990, all for *Among Schoolchildren.*

WRITINGS:

NONFICTION

The Road to Yuba City: A Journey into the Juan Corona Murders, Doubleday, 1974.
The Soul of a New Machine, Little, Brown, 1981.
House, Houghton Mifflin, 1985.
Among Schoolchildren, Houghton Mifflin, 1989.

OTHER

Also contributing editor, *Atlantic Monthly,* 1982—. Contributor to newspapers and magazines, including *New York Times Book Review, Science '83,* and *Country Journal.*

SIDELIGHTS: Tracy Kidder's *The Soul of a New Machine* proved by its critical reception that technical subjects can be comprehensible and intriguing to laymen when they are skillfully presented. The book details the eighteen-month-long struggle of engineers at Data General Corporation to create a competitive super-mini computer. Kidder, a newcomer to this highly technical world, spent months in a basement laboratory at the corporation's Massachusetts headquarters observing teams of young engineers at work: the hardware specialists, or "Hardy Boys," who put the computer's circuitry together, and the "Micro-kids," who developed the code that fused the hardware and software of the system. In telling the story of the assembly, setbacks, and perfection of the thirty-two "bit" prototype computer, the Eagle, Kidder exposes the inner workings of a highly competitive industry, illustrates both concentrated teamwork and moments of virtuosity on the part of the project's brilliant engineers, and produces what reviewer Edward R. Weidlein, in the *Washington Post Book World,* judged "a true-life adventure" and "compelling entertainment."

Many critics cited Kidder's masterful handling of the complex subject matter in *The Soul of a New Machine* as one of the book's strongest features. "Even someone like this reviewer," wrote Christopher Lehmann-Haupt of the *New York Times,* "who barely understood the difference between computer hardware and software when he began *The Soul of a New Machine,* was able to follow every step of the debugging mystery, even though it involves binary arithmetic, Boolean algebra, and a grasp of the difference between a System Cache and an Instruction Processor." Weidlin concurred, observing that Kidder "offers a fast, painless, enjoyable means to an initial understanding of computers, allowing us to understand the complexity of machines we could only marvel at before."

Kidder's portraits of the Eagle's engineers were applauded by critics as well. A *New Yorker* reviewer proclaimed that Kidder "gives a full sense of the mind and motivation, the creative genius of the computer engineer." And a *Saturday Review* critic claimed that *The Soul of a New Machine* "tells a human story of tremendous effort." Critics also lauded *The Soul of a New Machine* for its departure from the standard journalistic approach to nonfiction. Jeremy Bernstein, writing in the *New York Review of Books,* declared, "I strongly recommend Tracy Kidder's book. I do not know anything quite like it. It tells a story far removed from our daily experience, and while it may seem implausible, it has the ring of truth."

Following the working style he established in *The Soul of a New Machine,* Kidder immersed himself once again in the workaday world of a diverse group of individuals for his next book, *House.* Documenting the construction of a new home from blueprints to finished product, *House* presents the pleasures and pitfalls that occur at all phases of the building process. The book allows the reader to view that process through the eyes of the seven adults involved: architect and "Renaissance man in delirium" Bill Rawn, the quartet of counterculturist builders known as the Apple Corps, and the prospective homeowners, Jonathan and Judith Souweine. Kidder, who spent six months observing all aspects of the construction, as well as the lives of the people involved, traces their combined efforts to design, finance, and build the house, and places special emphasis on the parties' abilities to forge relationships under somewhat trying circumstances.

Reviewers noted that the theme of *House* centers on the building of these relationships, and of the lines of trust and communication necessary for the relationships to occur. Writing in the *Los Angeles Times*, Esther McCoy noted: "*House* . . . essentially is concerned with the people who build the house and their interaction with clients and architect." The ties do not come easily, however, as the participants haggle and argue about the various problems that arise. A rift develops between the Souweines and the Apple Corps over the final $660 of the $146,660 construction cost; in another instance, the builders are at odds with Rawn over his underdeveloped designs for a staircase. Commenting on the give-and-take nature of these dealings, Paul Goldberger of the *New York Times Book Review* stated: "The clients, the architect and the builders form a kind of triangle . . . and they push and pull each other in every possible way." Jonathan Yardley, writing in the *Washington Post Book World*, agreed, adding, "The construction of a house is an undertaking that puts human beings in an odd relationship of cooperation and conflict, a relationship that begins as business but invariably acquires intensely personal overtones."

To some reviewers, these "personal overtones" were also reflected in Kidder's quiet observations of the differences in the characters' social positions and the tensions that exist as those distinctions become more and more apparent. Though three members of the Apple Corps "had upbringings more white collar than blue collar," Goldberger wrote, "they are aware that their lives are different from those of people like Mr. and Mrs. Souweine." Kidder approached the situation democratically, claimed R. Z. Sheppard in *Time*, giving "equal time to client, architect and builders." Sheppard went on to find that "the interplay between confident professionals and self-conscious craftsmen conveys much about misunderstandings and bad feelings in a society stratified by education and status."

House does more than chronicle the relationships that developed over the course of the home's construction; it is also a nuts-and-bolts account of the construction itself. In addition, Kidder fills the book with a collection of short essays on topics as varied as the history of nails and a cost analysis of Henry Thoreau's Walden Pond shelter, so that *House* becomes more a study of architectural lore than a how-to of homebuilding. "The book keeps opening out into discourses on welcome, unexpected subjects," stated *Newsweek* reviewer David Lehman, "Kidder's book is filled with this kind of unobtrusive information." Affirming Kidder's inclusion of these asides, Adele Freedman of the Toronto *Globe and Mail* claimed: "After reading

House, no one will ever take the design of a staircase or the installation of a window for granted."

As with *The Soul of a New Machine*, Kidder earned praise for his clear presentation of unfamiliar terms and operations. Christopher Lehmann-Haupt of the *New York Times* found Kidder "a master at the difficult art of describing complex objects and processes." Citing the parallels in style between *The Soul of a New Machine* and *House, Chicago Tribune* reviewer Max J. Friedman declared that Kidder wrote *House* "with the same thoroughness, attention to detail and technical explanation that marked the earlier work. . . . Kidder's careful, precise reportage and brand of literary verite take us on a remarkable journey into the technical, mechanical and emotional world of housebuilding." Finally, Goldberger summarized the feelings of many critics with his statement that *House* "is told with such clarity, intelligence and grace it makes you wonder why no one has written a book like it before."

Kidder changed his subject matter but retained his reportorial methods for *Among Schoolchildren*, a record of the nine months he spent observing a Holyoke, Massachusetts, elementary school classroom. The book follows thirty-four-year-old Chris Zajac and her class of twenty fifth-grade students from their first day together at Kelly School to their last. In order to gather his material, Kidder placed himself at a desk in the front of the classroom, right next to Mrs. Zajac's own. He remained there, a silent observer on the scene, for nearly 180 schooldays. "I missed two days all year," Kidder told *Publishers Weekly* interviewer Amanda Smith. "One I just played hooky, and the other one, I was sick." The author eventually took over 10,000 pages of notes, compiled from his own observations and his frequent talks with Mrs. Zajac, which he then assembled, edited, and reworked into the finished book.

Written from Zajac's point of view, *Among Schoolchildren* serves as an account of the teacher's thoughts and feelings about her day-to-day teaching decisions and provides a first-hand look at what occurs in an American classroom. Kidder drew praise for his portrayals of the diminuitive, energetic Zajac and her "fragile rubber raft of children," as *New York Times Book Review* contributor Phyllis Theroux called them. Students like the hyperactive, destructive Clarence, the barely literate Pedro, who was "born and raised with my grandmother, because I was cryin' too much," and the intelligent, introverted Judith test the limits of Zajac's teaching skills and patience. Because of his proximity to the participants, especially Zajac, Kidder was able to get "inside her head and inside the heads of the children," reflected Gerald Grant in the *Chicago Tribune Books*, adding that the author's "close observations of the children in their many moods tie us into the emotional networks that make up classroom life." Those thoughts were echoed by *New York Times* reviewer Eva Hoffman, who asserted: "By the end of the book, we appreciate Mrs. Zajac's skills and strengths, and we come to care about the children's small hurts and triumphs."

Aside from providing insights into these characters, *Among Schoolchildren* also tackles some of the difficult issues facing the American educational system. Talking about the progress of reform with Smith, Kidder noted that "most efforts at reform usually are conducted independently of the experience, knowledge, wishes of teachers. And that's a *terrible* mistake, of course, since, for better or worse, education *is* what happens in these little rooms." Several reviewers found Kidder's observations worthy of praise. "Kidder writes with sensitivity . . . of the need for educational reform," a *Publishers Weekly* reviewer judged. "We see Kelly School as a compelling microcosm of what is wrong—and right—with our educational system." Grant concurred, adding: "Tracy Kidder has written a wonderful, compassionate book about teaching. While we have some cause for despair about the operation of the system, we have grounds for hope if his book helps draw more Mrs. Zajacs into our classrooms." And Phillip Lopate in the *Washington Post Book World* stressed: "At a time when public education seems to be fair game for attacks from all sides, Tracy Kidder has written a celebration of the work of one good schoolteacher."

In his best-known books, Tracy Kidder has shown himself to be adept at creating works of nonfiction that, as he told Smith, "do a lot of the things that novels do." By using similar research and writing techniques for all of his works, Kidder has discovered a formula for success, yet his books are far from formulaic. Critics have complimented Kidder's ability to transform the ordinary and everyday into something fascinating, a talent that Friedman termed Kidder's "penchant . . . for taking the reader on a journey into undiscovered knowledge." But as informative and entertaining as those journeys may be, the focus of Kidder's energy is on the people who inhabit his books. Speaking of his writing to Smith, Kidder admits that one of his purposes is "to bring people to life on the page." According to reviewers, who agree with Theroux's summation that Kidder's works are "full of the author's genuine love, delight and celebration of the human condition," he does so successfully.

BIOGRAPHICAL/CRITICAL SOURCES:

PERIODICALS

Chicago Tribune, September 29, 1985.
Globe and Mail (Toronto), December 14, 1985.
Los Angeles Times, November 12, 1985.
Newsweek, October 28, 1985.
New Yorker, October 19, 1981.

New York Review of Books, October 8, 1981.
New York Times, August 11, 1981; September 5, 1985; October 3, 1985; August 30, 1989.
New York Times Book Review, August 23, 1981; November 29, 1981; October 6, 1985; September 17, 1989.
Publishers Weekly, July 21, 1989; September 15, 1989.
Saturday Review, December, 1981.
Time, October 14, 1985.
Tribune Books (Chicago), August 13, 1989.
Washington Post Book World, September 9, 1981; October 6, 1985; September 3, 1989.

*   *   *

KING, Norman A.
See TRALINS, S(andor) Robert

*   *   *

KING, Richard H. 1942-

PERSONAL: Born March 2, 1942, in Knoxville, TN; son of Dewey Dawson (a contractor) and Dorothy Grace (a teacher; maiden name, Howell) King; married Nancy K. Landreth (a teacher), August 14, 1967 (divorced, August, 1979); married Charlotte D. C. Fallenius (a teacher and businesswoman), September 3, 1988. *Education:* University of North Carolina, A.B. (honors), 1963; Yale University, M.A., 1966; University of Virginia, Ph.D., 1971. *Politics:* Democrat. *Religion:* Presbyterian. *Avocational interests:* Sports, music (country and western, bluegrass).

ADDRESSES: Home—3 Grange Ave., Beeston, Nottingham NG9 1GJ, England. *Office*—American and Canadian Studies, University of Nottingham, University Park, Nottingham NG7 2RD, England.

CAREER: Stillman College, Tuscaloosa, AL, instructor in history, 1965-66; Federal City College, Washington, D.C., 1968-83, began as instructor, became professor of history and philosophy; University of Nottingham, Nottingham, England, reader and lecturer in American studies and critical theory, 1983—. Instructor in history, Lane College, 1965; acting instructor in honors program, University of Maryland, 1972-74. Fulbright lecturer at University of Nottingham, 1977-78. Visiting professor of history and Southern studies, University of Mississippi. D.C. Community Humanities Council, member, 1979-82, co-chairperson, 1981-82.

MEMBER: British Association of American Studies (chairperson, 1992-95), Phi Beta Kappa.

AWARDS, HONORS: Fulbright fellow in West Germany, 1963-64; Danforth graduate fellowship, 1964-67.

WRITINGS:

The Party of Eros, University of North Carolina Press, 1972.
A Southern Renaissance, Oxford University Press, 1980.
Civil Rights and the Idea of Freedom, Oxford University Press, 1992.

Contributor of articles and reviews to scholarly and popular journals, including *New Leader, Southern Literary Journal, American Quarterly, History and Theory, Salmagundi,* and *New South.* Member of editorial board, *Open Here, Journal of American Studies,* and *Mississippi Quarterly.*

WORK IN PROGRESS: Post World War II developments in history; researching theories of anti-Semitism and race.

SIDELIGHTS: Richard H. King told *CA* that his main interests are Freud and psychological thought, and Southern politics and culture.

*   *   *

KIRKWOOD, James   1930(?)-1989
(Jim Kirkwood)

PERSONAL: Born August 22, 1930 (some sources say 1924), in Los Angeles, CA; died of cancer, April 21, 1989, in New York, NY; son of James, Sr. (an actor and director) and Lila (a silent film star; maiden name, Lee) Kirkwood. *Education:* Studied acting for three years with Sanford Meisner Professional Classes in New York; attended New York University and University of California, Los Angeles. *Religion:* Catholic.

ADDRESSES: Home—58 Oyster Shores Rd., East Hampton, NY 11937; or, 1023 Catherine St., Key West, FL 33040. *Office*—484 West 44th St., No. 45R, New York, NY 10036. *Agent*—(Novels) Jed Mattes, International Creative Management, 40 West 57th St., New York, NY 10019; (screenplays) Ron Mardigan, William Morris Agency, 151 El Camino Real, Beverly Hills, CA 90069.

CAREER: Actor, novelist, and playwright. Made acting debut at an early age; many minor acting roles; appeared on tour in *Joan of Lorraine* (stage debut, 1947), *Call Me Madame, Wonderful Town, Welcome Darling, The Rainmaker, Oh Men, Oh Women, The Tender Trap,* and *Mary, Mary,* all U.S. Cities; also appeared on stage in *Small Wonder* (Broadway debut, 1949), *Junior Miss, Panama Hattie,* and *Dance Me a Song;* made South African tour in cast of *Never Too Late;* featured on television in *Garry Moore Show, Ed Sullivan Show, Alfred Hitchcock Presents, Valiant Lady,* and *Kraft Theatre;* film appearances include *Oh God, Book II, Mommie Dearest,* and *The Supernatu-*

rals; nightclub appearances with Lee Goodman as comedy-satire team include the Bon Soir, Le Ruban Bleu, the Blue Angel, the Embassy Club, and the Mocambo (Hollywood); radio work includes a week-day program with Goodman, *Kirkwood-Goodman Show,* running for two years over WOR, New York, and a twenty-six week series, *Teenager Unlimited,* on Mutual network, with other appearances on *Henry Aldrich,* and *Theatre Guild of the Air. Military service:* U.S. Coast Guard Reserve.

MEMBER: Actor's Equity Association, American Federation of Television and Radio Artists, Screen Actors Guild, American Guild of Variety Artists, Dramatists Guild, Authors League, PEN.

AWARDS, HONORS: Pulitzer Prize in Drama, Antoinette Perry (Tony) Award for best play, Drama Desk Award, Drama Critics Circle Award, and Theatre World Award, all 1976, all for *A Chorus Line.*

WRITINGS:

There Must Be a Pony! (novel; also see below), Little, Brown, 1960.
Good Times/Bad Times (novel; also see below), Simon & Schuster, 1968.
American Grotesque (nonfiction), Simon & Schuster, 1970.
P.S. Your Cat Is Dead (novel; also see below), Stein & Day, 1972.
Some Kind of Hero (novel; also see below), Crowell, 1975.
Hit Me with a Rainbow (novel), Delacorte, 1980.
Diary of a Mad Playwright (nonfiction), Dutton, 1989.

PLAYS

There Must Be a Pony! (based on novel of same title), touring production, 1962.
U.T.B.U. (Unhealthy to Be Unpleasant) (produced on Broadway, 1965), Samuel French, 1966.
P.S. Your Cat Is Dead (based on novel of same title; first produced on Broadway, 1975; revised and produced Off-Broadway, 1978), Samuel French, 1976.
(With Nicholas Dante) *A Chorus Line* (musical; also see below), first produced by New York Shakespeare Festival, 1975, produced on Broadway, 1975.
Surprise, produced in Long Island, NY, at John Drew Theatre, 1981.
Legends!, first produced in Los Angeles at the Ahmanson Theatre, then touring production, both 1986.
(With Jim Piazza) *Stage Struck,* produced in Jupiter, FL, at the Burt Reynolds Jupiter Theater, 1989.

SCREENPLAYS

Good Times/Bad Times (based on novel of same title), United Artists, 1968.

Some Kind of Hero (based on novel of same title), Paramount, 1982.

A Chorus Line (based on play of same title), Universal, 1985.

TELEPLAYS

There Must Be a Pony! (based on novel of same title), Columbia Pictures Television, 1986.

WORK IN PROGRESS: *Murder at the Vanities,* an original musical; *I Teach Flying,* a novel.

SIDELIGHTS: James Kirkwood's best known work is the highly acclaimed musical, *A Chorus Line.* The musical, presented in the form of an audition in which the dancers are asked to tell something about themselves, was conceived by director Michael Bennett, who had tape recorded some all night talk sessions with a group of dancers. Bennett and Kirkwood's co-author, Nicholas Dante, edited the tapes and then developed the play in Joseph Papp's Theater Workshop. They found, however, that the musical needed much more work, so they brought in Kirkwood. Kirkwood's appearance marked the beginning of a great deal of rewriting, for as Bennett told Robert Berkvist in the *New York Times,* "We reworked the material so often, I think we must have discarded six versions of the show."

Walter Kerr of the *New York Times* praised the final result, calling it a "brilliant" accomplishment. At the same time, Kerr found that "rather too many [of the dancer's life stories] are familiar and thin: the girl who was born just to keep a marriage together (no dice); the girl who compensated for a dreary life by dancing because 'everyone is beautiful in ballet. . . .'" On the other hand, Kerr recognized that the ordinariness of their everyday lives strengthens the contrast with their professional lives, with the magic they feel when dancing. As Kerr commented, "[Bennett] wants us to feel the happiness that overtakes these nonentities so long as toes slap the ground or fly in air—at the same time that we recognize the essential hopelessness of their lot." Catherine Hughes, writing in *America,* claimed, "[A Chorus Line] prompts both laughter and tears."

In 1983, *A Chorus Line* became the longest running musical in Broadway history, and two years later it was made into a film. Directed by Richard Attenborough (*Ghandi*), the movie version of *A Chorus Line* stars Michael Douglas as Zach, the show's choreographer, and Alyson Reed as Cassie, a former lead dancer trying to revive her career in the chorus. A reviewer for the *Chicago Tribune* commented, "A classic play has been reduced [to] a decent movie. It's a shame it couldn't be as good as the play; it's a small pleasure that it's as entertaining as it is."

One of Kirkwood's later plays, *Legends!,* also relies on the theatre world for its subject matter. The play concerns two movie stars (portrayed by Mary Martin and Carol Channing), now old and near poverty—once rivals and enemies—reunited as leads in a play. One is the sweet, genteel Leatrice Monsee (Martin), and the other the aggressive, cursing Sylvia Glenn (Channing). The plot revolves around the tension between these two women—will they perform well, or kill each other? While most reviewers were critical, audiences generally loved the play, which grossed over ten million dollars after slightly more than one year of touring. David Richards of the *Washington Post* wrote, "*Legends!* is what is generally termed an audience show . . . its deficiencies of plot, character and taste will be supremely irrelevant" to many theater goers and fans of Channing and Martin. One of the major criticisms among reviewers was that Martin and Channing deserved a better play, "commensurate with their status as Broadway greats," as Richards phrased it. A *Variety* reviewer quoted by Dan Sullivan in the *Los Angeles Times* summed up the play as " 'a generally agreeable, frequently witty comedy that allows these two theatrical favorites to both amuse and surprise their legions of fans.' "

Kirkwood's involvement with *Legends!* continued with the posthumous publication of *Diary of a Mad Playwright* in 1989. A chronicle of his experiences with *Legends!,* *Diary of a Mad Playwright* follows the play's development from its early beginnings to its closing night. Kirkwood discusses his chance meeting with the play's producers, his struggles in casting Mary Martin and Carol Channing, conflicts among the people involved with the play, repeated rewrites, and threats by one producer to end the tour. *Diary of a Mad Playwright* is a "behind the scenes" look at the makeup of a play—beyond rehearsals and press conferences and into the struggles a playwright endures to see his play on stage. Richards, writing in the *Washington Post Book World,* called *Diary of a Mad Playwright* "brisk and breezy," explaining that "Kirkwood had an observant eye for the foibles of performers (having been one himself), the zest of an incorrigible gossip and a crisp sense of humor that stopped short of bitchiness." In the *New York Times Book Review,* Wendy Wasserstein concluded: "James Kirkwood was a delightful companion and theatrical raconteur. As a reader, I had a wonderful time with *Diary of a Mad Playwright.* But as a playwright and colleague of his, I'm so very happy I didn't have to be there."

BIOGRAPHICAL/CRITICAL SOURCES:

BOOKS

Authors in the News, Volume 2, Gale, 1976.
Contemporary Literary Criticism, Volume 9, Gale, 1978.

PERIODICALS

America, January 17, 1976, p. 41.
Chicago Tribune, December, 20, 1985.
Los Angeles Times, November 29, 1985; December 13, 1985; January 22, 1986.
New York Times, June 1, 1975; June 15, 1975; October 26, 1975; May 4, 1976; April 2, 1982; August 13, 1982; December, 1986; January 2, 1987; February 17, 1989.
New York Times Book Review, September 24, 1989.
Washington Post, April 3, 1982; August 14, 1986.
Washington Post Book World, January 8, 1989; September 10, 1989.

OBITUARIES:

PERIODICALS

Los Angeles Times, April 23, 1989.
New York Times, April 23, 1989.
Times (London), April 24, 1989.
Washington Post, April 23, 1989.

* * *

KIRKWOOD, Jim
See KIRKWOOD, James

* * *

KLEIN, David 1919-

PERSONAL: Born March 30, 1919, in New York, NY; son of Solomon (a manufacturing jeweler) and Helen (Schoenberg) Klein; married Marymae Endsley (a textbook editor), December 6, 1942; children: Helen Leslie, Edith Sarah. *Education:* City College of New York (now City College of the City University of New York), B.A., 1940; Columbia University, M.A., 1941; attended New York University, 1962-65. *Politics:* Social Democrat. *Religion:* Humanist. *Avocational interests:* Clock collecting, psychology, sociology, conducting research on risk-taking and consumer behavior.

ADDRESSES: Home—1130 Fifth Avenue South, No. 300, Edmonds, WA 98020. *Agent*—Frances Collin, 110 West 40th Street, New York, NY 10018.

CAREER: McGraw-Hill Book Co., New York City, technical editor, 1940-1942; Henry Holt & Co., New York City, college textbook editor, 1946-48; Dryden Press, New York City, executive vice-president, 1948-56; Basic Books, Inc., New York City, vice-president, 1956-58; Association for the Aid of Crippled Children, New York City, director of publications, 1958-65; Michigan State University, East Lansing, associate professor, 1965-68,

professor of social science, 1968-83, professor of human development, 1970-83, professor emeritus in department of social science, 1983—. Instructor and lecturer in English and adult education, City College of New York (now City College of the City University of New York), 1946-56; exchange professor, University of Ryukyus, Okinawa, Japan, 1966; visiting professor, Hofstra University, 1970-71; senior lecturer, University of New South Wales, 1972-73; chairman designate at University of Sydney, 1979. *Military service:* U.S. Army, 1942-46; became warrant officer junior grade.

AWARDS, HONORS: Ford Foundation travel grant, 1966; certificate of recognition, National Safety Council, 1966; Fulbright grant, Australian-American Education Foundation, 1972, 1979.

WRITINGS:

The Army Writer, Military Service Publishing Co., 1946.
(With Mary Louise Johnson) *They Took to the Sea,* Rutgers University Press, 1948.
Your First Boat, Funk, 1953.
Your Outboard Cruiser, Norton, 1954.
Beginning with Boats, Crowell, 1962.
Helping Your Teenager Choose a College, Child Study Association, 1963.
(With W. Haddon and E. A. Suchman) *Accident Research: Methods and Approaches,* Harper, 1964.
(With S. A. Richardson and B. S. Dohrenwend) *Interviewing: Its Forms and Functions,* Basic Books, 1965.
When Your Teen-ager Starts to Drive, Association for Aid of Crippled Children, 1965.
(With Theodore E. Hughes) *A Family Guide to Estate Planning, Funeral Arrangements, and Settling an Estate after Death,* Scribner, 1983.
(With Hughes), *Ownership,* Scribner, 1984.
(With Hughes) *The Parents' Financial Survival Guide,* H. P. Books, 1987.
(With Douglas Walsh and Marymae E. Klein) *Getting Unscrewed,* Henry Holt, in press.

WITH WIFE, MARYMAE E. KLEIN

Yourself and Others, McDougal, Littell, 1970.
Supershopper, Praeger, 1971.
Yourself Ten Years from Now, Harcourt, 1977.
More for Your Money, Penguin, 1979.
How Do You Know It's True?, Scribner, 1984.
Your Parents and Yourself, Scribner, 1986.

Contributor of articles on recreation, education, and consumer topics to periodicals including *Consumer Reports, Ladies' Home Journal, Mademoiselle, New York Times, Fifty Plus,* and *North Carolina Independent.*

WORK IN PROGRESS: Popular and professional writing on accidents and research methods in the social sciences.

KLEIN, Marymae E. 1917-

PERSONAL: Born October 16, 1917, in Indianapolis, IN; daughter of E. Prichett and Bernice Leslie Endsley; married David Klein (a professor of social sciences and writer), 1942; children: Helen Leslie, Edith Sarah. *Education:* MacMurray College, B.A., 1939; Columbia University, M.S., 1959.

ADDRESSES: Home—1130 Fifth Avenue South, No. 300, Edmonds, WA 98020. *Agent*—Marie Rodell-Francis Collins Literary Agency, 110 West 40th Street, New York, NY 10018.

CAREER: Free-lance textbook editor, 1951-75; Michigan State University School of Medicine, East Lansing, librarian, 1975-83.

WRITINGS:

WITH HUSBAND, DAVID KLEIN

Yourself and Others, McDougal, Littell, 1970.
Supershopper, Praeger, 1971.
Yourself Ten Years from Now, Harcourt, 1977.
More for Your Money, Penguin, 1979.
How Do You Know It's True?, Scribner, 1984.
Your Parents and Yourself, Scribner, 1986.
(With coauthor Douglas Walsh) *Getting Unscrewed,* Henry Holt, in press.

WORK IN PROGRESS: Research on consumerism; research on how health services are delivered in the community, especially to the chronically ill and elderly.

SIDELIGHTS: Marymae Klein once told *CA:* "My husband [David Klein] and I are trying to introduce teenagers to the real world of money, work, and life in our society without either preaching or talking down to them. We are trying to show young people how to think clearly and how to cope with people who don't."

*   *   *

KLEIN, Robin 1936-

PERSONAL: Born February 28, 1936, in Kempsey, Australia; daughter of Leslie Macquarie (a farmer) and Mary (a homemaker; maiden name, Cleaver) McMaugh; married Karl Klein, August 18, 1956 (divorced April, 1978); children: Michael, Peter, Ingrid, Rosalind. *Education:* Attended Newcastle Girl's High School in Newcastle, Australia.

ADDRESSES: Home—P.O. Box 123, Belgrave, Victoria, Australia. *Agent*—Curtis Brown, 86 William St., Paddington, Sydney NSW 2021, Australia.

CAREER: Writer, 1981—. Worked as a "tea lady" at a warehouse, and as a bookshop assistant, library assistant,

nurse, copper enamelist, and program aide at a school for disadvantaged children.

AWARDS, HONORS: Special Mention in Critici in Erba Awards, Bologna Children's Book Fair, 1979, for *The Giraffe in Pepperell Street;* Australian Junior Book of the Year Award, Children's Book Council of Australia, 1983, for *Thing;* "highly commended" book of the year award, Children's Book Council of Australia, 1984, for *Penny Pollard's Diary;* Children's Book Council of Australia Award nominations, 1984, for *Junk Castle* and *People Might Hear You,* 1985, for *Penny Pollard's Letters,* 1986, for *Halfway across the Galaxy and Turn Left* and *The Enemies,* 1987, for *Boss of the Pool,* and 1988, for *Birk the Berserker;* senior fellowship grant, Arts Council of Australia literature board, 1985; Special Award, West Australian Young Reader's Book Awards, winner of senior category, KOALA Awards, both 1987, and Children's Book Council of Australia Award nomination, all for *Hating Alison Ashley;* Australian Human Rights Award for Literature, 1989, Australian Book of the Year, Children's Book Council of Australia, and N.S.W. and Vic. Premiers' Awards nominations, both 1990, all for *Came Back to Show You I Could Fly;* Honour Book Award, Children's Book Council of Australia, 1991, for *Boris and Borsch;* Dromkeen Medal for services to children's literature, 1991.

WRITINGS:

CHILDREN'S BOOKS

The Giraffe in Pepperell Street, illustrated by Gill Tomblin, Hodder & Stoughton, 1978.
Honoured Guest, illustrated by Margaret Power, Macmillan, 1979, revised edition, 1987.
Sprung!, illustrated by Power, Rigby Young Magpie Series, 1982.
Thing (also see below), illustrated by Alison Lester, Oxford University Press, 1982.
Junk Castle (also see below), illustrated by Rolf Heimann, Oxford University Press, 1983.
Penny Pollard's Diary (also see below), illustrated by Ann James, Oxford University Press, 1983.
Oodoolay, illustrated by Vivienne Goodman, Era Publications, 1983.
People Might Hear You, Viking Kestrel, 1984.
Hating Alison Ashley, Penguin, 1984.
Brock and the Dragon, illustrated by Rodney McRae, Hodder & Stoughton, 1984.
Thalia the Failure, illustrated by Rhyll Plant, Ashton Scholastic, 1984.
Thingnapped! (also see below), illustrated by Lester, Oxford University Press, 1984.
Penny Pollard's Letters (also see below), illustrated by James, Oxford University Press, 1984.

The Tomb Comb, illustrated by Heather Potter, Rigby Magpie Series, 1984.

Ratbags and Rascals, illustrated by Lester, Dent, 1984.

Halfway across the Galaxy and Turn Left, Viking Kestrel, 1985.

The Enemies, illustrated by Noela Young, Angus & Robertson, 1985.

Annabel's Ghost (thematic pack), edited by Ron Thomas, Oxford University Press, 1985.

Separate Places, illustrated by Anna Lacis, Kangaroo Press, 1985.

Snakes and Ladders, illustrated by James, Dent, 1985.

Battlers (kit of cassettes and books; includes *Good for Something, Serve Him Right!,* and *You're on Your Own!*), Audiobooks, 1985.

Penny Pollard in Print, illustrated by James, Oxford University Press, 1986.

The Princess Who Hated It, illustrated by Maire Smith, Omnibus Books, 1986.

Boss of the Pool, illustrated by H. Panagopoulos, Omnibus Books, 1986, illustrated by Paul Geraghty, Viking Kestrel, 1987.

Games, illustrated by Melissa Webb, Viking Kestrel, 1986.

(With Max Dann) *The Lonely Hearts Club,* Oxford University Press, 1987.

Robin Klein's Crookbook, illustrated by Kristen Hilliard, Methuen, 1987.

Get Lost ("Southern Cross" series), illustrated by June Joubert, Macmillan, 1987.

The Last Pirate, illustrated by Rick Armor, Rigby Education, 1987.

Parker-Hamilton, illustrated by Gaston Vanzet, Rigby Education, 1987.

Christmas, illustrated by Hilliard, Methuen, 1987.

I Shot an Arrow, illustrated by Geoff Hocking, Viking Kestrel, 1987.

Birk the Berserker, illustrated by Lester, Omnibus Books, 1987.

Into Books (includes *Junk Castle, Penny Pollard's Diary, Penny Pollard's Letters, Thing,* and *Thingnapped!*), Oxford University Press, 1988.

Stanley's Smile, Rigby Education, 1988.

Annabel's Party, illustrated by Mark Payne, Rigby Education, 1988.

Irritating Irma, illustrated by Chris Johnston and Rowena Cory, Rigby Education, 1988.

The Kidnapping of Clarissa Montgomery, illustrated by Jane Wallace-Mitchell, Rigby Education, 1988.

Jane's Mansion, illustrated by Webb, Rigby Education, 1988.

Laurie Loved Me Best, Viking Kestrel, 1988.

Penny Pollard's Passport, illustrated by James, Oxford University Press, 1988.

Dear Robin, Allen & Unwin, 1988.

Against the Odds, illustrated by Bill Woods, Viking Kestrel, 1989.

The Ghost in Abigail Terrace, illustrated by Power, Omnibus Books, 1989.

Came Back to Show You I Could Fly, Viking Kestrel, 1989.

Penny Pollard's Guide to Modern Manners, illustrated by James, Oxford University Press, 1989.

Tearaways, Viking, 1990.

Boris and Borsch, illustrated by Cathy Wilcox, Allen & Unwin, 1990.

All in the Blue Unclouded Weather, Penguin Books, 1991.

Dresses of Red and Gold, Penguin Books, 1992.

OTHER

Contributor to books, including *Don't Tell Lucy* ("Storyteller" series), illustrated by Kristen Hilliard, Methuen, 1987; *The Story Makers,* edited by Margaret Dunkle, Oxford University Press, 1987; *How Writers Write,* by Pamela Lloyd, Methuen, 1987; *The Inside Story—Creating Children's Books,* edited by Belle Alderman, Children's Book Council of Australia, A. C. T. Branch, 1987; *Coming out from Under—Contemporary Australian Women Writers,* by Pam Gilbert, Pandora Press, 1988. Also contributor of stories, poems, and plays to *New South Wales School Magazine* and publications of the Victorian Department of Education.

ADAPTATIONS: Thing and *Penny Pollard's Diary* were both adapted for the television series *Kaboodle* by the Australian Children's Television Foundation, both 1987; *Hating Alison Ashley* was adapted for the stage by Richard Tulloch, Puffin Books, 1988; *Boss of the Pool* was adapted for the stage by Mary Morris, 1990; *Halfway across the Galaxy and Turn Left* was adapted into a television series by Crawford Productions, 1992.

SIDELIGHTS: Robin Klein once told *CA:* "I write for children because I adore their company, honesty, and sense of fun. I'm addicted to writing and can feel quite physically ill if more than three days go by and I haven't been able to get to a typewriter (it makes me a dreadful hostess!). The letters I receive from children more than make up for the long hours of isolated work, and I've never wanted to move into any other field of writing.

"I wrote my first book, *The Giraffe in Pepperell Street,* while sitting in a railway station watching a kid trying to entice an enormous stray dog home with her. Since then I've become an eager 'child watcher' and get many ideas from incidents I see on public transport and at shopping centers. I also use material gathered from bringing up my own four children and working in various jobs where children were involved. However, I don't sit down and write consciously for children as a particular audience, or use modified vocabulary for their benefit.

"Most of my books seem to have a strong female character, capable of dealing with any problem that arises, perhaps because I was a very cowardly child and admired people like that. I also have a soft spot for the 'underdog,' and many of my characters are awkward misfits who still manage to achieve goals. Without really meaning to, I find that I'm most at ease writing in a humorous vein. I suppose that what I admire most in people is their ability to laugh when facing quite sad circumstances in their lives; it seems to me a very moving gallantry that often goes unpraised."

*　　*　　*

KNIGHT, Max 1909-
(Peter Fabrizius, a joint pseudonym)

PERSONAL: Born June 8, 1909, in Austria; immigrated to United States, May, 1941; naturalized U.S. citizen, 1942; son of Bernhard (a bank vice-president) and Margarethe (Hoffer) Kuehnel; married Charlotte Lowes, July 11, 1942; children: Anthony C., Martin L. *Education:* University of Vienna, J.Sc.D., 1933; post-graduate study at University of California, Berkeley, 1942-43, 1948-50.

ADDRESSES: Home and office—760 Grizzly Peak Boulevard, Berkeley, CA 94708.

CAREER: Newspaper editor and feature writer, *Neues Wiener Tagblatt,* Vienna, Austria, *Daily Herald,* London, and *North China Daily News,* Shanghai, China, 1935-41; Office of War Information, San Francisco, CA, script writer and analyst, 1943-45; *San Francisco Daily Commercial News,* San Francisco, financial editor, 1945-47; Hoover Institute, Stanford University, Stanford, CA, deputy executive secretary of RADIR Carnegie Project, 1949; University of California, Berkeley, research assistant in political science, 1950; University of California Press, Berkeley, principal editor, 1950-76. Writer, 1976—.

MEMBER: American Council of Learned Societies fellow.

AWARDS, HONORS: Golden Honor Award of the Republic of Austria, 1986; first prize, Annual Poetry Contest, Berkeley, CA, 1991.

WRITINGS:

The German Executive 1890-1933, Stanford University Press, 1952.
Return to the Alps, Friends of the Earth, 1970.
The Original Blue Danube Cookbook, Lancaster-Miller, 1979.
(With Ernst Friese) *Lisa, benimn dich* (musical comedy in four acts), first produced in Vienna, Austria, at Kammerspiele Theatre, March, 1939.

(Contributor) Gerhard Friesen, editor, *Deutsche Literatur in den U.S.A.,* Volume 5: *Auslandsdeutsche Literatur der Gegenwart,* edited by Alexander Ritter, Olms Presse, 1983.
(With Joseph B. Fabry under joint pseudonym Peter Fabrizius) *One and One Make Three: Story of a Friendship* (autobiography), Benmir Books, 1988.

WITH JOSEPH B. FABRY; UNDER JOINT PSEUDONYM PETER FABRIZIUS; COLLECTIONS OF SHORT STORIES IN GERMAN

Der schwarze Teufel, J. Murray, 1942.
Der Kommet, J. Murray, 1942.
Die Siebzehn Kamele, J. Murray, 1949.
Wer zuletzt lacht. . ., edited by Claire Hayden Bell, Appleton, 1952.
. . . lacht am besten, edited by Bell, Appleton, 1957.

TRANSLATOR FROM THE GERMAN

Christian Morgenstern, *Christian Morgenstern's Galgenlieder,* University of California Press, 1963.
(With Joseph B. Fabry) *Johann Nestroy: Three Comedies,* Ungar, 1967.
Hans Kelsen, *The Pure Theory of Law,* University of California Press, 1967.
Heinrich Kuenzel, *Upper California,* Book Club of California, 1967.
Morgenstern, *Three Sparrows,* Scribner, 1968.
(With Fabry) Willy Haas, *Bert Brecht,* Ungar, 1968.
Morgenstern, *The Great Lalula,* Putnam, 1969.
(With Edward Gans) *Goethe's Italian Renaissance Medals,* Malter-Westerfield, 1969.
Galgenlieder/Gallows Songs, Piper, 1972.
Morgenstern, *The Daylight Lamp,* Houghton, 1973.
(With Fabry) Helen Mustard, editor, *Heinrich Heine: Selected Works,* Random House, 1973.
(Contributor of translation) Ralph Manheim, editor, *Bertold Brecht: Collected Works,* Volume 7, Random House, 1975.
A Confidential Matter: The Letters of Richard Strauss and Stefan Zweig, University of California Press, 1977.
(Contributor of translation) Karl Kraus, *In These Great Times,* edited by Harry Zohn, Engendra Press, 1977.
(And editor) Albert Friedemann, *The Stamps of the German Colonies,* Part I: *Offices in China,* German Colonies Collectors Group, 1978.
(Contributor of translation) Douglas Russell, editor, *Anthology of Austrian Drama,* Fairleigh Dickinson Press, 1981.
(Translator of poems) Jost Herman, editor, *Heinrich Heine: Poetry and Prose,* Continuum, 1983.
(Translator of section on Christian Morgenstern), *The German Library,* Volume 50: *German Satirical Writings,* edited by Dieter Lotze, Continuum, 1984.
Volkmar Sander, *The German Library,* Volume 73: *Gottfried Benn,* Continuum, 1987.

Morgenstern, *Igel and Agel: Stickly and Stackly* (gallows and children's poems), Piper, 1992.

Contributor of translations to proceedings of International Josquin Festival Conference, 1980.

TRANSLATOR INTO GERMAN

Lawrence Price, *Die Aufnahme englischer Literatur in Deutschland,* Francke, 1962.

(With Karl Ross) Ogden Nash, *Der Kuckuck fuehrt ein Lotterleben,* Paul Zsolnay Verlag, 1977.

Edward Teller, "Technik, Krieg und Kriegsverhuetung," *Naturwissenschaften,* Springer Verlag, 1984.

Yoav Lorch, *Wichtige Sachen* (children's poetry), Paul Zsolnay Verlag, 1985.

TRANSLATOR FROM MEDIEVAL FRENCH

(Translator of poems) Howard Mayer Brown, editor, *Monuments of Renaissance Music,* Volumes 7-8: *A Florentine Chansonnier from the Time of Lorenzo the Magnificent,* University of Chicago Press, 1983.

Knights and Valentines, Harold Berliner, 1989.

EDITOR

Otto Maenchen-Helfen, *The World of the Huns,* University of California Press, 1973.

Albert Ehrenzweig, *Law: A Personal View,* Sijthoff, 1977.

Yizhak Oren, *The Imaginary Number,* Benmir Books, 1986.

WORK IN PROGRESS: Looney Zoo: Children's Verses for Grown-ups, a collection of animal poetry.

SIDELIGHTS: Max Knight once told *CA:* "Raised in the German-language orbit, yet living most of my adult life in the United States, I am thoroughly bilingual. I consider myself as part of a bridge between the two cultures, an attitude that finds expression in my translations. I travel to Europe frequently; whether I arrive in Austria or California, I am always 'coming home.' I am happiest in the mountains, as indicated in my *Return to the Alps.*"

* * *

KNOWLES, John 1926-

PERSONAL: Born September 16, 1926, in Fairmont, WV; son of James Myron and Mary Beatrice (Shea) Knowles. *Education:* Graduate of Phillips Exeter Academy, 1945; Yale University, B.A., 1949.

ADDRESSES: Home—New York, NY. *Office*—P.O. Box 939, Southampton, Long Island, NY 11968.

CAREER: Hartford Courant, Hartford, CT, reporter, 1950-52; free-lance writer, 1952-56; *Holiday,* associate editor, 1956-60; full-time writer, 1960—. Writer in residence at University of North Carolina at Chapel Hill, 1963-64, and Princeton University, 1968-69. *Military service:* U.S. Army Air Force, 1954.

AWARDS, HONORS: Richard and Hinda Rosenthal Foundation Award, American Academy and Institute of Arts and Letters, and William Faulkner Foundation Award, both 1960, both for *A Separate Peace;* National Association of Independent Schools Award, 1961.

WRITINGS:

NOVELS

A Separate Peace, Macmillan, 1960.
Morning in Antibes, Macmillan, 1962.
Indian Summer, Random House, 1966.
The Paragon, Random House, 1971.
Spreading Fires, Random House, 1974.
A Vein of Riches, Little, Brown, 1978.
Peace Breaks Out, Holt, 1981.
A Stolen Past, Holt, 1983.
The Private Life of Axie Reed, Dutton, 1986.

OTHER

Double Vision: American Thoughts Abroad (travel), Macmillan, 1964.
Phineas (short stories), Random House, 1968.

A collection of Knowles's manuscripts is housed in Beinecke Library at Yale University.

ADAPTATIONS: A Separate Peace was adapted for film and released by Paramount Pictures in 1972.

WORK IN PROGRESS: A memoir of the author's friend, the late writer Truman Capote.

SIDELIGHTS: John Knowles is an acclaimed American novelist whose first—and most famous—novel, *A Separate Peace,* received both the William Faulkner Award for an outstanding first novel, and the Richard and Hinda Rosenthal Foundation Award. *A Separate Peace* is Knowles's most lyrical work, describing in rich, evocative language the idyllic lives of school boys during the first years of American involvement in World War II. The plot is deceptively simple. The narrator, Gene Forrester, and his friend, Phineas (Finny), are both students at Devon, an Eastern seaboard private school much like Exeter Academy that Knowles attended. Gene is the more conscientious student of the two, and Finny the more athletically and socially gifted. Though their bond is a strong one, it eventually suffers from competition. Gene, growing increasingly resentful of Finny's popularity, finally causes him a crippling injury by pushing him from a tree. A kangaroo court session ensues, with Gene accused of deliberately injuring Finny, who leaves suddenly, again injures himself, and dies during surgery.

From this episode, Gene eventually accepts the necessity of exploring himself based upon his admission of guilt. Jay L. Halio, writing about *A Separate Peace* in *Studies in Short Fiction,* observes that "the prevailing attitude seems to be that before man can be redeemed back into social life, he must first come to terms with himself."

The setting and plot of *A Separate Peace* play upon a series of contrasts between negative and positive elements, the combination of which stresses the need to tolerate, understand, and integrate radically opposing perceptions and experiences. The school itself stands between two rivers, the Devon and the Naguamsett, one pure and fresh, the other ugly and dirty. As James Ellis concludes in the *English Journal,* the Devon symbolizes Eden, a place of joy and happiness, while the Naguamsett indicates a landscape destroyed by personal greed and callousness toward the environment. The winds of war, blowing just beyond the lives of the boys, and the battle between Gene and Finny encapsulate Knowles's twin purposes—to both explore the competing sides of an individual's personality and to imply, as McDonald has noted, that the conflict of nations is an extension of self-conflict and the antipathy one person feels toward another.

These internal and external conflicts result from fear, whether based on hatred, inadequacy, exposure, or rejection. This view of life as a battle between two opposing selves, persons, or camps—the solution being acceptance and love of others—is the most dominant theme of Knowles's fiction. It first appears in *A Separate Peace,* but it is never far from the center of later works.

Published over twenty years after *A Separate Peace, Peace Breaks Out* will "take its place alongside the earlier books as a fine novel," Dick Abrahamson argues in the *English Journal.* Knowles's second Devon School novel takes place in 1945, and its main character and center of consciousness is Pete Hallam, a young teacher of history and physical education who has just returned from World War II. Hallam has not only been wounded, captured, and incarcerated in a prison camp, but has also been abandoned by his wife. Because of the traumas he has suffered, he is not always articulate and tends to be somewhat cynical in his attempt to retreat into the past. Although also essentially romantic in nature, he has lost the ability to love, and he returns to Devon to lay the past to rest and to regain some sense of love and compassion.

At Devon, the innocence Hallam remembers is missing. Schoolboys, too, have been affected by the war—or perhaps Pete has simply matured enough through his own suffering to recognize the flaws in human nature. The conflict that helps Pete to understand himself is between two

bright, articulate, and bitter students: "[Hochschwender and Wexford] hated each other. But also and simultaneously they seemed to hate something about themselves. There was a curious, fundamental similarity between them which made their mutual aversion almost incendiary." Bright and insecure, Eric Hochschwender riles the other students with his outrageous statements about German superiority and his denial of the atrocities of World War II. Motivated in part by his insignificant Wisconsin background, his obviously Germanic name, and his fears of rejection, Eric primarily assumes this position to test the tolerance of others, believing that under the surface of American liberalism is a strong strain of intolerance and bigotry. He is correct, and he himself becomes the target of that bigotry.

Never called by his first name, Wexford is equally bright, but, as the scion of a wealthy Massachusetts family and as the editor of the student newspaper, he is given considerable respect. This respect is not well-deserved, for his collection of money for a memorial window in the chapel is designed only to enhance his own reputation. Dishonest, intolerant, and elitist, Wexford tries to convince others that Eric is a threat to the Devon spirit and the traditional New England, prep school way of life. He incites the other boys into thinking that Hochschwender broke the memorial window and they attack Eric, causing him to have a fatal heart seizure.

The situation in *Peace Breaks Out* strongly resembles that of the earlier *A Separate Peace,* but Knowles's message is now more bleak. Whereas Gene's crime is discovered and he suffers personal guilt, thereby maturing in his understanding of himself and others, Wexford is not found out and gains no self-knowledge. Pete believes that Wexford himself has broken the window and sowed the seeds of hatred against Eric, but the teacher takes no measure to expose Wexford as a fraud and a cheat. The book suggests that Wexford will continue to go through life cheating. The plunge that Knowles's characters take into the maelstrom of desires and conflicts thus does not always result in illumination and insight.

A second group of novels—*Indian Summer, A Stolen Past,* and *The Paragon*—deals with Wexford-like figures who have power and authority generated by money, which becomes a substitute for human warmth and sexual expression. The forum for this exploration is no longer Devon but Yale and its immediate environs. All three novels depend upon the mutually reinforcing oppositions between the rich and the middle class, the quest for money and the desire for a good life, and excessive rationality and healthy sexuality.

Second only to *A Separate Peace* in critical acclaim, *Indian Summer* concerns Cleet Kinsolving and his gradual realization of the emptiness of wealth and position. The spontaneous, impulsive, and intuitive Cleet, grandson of an Indian woman, contrasts with the more controlled, rational, spoiled, and mercantile Neil Reardon. Unlike many of Knowles's characters, Cleet understands himself: to "roll out his life full force" meant "to be strong, to be happy, to be physically tired at night, to have love and sex at one and the same time, to be proud of himself." When Cleet follows his native instincts, he feels complete and satisfied; when he becomes trapped in the rationalist-mercantile pursuits of others, he nearly destroys himself. Related to this view of the self is the perception of place. The Midwest and West are equated with personal freedom and lack of social restraint; Connecticut and the East are equated with acquisitiveness, self-denial, and atrophying social conventions.

After his discharge from the Army Air Force in 1946, Cleet takes a job in Kansas, working for a small crop-dusting firm and living in a tiny motel cabin. This Thoreau-like existence under the "vaults and domes of sky" emphasizes a simple, natural life, undiminished by material possessions. Here, in the Midwest, Cleet's feelings and senses—his sight, hearing, taste, and sexuality—are at their finest.

What Cleet fears most is the entrapment symbolized by the East. The appearance in Kansas of his childhood friend, Cornelius (Neil) Reardon, realizes those fears. Cleet, in accepting Neil's offer of a two-hundred-dollars weekly job in Cleet's home town of Wetherford, sells himself out to the Eastern establishment. Neil embodies the lust for acquisition, and he uses emotional attachments, generosity, loyalty, and philanthropy for his own ends so that they become deception, bribery, ambition, and willfulness. His marriage is empty, and his books and lectures merely hide his fear of failure. Even his desire to have a son is born of fear—to perpetuate himself and ensure material immortality against an uncertain future.

To be true to his vision of himself, Cleet is obliged to leave the Reardons and return to the Midwest, where he can put the dishonesty and stifling conventions of the East behind him. Before he returns to Kansas, he seduces Neil's wife, but since he means no ill toward her and is primarily responding to her own unrepressed sexual desires, he suffers no guilt about his conduct. His departure for Kansas reaffirms the fundamental nineteenth-century American romantic view: truth to oneself depends upon responding to spirituality rather than materialism.

Although the narrator of the 1983 novel *A Stolen Past* has also been born in the East (Maryland) and educated there (at Devon and Yale), he has been no more faithful to it than Cleet. As a mature adult recalling his college experiences, Allan Prieston is realistic, knowing that he can never totally recapture the past; but he is also philosophical, understanding that the past will take its toll unless fully recognized and incorporated. A writer, Allan attempts to find his own literary voice and separate himself from his formative influences, notably mentor Reeves Lockhart. Allan recalls Reeves as an exceptional teacher, but in dignifying Reeve's memory, Allan failed to understand the loneliness, alcoholism, and crippling perfectionism that also plagued Reeves the man. By coming to terms with Reeves's weaknesses, however, Allan is better able to deal with his own limitations and feelings of inadequacy so that he can finally affirm himself as a "mischievous, conniving rascal and a cheat: a writer."

Whereas Allan's friendship with Reeves represents the possibilities and limitations of the mentor-student relationship, Allan's friendship with Greg Trouvenskoy addresses peer admiration. Initially Allan idolizes Greg's maturity, good looks, popularity with men and women, and background. The son of parents belonging to the Russian nobility who had escaped the Bolshevik revolution, Greg conveys a sense of wealth and prestige, punctuated by his family's possession of the wonderful Militsa Diamond, their sole remaining treasure from the grand days in St. Petersburg. Handsome and elegant, full of wonderful stories of the Romanoffs and other Russian figures, Greg's parents fulfill Allan's every exotic impulse. They also make him aware of the weaknesses of the aristocratic, feudal system, for they have been dispossessed and are now American citizens and New Deal Democrats. They have survived because they have the inner resources to make the transition from wealth and power to more average social positions.

Greg, however, is weaker than Allan imagined, proving secretly jealous, especially of Allan's relation with Reeves. In certain respects, Greg is adversely affected by his Russian roots—he has his parents' temper, passions, and recklessness without their versatility. He is also more affected by the loss of wealth than are his parents. His failure to come to terms with their past and his present forces him to steal their diamond, an act that eventually causes the death of his father.

In *The Paragon*, main character Louis Colfax learns that individual people and events together create history. Of a family that had been rich in the nineteenth century, Louis grows up with few material advantages and is surrounded by family members who are psychologically and socially damaged—passive, pious, repressive, oppressive, and alcoholic. Louis feels himself psychologically impaired by his environment. In his many despairing moments he withdraws and hopes to put an end to the cycle of biological and environmental determinism. In the end, he recognizes that his problems have been determined not only by his bizarre family but also by his own independent character and actions.

In *The Paragon* Knowles suggests that each person and culture has a repressed side referred to as "the animal inside the human." Indeed, in talking with his fiancee Charlotte Mills, Louis says, "I love you too much, like a man *and* like a woman. . . . I think I'm a lesbian." He believes that she has her masculine side, just as he has his feminine side, and that both must be recognized and embraced. Knowles implies that all human beings have these opposing characteristics, one often suppressing another and destroying the balanced personality, and he suggests that this is even true of institutions and nations. Juxtaposed against male institutional power in *The Paragon* is the power of nature. The image of an Hawaiian volcano represents for Lou all of nature's raw power: "This was the ultimate, uncontrollable force on earth. No fence could stop it, no wall, no channel. No will could stop it, no bomb." *The Paragon,* then, pits the masculine against the feminine, the rational against the emotional, and the institutional against the natural.

Despite *The Paragon's* complexity, critics have not been altogether appreciative of the book. Jonathan Yardley states in the *New Republic* that he likes the novel but finds it derivative of *A Separate Peace* and inherently false in tone. James Aronson in the *Antioch Review* agrees: "The dialogue is faked and stagey, the characters are stereotyped, the parallels between 1950 and 1970 are tritely obvious, and the shape of the novel is curiously disjointed." However, Webster Schott, writing in the *New York Times Book Review,* finds much to admire, especially in the conception of the protagonist: "the title is important. It's not 'A Paragon.' It's '*The Paragon*.' And Knowles's model or pattern of perfection for youth and manhood is a seeking, nonconforming, erratically brilliant and socially maladjusted college student. For Knowles the perfect model must be less than perfect. Not an irony. A moral position."

In *A Vein of Riches* Knowles's presents his strongest indictment of the rich by sympathetically portraying West Virginia miners who struck against rapacious coal barons between 1918 and 1921. The Catherwood family—Clarkson, Minnie, and Lyle—represent the attitudes of other mine-owner families towards the laboring classes and their own family affairs. The first part of the book primarily centers on the Catherwoods' views of the strikers, black servants, and the economy; the second, on the family's increasing financial difficulties and their problems in discovering personal fulfillment and meaning. In their personal roles and attitudes to others, the Catherwoods become a microcosm of the ownership class—what the strikers call "bloated capitalists" and "economic royalists." Shortsighted and greedy, they do not have the ability

to manage the mines and guarantee prosperity and calm in both good times and bad.

In *A Vein of Riches,* then, Knowles discloses the viciousness that lies beneath the surface of American capitalism. The true vein of riches, he suggests, may be a vivid imagination, powerful emotions, and a sharp conscience.

Morning in Antibes, the first of Knowles's Mediterranean novels, treats class conflict, marital issues, and international relations. Here the setting is Juan-les-Pins on the Riviera, the playground of the rich from America (Nicholas and Liliane Bodine and Jimmy Smoot), France (Marc, Constance, and Titou de la Croie), and elsewhere. In contrast to the rich, those who work on the Riviera—the restaurateurs and servants, even the transvestites who participate in nightclub acts—are faced with hard daily schedules, little money, and the scorn of their patrons.

Also set in Southern France, *Spreading Fires* is a gothic tale of insanity and guilt, and in it Knowles explores deeply seated sexual attitudes. The book's protagonist is Brendan Lucas, a well-heeled American diplomat who rents a spacious villa overlooking the Mediterranean near Cannes. This area exudes sexuality in "the musky air, the sticky sea, the sensuous food, the sensual wine." Although Brendan does not overtly share in that pervasive sensuality, he has, as Christopher Lehmann-Haupt puts it in the *New York Times*, "unresolved Oedipal rage" and homosexual anxieties. The conflict between sexuality and repression serves as the central issue of the book. For Knowles, sexual emotion is a side of the self that must be recognized.

Though best known for his novels, Knowles also produced *Phineas,* a collection of stories about adolescent boys and young men reaching a greater understanding of life. James P. Degman of the *Kenyon Review* admires Knowles's dramatization of the torments of sensitive and intelligent adolescents, particularly in "Phineas," "A Turn with the Sun," and "Summer Street." An early version of the scene from *A Separate Peace* in which the narrator causes Finny to fall from a tree, "Phineas" focuses upon the narrator's attempts at confession and reconciliation. "A Turn with the Sun," set like "Phineas" at the Devon School, portrays an alienated young protagonist whose beautiful dive into a cold river ironically consolidates his relationship with his comrades and brings on his death. "Summer Street," in which a young boy copes with his anxieties about the birth of a sister, treats the development of imagination—both the quality of wonder and enchantment, as well as the fear of the unknown. Some people, the story implies, have little imagination and will be mired in their environment; others suppress their imagination and lose access to a rich world; still others have this talent but need to foster and channel it so that it does not prove an instrument of evasion.

Conflicting personality traits, genders, and ways of functioning infuse all of Knowles's work. These themes are reinforced in Knowles's nonfiction book, *Double Vision: American Thoughts Abroad*. In this travel account, Knowles regales the reader with his impressions of Arab spontaneity and Greek hospitality, but he also criticizes America's puritanical Protestant habits, repressed sexuality, tendency toward violence in its cities, and unfair distribution of jobs and wealth. Knowles's own personal apprehensions and fear about the strangeness of Arab culture, its "paralyzed battlefield," raises another concern, the American fear of other cultures. This fear of the unknown, the strangeness of other people, is, the author implies, deeply human, but especially characteristic of Americans. Yet Knowles is not altogether negative about America and its ideals. He likes American directness and honesty, the great energy of its people, and the feeling of governmental stability. He is hopeful that America will, with time, create a civilization in harmony with nature, one that stresses tolerance and equal rights for blacks and women, that erases oppositions.

Throughout his fiction, Knowles shows a concern for middle- and upper-class Americans. He sees, and perhaps shares, their hunger for wealth, but he also knows their weaknesses and those of the American system. He exposes the effects of greed, obsessive social propriety, puritanical religion, and stifled emotions, qualities that lead to rivalry, suppression, and self-destruction. Yet these forces can be countered, Knowles suggests, by letting go—by abandoning urban competition, by restoring the primacy of emotions, by allowing love to flourish, and by returning to nature.

BIOGRAPHICAL/CRITICAL SOURCES:

BOOKS

Concise Dictionary of Literary Biography: Broadening Views, 1968-1988, Gale, 1989, pp. 120-135.
Contemporary Literary Criticism, Gale, Volume 1, 1973, p. 169, Volume 4, 1975, pp. 302-304, Volume 10, 1979, pp. 302-304, Volume 26, 1983, pp. 245-265.
Dictionary of Literary Biography, Volume 6: *American Novelists since World War II, Second Series,* Gale, 1980, pp. 167-177.
Knowles, John, *A Separate Peace,* Macmillan, 1960.
Knowles, *Double Vision: American Thoughts Abroad,* Macmillan, 1964.
Knowles, *Indian Summer,* Random House, 1966.
Knowles, *The Paragon,* Random House, 1971.
Knowles, *Spreading Fires,* Random House, 1974.
Knowles, *A Vein of Riches,* Little, Brown, 1978.
Knowles, *Peace Breaks Out,* Holt, 1981.

Knowles, *A Stolen Past,* Holt, 1983.

PERIODICALS

Antioch Review, spring, 1971, pp. 131-132.
Arizona Quarterly, winter, 1967, pp. 335-342.
Atlantic Monthly, March, 1962, pp. 148-149; August, 1964, p. 116.
Book Week, July 24, 1966.
Chicago Tribune, September 21, 1986.
Chicago Tribune Book World, March 29, 1981, p. 3.
Clearing House, September, 1973.
Commonweal, December 9, 1960.
Critique: Studies in Short Fiction, winter, 1974, pp. 107-112.
English Journal, May, 1964, pp. 313-318; April, 1969; December, 1969; September, 1981, pp. 75-77; February, 1984, p. 107.
Harper's, July, 1966.
Kenyon Review, Volume 31, 1969, pp. 275-276.
Life, August 5, 1966.
Los Angeles Times, April 2, 1981, p. 22; May 2, 1986; August 27, 1986, pp. 1, 10.
Los Angeles Times Book Review, August 28, 1983, p. 4.
Manchester Guardian, May 1, 1959.
Minnesota Review, summer, 1962, p. 564.
New Republic, February 13, 1971, pp. 29-30.
New Statesman, May 2, 1959.
Newsweek, April 20, 1981, p. 92.
New York Times, June 11, 1974, p. 39; February 3, 1978; September 4, 1981; April 16, 1986.
New York Times Book Review, February 7, 1960; August 14, 1966; January 31, 1971, p. 6; June 4, 1978, p. 15; March 22, 1981, pp. 3, 37; October 17, 1982, p. 45; October 30, 1983, p. 32; May 11, 1986, p. 19.
Saturday Review, August 13, 1966; February 18, 1978, p. 33.
Studies in Short Fiction, winter, 1974, pp. 107-112.
Time, April 6, 1981, p. 80.
Times Literary Supplement, May 1, 1959; August 31, 1984, p. 964.
Washington Post, June 1, 1983.
Washington Post Book World, February 19, 1978, p. E4; March 15, 1981, p. 8.*

—*Sidelights by Gordon E. Slethaug*

*   *   *

KOENNER, Alfred 1921-

PERSONAL: Born December 2, 1921, in Schalkendort, Germany; married; children: Stephan, Henry. *Education:* Attended University of Berlin. *Religion:* Catholic.

ADDRESSES: Home—Valwigerstrasse 32, 1140 Berlin, Germany.

CAREER: Assistant at institute for practical pedagogy in East Berlin, Germany, 1946-49; lecturer in German language and literature, 1953; assistant with writers' association in East Berlin, 1954; Altberliner Verlag (publisher), East Berlin, chief reader, 1959-85.

WRITINGS:

IN ENGLISH TRANSLATION; JUVENILES

Jolli, Parabel Verlag, c. 1960, translation by Regina Waldman published as *Jolli,* Lenner Publications, 1967.

The Clever Coot, translated from the original German, Carolrhoda Books, 1971.

Die Hochzeit des Pfaus, [East Germany], 1972, translation by Marion Koenig published as *The Peacock's Wedding,* Chatto & Windus, 1973.

Silko, [East Germany], 1975, translation by Richard Sadler published as *Silko: A Day in the Life of a Heron,* illustrated by Gerhard Lahr, [England], 1977.

Kleiner Bruder Namenlos, [East Germany], 1981, translation published as *Little Brother without a Name,* Macdonald, 1983.

Eines Tages frueh am Morgen, Altberliner Verlag, 1981, translation published as *Early One Morning,* 1984.

Flieg, Schirmchen, Flieg, Altberliner Verlag, 1981, translation published as *Fly, Little Umbrella, Fly,* 1984.

Pfefferchen, [East Germany], 1982, translation published as *The Little Boy and the Fishes,* Macdonald, 1985.

Der Riese im Schnee, [East Germany], 1985, translation by Helen East published as *Attu and the Snow Giant,* Macdonald, 1985.

Die Perle des Gluecks, Altberliner Verlag, 1988, translation by Helen East published as *The Lucky Pearl,* Macdonald, 1988.

IN GERMAN; JUVENILES

Kiek in die Welt (stories), [East Germany], 1964.

Als Robert aus dem Fenster sah (cantata), [East Germany], 1979.

IN GERMAN; JUVENILE PICTURE BOOKS

Wenn ich gross bin, lieber Mond, Buchheim Verlag, 1961.
Das Pony mit dem Federbusch, [East Germany], 1962.
Tappelpit, [East Germany], 1964.
Fertig macht sich Nikolaus, Altberliner Verlag, 1967.
Der Raeuberhase, [East Germany], 1969.
Wer maeuschen still am Bache sitzt, [East Germany], 1971.
Eine Wolke schwarz und schwer, [East Germany], 1973.
Pusteblumen, [East Germany], 1973.
Kieselchen, [East Germany], 1975.
Olrik, [East Germany], 1976.
Drei kleine Baeren, [East Germany], 1976.
Der verwandelte Wald, [East Germany], 1976.
Ein Bagger geht spazieren, [East Germany], 1978.

Ich reise ins Blaue, [East Germany], 1979.
Es tanzen die Flocken, [East Germany], 1979.
Ein schoener Hahn, [East Germany], 1979.
Der blaue Traktor, [East Germany], 1980.
Weine nicht, sagte der Baum, [East Germany], 1980.
Weit fliegt der Ball, [East Germany], 1982.
Wo schlafen die Hasen, [East Germany], 1982.
Wer darf schwarz sein jeden Tag, [East Germany], 1983.
Herr Dickbauch und Frau Duennebein, [East Germany], 1983.
Wir pfeifen auf das Krokodil, [East Germany], 1983.
Drei kleine Hasen, [East Germany], 1983.
Koch im Baum schlief der Kater, [East Germany], 1984.
Da waren sieben Hasen, [East Germany], 1984.
Der dicke grosse Fisch, [East Germany], 1984.
Ein Maedchen namens Rosamund, Altberliner Verlag, 1985.
Das Apfelsinenmaedchen, Altberliner Verlag, 1986.
Vom goldenen Handwerk, Altberliner Verlag, 1986.
Wo ist Anne?, Altberliner Verlag, 1988.
Der rote Cowboyhut, Altberliner Verlag, 1990.

IN GERMAN; JUVENILE POETRY

Mein bunter Zoo, [East Germany], 1962.
Der Rummelpott, Alterberliner Verlag, 1967.
Auf dem Hofe tut sich was, [East Germany], 1972.
(Editor) *Der Plumpsack,* Altberliner Verlag, 1975.
Schnick und Schnack und Schabernack, [East Germany], 1978.
Bilderzoo, [East Germany], 1983.
(Editor) *Eene meene mopel* (rhymes of Berlin children), Altberliner Verlag, 1986.

SIDELIGHTS: Alfred Koenner told *CA* that his writings and other literary activities are concerned with the development and furtherance of books for pre- and school-age children. He is interested in this age group because of their spontaneity and sizable attention span. Consequently, he creates picture books with short stories about animals, often with characters taken from popular fables. He added that a major feature of his work is the linking of poetic fantasy with educational theory.

*   *   *

KONDRASHOV, Stanislav (Nikolaevich) 1928-

PERSONAL: Born December 25, 1928, in the Soviet Union (now Commonwealth of Independent States); son of Nikolai Petrovich (an engineer) and Taisia (Mikhailovna) Kondrashov; married Klara Mikhailovna Kurikova, February 9, 1950; children: Natalia, Tatiana, Nikolai. *Education:* Attended Moscow's Institute of International Relations, 1946-51.

ADDRESSES: Home—Begovaya Ulica 13, Moscow, Russia, Commonwealth of Independent States. *Office*—*Izvestia,* Pushkinskaya Sq. 5, Moscow, Russia, Commonwealth of Independent States.

CAREER: Izvestia, Moscow, Russia, Commonwealth of Independent States, in foreign department, 1951-57, correspondent from Cairo, 1957-61, and New York City, 1961-68, foreign commentator, 1968-71, correspondent from Washington DC, 1971-76, dep. editor in chief, 1976-77, senior political commentator, 1977—.

MEMBER: Union of Journalists, Union of Writers.

AWARDS, HONORS: Vorovskii Prize from Union of Journalists, 1968, for international reporting (from the United States); Decorated Order Lenin, Order of Honor.

WRITINGS:

Na Beregakh Nila (title means "On the Banks of the Nile"), Izvestia Publishing House, 1958.
Perekresti Ameriki (title means "American Crossroads"), Politizdat, 1969.
Zhiznj i Smertj Martina Lutera Kinga (title means "The Life and Death of Martin Luther King"), Molodaya Gvardia, 1970.
Amerikancy y Amerike (title means "Americans in America"), Izvestia Publishing House, 1970.
Svidanie s Kaliforniei (title means "Rendezvous with California"), Publishing House (Moscow, Russia, Commonwealth of Independent States), 1975.
Po Vtoromu Krugu: Zametki ob Amerike (title means "On the Second Circle"), Izvestia Publishing House, 1978.
Kontury Vremeni, Izvestia Publishing House, 1981.
V Arizone, u Indeltsev, Sovetskaya Rossiya', 1982.
Bliki N' Tu-Torka, Sovetskii Pisatel, 1982.
Puteshestvie Amerikanista, Sovetskii Pisatel, 1986.

Also author of *My i Oni v Etom Tesnom Mire: Dnevnik Politicheskogo Obozrevatelia,* 1984. Contributor of articles and stories on the United States and on the Middle East to Soviet magazines, including *Novyi Mir, Inostrannaya Literatura, Znamya,* and *New Times.*

BIOGRAPHICAL/CRITICAL SOURCES:

PERIODICALS

Zhurnalist, December, 1971.
Kommunist, March, 1972.

*   *   *

KOSSLYN, Stephen Michael   1948-

PERSONAL: Born November 30, 1948, in Santa Monica, CA; son of S. Duke and Rhoda (Rosenberg) Kosslyn; married Robin Sue Rosenberg (a clinical psychologist), March 28, 1982. *Education:* University of California, Los Angeles, B.A., 1970; Stanford University, Ph.D., 1974.

ADDRESSES: Office—Department of Psychology, 832 William James Hall, Harvard University, Cambridge, MA 02138.

CAREER: Johns Hopkins University, Baltimore, MD, assistant professor of psychology, 1974-77; Harvard University, Cambridge, MA, associate professor, 1977-83, professor of psychology, 1983—.

MEMBER: American Psychological Association (fellow), American Psychological Society, Psychonomic Society, Society for Neuroscience, Cognitive Science Society, American Association for the Advancement of Science.

AWARDS, HONORS: Boyd R. McCardless Young Scientist Award, American Psychological Association, 1978; Initiatives in Research Award, National Academy of Sciences, 1983; honorary M.A., Harvard University, 1983.

WRITINGS:

Image and Mind, Harvard University Press, 1980.
Ghosts in the Mind's Machine: Creating and Using Images in the Brain, Norton, 1983.
(Editor with J. R. Anderson) *Tutorials in Learning and Memory: Essays in Honor of Gordon H. Bower,* W. H. Freeman, 1983.
(With Oliver Koenig) *Wet Mind: The New Cognitive Neuroscience,* Free Press, 1992.
(Editor with Richard Andersen) *Frontiers in Cognitive Neuroscience,* MIT Press, 1992.
Elements of Graph Style, W. H. Freeman, 1993.
Image and Brain, MIT Press, 1993.

Contributor of about seventy-five articles to psychology journals.

SIDELIGHTS: Stephen Michael Kosslyn once told *CA:* "*Image and Mind* grew out of mistakes two people made in a psychology experiment. People were asked to decide whether statements were true or false as quickly as possible (reaction times were measured), and two people happened to say 'false' to the statement 'A flea can bite.' When interviewed afterwards, one said he couldn't 'see' any teeth on a flea, and the other said something similar (the whole story is recounted in *Image and Mind*'s preface). All of the people who participated were then asked if they had used visual imagery in the experiment, and the data were analyzed separately for those who did and did not claim to use this method of evaluating the statements; the results were very different for the two groups. Explaining why the results were so different took about ten years, and *Image and Mind* was the result.

"*Ghosts* was written to make the material in the first book more accessible and to put it in a broader context. Indeed, *Ghosts* uses the work on imagery as a way of introducing the central concepts in the new discipline called cognitive science. The book on charts and graphs takes psychological findings and shows how they can be used to improve the design of visual displays. This book shows how 'pure' research in psychology can result in a useful technology. The urge to be useful should be apparent in *Wet Mind,* which has straightforward implications for neuropsychological testing and the rehabilitation of brain-damaged people."

He added, "It should also be apparent in *Elements of Graphic Style,* which uses results of psychological research to generate recommendations for the design of visual displays."

* * *

KRANTZ, Hazel (Newman)

PERSONAL: Born January 29, in Brooklyn, NY; daughter of Louis John and Eva Newman; married Michael Krantz, 1942; children: Laurence Ira, Margaret Ann, Vincent. *Education:* New York University, B.S., 1942; Hofstra College (now University), M.S., 1959. *Avocational interests:* Gardening, sewing, swimming, cooking, tennis, hand weaving.

ADDRESSES: Home—1306 Stoney Hill Dr., Fort Collins, CO 80525; winter: 13767A Via Aurora, Delray Beach, FL 33484.

CAREER: McGreevey, Werring & Howell, New York City, home-furnishings coordinator, 1942-43; Felix Lilienthal, New York City, fashion coordinator, 1944-45; Nassau County Schools, Nassau County, NY, elementary school teacher in public schools, 1957-68; *True Frontier* (magazine), Valley Stream, NY, full charge editor, 1970-72; *db: The Sound Engineering Magazine,* Plainview, NY, copy editor, 1973-78; free-lance writer, specializing in educational materials.

MEMBER: Society of Children's Book Writers, Emissary Society, Northern Colorado Weavers Guild.

WRITINGS:

JUVENILES

One Hundred Pounds of Popcorn, Vanguard, 1961.
Freestyle for Michael, Vanguard, 1964.
The Secret Raft, Vanguard, 1965.
Tippy, Vanguard, 1968.
A Pad of Your Own, Pyramid Publications, 1973.
Complete Guide to Success and Happiness, Merit Publications, 1980.

Pink and White Striped Summer, Berkley Publishing, 1984.
None but the Brave, Silhouette Books, 1986.
Daughter of My People: The Story of Henrietta Szold, Dutton/Lodestar, 1987.
For Love of Jeremy, Dutton/Lodestar, 1990.

SIDELIGHTS: Hazel Krantz once told *CA:* "Most of my books have been written for young people. They emanate from a place called the Aquarius Room, which has actually been a series of rooms: Aquarius Room East, on Long Island, New York, Aquarius Room South, in Delray Beach, Florida, and Aquarius Room West, in Fort Collins, Colorado. This denotes not only my [astrological] sign but also a subliminal search for the Age of Aquarius. Somewhere, hidden in the depths of my word processor are these bits and pieces of gold, the clear and glowing truth of life.

"It all starts with stories, of course. A tale takes shape, something is going to happen. It will start somewhere and have a certain conclusion. All these things are tentative. The tale must have people, of course, especially a main character who has problems to solve and adventures to experience. There are other characters who give spice to the protagonist's life; in a teen romance, closely following the heroine, is the elusive hero.

"As these people come to life, emerging from that word processor, they tell me what they want to do, and I write it down, recounting their conversations and private thoughts.

"When it is over, the story is like a memory, the same as all the episodes in our lives, a parable that illuminates some part of the truth. The story, of course, does not start with this, any more than we commence life's experiences in order to learn something about the design. The pattern becomes evident only upon completion. The reader may be told the secret, or it may be left to her (usually) to sense what has been told and to see parallels in her own life."

BIOGRAPHICAL/CRITICAL SOURCES:

PERIODICALS

Young Readers' Review, September, 1968.

* * *

KULKIN, Mary-Ellen
See SIEGEL, Mary-Ellen (Kulkin)

KYGER, Joanne (Elizabeth) 1934-

PERSONAL: Born November 19, 1934, in Vallejo, CA; daughter of Jacob Holmes (a career navy officer) and Anne (Lamont) Kyger; married Gary Snyder (a poet), 1960 (divorced, 1964); married John Boyce (a painter), 1966 (died, 1972). *Education:* Attended Santa Barbara College (now University of California, Santa Barbara), 1952-56.

ADDRESSES: Home—Box 688, Bolinas, CA 94924.

CAREER: Poet. Teaches at Naropa Institute, Boulder, CO, and at New College, San Francisco, CA. Performer and poet in an experimental television project, 1967-68.

AWARDS, HONORS: Grant from National Endowment for the Arts, 1968.

WRITINGS:

POETRY

The Tapestry and the Web, Four Seasons Foundation, 1965.
The Fool in April: A Poem, Coyote Books, 1966.
Places to Go, Black Sparrow Press, 1970.
Joanne, Angel Hair Books, 1970.
Desecheo Notebook, Arif, 1971.
Trip Out and Fall Back, Arif, 1974.
All This Every Day, Big Sky, 1975.
The Wonderful Focus of You, Z Press, 1980.
Up My Coast, Floating Island, 1979.
The Japan-India Journals, Tombouctou Books, 1981.
Mexico Blonde, Evergreen Press, 1981.
Going On: Selected Poems 1958-80, Dutton, 1983.
The Dharma Committee, Smithereens Press, 1986.
Phenomenological: A Curriculum of the Soul, Institute of Further Studies, 1989.
Just Space: Poems 1979-89, Black Sparrow Press, 1991.

OTHER

Contributor to books, including *Rising Tides,* edited by Laura Chester and Sharon Barba, Pocket Books, 1973. Contributor to anthologies, including *The American Liter-* *ary Anthology,* edited by George Plimpton and Peter Ardery, Random House, 1969; and *The World Anthology,* edited by Anne Waldman, Bobbs-Merrill, 1969. Contributor to numerous periodicals, including *Paris Review, Poetry, Coyote's Journal, Peninsula, Intent, Rockey Ledge,* and *World.* Kyger's papers are deposited at the Archive for New Poetry, University of California, San Diego.

SIDELIGHTS: A leading figure in San Francisco poetry circles, Joanne Kyger was a member of some of the groups which formed around senior poets Robert Duncan and Jack Spicer in the late 1950s and fostered such writers as Richard Brautigan, Michael McClure, and George Stanley.

From 1970 on, notes Bill Berkson in *Dictionary of Literary Biography,* "Kyger's poems have dealt with a number of set themes: Buddhist and American Indian figures and myths, the relationship of the individual psyche to the social-political life of the town, love and marriage, and travel." According to Berkson, during a 1974 panel discussion at Kent State University, Kyger "spoke of her change from what she termed 'the linear line': 'at this point the kind of space that interests me is the kind of space that vibrates its meaning. It's the one-liner or the sampler on the wall. . . . It just stays there for a long time. You can go back into the one line and it will keep giving off overtones.' "

BIOGRAPHICAL/CRITICAL SOURCES:

BOOKS

Dictionary of Literary Biography, Volume 16: *The Beats: Literary Bohemians in Postwar America,* Gale, 1983.

PERIODICALS

Credences 4, Volume 2, number 1, 1977.
Los Angeles Times Book Review, November 13, 1983.
Occident, spring, 1974.
Partisan Review, spring, 1972.
San Francisco Review of Books, February, 1976.
Tomales Bay Times, July 16, 1976.

L

LADY of QUALITY, A
See BAGNOLD, Enid

*   *   *

L'AMOUR, Louis (Dearborn)   1908-1988
(Jim Mayo; Tex Burns, a house pseudonym)

PERSONAL: Born March 28, 1908, in Jamestown, ND; died June 10, 1988, of lung cancer in Los Angeles, CA; son of Louis Charles (a veterinarian and farm-machinery salesman), and Emily (Dearborn) LaMoore; married Katherine Elizabeth Adams, February 19, 1956; children: Beau Dearborn, Angelique Gabrielle. *Education:* Self-educated.

CAREER: Author and lecturer. Held numerous jobs, including positions as longshoreman, lumberjack, miner, elephant handler, hay shocker, boxer, flume builder, and fruit picker. Lecturer at many universities including University of Oklahoma, Baylor University, University of Southern California, and University of Redlands. *Military service:* U.S. Army, 1942-46; became first lieutenant.

MEMBER: Writers Guild of America (West), Western Writers of America, Academy of Motion Picture Arts and Sciences, American Siam Society, California Writers Guild, California Academy of Sciences.

AWARDS, HONORS: Western Writers of America Award-Novel, 1969, for *Down the Long Hills;* LL.D., Jamestown College, 1972; Theodore Roosevelt Rough Rider award, North Dakota, 1972; American Book Award, 1980, for *Bendigo Shafter;* Buffalo Bill Award, 1981; Distinguished Newsboy Award, 1981; National Genealogical Society Award, 1981; Congressional Gold Medal, 1983; Presidential Medal of Freedom, 1984; LL.D., Pepperdine University, 1984.

WRITINGS:

NOVELS

Westward the Tide, World's Work (Surrey, England), 1950.

Hondo (expanded version of his story, "The Gift of Cochise"; also see below), Gold Medal, 1953, reprinted with introduction by Michael T. Marsden, Gregg, 1978.

Crossfire Trail (also see below), Ace Books, 1954, reprinted with introduction by Keith Jarrod, Gregg, 1980.

Heller with a Gun (also see below), Gold Medal, 1954.

Kilkenny (also see below), Ace Books, 1954, reprinted with introduction by Wesley Laing, Gregg, 1980.

To Tame a Land, Fawcett, 1955.

Guns of the Timberlands, Jason, 1955.

The Burning Hills, Jason, 1956.

Silver Canyon (expanded version of his story, "Riders of the Dawn"), Avalon, 1956.

Last Stand at Papago Wells (also see below), Gold Medal, 1957.

The Tall Stranger (also see below), Fawcett, 1957.

Sitka, Appleton, 1957.

Radigan, Bantam, 1958.

The First Fast Draw (also see below), Bantam, 1959.

Taggart, Bantam, 1959.

Flint, Bantam, 1960.

Shalako, Bantam, 1962.

Killoe (also see below), Bantam, 1962.

High Lonesome, Bantam, 1962.

How the West Was Won (based on the screenplay by James R. Webb), Bantam, 1963.

Fallon, Bantam, 1963.

Catlow, Bantam, 1963.

Dark Canyon, Bantam, 1963.

Hanging Woman Creek, Bantam, 1964.

Kiowa Trail (also see below), Bantam, 1965.
The High Graders, Bantam, 1965.
The Key-Lock Man (also see below), Bantam, 1965.
Kid Rodelo, Bantam, 1966.
Kilrone, Bantam, 1966.
The Broken Gun, Bantam, 1966.
Matagorda, Bantam, 1967.
Down the Long Hills, Bantam, 1968.
Chancy, Bantam, 1968.
Conagher, Bantam, 1969.
The Empty Land, Bantam, 1969.
The Man Called Noon, Bantam, 1970.
Reilly's Luck, Bantam, 1970.
Brionne, Bantam, 1971.
Under the Sweetwater Rim, Bantam, 1971.
Tucker, Bantam, 1971.
North to the Rails, Bantam, 1971.
Callaghen, Bantam, 1972.
The Ferguson Rifle, Bantam, 1973.
The Quick and the Dead, Bantam, 1973, revised edition, 1979.
The Man from Skibbereen, G. K. Hall, 1973.
The Californios, Saturday Review Press, 1974.
Rivers West, Saturday Review Press, 1974.
Over on the Dry Side, Saturday Review Press, 1975.
The Rider of the Lost Creek (based on one of his short stories), Bantam, 1976.
Where the Long Grass Blows, Bantam, 1976.
Borden Chantry, Bantam, 1977.
The Mountain Valley War (based on one of his short stories), Bantam, 1978.
Fair Blows the Wind, Bantam, 1978.
Bendigo Shafter, Dutton, 1978.
The Iron Marshall, Bantam, 1979.
The Proving Trail, Bantam, 1979.
The Warrior's Path, Bantam, 1980.
Comstock Lode, Bantam, 1981.
Milo Talon, Bantam, 1981.
The Cherokee Trail, Bantam, 1982.
The Shadow Riders, Bantam, 1982.
The Lonesome Gods, Bantam, 1983.
Son of a Wanted Man, Bantam, 1984.
The Walking Drum, Bantam, 1984.
Passin' Through, Bantam, 1985.
Last of the Breed, Bantam, 1986.
West of the Pilot Range, Bantam, 1986.
A Trail to the West, Bantam, 1986.
The Haunted Mesa, Bantam, 1987.

Also author of *Man Riding West,* Carroll & Graf.

"SACKETT FAMILY" SERIES; NOVELS

The Daybreakers, Bantam, 1960.
Sackett, Bantam, 1961.
Lando, Bantam, 1962.

Mojave Crossing, Bantam, 1964.
The Sackett Brand, Bantam, 1965.
Mustang Man, Bantam, 1966.
The Skyliners, Bantam, 1967.
The Lonely Men, Bantam, 1969.
Galloway, Bantam, 1970.
Ride the Dark Trail, Bantam, 1972.
Treasure Mountain, Bantam, 1972.
Sackett's Land, Saturday Review Press, 1974.
The Man from the Broken Hills, Bantam, 1975.
To the Far Blue Mountains, Dutton, 1976.
Sackett's Gold, Bantam, 1977.
The Warrior's Path, Bantam, 1980.
Lonely on the Mountain, Bantam, 1980.
Ride the River, Bantam, 1983.
Jubal Sackett, Bantam, 1985.

"HOPALONG CASSIDY" SERIES; NOVELS; PUBLISHED UNDER HOUSE PSEUDONYM TEX BURNS

Hopalong Cassidy and the Riders of High Rock, Doubleday, 1951.
Hopalong Cassidy and the Rustlers of West Fork, Doubleday, 1951.
Hopalong Cassidy and the Trail to Seven Pines, Doubleday, 1951.
Hopalong Cassidy: Trouble Shooter, Doubleday, 1952.

ORIGINALLY PUBLISHED UNDER PSEUDONYM JIM MAYO; REPRINTED UNDER AUTHOR'S REAL NAME; NOVELS

Showdown at Yellow Butte (also see below), Ace Books, 1954, reprinted with introduction by Scott R. McMillan, Gregg, 1980.
Utah Blaine (also see below), Ace Books, 1954, reprinted with introduction by Wayne C. Lee, Gregg, 1980.

OMNIBUS VOLUMES

Kiowa Trail [and] *Killoe,* Ulverscroft, 1979.
The First Fast Draw [and] *The Key-Lock Man,* Ulverscroft, 1979.
Four Complete Novels (includes *The Tall Stranger, Kilkenny, Hondo,* and *Showdown at Yellow Butte*), Avenal Books, 1980.
Five Complete Novels (includes *Crossfire Trail, Utah Blaine, Heller with a Gun, Last Stand at Papago Wells,* and *To Tame a Land*), Avenel Books, 1981.
L'Amour Westerns (four volumes), Gregg, 1981.

SHORT STORIES

War Party, Bantam, 1975.
Yondering, Bantam, 1980, revised edition, 1989.
The Strong Shall Live, Bantam, 1980.
Buckskin Run, Bantam, 1981.
Law of the Desert Born, Bantam, 1983.
Bowdrie, Bantam, 1983.
The Hills of Homicide, Bantam, 1984.

Bowdrie's Law, Bantam, 1984.
Riding for the Brand, Bantam, 1986.
Dutchman's Flat, Bantam, 1986.
The Trail to Crazy Man, Bantam, 1986.
The Rider of the Ruby Hills, Bantam, 1986.
Night over the Solomons, Bantam, 1986.
West from Singapore, Bantam, 1987.
Lonigan, Bantam, 1988.
The Outlaws of Mesquite, Bantam, 1991.

OTHER

Smoke from This Altar (poetry), Lusk (Oklahoma City, OK), 1939.
Frontier (essays), Bantam, 1984.
(Author of foreword) Frank C. McCarthy, *Frank C. McCarthy: The Old West,* Greenwich Press, 1981.
The Sackett Companion: A Personal Guide to the Sackett Novels (nonfiction), Bantam, 1988.
A Trail of Memories: The Quotations of Louis L'Amour (excerpts from L'Amour's fiction), compiled by daughter, Angelique L'Amour, Bantam, 1988.
The Education of a Wandering Man (autobiography), Bantam, 1989.

Also author of filmscripts and more than sixty-five television scripts. Contributor of more than four hundred short stories and articles to more than eighty magazines in the United States and abroad, including *Argosy, Collier's,* and *Saturday Evening Post.*

ADAPTATIONS: More than forty-five of L'Amour's novels and short stories have been adapted into feature films and television movies, including *Hondo,* Warner Bros., 1953; *East of Sumatra,* Universal, 1953; *Four Guns to the Border,* Universal, 1954; *Treasure of the Ruby Hills,* Allied Artists, 1955; *Kilkenny,* Columbia, 1956; *The Burning Hills,* Warner Bros., 1956; *Utah Blaine,* Columbia, 1956; *Walk Tall,* Allied Artists, 1957; *Last Stand at Papago Wells,* Columbia, 1958; *Heller with Pink Tights* (based on his *Heller with a Gun*), Paramount, 1960; *Guns of the Timberlands,* Warner Bros., 1960; *Taggart,* Universal, 1964; *Kid Rodelo,* Paramount, 1966; *Shalako,* Cinerama Releasing Corp., 1968; *Catlow,* Metro-Goldwyn-Mayer, 1971; *The Broken Gun,* Warner Bros., 1972; *The Man Called Noon,* Scotia-Barber, 1973; *Down the Long Hills,* Disney Channel, 1986; and *The Quick and the Dead,* Home Box Office, 1987; the *Sackett Family* series was made into a television miniseries, *The Sacketts.*

Many of L'Amour's novels and short stories have been adapted for presentation on audio cassettes, including "Riding for the Brand" (adapted from a short story from *Riding for the Brand*), Bantam, 1987; "Bowdrie Passes Through," (adapted from a short story from *Bowdrie*), Bantam, 1988; "Keep Travelin' Rider" (adapted from a short story from *Dutchman's Flat*), Bantam, 1988; and "One for the Mojave Kid" (adapted from a short story from *Dutchman's Flat*), Bantam, 1988.

SIDELIGHTS: When describing someone like Western writer Louis L'Amour it was necessary to use terms as wide and grand as the West about which he wrote. He sold more books than nearly every other contemporary novelist. He wrote more million-copy bestsellers than any other American fiction writer. He was the only novelist in this nation's history to be granted either of the country's highest honors—the Congressional Gold Medal and the Presidential Medal of Freedom—and L'Amour received them both. When he died, nearly two hundred million copies of his books were in print.

L'Amour's achievements were even more remarkable when one considered the obstacles that he overcame to achieve popularity. He had no formal education, spent much of his youth wandering from job to job, and was over forty by the time he published his first novel. Among his first published books were some volumes of poetry and stories about the Far East. "I also wrote some sport stories, some detective stories, and some Western stories," L'Amour told *CA.* "It so happens that the Westerns caught on and there was a big demand for them. I grew up in the West, of course, and loved it, but I never really intended to write Westerns at all." After he started publishing his work, his novels were often not even reviewed by critics. As Ned Smith of *American Way* noted, L'Amour suffered the same fate as the majority of Western writers who found themselves "largely greeted with indifference . . . by the critics." James Barron, writing in the *New York Times,* cited L'Amour's comment that explained how he felt about being labeled a writer of "Westerns": "If you write a book about a bygone period that lies east of the Mississippi River, then it's a historical novel. . . . If it's west of the Mississippi, it's a western, a different category. There's no sense to it."

L'Amour ignored criticism—or the lack of it—and decided to do what hardly anyone had ever done before: make a living as a Western writer. Surprisingly, L'Amour's determination to persevere led to increased critical interest in his work; the literary establishment eventually could no longer continue to disregard such a popular writer. *Newsweek* contributor Charles Leerhsen noted that as L'Amour entered his fourth decade as a novelist "the critics back East [were] finally reviewing his work—and praising his unpretentious, lean-as-a-grass-fed-steer style."

Some critics maintained that L'Amour's style was the key to his appeal. They applauded his ability to write quick-paced action novels filled with accurate descriptions of the Old West—or other locales in which his protagonists found themselves. "Probably the biggest reason for

L'Amour's success . . . ," wrote Ben Yagoda in *Esquire,* was "his attention to authenticity and detail. . . . His books are full of geographical and historical information."

Because of what *People* contributor Joseph Pilcher called L'Amour's "painstaking respect for detail," a typical L'Amour novel often seemed to contain as many factual elements as fictional ones. Writing in *Arizona and the West* about L'Amour's novel *Lando,* Michael T. Marsden noted that in that book alone the writer "instruct[ed] his readers on the historical and cultural importance of Madeira wine, the nature of longhorn cattle, the Great Hurricane of 1844, and the several cultural functions of a Western saloon, all the while providing them with an entertaining romance." In other L'Amour works readers learned such things as how Native Americans made mocassins, how to pan for gold, and the finer points of Elizabethan decor.

Some critics felt that all the factual material in L'Amour's novels detracted from their narrative continuity. They also felt that L'Amour's energies might have been better spent developing his characters or varying his plots rather than on research. *New York Times Book Review* contributor Richard Nalley, for example, wrote: "There is wonderful information [in L'Amour's novel, *The Walking Drum,*] . . . but the author's historical research is presented textbook style, in great, undigested chunks. Although the adventure plot is at times gripping, the uneasy integration of Mathurin [the protagonist] with his surroundings prevents the reader from being entirely swept up in the romance."

In *Western American Literature* John D. Nesbitt observed a similar flaw in L'Amour's *Over on the Dry Side.* According to Nesbitt, in the novel "entertaining narrative effect is lost in favor of flat introduction of historical details and moral speeches." Despite such criticism, L'Amour had an enormous following of readers. In the *Lone Star Review* Steve Berner wrote: "It [was], in fact, pointless to discuss the merits or weaknesses of L'Amour's writings . . . since it [had] little or no effect on either author or his public." According to the *Washington Post*'s Richard Pearson, despite what he called "plots [that] could be predictable" and a technique of narrating that was "wooden," L'Amour was a skilled story teller. L'Amour's agent, C. Stuart Applebaum, observed in a *Detroit News* interview: "For many of his readers, he was the living embodiment of the frontier because of the authenticity of his stories and characters. His readers felt L'Amour walked the land his characters had walked. That was one of the major reasons for his enduring popularity."

L'Amour identified himself as a storyteller in the tradition of Geoffrey Chaucer (fourteenth-century author of *The Canterbury Tales*). Barron cited L'Amour's comment, "I don't travel and tell stories, because that's not the way

these days. . . . But I write my books to be read aloud and I think of myself in that oral tradition."

One story that L'Amour seemed not to want to stop telling was the story of the Sackett family, continued in more than a dozen novels. These books explore the lives of the two branches of the Sackett clan and, to a lesser extent, two other frontier families, the Chantrys and the Talons, across three hundred years of history. In a *North Dakota Quarterly* article, Marsden commented that L'Amour's "formal family groupings may well constitute the most ambitious and complex attempt to date to create a Faulknerian series of interrelated characters and events in the popular Western tradition."

The publication of L'Amour's 1984 novel, *The Walking Drum,* caused a stir in literary circles because L'Amour had written a saga of medieval life in Europe instead of a Western. Apparently L'Amour's change of locale did not intimidate his readers, for the book appeared on the *New York Times* hardcover bestseller list five days before its official publication date. In *People* L'Amour explained to Pilcher that he was irritated that most books about the twelfth century dealt only with the Crusades, so he "decided to tell a swashbuckling adventure story about the period which would also show the history of the times—how people lived and how they worked."

According to *Los Angeles Times* writer Garry Abrams, L'Amour saw the publication of this non-Western novel as "a turning point" in his development as a writer. "From now on, he said, he want[ed] to concentrate less on promotion and more on 'improving my writing. I know how to write and I write fairly well. But you can never learn enough about writing.'" L'Amour concentrated on his writing by branching out in several directions. In 1987, he published *The Haunted Mesa,* which *Washington Post Book World* contributor Tony Hillerman referred to as "part western, part adventure, [and] part fantasy." He wrote *The Sackett Companion: A Personal Guide to the Sackett Novels,* which includes a Sackett family tree as well as background information on the sources behind the novels in the series, and completed his long-planned autobiography, *The Education of a Wandering Man.*

Explaining his approach to fiction writing to Clarence Petersen in the *Chicago Tribune,* L'Amour remarked: "A reader of my books expects to get an entertaining story, and he expects a little bit more. I've got to give him something of the real quality of the West, and I can do that because I'm a storyteller, and I don't have to imagine what happened in the Old West—I know what happened." Descended from pioneers who fought with the Sioux Indians and in the Civil War, L'Amour spent much of his early life traveling the west, working alongside the cattlemen and homesteaders who knew the most about the local history.

L'Amour's informers included one of his employers, a man who had been raised as an Apache Indian, who taught him much about the Indian experience of the American west. The novelist's characters also know much about Indian life, but the claims of their own culture exert a stronger hold. Pearson observed in the *Washington Post,* "Though Mr. L'Amour was often faulted by critics for cardboard, simplistic characters, his western heroes often fought an inner struggle against admiration for the Indian and his way of life on one hand and the need to advance 'civilization' on the other. His were often stories of culture in conflict." The title character of *Bendigo Shafter* describes the conflict felt by many of L'Amour's frontier heroes: "I could have lived the Indian way and loved it. I could feel his spirits move upon the air, hear them in the still forest and the chuckling water of the mountain streams, but other voices were calling me, too, the voices of my own people and their ways. For it was our way to go onward; to go forward and to try to shape our world into something that would make our lives easier, even if more complicated."

L'Amour wrote three novels a year for his publisher for more than thirty years. Even so, by the late 1980s, he had come nowhere near to exhausting the store of research he had gathered as a connoisseur of historical details. At the time of his death in 1988, he had developed outlines for fifty more novels. A year before he died, L'Amour told *CA,* "There's a lot of Western material out there that's very fresh. And the Western novel is not dying, it's doing very well. It's selling every place but in the movies. . . . There seem to be some misconceptions about me and my type of writing, which have been perpetuated by several articles that weren't written too well. . . . Too often people start with a cliched idea of a Western writer. That automatically eliminates an awful lot of things that interest me. There's no difference in the Western novel and any other novel, as I said earlier. A Western starts with a beginning and it goes to an end. It's a story about people, and that's the important thing to always remember. Every story is about people—people against the canvas of their times."

BIOGRAPHICAL/CRITICAL SOURCES:

BOOKS

Authors in the News, Volume 2, Gale, 1976.
Contemporary Literary Criticism, Volume 25, Gale, 1983.
Dictionary of Literary Biography Yearbook: 1980, Gale, 1981.
L'Amour, Louis, *Bendigo Shafter,* Dutton, 1978.
Pilkington, William T., editor, *Critical Essays on the Western American Novel,* G. K. Hall, 1980.

PERIODICALS

American Way, April, 1976.
Arizona and the West, autumn, 1978.
Chicago Tribune, June 5, 1984; June 23, 1985; February 25, 1987.
Chicago Tribune Book World, September 9, 1984.
Detroit News, March 31, 1978; June 30, 1985.
Esquire, March 13, 1979.
Globe and Mail (Toronto), May 19, 1984; October 17, 1987.
Lone Star Review, May, 1981.
Los Angeles Times, July 9, 1983; May 30, 1984; August 3, 1986; November 7, 1989.
Los Angeles Times Book Review, March 20, 1983; August 25, 1985; April 3, 1986; August 3, 1986.
Newsweek, November 10, 1975; July 14, 1986.
New Yorker, May 16, 1983.
New York Times, October 21, 1971; September 23, 1983.
New York Times Book Review, November 24, 1974; April 6, 1975; November 30, 1975; January 2, 1977; March 22, 1981; April 24, 1983; July 1, 1984; June 2, 1985; July 6, 1986.
North Dakota Quarterly, summer, 1978.
People, June 9, 1975; July 23, 1984.
Publishers Weekly, October 8, 1973; November 27, 1978; November 4, 1978.
Southwest Review, winter, 1984.
Time, April 29, 1974; December 1, 1980; August 19, 1985; July 21, 1986; August 4, 1986.
Times Literary Supplement, August 26, 1977.
Us, July 25, 1978.
USA Weekend, May 30-June 1, 1986.
Washington Post, March 20, 1981; June 23, 1983; November 30, 1989.
Washington Post Book World, December 12, 1976; March 1, 1981; April 17, 1983; December 2, 1984; June 16, 1985; July 6, 1986; June 14, 1987.
West Coast Review of Books, November, 1978.
Western American Literature, May, 1978, February, 1982.

OBITUARIES:

PERIODICALS

Chicago Tribune, June 19, 1988.
Detroit News, June 13, 1988.
Los Angeles Times, June 13, 1988.
New York Times, June 13, 1988.
Times (London), June 14, 1988.
Washington Post, June 13, 1988.*

LANGE, John
   See CRICHTON, (John) Michael

*   *   *

LANGHORNE, Elizabeth (Coles)   1909-

PERSONAL: Born in 1909 in Bryn Mawr, PA; daughter of Stricker (a physician) and Bertha (Lippincott) Coles; married Harry F. Langhorne, July 18, 1941 (divorced November, 1963); children: John Coles, Elizabeth L., Harry F., Jr. *Education:* Attended Vassar College, 1931. *Politics:* Democrat. *Religion:* Episcopal.

ADDRESSES: Home—Box 186, Route 2, Charlottesville, VA 22901.

CAREER: Thoroughbred horse breeder and sales stable owner in Keene, VA, 1934-42; real estate broker in Vieques, PR, 1964—. Member of executive boards of Girl Scouts of America, Visiting Nurse Association, and Prestwould Foundation; president of Virginia Center for the Creative Arts, 1971.

MEMBER: Farmington Hunt Club, Keswick Hunt Club, Greencroft Club.

WRITINGS:

A History of Christ Church, Glendower, and the Early History of St. Anne's Parish, King Lindsay, 1957.
Jean Skipwith: A Virginia Blue Stocking, Prestwould Foundation, 1966.
Nancy Astor and Her Friends, Praeger, 1974.
The Golden Age of Albemarie, Charlottesville Museum, 1984.
Monticello: A Family Story, Algonquin Books of Chapel Hill, 1987.
A Virginia Family and Its Plantation Houses, University Press of Virginia, 1987.

Contributor to *Saturday Evening Post, New Mexico Quarterly, Virginia Cavalcade,* and *Vassar Quarterly.*

WORK IN PROGRESS: Life at Monticello, a family story.

SIDELIGHTS: Elizabeth Langhorne once told *CA:* "Life seems worth living when there is a work in progress. This includes history and fiction. I write best when I can get away to a colony, preferably the MacDowell Colony in Peterborough, NH. People are my vital interest, individually (fiction) and in the mass (history). Horses and airplanes have long been my major sport interests; now I am declining (gracefully?) into archaeology, land use, walking, and some tennis. I speak French, and always say that one day I will 'really learn' German and Spanish. I have travelled in Europe, and [taken] one trip each to Africa and the Far East. Hopefully South America next."*

LANGTON, Jane (Gillson)   1922-

PERSONAL: Born December 30, 1922, in Boston, MA; daughter of Joseph Lincoln (a geologist) and Grace (Brown) Gillson; married William Langton (a physicist), 1943; children: Christopher, David, Andrew. *Education:* Attended Wellesley College, 1940-42; University of Michigan, B.S., 1944, M.A., 1945; Radcliffe College, M.A., 1948; Boston Museum School of Art, graduate study, 1958-59. *Politics:* Democrat.

ADDRESSES: Home—9 Baker Farm Rd., Lincoln, MA 01773.

CAREER: Writer. Teacher of writing for children at Graduate Center for the Study of Children's Literature, Simmons College, 1979-80, and at Eastern Writers' Conference, Salem State College. Prepared artwork and visual material for "Discovery," an educational program in the natural sciences, WGBH-Channel 2, Boston, 1955-56. Volunteer worker for school and church.

MEMBER: Phi Beta Kappa.

AWARDS, HONORS: Edgar Award nomination, Mystery Writers of America, 1962, for *The Diamond in the Window;* Newbery Honor Book Award, Children's Services Division of American Library Association, 1980, and American Book Award nomination, 1982, both for *The Fledgling;* Nero Wolfe Award, 1984, and Edgar Award nomination, Mystery Writers of America, 1985, both for *Emily Dickinson Is Dead.*

WRITINGS:

JUVENILES

The Majesty of Grace, Harper, 1961, published as *Her Majesty, Grace Jones,* 1972.
The Diamond in the Window, Harper, 1962.
The Swing in the Summerhouse, Harper, 1967.
The Astonishing Stereoscope, Harper, 1971.
The Boyhood of Grace Jones, Harper, 1972.
Paper Chains, Harper, 1977.
The Fledgling, Harper, 1980.
The Fragile Flag, Harper, 1984.
The Hedgehog Boy (picture book), illustrated by Ilse Plume, Harper, 1985.
Salt (picture book), illustrated by Plume, Hyperion Press, 1992.

ADULT SUSPENSE NOVELS

The Transcendental Murder, Harper, 1964, published as *The Minuteman Murder,* Dell, 1976.
Dark Nantucket Moon, Harper, 1975.
The Memorial Hall Murder, Harper, 1978.
Natural Enemy, Ticknor & Fields, 1982.
Emily Dickinson Is Dead, St. Martin's, 1984.

Good and Dead, St. Martin's, 1986.
Murder at the Gardner, St. Martin's, 1988.
The Dante Game, Viking, 1991.
God in Concord, Viking, 1992.

OTHER

Contributor to *Acts of Light,* New York Graphic Society, 1980. Former children's book reviewer for *New York Times Book Review.*

SIDELIGHTS: Jane Langton once told *CA:* "My books start with an interest in a place. This has been most often Concord, Massachusetts, with its several layers of history, both from revolutionary times and from nineteenth-century transcendental times. But it is the present time, littered about with the past, that I seem to want to write about. Putting real children (as real as I can make them) into a real setting (as real as I can copy it) and then pulling some sort of fantasy out of that litter of the past that lies around them—this is what particularly interests me.

"I am lucky [to be] living in the town next to Concord. We go there very often for shopping, and [while] walking or driving one is wading through air which to me seems thick with meaning. The thing I am most afraid of is making a muddle of too many things which are not pulled together into a single unit. But the think I like best is taking a great many things and managing them all somehow in one fist like a complicated sort of cat's cradle."

Langton's *The Fledgling* deals with a group of children from Concord who attempt to persuade the President of the United States to cancel his new "Peace Missile." *New York Times* reviewer Nicholas Lemann describes the book as "completely charming" and adds, "the portrayals of the children themselves are so effortless and true that it seems momentarily impossible that other writers could find it difficult to endow characters that young with distinctive personalities."

BIOGRAPHICAL/CRITICAL SOURCES:

BOOKS

Carr, John C., *The Craft of Crime,* Houghton, 1983.
Something about the Author Autobiography Series, Volume 5, Gale, 1988.

PERIODICALS

New York Times, May 21, 1978.
New York Times Book Review, August 20, 1967; May 16, 1982; November 11, 1984.
Times Literary Supplement, December 4, 1969; April 16, 1970.
Washington Post Book World, December 21, 1980.

LATHROP, Francis
See LEIBER, Fritz (Reuter, Jr.)

*   *   *

LATOW, (Muriel) Roberta   1931-

PERSONAL: Born September 27, 1931, in Springfield, MA; daughter of Sol (in business) and Rose (a housewife; maiden name, Teitelbaum) Latow. *Education:* Whitney School of Interior Design, graduated, 1950.

ADDRESSES: *Home*—Wiltshire, England. *Agent*—Curtis Brown Ltd., 575 Madison Ave., New York, NY 10022.

CAREER: International interior designer in the United States, the Middle East, Europe, and Africa, 1952-81; writer of romance novels, 1981—. Owner of galleries of modern art in Springfield, MA, and New York, NY, 1954-62; collector of artifacts and handcrafts for Brooklyn Museum and Hallmark Card Co.

MEMBER: Authors Guild.

AWARDS, HONORS: Award from *Romantic Times,* 1984, for *Tidal Wave.*

WRITINGS:

ROMANCE NOVELS

Three Rivers, Ballantine, 1981.
Tidal Wave, Ballantine, 1983.
The Soft Warm Rain, Bantam, 1985.
This Stream of Dreams, Bantam, 1987.
White Moon Black Sea, Bantam, 1989.
Cheyney Fox, Fawcett, 1991.
Those Wicked Pleasures, Fawcett, 1992.

WORK IN PROGRESS: A novel.

SIDELIGHTS: Roberta Latow told *CA:* "I have always been deeply involved with art, the art world, and design. My sense of adventure in these fields opened up new horizons for me in my travels. In 1967 I left the United States to live in Greece, and it was there, in 1970, that writing became a focal point.

"My lifetime of interesting work has led me to adventures in foreign places and associations with people from many countries and various walks of life, and my knowledge of ancient and modern art and architecture, artifacts, places, and relationships of my own and others is reflected in my writing. My fascination with heroic men and women and how and why they create the lives they do for themselves, the romantic and erotic core within, the link between the past and the immediate present that affects behavior, and the questions of love and continuity are endlessly interesting to me."

Latow's travels have taken her through Greece, Turkey, the Middle East, Egypt, the Sudan, and Ethiopia. She spent a considerable length of time in Egypt, assembling a vast collection of Coptic art.

* * *

LAURANCE, Alfred D.
See TRALINS, S(andor) Robert

* * *

LAVENDER, David (Sievert) 1910-

PERSONAL: Born February 4, 1910, in Telluride, CO; son of Edgar Norfolk and Edith (Garrigues) Lavender; married Muriel Sharkey, 1990; children: seven children and stepchildren. *Education:* Princeton University, A.B., 1931; Stanford University, graduate study, 1931-32.

ADDRESSES: Home—4771 Thacher Rd., Ojai, CA 93023. *Agent*—Carl Brandt, Brandt & Brandt Literary Agents, Inc., 1501 Broadway, New York, NY 10036.

CAREER: Thacher School, Ojai, CA, faculty member, 1943-70. Consultant to special collections at the library of the University of California, Santa Barbara, 1982-91, and to the California history section of Oakland Museum, 1983-84.

MEMBER: American Society of Historians, Southwest National Parks and Monuments Association (member of board, 1981-91).

AWARDS, HONORS: Commonwealth Club of California medals, 1948, for *The Big Divide,* 1958, for *Land of Giants,* 1975, for *Nothing Seemed Impossible,* and 1989, for *The Way to the Western Sea;* Buffalo Award of New York Westerners, Spur Award of Western Writers of America, and Rupert Hughes Award of Los Angeles Authors Club, all for *Bent's Fort;* Guggenheim fellowship, 1961-62, to study American Fur Co., and 1968-69, to study aspects of the Canadian fur trade; Western Writers of America and American Heritage awards for *The Great West;* Award of Merit, American Association for State and Local History, 1968, for *The Rockies;* Award of Merit, California Historical Society, 1980, for outstanding contributions to California history.

WRITINGS:

One Man's West, Doubleday, 1943, 2nd edition, 1956, reprinted, Bison Books, 1977.
Andy Claybourne (novel), Doubleday, 1946.
The Big Divide, Doubleday, 1948.
Bent's Fort, Doubleday, 1954, reprinted, Bison Books, 1972.

Land of Giants, Doubleday, 1958, reprinted, Bison Books, 1979.
The Story of Cyprus Mines Corporation, Huntington Library, 1962.
Red Mountain (novel), Doubleday, 1963.
Westward Vision, McGraw, 1963, reprinted, Bison Books, 1985.
The First in the Wilderness, Doubleday, 1964, reprinted, University of New Mexico Press, 1979.
The Great West, American Heritage, 1965.
Climax at Buena Vista, Lippincott, 1966.
The Rockies, Harper, 1968, reprinted, Bison Books, 1981.
The Great Persuader, Doubleday, 1970.
California: Land of New Beginnings, Harper, 1972.
Nothing Seemed Impossible, American West, 1975,
California: A Bicentennial History, Norton, 1976.
David Lavender's Colorado, Doubleday, 1976.
Winner Take All, McGraw, 1977.
The Southwest, Harper, 1979.
Colorado River Country, Dutton, 1982.
River Runners of the Grand Canyon, Grand Canyon History Association/University of Arizona Press, 1985.
The Way to the Western Sea, Harper, 1988.
Let Me Be Free: The Nez Perce Tragedy, Harper, 1992.

JUVENILES

Trouble at Tamarack, Westminster, 1943.
Mike Maroney, Raider, Westminster, 1946.
Golden Trek, Westminster, 1948.
The Trail to Santa Fe, Houghton, 1958.
The Story of California, Harper, 1969.

OTHER

Also author of pamphlets for National Park Service. Contributor to *Growing Up Western,* Knopf, 1989. Contributor to *Encyclopaedia Britannica.* Contributor to periodicals, including *Arizona Highways, Wilderness Magazine, National Geographic Traveler, New York Times,* and *New York Herald-Tribune.*

SIDELIGHTS: David Lavender once told *CA:* "This job of mine could hardly be better. I explore the best parts of the American West—backpacking, riding horseback, and sometimes [travelling] in jeeps or rafting, in order to acquire for my writing a sense of immediacy and reality. Then, as I read what others have said on the subject and as I refine my own thoughts during the process of writing, a new sort of energizing takes over, and I find myself looking with new eyes and a new understanding at old scenes, a constant sequence of rediscoveries as it were. No, I don't get too tired of the West; it is too big and too dynamic, and filled with too many choice inhabitants for that."

BIOGRAPHICAL/CRITICAL SOURCES:

PERIODICALS

New York Times, May 9, 1968.
New York Times Book Review, May 10, 1970; August 5, 1973.

*   *   *

LEDBETTER, Ken(neth Lee) 1931-

PERSONAL: Born December 3, 1931, in Willow Springs, MO; son of Isaac Lovejoy Ledbetter and Cynthia Priscilla (Baker) Smith; married Sally Melville; children: Max, Anna Lee, Gary, Jeremy, Caddy. *Education:* Central College (now Central Methodist), A.B., 1956; University of Illinois at Urbana-Champaign, M.A., 1957, Ph.D., 1963.

ADDRESSES: Office—Department of English, University of Waterloo, Ontario, Canada N2L 3G1.

CAREER: Illinois State Normal University (now Illinois State University), Normal, associate professor of American literature, 1959-66; University of Waterloo, Waterloo, Ontario, professor of American literature, 1966—. Visiting professor at American University in Cairo, 1969-71. *Military service:* U.S. Army, 1953-55.

WRITINGS:

(Contributor) Victor Hoar, editor, *The Great Depression,* Copp Clark, 1969.
Too Many Blackbirds (novel), Beaufort Books, 1984.
Not Enough Women (novel), Mosaic, 1986.

Author of novels, *Just Like a Man* and *Valentine.* Also author of screenplay, *Eyes that Went Away.* Contributor of articles and stories to literature journals.

WORK IN PROGRESS: Additional novels.

SIDELIGHTS: Ken Ledbetter once told *CA:* "The only agony greater than writing is the agony I must endure if I don't."

*   *   *

LEIBER, Fritz (Reuter, Jr.) 1910-1992
(Francis Lathrop)

PERSONAL: Born December 24, 1910, in Chicago, IL; died September 5, 1992; son of Fritz (a Shakespearean actor) and Virginia (a Shakespearean actress; maiden name, Bronson) Leiber; married Jonquil Stephens (a writer), January 16, 1936 (died September, 1969); married Margo Skinner, May 15, 1992 (died January 16, 1993); children: (first marriage) Justin. *Education:* University of

Chicago, Ph.B., 1932; attended Episcopal General Theological Seminary.

CAREER: Episcopal minister at two missionary churches in New Jersey, 1932-33; Shakespearean actor with father's company under name Francis Lathrop, 1934-36; Consolidated Book Publishers, Chicago, IL, editor, 1937-41; Occidental College, Los Angeles, CA, instructor in speech and drama, 1941-42; Douglas Aircraft Co., Santa Monica, CA, precision inspector, 1942-44; *Science Digest,* Chicago, associate editor, 1944-56; free-lance writer, 1956-92. Lecturer at science fiction and fantasy writing workshops, Clarion State College, summers, 1968, 1969, 1970, and at San Francisco State University.

MEMBER: Science Fiction Writers of America.

AWARDS, HONORS: Guest of honor at World Science Fiction Convention, 1951, 1979; Hugo Award, World Science Fiction Convention, best novel, 1958, for *The Big Time,* and 1965, for *The Wanderer,* best novelette, 1968, for "Gonna Roll the Bones," best novella, 1970, for "Ship of Shadows," and 1971, for "Ill Met in Lankhmar," and best short story, 1975, for "Catch That Zeppelin"; Nebula Award, Science Fiction Writers of America, best novelette, 1968, for "Gonna Roll the Bones," best novella, 1971, for "Ill Met in Lankhmar," best short story, 1975, for "Catch That Zeppelin," and Grand Master, 1981, for lifetime contribution to the genre; Mrs. Ann Radcliffe Award, Count Dracula Society, 1970; Gandalf Award, World Science Fiction Convention, 1975; August Derleth Fantasy Award, 1976, for "Belsen Express"; World Fantasy Award, World Fantasy Convention, best short fiction, 1976, for "Belsen Express," and best novel, 1978, for *Our Lady of Darkness;* World Fantasy Life Award, World Fantasy Convention, 1976, for life achievement; Locus Award for best collection, 1986, for *The Ghost Light.*

WRITINGS:

SCIENCE FICTION AND FANTASY NOVELS

Gather, Darkness! (originally published in *Astounding Stories,* 1943), Pellegrini & Cudahy, 1950, new edition, Grosset, 1951.
(With James Blish and Fletcher Pratt) *Witches Three,* Twayne, 1952.
Conjure Wife (originally published in *Unknown Worlds,* 1943; also see below), Twayne, 1953, published as *Burn, Witch, Burn,* Berkley, 1962.
The Green Millennium, Abelard, 1953.
The Sinful Ones (bound with *Bulls, Blood, and Passion,* by David Williams), Universal Publishing, 1953, published separately as *You're All Alone,* Ace Books, 1972.
Destiny Times Three, Galaxy, 1957, bound with *Riding the Torch,* by Norman Spinrad, Dell, 1978.

The Silver Eggheads (originally published in *Magazine of Fantasy and Science Fiction*, 1958), Ballantine, 1961.

The Big Time [and] *The Mind Spider and Other Stories* (also see below), Ace Books, 1961.

The Wanderer, Ballantine, 1964.

Tarzan and the Valley of Gold, Ballantine, 1966.

A Specter Is Haunting Texas, Walker, 1969.

The Big Time, Gregg, 1976.

Our Lady of Darkness (also see below), Berkley, 1978.

Conjure Wife [and] *Our Lady of Darkness*, Tor Books, 1991.

SCIENCE FICTION AND FANTASY SHORT STORIES

Night's Black Agents, Arkham, 1947, abridged edition published as *Tales from Night's Black Agents*, Ballantine, 1961.

The Girl with Hungry Eyes and Other Stories, Avon, 1949.

Shadows with Eyes, Ballantine, 1962.

A Pail of Air, Ballantine, 1964.

Ships to the Stars (bound with *The Million Year Hunt*, by K. Bulmer), Ace Books, 1964.

The Night of the Wolf, Ballantine, 1966.

The Secret Songs, Hart-Davis, 1968.

Night Monsters, Ace Books, 1969, revised edition, Gollancz, 1974.

The Best of Fritz Leiber, edited by Angus Wells, Doubleday, 1974, revised edition, Sidgwick & Jackson, 1974.

The Book of Fritz Leiber, DAW Books, 1974.

The Second Book of Fritz Leiber, DAW Books, 1975.

The Worlds of Fritz Leiber, Ace Books, 1976.

The Mind Spider and Other Stories, Ace Books, 1976.

Heroes and Horrors, edited by Stuart D. Schiff, Whispers Press, 1978.

The Change War, Gregg Press, 1978.

Bazaar of the Bizarre, Donald Grant, 1978.

Ship of Shadows, Gollancz, 1979, (bound with *No Truce with Kings*, by Poul Anderson), Tor Books, 1989.

The Ghost Light: Masterworks of Science Fiction and Fantasy, Berkley, 1984.

"FAFHRD AND THE GRAY MOUSER" SERIES

Two Sought Adventure: Exploits of Fafhrd and the Gray Mouser (short stories), Gnome Press, 1957.

Swords against Wizardry (short stories), Ace Books, 1968.

Swords in the Mist (short stories), Ace Books, 1968.

The Swords of Lankhmar (novel), Ace Books, 1968.

Swords and Deviltry (novel), Ace Books, 1970.

Swords against Death (short stories), Ace Books, 1970.

Swords and Ice Magic (short stories), Gregg, 1977.

Rime Isle (short stories), Whispers Press, 1977.

The Knight and Knave of Swords (short stories), Morrow, 1988.

OTHER

The Demons of the Upper Air (verse), Roy A. Squires, 1969.

(With wife, Jonquil Leiber) *Sonnets to Jonquil and All* (verse), Roy A. Squires, 1978.

(Editor with Stuart D. Schiff) *The World Fantasy Awards 2*, Doubleday, 1980.

In the Beginning, illustrated by Alicia Austin, Cheap Street, 1983.

Ill Met in Lankhmar [and] *The Fair in Emain Macha*, Tor Books, 1990.

The Leiber Chronicles: Fifty Years of Fritz Leiber, edited by Martin H. Greenberg, Dark Harvest, 1990.

Work appears in numerous anthologies. Contributor to books, including *The Howard Phillips Lovecraft Memorial Symposium*, edited by Steven Eisner, privately printed, 1958, Science Fiction Society, 1963; *In Memoriam: Clark Ashton Smith*, edited by Jack L. Chalker, Mirage Press, 1963; *The Conan Swordbook*, edited by L. Sprague de Camp and George H. Scithers, Mirage Press, 1969; *Essays Lovecraftian*, edited by Darrell Schweitzer, T-K Graphics, 1976; and *Robert Bloch: A Bio-Bibliography*, Graeme Flanagan (Canberra City), 1979. Author of introduction of *The Creature Feature Movie Guide; or, An A to Z Encyclopedia of Fantastic Films; or, Is There a Mad Doctor in the House?*, by John Stanley, illustrated by Ken Davis, Creatures at Large, 1981, and of the introduction of *As Green as Emeraude: Collected Poems of Margo Skinner*, by Margo Skinner, Dawn Heron Press, 1990. Contributor of over two hundred short stories to *Unknown, Fantastic, Weird Tales, Magazine of Fantasy and Science Fiction*, and other magazines.

ADAPTATIONS: Conjure Wife was adapted for film as *Weird Woman*, Universal, 1944, as *Conjure Wife* (television film), NBC-TV, 1960, and as *Burn, Witch, Burn*, American International, 1962; Leiber's short stories, "The Girl with the Hungry Eyes," 1970, and "The Dead Man," 1971, were adapted for Rod Sterling's *Night Gallery* television series; *The Big Time* was adapted into a stage play; the "Fafhrd and the Gray Mouser" series was adapted into a board game by TSR Games.

SIDELIGHTS: Award-winning fantasy and science fiction writer Fritz Leiber was renowned for his adept depictions of the human condition in the various future worlds he created. His numerous short stories and novels are filled with solid characterizations and distinct imagery, and are skillfully set in rational and modern atmospheres brimming over with horror and superstition. "While other science fiction writers were producing adventures that spanned the galaxies," maintained Jeff Frane in his *Fritz Leiber*, "Leiber dealt with *people*, not in the mass but as individuals. It is perhaps this, his concern with and empathy for people as thinking, feeling, *unique* entities . . . that has made Fritz Leiber one of the best-loved creators of speculative fiction."

Although Leiber wrote a wide variety of science fiction, fantasy, and horror stories, he was best known for his sword and sorcery adventures featuring the two swashbuckling characters Fafhrd and the Gray Mouser. These adventures, written over a period of some forty years, are noted for their witty and colorful language, fast-paced plots, tongue-in-cheek humor, and eroticism. Leiber, writing in the author's note to *The Swords of Lankhmar,* described the pair of adventurers as "rogues through and through, though each has in him a lot of humanity and at least a diamond chip of the spirit of true adventure. They drink, they feast, they wench, they brawl, they steal, they gamble, and surely they hire out their swords to powers that are only a shade better, if that, than the villains."

Fafhrd, a tall, brawny warrior from the Cold Waste, and the Gray Mouser, a small, quick-moving thief, together seek adventure, romance, and treasure in the world of Nehwon, and invariably encounter crafty wizards, beautiful women, dark horrors, and plenty of sword-wielding adversaries. "In story after story," Lin Carter said of the series in his *Imaginary Worlds,* "[Leiber] has captained us on a voyage of exploration and discovery through the magical lands where his fascinating pair of delicious rogues dwell." "These adventure fantasies," Diana Waggoner wrote in *The Hills of Faraway,* "are distinguished by a sophisticated style and an excellent sense of humor."

Fafhrd and the Gray Mouser grew out of a correspondence between Leiber and his friend Harry Fisher during the 1930s. "Harry and I began to create imaginary worlds," Leiber recalled in an interview with Darrell Schweitzer for *Science Fiction Voices #1,* "solely for the purpose of writing about them in our letters. . . . One of the imaginary worlds originally invented by Harry was the world of Fafhrd and the Gray Mouser." Leiber's son, Justin Leiber, wrote in *Starship* that the two characters were loosely based on his father (as Fafhrd) and Fisher (as the Gray Mouser). "When I was a kid," Justin remembered, "both my mother Jonquil and I called Fritz 'Faf' or 'Fafhrd' more than anything else." Leiber and Fisher also invented the pair's home base, the city of Lankhmar, a treacherous, labyrinthian metropolis of evil sorcerers, corrupt priests, and numerous back-alley thieves (organized into a "thieves' guild," of course), widely noted for its easy accommodation of nefarious activity. Their world of Nehwon, vaguely reminiscent of both ancient Rome and medieval Europe, is thought by its inhabitants to be contained within a bubble of air floating in a cosmic sea. Perhaps it is, since Nehwon is a world in which magic works and magical events are commonplace.

The first Fafhrd and the Gray Mouser story, written in 1937, was read and commented upon by the late horror story writer H. P. Lovecraft. Leiber had written to Lovecraft after reading and admiring some of his stories and the two men began a regular correspondence. When Leiber mentioned that he also wrote, Lovecraft asked to see one of his stories. After reading it, Lovecraft circulated it among several editors and introduced Leiber to such writers as Robert Bloch and August Derleth. In his interview with Schweitzer, Leiber admitted that Lovecraft "had a big effect on my writing and continues to do so." Lovecraft's influence can particularly be seen in Leiber's novel *Our Lady of Darkness.* Raymond L. Hough, writing in *Library Journal,* noted that in *Our Lady* Leiber, like Lovecraft, uses "increasingly fantastic events [to] slowly reveal a brooding, and unnatural horror." In other ways, Leiber modified the standard elements of a Lovecraftian horror story. He set the story in urban California, for example, rather than in Lovecraft's inevitable rural New England. A Lovecraft-style ancient curse is blended with the ideas of modern psychology. "Lovecraft fans will recognize the debt," Hough observed, "but they'll enjoy the differences too." Algis Budrys of the *Magazine of Fantasy and Science Fiction* called *Our Lady* "a major work of fantasy, skillfully created and unimaginably imagined. . . . There are things in this book that no one has ever thought of before."

Before beginning his writing career, Leiber appeared in the films *Camille,* produced by Metro-Goldwyn-Mayer in 1937, and *Equinox.* His father, Fritz Leiber, Sr., was a professional actor who appeared on the stage and in some forty films. Leiber noted the theatrical influence in his writing. Speaking to Schweitzer, he remembered that "when I was just a little kid I was exposed to the plays of Shakespeare. . . . I do at times tend to fall into a kind of Shakespearean poetry in my writing. And also I tend to cast stories in a dramatic form. I visualize scenes in my stories as if they were scenes in a play on the stage."

Describing Leiber's place in contemporary science fiction, Budrys wrote: "Leiber is one of the best science fiction writers in the world. [He is] one SF writer who has somehow made the Hugo and the Nebula [Awards] seem inadequate." Budrys believed that Leiber's place belonged in mainstream literature. "Leiber is a giant," he maintained, "[a] figure of stature in 20th century literature."

BIOGRAPHICAL/CRITICAL SOURCES:

BOOKS

Carter, Lin, *Imaginary Worlds,* Ballantine, 1973.
Contemporary Literary Criticism, Volume 25, Gale, 1983.
Dictionary of Literary Biography, Volume 8: *Twentieth-Century American Science Fiction Writers,* Gale, 1981.

Frane, Jeff, *Fritz Leiber,* Starmont House, 1980.

Leiber, Fritz, *The Swords of Lankhmar,* Ace Books, 1968.

Morgan, Chris, *Fritz Leiber: A Bibliography, 1934-1979,* Morgenstern, 1979.

Moscowitz, Sam, *Seekers of Tomorrow,* World Publishing, 1966.

Schweitzer, Darrell, *Science Fiction Voices #1,* Borgo Press, 1979.

Staircar, Tom, *Fritz Leiber,* Ungar, 1983.

Waggoner, Diana, *The Hills of Faraway: A Guide to Fantasy,* Atheneum, 1978.

Walker, Paul, *Speaking of Science Fiction: The Paul Walker Interviews,* Luna, 1978.

PERIODICALS

Amazing Stories, October, 1951.

Analog, May, 1951.

Anduril, Number 6, 1976.

Books and Bookmen, February, 1970.

Fantastic Stories, February, 1970.

Fantasy Crossroads, Number 8, 1976.

Future Science Fiction, November, 1950.

Galaxy, May, 1954.

Library Journal, February 15, 1977.

Luna Monthly, July, 1969.

Magazine of Fantasy and Science Fiction, September, 1968; July, 1969 (special Fritz Leiber issue); September, 1978; February, 1979.

New Statesman, June 6, 1969.

New Worlds, March, 1969.

New York Herald Tribune Book Review, December 21, 1952.

New York Times Book Review, April 14, 1974.

Observer, November 9, 1969.

Punch, November 13, 1968.

Saturday Review, January 10, 1953.

Science Fiction Review, August, 1970; February, 1978; September/October, 1978.

Starship, summer, 1979.

Times (London), April 26, 1990.

Times Literary Supplement, June 15, 1967; January 8, 1970; May 31, 1974.

Venture Science Fiction, August, 1969.

Washington Post Book World, March 5, 1978.

OBITUARIES:

PERIODICALS

Locus, October, 1992; November, 1992 (memorial issue).

Time, September 21, 1992, p. 21.*

LEITCH, Maurice   1933-

PERSONAL: Born July 5, 1933, in Muckamore, Antrim County, Northern Ireland; son of Andrew (a linen worker) and Jean Leitch. *Education:* Attended Stranmillis Training College, 1950-53.

ADDRESSES: Home—32 Windermere Ave., London NW6 6LN, England. *Agent*—Deborah Rogers Ltd., 20 Powis Mews, London W11, England.

CAREER: Antrim Primary School, Antrim County, Northern Ireland, instructor of general subjects, 1954-62; British Broadcasting Corporation, Belfast, Northern Ireland, features producer, 1962-70, radio drama producer in London, England, 1970-89; writer.

AWARDS, HONORS: Fiction Prize, *Guardian* (London), 1969, for *Poor Lazarus;* Whitbread Prize for Fiction, 1981, for *Silver's City;* Pye Award for most promising writer new to television, 1981.

WRITINGS:

NOVELS

The Liberty Lad, MacGibbon & Kee, 1965, Pantheon, 1966.

Poor Lazarus, MacGibbon & Kee, 1969.

Stamping Ground, Secker & Warburg, 1975.

Silver's City, Secker & Warburg, 1981.

Burning Bridges, Hutchinson, 1989.

Also author of *In Beulah Land,* 1993.

TELEPLAYS

Rifleman, British Broadcasting Corporation (BBC-TV), 1980.

Guests of the Nation, BBC-TV, 1983.

Gates of Gold, BBC-TV, 1983.

Chinese Whispers, BBC-TV, 1989.

OTHER

A Little Bit of Heaven (radio play), BBC-Radio, 1978.

Chinese Whispers (novella), Hutchinson, 1987.

The Hands of Cheryl Boyd and Other Stories, Hutchinson, 1987.

SIDELIGHTS: In a succession of novels and short stories, Maurice Leitch has rendered a uniformly dark portrait of his native Northern Ireland. *Times Literary Supplement* reviewer Patricia Craig noted that "Leitch's subjects are viciousness, corruption, and varieties of power," and that he is "adept at evoking a mood of dust and ashes." Leitch sets his writing amidst the civil strife of Northern Ireland (an area also known as Ulster). His characters come from the Protestant side of the region's religious and political division, and they are on intimate terms with the violence and destruction that has marked Ulster's recent history.

Despite their Protestant identity, the individuals in Leitch's fiction experience an isolated existence. "His heroes are always in some sense outsiders, even in their native province," wrote Anne-Marie Conway in the *Times Literary Supplement.* Kenny, the protagonist of *Chinese Whispers,* lives within the walls of an insane asylum and has difficulty interacting with both the outside world and with the patients he takes care of; Sonny and Hazel in *Burning Bridges* have thrown over their past obligations to wander through England in a haze of drugs and alcohol; Silver, a former Protestant terrorist and the outlaw hero of *Silver's City,* escapes from jail but is unable to fully embrace his cause or his past actions. Plagued by their isolation and by the destructive conditions that surround them, the people who inhabit Leitch's writing find few happy endings. As Craig wrote, "Leitch sees to it that his characters' facile expectations are not fulfilled."

Reviewers have, at times, criticized the unremitting harshness of Leitch's fictional world. Conway's review of *Burning Bridges* suggested that Leitch's dim view of events left the novelist "unable to work up much sympathy or affection for his characters." Likewise, Craig, in her review of *Silver's City,* complained that the author "eschews every device that might make the bleakness, the violence, and the bad ends more palatable." Despite this reservation, Craig found *Silver's City* to be a "striking addition to a body of work which is engaged in exposing and dramatizing the characteristic defects of the Northern Irish." Further praise for Leitch's depiction of Ulster came from Paul Theroux when he announced that *Silver's City* had received the Whitbread Literary Award: "This is an unusual book about a difficult subject, . . . but it is written with such insight and compassion, bringing art to bear on the lives of people living in a beleaguered city, that it is impossible not to admire this novel."

Though he is noted for his emphasis on Northern Ireland, Leitch feels a strong connection to several authors from the southern United States. He once told *CA:* "All my novels deal with Ulster's 'poor whites,' the Protestant working people. Thus, my influences are not Irish as such, but more Faulkner, Flannery O'Connor, and Eudora Welty, for obvious reasons. My ancestral links are very strong in the southern United States, culturally and ethnically speaking, because my forebears became the Scotch-Irish Americans of the eighteenth and nineteenth centuries. I'd like to pursue this thread in another book."

BIOGRAPHICAL/CRITICAL SOURCES:

PERIODICALS

Times (London), October 28, 1981; November 26, 1981; March 23, 1989.
Times Literary Supplement, October 2, 1981, p. 1119; November 6-12, 1987, p. 1226; April 14-20, 1989, p. 403.

LEMESURIER, Peter
See BRITTON, Peter Ewart

*   *   *

LEROE, Ellen W(hitney) 1949-

PERSONAL: Born April 26, 1949, in Newark, NJ; daughter of Bernard William (a mechanical engineer) and Iris (an educational secretary; maiden name, Brienza) Leroe. *Education:* University of Leicester, certificate, 1970; Elmira College, B.A., 1971.

ADDRESSES: Home and office—2211 Stockton St., No. 409, San Francisco, CA 94133. *Agent*—Linda Allen Literary Agency, 1949 Green St., No. 5, San Francisco, CA 94123.

CAREER: Hahne's (retail store), Newark, NJ, fashion buyer, 1971-74; free-lance writer and illustrator, 1974-76; International Engineering Co., San Francisco, CA, editorial assistant, 1976-77; San Francisco Junior Chamber of Commerce, San Francisco, administrative manager, 1977-79; full-time free-lance writer, 1979—.

MEMBER: Media Alliance, Society of Children's Book Writers.

AWARDS, HONORS: First prize, San Francisco Fair Poetry Competition, 1985.

WRITINGS:

Single Bed Blues (poems), Tandem Press, 1982.
Confessions of a Teenage TV Addict (young adult), Lodestar, 1982.
Enter Laughing (romance novel), Silhouette, 1983.
The Plot against the Pom-Pom Queen (young adult), Lodestar, 1983.
Give and Take (romance novel), Silhouette, 1984.
Robot Romance (young adult science fiction novel), Harper, 1984.
Robot Raiders (young adult science fiction), Harper, 1985.
Have a Heart, Cupid Delaney (young adult), Lodestar, 1985.
The Peanut Butter Poltergeist (juvenile), Lodestar, 1986.
Personal Business (young adult; novelization of ABC-TV *Afterschool Special*), Bantam, 1986.
H.O.W.L. High (juvenile), Archway, 1989.
Meet Your Match, Cupid Delaney (young adult), Lodestar, 1990.
Love's in Harmony (romance novel), Cora-Verlag (Germany), 1990.
Leap Frog Friday (juvenile), Lodestar, 1991.
Heebie Jeebies at H.O.W.L. High (juvenile), Archway, 1991.
Ghost Dog (juvenile), Hyperion Books, 1992.
H.O.W.L. High Goes Bats! (juvenile), Archway, 1992.

Contributor of articles, poems, and short stories to periodicals, including *Cosmopolitan, National Business Woman, Highlights for Children, Good Housekeeping, Frequent Flyer, Total Fitness,* and *California Living.*

WORK IN PROGRESS: An adult farce action novel, *Involved;* a children's series involving "Ghost Dog," based on her 1992 book of the same title; an adult murder mystery series starring magician sleuth Jeremy Dare.

SIDELIGHTS: Ellen W. Leroe once told *CA:* "After getting off the roller coaster of my own adolescence in the late 1960s—shaken and somewhat thankful—I've decided that the ride was fun after all and definitely worth writing about. Through re-reading my old high school diaries and happily befriending a family of four teenagers I have become a Born Again Teen. I enjoy reading about young adults, writing about them, and, most importantly, talking and listening to them.

"Because I put so much of myself and my own experiences into my novels I tend to focus on main characters confronting, and eventually successfully altering, their insecure and vulnerable self-images. I start with a crisis—a girl who's hopelessly addicted to soap operas (*Confessions of a Teenage TV Addict*), a boy who bucks authority in a computer high school (*Robot Romance*), a teen whose use of sarcasm is shutting out friends and dates (*Enter Laughing*)—and then I mix in complications such as well-meaning but misguided friends, strict parents, and tension with the opposite sex. But the true growth and action come with the main character's discovery that the answers have been hidden within himself the whole time.

"Humor plays a strong part in all my writing, as it does in my own life. I strive to make my dialogue as realistic and as natural as possible. Basically I write about the subjects that interest me most. Those seem to be the subjects that also interest teens: becoming popular without selling yourself short, realizing that other things in life are more important than popularity, and learning to cope with such problems as being overweight, possessing a hyperactive funnybone, having a less than loving and supportive brother or sister, or parents that are too demanding. I try to impart a personal message with my books, but not a heavy-handed moralistic one. I respect young adults; they are bright and intelligent enough to ask the right questions. I don't write to preach but to entertain. And, hopefully, in the entertaining I can give my readers a new perspective about their problems, which will enable them to form their own conclusions.

"Taking the plunge into full-time writing was the most difficult thing I ever chose to do. Now, ten years and sixteen published books later, it is still the most difficult thing I chose to do, but it is also the most rewarding, the most personally satisfying, and the most liberating. The nine-to-five job syndrome is one I consciously set out to avoid. Though I often become discouraged when checks are late or when publishers reject my material, an inner voice still urges me to keep going. As Henry Ford so succinctly put it, 'You can't build a reputation on what you are GOING to do.'"

* * *

LEVOY, Myron

PERSONAL: Born in New York, NY; married; wife's name, Beatrice; children: Deborah, David. *Education:* Purdue University, M.Sc.

CAREER: Writer. Previously worked as chemical engineer.

AWARDS, HONORS: *Book World* honor book, 1972, and Children's Book Showcase selection, 1973, both for *The Witch of Fourth Street, and Other Stories; Alan and Naomi* was named a *Boston Globe-Horn Book* Award honor book and an American Book Award finalist, both in 1978, and in translation was awarded the Dutch Silver Pencil Award, 1981, the Austrian State Prize for Children's Literature, 1981, and the German State Prize for Children's Literature, 1982; best book for young adults, American Library Association, 1981, for *A Shadow like a Leopard,* and 1986, for *Pictures of Adam.*

WRITINGS:

A Necktie in Greenwich Village (novel), Vanguard, 1968.

JUVENILES

Penny Tunes and Princesses, Harper, 1972.
The Witch of Fourth Street, and Other Stories, Harper, 1972.
Alan and Naomi, Harper, 1977.
A Shadow like a Leopard, Harper, 1981.
Three Friends, Harper, 1984.
The Hanukkah of Great-Uncle Otto, Jewish Publication Society, 1984.
Pictures of Adam, Harper, 1986.
The Magic Hat of Mortimer Wintergreen, Harper, 1988.
Kelly 'n' Me, HarperCollins, 1992.

PLAYS

Eli and Emily, produced in New York City, 1969.
The Sun Is a Red Dwarf (one-act), produced Off-Off Broadway at New York Theatre Ensemble, 1969.
Sweet Tom (two-act), produced Off-Off Broadway at the Playbox, 1969.
Footsteps (produced in New York City, 1970), Breakthrough, 1971.
Smudge, produced in New York City, 1971.

OTHER

Contributor of short stories and poems to periodicals, including *Antioch Review, Massachusetts Review,* and *New York Quarterly.*

Alan and Naomi has been published in German and Dutch.

ADAPTATIONS: A theatrical film, *Alan and Naomi,* based on his juvenile novel of the same title, was released throughout the United States in early 1992.

SIDELIGHTS: Myron Levoy's *The Witch of Fourth Street, and Other Stories* consists of eight short stories about the immigrants who settled in New York City's lower East Side in the 1920s. Natalie Babbit observes in *Book World:* "[These stories] have extraordinary freshness and charm. . . . But Myron Levoy does not compromise with truth: there is pain too, and frustration—and in the final story, death. What makes this such a good book is the author's compassion, imagination, and humor; his clear eye for detail and craftsman's sense of what language means and can be made to do. It is a first book for children by a first-rate writer."

Levoy once told *CA:* "In my work for children and adults, my continuing concern has been for the 'outsider,' the loner. The Jewish boy facing anti-Semitism and the deeply troubled refugee girl he befriends (*Alan and Naomi*); the bisexual girl who believes she's losing her only friend and the sensitive chess prodigy who feels alone and strange (*Three Friends*); the ghetto boy, torn between two worlds, who carries a knife but writes poetry (*A Shadow like a Leopard*)—all must come to terms with and face their own uniqueness. Their stories are open-ended; there are no pat solutions, but rather, growth and discovery, with more struggles ahead to be met, one hopes, with greater strength and insight."

BIOGRAPHICAL/CRITICAL SOURCES:

BOOKS

Donelson, Kenneth L., and Alleen Pace Nilsen, *Literature for Today's Young Adults,* 2nd edition, Scott, Foresman, 1985.
Gallo, Donald R., *Speaking for Ourselves,* National Council of Teachers of English, 1990.
Lipson, Eden Ross, *The New York Times Parent's Guide to the Best Books for Children,* Times Books, 1988.
Trelease, Jim, *The Read-Aloud Handbook,* Penguin Books, 1985.

PERIODICALS

Book World, May 7, 1972.
Horn Book, December, 1977; July/August, 1986; September/October, 1988.

New York Times Book Review, June 18, 1972; November 13, 1977.

*   *   *

LIBERMAN, Anatoly   1937-

PERSONAL: Born March 10, 1937, in Leningrad, U.S.S.R. (now St. Petersburg, Russia); immigrated to United States, 1975, naturalized citizen, 1981; son of Simon (an engineer) and Ida (a music teacher; maiden name, Ashmyan) Liberman; married Sofya Slavina (a painter), April 30, 1969; children: Mark. *Education:* Hertzen Pedagogical Institute, Leningrad, B.A., 1959; graduate study at University of Leningrad, 1965; Academy of Science, Leningrad, D.Phil., 1972.

ADDRESSES: Home—312 Seymour Pl. S.E., Minneapolis, MN 55141. *Office*—Department of German, University of Minnesota, 9 Pleasant St. S.E., Minneapolis, MN 55455.

CAREER: Nazia Boarding School, Zhikharevo, U.S.S.R., teacher of English, 1959-62; Polytechnic Institute, Leningrad, U.S.S.R., instructor in English, 1962-65; Academy of Sciences, Leningrad, research fellow in Scandinavian at Institute of Linguistics, 1965-75; University of Minnesota—Twin Cities, Minneapolis, Hill Visiting Professor, 1975-76, associate professor, 1976-78, professor of Germanic philology, 1978—. Visiting professor at Harvard University, 1977, and at the Albert-Ludwigs Universitaet, Freiburg, Germany, 1988. Gives readings of poetry translations.

MEMBER: International Association of Phonetic Science, Modern Language Association of America, Linguistic Society of America, Society for the Advancement of Scandinavian Study, American Lexicographical Society, European Association for Lexicography.

AWARDS, HONORS: Guggenheim fellow, 1981; Cambridge University fellow, 1984; second prize, International Garik Contests of Russian Emigre Poetry, 1984, for the lyric "Proshchaite, slovno Sirano"; Fulbright fellow, 1988.

WRITINGS:

(With V. P. Beliatskaia) *Talks on Art,* Uchpedgiz (Leningrad), 1963.
Trade, Uchpedgiz, 1966.
Islandkaja Prosodika (title means "Icelandic Prosody"), Nauka (Leningrad), 1971.
Germanic Accentology, Volume 1, University of Minnesota Press, 1982.
(Editor, translator, and author of introductory essay and commentary) Mikhail Lermontov, *Mikhail Lermon-*

tov: *Major Poetical Works,* University of Minnesota Press, 1983.

(Editor and author of introduction and commentary) Vladimir Propp, *Vladimir Propp: The Theory and History of Folklore,* University of Minnesota Press, 1984.

(Editor and author of notes and introductory essay) Stefan Einarsson, *Stefan Einarsson: Studies in Germanic Philology,* H. Buske (Hamburg, Germany), 1986.

(Editor, translator, and author of introductory essay) N. S. Trubetzkoy, *N. S. Trubetzkoy: Writings on Literature,* University of Minnesota Press, 1990.

(Editor, cotranslator, and author of postscript) N. S. Trubetzkoy, *N. S. Trubetzkoy: The Legacy of Genghis Khan,* Michigan Slavic Publications, 1991.

(Editor, translator, and author of introductory essay and commentary) Fedor Tyutchev, *On the Heights of Creation: Lyrics of Fedor Tyutchev,* JAI Press, 1992.

Contributor to journals, including *Journal of English and Germanic Philology, Scandinavian Studies, Semiotica, Phonetica, Linguistics,* and *General Linguistics.*

WORK IN PROGRESS: Editing, translating, and writing commentary and introduction for *The Best of Evgeny Boratynsky.*

SIDELIGHTS: In *Mikhail Lermontov: Major Poetical Works,* editor and translator Anatoly Liberman presents the poetry of Mikhail Lermontov, an early nineteenth-century writer whose poetic legacy is considered second only to that of his contryman Aleksander Pushkin in their native Russia. Reviewing the volume for the *New York Times Book Review,* David Bethea called Liberman's translations "remarkable . . . a transposition of Lermontov's lyric and narrative poetry, a poetry that is all atmosphere and ensemble, to a linguistic environment long hostile to romantic formulas—in English that does justice to the original." The critic remarked that while purists would take issue with some of Liberman's departures from the literal text, "the majority of the translator's solutions are ingenious and successful. Many of Lermontov's best-loved and most-anthologized works . . . are rendered with their elusive ensembles, their rhythm, rhyme sense and central meaning, intact." Bethea concluded that Liberman's work "is the first successful rendering of the major part of Lermontov's poetic legacy into English, and he has supplied a fine introduction, an informed commentary and helpful facing text in Russian."

Liberman told *CA:* "I have been writing and translating poetry all my life. My native language is Russian; my first acquaintance with English goes back to 1945, when I was eight. I added German at college and French and the Scandinavian languages (especially Icelandic) still later. In the Soviet Union, I translated English and Icelandic poetry into Russian (Shakespeare, Coleridge, Robert Louis

Stevenson, Oscar Wilde, Jon Helgason, Old English and Old Icelandic poetry), but only a few translations of Shakespeare's sonnets and three lyrics from modern Icelandic were published there (in *Sever;* later, another batch of sonnets appeared in *Vremia i my,* published in Israel). My scholarly life began in 1954, in my freshman year at the Hertzen Pedagogical Institute and continued at the university and at the Academy of Sciences, all in Leningrad—linguistics, medieval literature, folklore, and poetics. In the United States, I continued to work in Germanic philology and finally, for the first time, met my colleagues from all over the world.

"In the United States, I decided to try to translate into English. I started with Lermontov (1814-41) because I remembered most of his poems by heart. As the number of translated lines grew, I realized that without extensive commentary Lermontov's texts could not be appreciated as much as they deserved. *Mikhail Lermontov: Major Poetical Works* is the result of my work with this poet. Like all translators from the Russian, I had to decide for myself whether I wanted my verse to sound more like modern (or nineteenth-century) English poetry or more like the original—in its metrical and rhyme scheme. I chose the second alternative. Some of my critics disagreed with my method, while others accepted the book on my terms; there have been over twenty reviews of *Mikhail Lermontov,* and most of them are favorable (the most visible of them, even laudatory).

"My next major project was the translation of Fedor Tyutchev (1803-73), one of the subtlest masters of short lyrics in any language but little-known in the West outside Slavic circles. He is one-third of the golden age of Russian poetry (the other two-thirds are Pushkin and Lermontov). My new translations are more faithful to the original wording and, I hope, faithful to the spirit of Tyutchev's poetry. This time the introductory essay and commentary are also addressed to scholars and not only to the general public. Eight lyrics from this volume appeared in *Poetry World* (Volume 1, 1986). I discussed my method of translation in two articles (*Poetry World,* Volume 1, 1986, and *International Journal of Slavic Linguistics and Poetics,* Volume 33, 1986); my analyses of Tyutchev's style can be found in the book *In Honorem Georgii Lotman* (1984) and in *Russian Language Journal* (Volume 41, 1987, Volume 43, 1989).

"In this country, I constantly feel that I am a messenger from another world. An edition of [the works of Vladimir] Propp, an outstanding Russian folklorist, is an outcome of this missionary spirit. The book was received very well and became a local bestseller. Putting a distinguished scholar 'in context' and evaluating his activities from several points of view is an activity that has great appeal to me. I have also written a monograph-length essay on the famous Russian scholar M. I. Steblin-Kamenskij (a supplement to the American edition of his *Myth*) and *Stefan Einarsson: Studies in Germanic Philology* (Einarsson was an outstanding Icelandic philologist who worked at Johns Hopkins University for thirty-five years). I have similar plans for another great Russian scholar.

"In 1990 and 1991 I brought out two volumes of N. S. Trubetzkoy's writing—the first on literature, the second on history and politics. Trubetzkoy (1891-1938) was one of the founders of European structuralism, a man of genius, and it was especially interesting to acquaint readers in the English-speaking world with his works on non-linguistic matters (he wrote in Russian, German, and French). The collapse of the Soviet Union makes his articles and books collected under the title *The Legacy of Genghis Khan* 'topical' reading.

"The Russian poet that I chose to translate after Lermontov and Tyutchev is Evgeny Boratynsky (or Baratynsky) (1800-44). His elegies made an epoch. His works are still the joy of those who can read Russian; it is my goal to make him accessible in the countries where English is understood. Although *Lermontov, Propp,* and, more recently, *Tyutchev* and *Trubetzkoy* have suddenly made my writings interesting to a rather broad audience, my main work remains the same as always, namely, linguistics—especially historical linguistics—which has been enriched greatly by my close contacts with poetics and literary criticism. Since I came to the United States, I have regularly worked on three books simultaneously, and I expect to maintain the same rhythm in the future. Articles, reviews, papers, and since 1988 work on a new etymological dictionary of English, are integral parts of this rhythm.

"In translation, my main ambition is to produce poetry whose aesthetic value is commensurate with that of the originals. Now that I have translated two poets and work on a third is in full swing, I strive to make the authors I love so much as distinct in English as they are in Russian. This is a difficult task, for the temptation is great to teach the masters of the past to speak your own uniform idiom, a temptation that even Pasternak was unable to resist. In editorial work and monographs on great scholars, I attempt to lift them from their national obscurity and introduce them to the world at large. In philology, I strive to reconstruct the origin of words, the meaning of old myths, and phonetic systems that have long since vanished."

BIOGRAPHICAL/CRITICAL SOURCES:

BOOKS

Lermontov, Mikhail, *Mikhail Lermontov: Major Poetical Works,* edited and translated by Anatoly Liberman, University of Minnesota Press, 1983.

Liberman, Anatoly, *Germanic Accentology,* Volume 1, University of Minnesota Press, 1982.

PERIODICALS

CLR Today (University of Minnesota), spring, 1986.
Minneapolis Star, May 26, 1981.
Minnesota, May, 1979.
Minnesota Daily, January 22, 1980; October 6, 1983; February 12, 1985.
Morgunbladid (Iceland), January 15, 1982.
New York Review of Books, May 31, 1984.
New York Times Book Review, October 21, 1984.
Report (University of Minnesota), June, 1980.
Times Literary Supplement, January 25, 1985.
University of Minnesota Update, Number 1, 1984; Number 3, 1990.

*   *   *

LINDSEY, (Helen) Johanna 1952-

PERSONAL: Born March 10, 1952, in Frankfurt, Germany; daughter of Edwin Dennis (a professional soldier) and Wanda (a personnel management specialist; maiden name, Donaldson) Howard; married Ralph Lindsey (an estimator), November 28, 1970; children: Alfred, Joseph, Garret. *Education:* Attended high school in Kailua, Hawaii.

ADDRESSES: Home—Ahuimanu Hills, 47-598 Puapoo Place, Kaneohe, HI 96744.

CAREER: Writer, 1975—.

AWARDS, HONORS: Historical romance writer of the year award, 1984, and numerous Reviewer's Choice Awards, *Romantic Times;* bronze award, *West Coast Review of Books,* for *So Speaks the Heart;* Waldenbooks Best Historical, 1986-1991; Outstanding Achiever award, 1991, and numerous Favorite Author Awards and Silver Pen Awards, *Affaire de Coeur.*

WRITINGS:

HISTORICAL ROMANCES

Captive Bride, Avon, 1977.
A Pirate's Love, Avon, 1978.
Fires of Winter, Avon, 1980.
Paradise Wild, Avon, 1981.
Glorious Angel, Avon, 1982.
So Speaks the Heart, Avon, 1983.
Heart of Thunder, Avon, 1983.
A Gentle Feuding, Avon, 1984.
Brave the Wild Wind, Avon, 1984.
Tender Is the Storm, Avon, 1985.
Love Only Once, Avon, 1985.
When Love Awaits, Avon, 1986.

A Heart So Wild, Avon, 1986.
Hearts Aflame, Avon, 1987.
Secret Fire, Avon, 1987.
Tender Rebel, Avon, 1988.
Silver Angel, Avon, 1988.
Defy Not the Heart, Avon, 1989.
Savage Thunder, Avon, 1989.
Warrior's Woman, Avon, 1990.
Gentle Rogue, Avon, 1990.
Once a Princess, Avon, 1991.
Prisoner of My Desire, Avon, 1991.
Man of My Dreams, Avon, 1992.
Angel, Avon, 1992.

SIDELIGHTS: "Since I was old enough to appreciate a good novel, I've been a romantic," Johanna Lindsey tells Kathryn Falk in *Love's Leading Ladies.* After years of being an avid reader of historical romances, Lindsey began writing them herself. Her books have appeared on the *New York Times* Paperback Best-Seller List and have sold over forty million copies. In addition to being successful, Lindsey feels she is well suited to her profession: "I enjoy happy-ending love stories more than any other type of reading. Romance is what comes out of me."

Lindsey's books are noted for their accurate portrayal of historic periods and foreign settings. A *Publishers Weekly* contributor notes that in *So Speaks the Heart,* set in tenth-century France, Lindsey manages realistically to "recreate the ferocity of the period and [give] a very real sense of the limited power of medieval warlords and the workings of the feudal system." Lindsey relies primarily on library research to achieve this realism. "I take care of research before I begin my story, once a century and a continent are decided upon," Lindsey explains to Falk. Despite the realism of her fiction, Lindsey has never traveled to the foreign settings she depicts. "I would love to visit the areas that I write about," she relates to Falk, "but unfortunately, the only traveling I do is to the library."

Summarizing the impact of writing on her life, Lindsey says to Falk that "other than a change in family finances, and the pride of accomplishment, success hasn't changed my life." Yet, she admits to Falk that her profession is important to her. "I would be literally *lost* if I had to give it up," Lindsey explains.

BIOGRAPHICAL/CRITICAL SOURCES:

BOOKS

Falk, Kathryn, *Love's Leading Ladies,* Pinnacle Books, 1982.

PERIODICALS

Affaire de Coeur, January, 1984.
Publishers Weekly, July 11, 1980; March 25, 1983.

LINGARD, Joan 1932-

PERSONAL: Born in 1932, in Edinburgh, Scotland; married; children: Bridget, Jenny, Kersten. *Education:* Moray House Training College, general teaching diploma.

ADDRESSES: Home—72 Gt. King St., Edinburgh EH3 6QU, Scotland.

CAREER: Teacher and writer.

WRITINGS:

NOVELS

Liam's Daughter, Hodder & Stoughton, 1963.
The Prevailing Wind, Hodder & Stoughton, 1964.
The Tide Comes In, Hodder & Stoughton, 1966.
The Headmaster, Hodder & Stoughton, 1967.
A Sort of Freedom, Hodder & Stoughton, 1969.
The Lord on Our Side, Hodder & Stoughton, 1970.
The Twelfth Day of July, Hamish Hamilton, 1970.
Across the Barricades, Hamish Hamilton, 1972.
Into Exile, Thomas Nelson, 1973.
Frying as Usual, Thomas Nelson, 1973.
The Clearance, Thomas Nelson, 1974.
A Proper Place, Thomas Nelson, 1975.
The Resettling, Thomas Nelson, 1976.
No Place for Love, Scholastic Book Services, 1976.
Hostages to Fortune, Thomas Nelson, 1977.
Snake among the Sunflowers, Thomas Nelson, 1977.
The Pilgrimage, Thomas Nelson, 1977.
The Reunion, Thomas Nelson, 1978.
The Gooseberry, Hamish Hamilton, 1978.
The Second Flowering of Emily Mountjoy, St. Martin's, 1979.
The File on Fraulein Berg, Julia McRae, 1980.
Greenyards, Putnam, 1981.
Strangers in the House, Hamish Hamilton, 1981.
Maggie Omnibus, Hamish Hamilton, 1982.
The Winter Visitor, Hamish Hamilton, 1983.
Sisters by Rite, St. Martin's, 1984.
Reasonable Doubts, Hamish Hamilton, 1986.
The Freedom Machine, Hamish Hamilton, 1986.
The Guilty Party, Hamish Hamilton, 1987.
Rags and Riches, Hamish Hamilton, 1988.
Tug of War, Dutton, 1989.
The Women's House, St. Martin's, 1989.
Glad Rags, Hamish Hamilton, 1990.
Between Two Worlds, Dutton, 1991.

OTHER

Also author of novel *Odd Girl Out,* 1978; also author of television scripts for Scottish television and British Broadcasting Corp. (BBC), Scotland.

WORK IN PROGRESS: A young adult novel set in contemporary Scotland.

SIDELIGHTS: Joan Lingard and her family moved to Belfast, Northern Ireland when she was very young. She lived in Belfast until she turned eighteen. Lingard once told *CA:* "I began to write because I couldn't get enough to read, and I was an avid reader. I was eleven years old and living in Belfast. The choice of books at my local library was poor, and the books themselves were in pretty bad shape though I read them, regardless of dirt and smell, until the day came when I had nothing to read at all, and so I sat down and wrote my own book, my first book."

Through different books, some of Lingard's fiction traces the same characters from late childhood through adolescence to early adulthood. She explores such themes as family tensions, young love, and the effects of prejudice on children and teens. In *The Twelfth Day of July,* she focuses on the Catholic-Protestant strife in Northern Island through the actions of several fictitious children caught in the crisis. As Lingard explained in the *Times Literary Supplement,* "The theme of prejudice is a vitally important one to present to children, who so often inherit the views of their parents at a very young age." *Times Literary Supplement* reviewer Lesley Croome notes that Lingard's books "reflect the complexities of the inflammable situation in Northern Ireland with a rare accuracy."

BIOGRAPHICAL/CRITICAL SOURCES:

BOOKS

Something about the Author Autobiography Series, Volume 5, Gale, 1988.

PERIODICALS

Spectator, April 12, 1975.
Times Literary Supplement, November 13, 1970; December 11, 1970; July 14, 1972; July 5, 1974; July 11, 1975; July 16, 1976; December 10, 1976; July 15, 1977; March 28, 1980; November 20, 1981; June 29, 1984.

*　　*　　*

LINNEY, Romulus 1930-

PERSONAL: Born September 21, 1930, in Philadelphia, PA; son of Romulus Zachariah Linney and Maitland Linney Clabaugh; married Margaret Andrews (an actress); children: Laura, Susan. *Education:* Oberlin College, A.B., 1953; Yale University, M.F.A., 1958; New School of New York City, novel workshop, 1960. *Avocational interests:* The arts and sports, especially water sports.

ADDRESSES: Home—235 West 76th St., New York, NY 10023. *Agent*—Gilbert Parker, William Morris Agency, 1350 Avenue of the Americas, New York, NY 10019.

CAREER: Writer, 1954—. Actor and director in professional Equity stock companies; Actors' Studio, New York City, stage manager, 1960. Visiting associate professor of English and drama at University of North Carolina at Chapel Hill, 1961, and visiting professor at University of Pennsylvania, Connecticut College, Brooklyn College of the City University of New York, and Columbia University; director of fine arts at North Carolina State College of Agriculture and Engineering of the University of North Carolina (now North Carolina State University at Raleigh), 1963; faculty member at Manhattan School of Music, 1964-72. Panel consultant to Creative Artists Public Service Program, National Endowment for the Arts Literary Panel, and New York State Council for the Arts Theatre Panel. *Military service:* U.S. Army, 1954-56.

MEMBER: Authors Guild, Authors League of America, Actor's Equity Association, Dramatists Guild, PEN.

AWARDS, HONORS: National Endowment for the Arts fellow, as playwright and librettist; National Endowment for the Arts grant, 1974; Obie Award, *Village Voice,* 1980, for *Tennessee;* Guggenheim Foundation fellow, 1980; Mishima Prize, 1981, for fiction; American Academy and Institute of Arts and Letters Award in Literature, 1984; Rockefeller Foundation fellow, 1986. Commissions for plays from the Appalachian Regional Commission, the Kennedy Center for the Performing Arts, Phoenix Theatre, Actor's Theatre of Louisville, and the Virginia Museum Theatre.

WRITINGS:

NOVELS

Heathen Valley (also see below), Atheneum, 1962.
Slowly, by Thy Hand Unfurled (also see below), Harcourt, 1965.
Jesus Tales (also see below), North Point Press, 1980.

PLAYS

(Editor with Norman A. Bailey and Domenick Cascio) *Ten Plays for Radio,* Burgess, 1954.
(Editor with Bailey and Cascio) *Radio Classics,* Burgess, 1956.
The Sorrows of Frederick (produced in Los Angeles at the Mark Taper Forum, 1967; also see below), Harcourt, 1966.
Democracy, (later published as *Democracy and Esther;* produced Off-Off Broadway, 1968; also see below) Dramatists Play Service, 1976.
Man's Estate: Five Plays (contains *Carnal Knowledge, Who Is Buried in Grant's Tomb?, The Death of King Phillip, Man's Estate,* and *Goodbye, Howard* [also see below]), Studio Duplicating Service, 1969.
The Love Suicide at Schofield Barracks [and] *Democracy and Esther* (adaptation of two novels by Henry

Adams; *The Love Suicide at Schofield Barracks* first produced in New York at Herbert Berghoff Playwrights Workshop, 1971, then on Broadway, 1972; also see below), Harcourt, 1973.

Holy Ghosts (first produced in Greenville, NC, at East Carolina University, 1971, then Off-Off Broadway, 1976; also see below), Studio Duplicating Service, 1976.

The Love Suicide at Schofield Barracks, Dramatists Play Service, 1972, one-act version published in *The Best Short Plays 1986,* edited by Ramon Delgado, Applause, 1986.

Appalachia Sounding, produced on tour in Appalachia by the Carolina Readers Theatre, 1975.

The Sorrows of Frederick [and] *Holy Ghosts,* Harcourt, 1977.

Childe Byron (two-act; first produced in Richmond, VA, at Virginia Museum Theatre, 1977, then Off-Broadway, 1981), Dramatists Play Service, 1981.

Just Folks (commissioned by the Kennedy Center for the Performing Arts), produced in New York, 1978.

Old Man Joseph and His Family (two-act; based on author's novel *Jesus Tales;* produced Off-Broadway, 1978), Dramatists Play Service, 1978.

The Death of King Phillip, (produced in Boston, 1979), Dramatists Play Service, 1984.

Tennessee (one-act; produced Off-Broadway, 1979; also see below), Dramatists Play Service, 1980, published in *Best Short Plays 1980,* Chilton Press, 1980.

The Captivity of Pixie Shedman (two-act; produced Off-Broadway, 1981), Dramatists Play Service, 1981.

El Hermano (one-act; produced in New York at Ensemble Studio Theatre, 1981), Dramatists Play Service, 1981.

Laughing Stock (three one-acts; includes *Goodbye, Howard* [produced Off-Off Broadway, 1982], *F.M.* [produced in Philadelphia, 1982], and *Tennessee;* produced together Off-Broadway, 1984), Dramatists Play Service, 1984.

Gardens of Eden, produced in New York, 1982.

April Snow, first produced in Los Angeles at South Coast Repertory's Second Stage, 1983, then Off-Broadway in *Marathon 87* at Ensemble Studio Theatre, 1987.

Why the Lord Come to Sand Mountain (also see below), Theatre Communications Group, 1984.

(And director) *Sand Mountain* (two one-acts; includes *Sand Mountain Matchmaking* and *Why the Lord Come to Sand Mountain;* produced in Montclair, NJ, at the Whole Theater, 1986), Dramatists Play Service, 1985.

A Woman without a Name (two-act; based on *Slowly, by Thy Hand Unfurled;* produced by the Denver Center Theatre Company, 1986), Dramatists Play Service, 1986.

Pops (six one-acts; includes *Tonight We Love* and *Ave Maria;* produced in New York, 1986), Dramatists Play Service, 1987.

(And director) *Heathen Valley* (based on novel of same title), first produced at the Philadelphia Festival Theater for New Plays, 1987, then Off-Broadway, 1988.

Juliet (one-act), produced Off-Broadway, 1988.

(And director) *Three Poets* (includes *Komachi, Hrosvitha,* and *Akhmatova*), produced in New York at the Theater for the New City, 1989.

2, produced in Louisville, KY, at the Actors' Theatre of Louisville, 1990.

Unchanging Love (adaptation of short story "In the Ravine," by Anton Chekhov), produced Off-Broadway, 1991.

Also author of *Choir Practice,* produced Off-Broadway; and *Southern Comfort* (two one-acts), produced at H. B. Playwrights Foundation.

OTHER

Also author of television script, *The Thirty-Fourth Star,* for CBS's *American Parade,* 1976; author of episodes for the series *Feelin' Good,* PBS, 1976-77. Contributor of several short works to literary publications. A collection of Linney's manuscripts is housed in the Lincoln Center Library for the Performing Arts, New York.

SIDELIGHTS: Romulus Linney has been writing and directing plays Off-Broadway and in regional repertory theatres for more than twenty years. The recipient of Guggenheim and Rockefeller foundation grants and a 1980 Obie Award, Linney has combined his work in the theatre with teaching at such institutions as Columbia University and the University of Pennsylvania. *New Yorker* contributor Mimi Kramer notes of the author: "One of his signatures as a playwright is the intellectual about-face. . . . Linney has a gift for dramatizing the potential metaphorical content of a ludicrous character, premise, or situation. He also has an instinct for finding just the right image— one sufficiently far out to be comic but expressive of a truth sufficiently universal to make us want to accept it."

New York Times correspondent Mel Gussow calls Linney "a poet of America's heartland." Although he was born in Philadelphia and educated at Oberlin College and Yale University, Linney spent part of his childhood near Nashville, Tennessee. His experiences there with the people— and especially with their revivalist religion—have helped to shape the characters and situations in his plays. "When it comes to writing about the 'hot blood and high jinks' of country people in our border states, no one can touch Romulus Linney," writes Gussow. "Himself a transplanted Tennessean, Mr. Linney never patronizes his earthy source material. With generosity and humor, he shows his people in their natural plumage, living full lives in the shadow of desperation and poverty."

A number of Linney's plays are set in the South, including one-acts such as *Tennessee, Sand Mountain Matchmaking,* and *Why the Lord Come to Sand Mountain.* He has also written full-length plays about the region, earning his biggest success with *Holy Ghosts* and *Heathen Valley.* Gussow notes that Linney "is a playwright with a rich, Faulknerian sense of humor. In the best tradition, he is a local colorist, taking regional characters and showing us how their lives are inextricably bound up with land, family and ancestral roots." In another review, the critic adds that the author "has an intimate understanding of those who live in rural America and are shadowed by their environment and their ritualistic past."

Linney has also found themes in the lives of complex historical figures. Two of his plays, *The Sorrows of Frederick* and *Childe Byron,* concern Frederick the Great of Russia and the poet Lord Byron. Another better-known Linney work is his novel *Jesus Tales* and its theatrical adaptation, *Old Man Joseph and His Family.* Both pieces explore the exploits of Jesus, his followers, and his family from a folk tale perspective not necessarily found in the standard Gospels. In a review of *Old Man Joseph,* Gussow claims that the play "poses and answers two questions: how did Joseph feel about being the father of the son of God, and what was Jesus like as a boy?" The critic praises the work for its "attempt to humanize the Holy Family."

Productions of Linney's work have appeared in nearly every large American city, sometimes directed by the playwright himself. Since 1980 many of his one-acts and most of his longer dramas have been staged Off-Broadway, earning him an Award in Literature from the American Academy and Institute of Arts and Letters. In the *New York Times,* Mervyn Rothstein maintains that, despite his awards and fellowships, Linney is "perhaps the most underrated, underrecognized American playwright today." This low visibility is changing as new productions of Linney plays are staged in one-act marathons, in larger Off-Broadway theatres, and in important regional repertory companies. "I'm happy with what I'm doing," the author told the *New York Times.* "I'm not unhappy with my career. I've noticed that a lot of people who have great successes early on have a great deal of trouble later, and I feel that I am more enamored and obsessed with writing plays than ever." Linney concluded: "Ford Madox Ford said a very nice thing—he said, 'I'm an old man crazy about writing.' And I hope that's what's going to happen to me."

BIOGRAPHICAL/CRITICAL SOURCES:

PERIODICALS

Chicago Tribune, October 16, 1981.

Los Angeles Times, June 10, 1983; November 21, 1987; August 17, 1989; April 7, 1990.
Nation, February 21, 1981.
Newsweek, February 2, 1981.
New Yorker, March 9, 1981; July 25, 1988.
New York Times, February 10, 1972; February 13, 1972; January 20, 1978; February 3, 1981; February 27, 1981; May 24, 1982; April 13, 1984; February 28, 1986; May 12, 1987; June 3, 1987; June 14, 1987; August 9, 1987; August 12, 1987; December 24, 1988; June 25, 1989; November 23, 1989; December 3, 1989; April 5, 1990; February 10, 1991.
Publishers Weekly, October 31, 1980, p. 77.
Southern Review, winter, 1983.
Washington Post Book World, March 1, 1981.*

*   *   *

LIPSEY, Robert E(dward) 1926-

PERSONAL: Born August 14, 1926, in New York, NY; son of Meyer A. and Anna (Weinstein) Lipsey; married Sally Rothstein (a retired associate professor of mathematics at Brooklyn College of the City University of New York), November 24, 1948; children: Marion, Carol, Eleanor. *Education:* Columbia University, B.A., 1944, M.A., 1946, Ph.D., 1961.

ADDRESSES: Home—70 East Tenth St., New York, NY 10003. *Office*—National Bureau of Economic Research, 269 Mercer, New York, NY 10003; and Department of Economics, Queens College of the City University of New York, Flushing, NY 11367.

CAREER: National Bureau of Economic Research, New York City, 1945—, director of international and financial studies and vice-president of research, currently research associate and director of New York office; City University of New York, professor of economics at Queens College, Flushing, NY, 1967—, and at Graduate School and University Center, New York City. Member of Conference on Research in Income and Wealth. Lecturer in economics at Columbia University, 1961-64. Consultant to Federal Reserve Board, U.S. Department of Commerce.

MEMBER: International Association for Research in Income and Wealth, International Trade and Finance Association, Academy of International Business, American Economic Association, American Statistical Association (fellow), National Association of Business Economists, Econometric Society, European Economic Association.

WRITINGS:

Price and Quantity Trends in the Foreign Trade of the United States, Princeton University Press, 1963.

Studies in the National Balance Sheet of the United States, Princeton University Press, 1963, Volume 1 (with Raymond W. Goldsmith), Volume 2 (with Goldsmith and Morris Mendelson).

(With Irving B. Kravis and Philip J. Bourque) *Measuring International Price Competitiveness: A Preliminary Report,* National Bureau of Economic Research, 1965.

(With Doris Preston) *Source Book of Statistics Relating to Construction,* National Bureau of Economic Research, 1966.

(With Kravis) *Comparative Prices of Nonferrous Metals in International Trade,* National Bureau of Economic Research, 1966.

(With Kravis) *Price Competitiveness in World Trade,* National Bureau of Economic Research, 1971.

(With Phillip Cagan) *The Financial Effects of Inflation,* Ballinger, 1978.

(Author of foreword) Anne O. Krueger, *Liberalization Attempts and Consequences,* Ballinger, 1978.

(Author of foreword) Jagdish Bhagwati, *Anatomy and Consequences of Exchange Control Regimes,* Ballinger, 1978.

(With Kravis) *Toward an Explanation of National Price Levels,* International Financial Section, Princeton University, 1983.

(With Kravis) *Saving and Economic Growth: Is the U.S. Really Falling Behind?,* The Conference Board, 1987.

(Editor with Helen S. Tice) *The Measurement of Saving, Investment, and Wealth,* University of Chicago Press, 1989.

(With Blomstroem and Lennart Ohlsson) *Economic Relations Between the United States and Sweden,* Svenska Handelsbamken and the Federation of Swedish Industries, 1989.

Contributor to over twenty books, including *Price Indexes and Quality Change,* edited by Kravis, Harvard University Press, 1971; *A Retrospective on the Classical Gold Standard,* University of Chicago Press, 1984; *Trade Policy Issues and Empirical Analysis,* edited by Robert Baldwin, University of Chicago Press, 1988; *International Economic Transactions,* edited by Peter Hooper and Richardson, University of Chicago Press, 1991; and *Direct Foreign Investment in the Asia-Pacific Region,* Westview Press, 1991.

Also author of reports and working papers. Contributor to *Proceedings of the Business and Economic Statistics Section, American Statistical Association,* 1967, 1969, 1971, and 1972. Contributor of articles and reviews to professional journals, including *American Economic Review, Journal of International Economics, Economic Journal, Review of Income and Wealth, Scandinavian Journal of Economics, Banca Nazionale del Lavoro Quarterly Review,*

and *World Development.* Member of editorial board of *Review of Income and Wealth;* associate editor of *Review of Economics and Statistics.*

WORK IN PROGRESS: Studies of multinational firms, technology, and trade, of international price levels, of takeovers of U.S. firms, and of nineteenth century U.S. trade.

* * *

LUSTICK, Ian Steven 1949-

PERSONAL: Born October 4, 1949, in Syracuse, NY; son of Bernard R. and Renee Lustick. *Education:* Brandeis University, B.A., 1971; University of California, Berkeley, M.A., 1972, Ph.D., 1976.

ADDRESSES: Office—Department of Political Science, 217 Stiteler Hall, University of Pennsylvania, Philadelphia, PA 19104-6215.

CAREER: Dartmouth College, Hanover, NH, assistant professor, 1976-81, associate professor, 1981-88, professor of government, 1988-91; University of Pennsylvania, Philadelphia, professor of political science, 1991—. Member of Council on Foreign Relations.

MEMBER: American Political Science Association, Association for Israel Studies, Middle East Studies Association.

WRITINGS:

Arabs in the Jewish State: Israel's Control of a National Minority, University of Texas Press, 1980.

State-Building Failure in British Ireland and French Algeria, Institute of International Studies, University of California, 1985.

For the Land and the Lord: Jewish Fundamentalism in Israel, Council on Foreign Relations, 1988.

States and Territories: British, French, and Israeli Ties to Ireland, Algeria, and the West Bank and Gaza, Cornell University Press, 1993.

* * *

LYNCH, James 1936-

PERSONAL: Born August 25, 1936, in Bradford, England; married Margaret Ann Smith, 1958; children: Mark Andrew, Angela Margaret, Colette Elizabeth. *Education:* University of Hull, B.A. (with honors), 1957, certificate in education, 1958, advanced diploma in education, 1962, M.Ed., 1966; University of Durham, Ph.D., 1974.

ADDRESSES: Home—9 Ghyll Wood, Ilkley, West Yorkshire LS29 9NR, England; and 3808 Porter St. N.W.

#202, Washington, DC 20016-2949. *Office*—E9043 The World Bank, Washington, DC.

CAREER: High school teacher in Hull, England, 1958-63, head of department, 1960-63; British Ministry of Defence, Higher Education Centre, assistant lecturer in modern languages, 1963-65; Bede College of Education, lecturer, 1965-67, senior lecturer in education, 1967-68; Southampton School of Education, Southampton, England, lecturer in education, 1968-75; Bradford College, Bradford, England, head of Margaret McMillan School of Education, 1976-79; Newcastle College of Advanced Education, Newcastle, Australia, head of School of Education, 1979-80; Sunderland Polytechnic, Sunderland, England, professor, 1982, head of department of teaching studies, 1981-89, dean of Faculty of Education, 1982-89; staff member and education specialist at World Bank, Washington, DC. Visiting professor, University of Frankfort, 1975; teacher at schools for adult education. Consultant to UNESCO, German Institute for International Educational Research, Ministry of Education (Malta), Ministry for Overseas Development (London), and University of Graz Institute of Education.

MEMBER: Royal Society of the Arts (fellow).

WRITINGS:

(With H. D. Plunkett) *Teacher Education and Cultural Change,* Allen & Unwin, 1973.

(With John Pimlott) *Parents and Teachers: An Action Research Approach,* Macmillan (London), 1976.

Lifelong Education and the Preparation of Educational Personnel, UNESCO, 1977.

The Reform of Teacher Education in the United Kingdom, Society for Research into Higher Education, 1979.

Education for Community, Macmillan (London), 1979.

(Translator) Wolfgang Mitter, *Educational Research and Teacher Education in the Perspective of Comparative Education,* German Institute for International Education Research, 1979.

Policy and Practice in Lifelong Education, Nafferton (England), 1982.

The Multicultural Curriculum, Batsford, 1983.

Multicultural Education: Principles and Practice, Routledge & Kegan Paul, 1986.

Prejudice Reduction and the Schools, Holt, Saunders, 1987.

Multicultural Education for a Global Society, Falmer Press, 1989.

Education for Citizenship in a Multicultural Society, Cassell, 1992.

EDITOR

(And contributor) *Teaching in the Multicultural School,* Ward, Lock, 1981.

(With Peter Doebrich, Christoph Kodron, and Mitter, and contributor) *Lehrerbildung fuer den Unterricht behinderter Kinder in ausgewaehlten Laendern,* Bohlau Verlag (Cologne), 1984.

(With Doebrich, Kodron, and Mitter, and contributor) *Lehrerbildung fuer multikulturelle Schulen in ausgewaehlten Laendern,* Bohlau Verlag, 1984.

(With Robin Alexander and Maurice Craft) *Change in Teacher Education: Context and Provision since Robbins,* Holt, Saunders, 1984.

(And contributor, with James Banks) *Multicultural Education in Western Societies,* Holt, Saunders, 1986.

(With Sohan and Celia Modgil) *Cultural Diversity and the Schools,* Falmer Press, 1992.

OTHER

Also author of reports for governmental and intergovernmental agencies. Contributor to books, including *The History of Education in Europe,* edited by T. G. Cook, Methuen, 1974; *Linking Home and School,* by Craft and others, 3rd edition, Longman, 1980; and *Teachers for a Multicultural Society,* by A. Carter, Longman/Schools Council, 1985. Contributor of articles and reviews to periodicals in Great Britain, Europe, Canada, Australia, and the United States, including *International Review of Education, Comparative Education Review, Education for Teaching, Gesamtschule, Comparative Education, History of Education,* and *Phi Delta Kappan.* Member of editorial board, *Multicultural Education.* Several of Lynch's books have been translated into foreign languages, including Arabic, French, Japanese, Spanish, and German.

WORK IN PROGRESS: A study of strategies for the linking of human rights and development education.

SIDELIGHTS: James Lynch once told *CA:* "Writing is an important contribution to social and educational change. It is an expression of man's wish both to create and to liberate himself and others. Problems of emancipatory education in the multicultural society are a central theme of my contemporary work and aspiration, focused on what I see as a central feature of current educational provision, namely its implicit racial prejudice and social inequity."

He adds, "My current efforts are aimed at making human rights actual for all children and in all schools throughout the world."

M

MacLEOD, Charlotte 1922-
(Alisa Craig, Matilda Hughes)

PERSONAL: Born November 12, 1922, in Bath, New Brunswick, Canada; immigrated to United States, 1923, naturalized citizen, 1952; daughter of Edward Phillips (a contractor) and Mabel Maud (a housewife; maiden name, Hayward) MacLeod. *Education:* Attended School of Practical Art (now the Art Institute of Boston). *Politics:* Liberal Democrat.

ADDRESSES: Agent—Jed Mattes, 200 West 72nd St., No. 50, New York, NY 10023.

CAREER: Writer. Stop and Shop Supermarkets, Boston, MA, staff artist and copy writer, 1945-52; N. H. Miller & Co., Inc. (advertising firm), Boston, copy chief, 1952-82. Library trustee, Sundbury, MA, 1976-82.

MEMBER: American Crime Writers League (co-founder and president, 1989-90; editor, 1991—), Crime Writers of Canada.

AWARDS, HONORS: Guest of Honor at Bouchercon 19, 1988, and at Malice Domestic, 1991; Lifetime Achievement Award, Bouchercon 23, 1992; five American Mystery Awards; two Edgar Award nominations; Nero Wolfe Award.

WRITINGS:

Astrology for Skeptics, Macmillan, 1972.
(Under pseudonym Alisa Craig) *The Terrible Tide,* Doubleday, 1983.
Grab Bag (short stories), Avon, 1987.
(Editor) *Mistletoe Mysteries* (anthology), Mysterious Press, 1989.
(Editor) *Christmas Stalkings* (anthology), Mysterious Press, 1991.

JUVENILE

Mystery of the White Knight, Bouregy, 1964.
Next Door to Danger, Bouregy, 1965.
(Under name Matilda Hughes) *The Food of Love,* Bouregy, 1965.
(Under name Matilda Hughes) *Headlines for Caroline,* Bouregy, 1967.
The Fat Lady's Ghost, Weybright, 1968.
Mouse's Vineyard, Weybright, 1968.
Ask Me No Questions, Macrae, 1971.
Brass Pounder, Little, Brown, 1971.
King Devil, Atheneum, 1978.
We Dare Not Go A-Hunting, Atheneum, 1980.
Cirak's Daughter, Atheneum, 1982.
Maid of Author, Atheneum, 1984.

"PETER SHANDY" SERIES

Rest You Merry, Doubleday, 1978.
The Luck Runs Out, Doubleday, 1979.
Wrack and Rune, Doubleday, 1982.
Something the Cat Dragged In, Avon, 1984.
The Curse of the Giant Hogweed, Doubleday, 1985.
The Corpse in Oozak's Pond, Mysterious Press, 1987.
Vane Pursuit, Mysterious Press, 1989.
An Owl Too Many, Mysterious Press, 1991.

"SARAH KELLING" SERIES

The Family Vault, Doubleday, 1979.
The Withdrawing Room, Doubleday, 1980.
The Palace Guard, Doubleday, 1981.
The Bilbao Looking Glass, Doubleday, 1983.
The Convivial Codfish, Doubleday, 1984.
The Plain Old Man, Doubleday, 1985.
The Recycled Citizen, Mysterious Press, 1988.
The Silver Ghost, Mysterious Press, 1988.
The Gladstone Bag, Mysterious Press, 1990.

The Resurrection Man, Mysterious Press, 1992.

"MADOC RHYS" SERIES; UNDER PSEUDONYM ALISA CRAIG

A Pint of Murder, Thorndike Press, 1980.
Murder Goes Mumming, Doubleday, 1981.
A Dismal Thing to Do, Doubleday, 1986.
Trouble in the Brasses, Avon, 1989.
The Wrong Rite, Morrow, 1992.

"GRUB AND STAKERS" SERIES; UNDER PSEUDONYM ALISA CRAIG

The Grub and Stakers Move a Mountain, Doubleday, 1981.
The Grub and Stakers Quilt a Bee, Doubleday, 1985.
The Grub and Stakers Pinch a Poke, Avon, 1988.
The Grub and Stakers Spin a Yarn, Avon, 1990.
The Grub and Stakers House a Haunt, Morrow, 1993.

OTHER

Contributor of short stories to anthologies; former contributor of short stories and articles, some self-illustrated, to magazines for both adults and children in the United States and abroad, including *Good Housekeeping, Yankee, Edgar Wallace Mystery Magazine, Criminologist, Alfred Hitchcock's Mystery Magazine,* and *Cricket.*

WORK IN PROGRESS: A biography of Mary Roberts Rinehart, for Mysterious Press.

*   *   *

MacMANUS, Susan A(nn) 1947-

PERSONAL: Born August 22, 1947, in Tampa, FL; daughter of Harold Cameron (a salesperson) and Elizabeth (a housewife; maiden name, Riegler) MacManus. *Education:* Florida State University, B.A. (cum laude), 1968, Ph.D., 1975; University of Michigan, M.A., 1969. *Politics:* Republican. *Religion:* Methodist. *Avocational interests:* Sports, politics.

ADDRESSES: Home—2506 Collier Parkway, Land O' Lakes, FL 34639. *Office*—Department of Government and International Affairs, University of South Florida, 4202 East Fowler Ave., Tampa, FL 33620.

CAREER: Valencia Community College, Orlando, FL, instructor in political science, 1969-73; University of Houston, Houston, TX, assistant professor, 1975-79, associate professor of political science, 1979-84, director of Masters in Public Administration Program, 1983-84; Cleveland State University, Cleveland, OH, professor of urban affairs and political science, and director of doctoral urban studies program, both 1984-87; University of South Florida, Tampa, FL, professor of public administration and political science, 1987—, and chair of Department of

Government and International Affairs, 1990—. Visiting professor at University of Oklahoma, 1981—; research associate, Rice Institute for Policy Analysis, Rice University, 1985—. Member of executive council of Florida Political Science Association, 1972-75; member of Herbert Simon Award Committee for *International Journal of Public Administration,* 1981-82; member of advisory board of James Madison Institute for Public Policy Studies, 1987—; member of advisory council of Florida Institute of Government, 1988-89; member of Governor's Council of Economic Advisors, 1988-91; member of board of directors of USF Research Foundation, Inc., 1990—; and member of advisory board of the Nelson A. Rockefeller Institute of Government, State University of New York at Albany, Center for the Study of States, 1990—. Houston Area Women's Center, vice-president of finance, 1979-80, 1983, president, 1980; guest on radio and television programs; public speaker; consultant to numerous firms, institutions, and departments of the United States Government, including Brookings Institution, National Academy of Public Administration, Westat, Inc., Princeton University Urban and Regional Research Center, Columbia University Conservation of Human Resources, Rice University Center for Community Design and Research, University of Houston Center for Public Policy, city of Norfolk, VA, city of Pittsburgh, PA, National Broadcasting Company (NBC) News Election, South Carolina State Senate, U.S. Department of Commerce, and U.S. Department of Housing and Urban Development.

MEMBER: American Political Science Association (chairperson of section on intergovernmental relations, 1983-84), American Society for Public Administration (president of Suncoast Chapter, 1991-92), National Women's Political Caucus, Academy of Political Science, Policy Studies Organization (member of executive council, 1983-85), Government Finance Officers Association, Women's Caucus for Political Science, League of Women Voters, Southern Political Science Association (vice-president elect, 1989-90; vice-president, 1990-91), Midwest Political Science Association, Western Political Science Association, Southwestern Political Science Association, International Political Science Association, National Association of Schools of Public Affairs and Administration (member of executive council, 1985-88), National Tax Association, Phi Beta Kappa, Phi Kappa Phi, Pi Sigma Alpha.

AWARDS, HONORS: Valencia Community College grant, 1972; University of Houston, Faculty Research Initiation grant, 1976; Teaching Excellence Award, University of Houston, College of Social Sciences, 1977; University of Houston, Academic Enrichment Council Classroom-Oriented Project grant, 1977, and Office of

Research Development limited grant-in-aid, 1979; Outstanding Young Women of America, 1980; Herbert J. Simon Award, *International Journal of Public Administration,* 1981, for article "The Impact of Functional Responsibility and State Legal Constraints on the 'Revenue-Debt' Packages of the U. S. Central Cities"; University of Houston, Center for Public Policy research grant, 1983; Cleveland State University, College of Urban Affairs academic enhancement grant, 1985 and 1986; Northeast Ohio Inter-Institutional Program grant, 1985-86; Best Paper on Women & Politics, Southern Political Science Association Annual Meeting, 1988; Mentor to Women Award, Women's Caucus for Political Science, American Political Science Association, 1989; Fulbright Research Scholar, 1989; first place in Administrative Category, William Beaumont Army Medical Center Scientific Research Awards Competition, 1991, for (with Capt. K. C. Strunz) "Employee Surveys as a Strategic Management Tool: The Case of Army Physician Retention"; Theodore and Venette Askounes-Ashford Distinguished Scholar Award, USF, 1991.

WRITINGS:

Revenue Patterns in U.S. Cities and Suburbs: A Comparative Analysis, Praeger, 1978.

Selected Bibliography of State Government, 1973-1978, Council of State Governments, 1979.

(With Richard P. Nathan, Robert F. Cook, V. Lane Rawlings, and others) *Public Service Employment: A Field Evaluation,* Brookings Institution, 1981.

(Editor with Walter Williams and others) *Studying Implementation: Methodological and Administrative Issues,* Chatham House, 1982.

Federal Aid to Houston, Brookings Institution, 1983.

(With Nathan, Fred C. Doolittle, and others) *The Consequences of Cuts,* Urban and Regional Research Center, Princeton University, 1983.

(With Charles S. Bullock III and Donald M. Freeman) *Governing a Changing America,* Wiley, 1984.

(With Cook, Rawlins, Charles F. Adams, Jr., and others) *Public Service Employment: The Experience of a Decade,* W. E. Upjohn Institute for Employment Research, 1985.

(With Francis Borkowski) *Visions for the Future: Creating Institutional Relationships among Academia, Business, Government and Community,* University Presses of Florida, 1989.

(Editor) *Reapportionment and Representation in Florida: A Historical Collection,* Interbay Innovation Institute, University of South Florida, 1991.

Doing Business with Government: Federal, State, Local & Foreign Government Purchasing Practices for Every Business and Public Institution, Paragon House, 1992.

Also author of instructor's manuals. Contributor to numerous books, including *Readings in Women's Studies: An Interdisciplinary Collection,* edited by Kathleen O'Connor and Walter Johnson, Greenwood Press, 1978; *Perspectives on Taxing and Spending Limitations in the United States,* edited by Charlie B. Tyer and Marcia W. Taylor, Bureau of Government Research and Services, University of South Carolina at Columbia, 1981; *Reductions in U.S. Domestic Spending: How They Affect State and Local Governments,* edited by John W. Ellwood, Transaction Books, 1982; *The Municipal Money Chase: The Politics of Local Government Finance,* edited by Alberta Sbragia, Westview, 1983; *The Future of the Sunbelt: Issues in Managing Growth and Change,* edited by Steven Ballard and Tom James, Praeger, 1983; *Administering the New Federalism,* edited by Lewis G. Bender and James A Stever, Westview, 1986; *Latinos and the Political System,* edited by F. Chris Garcia, University of Notre Dame Press, 1988; *Women and the Constitution,* Haworth Press, 1990; *Governors, Legislatures, and Budgets: Diversity across the American States,* edited by Edward J. Clynch and Thomas P. Lauth, Greenwood Press, 1991; and *Women and Politics: Have the Outsiders Become the Insiders?,* edited by Lois L. Duke, Prentice-Hall, 1992. Contributor to *Political Parties and Elections in the United States: An Encyclopedia.* Contributor of articles and reviews to journals, including *American Journal of Political Science, Social Science Quarterly, Texas Business Review, Western Political Quarterly, Society/Transaction, Journal of Politics, Urban Fiscal Ledger, Journal of Urban Affairs,* and *National Civic Review.* Book review editor for *Urban Affairs Quarterly,* 1986-88. Member of the editorial boards of *State and Local Government Review,* 1980-83, 1990-93; *Southern Review of Public Administration* (now *Public Administration Quarterly*), 1981—; *Policy Studies Journal,* 1981—; *Administration and Policy Journal* (now *Administrative Comments and Letters*), 1982-87; *Journal of Politics,* 1982—; *Journal of Urban Affairs,* 1985-88, 1989—; *Ohio Economic Trends Review,* 1986-87; *Public Administration Review,* 1987-1990; *Public Budgeting and Financial Management,* 1988—; *Journal of Public Administration Research and Theory,* 1989-91; and *International Journal of Public Administration,* 1989—.

SIDELIGHTS: Susan A. MacManus once told *CA* that her goal is "making complex and traditionally boring subjects interesting, understandable, and relevant to students and the public at large." She continued: "American cities, like the federal government, have been challenged by taxpayers to do more with less. On the revenue side of the budgetary ledger, many cities have adopted revenue enhancement strategies (increasing user fees and service charges) along with productivity and privatization strategies. On the expenditure side, common strategies have included across-the-board cuts, cutting functions that are lower in the citizen priority hierarchy, cutting functions with few federal or state mandates, reducing functions transferable to the private sector, and cutting capital-intensive functions, or alternately, labor-intensive functions. Most have met the challenge, although it has been difficult. Particularly hard pressed have been the cities in regions of the country characterized by industrial decline, technological obsolescence, and stagnant, non-diversified economic bases."

*   *   *

MAGORIAN, James   1942-

PERSONAL: Born April 24, 1942, in Palisade, NE; son of Jack and Dorothy (Gorthey) Magorian. *Education:* University of Nebraska, B.S., 1965; Illinois State University, M.S., 1969; attended Oxford University, 1971, and Harvard University, 1972.

ADDRESSES: Home—Helena, MT. *Office*—1225 North 46th St., Lincoln, NE 68503.

CAREER: Writer.

WRITINGS:

POETRY

Almost Noon, Ibis Press, 1969.
Ambushes and Apologies, Ibis Press, 1970.
The Garden of Epicurus, Ibis Press, 1971.
The Last Reel of the Late Movie, Third Eye Press, 1972.
Distances, Ibis Press, 1972.
Mandrake Root Beer, Cosmic Wheelbarrow Chapbooks, 1973.
The Red, White and Blue Bus, Samisdat Press, 1975.
Bosnia and Herzegovina, Third Eye Press, 1976.
Alphabetical Order, Amphion Press, 1976.
Two Hundred Push-Ups at the Y.M.C.A., Specific Gravity Publications, 1977.
The Ghost of Hamlet's Father, Peradam Publishing House, 1977.
Safe Passage, Stone Country Press, 1977.
Notes to the Milkman, Black Oak Press, 1978.
Phases of the Moon, Black Oak Press, 1978.
Piano Tuning at Midnight, Laughing Bear Press, 1979.
Revenge, Samisdat Press, 1979.
The Night Shift at the Poetry Factory, Broken Whisker Studio Press, 1979.
Spiritual Rodeo, Toothpaste Press, 1980.
Ideas for a Bridal Shower, Black Oak Press, 1980.
Tap Dancing on a Tightrope, Laughing Bear Press, 1981.
Training at Home to Be a Locksmith, Black Oak Press, 1981.
The Great Injun Carnival, Black Oak Press, 1982.
Taxidermy Lessons, Black Oak Press, 1982.

The Walden Pond Caper, Black Oak Press, 1983.
Travel Expenses, Laughing Bear Press, 1984.
The Emily Dickinson Jogging Book, Black Oak Press, 1984.
Weighing the Sun's Light, Centaur, 1985.
Charles Darwin and the Theory of Evolution, Black Oak Press, 1985.
Summer Snow, Black Oak Press, 1985.
The Magician's Handbook, Centaur, 1986.
Karl Marx and International Communism, Black Oak Press, 1986.
Squall Line, Black Oak Press, 1986.
The Hideout of the Sigmund Freud Gang, Black Oak Press, 1987.
Mountain Man, Black Oak Press, 1989.
Amelia Earhart Playing Video Games, Centaur Books, 1990.
Saudi Arabia, Centaur Books, 1991.
Borderlands, Black Oak Press, 1992.

CHILDREN'S BOOKS

School Daze, Peradam Publishing House, 1978.
Seventeen Percent, Black Oak Press, 1978.
The Magic Pretzel, Black Oak Press, 1979.
Ketchup Bottles, Peradam Publishing House, 1979.
Imaginary Radishes, Black Oak Press, 1979.
Plucked Chickens, Black Oak Press, 1980.
Fimperings and Torples, Black Oak Press, 1981.
Floyd, Black Oak Press, 1982.
The Three Diminutive Pigs, Black Oak Press, 1982.
Kumquats, Black Oak Press, 1983.
Fouled Spark Plugs, Black Oak Press, 1983.
Griddlemort and the Questionists, Black Oak Press, 1983.
The Witches' Olympics, Black Oak Press, 1983.
Piffle, Black Oak Press, 1983.
Cucumber Cake, Black Oak Press, 1984.
The Lion and the Mouse, Black Oak Press, 1984.
Keeper of Fire, Council for Indian Education, 1984.
Bad Report Cards, Black Oak Press, 1985.
Ground Hog Day, Black Oak Press, 1987.
Magic Spell #207, Centaur Books, 1988.
The Beautiful Music, Black Oak Press, 1988.
The Bad Eggs, Centaur Books, 1989.
Spoonproof Jello, Black Oak Press, 1990.
Mud Pies, Black Oak Press, 1991.

OTHER

America First (novel), Black Oak Press, 1992.

Contributor of poems to more than 150 literary magazines, including *American Poet, Ararat, Bitterroot, Haiku Journal, Kansas Quarterly, New Earth Review, Spoon River Review, Black River Review, Bogg, Calypso, Different Drummer, Gulf Stream, Huron Review, Illinois Quarterly, Laughing Bear, Montana Gothic, Nebraska Review,*

Oxford Magazine, Plastic Tower, Rolling Stone, Slant, Stone Country, and *Whole Notes.*

SIDELIGHTS: James Magorian told *CA:* "My children's stories and satirical poems deal with everyday obsessions and absurdities that I find amusing and horrifying. My other poems reflect rural Nebraska and Montana where I have lived most of my life. These are simple poems of place."

*   *   *

MAJOR, Jean-Louis 1937-

PERSONAL: Born July 16, 1937, in Cornwall, Ontario, Canada; son of Joseph (a businessman) and Noella (Daoust) Major; married Bibiane Landry, June 4, 1960; children: Marie-France. *Education:* University of Ottawa, B.Ph., 1959, B.A. (with honors), 1960, L.Ph., 1960, M.A., 1961, Ph.D., 1965; Ecole Pratique des Hautes Etudes, research fellow, 1968-69.

ADDRESSES: *Home*—St.-Isidore, Ontario, Canada. *Office*—Lettres francaises, University of Ottawa, Ottawa, Ontario, Canada.

CAREER: University of Ottawa, Ottawa, Ontario, lecturer, 1961-64, assistant professor of philosophy, 1964-65, assistant professor, 1965-67, associate professor, 1967-70, professor of French-Canadian literature, 1971—, associate dean of research, 1991—. University of Toronto, visiting professor, 1970-71. Royal Society of Canada, fellow. Ontario Council on University Affairs, chairman of academic advisory committee.

WRITINGS:

Saint-Exupery: L'ecriture et la pensee (title means "Saint-Exupery: Style and Logic"), Editions de l'Universite d'Ottawa, 1968.

Edition critique de "Leone" de Jean Cocteau (title means "A Critical Edition of Jean Cocteau's 'Leone,' "), Editions de l'Universite d'Ottawa, 1975.

Anne Hebert et le miracle de la parole (title means "Anne Hebert and the Miracle of the Word"), Presses de l'Universite de Montreal, 1976.

Radiguet, Cocteau, "Les joues en feu," Editions de l'Universite d'Ottawa, 1977.

La Litterature francaise par les textes theoriques: XIXe siecle, Lettres francaises, 1977.

Paul-Marie Lapointe: La nuit incendiee, Presses de l'Universite de Montreal, 1978.

Le Jeu en etoile: Etudes et essais, Editions de l'Universite d'Ottawa, 1978.

Entre l'ecriture et la parole, Hurtubisc HMH, 1984.

Journal d'Henriette Dessaulles, Presses de l'Universite de Montreal, 1989.

Trente arpents de Ringuet, Presses de l'Universite de Montreal, 1991.

Contributor to numerous books, including *Histoire de la litterature francaise du Quebec,* Volume 4, edited by de Grandpre, Beauchemin, 1969; *Teaching in the Universities: No One Way,* edited by Sheffield, McGill-Queen's University Press, 1974; *La Poesie,* edited by Denoel, Gallimard, 1977; and *Cremazie et Nelligan,* edited by Robidoux and Wyczynski, Fides, 1981. Contributor to anthologies, encyclopedias, and dictionaries. Co-editor, "Cahiers inedits" series, Editions de l'Universite d'Ottawa. Author of regular column on autobiographical writings, *Lettres quebecoises.* Contributor to periodicals, including *Canadian Author and Bookman, Citizen, Le Devoir, Dialogue, Liberte, University of Toronto Quarterly,* and *Incidences.* Literary critic, *Le Droit,* 1963-65.

WORK IN PROGRESS: Coordinator of "Corpus d'editions critiques," a project subsidized by the Social Sciences and Humanities Research Council of Canada to prepare and publish critical editions of major works of French-Canadian literature; director of Canadian section in *Dictionnaire universel des litteratures,* for Presses Universitaires de France (Paris).

SIDELIGHTS: Jean-Louis Major once told *CA:* "My writings cover a variety of fields, French and French-Canadian literature, philosophy, semiotics, but I have persistently explored one main question: What is the meaning of literature?

"Whatever the topic or the technical difficulties involved, the essay can be an act of literature: as much as a novel or a poem, it pertains to creative writing. An essay writer is never tempted by the attractions of film, television, or song adaptations; only what he has to say matters. Perhaps it is an advantage."

BIOGRAPHICAL/CRITICAL SOURCES:

PERIODICALS

Voix et images, April, 1979.

*   *   *

MALGONKAR, Manohar (Dattatray) 1913-

PERSONAL: Born July 12, 1913, in Bombay, India; son of Dattatray Sakharam and Parvati (Walawalkar) Malgonkar; married, 1947; wife's name, Manorama; children: Sunita. *Education:* Bombay University, B.A., 1936. *Avocational interests:* Fishing, cooking, music.

ADDRESSES: *Home*—P.O. Jagalbet, Londa, R. Rly, Mysore, India.

CAREER: Big-game hunter in India, 1936-38; executive officer with Indian Government Service, 1938-43; proprietor of mining company in Mysore, India, 1952—. Independent candidate for the Indian Parliament. *Military service:* Indian Army Infantry, 1943-52; became lieutenant colonel.

WRITINGS:

The Sea Hawk: Life and Battles of Kanhoji Angrey, Asia Publishing House, 1959, reprinted, Vision Books (New Delhi), 1978.
Distant Drum, Asia Publishing House, 1961.
Combat of Shadows, Hamish Hamilton, 1962, Inter Culture Association, 1966.
The Puars of Dewas Senior, Longmans, Green, 1963.
The Princes (a Literary Guild selection), Viking, 1963.
A Bend in the Ganges, Hamish Hamilton, 1964, Viking, 1965.
Spy in Amber, Orient (New Delhi), 1970.
Chhatrapatis of Kolhapur, Popular Prakashan (Bombay), 1971.
The Devil's Wind, Viking, 1972.
A Toast in Warm Wine (short stories), Orient, 1973.
Bombay Beware (short stories), Orient, 1975.
Rumble-Tumble (short stories), Orient, 1977.
Line of Mars (play), Hind, 1977.
Dead and Living Cities, Hind, 1978.
Shalimar, Vikas (India), 1978.
The Men Who Killed Ghandi, Macmillan (London), 1978.
The Garland Keepers, Vision Books, 1979.
Cue from the Inner Voice: The Choice before Big Business, Vikas, 1980.
Bandicoot Run, Vision Books, 1981.
Inside Goa, Goa Government, 1982.
Princess (biography), Century-Hutchinson, 1985.
Four Graves (short stories), Penguin Books, 1990.
Cactus Country (novel), Viking, 1992.

Contributor to *John Kenneth Galbraith Introduces India,* Deutsch, 1973. Also author of weekly column "Time Off," syndicated in national newspapers in five major cities.

SIDELIGHTS: Manohar Malgonkar has spent most of his life in a village deep in the jungles of Canara, the site of his family's home for over one hundred years. He currently operates manganese mines which he and a brother own. Though he once worked for several years as a professional big-game hunter, Malgonkar is now a wildlife conservationist.

BIOGRAPHICAL/CRITICAL SOURCES:

PERIODICALS

Antioch Review, June, 1973.
Times Literary Supplement, January 3, 1986.

MARGETSON, Stella 1912-

PERSONAL: Born March 6, 1912, in London, England; daughter of Laurence (a business executive) and Florence (an actress; stage name, Collingbourne) Margetson. *Education:* Educated privately. *Avocational interests:* Conservation of the environment.

ADDRESSES: Home—15 Hamilton Ter., London, England. *Agent*—A. P. Watt, 20 John Street, London WC1N 2DL, England; and Collins-Knowlton-Wing, 575 Madison Ave., New York, NY 10022.

CAREER: Writer.

WRITINGS:

Flood Tide, and Other Stories, J. Crowther, 1943.
Peter's Wife (fiction), Heinemann, 1948.
The Prisoners (novel; also see below), Heinemann, 1949.
Journey by Stages: An Account of Travelling by Stage Coach and Mail between 1660 and 1840, Cassell, 1967.
Leisure and Pleasure in the Nineteenth Century, Coward, 1969.
Victorian London: An Illustrated Survey, Hastings House, 1969, published in England as *Fifty Years of Victorian London, from the Great Exhibition to the Queen's Death,* Macdonald & Co., 1969.
Leisure and Pleasure in the Eighteenth Century, Cassell, 1970.
Regency London, Praeger, 1971.
The Long Party: High Society in the Twenties and Thirties, Saxon House, 1974.
Victorian People, Batsford, 1977.
Victorian High Society, Batsford, 1980.
St. John's Wood: An Abode of Love and the Arts, Home and Law, 1988.

RADIO PLAYS

The Prisoners (adapted from her novel of the same title), British Broadcasting Corp. (BBC), 1952.
Lucertola, BBC, 1953.
Leading Lady, BBC, 1954.
These Quickening Years, BBC, 1954.
Village in the Stars, BBC, 1955.
Seven Stages, BBC, 1955.

OTHER

Contributor of fiction and historical features to *Homes and Gardens, Country Life,* and other publications.

WORK IN PROGRESS: Research into nineteenth-century social history.

SIDELIGHTS: Stella Margetson once told *CA:* "In writing social history, I believe passionately in the importance of the past as seen through the eyes of the individual people who lived at any specific time. Their diaries, letters, and comments reveal far more to me than facts and statistics: how they really lived, what they thought and felt. And I believe that in trying to understand their lives we cannot fail to enhance our own, for it is only by discovering how people coped with their problems in other days that we can put ours into perspective."

BIOGRAPHICAL/CRITICAL SOURCES:

PERIODICALS

Books and Bookmen, July, 1967.
Canadian Forum, August, 1969.
Punch, April 16, 1969.*

* * *

MASSIE, Robert K(inloch)   1929-

PERSONAL: Born January 5, 1929, in Lexington, KY; son of Robert K. and Mary (Kimball) Massie; married Suzanne Rohrbach (a writer), December 18, 1954 (divorced, 1990); children: Robert Kinloch, Susanna, Elizabeth. *Education:* Yale University, B.A., 1950; Oxford University, B.A. (Rhodes scholar), 1952. *Avocational interests:* Sailing.

ADDRESSES: Home—60 West Clinton Avenue, Irvington, NY 10533.

CAREER: Collier's, New York City, reporter, 1955-56; *Newsweek,* New York City, writer and correspondent, 1956-62; *USA-1,* New York City, writer, 1962; *Saturday Evening Post,* New York City, writer, 1962-65; free-lance writer, 1965—. Princeton University, Ferris Professor of Journalism, 1977, 1985; Tulane University, Mellon Professor of Humanities, 1981. *Military service:* U.S. Naval Reserves, 1952-55; became lieutenant, junior grade.

MEMBER: Authors Guild (vice-president, 1985-87, president, 1987—), Authors League of America, PEN, Society of American Historians.

AWARDS, HONORS: Christopher Award, 1976, for *Journey;* American Book Award nomination, American Library Association Notable Book citation, and Pulitzer Prize for Biography, all 1981, all for *Peter the Great: His Life and World.*

WRITINGS:

Nicholas and Alexandra (biography), Atheneum, 1967.
(With wife, Suzanne Massie) *Journey,* Knopf, 1975.
Peter the Great: His Life and World (biography), Knopf, 1980.
(Author of introduction) Jeffrey Finestone, *The Last Courts of Europe: A Royal Family Album, 1860-1914,* Dent, 1981, Crown, 1983.

Dreadnought: Britain, Germany, and the Coming of the Great War, Random House, 1991.

Massie's works have been translated into Spanish and German.

ADAPTATIONS: Nicholas and Alexandra was adapted into a motion picture by James Goldman and Edward Bond and released by Columbia, 1971; *Peter the Great* was adapted for television as a four-part mini-series for NBC-TV, 1986.

SIDELIGHTS: Robert K. Massie worked as a journalist for ten years before the circumstances of his personal life led him to the serious examination of Russian history. Soon after joining *Newsweek* as a book reviewer, Massie and his wife Suzanne discovered that their six-month-old son Bobbie suffered from hemophilia, a hereditary and incurable blood disease. Investigating his son's condition led Massie to spend many hours in the New York Public Library where he became caught up in the story of Alexei Romanov, heir of the last ruling family of Russia, who had been stricken with hemophilia through his mother, the Empress Alexandra. Familiarity with the devastating effects resulting from such a family tragedy prompted Massie to study the short, tragic reign of Alexei's father, Czar Nicholas II, from a unique perspective. As Massie told *CA:* "When something unusual happens in your life, you are curious to see what has happened before. We were busy trying to find out how to deal with this disease, talking to a lot of other families, to doctors and social workers and people like that about hemophilia in mid-twentieth-century America. But I knew a bit of the story of the Tsarevich Alexis and I was curious to find out how his family had dealt with it, what was all this business about hypnotism and so forth.

"There was no thought of a book," recalled Massie. "I was just curious to know what happened. I read whatever I could find and I began to notice a discrepancy. The general narrative historians swept pretty quickly by this whole business of the boy's illness with a sentence or two. I found that it was much more complicated than that. The links that even I could find, with very little background in the field, between the illness and what was happening politically were very much in evidence and were important." *Nicholas and Alexandra* was published ten years later to much critical acclaim. Robert Payne praised the book in the *New York Times Book Review:* "Massie's canvas is the whole of Russia, the Czar and Czarina merely the focal points. . . . What emerges is a study in depth of the reign of Nicholas, and for perhaps the first time we meet the actors in the drama face to face in their proper setting."

The profits from *Nicholas and Alexandra,* along with royalties from the film that would later be based upon it, provided Massie with sufficient funds to help his son Bobbie cope with life as a hemophiliac. In 1975, Massie and his wife coauthored *Journey,* chronicling their young son's courage in facing his condition, and describing how the disease affected their own lives as parents. "The substance of the book shifts from the mastery of pain to the mastery of life, and it is done in part by a turning outward in contrast to the Romanovs' [*Nicholas and Alexandra*] secretiveness and withdrawal," commented *New York Times Book Review* critic Elizabeth Hegeman.

Journey contains a harsh indictment of America's "pitifully inadequate health plans, the workings of hospitals and the politics of the Red Cross which, charged the Massies, places the welfare of drug companies above that of hemophilia victims," according to *Newsweek* reviewer Margo Jefferson. Hegeman echoed the authors' frustration in describing "the grotesque folly of trying to raise enough money for the Hemophilia Society through charity balls and premieres and the inadequacy of the 'patchwork' of uncoordinated charities and agencies set up to help special need groups." She added that Massie's impassioned criticism should not be construed as self-serving: "It is the statement of a father who feels guilty over using so much of the precious blood derivative *even though he pays for it,* because he has carefully thought out his connection to society and he knows that something is deeply wrong with our social policy if blood is treated as a commodity to be exchanged for money."

After completing *Journey,* Massie once again turned his attention to the lush panorama of the Russian past. Although now familiar with the time-period encompassing the life of the Tsarevich, there were still many areas of history with which Massie was unfamiliar. "While I was working on *Nicholas and Alexandra,* I was giving myself a course and reading as much as I could," Massie remembered. "I was fascinated by Peter [I]. There were glimpses of his character, stories and legends about him, but I couldn't find any biography which really captured him. After thinking about it for a while, I thought I could try one." Massie made frequent trips to Russia to do research for *Peter the Great: His Life and World.* He was fortunate in receiving a great deal of both official and scholarly assistance from the Soviet people who continue to have great reverence for Peter as one of the greatest of Russian heroes.

Considered the architect of modern Russia, Peter the Great was an imposing figure obsessed with forcing a backward Russian society into step with seventeenth-century Europe. Off came the flowing beards, gone were the long robes with their drooping sleeves; the monarch abolished such traditional emblems of the old order in favor of a "German" style of dress that allowed for the freedom of movement necessary for an active, forward-

thinking people. Peter the Great went on to establish Russia as a major power. Imbuing his homeland with Western technology through the importation of thousands of craftsmen and military personnel, raising the educational standards of his fellow Russians by setting up schools and sending young men abroad to study arts and sciences yet unknown in Russia, and defeating longtime opponent Charles XII of Sweden in the battle of Poltava in 1709, Peter crowned his growing empire with the city of St. Petersburg, capital of the new Russia and his "window into Europe," which he commanded be built upon the northern marshes bordering the Gulf of Finland.

A London *Times* critic felt that Massie's obvious admiration for his subject tended to color his view of the facts and remarked that "the urge to show Peter in the best light must spring partly from the relief of writing about a monarch who could, and did, do everything for himself, after devoting so many years to Peter's descendants who, between them, barely seemed able to tie up a ribbon or fasten a stud." And John Leonard of the *New York Times* criticized Massie for the fact that "there is, in [*Peter the Great*], no thesis. . . . Peter's spotty education, his voracious curiosity, his epileptic convulsions, his talent with his hands, his ignorance of literature, his humor and his terror—all are merely reported and forgiven, like the weather." However, while noting in the *New York Times Book Review* the book's somewhat daunting length, Kyril Fitzlyon hailed *Peter the Great* as "an enthralling book, beautifully edited, with a first-rate index and excellent illustrations," and later added: "It would be surprising if it did not become the standard biography of Peter the Great in English for many years to come, as fascinating as any novel and more so than most."

"I had done enough about Russia," Massie acknowledged in a 1991 interview with Joseph A. Cincotti in the *New York Times Book Review,* "so I decided to come home from Russia by way of western Europe." *Fin de siecle* western Europe was the route that Massie chose to travel, and the one that provided the subject for his next book, *Dreadnought: Britain, Germany, and the Coming of the Great War.* A narrative account of Britain's retreat from "splendid isolationism" after the crisis at Fashoda, the battle that resulted in France's cessation of efforts towards building a rival colonial empire after 1898, *Dreadnought* covers the period from 1897 to August, 1914, as Britain came to France's aid in World War I. Taking its title from the name given to the heavily armored and gunned battleship, H.M.S Dreadnought, designed by the British to render all other navies obsolete, Massie's lengthy volume uses the naval antagonism between Britain and Germany as a point of departure. Organizing such a broad range of cataclysmic events into a comprehensive format is no easy task, and some reviewers found fault with the book's areas of concentration. Stanley Weintraub commented in the *New York Times Book Review:* "Since Massie uses the lens of the British-Germany rivalry, the picture that emerges of the European powder keg and its multiple fuses, all sputtering at different speeds, is out of focus, although dramatic nevertheless."

However, *Dreadnought* was praised for the characteristically engaging narrative style of its author. Commending Massie's sharp eye for detail and his ability to vividly portray characters, Geoffrey Moorhouse observed in *Los Angeles Times Book Review,* "one will not forget . . . Bismarck working in his office, watched by his dog Tiras, who terrorized all visitors . . . or Lord Salisbury, who 'treated his children like small foreign powers: not often noticed, but when recognized, regarded with unfailing politeness.' " "*Dreadnought* is a saga elegantly spun out in palaces and cabinet rooms, on the decks of royal yachts and the bridges of battleships, in Europe's spas and rambling country houses," agreed Douglas Porch in *Washington Post Book World.* "Massie traces the development of naval forces and the calculations of European diplomats with clarity and humor," he added. "He has a subtle appreciation for interplay of personalities in an era when the ruling houses of England and Germany were blood relations, and their political leaders shared a strong sense of cultural communality."

BIOGRAPHICAL/CRITICAL SOURCES:

PERIODICALS

Los Angeles Times Book Review, December 8, 1991, pp. 4, 15.
Newsweek, August 28, 1967; May 26, 1975; October 20, 1980.
New York Times, October 7, 1980.
New York Times Book Review, August 20, 1967, pp. 1, 26; May 11, 1975, pp. 5-6; November 10, 1991, pp. 7, 9.
Punch, April 1, 1981, pp. 534-35.
Time, November 10, 1980, pp. 107-08.
Times (London), February 5, 1981.
Times Literary Supplement, April 28, 1981, p. 467.
Washington Post Book World, November 24, 1991, p. 5.

* * *

MATHEWS, Harry 1930-

PERSONAL: Born February 14, 1930, in New York, NY. *Education:* Studied music at Princeton and Harvard Universities and at L'Ecole Normale de Musique in Paris, France.

ADDRESSES: Home—Le Haut du Peuil, Lans-en-Vercors, 38250 Villard-de-Lans, France. *Agent*—Maxine Groffsky, 2 Fifth Ave., New York, NY 10011.

CAREER: Poet, novelist, and translator. Has taught at Bennington College, Hamilton College, and Columbia University. Member of Ouvroir de Litterature Potentielle, Paris, France.

AWARDS, HONORS: National Endowment for the Arts grant for fiction writing, 1982; National Academy and Institute of Arts and Letters fiction writing award, 1991.

WRITINGS:

The Conversions (novel; also see below), Random House, 1962.
Tlooth (novel; also see below), Paris Review/Doubleday, 1966.
The Planisphere (poetry), Burning Deck, 1974.
The Sinking of the Odradek Stadium and Other Novels (includes *The Conversions* and *Tlooth*), Harper, 1975.
Trial Impressions (poetry), Burning Deck, 1977.
Selected Declarations of Dependence, 2 Press, 1977.
Country Cooking and Other Stories, Burning Deck, 1980.
Armenian Papers (poetry), Princeton University Press, 1987.
Cigarettes (novel), Weidenfeld & Nicolson, 1987.
The Orchard (memoirs), Bamberger Books, 1988.
20 Lines a Day (journal), Dalkey Archive Press, 1988.
Singular Pleasures (fiction), Grenfell Press, 1988, Dalkey Archive Press, 1993.
Out of Bounds (poetry), Burning Deck, 1989.
The Way Home: Collected Longer Prose (contains *Singular Pleasures* and *Country Cooking*), Atlas Press (London), 1989.
The American Experience (fiction), Atlas Press, 1991.
Immeasurable Distances (criticism), Lapis Press, 1991.

Contributor of criticism to *American Book Review, Bomb, Grand Street, New York Review of Books, Parnassus, Review of Contemporary Fiction,* and *Shiny International;* contributor of poetry to *Art and Literature, Grand Street, o.blek, Paris Review,* and *Partisan Review.* Founding editor (with others) of *Locus Solus.*

SIDELIGHTS: Harry Mathews's early experimental novels, *The Conversions, Tlooth,* and *The Sinking of the Odradek Stadium,* "have long been cult classics admired for their humor, linguistic inventiveness and narrative ingenuity," a *Washington Post Book World* reviewer commented. *The Conversions,* in which the narrator must possess a ritual golden adze and solve three riddles to inherit an enormous fortune, is "a kind of literary hopscotch, one foot in the air, always nearly off balance, but at no matter what cost abandoning one position speedily for another," according to a *New York Herald Tribune Book Review* contributor. A *Times Literary Supplement* critic found it "fertile in linguistic skylarkings and fantastic invention" and "as exhilarating to read as a fireworks set-piece is to watch."

Tlooth is an "elaborate game, a compound of absurd adventures, faked documents, diagrams and word puzzles," Peter Buitenhuis wrote in the *New York Times Book Review.* "There is little pretense of realism. Mathews has abandoned himself to an imagination full of strange lore and miscellaneous literary allusions. . . . The imagination of the artist projected into the work of art has taken the real and the fantastic as related, even interchangeable, perceptions of life." A *Tri-Quarterly* reviewer found *Tlooth's* "ingenious plot is that of travelogue-adventure in which all places are very much the same, even if they are called Afghanistan, Russia, India, Morocco; and in this respect *Tlooth* very much descends from Apollinaire's *Zone* (1913) with its unbounded sense of literary space and the higher nonsense fiction of Lewis Carroll and especially, the Frenchman Raymond Roussel." *The Conversions* and *Tlooth* are contained in *The Sinking of the Odradek Stadium and Other Novels*; the title story, described by Edmund White in the *New York Times Book Review* as "a comic masterpiece," relates a couple's search for treasure in a ship sunk in the 16th century off the coast of Florida. White observed, "As Mathew's art has matured he has moved away from pearls of exotic narration strung on a slender thread of continuity. In *The Sinking of the Odradek Stadium,* he has created a seamless fabric, as tense, light, and strong as stretched silk."

In *Cigarettes,* which appeared after a seven-year break in publication, the author follows thirteen characters through their contacts with Elizabeth, "who winds through the novel like a plume of smoke," Lisa Zeidner noted in the *New York Times Book Review. Cigarettes* shows that "one reason complete happiness isn't possible . . . is that knowledge can be acquired but not lost," *Partisan Review's* Rachel Hadas commented. "Answers to many enigmas are teased out by the reader as well as the characters; the truth is like the seminal portrait of Elizabeth, which is cherished, stolen, forged, destroyed, bought, sold, restored—but about which we chiefly learn that it doesn't resemble her."

BIOGRAPHICAL/CRITICAL SOURCES:

BOOKS

Contemporary Literary Criticism, Volume 6, Gale, 1976.

PERIODICALS

Book Week, November 27, 1966.
Harper's, November, 1966.
Library Journal, June 1, 1962; December 1, 1966.
Los Angeles Times, October 11, 1987.
Nation, September 29, 1962.
New Leader, October 14, 1963.
New York Herald Tribune Book Review, September 2, 1962.

New York Review of Books, August 7, 1975.
New York Times, May 18, 1975; November 29, 1987; January 21, 1988.
New York Times Book Review, October 30, 1966; May 18, 1975; November 29, 1987, p. 23.
Partisan Review, February, 1989, p. 310.
Saturday Review, November 12, 1966.
Time, June 15, 1962.
Times Literary Supplement, September 14, 1962; September 15, 1989, p. 997.
Tri-Quarterly, winter, 1967.
Village Voice, January 26, 1967.
Washington Post Book World, December 29, 1991, p. 13.

*   *   *

MAUGHAM, Robert Cecil Romer   1916-1981
(David Griffin, Robin Maugham)

PERSONAL: Born May 17, 1916, in London, England; died March 13, 1981, in Brighton, England; son of Frederic Herbert (a judge and Lord High Chancellor of England) and Helen Mary (Romer) Maugham. *Education:* Attended Eton and Trinity Hall, Cambridge. *Religion:* Church of England.

CAREER: Writer, 1945-81. Barrister, Lincoln's Inn. Became second Viscount Maugham of Hartfield, 1958, took seat in House of Lords, 1960. Lecturer on the Middle East to the Royal Institute of International Affairs and other institutions in England. *Military service:* British Army, 1939-45; served in North Africa with Eighth Army, wounded, 1942; served with Middle East Intelligence Centre, 1943; invalided out with honorary rank of captain; mentioned in dispatches.

MEMBER: Garrick Club.

WRITINGS:

UNDER NAME DAVID GRIFFIN

The Wrong People, Paperback Library, 1967, revised edition published under name Robin Maugham, Heinemann, 1970, McGraw, 1971.

ALL UNDER NAME ROBIN MAUGHAM

STORY COLLECTIONS

The 1946 MS., War Facts Press, 1943.
Testament: Cairo, 1898, Michael de Hartington, 1972.
The Black Tent and Other Stories (also see below), edited by Peter Burton, W. H. Allen, 1972.

NOVELS

The Servant, Falcon Press, 1948, Harcourt, 1949.
Line on Ginger, Chapman and Hall, 1951.
The Rough and the Smooth, Chapman and Hall, 1951.

Behind the Mirror, Harcourt, 1955.

The Man with Two Shadows, Longman, 1958, Harcourt, 1959.

November Reef: A Novel of the South Seas, Longman, 1962.

The Green Shade, New American Library, 1966.

The Second Window, McGraw, 1968.

The Link: A Victorian Mystery, McGraw, 1969.

The Last Encounter, W. H. Allen, 1972, McGraw, 1973.

The Barrier: A Novel Containing Five Sonnets by John Betjeman Written in the Style of the Period, W. H. Allen, 1973, McGraw, 1974.

The Sign, McGraw, 1974.

Knock on Teak, W. H. Allen, 1976.

The Dividing Line, W. H. Allen, 1979.

PLAYS

The Rising Heifer, first produced in Dallas, Texas, 1952, produced in High Wycombe, Buckinghamshire, 1955.

The Leopard, first produced in Worthing, Sussex, 1956.

Mr. Lear (three-act; first produced in Worthing, Sussex, 1956), English Theatre Guild, 1963.

The Last Hero, first produced in London, England, 1957.

(With Philip King) *A Lonesome Road* (three-act; first produced in London, 1957), Samuel French, 1959.

Odd Man In (adapted from play *Monsieur Masure* by Claude Magnier; first produced in London, 1957), Samuel French, 1958.

The Servant (based on the novel of same title; first produced in Worthing, Sussex, 1958; produced in New York, 1974), Davis-Poynter, 1972.

(With P. King) *The Hermit,* first produced in Harrogate, Yorkshire, 1959.

It's in the Bag (adapted from the play *Oscar* by Magnier), first produced in Brighton, England, 1959, produced in London, 1960.

The Claimant, first produced in Worthing, Sussex, 1962; produced in London, 1964.

(With Willis Hall) *Azouk* (adapted from a play by Alexandre Rivemale), first produced in Newcastle upon Tyne, England, 1962.

Winter in Ischia, first produced in Worthing, Sussex, 1964.

Enemy! (two-act; first produced in Guildford, Surrey, 1969, and in London, 1969), Samuel French, 1971.

SCREENPLAYS

(With John Hunter) *The Intruder,* British Lion, 1953.

(With Bryan Forbes) *The Black Tent,* Rank Organization, 1956.

Also author of screenplays *The Man with Two Shadows,* 1960, *November Reef,* 1962, *How Are You Johnnie?, Willie,* 1969, *The Barrier,* 1972, and *The Joyita Mystery* (also see below), *Curtains, Cakes and Ale.*

TELEVISION SCRIPTS

Rise above It, British Broadcasting Corp. (BBC), 1957.

The Last Hero, BBC, 1966.

Also author of television script *Wise Virgins of Hove,* 1960.

OTHER

Come to Dust, Chapman and Hall, 1945.

(Editor) *Convoy Magazine: Stories, Articles, Poems from the Forces, Factories, Mines and Fields,* Collins, 1945.

Approach to Palestine, Grey Walls Press, 1947.

Nomad, Chapman and Hall, 1947, Viking, 1948.

North African Notebook, Chapman and Hall, 1948, Harcourt, 1949.

Journey to Siwa, Chapman and Hall, 1950, Harcourt, 1951.

The Slaves of Timbuktu, Harper, 1961.

The Joyita Mystery, Parrish, 1962.

Somerset and All the Maughams, New American Library, 1966.

Escape from the Shadows: An Autobiography, Hodder and Stoughton, 1972, McGraw, 1973.

Search for Nirvana, W. H. Allen, 1975.

Lovers in Exile (story collection), W. H. Allen, 1977.

Conversations with Willie: Recollections of W. Somerset Maugham, Simon & Schuster, 1978.

Contributor to periodicals, including *People, Chambers' Journal, Today, Argosy,* and *Oggi* (Italy). Editor, *Convoy* series of booklets, Collins, beginning 1944.

SIDELIGHTS: Robin Maugham, nephew of the novelist W. Somerset Maugham, was also a novelist, as well as a playwright and short story writer. Among his novels *The Rough and the Smooth* was a particular success, selling over one hundred thousand copies in its German translation alone, while *The Servant* was adapted as a popular film in 1966. In *Somerset and All the Maughams* Maugham wrote of his illustrious family, while in *Conversations with Willie* he remembered his famous uncle.

After attending Cambridge University, where he studied law, Maugham entered military service during the Second World War. He fought in North Africa with the British Eighth Army, was wounded, and invalided out. His injuries left him with occasional bouts of amnesia for the rest of his life. While recuperating from his wounds in an army hospital Maugham wrote *Come to Dust,* a description of his war experiences and rehabilitation. The book was such a success that Maugham decided to drop his budding law career and turn to free-lance writing.

His wartime knowledge of North Africa and the Middle East, and his many later travels throughout Asia and Africa, provided Maugham with the material he needed for his many books. Perhaps the most controversial of these was 1961's *The Slaves of Timbuktu,* an exploration of the contemporary slave trade in North Africa. Making a three thousand mile journey from the port of Dakar on the West African coast to the desert city of Timbuktu, Maugham discovered that slavery still exists in that part of the world, even going so far as to buy a slave himself and setting him free. Although Walter Schwarz in the *Guardian* suggested that Maugham may have been hoodwinked into buying and freeing a man who was never really a slave, many critics applauded the expose for its blend of personal narrative and historical perspective. M. I. Finley of the *New Statesman* noted that *The Slaves of Timbuktu* "is an account of a highly personal experience, told in Lord Maugham's easy prose, which makes much use of dialogue to evoke the people with whom he dealt and suggest the complicated historical and tribal background, not only of slavery but of this part of western Africa in general." Anthony Smith of the *Spectator* commented that Maugham's mixture of past and present was "a skilful piece of literary chemistry."

In his novels, Maugham displayed an ability to write succinctly, delineating characters and settings with a minimum of words. Speaking of *The Servant,* the story of a scheming servant who destroys his master by playing to his desire for comfort, the critic for the *Times Literary Supplement* found that "its merit lies in the economy with which it is told; there is little in it that does not directly affect the plot and little that could be spared." In his review of *Line on Ginger,* N. L. Rothman noted that Maugham "tells his tale with deceptive ease, he illumines it with meticulously chosen bits of dialogue. Everything contributes, everything builds toward the planned effect. There isn't a wasted word or moment."

In *Somerset and All the Maughams* Maugham chronicled his prominent family's history, tracing them back to the seventeenth century and providing glimpses of various Maughams who served in the English Navy, lived in poverty in London, and pioneered the American wilderness. But Maugham focuses his attention on his father and uncle in particular. His father, a Lord High Chancellor and viscount, played a substantial role in English government and law. Maugham's uncle Somerset was a writer of great distinction who is presented in this book "with all his warts, with all his distasteful perversities" as a critic for the *Christian Science Monitor* noted. As Francis King commented in the *New Statesman,* "this book is likely to be read chiefly for the frankness of its revelations about 'Uncle Willie.' "

In 1978, Maugham presented more revelations about his uncle in *Conversations with Willie.* Selected from diaries the younger Maugham kept from 1944 to 1965, the book explores the relationship between the celebrated writer and his family. It also gives insight into the later years

when Maugham was ill, senile and suffering. H. M. Hyde in the *Times Literary Supplement* found that *Conversations with Willie* "perhaps sheds more light than has appeared hitherto on the elder man's domestic life," while S. J. Laut in *Best Sellers* argued that it was "scarcely a flattering or cheerful portrait" of Somerset Maugham.

With *Escape from the Shadows,* Maugham wrote of his own life and his continuous struggle to emerge from the shadows of his famous father and uncle and establish his own career. The book also reveals for the first time Maugham's homosexuality. So prevalent was the homosexual nature of the memoir that the *Times Literary Supplement* critic claimed that "when heterosexual relationships develop they seem, in this context, almost improper." J. S. Phillipson in *Best Sellers* complained that *Escape from the Shadows* too often "reads like a collection of anecdotes strung together," although he occasionally found "a touching and memorable scene well told." Referring to Maugham's efforts to escape from his relatives' shadows, Helen Gregory in *Library Journal* stated that "this exorcism of private devils offers an account of the interesting adventures of an intelligent traveler, as well as stories of the war, Churchill, Coward, Eliot, and others."

BIOGRAPHICAL/CRITICAL SOURCES:

BOOKS

Maugham, Robin, *Escape from the Shadows: An Autobiography,* McGraw, 1973.

PERIODICALS

America, July 9, 1966, p. 38.
Atlantic, April, 1973, p. 128.
Best Sellers, June 15, 1966, p. 109; October 1, 1968; October 15, 1969; April 1, 1973, p. 16; September, 1978.
Books and Bookmen, May, 1966, p. 27; January, 1970, p. 10; May, 1972, p. 65; June, 1973, p. 93; July, 1978, p. 24.
Bookseller, September 5, 1970.
Christian Science Monitor, February 21, 1951; June 16, 1966, p. 5; October 10, 1968, p. 13.
Commonweal, January 6, 1950; September 7, 1951.
Economist, April 9, 1966, p. 152.
Esquire, June 20, 1978, p. 93.
Guardian, June 2, 1961, p. 9.
Library Journal, February 1, 1949; April 15, 1955; June 15, 1961; July, 1966; September 1, 1969; February 1, 1973, p. 416.
Listener, October 10, 1968, p. 479; January 1, 1970; January 22, 1970; April 6, 1972, p. 458; October 5, 1972, p. 447; April 19, 1973, p. 520; December 11, 1980, p. 804.
Manchester Guardian, November 29, 1947; September 24, 1948; October 17, 1950.

Nation, February 12, 1949; November 12, 1955.

New Leader, September 25, 1978, p. 20.

New Statesman, November 12, 1955; November 29, 1958; May 12, 1961, p. 760; April 8, 1966, p. 504; July 29, 1966, p. 174; October 11, 1968, p. 468; December 26, 1969.

Newsweek, May 9, 1966, p. 102.

New Yorker, April 10, 1948; February 10, 1951; September 8, 1951; April 9, 1955; July 18, 1959.

New York Herald Tribune Book Review, February 13, 1949; March 26, 1950; July 17, 1955.

New York Review of Books, November 23, 1978, p. 26.

New York Times, July 11, 1948; February 20, 1949; December 4, 1949; April 2, 1950; September 9, 1951; April 17, 1955; May 31, 1959; May 5, 1966, p. 45; June 15, 1978, p. 57.

New York Times Book Review, May 22, 1966, p. 32; June 19, 1966, p. 34; November 3, 1968, p. 54; October 21, 1973, p. 51; May 26, 1974, p. 19; June 25, 1978, p. 10.

Observer, April 3, 1966, p. 26; July 24, 1966, p. 22; October 6, 1968, p. 33; November 16, 1969, p. 31; March 19, 1972, p. 32; October 1, 1972, p. 40; April 15, 1973, p. 39; May 16, 1976, p. 31.

Plays and Players, February, 1970.

Punch, April 27, 1966, p. 633; August 3, 1966, p. 200; October 9, 1968, p. 521; November 12, 1969, p. 803; December 31, 1969.

Saturday Review, May 1, 1948; March 12, 1949; April 8, 1950; April 16, 1955; July 9, 1966, p. 28; September 21, 1968, p. 38; November 29, 1969, p. 54; June 10, 1978, p. 41.

Spectator, September 24, 1948; May 26, 1961, p. 768; April 8, 1966, p. 439; July 29, 1966, p. 153; October 7, 1972, p. 543; April 28, 1973, p. 524; May 6, 1978, p. 21; November 29, 1980, p. 22.

Stage, September 28, 1972.

Time, May 20, 1966, p. 126; July 24, 1978, p. 78.

Times Literary Supplement, October 2, 1948; March 5, 1949; November 18, 1955; December 5, 1958; June 2, 1961; April 7, 1966, p. 296; November 27, 1969, p. 1355; April 14, 1972, p. 409; October 20, 1972, p. 1259; April 20, 1973, p. 451; May 21, 1976, p. 601; May 26, 1978, p. 578; December 12, 1980, p. 1408; August 14, 1981, p. 943.

Variety, January 28, 1970.

Washington Post, June 27, 1978, p. C12.

OBITUARIES:

PERIODICALS

AB Bookman, May 25, 1981, pp. 4114-4115.

Chicago Tribune, March 14, 1981.

New York Times, March 14, 1981.

Publishers Weekly, April 3, 1981, p. 22.

Time, March 23, 1981, p. 61.

Washington Post, March 15, 1981.*

*   *   *

MAUGHAM, Robin
See MAUGHAM, Robert Cecil Romer

*   *   *

MAUGHAM, W. S.
See MAUGHAM, W(illiam) Somerset

*   *   *

MAUGHAM, W(illiam) Somerset   1874-1965
(W. S. Maugham, William Somerset Maugham)

PERSONAL: Surname is pronounced "Mawm"; born January 25, 1874, in Paris, France; died December 16, 1965, in Nice, France; buried on the grounds of Canterbury Cathedral, Canterbury, Kent, England; son of Robert Ormond (solicitor to the British Embassy in Paris) and Edith Mary (Snell) Maugham; married Gwendolen Maud Syrie Barnardo Wellcome, May 26, 1917 (divorced, 1927; died, 1955); children: Liza. *Education:* Attended University of Heidelberg, 1891-92; briefly studied accountancy in Kent, England; St. Thomas Hospital, M.R.C.S., L.R.C.P., 1897. *Religion:* Rationalist. *Avocational interests:* Bridge, music, gardening, and collecting paintings.

CAREER: Writer, 1896-1965. Created annual prize for promising young British writer, 1947; narrator for American television series, 1950-51. *Wartime service:* Served with Red Cross ambulance unit, as medical officer, and with British Secret Service in Switzerland and Russia during World War I; served with the British Ministry of Information in Paris during World War II.

MEMBER: Royal Society of Literature (fellow), American Academy of Arts and Letters (honorary member), Garrick Club.

AWARDS, HONORS: Chevalier of the Legion of Honor, 1929, Commander, 1939; D. Litt., Oxford University, 1952; Companion of Honour, 1954; Companion of Literature, Royal Society of Literature, 1961; named honorary senator of Heidelberg University, 1961; D. Litt., University of Toulouse; honorary fellow, Library of Congress, Washington, D.C.

WRITINGS:

NOVELS; OFTEN PUBLISHED UNDER NAME W. SOMERSET MAUGHAM

Liza of Lambeth, Unwin, 1897, revised edition, 1904, Doran, 1921, reprinted, Penguin Books, 1978.

The Making of a Saint, L. C. Page & Co., 1898, published as _The Making of a Saint: A Romance of Medieval Italy,_ Farrar, Straus, 1966, reprinted, Arno, 1977.

The Hero, Hutchinson, 1901, reprinted, Arno, 1977.

Mrs. Craddock, Heinemann, 1902, Doran, 1920, reprinted, Penguin Books, 1979.

The Merry-Go-Round, Heinemann, 1904, reprinted, Penguin Books, 1978.

The Bishop's Apron: A Study in the Origins of a Great Family, Chapman & Hall, 1906, reprinted, Arno, 1977.

The Explorer, Heinemann, 1907, Baker & Taylor, 1909.

The Magician, Heinemann, 1908, Duffield & Co., 1909, reprinted, Penguin Books, 1978, bound with _A Fragment of Autobiography,_ Heinemann, 1956, Doubleday, 1957.

Of Human Bondage, Doran, 1915, reprinted, Penguin Books, 1978.

The Moon and Sixpence, Doran, 1919, reprinted, Arno, 1977.

The Painted Veil, Doran, 1925, reprinted, Penguin Books, 1979.

Cakes and Ale; or, The Skeleton in the Cupboard, Doubleday, Doran & Co., 1930, reprinted, Arno, 1977, published as _Cakes and Ale,_ Modern Library, 1950.

The Book-Bag, G. Orioli, 1932.

The Narrow Corner, Doubleday, Doran & Co., 1932, reprinted, Pan, 1978.

Theatre, Doubleday, Doran & Co., 1937.

Christmas Holiday, Doubleday, Doran & Co., 1939, reprinted, Pan, 1978.

Up at the Villa, Doubleday, Doran & Co., 1941, reprinted, Penguin Books, 1978.

The Hour before the Dawn, Doubleday, Doran & Co., 1942, reprinted, Arno, 1977.

The Razor's Edge, Doubleday, Doran & Co., 1944, reprinted, Penguin Books, 1978.

Then and Now, Doubleday, 1946, published as _Fools and Their Folly,_ Avon, 1949, reprinted, Pan, 1979.

Catalina: A Romance, Doubleday, 1948, reprinted, Pan, 1978.

Selected Novels, three volumes, Heinemann, 1953.

SHORT STORIES; OFTEN PUBLISHED UNDER NAME W. SOMERSET MAUGHAM

Orientations, Unwin, 1899.

The Trembling of the Leaf: Little Stories of the South Sea Islands, Doran, 1921, reprinted, Arno, 1977, published as _Sadie Thompson and Other Stories of the South Seas,_ Readers Library, 1928, published as _Rain, and Other Stories,_ Grosset, 1932.

The Casuarina Tree: Six Stories, Doran, 1926, reprinted, Arno, 1977, published as _The Letter: Stories of Crime,_ Collins, 1930.

Ashenden; or, The British Agent, Doubleday, Doran & Co., 1928, reprinted, Penguin Books, 1977.

Six Stories Written in the First Person Singular, Doubleday, Doran & Co., 1931, reprinted, Arno, 1977.

Ah King, Doubleday, Doran & Co., 1933 (published in England as _Ah King: Six Stories,_ Heinemann, 1933), reprinted, Arno, 1977.

East and West: The Collected Short Stories, Doubleday, Doran & Co., 1934 (published in England as _Altogether; Being the Collected Stories of W. Somerset Maugham,_ Heinemann, 1934).

The Judgement Seat, Centaur, 1934.

Cosmopolitans, Doubleday, Doran & Co., 1936, reprinted, Arno, 1977, published as _Cosmopolitans: Very Short Stories,_ Heinemann, 1936, Avon, 1943.

The Favorite Short Stories of W. Somerset Maugham, Doubleday, Doran & Co., 1937.

Princess September and the Nightingale (fairy tale; first published in _The Gentleman in the Parlour_), Oxford University Press, 1939, published as _Princess September,_ Harcourt, 1969.

The Mixture as Before, Doubleday, Doran & Co., 1940, reprinted, Arno, 1977.

The Unconquered, House of Books, 1944.

"Ah King" and Other Romance Stories of the Tropics (contains selections from _Ah King_), Avon, 1944.

Creatures of Circumstance, Doubleday, 1947, reprinted, Arno, 1977.

Stories of Love and Intrigue from "The Mixture as Before," Avon, 1947.

East of Suez: Great Stories of the Tropics, Avon, 1948.

Here and There, Heinemann, 1948.

The Complete Short Stories, three volumes, Heinemann, 1951, Doubleday, 1952, published as _Collected Short Stories,_ Pan, 1976.

The World Over: Stories of Manifold Places and People, Doubleday, 1952.

The Best Short Stories, selected by John Beecroft, Modern Library, 1957.

Favorite Stories, Avon, 1960.

Collected Short Stories, Penguin Books, 1963.

Husbands and Wives: Nine Stories, edited by Richard A. Cordell, Pyramid, 1963.

The Sinners: Six Stories, edited by Richard A. Cordell, Pyramid, 1964.

A Maugham Twelve, edited by Angus Wilson, Heinemann, 1966.

The Complete Short Stories of W. Somerset Maugham, four volumes, Washington Square Press, 1967.

The Kite and Other Stories, introduction by Ian Serriallier, Heinemann Educational, 1968.

Maugham's Malaysian Stories, edited by Anthony Burgess, Heinemann, 1969.

Seventeen Lost Stories, edited by Craig V. Showalter, Doubleday, 1969.

A Baker's Dozen: Thirteen Short Stories, Heinemann, 1969.

Four Short Stories, illustrations by Henri Matisse, Hallmark Editions, 1970.

A Second Baker's Dozen: Thirteen Short Stories, Heinemann, 1970.

The Hairless Mexican [and] *The Traitor,* Heinemann Educational, 1974.

"Footprints in the Jungle" and Two Other Stories, edited by Rod Sinclair, Heinemann Educational, 1975.

Sixty-five Short Stories, Octopus Books, 1976.

A short story, "The Vessel of Wrath," was published by Dell as *The Beachcomber.*

PLAYS; OFTEN PUBLISHED UNDER NAME W. S. MAUGHAM

Marriages Are Made in Heaven (produced in Berlin as *Schiffbruechig,* January 3, 1902), in *The Venture Annual of Art and Literature,* edited by Maugham and Laurence Housman, Baillie, 1903.

A Man of Honour: A Tragedy in Four Acts (produced in Westminster, England, at the Imperial Theatre, February 22, 1903), Dramatic Publishing, 1903.

Mademoiselle Zampa, produced in London at the Avenue Theatre, February 18, 1904.

Lady Frederick: A Comedy in Three Acts (first produced in London at the Royal Court Theatre, October 26, 1907; produced in New York, 1908), Heinemann, 1911, Dramatic Publishing, 1912.

A Trip to Brighton (adaptation of a play by Abel Tarride), produced in London, 1911.

Jack Straw: A Farce in Three Acts (produced in London at the Vaudeville Theatre, March 26, 1908; produced in New York, 1908), Heinemann, 1911, Dramatic Publishing, 1912.

Penelope: A Comedy in Three Acts (produced in London at the Comedy Theatre, January 9, 1909), Dramatic Publishing, 1912.

The Explorer: A Melodrama in Four Acts (produced in London at the Lyric Theatre, June 13, 1908), Heinemann, 1912, Doran, 1920, reprinted, Arno, 1977.

Mrs. Dot: A Farce in Three Acts (produced in London at the Comedy Theatre, April 27, 1908), Dramatic Publishing, 1912.

Smith: A Comedy in Four Acts (first produced in London at the Comedy Theatre, September 30, 1909; produced in New York, 1910), Dramatic Publishing, 1913.

Landed Gentry: A Comedy in Four Acts (produced as *Grace* in London at the Duke of York's Theatre, October 15, 1910), Dramatic Publishing, 1913.

The Tenth Man: A Tragic Comedy in Three Acts (produced in London at the Globe Theatre, February 24, 1910), Dramatic Publishing, 1913.

The Land of Promise: A Comedy in Four Acts (first produced in New York at the Lyceum Theatre, December 25, 1913; produced in London at the Duke of York's Theatre, February 26, 1914), Bickers & Son, 1913.

Caroline, produced in London at the New Theatre, February 8, 1916.

Love in a Cottage, produced in London at the Globe Theatre, January 26, 1918.

The Unknown: A Play in Three Acts (produced in London at the Aldwych Theatre, August 9, 1920), Doran, 1920.

The Circle: A Comedy in Three Acts (produced in London at the Haymarket Theatre, March 3, 1921; produced in New York), Doran, 1921.

Caesar's Wife: A Comedy in Three Acts (produced in London at the Royalty Theatre, March 27, 1919), Heinemann, 1922, Doran, 1923.

East of Suez: A Play in Seven Scenes (produced in London at His Majesty's Theatre, September 2, 1922), Doran, 1922, reprinted, Arno, 1977.

Loaves and Fishes: A Comedy in Four Acts (produced in London at the Duke of York's Theatre, February 24, 1911), Heinemann, 1923.

The Unattainable: A Farce in Three Acts (produced in New York and London, 1916), Heinemann, 1923.

Our Betters: A Comedy in Three Acts (first produced in New York at the Hudson Theatre, March 12, 1917; produced in London at the Globe Theatre, September 12, 1923), Heinemann, 1923, Doran, 1924.

Home and Beauty: A Farce in Three Acts (produced in New York and London at the Playhouse, August 30, 1919; produced as *Too Many Husbands* in New York at the Booth Theatre, October 8, 1919), Heinemann, 1923.

The Camel's Back, first produced in Worcester, Mass., 1923; produced in New York at the Vanderbilt Theatre, November 13, 1923; produced in London at the Playhouse, January 31, 1924.

The Letter: A Play in Three Acts (based on *The Casuarina Tree;* produced in London at the Playhouse, February 24, 1927), Doran, 1925, reprinted, Arno, 1977.

The Constant Wife: A Comedy in Three Acts (first produced in New York at Maxine Elliott's Theatre, November 29, 1926; produced in London at the Strand Theatre, April 6, 1927), Doran, 1926.

The Sacred Flame: A Play in Three Acts (produced in New York at Henry Miller's Theatre, November 19, 1928; produced in London at the Playhouse, February 8, 1929), Doubleday, Doran & Co., 1928, reprinted, Arno, 1977.

The Breadwinner: A Comedy in One Act (first produced in London at the Vaudeville Theatre, September 30, 1930; produced in New York, 1931), Heinemann,

1930, published as *The Breadwinner: A Comedy,*
Doubleday, Doran & Co., 1931.

Plays, Heinemann, 1931, reprinted, 1966.

Dramatic Works, six volumes, Heinemann, 1931-34, published as *Collected Plays,* three volumes, 1952, published as *The Collected Plays of W. Somerset Maugham,* 1961.

For Services Rendered: A Play in Three Acts (produced in London at the Globe Theatre, November 1, 1932), Heinemann, 1932, Doubleday, Doran & Co., 1933, reprinted, Arno, 1977.

Sheppey: A Play in Three Acts (produced in London at Wyndham's Theatre, September 14, 1933), Heinemann, 1933, Baker, 1949, reprinted, Arno, 1977.

The Mask and the Face (adaptation of a play by Luigi Chiarelli), produced in Boston, 1933; produced in New York at the Fifty-Second Street Theatre, May 8, 1933.

Six Comedies, Doubleday, Doran & Co., 1937, reprinted, Arno, 1977.

(With Guy Reginald Bolton) *Theatre: A Comedy in Three Acts,* French, 1942, reprinted, Arno, 1977.

The Noble Spaniard: A Comedy in Three Acts (adapted from Ernest Grenet-Dancourt's *Les gaites du veuvage*; produced in London at the Royalty Theatre, March 20, 1909), Evans, 1953.

The Perfect Gentleman (adaptation of a play by Moliere; produced in London at His Majesty's Theatre, May 27, 1913), published in *Theatre Arts,* November, 1955.

Selected Plays, Penguin Books, 1963.

Three Dramas: "The Letter," "The Sacred Flame," "For Services Rendered," Washington Square Press, 1968.

Three Comedies: "The Circle," "Our Betters," "The Constant Wife," Washington Square Press, 1969.

Also author of *Mrs. Beamish,* 1917; *The Keys to Heaven,* 1917; *Not To-Night, Josephine!* (farce), 1919; *The Road Uphill,* 1924; *The Force of Nature,* 1928.

EDITOR; OFTEN UNDER NAME W. SOMERSET MAUGHAM

(With Laurence Housman) *The Venture Annual of Art and Literature,* Baillie, 1903.

(With Laurence Housman) *The Venture Annual of Art and Literature 1905,* Simpkin Marshall, 1904.

Charles Henry Hawtrey, *The Truth at Last,* Little, 1924.

Traveller's Library, Doubleday, Doran & Co., 1933, reissued as *Fifty Modern English Writers,* Doubleday, Doran & Co., 1933.

(With Joseph Frederick Green) *Wisdom of Life: An Anthology of Noble Thoughts,* Watts, 1938.

(With introduction) George Douglas, *The House with the Green Shutters,* Oxford University Press, 1938.

Tellers of Tales: One Hundred Short Stories from the United States, England, France, Russia and Germany, Doubleday, Doran & Co., 1939, published as *The*

Greatest Stories of All Times, Tellers of Tales, Garden City Publishing, 1943.

Great Modern Reading: W. Somerset Maugham's Introduction to Modern English and American Literature, Doubleday, 1943.

Charles Dickens, *David Copperfield,* Winston, 1948.

Henry Fielding, *The History of Tom Jones, a Foundling,* Winston, 1948.

Jane Austen, *Pride and Prejudice,* Winston, 1949.

Honore de Balzac, *Old Man Goriot,* Winston, 1949.

Emily Bronte, *Wuthering Heights,* Winston, 1949.

Fyodor Dostoyevski, *The Brothers Karamazov,* Winston, 1949.

Gustave Flaubert, *Madame Bovary,* Winston, 1949.

Herman Melville, *Moby Dick,* Winston, 1949.

Stendhal, *The Red and the Black,* Winston, 1949.

Leo Tolstoy, *War and Peace,* Winston, 1949.

A Choice of Kipling's Prose, Macmillan, 1952, reprinted, Telegraph Books, 1981, published as *Maugham's Choice of Kipling's Best,* Doubleday, 1953.

OTHER

The Land of the Blessed Virgin: Sketches and Impressions in Andalusia (travel), Heinemann, 1905, Knopf, 1920.

On a Chinese Screen (travel), Doran, 1922, reprinted, Arno, 1977.

The Gentleman in the Parlour: A Record of a Journey from Rangoon to Haiphong, Doubleday, Doran & Co., 1930, reprinted, Paragon, 1989.

The Non-Dramatic Works, twenty-eight volumes, Heinemann, 1934-69.

Don Fernando; or, Variations on Some Spanish Themes (travel), Doubleday, Doran & Co., 1935, reprinted, Arno, 1977, revised edition, Heinemann, 1961.

Works, collected edition, Heinemann, 1935.

My South Sea Island, privately printed, 1936.

The Summing Up (autobiography), Doubleday, Doran & Co., 1938, reprinted, Penguin Books, 1978.

Books and You, Doubleday, Doran & Co., 1940, reprinted, Arno, 1977.

France at War, Doubleday, Doran & Co., 1940, reprinted, Arno, 1977.

Strictly Personal, Doubleday, Doran & Co., 1941, reprinted, Arno, 1977.

The W. Somerset Maugham Sampler, edited by Jerome Weidman, Garden City Publishing Co., 1943, published as *The Somerset Maugham Pocket Book,* Pocket Books, 1944.

W. Somerset Maugham's Introduction to Modern English and American Literature, New Home Library, 1943.

Great Novelists and Their Novels: Essays on the Ten Greatest Novels of the World and the Men and Women Who Wrote Them, Winston, 1948, revised edition published as *Ten Novels and Their Authors,* Heinemann,

1954, published as *The Art of Fiction: An Introduction to Ten Novels and Their Authors,* Doubleday, 1955, published as *The World's Ten Greatest Novels,* Fawcett, 1956, published as *W. Somerset Maugham Selects the World's Ten Greatest Novels,* Fawcett, 1962.

Quartet: Stories by W. Somerset Maugham, Screen-Plays by R. C. Sheriff, Heinemann, 1948, Doubleday, 1949.

A Writer's Notebook, Doubleday, 1949, reprinted, Penguin, 1984.

The Maugham Reader, introduction by Glenway Wescott, Doubleday, 1950.

Trio: Original Stories by W. Somerset Maugham; Screenplays by W. Somerset Maugham, R. C. Sherriff and Noel Langley, Doubleday, 1950.

Cakes and Ale, and Other Favorites, Pocket Books, 1951.

Encore: Original Stories by W. Somerset Maugham, Screenplays by T. E. B. Clarke, Arthur Macrae and Eric Ambler, Doubleday, 1952.

The Vagrant Mood: Six Essays, Heinemann, 1952, Doubleday, 1953.

The Partial View (contains *The Summing Up* and *A Writer's Notebook*), Heinemann, 1954.

Mr. Maugham Himself, selected by John Beecroft, Doubleday, 1954.

The Travel Books, Heinemann, 1955.

The Magician: A Novel, Together with A Fragment of Autobiography, Heinemann, 1956, published as *The Magician: Together with A Fragment of Autobiography,* Doubleday, 1957.

Points of View (essays), Heinemann, 1958, Doubleday, 1959.

Purely for My Pleasure, Doubleday, 1962.

Selected Prefaces and Introductions of W. Somerset Maugham, Doubleday, 1963.

Wit and Wisdom of Somerset Maugham, edited by Cecil Hewetson, Duckworth, 1966.

Essays on Literature, New American Library, 1967.

Cakes and Ale, and Twelve Short Stories, edited by Angus Wilson, Doubleday, 1967.

Man from Glasgow and Mackintosh, Heinemann Educational, 1973.

Selected Works, Heinemann, 1976.

The Works of Somerset Maugham, forty-seven volumes, Arno, 1977.

The Letters of William Somerset Maugham to Lady Juliet Duff, edited and with an introduction by Loren R. Rothschild, Rasselas Press, 1983.

A Traveller in Romance: Uncollected Writings, 1901-1964, edited by John Whitehead, C. N. Potter, 1985.

A Maugham archive is maintained by the Yale University Library. Maugham's papers are also housed at the Humanities Research Center at the University of Texas at Austin, the Berg Collection of the New York Public Library, the Lilly Library at Indiana University, Stanford University, the Houghton Library at Harvard University, the Fales Collection at New York University, the Butler Library at Columbia University, the Olin Library at Cornell University, the Beaverbrook Papers at the House of Lords Records Office, London, and at the University of Arkansas Library.

ADAPTATIONS: The following films were based on Maugham's works: *Smith,* 1917; *The Land of Promise,* Famous Players, 1917, remade under the title *The Canadian,* Paramount, 1926; *The Divorcee* (based on *Lady Frederick*), Metro Pictures, 1919; *Jack Straw,* Famous Players/Lasky, 1920; *The Circle,* Metro-Goldwyn-Mayer, 1925, remade under the title *Strictly Unconventional,* Metro-Goldwyn-Mayer, 1930; *Sadie Thompson,* 1928, remade under the title *Rain,* United Artists, 1932, remade under the title *Miss Sadie Thompson,* Columbia, 1954; *Charming Sinners* (based on *The Constant Wife*), Paramount, 1929; *Our Betters,* RKO, 1933; *Of Human Bondage,* RKO, 1934, remade by Warner Bros., 1946, and Metro-Goldwyn-Mayer, 1964; *The Painted Veil,* Metro-Goldwyn-Mayer, 1934; *The Tenth Man,* Wardour Films, 1937; *The Beachcomber* (based on *The Vessel of Wrath*), Paramount, 1938; *Too Many Husbands* (based on *Not To-Night, Josephine!*), Columbia, 1940, remade under the title *Three for the Show,* Columbia, 1955; *The Letter,* Warner Bros., 1940; *The Moon and Sixpence,* United Artists, 1943; *The Razor's Edge,* Twentieth Century-Fox, 1947, and Columbia, 1984; *Quartet* (based on *The Facts of Life, The Alien Corn, The Kite,* and *The Colonel's Lady*), J. Arthur Rank, 1949; *Trio,* Paramount, 1951; *Encore* (based on *The Ant and the Grasshopper, Winter Cruise,* and *Gigolo and Gigolette*), J. Arthur Rank, 1952.

Plays based on Maugham's works: *Rain* (based on *Miss Thompson*), by John B. Colton and Clemence Randolph, produced in New York, 1922, published by Boni & Liveright, 1923, Samuel French, 1948; *Sadie Thompson,* musical adaptation, produced in New York, 1944; *Before the Party* (based on a short story), by Rodney Ackland, S. French, 1950; *Larger Than Life* (based on the novel *Theatre*), by Guy Bolton, Samuel French, 1951; *Jane* (based on a short story), by S. N. Behrman, produced in New York, 1952, published by Random, 1952.

SIDELIGHTS: W. Somerset Maugham was one of the most prolific, versatile and popular authors of the twentieth century. For some thirty years his plays dominated the London stage; Maugham still holds the record for having four plays running simultaneously. Maugham's short stories, according to Robert L. Calder in the *Dictionary of Literary Biography,* "have made him one of the foremost English exponents of that genre in the twentieth century." His collection of spy stories, *Ashenden; or, The British Agent,* based on his own experiences as a British agent during the First World War, set the tone for a new, more cynical type of espionage fiction. *Of Human Bondage, The Moon and Sixpence,* and *The Razor's Edge* are among Maugham's most widely-known novels; since it first appeared in 1915, *Of Human Bondage* has never been out of print. During his lifetime, Maugham's books sold over eighty million copies in virtually every language on Earth. Despite his enormous success as a writer, many academic critics have belittled Maugham's accomplishments. "The critic I am waiting for," Maugham once commented, "is the one who will explain why, with all my faults, I have been read for so many years by so many people. . . . I should have thought it would interest a critic to inquire into what qualities my work must have in order to interest such vast numbers of people in so many countries. I myself haven't the smallest idea."

Maugham was born in the British Embassy in Paris, where his father worked as a lawyer. His parents were British subjects who arranged the place of his birth so that Maugham could be born on British soil, thereby avoiding French citizenship. For several years, he lived a comfortable existence. The youngest of four sons, and prone to health afflictions, Maugham enjoyed a particularly close relationship with his doting mother. This idyllic life ended with the death of his mother from tuberculosis when he was eight years old. His father died two years later of stomach cancer, leaving the family in dire financial straits. Maugham was sent to live with an uncle, a vicar, in Whitestable, England. The move from France to England was traumatic for the young boy. Until the move, Maugham had only spoken a faltering French; now he developed a lifelong stammer as well. In addition, the lifestyle of his provincial, very religious, relatives was a drastic and restrictive change.

An introspective and shy young man, who thought he was physically ugly, Maugham shielded himself from the taunting of fellow students at the King's School by adopting an outwardly hostile persona. On the advice of his relatives, he studied medicine at St. Thomas's Hospital in London. From the age of fifteen, however, Maugham had secretly been writing stories and plays, hoping to become a full-time writer. He began publishing his work in 1903, although he was obliged to live on a slim allowance to supplement his income. After years of failure, Maugham achieved a career breakthrough in 1908 when four of his plays—*Lady Frederick, Jack Straw, Mrs. Dot,* and *The Explorer*—ran simultaneously on the London stage. In the years that followed, Maugham focused most of his writing efforts on the theatre. In doing so he became, as Calder states, "one of the most popular dramatists in the English-speaking world."

Maugham set out to become a playwright by reading, and copying out in longhand, a number of popular plays of the day. This method, he claimed, taught him how to construct a workable play. As Sewell Stokes commented in *Theatre Arts,* Maugham's ambition "was to become a successful playwright; not a playwright who might, if chance favoured him, turn out to be a success." To insure success, Maugham took a workmanlike approach to his craft, becoming, as Stokes noted, "a manufacturer of smart plays for smart audiences. . . . Instinctively, he knew the value of an amusing epigram, and if a finished work of his had not a sufficient number of these, he decorated the manuscript with additional ones." A concern for the tastes of his audience also marked Maugham's dramatic work. "All the best dramatists," Maugham once observed, "have written with their eye on [the audience] and though they have more often spoken of it with contempt than with good will they have known that they were dependent on it. It is the public that pays, and if it is not pleased with the entertainment that is offered, stays away."

Because of his commercial orientation, Maugham usually wrote comedies. "He did variations on a commonly appreciated theme—primarily comedies that turned upon the question of whether someone would marry (or stay married) or not," Archie K. Loss commented in his study *W. Somerset Maugham.* Although Maugham's plays are not known for thematic innovation, they made him for several decades one of England's most popular playwrights. As Loss observed, Maugham "produced in his thirty-two plays probably the most significant body of work in English drama after George Bernard Shaw and before Noel Coward."

Of the plays Maugham wrote and staged, nearly all of them were successes. Three of them, in the judgment of Walter Allen in the *New York Times,* are "the peaks of Maugham triumphs." *The Circle, The Constant Wife,* and *The Breadwinner,* Allen believed, "are of a kind madly unfashionable today, instances of conspicuously well-made artificial comedy in the line of descent from the Restoration through Oscar Wilde. To say this is not to imply that they are in any way derivative. The wit is their own, and so is the point of view from which character and action are seen." Despite the success of his plays, Maugham was unhappy with his work. He "raked in the takings from his brilliant comedies . . . ," Cyril Connolly explained in the *Sunday Times,* "while the artist groaned at the shallowness of his reputation." When theatrical fashion changed in the 1930s, threatening the type of sophisticated social comedy he wrote, Maugham stopped writing plays altogether.

While Maugham's light, entertaining plays attracted a large audience, they also provided him with an enormous income. This income allowed him to enjoy a lavish lifestyle. In 1928 he bought the luxurious Villa Mauresque on the Cote d'Azur in southern France, once owned by Leopold II, where he would live for the rest of his life. His extensive art collection was worth over half a million pounds. Wealth also allowed Maugham to travel the world. He visited the United States, the Far East, Africa, India, and South America in his quest for exotic locales and characters for his stories, novels and plays.

Maugham's early novels were admitted potboilers aimed at a popular audience. *Liza of Lambeth* tells the story of an unwed woman who dies after a miscarriage; *The Making of a Saint* is an historical novel set in Italy during the fifteenth century; *The Hero* concerns a disillusioned veteran of the Boer War. None of these books sold well. Of Maugham's early novels, only *The Magician* still enjoys a readership today. The story of ruthless occult master Oliver Haddo who, like Baron Frankenstein, seeks to create life from dead matter, *The Magician* is a macabre thriller unlike any of Maugham's other works. Oddly enough, the novel is based on a real-life figure. In his *A Fragment of Autobiography,* printed in the 1956 edition of *The Magician,* Maugham explained that Oliver Haddo was based on the notorious Aleister Crowley, a drug-addicted Satanist and occult writer of the turn of the century whose name was linked in the popular press with orgies, financial scams and even child murder. Maugham had met Crowley while visiting his close friend, landscape painter Gerald Kelly, in Paris in 1905. Crowley had married Kelly's daughter.

When *The Magician* appeared, it received a scathing review in *Vanity Fair.* A vindictive Crowley, writing under the name Oliver Haddo and aware that the mad villain of Maugham's novel was a disguised version of himself, accused Maugham of plagiarism and listed alleged similarities between passages in *The Magician* and such books as *The Island of Dr. Moreau* by H. G. Wells. *The Magician* was to be the last Maugham novel for several years. With the success of his dramatic work on the London stage, Maugham would devote his time exclusively to that genre until 1915.

In that year, Maugham's most popular novel appeared. *Of Human Bondage* tells the story of a crippled man's hopeless love for a woman who abuses him. The book's sordid realism repelled many critics of the time. American publishers were reluctant to publish the novel at all. Not until a manuscript reader at Doran named Sinclair Lewis recommended the book did it see American publication. Most American critics greeted the book with dismay. But Theodore Dreiser, writing in the *New Republic,* gave *Of Human Bondage* an enthusiastic review. Dreiser compared the novel's effect on the reader to an intricate Persian carpet: "One feels as though one were sitting before a splendid Shiraz or Daghestan of priceless texture and intricate weave, admiring, feeling, responding sensually to its colours and tones. Or better yet, it is as though a symphony of great beauty by a master, Strauss [or] Beethoven,

had just been completed, and the bud notes and flower tones were filling the air with their elusive message, fluttering and dying." Impressed by Maugham's depiction of tragic characters, Dreiser called him "a genius endowed with an immense capacity for understanding and pity." By 1925 Marcus Aurelius Goodrich in the *New York Times* could label *Of Human Bondage* "a classic," a status it had attained despite critical indifference. Although some critics still disparage *Of Human Bondage*—Gore Vidal wrote in the *New York Review of Books:* "The best that can be said of this masterpiece is that it made a good movie and launched Bette Davis's career"—the novel has been constantly in print for over seventy-five years. In addition, as Scott Simpkins noted in the *Dictionary of Literary Biography,* "Maugham's persistent themes of misery, loneliness, alienation, loss of religious faith, and self-doubt reach a climax of sorts in *Of Human Bondage.*"

Of Human Bondage "was written in pain," as Maugham once said. Its principal character, Philip Carey, sensitive and plagued with a clubfoot, was so like the author, who was afflicted with a life-long stutter, that Maugham was unable to read the book after it was published. Perhaps because of this uncomfortable familiarity, Maugham preferred to base many of his later characters on people he met during his many travels. He wrote in his autobiography *The Summing Up,* "I am almost inclined to say that I could not spend an hour in anyone's company without getting the material to write at least a readable story about him." Always modest about his achievement as a writer, Maugham often claimed that he possessed a weak imagination. His plots and characters, he explained, came directly from real life. Their seeming variety was simply the result of the many people and places he had come to know.

In all of his writing, Maugham displayed a characteristic attitude toward life and humanity. This attitude, Allen remarked, "is that of an aloof, sardonic clinician who expects little from existence, is surprised at nothing, is skeptical of aspirations and amused by the spectacle of the follies of mankind." This attitude allowed Maugham to create, as Vidal stated in the *New York Review of Books,* "sensuous, exotic imaginings of a duplicitous world." In story after story, Maugham wrote of infidelities, betrayals, and hidden crimes. In *The Summing Up* he wrote: "I have been called cynical. I have been accused of making men out worse than they are. I do not think I have done this. All I have done is to bring into prominence certain traits that many writers shut their eyes to. I think what has chiefly struck me in human beings is their lack of consistency." He also commented: "I've always been interested in people, but I don't like them."

Particularly in his short stories, many of which are set in British colonial outposts of the Far East, Maugham created a world distinctly his own. Connolly believed that if all of Maugham's other writings were forgotten, "there will remain a story-teller's world from Singapore to the Marquesas that is exclusively and for ever Maugham, a world of verandah and prahu which we enter, as we do that of Conan Doyle's Baker Street, with a sense of happy and eternal homecoming." Speaking of these stories set in the East, Christopher Isherwood noted in *Great English Short Stories* that "there must be many thousands of readers who have wished themselves, as I often have, at Maugham's side on board some small slow freighter, as it steams up a tropical river or into the harbor of a Pacific island. On the jetty, the Maugham characters are waiting: the cynical District Commissioner with the secret sorrow, the prim adulterous Married Lady, the handsome curly-haired callow Secretary, the drunken Doctor. . . . Now that you have arrived, their drama can begin."

In some stories, Maugham drew upon his wartime experience for plot ideas. During the First World War, for example, he served as an interpreter for the Red Cross in France. Later, the British government recruited him to be a secret agent, posting him first in Geneva, Switzerland, and then in Russia during the revolution. These experiences were turned into a collection of short stories entitled *Ashenden; or, The British Agent* in 1928. As Maugham pointed out, "The work of an agent in the Intelligence Department is on the whole extremely monotonous. A lot of it is uncommonly useless. The material it offers for stories is scrappy and pointless; the author has himself to make it coherent, dramatic and probable." Maugham's espionage stories were drastically different from the usual spy fiction of the time. Containing no acts of derring-do and no heroic characters, Maugham's stories tell of the private tragedies and moral dilemmas of espionage work. His work set an example later followed by Eric Ambler and John le Carre. "The element of moral ambiguity, which Ashenden's consciousness brings into the stories," Frank Occhiogrosso wrote in the *Dictionary of Literary Biography*, "is one of Maugham's greatest contributions to the genre of spy fiction. . . . Maugham's place as innovator in and shaper of the genre of spy fiction would therefore seem to be established."

Time and again, critics point out that Maugham was a phenomenally popular writer because he was a natural story-teller. As Peter Levi noted in the *Spectator*, Maugham "was a remarkable and psychologically acute story-teller. His strength was in plot and motive. Perhaps he had no other, as his style was always somewhat stiff by our standards. Yet it was lucid and had a dandy crispness and simplicity. . . . Maugham is magnificently readable." Maugham's readability came only with hard work. "I knew," he once said, "that I should never write as well as I could wish, but I thought with pains I could arrive at writing as well as my natural defects allowed. On taking

thought it seemed to me that I must aim at lucidity, simplicity and euphony." The approach worked. As Alan Pryce-Jones wrote: "Of [Maugham's] popular success there can be no question. In the history of literature there is nobody whose work has been more widely sold, translated and devoured—partly because of his real merit as a storyteller, partly because the functional simplicity of his writing made his books unusually accessible."

Summing up Maugham's life in his biography *Maugham,* Ted Morgan wrote: "Maugham was all of these: an alienated child, a medical student, an avant-garde novelist and playwright, a bohemian in Paris, a successful West End dramatist, a London social lion, an ambulance driver on the Flanders front, a spy in Russia, a promiscuous homosexual who paid for the favors of boys in remote lands, a cuckolded husband, a host to the famous persons of his time, a World War II propagandist, the most widely read novelist since Dickens, a living legend kept alive by cellular therapy, and a senile old man."

"In my twenties," Maugham once wrote, "the critics said I was brutal. In my thirties they said I was flippant, in my forties they said I was cynical, in my fifties they said I was competent, and in my sixties they say I am superficial." By 1959 this compulsive writer was writing, he said, only for himself, and at the time of his death he was reportedly working on an autobiography that was to be published posthumously. A few years before his death, however, he destroyed all of his old notebooks and unfinished manuscripts.

"Looking back upon my work in my old age," Maugham wrote, "I am disposed to regard it very modestly and to admit frankly some of its shortcomings. In my youth I had accepted the challenge of writing and literature to idealize them; in my age I see the magnitude of the attempt and wonder at my audacity." He added: "I wrote stories because it was a delight to write them."

BIOGRAPHICAL/CRITICAL SOURCES:

BOOKS

Aldington, Richard, *W. Somerset Maugham: An Appreciation,* Doubleday, Doran, 1939.

Barnes, Ronald E., *The Dramatic Comedy of William Somerset Maugham,* Mouton, 1969.

Bason, F. T., *A Bibliography of the Writings of William Somerset Maugham,* Haskell, 1974.

Bates, H. E., *The Modern Short Story: A Critical Survey,* T. Nelson, 1941, pp. 122-147.

Brander, Lawrence, *Somerset Maugham: A Guide,* Barnes & Noble, 1963.

Breit, Harvey, editor, *The Writer Observed,* World Publishing, 1956.

Brophy, Brigid, Michael Levey and Charles Osborne, *Fifty Works of English Literature We Could Do Without,* Stein & Day, 1968, pp. 125-127.

Brophy, John, *Somerset Maugham,* Longmans, Green, 1952, revised edition, 1958.

Brown, Ivor, *W. Somerset Maugham,* Barnes & Noble, 1970.

Burt, Forrest D., *W. Somerset Maugham,* Macmillan, 1985.

Calder, Robert Lorin, *W. Somerset Maugham and the Quest for Freedom,* Heinemann, 1972.

Calder, Robert Lorin, *Willie: The Life of W. Somerset Maugham,* St. Martin, 1990.

Contemporary Literary Criticism, Gale, Volume 1, 1973, Volume 11, 1979, Volume 15, 1980, Volume 67, 1992.

Cordell, Richard Albert, *Somerset Maugham: A Biography and Critical Study,* Indiana University Press, 1961, revised edition published as *Somerset Maugham, A Writer for All Seasons: A Biographical and Critical Study,* 1969.

Curtis, Anthony, *The Pattern of Maugham: A Critical Portrait,* Hamilton, 1974.

Curtis, Anthony, *Somerset Maugham,* Macmillan, 1977.

Curtis, Anthony and John Whitehead, editors, *W. Somerset Maugham: The Critical Heritage,* Routledge & Kegan Paul, 1987.

Dictionary of Literary Biography, Gale, Volume 10: *Modern British Dramatists, 1940-1945,* 1982; Volume 36: *British Novelists, 1890-1929: Modernists,* 1985; Volume 77: *British Mystery Writers, 1920-1939,* 1989; Volume 100: *Modern British Essayists,* Second Series, 1990.

Dobrinsky, Joseph, *La Jeunesse de Somerset Maugham, 1874-1903,* Etudes Anglaises, 1977.

Dottin, Paul, *Le Theatre de William Somerset Maugham,* Perrin, 1937.

Harrison, Gilbert A., editor, *The Critic as Artist: Essays on Books, 1920-1970,* Liveright, 1972, pp. 228-232.

Henry, William H., Jr., *A French Bibliography of W. Somerset Maugham,* Bibliographical Society of the University of Virginia, 1967.

Horne, Pierre L. and Mary Beth Pringle, editors, *The Image of the Prostitute in Modern Literature,* Ungar, 1984, pp. 9-18.

Isherwood, Christopher, editor, *Great English Short Stories,* Dell, 1957, pp. 294-296.

Jonas, Klaus W., *The Maugham Enigma,* Citadel Press, 1954.

Jonas, Klaus W., *The World of Somerset Maugham,* British Book Centre, 1959.

Kanin, Garson, *Remembering Mr. Maugham,* Atheneum, 1966.

Loss, Archie K., *W. Somerset Maugham,* Continuum, 1988.

Loss, Archie K., editor, *Of Human Bondage: Coming of Age in the Novel,* Macmillan, 1989.

MacCarthy, Desmond, *William Somerset Maugham: The English Maupassant,* [London], 1934, reprinted, Norwood Editions, 1977.

Mander, Raymond and Joe Mitchenson, *Theatrical Companion to Maugham: A Pictorial Record of the First Performance of the Plays of W. Somerset Maugham,* Rockliff, 1955.

Maugham, Robin, *Somerset and All the Maughams,* New American Library, 1966.

Maugham, Robin, *Conversations With Willie: Recollections of W. Somerset Maugham,* Simon & Schuster, 1978.

Maugham, W. Somerset, *The Summing Up,* Doubleday, Doran & Co., 1938, reprinted, Penguin Books, 1978.

Maugham, W. Somerset, *A Writer's Notebook,* Doubleday, 1949, reprinted, Penguin, 1984.

McIver, C. S., *William Somerset Maugham,* Richard West, 1978.

Menard, W., *The Two Worlds of Somerset Maugham,* Sherbourne Press, 1965.

Morgan, Ted, *Maugham,* Simon & Schuster, 1980.

Naik, M. K., *W. Somerset Maugham,* University of Oklahoma Press, 1966.

Nichols, Beverly, *A Case of Human Bondage,* Secker & Warburg, 1966.

Pfeiffer, Karl Graham, *W. Somerset Maugham: A Candid Portrait,* Norton, 1959.

Raphael, Frederic, *W. Somerset Maugham and His World,* Thames & Hudson, 1976.

Sanders, Charles and others, *W. Somerset Maugham: An Annotated Bibliography of Writings about Him,* Northern Illinois University Press, 1970.

Savini, Gertrud, *Das Weltbild in William Somerset Maughams Dramen,* Junge & Sohn, 1939.

Sutton, Graham, *Some Contemporary Dramatists,* L. Parsons, 1925, reprinted, Kennikat, 1967, pp. 95-117.

Swinnerton, Frank, *The Saturday Review Gallery,* Simon & Schuster, 1959.

Symons, Julian, *Mortal Consequences,* Schocken, 1973.

Toole, Raymond Stott, *A Bibliography of the Works of W. Somerset Maugham,* Kaye & Ward, 1973.

Ward, A. C., *Twentieth-Century English Literature, 1901-1960,* Methuen, 1964.

Whitehead, John, *Maugham: A Reappraisal,* Vision Press, 1987.

Wilson, Edmund, *Classics and Commercials: A Literary Chronicle of the Forties,* Farrar, Straus, 1950, pp. 319-326.

PERIODICALS

Armchair Detective, Number 14, 1981, pp. 190-191.

Athenaeum, May 9, 1919, p. 302.

Atlantic, May, 1944, p. 173.

Books and Bookmen, February, 1967, p. 57; January, 1973, pp. 19-23; March, 1985, p. 37.

Book Week, April 23, 1944, p. 4.

British Book News, May, 1987, p. 296; June, 1987, p. 365.

Chicago Tribune, April 30, 1980; October 19, 1984; May 6, 1987.

Christian Science Monitor, May 13, 1944, p. 10; October 14, 1969, p. 13; July 6, 1970.

Commonweal, April 28, 1944, p. 40; May 23, 1969, p. 302.

Detroit News, February 17, 1985.

Dial, September 16, 1915, p. 59; November 29, 1919, p. 67.

Graphic, October 15, 1930, p. 426.

Life, December 16, 1926, p. 19.

Listener, October 17, 1968.

Literary Half-Yearly, January, 1977, pp. 165-186.

Literature/Film Quarterly, summer, 1978, pp. 262-273.

London Magazine, August/September, 1992, pp. 67-78.

London Mercury, September, 1935, pp. 485-486.

London Review of Books, July 18, 1985, p. 22.

Los Angeles Times, October 19, 1984.

Los Angeles Times Book Review, June 2, 1985.

Modern Drama, December, 1987, pp. 549-559.

Nation, August 16, 1919, p. 109.

New Criterion, November, 1985, pp. 1-13.

New Republic, December 25, 1915, p. 5; December 10, 1919, p. 21; March 30, 1938, pp. 227-228; May 1, 1944, p. 110.

New Statesman, November 5, 1921, p. 140; August 26, 1944, p. 140; September 6, 1985.

New Statesman & Nation, August 25, 1934, pp. 243-44; June 15, 1940; August 26, 1944, p. 140; October 8, 1949, p. 401.

Newsweek, January 27, 1958.

New Yorker, April 22, 1944, p. 20; June 8, 1946, pp. 96-99; October 18, 1969, p. 214; July 15, 1985, p. 85.

New York Review of Books, December 22, 1983, p. 52; February 1, 1990, pp. 39-44.

New York Times, August 1, 1915, p. 20; August 3, 1919, p. 24; April 23, 1944, p. 3; October 23, 1949; April 5, 1953, p. 5; January 19, 1964; September 6, 1969, p. 45; February 18, 1986; February 21, 1986.

New York Times Book Review, October 8, 1950, p. 3; December 3, 1967, p. 103; May 4, 1969, p. 50.

New York Times Magazine, January 25, 1959; June 2, 1968.

Notes & Queries, October, 1974, p. 370.

Playboy, January, 1966.

Punch, March 8, 1911, pp. 177-178; July 5, 1967, p. 30; October 16, 1968.

Quarterly Review, October, 1966, pp. 365-378.

Saturday Night, March, 1978.

Saturday Review, March 5, 1904, pp. 207-208; April 4, 1908, pp. 431-432; June 20, 1908, pp. 782-783; September 4, 1915, p. 120; May 17, 1919, p. 127; October 14, 1961; November 5, 1966; March 22, 1969, p. 62; November 22, 1969, p. 87.

Saturday Review of Literature, November 1, 1930, p. 299; April 22, 1944, p. 27.

South Atlantic Review, November, 1981, pp. 54-63.

Spectator, August 31, 1934, p. 297; February 17, 1939, p. 274; July 21, 1944, p. 173; May 9, 1970, p. 624.

Stage, June 4, 1970; June 18, 1970; July 2, 1970; July 23, 1970.

Time, April 24, 1944, p. 43; April 20, 1962.

Times (London), March 28, 1988.

Times Literary Supplement, May 26, 1905; April 24, 1919, p. 224; July 15, 1944, p. 341; December 8, 1966, p. 1156; April 16, 1970, p. 420; May 26, 1978, p. 577; April 5, 1985.

Vanity Fair, December 30, 1908, pp. 838-840.

Variety, July 8, 1970.

Vogue, July 20, 1928.

Washington Post, October 8, 1969; October 19, 1984.

Weekly Book Review, April 23, 1944, p. 2.

OBITUARIES:

PERIODICALS

Books Abroad, spring, 1966.

Listener, December 23, 1965, p. 1033.

New York Herald Tribune, December 17, 1965.

New York Times, December 16, 1965.

Publishers Weekly, December 27, 1965.

Reporter, December 30, 1965.

Sunday Times (London), December 19, 1965.*

* * *

MAUGHAM, William Somerset
See MAUGHAM, W(illiam) Somerset

* * *

MAYNARD, John (Rogers) 1941-

PERSONAL: Born October 6, 1941, in Williamsville, NY; son of A. Rogers (an insurance executive) and Olive (Fisher) Maynard; married Florence Michelson (an artist), July 1, 1967 (divorced, 1981); children: Alex Stevens. *Education:* Harvard University, B.A. (summa cum laude), 1963, Ph.D., 1970. *Politics:* Democrat. *Religion:* Agnostic. *Avocational interests:* Fixing up old city houses, relaxing in the Massachusetts woods.

ADDRESSES: Office—Department of English, New York University, 19 University Pl., Room 235, New York, NY 10003.

CAREER: Harvard University, Cambridge, MA, assistant professor of English, history, and literature, 1969-74; New York University, New York, NY, assistant professor, 1974-76, associate professor, 1976-84, professor of English, 1984—, chairperson of English department, 1985-89. Director of Browning Institute. Sponsor of Concord Housing, a Boston community development project.

MEMBER: Modern Language Association of America, Phi Beta Kappa.

AWARDS, HONORS: Frederick Sheldon traveling fellowship, 1963-64; Woodrow Wilson fellowship, 1964-65; American Philosophical Society grant, 1972-73; National Endowment for the Humanities grant, 1972-73; Thomas J. Wilson Prize from Harvard University Press, 1975, for *Browning's Youth;* Guggenheim fellowship, 1980-81.

WRITINGS:

Browning's Youth, Harvard University Press, 1976.
Charlotte Bronte and Sexuality, Cambridge University Press, 1984.
(Co-editor) *Nineteenth Century Lives,* Cambridge University Press, 1989.
Victorian Discourses on Sexuality and Religion, Cambridge University Press, 1992.

Contributor of articles and reviews to literature journals. Editor, *Victorian Literature and Culture.*

WORK IN PROGRESS: Co-editing *The Journals and Letters of Anne Thachery Ritchie.*

SIDELIGHTS: John Maynard told *CA:* "Literary biography can be much more than the usual day by day record of things done, people seen, meals eaten, with occasional stops for discussion of major texts; and it can be more than the imposition of one or a few key explanations, psychological or pathological, that we find in Strachey's lesser followers. The challenge is to understand that complex thing, the emergence of genius. Biography is a meaningful nexus in our world of necessarily fragmented ways of looking at reality. It is not a gimcrack for making complexity into one simplicity of explanation. It is the human center that demands focus and appropriate integration of perspectives—a matter of judgment, imagination, and good sense. It is where the last new view must take its place among the rest, establish its claim to space as best it can in the full portrait. It is one way for my generation to put its badly traversed and centrifugal mind together."

*   *   *

MAYO, Jim
  See L'AMOUR, Louis (Dearborn)

McCAMMON, Robert R(ick) 1952-

PERSONAL: Born July 11, 1952, in Birmingham, AL; son of Jack (a musician) and Barbara (Bundy) McCammon. *Education:* University of Alabama, B.A., 1974. *Religion:* Methodist. *Avocational interests:* Antique automobile restoration.

ADDRESSES: Home—8912 Fourth Ave. S., Birmingham, AL 35206. *Office*—4321 Fifth Ave. S., Birmingham, AL 35214.

CAREER: Writer. Loveman's Department Store, Birmingham, AL, in advertising, 1974-75; B. Dalton Booksellers, Birmingham, in advertising, 1976; *Birmingham Post-Herald,* Birmingham, copy editor, 1976-78.

WRITINGS:

Baal, Avon, 1978.
Bethany's Sin, Avon, 1979.
Diana's Daughters, Avon, 1979.
The Hungry, Avon, 1980.
The Night Boat, Avon, 1980.
They Thirst, Avon, 1981, illustrated by Wendy and Charles Lang, Dark Harvest, 1991.
Mystery Walk, Holt, 1983.
Usher's Passing, Holt, 1984.
Swan Song, Pocket, 1987.
Stinger, Pocket, 1988.
The Wolf's Hour, Pocket, 1989.
Blue World, Pocket, 1990.
Mine, Pocket, 1990.
Boy's Life, Pocket, 1991.
(Editor and contributor) *Under the Fang* (short stories), Pocket, 1991.

SIDELIGHTS: Robert R. McCammon enjoys life's most frightening elements. "I'm interested in fear: the things that go bump in the night, that leer from the realm of dreams, that slither behind our backs on the stairway when we're not looking," McCammon once commented. "Why? Because probing the counterfeit fears, the fun fears, can tell us a lot about how we tick and define the things that *really* make us afraid. Horror fiction is one of the oldest of literary forms—if not *the* oldest—and it relates to the psychology of man as surely as our dreams relate to our waking hours. Nothing makes me feel better than getting a good scare out of a novel, or putting a good scare *into* a novel."

McCammon established a reputation as a horror-fiction writer with works such as *They Thirst,* set in modern-day Los Angeles, in which a vampire assembles an army and attempts a world takeover. "McCammon's ability to frighten the reader with a minimum of gore and a maximum of suspense has earned him a place in the modern horror pantheon with Stephen King, Dan Simmons, Dean

R. Koontz and Anne Rice," a reviewer for the *Los Angeles Times Book Review* wrote. Holocaust is again the topic in *Swan Song,* the story of a young girl with healing powers stalked by the evil character—the Man with the Scarlet Eyes—with whom she must eventually do battle. Still in the realm of the supernatural, McCammon chose werewolves to populate *The Wolf's Hour.* "Too long shunned by his peers in the horror genre, McCammon deftly validates his ability to spin an excellent yarn with three simultaneous threads: historical, horror, and espionage-suspense," James Blair Lovell remarked in *Washington Post Book World.* Lovell praised *The Wolf's Hour,* describing it as "a genuine triumph" that "breaks new ground" in its genre. "After *The Wolf's Hour,* werewolf stories can never be the same," Lovell declared.

McCammon surprised many readers and critics with *Boy's Life,* with which he left behind the horror genre. As Sam Staggs noted in a *Publishers Weekly* interview, "The Steven evoked by *Boy's Life* is Spielberg, not King." The book has supernatural overtones as well as a murder, but is for the most part a story about growing up in a small Southern town. McCammon told Staggs that he "probably won't be writing any more supernatural horror novels," but he is confident that his readers will remain loyal. "My real fans believe that wherever I take them, it will be a good trip," he commented to Staggs. "It doesn't have to be across dark and bloody ground. It can be across green hills." He told Staggs that part of his reason for withdrawing from writing horror novels was that "reality has become so horrific, there's no point in trying to compete with the evening news." Confinement was another factor in the decision, he said. "I just can't be happy as a one-note, one-genre writer."

BIOGRAPHICAL/CRITICAL SOURCES:

PERIODICALS

Los Angeles Times Book Review, May 22, 1983; June 30, 1991.
Publishers Weekly, August 2, 1991, pp. 54-55.
Washington Post Book World, June 14, 1987; June 18, 1989.*

*   *   *

McCORD, Howard   1932-

PERSONAL: Born November 3, 1932, in El Paso, TX; son of Frank Edward and Sylvia Joy (Coe) McCord; married Dora Garcia Ochoa, April 19, 1953; married Jennifer Sue Revis, July 26, 1975; children: (first marriage) Colman Garcia, Robert Ochoa; (second marriage) Susannah Leigh, Julia Eden, Wyatt Edward Asher, Eva Ariella Siobhan. *Education:* Texas Western College (now University of Texas at El Paso), B.A., 1957; University of Utah, M.A., 1960. *Politics:* Libertarian. *Religion:* None.

ADDRESSES: Home—15431 Sand Ridge, Bowling Green, OH 43402. *Office*—Department of English, Bowling Green State University, Bowling Green, OH 43403.

CAREER: Washington State University, Pullman, 1960-71, began as assistant professor, became associate professor of English; Bowling Green State University, Bowling Green, OH, 1971—, currently professor of English, director of M.F.A. program and of creative writing program, 1971-80. Visiting professor at Navaho Community College, 1975, California State University, Northridge, 1976, and University of Alaska, Juneau, 1978-80. Secretary and member of executive committee, Coordinating Council of Literary Magazines, 1972-77; member of literature panel of National Endowment for the Arts, 1977-79; chairman of literature panel of Ohio Arts Council, 1978-81. *Military service:* U.S. Navy, 1951-53.

MEMBER: Western Writers of America, Federation of Old Cornwall Societies.

AWARDS, HONORS: National Woodrow Wilson fellowship, 1957-58; Fulbright award, 1965; E. O. Holland fellow, 1967; Helen Wurlitzer Foundation Award, 1968; Washington State Governor's Award, 1968, 1970; Borestone Mountain Poetry award, 1969; Hart Crane Memorial Award, 1970; D. H. Lawrence fellow, University of New Mexico, 1971; Distinguished Achievement Award, Bowling Green State University, 1975; National Endowment for the Arts fellow, 1976, 1983; Ohio Arts Council fellow, 1982; Ohioana Award for Poetry, 1990; Golden Nugget Award, University of Texas at El Paso, 1990.

WRITINGS:

(Editor) Gordon Curtis, *Fire Prayers,* Tribal Press, 1966.
(With Walter Lowenfels) *The Life of Fraenkel's Death,* Washington State University Press, 1970.
The Fire Visions, Twowindows, 1970.
Maps, Kayak, 1971.
Gnomonology: A Handbook of Systems, Sand Dollar Press, 1971.
Some Notes to Gary Snyder's "Myth and Texts," Sand Dollar Press, 1971.
The Diary of a Lost Girl, Lillabulero Press, 1972.
The Old Beast, Copper Canyon, 1975.
The Arctic Desert, Figures, 1975.
Peach Mountain Smoke Out, Salt Works Press, 1978.
The Arcs of Lowitz, Salt Works Press, 1979.
The Great Toad Hunt and Other Expeditions, Crossing Press, 1980.
Walking Edges, Raincrow Press, 1983.
Jennifer, Salt Works Press, 1984.

Megadeath, Academic Arts Press, 1991.
Intemperance, Malpais Press, 1991.

POETRY

Precise Fragments, Dolman Press, 1963.
Twelve Bones, Goosetree Press, 1964.
The Spanish Dark, and Other Poems, Washington State University Press, 1965.
Fables and Transfigurations, Kayak, 1967.
Lonjaunes, His Periplus, Kayak, 1968.
Selected Poems: 1955-1971, Crossing Press, 1975.
The Duke of Chemical Birds, Bloody Twin Press, 1989.

OTHER

Also author of *Ovens: Poems against the War and Tyranny,* 1971, *Mirrors,* 1973, *Friend,* 1974, and *Perfecting an Unspeakable Act,* 1975. Contributor to anthologies, including *Poets of Today,* International Publishers, 1964; *The Young American Poets,* Follett, 1968; *I Love You All Day It Is That Simple,* Abbey Press, 1970; *The Sensuous President,* New Rivers Press, 1972; *Search the Silence,* Scholastic, 1974; *John Keats' Porridge: Favorite Recipes of American Poets,* University of Iowa Press, 1975; *Travois: An Anthology of Texas Poetry,* Contemporary Arts Museum of Houston, 1976; *Southwest: A Contemporary Anthology,* Red Earth Press, 1977; *A Geography of Poets,* Bantam, 1979; and *Vietnam Flashbacks,* Pig Iron, 1985. Also contributor to periodicals, including *International Poetry Number 1, Research Studies, New York Times, Harper's Bazaar, Arena, Partisan Review, Iowa Review, New Mexico Quarterly, Classical Journal, Caterpillar, Exquisite Corpse,* and *Tree.* Editor of the *Regulator,* 1991—.

WORK IN PROGRESS: The Second Arctic: Notes on Distance; a book on walking the Jornada del Muerto.

SIDELIGHTS: Howard McCord once told *CA:* "I began writing when a wise high school teacher told me it was perfectly reasonable to respond *to* a poem *with* a poem. I felt at once liberated from the burden of criticism and exegesis and was delighted to be told to trust myself. I have continued to trust myself and follow my own inclination, whether it be a ten year detour through Catholicism, or two years' immersion in Sanskrit, walking in Lapland and Iceland, and on the glaciers of Alaska, or a complete and deliberate ignorance of semiotics. I read Wittgenstein for his poetry, and try to learn Homeric Greek just to make the sounds, and not to be dependent. It seems important not to be dependent, to be free. Some of my work has been translated into Spanish, Polish, and Hindi and I like the curiosity of that triad." Looking back at his career as a writer and a teacher, McCord continues: "The words have been as stubborn as the students and it is not my place to say what any of it has been worth. I like my Jennifer best, and the kids we have. . . . I run marathons now, and

ultramarathons. I like the distances beyond the hundred kilometers, where the most surprises are, and the greatest freedom."

BIOGRAPHICAL/CRITICAL SOURCES:

PERIODICALS

Chicago Review, Volume 20, number 1, 1968; January-February, 1971.
Concerning Poetry, spring, 1969.
Lillabulero, winter, 1970.

*   *   *

McDERMOTT, Alice   1953-

PERSONAL: Born June 27, 1953, in Brooklyn, NY; daughter of William J. and Mildred (Lynch) McDermott; married David M. Armstrong (a research neuroscientist), June 16, 1979. *Education:* State University of New York, B.A., 1975; University of New Hampshire, M.A., 1978.

ADDRESSES: Home—8674-3 Villa La Jolla Drive, La Jolla, CA 92037. *Agent*—Harriet Wasserman Literary Agency, 137 East 36th St., New York, NY 10016.

CAREER: Writer. Lecturer in English at the University of New Hampshire, Durham, 1978-79; fiction reader for *Redbook* and *Esquire,* 1979-80; consulting editor of *Redbook*'s Young Writers Contest; lecturer in writing at the University of California, San Diego.

MEMBER: Writer's Guild, PEN, Associated Writing Programs, Poets and Writers.

AWARDS, HONORS: Whiting Writers Award, 1987; National Book Award nomination, 1987, and PEN/Faulkner Award for Fiction nomination, 1988, both for *That Night.*

WRITINGS:

NOVELS

A Bigamist's Daughter, Random House, 1982.
That Night, Farrar, Straus, 1987.
At Weddings and Wakes, Farrar, Straus, 1991.

OTHER

Contributor of short stories to *Redbook, Mademoiselle, Seventeen,* and *Ms.*

WORK IN PROGRESS: A novel.

SIDELIGHTS: Award-winning novelist Alice McDermott deals with many aspects of love and family life in her novels, including a love affair between a cynical editor and a novelist, a romance between two teenagers in the early 1960s, and the many nuances of an Irish American family. She infuses her works with a great deal of inventiveness and originality, and is praised for her storytelling skills, her lyrical writing, and her descriptive detail and imagery. "A formidably gifted prose stylist, [McDermott] can make each sentence a bell of sound, a prism of sight," relates a *Publishers Weekly* contributor. And Michael J. Bandler, writing in *Tribune Books,* asserts: "McDermott is a spellbinder, adding a cachet of mystery and eloquence to common occurrences."

McDermott's first novel, *A Bigamist's Daughter,* concerns Elizabeth Connelly, a twenty-six-year-old editor at a vanity publisher. Her job consists of reading the summaries of books (instead of the entire thing), heaping enthusiasm and praise on the author, extracting payments of $5,000 or more from them, and then trying to explain why the book was never published. Two years of this kind of work at Vista Books has turned Elizabeth into a cynic, and it is at this point in her life that she meets and becomes involved with a Southern client still in search of an ending for his novel about a bigamist. Consequently, Connelly ponders her own father's frequent absences from home as she was growing up. As Elizabeth's memories of her father begin to resurface "she becomes more appealing; she loses the harshness and superficiality that initially alienate the reader," maintains Anne Tyler in the *New York Times Book Review.* LeAnne Schreiber, writing in the *New York Times,* praises the humor in *A Bigamist's Daughter:* "The laughter is wicked but not cruel." And Tyler concludes that the novel "is impressive," adding that at certain moments "McDermott sounds like anything but a first-time novelist. She writes with assurance and skill, and she has created a fascinatingly prismatic story."

A National Book Award finalist, McDermott's second novel, *That Night,* examines love and the loss of innocence through the story of two teenage lovers and their separation. Set in suburbia during the early 1960s, the novel begins with the story of the night referred to in the title. Rick, one of the neighborhood boys, has been trying to get in touch with his girlfriend Sheryl for a number of days, only to be put off by her mother, who will not tell him where she is. His anxiety and rage finally culminate with a visit to Sheryl's house. Accompanied by a bunch of drunk friends, Rick pulls Sheryl's mother from the house, threatening her and demanding to see her daughter. The men in the neighborhood come to her rescue and a battle (in which no one is injured) ensues, with Rick ending up in jail. What Rick does not know is that a few days earlier Sheryl discovered she was pregnant and was whisked away to a cousin's house in a different state. All of this is recalled by a grown woman who was a child of ten during the time of Rick and Sheryl's romance. The incident becomes her initiation (and that of many others in the neighborhood) into the failures of love and the realities and many disappointments of the adult world.

That Night "is concerned not only with . . . [the] loss of innocence but also with the mundane disillusionments that go with adolescence and the rites of growing up," describes Michiko Kakutani in the *New York Times.* Bandler maintains that McDermott "has taken as mundane a subject as one can find, a suburban teenage romance and pregnancy, and infused it with the power, the ominousness and the star-crossed romanticism of a contemporary Romeo and Juliet." What separates *That Night* "from the mass of literature that takes on the barely middle-class suburban experience is the almost baroque richness of . . . McDermott's sentences, the intellectual complexity of her moral vision and the explicit emotion of her voice," asserts David Leavitt in the *New York Times Book Review.* "*That Night* gloriously rejects the notion that this betrayed and bankrupt world can be rendered only in the spare, impersonal prose that has become the standard of so much contemporary fiction, and the result is a slim novel of almost 19th-century richness, a novel that celebrates the life of its suburban world at the same moment that it mourns that world's failures and disappointments." Bandler concludes that through her descriptions of "suburban violence" and "loss by separation, McDermott has wrought a miracle, one that is enhanced even more in its telling."

In her 1991 novel *At Weddings and Wakes,* "McDermott's strategy is to use family gatherings to tell the tales of individual family members and the tale of the family as a whole," points out Catherine Petroski in *Tribune Books.* The family that McDermott presents is Irish American and consists of four sisters, only one of whom (Lucy) is married and living with her own family in Long Island. The other three—May, an ex-nun; Agnes, a businesswoman; and Veronica, an introverted alcoholic—still live at home with their stepmother in Brooklyn. The wedding referred to in the title is between May and the mailman Fred, and the wake is also for May, who dies very suddenly shortly following her wedding. Through her presentation of such a fractured immigrant family, McDermott examines the many tensions that can arise, including the question of how their heritage should be honored. "Many of the Townes' antics are straight out of the prototypical dysfunctional family," observes Petroski. "Its members play their self-destructive and self-limiting roles; they deny the truth and themselves; they are often (usually unwittingly but sometimes not) as cruel to each other as they are tender." Petroski goes on to conclude that "it is the actual words of this novel that I will remember—words that bring us a generously imagined, flawlessly realized, extraordinarily complex story of memorable characters whom otherwise we would never have known."

Commenting on her chosen profession in an interview with Mervyn Rothstein for the *New York Times,* McDermott contends: "There has to be an obsession with the act of writing. . . . It's too hard, too unpleasant too often, without that. I suppose I don't know any other way of living. . . . It's organic, as we say in California—it's just there. I've always done it. When I'm not writing—and I have considered many times trying something else—I can't make sense out of anything. I feel the need to make some sense and find some order, and writing fiction is the only way I've found that seems to begin to do that. Even if the story or the novel ends up saying there is no sense and there is no order, at least I've made that much of an attempt."

BIOGRAPHICAL/CRITICAL SOURCES:

PERIODICALS

Chicago Tribune Book World, January 2, 1983.
Los Angeles Times, February 18, 1982.
Los Angeles Times Book Review, April 26, 1987, p. 3.
Newsweek, March 22, 1982.
New York Times, February 1, 1982; March 28, 1987; May 9, 1987.
New York Times Book Review, February 21, 1982, pp. 1, 28-29; April 19, 1987, pp. 1, 29-31.
People, June 1, 1987.
Publishers Weekly, January 27, 1992, p. 88.
Time, July 27, 1987.
Times Literary Supplement, March 11, 1988, p. 276.
Tribune Books (Chicago), April 30, 1987; March 29, 1991, pp. 1, 4.
Washington Post Book World, April 12, 1987, pp. 1, 3.*

—Sketch by Susan M. Reicha

*   *   *

McEVOY, Marjorie Harte
(Marjorie Harte)

PERSONAL: Born in York, Yorkshire, England; daughter of William Hinds (a cabinetmaker) and Margaret (Pratt) Harte; married William Noel McEvoy (deceased); children: Peter, Sheila Margaret (Mrs. Bryan Large). Education: Educated privately. Religion: Church of England. Avocational interests: Mountaineering in Great Britain, trailer travel, world exploration.

ADDRESSES: Home—54 Miriam Ave., Somersall, Chesterfield, S40 3NF, England.

CAREER: Novelist. Writer for Fleetway Publications. Has worked as assistant matron at girls' boarding school and as an auxiliary nurse.

MEMBER: Romantic Novelists Association.

WRITINGS:

No Castle of Dreams, Jenkins, 1960.

A Red Red Rose, Jenkins, 1961.
The Meaning of a Kiss, Jenkins, 1961.
Forever Faithful, Jenkins, 1962.
Softly Treads Danger, Jenkins, 1963.
Calling Nurse Stewart, Jenkins, 1963.
Moon over the Danube, Jenkins, 1966.
Brazilian Stardust, Arcadia, 1967.
Dusky Cactus, Jenkins, 1968.
The Grenfell Legacy, Jenkins, 1968.
Who Walks by Moonlight, Arcadia, 1969.
The White Castello, Lenox, 1970.
Enchanted Isle, Lenox, 1971.
Peril at Polvellyn, Lenox, 1972.
The Hermitage Bell, Lenox, 1972.
The Chinese Box, Lenox, 1973.
Castle Doom, Ballantine, 1973.
Ravensmount, Ballantine, 1974.
The Wych Stone, Ballantine, 1974.
Queen of Spades, Ballantine, 1975.
Echoes from the Past, Doubleday, 1979.
Calabrian Summer, Doubleday, 1980.
The Sleeping Tiger, Doubleday, 1983.
Star of Randevi, Doubleday, 1984.
Temple Bells, Doubleday, 1985.
Camelot Country, Doubleday, 1986.

UNDER NAME MARJORIE HARTE

A Call for the Doctor, R. Hale, 1961.
Goodbye Doctor Garland, R. Hale, 1962.
Nurse in the Orient, R. Hale, 1962.
Doctors in Conflict, R. Hale, 1963.
Masquerade for a Nurse, R. Hale, 1964.
Doctor Mysterious, R. Hale, 1965.
Cover Girl, R. Hale, 1968.
No Orchids for a Nurse, R. Hale, 1968.
The Gulf Between, R. Hale, 1969.

OTHER

Contributor to Modern Caravan, Caravan, Weekend, and Country Gentleman's Estate Magazine.

SIDELIGHTS: Marjorie Harte McEvoy told CA: "Being an enthusiastic world traveller has proved a great asset by giving me firsthand experience of exotic backgrounds for my novels. My books have been translated into a dozen foreign languages. An authentic background is essential if novels set in these countries are to have good sales there."

*   *   *

McGOVERN, Arthur F(rancis) 1929-

PERSONAL: Born December 4, 1929, in Columbus, OH; son of Arthur F. (a sales engineer) and Philomena (a homemaker and poet; maiden name, Ambrose) McGovern. *Education:* Georgetown University, A.B., 1951; Loyola University of Chicago, M.A., 1959; West Baden College, S.T.L., 1962; University of Paris, Ph.D., 1967. *Politics:* Democrat.

ADDRESSES: Home—4001 West McNichols, Detroit, MI 48221. *Office*—Department of Philosophy, University of Detroit, Detroit, MI 48221.

CAREER: Entered Society of Jesus (Jesuits), 1951, ordained Roman Catholic priest, 1962; Bellarmine School of Theology, North Aurora, IL, assistant professor of philosophy, 1967-70; University of Detroit, Detroit, MI, assistant professor, 1970-73, associate professor, 1973-80, professor of philosophy, 1980—, director of humanities program, 1972-77, faculty director of honors program, 1980—, chair of university core curriculum committee, 1982-87. Lecturer and public speaker.

MEMBER: Jesuit Philosophical Association (president, 1977-78), Christians Association for Relationships with Eastern Europe, Latin American Studies Association.

AWARDS, HONORS: Essay prize, *Science and Society,* 1970, for "The Young Marx on the State"; award from president of University of Detroit, 1980, for excellence in teaching and research.

WRITINGS:

Marxism: An American Christian Perspective, Orbis, 1980.
(With Gerald F. Cavanagh) *Ethical Dilemmas in the Modern Corporation,* Prentice-Hall, 1988.
Liberation Theology and Its Critics, Orbis, 1989.

Contributor to books, including *Demythologizing Marxism,* edited by Frederick Adelmann, Boston College Press, 1969; *American Business Values in Transition,* edited by G. F. Cavanagh, Prentice-Hall, 1986; and *Three Worlds of Marxist-Christian Dialogue,* edited by Nicholas Piediscalzi and Robert Thobaben, Fortress, 1985. Contributor to numerous periodicals.

WORK IN PROGRESS: Studies on Catholic social thought, with a particular reference to Latin America.

SIDELIGHTS: Arthur F. McGovern told *CA:* "Except for a few scholarly articles, I wrote very little until I reached my late forties. Long years of seminary training accounted for the delay in part, but lack of confidence in my own writing ability played a more significant part. I knew that I had gifts as a successful teacher. But good writing, I believed, required creative imagery and a skillful use of words—gifts I found lacking in myself.

"Then a friend of mine, whose writing style was quite simple and direct, published a very successful book on American business values. 'That kind of writing,' I said, 'I think

I can do.' I also saw a great need for a book that would explain Marxism to a Christian audience. Through teaching and research I had the necessary qualifications for writing such a book.

"The completed book, *Marxism: An American Christian Perspective,* received gratifying endorsements and reviews and has gone through six printings. My own giftedness for writing, I came to realize, consisted of clarity, integrity, and balance in presenting and evaluating controversial issues. The success of the first book encouraged me to undertake two others. It also brought requests to contribute chapters to other books and led to numerous speaking engagements.

"My advice, then, for those who question whether they have the ability to write: 'Go with your own gifts; if you have something important to say, rely on the talents you have.' "

BIOGRAPHICAL/CRITICAL SOURCES:

PERIODICALS

America, July 21, 1990.
Christian Century, October 1, 1980; December 12, 1990.
Commonweal, May 22, 1981; February 26, 1982; January 26, 1990; March 8, 1991.
Horizons, fall, 1982.
Journal of Church and State, autumn, 1990.
Journal of Religion, April 20, 1981.
Monthly Review, June, 1984.
New Oxford Review, April, 1981; July-August, 1990.
Religious Studies Review, October, 1982.
Studies in Soviet Thought, May 29, 1984.
Telos, winter, 1983-84.
Theological Studies, March, 1991.
Theology Today, July, 1981.

*   *   *

McKUEN, Rod 1933-

PERSONAL: Born April 29, 1933, in Oakland, CA; son of Clarice Woolever (a dancer); children: one son and one daughter. *Education:* Less than four years, mostly in one-room schoolhouses and rural country schools in Nevada, California, Washington, and Oregon; attended high school in Oakland, CA.

ADDRESSES: P.O. Box G, Beverly Hills, CA 90213.

CAREER: Author, poet, singer, songwriter, and composer. Has appeared in films, on television, and in concerts. President of Stanyan Records, Discus Records, Mr. Kelly Productions, Montcalm Productions, Stanyan Books, Cheval Books, Biplane Books, and Rod McKuen

Enterprises; vice president of Tamarack Books. Member of board of directors of Animal Concern and American National Theatre of Ballet; member of advisory board of International Education and Fund for Animals. *Military service:* U.S. Army, 1953-57; served in Korea; was Psychological Warfare scriptwriter and military assistant to Korean Civil Assistance Command; decorated by Syngman Rhee for bringing friendship and understanding to the Korean people.

MEMBER: American Society of Composers, Authors and Publishers, American Federation of Television and Radio Artists, American Guild of Variety Artists, American Human Society (member of board of directors), National Academy of Recording Arts and Sciences (member of board of directors; vice president), Modern Poetry Association, Writers Guild, New Gramophone Society (president).

AWARDS, HONORS: Grand Prix du Disc (Paris), 1966, 1974, 1975, 1982; National Academy of Recording Arts and Sciences, eleven nominations, and Grammy Award for best spoken-word album for "Lonesome Cities," 1969; Motion Picture Academy Award nominations for musical score for the films *The Prime of Miss Jean Brodie,* 1969, and *A Boy Named Charlie Brown,* 1970; Golden Globe Award, 1969; *Motion Picture Daily* Award, 1969; Emmy Award, Academy of Television Arts and Sciences, for musical scores "Say Goodbye," 1970, and "Hello Again," 1977; Pulitzer Prize nomination in classical music, 1973, for composition "Suite for Narrator and Orchestra: The City"; Freedoms Foundation Medal of Honor, 1975; Entertainer of the Year award, Shriners Club of Los Angeles, 1975; Horatio Alger Award, 1975; Humanitarian Award, First Amendment Society, 1977; Outstanding Poet Award, Carl Sandburg Society, 1978; Man of the Year award, University of Detroit, 1978; Literary Trust Award, Brandeis University, 1981; Sylvester Pat Weaver Award for Public Service Broadcasting, 1981; Freedoms Foundation Patriot Medal, 1981; Man of the Year award, Salvation Army, 1982.

WRITINGS:

POETRY

And Autumn Came, Pageant, 1954.
Stanyan Street and Other Sorrows (also see below), Stanyan Music Co., 1966.
Listen to the Warm (also see below), Random House, 1967.
Twelve Years of Christmas, Stanyan/Cheval, 1968.
Lonesome Cities (also see below), Random House, 1968.
Sea Cycle, Montcalm Productions, 1969.
In Someone's Shadow, Stanyan/Cheval, 1969.
With Love . . . , Random House, 1970.
Caught in the Quiet, Random House, 1970.

Rod McKuen at Carnegie Hall, Grosset, 1970.
Moment to Moment, Stanyan/Cheval, 1971.
The Carols of Christmas, Random House, 1971.
So My Sheep Can Safely Graze, Random House, 1971.
Pastorale: A Collection of Lyrics, Random House, 1971.
And to Each Season, Simon & Schuster, 1972.
Grand Tour, Random House, 1972.
Beyond the Boardwalk, Stanyan/Cheval, 1972.
Fields of Wonder, W. H. Allen, 1972.
Come to Me in Silence, Simon & Schuster, 1973.
Seasons in the Sun, Pocket Books, 1974.
Celebrations of the Heart, Simon & Schuster, 1975.
The Rod McKuen Omnibus (includes *Stanyan Street and Other Sorrows, Listen to the Warm,* and *Lonesome Cities*), W. H. Allen, 1975.
Hand in Hand, Pocket Books, 1976.
The Sea around Me, Simon & Schuster, 1977.
Coming Close to the Earth, Simon & Schuster, 1978.
We Touch the Sky, Simon & Schuster, 1979.
Love's Been Good to Me, Pocket Books, 1979.
The Power Bright and Shining: Images of My Country, Simon & Schuster, 1980.
Looking for a Friend, Pocket Books, 1980.
The Beautiful Strangers, Simon & Schuster, 1981.
Too Many Midnights, Pocket Books, 1981.
Watch for the Wind, Pocket Books, 1983.
(And illustrator) *The Sound of Solitude,* Harper & Row, 1983.
Suspension Bridge, Harper & Row, 1984.
Valentines, Cheval, 1986.
(And illustrator) *Intervals,* Harper & Row, 1986.

MUSIC COLLECTIONS

New Ballads, Random House, 1970.
Seasons in the Sun (libretto), Pioneer Drama Service, 1982.

Also author of *New Carols for Christmas, The McKuen/Sinatra Songbook, At Carnegie Hall, 28 Greatest Hits, Through European Windows, The Songs of Rod McKuen, Vol. 1,* and *The Songs of Rod McKuen, Vol. 2.*

OTHER

The World of Rod McKuen (illustrated songbook), Random House, 1968.
Frank Sinatra, a Man Alone, Cheval, 1969.
(Editor and author of introduction) Henry David Thoreau, *The Wind That Blows Is All That Anybody Knows,* illustrated by Helen Miljakovich, Stanyan, 1970.
(Compiler) Robert Allen, editor, *Here's Another Book, My Friend,* Stanyan/Cheval, 1971.
(Contributor) *Never Let the Sun Set on a Quarrel,* Stanyan/Cheval, 1971.

(Editor and compiler) *The Will to Win,* Stanyan/Cheval, 1971.

Rod McKuen Calendar and Datebook, 1973, Cheval, 1972.

Finding My Father: One Man's Search for Identity (autobiography), Stanyan/Cheval, 1976.

An Outstretched Hand: Poems, Prayers, and Meditations, Cheval, 1980.

Rod McKuen's Book of Days and a Month of Sundays, Harper & Row, 1981.

Composer of musical scores for films and television, including *Joanna,* 1968; *The Prime of Miss Jean Brodie,* 1969; *Travels with Charlie,* 1969; *Me, Natalie,* 1969; *The Loner,* 1969; *A Boy Named Charlie Brown,* 1970; *Come to Your Senses,* 1971; *Scandalous John,* 1971; *Wildflowers,* 1971; *The Seagull,* 1972; *Lisa, Bright and Dark,* 1973; *Big Mo,* 1973; *The Borrowers,* 1973; *Hello Again,* 1974; *Emily,* 1975; *The Unknown War,* 1979; *Man to Himself,* 1980; *Portrait of Rod McKuen,* 1982; *The Living End,* 1983; and *Death Rides This Trail,* 1983.

Also author of annual datebook and calendar. Author of numerous concertos, symphonies, and ballets, and of more than one thousand songs, including "Jean," "If You Go Away," "Seasons in the Sun," "I'm Not Afraid," "The Lovers," and "Love's Been Good to Me." Coauthor and composer of music for television documentary *The Unknown War,* 1978. Author of monthly poetry column for *Cosmopolitan,* 1970-71.

SIDELIGHTS: "I never meant to be a conglomerate, but my interests are varied," author, poet, actor, singer, composer, and lecturer Rod McKuen once told *CA.* "When anyone suggests I cut back on some of my activity, it would be like cutting off my arm. . . . I want to work. Without working, you go bananas." McKuen's poems, essays and songs are therapeutic for him as well as his fans. Many of his books, such as *Finding My Father: One Man's Search for Identity,* chronicle the difficulties of the author's life and his efforts to overcome them.

McKuen was born during the Depression in a California Salvation Army hospital. Several birth certificates with conflicting dates have been found; McKuen chose to accept the earliest date among them. Raised by his mother and abusive stepfather, McKuen ran away from home several times but was always caught. He finally escaped at age eleven, after three years of trying, and set out walking, hitchhiking, and train-hopping, putting mile after mile between him and his painful past. Much of his writing and his work with the National Committee for the Prevention of Child Abuse have helped McKuen exorcise the misery embedded in him by those early experiences. "The fact that my stepfather had beaten me up when I was a kid wasn't hard for me to talk or write about," McKuen wrote

in a 1982 article for *People.* "I had both arms broken and my ribs caved in several times, but physical injuries on the outside heal. Before now, though, I have never been able to come forward and talk about having been sexually abused when I was a child. Those scars have never healed, and I expect they never will." McKuen's aunt and then his uncle each molested their seven-year-old nephew within two weeks' time. Like most abused children, McKuen believed that he was somehow to blame for the actions of his attackers. He carried overwhelming feelings of guilt and shame well into adulthood, finally finding some relief close to age fifty when he chose to share his experiences in a speech delivered at the 1982 National Conference on Sexual Victimization of Children. Since then McKuen has remained an active spokesman for children's rights.

Ironically, McKuen's abuse at the hands of his relatives played a part in his later success. "I've always had an inferiority complex, and that childhood incident was one of the things that intensified it, for sure," McKuen related in *People.* "I think that's one of the reasons I've always worked and never taken vacations. I'm always trying to be as good as everybody else." In *Finding My Father: One Man's Search for Identity,* McKuen chronicles his search for his biological father, a man whose existence gave McKuen hope for happiness in his childhood. When his mother died in 1972, McKuen realized that his best chance of discovering his father's identity had died as well. He launched a worldwide search for "Mac McKuen," using every tactic from private investigators to personal ads, and found who he believes was his father, "a man 10 years deceased . . . Rodney Marion McKune, a lumberman in Utah, twice married . . . , who at the close of his life was an iceman in Santa Monica, Calif., 20 miles from where McKuen was living," Betty Jean Lifton reported in the *New York Times Book Review.* McKuen bases his certainty on a number of similarities of character and physique, and wrote in *Finding My Father,* "I knew, of course, that he was my father the moment I saw the first photographs." "In no way does McKuen try to get beneath the surface of his revelations, or himself " in *Finding My Father,* Lifton remarked. "But the pain is there—and the importance of a father to a man's identity."

Although critics often lambaste his work, the sales figures of his books and albums attest to McKuen's vast popularity. Despite her contention that McKuen is "so devitalized a singer, so bad a poet, so without wit or tune," Margot Hentoff conceded in a 1971 *New York Review of Books* article that "McKuen's records do wonderfully well, and a Random House ad tells us that over three and a half million copies of his books of poetry and songs are currently in print." In a 1975 *Times Literary Supplement* article, David Harsent found McKuen's popularity frightening, describing his style as "a formula likely to appeal to the groupies and the grannies alike. But to teachers, lecturers and students all over the world? And to the tune of 1.8 million sales each year for five years; or 150,000 a month; or, to make it really scary, almost 5,000 a day?"

Remarking in *Book World* on the "pastel mistiness of image" which permeates McKuen's poetry, Tom Disch noted, "Fogs are dear to him as emblems of the state of reverie that is the source of his poetry, a state in which (and this may be the secret of his success) he and his reader are most closely akin." Disch concluded that, for McKuen, conventional training would have been a mistake. "Had Rod McKuen been sent to one of the creative writing schools, [one of his lessons] would have been to abjure his love of imprecision and ineffability for a sparrow's eye view that concentrates on clear outlines and telling details—and the writing school would have been wrong."

BIOGRAPHICAL/CRITICAL SOURCES:

BOOKS

Contemporary Literary Criticism, Gale, Volume 1, 1973, Volume 3, 1975.

PERIODICALS

American Poetry Review, May/June, 1973.
Book World, November 24, 1968; December 30, 1984.
Denver Post, August 14, 1974.
Detroit News, May 1, 1969.
Esquire, June, 1971.
Journal of Popular Culture, spring, 1970.
Life, February 9, 1968.
Miami Herald, January 10, 1975.
New York Review of Books, November 4, 1971.
New York Times, May 1, 1969.
New York Times Book Review, October 22, 1967; September 5, 1976, p. 8.
Publishers Weekly, July 5, 1976, p. 73; March 5, 1979, p. 104; January 3, 1986, p. 49.
Time, November 24, 1967; May 16, 1969.
Times Literary Supplement, January 31, 1975.
Writer's Digest, October, 1972.*

—*Sketch by Deborah A. Stanley*

*   *   *

McWILLIAMS, Wilson Carey   1933-

PERSONAL: Born September 2, 1933, in Santa Monica, CA; son of Carey and Dorothy Janet (Hedrick) McWilliams; married Carol Golder, June, 1955 (marriage ended, 1961); married Nancy Riley (a psychoanalyst), September 16, 1966; children: Susan Jane, Helen Elizabeth. *Education:* University of California, Berkeley, A.B., 1955, M.A.,

1960, Ph.D., 1966. *Politics:* Democrat. *Religion:* Presbyterian.

ADDRESSES: Home—9 Mine St., Flemington, NJ 08222. *Office*—Department of Political Science, Rutgers University, New Brunswick, NJ 08903.

CAREER: Oberlin College, Oberlin, OH, instructor, 1961-67; Brooklyn College of the City University of New York, Brooklyn, NY, assistant professor, 1967-70; Rutgers University, New Brunswick, NJ, professor of political science, 1970—. Vice president of Institute for the Study of Civic Values. *Military service:* U.S. Army, 1955-57; became first lieutenant.

MEMBER: American Political Science Association.

AWARDS, HONORS: National Historical Society prize, for *The Idea of Fraternity In America;* John Witherspoon Award, New Jersey Committee for the Humanities, for distinguished service to the humanities.

WRITINGS:

(Editor with George A. Lanyi) *Crisis and Continuity in World Politics: Readings in International Relations,* Random House, 1965, 2nd edition, 1973.
(Editor) *Garrisons and Government,* Chandler & Sharp, 1967.
Military Honor after Mylai, Council on Religion and International Affairs, 1972.
The Idea of Fraternity in America, University of California Press, 1973.
(With Gerald M. Pomper and others) *The Election of 1976: Reports and Interpretations,* edited by Marlene M. Pomper, McKay, 1977.
(With G. Pomper and others) *The Election of 1980: Reports and Interpretations,* edited by M. Pomper, Chatham House, 1981.
(With G. Pomper and others) *The Election of 1984: Reports and Interpretations,* Chatham House, 1985.
(With G. Pomper and others) *The Election of 1988: Reports and Interpretations,* Chatham House, 1989.
(Editor with Michael Gibbons) *The Federalists, the Antifederalists and the American Political Tradition,* Greenwood, 1992.
(With G. Pomper and others) *The Election of 1992: Reports and Interpretations,* Chatham House, 1993.

Contributor to magazines, including *Commonweal.* Member of editorial board of *Society.*

*   *   *

MEREDITH, William (Morris)   1919-

PERSONAL: Born January 9, 1919, in New York, NY; son of William Morris and Nelley Atkin (Keyser) Meredith. *Education:* Princeton University, A.B. (magna cum laude), 1940. *Politics:* Democrat.

CAREER: New York Times, New York City, 1940-41, began as copy boy, became reporter; Princeton University, Princeton, NJ, instructor in English and Woodrow Wilson fellow in writing, 1946-50; University of Hawaii, Honolulu, associate professor of English, 1950-51; Connecticut College, New London, associate professor, 1955-65, professor of English, 1965-83. Middlebury College, Middlebury, VT, instructor at Breadloaf School of English, 1958-62. Member of Connecticut Commission on the Arts, 1963-65; director of the humanities, Upward Bound Program, 1964-68; poetry consultant, Library of Congress, 1978-80. *Military service:* U.S. Army Air Forces, 1941-42; U.S. Navy, Naval Aviation, 1942-46; served in Pacific Theater; became lieutenant. U.S. Naval Reserve, active duty in Korean War as naval aviator, 1952-54; became lieutenant commander; received two Air Medals.

MEMBER: National Institute of Arts and Letters, Academy of American Poets (chancellor), American Choral Society (second vice-president).

AWARDS, HONORS: Yale Series of Younger Poets Award for *Love Letter from an Impossible Land,* 1943; Harriet Monroe Memorial Prize, 1944, and Oscar Blumenthal Prize, 1953, for poems published in *Poetry;* Rockefeller grant, 1948, 1968; *Hudson Review* fellow, 1956; National Institute of Arts and Letters grant in literature, 1958; Ford Foundation fellowship for drama, 1959-60; Loines Prize from National Institute of Arts and Letters, 1966; Van Wyck Brooks Award, 1971; National Endowment for the Arts grant, 1972, fellow, 1984; Guggenheim fellow, 1975-76; International Vaptsarov Prize for Literature, Bulgaria, 1979; *Los Angeles Times* Prize, 1987; Pulitzer Prize for poetry, 1988, for *Partial Accounts: New and Selected Poems.*

WRITINGS:

POETRY

Love Letter from an Impossible Land, Yale University Press, 1944.
Ships and Other Figures, Princeton University Press, 1948.
The Open Sea and Other Poems, Knopf, 1958.
The Wreck of the Thresher and Other Poems, Knopf, 1964.
Winter Verse, privately printed, 1964.
Year End Accounts, privately printed, 1965.
Two Pages from a Colorado Journal, privately printed, 1967.
Earth Walk: New and Selected Poems, Knopf, 1970.
Hazard, the Painter, Knopf, 1975.
The Cheer, Knopf, 1980.
Partial Accounts: New and Selected Poems, Knopf, 1987.

OTHER

(Librettist) *The Bottle Imp* (opera; music by Peter Whiton), first produced in Wilton, CT, 1958.
(Editor) *Shelley: Poems,* Dell, 1962.
(Translator) Guillaume Apollinaire, *Alcools: Poems, 1898-1913,* Doubleday, 1964.
(Editor) *University and College Poetry Prizes, 1960-66,* Academy of American Poets, 1966.
(Editor with Mackie L. Jarrell) *Eighteenth-Century Minor Poets,* Dell, 1968.
Selected Poems, 1977 (recording), Watershed, 1977.
Reasons for Poetry and the Reason for Criticism (lectures), Library of Congress, 1982.
(Editor) Denise Levertov and others, translators, *Poets of Bulgaria,* Unicorn Press, 1985.
Poems Are Hard to Read, University of Michigan Press, 1991.

Contributor to magazines. Opera critic, *Hudson Review,* 1955-56.

SIDELIGHTS: William Meredith writes a formal, disciplined poetry concerned with the proper balance between the natural and civilized worlds. His poems, Matthew Flamm comments in the *Village Voice,* are "polished and direct, formal and natural, in equal measure," while his poetic voice is that "of someone who has been thinking for years about his place in the world, with no illusions of importance." A *Publishers Weekly* critic explains that Meredith's poems are "exercises in discipline and craft—objective in the choice and handling of theme, clear and simple in style and restrained in tone. He is a master in the use of meter, rhyme and stanzaic structure. . . . The perfectly achieved formal aspects of Meredith's poetry mark him as a writer whose bedrock values transcend time and place." In 1988, Meredith received a Pulitzer Prize for his collection *Partial Accounts: New and Selected Poems.*

Meredith first began writing poetry in college. After graduating in 1940, he worked for a year as a reporter with the *New York Times* before joining the army. In 1942 he transferred to the U.S. Navy to become a pilot, serving on aircraft carriers in the Pacific Theatre for the duration of World War II. In 1952, he re-enlisted to fly missions in the Korean War as well. Following his military service Meredith pursued an academic career, teaching English at Connecticut College from 1955 to 1983. A severe stroke in 1983 forced an early retirement from teaching and months of rehabiliation to regain his speech.

Meredith has always written a personal poetry rendered in traditional poetic forms, using these forms as frameworks for individual expression. Like fellow New Englander Robert Frost, to whom he is often compared, Meredith writes unadorned, formal verse. As Moul explains, the poet believes that "immediacy of image and idea, spoken in the poet's own voice, are and should be the poet's object." A critic for the *Antioch Review* describes Meredith's poems as "beautifully worked, distinct objects, the language at once exciting and unobtrusive—what keeps them together is a tone wistful and ironic, which gives them the air of events as inevitable to the reader as to the poet." James Dickey, writing in his *Babel to Byzantium,* notes a "certain ingroup variety of bookish snobbery that is probably Meredith's one outstanding weakness as a writer," but nonetheless finds that "at his best he is a charming poet, cultivated, calm, quietly original, expansive and reflective, moving over wide areas slowly, lightly, mildly and often very memorably."

Over the years, Meredith's production of poetry has been modest in size. Writing in *Corgi Modern Poets in Focus 2,* the poet comments: "Chiefly I think my poverty of output stems from the conviction that an unnecessary poem is an offense to the art." But Moul disagrees: "Meredith's 'poverty of output' is instead a rare thing among poets, a discriminating taste."

Meredith's first collection of poems, *Love Letter from an Impossible Land,* was chosen by Archibald MacLeish for publication in the Yale Series of Younger Poets in 1944. Half the poems in the collection were written while Meredith was still in college; many of these were derivative of other poets' work. But critics felt that the poems based on Meredith's war experiences as a pilot displayed emotional honesty. The *Christian Century* reviewer explains that the "poems born out of the war are true, and often eloquent and revealing." Ruth Lechlitner in *Poetry* finds: "When William Meredith leaves the book-shelves and becomes the flyer, he becomes also a poet in his own right."

In 1948, Meredith's second collection of poems was published. *Ships and Other Figures* again draws upon Meredith's time in the Navy for subject matter. Milton Crane, writing in the *New York Times,* finds the poems to be "cool, intellectual, and self-contained. . . . [Meredith's] detachment bespeaks no incapacity for more overt emotional expression, but a deliberate decision to set down his observations and conclusions as clearly and succinctly as possible." Writing in the *Saturday Review of Literature,* G. P. Meyer notes: "That a poet today can still write with affection of people and things and communicate that feeling to others, is something to celebrate."

Open Sea and Other Poems appeared in 1958, displaying a poetry more adventurous than previously suspected of Meredith. As Richard Howard states in his *Alone with America: Essays on the Art of Poetry in the United States since 1950,* with *Open Sea and Other Poems,* Meredith "insisted on play, on a response to selfhood as pleasure, on the morality of virtuosity." At the same time, Howard admits that for Meredith, "all art, poetic or otherwise, is an act of self-defense against the world changing its meaning from moment to moment, against the difference, against things becoming *other,* against their loss of identity. For him, poetry is a way of asserting that things are what they are—the insight of self-reference—and that when they mean something else, order as well as delight is endangered."

In 1964, Meredith published *The Wreck of the Thresher and Other Poems,* a book whose title poem is an elegy to an American submarine lost at sea in 1963. Despite the shift in tone, Meredith's handling of the tragic theme was met with critical applause. According to D. R. Slavitt in *Book Week,* "If any one could write a poem on the wreck of the Thresher, it would be Meredith; that elegiac honesty, that speculative gentleness of his are worthy of the subject." Fred Bornhauser in the *Virginia Quarterly Review* praises "the elegance which is compounded of compassion, intelligence, and linguistic precision," while S. F. Morse in the *New York Times Book Review* states that " 'The Wreck of the Thresher' is an accomplishment of a very high order. . . . The title poem may well come to stand as a model of the elegy in our time." Keith Moul in the *Dictionary of Literary Biography* finds that "the consensus is that Meredith attains a consistently high level of performance" in *The Wreck of the Thresher.*

Gathering poems from the previous twenty-five years, *Earth Walk* reveals the range of Meredith's early work. As Chad Walsh of *Book World* comments, "the poems move toward freer forms with the passage of time, but one is more impressed by the continuities—the sober intelligence, the perceptive sensibility exploring a world waiting to have its latent poetry revealed to it." Victory Howes in the *Christian Science Monitor* calls Meredith "a poet of hairline precisions, minute discriminations, and subtle observings. . . . How quickly the strangeness, the wonder, would pass from things were it not for poets like William Meredith." *Earth Walk,* according to Moul, is "a just selection that as much emphasizes [Meredith's] variety as his quirks. Much of his best writing is here."

With *Partial Accounts: New and Selected Poems,* Meredith gathered poems from throughout his long writing career to give an overview of his poetic achievement. Publication of the book provided an opportunity for critics to access Meredith's contribution to the genre. Among those critics is Linda Gregerson in *Poetry.* She finds that *Partial Accounts* documents Meredith's serious use of formal poetic structures. Meredith, Gregerson writes, "is a poet who asks us seriously to consider the rhymed quatrain as a unit of perceptual pacing, the villanelle as the ambivalent and ritual simulation of fate, the sestina as a scaffolding for directed rumination, the sonnet as an instrument for testing the prodigious or the ineffable against the longing-for-shapeliness we know as 'argument'." She concludes:

"Touched as they are by goodness, rich in craft and thoughtfulness, the poems collected here should find themselves well-treated by their readers." Edward Hirsch, in his evaluation of *Partial Accounts* for the *New York Times Book Review,* sees Meredith as a poet who has "emphasized the need for a civilizing intelligence and humane values. In one sense, all of his work constitutes a desire to recognize and then move beyond catastrophe and despair—whether personal, social or historical. Book by book, he has evolved into a poet by sly wit and quiet skill, working out a thoughtful esthetic of orderliness."

BIOGRAPHICAL/CRITICAL SOURCES:

BOOKS

Contemporary Authors Autobiography Series, Volume 14, Gale, 1991.
Contemporary Literary Criticism, Gale, Volume 4, 1975, Volume 13, 1980, Volume 22, 1982, Volume 55, 1989.
Dickey, James, *Babel to Byzantium,* Farrar, Straus, 1968, pp. 197-198.
Dictionary of Literary Biography, Volume 5: *American Poets since World War II,* Gale, 1980.
Howard, Richard, *Alone with America: Essays on the Art of Poetry in the United States since 1950,* Atheneum, 1971, revised edition, 1980.
Robson, Jeremy, *Corgi Modern Poets in Focus 2,* Transworld Publishers, 1971, pp. 117-125.
Rotella, Guy, *Three Contemporary Poets of New England,* Twayne, 1983.

PERIODICALS

American Scholar, autumn, 1965, pp. 646-658.
Antioch Review, spring, 1970, p. 134.
Atlantic, February, 1981, p. 94.
Christian Century, April 19, 1944, p. 498.
Christian Science Monitor, October 15, 1970, p. 9.
Commonweal, January 24, 1958, pp. 437-439; December 4, 1981, p. 692.
Georgia Review, spring, 1976, p. 205.
Hollins Critic, February, 1979, pp. 1-15.
Hudson Review, autumn, 1970, p. 564; autumn, 1975, p. 455; spring, 1981, pp. 141-154.
Kenyon Review, summer, 1988, p. 127.
Los Angeles Times Book Review, November 30, 1980.
Nation, June 15, 1970, p. 695.
New Republic, June 14, 1975, p. 25.
New York Review of Books, June 15, 1972, p. 32.
New York Times Book Review, September 27, 1964, p. 53; September 21, 1975, p. 39; March 22, 1981, p. 14; July 31, 1988, p. 20.
Parnassus: Poetry in Review, spring-summer, 1976, pp. 220-224; fall, 1981, p. 169.
Partisan Review, winter, 1971-72, pp. 474-475.

Poetry, July, 1944, pp. 227-229; November, 1948, pp. 111-116; September, 1958, pp. 380-382; February, 1966, pp. 320-330; July, 1971, p. 228; January, 1976, p. 234; December, 1981, p. 171; February, 1988, p. 423.
Publishers Weekly, April 10, 1987, p. 90.
Saturday Review, August 8, 1970, p. 34.
Saturday Review of Literature, April 29, 1944, p. 24; May 15, 1948, pp. 24-25; March 22, 1958, p. 23.
Sewanee Review, winter, 1972, p. 137; winter, 1973, pp. 147-150.
Shenandoah, winter, 1971, pp. 82-83.
Village Voice, August 18, 1987, p. 52.
Virginia Quarterly Review, summer, 1975, p. 110; summer, 1981, p. 94; autumn, 1987, p. 138.
Washington Post, October 11, 1978.
World Literature Today, spring, 1989, p. 330.
Yale Review, December, 1944, pp. 342-343; June, 1958, pp. 608-610; winter, 1971, p. 284.*

*   *   *

MERLIN, Christina
See HEAVEN, Constance

*   *   *

MILES, Keith
See TRALINS, S(andor) Robert

*   *   *

MILLER, E(ugene) Willard 1915-

PERSONAL: Born May 17, 1915, in Turkey City, PA; son of Archie H. (a petroleum engineer) and Tessie (Master) Miller; married Ruby M. Skinner (a librarian), June 28, 1941. *Education:* Clarion State College, B.S., 1937; University of Nebraska, M.A., 1939; Ohio State University, Ph.D., 1942. *Religion:* United Church of Christ.

ADDRESSES: Home—845 Outer Dr., State College, PA. *Office*—Department of Geography, Pennsylvania State University, University Park, PA 16802.

CAREER: Ohio State University, Columbus, instructor in geography, 1942-43; Western Reserve University (now Case Western Reserve University), Cleveland, Ohio, assistant professor of geography and geology, 1943-44; Office of Strategic Services, Washington, D.C., geographer, 1944-45; Pennsylvania State University, University Park, associate professor, 1945-49, professor of geography, 1949-80, professor emeritus, 1980—, head of department, 1945-63, assistant dean, 1964-72, associate dean for resident instruction, 1972-88, dean emeritus, 1988—. U.S. member of committee on natural resources of Commission of Geography, Pan American Institute of Geography and History. Geographic editor, Thomas Y. Crowell Co. President, Geographical Slide Service.

MEMBER: American Association for the Advancement of Science (fellow), American Geographical Society (fellow), National Council for Geographic Education (fellow), Association of American Geographers, American Association of University Professors (president, Pennsylvania State University chapter, 1958-59), American Society for Professional Geographers (president, 1948), Pennsylvania Council for Geographic Education (president, 1948), Pennsylvania Academy of Science (president, 1966-68), Explorers Club (fellow).

AWARDS, HONORS: Ray Hughes Whitbeck Award, 1950, for outstanding article on economic geography in *Journal of Geography;* certificate of merit, Office of Strategic Services; National Science Foundation travel grant, 1960, 1963; meritorious service award, Pennsylvania Department of Commerce, 1975; citation for service to the commonwealth, Governor of Pennsylvania, 1975; distinguished service award, Pennsylvania Academy of Science, 1985; named distinguished alumnus, Clarion State College, 1987; honor award, Association of American Geographers, 1989.

WRITINGS:

Careers in Geography, Institute for Research, 1948, 2nd edition, 1955.
(Contributor) *Conservation of Natural Resources,* Wiley, 1950, 3rd edition, 1970.
(Contributor) *Outside Readings in Geography,* Crowell, 1955.
(Editor) *Global Geography,* Crowell, 1957.
(With others) *The World's Nations: An Economic and Regional Geography,* Lippincott, 1958.
A Geography of Manufacturing, Prentice-Hall, 1962.
An Economic Atlas of Pennsylvania, Pennsylvania State Planning Board, 1964.
Exploring Earth Environments: A World Geography, Crowell, 1964.
Mineral Resources of the United States, Rand McNally, 1968.
Energy Resources of the United States, Rand McNally, 1968.
A Geography of Industrial Location, William C. Brown, 1970.
Socioeconomic Patterns of Pennsylvania: An Atlas, Bureau of Management Services, Commonwealth of Pennsylvania, 1975.
Manufacturing: A Study of Industrial Location, Pennsylvania State University Press, 1977.

(With wife, Ruby M. Miller) *Economic, Political, and Regional Aspects of the World's Energy Problems,* Vance Bibliographies, 1979.
(Editor with S. K. Majumdar) *Hazardous and Toxic Wastes,* Pennsylvania Academy of Science, 1984.
(Editor with Majumdar) *Liquid and Solid Wastes,* Pennsylvania Academy of Science, 1984.
(With R. M. Miller) *Industrial Location and Planning: Theory, Models and Factors of Localization, a Bibliography,* Vance Bibliographies, 1984.
(With R. M. Miller) *Industrial Location and Planning: Localization, Growth and Organization, a Bibliography,* Vance Bibliographies, 1984.
(With R. M. Miller) *Industrial Location and Planning: Industries, a Bibliography,* Vance Bibliographies, 1984.
(Editor with Majumdar) *Radioactive Materials and Wastes,* Pennsylvania Academy of Science, 1985.
Physical Geography: Earth Systems and Human Interactions, C. E. Merrill, 1985.
(With R. M. Miller) *Environmental Hazards: Air Pollution, a Bibliography,* Vance Bibliographies, 1985.
(With R. M. Miller) *Environmental Hazards: Solid Wastes, a Bibliography,* Vance Bibliographies, 1985.
(With R. M. Miller) *Environmental Hazards: Liquid Wastes, a Bibliography,* Vance Bibliographies, 1985.
(With R. M. Miller) *Environmental Hazards: Industrial and Toxic Wastes, a Bibliography,* Vance Bibliographies, 1985.
(With R. M. Miller) *Environmental Hazards: Radioactive Materials and Wastes, a Bibliography,* Vance Bibliographies, 1985.
Pennsylvania: Keystone to Progress, Windsor Publications, 1986.
(Editor with Majumdur and F. J. Brenner) *Environmental Consequences of Energy Production,* Pennsylvania Academy of Science, 1987.
(With R. M. Miller) *Doing Business In and With Latin America,* Gryx Press, 1987.
(Editor with Majumdar and L. E. Sage) *Ecology and Restoration of the Delaware River Basin,* Pennsylvania Academy of Science, 1988.
(Editor with Majumdar and R. Parizch) *Water Resources in Pennsylvania,* Pennsylvania Academy of Science, 1989.
(With R. M. Miller) *Contemporary World Issues: Environmental Hazards, Air Pollution,* Clio, 1989.
(Editor with Majumdur and R. F. Schmatz) *Management of Hazardous Materials and Wastes,* Pennsylvania Academy of Science, 1989.
(With Majumdur and Schmatz) *Environmental Radon,* Pennsylvania Academy of Science, 1990.
(With R. M. Miller) *Contemporary World Issues: Environmental Hazards, Radioactive Materials, and Wastes,* Clio, 1990.

(Editor with Majumdar, L. M. Rosenfeld, P. A. Rubba, and Schmatz) *Science Education in the United States,* Pennsylvania Academy of Science, 1991.
(Editor with Majumdar and J. Calrir) *Air Pollution,* Pennsylvania Academy of Science, 1991.
(With R. M. Miller) *Contemporary Issues: Environmental Hazards, Hazardous Wastes, and Toxic Materials,* Clio, 1991.

Also author with R. M. Miller, of *Industrial Location: A Bibliography,* 1978, and *The American Coal Industry,* 1980. Contributor to proceedings. Contributor to *Journal of Geography, Economic Geography, Scientific Monthly,* and other periodicals. Associate editor, *Producers Monthly,* 1948-68; associate editor, *Pennsylvania Geographer,* 1965—; general editor, *Earth and Mineral Sciences Bulletin,* 1966-68. Member of editorial committee, *Journal of the Pennsylvania Academy of Science.*

*   *   *

MILLER, Roy Andrew 1924-

PERSONAL: Born September 5, 1924, in Winona, MN; son of Andrew and Jessie (Eickelberry) Miller. *Education:* Gustavus Adolphus College, B.A., 1946; Columbia University, M.A., 1950, Ph.D., 1953.

ADDRESSES: Home—555 University Ave., Apt. 2606, Honolulu, HI 96826.

CAREER: Central Intelligence Group, Washington, DC, research analyst, 1946-48; field research in spoken Tibetan in northern India and Kyoto, Japan, 1953-54; University of California, Berkeley, lecturer in Japanese, 1955; International Christian University, Tokyo, Japan, assistant professor, 1955-58, associate professor, 1958-61, professor of linguistics, 1961-62, acting vice-president for education, 1959-60; Yale University, New Haven, CT, associate professor and director of Institute of Far Eastern Languages, 1962-64, professor of Far Eastern languages and chairman of department of East and South Asian languages and literature, 1964-72; University of Washington, Seattle, professor of Asian languages and literature, 1972-89.

Lecturer, University of Maryland Far Eastern Program, Japan, 1956-62, and Stanford University, summer, 1961; guest scholar, University of Hawaii, Honolulu, Institute of Advanced Projects, East-West Center, 1961; visiting professor of linguistics, International Christian University, 1964-65; visiting professor, University of Vienna, 1990. Director, Inter-University Center for Japanese Studies, Tokyo, 1964-65. *Military service:* U.S. Naval Reserve, 1944-46; served with Office of Naval Intelligence.

AWARDS, HONORS: Research prize, Alexander von Humboldt Foundation (Germany), 1991-92.

WRITINGS:

Problems in the Study of Shuo-wen Chiehtzu, [Ann Arbor], 1953.
The Tibetan System of Writing, American Council of Learned Societies, 1956.
(Translator) M. Kawakita, *Kobayashi Kobei, 1883-1957,* Tuttle, 1957.
(Translator) *Utagawa Toyokuni, 1769-1875,* Tuttle, 1957.
(Editor and translator) *Bunraku Puppet Head Masterpieces,* Tuttle, 1958.
(Translator and annotator) *Accounts of Western Nations in the History of the Northern Chou Dynasty,* University of California Press, 1959.
Japanese Ceramics, Toto Shuppan Co., 1960.
(Translator) F. Miki, *Haniwa: The Clay Sculptures of Protohistoric Japan,* Tuttle, 1960.
(Translator) I. Kondo, *Japanese Genre Painting: The Lively Art of Renaissance Japan,* Tuttle, 1961.
Japanese Ceramics, Crown, 1962.
(Editor) *A Japanese Reader,* Tuttle, 1962.
The Japanese Language, University of Chicago Press, 1967.
(Editor) *Bernard Bloch on Japanese,* Yale University Press, 1970.
Japanese and the Other Altaic Languages, University of Chicago Press, 1971.
The Footprints of the Buddha: An Eighth-Century Old Japanese Poetic Sequence, American Oriental Society, 1975.
Studies in the Grammatical Tradition in Tibet, John Benjamins, 1976.
Japanese Language in Contemporary Japan: Some Sociolinguistic Observations, American Enterprise Institute for Public Policy Research, 1977.
Origins of the Japanese Language, University of Washington Press, 1980.
Japan's Modern Myth, the Language and Beyond, Tuttle, 1982.
Nihongo: In Defense of Japanese, Athlone Press, 1986.
(With Nelly Naumann) *Altjapanisch Fafuri, Zu Priestertum und Schamanismus im vorbuddhistischen Japan,* [Hamburg], 1991.
Prolegomena to the First Two Tibetan Grammatical Treatises, University of Vienna, 1993.

Contributor of over one hundred articles and reviews to professional journals. Some of Miller's books have been translated into Japanese and Korean.

WORK IN PROGRESS: A comparative grammar of Old Japanese on historical principles.

MITCHELL, Allison
See BUTTERWORTH, W(illiam) E(dmund III)

*　　*　　*

MITCHELL, Judith Paige

PERSONAL: Original name, Judith Segel; name legally changed; born in New Orleans, LA; daughter of George J. (an engineer) and Esther (a teacher; maiden name, Finerowsky) Segel.

ADDRESSES: Home—Bel Air, CA. *Agent*—Wendy Weil Agency, 232 Madison Ave., New York, NY 10016.

CAREER: Writer and television producer.

WRITINGS:

A Wilderness of Monkeys (novel), Dutton, 1965.
Love Is Not a Safe Country (novel), Dutton, 1967.
The Mayfly (novel), Bantam, 1971.
The Covenant (novel), Atheneum, 1973.
Act of Love: The Killing of George Zygmanik (nonfiction), Knopf, 1976.
Wild Seed (novel), Doubleday, 1982.
American Geisha (television film), Columbia Broadcasting System (CBS-TV), 1985.
Roses Are for the Rich (television miniseries), CBS-TV, 1987.
Desperate for Love (television film), CBS-TV, 1989.
Burning Bridges (television film), American Broadcasting Companies (ABC-TV), 1990.
Island Son (drama series), CBS-TV, 1990.
Black Widow (television film), National Broadcasting Company (NBC-TV), 1992.

Also author of other screenplays and a television series pilot.

BIOGRAPHICAL/CRITICAL SOURCES:

PERIODICALS

Best Sellers, June, 1976.
Critic, fall, 1976.
Library Journal, June 15, 1976.
New York Times Book Review, May 27, 1973; April 4, 1976.*

*　　*　　*

MODIANO, Patrick (Jean) 1945-

PERSONAL: Born July 30, 1945, in Boulogne-Billancourt, France; son of Albert (a financier) and Luisa (an actress; maiden name, Colpyn) Modiano; married Dominique Zehrfuss, 1970; children: Zenaide, Maria. *Education:* Attended high school in Thones, France.

ADDRESSES: Home—Paris, France. *Agent*—Georges Beaume, 3 quai Malaquais, 75006 Paris, France.

CAREER: Novelist, 1968—.

AWARDS, HONORS: Prix Roger Nimier, 1968, and Prix Felix Feneon, 1969, both for *La Place de l'etoile;* Grand Prix Roman, L'Academie Francaise, 1972, for *Les Boulevards de ceinture;* Prix Goncourt, 1978, for *Rue des boutiques obscures.*

WRITINGS:

La Place de l'etoile (novel), Gallimard, 1968.
La Ronde de nuit, Gallimard, 1969, translation by Patricia Wolf published as *Night Rounds,* Knopf, 1971.
Les Boulevards de ceinture, Gallimard, 1972, translation by Caroline Hillier published as *Ring Roads,* Gollancz, 1974.
(With Louis Malle) *Lacombe Lucien* (screenplay; released by Louis Malle, 1974), Gallimard, 1974, translation by Sabine Destree published as *Lacombe Lucien,* Viking, 1975.
Villa Triste (novel), Gallimard, 1975, translation by Hillier published as *Villa Triste,* Gollancz, 1977.
(With Emmanuel Berl) *Interrogatoire par Patrick Modiano suivi de Il fait beau, allons au cimetiere,* Gallimard, 1976.
Livret de famille (novel; title means "Family Book"), Gallimard, 1977.
Rue des boutiques obscures (novel), Gallimard, 1978, translation by Daniel Weissbort published as *Missing Person,* J. Cape, 1980.
Une Jeunesse (novel; title means "A Youth"), Gallimard, 1981.
Memory Lane (novel), Hachette, 1981.
De si braves garcons (title means "Such Good Fellows"), Gallimard, 1982.
Poupee blonde (title means "Blonde Doll"), P.O.L., 1983.
Quartier perdu, Gallimard, 1985.
Dimanches d'Aout (novel), Gallimard, 1986.
Remise de Peine (novel), Seuil, 1988.
Catherine Certitude (novel), Gallimard, 1988.
Vestiaire de l'Enfance (novel), Gallimard, 1989.
Voyage de Noces (novel), Gallimard, 1990.
Fleurs de Ruine (novel), Seuil, 1991.

SIDELIGHTS: "What did the last generation get up to when it was the present generation? That is the simple yet unsettling question out of which Patrick Modiano has . . . made . . . expert and intriguing novels," writes John Sturrock in the *Times Literary Supplement.* French novelist Modiano published his first book at the age of twenty-three, in 1968. Since then his work has won several major

French awards, including the Grand Prix Roman from the Academie Francaise and the Prix Goncourt. Modiano, described by Joyce Carleton in the *French Review* as "a young author particularly haunted by the grey years of the nineteen-forties," has set many of his novels, as well as *Lacombe Lucien*—the highly acclaimed screenplay he co-authored with French director Louis Malle—in Occupied France. His technique, notes Anne Duchene in the *Times Literary Supplement,* relies upon "delicately superimposing past upon present, grafting the 'then' on the 'now,' in a thin yet infinitely hurtful threnody."

Although Modiano is too young to have directly experienced France during the Occupation, John Weightman suggests in the *Times Literary Supplement* that "something romantically mysterious in his past," perhaps "some unhappy family link," ties him to that period. Weightman feels that Modiano is "obsessed with Jewishness" and the dubious or ambiguous roles French Jews assumed to survive the Occupation. Indeed, Modiano's novel that won the Grand Prix Roman, *Les Boulevards de ceinture,* tells the story of a young man whose father is a Jew in Occupied France. Jewish characters also play central roles in Modiano's screenplay for *Lacombe Lucien,* a film that Weightman praises as "possibly the most brilliant imaginative evocation of wartime France that has yet appeared, and a very delicate account of a certain kind of relationship between Jews and non-Jews."

If, as Weightman suggests, an obsession with Jewishness motivates Modiano, the idea does not serve as Modiano's sole fictive theme. The author is also fascinated by the casual attitudes of some of those who cooperated with the Nazis during the Occupation. "His characters are chiefly the Nazi occupiers and their French and international hangers-on," notes Francis Steegmuller in the *Times Literary Supplement.* This is particularly evident in *Lacombe Lucien* when the teenaged Lucien is attracted to the Nazis chiefly because they are well-dressed and living in sumptuous comfort. Jay Cocks writes in *Time* magazine: "As with Lucien, the foundation for national tragedy is laid quietly, and is built upon with a terrible ease."

Several of Modiano's novels have dealt with another recurring theme, that of looking back to Paris of the early 1960s. In *Une Jeunesse,* a "flagrantly nondescript bourgeois" couple, Louis and Odile, are "rejoined by their past," according to Sturrock, who comments: "*Une Jeunesse* has the trappings of naturalism, with the brevity of a fable; it is a more devious story than it seems. Louis and Odile's past does not explain their present; its apparent recovery invests them merely with the pathos of a third dimension, of time." *Quartier perdu,* too, traces the mysterious memories of an expatriate Frenchman returning to Paris after an absence of twenty years. His memories revolve around boyhood friends, described by Duchene as

"a fairly dispirited group, compulsively aimless, aware that the mythic Paris was dead, that 'le temps de monde fini' had begun, but still nightly seeking what passed for pleasure." In *Villa Triste,* the character Victor Chamara describes his eighteenth summer, and, as David Leich notes in the *Times Literary Supplement,* "it is not all that long ago: but the tone is one of infinite distance, infinite regret. It might be the memoir of a very old man striving painfully to re-create a moment of youth or some vanished Edwardian season lost in the mists of half a dozen decades."

Critics such as Duchene occasionally suggest that through the repetition of Modiano's themes, his technique is becoming "rather dangerously sleek, . . . at moments a matter of formula." "Patrick Modiano . . . has only a few suits which are beginning to look a little threadbare," comments Barbara Wright in the *Times Literary Supplement.* "All [his] heroes are a variation on those in his first two books." Critical consensus, however, accords Modiano high praise for his contributions to modern French letters. Steegmuller writes: "Modiano is one of the few young novelists writing today in any language to whose new books one looks forward; and whose past work, re-read, does not disappoint." His method, as a *Times Literary Supplement* reviewer describes it, is "both delicate and cunning: it is to sidle up to subjects of mystery and horror, indicating them without broaching them, as if gingerly fingering the outer surface of a poison bottle." "Modiano's way," claims Sturrock, "has always been to open dark doors into the past out of a sunlight present."

BIOGRAPHICAL/CRITICAL SOURCES:

BOOKS

Contemporary Literary Criticism, Volume 18, Gale, 1981.
Dictionary of Literary Biography, Volume 83: *French Novelists since 1960,* Gale, 1989.

PERIODICALS

French Review, March, 1979.
Time, October 14, 1974.
Times Literary Supplement, January 1, 1969; December 4, 1969; May 5, 1972; December 15, 1972; December 12, 1975; July 15, 1977; October 27, 1978; September 5, 1980; May 8, 1981; August 2, 1985; October 3, 1986.

*   *   *

MONTGOMERY, Herbert J. 1933-

PERSONAL: Born June 26, 1933, in Deer River, MN; married; wife's name, Mary A.

ADDRESSES: Home—5309 West 56th St., Edina, MN 55436.

CAREER: Professional writer.

AWARDS, HONORS: First prize in *Writer's Digest* contest, 1965, for article co-authored with wife.

WRITINGS:

The Apple and the Envelope, Holt, 1973.
(With Armand Maanum) *The Complete Book of Swedish Massage,* Harper, 1988.

WITH WIFE, MARY A. MONTGOMERY

Rodeo Road, Scholastic, 1973.
The Jesus Story, Winston Press, 1974.
The Chase, Scholastic, 1974.
The Splendor of the Psalms: A Photographic Meditation, Winston Press, 1977.
On the Run, Scholastic, 1990.
Beyond Sorrow: Reflections on Death and Grief, Montgomery Press, 1991.
What Will We Make? What Can We Do?, Franciscan Communications, 1992.

WITH MONTGOMERY, AND RON DelBENE

Into the Light, Upper Room Books, 1988.
Christmas Remembered, Upper Room Books, 1991.
From the Heart, Upper Room Books, 1991.
Alone With God, Upper Room Books, 1992.
The Hunger of the Heart, Upper Room Books, 1992.
The Breath of Life, Upper Room Books, 1992.

SIDELIGHTS: Montgomery began writing at the age of 22 after serving in the military during the Korean War. It took him four years to make his first sale, so to support himself he became an editor and wrote part time. "I discovered," he told *CA,* "that there are two kinds of writers: those who live to write and those who write to live. I did not want to become a starving artist, so I made the choice to write for a living." Most of Montgomery's writing now is done in collaboration, and he specializes in non-fiction.

*   *   *

MORGAN, H(oward) Wayne 1934-

PERSONAL: Born May 16, 1934, in Ashland, OK; son of Lee P. and Ura (Howard) Morgan; married Anne Hodges, October 16, 1971. *Education:* Arizona State University, B.A., 1955; Claremont Graduate School, M.A., 1956; University of California, Los Angeles, Ph.D., 1960. *Politics:* Independent.

ADDRESSES: Home—4701 Fountaingate, Norman, OK 73072. *Office*—Department of History, University of Oklahoma, Norman, OK 73019.

CAREER: San Jose State College (now California State University, San Jose), instructor in history, 1960-61; Uni-

versity of Texas at Austin, assistant professor, 1961-63, associate professor, 1963-64, professor of history, 1964-72; University of Oklahoma, Norman, professor of history, 1972—, George Lynn Cross Research Professor, 1976—, department chair, 1991—. Visiting professor, University of California, Los Angeles, summer, 1963; and University of British Columbia, summer, 1965. Oklahoma Governor's Conference on Libraries and Information Services, steering committee chairman, 1977-78. Lecturer, public speaker, and consultant for several national cultural projects.

MEMBER: Organization of American Historians.

AWARDS, HONORS: American Philosophical Society grant, 1963; Elizabeth Clay Howald Fellow in History, Ohio State University, 1963-64; Ohioana Book Award, Martha Kinney Cooper Ohioana Library Association, 1964, for *William McKinley and His America;* National Award of Merit, American Association of State and Local History, for *Newcomers to a New Land;* Harry E. Pratt Memorial Award, Illinois Historical Society, 1990, for best article.

WRITINGS:

Eugene V. Debs: Socialist for President, Syracuse University Press, 1962.
Writers in Transition: Seven Americans, Hill & Wang, 1963.
(Editor) *The Gilded Age: A Reappraisal,* Syracuse University Press, 1963, revised edition, 1970.
William McKinley and His America, Syracuse University Press, 1963.
America's Road to Empire: The War with Spain and Overseas Expansion, Knopf, 1963.
(Editor) *American Socialism: 1900-1960,* Prentice-Hall, 1964.
(Editor) *Making Peace with Spain: The Diary of Whitelaw Reid, September-December, 1898,* University of Texas Press, 1965.
American Writers in Rebellion: From Mark Twain to Dreiser, Hill & Wang, 1965.
From Hayes to McKinley: National Party Politics, 1877-1896, Syracuse University Press, 1969.
Unity and Culture: The United States, 1877-1900, Penguin, 1971.
(Editor) *Victorian Culture in America, 1865-1900,* Peacock, 1973.
(Editor) *Industrial America: Readings in the Environment and Social Problems, 1865-1914,* Rand McNally, 1973.
(Editor) *Yesterday's Addicts: American Society and Drug Abuse, 1865-1920,* University of Oklahoma Press, 1974.

(With wife, Anne Hodges Morgan) *Oklahoma: A Bicentennial History,* Norton, 1977.

New Muses: Art in American Culture, 1865-1920, University of Oklahoma Press, 1978.

(Editor) *Newcomers to a New Land,* ten volumes, University of Oklahoma Press, 1980.

Drugs in America: A Social History, 1800-1980, Syracuse University Press, 1981.

(Editor with A. H. Morgan) *Oklahoma: New Views of the Forty-Sixth State,* University of Oklahoma Press, 1982.

(Editor) *An American Artist in Paris: The Letters of Kenyon Cox, 1877-1882,* Kent State University Press, 1986.

Keepers of Culture: The Art-Thought of Kenyon Cox, Royal Cortissoz and Frank Jewett Mather, Jr., Kent State University Press, 1989.

Kenyon Cox, a Life in American Art, 1856-1919, Kent State University Press, 1993.

(Editor) *An Artist in New York: The Letters of Kenyon Cox, 1883-1919,* Kent State University Press, in press.

Contributor to books, including *The Gilded Age,* revised edition, Syracuse University Press, 1970; *History of American Presidential Elections,* four volumes, edited by Arthur M. Schlesinger, Jr., and Fred L. Israel, Chelsea House, 1971; *History of U.S. Political Parties,* four volumes, edited by Schlesinger, Chelsea House, 1973; *Essays on the Gilded Age,* edited by Margaret Francine Morris, University of Texas Press, 1973; *Issues and Ideas in America,* edited by Benjamin Taylor and Thurman White, University of Oklahoma Press, 1976; and *The Twentieth–Century West,* edited by Gerald Nash and Richard Etulain, University of New Mexico Press, 1989. Also contributor to history and literary journals, including *Historian, American Heritage,* and *Review of Politics.* Member of editorial board, *Pacific Historical Review,* 1977-90, and *Social Science Quarterly,* 1982—.

WORK IN PROGRESS: A history of drug cures and treatment programs from about 1865 to 1950.

*   *   *

MORGAN-WITTS, Max 1931-

PERSONAL: Born September 27, 1931, in Detroit, MI; son of George Frederick (a businessman) and Cassie (Davis) Morgan-Witts; married Pauline Lawson, January 4, 1958; children: Paul, Michele. *Education:* Attended Mount Royal College, Calgary, Alberta, 1947-50; Academy of Radio and Television Arts, Toronto, graduate (with honors), 1952.

ADDRESSES: Home—London, England; and South of France. *Agent*—A. M. Heath & Co. Ltd., 79 St. Martin's Lane, London WC2N 4AA, England.

CAREER: Worked in the broadcasting/communications industry in Canada, the United States, Australia, Sri Lanka, and India; British Broadcasting Corporation, London, England, executive editor of television documentary film series, 1963-72; writer, 1970—; independent producer/director of films and videos, 1983—.

MEMBER: Society of Authors, Association of Cinematic and Television Technicians.

AWARDS, HONORS: Mark Twain Award, 1970 and 1974; Edgar Allan Poe Award, 1974.

WRITINGS:

WITH GORDON THOMAS

The Day the World Ended (Literary Guild selection), Stein & Day, 1969.

The San Francisco Earthquake (Book-of-the-Month Club selection), Stein & Day, 1971, published in England as *Earthquake: The Destruction of San Francisco,* Souvenir Press, 1971.

Shipwreck: The Strange Fate of the Morro Castle, Stein & Day, 1972.

Voyage of the Damned (Literary Guild selection), Stein & Day, 1974.

Guernica: The Crucible of World War II, Stein & Day, 1975, published in England as *The Day Guernica Died,* Hodder & Stoughton, 1975.

Enola Gay (Book-of-the-Month club selection), Stein & Day, 1977, published in England as *Ruin from the Air: The Atomic Mission to Hiroshima,* Hamish Hamilton, 1977.

The Day the Bubble Burst: A Social History of the Wall Street Crash of 1929, Doubleday, 1979.

Trauma: The Search for the Cause of Legionnaires' Disease, Hamish Hamilton, 1981, published in the United States as *Anatomy of an Epidemic,* Doubleday, 1982.

Pontiff (Book-of-the-Month club alternate selection), Doubleday, 1983.

Averting Armageddon, Doubleday, 1984, published in England as *The Year of Armageddon: The Pope and the Bomb,* Granada Publishing, 1984.

OTHER

The Golden Opportunity of a Thousand Years, Reader's Digest Press, 1986.

Contributor to periodicals, including *Reader's Digest* and *Listener.*

ADAPTATIONS: The Day the World Ended was adapted for film by Warner Brothers; *Voyage of the Damned* was adapted for film by Embassy; *Enola Gay* was adapted for television by the National Broadcasting Company (NBC-TV); *The Day the Bubble Burst* was adapted for television by Fox/NBC.

WORK IN PROGRESS: A novel, and more television film work.

SIDELIGHTS: Max Morgan-Witts has combined a penchant for world travel with the experience of a documentary filmmaker to create a series of best-selling social histories, including *Voyage of the Damned* and *The Day the Bubble Burst.* His books have sold more than thirty-five million copies in all editions in some three dozen countries worldwide, and have been optioned by film companies and book club distributors alike. To date, Morgan-Witts's work has been translated into fifteen languages.

Chicago Tribune reporter Bill Neikirk calls the writing team of Gordon Thomas and Morgan-Witts "an institution," noting that the pair have been known to spend as much as $600,000 in research fees and travel expenses before they even begin writing a book. *Washington Post* contributor Joseph McLellan observes: "Gordon Thomas and Max Morgan-Witts have established a substantial reputation for reporting that is as solid as it is vivid. Their efforts have enjoyed a Hollywood success that is rare for nonfiction—undoubtedly because they clothe their facts in the kind of small, concrete detail that is one of the virtues of good fiction; because they take the reader into the minds and feelings of the real people they write about as though these characters were their own creations." McLellan concludes that the authors have "assembled an enormous mass of complex material in a readable, credible form."

BIOGRAPHICAL/CRITICAL SOURCES:

PERIODICALS

Atlantic, September 1971.
Best Sellers, April 15, 1969; September 1, 1971; January 1, 1973.
Chicago Tribune, March 17, 1980.
Economist, January 24, 1976.
Globe and Mail (Toronto), September 8, 1984.
New Statesman, February 13, 1976.
New Yorker, October 23, 1971.
New York Times, April 15, 1969.
New York Times Book Review, June 30, 1974; February 15, 1976; August 14, 1977; October 14, 1979.
Spectator, January 24, 1976.
Times Literary Supplement, July 24, 1969; January 23, 1976; November 2, 1984.
Washington Post, June 21, 1983.

MORRISON, James Douglas   1943-1971
(Jim Morrison)

PERSONAL: Born December 8, 1943, in Melbourne, FL; died July 3, 1971, of a heart attack, in Paris, France; buried in the Poet's Corner of the Pere Lachaise Cemetery in Paris; son of George Stephen (a rear admiral in the U.S. Navy) and Clara (Clarke) Morrison; married Pamela Susan Courson (died of a heroin overdose, April 25, 1974). *Education:* Attended St. Petersburg Junior College, 1961-62, Florida State University, 1962-63, and University of California at Los Angeles, 1964-65.

CAREER: Singer, songwriter, poet and filmmaker. Founding member, with Ray Manzarek, John Densmore, and Robbie Krieger, of the "Doors" (rock band), 1965-71. Appeared in films *Unknown Soldier,* 1968, and *Machine Gun McGain,* 1970.

WRITINGS:

UNDER NAME JIM MORRISON

BOOKS

The Lords and the New Creatures, privately printed, 1969, Simon & Schuster, 1970.
The Bank of America of Louisiana, Zeppelin Publishing, 1975.
Light My Fire, edited by Jim Mooney, Zeppelin Publishing, 1978.
American Prayer, Zeppelin Publishing, 1983.
CIA Psychic, edited by Mooney, Zeppelin Publishing, 1986.
Eyes: Poetry of Jim Morrison, 1967-1971, Zeppelin Publishing, 1986.
Wilderness: The Lost Writings of Jim Morrison, Volume 1, edited by Frank Lisciandro, Random House, 1988.
The American Night: The Writings of Jim Morrison, Volume 2, Random House, 1990.

OTHER

An American Prayer (recording of Morrison reading his poetry set to new music by the Doors), 1979.

Also author of screenplay *Feast of Friends,* 1970. Contributor of poems to *Us, Aum,* and other publications.

SONGWRITER OF RECORDINGS BY THE DOORS

The Doors, Elektra, 1967.
Strange Days, Elektra, 1967.
Waiting for the Sun, Elektra, 1968.
The Soft Parade, Elektra, 1969.
Absolutely Live, Elektra, 1970.
The Doors' Greatest Hits, Elektra, 1970.
Morrison Hotel, Elektra, 1970.
L. A. Woman, Elektra, 1971.
Other Voices, Elektra, 1971.

Full Circle, Elektra, 1972.
Weird Scenes Inside the Gold Mine, Elektra, 1972.
The Best of the Doors, Elektra, 1973.

SIDELIGHTS: Jim Morrison was lead singer and song-writer for the Doors, one of the most successful acts in rock and roll music history. During the band's brief rise and fall, spanning some four years, Morrison became internationally known as "an ikon of wasted youth and beautiful druggy doom," as Robert Carver stated in *New Statesman and Society.* In 1971, Morrison died of a heart attack at the age of twenty-seven, the result of alcoholism and drug abuse. Over twenty years after Morrison's death, Elektra Records, the Doors recording company, still sells over 100,000 Doors records, cassettes and compact discs every year.

Born into a family with a tradition of career militarism, Morrison spent his youth travelling the country as his father, a career Navy man, was transferred from one military base to the next. The family finally settled in Alexandria, Virginia, where Morrison finished high school. In 1961 he enrolled at St. Petersburg Junior College, then transferred to Florida State University the following year. By 1964 he had dropped out of school entirely, heading to California to study film at the University of California at Los Angeles (UCLA).

Largely self-taught, Morrison read poetry and philosophy copiously, particularly the works of Friedrich Nietzsche and William Blake. A fellow student recalled: "Morrison was a genius—he knew all about the poets, he knew all about poetry and all about books. He knew more than the teacher even, like sometimes someone would ask a question and the teacher wouldn't know the answer, and Morrison would just blurt it out." Frank Lisciandro, a friend of Morrison, admitted in the *Chicago Tribune:* "He was as well read as anybody I've ever met."

It was in an art class at UCLA that Morrison met Ray Manzarek, a young musician playing in a blues band on weekends. While the two friends were on the beach at Venice, California, Morrison mentioned that he had written some songs. "So we sat on the beach and I asked him to sing some of them," Manzarek recalled. "When he sang those first lines—'Let's swim to the moon / Let's climb through the tide / Penetrate the evening / That the city sleeps to hide'—I said, 'That's it.' I'd never heard lyrics to a rock song like that before. We talked a while before we decided to get a group together and make a million dollars." With friends John Densmore and Robbie Krieger, whom they met at a Maharishi Yogi meditation class, Morrison and Manzarek formed the Doors. Morrison took the name from a William Blake quote: "There are things that are known and things that are unknown; in between are the doors."

After practicing for five months, the Doors made their debut at the London Fog on Sunset Strip, working for five dollars apiece on weekdays and ten dollars on weekends. The job lasted only four months. On the verge of breaking up, the Doors were hired at the last minute to play as a back-up band at the Whiskey A-Go-Go. At first they were hardly noticed, but as they added more original songs to their nightly performance, and Morrison developed into a powerful, erotic stage performer, the Doors began to attract attention. When Elektra Records president Jac Holzman stopped by the club to see the main act, the Love, he happened to see the Doors as well. In late 1966, he signed them to a recording contract.

The band's first record, simply called *The Doors,* was produced by Paul Rothschild, who remembered: "I have never been as moved in a recording studio. I was impressed by the fact that for one of the very first times in rock and roll history sheer drama had taken place on tape. I felt emotionally washed. There were four other people in the control room at the time, when the take was over we realized the tape was still going. And all of us were audience, there was nothing left, the machines knew what to do." Rapidly selling one million copies, the album made the Doors an overnight success. Speaking of the album, a critic for *Disk Review* commented: "In it the Doors laid down their style—hard rock with slippery, psychedelic overtones. Morrison got some of his lyrics from Nietzsche—he always said his main guide to his poetry is 'The Birth of Tragedy' from the 'Spirit of Music'—he combined Nietzsche with a little freshman psychology and a lot of very broad images (the sea, the sun, the earth, death) and came up with Morrison therapy: to become more real, to become a better person, cut your ties to the establishment past, swim in your emotions, suffer symbolic death and rebirth, rebirth as a new man, psychologically cleansed."

The single "Light My Fire" became a number one hit during the summer of 1967, pulling the album to the number one position on the album charts as well. Later that year, "People Are Strange" and "Love Me Two Times" also made the charts, establishing the Doors as a favorite both with the critics and with the teenybopper music audience. The Doors music drew heavily from blues and jazz, adding an uncharacteristic, for rock and roll, hypnotic organ accompaniment. Morrison's throaty renditions of his own evocative, poetic lyrics (borrowed liberally from Blake, Coleridge and other writers) ranged from a sinister whisper to an incoherent scream. Compared to the commercial rock and roll of the time, the Doors' music seemed dark, moody, and disturbing.

Always influenced by the nihilistic visions of Nietzsche and Blake, Morrison began to live the lifestyle of a visionary artist once the Doors achieved success. He indulged in drugs and alcohol, which made his stage antics more frenzied, ritualistic, and incoherent. With the release of the band's third album, *Waiting for the Sun,* Morrison had styled himself the "Lizard King," a figure who appears in some of his poetry and in the song "Not to Touch the Earth." He told reporter Salli Stevenson: "I've always liked reptiles. I used to see the universe as a mammoth peristaltic snake and I used to see all the people and objects and landscapes as little pictures of the facets of their skins, their scales. I think the peristaltic motion is the basic life movement. It's swallowing, digestion, the rhythms of sexual intercourse, and even your basic unicellular structures have the same motion."

In December of 1967, Morrison was arrested for obscenity at a concert at the New Haven Arena. Later that year Doors concerts in Phoenix and Long Island ended in audience riots, and the band was prohibited from returning to those auditoriums. "I always try to get them to stand up," Morrison said of the disruptions, "to feel free to move around anywhere they want to. It's not to precipitate a chaos situation. It's . . . how can you stand the anchorage of a chair and be bombarded with all this intense rhythm and not want to express it physically in movement? I like people to be free."

On March 2, 1969, the Doors played a concert to twelve thousand fans in Miami's Dinner Key Auditorium. During the concert, an incoherent Morrison partially undressed and exposed himself to the audience. Six charges were brought against him and, after a two month trial, he was convicted of public drunkenness and indecent exposure. Because of the trial and resulting notoriety, the Doors lost at least a half a million dollars in future bookings.

Because of his increasing dependence on drugs and alcohol, and a personal life which included frequent beatings of his common law wife, Morrison grew estranged from other band members. A sign of how far he had gone is found in a phone call Morrison made to poet Michael McClure one evening. "In his wasted voice," as Nick Tosches described the episode in *Rolling Stone,* "[Morrison] told McClure that he'd just killed somebody out in the desert: 'I don't know how to tell ya, but, ah, I killed somebody. No. . . . It's no big deal, y'know.' "

Despite Morrison's physical and mental decline, during 1970 and 1971 the Doors recorded three new albums and scored a hit single with "Love Her Madly." Morrison began looking into film work, as well, and wrote the screenplay *Feast of Friends.* He also published a book of his poetry, *The Lords and the New Creatures.* "Real poetry," Morrison claimed, "doesn't say anything, it just ticks off the possibilities. Opens all doors. You can walk through any one that suits you." Though critical reaction was unfavorable, Morrison's poetry sold well. Since his

death, further volumes of Morrison's unpublished poetry have appeared. Writing in *New Statesman and Society* about the collection *Wilderness: The Lost Writings of Jim Morrison,* Carver found the poems to be "angst-laden, self-indulgent and West Coast-subjective. . . . It's difficult not to conclude that had he not been so famous and died so young these adolescent ramblings from a hippy Sid Rumpole would have been consigned to oblivion."

Late in 1970, Morrison and his wife traveled overseas for a lengthy vacation in Morroco, Spain and Corsica, settling in Paris so he could work on a screenplay. The trip was inspired in part by friction with fellow band members. The Doors, growing increasingly troubled by his behavior, had begun recording their next album without Morrison. On July 3, 1971, Morrison was found dead in his hotel bathtub in Paris. "No autopsy was performed," Wayne A. Saroyan noted in the *Chicago Tribune,* "and though Parisian authorities suspected that drugs were involved, the official cause of death was listed as a heart attack." Ironically, one of the Doors' biggest hits, "Riders on the Storm," hit the charts the same month that Morrison died.

Since his death, Morrison has remained a cult figure among rock and roll fans around the world. His image as a poetic messiah whose uncompromising vision led to an early death is still popular with some. Others claim that Morrison is not really dead but only faked his death in order to devote himself to writing poetry undisturbed. Over twenty years after his death, fans continue to flock to Morrison's grave, buy his records and read his poetry. In 1991, filmmaker Oliver Stone even released *The Doors,* a fawning docudrama about the late rock singer. Perhaps Morrison's life best embodied what his revered idol William Blake once claimed: "The road of excess leads to the palace of wisdom."

BIOGRAPHICAL/CRITICAL SOURCES:

BOOKS

Contemporary Literary Criticism, Volume 17, Gale, 1981.
Dalton, David and Lenny Kaye, *Rock 100,* Grosset, 1977, pp. 163-166.
Jahn, Mike, *Rock: From Elvis Presley to the Rolling Stones,* Quadrangle Books, 1973, pp. 200-215.
Miller, Jim, editor, *The Rolling Stone Illustrated History of Rock and Roll,* Random House, 1976, pp. 262-263.
Williams, Paul, *Outlaw Blues,* Dutton, 1969, pp. 93-115.

PERIODICALS

Chicago Tribune, March 22, 1989.
Crawdaddy, January, 1968, pp. 21-25, 36-39; April, 1969.
Disk Review, fall, 1967.
Down Beat, May 28, 1970, pp. 13, 32.
Esquire, June, 1972.
Feature, February, 1979, p. 72.

Inside Books, November, 1988, p. 43.

Jazz & Pop, October, 1969, pp. 40-41; October, 1970, p. 60.

Melody Maker, August 3, 1968, p. 11; July 10, 1971, p. 43; March 11, 1972, p. 26; October 20, 1973, p. 41.

New Statesman and Society, March 30, 1990, p. 40.

Rolling Stone, January 20, 1968; October 26, 1968, p. 1; April 5, 1969; April 19, 1969; July 12, 1969, p. 8; August 23, 1969, p. 35; April 30, 1970, pp. 48, 53; October 1, 1970, p. 44; October 15, 1970; January 7, 1971, p. 52; March 4, 1971; May 27, 1971, p. 48; August 5, 1971; January 25, 1979, pp. 94, 96.

Stereo Review, April, 1979, pp. 70-71.

Times Educational Supplement, April 13, 1990, p. 24.

Trouser Press, April, 1979, p. 29; September-October, 1980.

Village Voice, January 8, 1979, pp. 46, 51.*

*   *   *

MORRISON, Jim
   See MORRISON, James Douglas

*   *   *

MUNSON, Henry (Lee), Jr. 1946-

PERSONAL: Born November 1, 1946, in New York, NY; son of Henry Lee and Monique (Ruzette) Munson; married Fatima Bernikho, June 26, 1971; children: Leila, John, Michael, Nadia. *Education:* Columbia University, B.A., 1970; University of Chicago, M.A., 1973, Ph.D., 1980. *Religion:* None.

ADDRESSES: Office—Department of Anthropology, University of Maine at Orono, Orono, ME 04469.

CAREER: University of Maine at Orono, assistant professor, 1982-88, associate professor of anthropology, 1988—.

MEMBER: American Anthropological Association, Middle East Studies Association, Society for Moroccan Studies.

AWARDS, HONORS: Fulbright fellow, 1976-77; Social Science Research Council fellow, 1976-77, 1987; National Endowment for the Humanities fellow, 1984; Program on Peace and International Cooperation research and writing grant, John D. and Catherine T. MacArthur Foundation, 1990-91.

WRITINGS:

The House of Si Abd Allah: The Oral History of a Moroccan Family, Yale University Press, 1984.

Islam and Revolution in the Middle East, Yale University Press, 1988.

Religion and Power in Morocco, Yale University Press, 1992.

Contributor to anthropology and Middle East studies journals.

SIDELIGHTS: In *The House of Si Abd Allah: The Oral History of a Moroccan Family* Henry Munson presents contrasting views of the history of Morocco over the past century as witnessed by two very different members of a Moroccan clan. Amal Rassam comments in the *New York Times Book Review* that this "juxtaposition of the two different perspectives makes for a rich account of life in a Muslim society today." Each chapter describes two accounts of the same events and the same people, from the point of view first of the middle-aged, streetwise al-Hajj Muhammad and then of the young, college-educated Fatima Zohra. The book, writes Edmund Leach in the *London Review of Books,* has "really three authors. The two principal narrators, both born in Tangier, are first cousins" who "have made extensive tape-recordings for Munson in which they discuss their past lives, their general views of religion and society, and their kinsfolk. The third author is of course Munson himself, who provides an edited translation and a long and lucid Introduction." Leach also suggests that Munson's greater attention in that introduction to the conservative orthodoxy of al-Hajj Muhammad than to the liberal modernism of Fatima Zohra was intended to enlighten the American audience as to "how the Iranian masses could have preferred the fundamentalist tyranny of the Ayatollah Khomeini to the corrupt but Westernized (and therefore comprehensible) tyranny of the Shah." Although al-Hajj Muhammad never read the works of the Ayatollah or of other fundamentalists, his perspective, according to *Worldview* writer Sterret Pope, "epitomizes the Zealotism of Khomeini and his 'Party of God'."

Additionally, Leach commends Munson for his demonstration that the apparently dissimilar idealogies of the two cousins mask their common heritage and shared values: they both come form the same impoverished background and, according to Leach, "clearly share many family affections as well as a deeply felt conviction that all the misfortunes of Morocco as they know it derive from the colonial experience and from the Moroccan elite." Similarly, Pope comments: "One of the virtues of *The House of Si Abd Allah* is that it shows, particularly through Fatima Zohra's narrative, that Westernized Muslims still prize their Islamic heritage as a vital component of their political and cultural identity, even as they criticize it."

Critics praised *The House of Si Abd Allah.* Rassam assessed it "a valuable book for those interested in Moroccan culture." Pope concurred, adding that Munson's "book has much to say about the travails of rural indigence and urban migration, the problems and the joys of marriage and childbearing, and the trauma of modernization and cultural dependence in modern Morocco," and Leach lauded the work's "original manner," its "clear, uncluttered style," and its appeal even to "people who have no professional interest in anthropology."

BIOGRAPHICAL/CRITICAL SOURCES:

PERIODICALS

London Review of Books, August 2, 1984, p. 18.
New York Times Book Review, April 15, 1984, p. 23.
Times Literary Supplement, September 7, 1984, p. 1002.
Worldview, July, 1984.

N

NAIFEH, Steven Woodward 1952-

PERSONAL: Surname is pronounced "*Nay*-fee"; born June 19, 1952, in Tehran, Iran; U.S. citizen; son of George Amel (a consultant) and Marion (a professor; maiden name, Lanphear) Naifeh. *Education:* Princeton University, A.B. (summa cum laude), 1974; Harvard University, J.D., 1977, M.A., 1978.

ADDRESSES: Home—Aiken, SC. *Office*—Sabbagh, Naifeh & Associates, Inc., 4600 Reno Rd. N.W., Washington, DC 20008. *Agent*—Connie Clausen, Connie Clausen Associates, 250 East 87th St., New York, NY 10028.

CAREER: National Gallery of Art, Washington, DC, staff lecturer, summer, 1976; Milbank, Tweed, Hadley & McCloy (law firm), New York City, associate, summer, 1976; Sabbagh, Naifeh & Associates, Inc. (consulting and public relations firm), Washington, DC, vice-president, 1980—. Art exhibited in solo shows in the United States, United Arab Emirates, Nigeria, and Pakistan; lecturer in art.

MEMBER: Phi Beta Kappa.

AWARDS, HONORS: (With Gregory White Smith) National Book Award nomination for nonfiction, 1990, and Pulitzer Prize, 1991, both for *Jackson Pollock: An American Saga.*

WRITINGS:

Culture Making: Money, Success, and the New York Art World, Princeton University, 1976.

WITH GREGORY WHITE SMITH

Moving Up in Style, St. Martin's 1980.
Gene Davis, Arts Publisher, 1981.

(With Michael Morgenstern) *How to Make Love to a Woman,* C.N. Potter, 1982.

What Every Client Needs to Know about Using a Lawyer, Putnam, 1982.

The Bargain Hunter's Guide to Art Collecting, Morrow, 1982.

The Best Lawyers in America, Woodward/White, 1983, revised edition published as *The Best Lawyers in America: 1989-1990,* 1989.

Why Can't Men Open Up?: Overcoming Men's Fear of Intimacy, C.N. Potter, 1984.

The Mormon Murders: A True Story of Greed, Forgery, Deceit, and Death, Weidenfeld & Nicolson, 1988.

Jackson Pollock: An American Saga, C.N. Potter, 1989.

The Best Lawyers in America: Directory of Expert Witnesses, Woodward/White, 1990.

OTHER

Contributor to *Arts, Art International,* and *African Arts.*

ADAPTATIONS: Film rights to *Jackson Pollock: An American Saga* have been sold to Keith Barish Productions; film rights to *The Mormon Murders: A True Story of Greed, Forgery, Deceit, and Death* were also sold.

WORK IN PROGRESS: Two "true crime" books for New American Library.

SIDELIGHTS: Exhaustive research and a highly readable style are the hallmarks of the most well-known and widely-reviewed books by Steven Woodward Naifeh and his collaborator, Gregory White Smith. The two men met as students at Harvard University, where both were enrolled in the School of Law. Each of them graduated, but neither pursued a career as a lawyer. Naifeh's avocation, painting, led him to write his first book, *Culture Making: Money, Success, and the New York Art World,* a scholarly examination of the complex relationship between artists, the general public, and dealers of fine art. The art world also provided the basis for one of Naifeh and Smith's first collaborations, a short biography of the painter Gene Davis.

Finding that they worked well together, the two friends settled on a more ambitious subject: a definitive biography of the man some consider the greatest American artist of this century, Jackson Pollock. Pollock was a leader of the Abstract Expressionism movement of the 1940s and 1950s, and through his painting he sought to depict the inner landscape of the mind. He became known as an "action painter" due to his revolutionary technique of placing his canvases on the floor and splattering paint on them from above. Naifeh and Smith began researching Pollock's life in 1982, never dreaming that they would publish six other books before completing the biography.

The co-authors studied every Pollock canvas to which they could gain access, read everything previously written about him, and interviewed 2,500 people connected with the artist, including his widow, the painter Lee Krasner; his brothers; and many of his close friends. Their research yielded 40,000 single-spaced half-pages of notes. Interpreting and organizing such a mass of information was a formidable and lengthy task, and Naifeh and Smith supported themselves while working on it by publishing moneymaking titles such as *How to Make Love to a Woman* and consumer guides based on their backgrounds in law.

Their best-known collaboration published before the Pollock biography was *The Mormon Murders: A True Story of Greed, Forgery, Deceit, and Death.* This true crime book details the strange case of Mark Hofmann, a master forger who in October 1985 was arrested for murder. Hofmann, raised in the Church of the Latter-Day Saints (Mormon), had privately renounced his religion and then gone on to create false documents discrediting the church's founder, Joseph Smith. Mormon leaders found the forgeries so threatening that they were willing to pay huge sums in order to possess them, intending to hide them away in secret archives. When Hofmann's elaborate schemes began to crumble and it looked as though his forgeries might be exposed, he bombed the homes of two prominent Mormons in order to divert attention from himself, then seriously wounded himself with a third bomb.

Naifeh and Smith drew on court records, police investigations, and personal interviews to produce a book that was laden with forensic, financial, and legal details. Some reviewers faulted the authors for a somewhat sensationalistic style, but John Katzenbach, writing in the *New York Times Book Review,* praised Naifeh and Smith for their perceptive examination of Hofmann's youth and the bearing it had on his later actions; for their characterizations of the police officers who built the case against Hofmann;

and for their delineation of the tangle of deception that surrounded the investigation.

Even when engaged in work on *The Mormon Murders* and other titles, the co-authors continued to research and speculate on the life of Jackson Pollock. "Pollock was our life," Smith told Judith Weintraub of the *Washington Post.* "We had no social life. We had to be obsessed with the material." Finally, after spending some $100,000 on research and travel and devoting ten hours a day, five days a week, for three full years to writing, the book was finished: 934 pages covering even the most minor details of Pollock's life and the authors' theories on the psychological underpinnings of his work. The result was as controversial as it was long. *Washington Post Book World* contributor William Drozdiak called *Jackson Pollock: An American Saga* "monumental and impressive," and he praised the authors for their efforts to "achieve nothing less than a full understanding of the complex social and psychological forces that lay behind the work of an artist considered by many to be America's greatest abstract painter." He further credited Naifeh and Smith with having "marshalled an exhaustive array of material to buttress their interpretation of Pollock's life."

On the other end of the critical spectrum, however, were reviewers such as Elizabeth Frank, who stated in the *New York Times Book Review* that the authors' collaborative style was "based on the kind of glib, reckless, off-the-rack psychobiography that is dazzling in its lack of speculative humility and intellectual caution. There are no questions in this book, only answers." Frank went on to add that Naifeh and Smith "proceed as if diving into the unconscious of a great artist were as easy as diving into a swimming pool. They are too literal, too positive, too contemptuous of Pollock and too ignorant of the ways in which the unconscious remains just that to explain his life or work in terms satisfactory from either an art-historical or a psychological perspective."

Speaking with *Los Angeles Times* writer Suzanne Muchnic, Naifeh and Smith explained that "an anti-biographical bias in the art field" was the source of much of the negative reaction to their book. By delving into questions of Pollock's sexual orientation and exposing some of the less-attractive aspects of his life—such as his violent streak, his heavy drinking and his obsession with urinating in public—the authors broke many taboos of the art history world. "There's very little written about incredibly important artists," Naifeh told Muchnic. "And because it's never done, it seems unethical. Fifty percent of the people we talked to spent all of their spare time gossiping about everybody else's sex life, but the idea that you would actually talk about sex in a book, no matter how relevant that might be to the works of art, is somehow unseemly. . . . We knew we would get flak from certain quarters for writing a book that was readable. There's no jargon in it. . . . Someone writing about a literary figure would be excused the effort to make the product a literary experience in its own right, whereas the art world will not make such allowances."

Naifeh rejected the notion, advanced by some reviewers, that because he and Smith showed Pollock as somewhat uncontrolled and inarticulate, they did not respect the artist. "Some educated people have a hard time seeing that people can be intelligent without being verbal, without being articulate, without being logical, that there is an intelligence that is intuitive and emotional and visual without being translated into words," Naifeh told Muchnic. "What's wonderful about Jackson is the triumph over vulgarity of human life and his own desires and the coarseness and brutishness of his own life to create these incredible, lyrical, magical images. Jackson took the most tormented aspects of his daily life and worked them into his masterpieces."

BIOGRAPHICAL/CRITICAL SOURCES:

PERIODICALS

Chicago Tribune, March 24, 1985.
Los Angeles Times, February 1, 1990.
New York Times, November 12, 1988; January 25, 1990.
New York Times Book Review, October 9, 1988; January 28, 1990.
Times (London), March 24, 1990.
Times Literary Supplement, November 25, 1977; June 9, 1989; March 16, 1990.
Washington Post, January 30, 1990.
Washington Post Book World, October 9, 1988; January 21, 1990.*

—*Sketch by Joan Goldsworthy*

*   *   *

NEWMAN, Judie 1950-

PERSONAL: Born May 9, 1950, in Preston, England; daughter of Ellis Edward (a chemist) and Alice (Herringshaw) Newman; married Ian Revie (a university lecturer), July 10, 1978; children: James; stepchildren: Christopher Revie. *Education:* Edinburgh University, M.A. (with honors; English literature), 1972, M.A. (with honors; French), 1974; Cambridge University, Ph.D., 1982. *Politics:* Labour. *Religion:* Atheist.

ADDRESSES: Office—School of English, University of Newcastle upon Tyne, Newcastle upon Tyne NE1 7RU, England.

CAREER: University of Metz, Metz, France, lectrice in English, 1972-73; University of Newcastle upon Tyne,

Newcastle upon Tyne, England, lecturer in English, 1976-91, reader in American and post-colonial literature, 1991—.

MEMBER: British Association for American Studies (member of executive committee; chair of publications sub-committee), Saul Bellow Society (member of executive committee).

WRITINGS:

Saul Bellow and History, Macmillan, 1984.
John Updike, Macmillan, 1988.
Nadine Gordimer, Routledge & Kegan Paul, 1988.
(Editor) Harriet Beecher Stowe, *Dred: A Tale of the Great Dismal Swamp,* Ryburn, 1992.

Also contributor of chapters to books. Associate editor, "Pamphlets in American Studies," British Association for American Studies. Contributor to numerous periodicals, including *Journal of American Studies, Critique: Studies in Modern Fiction, Canadian Review of American Studies, Journal of Commonwealth Literature, Commonwealth, Saul Bellow Journal,* and *Etudes Anglaises.*

WORK IN PROGRESS: Post-Colonial Fiction, for Edward Arnold; *Alison Lurie,* a research project.

SIDELIGHTS: Judie Newman told *CA:* "My interests range over most contemporary fiction, particularly American, South-African, Indian, and Caribbean, with research in progress on a book on intertextuality in post-colonial fiction and a research project on the words of contemporary women novelists, especially Alison Lurie. I have recently become involved in a series of reprints of American titles, for which I edited *Dred: A Tale of the Great Dismal Swamp* by Harriet Beecher Stowe. I hope to edit further works by neglected women writers and invite suggestions for titles and editors for the present series (novels, travelogues, autobiographies by American writers)."

BIOGRAPHICAL/CRITICAL SOURCES:

PERIODICALS

Journal of American Studies, August, 1985.
Modern Fiction Studies, winter, 1984.
Times Literary Supplement, June 22, 1984.

*   *   *

NEWMAN, Michael 1946-

PERSONAL: Born March 4, 1946, in London, England; son of Henry (a chartered accountant) and Ruby (a secretary; maiden name, Horwood) Newman; married Ines Marian Oppenheimer (a town planner), January 25, 1970; children: Kate, Hannah, Zachary. *Education:* Exeter College, Oxford, B.A., 1967, D.Phil., 1972. *Politics:* Labour. *Religion:* Jewish.

ADDRESSES: Home—3 Langbourne Ave., London N6 6AJ, England. *Office*—School of Languages and European Studies, Polytechnic of North London, Holloway, London N7 8DB, England.

CAREER: Polytechnic of North London, London, England, lecturer, 1972-74, senior lecturer, 1974-81, principal lecturer, 1981-92, professor of politics, 1992—.

MEMBER: Royal Institute of International Affairs, Association for the Study of Contemporary and Modern France, Association for the Study of Modern Italy.

AWARDS, HONORS: British Academy fellow in Europe, 1978-79; Nuffield Foundation research grant and U.S. Embassy research grant, both 1988, both for work in U.S. on Harold Laski.

WRITINGS:

Socialism and European Unity: The Dilemma of the Left in Britain and France, C. Hurst, 1983.
(Coeditor, with Sonia Mazey) *Mitterrand's France,* Croom Helm, 1987.
John Strachey, Manchester University Press, 1989.
Harold Laski: A Political Biography, Macmillan, 1993.

Contributor to history, political, and European studies journals.

WORK IN PROGRESS: National Sovereignty and the Nation-State in Europe.

SIDELIGHTS: Michael Newman once told *CA:* "In general I choose to write on subjects that seem to have some contemporary political relevance for the Left. My motivation is normally, therefore, both academic and political. I began research for *Socialism and European Unity* because I was dissatisfied with the British Labour party's wholly negative attitude towards West European integration. I wanted to analyze it in contrast with the differing stance of the French Left and to understand it in terms of British political development since World War II.

"I concluded that the attitudes of the political parties are a complex amalgam of considerations influenced both by national factors and socialist arguments. Both British and French parties of the Left have therefore found it extremely difficult to formulate and maintain consistent policies.

Newman later commented on the reasons for his interest in the socialist political figures outlined in *John Strachey* and *Harold Laski: A Political Biography:* "Laski is interesting because of his evolution from liberal pluralism to socialism and also because of his role as an academic theoretician and a participant in the Labour movement. He

has been misrepresented as a person and as a theorist and merits more serious attention than he has received in recent years. John Strachey—a major influence on left-wing thought in Great Britain during the 1930s—and his 'revisionist' socialism in the 1950s is of great interest because of his attempt to combine Marxism and Keynesianism."

Newman continues to study topics that relate to trends in contemporary politics. "My current research on the nation-state and national sovereignty in Europe arises from a long-standing interest in a subject which seems to me to have enormous contemporary importance in the new era of instability and uncertainty following the collapse of the post-war division between the two blocs. I want to try to understand what is now happening to the nation-state particularly within the European community."

*   *   *

NORDAN, Lewis 1939-

PERSONAL: Born August 23, 1939, in MS; son of Lemuel Alonzo and Sara (a teacher; maiden name, Hightower) Bayles; married Alicia Blessing; children: Russell Ammon (deceased), Lewis Eric, John Robert (deceased). *Education:* Millsaps College, B.A., 1963; Mississippi State University, M.A., 1966; Auburn University, Ph.D., 1973. *Politics:* Democrat. *Religion:* Episcopalian.

ADDRESSES: Home—Pittsburgh, PA. *Office*—Department of English, University of Pittsburgh, Pittsburgh, PA 15260.

CAREER: Teacher at public schools in Titusville, FL, 1963-65; Auburn University, Auburn, AL, instructor in English, 1966-71; University of Georgia, Athens, instructor in English, 1971-74; worked variously as an orderly, nightwatchman, and clerk, 1975-81; University of Arkansas, Fayetteville, assistant professor of English, 1981-83; University of Pittsburgh, Pittsburgh, PA, assistant professor of English, 1983—. *Military service:* U.S. Navy, 1958-60.

AWARDS, HONORS: John Gould Fletcher Award for fiction, University of Arkansas, 1977, for short story "Rat Song"; National Endowment for the Arts grant, 1978-79; Porter Fund Prize, 1987; Notable Book Award, American Library Association, 1992; Best Fiction Award, Mississippi Institute of Arts and Letters, 1992.

WRITINGS:

Welcome to the Arrow-Catcher Fair (short stories), Louisiana State University Press, 1983.
The All-Girl Football Team (short stories), Louisiana State University Press, 1986.
Music of the Swamp, Algonquin Books, 1991.
Wolf Whistle, Algonquin Books, 1993.

Contributor to *Harper's, Redbook, Playgirl,* and small literary magazines.

SIDELIGHTS: Welcome to the Arrow-Catcher Fair is Lewis Nordan's first published collection of short fiction. Critiquing the volume for the *New York Times Book Review,* Edith Milton pronounced its stories "splendid," an illustration of the diversity that the short story form can take. While the reviewer commented that the stories' variety worked against the book as a collection, she did note a recurrent theme that played throughout the volume: "the juxtaposition of an unglamorous *modern* reality, comically reduced, against an equally comic but larger-than-life mythology about the past that surrounds it."

Nordan told *CA:* "I was a storyteller a long time before I became a writer. Everyone in my family is a storyteller, though none of the others are writers. For a long time I thought I was somehow defective for not being able to tell the truth—the 'truth,' I should say—without changing it, amplifying it, or romanticizing it. This seemed to be a flaw in my character. Now I think that it may be a flaw, but it is also a gift for which I am grateful."

BIOGRAPHICAL/CRITICAL SOURCES:

PERIODICALS

New York Times Book Review, January 15, 1984.

* * *

NORDEN, Charles
See DURRELL, Lawrence (George)

* * *

NORTH, Rick
See BONANNO, Margaret Wander

* * *

NORTH, Sterling 1906-1974

PERSONAL: Born November 4, 1906, in Edgerton, WI; died of a stroke, December 22, 1974, in Morristown, NJ; son of David Willard (a real estate salesman, farm owner, and expert on Indian artifacts) and Elizabeth (a linguist, biologist, and history teacher; maiden name, Nelson) North; married Gladys Dolores Buchanan, June 23, 1927; children: David Sterling, Arielle (Mrs. C. E. Olson). *Education:* University of Chicago, A.B., 1929.

CAREER: Chicago *Daily News,* Chicago, IL, reporter, 1929-31, literary editor, 1932-43; *Post,* New York City, lit-

erary editor, 1943-49; *World Telegram and Sun,* New York City, literary editor, 1949-56; Houghton Mifflin Co. (publishers), founder and general editor of North Star Books (historical series for children), 1957-64; author. Master of ceremonies for radio program, "Books on Trial," four years.

MEMBER: Authors League of America.

AWARDS, HONORS: Spring Book Festival honor book award, *New York Herald Tribune,* 1956, for *Abe Lincoln: Log Cabin to White House;* Animal Book Award, E. P. Dutton, and Authors Award, New Jersey Institute of Technology, both 1963, Newbery Honor Book, American Library Association, 1964, Lewis Carroll Shelf Award, 1964, Dorothy Canfield Fisher Children's Book Award, Vermont PTA, 1965, Aurianne Award, 1965, William Allen White Children's Book Award, 1966, Young Readers' Choice Award, Pacific Northwest Library Association, 1966, Sequoyah Children's Book Award, Oklahoma Library Association, 1966, Notable Book citation, American Library Association, and honor citation, *Horn Book,* all for *Rascal: A Memoir of a Better Era;* Authors Award, New Jersey Institute of Technology, 1965, for *Little Rascal;* Children's Book Writer of the Year Award, New Jersey Institute of Technology, 1966; Dutton Animal Book Award, 1969, for *The Wolfling: A Documentary Novel of the Eighteen-Seventies;* Witter Bynner Poetry Award; Young Poet's Prize, *Poetry* magazine.

WRITINGS:

FOR CHILDREN

The Five Little Bears, illustrated by Clarence Biers and Hazel Frazee, Rand McNally, 1935.
The Zipper ABC Book, illustrated by Keith Ward, Rand McNally, 1937.
Greased Lightning, illustrated by Kurt Wiese, Winston, 1940.
Midnight and Jeremiah, illustrated by Wiese, Winston, 1943.
So Dear to My Heart, illustrated by Brad Holland, Doubleday, 1947.
The Birthday of Little Jesus, illustrated by Valenti Angelo, Grosset, 1952.
Son of the Lamp Maker: The Story of a Boy Who Knew Jesus, illustrated by Manning Lee, Rand McNally, 1956.
The First Steamboat on the Mississippi, illustrated by Victor Mays, Houghton, 1962.
Rascal: A Memoir of a Better Era, illustrated by John Schoenherr, Dutton, 1963, published in England as *Rascal: The True Story of a Pet Raccoon,* Hodder & Stoughton, 1963.
Little Rascal (based on *Rascal: A Memoir of a Better Era*), illustrated by Carl Burger, Dutton, 1965.

Raccoons Are the Brightest People, Dutton, 1966, published in England as *The Raccoons of My Life,* Hodder & Stoughton, 1967.
The Wolfling: A Documentary Novel of the Eighteen-Seventies, illustrated by Schoenherr, Dutton, 1969.

BIOGRAPHIES; FOR CHILDREN

Abe Lincoln: Log Cabin to White House, illustrated by Lee Ames, Random House, 1956.
George Washington, Frontier Colonel, illustrated by Ames, Random House, 1957.
Young Thomas Edison, illustrated by William Barss, Houghton, 1958.
Thoreau of Walden Pond, illustrated by Harve Stein, Houghton, 1959.
Captured by the Mohawks, and Other Adventures of Radisson, illustrated by Mays, Houghton, 1960.
Mark Twain and the River, illustrated by Mays, Houghton, 1961.

EDITOR

(With Carl Kroch) *So Red the Nose, or Breath in the Afternoon: Literary Cocktails,* Farrar & Rinehart, 1935.
(With C. B. Boutell) *Speak of the Devil: An Anthology of the Appearances of the Devil in the Literature of the Western World,* Doubleday, 1945.

Editor of about twenty-three other books.

OTHER

(With Harry Dean) *The Pedro Gorino: The Adventures of a Negro Sea-Captain in Africa* (autobiography of H. Dean), Houghton, 1929, published in England as *Umbala,* Harrap, 1929.
Midsummer Madness, Grosset, 1933.
Tiger, Reilly & Lee, 1933.
Plowing on Sunday (novel), Reilly & Lee, 1933.
Night Outlasts the Whippoorwill (novel), Macmillan, 1936.
Seven against the Years (novel), Macmillan, 1939.
(With wife, Gladys North) *Being a Literary Map of These United States Depicting a Renaissance No Less Astonishing Than That of Periclean Athens of Elizabethan London,* Putnam, 1942.
Reunion on the Wabash (novel), Doubleday, 1952.
Hurry, Spring!, illustrated by Burger, Dutton, 1966.

Also author of a book of lyric poems, published by University of Chicago Press, 1925, and *The Writings of Mazo De La Roche,* published by Little, Brown. Contributor of poems, articles, and stories to anthologies and periodicals, including *Dial, Atlantic Monthly, Esquire, Saturday Review, Harper's, Yale Review, Poetry, Nation, Reader's Digest,* and *Holiday.* Syndicated columnist for several years before 1957.

ADAPTATIONS: So Dear to My Heart was made into a motion picture by RKO in 1948; *Rascal: A Memoir of a Better Era* was filmed by Disney Studios in 1969 and made into a record/cassette by Miller-Brody, 1979.

SIDELIGHTS: Sterling North was a serious literary editor, essayist, and critic who showed his light side in his books for children. A nature-lover who lived most of his life on farms in the Midwest and New Jersey, North earned recognition for books about the relationships between animals and people. His best-known work, *Rascal: A Memoir of a Better Era,* won numerous prestigious awards and was adapted as a film by Walt Disney Studios.

North held great disdain for such distractions as television and comic books. His own works often recalled earlier times, when children found amusement among the wildlife and the animals of the farmyard. The author told *Reader's Digest:* "I feel that I was blessed by a richly rewarding childhood in a far off time before the genocide of the human race seemed probable. There were in those days certain 'enduring' values, only a few of which still survive. If I have captured the ear and the imagination of a few million children around the globe I feel I have not lived in vain." North's estimate of his readership may have been low. To date some of his books have been translated into fifty different languages and have sold many millions of copies.

North was born on a farm in southern Wisconsin in 1906. Both of his parents were college-educated, and both were fascinated by the natural world. His father, a real-estate speculator, also studied American Indian cultures and tribal lore. His mother was well versed in linguistics, biology, and history, and she taught North to read at an early age. When North was seven his mother died. He was raised by his father and his older sister, the poet Jessica Nelson North. Business ventures often occupied his father, so North led a somewhat solitary life. He began writing poetry at the age of eight and published his first piece in *St. Nicholas* magazine in 1914.

North's favorite childhood companions were his pets. At various times he kept cats, dogs, a crow named Edgar Allan Poe, baby skunks, and a raccoon—Rascal. North remembered Rascal in *Reader's Digest:* "I had raised him from a kit, and now he ate at the table with Dad and me, occupying my old high chair and drinking warm milk from a bowl. . . . Rascal slept with me, too, and at night his comforting furry presence made me feel less lonesome when my father was away." Rascal learned to ride on the front of North's bike, and the youngster took him everywhere.

Eventually Rascal returned to the wild, and North grew into young adulthood. He attended the University of Chicago, where he kept a dizzying schedule of on- and off-campus activities. While still a student North married his childhood sweetheart, Gladys Buchanan. He also published his first collection of poetry, most of which had appeared in magazines such as *Dial, Nation,* and *Harper's.* After college North took a job as a cub reporter with the Chicago *Daily News.* His first child and his first full-length book, *The Pedro Gorino: The Adventures of a Negro Sea-Captain in Africa,* arrived simultaneously in 1929.

Within three years North had been promoted to literary editor of the *Daily News.* In addition to reviewing books and writing essays on the issues of the day, he continued to publish novels and poetry of his own. He began creating children's books for the amusement of his own son and daughter, only later releasing some of the works to the public. In 1943 North moved to New York City, where he served as literary editor for the *Post* and later for the *World Telegram and Sun.* His success as a writer enabled him to buy a farm on a lake near Morristown, New Jersey. Beginning in 1947, North spent more and more time writing books for children. One of his early children's novels, *So Dear to My Heart,* was adapted for film in 1948. *So Dear to My Heart* tells the story of a young boy who raises a prize-winning ram on a Midwestern farm. Other North works also explored the ties between child and animal: *Rascal* is a memoir of North's own adventures with his dear pet raccoon, and *The Wolfling* is a fictional tale of a pioneer family and a half-wolf they adopt.

North quit newspaper work in 1957 to become general editor of Houghton-Mifflin's North Star Books. North Star became a highly-regarded name in American history books for children, and North himself published several titles under the imprint. His best-known biography, *Abe Lincoln: Log Cabin to White House,* was published in 1956. Other North biographies included works on George Washington, Mark Twain, and the naturalist Henry David Thoreau. *Rascal* is the book for which North will be remembered, however. In the years since its publication, it has sold more than two million copies in fourteen countries and has been adapted for both film and recording. Critics have praised the story for its sensitive portrayal of a rural region in a bygone era, its unusual family relationships, and its honesty about the treatment of wild animals.

North died of a stroke in 1974, at home on his New Jersey farm. A decade before his death, he told *Reader's Digest:* "The impulse to write, I believe, is the desire to communicate a memory, a mood, a distillation of delight that might otherwise be lost forever. It is mortal man's feeble attempt to stay the hand of time. . . . In children we have an innocent audience not yet hardened and brutalized and made cynical. They look to us trustingly for information and enchantment. How very few of us are worthy of such trust."

BIOGRAPHICAL/CRITICAL SOURCES:

BOOKS

Fitzgibbon, Robert, and Ernest V. Heyn, editors, *My Most Inspiring Moment,* Doubleday, 1965.
Twentieth-Century Children's Writers, 3rd edition, St. James Press, 1989.
Warfel, Harry R., *American Novelists of Today,* American Book, 1951.

PERIODICALS

New York Times, December 23, 1974.
New York Times Book Review, August 25, 1963; August 22, 1965; April 24, 1966; February 12, 1989.
Publishers Weekly, January 13, 1975.
Reader's Digest, September, 1963.
Saturday Review, January 15, 1966.
Time, January 6, 1975.*

O

O'BRIEN, Tim 1946-

PERSONAL: Original name, William Timothy O'Brien; born October 1, 1946, in Austin, MN; son of William T. (an insurance salesman) and Ava E. (a teacher; maiden name, Schultz) O'Brien; married, 1973; wife's name, Ann (a magazine production manager). *Education:* Macalester College, B.A. (summa cum laude), 1968; graduate study at Harvard University.

ADDRESSES: Home—Boxford, MA. *Agent*—Lynn Nesbit, International Creative Management, 40 West 57th St., New York, NY 10019.

CAREER: Writer. *Washington Post,* Washington, DC, national affairs reporter, 1973-74; Breadloaf Writer's Conference, Ripton, VT, teacher. *Military service:* U.S. Army, 1968-70, served in Vietnam; became sergeant; received Purple Heart.

MEMBER: Phi Beta Kappa.

AWARDS, HONORS: O. Henry Memorial Awards, 1976 and 1978, for chapters of *Going after Cacciato;* National Book Award, 1979, for *Going after Cacciato;* Vietnam Veterans of America award, 1987; Heartland Prize, *Chicago Tribune,* 1990, for *The Things They Carried;* has also received awards from the National Endowment for the Arts, the Massachusetts Arts and Humanities Foundation, and the Bread Loaf Writers' Conference.

WRITINGS:

If I Die in a Combat Zone, Box Me Up and Ship Me Home (anecdotes), Delacorte, 1973.
Northern Lights (novel), Delacorte, 1975.
Going after Cacciato (novel), Delacorte, 1978.
The Nuclear Age, limited edition, Press-22, 1981, 1st trade edition, Knopf, 1985.

The Things They Carried: A Work of Fiction, Houghton, 1990.

Contributor to magazines, including *Playboy, Esquire,* and *Redbook.*

WORK IN PROGRESS: The Lake of the Woods, a novel for Houghton.

SIDELIGHTS: Award-winning author Tim O'Brien is perhaps best known for his fictional, yet gripping, portrayals of the Vietnam conflict, especially of its people. Based on his own combat exposure, O'Brien delves into the American psyche and the human experience as he writes of not only what may have happened physically, but emotionally and mentally. Drafted immediately following his graduation from Macalester College in 1968, he served two years with the U.S. infantry. In a *Publishers Weekly* interview with Michael Coffey, O'Brien explained his motivation in writing about the war as his need to write with "passion," and commented that to write "good" stories "requires a sense of passion, and my passion as a human being and as a writer intersect in Vietnam, not in the physical stuff but in the issues of Vietnam—of courage, rectitude, enlightenment, holiness, trying to do the right thing in the world."

"Writing fiction is a solitary endeavor," explained O'Brien in an excerpt of an essay from an anthology quoted in the *Dictionary of Literary Biography Documentary Series (DLBDS).* He elaborated: "You shape your own universe. You practice all the time, then practice some more. You pay attention to craft. You aim for tension and suspense, a sense of drama, displaying in concrete terms the actions and reactions of human beings contesting problems of the heart. You try to make art. You strive for wholeness, seeking continuity and flow, each element performing both as cause and effect, always hoping to create, or to re-create, the great illusions of life."

"It's kind of a semantic game: lying versus truth-telling," described O'Brien, discussing his attitude towards writing in an interview with Ronald Baughman in *DLBDS*. "But I think it's an important game that writers and readers and anyone interested in art in general should be fully aware of. One doesn't lie for the sake of lying; one does not invent merely for the sake of inventing. One does it for a particular purpose and that purpose always is to arrive at some kind of spiritual truth that one can't discover simply by recording the world-as-it-is. We're inventing and using imagination for sublime reasons—to get at the essence of things, not merely the surface."

O'Brien's first novel, *If I Die in a Combat Zone, Box Me Up and Ship Me Home,* is an anecdotal account of an infantryman's year in Vietnam. A semi-fictionalized recounting of his own experiences, O'Brien tells the tale of a college educated young man who is drafted, trained for war, and shipped overseas to fight the Vietcong. He relates the story "with as much attention to his own feelings and states of mind as to the details of battle," declared a reviewer in the *Times Literary Supplement.* An "interesting and highly readable book," remarked another critic in the *New Republic.* Joseph McLellan, writing in the *Washington Post Book World,* called *If I Die in a Combat Zone* "powerfully written." And *New York Times Book Review* contributor Annie Gottlieb ended her review with more praise: "Tim O'Brien writes—without either pomposity or embarrassment—with the care and eloquence of someone for whom communication is still a vital and serious possibility, not a narcissistic vestige. It is a beautiful, painful book, arousing pity and fear for the daily realities of modern disaster."

Northern Lights, O'Brien's next book, creates a progression in the Vietnam tale—the story of the Vietnam soldier coming home to his family. Harvey Perry is the "hero," the soldier who fought for his country, lost an eye in battle, and seems to be all that his father wanted. Paul Perry, on the other hand, is the stay-at-home brother, the "failure" of the family who is married and employed as a farm agent in their hometown of Sawmill Landing, Minnesota. *Northern Lights* is about the two brothers' relationship, and the changes that occur during a long and difficult cross-country ski trip. Paul emerges as the "hero" after Harvey, upset over the abrupt end of a romance and physically ill, proves to be less adept at survival than his cunning brother. It is Paul who rescues Harvey, much to the surprise of everyone, including himself. The book received mixed reviews, with several critics commenting on O'Brien's style; Duncan Fallowell, writing in the *Spectator,* called *Northern Lights* "indigestible, as if [the author] is having a crack at raising the great American novel fifty years after it sank." Alasdair Maclean, writing in the *Times Literary Supplement,* expressed a similar view,

claiming "O'Brien's ambition outreaches his gifts." *New York Times Book Review* contributor John Deck, however, concluded that O'Brien "tells the story modestly and neatly . . . [in] a crafted work of serious intent with themes at least as old as the Old Testament—they still work."

O'Brien turns to a new slant on his Vietnam theme in *Going after Cacciato,* winner of the National Book Award in 1979. The chapters can stand alone as short stories; several were published as such before the book's completion, with two tales winning O. Henry Awards. *Cacciato* records the dream journey of Paul Berlin, an infantryman in Vietnam, and alternates this with the "dreamlike" actualities of war. The story begins in reality when a fellow platoon member, Cacciato (which means "the pursued" in Italian), decides to leave South East Asia and walk to Paris. He never makes it, being found near the Laotian border by a search party that includes Berlin. But, Berlin later wonders during guard duty one night, what if Cacciato was never found and the group had to track him all the way to Paris? Here, Berlin's imagination roams free as fantasies of travel, beautiful women, and, ultimately, Paris, alternate with memories of battle, death, and war. "The fantasy journey is an unworkable idea that nearly sinks the book," claimed a reviewer in *Newsweek.* And Mary Hope, writing in the *Spectator,* labeled *Going after Cacciato* a "strained effort." Other critics issued more positive reviews, praising the writing style and the author's abilities. "Tim O'Brien's writing is crisp, authentic and grimly ironic," declared Richard Freedman in the *New York Times Book Review. Washington Post Book World* contributor Robert Wilson also commented on the dream elements, calling them "out of place, hard to reconcile with the evocative realism of the rest of the narrative," but closed by writing that "Tim O'Brien knows the soldier as well as anybody, and is able to make us know him in the unique way that the best fiction can."

In *The Nuclear Age,* O'Brien shifts his focus to a civilian's perspective. William Cowling, a Vietnam era anti-war radical, terrorist, and draft dodger, is the protagonist who traded in his radicalism for profits in uranium speculation in the 1990s. A product of the "nuclear age," his childhood fear of nuclear annihilation, a concern rampant during the 1950s, has turned into paranoia in his adulthood. The story opens in 1995, with Cowling digging a bomb shelter in his backyard, but most of the story is told through flashbacks illustrating his childhood and radical young adult years. Eventually, Cowling must accept that the bombs exist and learn to ignore them, ultimately choosing the love of his family over his paranoia. "O'Brien never makes William's hysteria real or convincing," judged Michiko Kakutani in the *New York Times.* Richard Lipez, writing in the *Washington Post Book World,* called *The Nuclear Age* an "imperfect but very lively novel," an opinion several other reviewers seemed to share. Lipez praised the "marvelous character" of William Cowling, but noted that the impact of O'Brien's "main message" about the craziness of the nuclear age gets lost in the radical actions of another era. *Times Literary Supplement* contributor David Montrose also noted several flaws in the novel, including the characterization of Cowling's friends, but wrote in his conclusion: "Taken as *roman, The Nuclear Age* is notable for the lean clarity of O'Brien's prose and the finesse with which, as ever, he evokes states of mind."

O'Brien returns to the subject of Vietnam and the soldier's viewpoint with *The Things They Carried,* a fictional memoir filled with interconnected stories about the conflict and the people involved. The volume is narrated by a character named "Tim O'Brien," whom the author states is not himself, although there are many similarities. One tale records the visit of an All-American girl made to her boyfriend in South East Asia, where she eventually becomes so caught up in the war that she wanders off into combat wearing a necklace of human tongues. Another relates the death of a friend whose misstep while playing catch with hand grenades causes him to be blown up by a land mine. The title, *The Things They Carried,* refers to the things a soldier takes into combat with him—not necessarily all physical items, like weapons, but also intangibles such as fear, exhaustion, and memories. Many reviewers had only praise for O'Brien's work, with *New York Times Book Review* editor Robert R. Harris proclaiming it "a stunning performance. The overall effect of these original tales is devastating." "O'Brien convinces us that such incredible stories are faithful to the reality of Vietnam," declared Julian Loose in the *Times Literary Supplement.* Kakutani praised O'Brien's prose, describing it a as a style "that combines the sharp, unsentimental rhythms of Hemingway with gentler, more lyrical descriptions . . . [giving] the reader a shockingly visceral sense of what it felt like to tramp through a booby-trapped jungle," and concluded, "With *The Things They Carried,* Mr. O'Brien has written a vital, important book—a book that matters not only to the reader interested in Vietnam, but to anyone interested in the craft of writing as well."

"What can you teach people, just for having been in a war?," O'Brien once pondered, having been asked a similar question by Larry McCaffery in a *Chicago Review* interview. He answered by summing up his personal writing strategy: "By 'teach,' I mean provide insight, philosophy. The mere fact of having witnessed violence and death doesn't make a person a teacher. Insight and wisdom are required, and that means reading and hard thought. I didn't intend *If I Die* to stand as a profound statement, and it's not. Teaching is one thing, and telling stories is

another. Instead I wanted to use stories to alert readers to the complexity and ambiguity of a set of moral issues—but without preaching a moral lesson."

BIOGRAPHICAL/CRITICAL SOURCES:

BOOKS

Contemporary Literary Criticism, Gale, Volume 7, 1977, Volume 19, 1981, Volume 40, 1986.
Dictionary of Literary Biography Documentary Series, Volume 9, Gale, 1991.
Dictionary of Literary Biography Yearbook: 1980, Gale, 1981.

PERIODICALS

America, September 1, 1973; November 17, 1973.
Antioch Review, spring, 1978.
Atlantic, May, 1973.
Books and Bookmen, December, 1973.
Chicago Review, number 2, 1982, pp. 129-49.
Chicago Tribune, April 27, 1990; August 23, 1990.
Chicago Tribune Book World, October 6, 1985, p. 39.
Christian Science Monitor, March 9, 1978.
Commonweal, December 5, 1975.
Guardian Weekly, October 20, 1973.
Harper's, March, 1978.
Library Journal, December 18, 1977.
Listener, April 1, 1976.
Los Angeles Times, March 22, 1979; March 11, 1990.
Los Angeles Times Book Review, November 3, 1985, p. 16; April 1, 1990, p. 3.
Nation, January 29, 1977; March 25, 1978.
New Republic, May 12, 1973, p. 30; February 7, 1976.
New Statesman, January 4, 1974.
Newsweek, February 20, 1978.
New Yorker, July 16, 1973; March 27, 1978.
New York Review of Books, November 13, 1975.
New York Times, February 12, 1978; March 19, 1979; April 24, 1979; September 28, 1985; April 4, 1987; August 4, 1987; March 6, 1990; April 3, 1990.
New York Times Book Review, July 1, 1973, pp. 10, 12; December 2, 1973; October 12, 1975, p. 42; February 12, 1978, pp. 1, 22; November 3, 1985, p. 16; November 17, 1985, p. 7; August 16, 1987, p. 28; March 11, 1990, p. 8.
Publishers Weekly, August 9, 1985, p. 65; December 15, 1989, p. 35; January 26, 1990, p. 404; February 16, 1990, pp. 60-61.
Saturday Review, February 18, 1978; May 13, 1978.
Spectator, April 3, 1976, p. 22; November 25, 1978, p. 23.
Times Literary Supplement, October 19, 1973, p. 1269; April 23, 1976, p. 498; March 28, 1986, p. 342; June 29, 1990, p. 708.
Tribune Books (Chicago), March 11, 1990, p. 5.
Virginia Quarterly Review, summer, 1978.

Washington Post, July 31, 1987; April 23, 1990.
Washington Post Book World, May 27, 1973; June 3, 1973, p. 14; June 30, 1974, p. 4; February 19, 1978, p. E4; October 13, 1985, p. 9; April 7, 1991, p. 12.*

—*Sketch by Terrie M. Rooney*

*   *   *

OSBORNE, Maggie
See OSBORNE, Margaret Ellen

*   *   *

OSBORNE, Margaret Ellen 1941-
(Maggie Osborne, Margaret St. George)

PERSONAL: Born June 10, 1941, in Hollywood, CA; daughter of William Edward and Lucille Prather; married George M. Osborne II (an insurance agent), April 29, 1972; children: (from previous marriage) Zane Carter. *Education:* Attended Fort Lewis Junior College. *Religion:* Protestant. *Avocational interests:* Travel, gardening, playing the organ, reading.

ADDRESSES: Home—Box E, Dillon, CO 80435. *Agent*—Meg Ruley, Jane Rotrosen Agency, 318 East 51st St., New York, NY 10022.

CAREER: United Airlines, Denver, CO, flight attendant, 1963-67; Welcome Service, Denver, owner and operator, 1970-72; State Farm Insurance, Denver, secretary, 1972-76; writer, 1977—.

MEMBER: Romance Writers of America (president, 1984-86), Novelist's Inc. (co-founder; national secretary, 1989-90), Colorado Authors League, Mensa.

AWARDS, HONORS: Named writer of the year, Rocky Mountain Writers Guild, 1980; Master of Letters, Rocky Mountain Writers Guild, 1984; *Romantic Times* finalist for best intrigue, 1990, for best historical romantic adventure, and for Reviewer's Choice Award, both 1991; *Romantic Times* Career Achievement Award, 1991.

WRITINGS:

HISTORICAL NOVELS UNDER NAME MAGGIE OSBORNE

Alexa, Signet, 1980.
Salem's Daughter, Signet, 1981.
Portrait in Passion, Signet, 1982.
Yankee Princess, Signet, 1983.
Rage to Love, Signet, 1984.
Chase the Heart, Morrow, 1987.
Lady Reluctant, St. Martin's, 1990.
Emerald Rain, St. Martin's, 1991.

UNDER NAME MARGARET St. GEORGE

Winter Magic, Harlequin, 1986.
Castles and Fairy Tales, Harlequin, 1986.
The Heart Club, Harlequin, 1987.
Where There's Smoke . . . , Harlequin, 1987.
Heart's Desire, Harlequin, 1988.
Dear Santa, Harlequin, 1989.
Jigsaw, Harlequin, 1990.
American Pie, Harlequin, 1990.
Happy New Year, Darling, Harlequin, 1992.
Murder by the Book, Harlequin, 1992.
The Pirate and His Lady, Harlequin, 1992.

OTHER

Contributor to magazines, including *McCall's* and *Guideposts.*

SIDELIGHTS: Margaret Ellen Osborne once told *CA:* "I've been very fortunate. Unlike many writers I have no first novel tucked into a desk drawer somewhere. My first novel sold, thankfully, and I feel as if I've lived a Cinderella existence since, with autographs and speaking engagements. It's been unforgettable. I've had the pleasure of addressing writers' groups (beginners mostly) and one question continually arises: 'What would you advise the beginner?' I think the key is never to give up. Finer writers than I continue to go unpublished. This is a tough business with a great deal of rejection, but those who develop discipline and determination will eventually make it.

"My own most difficult problem is confidence. For reasons I can't even guess, the more success I have, the less confident I become. I want each published effort to reflect the best work I can do, but I'm never satisfied.

"I love writing. It frustrates me, maddens me, drives me wild, but I love it. I'm amazed when I receive a check for doing something I would do if I never received another penny. I get paid for daydreaming in print. What could be lovelier?"

*   *   *

O'SHEA, Sean
See TRALINS, S(andor) Robert

*   *   *

O'TOOLE, Rex
See TRALINS, S(andor) Robert

OUTLAND, Charles (Faulkner) 1910-1988

PERSONAL: Born August 30, 1910, in Santa Paula, CA; died after a long illness, March 21, 1988, in Santa Paula, CA; son of Elmer Garfield (a rancher) and Stella Martha (Faulkner) Outland; married Harriet Roberts (a nurse), August 1, 1933 (divorced, 1966); children: Richard, Barbara. *Education:* Attended Whittier College and Boston University. *Politics:* Republican. *Religion:* Protestant. *Avocational interests:* History of the American West and Ventura County, California.

CAREER: Rancher, Santa Paula, CA, 1933-66; historian, Santa Paula, 1953-88. Member of first Ventura County Board of Directors, 1955-64, 1968-71. *Military service:* U.S. Naval Reserve, 1936-40.

MEMBER: Ventura County Historical Society, Ventura County Cultural Heritage Board, Santa Barbara Corral of Westerners, E. Clampus Vitus (Los Angeles chapter), Santa Clarita Historical Society, Kern County Historical Society.

AWARDS, HONORS: American Association for State and Local History, Certificate of Commendation, 1980; named Honorary County Historian by Ventura County Board of Supervisors, 1984.

WRITINGS:

Man-Made Disaster: The Story of St. Francis Dam, Its Place in Southern California's Water System, Its Failure and the Tragedy in the Santa Clara River Valley, March 12 and 13, 1928, Arthur H. Clark, 1963, revised and enlarged edition, 1977.
(Editor) George Washington Faulkner, *Ho for California: The Faulkner Letters, 1875-1876,* privately printed, 1964.
Mines, Murders, and Grizzlies: Tales of California's Ventura Back Country, Ventura County Historical Society, 1969, revised edition, Arthur H. Clark, 1986.

Stagecoaching on El Camino Real, Los Angeles to San Francisco, 1861-1901, Arthur H. Clark, 1973.
An Old Shoe Box: The Story of the Discovery of a Drawing by Charles M. Russell, Grant Dahlstrom, 1975.
Sespe Gunsmoke: An Epic Case of Rancher versus Squatters, Arthur H. Clark, 1991.

First Editor and contributor, *Ventura County Historical Society Quarterly,* 1955-64.

Some of Outland's papers are held at the Ventura County Historical Museum Library.

SIDELIGHTS: Ynez Haase, executor of the estate of Charles Outland, told *CA:* "A third-generation Californian, Mr. Outland contributed more to the history of Ventura County than any other person. His interest in history probably began early in life. He was already a history major when he entered Boston College.

"Long before computers became common, he began and completed indexing Ventura County newspapers from 1871 to 1915, as well as the *LA Star* from 1853 to 1871. In order to promote interest in local and state history, he generously gave of his private library more than 150 rare books, pamphlets, and programs to the Ventura County Library system, as well as a collection of slide and tape programs depicting certain phases of history in the county. He also gave history talks to local county-wide business and social organizations to further this interest.

"[Outland] freely gave his time, knowledge, and the use of his extensive notes to anyone interested in local history. He had a commanding historical knowledge of California, the West, and World Wars I and II, particularly naval history. He was a historian to the very last. His *Sespe Gunsmoke: An Epic Case of Rancher versus Squatters* was published posthumously."

[Sketch reviewed by Ynez Haase.]

P

PANITZ, Esther L(eah)

PERSONAL: Born in New York, NY; daughter of Robert and Gittel (a translator; maiden name, Halkin) Allentuck; married David H. Panitz (a rabbi and educator), June, 1942 (died, 1991); children: Jonathan, Raphael, Michael. *Education:* Hunter College (now Hunter College of the City University of New York), B.A., 1942; Jewish Theological Seminary, B.H.L., 1943; Columbia University, M.A., 1951. *Avocational interests:* Exercise, swimming, attending concerts, visiting museums, spending time with her grandchildren, travel, reading, collecting rare books and old china.

ADDRESSES: Home—1204 Williams Dr., Shrub Oak, NY 10588.

CAREER: Ghostwriter in New York City, 1946; worked as instructor in Hebrew and history at private day school in Syracuse, NY, 1943-45; instructor in English, Washington, DC, Public Schools, 1957-59; Park Ridge High School, Park Ridge, NJ, instructor in English, 1968-70; Northern Valley Regional High School, Old Tappan, NJ, instructor in English, beginning 1970. William Paterson College, Wayne, NJ, adjunct member of English faculty, 1990, 1991. Lecturer in American Jewish history at Temple Adas Israel, Washington, DC, 1951-59, Judeo-Christian Institute of Seton Hall University, South Orange, NJ, 1973, Temple Emanuel, Paterson, NJ, 1965 and 1976-84, and at Temple Emanuel, New Rochelle, NY, 1981. Speaker for Hadassah, Women's Zionist Organization of America, 1943-59. United Jewish Appeal, chairman of Women's Division, Greater Paterson (NJ) area, 1963-65.

MEMBER: National Education Association, National Council of Teachers of English, Modern Language Association of America, Columbia University Alumni Association, Hunter College Alumni Association, Jewish Theological Seminary Alumni Association, Phi Beta Kappa.

WRITINGS:

(With husband, David H. Panitz) *Liberty under Law: The Life and Contributions of Simon Wolf* (monograph), American Jewish Tercentenary Committee, 1955.

The Alien in Their Midst: Images of Jews in English Literature, Fairleigh Dickinson University Press, 1981.

Simon Wolf: Private Conscience and Public Image, Fairleigh Dickinson University Press, 1987.

Contributor to books, including *The Jewish Experience in America,* Volumes 4 and 5, edited by Abraham J. Karp, Ktav, 1969; *Herzl Yearbook,* Volume 8, edited by Melvin I. Urofsky, Herzl Press, 1978; and *Essays in American Zionism.* Contributor to periodicals, including *American Jewish Historical Quarterly.* Editor of alumni journal of Teacher's Institute, 1988.

WORK IN PROGRESS: Max James Kohler: The Pursuit of God in Freedom; researching a projected volume, *The English Romantics and the Medieval Tradition,* for Fairleigh Dickinson University Press.

SIDELIGHTS: Esther L. Panitz once told *CA:* "I measure the level of civilization in any society by the ways in which it cares for its children, its aged and infirm, and the strangers who come to sojourn in its midst. This has been the rationale for all my writings. In works dealing with the Jewish immigrant, I have shown how the nativist in America and strangers—who in the process of residence themselves acquire nativist tendencies—reject the alien.

"Unfortunately, exceptions do not prove the rule. The few valiant leaders who battle for civil and religious rights on the strangers' behalf ultimately go down to defeat. But the story of their courageous stand against the tendency to close America's gates of opportunity to the newcomer deserves a fair hearing. Two of my articles, 'The Polarity of Jewish Attitudes to Immigration, 1870-1891' and 'In Defense of the Jewish Immigrant,' fulfill that need. In them we learn how communal worker and attorney Simon Wolf and his colleagues—at the bar, on the bench, and in institutions of learning—marshal their forces to reverse the trend in American history which would deny Emma Lazarus's cry, so boldly engraved in stone on the base of the Statue of Liberty: 'Give me your tired, your poor, your huddled masses. . . .'

"Efforts by Jacob Schiff, an internationally famous banker, and others to maintain America's early tradition of welcome for the newcomer were shattered by a combination of time and circumstance. The means they used to delay the inevitable rush to restriction became the focus of my works on immigration. These articles expand on a hitherto unpublicized segment of American history, clarify the nature of the personalities involved in the struggle for human freedoms, and shed new light on the directions the Jewish-American community took in its comprehensions of social welfare.

"By 1924, however, the confrontations these Jewish-American leaders had had with federal administrators in the immigration system and with American legislators proved useless. For at that time the alien would either be barred from entering the New World, or his admission would be so hedged about with obstacles that such legal rights as he might have enjoyed under the Constitution would not be clearly defined.

"Topically then, these works deal with political, social, and legal issues. More poignantly, they concern themselves with the never-ending drama of how to save the lives of refugees from Old World persecution.

"My concern for the immigrant's adjustment and acculturation to his new environment has also led me to study Simon Wolf's ascent up the social ladder. A German immigrant who was responsible for saving more than 103,000 immigrants from deportation, he was appointed to the United States Diplomatic Corps in 1881. At that time he held the post of United States consul in Egypt. How he fared at this task is a subject I wrote about in collaboration with my late husband, Dr. David H. Panitz. This article, 'Wolf as United States Consul to Egypt,' followed shortly after another joint effort to analyze one of Wolf's overriding passions had appeared in print. That publication was a monograph called *Liberty under Law: The Life and Contributions of Simon Wolf.*

"Max James Kohler (1871-1934) inherited Wolf's mantle and expanded an attorney's interest beyond immigration to minority rights. My work in progress on Kohler also addresses the issues of minority rights at Versailles and the danger of racism with the advent of the Nazi period.

"Closely allied to the problems inherent in the immigrant's acclimation to his new surroundings are the questions of old loyalties and nationalisms the newcomer brings with him to the land of his adoption. Within the Jewish-American community, the millennia-old dream of Zion, or reestablishing a homeland for the Jew in what was once called Palestine, remained constant. Though there was a significant number of Jewish-American leaders—and Simon Wolf was one of them—who feared a recrudescence of political Zionism in the United States would impugn their loyalties to this country, the mass of Jewish immigrants who came here saw no discrepancies between being good Americans and faithful Zionists. This was the rallying cry of Justice Louis Dembitz Brandeis.

"For this reason, I analyzed two essays detailing the conflicts between European and American Zionists whose concepts of nationalism forced them to approach the matter of Jewish settlement in Palestine in two diametrically opposite fashions. The results of these struggles has now been lucidly evoked in '*Washington vs. Pinsk': The Brandeis-Weizmann Dispute,* which appeared in Volume 8 of *Essays in American Zionism,* and in 'Louis Dembitz Brandeis and the Cleveland Conference,' published in the *American Jewish Historical Quarterly* in 1975. Here too, as in my works dealing with problems confronting newcomers to the country, I have tried to bring new insights to bear on a struggle which ultimately determined the paths worldwide Zionism was to take.

"Having taught courses in English literature for eighteen years and lectured extensively on the adult level in the field of American Jewish history, it was but natural for me to turn to the question of how Jews were perceived by Christian authors in works ranging from the writings of Geoffrey Chaucer to those of C. P. Snow in the 1970s. My book *The Alien in Their Midst: Images of Jews in English Literature* posits the theory that from the fourteenth century until the present, Jews have been regarded basically as aliens in fictional, nonfictional, and dramatic presentations. To have included literary creations of Jews by Jewish authors might have resulted in a series of distorted self-images. Consequently, *The Alien in Their Midst* is confined to the novels, essays, and plays of more than thirty well-known British writers who were not Jews. Likewise, I have omitted biblical recreations of Jewish characters in English literary works, for scriptural portrayals tend always to be universal in character and outlook.

"While writing the book, I discovered that whether British writers exhibited anti-Semitic or philo-Semitic attitudes to their fictional creations was quite beside the point. In the main, a whole variety of literary geniuses, ranging from Chaucer to Shakespeare to Milton, Swift, Pope, Dickens, Trollope, Thackeray, and the moderns of the twentieth century, regarded the Jew as some unique, distinct, or strange creation in whatever specific milieu he had been shaped. The only exception to this general thesis seemed to have been Robert Browning, whose psychological insights allowed him to see Jews whole, and James Joyce, whose characters, like the Jew to begin with in this literary saga, were themselves alienated."

Panitz adds: "Recently, after I resumed teaching, this time as an adjunct at William Paterson College, Wayne, New Jersey, my interest in literature turned to the English Romantics and their relationships to the medieval tradition. Papers read at college conferences at Plymouth State College, New Hampshire, West Point Academy, New York, Middlesex County College, New York, and the University of Delaware, Newark, Delaware, now include sections on 'Chaucer's Lady Prioress Revisited,' 'Coleridge's Medievalism,' 'Romanticist Refractions on Medieval Perspectives,' and 'Byron's Skewed Heroes: Their Real and Imaginary Voyages.' This material will be the nexus for a volume dealing with the English Romantic poets and the medieval tradition."

*   *   *

PARADIS, Adrian A(lexis) 1912-

PERSONAL: Born November 3, 1912, in Brooklyn, NY; son of Adrian Frederick (a businessman) and Marjorie (Bartholomew) Paradis; married Grace Dennis, October 8, 1938; children: Steven, Joel, Andrea. *Education:* Dartmouth College, A.B., 1934; Columbia University, B.S., 1942. *Politics:* Democratic.

ADDRESSES: Home—Sugar Hill, NH 03585. *Office*—Phoenix Publishing, Sugar Hill, NH.

CAREER: Worked in hotel business, 1935-39; Chadbourne, Wallace, Parke & Whiteside, New York City, law librarian, 1940-42; American Airlines, Inc., New York City, 1942-68, worked as librarian, office manager of department of economic planning, economic analyst, assistant to the secretary, and assistant secretary in charge of contributions, memberships, and security; New England Writing Associates (editorial and public relations firm), Westchester County, NY, owner and director, 1968-72; Phoenix Publishing, Sugar Hill, NH, editor, 1972—. Secretary, Sky Chefs, Inc. Deputy director of Civil Defense, Westchester County, 1952-56; director and chairman of Attaquechee (Vermont) Planning and Development Commission, 1969-76.

WRITINGS:

75 Ways for Boys to Earn Money, Greenburg, 1950.
Never Too Young to Earn, McKay, 1954.
For Immediate Release, McKay, 1955.
From High School to a Job, McKay, 1956.

Americans at Work, McKay, 1958.
Dollars for You, McKay, 1958.
(With wife, Grace D. Paradis) *Grow in Grace,* Abingdon, 1958.
Librarians Wanted, McKay, 1959.
The New Look in Banking, McKay, 1961.
Business in Action, Messner, 1962.
(With Betsy Burke) *The Life You Save,* McKay, 1962.
Labor in Action, Messner, 1963.
The Problem Solvers, Putnam, 1964.
Gail Borden: Resourceful Boy, Bobbs-Merrill, 1965.
Government in Action, Messner, 1965.
You and the Next Decade, McKay, 1965.
Toward a Better World, McKay, 1966.
The Research Handbook, Funk, 1966.
Economics in Action Today, Messner, 1967.
Hungry Years, Chilton, 1967.
Henry Ford, Putnam, 1967.
Bulls and Bears, Hawthorn, 1967.
Harvey Firestone, Bobbs-Merrill, 1968.
Jobs That Take You Places, McKay, 1968.
(With G. D. Paradis) *Your Life: Make It Count,* Funk, 1968.
Trade: The World's Lifeblood, Messner, 1969.
Job Opportunities for Young Negroes, McKay, 1969.
Two Hundred Million Miles a Day, Chilton, 1969.
Encyclopedia of Economics, Chilton, 1970.
Economics Reference Book, Chilton, 1970.
Gold: King of Metals, Hawthorn, 1970.
From Trails to Superhighways, Messner, 1971.
How Money Works: The Federal Reserve System, Hawthorn, 1972.
Labor Reference Book, Chilton, 1972.
International Trade in Action, Messner, 1973.
Inflation in Action, Messner, 1974.
(With R. Wood) *Social Security in Action,* Messner, 1975.
Opportunities in Banking, Vocational Guidance Manuals, 1980.
Opportunities in Airline Careers, Vocational Guidance Manuals, 1981.
(With G. D. Paradis) *Labor Almanac,* Libraries Unlimited, 1983.
Opportunities in Transportation, Vocational Guidance Manuals, 1983.
Planning Your Military Career, Vocational Guidance Manuals, 1984.
Opportunities in Your Own Service Business, Vocational Guidance Manuals, 1985.
Ida Tarbell, Children's Press, 1986.
Job Opportunities in the Twenty-First Century, Vocational Guidance Manuals, 1986.
Small Business Information Source Book, Betterway, 1987.

Opportunities in Part-time and Summer Jobs, Vocational Guidance Manuals, 1987.

Opportunities in Vocational & Technical Careers, Vocational Guidance Manuals, 1992.

Opportunities in Cleaning Service Careers, Vocational Guidance Manuals, 1992.

Opportunities in Non-Profit Organization Careers, Vocational Guidance Manuals, in press.

SIDELIGHTS: Adrian Paradis told CA: "I have found writing information books for young people most satisfying because I try to present data and advice in an interesting way that should help readers choose their life work. I like to pretend I am sitting opposite a young man or woman and assisting with this all-important career decision. A writer experiences joy and personal satisfaction by sharing his or her knowledge and experience with others."

*　　*　　*

PASACHOFF, Jay M(yron)   1943-

PERSONAL: Surname is pronounced Pa-sa-koff; born July 1, 1943, in New York, NY; son of Samuel S. (a doctor) and Anne (a teacher; maiden name, Traub) Pasachoff; married Naomi Schwartz (a writer), March 31, 1974; children: Eloise Hilary, Deborah Donna. Education: Harvard University, A.B. (cum laude), 1963, A.M., 1965, Ph.D., 1969.

ADDRESSES: Home—1305 Main St., Williamstown, MA 01267. Office—Hopkins Observatory, Williams College, Williamstown, MA 01267.

CAREER: Air Force Cambridge Research Laboratories, Bedford, MA, research physicist, 1968-69; Harvard University, Cambridge, MA, Menzel research fellow at Harvard College Observatory, 1969-70; Williams College, Williamstown, MA, assistant professor, 1972-77, associate professor, 1977-84, professor, 1984-85, Field Memorial Professor of Astronomy, 1985—, chairman of department, 1972-77, 1990-93, director of Hopkins Observatory, 1972—. University of Massachusetts at Amherst, adjunct assistant professor, 1975-77, adjunct associate professor, 1977-85, adjunct professor, 1985—; Lockhart Lecturer at University of Manitoba, 1979; visiting associate professor and visiting colleague at University of Hawaii at Manoa, 1980-81, 1984-85. Research fellow at Hale Observatories, Carnegie Institution of Washington, and California Institute of Technology, 1970-72, Owens Valley Radio Observatory, summer, 1973, and Australian National Radio Astronomical Observatory, 1974. Visiting scientist, Institut d'Astrophysique, 1988. Member of National Science Foundation expedition to Kenya, 1973; assistant director of Harvard-Smithsonian-National Geographic expedition

to Mexico, 1970, and Harvard-Smithsonian-Williams expedition to Canada, 1972; participated in eclipse expeditions to Massachusetts, 1959, Quebec, 1963, Kenya, 1973, Colombia, 1973, Australia, 1974, the Pacific Ocean, 1977, Canada, 1979, India, 1980, Hawaii and the Pacific, 1981, Indonesia, 1983, 1984, Mississippi, 1984, Papua New Guinea, 1984, Finland, 1990, Hawaii, 1991, California, 1992, and South Africa, 1992. Member of Institute for Advanced Study, 1989-90. Guest investigator with the Laboratoire de Physique Stellaire et Planetaire, Verrieres-le-Buisson, France, on the National Aeronautics and Space Administration's Orbiting Solar Observatory 8, 1975-79.

MEMBER: International Astronomical Union (U.S. national representative to Commission of Teaching Astronomy, 1976—; chairperson of Working Group on Eclipses, 1991—), International Union of Radio Science, American Association for the Advancement of Science (fellow), American Astronomical Society, American Physical Society (fellow), American Association of University Professors (Williams College chapter president, 1977-80), Royal Astronomical Society (fellow), Astronomical Society of the Pacific, New York Academy of Sciences, Sigma Xi (Williams College club president, 1973-74).

AWARDS, HONORS: Bronze medal from Nikon Photo Contest International, 1971; grants from National Science Foundation, National Geographic Society, National Aeronautics and Space Administration, and Research Corp., 1973—.

WRITINGS:

Contemporary Astronomy, Saunders College, 1977, 4th edition, 1989.

Astronomy Now, Saunders College, 1978.

(With Marc L. Kutner) University Astronomy, Saunders College, 1978.

Astronomy: From the Earth to the Universe, Saunders College, 1979, 4th edition, 1993.

(With Kutner) Invitation to Physics, Norton, 1981.

(With wife, Naomi Pasachoff) Physical Science, Scott, Foresman, 1983, 2nd edition, 1989.

(With N. Pasachoff) Earth Science, Scott, Foresman, 1983, 2nd edition, 1989.

(With Donald H. Menzel) A Field Guide to the Stars and Planets, 2nd edition, Houghton, 1983, 3rd edition, 1992.

A Brief View of Astronomy, Saunders College, 1986.

(With Richard Wolfson) Physics, Little, Brown, 1987, 2nd edition, in press.

First Guide to Astronomy, Houghton, 1988.

(With N. Pasachoff) Discover Science (seven volumes), Scott, Foresman, 1989.

(Editor with John R. Percy) The Teaching of Astronomy, Cambridge University Press, 1990.

First Guide to the Solar System, Houghton, 1990.
Journey Through the Universe, Saunders College, 1992.
(Editor with Sybil Parker) *Encyclopedia of Astronomy,* McGraw, 1993.
(With L. Holder and J. DeFranze) *Calculus,* Brooks/Cole, in press.

Contributor to encyclopedias. Contributor of articles and photographs to scientific journals and popular magazines, including *National Geographic, Scientific American,* and *Sky and Telescope.* Associate editor of *Journal of Irreproducible Results,* 1972—. Astronomy consultant to *McGraw-Hill Encyclopedia of Science and Technology,* 1984—, and to *Random House Dictionary,* unabridged edition, 1984—.

SIDELIGHTS: Jay M. Pasachoff's research specialty is solar eclipses. He has been able to observe more than a dozen of them from Canada, Mexico, Colombia, Australia, Kenya, Indonesia, Papua New Guinea, Finland, Africa, and the United States. His scientific studies of the corona have been supplemented by articles and photographs that have appeared in *National Geographic, Sky and Telescope,* and *Scientific American,* and other publications. His books are noted for their numerous high-quality drawings and photographs, among them a few of his own.

Pasachoff told *CA:* "I have been very interested, in my writing, in showing laymen the vitality of contemporary astronomy and physics by discussing the most up-to-date and exciting topics."

*   *   *

PASTAN, Linda (Olenik) 1932-

PERSONAL: Born May 27, 1932, in New York, NY; daughter of Jacob L. (a physician) and Bess (Schwartz) Olenik; married Ira Pastan (a molecular biologist), June 14, 1953; children: Stephen, Peter, Rachel. *Education:* Radcliffe College, B.A., 1954; Simmons College, M.L.S., 1955; Brandeis University, M.A., 1957. *Religion:* Jewish.

ADDRESSES: Home—11710 Beall Mountain Rd., Potomac, MD 20854.

CAREER: Writer. Lecturer at Breadloaf Writers Conference, Ripton, VT.

AWARDS, HONORS: Dylan Thomas Poetry Award, 1958, *Mademoiselle;* National Endowment for the Arts fellow; Maryland Arts Council grant; De Castagnola Award, 1978, for *The Five Stages of Grief;* American Book Award poetry nomination, 1983, for *PM/AM: New and Selected Poems;* Bess Hokin Prize, *Poetry;* Maurice English Award; Virginia Faulkner Award, *Prairie Schooner,* 1992.

WRITINGS:

POETRY

A Perfect Circle of Sun, Swallow Press, 1971.
On the Way to the Zoo, Dryad, 1975.
Aspects of Eve, Liveright, 1975.
The Five Stages of Grief, Norton, 1978.
Setting the Table, Dryad, 1980.
Waiting for My Life, Norton, 1981.
PM/AM: New and Selected Poems, Norton, 1983.
A Fraction of Darkness: Poems, Norton, 1985.
The Imperfect Paradise, Norton, 1988.
Heroes in Disguise, Norton, 1991.

SIDELIGHTS: One of the prevailing themes of Linda Pastan's poetry is the complexity of domestic life. In what she terms "the war between desire and dailiness," Pastan "dissects the tension that divides womanly rituals of motherhood and housekeeping from the solitary rites of the poet," writes Phoebe Pettingell in the *New Leader.* Pastan relies on imagery and metaphor to infuse ordinary domestic matters with mystery and magic in a style reminiscent of Emily Dickinson, who, according to Dave Smith in the *American Poetry Review,* "took her dailiness to the heights of metaphysical vision. . . . It may be, Dickinson is Pastan's ghost, though less perhaps in sound than in what to look at and how to show it." Pastan's style is simple and understated; her poetry, therefore, is "never baroque, never sentimental, never suffused with a militant feminism," observes Samuel Hazo in the *Hudson Review.* Commenting on the economy of her language, *Chicago Tribune Book World* contributor L. M. Rosenberg writes that Pastan "knows the force of what's left unsaid, the importance of the white space around the written word. This makes her a poet of elegant spareness."

Pastan's "material chose her," according to Pettingell, "when she interrupted her writing career to [marry and] raise a family." The interruption immediately followed Pastan's graduation from Radcliffe, where, in her senior year, she won the *Mademoiselle* poetry contest. The runner-up was Sylvia Plath. Unlike Plath, however, Pastan relinquished her writing. "I was into the whole '50s thing, kids and the clean floor bit," she told *Washington Post* writer Michael Kernan. "I was unhappy because I knew what I should be doing." Pastan explained that her husband, tired "of hearing what a great writer I would have been if I hadn't got married," urged her to take her work seriously and write while the children were in school. Since that time, Pastan has dedicated herself to her poetry; her efforts were rewarded in 1983 when *PM/AM: New and Selected Poems* was nominated for an American Book Award.

In *Waiting for My Life,* a title that alludes to Pastan's interrupted writing career, "she broods on the rewards as well as the risks of domesticity," comments Sandra M. Gilbert in *Parnassus*. One of those risks, according to Pastan, is that those who are unfamiliar with domesticity will equate it with mundaneness. Gilbert, for example, wonders, "Is it because she is quite self-consciously a *woman* poet that Pastan so austerely ordains the necessity of acquiescence in the ordinary?" In "Who Is It Accuses Us?" Pastan defends both her lifestyle and her poetry by suggesting that domesticity is hazardous and requires physical and emotional fortitude. Another poem, "The War between Desire and Dailiness," explores the conflict "between longing and order, body and soul, the woman and the poet," according to J. D. McClatchy in *Poetry*. At the end of the poem Pastan declares, "Let dailiness win," and though "it sounds as if she has chosen safety, . . . the line ends [the] poem with anything but conviction," observes Smith.

Waiting for My Life also depicts "parents musing on the lives of grown children, on their own altered flesh, the weather, the slackened but not dead fevers of desire, those moments spent at windows in kitchens or gardens where we are astonished at the speed and movement that is all the not-us," Smith explains. In "Meditation by the Stove," for instance, Pastan describes a housewife who contemplates neglecting her duties. Pettingell remarks that while there is "menace implicit" in the concluding lines "And I have banked the fires of my body / into a small domestic flame for others / to warm their hands on for a while," Pastan "knows what price men and women pay for domesticity, while realizing that not even poets want to live entirely alone, without responsibilities."

Both her subject matter and unaffected writing style make Pastan an accessible poet. Several critics note, however, that Pastan sometimes sacrifices subtly for accessibility. Mary Jo Salter, for example, comments in the *Washington Post Book World* that *Waiting for My Life* "is sometimes simple to a fault," citing the simile "the white curtains blow / like ghosts of themselves." Similarly, *Chicago Tribune Book World* contributor L. M. Rosenberg describes Pastan's poetry as "occasionally too easy" but later concedes that her "work is its own argument against charges of insufficiency." Peter Stitt, on the other hand, maintains in the *Georgia Review* that Pastan "does not cause brain strain, like the early Mark Strand, and she does not leave us breathless, sweating, far from civilization, like Galway Kinnell—but she is a wonderful writer nevertheless and works in a rich, human vein." *Waiting for My Life* "is full of surprises that make it far from daily," concludes Smith. "It keeps a low heat, but it is radiant heat nonetheless."

One way that Pastan elevates her subject matter is through metaphor. As Stephen Dobyns observes in the *Washington Post Book World:* "It is metaphor that drives all her poems, that lifts them from the mundane and gives them

their degree of magic. . . . The poems are strongest when the commentary combines with the mysterious through metaphor to give us a new sense of the world, to make us see what has become commonplace as if for the first time." In *The Five Stages of Grief,* arranged according to the stages outlined in Elisabeth Kuebler-Ross's *On Death and Dying,* Pastan writes not only about death, but about death as a metaphor for "loss through divorce, adultery, argument, aging, children leaving home, identity crisis, silence, and innocence/wisdom," writes Karla Hammond in the *Prairie Schooner*. Several of the poems describe a discontented married woman who, after experiencing denial, anger, bargaining, and depression, finally reaches acceptance when she realizes that "even though their relationship has been strained to the point that it is no longer satisfactory to [her], she can find comfort only with her husband, with the familiar, with the imperfect," observes Benjamin Franklin V in the *Dictionary of Literary Biography*.

This metaphor "of the breaking marriage . . . is not a literal truth referring to the poet's life (other poems make this unmistakably clear) but a metaphor standing for the issue of loss and abandonment generally, as our children disappear from us into their own lives, as our parents disappear into their deaths, and so on," notes Stitt. "If there is an ultimate truth" in *The Five Stages of Grief,* "it is that grief (embodied in loss, separation, and death) like history, is a 'circular staircase' from which there is no human escape," comments Hammond, who later concludes that "this is a moving work in its subtlety, intensity and matter-of-factness. . . . It touches the lives of each of us on our journey from denial to acceptance."

In *PM/AM: New and Selected Poems* Pastan again "stresses the mystery of the ordinary, the strangeness to which we wake each 'AM' and out of which we lapse each 'PM,' " writes Gilbert. The early morning hours are especially important to Pastan, for she begins to write as soon as she wakes, hoping to "surprise her mind before the visions melt, while it is still running loose in that landscape of wishes, still detached from the engines of reason," according to Michael Kernan in the *Washington Post*. These fragments of dreams play a significant role in Pastan's writing, although, as she explained to Kernan, "it's not a matter of transcribing actual dreams, . . . but of using the unconscious state and its strange associations and the insights you get from them." Pastan's interest in the dream state manifests itself in several of the poems in *PM/AM: New and Selected Poems*. "Waking," for example, describes the process of awakening as "watching our dreams move / helplessly away like fading / lantern fish." And in "Dreams," originally published in *Waiting for My Life,* Pastan observes that dreams transport us to "the place where the children / we were / rock in the arms of the children / we have become." It is poems like these that "reveal a complex, original imagination finding magic in the commonplace and making dreams universally intelligible," writes *Detroit News* contributor Edward Morin.

The publication of *PM/AM: New and Selected Poems* has prompted several critics to review Pastan's progress as a writer. Kernan comments that in this book, "the sense of self-observation seems to have grown more acute, both in the quality of the observations and in the merciless cutting of lines and words . . . to clutch at some essence." *New York Times Book Review* contributor Hugh Seidman remarks: "One cannot deny that [Pastan's] vision has gained in depth over the years. [*PM/AM*] has a stateliness and solidity of tone not reached in earlier [books], and there is evidence of more emotional opening out in some of her newest pieces." Even those earlier poems "that seemed minor and fragmentary [the] first time around," writes a *Publishers Weekly* critic, "are transformed by the unity of their context" in *PM/AM.* Pastan's voice, however, remains calm yet penetrating. Her poems, concludes *Voyages* critic Roderick Jellema, continue to "quietly unmake the set of the mind as they cut apart, deepen, and then reunify the ingredients of simple experience. And that's where discoveries about our lives and our world are made."

One of Pastan's more recent books, *The Imperfect Paradise,* is a collection of poems in which she writes of love and grief. Mortality, death, loss of a loved one, happiness, spiritual and physical love, and marital crisis are among the topics she explores, revealing her deepest thoughts, beliefs, and fears. Grace Bauer in the *Library Journal* calls Pastan's poems "direct and passionate, yet controlled." Bruce Bennett, writing in the *New York Times Book Review,* comments that "Ms. Pastan's unfailing mastery of her medium holds the darkness firmly in check," continuing on to conclude: "Enmeshed in the 'imperfect paradise' that constitutes our common life, Ms. Pastan sounds these depths ['whose measure we only guess'] in subtle and delicate ways."

BIOGRAPHICAL/CRITICAL SOURCES:

BOOKS

Contemporary Literary Criticism, Volume 27, Gale, 1984.
Dictionary of Literary Biography, Volume 5: *American Poets since World War II,* Gale, 1980.
Pastan, Linda, *Waiting for My Life,* Norton, 1981.
Pastan, *PM/AM: New and Selected Poems,* Norton, 1983.

PERIODICALS

American Poetry Review, January, 1982.
Chicago Tribune Book World, September 13, 1981; June 12, 1983.
Detroit News, September 27, 1981.

Georgia Review, winter, 1979; spring, 1983.
Hudson Review, autumn, 1978.
Library Journal, May 15, 1988, p. 85.
New Leader, December 27, 1982.
New York Times, August 18, 1972.
New York Times Book Review, February 20, 1983; September 18, 1988, pp. 42-44.
Parnassus, fall/winter, 1972; spring, 1983.
Poetry, September, 1982; June 12, 1983.
Prairie Schooner, fall, 1979.
Publishers Weekly, September 10, 1982.
Shenandoah, summer, 1973.
Voyages, spring, 1969.
Washington Post, December 17, 1983.
Washington Post Book World, May 21, 1978; July 5, 1981; November 7, 1982; February 2, 1986.

*   *   *

PEARL, Esther Elizabeth
See RITZ, David

*   *   *

PEESLAKE, Gaffer
See DURRELL, Lawrence (George)

*   *   *

PELLEGRINI, Angelo   1904-1991

PERSONAL: Born April 20, 1904, in Casabianca, near Florence, Italy; died November 1, 1991; immigrated to the United States in 1913; son of Piacentino (a peasant) and Annunziata (Palidoni) Pellegrini; married Virginia Thompson, August 27, 1934; children: Angela (Mrs. Tom Owens), Toni (Mrs. Denis Lucey III), Brent. *Education:* University of Washington, Seattle, Ph.D., 1942. *Politics:* Democrat.

ADDRESSES: Office—Department of English GN-30, University of Washington, Seattle, WA 98195.

CAREER: University of Washington, Seattle, associate professor, 1951-58, professor of English, 1958—.

AWARDS, HONORS: Guggenheim fellowship, 1949-50; Freedoms Foundation Award, 1951; James Beard Foundation Award nomination, 1992, for *Vintage Pellegrini.*

WRITINGS:

The Unprejudiced Palate, Macmillan, 1948.
Immigrant's Return, Macmillan, 1951.
Americans by Choice, Macmillan, 1956.

Wine and the Good Life, Knopf, 1965.
Washington: Profile of a State, Coward, 1967.
The Food Lover's Garden, Knopf, 1970.
Lean Years, Happy Years, Madrona Publishers, 1983.
American Dream: An Immigrant's Quest, North Point Press, 1986.
Vintage Pellegrini: The Collected Wisdom of an American Buongustaio, edited by Schuyler Ingle, Sasquatch Books, 1991.

Contributor of essays to magazines and professional journals.

SIDELIGHTS: Angelo Pellegrini's writings on gardening, the enjoyment of life, and his family's experiences as immigrants in early twentieth-century have extolled simple living for almost half a century. "I suggest," Pellegrini writes in his *Contemporary Authors Autobiography Series* entry, "that the very essence of living appropriately, especially in an age of scarcity, is living in harmony with Nature. . . . This credo, which has given my life a meaningful direction, is also in accord with what I learned from my immigrant father: 'It is the duty of every member of the human family to leave that section of land whence he draws his sustenance in better condition than it was when he acquired it.' This I have done by cultivating a kitchen garden, fifteen hundred square feet. . . . May I suggest you do the same? And bless you for the effort."

BIOGRAPHICAL/CRITICAL SOURCES:

BOOKS

Contemporary Authors Autobiography Series, Volume 11, Gale, 1990.
Heiney, Donald, *America in Modern Italian Literature,* Rutgers University Press, 1964.

PERIODICALS

Washington Post Book World, December 23, 1984, p. 12.
[Death date provided by wife, Virginia Pellegrini]

*   *   *

PETERS, Edward (Murray) 1936-

PERSONAL: Born May 21, 1936, in New Haven, CT; son of Edward Murray and Marjorie (Corcoran) Peters; married Patricia Ann Knapp, July 8, 1961; children: Nicole, Moira, Edward. *Education:* Yale University, B.A., 1963, M.A., 1965, Ph.D., 1967.

ADDRESSES: Home—4225 Regent Sq., Philadelphia, PA 19104. *Office*—Department of History, University of Pennsylvania, Philadelphia, PA 19104.

CAREER: Quinnipiac College, Hamden, CT, instructor in English and history, 1964-67; University of Califor-

nia—San Diego, La Jolla, assistant professor of history, 1967-68; University of Pennsylvania, Philadelphia, Henry Charles Lea Assistant Professor of Medieval History, 1968-70, Henry Charles Lea Associate Professor of Medieval History, 1970-81, Henry Charles Lea Professor of Medieval History, 1981—. Curator of Henry Charles Lea Library, 1968—. High school French and Spanish instructor, summer, 1964; visiting professor of history, Moore College of Art, 1970-71; visiting professor of history, Katholieke Universiteit, Leuven, Belgium, 1992. *Military service:* U.S. Army, 1956-59.

MEMBER: Iuris Canonici Medii Aevi Consociatio (ICMAC), American Historical Association, Mediaeval Academy of America, Royal Historical Society (fellow), American Society of Legal History.

AWARDS, HONORS: Woodrow Wilson fellow, 1963-64; Foote fellowship, 1963-64; Woodrow Wilson dissertation fellowship, 1966-67; honorary Sterling fellowship, 1966-67; John Addison Porter dissertation prize, 1967; University of Pennsylvania faculty research grants, 1969 and 1970; American Philosophical Society research grant, 1972; honorary M.A., University of Pennsylvania, 1973; American Council of Learned Societies fellowship, 1981-82.

WRITINGS:

The Shadow King, Yale University Press, 1970.
The First Crusade, University of Pennsylvania Press, 1971.
Christian Society and the Crusade, 1198-1229, University of Pennsylvania Press, 1971.
(Editor with Alan C. Kors) *Witchcraft in Europe, 1100-1750: A Documentary History,* University of Pennsylvania Press, 1972.
Monks, Bishops, and Pagans, University of Pennsylvania Press, 1975.
Europe: The World of the Middle Ages, Prentice-Hall, 1977.
The Magician, the Witch, and the Law, University of Pennsylvania Press, 1978.
(Editor and author of introduction) *Heresy and Authority in Medieval Europe: Documents in Translation,* University of Pennsylvania Press, 1980.
Europe and the Middle Ages: A Short History, Prentice-Hall, 1983, reprinted, 1989.
Torture, Basil Blackwell, 1985.
Inquisition, The Free Press, 1988.

Also author of *The World around the Revolution* (television series), 1977.

WORK IN PROGRESS: Research on medieval cultural history.

BIOGRAPHICAL/CRITICAL SOURCES:

PERIODICALS

New York Times Book Review, September 15, 1985.
Times Literary Supplement, July 26, 1985.

* * *

PHILLIPS, E(ugene) Lee 1941-

PERSONAL: Born October 13, 1941, in St. Joseph, MO; son of Samuel Maxwell (a grocer) and Eulah (Sanders) Phillips. *Education:* Southwest Baptist College, A.A., 1961; Howard Payne College, B.A., 1963; Southwestern Baptist Theological Seminary, B.D. and M.A., both 1968; Institute of Religion at Texas Medical Center, certificate of completion, 1969; Vanderbilt University, D.Min., 1976. *Avocational interests:* Reading, travel, floriculture.

ADDRESSES: Home—Lemon Grove, 791 Marstevan Dr. N.E., Residence A, Atlanta, GA 30306.

CAREER: Ordained Baptist minister, June, 1968; Memorial Hospital, Houston, TX, chaplain-intern, 1968-69; part-time nursing home chaplain and substitute schoolteacher in Louisville, KY, 1970-73; Crescent Hill Baptist Church, Louisville, assistant to the pastor, 1973-74; First Presbyterian Church, Mt. Pleasant, TN, guest minister, 1975-76; supply preacher for churches in the Nashville, TN, area, 1976-77; writer, 1978—. Guest lecturer and preacher.

AWARDS, HONORS: Dixie Council of Authors and Journalists, Merit Award, 1982, for *Prayers for Our Day,* and Georgia Author of the Year Award in Inspirational Literature, 1987, for *Breaking Silence before the Lord.*

WRITINGS:

Prayers for Worship, Word Books, 1979.
Prayers for Our Day, John Knox, 1982.
Breaking Silence before the Lord, Baker Book, 1986.

Contributor to *Old Stone Worship Book,* Old Stone Presbyterian Church (Delaware, OH), 1982; and *Leadership Handbooks of Practical Theology,* Volume 1, edited by James D. Berkley, Christianity Today and Baker Book, 1992. Contributor of prayers to anthologies and annuals, including *Rejoice,* edited by Ronald E. Garman, Word Books, 1982; *The Minister's Manual,* edited by James Cox, HarperCollins, 1984—; and *101 Meal Prayers for Christians,* compiled by Theresa Cotter, St. Anthony Messenger Press, 1991. Contributor to periodicals, including *Anglican Digest, Christian Index, alive now!, These Days, Vista, Guideposts,* and *Decision.*

WORK IN PROGRESS: Prayers in Praise of God; Prayers for Every Day; musical adaptations of prayers with various composers.

SIDELIGHTS: E. Lee Phillips told *CA:* "One writes to find out what one knows. The more one writes the more one knows. Write what you know. Writing does not make your life easier, only wiser. If you write just to get rich that is one use of the gift; if you write to shape truth into verbiage worthy of the human condition and thoughtful consideration, that is a wiser use of the gift.

"If you can do anything else besides writing, you should; if you can shake the thing then it wasn't the real thing in the beginning. Writing can take you to the door of starvation, deprivation, exasperation, depression, rejection, and tears, make your nights restless and your days fitful. Writing can also transport you to ecstasies few mortals ever enjoy because you have seen things, heard voices, felt feelings, tapped the magic of imagination, filled words with vibrant life, birthed something substantive that for generations ought to be pondered. There is nobility in that.

"Don't apologize for your sensitivities. If you feel and hear and see more than most mortals, make that work for you: soundproof the walls, head to the woods, take a cabin at the beach, climb a tree, rent an island, confiscate a large closet—whatever it takes roll your own! Your honest word is every bit as valuable as many another's word. In writing religious books try to make the pages sing with the unforgettable. Give voice to the irrevocable. Prod faith to the fore and love to the center. Couch it plainly, say it clearly, bring it home swiftly, that it may linger undeniably.

"Do not deprecate yourself if what you write is not best-selling. If it is of truth, well said, born of the turmoils, woes, and joys of life, couched in genuine and poignant words, pregnant with that which outlasts life, then you have done what it is your duty to do as a writer, whether you are ever greatly recognized or not. Your hour will come. Someone you never met and may never meet needs to read what you have to write."

BIOGRAPHICAL/CRITICAL SOURCES:

PERIODICALS

Atlanta Journal and Constitution, July 14, 1979; October 2, 1982; December 18, 1983; November 2, 1987.
Chronicle (Anderson, SC), November 16, 1983.
Paris Enterprise (Paris, KY), October 7, 1982; October 21, 1982.
Pearl Press (Pearl, MS), November 1, 1979.
St. Joseph News Press and Gazette (St. Joseph, MO), April 26, 1975; October 24, 1975; May 16, 1976; March 15, 1977; September 29, 1979; May 22, 1982; May 24, 1982; September 17, 1983; January 3, 1987; May 23,

1987; November 14, 1987; March 16, 1991; October 19, 1991; November 9, 1991.

*   *   *

PHILLIPS, Kevin (Price) 1940-

PERSONAL: Born November 30, 1940, in New York, NY; son of William Edward (a state administrator) and Dorothy (Price) Phillips; married Martha Henderson (Republican staff director of the U.S. House of Representatives Budget Committee), September 23, 1968; children: Andrew, Alexander. *Education:* Colgate University, A.B., 1961; Harvard University, LL.B., 1964; also attended University of Edinburgh, 1959-60. *Politics:* Republican. *Religion:* Protestant.

ADDRESSES: Home—5115 Moorland Rd., Bethesda, MD 20014. *Office*—American Political Research Corp., 7316 Wisconsin Ave., Bethesda, MD 20014.

CAREER: Administrative assistant to Congressman Paul Fino, 1964-68; special assistant to campaign manager of "Nixon for President" committee, 1968-69; special assistant to U.S. Attorney General, 1969-70; American Political Research Corp., Bethesda, MD, president, 1971—. Commentator on National Public Radio, CBS Radio Network, and CBS Television.

MEMBER: New York Bar Association, Washington D.C. Bar Association, Phi Beta Kappa, Pi Sigma Alpha.

AWARDS, HONORS: National Book Critics Circle award nomination, 1991, for *The Politics of Rich and Poor: Wealth and the American Electorate in the Reagan Aftermath.*

WRITINGS:

The Emerging Republican Majority, Arlington House, 1969.
(With Paul H. Blackman) *Electoral Reform and Voter Participation: Federal Registration, a False Remedy for Voter Apathy,* American Enterprise Institute for Public Policy Research, 1975.
Mediacracy: American Parties and Politics in the Information Age, Doubleday, 1975.
Post-Conservative America: People, Politics, and Ideology in a Time of Crisis, Random House, 1982.
Staying on Top: The Business Case for a National Industrial Strategy, Random House, 1984, published as *Staying on Top: Winning the Trade War,* Vintage Books, 1986.
The Politics of Rich and Poor: Wealth and the American Electorate in the Reagan Aftermath, Random House, 1990.
Boiling Point: Republicans, Democrats and the Decline of Middle Class Prosperity, Random House, 1993.

Also author of columns for King Features Syndicate, 1970—. Columnist for *Los Angeles Times;* contributor to *New York Times* and *Washington Post.* Editor and publisher of *The American Political Report.*

SIDELIGHTS: Kevin Phillips is considered one of America's premier political analysts. He skyrocketed to public notice with his first book, *The Emerging Republican Majority.* Only 28 years old when the book was published, Phillips already had political experience—he served as a special assistant in voting trends analysis to Richard Nixon's campaign manager John N. Mitchell in the successful Republican campaign of 1968. Phillips later followed Mitchell to the Attorney General's office, again working as a special assistant. *The Emerging Republican Majority* correctly predicted the shift from liberalism to conservativism that took place beginning with Nixon's reelection in 1972, as well as coining the term "Sun Belt," and recognizing the political reemergence of the South. In the book, Phillips suggested new ways in which Republicans could gain the political support they needed to dominate American politics.

Political dogma in the late 1960s mandated that Republicans could not come to power without appealing to liberal voters, especially young people and minorities—groups already aligned with the Democratic party, or unaffiliated. Phillips saw Nixon's election in 1968 as the end of a Democratic preeminence in American politics that had begun with Franklin D. Roosevelt's New Deal in the 1930s. He also saw that the Republican party could create an alliance between dissatisfied conservatives in the South, in the Midwest, and on the West Coast, in combination with Roman Catholics, blue-collar workers, and prosperous suburbanites—a section of the voting public that could give Republicans victory without appealing to liberals. By 1972, a version of Phillips's plan was in effect, and conservatives returned to power in America.

Phillips left the Attorney General's office in 1970, and became president of the American Political Research Corporation in 1971. He continued to state his views through *The American Political Report* and *The Business and Public Affairs Fortnightly,* periodicals he edited and published himself. In addition, he wrote several more examinations of contemporary American politics. *Mediacracy: American Parties and Politics in the Communications Age,* published in 1975, examined the emerging importance of the information industry in American politics. In *Post-Conservative America: People, Politics, and Ideology in a Time of Crisis* (1982), Phillips drew parallels between contemporary America, Weimar Germany, and 16th-century Europe, in order to look at two possible political futures for the United States: a shift toward authoritarianism, or disintegration of the two-party political system. *Staying on Top: The Business Case for a National Industrial Strategy*

(1984) suggested possible solutions for the trading and industrial problems of the United States, including a more agressive trade policy and expansion of "economic nationalism."

In *The Politics of Rich and Poor,* Phillips contends that throughout the past twenty years, and especially during Ronald Reagan's presidency—years dominated by conservative Republican politics—the rich have gotten richer and the poor have gotten poorer. Citing data from national magazines and government reports, Phillips shows that during the 1980s average incomes from the poorest 10% of the population dropped 10.5%. At the same time, the average incomes from the wealthiest 10% rose 24.4%, and the average incomes of the top 1% increased over 74%. In addition, the economic policies of the 1980s produced record numbers of millionaires and billionaires, while farmers, middle-income workers, inner-city poor, and the unemployed saw prosperity recede from their grasp.

Phillips sees two historical precedents and a political effect in this accumulation of wealth in the hands of the rich. The precedents lie in the "Gilded Age" (roughly the 1890s) and the "Roaring 20s," both eras of laissez-faire economics marked by government deregulation and low taxes, and directed by conservative Republicans. They were also marked, says Phillips, by hard times for farmers and an increase in indigent poor. Both eras ended in periods of Populist upheaval. The political effect of the Reagan years, Phillips believes, will be similar: a backlash of Populist origins—farmers, middle-income white-collar workers, and the poor—against the politicians in power. These predictions were realized in the presidential elections of 1992, which brought a Democratic president into office for the first time in 12 years.

"The 1980s were a second Gilded Age," writes Phillips in *The Politics of Rich and Poor,* "in which many Americans made and spent money abundantly. Yet as the decade ended, too many stretch limousines, too many enormous incomes and too much high fashion foreshadowed a significant shift of mood. A new plutocracy—some critics were even using the word 'oligarchy'—had created a new target for populist reaction. A small but significant minority of American liberals had begun to agitate the economy's losers—minorities, young men, female heads of households, farmers, steelworkers and others. Television audiences were losing their early-eighties fascination with the rich. And many conservatives, including President George Bush himself, were becoming defensive about great wealth, wanton moneymaking and greed. . . . The 1980s boom in the Boston-Washington megalopolis, coupled with hard times on the farm and in the Oil Patch, produced a familiar economic geography—a comparative

shift of wealth toward . . . income groups already well off."

Reviews of *The Politics of Rich and Poor* were mixed. Priscilla Painton, writing in *Time,* states that "Phillips brings the authority of statistics and history to his argument: with an elegant weaving of charts and cultural observations, he paints a picture of the Reagan decade as America's third period of 'heyday capitalism,' when the poor got poorer, the middle class has to get rich in order to retain a middle-class life-style, and being rich had to be redefined to account for the tripling in the number of multimillionaires." Ronald Reagan, writes Garry Wills in the *New York Review of Books,* "brought in a new elite of glitterati whom Phillips denounces, here, as betrayers of right-wing populism. The [Republican] party has given itself back to those 'economic royalists' Phillips denounced in 1968. He is admirably consistent. No one else has assembled a more scathing assault on the 1980s as a time of economic exploitation."

Other reviewers were not so enthusiastic. *Fortune* magazine reviewer Walter Olson, and Allen Randolph, writing for the *National Review,* both point out that, contrary to Phillips' contention, the tax structure as revised under President Reagan actually resulted in an increase in tax revenues from the taxpayers in the highest brackets. Olson further declares that the dip in unemployment in Reagan's second term helped create higher wages for lower income workers in restaurants—resulting in costs (which Phillips decries) that were in turn passed to consumers. Randolph states that "the author's curious resentment of the prosperity of the Reagan Era is omnipresent and burdensome—but . . . if there is one thing that we have learned from recent events it is that resentment does not make for sound economics."

Phillip's own political stance in this book has attracted as much attention as his views. "Phillips' biting polemic against the Reagan years is . . . most surprising," writes Ronald Brownstein in the *Los Angeles Times Book Review.* "As a former aide to Richard Nixon, Phillips usually is described as a Republican analyst. But in recent years he has actually assumed a new role; the conservative who dares to say that liberals are right. This book should confirm him in that improbable position." Olson in particular perceives Phillips as a liberal Democrat in Republican's clothing, stating that "His current book represents a sort of wet-winged emergence from the ideological chrysalis." "It may be that a Democratic comeback will have to wait for a severe economic downturn," states Michael Waldman in the *Nation.* "Phillips makes a persuasive case that, should this occur, principled progressives will have an opportunity to reshape the political landscape." But Phillips himself states in *Newsweek,* "I don't see any reason to concede the conservative label to those people who are survival-of-the-fittest disrupters of a lot of ordinary Americans' lives."

BIOGRAPHICAL/CRITICAL SOURCES:

PERIODICALS

Business Week, September 17, 1984, pp. 12, 16.
Christian Science Monitor, September 4, 1969.
Fortune, July 16, 1990, pp. 113-14.
Los Angeles Times, January 1, 1985.
Los Angeles Times Book Review, June 10, 1990, pp. 1, 8.
Nation, July 3, 1982, pp. 20-22; August 13-20, 1990, pp. 175-76.
National Observer, December 22, 1969.
National Review, August 6, 1990. p. 44.
Newsweek, July 23, 1990, p. 19.
New Republic, September 6, 1982, pp. 28-30.
New York Times, June 21, 1990.
New York Times Book Review, May 24, 1975, p. 10; October 21, 1984, pp. 37-38; June 24, 1990, pp. 1, 26-27.
Saturday Review, September 13, 1969.
Time, August 1, 1969; June 25, 1990, p. 69.
Washington Post Book World, August 15, 1982, p. 7; November 25, 1984, pp. 4, 6; July 8, 1990, pp. 1, 9.

—*Sketch by Kenneth R. Shepherd*

* * *

PILKEY, Orrin H. 1934-

PERSONAL: Born September 19, 1934, in New York, NY; son of Orrin H. and Elizabeth (Street) Pilkey; married Sharlene Greenaa (a researcher), December 31, 1956; children: Charles, Linda, Diane, Keith, Kerry. *Education:* Washington State University, B.S., 1957; Montana State University, M.S., 1959; Florida State University, Ph.D., 1962.

ADDRESSES: Home—3303 Highway 70 E, Hillsborough, NC 27278. *Office*—Department of Geology, Duke University, Old Chemistry Bldg., Durham, NC 27706. *Agent*—Virginia Barber Literary Agency, Inc., 44 Greenwich Ave., New York, NY 10011.

CAREER: University of Georgia, Athens, research associate at Marine Lab and assistant professor of geology, 1962-65; Duke University, Durham, NC, assistant professor of geology, 1965-67, associate professor of geology, 1967-75, professor of geology, 1975-83, James B. Duke professor of geology, 1983—. Visiting professor at University of Puerto Rico, Mayaguez, 1972-73. Research geologist with U.S. Geological Survey, 1975-76. Co-producer of PBS-Television documentary *The Beaches Are Moving,* 1990. *Military service:* U.S. Army; became captain.

MEMBER: International Association of Sedimentologists, American Association of Petroleum Geologists, American Association for the Advancement of Science (fellow, 1983), Association of Earth Science Editors, Society for Sedimentary Geology, Geological Society of America, Explorers Club, North Carolina Academy of Science (President, 1982), Sigma Xi.

AWARDS, HONORS: Francis Shepard medal, 1987, for excellence in marine geology; Conservation Educator of the Year, North Carolina Wildlife Federation, 1991.

WRITINGS:

(With D. J. P. Swift and D. B. Duane, and editor) *Shelf Sediment Transport, Process and Pattern,* Dowden, Hutchinson and Ross, Inc., 1972.
(With father, Orrin H. Pilkey, Sr., and Robb Turner) *How to Live With an Island,* North Carolina Scientific and Technical Research Center, 1975.

"LIVING WITH THE SHORE" SERIES

(With O. H. Pilkey, Sr., and William J. Neal) *From Currituck to Calabash,* North Carolina Scientific and Technical Research Center, 1978.
(With W. Kaufman) *The Beaches Are Moving; The Drowning of America's Shoreline,* Doubleday, 1979.
(With R. Morton and W. J. Neal) *Living With the Texas Shore,* Duke University Press, 1983.
(With Sharma Dinesh, H. Wanless, L. J. Doyle, W. J. Neal, and B. Gruver) *Living with the East Florida Shore,* Duke University Press, 1984.
(With W. J. Neal and C. Blakeney) *Living with the South Carolina Shore,* Duke University Press, 1984.
(With L. J. Doyle et al) *Living with the West Florida Shore,* Duke University Press, 1984.
(With J. R. Kelley, A. R. Kelley, and A. A. Clark) *Living with the Louisiana Shore,* Duke University Press, 1984.
(With L. R. McCormick, W. J. Neal, and O. H. Pilkey, Sr.) *Living with Long Island's South Shore,* Duke University Press, 1984.
(With W. F. Canis, W. J. Neal, and O. H. Pilkey, Sr.) *Living with the Mississippi-Alabama Shore,* Duke University Press, 1985.
(With K. F. Nordstrom et al) *Living with the New Jersey Shore,* Duke University Press, 1986.
(With C. Carter et al) *Living with the Lake Erie Shore,* Duke University Press, 1987.
(With J. T. Kelley and A. R. Kelley) *Living with the Coast of Maine,* Duke University Press, 1989.
(With Larry G. Ward, Peter S. Rosen, W. J. Neal, O. H. Pilkey, Sr., Gary L. Anderson, and Stephen J. Howie) *Living with Chesapeake Bay and Virginia's Ocean Shore,* Duke University Press, 1989.

Also coeditor with W. J. Neal of *Living with the California Coast, Living with the Connecticut Coast, Living with the*

Georgia Shore, and *Living with Puget Sound and Georgia Straight.*

Editor of *Journal of Sedimentary Petrology* (1978-83); associate editor of *Marine Geology, Journal of Coastal Research,* and *Geology.* Author or co-author of over 150 articles for scholarly journals and periodicals.

SIDELIGHTS: Pilkey told *CA:* "My primary motivation is the need for public education concerning the interaction of man and nature at the shoreline."

*   *   *

PLISCHKE, Elmer 1914-

PERSONAL: Born July 15, 1914, in Milwaukee, WI; son of Louis J. W. and Louise (Peterleus) Plischke; married Audrey Alice Siehr, May 30, 1941; children: Lowell, Julianne. *Education:* Marquette University, Ph.B. (cum laude), 1937; American University, M.A., 1938; University of Michigan, certificate from Carnegie Summer Session in International Law, 1938; Clark University, Ph.D., 1943; Columbia University, certificate from Naval School of Military Government and Administration, 1944.

ADDRESSES: Home—227 Ewell Ave., Gettysburg, PA 17325.

CAREER: Springfield College, Springfield, MA, instructor, 1940; Wisconsin Historical Records Survey, district supervisor, 1940-42, state director, 1942; executive secretary, Wisconsin War Records Commission of the Wisconsin State Council of Defense, 1942; DePauw University, Greencastle, IN, assistant professor, 1946-48; University of Maryland, College Park, assistant professor, 1948-49, associate professor, 1949-52, professor of government and politics, 1952-79, professor emeritus, 1979—, head of department, 1954-68; Gettysburg College, Gettysburg, PA, adjunct professor of political science, 1979-86. Guest professor, Goucher College, spring, 1971, and U.S. Army War College, spring, 1972, fall, 1973; adjunct scholar, American Enterprise Institute, 1978—. Special historian, Office of the U.S. High Commissioner for Germany, 1950-52. Chairman of several conferences on politics. Consultant, U.S. Department of State, 1952. *Military service:* U.S. Naval Reserve, 1943-46; became lieutenant.

MEMBER: American Association of University Professors, American Political Science Association (member of council, 1958-60), American Society of International Law, Committee for the Study of Diplomacy (charter member), Southern Political Science Association (member of executive council, 1961-64), Northeast Political Science Association, Pennsylvania Political Science Association, District of Columbia Political Science Association

(former member of council; president, 1962), Phi Kappa Phi, Pi Sigma Alpha, Sigma Tau Delta, Phi Beta Kappa.

AWARDS, HONORS: Eliza D. Dodd and Henry White Field research fellowships, 1940-41; University of Maryland Research Board grants, 1957, 1958, and 1969; Recognition Award, Pi Sigma Alpha, 1966; Earhart Foundation fellowship research grant, 1982-83, for study on the president as diplomat-in-chief, and 1985-86, for study of analysis of the anatomy of foreign relations; Plischke was honored by establishment of the Elmer Plischke Award in Political Science to be awarded annually by the Munich Center of the University of Maryland.

WRITINGS:

History of the Allied High Commission for Germany, Office of the U.S. High Commissioner for Germany, 1951.

Revision of the Occupation Statute for Germany, Office of the U.S. High Commissioner for Germany, 1952.

Allied High Commission Relations with the West German Government, Office of the U.S. High Commissioner for Germany, 1952.

The West German Federal Government, Office of the U.S. High Commissioner for Germany, 1952.

Berlin: Development of Its Government and Administration, Office of the U.S. High Commissioner for Germany, 1952, reprinted, Greenwood Press, 1970.

(With Henry Pilgert) *United States Information Programs in Berlin,* Office of the U.S. High Commissioner for Germany, 1953.

The Allied High Commission for Germany, Office of the U.S. High Commissioner for Germany, 1953.

American Foreign Relations: A Bibliography of Official Sources, Bureau of Governmental Research, University of Maryland, 1955.

American Diplomacy: A Bibliography of Biographies, Autobiographies, and Commentaries, Bureau of Governmental Research, University of Maryland, 1957.

Summit Diplomacy: Personal Diplomacy of the President of the United States, Bureau of Governmental Research, University of Maryland, 1958, reprinted, Greenwood Press, 1974.

(Author of foreword) Elber M. Byrd, Jr., *Treaties and Executive Agreements in the United States,* Nijhoff, 1960.

(Author of foreword) E. Wilder Spaulding, *Ambassadors Ordinary and Extraordinary,* Public Affairs Press, 1961.

Government and Politics of Contemporary Berlin, Nijhoff, 1963.

(Editor and contributor) *Systems of Integrating the International Community,* Van Nostrand, 1964.

(Author of foreword) David B. Michaels, *International Privileges and Immunities,* Nijhoff, 1971.

(Author of foreword) Lee H. Burke, *Ambassador at Large: Diplomat Extraordinary,* Nijhoff, 1972.

Foreign Relations Decision Making: Options Analysis, Institute of Middle Eastern and North African Affairs, 1973.

United States Diplomats and Their Missions: A Profile of American Diplomatic Emissaries since 1778, American Enterprise Institute, 1975.

Microstates in World Affairs: Policy Problems and Options, American Enterprise Institute, 1977.

Neutralization as an American Strategic Option, Strategic Studies Institute, U.S. Army War College, 1978.

(Author of foreword) Robert Ghobad Irani, *American Diplomacy: An Options Analysis of the Azerbaijan Crisis, 1945-1946,* Institute of Middle Eastern and North African Affairs, 1978.

Modern Diplomacy: The Art and the Artisans, American Enterprise Institute, 1979.

Conduct of United States Foreign Relations: A Guide to Information Sources, Gale, 1980.

Presidential Diplomacy: A Chronology of Summit Visits, Trips, and Meetings, Oceana, 1985.

Diplomat-in-Chief: The President at the Summit, Praeger, 1986.

Foreign Relations: Analysis of Its Anatomy, Greenwood Press, 1988.

Contemporary U.S. Foreign Policy: Documents and Commentary, Greenwood Press, 1991.

TEXTBOOKS

(Compiler with Robert G. Dixon, Jr.) *American Government: Basic Documents and Materials,* Van Nostrand, 1950, reprinted, Greenwood Press, 1971.

Conduct of American Diplomacy, Van Nostrand, 1950, 3rd edition, 1967.

International Relations: Basic Documents, Van Nostrand, 1953, 2nd edition, 1962.

Contemporary Governments of Germany, Houghton, 1961, revised edition, 1969.

OTHER

Also author of *Conduct of United States Foreign Relations,* U.S. Army War College. Contributor to numerous books, including *Inventory of the City Archives of Wisconsin: City of Wauwatosa,* Wisconsin Historical Records Survey, 1942; *European Politics I: The Restless Search,* by William G. Andrews, Van Nostrand, 1966; *Selected Readings in International Relations,* U.S. Naval War College, 1972; and *Americans as Proconsuls: United States Military Government in Germany and Japan, 1944-1952,* edited by Robert Wolfe, Illinois University Press, 1984. Contributor of thirty articles of encyclopedias. Contributor of eighty articles to periodicals. Editor, *Style Manual,* 1957; member of editorial board, *Journal of Politics,* 1966-68, and *Commonwealth: A Journal of Political Science,* 1987—.

SIDELIGHTS: Elmer Plischke once told *CA,* "To maintain a flow of scholarly interest and production—aside from the generation of ideas and the refinement of treatment and craftsmanship—it is essential to identify and frame the parameters of the subject of each inquiry, to define one's objectives, sources, and readership for each research and publication venue, to cultivate qualities of dedication and self-discipline, and to establish and maintain a managed program and momentum."

BIOGRAPHICAL/CRITICAL SOURCES:

BOOKS

Piper, Don C. and Ronald J. Terchek, editors, *Interaction: Foreign Policy and Public Policy,* American Enterprise Institute, 1983.

*   *   *

POET OF TITCHFIELD STREET, The
See POUND, Ezra (Weston Loomis)

*   *   *

POIRIER, Richard   1925-

PERSONAL: Born September 9, 1925, in Gloucester, MA; son of Philip (a fisherman) and Annie Veronica (a housewife; maiden name, Kiley) Poirier. *Education:* Attended University of Paris, 1944-45; Amherst College, B.A., 1949; Yale University, M.A., 1951; Harvard University, Ph.D., 1960. *Politics:* Democrat. *Avocational interests:* Travel, film, ballet, New York City.

ADDRESSES: Office—*Raritan Quarterly,* 31 Mine St., New Brunswick, NJ 08903.

CAREER: Williams College, Williamstown, MA, instructor, 1950-52; Harvard University, Cambridge, MA, instructor, 1958-60, assistant professor of English, 1960-63; Rutgers University, New Brunswick, NJ, Marius Bewley Professor of American and English Literature, 1963—, chairman of department, 1963-72, director of graduate studies, 1970—; *Raritan: A Quarterly Review,* New Brunswick, NJ, founder and editor, 1981—. Stanford University, member of faculty, summer, 1961; University of Leicester, Sir George Watson Lecturer, 1974; University of California, Berkeley, Beckman Lecturer, 1976; Stanford University, Harry Camp Lecturer, 1987; Princeton University, Gauss Seminars Lecturer, 1990; University of Kent, T. S. Eliot Memorial Lecturer, 1991; New York University, Henry James Lecturer, 1992. Has lectured throughout the United States, England, Germany, and Japan.

Literary Classics of the United States (publisher of Library of America), co-founder, 1983, chairman of board, 1983—; chair of advisory committee on English, Harvard University, 1988—. Past director, English Institute and National Book Critics Circle; past member of nominating committee for National Medal for Literature. Consultant to National Public Radio. *Military service:* U.S. Army, 1943-46; served in infantry in European Theater.

MEMBER: American Academy of Arts and Sciences, Phi Beta Kappa, Century Club.

AWARDS, HONORS: Fulbright scholar, Cambridge University, 1952-53; Bollingen Foundation grant, 1962-63; Guggenheim Foundation grant, 1974-75; Doctor of Humane Letters (honorary), Amherst College, 1978; National Endowment for the Humanities grant, 1978-79; achievement award in literary criticism, American Academy and Institute of Arts and Letters, 1979; Jay B. Hubbell Award, 1988, for contributions to American criticism.

WRITINGS:

The Comic Sense of Henry James, Oxford University Press, 1960.
(Editor with Reuben A. Brower) *In Defense of Reading,* Dutton, 1962.
A World Elsewhere: The Place of Style in American Literature, Oxford University Press, 1966, reprinted, University of Wisconsin Press, 1989.
The Performing Self: Compositions and Decompositions in Languages of Contemporary Life, Oxford University Press, 1970, reprinted, Rutgers University Press, 1991.
(Editor with W. L. Vance) *American Literature,* two volumes, Little, Brown, 1970.
(Editor with Frank Kermode) *The Oxford Reader,* Oxford University Press, 1971.
Norman Mailer, Viking, 1972.
Robert Frost: The Work of Knowing, Oxford University Press, 1978, new edition, Stanford University Press, 1989.
(Editor) *Raritan Reading,* Rutgers University Press, 1990.
The Oxford Author's Ralph Waldo Emerson, Oxford University Press, 1990.
The Renewal of Literature: Emersonian Reflections, Random House, 1987.
Poetry and Pragmatism, Harvard University Press, 1992.

Contributor to *William Faulkner: Two Decades of Criticism,* University of Michigan Press, 1951. Editor of annual *Prize Stories: The O. Henry Awards,* Doubleday, 1959-64, with William Abrahams, 1965-66. Contributor to numerous periodicals, including *London Review of Books, New Republic, New York Times Book Review, Nineteenth-Century Fiction, Daedalus, Yale Review,* and *Harper's.* Co-

editor, *Partisan Review,* 1962-71; member of editorial board, *PMLA,* 1977-79.

WORK IN PROGRESS: A study of "genuis."

BIOGRAPHICAL/CRITICAL SOURCES:

PERIODICALS

Commentary, October, 1967.
National Review, March 9, 1967; May 15, 1971.
New Leader, May 17, 1971.
New Republic, May 1, 1971.
New Statesman, May 12, 1967.
New York Review, March 9, 1967.
New York Times, October 16, 1972; October 5, 1977.
South Atlantic Quarterly, autumn, 1967.
Times Literary Supplement, May 18, 1967.
Yale Review, spring, 1967.

*   *   *

POLLOCK, John (Charles)   1923-

PERSONAL: Born October 9, 1923, in London, England; son of Robert (a lawyer) and Ethel (Powell) Pollock; married Anne Barrett-Lennard, May 4, 1949. *Education:* Attended Charterhouse, Godalming, England, and Ridley Hall, Cambridge; Trinity College, Cambridge, B.A., 1946, M.A., 1948. *Avocational interests:* Walking in the mountains and moorland, tennis.

ADDRESSES: Home—Rose Ash House, South Molton, Devonshire EX36 4RB, England.

CAREER: Writer. Wellington College, Berkshire, England, assistant master of history and divinity, 1947-49; ordained Anglican deacon, 1951, priest, 1952; St. Paul's Church, Portman Square, London, England, curate, 1951-53; Horsington, Somerset, England, rector, 1953-58. *Military service:* British Army, Coldstream Guards, 1943-45; became captain.

MEMBER: English Speaking Union Club.

WRITINGS:

Candidate for Truth, Church Book Room Press, 1950.
A Cambridge Movement, J. Murray, 1953.
The Cambridge Seven, Inter-Varsity Press, 1955, revised edition, Marshall Pickering, 1985.
Way to Glory (biography of Havelock of Lucknow), J. Murray, 1957.
Shadows Fall Apart (story of Zenana Bible and medical mission in India), Hodder & Stoughton, 1958.
The Good Seed (story of the Scripture Union), Hodder & Stoughton, 1959.
Earth's Remotest End, Hodder & Stoughton, 1960, Macmillan, 1961.

Hudson Taylor and Maria, McGraw, 1962, reprinted, Kingsway Publications, 1983.

Moody, Macmillan, 1963, revised edition, Moody, 1984 (published in England as *Moody without Sankey,* Hodder & Stoughton, 1963).

The Keswick Story, Moody, 1964.

The Faith of the Russian Evangelicals, McGraw, 1964 (published in England as *The Christians from Siberia,* Hodder & Stoughton, 1964), published as *Faith and Freedom in Russia,* Zondervan, 1971.

Billy Graham, McGraw, 1966, revised edition, World Wide Publications, 1969.

The Apostle: A Life of Paul, Doubleday, 1969, revised edition, Victor Books, 1985.

Victims of the Long March, Word Books, 1970.

A Foreign Devil in China: The Life of Nelson Bell, Zondervan, 1971, new edition, World Wide Publications, 1988.

George Whitefield and the Great Awakening, Hodder & Stoughton, 1972, Doubleday, 1973.

Wilberforce, Constable, 1977, St. Martin's, 1978, new edition, Lion, 1988.

Billy Graham: Evangelist to the World, Harper, 1979.

The Siberian Seven, Hodder & Stoughton, 1979, Word Books, 1980.

Amazing Grace: John Newton's Story, Harper, 1981.

The Master: A Life of Jesus, Hodder & Stoughton, 1984, new edition with foreword by Charles W. Colson, Victor Books, 1985, new edition, 1992.

Billy Graham: Highlights of the Story, Marshall Pickering, 1984, published as *To All the Nations: The Billy Graham Story,* Harper, 1985.

Shaftesbury: The Poor Man's Earl, Hodder & Stoughton, 1985, Lion, 1986.

A Fistful of Heroes: Great Reformers and Evangelists, Marshall Pickering, 1988.

John Wesley, Victor Books, 1989.

On Fire for God: Great Missionary Pioneers, Marshall Pickering, 1990.

Fear No Foe: A Brother's Story, Hodder & Stoughton, 1992.

Gordon: The Man behind the Legend, Constable & Co., in press.

Contributor to *New International Dictionary of the Christian Church,* edited by J. D. Douglas, Zondervan, 1974; *Great Leaders of the Christian Church,* edited by John D. Woodbridge, Moody, 1988; and *More Than Conquerors,* edited by Woodbridge, Moody, 1992. Contributor to religion journals. Editor, *Churchman,* 1953-58; contributing editor, *Christianity Today.*

SIDELIGHTS: John Pollock told *CA:* "Using manuscript sources and on-the-spot research, with the resources of modern scholarship to ensure accuracy, I seek by a strong narrative style to reach the general reader with historical biography.

"I aim to tell how God takes ordinary men and women of the past and present (sometimes most unlikely characters) and transforms them to be Christian leaders in their generation.

"I seek to get inside a character so that the reader comes to know him as a friend. I try not to get between the subject and the reader by tiresome comment and analysis but to let the story tell itself."

BIOGRAPHICAL/CRITICAL SOURCES:

PERIODICALS

Baptist Timees, March 5, 1992.
Church of England Newspaper, June 12, 1992.
Los Angeles Times Book Review, June 17, 1979.

*   *   *

PONGE, Francis (Jean Gaston Alfred) 1899-1988

PERSONAL: Surname is pronounced "ponzh"; born March 27, 1899, in Montpellier, France; died August 6 (some sources say August 7), 1988, in Le Bar-sur-Loup, France; son of Armand (a bank director) and Juliette (Saurel) Ponge; married Odette Chabanel, July 4, 1931; children: Armande. *Education:* Educated in France.

CAREER: Poet and essayist. Editions Gallimard (publisher), Paris, France, secretary, 1923; Hachette (publisher), Paris, secretary, 1931-37; Progress de Lyon, Bourg-en-Bresse, France, head of center, 1942; Alliance Francaise, Paris, professor, 1952-64. Editor of *Progres* (newspaper), Lyon, France. Political traveler for National Committee of Journalists, 1942-44; literary and artistic director of *Action,* 1944-46; Virginia C. Gildersleeve Visiting Professor at Barnard College and Columbia University, 1966-67. Lecturer in France and abroad. *Military service:* Member of French Resistance during World War II.

MEMBER: Bayerischen Akademie der Schoenen Kuenste, American Academy and Institute of Arts and Letters (honorary member).

AWARDS, HONORS: International Poetry Prize, 1959; Ingram Merrill Foundation award, 1972; Grand Prize for Poetry from French Academy, 1972; Books Abroad Neustadt International Prize for Literature, 1974; French National Poetry Prize, 1981; Grand Prize from Societe de Glees de Lettres, 1985; became officer and commander in French Legion of Honor.

WRITINGS:

IN ENGLISH

Le Parti pris des choses (poetry), Gallimard, 1942, revised edition, 1949, translation by Beth Archer published as *The Voice of Things,* McGraw, 1972.

Le Savon (poetry), Gallimard, 1967, translation by Lane Dunlop published as *Soap,* J. Cape, 1969.

Two Prose Poems, translated from the French by Peter Hoy, Black Knight Press, 1968.

Rain: A Prose Poem, translated from the French by Peter Hoy, Poet & Printer, 1969.

Things, translation by Cid Corman, Grossman, 1971, published as *Things: Selected Writings of Francis Ponge,* White Pine, 1986.

(With Pierre Descargues and Andre Malraux) *G. Braque, de Draeger,* Draeger, 1971, translation by Richard Howard and Lane Dunlop published as *G. Braque,* Abrams, 1971.

La Fabrique du "pre," Albert Skira, 1971, translation by Lee Fahnestock published as *The Making of the "Pre,"* University of Missouri Press, 1979.

The Sun Placed in the Abyss and Other Texts, translation by Serge Gavronsky, SUN, 1977.

The Power of Language: Texts and Translations, translation by Serge Gavronsky, University of California Press, 1979.

Vegetation, translation by Lee Fahnestock, Red Dust, 1987.

OTHER

L'Oeillet, le guepe, le mimose (poetry), Mermod, 1946.

Le Carnet du bois de pins, Mermod, 1947.

Liasse: Vingt-et-un Textes suivis d'une bibliographie, Ecrivains reunis, 1948.

Le Peintre a l'etude, Gallimard, 1948.

Proemes, Gallimard, 1948.

Germaine Richier, Adrien Maeght, 1948.

La Seine, Guilde du livre, 1950.

La Rage de l'expression, Mermod, 1952, Schoenhof, 1976.

Le Grand Recueil, Volume I: *Lyres,* Volume II: *Methodes,* Volume III: *Pieces,* Gallimard, 1961; revised edition, 1976-78.

Francis Ponge, edited by Philippe Sollers, P. Seghers, 1963.

De la nature morte et de Chardin, Hermann, 1964.

Pour un Malherbe, Gallimard, 1965.

Tome premier, Gallimard, 1965.

Nouveau Recueil, Gallimard, 1967.

Ponge, edited by Jean Thibaudeau, Gallimard, 1967.

Le Parti pris des choses, precede de douze petits ecrits et suivi de proemes, Gallimard, 1967.

Entretiens de Francis Ponge avec Philippe Sollers, edited by Sollers, Gallimard, 1970.

Ici haute, R. G. Cadou, 1971.

(With Pierre Descargues and Edward Quinn) *Picasso de Draeger,* Draeger, 1974.

(Contributor) *A Phillipe Jaccottet,* La Revue de belles-lettres, 1976.

Abrege de l'aventure organique: Developpement d'un detail de celle-ci, R. Dirieux, 1976.

L'Atelier contemporain, Gallimard, 1977.

Ponge: Inventeur et classique, Union generale d'editions, 1977.

Comment une figue de paroles et pourquoi, Flammarion, 1977.

L'Ecrit Beaubourg, Centre Pompidou, 1977.

Nioque de l'avant-printemps, Gallimard, 1983.

Petite suite vivaraise, Fata Morgana, 1983.

Dix poemes, Greenwood Press, 1983.

Pratiques d'ecriture; ou, L'Inachevement perpetuel, Hermann, 1984.

Also author of *Douze Petits Ecrits,* 1926; *La Crevette dans tous ses etats,* 1948; *L'Araignee,* 1952; *Nous mots francais,* 1978; *Souvenirs interrompus,* 1979; *Tombeaux et hommages divers 1980,* 1981; (with Jean Paulhan) *Correspondance, 1923-1968,* 1984; *La Table,* 1983; *La Facon de faner des tulipes, des etrangetes naturelles,* 1983; *Des cristaux naturels,* P. Bettencourt. Contributor of poems and essays to literary journals.

SIDELIGHTS: Francis Ponge has been called "the poet of things" because simple objects like a plant, a shell, a cigarette, a pebble, or a piece of soap are the subjects of his prose poems. For Ponge, all objects "yearn to express themselves, and they mutely await the coming of the word so that they may reveal the hidden depths of their being," as Richard Stamelman explained it in *Books Abroad.* "What has an imperious fascination for [Ponge]," observed Betty Miller of the late poet, "is the essence of the interior life of the plant or shell, so that we feel in reading him almost as though it were the plant which spoke to express miraculously, without human intervention, its personality." Robert Bly noted in the *Georgia Review* that Ponge's prose poems also exposed the hidden relationship between the inner life of human beings and the world of objects. "It is as if," Bly wrote, "the object itself, a stump or an orange, has links with the human psyche, and the unconscious provides material it would not give if asked directly. The unconscious passes into the object and returns."

Throughout his forty-five year writing career, Ponge was faithful to his unique approach to poetic subject. Speaking of the poet's collected works, Sarah N. Lawall in *Contemporary Literature* found that "what Ponge has to say remains quite consistent, and his collected works juxtapose texts from 1921 to 1967 without any contradiction whatsoever. He still goes to the 'mute world' of things for his peculiar dialectic, and he still celebrates the creative power of speech." Lawall found, too, that Ponge's work served as an "example of systematically *individual* perception and expression in a world threatened by group morality and intellectual totalitarianism."

Perhaps the most obsessive example of Ponge's approach is to be found in his collection *Le Savon,* translated as *Soap.* In this collection, each prose poem considers a different aspect of the life of a bar of soap, detailing each one from the soap's perspective. When used for washing, the soap becomes sudsy with joyous exuberance; when left alone, it grows hard, dry and cracked. In addition, Ponge makes clear to the reader that their shared experience in the text has been nothing more than a linguistic experience having nothing to do with the object ostensibly being discussed. As Lawall explained, Ponge "develops a series of comparisons to show how the reader's pleasure has come from his sense of playing a game, that the extreme form of this game is 'poetry, the purely verbal game which neither imitates nor represents "life,"' and that 'words and figures of speech' resemble other human concoctions like bread, soap, and electricity."

This close relationship between Ponge's poems and the objects they discuss is also noted by other critics. Michael Benedikt, writing in *The Prose Poem: An International Anthology,* concluded that Ponge's poems are "as 'objective' as objects in the world themselves." Robert W. Greene, in his book *Six French Poets of Our Time: A Critical and Historical Study,* argued that in many of his poems, Ponge tries "to create a verbal machine that will have as much local intricacy as its counterpart in the world of objects." Stamelman went even further in analyzing this relationship. "In Ponge's poetry," he wrote, "the text refers to itself and to itself alone. . . . The only thing the text 'represents' is its own surging into being through language, its own act of expression. Ultimately, the text signifies itself."

Ponge's prose poems follow no set formula. They develop instead in a seemingly spontaneous manner, following a meandering path to their completion. "Ponge may be the first poet," James Merrill wrote in the *New York Review of Books,* "ever to expose so openly the machinery of a poem, to present his revisions, blind alleys, critical asides, and accidental felicities as part of a text perfected, as it were, without 'finish' ". Greene acknowledged that Ponge's "texts hardly conform to most conceptions of what poems, even prose poems, are or should be. They contain puns, false starts, repetitions, agendas, recapitulations, syllogistic overtones, a heavy ideological content, and other features that one normally associates with prose—and the prose of argumentation at that—rather than with poetry."

"Francis Ponge, compared to Valery, is a minor poet," John Weightman observed in *Encounter,* "but a very charming one, who has made it his business for the last fifty years to compose prose poems about objects, any objects—a glass of water, an open door, a wasp, a piece of soap, etc. The point about this, of course, is that for someone with what we might call an Existentialist sensibility, there are no privileged objects, as there were in traditional poetry. . . . This is because everything outside the consciousness is object, and the lyrical emotion can be engendered by establishing a sufficiently subtle linguistic web between the sense-perceptions relating to any particular object and the rest of the consciousness." Similarly, Bly concluded that "Ponge doesn't try to be cool, distant, or objective, nor does he 'let the object speak for itself.' His poems are funny, his vocabulary immense, his personality full of quirks, and yet the poem remains somewhere in the place where the senses join the object." Benedikt noted that, "with Michaux, Ponge is regarded as one of the most significant mid-century French poets."

BIOGRAPHICAL/CRITICAL SOURCES:

BOOKS

Aspel, Alexander and D. R. Justice, editors, *Contemporary French Poetry: Fourteen Witnesses of Man's Fate,* University of Michigan, 1965.
Benedikt, Michael, editor, *The Prose Poem: An International Anthology,* Dell, 1976, pp. 590-591.
Contemporary Literary Criticism, Gale, Volume 6, 1976, Volume 18, 1981.
Greene, Robert W., *Six French Poets of Our Time: A Critical and Historical Study,* Princeton University Press, 1979, pp. 59-98.
Higgins, Ian, *Ponge,* Athlone Press, 1979.
Sorrell, Martin, *Ponge,* Twayne, 1981.
Willard, Nancy, *Testimony of the Invisible Man: William Carlos Williams, Ponge, Rainer Maria Rilke, Pablo Neruda,* University of Missouri Press, 1970.

PERIODICALS

American Poetry Review, January, 1984, p. 40.
Books Abroad, autumn, 1974, pp. 688-694, 715-717.
Book World, March 12, 1978.
Contemporary Literature, winter, 1970, pp. 192-216.
Encounter, December, 1970.
Georgia Review, spring, 1980, pp. 105-109.
Hudson Review, spring, 1973, p. 192.
L'Esprit, summer, 1980, p. 84.
Listener, August 28, 1969, p. 285.
Modern Language Review, April, 1981, p. 481.
National Observer, December 18, 1971.
New York Review of Books, November 30, 1972, pp. 31-34.
New York Times, October 28, 1971, p. 39; October 30, 1971, p. 39.

Nouvelle Revue Francaise, September, 1956.
Observer, June 8, 1969, p. 27.
Parnassus: Poetry in Review, spring/summer, 1973, pp. 60-68.
Prairie Schooner, spring, 1975, p. 90; winter, 1978, p. 425.
Time, December 20, 1971, p. 90.
Times Literary Supplement, May 4, 1962; September 30, 1965, p. 866; May 18, 1967, p. 420; September 12, 1968, p. 1022; August 28, 1969, p. 959; August 5, 1983, p. 840.
World Literature Today, autumn, 1974; spring, 1978; spring, 1978, p. 256; autumn, 1978, p. 594; spring, 1980, p. 256.

OBITUARIES:

PERIODICALS

Chicago Tribune, August 10, 1988.
New York Times, August 9, 1988.
Times (London), August 11, 1988.
Washington Post, August 10, 1988.*

*   *   *

POUND, Ezra (Weston Loomis)   1885-1972 (William Atheling, The Poet of Titchfield Street, Alfred Venison)

PERSONAL: Born October 30, 1885, in Hailey, Idaho; died November 1, 1972, in Venice, Italy; buried in San Michele Cemetery on the island of San Giorgio Maggiore, Italy; son of Homer Loomis (a mine inspector in Idaho, later an assayer at the Philadelphia mint) and Isabel (Weston) Pound; married Dorothy Shakespear, 1914; lived with Olga Rudge for 12 years; children: Omar Shakespear, Mary Rachewilz. *Education:* Attended University of Pennsylvania, 1901-03; Hamilton College, Ph.B., 1905; University of Pennsylvania, fellow in Romantics, received M.A,, 1906.

CAREER: Writer, poet, critic. Wabash College, Crawfordsville, Ind., lecturer in French and Spanish, 1906; Regent Street Polytechnic Institute, London, England, teacher of literature; foreign correspondent in London for *Poetry* (Chicago), 1912-19; associated with H. L. Mencken's *Smart Set;* W. B. Yeats's unofficial secretary in Sussex, England, 1913-16; unofficial literary executor for Ernest Fenollosa, London, 1914; member of the editorial staff of *Mercure de France,* Paris, and of the British publications, *Egoist* and *Cerebralist;* founder, with Wyndham Lewis, of the Vorticist magazine, *BLAST!,* 1914; London editor of *The Little Review,* 1917-19; left London, 1921, and settled in Paris; Paris correspondent for *The Dial,* 1922; moved to Rapallo, Italy, 1925; founder and editor of *The Exile,* 1927-28; radio broadcaster in Rome until

1945; arrested by the U.S. Army in 1945 and charged with treason; after being declared insane and unfit to stand trial for his life, committed to St. Elizabeths Hospital, Washington, D.C., until 1958; lived in Italy, 1958-72.

AWARDS, HONORS: Honorary degree from Hamilton College, 1939; *Dial* Award for distinguished service to American letters; Bollingen Library of Congress Award, 1949, for *The Pisan Cantos;* Academy of American Poets fellowship, 1963.

WRITINGS:

POETRY

A Lume Spento (also see below), privately printed in Venice by A. Antonini, 1908.
A Quinzaine for This Yule, Pollock (London), 1908.
Personae, Elkin Mathews (London), 1909.
Exultations, Elkin Mathews, 1909.
Provenca, Small, Maynard (Boston), 1910.
Canzoni, Elkin Mathews, 1911.
Ripostes of Ezra Pound, S. Swift (London), 1912, Small, Maynard, 1913.
Personae and Exultations of Ezra Pound, [London], 1913.
Canzoni and Ripostes of Ezra Pound, Elkin Mathews, 1913.
Lustra of Ezra Pound, Elkin Mathews, 1916, Knopf, 1917.
Quia Pauper Amavi, Egoist Press (London), 1918.
The Fourth Canto, Ovid Press (London), 1919.
(And translations) *Umbra,* Elkin Mathews, 1920.
Hugh Selwyn Mauberley, Ovid Press, 1920.
Poems, 1918-1921, Boni & Liveright, 1921.
A Draft of XVI Cantos, Three Mountains Press, 1925.
Personae: The Collected Poems of Ezra Pound, Boni & Liveright, 1926.
Selected Poems, edited and with an introduction by T. S. Eliot, Faber & Gwyer, 1928, Laughlin, 1957.
A Draft of the Cantos 17-27, John Rodker (London), 1928.
A Draft of XXX Cantos, Hours Press (Paris), 1930, Farrar & Rinehart, 1933.
Homage to Sextus Propertius, Faber, 1934.
Eleven New Cantos: XXXI-XLI, Farrar & Rinehart, 1934, published in England as *A Draft of Cantos XXXI-XLI,* Faber, 1935.
(Under pseudonym The Poet of Titchfield Street) *Alfred Venison's Poems: Social Credit Themes,* Nott (London), 1935.
The Fifth Decade of Cantos, Farrar & Rinehart, 1937.
Cantos LII-LXXI, New Directions, 1940.
A Selection of Poems, Faber, 1940.
The Pisan Cantos (also see below), New Directions, 1948.
The Cantos of Ezra Pound (includes *The Pisan Cantos*), New Directions, 1948, revised edition, Faber, 1954.
Selected Poems, New Directions, 1949.

Personnae: The Collected Poems of Ezra Pound, New Directions, 1950, published in England as *Personnae: Collected Shorter Poems,* Faber, 1952, new edition published as *Collected Shorter Poems,* Faber, 1968.

Seventy Cantos, Faber, 1950.

Section Rock-Drill, 85-95 de los Cantares, All'Insegna del Pesce d'Oro (Milan), 1955, New Directions, 1956.

Thrones: 96-109 de los Cantares, New Directions, 1959.

The Cantos (1-109), new edition, Faber, 1964.

The Cantos (1-95), New Directions, 1965.

A Lume Spento, and Other Early Poems, New Directions, 1965.

Selected Cantos, Faber, 1967.

Drafts and Fragments: Cantos CX-CXVII, New Directions, 1968.

From Syria: The Worksheets, Proofs, and Text, edited by Robin Skelton, Copper Canyon Press, 1981.

The Collected Early Poems of Ezra Pound, New Directions, 1982.

PROSE

The Spirit of Romance, Dent, 1910, New Directions, 1952, revised edition, P. Owen, 1953, reprinted, New Directions, 1968.

Gaudier-Brzeska: A Memoir Including the Published Writings of the Sculptor and a Selection from His Letters, John Lane, 1916, New Directions, 1961.

(With Ernest Fenollosa) *Noh; or, Accomplishment: A Study of the Classical Stage of Japan,* Macmillan (London), 1916, Knopf, 1917, published as *The Classic Noh Theatre of Japan,* New Directions, 1960.

Pavannes and Divisions, Knopf, 1918.

Instigations of Ezra Pound, Together with an Essay on the Chinese Written Character by Ernest Fenollosa, Boni & Liveright, 1920.

Indiscretions, Three Mountains Press (Paris), 1923.

(Under pseudonym William Atheling) *Antheil and the Treatise on Harmony,* Three Mountains Press, 1924, published under his own name, P. Covici, 1927, 2nd edition, Da Capo, 1968.

Imaginary Letters, Black Sun Press (Paris), 1930.

How to Read, Harmsworth, 1931.

ABC of Economics, Faber, 1933, New Directions, 1940, 2nd edition, Russell, 1953.

ABC of Reading, Yale University Press, 1934, New Directions, 1951, new edition, Faber, 1951.

Make It New, Faber, 1934, Yale University Press, 1935.

Social Credit: An Impact (pamphlet), Nott, 1935, reprinted, Revisionist Press, 1983.

Jefferson and/or Mussolini, Nott, 1935, Liveright, 1936.

Polite Essays, Faber, 1937, New Directions, 1940.

Culture, New Directions, 1938, new edition published as *Guide to Kulchur,* New Directions, 1952.

What is Money For?, Greater Britain Publications, 1939, published as *What Is Money For?: A Sane Man's Guide to Economics,* Revisionist Press, 1982.

Carla da Visita, Edizioni di Lettere d'Oggi (Rome), 1942, translation by John Drummond published as *A Visiting Card,* Russell, 1952, published as *A Visiting Card: Ancient and Modern History of Script and Money,* Revisionist Press, 1983.

L'America, Roosevelt e le Cause della Guerra Presente, Edizioni Popolari (Venice), 1944, translation by Drummond published as *America, Roosevelt and the Causes of the Present War,* Russell, 1951, reprinted, Revisionist Press, 1983.

Introduzione alla Natura Economica degli S.U.A., Edizioni Popolari, 1944, English translation by Carmine Amore published as *An Introduction to the Economic Nature of the United States,* Russell, 1958.

Oro e Lavoro, Tip. Moderna (Rapallo, Italy), 1944, translation by Drummond published as *Gold and Work,* Russell, 1952, reprinted, Revisionist Press, 1983.

Orientamenti, Edizioni Popolari, 1944.

"If This Be Treason . . . " (four original drafts of Rome radio broadcasts), privately printed for Olga Rudge, 1948.

The Letters of Ezra Pound, 1907-1941, edited by D. D. Paige, Harcourt, 1950.

Patria Mia (written in 1913), R. F. Seymour (Chicago), 1950 (published in England as *Patria Mia and The Treatise on Harmony,* Owen, 1962).

Literary Essays of Ezra Pound, edited and with an introduction by T. S. Eliot, New Directions, 1954.

Lavoro ed Usura, All'Insegna del Pesce d'Oro, 1954.

Brancusi, [Milan], 1957.

Pavannes and Divagations, New Directions, 1958.

Impact: Essays on Ignorance and the Decline of American Civilization, edited and with an introduction by Noel Stock, Regnery, 1960.

EP to LU: Nine Letters Written to Louis Untermeyer, edited by J. A. Robbins, Indiana University Press, 1963.

Pound/Joyce: The Letters of Ezra Pound to James Joyce, edited by Forrest Read, New Directions, 1967.

Selected Prose, 1909-1965, edited by William Cookson, New Directions, 1973.

Ezra Pound and Music: The Complete Criticism, edited by R. Murray Schafer, New Directions, 1977.

"Ezra Pound Speaking": Radio Speeches of World War II, edited by Leonard W. Doob, Greenwood Press, 1978.

Letters to Ibbotsom, 1935-1952, National Poetry Foundation, 1979.

Ezra Pound and the Visual Arts, edited by Harriet Zinnes, New Directions, 1980.

Letters to John Theobald, Black Swan Books, 1981.

Pound-Ford, the Story of a Literary Friendship: The Correspondence between Ezra Pound and Ford Madox Ford and Their Writings about Each Other, New Directions, 1982.

Ezra Pound and Dorothy Shakespear: Their Letters, 1909-1914, New Directions, 1984.

Pound-Lewis: The Letters of Ezra Pound and Wyndham Lewis, New Directions, 1985.

Selected Letters of Ezra Pound and Louis Zukofsky, New Directions, 1987.

Pound the Little Review: The Letters of Ezra Pound to Margaret Anderson, New Directions, 1988.

A Walking Tour in Southern France: Ezra Pound among the Troubadours, with introduction by Richard Sieburth, New Directions, 1992.

TRANSLATOR

The Sonnets and Ballate of Guido Cavalcanti, Small, Maynard (Boston), 1912, published as *Ezra Pound's Cavalcanti Poems* (includes "Mediaevalism" and "The Other Dimension," by Pound), New Directions, 1966.

(Contributor of translations) *Selections from Collection Yvette Guilbert,* [London], 1912.

Cathay, Elkin Mathews, 1915.

Certain Noh Plays of Japan, Cuala Press (Churchtown), 1916.

Remy de Gourmount, *The Natural Philosophy of Love,* Boni & Liveright 1922.

Confucius, *To Hio: The Great Learning,* University of Washington Bookstore, 1928.

Confucius: Digest of the Analects, edited and published by Giovanni Scheiwiller, 1937.

Odon Por, *Italy's Policy of Social Economics, 1930-1940,* Istituto Italiano D'Arti Grafiche (Bergamo, Milan and Rome), 1941.

(Translator into Italian, with Alberto Luchini) *Ta S'eu Dai Gaku Studio Integrale,* [Rapallo], 1942.

Confucius, *The Great Digest [and] The Unwobbling Pivot,* New Directions, 1951.

Confucius, *Analects,* Kasper & Horton (New York), 1951, published as *The Confucian Analects,* P. Owen, 1956, Square $ Series, 1957.

The Translations of Ezra Pound, edited by Hugh Kenner, New Directions, 1953, enlarged edition published as *Translations,* New Directions, 1963.

The Classic Anthology, Defined by Confucius, Harvard University Press, 1954.

Richard of St. Victor, *Pensieri sull'amore,* [Milan], 1956.

Enrico Pea, *Moscardino,* All' Insegna del Pesce d'Oro (Milan), 1956.

Sophocles, *Women of Tiachis* (play; produced in New York at Living Theatre, June 22, 1960), Spearman, 1956, New Directions, 1957.

Rimbaud, All' Insegna del Pesce d'Oro, 1957.

(With Noel Stock) *Love Poems of Ancient Egypt,* New Directions, 1962.

Also translator of *Twelve Dialogues of Fontenelle,* 1917, and (with Agnes Bedford) *The Troubadour Sings,* 1920.

EDITOR

(And contributor) *Des Imagistes* (anthology; published anonymously), A. & C. Boni, 1914.

(And contributor) *Catholic Anthology, 1914-1915,* Elkin Mathews, 1915.

Passages from the Letters of John Butler Yeats, Cuala Press, 1917.

Ernest Hemingway, *In Our Time,* Three Mountains Press, 1924.

The Collected Poems of Harry Crosby, Volume Four, Torchbearer, [Paris], 1931.

Guido Cavalcanti, *Rime,* Marsano (Genoa), 1932.

Profiles (anthology), [Milan], 1932.

(And contributor) *Active Anthology,* Faber, 1933.

Ernest Fenollosa, *The Chinese Written Character as a Medium for Poetry,* Square $ Series, 1935.

(With Marcella Spann) *Confucius to Cummings: An Anthology of Poetry,* New Directions, 1964.

OTHER

Contributor to *British Union Quarterly, Townsman, Hudson Review, National Review, New Age* (under the pseudonym Alfred Venison), and other periodicals. Also wrote the score for "Le Testament," a ballet and song recital based on the poem by Francois Villon, 1919-21, first produced in its entirety at Gian Carlo Menotti's Festival of Two Worlds, Spoleto, July 14, 1965; wrote opera, "Villon," in the early 1920s, portions performed in Paris, 1924, and broadcast on the B.B.C., 1931 and 1962; wrote an unfinished opera, "Cavalcanti"; composer of several short pieces for the violin; transcribed medieval troubadour songs.

SIDELIGHTS: Of all the major literary figures in the twentieth century, Ezra Pound has been the most controversial; he has also been one of modern poetry's most important contributors. In an introduction to the *Literary Essays of Ezra Pound,* T. S. Eliot declared that Pound "is more responsible for the twentieth-century revolution in poetry than is any other individual." Four decades later, Donald Hall reaffirmed in remarks collected in *Remembering Poets* that "Ezra Pound is the poet who, a thousand times more than any other man, has made modern poetry possible in English." The importance of Pound's contributions to the arts and to the revitalization of poetry early in this century has been widely acknowledged; yet in 1950, Hugh Kenner could claim in his groundbreaking study *The Poetry of Ezra Pound,* "There is no great contemporary writer who is less read than Ezra Pound." Pound never sought, nor had, a wide reading audience; his technical innovations and use of unconventional poetic materials often baffled even sympathetic readers. Early in his career, Pound aroused controversy because of his aesthetic views; later, because of his political views. For the greater part of this century, however, Pound devoted his energies to advancing the art of poetry and maintaining his aesthetic standards in the midst of extreme adversity.

In his article "How I Began," collected in *Literary Essays,* Pound claimed that as a youth he had resolved to "know more about poetry than any man living." In pursuit of this goal, he settled in London from 1908 to 1920, where he carved out a reputation for himself as a member of the literary avant-garde and a tenacious advocate of contemporary work in the arts. Through his criticism and translations, as well as in his own poetry, particularly in his *Cantos,* he explored poetic traditions from different cultures ranging from ancient Greece, China, and the continent, to current-day England and America. In *The Tale of the Tribe* Michael Bernstein observed that Pound "sought, long before the notion became fashionable, to break with the long tradition of Occidental ethnocentrism." In his efforts to develop new directions in the arts, he also promoted and supported such writers as James Joyce, T. S. Eliot and Robert Frost. The critic David Perkins, writing in *A History of Modern Poetry,* summarized Pound's enormous influence: "The least that can be claimed of his poetry is that for over fifty years he was one of the three or four best poets writing in English"; and, Perkins continues, his "achievement in and for poetry was threefold: as a poet, and as a critic, and as a befriender of genius through personal contact." In a 1915 letter to Harriet Monroe, Pound himself described his activities as an effort "to keep alive a certain group of advancing poets, to set the arts in their rightful place as the acknowledged guide and lamp of civilization."

Arriving in Italy in 1908 with only $80, Pound spent $8 to have his first book of poems, *A Lume Spento,* printed in June, 1908, in an edition of 100 copies. An unsigned review appearing in the May, 1909 *Book News Monthly* (collected in *Ezra Pound: The Critical Heritage*) noted, "French phrases and scraps of Latin and Greek punctuate his poetry. . . . He affects obscurity and loves the abstruse." William Carlos Williams, a college friend and himself a poet, wrote to Pound, criticizing the bitterness in the poems; Pound objected that the pieces were dramatic presentations, not personal expressions. On October 21, 1909, he responded to Williams, "It seems to me you might as well say that Shakespeare is dissolute in his plays because Falstaff is . . . or that the plays have a criminal tendency because there is murder done in them." He insisted on making a distinction between his own feelings and ideas and those presented in the poems: "I catch the

character I happen to be interested in at the moment he interests me, usually a moment of song, self-analysis, or sudden understanding or revelation. I paint my man as I *conceive* him," explaining that "the sort of thing I do" is "the short so-called dramatic lyric." Pound continued to explore the possibilities of the dramatic lyric in his work, later expanding the technique into the character studies of *Homage to Sextus Propertius* and *Selwyn Mauberley* and of the countless figures who people the *Cantos.*

Pound carried copies of *A Lume Spento* to distribute when he moved to London later that year; the book convinced Elkin Mathews, a London bookseller and publisher, to bring out Pound's next works: *A Quinzaine for this Yule, Exultations* and *Personae.* Reviews of these books were generally favorable, as notices collected in *The Critical Heritage* reveal: Pound "is that rare thing among modern poets, a scholar," wrote one anonymous reviewer in the December, 1909 *Spectator,* adding that Pound has "the capacity for remarkable poetic achievement." British poet F. S. Flint wrote in a May, 1909 review in the *New Age,* "we can have no doubt as to his vitality and as to his determination to burst his way into Parnassus." Flint praised the "craft and artistry, originality and imagination" in *Personae,* although several other unsigned reviews pointed out difficulties with Pound's poems.

His first major critical work, *The Spirit of Romance,* was, Pound said, an attempt to examine "certain forces, elements or qualities which were potent in the mediaeval literature of the Latin tongues, and are, I believe, still potent in our own." The writers he discussed turn up again and again in his later writings: Dante, Cavalcanti, and Villon, for example. Pound contributed scores of reviews and critical articles to various periodicals such as the *New Age,* the *Egoist,* the *Little Review* and *Poetry,* where he articulated his aesthetic principles and indicated his literary, artistic, and musical preferences, thus offering information helpful for interpreting his poetry. In his introduction to the *Literary Essays of Ezra Pound,* T. S. Eliot noted, "It is necessary to read Pound's poetry to understand his criticism, and to read his criticism to understand his poetry." His criticism is important in its own right; as David Perkins pointed out in *A History of Modern Poetry,* "During a crucial decade in the history of modern literature, approximately 1912-1922, Pound was the most influential and in some ways the best critic of poetry in England or America." Eliot stated in his introduction to Pound's *Literary Essays* that Pound's literary criticism was "the most important contemporary criticism of its kind. He forced upon our attention not only individual authors, but whole areas of poetry, which no future criticism can afford to ignore."

Around 1912, Pound helped to create the movement he called "Imagisme," which marked the end of his early poetic style. In remarks first recorded in the March, 1913 *Poetry* and later collected in his *Literary Essays* as "A Retrospect," Pound explained his new literary direction. Imagism combined the creation of an "image"—what he defined as "an intellectual and emotional complex in an instant of time" or an "interpretative metaphor"—with rigorous requirements for writing. About these requirements, Pound was concise but insistent: "1) Direct treatment of the 'thing' whether subjective or objective 2) To use absolutely no word that did not contribute to the presentation 3) As regarding rhythm: to compose in sequence of the musical phrase, not in sequence of a metronome." These criteria meant 1) To carefully observe and describe phenomena, whether emotions, sensations, or concrete entities, and to avoid vague generalities or abstractions. Pound wanted "explicit rendering, be it of external nature or of emotion," and proclaimed "a strong disbelief in abstract and general statement as a means of conveying one's thought to others." 2) To avoid poetic diction in favor of the spoken language and to condense content, expressing it as concisely and precisely as possible. 3) To reject conventional metrical forms in favor of individualized cadence. Each poem, Pound declared, should have a rhythm "which corresponds exactly to the emotion or shade of emotion to be expressed."

The original Imagist group included just Pound, H. D. (Hilda Doolittle), Richard Aldington, F. S. Flint, and later William Carlos Williams. American poet Amy Lowell also adopted the term, contributing one poem to the 1914 anthology *Des Imagistes,* edited by Pound. In following years, Lowell sponsored her own anthologies that Pound thought did not meet his Imagist standards; and wishing to dissociate himself from what he derisively called "Amygism," he changed the term "Image" to "Vortex," and "Imagism" to "Vorticism." Writing in the *Fortnightly Review* of September 1, 1914, Pound expanded his definition of the image: "a radiant node or cluster, it is what I can, and must perforce call a VORTEX, from which, and through which, and into which ideas are constantly rushing." As a much more comprehensive aesthetic principle, Vorticism also extended into the visual arts and music, thus including such artists as the Englishman Wyndham Lewis and Henri Gaudier-Breska, a French sculptor.

Another important facet of Pound's literary activity was his tireless promotion of other writers and artists. He persuaded Harriet Monroe to publish T. S. Eliot's "The Love Song of J. Alfred Prufrock," calling it in a 1914 letter to Monroe "the best poem I have yet had or seen from an American." In 1921, he edited Eliot's *The Waste Land* (published 1922), possibly the most important poem of the modernist era. In a circular (reprinted in Pound's *Letters*) for Bel Esprit, the well-intentioned but ill-fated scheme to

help support artists in need, Pound described the poetic sequence of Eliot's poem as "possibly the finest that the modern movement in English has produced." Eliot in turn dedicated the poem to "Ezra Pound, *il miglior fabbro*" (the better craftsman), and in his introduction to Pound's *Selected Poems* (1928) declared, "I sincerely consider Ezra Pound the most important living poet in the English language."

Pound was also an early supporter of the Irish novelist James Joyce, arranging for the publication of several of the stories in *Dubliners* (1914) and *A Portrait of the Artist as a Young Man* (1916) in literary magazines before they were published in book form. Forrest Read, in his introduction to *Pound/Joyce: The Letters of Ezra Pound to James Joyce,* reported that Pound described Joyce to the Royal Literary Fund as "*without exception* the best of the younger prose writers." Read declared that Pound "got Joyce printed" and "at critical moments Pound was able to drum up financial support from such varied sources as the Royal Literary Fund, the Society of Authors, the British Parliament, and the New York lawyer John Quinn in order to help Joyce keep writing." Richard Sieburth in *Istigatios: Ezra Pound and Remy de Gourment* noted, "Ever concerned about the state of Joyce's health, finances, and masterpiece-in-progress, Pound prevailed upon him to quit Trieste for Paris, thus setting in motion one of the major forces that would make Paris the magnet of modernism over the next decade. When Joyce and family arrived in Paris in July, Pound was there to help them settle: he arranged for lodgings, and loans . . . and introduced Joyce . . . to the future publisher of *Ulysses* (1922), Sylvia Beach."

Other writers Pound praised while they were still relatively unknown included D. H. Lawrence, Robert Frost, H. D., and Ernest Hemingway. In his *Life of Ezra Pound,* Noel Stock recalled that in 1925, the first issue of *This Quarter* was dedicated to "Ezra Pound who by his creative work, his editorship of several magazines, his helpful friendship for young and unknown . . . comes first to our mind as meriting the gratitude of this generation." Included among the tributes to Pound was a statement of appreciation from Ernest Hemingway: "We have Pound the major poet devoting, say, one-fifth of his time to poetry. With the rest of his time he tries to advance the fortunes, both material and artistic, of his friends. He defends them when they are attacked, he gets them into magazines and out of jail. He loans them money. He sells their pictures. . . . He advances them hospital expenses and dissuades them from suicide. And in the end a few of them refrain from knifing him at the first opportunity."

Pound's contributions to translation and his rapid critical and poetic development during the Vorticist years are reflected in *Cathay* (1915), translations from the Chinese. In a June, 1915 review in *Outlook,* reprinted in *The Critical Heritage,* Ford Madox Ford declared it "the best work he has yet done;" the poems, of "a supreme beauty," revealed Pound's "power to express emotion . . . intact and exactly." Sinologists criticized Pound for the inaccuracies of the translations; Wi-lim Yip, in his *Ezra Pound's Cathay,* admitted, "One can easily excommunicate Pound from the Forbidden City of Chinese studies"; yet he believed that Pound conveyed "the central concerns of the original author" and that no other translation "has assumed so interesting and unique a position as *Cathay* in the history of English translations of Chinese poetry." In *The Pound Era,* Kenner pointed out that *Cathay* was an interpretation as much as a translation; the "poems paraphrase an elegiac war poetry. . . . among the most durable of all poetic responses to World War I." Perhaps the clearest assessment of Pound's achievement was made at the time by T. S. Eliot in his introduction to Pound's *Selected Poems;* he called Pound "the inventor of Chinese poetry for our time" and predicted that *Cathay* would be called a "magnificent specimen of twentieth-century poetry" rather than a translation.

Hugh Selwyn Mauberley (1920) avoided the problems of being evaluated as a translation, since the title refers to a fictional rather than an historical poet. Yet this poem also suffered at the hands of readers who misunderstood the author's intent. In a July, 1922 letter to his former professor, Felix Schelling, Pound described *Propertius* and *Mauberley* as "portraits," his rendering of sensibilities. Propertius represents the character of a Roman writer responding to his age; Mauberley, the character of a contemporary British critic-poet. Both poems were, Pound told Schelling, his attempt "to condense a James novel" and both were extended dramatic lyrics. "Mauberley is a learned, allusive, and difficult poem, extra-ordinarily concentrated and complex," Michael Alexander observed in *The Poetic Achievement of Ezra Pound;* a central difficulty the poetic sequence presents is point of view. Most importantly, however, *Mauberley* served as Pound's "farewell to London" and showed, according to Alexander, "how profoundly Pound wished to reclaim for poetry areas which the lyric tradition lost to the novel in the nineteenth century—areas of social, public, and cultural life." The poem thus points toward the work that was to occupy Pound for the remainder of his life: the *Cantos.*

By the time Pound left London for Paris in December, 1920, he had already accomplished enough to assure himself a place of first importance in twentieth-century literature. Yet his most ambitious work, the *Cantos,* was scarcely begun. And for a time, it seemed that his long poem was stalled. He had written to Joyce in 1917, "I have begun an endless poem, of no known category . . . all about everything." His original first *Three Cantos* had

been published in *Poetry* (1917) and his *Fourth Canto* in 1919. Cantos V, VI, and VII appeared in the *Dial* (1921) and "The Eighth Canto" appeared in 1922, but except for limited editions, no new poems appeared in book form for the next decade. *A Draft of XVI. Cantos* (1925) in an edition of only 90 copies came out in Paris, and *A Draft of XXX Cantos* in 1930; but commercial editions of the first thirty *Cantos* were not published in London and New York until 1933.

The significance of Pound's undertaking was recognized early. In a 1931 review for *Hound and Horn,* reprinted in *The Critical Heritage,* Dudley Fitts called the *Cantos* "without any doubt, the most ambitious poetic conception of our day." Three decades later, in "The Cantos in England," also reprinted in *The Critical Heritage,* Donald Hall concluded, "Pound is a great poet, and the *Cantos* are his masterwork." The long poem, however, presented innumerable difficulties to its readers. When *A Draft of XVI. Cantos* appeared, William Carlos Williams lamented in a 1927 issue of the *New York Evening Post Literary Review* (comments reprinted in *The Critical Heritage*), "Pound has sought to communicate his poetry to us and failed. It is a tragedy, since he is our best poet." Pound himself worried: "Afraid the whole damn poem is rather obscure, especially in fragments," he wrote his father in April, 1927. With fragmentary, telescoped units of information arranged in unfamiliar ways, the *Cantos* confounded critics. Fitts summarized two common complaints: "The first of these is that the poem is incomprehensible, a perverse mystification; the second that it is structurally and melodically amorphous, not a poem, but a macaronic chaos." And George Kearns in his *Guide to Ezra Pound's Selected Cantos* warned that "a basic understanding of the poem requires a major investment of time" since if "one wants to read even a single canto, one must assemble information from a great many sources." The first major critical treatment of Pound's work, Kenner's *The Poetry of Ezra Pound* (1951) paved the way for other serious scholarly attention, and intense critical activity in recent years has produced a host of explanatory texts designed to help readers understand and evaluate the *Cantos.*

Reestablishing a poetic tradition traced from Homer's *Odyssey* and Dante's *Divine Comedy,* the *Cantos* are a *modern* epic. In his 1934 essay "Date Line" (in *Literary Essays of Ezra Pound*), Pound defined an epic as "a poem containing history." He further declared, in *An Introduction to the Economic Nature of the United States* (1944; reprinted in *Selected Prose, 1909-1965*), "For forty years I have schooled myself, not to write an economic history of the U.S. or any other country, but to write an epic poem which begins 'In the Dark Forest,' crosses the Purgatory of human error, and ends in the light and 'fra i maestri di color che sanno' [among the masters of those who know]."

Bernstein explained that Pound's concept of an epic determined many of the characteristics of the *Cantos:* "the principle emotion aroused by an epic should be admiration for some distinguished achievement," rather than "the pity and fear aroused by tragedy." Thus, the *Cantos* are peopled with figures Pound considers heroic. Historical characters such as the fifteenth century soldier and patron of the arts Sigismundo Malatesta, the Elizabethan jurist Edward Coke, Elizabeth I, John Adams, and Thomas Jefferson speak through fragments of their own writings. Embodying the ideals of personal freedom, courage, and independent thinking, they represented to Pound heroic figures whose public policies led to enlightened governing. Pound searched through the historical and mythical past as well as the modern world to find those who embodied the Confucian ideals of "sincerity" and "rectitude" in contrast to those who through greed, ignorance, and malevolence worked against the common good.

An epic also encompasses the entire known world and its learning; it is "the tale of the tribe." Thus, the *Cantos* were designed to dramatize the gradual acquisition of cultural knowledge. Pound's poem follows other epic conventions, such as beginning *in medias res* (in the middle) and including supernatural beings in the form of the classical goddesses. The structure is episodic and polyphonic, but the form is redefined to be appropriate for the modern world. Christine Froula in *A Guide to Ezra Pound's Selected Poems* suggested that Pound's poem, "in its inclusion of fragments of many cultures and many languages, its multiple historical lines, its anthropological perspectives, remains a powerfully and often movingly expressive image of the modern world. It marks the end of the old idea of the tribe as a group who participate in and share a single, closed culture, and redefines it as the human community in all its complex diversity." The *Cantos* are, thus, "truly expressive of our perpetually unfolding perception and experience."

In an often quoted letter to his father in April, 1927, Pound explained that the "outline or main scheme" of the *Cantos* is "Rather like, or unlike, subject and response and counter subject in fugue: A.A. Live man goes down into world of Dead/C.B. The 'repeat in history'/B.C. The 'magic moment' or moment of metamorphosis, bust thru from quotidien into 'divine or permanent world.' Gods., etc." In the same letter, Pound also briefly outlined the themes—the visit to the world of the dead, the repetition in history, and the moment of metamorphosis—all of which have correspondences in three texts that served as his major inspiration: Dante's *Divine Comedy,* Homer's *Odyssey,* and Ovid's *Metamorphosis.* To these models, Pound added the teachings of Confucius, historical material, and information from his immediate experience. In *The Spirit of Romance* (1910), Pound had earlier inter-

preted the *Divine Comedy* both as a literal description of Dante's imagining a journey "through the realms inhabited by the spirits of the men after death" and as the journey of "Dante's intelligence through the states of mind wherein dwell all sorts and conditions of men before death." The *Cantos* also dramatize such a journey. "By no means an orderly Dantescan rising/but as the winds veer" (Canto LXXIV), the *Cantos* record a pilgrimage—an intellectual and spiritual voyage that parallels Dante's pursuit of enlightenment and Ulysses's search for his proper home. Alexander noted, "If the *Cantos* are not cast consistently in the form of a voyage of discovery, they are conducted in the spirit of such a venture, and continents or islands of knowledge, like Enlightenment America or Siena, or corners of Renaissance Italy, or China as seen via Confucianism, are explored and reported on." The journey in the *Cantos* occurs on two levels: one, a spiritual quest for transcendence, for the revelation of divine forces that lead to individual enlightenment; the other, an intellectual search for worldly wisdom, a vision of the Just City that leads to civic order and harmony. These goals, personal and public, are present throughout the poem; they also sustained the poet throughout his life.

Canto I introduces these controlling themes, presenting Odysseus's visit to the underworld, where he is to receive information from the spirits of the dead that will enable him to return home. The scene also serves as an analogy to the poet's exploration of the literature from the past in hopes of retrieving information that may be significant in his own time. Later Cantos present historical figures such as Sigismundo Malatesta and explore the relationship between creativity in the political and literary realms. By the 1930s, Pound was writing about banking and economic systems, and incorporating into the *Cantos* his own ideas about usury, which he identified as an exploitative economic system. Froula noted that the *Cantos* was "a verbal war against economic corruption, against literal wars, against materialism, against habits of mind that permit the perpetuation of political domination. It advocates economic reform as the basis of social and cultural reform, and it could not have held aloof from political reality."

Pound himself was also not aloof from political reality. An admirer of Mussolini, he lived in fascist Italy beginning in 1925. When the Second World War broke out, Pound stayed in Italy, retaining his American citizenship, and broadcasting a series of controversial radio commentaries. These commentaries often attacked Roosevelt and the Jewish bankers whom Pound held responsible for the war. By 1943, the United States government deemed the broadcasts to be treasonous. At war's end Pound was arrested by the United States Army and kept imprisoned in a small, outdoor wire cage at an Army compound near Pisa, Italy. For several weeks during that hot summer, Pound was confined to the cage. At night, floodlights lit his prison. Eventually judged to be mentally incompetent to stand trial, Pound was incarcerated in St. Elizabeth's Hospital in Washington, D.C. He was to stay in the hospital until 1958 when Robert Frost led a successful effort to free the poet. Ironically, while imprisoned by the Army in Italy, Pound completed the "Pisan Cantos," a group of poems that Paul L. Montgomery of the *New York Times* called "among the masterpieces of this century." The poems won him the Bollingen Prize in 1949.

Upon his release from St. Elizabeth's in 1958, Pound returned to Italy where he was to live quietly for the rest of his life. In 1969, *Drafts and Fragments of Cantos CX-CXVII* appeared, including the despairing lines: "My errors and wrecks lie about me/ . . .I cannot make it cohere." Speaking to Donald Hall, Pound described his *Cantos* as a "botch. . . . I picked out this and that thing that interested me, and then jumbled them into a bag. But that's not the way to make a *work of art*." Poet Allen Ginsberg reported in *Allen Verbatim: Lectures on Poetry, Politics, Consciousness* that Pound had "felt that the Cantos were 'stupidity and ignorance all the way through,' and were a failure and a 'mess.' " Ginsberg responded that the *Cantos* "were an accurate representation of his mind and so couldn't be thought of in terms of success or failure, but only in terms of the actuality of their representation, and that since for the first time a human being had taken the whole spiritual world of thought through fifty years and followed the thoughts out to the end—so that he built a model of his consciousness over a fifty-year time span—that they were a great human achievement." In the end, Pound fulfilled his own requirement for a poet, as stated in his *Selected Prose, 1909-1965*: "The essential thing about a poet is that he build us his world."

BIOGRAPHICAL/CRITICAL SOURCES:

BOOKS

Ackroyd, Peter, *Ezra Pound,* Thames Hudson, 1987.

Alexander, Michael, *The Poetic Achievement of Ezra Pound,* University of California Press, 1979.

Bernstein, Michael A., *The Tale of the Tribe: Ezra Pound and the Modern Verse Epic,* Princeton University Press, 1980.

Bloom, Harold, *Ezra Pound,* Chelsea House, 1987.

Bornstein, George, editor, *Ezra Pound among the Poets,* University of Chicago Press, 1988.

Brooke-Rose, Christine, *A ZBC of Ezra Pound,* University of California Press, 1971.

Bush, R., *The Genesis of Ezra Pound's Cantos,* Princeton University Press, 1989.

Carpenter, Humphrey, *A Serious Character: The Life of Ezra Pound,* Houghton, 1988.

Chace, William M., *The Political Identities of Ezra Pound and T. S. Eliot,* Stanford University Press, 1973.

Concise Dictionary of American Literary Biography: The Twenties, 1917-1929, Gale, 1989.

Contemporary Literary Criticism, Gale, Volume 1, 1973, Volume 2, 1974, Volume 3, 1975, Volume 4, 1976, Volume 5, 1976, Volume 7, 1977, Volume 10, 1979, Volume 13, 1980, Volume 18, 1981, Volume 34, 1985, Volume 48, 1988, Volume 50, 1988.

Cookson, William, *A Guide to the Cantos of Ezra Pound,* Persea Books, 1985.

Dasenbrock, Reed W., *The Literary Vorticism of Ezra Pound and Wyndham Lewis: Towards the Condition of Painting,* Johns Hopkins University Press, 1985.

Davie, Donald, *Ezra Pound: Poet as Sculptor,* Oxford University Press, 1964.

Davie, Donald, *Ezra Pound,* University of Chicago Press, 1982.

Davie, Donald, *Studies in Ezra Pound,* Carcanet, 1991.

Dekker, George, *The Cantos of Ezra Pound: A Critical Study,* Barnes & Noble, 1963.

De Rachewiltz, Mary, *Discretions,* Little, Brown, 1971.

Dictionary of Literary Biography, Gale, Volume 4: *American Writers in Paris, 1920-1939,* 1980, Volume 45: *American Poets, 1880-1945, First Series,* 1986, Volume 63: *Modern American Critics, 1920-1955,* 1988.

Dilligan, Robert J. and others, editors, *A Concordance to Ezra Pound's Cantos,* Garland, 1981.

Doolittle, Hilda, *End to Torment: A Memoir of Ezra Pound,* New Directions, 1979.

Edwards, John H. and William Vasse, *Annotated Index to the Cantos of Ezra Pound,* University of California Press, 1957.

Eliot, T. S., *Ezra Pound: His Metric and Poetry,* Knopf, 1917.

Farmer, David, compiler, *Ezra Pound: An Exhibition,* University of Texas, Humanities Research Center, 1967.

Flory, Wendy S., *Ezra Pound and the Cantos: A Record of Struggle,* Yale University Press, 1980.

Flory, Wendy S., *The American Ezra Pound,* Yale University Press, 1989.

Fraser, G. S., *Ezra Pound,* Grove, 1961.

Froula, Christine, *A Guide to Ezra Pound's Selected Poems,* New Directions, 1982.

Furbank, P. N., *Pound,* Taylor & Francis, 1985.

Gallup, Donald, *Ezra Pound: A Bibliography,* University Press of Virginia, 1983.

Ginsberg, Allen, *Allen Verbatim: Lectures on Poetry, Politics, Consciousness,* McGraw, 1975.

Goodwin, K. L., *The Influence of Ezra Pound,* Oxford University Press, 1966.

Grover, Philip, editor, *Ezra Pound: The London Years, 1908-1920,* AMS Press, 1978.

Hall, Donald, *Remembering Poets,* Harper, 1978.

Heyman, C. David, *Ezra Pound: The Last Rower,* Viking, 1976.

Homberger, Eric, editor, *Ezra Pound: The Critical Heritage,* Routledge & Kegan Paul, 1972.

Kearns, George, *Guide to Ezra Pound's Selected Cantos,* Rutgers University Press, 1980.

Kearns, George, *Pound: The Cantos,* Cambridge University Press, 1990.

Kenner, Hugh, *The Poetry of Ezra Pound,* New Directions, 1950.

Kenner, Hugh, *The Pound Era,* University of California Press, 1971.

Knapp, James F., *Ezra Pound,* Macmillan, 1979.

Lane, Gary, *A Concordance to the Poems of Ezra Pound,* Haskell, 1972.

Mullins, Eustace, *Ezra Pound: This Difficult Individual,* AMS Press, 1983.

Norman, Charles, *Ezra Pound,* Minerva, 1969.

Olson, Charles, *Charles Olson and Ezra Pound at St. Elizabeths,* edited by Catherine Seelye, Grossman, 1975.

Perkins, David, *A History of Modern Poetry: From the 1890's to the High Modernist Mode,* Harvard University Press, 1976.

Poetry Criticism, Volume 4, Gale, 1992.

Pound, Ezra, *The Spirit of Romance,* Dent, 1910, New Directions, 1952, revised edition, P. Owen, 1953.

Pound, Ezra, *Selected Poems,* edited and with an introduction by T. S. Eliot, Faber & Gwyer, 1928, Laughlin, 1957.

Pound, Ezra, *Literary Essays of Ezra Pound,* edited and with an introduction by T. S. Eliot, New Directions, 1954.

Pound, Ezra, *Pound/Joyce: The Letters of Ezra Pound to James Joyce,* edited by Forrest Read, New Directions, 1967.

Pound, Ezra, *Drafts and Fragments: Cantos CX-CXVII,* New Directions, 1968.

Pound, Ezra, *Selected Prose, 1909-1965,* edited by William Cookson, New Directions, 1973.

Quinn, Bernetta, *Ezra Pound: An Introduction to the Poetry,* Columbia University Press, 1973.

Redman, Tim, *Ezra Pound and Italian Fascism,* Cambridge University Press, 1991.

Rosenthal, M. L., *A Primer of Ezra Pound,* Macmillan, 1960.

Rusell, Peter, editor, *An Examination of Ezra Pound,* New Directions, 1950.

Schwartz, Sanford, *The Matriz of Modernism: Pound, Eliot and Early Twentieth Century Thought,* Princeton University Press, 1988.

Sieburth, Richard, *Instigations: Ezra Pound and Remy de Gourmont,* Harvard University Press, 1978.

Stock, Noel, *The Life of Ezra Pound,* Pantheon, 1970.

Sutton, Walter, editor, *Ezra Pound: A Collection of Critical Essays,* Prentice-Hall, 1963.

Tate, Allen, *Reactionary Essays on Poetry and Ideas,* Scribner, 1936, pp. 3-63.

Terrell, Carroll F., *A Companion to the Cantos of Ezra Pound,* University of California Press, Volume 1, 1980, Volume 2, 1984.

Torrey, E. Fuller, *The Roots of Treason: Ezra Pound and the Secret of St. Elizabeths,* McGraw, 1984.

Tytell, John, *Ezra Pound: The Solitary Volcano,* Doubleday, 1987.

Wilhelm, J. J., *Ezra Pound in London and Paris, 1908-1925,* Pennsylvania State University Press, 1990.

Wilhelm, James H., *The American Roots of Ezra Pound,* Garland, 1985.

Witemeyer, Hugh, *The Poetry of Ezra Pound: Form and Renewal, 1908-1920,* University of California Press, 1969.

World Literature Criticism, Gale, 1992.

PERIODICALS

Agenda, autumn-winter, 1985-86, pp. 153-163.

Athenaeum, October 24, 1919, pp. 1065-1066.

Boundary 2, fall-winter, 1982-83, pp. 103-128.

Criterion, July, 1935, pp. 649-651.

Critical Inquiry, winter, 1986, pp. 347-364; autumn, 1988, pp. 1-25.

Critical Quarterly, summer, 1985, pp. 39-48; spring-summer, 1986, pp. 154-166.

Journal of Modern Literature, spring, 1990, pp. 511-533.

London Magazine, October, 1955, pp. 55-64.

New Directions in Prose and Poetry, November 30, 1961, pp. 159-184.

New York Review of Books, March 13, 1986, pp. 16-24; October 9, 1986, pp. 53-55.

New York Times, July 9, 1972; November 4, 1972; November 5, 1972.

New York Times Book Review, November 10, 1985, p. 1.

Paideuma, fall, 1979, pp. 243-247; fall, 1981, pp. 331-345.

Paris Review, summer-fall, 1962, pp. 22-51.

Rendezvous, fall, 1986, pp. 34-47.

Yale Review, summer, 1986, pp. 635-640.

OBITUARIES:

PERIODICALS

Newsweek, November 13, 1972.

New York Times, November 2, 1972.

Publishers Weekly, November 13, 1972.

Time, November 13, 1972.*

—Sidelights by Jo Brantley Berryman

POYER, Joe
See POYER, Joseph John (Jr.)

* * *

POYER, Joseph John (Jr.) 1939-
(Joe Poyer)

PERSONAL: Born November 30, 1939, in Battle Creek, MI; son of Joseph John (a salesman) and Eileen (Powell) Poyer; married Susan Pilmore; married Bonnie Johnson; children: (first marriage) Joseph John III, Geoffrey; (stepchildren) Amy, Bradley. *Education:* Kellogg Community College, A.A., 1959; Michigan State University, B.A., 1961. *Politics:* Independent. *Religion:* None. *Avocational interests:* Travel, photography, antique firearms.

ADDRESSES: *Home*—Tustin, CA. *Agent*—Diane Cleaver Inc., Literary Agent, 55 Fifth Ave., New York, NY 10003; and Anthony Sheil Associates Ltd., 2-3 Morewell St., London WC1B 3AR, England.

CAREER: Michigan Tuberculosis and Respiratory Disease Association, Lansing, assistant director of public information, 1961-62; Pratt & Whitney Aircraft, East Hartford, CT, proposals writer, 1963-65; Beckman Instruments, Fullerton, CA, proposals writer, 1965-67; Bioscience Planning, Anaheim, CA, manager of interdisciplinary communications, 1967-68; Allergan Pharmaceuticals, Irvine, CA, senior project manager and research administrator, 1968-77; full-time novelist, 1977—. North Cape Publications, owner and publisher. KCAL-TV, Los Angeles, military affairs consultant.

WRITINGS:

UNDER NAME JOE POYER; NOVELS

Operation Malacca, Doubleday, 1968.
North Cape (Book-of-the-Month Club selection in England), Doubleday, 1969.
The Balkan Assignment, Doubleday, 1971.
The Chinese Agenda (Junior Literary Guild selection; Book-of-the-Month Club selection in Sweden), Doubleday, 1972.
The Shooting of the Green, Doubleday, 1973.
Day of Reckoning, Weidenfeld & Nicolson, 1976.
The Contract, Atheneum, 1978.
Tunnel War, Atheneum, 1979.
Vengeance 10, Atheneum, 1980.
Devoted Friends, Atheneum, 1982.

UNDER NAME JOE POYER; NONFICTION

The Illustrated History of Tanks, Publications International, 1989.
U.S. Combat: America's Landbased Weaponry, Beekman House, 1990.
The Illustrated History of Helicopters, Publications International, 1990.
Helicopter Fighters, Publications International, 1990.
Submarines: Hunter/Killers and Boomers, Beekman House, 1990.
The Great Book of Fighter Planes, Beekman House, 1990.
The Complete Book of U.S. Fighting Power, Publications International, 1990.
The Complete Book of Top Gun, Publications International, 1990.
The Complete Book of U.S. Naval Power, Publications International, 1991.

UNDER NAME JOE POYER; "A TIME OF WAR" SERIES

A Time of War: The Transgressors, Sphere Books, 1983.
. . . *: Come Evil Days,* Sphere Books, 1985.

UNDER NAME JOE POYER; EDITOR

Instrumentation Methods for Predictive Medicine, Instrument Society of America, 1966.
Biomedical Sciences Instrumentation, Plenum, 1967.

OTHER

Contributor of about a dozen short stories and over two hundred articles on military affairs to periodicals. Editor, *International Military Review* and *International Naval Review;* field editor, *International Combat Arms,* 1986-89.

WORK IN PROGRESS: A sequel to *North Cape;* a series of books for collectors of antique firearms; *Media Guide to the U.S. Military.*

BIOGRAPHICAL/CRITICAL SOURCES:

PERIODICALS

Los Angeles Times Book Review, December 9, 1979; November 24, 1980.
Spectator, February 28, 1970.
Washington Post, November 30, 1979.

* * *

PRATT, John Clark 1932-

PERSONAL: Born August 19, 1932, in St. Albans, VT; son of John Lowell (a publisher) and Katharine (Jennison) Pratt; married second wife, Doreen K. Goodman, June 28, 1968; children: Karen, Sandra, Pamela, John Randall; stepchildren: Lynn Goodman, Christine Goodman. *Education:* Attended Dartmouth College, 1950-53; University of California, Berkeley, B.A., 1954; Columbia University, M.A., 1960; Princeton University, Ph.D., 1965. *Politics:* Variable.

ADDRESSES: *Office*—Department of English, Colorado State University, Ft. Collins, CO 80523.

CAREER: U.S. Air Force, regular officer; commissioned second lieutenant, retired as lieutenant colonel, 1974; served in Vietnam, 1969-70. U.S. Air Force Academy, Colorado Springs, CO, assistant professor, 1960-68, associate professor, 1968-73, professor of English, 1973-74; Colorado State University, Ft. Collins, chairman of department of English, 1974-80, professor of English, 1980—; Pratt Publishing Company, Ft. Collins, CO, founder and president, 1988—. Fulbright lecturer, University of Lisbon, 1974-75, and Leningrad State University, 1980. Consultant in remedial English, United States Industries, Inc.

MEMBER: Coffee House (New York).

WRITINGS:

The Meaning of Modern Poetry, Doubleday, 1962.
John Steinbeck, Eerdmans, 1970.
(Editor) Ken Kesey, *One Flew Over the Cuckoo's Nest,* Viking, 1973.
The Laotian Fragments, Viking, 1974.
(Contributor) *Hemingway in Our Time,* Oregon State University, 1974.
(Author of introduction) *Kesey,* Northwest Review Books, 1977.
(Editor with Victor A. Neufeldt) *George Eliot's "Middlemarch" Notebooks: A Transcription,* University of California Press, 1979.
(Author of foreword) *Vietnam War Literature,* Scarecrow, 1982.
(Author of foreword) *Vietnam-Perkasie,* McFarland, 1983.
Vietnam Voices: Perspectives on the War Years, 1941-1982, Viking, 1984.
(With Timothy Lomperis) *Reading the Wind: The Literature of the Vietnam War,* Duke University Press, 1986.
Writing from Scratch: The Essay, Hamilton Press, 1987.
(Editor) *The Key to Failure: Laos and the Vietnam War,* Madison Books, 1988.
(Contributor) *The Frontier Experience and the American Dream,* Texas A & M University Press, 1989.
(Author of preface and annotated bibliography) *Unaccustomed Mercy: Soldier-Poets of the Vietnam War,* Texas Tech University Press, 1989.
(Editor) *Writing from Scratch: For Business,* Rowman and Littlefield, 1990.
(Contributor) *Fourteen Landing Zones,* University of Iowa Press, 1991.
(Editor) *Writing from Scratch: Freelancing,* Rowman and Littlefield, 1991.

WORK IN PROGRESS: Two novels, *American Affairs* and *Academe;* a musical; numerous editing and publishing projects; an interactive humanities computer program for hypertext.

SIDELIGHTS: As a Vietnam veteran, John Clark Pratt witnessed the events of the controversial war first-hand. "Looking back," Pratt recalled in a letter to *CA,* "I remember thinking that by writing a novel about the Vietnam War, I could at least get the war off my back—but it never happened." Instead, Pratt continued to draw upon his experiences to write and edit numerous books about this volatile period in American history.

Pratt's first book about the Vietnam War, *The Laotian Fragments,* tells the story of Bill Blake, a forward air controller. Mixed with diary entries, actual articles, documents and military reports, the narrative follows the protagonist from his first impressions of Vietnam to his disappearance during a flying mission over Laos. Calling it a "formidable accomplishment," in *Impact,* Tom Mayer went on to classify *The Laotian Fragments* as "one of the most ambitious books in scope and literary design to come out of the war."

Expanding on the historical montage technique of *The Laotian Fragments,* Pratt wrote what many critics thought was a nonfiction book, but was actually a postmodern collage novel. Pratt told *CA* he only admitted that *Vietnam Voices* was a novel to his editor once, who replied "I didn't hear that. If we'd thought it was a novel, we wouldn't have published it." Pratt's unique approach, both praised and criticized by reviewers, juxtaposes excerpts of diaries, press releases, poems, journalism, and graffiti with brief passages of prose. The result, found Mark Barent in the *National Vietnam Veterans Review,* is a book which covers the war "the way it really was . . . from all points of view."

In addition to writing books about the Vietnam experience, Pratt has used Pratt Publishing Company, which he founded, as a springboard for other authors writing on the topic. "Starting the first truly on-demand publishing company in the world was fun, but I immediately found that Vietnam was still riding my shoulders," he told *CA.*

Pratt's experiences at Pratt Publishing gave him insight into the process of editing from a writer's perspective. "Over and over again, writers of the 80s and 90s decry the lack of understanding shown them by the corporate, conglomerate, market-oriented editors," Pratt explained to *CA.* "But as authors, we must not only live with what we deplore, but also figure out a way to use and transcend it. Thanks to computers, we have the capability of doing it all—including marketing. There are, I think, no more undiscovered authors—only undiscovering authors. What we write about we must also be able to do. My main interest is in getting important words and thoughts—mine or someone else's—about important human experiences in front of readers. To me, figuring out how to make this happen is what being a truly contemporary author is all about."

BIOGRAPHICAL/CRITICAL SOURCES:

BOOKS

Jason, Philip K., *Fourteen Landing Zones,* University of Iowa Press, 1991.
Stephens, Michael, *The Dramaturgy of Style,* Southern Illinois University Press, 1986.

PERIODICALS

Impact (magazine of the *Albuquerque Journal*) July 30, 1985.
Los Angeles Times Book Review, December 9, 1984.
Modern Fiction Studies, spring, 1984.
National Vietnam Veterans Review, January, 1986, p. 15.
New York Times Book Review, October 7, 1984.
Playboy, January, 1985.
Times Literary Supplement, August 15, 1980; February 15, 1985.
Washington Post Book World, September 23, 1984.

Q-R

QUARTERMAIN, Peter (Allan) 1934-

PERSONAL: Born April 6, 1934, in Evesham, Worcester, England; son of Clifford Philip (a store manager) and Ada Bessie (Wilson) Quartermain; married Carol Munro (divorced); married Meredith Andrea Yearsley (a writer), August 4, 1984; children: (first marriage) Ian Mark, David Allan. *Education:* University of Nottingham, B.A., 1955, Ph.D., 1959.

ADDRESSES: Home—128 East 23rd Ave., Vancouver, British Columbia, Canada V5V 1X2. *Office*—Department of English, University of British Columbia, Vancouver, British Columbia, Canada V6T 1W5.

CAREER: University of Pennsylvania, Philadelphia, postdoctoral fellow in American civilization, 1959-60; University of British Columbia, Vancouver, assistant professor, 1961-68, associate professor, 1968-91, professor of English, 1991—. Visiting assistant professor of English at Mills College, 1960-62. Proprietor with wife, Meredith Quartermain, of Slug Press, c. 1979—.

MEMBER: Association of Canadian University Teachers of English, Modern Language Association of America, American Printing History Association, William Carlos Williams Society, Ezra Pound Society, Printing Historical Society, Alcuin Society (president, 1981-82).

AWARDS, HONORS: Fulbright-Rockefeller Fellow, 1956; Mountjoy Fellow, University of Durham (U.K.), 1990.

WRITINGS:

(Editor) *Dictionary of Literary Biography,* Gale, Volume 45: *American Poets, 1880-1945, First Series,* 1986, Volume 48: *American Poets, 1880-1945, Second Series,* 1986, Volume 54: *American Poets, 1880-1945, Third Series,* 2 parts, 1987.

Basil Bunting: Poet of the North, University of Durham, 1990.
Disjunctive Poetics: From Gertrude Stein and Louis Zukofsky to Susan Howe, Cambridge University Press, 1992.

Contributor to books, including *Louis Zukofsky: Man and Poet,* edited by Carroll F. Terrell, National Poetry Foundation, 1980; *Louis Zukofsky, or Whoever Someone Else Thought He Was,* edited by Harry Gilonis, North and South Press, 1988; and *Lorine Niedecker: Woman and Poet,* edited by Jenny Penberthy, National Poetry Foundation, 1993. Contributor to periodicals, including *Chicago Review, Canadian Literature, Southern Review, Parnassus, American Literature, Writing,* and *Paideuma.*

WORK IN PROGRESS: A memoir and study of Basil Bunting; an edition of the collected prose of Basil Bunting; a study of language poetry; a meditation on poetics; miscellaneous essays.

SIDELIGHTS: Peter Quartermain once told *CA:* "Most of my writing is promotional in the sense that my ideal reader will, halfway through one of my essays, stop reading my work and start reading the poet I am talking about. I cultivate the acquaintance of poets whose work I enjoy, correspond with them if I can, and try in my writing—in recording the news their work gives me—to give them some sort of news back. Poets are, especially in this century and on this benighted continent, a beleaguered species. As a writer and teacher I try to alleviate that deplorable state of affairs.

"As the proprietor (with my wife) of Slug Press since 1979 or so, we publish decent limited editions (sometimes as pamphlets, sometimes as broadsides; sometimes for sale, sometimes as giveaways) of the work of contemporary writers whose work is perhaps neglected, or whose work we very much admire, or who are indeed completely unknown outside a very small circle of readers. Most of our publications go out of print very quickly. We turn a very small profit, which we use to finance the next publication or to buy type or equipment. We pay a small royalty in advance of publication, and we never consider unsolicited manuscripts. What we do is, we think, useful as well as pleasing."

*   *   *

RACHLEFF, Owen S(pencer)   1934-

PERSONAL: Surname is pronounced "*rack*-leff "; born July 16, 1934, in New York, NY; son of Harold Kirman (a banker) and Theresa (Friedman) Rachleff. *Education:* Columbia University, B.F.A., 1956; University of London, M.A., 1958.

ADDRESSES: Home—135 East 71st St., New York, NY 10021. *Office*—c/o Marvin Starkman Agency, 1501 Broadway, New York, NY 10036.

CAREER: Writer. Harry N. Abrams, Inc. (publisher), New York City, house writer and editor, 1963-67; American Heritage Publishing Co., New York City, staff writer and editor, 1967-68; New School for Social Research, teacher in religion and humanities, beginning 1968; New York University, New York City, assistant professor of humanities, 1968-74; Hofstra University, adjunct assistant professor, 1972-78; *Midstream* (magazine), film and theater critic, 1972-77. Anti-Defamation League, New York, European Affairs Director, 1969-74.

Professional actor, 1975—, appearing in Off-Broadway productions, including *Catsplay,* 1978, *The Lesson,* 1978, *Arms and the Man,* 1980, *Waltz of the Toreadors,* 1980, *Escoffier: King of Chefs* (also see below), 1981-88, *A New Way to Pay Old Debts,* 1983, *The Imaginary Invalid,* 1985, *The Jew of Malta,* 1987, *The Sunday Promenade,* 1989, and *Variations without Fugue,* 1992; appeared in films, including *The Dain Curse,* 1977, *Night Flowers,* 1979, *A Question of Honor,* 1981, and *The Murder of Mary Phagan,* 1988; also appeared on television in series *The Bloodhound Gang,* Public Broadcasting Service, and soap operas, including *Ryan's Hope,* America Broadcasting Companies, Inc.

MEMBER: Actors Equity Association, Screen Actors Guild, American Federation of Television and Radio Artists, Dramatists Guild, Authors League.

AWARDS, HONORS: MacDowell Colony fellow, 1965; A.B.A. White House Selection, 1970.

WRITINGS:

Rembrandt's Life of Christ, Abradale Press, 1966.

Young Israel: A History of the Modern Nation, Lion Press, 1968.
Great Bible Stories and Master Paintings: A Complete Narration of the Old and New Testaments, Abrams, 1968.
An Illustrated Treasury of Bible Stories, Abradale Press, 1970.
The Occult Conceit: A New Look at Astrology, Witchcraft and Sorcery, Cowles Book Co., 1971.
The Magic of Love, C. R. Gibson, 1972.
Sky Diamonds: The New Astrology, illustrated by Robert Rappaport, Hawthorn, 1973.
The Secrets of Superstitions: How They Help and How They Hurt, Doubleday, 1976.
Exploring the Bible, Abbeville Press, 1980.
Eric's Image (novel), Tower Books, 1982.
The Occult in Art, Alpine, 1983.
Enigma (novel), Tower Books, 1988.

PLAYS

Cain, produced in St. Petersburg, FL, 1965.
Javelin, produced Off-Broadway, 1966.
From the Classifieds, produced Off-Broadway, 1970.
Uncle Money, produced Off-Broadway, 1980.
Escoffier: King of Chefs, (produced in New York City, 1981), Broadway Play Publishing Co., 1983.
(Adaptor) *Tosca 1943* (based on the play *La Tosca,* by Victorien Sardou), produced Off-Broadway, 1984.
The Fabulous La Fontaine (musical), produced Off-Broadway, 1990.

*   *   *

RAFFINI, James O.   1941-

PERSONAL: Born April 23, 1941, in Montreal, WI; married Carol Seidl (a teacher), 1965; children: Leslie, Eric. *Education:* Wisconsin State University (now University of Wisconsin—Whitewater), B.Ed., 1964; University of Florida, M.Ed., 1967; Northern Illinois University, Ed.D., 1970.

ADDRESSES: Home—N1081 Cold Spring Rd., Fort Atkinson, WI 53538. *Office*—Department of Educational Foundations, University of Wisconsin—Whitewater, Whitewater, WI 53190.

CAREER: University of Wisconsin—Whitewater, professor of educational psychology, 1970—, chairperson of Department of Educational Foundations.

MEMBER: Association for Supervision and Curriculum Development, American Educational Research Association, Phi Delta Kappa, Phi Kappa Phi.

(Contributor) *Fundamentals of Research,* Kendall/Hunt, 1972.

Discipline: Negotiating Conflicts with Today's Kids, Prentice Hall, 1980.

Student Apathy: The Protection of Self-Worth, National Education Association, 1988.

Winners Without Losers: Structures and Strategies for Increasing Student Motivation to Learn, Allyn & Bacon, 1993.

Contributor to education journals.

WORK IN PROGRESS: Conflict Negotiation Skills for Educators.

*   *   *

RAPOPORT, Janis 1946-

PERSONAL: Born June 22, 1946, in Toronto, Ontario, Canada; daughter of Maxwell Lewis (a lawyer) and Roslyn (Cohen) Rapoport; married David J. Seager, December 22, 1966 (divorced February 21, 1980); married Douglas F. Donegani (a publisher), May 20, 1980; children: (first marriage) Jeremy, Sara, Julia; (second marriage) Renata. *Education:* University of Toronto, B.A., 1967. *Religion:* Jewish.

ADDRESSES: Office—c/o The Writers' Union of Canada, 24 Ryerson Ave., Toronto, Ontario, Canada.

CAREER: Which? (magazine), London, England, editorial assistant, 1968-69; Paul Hamlyn Ltd., London, assistant editor, 1969-70; Heinemann Educational Books, Scarborough, Ontario, assistant editor, 1971-73; Canadian Broadcasting Corp. (CBC), Toronto, Ontario, story editor in television drama, 1973-74; free-lance editor, writer, and broadcaster, Toronto, 1974-83. Part-time instructor in creative writing, Sheridan College, 1984-86, and University of Toronto, 1988—. Playwright-in-residence at Tarragon Theatre, Toronto, 1974-75, and Banff Centre, summer, 1976; writer-in-residence, St. Thomas (Ontario) Public Library, 1987, Beeton (Ontario) Public Library, 1988, Dundas (Ontario) Public Library, 1990, North York (Ontario) Public Library, 1991, and Toronto Board of Education, 1991. Participates in workshops and conferences and gives readings and talks at public and educational institutions across Canada, 1973—; work has been read at poetry festivals in Canada and Europe; writing has been broadcast on radio in Canada and the U.S. and on Canadian television.

MEMBER: League of Canadian Poets, Association of Canadian Television and Radio Artists, P.E.N., Playwrights Union of Canada, Writers' Union of Canada.

AWARDS, HONORS: Arts award, Canada Council, 1981-82; awards of merit, New York Art Director's Club,

both 1983, for *Imaginings,* and for poem on University of Guelph poster; certificate of excellence, American Institute of Graphic Arts, 1983, for *Imaginings;* Outstanding Achievement Award, American Poetry Association, 1986; research and development award, Toronto Arts Council, 1990, 1992.

WRITINGS:

(Co-author) *Imaginings,* Ethos Cultural Development Foundation, 1982.

POETRY

Within the Whirling Moment, House of Anansi Press, 1967.

Jeremy's Dream, Press Porcepic, 1974.

(Editor with Gay Allison and Karen Hood) *Landscape* (anthology), Women's Writing Collective, 1977.

Winter Flowers, Hounslow Press, 1979.

Upon Her Fluent Route, Hounslow Press, 1991.

PLAYS

And She Could Eat No Lean (three-act), produced in Toronto, Ontario, at Tarragon Theatre, 1975.

Gilgamesh (one-act), produced in Toronto at U.C. Playhouse, 1976.

Dreamgirls (two-act; produced in Toronto at Theatre Passe-Muraille, 1979), Playwrights Canada, 1979.

OTHER

Contributor to anthologies, including *Full Moon, Tributaries, Whale Sound, Essential Words,* and *La Traductiere.* Associate coordinator, "Words Alive" reading series, Ethos Cultural Development Foundation, 1980-84. Contributor to periodicals, including *Malahat Review, Canadian Fiction Magazine, Quarry, Canadian Forum, West Coast Review,* and *Black Cat.* Founding editor-in-chief, *Ethos,* 1983-87; associate editor, *Tamarack Review,* 1970-82.

ADAPTATIONS: One of the poems from Rapoport's *Upon Her Fluent Route* is being scored for voice and scalatron, in addition to voice and piano, for the world premier performance (planned by McMaster University professor Paul Rapoport), in Ontario, 1993.

WORK IN PROGRESS: Short stories; poetry.

SIDELIGHTS: Janis Rapoport once told *CA:* "I may not have become a writer were it not for the encouragement of Dave Godfrey, my creative writing instructor at the University of Toronto. I now write because I have to; in the act of writing I am following an inner compulsion. Through my artistic efforts—in whatever medium—I hope to take people, in a metaphoric sense, on new journeys and return them to reality with their sensibilities extended and enriched. I believe in the moral—that is, life affirming—value of art."

*　　*　　*

REARDEN, Jim 1925-

PERSONAL: Born April 22, 1925, in Petaluma, CA; son of Barton B. (a teacher) and Grace M. (a housewife; maiden name, Miller) Rearden; married Ursula R. Budde, 1943 (divorced, 1965); married Audrey A. Roberts (a business manager), January 27, 1966; children: Kathleen Rearden Richardson, Mary Rearden Bookman, Michael, Nancy Rearden Kleine, Jim K.; (stepchildren) Terry Sagmoen, Tamara Sagmoen, Michael Sagmoen. *Education:* Oregon State University, B.S., 1948; University of Maine, M.S., 1950. *Politics:* Independent. *Religion:* Protestant. *Avocational interests:* Wildlife conservation, World War II, Aleutian campaign of World War II, aviation.

ADDRESSES: Home and office—413 East Lee Dr., Homer, AK 99603. *Agent*—Jack Scagnetti, 5330 Lankershim Blvd., Suite 210, North Hollywood, CA 91601.

CAREER: University of Alaska, Fairbanks, assistant professor, 1950-51, professor of wildlife and fishery management, 1952-54, head of department of wildlife management, 1950-54; Alaska Department of Fish and Game, Homer, commercial fisheries biologist, 1959-69; *Alaska* (magazine), Homer, outdoors editor, 1968-88. *Outdoor Life*, Alaska field editor, 1976—. Member of Alaska Board of Fish and Game, 1970, 1973-75; member of Alaska Board of Game, 1970-82; member of National Advisory Committee on Oceans and Atmosphere, 1976-77. *Military service:* U.S. Navy, 1943-45; served as second class petty officer (sonar).

MEMBER: American Society of Journalists and Authors.

AWARDS, HONORS: Outstanding conservation communicator—Alaska, National Wildlife Federation and Alaska Sportsmen Council, 1980; distinguished alumnus, College of Forest Resources, University of Maine, 1987.

WRITINGS:

Wonders of Caribou (juvenile), Dodd, 1976.
Yukon: Kuskokwim Delta, Alaska Geographic, 1979.
Alaska Mammals, Alaska Geographic, 1981.
Alaska's Salmon Fisheries, Alaska Geographic, 1983.
Tales of Alaska's Big Bears, Wolfe Publishing, 1989.
Cracking the Zero Mystery, Stackpole, 1990.
Castner's Cutthroats (novel), Wolfe Publishing, 1990.
(With Lenora Conkle) *Trail of the Eagle,* Great Northwest, 1990.
(With Conkle) *Wind on the Water,* Great Northwest, 1991.

(With Rudy Billberg) *In the Shadow of Eagles: From Barnstormer to Alaska Bush Pilot, a Flyer's Story,* Alaska Northwest Publishing, 1992.
(Editor) Dolores Cline Brown, *White Squaw,* Wolfe Publishing, 1992.
(With Sydney Huntington) *Koyukuk Man: Sidney Huntington, Tale of an Alaskan,* Alaska Northwest Publishing, 1993.

Contributor of over two hundred articles to periodicals, including *International Wildlife, Audubon, Outdoor Life, Field and Stream, Sports Afield, National Wildlife,* and *National Geographic. Cracking the Zero Mystery* has been published in Japanese.

ADAPTATIONS: A screenplay Rearden wrote based on his novel *Castner's Cutthroats* is being considered for production in Hollywood.

WORK IN PROGRESS: More books; more magazine articles.

SIDELIGHTS: Jim Rearden told *CA:* "My father was an agriculture teacher in Petaluma, California, High School. I started college at Oregon State (Corvallis) when I was 17, dropped out, and enlisted in the U.S. Navy. Served aboard destroyer escort U.S.S. Lovering in Central Pacific as a sonarman. Fall 1945, reentered Oregon State, completed B.S. in fish and game conservation in 1948.

"While a junior at O.S.C. spent a summer as a temporary employee of the U.S. Fish and Wildlife Service in Alaska. Awarded a fellowship at the University of Maine. With M.S. degree in wildlife conservation from Maine, accepted professorship at University of Alaska to teach wildlife management.

"Left teaching to become free-lance writer-photographer. Have sold more than five hundred magazine articles, mostly about Alaska, to perhaps fifty different magazines worldwide, including *National Geographic, Audubon,* and the major hunting/fishing magazines.

"Spent eleven years as a commercial fisheries biologist for the new state of Alaska, 1959-69, then worked for twenty years as outdoors editor for *Alaska* magazine.

"Have written and sold eight books in the past five years since leaving *Alaska* magazine. *Cracking the Zero Mystery,* the story of a Japanese Zero found in the Aleutians during World War II, has been translated into Japanese and published in that country. *Castner's Cutthroats,* saga of the Alaska Scouts, is a novel based on the heroic performance of these scouts in the Aleutians during World War II. A screenplay I have written based on this novel is being considered by a major Hollywood producer.

"In my forty-two years in Alaska I have become a fisheries patrol agent, college professor, registered big game guide, full-time free-lance writer/photographer, clerk in a trading post, commercial fisherman, bounty hunter, construction laborer, and outdoors editor. I learned to fly at age fifty-nine and am currently building a kit airplane in my basement. I have half-a-dozen more books planned and continue to write an occasional magazine piece. I live in a log home I built myself in Homer, at the tip of the Kenai Peninsula."

*   *   *

RITZ, David   1943-
(Esther Elizabeth Pearl)

PERSONAL: Born December 2, 1943, in New York, NY; son of Milton M. (a stockbroker) and Pearl (Graver) Ritz; married Roberta Plitt (a comedienne); children: Alison, Jessica (twins). *Education:* University of Texas, B.A., 1966; State University of New York at Buffalo, M.A., 1969. *Religion:* Jewish.

ADDRESSES: Home—Los Angeles, CA.

CAREER: Bloom Advertising, Dallas, TX, copywriter, 1961-70; Houston/Ritz/Cohen/Jagoda (advertising agency), New York City, owner, 1971-75; writer, 1975—. Teacher at University of Pennsylvania, 1969.

AWARDS, HONORS: Fulbright scholar, 1968.

WRITINGS:

(With Ray Charles) *Brother Ray: Ray Charles' Own Story,* Dial, 1978.
Glory (novel), Simon & Schuster, 1979.
Search for Happiness (novel), Simon & Schuster, 1980.
The Man Who Brought the Dodgers Back to Brooklyn, Simon & Schuster, 1981.
(With Marvin Gaye) *Divided Soul: The Life of Marvin Gaye,* McGraw-Hill, 1985, edition with new introduction and updated discography, Da Capo Press, 1991.
Blue Notes under a Green Felt Hat (novel), Donald I. Fine, 1989.
(With Smokey Robinson) *Smokey: Inside My Life,* McGraw-Hill, 1989.
Barbells and Saxophones, Donald I. Fine, 1989.
Family Blood, Donald I. Fine, 1991.

Also author of novel, *Deeper than Shame,* under pseudonym Esther Elizabeth Pearl.

SIDELIGHTS: David Ritz is the author of popular novels and biographies of show business figures such as Ray Charles, Marvin Gaye, and Smokey Robinson of The Miracles. *Brother Ray,* Ritz's biography of the famed soul singer, impressed Marvin Gaye to commission a similar book. *Divided Soul: The Life of Marvin Gaye,* informed by

their long friendship and published after the singer's tragic death, "is a personal history and at the same time a sweeping saga of black music over the past three decades," Norman (Otis) Richmond observes in a Toronto *Globe and Mail* review. George de Stefano, like other reviewers, finds Ritz's presentation balanced between the brilliance of Gaye's musical talent and the darker aspects of his life. Explains de Stefano in the *Nation,* "*Divided Soul* started out in 1979 as a collaboration between Gaye and his long-time admirer. Ritz is sympathetic and loving toward the man whose friend and confidant he was for several years, but he doesn't hide Gaye's dark side, his self-absorption, his cruelties and violence. *Divided Soul* is often startlingly candid, but it manages to avoid lurid sensationalism, no mean feat given the particulars of the story: sex, drugs, child abuse, show-business scandal." This study of Gaye's growth from abused child to rebel to creative popular musician has been widely reviewed and generally well-received.

Novels by Ritz have also been favorably reviewed; readers say their plots take some interesting turns. *The Man Who Brought the Dodgers Back to Brooklyn,* for example, is a fantasy in which the Dodgers return to a reconstructed Ebbets Field with a female pitcher, yet the story falls just short of a fairy-tale ending. *Blue Notes under a Green Felt Hat*—the story of a jazz-loving hatmaker's son's vocational and romantic choices—"builds to a not-unpredictable trick ending, one [at] which he has dropped a few delectable hints along the way," writes Leonard Feather in the *Los Angeles Times Book Review.*

Ritz's 1980 offering, *Search for Happiness,* presents the problems that beset a writer of soap operas when he invents a character based on a real-life nun to save his slipping ratings. Burger King wants to build where her convent stands. In her fight to save the convent, she falls into the tempting arms of a married lawyer—an ethical problem for the real-life nun that sends her TV counterpart's ratings soaring. By the time the soap opera character is due for some requisite misery, the actress who plays her has identified so closely with the nun that the writer hesitates to cause the trouble that will again save the ratings. A *Washington Post Book World* reviewer comments, "What you got here, Sweetheart, is a soap within a soap, fast, funny, and sad. Also dirty like you wouldn't believe." *Los Angeles Times Book Review* contributor Leslie Raddatz remarks that the writer's "epic telling off of the network v.p. and his raffish views on such varied subjects as jogging and love are worth the price of admission."

BIOGRAPHICAL/CRITICAL SOURCES:

PERIODICALS

Chicago Tribune Book World, July 26, 1981.
Globe and Mail (Toronto), September 21, 1985.

Los Angeles Times, April 9, 1981.
Los Angeles Times Book Review, October 10, 1980; May 5, 1985; August 6, 1989.
Nation, October 5, 1985.
New York Times Book Review, June 2, 1985.
Time, July 6, 1981.
Times Literary Supplement, December 6, 1985.
Washington Post Book World, January 16, 1980.*

* * *

ROACH, Joyce Gibson 1935-

PERSONAL: Born December 18, 1935, in Jacksboro, TX; daughter of Dave (an independent grocer) and Ann (an independent insurance agent; maiden name, Hartman) Gibson; married Claude D. Roach (with U.S. Probation), June 15, 1957; children: Darrell, Delight. *Education:* Texas Christian University, B.F.A., 1958, M.A., 1964.

ADDRESSES: Home—Box 143, Keller, TX 76248. *Agent*—Nancy Crow, Cordovan Corp., 5314 Bingle Rd., Houston, TX 77092.

CAREER: Ann Gibson Insurance Agency, vice-president. Consultant, Texas Christian University Press, Educational Service Center, and Words in Season. Texas Christian University, Ft. Worth, TX, adjunct instructor in composition and Western Novel.

MEMBER: International Platform Association, Hymn Society of America, Western Writers of America, Western History Association, Western Literature Association, Texas Folklore Society (president, 1976), Texas Alliance for the Humanities (board member), Texas Institute of Letters, Texas State Historical Society.

AWARDS, HONORS: Spur Awards, Western Writers of America, for 1976 non-fiction work *The Cowgirls,* for short non-fiction work "A High-Toned Woman," and for short fiction work "Just As I Am"; Outstanding Educator, Texas Christian University Alumni Board, 1984; non-fiction award, Texas Institute of Letters, for *Eats: A Folk History of Texas Foods.*

WRITINGS:

The Cowgirls, Cordovan Press, 1977, revised edition, North Texas University Press.
C. L. Sonnichsen: Folk Historian, Boise State University Press, 1980.
(Contributor) *Women Who Made the West,* Doubleday, 1980.
(Editor) *Texas and Christmas,* Texas Christian University Press, 1983.
(With Ernestine Sewell Linck) *Eats: A Folk History of Texas Foods,* Texas Christian University Press, 1989.

MUSICAL DRAMAS

Nancy MacIntyre: A Tale of the Prairies, produced in Uvalde, TX, at Grand Op'ry House, 1989.
Legend of the Animals, produced in Uvalde, 1990.
Psalm 151 (fantasy), produced in Keller, TX, 1990.

Also *Texanna!* was produced in five Texas locations during the state's Sesquicentennial.

OTHER

(Editor) *This Place of Memory: A Texas Perspective* (anthology), University of North Texas Press, 1992.

Also contributor of articles to periodicals, including *Western Folklore, Publications of Texas Folklore Society, Horseman, Quarter Horse Journal, Western Treasures,* and *Southwest Heritage.*

WORK IN PROGRESS: Editing *Ride for the Brand,* a volume of poetry and song, for Texas cowboy-poet Rod Steagall.

SIDELIGHTS: Joyce Gibson Roach told *CA:* "I continue to find folklore a source for all my writing. Although I have turned to writing musical drama in the past few years, I continue to use folk materials as inspiration. The supply seems unlimited, rich, and waiting for the skill of writers and musicians to turn it into an artistic form which touches young and old, all levels of experience and social classes."

* * *

ROMULO, Beth Day
See DAY, Beth (Feagles)

* * *

ROSENBLUM, Martin J(ack) 1946-

PERSONAL: Born August 19, 1946, in Appleton, WI; son of Sander (a merchant) and Esther (Ressman) Rosenblum; married Maureen Rice (a psychotherapist), September 6, 1970; children: Sarah Terez. *Education:* University of Wisconsin—Madison, B.S. (with distinction), 1969; University of Wisconsin—Milwaukee, M.A., 1971, Ph.D., 1980. *Religion:* Jewish. *Avocational interests:* Music, martial arts, long-distance running.

ADDRESSES: Home—2521 East Stratford Ct., Shorewood, Milwaukee, WI 53211. *Office*—Department of Educational Opportunity, University of Wisconsin, Mitchell Hall 177F, P.O. Box 413, Milwaukee, WI 53201; American Ranger Inc., P.O. Box 71231, Milwaukee, WI 53211-7331.

CAREER: University of Wisconsin—Milwaukee, member of Midwest Poetry Reading Circuit, 1970—, poetry readings coordinator, 1971, lecturer in English, 1971-72, guest lecturer at Institute of World Affairs, spring, 1972, lecturer in English, 1973—, admissions specialist and academic advisor in department of educational opportunity, 1980—. Division of Continuing Education, Marquette University, Milwaukee, WI, instructor in English, 1971-72, director of division, summer, 1972; University of East Anglia, Norwich, England, guest lecturer and poetry reader, 1977; Interarts High School, Milwaukee, poetry instructor, 1977. Editor and publisher, Albatross Press, 1969-72, and Lionhead Publishing, 1972-78. Has conducted poetry workshops; has read own work over University of Wisconsin—Milwaukee radio station WUWM-FM, 1970—; has performed with his band in a British Broadcasting Corporation documentary, and on several television stations, including French public television, New Zealand television, and U.S. national television.

MEMBER: Modern Language Association of America, Committee of Small Magazine Editors and Publishers (COSMEP).

AWARDS, HONORS: Honorable mention, Academy of American Poets, 1971, for poem "The Logs"; Knapp fellowships in modern poetry research, 1977 and 1978.

WRITINGS:

POETRY

Halloween Evening, privately printed, 1969.
Bright Blue Coats (limited edition), Department of Art, University of Wisconsin—Madison, 1970.
First Words the Moon Sings Near Drowning, Albatross Press, 1970, 2nd edition, 1970.
Settling Attention and Other Poems, Albatross Press, 1970.
Home, Membrane Press, 1971, 2nd edition, Lionhead, 1991.
Sequence 50 from the Werewolf Sequence (also see below), Membrane Press, 1972.
Father for My Prayer, Monday Morning Press, 1972.
On:, Harpoon Press, 1972.
The Werewolf Sequence, Membrane Press, 1974.
Protractive Verse, Cat's Pajamas, 1976.
Scattered On: Omens and Curses, Pentagram Press, 1976.
as i magic, Morgan Press, 1976.
Divisions/One, Great Raven Press, 1978, published as *Divisions,* Lionhead, 1991.
Holy Screams, Pentagram Press, 1979.
Borne Out, Sutra, 1983.
Still Life, Morgan Press, 1986, limited edition, Lionhead, 1990.
(With Steven Lewis) *Geographics,* Lionhead, 1986.
(With Judith Marks) *Burning Oak,* Lionhead, 1986.

(With Steve Nelson-Raney) *Hocket Stutter,* Lionhead, 1987.
(With Laura Cairney-Winter) *Stone Fog,* Lionhead, 1987.
Conjunction, Lionhead, 1987.
The Holy Ranger: Harley-Davidson Poems, Lionhead, 1990.

POETRY ALBUMS

Backlit Frontier, Lionhead, 1987.
Music Lingo, Lionhead, 1989.

MUSIC ALBUMS

Other Symptoms (audio tape), Roar Recording, 1984.
I Am the Holy Ranger (cassette), Roar Recording, 1990.
The Holy Ranger's Free Hand (cassette), Flying Fish Records, 1991.
Outlaw, Roar Recording, 1992.

OTHER

(Editor with Bruce Borcherdt, Rod Clark, and Barry Russal, and contributor) *Albatross One* (anthology), Albatross Press, 1970.
(Editor, author of foreword, and contributor) *Brewing: 20 Milwaukee Poets,* Giligia Press, 1972.
Projective Verse (critical study), Dry Run Press, 1976.
Free Verse Self (critical study), Dry Run Press, 1979.

Contributor to books, including *Brite Shade,* Cody Books, 1984, with Nelson-Raney, Lionhead, 1987. Author of introduction, *The Round of Her Breast,* by Steven Lewis, Albatross Press, 1970. Work represented in anthologies, including *This Book Has No Title,* edited by Roger Mitchell and others, Third Coast/Amalgamated Holding Co., 1971; *Sorts,* edited by Tom Montag, Monday Morning Press, 1971; *The Freek Anthology of Poetry,* Volume 2, edited by Karl Young, Membrane Press, 1971; *The Wisconsin Review Anthology; Anthology of Poets,* edited by Victor Contoski; *Cassiopeia; Gathering Place of the Waters: 30 Milwaukee Poets; Younger Jewish Poets in America; Abraxas Anthology;* and *An Anthology of Blues, Look Quick* (songs).

Contributor of poetry and criticism to *Thistle, Cream City Review, Lakes and Prairies, Occurrence, Energy Review, Pembroke, Roadhouse, Hey Lady, Hawkwind, Wisconsin Review, Erratica, Monday Morning Wash, Stations, Daily Cardinal, Bugle-American, Shore Review, Modine Gunch, Harpoon, Margins, Small Press Review, Road Apple Review, Hanging Loose, Tempest,* and *Ziggurat.* Poetry editor and review columnist, *Bugle-American* (a Milwaukee weekly newspaper), 1971-72; editor, *Stations,* 1972-78; editor of third issue, *Monday Morning Wash,* 1972-73. Collections of Rosenblum's works are housed at the Murphy Library of the University of Wisconsin—La Crosse and at the Yale University Library.

WORK IN PROGRESS: A recording of *The Werewolf Sequence; Down on the Spirit Farm,* an album; *The Critical Biography of Carl Rakosi,* for University of Maine at Orono Press; *The Warrior Project,* a novel; a book on the white blues singers of the sixties; a volume of selected poems written from 1970 to 1980, for Membrane Press; *American Outlaw Visionary,* for Lionhead.

SIDELIGHTS: Martin J. Rosenblum once told *CA:* "Poetry and fiction—and even criticism—that does not expose the Self as the object but merely exorcises it by virtue of content that is all drama or structure is uninspired. But a work that is highly subjective is equally lacking imagination. The prime directive involved in writing must be to create an objective language that recreates the personality of the subject matter (which is originally experienced by the author). This Self (which may not be the author's) is the subject of all writing that is creative.

"This is not to say that such writing is simply a technical invention. Writing poetry, which is what I do most, is a craft—which is how it is effectively described; psychological or aesthetic terms can be applied only after the craft of a poem is understood—but it is an Image for the Self in transformation. Self requires form; flesh and bones make it recognizable as does a poem. Poems without this objective are formless (no matter what capricious ideological shape assumed) and intellectual and hysterical: the language composition of a personality is poetry in all its secret energy revealed, and anything else is something other than a poem."

Rosenblum recently added: "Poetry should not be removed from music. Poets can build 'music' into the line itself, but I am referring to poetry that combines with music in such a way as to make them both function in a mutually charged field of energy. I am contracted to a national record label, Flying Fish Records, Chicago, Illinois, and on this label have released *The Holy Ranger's Free Hand.* I am presently recording the album called *Down on the Spirit Farm.* Both albums present songs of mine, yes, but these are not just lyrics with music—they are Real Poems set on Music the way poetry is typeset for books. Critics have referred to my *Free Hand* album as 'poetry that rocks.'"

BIOGRAPHICAL/CRITICAL SOURCES:

BOOKS

Contemporary Authors Autobiography Series, Volume 11, Gale, 1990.

PERIODICALS

Appleton Post-Crescent View Magazine, June 24, 1973.
Bugle-American, May 6-12, 1971; January 26-February 2, 1972; March 22-April 5, 1972.

IMPACT, April, 1972.
Lakes and Prairies, fall/winter, 1979.
Milwaukee Journal, February, 1973.
Milwaukee Sentinel, August 19, 1972.
Northeast Post, August 15, 1979.
Plains Booklist, autumn, 1975.

*   *   *

ROSENFELD, Isadore   1926-

PERSONAL: Born September 7, 1926, in Montreal, Quebec, Canada; came to the United States in 1958, naturalized citizen, 1963; son of Morris and Vera (Friedman) Rosenfeld; married Camilla Master, August 19, 1956; children: Arthur, Stephen, Hildi, Herbert. *Education:* McGill University, B.Sc., 1947, M.D.C.M., 1951, diploma in internal medicine, 1956. *Politics:* Democrat. *Religion:* Jewish.

ADDRESSES: Office—125 East 72nd St., New York, NY 10021.

CAREER: Royal Victoria Hospital, Montreal, Quebec, junior rotating intern, 1951-52, junior assistant resident in medicine, 1952-53; Johns Hopkins Service, Baltimore, MD, assistant resident in Baltimore city hospitals, 1953-54; Jewish General Hospital, Montreal, Quebec, Mona B. Scheckman Research Fellow in Cardiology, 1954-55; Mount Sinai Hospital, New York City, fellow in cardiology, 1955-56; currently in private practice of medicine in New York City. Clinical assistant professor of medicine at Cornell University, 1964-71, clinical associate professor, 1971-79, clinical professor, 1979—, currently honorary fellow. Visiting professor, Baylor University College of Medicine, 1982; member of board of overseers, Cornell University Medical College, 1980—; member of board of visitors, University of California School of Medicine—Davis, 1983—. Certified specialist in cardiology, College of Physicians and Surgeons (Quebec); attending physician at New York Hospital, 1964—; attending physician at Memorial Hospital, 1989—.

President of Rosenfeld Heart Foundation, 1974—; member of board of trustees of Sackler School of Medicine, Tel Aviv University, 1977—. Member of National Heart Institute Task Force on Arteriosclerosis, 1970, 1971; member of National Task Force on Hypertension, 1975-77. Juror for Lasker Scientific Awards, 1972—. Chairman, Foundation for Bio-Medical Research, New York City, 1982-90; member, national advisory committee, Harriman Institute for the Advanced Study of the Soviet Union, 1982—; member, Practicing Physicians Advisory Council of the Health Care Financing Administration, 1992-96.

MEMBER: American College of Physicians (fellow), American College of Chest Physicians (fellow), American

College of Cardiology (fellow), American Heart Association (fellow of Council on Epidemiology), American Physicians Fellowship for Israel (chapter president, 1973-75; national president, 1973-74; honorary national president, 1975-88), American Therapeutic Society, American Public Health Association, Royal College of Physicians (Canada; fellow), New York Cardiological Society (fellow), New York Heart Association (board of directors, 1979-82), New York Academy of Sciences, New York County Medical Society (censor, 1975-78; vice-president, 1983-84; president, 1984-85; trustee, 1985-90), Cornell Alumni Association (honorary fellow).

AWARDS, HONORS: Sir Edward Beattie Scholarship from McGill University, 1955-56; Vera Award, Voice Foundation, 1981; Commendatore dell'Ordine al Merito della Repubblica Italiana, 1987; honorary surgeon of New York City Police Department.

WRITINGS:

(With Arthur M. Master, R. P. Lasser, and E. Donoso) *The Electrocardiogram and Chest Roentgenogram in Diseases of the Heart,* Lea & Febiger, 1963.
(Author of foreword) Richard G. Margoles, *A Doctor's Eat-Hearty Guide for Good Health and Long Life,* Parker Publishing, 1974.
The Complete Medical Exam: What Your Doctor Knows Is Critical; What YOU Know Is Critical, Simon & Schuster, 1978.
(Contributor) *Ann Landers Encyclopedia,* Doubleday, 1978.
Second Opinion, Linden Press/Simon & Schuster, 1981, revised and updated edition, Bantam, 1982, 2nd edition published as *Second Opinion: Your Comprehensive Guide to Treatment Alternatives,* Bantam, 1988.
Modern Prevention: The New Medicine, Linden Press/ Simon & Schuster, 1986.
Symptoms, Simon & Schuster, 1989.
Distress Signals, Poseidon Press, 1989.
The Best Treatment, Simon & Schuster, 1991.

Contributor of many articles to medical journals. Editorial consultant for *Journal of Electrocardiology,* 1973-85. Monthly health columnist for *Vogue* magazine, 1992—.

SIDELIGHTS: Dr. Isadore Rosenfeld once told *CA:* "*The Complete Medical Exam* was my first foray into the world of non-professional writing. I felt it was necessary because I believe the best informed patient gets the best medical care, and that the era of double-talk from doctor to patient is over, and none too soon. But how to find the time, in the midst of an 18 hour day practicing medicine, to write a book that (a) patients would read, understand, and enjoy; and (b) somebody would publish. It took me two years of weekend writing, editing, and re-writing alone. No ghost writer, no chapters written by guest editors. I

just closed my eyes and dictated a typical office visit by a patient coming for a check-up, complete with the pathos and the humor of everyday situations.

"When I first broached the subject of my proposed book, a publisher turned it down sight unseen. But my motivation was not royalties or income. I felt this was a book that needed to be written. When I was finished the same publisher who turned it down bought it with enthusiasm, and has guided it into its fourth printing and a very gratifying paperback sale. The point of all this is that you don't have to stop whatever else you're doing in order to write a book. Also, if you're convinced that an idea is good, you mustn't be discouraged by a rejection. Chances are that those who turn you down know less about what the reading public wants and needs than you do."

*   *   *

ROTTENBERG, Dan(iel) 1942-

PERSONAL: Born June 10, 1942, in New York, NY; son of Herman and Lenore (Goldstein) Rottenberg; married Barbara Rubin (a music teacher), January 4, 1964; children: Lisa, Julie. *Education:* University of Pennsylvania, B.A., 1964. *Religion:* Jewish.

ADDRESSES: Home—1618 Waverly St., Philadelphia, PA 19103. *Agent*—McIntosh & Otis, Inc., 310 Madison Ave., New York, NY 10017. *Office*—275 South 19th St., Philadelphia, PA 19103.

CAREER: Commercial Review, Portland, IN, sports editor, 1964-66, editor, 1966-68; *Wall Street Journal,* Chicago, IL, reporter, 1968-70; *Chicago Journalism Review,* Chicago, managing editor, 1970-72; *Philadelphia,* Philadelphia, PA, executive editor, 1972-75; free-lance writer, 1975—.

AWARDS, HONORS: Penney-Missouri Newspaper Award from J. C. Penney Co. and University of Missouri, 1976, for article, "Fernanda"; Clarion Award from Women in Communications, 1977, for article, "Edison's Nuclear Gamble"; Peter Lisagor Award for financial writing from Chicago Headline Club, 1982, for article "The Bank That Couldn't Say No"; Peter Lisagor Award for magazine reporting, 1984, for article "The Last Run of the Rock Island Line."

WRITINGS:

Finding Our Fathers, Random House, 1977.
(Contributor) Murray Friedman, editor, *Jewish Life in Philadelphia,* Institute for the Study of Human Issues, 1983.
Fight On, Pennsylvania, University of Pennsylvania Press, 1985.
Wolf, Block, Schorr, 1988.

Main Line WASP, Norton, 1990.
Revolution On Wall Street, Norton, 1993.

Author of monthly film column syndicated to city magazines, 1971-83, and weekly column in *Philadelphia Inquirer,* 1978—. Contributing editor, *Chicago,* 1971-86, and *Town and Country,* 1976—. Editor, *Weicomat,* 1981—.

SIDELIGHTS: Dan Rottenberg described to *CA* his areas of expertise as "business, the law, news media, movies, the super-rich, and Judaica."

S

SACKVILLE-WEST, V(ictoria Mary) 1892-1962

PERSONAL: Born March 9, 1892, at Knole Castle, Sevenoaks, Kent, England; died of cancer, June 2, 1962, at Sissinghurst Castle, Cranbrook, Kent, England; daughter of Lionel Edward and Victoria Josepha Dolores Catalina Sackville-West; married Harold George Nicolson (a journalist and diplomat), October 1, 1912 (died, 1968); children: Benedict, Nigel. *Education:* Studied privately with tutors.

CAREER: Novelist and poet. *Observer,* London, England, author of column on gardening, 1946-61. Member of National Trust's Garden Committee. *Wartime service:* Organizer of Kent's Women's Land Army during World War II.

MEMBER: Royal Society (fellow).

AWARDS, HONORS: Hawthornden Prize, 1927, for *The Land;* Heinemann Prize, 1946, for *The Garden;* named Companion of Honor, 1948.

WRITINGS:

POETRY

Chatterton, privately printed, 1909.
Constantinople, privately printed, 1915.
Poems of West and East, John Lane, 1918.
Orchard and Vineyard, John Lane, 1921.
The Land, Heinemann, 1926, Doran & Coy, 1927.
King's Daughter, Hogarth Press, 1929, Doubleday, 1930.
Invitation to Cast Out Care, illustrated by Graham Sutherland, Faber, 1931.
Sissinghurst, Hogarth Press, 1931, reprinted, National Trust, 1972.
Collected Poems: Volume I, Hogarth Press, 1933, Doubleday, 1934.
Some Flowers, Cobden-Sanderson, 1937.

Solitude: A Poem, Hogarth Press, 1938, Doubleday, 1939.
Selected Poems, Hogarth Press, 1941.
The Garden, Doubleday, 1946.

NOVELS

Heritage, George H. Doran, 1919.
The Dragon in Shallow Waters, Collins, 1921, Putnam, 1922.
Challenge, George H. Doran, 1923, reprinted, Avon, 1976.
Grey Wethers: A Romantic Novel, George H. Doran, 1923.
Seducers in Ecuador, Hogarth Press, 1924, George H. Doran, 1925.
The Edwardians, Doubleday, Doran, 1930, reprinted, Virago, 1983.
All Passion Spent, Doubleday, Doran, 1931, reprinted, Hogarth Press, 1965.
Family History, Doubleday, Doran, 1932, reprinted, Penguin, 1987.
The Dark Island, Doubleday, Doran, 1934.
Grand Canyon, Doubleday, Doran, 1942.
The Devil at Westease: The Story as Related by Roger Liddiard (detective story), Doubleday, 1947.
The Easter Party, Doubleday, 1953, reprinted, Greenwood Press, 1972.
No Signposts in the Sea, Doubleday, 1961, reprinted, Penguin, 1985.

SHORT STORIES

The Heir: A Love Story (short story), privately printed, 1922.
The Heir: A Love Story (short story collection; contains "The Heir," "The Christmas Party," "Patience," "Her Son," and "The Parrot"), George H. Doran, 1922, reprinted, Cedric Chivers, 1973.
Thirty Clocks Strike the Hour and Other Stories (contains "Thirty Clocks Strike the Hour," "The Death of

Noble Godavary," "Gottfried Kuenstler," "The Poet," "Pomodoro," "Elizabeth Higginbottom," "Up Jenkins," and "An Unborn Visitant"), Doubleday, Doran, 1932.

"The Death of Noble Godavary" and "Gottfried Kuenstler," Benn, 1932.

BIOGRAPHIES

Aphra Ben: The Incomparable Astrea, G. Howe, 1927, Viking, 1928, reprinted, Russell, 1970.

Andrew Marvell, Faber, 1929, reprinted, Folcroft, 1969.

St. Joan of Arc, Doubleday, 1936, reprinted, M. Joseph, 1969.

Pepita, Doubleday, 1937, reprinted, Hogarth Press, 1970.

The Eagle and the Dove: A Study in Contrasts, St. Theresa of Avila and St. Theresa of Lisieux, M. Joseph, 1943, Doubleday, 1944, reprinted, M. Joseph, 1969.

Daughter of France: The Life of Anne Marie Louise d'Orleans, Duchesse de Montpensier, 1627-1693, La Grande Mademoiselle, Doubleday, 1959.

BOOKS ON GARDENING

Country Notes, M. Joseph, 1939, Harper, 1940, reprinted, Books for Libraries, 1971.

Country Notes in Wartime, Hogarth Press, 1940, Doubleday, 1941, reprinted, Books for Libraries, 1970.

In Your Garden, M. Joseph, 1951, published as *V. Sackville-West's Garden Book,* edited by Philippa Nicolson, Atheneum, 1968, published in England as *V. Sackville-West's Garden Book: A Collection Taken from 'In Your Garden,'* M. Joseph, 1968, reprinted, Macmillan, 1983.

In Your Garden Again, M. Joseph, 1953.

More for Your Garden, M. Joseph, 1955.

A Joy of Gardening: A Selection for Americans, edited by Hermine I. Popper, Harper, 1958.

Even More for Your Garden, M. Joseph, 1958.

The Illustrated Garden Book: A New Anthology, edited by Robin Lane Fox, Atheneum, 1986.

The Land and the Garden, Viking, 1989.

OTHER

Knole and the Sackvilles, George H. Doran, 1922, revised edition, Benn, 1950.

(Author of introduction and notes) *The Diary of Lady Anne Clifford,* Heinemann, 1923, reprinted, Norwood Editions, 1979.

Passenger to Teheran, Hogarth Press, 1926, George H. Doran, 1927, reprinted, Moyer Bell, 1991.

Twelve Days: An Account of a Journey Across the Bakhtiari Mountains in Southwestern Persia, Doubleday, 1928.

(Translator) Rainer Marie Rilke, *Duineser Elegien: Elegies from the Castle of Duino,* Hogarth Press, 1931.

English Country Houses, Collins, 1941.

The Women's Land Army, M. Joseph, 1944.

(With husband, Harold Nicolson) *Another World Than This* (anthology), M. Joseph, 1945.

Nursery Rhymes (a study of the history of nursery rhymes), Dropmore, 1947.

(Author of introduction) Alice Christiana Meynell, *Prose and Poetry,* J. Cape, 1947.

Faces: Profiles of Dogs, Harvill, 1961, Doubleday, 1962.

Berkeley Castle: The Historic Glouchestershire Seat of the Berkeley Family Since the Eleventh Century, English Life Publications, 1972.

Dearest Andrew: Letters from V. Sackville-West to Andrew Reiber, 1951-1952, edited by Nancy MacKnight, Scribner, 1979.

Contributor of critical essays to Royal Society of Literature of the United Kingdom, c. 1927-45.

SIDELIGHTS: Victoria Sackville-West was an award-winning poet, as well as a novelist, biographer, and writer of books about gardening. In addition, the gardens she designed, especially the all-white garden at Sissinghurst Castle, earned her an international reputation as a landscape designer. Since her death in 1962, details about Sackville-West's often dramatic personal life have emerged and given the author a reputation quite apart from her work as a writer and gardener.

Born into one of England's most socially prominent families, Sackville-West spent most of her life in Knole Castle, which her son Nigel Nicolson described in *Portrait of a Marriage* as "the largest house in England still in private hands." The castle had been given to her ancestor, Thomas Sackville, a sixteenth century poet and dramatist. To Sackville-West, Knole represented historical continuity and an ordered world. She lived there for much of her life. As a child growing up at Knole, her social milieu included people of noble birth and wealth, including Rudyard Kipling, Auguste Rodin, Pierpont Morgan, William Waldorf Astor, and Henry Ford. As a young girl, she was courted at the castle by nobility, including Lord Lascelles and Lord Granby.

Sackville-West began writing at an early age. "Through Knole and her preferred solitude," Nicolson revealed, "she discovered the joy of writing." Her first works, written at the age of eleven, were ballads in the Horatius manner, and the first money she ever earned was one pound for a poem published in the *Onlooker* when she was fifteen years old. *Chatterton,* her first collection of poetry, was privately printed in 1909, followed by *Constantinople* in 1915. In addition to poetry, Sackville-West wrote eight full-length novels (one in French) and five plays between 1906 and 1910. She chose early to publish her work under the name "V. Sackville-West," hoping thereby to avoid being labeled a "woman writer." She wanted her work to be judged on its own merits, without gender considerations.

In her poetry, Sackville-West often dealt with pastoral themes. Her most widely celebrated poem, *The Land,* was published in 1926 and won the Hawthornden Prize for that year. *The Land* is a 2,500-line evocation of the English countryside near Kent. The critic for the *Boston Transcript* called the work "a poetic saga of the land and the beauties of the changing seasons." Divided into four parts based on the seasons, *The Land* focuses on the daily life of ordinary country people, presenting their activities with a simple dignity. So accurate was Sackville-West's rendering of country folk that the reviewer for *Nation and Atheneum* found that "long stretches of 'The Land' could be read aloud in a country alehouse, and if it were not announced as poetry, its rough and racy wisdom would win a gruff assent." This realism was also commented on by C. H. Warren in the *Spectator. The Land* contains, Warren believed, "such wealth of coloured lore, such pictures of exact observation, and such a richness of intuitive understanding of the peasant-mind that we might say who carries [Sackville-West's] poem with him into a foreign land carries all the best of England in his pocket."

Although Sackville-West published other collections of poetry, it was *The Land* for which she was always best known. Speaking of the poem in the *New Statesman and Nation,* Richard Church noted that *The Land* is "one of the most complete and beautiful bucolics written in English. It is so satisfying a poem that one tends to neglect her other work, and to reread it again and again." A *Saturday Review* critic called *The Land* "a very simple, moving and intimate poem which will continue to find readers as long as there are English people who love to be reminded of the native beauty of their countryside, and of the ancient, and (it seems) unalterable life of the soil." Nature continued to be a prominent theme in Sackville-West's later poetry, expressing her deep love for the natural world. "Her poetry," John Sparrow remarked in *Spectator,* "does not merely describe nature; it does not merely express her feeling; she describes, and in what she writes Nature and her feeling are one."

Sackville-West's love of nature was reflected, too, in her books on gardening and in the gardening column she wrote for the *Observer* for fifteen years. Many of her books are collections of these columns. When writing about gardening, she wrote in a suitably lush and poetic style. Describing one plant specimen in her *The Illustrated Garden Book,* for example, Sackville-West reported: "The flowers of Magnolia grandiflora look like great white pigeons settling among dark leaves."

Combining a thorough knowledge of horticulture with a poetic style, Sackville-West's books on gardening remain among the most popular in the field. She "writes vividly and attractively," a *Times Literary Supplement* critic said of Sackville-West, "making what she describes come to life, and giving the reader a mental picture of a garden which is full of colour, form and scent." Margaret McClure of the *Chicago Sunday Tribune* found the book *Joy of Gardening* to be "a treasure. There are excellent books on horticulture and others to delight us with the beauty of gardens; but never before, to my knowledge, has there been a book that inspires and instructs us as well." Speaking of Sackville-West's literate presentation of gardening information, a *Christian Science Monitor* critic commented that the author "cannot help adding to literature even when writing on slugs or an irrigating hose."

In 1930, Sackville-West and her husband, Harold Nicolson, bought Sissinghurst Castle in England. In the following years, the couple planned and created a number of gardens on the castle's grounds. The most famous of these is the all-white garden designed by Sackville-West. Based on earlier ideas about "tonal" gardens, which emphasize the colors and shapes of the chosen plants rather than their placement within the garden, the Sissinghurst garden creates a soft and charming atmosphere and served as an inspiration for many similar gardens throughout the world.

A prolific writer in several genres, Sackville-West wrote novels and biographies as well as poetry and books on gardening. For her novels, she turned to the stories of Knole and the Sackville family. "The Sackvilles, who were on the whole a modest family given to lengthy bouts of melancholia," Nicolson reported, "were transformed by Vita into troubadors who played the most dramatic roles at the most dramatic moments of English history, and behaved in every situation with the utmost gallantry." Among the novels based on Sackville-West's family history are *The Edwardians, All Passion Spent,* and *Family History.* Speaking of the relationship between Sackville-West's poetry and novels, L. A. G. Strong observed in the *Spectator:* "Every novel written by a poet is in one sense an allegory. If it moves him as a poet—and he has no business with it otherwise—its characters and scenes will bear more than their literal meaning. Like a poem, it will contain more than the poet is consciously aware of as he writes. Miss Sackville-West's work has always had this double validity. Even where she is least conscious of her intentions, the truth of her work rings on more than one level."

In the novel *The Edwardians,* Sackville-West recreated England's aristocratic society of the turn of the century, basing the characters on herself as a young girl and on her mother's friends who visited the family. The novel is, the critic for the *Springfield Republican* stated, "a magnificent portrait of a class and an era," while Louis Kronenberger wrote in the *New York Times* that "as a picture, as a study in manners, as a record of social history, 'The Edwardians' could hardly be bettered." The first of three best-selling novels for Sackville-West, *The Edwardians* brought her work to a wider audience than she had previously enjoyed.

Sackville-West's next novel, *All Passion Spent,* was also a bestseller. Telling the story of a widowed aristocrat who wishes to express her individuality, the novel drew critical praise for its fully-realized central character as well as its delicate prose. "It is as formal, as stately, as measured as a minuet. . . . ," Margaret Wallace commented in the *New York Times.* "Sackville-West has borrowed in her prose writing some part of the function of poetry, the ability to suggest far more than she says." Sackville-West's voice, "unmistakable even in its lightest inflection," Strong believed, "speaks throughout with the authority and poise of an untroubled accomplishment."

In her third best-selling novel, *Family History* Sackville-West continued to focus her attention on the social dramas of the English upper classes. Telling of a middle-aged widow who falls in love with a much younger man, the novel gives a panoramic vision of several generations of a wealthy family. It is, R. E. Roberts claimed in *New Statesman and Nation,* "packed with keenly observed characters." The critic for the *Boston Transcript* found a deeper level to the novel as well. The story, he believed, "implies the age-long struggle between established customs and new ideas, and the ironical tragedy of a woman who could rely upon neither to control her heart." "Simply as entertainment," wrote Dorothea Brande in *Bookman,* "the book has very few equals."

The Sackville family also inspired the biography *Pepita,* which tells the life story of Sackville-West's grandmother, a popular Spanish dancer who was the mistress of the English diplomat Sir Lionel Sackville-West. Her many exploits form the first half of the book, while the life of her illegitimate daughter, Sackville-West's mother, form the second half. Sackville-West's style, Strong wrote, moves from a "cool, half-humorous detachment" when speaking of Pepita to a "no less humorous, no less controlled, but warmer, richer, and quite beautiful" style when speaking of her mother. Norma McCarty in *New Republic* also notes a dual tone to Sackville-West's writing: "Detached enough to see her mother's faults in their true perspective . . . Sackville-West was at the same time passionately fond of her. And this mixed approach gives the portrait the breath of life."

Sackville-West also wrote more experimental novels, particularly *Seducers in Equador,* a spare and surreal tale of Arthur Lomax, who dons a pair of unusual spectacles and sees the world in a different and more adventurous way. Because of this new insight, Lomax ends up killing a man and getting arrested for murder. The reviewer for the Lon-

don *Times* found *Seducers in Equador* to be "sparkling with terse, amusing irony and occasionally vibrant colour, and hinting mysterious abysses." The *Spectator* critic called the novel "a slim, fantastic *conte* in the best Bloomsbury manner—something of the form of 'Lady into Fox.' "

Seducers in Equador was written for Virginia Woolf and was first published by Woolf's Hogarth Press. In a letter written to Sackville-West on September 15, 1924, Woolf spoke about her reaction to the novel. "I like its texture," Woolf wrote, "the sense of all the fine things you have dropped into it, so that it is full of beauty in itself when nothing is happening—nevertheless such interesting things do happen, so suddenly—barely, too; and I like its obscurity so that we can play about with it—interpret it different ways, and the beauty and the fantasticality of the details."

A large part of Sackville-West's literary renown stems from her association with the Bloomsbury group, an English literary clique of the 1920s, and from her relationship with Virginia Woolf, the most prominent member of Bloomsbury. Sackville-West shared a deep, lasting emotional and sexual relationship with Woolf. Many critics believe that Sackville-West is the title character of *Orlando,* Woolf's experimental novel that follows its central character through several centuries and identities. "The usual boundaries of gender, time, and tragic consequence are transcended in a lighthearted Ovidian skating," according to J. J. Wilson in the *Concise Dictionary of British Literary Biography.* Some of the Sackville family history figures prominently in *Orlando,* while a portrait of Sackville-West was printed in the novel, identified as "Orlando, about the year 1840." Because of the novelists' close friendship, the novel took on unique importance in Sackville-West's life. Nicolson explained: "Virginia by her genius has provided Vita [Sackville-West] with a unique consolation for having been born a girl, for her exclusion from her inheritance, for her father's death earlier that year. The book, for her, was not simply a brilliant masque or pageant. It was a memorial mass." Wilson called the book "a kind of love letter tribute to Virginia and Vita's passionate friendship." The close relationship between the two women lasted until the late 1920s; thereafter the two women continued to correspond until Woolf's suicide in 1941.

After Sackville-West's own death in 1962, her son Nigel discovered an autobiography that his mother had written in 1920. The memoir, later incorporated into Nigel's book *Portrait of a Marriage,* revealed his mother's lesbian relationships with two other women, Rosamund Grosvenor, a relative of the Duke of Westminster, and Violet Keppel. Sackville-West's relationship with Violet led to the two women running away to France together. There, Sackville-West played out the masculine side of her nature, taking on the role of "Julian" and dressing in male clothes. She would escort Violet dining and dancing in Parisian nightspots. "When posing as a man," Priscilla Diaz-Dorr wrote in the *Dictionary of Literary Biography,* "Sackville-West felt most free." This relationship was also depicted in Sackville-West's novel *Challenge,* in which the character Julian Davenant loves a woman who is obviously based on Violet Keppel. The novel's "likenesses and the underlying Sapphic philosophy," Diaz-Dorr reported, "were apparent enough that the families of these two women suppressed [*Challenge*'s] publication in England."

Apart from disclosing the homosexuality within Britain's upper classes, Sackville-West's autobiography is the remarkable story of the author's relationship with her husband, Harold Nicolson. Their son called his parents' marriage "the strangest and most successful union that two gifted people have ever enjoyed." Theirs "is the story of two people who married for love and whose love deepened with every passing year, although each was constantly and by mutual consent unfaithful to the other. Both loved people of their own sex, but not exclusively. Their marriage not only survived infidelity, sexual incompatibility and long absences, but it became stronger and finer as a result. . . . Marriage succeeded because each found permanent and undiluted happiness only in the company of the other," he observed.

Sackville-West enjoys a reputation in several genres. Her gardening books are basic texts in that subject, while her novels and poetry are read with interest by feminist scholars. As Diaz-Dorr noted: "When placed in the tradition of twentieth-century British women novelists, [Sackville-West's] writings contribute to the history of women's thought during the turbulent years after emancipation when British women were seeking a new identity. The enduring value of her works comes from the honesty with which she portrays the emotional turmoil created by the changing social and intellectual environment of the 1920s and 1930s in England." In *Bookman,* Hugh Walpole stated: "I find among all the writers in England no one else who has achieved such distinction in so many directions. The novelists who are also poets, the poets who are also novelists, are very rare always."

BIOGRAPHICAL/CRITICAL SOURCES:

BOOKS

Bell, Quentin, *Virginia Woolf: A Biography,* Harcourt, 1972.

Brown, Jane, *Vita's Other World: A Gardening Biography of V. Sackville-West,* Viking, 1986.

Concise Dictionary of British Literary Biography, Volume 6: *Modern Writers, 1914-1945,* Gale, 1992.

Dictionary of Literary Biography, Volume 34: *British Novelists, 1890-1929: Traditionalists,* Gale, 1985.

Glendinning, Victoria, *Vita: The Life of Vita Sackville-West,* Knopf, 1983.

Glendinning, *Vita: A Bibliography of Vita Sackville-West,* Morrow, 1985.

Nicolson, Nigel, editor, *The Diaries and Letters of Harold Nicolson,* three volumes, Atheneum, 1966-68.

Nicolson, *Portrait of a Marriage,* Atheneum, 1973.

Nicolson and Joanne Trautmann, editors, *The Letters of Virginia Woolf: Volume III, 1923-1928,* Harcourt, 1977.

Philippe, Juliann, and John Phillips, *The Other Woman: A Life of Violet Trefusis,* Houghton, 1976.

Rule, Jane, *Lesbian Images,* Doubleday, 1975.

Sackville-West, V., *Dearest Andrew: Letters from V. Sackville-West to Andrew Reiber, 1951-1952,* edited by Nancy MacKnight, Scribner, 1979.

Scott-James, Anne, *Sissinghurst: The Making of a Garden,* M. Joseph, 1983.

Smaridge, Norah, *Famous British Women Novelists,* Dodd, 1967.

Stevens, Michael, *V. Sackville-West: A Critical Biography,* Scribner's, 1974.

Trautmann, Joanne, *The Jessamy Brides: The Friendship of Virginia Woolf and V. Sackville-West,* Pennsylvania State University Press, 1973.

Watson, Sarah Ruth, *V. Sackville-West,* Twayne, 1972.

PERIODICALS

America, October 17, 1936, p. 46.

Atlantic, July, 1961, p. 132.

Bookman, September, 1930; November, 1932, p. 734.

Books, May 5, 1929, p. 10; August 30, 1931, p. 3; June 12, 1932, p. 2; October 30, 1932, p. 6; November 25, 1934, p. 16; September 27, 1936, p. 3.

Book World, February 9, 1969, p. 5.

Boston Transcript, October 29, 1927, p. 8; November 2, 1932, p. 2.

British Book News, June, 1980, p. 375; May, 1982, p. 275.

Chicago Daily Tribune, August 29, 1931, p. 4; June 11, 1932, p. 8.

Chicago Sunday Tribune, February 23, 1958, p. 14.

Christian Science Monitor, June 11, 1932, p. 6; September 30, 1936, p. 11; March 2, 1940, p. 11; April 3, 1958, p. 7; January 14, 1980, p. 84; July 27, 1983, p. 11.

Economist, February 23, 1974, p. 116.

Horticulture, July, 1977; February, 1981, p. 8.

Independent, February 26, 1927, p. 118.

Listener, February 28, 1974, p. 280.

Los Angeles Times Book Review, December 8, 1985, p. 8.

Ms., April, 1984, p. 27.

Nation, October 21, 1931, p. 439; December 5, 1934, p. 656.

Nation and Atheneum, November 6, 1926, p. 188; December 3, 1927, p. 360; November 17, 1928, p. 270.

New Republic, September 24, 1930, p. 158; January 12, 1938, p. 290.

New Statesman, November 13, 1926; December 25, 1926, p. 347; December 3, 1927, p. 360; June 14, 1930, p. 308; February 24, 1961, p. 313; December 3, 1965, p. 896; February 22, 1974, p. 266; November 2, 1984, p. 33.

New Statesman and Nation, October 22, 1932, p. 490; May 12, 1934, p. 740.

Newsweek, April 24, 1961; November 5, 1973.

New Yorker, March 28, 1970, p. 125.

New York Times, September 7, 1930, p. 7; August 30, 1931, p. 7; June 12, 1932, p. 7; October 30, 1932, p. 7; November 25, 1934, p. 6; September 27, 1936, p. 1; April 7, 1940, p. 28; May 11, 1941, p. 12; February 23, 1958, p. 20; June 3, 1962; April, 16, 1987.

New York Times Book Review, April 16, 1961, p. 4.

Observer, February 17, 1974, p. 32.

Outlook, February 13, 1929, p. 267; October 1, 1930, p. 188.

PMLA, March, 1955; March, 1956.

Publishers Weekly, June 25, 1962.

Punch, June 1, 1983, p. 81.

Saturday Review, December 4, 1926, p. 682; July 19, 1930, p. 84; October 15, 1932, p. 399; November 3, 1934, p. 344; April 22, 1961, p. 24.

Saturday Review of Literature, October 17, 1931, p. 214; March 24, 1934, p. 580; October 10, 1936, p. 7; December 4, 1937, p. 7.

Spectator, January 3, 1925, p. 20; October 30, 1926; November 24, 1928; May 31, 1930, p. 913; May 30, 1931, p. 872; October 22, 1932, p. 556; January 26, 1934, p. 129; June 19, 1936, p. 1140; November 19, 1937; December 8, 1939, p. 836; June 2, 1953; March 2, 1974, p. 268.

Time, June 8, 1962; November 12, 1973.

Times (London), November 27, 1924, p. 794; May 14, 1983.

Times Literary Supplement, October 21, 1926, p. 716; November 4, 1926, p. 758; May 29, 1930, p. 454; October 13, 1932, p. 730; October 11, 1934, p. 692; June 6, 1936, p. 469; October 30, 1937, p. 796; December 2, 1939, p. 697; December 7, 1940, p. 618; October 3, 1968, p. 1135; March 15, 1974, p. 253.

Vogue, September 1, 1956; October 15, 1961; November, 1973.

Washington Post Book World, December 7, 1986, p. 15.

Wilson Library Bulletin, September, 1962.

Yale Review, autumn, 1930; winter, 1937.*

St. GEORGE, Margaret
See OSBORNE, Margaret Ellen

*   *   *

SAMBROOK, Arthur James 1931-

PERSONAL: Born September 5, 1931, in Nuneaton, Warwickshire, England; son of Arthur (a carpenter) and Constance Elizabeth (a local government officer; maiden name, Gapper) Sambrook; married Patience Ann Crawford (a librarian), March 25, 1961; children: John Arthur, William James, Robert Joseph, Thomas Daniel. *Education:* Worcester College, Oxford University, B.A. (first class honors), 1955, M.A., 1959; University of Nottingham, Ph.D., 1957.

ADDRESSES: Home—36 Bursledon Rd., Hedge End, Southampton SO9 5NH, England.

CAREER: St. David's College, Lampeter, Wales, lecturer in English, 1957-64; University of Southampton, Southampton, England, lecturer, 1964-71, senior lecturer in English, 1971-75, reader, 1975-81, professor, 1981—. Visiting research fellow, Newberry Library, Chicago, IL, 1969, Folger Shakespeare Library, Washington, D.C., 1974, 1982, Magdalen College, Oxford University, 1984, St. John's College, Oxford University, 1985, and Humanities Research Centre, Australian National University, 1988. *Military service:* Royal Air Force, 1950-52.

AWARDS, HONORS: Killam Senior Research Fellow, Dalhousie University, Nova Scotia, 1968-69; Leverhulme Research Fellow, 1974-75.

WRITINGS:

A Poet Hidden: The Life of Richard Watson Dixon, 1833-1900, Athlone Press, 1962.
(Editor) *The Scribleriad, 1742,* Augustan Reprint Society, 1967.
(Editor) James Thomson, *The Seasons and The Castle of Indolence,* Clarendon Press, 1972, 3rd edition, 1987.
William Cobbett: An Author Guide, Routledge, 1973.
(Editor) *Pre-Raphaelitism,* University of Chicago Press, 1974.
English Pastoral Poetry, Twayne, 1983.
(Editor) *Liberty, The Castle of Indolence, and Other Poems,* Clarendon Press, 1986.
The Eighteenth Century: The Intellectual and Cultural Context of English Literature, 1700-1789, Longman, 1986, 4th edition, 1990.
James Thomson, 1700-1748: A Life, Clarendon Press, 1992.

Contributor to numerous books, including *The Victorians,* edited by Arthur Pollard, Sphere Books, 1970, revised edition, 1987; *Alexander Pope,* edited by Peter Dixon, Bell, 1972; *The Romantic Period Excluding the Novel,* edited by Kenneth Muir, Macmillan, 1980; *British Poets, 1880-1914,* edited by D. E. Stanford, Gale, 1984; *British and American Gardens in the Eighteenth Century,* edited by R. P. Maccubbin and P. Martin, Colonial Williamsburg Foundation, 1984; and *The Blackwell Companion to the Enlightenment,* edited by John W. Yolton and others, Blackwell, 1991. Also contributor to *Yearbook of English Studies;* contributor of articles to *Notes and Queries, English, Review of English Studies, Etudes Anglaises, Church Quarterly Review, Eighteenth Century Studies, English Miscellany, Forum, Modern Philology, Studies in Bibliography, Studies in Burke and His Time, Studies on Voltaire and the Eighteenth Century, Times Literary Supplement, Garden History, Trivium,* and *Journal of the Warburg and Courtauld Institutes.*

*   *   *

SAMPSON, Fay (Elizabeth) 1935-

PERSONAL: Born June 10, 1935, in Plymouth, England; daughter of Edmar Ismail (a member of Royal Marine Staff Band) and Edith Maud (a hotel waitress; maiden name, Cory) Sampson; married Jack Greaves Priestley (principal of Westhill College), March 30, 1959; children: Mark Alan, Katharine Fay. *Education:* University College of the Southwest, B.A. (with honors), 1956; University of Exeter, certificate in education, 1957. *Politics:* Radical. *Religion:* Christian. *Avocational interests:* Walking, travel, Celtic history, mythology, exploring spirituality.

ADDRESSES: Home—45 Weoley Hill, Selly Oak, Birmingham B29 4AB, England; (vacation) Christie Cottage, Tedburn St. Mary, Exeter, Devon EX6 6AZ, England.

CAREER: Assistant mathematics teacher at high school in Mytholmroyd, England, 1957-58, bilateral school in Nottingham, England, 1959-60, and technical school in Eastwood, England, 1960-61; St. Peter's High School, Exeter, England, part-time assistant mathematics teacher, 1973-86; writer, 1979—. Volunteer librarian in Zambia, 1962-64; volunteer at work camps in Germany, Greece, France, Jordan, South Africa, and Ireland; organized dramatic readings. Member of international committee of Student Christian Movement, 1956-57; member of national executive of NALSO, 1956-57.

MEMBER: Amnesty International, Society of Authors, Fellowship of Christian Writers, West Country Writers Association.

WRITINGS:

JUVENILE

F.67, Hamish Hamilton, 1975.

Half a Welcome, Dobson, 1977.
The Watch on Patterick Fell, Dobson, 1978, Morrow, 1980.
The Empty House, Dobson, 1979.
Landfall on Innis Michael (sequel to *The Watch on Patterick Fell*), Dobson, 1980.
The Hungry Snow, Dobson, 1980.
The Chains of Sleep, Dobson, 1981.
SUS, Dobson, 1982.
Pangur Ban, the White Cat, Lion, 1983.
Jenny and the Wreckers, Hamish Hamilton, 1984.
Finnglas of the Horses, Lion, 1985.
Chris and the Dragon, Gollancz, 1985.
May Day, RMEP, 1985.
Finnglas and the Stones of Choosing, Lion, 1986.
Josh's Panther, Puffin, 1988.
Shapeshifter, Lion, 1988.
A Free Man on Sunday, Gollancz, 1989.
The Serpent of Senargad, Lion, 1989.
The White Horse Is Running, Lion, 1990.
The Christmas Glizzard, Lion, 1991.

ADULT NOVELS

Wise Woman's Telling (also see below), Headline, 1989.
White Nun's Telling (also see below), Headline, 1989.
Blacksmith's Telling (also see below), Headline, 1990.
Taliesin's Telling (also see below), Headline, 1991.
Herself (also see below), Headline, 1992.
Daughter of Tintagel (omnibus edition of *Wise Woman's Telling, White Nun's Telling, Blacksmith's Telling, Taliesin's Telling,* and *Herself*), Headline, 1992.
Lover and Lion, Headline, in press.

SIDELIGHTS: Fay Sampson once commented: "I was a solitary child, taking pleasure in reading and long walks with a dog on the hills above the fishing village where I lived. I loved writing, but no one ever suggested that I might earn a living by it. That had to wait until I had returned from Zambia and my younger child was starting school. Having made a break in my teaching career, I had to face the question, What next? It was my husband and the late Sidney Robbins, an enthusiast for children's literature in education, who encouraged me to take writing seriously.

"I spent five very enjoyable years writing books that almost, but not quite, got published. I finally struck lucky with *F.67.* At first I wrote out of a deep love of my native west-country, its landscape, history, and legends. But success came when I turned to the present and the near future (I regard *F.67* and *The Watch on Patterick Fell* not as science fiction, but as social fantasy—shaking the kaleidoscope of the present and seeing what new patterns might emerge from the chaos). I still have a strong attachment to the west-country, particularly its Celtic past, and this is reflected in my more recent books. But however old the theme, it must still speak to today.

"Every week of the year I come across a news item or a snippet of history that would make a good book. But nineteen times out of twenty I don't want to write it. It is too rounded, complete. For me the essential motivation in writing is curiosity. What would it be like if . . . ? What if they *had* . . . ? Or just, Why? My books are an exploration of these questions. For instance, *F.67* began with the influx of Ugandan Asian refugees when I visited one of their camps and asked, What would it be like if my own children were put into this situation? But if I have done my work well, the books themselves will raise more questions than they answer, so that at the end the reader is just beginning his own adventure of the mind."

*   *   *

SAMUELSON, Paul A(nthony) 1915-

PERSONAL: Born May 15, 1915, in Gary, IN; son of Frank (a pharmacist) and Ella (Lipton) Samuelson; married Marion E. Crawford, July 2, 1938 (died, 1978); married Risha Eckaus, 1981; children: (first marriage) Jane Kendall, Margaret Wray, William Frank, Robert James, John Crawford, Paul Reid. *Education:* University of Chicago, B.A., 1935; Harvard University, M.A., 1936, Ph.D., 1941. *Politics:* Democrat. *Avocational interests:* Tennis, reading detective novels.

ADDRESSES: Home—75 Clairemont Rd., Belmont, MA 02178. *Office*—Department of Economics, Massachusetts Institute of Technology, Cambridge, MA 02139.

CAREER: Massachusetts Institute of Technology, Cambridge, assistant professor, 1940-44, radiation laboratory staff member, 1944-45, associate professor, 1944-47, professor of economics, 1947—, institute professor and chairman of economics department, 1966—. Consultant to National Resources Planning Board, 1941-43, War Production Board and Office of War Mobilization and Reconstruction, both 1945, U.S. Treasury Department, 1945-52 and 1961—, Rand Corp., 1948-75, Bureau of the Budget, 1952, Research Advisory Panel to President's national goals committee for economic development, 1960, Federal Reserve Board, 1965—. Member, Council of Economic Advisors, 1960-68; member, National Task Force on Economic Education, 1960-61; chairman, President's Task Force on Maintaining American Prosperity, 1964. Senior advisor, Brookings Panel on Economic Activity. Fletcher School of Law and Diplomacy, part-time professor of international economic relations, 1945; Center for Japan/U.S. Business and Economic Studies, visiting professor of political economics, 1987. Has given numerous lectures in England, Sweden, and throughout the United States, including the Stamp Memorial Lecture, Wicksell Lecture, and Franklin Lecture.

MEMBER: International Economic Association (president, 1966-68, honorary president, 1968—), American Economic Association (president, 1961), American Academy of Arts and Sciences, National Science Foundation, National Academy of Sciences, American Philosophical Society (fellow), Econometric Society (vice-president, 1950, president, 1951), Economic society (past vice-president, now council member), National Association of Investment Clubs, British Academy (fellow), Leibniz-Akademie der Wissenschaften und der Literature, Phi Beta Kappa, Omicron Delta Kappa (trustee), Omicron Delta Epsilon (trustee).

AWARDS, HONORS: David A. Wells Prize, Harvard University, 1941; John Bates Clark Medal, American Economic Association, 1947; Guggenheim fellow, 1948-49; Ford Foundation research fellow, 1958-59; honorary LL.D., University of Chicago, and Oberlin College, both 1961, Boston College, 1964, Indiana University, 1966, University of Michigan, 1967, Claremont Graduate School, 1970, University of New Hampshire and Keio University, both 1971, Harvard University, 1972, Gustavius Adolphus College, 1977, Stonehill College, 1978, Catholic University at Riva Aguero University, 1980, Widener College, 1982; Alfred Nobel Memorial Prize in economic science, Swedish Royal Academy of Sciences, 1970; D.Sc., East Anglia University, 1966, University of Massachusetts and University of Rhode Island, both 1972, Tufts University, 1988; Litt.D., Rippon College, 1962, North Michigan University, 1973, Valparaiso University, 1987, Columbia University, 1988; Medal of Honor, University of Evansville, 1970; Albert Einstein Commemorative Award, 1971; L.H.D., Seton Hall College and Williams College, both 1971; Distinguished Service Award in investment education, National Association of Investment Clubs, 1974; Doctorate Honoris Causa, University Catholique de Louvain, 1976, City University of London, 1980, New University of Lisbon, 1985, Universidad National de Education a Distancia, 1989; Alumni medal, University of Chicago, 1983; Gordon Y. Billard fellow, Massachusetts Institute of Technology, 1986—; Britannica Award, 1989.

WRITINGS:

Foundations of Economic Analysis (thesis), Harvard University Press, 1947, revised edition, 1983.

Economics: An Introductory Analysis, McGraw, 1948, selections published as *Microeconomics: A Version of 'Economics,'* 13th edition, 1989, selections published as *Macroeconomics: A Version of 'Economics,'* 13th edition, 1989, 14th edition, coauthored with William Nordhaus, 1992.

(Editor, with Robert L. Bishop and John R. Coleman) *Readings in Economics,* McGraw, 1952, 13th edition, 1989.

(With Robert Dorfman and Robert M. Solow) *Linear Programming and Economic Analysis,* McGraw, 1958.

(With others) *Study Guide and Workbook,* McGraw, 1958, revised edition, 1980, published as *Study Guide to Accompany Samuelson-Nordhaus 'Economics,'* 13th edition, McGraw, 1989.

Problems of the American Economy (Stamp Memorial Lecture), Athlone Press, 1962.

The Collected Scientific Papers of Paul A. Samuelson, MIT Press, Volume 1 and 2, edited by Joseph Stiglitz, 1966, Volume 3, edited by R. C. Merton, 1972, Volume 4, edited by H. Nagatain and K. Crowley, 1978, Volume 5, 1986.

(With Arthur F. Burns) *Full Employment Guideposts and Economic Stability,* American Enterprise Institute for Public Policy Research, 1967.

(Editor) *International Economic Relations: Proceedings of the Third Congress of the International Economic Association,* St. Martin's, 1969.

The Samuelson Sampler, T. Horton, 1973.

(Editor, with James L. Bicksler) *Investment Portfolio Decision-Making,* Lexington Books, 1974.

(Editor) *Trade, Stability, and Macroeconomics: Essays in Honor of Lloyd A. Metzler,* Academic Press, 1974.

Economics from the Heart: A Samuelson Sampler (selection of columns from *Newsweek*), edited and with an introduction by Maryann O. Keating, Harcourt, 1983.

Also contributor of numerous articles to professional journals and periodicals including *Financial Times* (London), *New York Times,* and *Washington Post;* columnist for *Newsweek,* 1966-1981. Associate editor of periodicals, including *Journal of International Economics, Journal of Nonlinear Analysis,* and *Journal of Public Economics.* Senior editorial consultant, "The Basic Investor's Library" series, Chelsea House, 1988. Member of editorial board, *Econometrica.* Samuelson's work has been translated into a number of languages, including Russian, Japanese, German, Dutch, Greek, Spanish, French, Portuguese, Arabic and Korean.

SIDELIGHTS: Economist and educator Paul A. Samuelson stands foremost among the key twentieth-century proponents of post-Keynesian economic doctrine in the United States. Praised by his colleagues as one of the most respected modern economic theorists, Samuelson has also received great recognition from the public at large through his authorship of *Economics: An Introductory Analysis,* one of the most widely-read introductory college textbooks on the subject of economics. First published in 1948, this comprehensive text has sold more than four million copies and has been translated into nine languages, including Arabic and Korean. As Stephen Martin noted in *Thinkers of the Twentieth Century,* "Economists commonly indicate their vintage in terms of just which edition of Samuelson's *Economics* was used in their own principles of economics class."

Samuelson served as economic advisor to the presidential administrations of both John F. Kennedy and Lyndon B. Johnson during his years of government service. A key figure in forming the economic policies of the White House during the 1960s, he contributed his insights to such projects as the formation of tax legislation and to the war on poverty which was made manifest by Johnson's "Great Society" program during the middle years of that decade. Samuelson is credited for initiating tax cuts that would trigger an economic boom in the United States during the 1960s and usher in years of stable domestic economic growth. As a long-time proponent of traditional democratic ideology, Samuelson became critical of the economic policies of the Republican administration that followed Johnson into the White House in 1968. Commenting on the Nixon administration's lack of either an environmental agenda or a national health insurance policy in favor of involvement in the war in Southeast Asia, Samuelson exclaimed in the *New York Times* that there was so much to be done in the country that "the notion that we've got to put something down a rathole in Vietnam is ridiculous."

A teacher of economics at the Massachusetts Institute of Technology since 1940, Samuelson was named institute professor in 1966. In addition to being both a popular speaker and a consultant for numerous private and public concerns, the noted economist also served as a regular contributor to *Newsweek* magazine for fifteen years, with a writing style described as "breezy and lucid" by Robert Reinhold in the *New York Times.* A collection of his *Newsweek* articles was published in book form in 1973 as *Economics from the Heart: A Samuelson Sampler.* In addition, many of Samuelson's contributions to professional economic journals were anthologized by MIT Press in a series of volumes collectively titled *The Collected Scientific Work of Paul A. Samuelson.* Described by fellow economist and *Newsweek* columnist Milton Friedman as displaying "the clarity of exposition and felicity of expression that readers of his column have come to expect," Samuelson's numerous contributions to professional journals deal with such things as consumer behavior, international trade, business cycles, and related topics as they illustrate the validity of advanced mathematical economic theorems.

In awarding Samuelson the Alfred Nobel Memorial Prize in 1970, the Swedish Royal Academy of Sciences commended him, as Bernard Weintraub reported in the *New York Times,* for "extensive production, covering nearly all areas of economic theory, . . . characterized by an outstanding ability to derive important new theorems and to find new applications for existing ones. By his contributions, Samuelson has done more than any other contemporary economist to raise the level of scientific analysis in economic theory."

Samuelson's economic views are derived from the economic theories of the noted early twentieth-century economist John Maynard Keynes. From a Keynesian viewpoint, according to Samuelson, in a capitalist economic system it is the responsibility of government to stabilize both the level of employment—for example, through the creation of jobs during recessionary periods when the private sector has failed in that obligation—and the distribution of wealth. His classification as a Keynesian economist is also reflected in the political characterization of "liberal Democrat" which Samuelson has earned through his comments on matters of public policy. He himself was quoted by Reinhold as saying, "I'm a liberal but not a libertarian because I cannot agree that the free distribution of dollar votes in the market place represents any kind of ethical optimum, according to any ethical doctrine known to me. A laissez-faire system is a system of coercion by dollar votes. Anatole France said the last word that needs to be said on that: 'How majestic is the equality of the law which permits the rich and the poor alike to sleep under the bridges at night.' "

BIOGRAPHICAL/CRITICAL SOURCES:

BOOKS

Breit, William, and Roger W. Spencer, *Lives of the Laureates: Seven Nobel Economists,* MIT Press, 1986.
Brown, E. Cary, and Robert M. Solow, editors, *Paul Samuelson and Modern Economic Theory*, McGraw-Hill, 1983.
Feiwel, George R., editor, *Samuelson and Neoclassical Economics,* Kluwer, 1982.
Martin, Stephen, "Paul A. Samuelson," *Thinkers of the Twentieth Century,* St. James Press, 1987, pp. 670-672.

PERIODICALS

Atlantic, July, 1983, pp. 96-100.
Business Week, February 14, 1959.
Newsweek, January 11, 1965; November 9, 1970.
New York Times, October 27, 1970, pp. 1, 8.
Washington Post, November 4, 1970.

SARNOFF, Paul 1918-

PERSONAL: Born April 21, 1918, in Brooklyn, NY; son of Nathan (a salesman) and Rose (Goldberg) Sarnoff; married Lucille Levitt, October 13, 1940; children: Alan, Mitchell, Steven. *Education:* Attended Albright College, 1934-36; City College (now City college of the City University of New York), B.S., 1940, M.B.A., 1954. *Politics:* Liberal. *Religion:* Hebrew.

ADDRESSES: Home—3319 Poplar St., Oceanside, NY. *Office*—The Metals Consultancy, P.O. Box 178, Baldwin, NY 11510.

CAREER: Stockbroker with various companies, New York City, 1937-56; owner of investment advisory firm, 1956-57; Thomas Haab & Botts (put and call brokers), New York City, sales manager, beginning 1957; Herzog & Co., New York City, vice-president, 1971-76; Herzog Commodities, Inc., New York City, vice-president, 1973-76; Conti Commodity Services, New York City, director of New York research, and options director, 1976-80; Rudolf Wolff Commodity Brokers, Inc., New York City, research director, 1980-82; Paine Webber, Inc., Garden City, NY, corporate vice-president, 1982-86. Teacher of private class on puts and calls, New York City, 1957-67. President of Futures Industry Research Division, 1978-80; director of AMEX gold coin exchange, 1982-85; member of board of directors of Duggan's Distillers Ltd. and Oceanside Jewish Center, 1949-53. Member of Havana Stock Exchange (in absentia), Pacific Commodity Exchange, 1975—, and AMEX Commodities Exchange, 1979-80. *Military service:* U.S. Army, 1943-46; became second lieutenant.

MEMBER: International Precious Metals Institute, Authors League of America, Authors Guild, Northwest Mining Association.

WRITINGS:

Lessons in Leverage, Investor's Intelligence, 1959.
Wall Street Thesaurus, Obolensky, 1963, published as *Wall Street Wisdom,* Pocket Books, 1965.
Russell Sage, the Money-King, Obolensky, 1965.
(Co-author) *90 Days to Fortune,* Obolensky, 1965.
Ice Pilot, Messner, 1966.
Robert Abram Bartlett, Messner, 1966.
Samuel James Tilden, Scribner, 1967.
Jesse Livermore, Investors' Press, 1967.
Wall Street Careers, Messner, 1968.
Your Investment $: Using Puts and Calls, Prentice-Hall, 1968, published as *Puts and Calls: The Complete Guide,* Hawthorn, 1970.
Careers in Biological Science, Messner, 1968.
Your Investments, Prentice-Hall, 1968.
Careers in the Legal Profession, Messner, 1970.

New York Times Encyclopedia Dictionary of the Environment, Quadrangle, 1971.

Getting Rich with Other People's Money, Parker Publishing, 1971.

(With Frederik J. Zeehandelaar) *Zeebongo: The Wacky Wild Animal Business,* Prentice-Hall, 1971.

(Editor) *An Empirical Examination of the Options Business,* School of Business, Hofstra University, 1977.

Trading in Gold, Woodhead-Faulkner, 1980.

Silver Bulls, Arlington House, 1980.

Trading in Financial Futures, Woodhead-Faulkner/ Universe Books, 1985.

Trading in Gold II, Woodhead-Faulkner, 1989.

Super Leverage, Woodhead-Faulkner, 1990.

Trading in Silver, Woodhead-Faulkner, 1990.

Also author of *Profits with Puts and Calls,* 1958, and of thirty other books, 1986-92. Columnist for *Journal of Commerce.* Contributor to *Commodities* magazine.

WORK IN PROGRESS: Leaf-Looker's Guide; Gold Chrysanthemums.

BIOGRAPHICAL/CRITICAL SOURCES:

PERIODICALS

Albany Times Union, February 13, 1963.
New York Times, November 3, 1957.

*   *   *

SAUL, John (W. III) 1942-

PERSONAL: Born February 25, 1942, in Pasadena, CA; son of John W., Jr., and Elizabeth (Lee) Saul. *Education:* Attended Antioch College, 1959-60, Montana State University, 1961-62, and San Francisco State College (now University), 1963-65. *Politics:* "Mostly Democrat." *Religion:* "Sort of Swedenborgian."

ADDRESSES: Home—Bellevue, WA. *Agent*—Jane Rotrosen, 318 East 51st St., New York, NY 10022.

CAREER: Writer. Spent several years traveling about the United States, writing and supporting himself by odd jobs; worked for a drug and alcohol program in Seattle, WA; director of Tellurian Communities, Inc., 1976-78; Seattle Theater Arts, Seattle, director, 1978—.

MEMBER: Authors Guild, Authors League of America.

WRITINGS:

NOVELS

Suffer the Children, Dell, 1977.
Punish the Sinners, Dell, 1978.
Cry for the Strangers, Dell, 1979.
Comes the Blind Fury, Dell, 1980.

When the Wind Blows, Dell, 1981.
The God Project, Bantam, 1982.
Nathaniel, Bantam, 1984.
Brainchild, Bantam, 1985.
Hellfire, Bantam, 1986.
The Unwanted, Bantam, 1987.
The Unloved, Bantam, 1988.
The Fear Factor, Bantam, 1988.
Creature, Bantam, 1989.
Sleepwalk, Bantam, 1990.
Second Child, Bantam, 1990.
Darkness, Bantam, 1991.
Shadows, Bantam, 1992.

Also author of other novels under pseudonyms.

SIDELIGHTS: Best-selling horror novelist John Saul has produced a suspenseful thriller every year since 1977, but there is nothing mysterious about his rise to success. Saul, best known for eerie tales set in isolated locales and high-tech novels bordering on science fiction, has become especially popular among young adults who relish the author's adolescent characters as much as his frightening narratives. Today, with over twenty-three million copies of his novels in print, Saul continues to please his legion of fans with the successful formula he created early in his career.

As a youngster growing up in Whittier, California, Saul enjoyed a normal childhood. When the question comes up, the author denies having lived through anything as bizarre as the experiences his young characters confront. Instead, Saul directed his youthful energies towards school and recalled that, even as a youth, he was very focused on writing to please his audience. "If you had to write 300 words on a subject," he told Andrea Chambers in *People* magazine interview, "300 words was exactly what they got. I sat there and counted them." Although Saul continued to diligently hone his writing skills while in college by penning a "technically correct" twenty-line poem every day, after five years he left school without a degree.

College was followed a series of odd jobs, including stints as a technical writer and temporary office helper. Whatever he did by day, at night the aspiring author continued working on his unpublished books and stories. "Between the ages of 30 and 35 you really start to lose your dignity badly when you say you've been trying to be a writer for fifteen years," he admitted to Chambers. "I finally thought that by the time I was 35, I would no longer be a struggling writer, I'd be a failed writer."

After a number of works had been rejected by publishers, including comic murder mysteries and one novel about the citizen band radio craze of the 1970s, Saul finally received a suggestion that paid off. After a New York literary agent mentioned the tremendous popularity of horror novels, Saul visited a drugstore paperback rack for ideas, wrote an outline for *Suffer the Children,* signed a contract for the book and produced it in less than a month. "I'd never really tried writing horror before," Saul recalled in a *Publishers Weekly* interview with Robert Dahlin, "but when I began, I found it fascinating. There were times I was writing certain scenes that I had to stop because I even scared myself, but I'm convinced that it helps to be a total coward when it comes to writing a book like this. If you can't scare yourself, how can you scare anyone else?"

Saul's first novel, about a dysfunctional family in a small New England town whose disturbed daughter becomes a suspect in the gruesome and mysterious disappearance of several of the town's children, became an instant bestseller. *Suffer the Children* introduced the themes which have dominated almost all of the works that followed, including the use of children and teenagers as victims or perpetrators of crime and a marked ambiguity which leaves the reader uncertain "whether spooks are at work or merely morbid psychology," as a *Detroit News* reviewer observed. Despite the book's popularity, reviewers lambasted Saul's exceedingly violent tale. Upon the book's release, a *Publishers Weekly* reviewer criticized the novel for its "graphically violent scenes against children which are markedly tasteless."

The brutality of Saul's first novel was not matched in his later work. The author made a concentrated effort to focus less on violent acts and instead depended on mood to frighten readers. "After [*Suffer the Children*], my books got progressively less violent because I really saw no reason for gore for gore's sake . . . ," Saul explained in *Publishers Weekly.* "It seems to me that what makes a book good is the tension in wondering what's going to happen next." Saul did not, however, stray too far from the formula which propelled him to the top of the bestseller lists. His next novel, *Punish the Sinners,* involved bizarre sex rites within an order of priests. Once again, Saul was criticized by a *Publishers Weekly* reviewer for opening "the proceedings with a dual meat-cleaver slaying" and then writing "with cleaver in hand throughout." But once again, despite negative reviews, Saul's book enjoyed tremendous success and was followed by three more books with similar themes, all of which enjoyed equal success. In a typical plot, the ghost of a blind girl who was taunted and killed by classmates one hundred years earlier returns to seek revenge on the young descendents of her tormenters in *Comes the Blind Fury.*

Explaining his reasons for featuring children in his novels, Saul told *Publishers Weekly:* "Children are very imaginative. They share a lot of fear based on the unknown, or what might happen in the dark. I can remember everything that ever happened to me since I was three, and that certainly helps me write from a children's point of view. Also, children are very appealing, both as villains and as victims. It's hard to stay mad at a kid, no matter what he does."

Saul ventured into a new realm with his sixth book, *The God Project,* his first hardcover publication. "I'd begun to feel I was repeating myself, and I needed something new," he told Dahlin. Instead of focusing on ghosts from the past as he had in his previous novels, Saul looked toward the future and produced a "techno-thriller" about a secret government project called CHILD. The project involves the genetic engineering of unsuspecting women's fetuses. Once born, the children have amazing powers of regeneration, but when the project backfires, they begin to die. Discussing the plot with a *Detroit News* writer, Saul said: "I feel that the experiments in genetic engineering ought to be going on . . . but I'm also convinced that it can't be done with too much care. There is talk now about adjusting human beings genetically to fit certain job slots. Do you have to go any further than that for a scary idea?"

At the time it was released, Saul described *The God Project* as his most ambitious undertaking. "It seems as though I'm starting all over again," he told Dahlin. "I feel just like a first novelist waiting around and wondering how my book will do, but I'm looking forward to reading the professional criticism—constructive criticism, I hope—that will be written about it." The book, which Saul described in *Publishers Weekly* as containing "very little overt violence," didn't achieve quite the same level of popularity as some of his earlier books, but it did mark an expansion in the author's scope of themes and topics.

In 1985's *Brainchild,* Saul combined the centuries-old revenge plot formulas of his earlier works with the futuristic slant of *The God Project.* The result is the story of Alex Lonsdale, a teenager who suffers brain damage in a car accident and is operated on by renowned surgeon Raymond Torres, a fourth-generation Mexican-American whose ancestors were murdered when America acquired California in 1850. Although young Alex's recovery seems complete, his strange behavior disturbs his friends and family, who begin to suspect Alex's involvement when a series of brutal murders takes place. When Torres' hatred for *gringos* is revealed, the plot's revenge elements come into play. A *Kliatt* reviewer found *Brainchild* a fast-paced, "intriguing story with fascinating implications."

Not deviating from the successful premise of a ghost seeking revenge for the deeds of years past, Saul wrote *Hellfire* in 1986. Set in an isolated Massachusetts town, the story revolves around a wealthy family's plans to transform their empty mill into a shopping mall. When their renovations go awry, the family matriarch fears they have roused the spirit of a girl who died there in a fire one hundred years ago. True to his formula, Saul includes several young characters, including an amiable girl named Beth and her spoiled, snobby cousin, Tracy. A *Publishers Weekly* reviewer found "an inevitability about much of the novel," but conceded that "the bloody, tantalizing plot rushes forward, the setting and historical background are well-drawn and Tracy is memorably, startlingly nasty."

A wealthy family stirring old resentments is also at the center of *The Unloved.* The plot centers around elderly Helena Devereaux, who lures her estranged son and his family to her estate on a South Carolina island, where her sweet-natured daughter, Marguerite, cares for the cantankerous old woman. Helena finally dies, but her control extends beyond the grave in the form of a malicious will which ties her children to her estate. When frequent sightings of her ghost occur and the formerly pleasant Marguerite begins behaving more and more like her mother, the plot takes an expected turn into the supernatural. "Saul plays out the expected Southern gothic but does so with empathy for the lives caught in the Devereaux web, from the relatives and friends to the dispirited townspeople who are dependent on the family for their very homes," remarked a *Publishers Weekly* reviewer.

Saul's twelfth novel, *Creature,* mixed modern-day headlines about steroid abuse with the mad scientist motif of classic horror novels such as *Frankenstein.* In Saul's modern twist, the mad scientist is Dr. Marty Ames, an employee of the TarrenTech conglomerate, who poses as a high-tech athletic trainer at a local high school in order to conduct clandestine experiments upon unsuspecting jocks. In his attempt to create the perfect physical specimen, Ames accidentally turns his subjects into unmanageable, violent freaks. Critics weren't especially impressed with Saul's adaptation of the classic horror novel premise. "While Saul's storytelling is energetic and atmospheric, it can not mask the direction of this thinly drawn and predictable plot," commented Marc Shapiro in *Inside Books.* A *Publishers Weekly* reviewer also found the story formulaic, but added "it should please the author's fans as it continues Saul's focus on children as the vehicles and victims of unnatural forces."

Saul's next novel, *Sleepwalk,* contained themes and a plot line similar to *Creature.* Once again, a sleepy town is the setting for a mysterious experiment on teenagers, but this time Saul included an extra dimension through the use of Native American folklore. The characters include Judith Sheffield, the math teacher who first suspects that the students in her New Mexican hometown are in danger, teenaged Jed, and his Native American grandfather, Brown Eagle. A *Publishers Weekly* critic praised the book for its "compelling scenes in which Brown Eagle introduces Jed to Native American mysticism" and its climax, which includes "a spectacular display of man restoring nature to its rightful place—after having almost destroyed everything in the process."

Saul's novel *Second Child* appeared on the *New York Times* bestseller list just one month after publication, proving once again the author's bankable popularity. The story, featuring a teenage villain, centers around fifteen-year-old Teri MacIver, who finds herself living with her biological father after a fire kills her mother and stepfather. What Teri's father doesn't know is that Teri was responsible for the blaze which killed her mother and that she has come to live with him for the express purpose of propagating more evil. She finds the perfect victim in her shy, unstable half-sister, Melissa. An element of the supernatural is added when Melissa appears to become unknowingly manipulated by the ghost of D'Arcy, a young maidservant who committed hideous acts of violence one hundred years ago. Critics gave *Second Child* a reception typical of a Saul novel: "With a tired plot and boring dialogue, John Saul never deviates from the predictable in his new novel," wrote a *Detroit News and Free Press* reviewer.

Reviews were no better, but sales were just as good, for Saul's 1991 effort, *Darkness.* The story focused this time on a group of teenagers suffering from disturbing nightmares about a menacing old man. The prologue, described by a *Publishers Weekly* reviewer as "wonderfully scary," features the sacrifice of a newborn baby performed by none other than the Dark Man of the teens' dreams. Despite the novel's promising start, the mystery of the Dark Man is "revealed halfway through the book," continued the reviewer, who found Saul's ending "cozily sentimental."

In his 1992 novel, *Shadows,* Saul again features school-age children prominently. At the center of the story is a school for gifted children called The Academy, where a diabolical experiment is being carried out without anyone's knowledge. When strange things begin to happen, the bright students realize they are in danger of being destroyed by the evil presence behind the experiment and must join forces to escape the terror of The Academy. With all the elements of a successful Saul novel, *Shadows* quickly became a bestseller.

Saul's astounding popularity continues to grow in the face of rather harsh criticism. One point about which critics are especially contentious is Saul's tendency to feature young victims and villains, thereby making his novels especially attractive to young readers. Because of the disturbing subject matter he deals with, Saul has said he was reluctant, at first, to recommend them to a young audience. "Originally, I though they were a bit strong for children, for anyone under 15," Saul said in a *Publishers Weekly* interview, "but since then, I've talked to school librarians who are happy with them. Young people like my books, and as it turns out, in this way I've introduced many of them to the act of reading. Librarians aren't concerned that any of my violence is going to affect children.

They would rather have them reading, and these kids have told me they don't read the books for the violence. They read them for the plot."

With little regard for critical appraisal, Saul's fans continue to make each successive novel a bestseller. The author himself never denigrates his books or the people who enjoy them. "Hopefully," as he told Dahlin, "each of my books is better than the last. Each gets rewritten more." Saul certainly plans to continue writing in the genre which has made him so successful. Topics for future novels are unlimited in scope, since Saul has the ability to "find horror in the commonplace," he told Chambers. "In my books everything looks perfectly normal and wonderful at the beginning," he continued, "but there's some little thing that's wrong, and it gets out of control."

BIOGRAPHICAL/CRITICAL SOURCES:

BOOKS

Contemporary Literary Criticism, Volume 46, Gale, 1988.

PERIODICALS

Detroit News and Free Press, July 1, 1990.
Fantasy Review, October, 1985, p. 20.
Inside Books, August, 1989, p. 80.
Kirkus Reviews, March 1, 1989, p. 329.
Kliatt Young Adult Paperback Book Guide, fall, 1985, p. 20.
Los Angeles Times Book Review, October 10, 1982; August 10, 1986, p. 6.
People, June 26, 1989.
Publishers Weekly, April 25, 1977, p. 73; April 10, 1978, p. 70; April 23, 1979, p. 79; April 11, 1980, p. 75; June 27, 1980, p. 82; June 25, 1982, p. 104; August 13, 1982; April 29, 1988, p. 72; March 10, 1989, p. 74; December 14, 1990; April 12, 1991, p. 45.

—*Sketch by Cornelia A. Pernik*

*   *   *

SCALAPINO, Robert A(nthony) 1919-

PERSONAL: Born October 19, 1919, in Leavenworth, KS; son of Anthony and Beulah (Stephenson) Scalapino; married Ida Mae Jessen, August 23, 1941; children: Diane Jablon, Sharon Leslie, Lynne Thompson. *Education:* Santa Barbara College (now University of California, Santa Barbara), B.A., 1940; Harvard University, M.A., 1943, Ph.D., 1948. *Avocational interests:* Fishing, photography.

ADDRESSES: Home—2850 Buena Vista Way, Berkeley, CA 94708. *Office*—Institute of East Asian Studies, 2223 Fulton St., University of California, Berkeley, CA 94720.

CAREER: Santa Barbara College (now University of California, Santa Barbara), lecturer, 1940-41; Harvard University, Cambridge, MA, instructor, 1948-49; University of California, Berkeley, assistant professor, 1949-51, associate professor, 1951-56, professor of political science, 1956-77, Robson Research Professor of Government, 1978-90, professor emeritus, 1990—, chairman of Group in Asian Studies, 1959-61, chairman of Department of Political Science, 1962-65, director of Institute of East Asian Studies, 1978-90. Member of board of trustees, Asia Foundation; member of board of governors, Pacific Forum, CSIS; member of advisory council, National Bureau of Asian Research. *Military service:* U.S. Navy, Intelligence, 1943-46; became lieutenant junior grade.

MEMBER: Association for Asian Studies (member of board of directors, 1960-63), American Political Science Association, Foreign Policy Association, Council on Foreign Relations (member of board of directors), American Academy of Arts and Sciences, Western Political Science Association.

AWARDS, HONORS: Grants from Carnegie Foundation, 1951-53, Ford Foundation, 1955, Rockefeller Foundation, 1956-59, 1961, and Guggenheim Foundation, 1965-66; Social Science Research Council fellow, 1952-53; Woodrow Wilson Award, American Political Science Association, 1973, for *Communism in Korea;* Alumni Award, University of California, Santa Barbara, 1975; honorary LL.D., China Academy (Taiwan), 1976; honorary D.P.S., Hankuk University of Foreign Studies (Korea), 1983, and Kyunghee University (Korea), 1989; Order of the Sacred Treasure (Japan), 1988; Presidential Order (Korea), 1990; Berkeley Citation, University of California, Berkeley, 1990; also received awards from Luce Foundation, National Endowment for the Humanities, and others.

WRITINGS:

Democracy and the Party Movement in Pre-War Japan, University of California Press, 1953, 2nd edition, 1967.
(With George T. Yu) *The Chinese Anarchist Movement,* Institute of International Studies, University of California Press, 1961.
(With Junnosuke Masumi) *Parties and Politics in Contemporary Japan,* University of California, 1962.
(Editor and contributor) *North Korea Today,* Praeger, 1963.
The Japanese Communist Movement, 1920-1966, University of California Press, 1967.
(Editor and contributor) *The Communist Revolution in Asia,* Prentice-Hall, 1969, 2nd edition, Praeger, 1977.
(With Chong-Sik Lee) *Communism in Korea,* University of California Press, 1972.

(Editor) *Elites in the People's Republic of China,* University of Washington Press, 1972.

Asia and the Road Ahead, University of California Press, 1975.

(Editor) *The Foreign Policy of Modern Japan,* University of California Press, 1977.

The United States and Korea: Looking Ahead, Sage Publications, 1979.

(Editor with Jun-Yop Kim, and contributor) *North Korea Today: Strategic and Domestic Issues* (monograph), Institute of East Asian Studies, University of California, 1983.

The Early Japanese Labor Movement, Institute of East Asian Studies, University of California, 1984.

(With Yu) *Modern China and Its Revolutionary Process,* University of California Press, 1985.

The Politics of Development: Perspectives on Twentieth Century Asia, Harvard University Press, 1989.

Also contributor of numerous books, including *Modern Political Parties,* edited by Sigmund Neuman, University of Chicago Press, 1955; *Foreign Policies in a Changing World,* edited by Black and Thompson, Harper, 1963; and *The State and Economic Enterprise in Japan: Essays in the Political Economy of Growth,* edited by Lockwood, Princeton University Press, 1965.

Also author of monographs *American-Japanese Relations in a Changing Era,* 1972, *Asia and the Major Powers,* 1972, and *The United States and Korea: The Road Ahead,* 1979. Contributor to numerous journals, including *Orbis, Survey, Journal of Asian Studies, Foreign Affairs,* and *American Spectator.* Editor, *Asian Survey,* 1962—; member of editorial advisory board of various political science journals.

WORK IN PROGRESS: Volume two of *Modern China and Its Revolutionary Process,* covering the period 1921-1949.

*   *   *

SCHLEE, Susan
    See BAUR, Susan

*   *   *

SCHOLEFIELD, Edmund O.
    See BUTTERWORTH, W(illiam E(dmund III)

*   *   *

SCURO, Vincent 1951-

PERSONAL: Born September 28, 1951, in Jersey City, NJ; son of Joseph E. (en executive) and Phyllis (Amato) Scuro; married Katherine Anne Krettecos, 1978; children: Alexandra Maria, Elena Kristie. *Education:* St. Peter's College, A.B., 1973; Fairleigh Dickinson University, M.A.T., 1976. *Avocational interests:* Sports, music, movies, home electronics.

ADDRESSES: Home—8133 Breeze Cove Ln., Orlando, FL 32819.

CAREER: Writer. Has worked as newspaper correspondent, copywriter, editor, photographer, musician, teacher, and computer consultant. Has written and produced computer-animated commercials and computer-assisted instruction for business, industry, and government.

AWARDS, HONORS: Authors Citation, New Jersey Institute of Technology, 1983, for *Wonders of Mules,* and 1984, for *Wonders of Sheep.*

WRITINGS:

(Self-illustrated with photographs) *Presenting the Marching Band,* Dodd, 1974.

"WONDERS" SERIES; JUVENILES; SELF-ILLUSTRATED WITH PHOTOGRAPHS

(With Sigmund A. Lavine) *Wonders of the Bison World,* Dodd, 1975.

(With Lavine) *Wonders of Donkeys,* Dodd, 1979.

(With Lavine) *Wonders of Elephants,* Dodd, 1980.

(With Lavine) *Wonders of Goats,* Dodd, 1980.

Wonders of Cattle, Dodd, 1980.

(With Lavine) *Wonders of Pigs,* Dodd, 1981.

(With Lavine) *Wonders of Mules,* Dodd, 1982.

(With Lavine) *Wonders of Sheep,* Dodd, 1983.

Wonders of Zebras, Dodd, 1983.

(With Lavine) *Wonders of Turkeys,* Dodd, 1984.

Wonders of Dairy Cattle, Dodd, 1986.

OTHER

Contributor of photographs to books, including *Moon Landing: Project Apollo,* by James C. Sparks, Dodd, 1970; *Wonders of Bears* (jacket photo), by Bernadine Bailey, Dodd, 1975; *Wonders of Herbs,* by Lavine, Dodd, 1976; *Bells, Bells, Bells,* by Bailey, Dodd, 1977; and *Wonders of Ponies* (jacket photo), by Lavine and Brigid Casey, Dodd, 1980. Also contributor to numerous periodicals, including *Los Angeles Times, Satellite Orbit,* and *Orbit Video.*

WORK IN PROGRESS: A children's storybook; adult nonfiction; magazine articles; a computer-animated video.

SIDELIGHTS: Vincent Scuro told *CA:* "Some people hate writing but love having written. I love both. If you write because you enjoy it, writing becomes easier. If you look upon writing as work, you've built a mental wall inside your head that you have to knock down before you can get anything done. I rarely get writer's block.

"It's always a tremendous thrill seeing something I've written in print. Some people spend their whole lives trying to get a book or magazine article published. I made my first sale when I was twenty, and it seems like I've always got something coming out soon."

About the rewards of writing, Scuro observed: "Editors call me with assignments. Schoolchildren write to me about something they've read in one of my books. One of my daughter's friends does my zebra book for a book report—and the next time he sees me, I get a critique. That's what's fun about being an author."

*   *   *

SEBESTYEN, Ouida 1924-

PERSONAL: Name is pronounced "*Wee*-da See-best-yen"; born February 13, 1924, in Vernon, TX; daughter of James Ethridge (a teacher) and Byrd Grey (a teacher; maiden name, Lantrip) Dockery; married Adam Sebestyen, December 22, 1960 (divorced, 1966); children: Corbin. *Education:* Attended University of Colorado. *Avocational interests:* "Gardening, travel, hiking, all crafts, building new things and restoring old ones."

ADDRESSES: Home and office—115 South 36th St., Boulder, CO 80303.

CAREER: Writer; lecturer. Worked variously at a training school for military pilots and as a day-care provider, housekeeper, gardener, seamstress, carpenter, mason, and handyperson.

AWARDS, HONORS: Words by Heart was selected as one of the best books of the year by *New York Times* and *School Library Journal,* both 1979, named one of the best books for young adults and a notable children's book by American Library Association and a Library of Congress Children's Book, both 1979, and received International Reading Association Children's Book Award, 1980, and American Book Award, 1982; *Far from Home* was named one of the best books for young adults by American Library Association and one of the best books of the year by *School Library Journal,* both 1980, received American Book Award nomination and was a Child Study Association recommended title, both 1981, was included on William Allen White master list, 1982-83, and received Zilveren Griffel (Silver Pencil) Award, 1984; *IOU's* was named a National Council of Teachers of English Teacher's Choice-*Parents' Choice* Remarkable Book, and one of the best books for young adults by American Library Association, both 1982, was included on Child Study Children's Book Committee list, 1983, received Texas Institute of Letters Children's Book Award, 1983, and was a Mark Twain Award nominee, 1985; *The Girl in the Box* was

nominated for the Colorado Blue Spruce Young Adult Award.

WRITINGS:

NOVELS FOR YOUNG ADULTS

Words by Heart, Little, Brown, 1979.
Far from Home, Little, Brown, 1980.
IOU's, Little, Brown, 1982.
On Fire, Atlantic, 1985.
The Girl in the Box, Little, Brown/Joy Street Books, 1988.

Some of Sebestyen's novels have been translated into French, Dutch, Japanese, Danish, Norwegian, Spanish, and Swedish.

OTHER

Contributor of stories to magazines and anthologies under pseudonym Igen Sebestyen.

ADAPTATIONS: Words by Heart was adapted as a dramatic special under the same title for PBS-TV, 1985; the program received two Emmy nominations.

WORK IN PROGRESS: "A boy-and-dog novel for young adults"; a play.

SIDELIGHTS: Ouida Sebestyen is internationally known for her award-winning novels for young adults. Highly regarded as realistic and multi-dimensional, Sebestyen's works, which include *Words by Heart, On Fire, IOU's,* and *The Girl in the Box,* are appreciated for their convincingly drawn characters, thought-provoking themes, and touches of humor. Although her work is directed toward young adults, Sebestyen aspires to reach a broader audience. She told *Something about the Author (SATA)* that "I hope I write for readers of all ages, because I want to nourish the child's idealism and delight in life that we all have in us."

The main characters in Sebestyen's novels are usually spirited teenagers who overcome barriers such as prejudice, poverty, and the death of loved ones on their road to maturity. Sebestyen also focuses on families, particularly on relationships between parents and children. In the *ALAN Review* Sebestyen reflected that she likes to express all the joys, difficulties, and responsibilities inherent in being a part of a family; for her, a family not only shapes the lives of young people but is full of dramatic potential: "Certainly every family is a world, teeming with life, symbiotic, ancient and futuristic, sending little spaceships out, first to visit grandma, then off to college, and finally out to people other colonies."

Although she liked books and earned good grades, Sebestyen disliked school. She worked on the school newspaper and was in the honor society, "but a photo of that group shows me squashed nearly sideways in a row of sturdier types. I was a misfit and loner who loved learning, but was intimidated by the process," she told *Something about the Author Autobiography Series* (*SAAS*). Nevertheless, Sebestyen made "friends with a girl named Peggy who wrote poetry. . . . Knowing her made school easier to take." After their senior year of high school, the two "had bright plans for writing The Great American Novel and wallowing in fame and fortune, preferably within a few months."

The girls had grand hopes, but nothing went quite as planned. For a while other endeavors occupied their time; during World War II Peggy worked at an airfield in Oklahoma and Sebestyen took a job at a training school for military pilots. The author repaired holes torn in planes, "work that seemed off-the-wall, patriotic, and enlarging enough for a budding writer," she told *SAAS*. "I loved every day of my years there—the rough men, the hard dirty work, the night shift, the contrasts." She and Peggy eventually wrote a novel together, and although it was rejected by publishers, Sebestyen recalled that "we learned a lot, specifically that we weren't natural collaborators."

Sebestyen sold her first story to a women's magazine in 1950. "I couldn't believe it," she told *SAAS*. "I was really and truly a Published Author at last." Though two more of her stories were published, Sebestyen was headed for another long dry spell. Her spirits were buoyed, however, when a writer from New York wanted to adapt one of her stories as a television drama. Sebestyen went to New York to discuss the adaptation, and although the television play was never produced, she made friends who invited her to visit them in Iceland. "Girls from Vernon didn't do that in the '50s," she remarked in *SAAS*, "but I went."

She visited Ireland at the end of her Iceland trip and was so inspired by the country and its people that she sent a Dublin newspaper a thank-you note addressed "to Ireland in general," she explained in *SAAS*. When the note was published in the newspaper, Adam Sebestyen, a visiting Hungarian student, saw it and wrote her a letter. Their correspondence flowered into a romance; he moved to the United States and they were married in 1960. The relationship, however, ended in divorce. In *SAAS* Sebestyen commented, "Budapest and Vernon, Texas, kept colliding. . . . When we began to hurt each other constantly with our opposing expectations, we knew our marriage had been a tragic mistake."

So Sebestyen, her mother, and her son Corbin moved to Boulder, Colorado. Sebestyen started a new novel while supporting her three-generation family by taking on a variety of odd jobs, from day-care to trimming bushes. She remembered in *SAAS*: "I took jobs at church nurseries, rocking babies and chasing terrible-twos, not knowing I was collecting mood and material for [the novel] *IOU's* years later." Despite her difficulties in selling her stories,

Sebestyen continued writing and doing odd jobs, her family barely squeaking by. She said in *Innocence and Experience*: "I wasn't about to give up just because I couldn't write!" Sebestyen admitted that this attitude was impractical, but writing, with its freedom, flexibility, and creative outlet, was what she most wanted to do.

Since she had failed at writing adult novels, poetry, plays, articles, and true confessions, Sebestyen opted for a new approach. She had not yet tried to write books for children, but she found she did not feel comfortable writing about their simple, fairy-tale world. Sebestyen recalled in *SAAS*, "The talking animals and retold tales and jolly nonsense left me feeling adult and exiled." She then began reading books for young adults and remembered that "I came alive. . . . I didn't know all those skillful, pertinent, moving books were out there." A young-adult fiction editor to whom she sent one of her stories expressed interest in seeing a longer version. Sebestyen explained in *Innocence and Experience* that after years of frustrating rejections, the encouragement she received "absolutely electrified me. If she had asked me to write a sequel to *War and Peace*, I would have tried." So Sebestyen expanded her story to novel length. After weeks of waiting for a response to the book, titled *Words by Heart*, Sebestyen received a phone call from her editor. She recounted the call in *Innocence and Experience*: "A soft voice said, 'Did you know you've written a beautiful book? . . . I sobbed when I read it. The assistant editor sobbed. That doesn't happen very often in this business. And we want your book.'"

Set in 1910, *Words by Heart* is about a black family who moves to an all-white Western town in search of opportunity and a better life. The novel focuses on the relationship between Ben Sills and his twelve-year-old daughter Lena. Ben is a hardworking man who teaches Lena Christian ethics—forgiveness, especially—through Bible study. During the course of the book Lena learns that to know Bible verses "by heart" means not only to memorize them but to live by them, even in the face of injustice and racial prejudice. When Ben takes over the job of a lazy sharecropper and is shot and killed by the sharecropper's spiteful son, Tater, Lena makes the difficult choice to live by the values her father instilled in her; she decides to save the life of Tater, who was also shot in the scuffle with Ben. Though hailed by reviewers as a story showing the triumph of good over evil and regarded as a novel of literary merit, *Words by Heart* was nevertheless a controversial book. Some reviewers questioned the values Sebestyen promotes in the novel, claiming that her characterizations of Ben and Lena perpetuate the stereotype of meek, passive blacks who "turn the other cheek" when they encounter violence and racism. Still, Sebestyen commented in *Innocence and Experience* that the favorable reviews of *Words by Heart* "took my breath away."

Success began to come regularly for Sebestyen. Her second novel, *Far from Home,* published in 1980, begins with the death of thirteen-year-old Salty's deaf-mute mother. Salty, who has never known his father, is left with his great-grandmother, Mam. He is also left with a note from his mother instructing him to visit Tom Buckley, who she says will take Salty in. Salty gets a job at Tom's boarding house and rooms there with Mam, later discovering that Tom, who is married, is his father. This finding does not make life easier for Salty, for he must face the pain of having a father who will not acknowledge him. *Far from Home* was critically acclaimed; reviewers especially noted that Sebestyen's sense of humor serves to counteract the seriousness of the novel. In a *Bulletin of the Center for Children's Books* review, Zena Sutherland commented that "all of the characters are drawn in depth, in a moving story in which several of them change believably in response to the others. . . . [*Far from Home* is] a fine novel."

The author's next novel, *IOU's,* traces a relationship between an unorthodox mother and son that parallels Sebestyen's relationship with her own son. The mother, Annie, is divorced and is estranged from her father; she struggles to support her son, Stowe, by taking in day-care children. The two share a strong bond that endures poverty and other adversities only to become stronger. "This is a powerful story," remarked Hazel Rochman in the *New York Times Book Review.* "The young protagonist, strengthened by the love and integrity of a parent, takes on moral responsibility in a harsh world." Mary M. Burns, writing in the *Horn Book Magazine,* praised *IOU's,* "With feeling, but not without humor, the novel works on many levels. The characters, developed in action and dialogue, are remarkably well rounded, and the theme . . . is a substantial one."

Sebestyen followed *IOU's* with *On Fire,* a novel that tells the story of Tater Hanley, the boy who shot Ben Sills in *Words by Heart. On Fire* is told from the perspective of Sammy, Tater's younger brother who worships Tater and is unaware of his crime. When their father is imprisoned for drunkenness, Tater takes a hazardous position as a strikebreaker in the local mines to support their family. Both Tater and Sammy mature in the novel: Sammy forms a more realistic portrait of his brother's character, and Tater voices remorse for his wrongdoings. Their father's suicide in jail eventually brings the Hanleys closer together, giving them the strength to face the future with hope. Sebestyen was again praised by critics for her vivid characterizations and for presenting her characters with difficult choices and questions. In *Interracial Books for Children Bulletin* Rudine Sims praised *On Fire* as "a provocative book, worth reading, worth thinking about, worth discussing with young people."

In her next book, *The Girl in the Box,* Sebestyen deviates from the pattern of her earlier novels. Rather than focusing on families who weather adversity and eventually look toward a brighter future, Sebestyen tells the story of an isolated teenager whose future is at best uncertain. Jackie McGee is kidnapped on her way home from school one day. She is given no explanation and is left in a cellar with little food and water and the typewriter and paper she was carrying. The novel is structured as a series of letters that Jackie writes and slips out through the crack in the door, hoping someone will find them and rescue her. Through her letters, the reader experiences Jackie's panic, learns about the state of her personal relationships before her kidnapping, and witnesses a philosophical transformation that comes from hours of meditation. Whether or not Jackie is ever rescued cannot be determined—a departure from Sebestyen's typically optimistic endings. Like her earlier works, though, Sebestyen was praised for her powerful story and remarkable characterization. Sebestyen remarked in *SAAS* that a friend "said that *The Girl in the Box* had slammed her into her own box of self-examination, and that the strange view from it had given her new insights. I was so pleased, because that's the gift I wanted the book to give its readers."

Sebestyen commented further on the effect she hopes to produce through her writing in the *ALAN Review:* "I hope one out of every ten words in [my books] conjures up love, because in my mind love, and the miracles of acceptance and connection it generates, are the ultimate things to write about." Love and family are themes evident throughout Sebestyen's life as well as her works. The author commented in *SAAS* that "as I try to form a picture of my life-so-far, I see how much a love of family and home has shaped it." She continued, "Maybe each of my books is a home, too, where I come to stay a year or so, unpacking the baggage from my past and growing to love the family I move in with."

Reflecting upon her writing career, Sebestyen remarked in *Innocence and Experience* that "sometimes writing fiction is a struggle, sometimes a joy. Most of the time it's like a chronic backache or a ringing in the ears that won't go away." Her persistence, however, has led her to produce award-winning novels. Commenting on the numerous awards she has won for her books, Sebestyen noted in *SAAS,* "I am grateful for their encouragement, although books have no more business being ranked than people do—how can we judge a book's worth as it touches mind after mind?" The awards are, however, an indication of Sebestyen's achievements. Sebestyen has likened her success story to that of the magical rags-to-riches tale of Cinderella. Marvelling at her accomplishments, she hopes that her perseverance will be an inspiration to other writers; in *SATA* Sebestyen declared the hope that if her story "can keep another writer trying—never, never giving up—that will be frosting on the cake."

BIOGRAPHICAL/CRITICAL SOURCES:

BOOKS

Children's Literature Review, Volume 17, Gale, 1989.
Contemporary Authors, Volume 107, Gale, 1983.
Contemporary Literary Criticism, Volume 30, Gale, 1984.
Harrison, Barbara, and Gregory Maguire, editors, *Innocence and Experience: Essays and Conversations on Children's Literature,* Lothrup, 1987, pp. 440-42.
Something about the Author, Volume 39, Gale, 1985, p. 187.
Something about the Author Autobiography Series, Volume 10, Gale, 1990, pp. 289-303.

PERIODICALS

ALAN Review, spring, 1983; spring, 1984, pp. 1-3.
Bulletin of the Center for Children's Books, September, 1980, p. 21.
Horn Book, August, 1982, p. 418; November, 1988.
Interracial Books for Children Bulletin, Volume 17, numbers 3 & 4, 1986, pp. 34-5.
New York Times Book Review, September 19, 1982, p. 41.
Times Literary Supplement, November 3, 1989.

*   *   *

SHEEHAN, Neil   1936-

PERSONAL: Born Cornelius Mahoney Sheehan, October 27, 1936, in Holyoke, MA; son of Cornelius Joseph (a farmer) and Mary (O'Shea) Sheehan; married Susan M. Margulies (a staff writer for *New Yorker* magazine), March 30, 1965; children: Maria Gregory, Catherine Fair. *Education:* Harvard University, B.A. (cum laude), 1958.

ADDRESSES: Home—4505 Klingle St. N.W., Washington, DC 20016. *Agent*—Robert Lescher, 67 Irving Place, New York, NY 10003.

CAREER: United Press International, Saigon, Vietnam, bureau chief, 1962-64; *New York Times,* New York City, member of news staff, 1964-72, reporter in New York, 1964, foreign correspondent in Indonesia, 1965, and Vietnam, 1965-66, Pentagon correspondent, Washington, DC, 1966-68, White House correspondent, 1968-69, and special investigative reporter, Washington, DC, 1969-72; free-lance writer, 1972—. *Military service:* U.S. Army, 1959-62; received Army Commendation Medal.

MEMBER: Society of American Historians, American Academy of Achievement.

AWARDS, HONORS: Silver Medal, Poor Richard Club of Philadelphia, 1964; Louis M. Lyons Award for con-

science and integrity in journalism, 1964; certificate of appreciation, Overseas Press Club, 1967, for best article on Asia; Drew Pearson Prize for excellence in investigative reporting, 1971; honorary Doctor of Letters, Columbia College, 1972, American International College, 1990, and University of Lowell, 1991; Columbia Journalism Awards, 1972 and 1989; Sidney Hillman Foundation Awards, 1972 and 1988; Page One Award, Newspaper Guild of New York, 1972; distinguished service award and bronze medallion, Sigma Delta Chi, 1972; citation of excellence, Overseas Press Club, 1972; Guggenheim fellow, 1973-74; Adlai Stevenson fellow, 1973-74; Lehrman Institute fellow, 1975-76; Rockefeller Foundation fellow in humanities, 1976-77; Woodrow Wilson Center for International Scholars fellow, 1979-80; National Book Award for nonfiction, 1988, Pulitzer Prize for nonfiction and nominations for biography and history, Robert F. Kennedy Book Award, outstanding investigative reporting award, Investigative Reporters and Editors Inc. of the University of Missouri School of Journalism, Vetty Award, Vietnam Veterans Ensemble Theatre Company, achievement award, Vietnam Veterans of America, and Ambassador Award, English-Speaking Union, all 1989, all for *A Bright Shining Lie: John Paul Vann and America in Vietnam.*

WRITINGS:

The Pentagon Papers as Published by the New York Times, Quadrangle, 1971.
The Arnheiter Affair, Random House, 1972.
A Bright Shining Lie: John Paul Vann and America in Vietnam, Random House, 1988.
After the War Was Over: Hanoi and Saigon, Random House, 1992.

SIDELIGHTS: Almost sixteen years of Neil Sheehan's life were devoted to writing his Pulitzer Prize-winning bestseller, *A Bright Shining Lie: John Paul Vann and America in Vietnam.* Blending biography with history and personal memories, the book examines the evolution of the United States' role in the Vietnam War. When Sheehan first thought of writing the book, he supposed it would take three or four years to complete. But as he delved more deeply into his research, he found the history of the war, the personality of his subject, and his own feelings about the conflict becoming ever more complex. The project became his sole interest, leading some of his friends to dub him "the last casualty of Vietnam," according to *Washington Post Magazine* writer William Prochnau. The result of Sheehan's obsessive labor is a "massive, important and deeply unsettling" book, in the words of *Newsweek* reviewer Joseph Nocera. "Immensely long, enormously ambitious, told with an emotion that bursts through its pages, this is an impressive achievement. If there is one book that captures the Vietnam War in the sheer Homeric scale of its passion and folly, this book is it," maintains *New York Times Book Review* contributor Ronald Steel.

Sheehan's involvement with the war began in 1962, when he went to Saigon as a foreign correspondent for United Press International. At that time the United States had just 3,200 military advisers in Southeast Asia, whose role was to instruct the government forces of South Vietnam against the Communist-led Vietcong guerrillas. The Cold War was at its height, and Sheehan initially considered American involvement in the Vietnamese conflict "a glorious adventure," as Prochnau quotes him as saying. "We all believed in the American cause. . . . We were winners; we were invulnerable; we were right." But the war, and Sheehan's perceptions of it, changed rapidly and dramatically. Sheehan and his fellow reporters soon discovered that the American commanders in Saigon were not reliable sources of information; they constantly issued optimistic reports while shrouding their very real problems and defeats in secrecy and self-deception.

It was not long before Sheehan became acquainted with John Paul Vann, a thirty-seven-year-old lieutenant colonel and a top military adviser to the South Vietnamese. Vann gave the reporters the truth that the rest of the American command would not divulge: that the South Vietnamese troops under his instruction were unwilling or unable to fight effectively, and that they had suffered humiliating battle defeats. He openly criticized the U.S. policies of indiscriminate bombing and urged officials to adopt a new strategy that would address the social problems behind the war. For this he was sharply rebuked by his superiors, and when the reporters passed Vann's statements on to the public, they were accused of being unpatriotic. Vann left Vietnam and retired from the Army in 1963, leaving behind a corps of reporters who had come to idolize him for his battlefield bravery and his truthfulness. Like Vann, the reporters still believed in their country's cause, but they were deeply disillusioned with the leaders of the war effort.

Sheehan was hired away from United Press International by the *New York Times* in 1964, about the same time that Vann was preparing to return to Vietnam as a civilian pacification adviser. After another year in Vietnam himself, Sheehan returned to the United States in 1966 to join the newspaper's Washington Bureau and raise his family. By 1972 he had turned vehemently against the war and was faced with a possible trial for obtaining what would become known as the "Pentagon Papers"—a secret government history of the war and an archive of documents revealing the tangle of lies behind the U.S. involvement in Vietnam—for the *New York Times*. Sheehan's work in obtaining the Pentagon Papers and the *New York Times*'s courage in publishing them won the newspaper the Pulitzer Gold Medal for public service. Vann, meanwhile, re-

mained in Southeast Asia, where, as the war ballooned, his power and influence increased proportionately. In time he attained the status of a general, commanding an entire corps region in the mountains of the Central Highlands of South Vietnam until he was killed in a helicopter crash in 1972. While attending Vann's funeral in Washington, D.C., Sheehan realized that Vann had become a personification of America's long, complex commitment to the war. The idea for his book was born.

In the course of his research, Sheehan discovered that Vann, once revered by reporters for his commitment to truth, had eventually succumbed to the same willful blindness exhibited by the rest of the U.S. military leadership. He found that Vann had left the Army not in a noble gesture of protest, but because charges of statutory rape had made it impossible for him to advance to the rank of general. The man who in 1962 had decried the wanton waste of life was, by 1972, speaking in glowing terms of the "battlefield stench" arising from effective B-52 strikes that turned the countryside into "a moonscape," as Sheehan quotes Vann as saying. Sheehan's painstaking portrayal of the many facets of Vann's personality rivals "the most complex creations of fiction," asserts *Time* reviewer Laurence Zuckerman. "He was a brave soldier, a brilliant analyst, a born maverick and a savvy political infighter. He was also . . . a shameless hypocrite with a 'secret vice' he could not or would not control. To Sheehan . . . Vann is the very symbol of the U.S. in Viet Nam: a courageous do-gooder masking a dark streak of amorality."

The use of Vann as a symbol for all that was right and wrong with the United States involvement in Vietnam "brings together what are really two books: a graphic history of the war and the story of John Paul Vann," writes Steel. "They do not fully overlap, for at times Vann is the story, while at other times he fades away completely. This book is not so much a biography as it is a montage. But a dazzling montage it is: vividly written and deeply felt, with a power that comes from long reflection and strong emotions. The dramatic scenes of lonely men locked in combat, the striking portraits of those who made and reported the conflict, the clash of wills and egos, the palpable touch and feel of the war, the sensitivity to the politics and psychology behind the battles, the creation of a memorable, though still mysterious, man—all these combine in a work that captures the Vietnam War like no other."

Speaking to *Publishers Weekly* interviewer Walter Gelles, Sheehan offered his reflections on the reasons behind the tragic course of the war in Vietnam: "In World War II, our leadership was attuned to reality, but in the postwar period we became so rich and powerful that our leadership lost its ability to think creatively—and arrogance replaced reality. In Vietnam, our political and military leaders simply could not conceive the possibility that we could lose.

Successive administrations deluded themselves into the fantasy that we could somehow perpetuate an American presence in the country. The American soldier became a victim of his own leadership, which is a bitter lesson to face."

BIOGRAPHICAL/CRITICAL SOURCES:

BOOKS

Bestsellers 89, Issue 2, Gale, 1989.

PERIODICALS

Business Week, October 3, 1988.
Chicago Tribune, October 9, 1988.
Detroit Free Press, October 16, 1988; November 13, 1988.
Detroit News, February 20, 1972.
Los Angeles Times, October 12, 1988; October 17, 1988.
New Republic, October 24, 1988.
Newsweek, October 10, 1988.
New York Times, October 18, 1988.
New York Times Book Review, September 25, 1988.
Publishers Weekly, September 2, 1988.
Time, March 6, 1972; October 17, 1988.
Variety, June 28, 1972.
Washington Post, September 16, 1988.
Washington Post Magazine, October 9, 1988.

—*Sketch by Joan Goldsworthy*

*   *   *

SHEEHAN, Susan   1937-

PERSONAL: Born August 24, 1937, in Vienna, Austria; immigrated to the United States, 1941, naturalized citizen, 1946; daughter of Charles and Kitty C. (Herrmann) Sachsel; married Neil Sheehan (a writer), March 30, 1965; children: Maria Gregory, Catherine Fair. *Education:* Wellesley College, B.A., 1958.

ADDRESSES: Home—4505 Klingle St. N.W., Washington, DC 20016. *Agent*—Robert Lescher, 67 Irving Place, New York, NY 10003. *Office*—*New Yorker* Magazine, 20 West 43rd St., New York, NY 10036.

CAREER: Esquire-Coronet (magazines), New York City, editorial researcher, 1959-60; free-lance writer in New York City, 1960-1961; *New Yorker* (magazine), New York City, staff writer, 1961—. Member of advisory committee on employment and crime, Vera Institute of Justice, 1978-84; member of literature panel of the District of Columbia Commission on Arts and Humanities, 1979-84; consultant on 42nd St. redevelopment project for New York City Department of City Planning. Judge for Robert F. Kennedy Journalism Awards, 1980, 1984; chair of Pulitzer Prize nominating jury in general nonfiction, 1988; member of Pulitzer Prize nominating jury in general nonfiction, 1991.

MEMBER: National Mental Health Association (literary panel, 1982-83), American Society of Historians, Phi Beta Kappa.

AWARDS, HONORS: Guggenheim fellow, 1975-76; Sidney Hillman Foundation Award, 1976, for *A Welfare Mother;* Gavel Award, American Bar Association, 1978, for *A Prison and a Prisoner;* Woodrow Wilson Center for International Scholars fellow, 1981; Mental Health Media Award for individual reporting, National Mental Health Association, 1981, for article "The Patient"; Pulitzer Prize for best nonfiction work, 1982, and American Book Award nomination for general nonfiction, 1983, both for *Is There No Place on Earth for Me?;* Distinguished Alumni Award, Wellesley College, 1984; feature writing award, New York Press Club, 1984; honorary Doctor of Letters, University of Lowell, 1991; Ford Foundation fellow.

WRITINGS:

NONFICTION

Ten Vietnamese (collection of sketches), Knopf, 1967.
A Welfare Mother (first printed in *New Yorker*), introduction by Michael Harrington, Houghton, 1976.
A Prison and a Prisoner (first printed in *New Yorker*), Houghton, 1978.
Is There No Place on Earth for Me? (first printed as "The Patient" in *New Yorker*), Houghton, 1982.
Kate Quinton's Days (first printed in *New Yorker*), Houghton, 1984.
A Missing Plane (first printed in *New Yorker*), Putnam, 1986.

OTHER

Contributor to magazines, including *New York Times Sunday Magazine, Atlantic, New Republic, Harper's, Boston Globe Sunday Magazine, Washington Post Sunday Magazine,* and *Life.*

WORK IN PROGRESS: A book about foster care.

SIDELIGHTS: Journalist Susan Sheehan specializes in long, difficult stories that lay open the lives of people to whom her affluent *New Yorker* readers are not ordinarily exposed. Four of these accounts—of a welfare recipient, a convicted thief, a mental patient, and an elderly woman on Medicaid—have been published in book form. Sheehan's account of a schizophrenic woman, first published in the *New Yorker* as "The Patient," and then as a book entitled *Is There No Place on Earth for Me?,* won a Pulitzer Prize for general nonfiction in 1982 and received an American Book Award nomination.

In her work Sheehan attempts to examine systems and institutions through the presentation of an individual case. In *A Welfare Mother* Sheehan takes on the governmental public assistance programs, in *A Prison and a Prisoner* she looks at Green Haven maximum security prison and the New York penal system, in *Is There No Place on Earth for Me?* she scrutinizes Creedmoor Psychiatric Center as well as many of the methods for treating the mentally ill, and in *Kate Quinton's Days* she tackles the Medicaid program and the treatment of the elderly in the United States. In a *Village Voice* review of *Is There No Place on Earth for Me?*, Vince Aletti points out that in psychiatric patient Sylvia Frumkin, Sheehan "has found . . . a 'representative' figure whose history illuminates a system or an institution, not in a flash of revelation but through painstaking accumulation of data and insight. Sheehan's scrupulous, vivid case histories are constructed bit by bit, fine webs of evidence and observation dense with fact but charged with feeling. . . . Sheehan's focus on Sylvia is hardly a narrow one; Sylvia is the entry point, the key that begins to unlock the institution. Starting with her, Sheehan takes every tangent, follows every lead, and attempts to follow up every loose end—all with obvious delight in the serendipitous fact."

Writing about *A Prison and a Prisoner,* Kenneth Lamont states in the *Washington Post Book World:* "Susan Sheehan's cool and altogether admirable book does not describe an unusual prisoner in an unusual prison. Quite the contrary, I was reminded on almost every page of my own experience teaching school in San Quentin 25 years ago. I knew [George] Malinow in a half-dozen incarnations." *Newsweek*'s Peter S. Prescott observes that in *A Prison and a Prisoner* Sheehan "wisely has chosen as narrow a focus as possible; an intense look at a single prisoner is more likely to provide reliable insights into the whole system than is a broad and superficial survey."

Sheehan spends months researching her articles and, in order to catch and record the smallest details, she often stays with her subjects for stretches at a time, observing and interviewing them and everyone with whom they are involved. Before she began writing *Is There No Place on Earth for Me?*—a book Meg Rosenfeld of the *Washington Post* calls a "reportorial tour de force"—Sheehan had compiled 1000 pages of her own notes and observations as well as an additional 1000 pages of material on the treatment Sylvia Frumkin had received for the past seventeen years. Sheehan's technique, says Rosenfeld, "is a kind of total immersion, observation and interviews combined with extensive library research. At Creedmoor, she insinuated herself so completely that she became the proverbial fly on the wall. She calls it 'third person invisible.' " In an interview with *Chicago Tribune* reporter Peter Gorner, Sheehan recalls, "I literally live with my subjects when

I'm on a story. When I profiled Carmen Santana, the welfare mother, I slept in the same bed with her. I found myself in a room where heroin was being dealt, wondering all the time how I was going to explain my presence when the police came."

Sheehan writes her profiles in a straightforward, documentary style that Prescott refers to as her "plain gray worsted prose." For instance, in *A Welfare Mother* Sheehan spends seven pages recording Carmen Santana's purchases after she received her biweekly assistance check. In *A Prison and a Prisoner,* she details the events of inmate George Malinow's day, often recording it in minute-by-minute fashion. *Is There No Place on Earth for Me?* begins with a vivid account of one of Sylvia Frumkin's psychotic breakdowns. "Susan Sheehan is a master of the *New Yorker* style," comments Willard Gaylin in the *New Republic.* "[*Is There No Place on Earth for Me?*] is a written version of what in movies would be called cinema verite." The sparse unemotional prose Sheehan uses in her books is carried through in her approach to her material. "Massive research and clear, dry, unsentimental prose style characterize Sheehan's work," notes Gorner in his *Chicago Tribune* review of *Is There No Place on Earth for Me?* "[Sheehan] is a camera who reports on what she learns and observes, neither excoriating or lauding—'I try not to affix blame,' she says. 'Blame is not very useful.' "

All of Sheehan's profiles have been well-received, both by critics and the public. For example, Sara Sanborn, writing in *Saturday Review,* considers *A Welfare Mother* to be "a perfect little book. The excellence of *A Welfare Mother* lies in the sureness of vision, discipline, and patience that kept it small; a more self-indulgent writer could have made it twice as long and half as good. Its purity is its impact. . . . This is a book of life on its own terms; it makes the pious generalizations of both right and left look even more futile than usual. *A Welfare Mother* is a fine achievement, a book that should be read."

A number of critics, however, find that Sheehan's approach to her subject in *A Welfare Mother* detracts from the story she presents and that her style is too controlled and factual, thus lacking in emotion. "Unfortunately, Mrs. Santana seldom emerges as anyone other than a welfare recipient," says Susan Jacoby in the *New York Times Book Review.* "One of Mrs. Santana's sons is a drug addict, and her attitude toward that is disposed of in two quick sentences. Does a mother on welfare bleed less than other mothers when she learns her son is mainlining heroin? In this instance, as in many others, a major weakness of the piece is its lack of direct quotation." Richard Lingeman of the *New York Times* sees this as a possible problem of reprinting a magazine article as a book: "Mrs. Sheehan's style . . . is cool, objective, self-effacing, pitched in an even, controlled tone; the facts of Mrs. Santana's life, the comings-and-goings of her typical days, the highs and lows are all extruded through this mold in a smooth controlled flow," writes Lingeman. "While this style may have worked well in a magazine piece, in a book, out of the context of the magazine, it suddenly seems to shrink and flatten out. . . . Mrs. Sheehan's journalistic commitment is praiseworthy, and her book does offer some insight into the welfare system through the eyes of one of its victims—or beneficiaries, if you will. But laughter, tears and emotions are missing. The author has distanced the reader too much, providing neither emotional involvement nor material for thought." Despite raising similar objections in the *Washington Post Book World,* though, Kristen Hunter maintains: "Susan Sheehan has chosen to concentrate on only one life. Considering that life's scope, having distilled its essence into slightly more than 100 pages is a remarkable feat."

In a *New York Times Book Review* article in which he praises Sheehan for her insights into the penal system in *A Prison and a Prisoner,* Fred J. Cook states, "The bulging prisons of America incarcerate a full-sized criminal army, composed overwhelmingly of incorrigibles and growing at a rate that outstrips facilities to contain them." *A Prison and a Prisoner,* Cook continues, "is a marvelous work of detailed reporting, . . . [and] Sheehan presents this picture [of the prisons] in all its hopelessness. She not only delves into the mechanics of the prison system and the daily life of the prisoner, but she gets inside their skulls as well." *A Prison and a Prisoner* also examines the changes in philosophy of the correctional system from reformist (which aims at rehabilitation of the prisoners) to hard-line (which entails incarcerating prisoners simply to keep them off the streets and spurns rehabilitation programs such as job training). "George Malinow, 57, a payroll-robbing recidivist from Brooklyn, is a complex figure and living repository of correction history," observes James Lieber in the *Nation.* "Incarcerated all but three years since 1938, he participated in the state's early reform experiments in Walkill, hardened big-house years at Sing Sing, and survived Attica by nesting on a roof. . . . These institutions and others . . . have distinct, often bizarre rules and flavors that Sheehan understands. The prisons come to seem like strange city-states within a not always harmonious league."

Although Sheehan paints a vivid picture of prison life, the absence of emotion in her style once again works against her in some critics' minds. Her book lacks focus in that she does not present the reader with any conclusions, contends the *New York Times*'s Anatole Broyard. "I don't know quite what to make of 'A Prison and a Prisoner,'" declares Broyard. "Susan Sheehan is a good observer as well as a determined researcher, yet when I had finished her book, I felt at a loss to say what she thought—or

wanted me to think—about the prisons and the particular prisoner she describes. . . . [She] gives us an accurate but curiously passive picture of the current issues in prison management. When she tells us the prevalent view in penology now is that rehabilitation does not work, I was not sure whether she was reporting a trend or expressing an evaluation of her material."

Kenneth Lamont, writing in the *Washington Post Book World,* finds this absence of opinion one of the book's strengths rather than one of its weaknesses: "*A Prison and a Prisoner* . . . is not a reformer's book, complete with recommendations for an increased food budget, more vocational training, enlarged visiting hours, and all the dreary rest. It is a much better and more important book than that, for it comes to grips with reality and portrays it superbly. The world it describes is often absurd and shot through with black humor, precisely the sort of reality that reduces official society to muscle-bound helplessness." "Susan Sheehan never says . . . [that prisons do not work]," says *Newsweek*'s Prescott, who also observes that Sheehan offers the reader few conclusions of her own. "A cool reporter determined to be as objective as she can, she leaves it to her reader to infer her conclusions." Prescott concludes: "Thoughtless reviewers will doubtless complain that [Sheehan] offers no solutions to the dilemma of our prisons. Never mind; reporters are not social engineers. It is achievement enough that they describe a situation as it is—and this Sheehan has done remarkably well."

Also writing on the same issue of neutrality in *A Prison and a Prisoner, Nation* reviewer James Lieber differs from the other critics in believing that Sheehan comes to a conclusion and that "she manages without opining to make a point that is arguably reactionary, possibly dangerous." Lieber finds that in her presentation Sheehan offers a more than sympathetic view of prison officials' beliefs that few of the men in prisons like Green Haven are suffering, and that her choice of Malinow as her subject serves to confirm this view. And Malinow, says Lieber, is not necessarily representative of the prison population. "The message is clear that Malinow does best when given maximal structure, when put in a box," the critic notes. "Because [Sheehan] has chosen Malinow as opposed to equally valid counterimages available (rebellious, retarded, junkie, nonwhite, etc.), she is able to slip into easy generalizations about a population of 1,800 [at Green Haven]. . . . Something doesn't fit. In my job [as an assistant public defender] we try to keep defendants out of state pens even when the alternative is the county jail. The reason is that state time is hard time, and for reasons that range from noise to separation, those who draw it hit bottom and grow old before their years. Taking her cue from the administration, Sheehan regards the regular suicide attempts as ploys to get attention, drugs and transfers rather than as reflections of despair." Cook, writing in the *New York Times Book Review,* also believes that Sheehan is making some conclusions about the penal system, but suggests that "the most chilling aspect of Susan Sheehan's account is the conclusion that nothing has worked—and nothing in the foreseeable future is likely to work."

Of all of Sheehan's books, *Is There No Place on Earth for Me?* has gained the greatest attention. Its notoriety derives from its sometimes harrowing presentation of life in a psychiatric hospital, but especially from the bizarre and often darkly humorous personality of its main subject, Sylvia Frumkin. "I have schizophrenia—cancer of the nerves. My body is overcrowded with nerves. This is going to win me the Nobel Prize for medicine," declares Frumkin in one of her numerous highspeed monologues in *Is There No Place on Earth for Me?*

"Cancer of the nerves. Sylvia Frumkin is the lunatic poet of the nut house," writes Megan Rosenfeld in the *Washington Post,* "summoning from the dark mess of her mind amazing screeds that ring like a bell in the fog. 'The body is run by electricity. My wiring is all faulty,' she said once. On another day her vision was this: 'My skin is just like the lawn. I'm going to tear it off and pluck out the bed of dandelions. This isn't schizophrenia, it's terminal acne. . . .' " And it is Frumkin's vision of the world and of herself that keeps the reader so intensely interested, despite the fact that she is, as Maggie Scarf says in the *New York Times Book Review,* "an unlikely heroine, voraciously greedy (for food and attention), overweight, hostile and assaultive . . . [prone to] excesses of . . . speechifying, and . . . preposterous appearance and behavior." To Vince Aletti in the *Village Voice,* she "emerges as an unlikely and unforgettable heroine, at once the most appealing and appalling character you're likely to encounter in a book this year." According to Willard Gaylin in the *New Republic,* Sylvia Frumkin "is not a 'lovable eccentric.' She is not even very likable. But she will break your heart."

Sylvia Frumkin was first diagnosed as a schizophrenic at the age of fourteen, entering Creedmoor Psychiatric Center in Queens, New York, for the first time a year and a half later. By the time Sheehan met her seventeen years later, Frumkin had been in and out of mental institutions ten times; one hospitalization lasted two years. It is through Frumkin that Sheehan is able to enter the nightmarish world of the insane and to explore the labyrinth of hospitals, drugs, megavitamins, electroconvulsive treatment, and insulin shock therapy that comprise part of the darker side of America's approach to the mentally ill. "Susan Sheehan, with extraordinary explicitness, takes us through each hospitalization," explains Gaylin. "The central institution is Creedmoor, not one of the ornaments of the New York State mental health system. What happens

at Creedmoor is often infuriating: wrong medications wrongly administered, insensitivity, bureaucratic mess and meanness." The *New York Times*'s Christopher Lehmann-Haupt comments: "If Sylvia's plight is foremost in our awareness while reading 'Is There No Place on Earth for Me?,' Mrs. Sheehan's narrative handling of it is not far behind. What is especially impressive is how effortlessly she moves back and forth between this case in particular and the status of mental disease in general."

Is There No Place on Earth for Me? points out many of the changes in the approach to treating the mentally ill, as well as many of the shortfalls in the methods of those treatments and in the philosophies behind them. Creedmoor, says Gaylin, "is the kind of institution that has contributed to the recent crusade for 'deinstitutionalization' with its simplistic assumption that if only there were no institutions there would be no mental disease. Sylvia herself knows better. On reading in a Creedmoor form that their 'philosophy of treatment' is that 'the individual with a problem is best served in his own environment,' she responds, 'I'm against polluting the environment, always have been.' " At the same time, however, Sheehan is determined "not to affix blame" to any one person or institution. Meg Greenfield reports in the *Washington Post Book World* that "it is true that the book reveals some terrible lapses in institutional conduct, for instance, and some dangerous shortages of money, expertise and common sense among those charged with the care of Miss Frumkin when she is at her most violent or deranged." Greenfield goes on to point out that Frumkin has also "been the beneficiary, if that is the word for it, of all those many reforms and bright ideas we editorial writers like to pronounce the good and self-evident solution: halfway houses and rehabilitation programs and vocational training and God knows what all for nearly two decades. What we learn is humility, that there are some human conditions and complexities that we can't 'fix' with a bright idea."

Sheehan's book has been praised as perhaps a clearer portrait of mental illness than many of the books that have preceded it. "If only Ken Kesey had met Sylvia Frumkin before he took his fanciful flight over the cuckoo's nest," speculates Gaylin, adding: "To romanticize an illness as severe as schizophrenia is a sin against the sufferer. To minimize it by assuming that kindness and proper care are enough is to trivialize the problem. Susan Sheehan does neither. She honestly and directly indicates, with infinite detail and patience, the anguish and the agony that mental illness always wreaks on its victim, and on those in contact with her, particularly those who love her."

After completing her book on Sylvia Frumkin, Sheehan began yet another study of an individual trapped within an ineffective social system. Using the same technique as in her previous works—focusing on one individual to provide an overview of a whole segment of society—Sheehan illuminates the plight of America's elderly in *Kate Quinton's Days.* In the same careful, meticulous style that won her the Pulitzer Prize for Sylvia Frumkin's story, Sheehan describes one year in the life of Kate Quinton, an elderly woman who, after a lifetime of hard work and good health, found herself perilously close to becoming an unwilling resident of a nursing home. As a character, Kate Quinton lacks Sylvia Frumkin's flamboyance and intensity, but the story of her struggle to remain independent is just as compelling, according to several reviewers. "Not many of us will be hospitalized for schizophrenia, but most of us will get old," remarks Walter Clemons in a *Time* review that compared *Kate Quinton's Days* to *Is There No Place on Earth for Me?* "Sheehan quietly details the frustrations and delays of health-care services for the old in a society in which the family has dispersed." As in her previous books, Sheehan avoids emotional comment in her narrative, letting the often-depressing facts speak for themselves. The result "stands out as a work of great integrity and quality, a poignant and soundly constructed documentation of what it really means to be weak and old in New York City," declares Mark Kramer in the *Washington Post Book World.*

Sheehan departed from her usual subject matter with her 1986 publication, *A Missing Plane.* The plane mentioned in the title was a United States B-24 bomber that vanished mysteriously somewhere over New Guinea's dense jungles during World War II. Search parties were unable to find any wreckage, but the more than twenty men on board were soon declared dead. Many of their relatives continued to hope against hope that they had somehow survived, until 1982, when two tribesmen on a parrot-hunting expedition stumbled upon the remains of the craft and its crew. Sheehan's book, "a superbly reported reconstruction of a quirk of fate and its aftermath," according to *New York Times Book Review* contributor Eric Lax, highlights the skill and dedication of Tadao Furue, the forensics expert who took on the daunting task of identifying what remained of the victims' bodies. "Mr. Furue's skill is turning missing people into dead ones, thus laying them to rest. Mrs. Sheehan's is bringing them back to life through the story she weaves from the recollections of the relatives and friends of each of the 22 men on the missing plane," states Lax. "With a firm grasp on the scientific aspects and a deep understanding of the problems faced by Mr. Furue, [Sheehan] makes these pages as interesting as anything ever penned by Dorothy L. Sayers," asserts *New York Times* reviewer Drew Middleton. "Surely this is one of the most remarkable books of the year. . . . Although the book has the pace of a novel, it is clearly the result of the most thorough research and analysis. . . . This is real reporting by a master of the craft."

BIOGRAPHICAL/CRITICAL SOURCES:

BOOKS

Sheehan, Susan *Is There No Place on Earth for Me?*, Houghton, 1982.

PERIODICALS

America, July 31, 1982.
Chicago Tribune, May 17, 1982.
Chicago Tribune Book World, April 18, 1982.
Ms., June, 1982.
Nation, September 2, 1978.
National Review, September 17, 1976.
New Republic, May 12, 1982.
Newsweek, May 15, 1978; April 5, 1982; October 8, 1984.
New York Times, August 27, 1976; May 13, 1978; April 7, 1982; November 29, 1986.
New York Times Book Review, August 8, 1976; July 9, 1978; May 2, 1982; November 4, 1984; October 19, 1986.
Saturday Review, July 10, 1976.
Village Voice, April 20, 1982.
Washington Post, August 1, 1982.
Washington Post Book World, July 18, 1976; May 21, 1978; April 11, 1982; September 9, 1984; October 26, 1986.

*   *   *

SHERMAN, Kenneth 1950-

PERSONAL: Born July 3, 1950, in Toronto, Ontario, Canada; son of Ted and Eve Sherman; married Marie Goldstein; children: Justine, Adam. *Education:* York University, B.A., 1968; University of Toronto, M.A., 1972.

ADDRESSES: Home—10 Romney Rd., Downsview, Ontario, Canada M3H 1H2.

CAREER: Sheridan College, Brampton, Ontario, English teacher, 1971—.

WRITINGS:

POETRY

Snake Music, Mosaic Press/Valley Editions, 1978.
The Cost of Living, Mosaic Press/Valley Editions, 1981.
Words for Elephant Man, Mosaic Press/Valley Editions, 1983.
Black Flamingo, Mosaic Press, 1985.
(Editor) *Relations* (poetry anthology), Mosaic Press, 1986.
The Book of Salt, Oberon Press, 1987.
Jackson's Point, Oberon Press, 1989.
Open to Currents, Wolsak & Wynn, 1992.

OTHER

Work is represented in anthologies, including *Modern Poetry,* Heath; *Aurora,* Doubleday (Canada); and *Essential Words,* Oberon Press. Contributor to periodicals, including *Prism International, Descant,* and *Canadian Literature.*

WORK IN PROGRESS: Re-Visions, a collection of essays on various literary topics, including the works of Czeslaw Milosz, Primo Levi, and World War I British poets.

*   *   *

SHINN, Roger L(incoln)   1917-

PERSONAL: Born January 6, 1917, in Germantown, OH; son of Henderson L. V. and Carrie Margaret (Buehler) Shinn; married Katharine Cole, November 6, 1943; children: Carol Katharine, Marybeth. *Education:* Heidelberg College, A.B., 1938; Union Theological Seminary, B.D., 1941; Columbia University, Ph.D., 1951. *Religion:* United Church of Christ. *Avocational interests:* Theater and gardening.

ADDRESSES: Home—288 Cowles Rd., Woodbury, CT 06798; 501 West 123rd St., Apt. 6A, New York, NY 10027.

CAREER: Ordained to Evangelical and Reformed Church (now United Church of Christ), 1946; Union Theological Seminary, New York City, instructor in philosophy of religion, 1947-49; Heidelberg College, Tiffin, OH, 1949-54, began as associate professor, became professor of philosophy and religion and chairman of philosophy department; Vanderbilt University, Divinity School, Nashville, TN, professor of theology, 1954-57, professor of Christian ethics, 1957-59; Union Theological Seminary, professor of Christian ethics, 1959-60, William E. Dodge, Jr., Professor of Applied Christianity, 1960-70, dean of instruction, 1963-70, Reinhold Niebuhr Professor of Social Ethics, 1970-85, professor emeritus, 1985—, acting president, 1974-75. Adjunct professor of religion, Columbia University, 1962-86. Adjunct professor of economics, New York University Graduate School of Business Administration, 1979. Visiting professor of philosophies of Judaism, Jewish Theological Seminary of America, 1982. Lecturer at more than one hundred colleges and universities, including the Earle Lectures, Pacific School of Religion, 1957, the William Belden Noble lectures, Harvard University, 1960, the Harris Franklin Rall Lectures, Garrett Theological Seminary, 1967, and the Danforth Lectures, Association of American Colleges, 1970.

United Church of Christ, consultant on curriculum in Christian education, 1952-62, member of Commission to Prepare Statement of Faith, 1957-59, president of Board for Homeland Ministries, 1962-66, member of board of directors, 1962-72, member of Committee for Racial Justice Now, 1963-67. Consultant to numerous civic and ecumenical committees. Member of numerous conferences, committees, and councils on the role of the church in society. *Military service:* U.S. Army, 1941-45; became major, received Silver Star.

MEMBER: American Association of University Professors, Society for Values in Higher Education, American Theological Society (president, 1975-76), American Society of Christian Ethics (president, 1974-75), American Academy of Religion, American Veterans Committee, Americans for Democratic Action, League for Industrial Democracy, American Association for the United Nations, National Association for the Advancement of Colored People.

AWARDS, HONORS: Traveling fellow, Union Theological Seminary, 1945-46; Kent fellow, 1946; Martha Kinney Cooper Ohioana Library Award, 1954, for *Christianity and the Problem of History;* D.D. from Mission House Theological Seminary, 1960, and Franklin and Marshall College, 1963; D. Litt. from Heidelberg College, 1963; Fellow, Conference on Science, Philosophy and Religion, 1966; inducted into Infantry School Hall of Fame, Ft. Benning, GA, 1973; Award for Excellence, Graduate Faculties Alumni of Columbia University, 1981; L.H.D., Drury College, 1984; Doctor of Humanities, Blackburn University, 1985.

WRITINGS:

Beyond This Darkness, Association Press, 1946.
Christianity and the Problem of History, Scribner, 1953.
The Sermon on the Mount, Christian Education Press, 1954, revised edition, 1962.
Life, Death, and Destiny, Westminster, 1957.
The Existentialist Posture, Association Press, 1959, revised edition, 1970.
The Educational Mission of Our Church, United Church Press, 1962.
(Editor and co-author) *The Search for Identity: Essays on the American Character,* Harper, 1964.
Moments of Truth, United Church Press, 1964.
Tangled World, Scribner, 1965.
(With Daniel Day Williams) *We Believe: An Interpretation of the United Church Statement of Faith,* United Church Press, 1966.
Man: The New Humanism, Westminster, 1968.
(Editor and co-author) *Restless Adventure: Essays on Contemporary Expressions of Existentialism,* Scribner, 1968.
Wars and Rumors of Wars, Abingdon, 1972.

(Editor) *Faith and Science in an Unjust World: Report of the World Council of Churches' Conference on Faith, Science, and the Future,* Volume 1: *Plenary Presentations,* Fortress Press and the World Council of Churches, 1980.

Forced Options: Social Decisions for the Twenty-first Century, Harper, 1982, third edition, Pilgrim Press, 1991.

(Co-editor and co-author with James Luther Adams and Wilhelm Pauck) *The Thought of Paul Tillich,* Harper, 1985.

Confessing Our Faith, Pilgrim Press, 1990.

Also author and narrator of television series, *Tangled World.* Author of sound recording, *Learning to Live with Scarcity,* Thesis Theological Cassettes, 1975. Contributor of chapters and essays to over forty books. Contributor of articles and reviews to numerous magazines and scholarly journals, including *Saturday Review* and *Christian Century.* Contributing editor, *Christianity and Crisis.* Associate editor, *Bulletin of Science, Technology and Society.* Member of editorial board, *Journal of Religious Ethics.*

Shinn's writings have been translated into French, German, Spanish, Chinese, Japanese, Korean, Arabic and Turkish.

WORK IN PROGRESS: A Book on perception, belief, and decision.

SIDELIGHTS: Roger L. Shinn told *CA:* "On my seventy-fifth birthday it dawned on me that I was more than half-way through my literary career and would not be in this world long enough to write the many things I crave to do. I'm still eager and energetic, but I am asking, a little more wistfully than before, what I want my literary legacy to be."

*   *   *

SICINSKI, Andrzej 1924-

PERSONAL: Born May 20, 1924, in Warsaw, Poland; son of Antoni (a civil engineer) and Stanislawa Sicinski; married Barbara Laczkowska (an editor), 1959; children: Jacek Stebnicki (stepson), Marcin. *Education:* Warsaw Polytechnic Institute, Civil Engineer, 1952; University of Warsaw, M.A., 1952, Ph.D., 1961.

ADDRESSES: Home—Klaudyny 16-160, 01-684 Warsaw, Poland. *Office*—Division for Civil Society Studies, Institute of Philosophy and Sociology, Polish Academy of Science, Nowy Swiat 72, 00-330 Warsaw, Poland.

CAREER: Public Opinion Research Center, Warsaw, Poland, deputy director, 1958-64; Polish Academy of Sciences, Warsaw, professor of sociology and head of Division for Civil Society Studies (formerly Division for Life-

styles Studies and Division for Social Prognoses), Institute of Philosophy and Sociology, 1965—, scientific secretary of committee, Poland 2000, 1979-85. *Military service:* Polish Underground Army (AK), 1940-44.

MEMBER: International Sociological Association, World Future Studies Federation, Polish Sociological Association, Polish Philosophical Association, National Civic Committee, Rotary Club of Warsaw (president, 1990-91).

AWARDS, HONORS: Ford Foundation grant, 1968; Secretary of the Polish Academy of Science award, 1971, for study "Polish Simulation Model of Development of Schooling System."

WRITINGS:

(Editor with Helmut Ornauer, Hakan Wiberg, and Johan Galtung, and contributor) *Images of the World in the Year 2000: A Comparative Ten-Nation Study,* Humanities, 1976.

(Contributor) Ian Miles and John Irvine, editors, *The Poverty of Progress,* Pergamon, 1982.

(Contributor) Eleonora Masini, editor, *Visions of Desirable Societies,* Pergamon, 1983.

(Editor with Monica Wemegah, and contributor) *Alternative Ways of Life in Contemporary Europe,* United Nations University, 1983.

(Editor with Rolf Homann and Masini, and contributor) *Changing Lifestyles as Indicators of New and Cultural Values,* World Future Studies Federation, 1984.

(Editor with J. P. Roos, and contributor) *Ways of Life in Finland and Poland,* Averbury, 1987.

(Contributor) Raymond Breton, Gilles Houle, Gary Caldwell, Edmund Mokrzycki, Edmund Wnuk-Lipinski, editors, *National Survival in Dependent Societies: Social Change in Canada and Poland,* Carleton University Press, 1990.

(Contributor) Piotr Ploszajski, editor, *Philosophy of Social Choice,* IFIS Publishers, 1990.

IN POLISH

Literaci polscy (title means "Polish Writers"), Ossolinskich, 1971.

Technika a spoleczenstwe: Antologia (title means "Technology and Society: A Reader"), Instytut, 1974.

Dzis i jutre kultury polskiej (title means "Today and Tomorrow of Polish Culture"), Ksiazka i Wiedza, 1975.

Mlodzi o roku 2000 (title means "Youth About the Year Two Thousand"), Centralnej Rady Zwiazkow Zawodowych, 1975.

(Editor and contributor) *Styl zycia: Koncepcje i propozycje* (title means "Style of Life: Concepts and Proposals"), P.W.N., 1976.

(Editor and contributor) *Styl zycia: Przemiany we wspol-czesnej Polsce* (title means "Style of Life: Transformations in Contemporary Poland"), P.W.N., 1978.

(Editor and contributor) *Style zycia w miastach polskich (u progu kryzysu)* (title means "Styles of Life in Polish Cities [On the Verge of a Crisis]"), Ossolineum, 1988.

(Editor and contributor) *Badania "rozumiejace" stylu zycia: narzedzia* (title means " 'Understanding' Research of Styles of Life: Instruments"), IFIS Publishers, 1988.

(Editor and contributor) *Nazajutrz: Reakcje spoleczenstwa polskiego na katastrofe w Czarnobylu* (title means "The Next Day: Reactions of the Polish Population to the Tscharnobyl Catastrophe"), IFIS Publishers, 1989.

(Editor, and contributor with Jan Kopczynski) *Czlo-wiek—Srodowiski—Zdrowie* (title means "Man—Environment—Health"), Ossolineum, 1990.

Editor in chief of *Polska 2000* (magazine; title means "Poland 2000"); co-editor of *Kultura i Spoleczenstwe* (quarterly magazine; title means "Culture and Society").

WORK IN PROGRESS: Dom we wspolczesnej Polsce (title means "Home in Contemporary Poland"); writing chapter for *Socialism and Change: The Polish Perspective;* editing *Sens uczestnictwa* (title means "The Meaning of Participation").

SIDELIGHTS: Andrzej Sicinski told *CA:* "It is bad luck but also a privilege to live in the dramatic and fascinating social laboratory called Poland. How can an individual use his or her personal and national experience to understand what is going on in the world? That is the question.

"Despite my being a social scientist, I am interested more in social reality—or, in more general times, in human existence and its sense—than in any social theory. This, I believe, explains the 'future orientation' of many of my studies. From that point of view, both the present and the past are important. But, perhaps above all, the future is important, the future that to some extent could be shaped by us.

"I don't overestimate our influence on what is going on in our personal lives, in the lives of our countries, or, all the more, our influence on what is happening on a larger scale. I do appreciate, however, not only actual influence, but also any human efforts aiming at exerting such an influence, given many restraints. Because of that, next to my academic studies I am also involved in some social, and some political activities.

"In my recent studies, the crucial idea is a concept of the human making the choice. Our present choice, directed toward the future, is also coloring the meaning of our past. In fact, culture and styles of life—the main subjects of my studies—are both manifestations and results of choices being made, consciously or unconsciously, by individuals, groups, and societies.

"I am concerned above all with 'social reality,' its means, and with social practice. However, I want to stress that social sciences can contribute to that practice better through developing people's wisdom rather than trying to be directly 'useful' in decision-making processes."

*   *   *

SIEGEL, Beatrice

PERSONAL: Born in New York, NY; daughter of Samuel and Sophie (Kopp) Jacobson; married Samuel R. Siegel (a dentist); children: Andra Sigerson Patterson. *Education:* Brooklyn College (now of the City University of New York), B.A., 1932; Cornell University, M.A., 1936.

ADDRESSES: Home—New York, NY.

CAREER: Affiliated with Retail Drug Employees Union, Local 1199, 1950-55, and Neighborhood Youth Corps, 1966-68; writer, 1971—.

AWARDS, HONORS: Notable children's book citation, American Library Association, 1980, for *An Eye on the World: Margaret Bourke-White, Photographer;* notable children's trade book in the field of social studies citation, 1982, for *Fur Trappers and Traders: The Indians, the Pilgrims, and the Beaver,* and 1987, for *The Basket Maker and the Spinner.*

WRITINGS:

CHILDREN'S BOOKS

Indians of the Woodland: Before and after the Pilgrims, Walker & Co., 1972, revised edition published as *Indians in the Northeast Woodlands,* 1992.

Living with Mommy (story), Feminist Press, 1974.

A New Look at the Pilgrims: Why They Came to America, Walker & Co., 1977.

Alicia Alonso: The Story of a Ballerina (American Dance Guild Book Club selection), Warne, 1979.

An Eye on the World: Margaret Bourke-White, Photographer (Junior Literary Guild selection), Warne, 1980.

Fur Trappers and Traders: The Indians, the Pilgrims, and the Beaver, Walker & Co., 1981.

Lillian Wald of Henry Street (Junior Literary Guild selection), Macmillan, 1983.

The Sewing Machine ("Inventions That Changed Our Lives" series), Walker & Co., 1984.

Sam Ellis's Island (Junior Literary Guild selection), Four Winds, 1985.

The Steam Engine ("Inventions That Changed Our Lives" series), Walker & Co., 1986.

The Basket Maker and the Spinner, Walker & Co., 1987.

Cory: Corazon Aquino and the Philippines, Lodestar/Dutton, 1988.

George and Martha Washington at Home in New York, Four Winds/Macmillan, 1989.

Faithful Friend: The Story of Florence Nightingale, Scholastic, 1991.

The Year They Walked: Rosa Parks and the Montgomery Bus Boycott, Four Winds/Macmillan, 1992.

Murder on the Highway: Viola Liuzzo and the March to Montgomery, Four Winds/Macmillan, 1993.

WORK IN PROGRESS: A biography of a woman reformer of the late 1800s and early 1900s.

SIDELIGHTS: Beatrice Siegel once told *CA:* "I did my undergraduate college work in French and German. My graduation from college during the years of the Great Depression cancelled my interest in languages and turned me to more immediate interests, such as history and political theory."

"I have put these concerns of mine into writing biographies and social history for young readers," Siegel recently added. "I hope to kindle their interest in the world around them, and to help them understand that we all play a role in history, that we can be effective. In researching the life of Margaret Bourke-White, I was struck at how she changed from being a fashionable photographer to a socially aware one when she became conscious of the damaging economic and cultural effects of the Great Depression.

"My last two books deal with racism and the heroic struggles of everyday people against its insults and oppression. There is Rosa Parks, in *The Year They Walked,* fighting segregation in Alabama and igniting the dramatic Montgomery Bus Boycott of 1955-56 that brought an end to segregated seating on city buses. In *Murder on the Highway,* I tell about the courageous Viola Liuzzo who traveled from Detroit, Michigan, to Selma, Alabama, to participate in the historic March to Montgomery for Voting Rights. On the last day of the march she was slain by four members of the Ku Klux Klan.

"To communicate the struggles and ideas of valiant people as they change and help change the world compels me to write: to tell about Florence Nightingale, Lillian Wald of Henry Street, Rosa Parks, Viola Liuzzo, George and Martha Washington, and many others."

BIOGRAPHICAL/CRITICAL SOURCES:

PERIODICALS

New York Times Book Review, February 19, 1984; January 5, 1986; April 23, 1989.

SIEGEL, Mary-Ellen (Kulkin) 1932- (Mary-Ellen Kulkin)

PERSONAL: Born February 12, 1932, in New York, NY; daughter of Monroe E. (a urologist) and Miriam Baum (a hospital volunteer and homemaker) Greenberger; married Edgar Kulkin, 1951 (divorced, 1977); married Walter Siegel (in advertising sales), 1980; children: Betsy Kulkin Baldwin, Peter, Vicki; stepchildren. *Education:* City University of New York, A.B. (summa cum laude), 1974; Columbia University, M.S., 1976.

ADDRESSES: Home—75-68 195th St., Fresh Meadows, NY 11366.

CAREER: Actress and television columnist for the trade paper *Show Business,* 1949-54; homemaker, 1954-70; Mount Sinai Hospital, New York City, social worker, and co-director and moderator of "Understanding Chemotherapy and the Cancer Experience" program, 1976-84; Mount Sinai School of Medicine of the City University of New York, New York City, lecturer in department of community medicine, 1983—. Private practice of social work, 1978—. Lecturer at Hunter College of the City University of New York, spring, 1975, and State University of New York Empire State College, fall, 1983, and 1984; member of guest faculty at Columbia University's College of Physicians and Surgeons, 1982-84. Member of Foundation of Thanatology, American Jewish Committee. Presents workshops; guest on television and radio programs; public speaker. Consultant to Chemotherapy Foundation.

MEMBER: National Organization for Women, National Association of Social Workers, Academy of Certified Social Workers, American Medical Writers Association, National Council on Problem Gambling, Authors Guild, American Society of Journalists and Authors, National Association of Oncology Social Workers, National Association of Private Geriatric Care Managers.

WRITINGS:

(Under name Mary-Ellen Kulkin) *Her Way: Biographies of Women for Young People,* American Library Association, 1976, revised edition (under name Mary-Ellen Siegel) published as *Her Way: A Guide to Biographies of Women for Young People,* 1984.

(With Ezra M. Greenspan) *Chemotherapy: Your Weapon against Cancer,* Chemotherapy Foundation, 1978, revised edition, 1991.

(With father, Monroe E. Greenberger) *What Every Man Should Know about His Prostate,* Walker & Co., 1983, revised edition published as *Dr. Greenberger's What Every Man Should Know about His Prostate,* 1988.

(With sister, Hermine M. Koplin) *More Than a Friend: Dogs with a Purpose* (juvenile), Walker & Co., 1984.

Reversing Hair Loss, Simon & Schuster, 1985.

The Cancer Patient's Handbook, Walker & Co., 1986.

(Editor with others) *Suffering: Psychological and Social Aspects in Loss, Grief and Care,* Haworth Press, 1986.

(With O. Robin Sweet) *The Nanny Connection,* Atheneum, 1987.

(Editor with others and contributor) *Psychosocial Aspects of Chemotherapy in Cancer Care: The Patient, Family and Staff,* Haworth Press, 1987.

(With Elisa Ferri) *Finger Tips,* C. N. Potter, 1988.

(Editor with others) *Psychiatric Aspects of Terminal Illness,* Charles Press, 1988.

Safe in the Sun, Walker & Co., 1990.

(Editor with others and contributor) *For the Bereaved: The Road to Recovery,* Charles Press, 1990.

(Editor with others) *Communicating with Cancer Patients and Their Families,* Charles Press, 1990.

(Editor with others and contributor) *Unrecognized and Unsanctioned Grief,* C. C. Thomas, 1990.

(With Linda Berman) *Behind the 8-Ball: A Guide for Families of Gamblers,* Fireside, 1992.

Contributor to books, including *Grief and the Loss of an Adult Child,* by Margolis and others, Praeger, 1988; and *Euthanasia of the Companion Animal,* by William J. Kay and others, Charles Press, 1988.

WORK IN PROGRESS: A book on dizziness for Consumer Reports; a book on breast cancer for Pocket Books.

SIDELIGHTS: Mary-Ellen Siegel once told *CA:* "When young people look at my professional resume and note that I worked from 1949 until the early 1950s as a television columnist and actress, then seemed to 'disappear' until 1976, they wonder. They forget that I came of age at a time when many women didn't attend college and never worked. Instead, they married and raised children. That was what I did. And so, from 1954 until 1970, when I began college, I had a great time taking care of Betsy, Peter, and Vicki. Almost on a whim I began college (City University of New York) in 1970 and 'got hooked' on school. Four years later I graduated summa cum laude and then entered Columbia University School of Social Work, where I received my master in social work in 1976. My first 'real grown up job' started when I was forty-four years old and began work as a social worker at Mount Sinai Hospital in New York.

"The professional side of my life is closely intertwined with the personal side because my writing develops out of my own personal experiences. *Her Way* is a guide to biographies of women for young people. It began as a term paper for a women's studies course during my first year at college at a time when I lacked confidence in my ability to do anything very intellectual. I had been home so long with the children that the only thing I felt I knew much about was children. At that time my youngest daughter,

Vicki, was assigned to write a book report on a biography of someone from the Civil War or Reconstruction Period. All she could find were biographies of men and a few on Clara Barton and Mary Todd Lincoln. She couldn't believe there weren't any other women from that period who did anything important enough to have a book written about them. Thus began my search and a topic for *my* term paper.

"The term paper grew and grew until it eventually became the 1976 edition of *Her Way,* published by American Library Association. The [later] edition is an expanded, updated, and revised edition of the earlier guide, which again provides access to worthwhile reading on women for children and young people of both sexes and all ages.

"In 1978 I wrote *Chemotherapy: Your Weapon against Cancer* (co-authored with Ezra M. Greenspan, M.D.), making use of my social work experiences with cancer patients and their families. This booklet for patients and their families is now in its ninth printing and has been recommended by Jane Brody in the *New York Times* and in her book *Personal Health,* as well as by many physicians and social workers.

"*What Every Man Should Know about His Prostate* was written with my late father, Monroe E. Greenberger, M.D. Writing it was a wonderful experience because of the close professional collaboration we developed. We had always had a warm father-daughter relationship but writing together added a special dimension to our relationship. Unfortunately he died just before publication (he was eighty-six years old and still active as a urologist at the time of his sudden stroke and death), but the book continues as a tribute to his years of urological practice and special way with patients. In 1988 I revised the book, and it is now entitled *Dr. Greenberger's What Every Man Should Know about His Prostate.*

"*More Than a Friend: Dogs with a Purpose* was written with my sister, Hermine M. Koplin. Hermine's daughter, Stephanie B. Koplin, did all the photography for the book. It is a juvenile publication, but we think the book will be of interest to dog lovers of any age. Each of the nine chapters tells the 'story' of a special relationship between dogs and people. Dogs with children, the elderly, police, hearing ear dogs, guide dogs, rescue dogs, dogs with the handicapped are all highlighted in individual real-life stories. One of our favorite stories describes Hermine's own dog, Trumpet, who was a 'therapy dog.' Hermine and Trumpet went to nursing homes, hospitals, schools, and institutions for the handicapped.

"I've also written a book on hair loss for Simon & Schuster. It is a total guide to not being bald anymore and is for women as well as men. Hair loss is a serious problem for many people—far more than just an affront to vanity.

Although much of the book deals with 'male pattern baldness,' my work with cancer patients who have had chemotherapy and radiation gives me a special insight and knowledge into the psychological effects of baldness on anyone who experiences it.

"My book *The Cancer Patient's Handbook* is a practical handbook for cancer patients and their families and deals with all aspects of treatment. My experiences with patients and friends and family members who have had treatment for cancer pointed out the need for this book and stimulated me to write it.

"*The Nanny Connection* was fun to write, and I believe it is helpful to the millions of families who need to have in-home care for their children while they work. Day care and other alternatives such as family care, or someone in the family caring for a child is not an option available to everyone either because of their unique needs or because they prefer a hired caregiver in their home. This book helps people choose someone who is 'right' for their family.

"*Finger Tips* was a bit of a departure from my usual writing, in that it is really a book that helps women (although there is a section for men) give themselves manicures or pedicures, or if they choose to have a professional do it, know how to evaluate the salon and nail technician that is doing the work. In these days when people are conscious of hygiene, I do feel the book contributes something towards physical health. And certainly, looking attractive contributes to self-esteem and thus mental health, so I suppose it's not that much of a departure after all!

"*Safe in the Sun* came from the heart. I love the sun but recognized that the depletion of the ozone layer and easy availability of sun-filled activities was taking a heavy toll on the skin and increasing dramatically the rates of skin cancer, including the potentially deadly melanoma. This book really told readers how they could still enjoy themselves while protecting themselves from the sun and also described what you can do if damage does occur. I was able to bring these important messages to the public on radio, television, and in newspapers as well as the book, because in the spring and summer of 1990, I served as a spokesperson for Max Factor's PURE SPF, a product that protects people from that everyday, incidental sun that most of us don't think much about.

"*Behind the 8-Ball* is another book that came from the heart. For years I had wanted to write a book that would help families who have been impacted by the consequences of someone who is obsessed with gambling. These people who gamble too much are often problem or compulsive gamblers. Until I met Linda Berman, M.S.W., a recognized expert in the field, I kept putting off doing anything about the book. When we met, we just clicked and

decided the time was right. Fortunately, Simon & Schuster agreed that it was a good idea, and . . . we anticipate that we will get a chance to bring some important help to the millions of people affected by gambling.

"I often speak to professional groups and to the general public at meetings and on the radio and television. I especially like speaking to general audiences and have spoken on such diverse subjects as women as role models for young people, the impact of illness and aging on families, and children's reactions to death. Most of these talks are based on my clinical experiences, but I often cite reactions of my own family members. For instance, I have frequently spoken on the reactions of pre-school children to the death of a grandfather and great-grandfather, utilizing conceptual material and specific reactions of my grandson and my husband's grandsons to such losses. This 'case material' takes on a very immediate quality when professional and personal observations and interventions are integrated.

"Most of my work deals with the impact of external forces on people. These forces may have many determinants: cultural, gender, age, illness, or death, each of which can represent opportunity or constraints. In both my clinical social work practice and in my writing, I try to help people integrate these forces into their lives just as I have tried to integrate my own private roles as wife, mother, sister, daughter, grandmother, and step-parent with the professional roles of social worker and writer."

She added, "In February 1992, just as I was celebrating my sixtieth birthday, my husband and I welcomed my younger daughter's second baby (collectively we now have ten grandchildren), and a few days later I contracted to co-author two new books: one on dizziness for Consumer Reports and one on breast cancer for Pocket Books."

BIOGRAPHICAL/CRITICAL SOURCES:

BOOKS

Brody, Jane, *The New York Times Guide to Personal Health,* Times Books, 1982.

PERIODICALS

New York Times, May 14, 1984.

*   *   *

SIKORA, Frank J(oseph)   1936-

PERSONAL: Born March 19, 1936, in Byesville, OH; son of John George (a grocer) and Josephine Anne (a housewife; maiden name, Jurcak) Sikora; married Mildred Helms (a nurse), October 4, 1958; children: Deborah Sikora Carpenter, Victor, Frank J., Jr., Terry, Jan, Michelle.

Education: Attended Ohio State University. *Politics:* Independent. *Religion:* Roman Catholic.

ADDRESSES: *Home*—8137 Rugby Ave., Birmingham, AL 35202. *Office*—Birmingham News, P.O. Box 2553, Birmingham, AL 35206. *Agent*—Diane Cleaver, Sanford J. Greenburger Associates, Inc., 825 Third Ave., New York, NY 10022.

CAREER: Associated with the *Gadsden Times,* Gadsden, AL, 1964-67; *Birmingham News,* Birmingham, reporter, 1967—. *Military service:* U.S. Army, 1954-56.

AWARDS, HONORS: Award from Associated Press, 1977, for stories on black land loss in the South; U.S. Conference of Christians and Jews award, Author of the Year Award, Alabama Library Association, both 1980, and American Library Association award, 1981, all for *Selma, Lord, Selma: Girlhood Memories of the Civil-Rights Days;* Pulitzer Prize nomination, 1991, for *Until Justice Rolls Down, The Birmingham Bombing Case.*

WRITINGS:

(With Sheyann Webb and Rachel West Nelson) *Selma, Lord, Selma: Girlhood Memories of the Civil-Rights Days,* University of Alabama Press, 1980.
Until Justice Rolls Down, The Birmingham Bombing Case, University of Alabama Press, 1991.
The Second Lincoln: Judge Frank Johnson and the Civil Rights Movement, Black Belt Publishers, 1992.

Also contributor to magazines, including *Ebony, Time, Newsweek,* and *Parade.*

WORK IN PROGRESS: "A biography of a little-known black schoolteacher who tells of growing up in the segregated South and his early days of teaching in the 1950's."

SIDELIGHTS: Frank J. Sikora told *CA:* "As a news reporter in Alabama I covered some of the civil rights activities of the sixties. Following up on these stories has been my prime interest.

"Coming from Ohio, I found that one of the things that struck me about the Deep South is that the people in rural areas have some inner sense of determination that defies poverty and past repressions—that through the worst of times they have a spirit that seems to prevail. Some of this has come out in *Selma, Lord, Selma;* it's an innocence that goes with childhood but also reaches into the lives of most of the people. In researching the work on Judge Frank M. Johnson, Jr., I found this same human spirit in the people who came to him for redress of grievances.

"Of Johnson himself, I think I've found the most truly American hero since Abraham Lincoln, for in many ways Judge Johnson is like Lincoln: one freed the people from slavery, the other from segregation. The book on Judge

Johnson is a biography, but it is heavily autobiographical, with lots of space devoted to Johnson talking as he recalls events of the 1950s and 1960s. President Lyndon Johnson once remarked that he wouldn't have to be president, 'If my name was Frank Johnson,' which gives some idea of the esteem in which the Judge is held.

"*Until Justice Rolls Down, The Birmingham Bombing Case* is about the bombing of a Birmingham church which killed four little black girls in 1963, the worst single act of terrorism to occur in the civil rights movement. And yet, no one had ever written a book about it.

"The book currently in the works is another biography about an obscure black educator in Greene County, Alabama. It recounts growing up in a segregated society, facing the violence of the Ku Klux Klan, and finding the challenge of trying to educate black children when the only teaching aids he receives are an eraser, 144 pieces of chalk, and a register book.

"I'm certainly not an authority on the subject of writing. I've seen people in their early twenties who get books published. I never had a desire to write a book. It wasn't until I was nearly thirty-eight years old that the impulse suddenly hit me. I knew I had to do it when I first met Sheyann Webb, and later, Rachel West Nelson, and heard about their part in the civil rights movement of Selma, Alabama. I came home that evening and told my wife I was going to write a book. When I couldn't go to sleep that night, I knew that I was really going to. To me it was the most important thing I could be working on. I think anybody writing a book has to feel that way about the work—that it's the most important thing."

*   *   *

SKELTON, Geoffrey (David) 1916-

PERSONAL: Born May 11, 1916, in Springs, South Africa; son of Richard Hugh (a mining engineer) and Saizy (Watson) Skelton; married Gertrude Klebac, September 4, 1947; children: Stephen, Robert Piers. *Education:* Attended schools in England and Hong Kong. *Avocational interests:* "Enthusiastic piano player for own private amusement (serious music only)."

ADDRESSES: *Home*—49 Downside, Shoreham, Sussex BN43 6HF, England.

CAREER: Reporter and sub-editor for various newspapers and periodicals, 1935-38; free-lance writer and journalist, 1938-40; sub-editor, *Sussex Daily News,* 1946-48; Press Association, London, England, sub-editor, 1948-49; British Information Services, Foreign Office in Germany, controller on *Die Welt* in Hamburg, 1949, information officer in Dortmund and Hamburg, 1950-56; British Broadcasting Corp. (BBC), London, sub-editor in External Services News Department, 1956-58, program assistant in BBC German Service, 1958-66, program organizer, 1966-67; full-time writer and translator, 1967—. *Wartime service:* Conscientious objector; served in British Army Medical Corps, 1940-46.

MEMBER: Radiowriters Association (member of executive committee, 1969-72), Translators Association (member of executive committee, 1972—, chairman, 1974, 1979-81).

AWARDS, HONORS: American PEN Club translation award, 1965, for *The Persecution and Assassination of Jean-Paul Marat as Performed by the Inmates of the Asylum of Charenton under the Direction of the Marquis de Sade;* Schlegel-Tieck Translation Prize, 1973, for *Frieda Lawrence: The Story of Frieda von Richthofen and D. H. Lawrence;* Yorkshire Post Music Award, 1975, for *Paul Hindemith: The Man behind the Music.*

WRITINGS:

Wagner at Bayreuth: Experiment and Tradition, Barrie & Rockliff, 1965, Braziller, 1966, 2nd edition, White Lion Publishers, 1976, Da Capo Press, 1983.
Wieland Wagner: The Positive Sceptic (biography), St. Martin's, 1971.
(Editor with Robert L. Jacobs) *Wagner Writes from Paris,* John Day, 1973.
Paul Hindemith: The Man behind the Music, Crescendo Book, 1975.
Richard and Cosima Wagner: Biography of a Marriage, Houghton, 1982.
Wagner in Thought and Practice, Lime Tree, 1991.

ONE-ACT PLAYS

Flowers for the Leader, Samuel French, 1939.
Summer Night, published in *Twelve One-Acts,* edited by Elizabeth Everard, Allen & Unwin, 1939.
Have You Seen My Lady?, Muller, 1948.
Memories for Sale, published in *Twenty Minute Theatre,* J. Garnet Miller, 1955.

TRANSLATIONS FROM THE GERMAN

Theodor Storm, *The White Horseman* (short stories), New English Library, 1962.
Guenter Herburger, *A Monotonous Landscape* (short stories), Harcourt, 1968.
Friedrich Heer, *God's First Love: Christians and Jews over 2000 Years,* Weidenfeld & Nicolson, 1970, Weybright, 1971.
Robert Lucas, *Frieda Lawrence: The Story of Frieda von Richthofen and D. H. Lawrence,* Viking, 1973.
Heer, *Challenge of Youth,* Weidenfeld & Nicolson, 1974.

Max Frisch, *Sketchbook, 1966-1971,* Harcourt, 1974.
Frisch, *Montauk,* Harcourt, 1976.
Frisch, *Sketchbook, 1946-1949,* Harcourt, 1977.
(And author of introduction and notes) *Cosima Wagner's Diaries,* Harcourt, Volume 1, 1978, Volume 2, 1980.
Frisch, *Man in the Holocene,* Harcourt, 1980.
Frisch, *Bluebeard,* Harcourt, 1983.
Siegfried Lenz, *The Training Ground,* H. Holt, 1991.

PLAYS TRANSLATED FROM THE GERMAN

(With Adrian Mitchell) Peter Weiss, *The Persecution and Assassination of Marat as Performed by the Inmates of the Asylum of Charenton under the Direction of the Marquis de Sade* (English version by Skelton, verse adaptation by Mitchell; first produced by Royal Shakespeare Company on West End at Aldwych Theatre, August 20, 1964; produced on Broadway at Martin Beck Theatre, 1966), Calder & Boyars, 1965, 4th edition, 1969, published as *The Persecution and Assassination of Jean-Paul Marat . . . ,* Atheneum, 1966.
Erich Fried, *Arden Must Die* (opera; music by Alexander Goehr; first produced in London, England, at Sadler's Wells Theatre, April 17, 1974), Schott, 1967.
Ferdinand Raimund, *The Mountain King,* first produced in Nottingham, England, at Nottingham Theatre, 1968.
Bertolt Brecht, *Lesson on Consent* (cantata; music by Paul Hindemith; first produced in Brighton, England, at Brighton Festival, May 5, 1968), Schott, 1968.
Weiss, *Discourse on the Progress of the Prolonged War of Liberation in Viet Nam,* published with *Song of the Lusitanian Bogey* as *Two Plays,* Atheneum, 1970 (published in England as *Discourse on Vietnam,* Calder & Boyars, 1970).
Weiss, *Trotsky in Exile* (broadcast by BBC Radio Three, November, 1970), Methuen, 1971, Atheneum, 1972.
Frisch, *Triptych: Three Scenic Panels* (staged reading by Royal Shakespeare Company in London, England, at the Barbican Pit, February 24, 1983), Harcourt, 1981.
Michael Meschke and Gyoergy Ligeti, *Le Grand Macabre* (opera; music by Ligeti; first produced in London, England, at Coliseum Theatre, December 2, 1982), Schott, 1982, revised English version (given concert performance at Royal Festival Hall, London, October 30, 1989), Schott, 1989.
Pavel Kohout, *1984* (adaptation of novel of the same title by George Orwell), first produced in Edmonton, Canada, at the Citadel Theatre, October 19, 1984.

RADIO SCRIPTS

(With Christopher Sykes) *Return to the Shrine,* produced by British Broadcasting Corporation (BBC), 1961.

(With Sykes) *Bayreuth Backstage I,* BBC, 1962, . . . *II,*
1963, . . . *III,* 1965.
Pleasant Are the Tears Which Music Weeps, BBC, 1965.
Wagner's Comic Masterpiece: Die Meistersinger, BBC,
1968.
Music from the Dead Composers, BBC, 1969.
Winifred Wagner Remembers (interview), BBC, 1969.
Rossini and Wagner, BBC, 1970.
Wagner's Problem Child: Tannhaeuser, BBC, 1972.
The Art of Wagnerian Singing, BBC, 1974.
Preserving Wagner's Heritage, BBC, 1974.
How Wagner Wrote and Produced The Ring, BBC, 1976.
Parsifal: Wagner's Final Victory over Life, Suedwestfunk
(Baden-Baden, Germany), 1982.
Bluebeard (based on novel of the same title by Frisch),
BBC, 1984.

OTHER

Also contributor to Peter Burbridge and Richard Sutton,
editors, *The Wagner Companion,* Faber, 1979; *The New
Grove Dictionary of Music and Musicians,* Macmillan,
1980; Nicholas John, editor, *Wagner's "The Valkyrie,"*
Riverrun Press, 1983; *The International Dictionary of
Opera,* Gale, 1993; and *The New Grove Dictionary of
Opera,* Macmillan, in press.

Contributor of short stories to periodicals, including *New
Writing, Penguin Parade, English Story, Bugle Blast, Adelphi,* and *London Magazine,* and of articles on music and
theatre to *World Review, Musical Times, Musical Opinion,
Music and Musicians, Plays and Players,* and other publications.

SIDELIGHTS: Geoffrey Skelton has written extensively
on the composer Richard Wagner. He has also translated
over a million words of the diaries of Wagner's second
wife, Cosima, and has devoted an entire book to Wagner's
marriage to this illegitimate daughter of Franz Lizst. "His
concern is primarily with facts: to examine them in their
confusing abundance, to sift from that abundance what is
most useful and interesting and to present it in a reasonable, orderly style," writes *Washington Post* reviewer Joseph McLellan of Skelton's *Richard and Cosima Wagner:
Biography of a Marriage.* "He has done it well, keeping the
material of permanent interest. . . . The work is largely
a condensation—and thereby an enrichment—of the diaries he has already translated, and in addition, he has a
critical detachment that is both necessary and refreshing."

BIOGRAPHICAL/CRITICAL SOURCES:

PERIODICALS

Time, June 28, 1982.
Times (London), February 25, 1982.
Washington Post, July 26, 1982.

SKLAR, Kathryn Kish 1939-

PERSONAL: Born December 26, 1939, in Columbus,
OH; daughter of William Edward and Elizabeth Sue
(Rhodes) Kish; married Robert Sklar (a historian), 1958
(divorced, 1979); married Thomas Dublin, 1988; children:
(first marriage) Leonard, Susan. *Education:* Radcliffe College, A.B., 1965; University of Michigan, Ph.D., 1969.

ADDRESSES: Office—Department of History, State University of New York, Binghamton, NY 13902.

CAREER: University of Michigan, Ann Arbor, lecturer
and assistant professor of history, 1969-74; University of
California, Los Angeles, associate professor, 1974-81, professor of history, 1981-88; State University of New York
at Binghamton, distinguished professor of history,
1988—.

MEMBER: American Historical Association, Organization of American Historians, American Studies Association, Conference Group in Women's History, West Coast
Association of Women Historians, Berkshire Conference
of Women Historians, Phi Beta Kappa.

AWARDS, HONORS: Woodrow Wilson fellowship,
1965-67; Danforth Foundation fellowship, 1967-69; Ford
Foundation fellowship for study of the role of women in
society, 1973-74; Radcliffe Institute of Harvard University fellowship, 1973-74; National Book Award nomination, 1974, for *Catharine Beecher;* annual prize, Berkshire
Conference of Women Historians, 1975; National Humanities Institute fellowship, 1975-76; Rockefeller Foundation humanities fellowship, 1981-82; Guggenheim fellowship, 1984-85; Center for Advanced Studies in the Behavioral and Social Sciences (Stanford) fellowship,
1987-88; American Association of University Women fellowship, 1990-91; Woodrow Wilson International Center
for Scholars fellowship, 1992-93.

WRITINGS:

Catharine Beecher: A Study of American Domesticity, Yale
University Press, 1973.
(Author of introduction) Catharine Beecher, *A Treatise on
Domestic Economy,* Schocken, 1977.
(Editor) *The Writings of Harriet Beecher Stowe: "Uncle
Tom's Cabin; or, Life among the Lowly," "The Minis-
ter's Wooing," "Oldtown Folks,"* Library of America,
1981.
(Editor) *Notes of Sixty Years: The Autobiography of Flor-
ence Kelley, 1859-1926,* Charles Kerr, 1985.
(Editor with husband, Thomas Dublin, and contributor)
Women and Power in American History, Prentice-
Hall, 1990.
(Editor with Martin Bulmer and Kevin Bales, and con-
tributor) *The Social Survey Movement in Historical
Perspective,* Cambridge University Press, 1992.

Also author of pamphlet, *Recent Scholarship by U.S. Historians on the History of Women,* American Historical Association; co-author with Gerda Lerner of *Graduate Training in U.S. Women's History: A Conference Report,* 1990, American Historical Association. Contributor to books, including *Women in America: Original Essays and Documents,* edited by Carol Berkin and Mary Beth Norton, Houghton, 1979; *Rights of Passage: The Past and Future of the ERA,* edited by Joan Hoff-Wilson, Indiana University Press, 1986; and *Writing Women's Lives: The Challenge of Feminist Biography,* edited by Joyce Antler, Elizabeth Perry, and Sara Alpern, University of Illinois Press, 1992. Contributor to periodicals, including *University of Michigan Papers in Women's Studies, Pacific Historical Review, Feminist Studies, American Historical Review,* and *Journal of American History.*

WORK IN PROGRESS: Florence Kelley and the Rise and Fall of Women's Political Culture: "Doing the Nation's Work," 1830-1930, for Yale University Press; contributing to *Gender and the Origins of Welfare States in Western Europe and North America,* edited by Seth Koven and Sonya Michel, for Routledge & Kegan Paul.

BIOGRAPHICAL/CRITICAL SOURCES:

PERIODICALS

Washington Post Book World, April 25, 1982; May 2, 1982.

* * *

SLATER, Philip E(lliot) 1927-

PERSONAL: Born May 15, 1927, in Riverton, NJ; son of John Elliot (a consulting engineer) and Pauline (Holman) Slater. *Education:* Harvard University, A.B., 1950, Ph.D., 1955. *Avocational interests:* Acting.

ADDRESSES: Agent—Susan Zilber, Los Angeles, CA.

CAREER: Harvard University, Cambridge, MA, lecturer in sociology, 1958-61; Brandeis University, Waltham, MA, 1961-71, began as assistant professor, professor of sociology, 1968-71; associated with Greenhouse, Inc., Cambridge, 1971-75.

AWARDS, HONORS: Named a "Male Hero" by *Ms.,* 1980.

WRITINGS:

Microcosm, Wiley, 1966.
(With Warren G. Bennis) *The Temporary Society,* Harper, 1968.
The Glory of Hera: Greek Mythology and the Greek Family, Beacon Press, 1968.

The Pursuit of Loneliness: American Culture at the Breaking Point, Beacon Press, 1970, revised edition with introduction by Todd Gitlin, 1990.
Earthwalk, Anchor, 1974.
Footholds: Understanding the Shifting Family and Sexual Tensions in our Culture, edited by Wendy Slater Palmer, Dutton, 1977.
The Wayward Gate: Science and the Supernatural, Beacon Press, 1977.
Wealth Addiction, Dutton, 1980.
How I Saved the World: A Novel, Dutton, 1985.
A Dream Deferred: America's Discontent and the Search for a New Democratic Ideal, Beacon Press, 1991.

Also author of the play "To the Dump," a comedy produced in 1993, and "Desperation Comedies" (two one-act plays), produced at Actors' Theatre in Santa Cruz, CA.

WORK IN PROGRESS: "Currently at work on a number of plays and novels."

SIDELIGHTS: Sociologist Philip E. Slater's best-known work, *The Pursuit of Loneliness: American Culture at the Breaking Point,* is "an analysis of the American ideal of individualism and its effects on society at large," *Publishers Weekly* reviewer Maria Simson wrote. With 500,000 copies sold, the book established Slater as an authority on American society. *A Dream Deferred: America's Discontent and the Search for a New Democratic Ideal,* billed by Beacon Press director Wendy Strothman as "really like *The Pursuit of Loneliness*—only taken one step further," focuses on "the authoritarian way of being," Strothman told Simson.

In *A Dream Deferred,* "Slater, a wide-ranging social critic, asks, 'How can the United States move more genuinely beyond the era of authoritarianism to a fuller democratic megaculture?'" Neal Riemer wrote in the *American Political Science Review.* "His thesis is that the democratic megaculture requires the complete rout of authoritarianism in its many forms—military, political, economic, social, religious, educational, medical, and psychological. . . . Slater's attack on authoritarianism (and its four pillars: institutionalized submissiveness, systematic oppression, secrecy, and deflected hate) is hard-hitting and cogent, even when sometimes exaggerated or overstated. His defense of democracy as efficient, flexible, innovative, and participatory is heartening (if sometimes open to challenge)."

In *Wealth Addiction,* Slater advocates a system of "voluntary simplicity" in which Americans gain happiness not by acquiring more money and goods, but by wanting less. He admits that convincing readers of this philosophy will always be difficult. "It's not that Slater doesn't do a rousing job of selling in *Wealth Addiction.* He does," Bill Bridges commented in the *Los Angeles Times.* "It's just that the other side has money, greed and temptation going for it—hard acts to top." The *New York Times*'s Christopher Lehmann-Haupt also found fault with the applicability of Slater's plan. "Unfortunately, the American system of government has lately come to reflect and promote this addiction to wealth," Lehmann-Haupt wrote. As Slater noted in *Wealth Addiction,* "The majority of us go along because those of us who aren't actually wealthy are 'closet addicts' of wealth, meaning that we secretly believe that as long as an unjust system stays the same, we, too, may eventually become rich."

Slater's first novel, *How I Saved the World,* satirizes the United States government in general and the Defense Department in particular. Slater's hero, an out-of-body-traveling former mental patient, narrowly averts an atomic disaster and exposes a government project in which a vagrant with psychic powers is hypnotized to de-activate fail-safe systems around the world when the president shouts "I love Lenin!" or "Abortion on demand!" Slater's approach is effective, *Washington Post Book World* reviewer Wray Herbert noted: "*How I Saved the World* is about our precariously balanced nuclear world, but happily Slater seems really to have left the podium far behind; he makes his point not by lecturing but by telling an outrageous and thoroughly enjoyable modern-day adventure story."

BIOGRAPHICAL/CRITICAL SOURCES:

PERIODICALS

American Political Science Review, March, 1992, pp. 221-222.
Harvard Law Review, May, 1992, p. 1819.
Library Journal, October 1, 1985, p. 71.
Los Angeles Times, June 24, 1980.
New York Times, March 14, 1980.
New York Times Book Review, November 10, 1985, p. 28.
Publishers Weekly, November 2, 1990, p. 42.
Village Voice, December 24, 1985, p. 68.
Washington Post Book World, April 17, 1980; January 5, 1986, p. 11.

*   *   *

SLOYAN, Gerard Stephen 1919-

PERSONAL: Born December 13, 1919, in New York, NY; son of Jerome James (a mechanical engineer) and Marie Virginia (Kelley) Sloyan. *Education:* Seton Hall University, A.B., 1940; Catholic University of America, S.T.L., 1944, Ph.D., 1948. *Politics:* Democrat.

ADDRESSES: Home—2313 Sansom St., Philadelphia, PA 19103. *Office*—Department of Religion, Temple University, Philadelphia, PA 19122.

CAREER: Roman Catholic priest in diocese of Trenton, NJ, 1944—; assistant pastor in Trenton and Maple Shade, NJ, 1947-50; Catholic University of America, Washington, DC, 1950-67, head of department of religious education, 1957-67; Temple University, Philadelphia, PA, professor in department of religion, 1967-91, professor emeritus, 1991—. Liturgical Conference, president, 1962-64, chairman of board of directors, 1980-88.

MEMBER: Society of Biblical Literature, American Theological Society, College Theology Society (president, 1966-68), Catholic Biblical Association, Catholic Theological Society of America (president, 1993-94).

WRITINGS:

(Editor) *Shaping the Christian Message,* Macmillan, 1958.
The Gospel of St. Mark, Liturgical Press, 1960.
Christ the Lord, Herder & Herder, 1962.
The Three Persons in One God, Prentice-Hall, 1963.
(Editor) *Modern Catechetics,* Macmillan, 1963.
Liturgy in Focus, Deus, 1964.
To Hear the Word of God, Herder & Herder, 1965.
Worship in a New Key, Liturgical Conference, 1965.
Nothing of Yesterday Preaches, Herder & Herder, 1966.
How Do I Know I'm Doing Right?, Pflaum, 1967, revised edition, 1976.
(Editor) *Secular Priest in the New Church,* Herder & Herder, 1967.
Speaking of Religious Education, Herder & Herder, 1968.
Jesus on Trial, Fortress, 1973.
A Commentary on the New Lectionary, Paulist, 1975.
Is Christ the End of the Law?, Westminster, 1978.
Jesus in Focus, Twenty-Third, 1983.
Worshipful Preaching, Fortress, 1984.
Rejoice and Take It Away, two volumes, Michael Glazier, 1984.
Advent-Christmas, Fortress, 1985.
John: An Interpretation Commentary, Westminster/John Knox Press, 1988.
Jesus, Redeemer and Divine Word, Michael Glazier, 1989.
(With L. Swidler, L. J. Aron, and L. Dean) *Bursting the Bonds? A Jewish-Christian Dialogue on Jesus and Paul,* Orbis, 1990.
What Are They Saying about John?, Paulist, 1991.

*   *   *

SMITH, Ward
See GOLDSMITH, Howard

SODARO, Craig 1948-

PERSONAL: Born May 25, 1948, in Chicago, IL; son of Eugene J. (a physician) and Eleanore (Klasen) Sodaro; married Suzanne Cooper (a teacher), 1972; children: Sally, Amy, Katie, Elizabeth. *Education:* Marquette University, B.A., 1970. *Religion:* Roman Catholic.

ADDRESSES: Home and office—P.O. Box 1648, Silverthorne, CO 80498.

CAREER: English, journalism, and art teacher in Glennallen, AK, 1970-71; Appel Farm Art and Music Center, Elmer, NJ, art specialist, 1971; English and journalism teacher in Marty, SD, 1972-73; Torrington Middle School, Torrington, WY, English teacher and chairman of department, beginning 1973; Summit Middle School, English teacher, 1991—. Member of Goshen County Fine Arts Council Board, 1980-82.

MEMBER: National Educational Association, Mystery Writers of America, Wyoming Writers, Wyoming Educational Association, Goshen County Educational Association, Kappa Tau Alpha.

AWARDS, HONORS: Dretzka Award, Marquette University, 1969, for *The Plants;* Art Core radio drama honorary mention, 1979, American Radio Theatre Award, 1980, and Wyoming Writers Success Award, 1980, all for *No Chance of Error;* Wyoming Writers Success Award, 1980, for *Be Our Guest;* National History Association commendation, for *Frontier Spirit;* Art Core Playwrighting Awards, 1989, for *A Corner Table in Paradise,* and 1990, for *Happy Anniversary.*

WRITINGS:

Joint Return, Heuer, 1976.
(With Rocky Adams) *Frontier Spirit: The Story of Wyoming,* Johnson Books, 1986.
Million Dollar Baby: A Hot Time in the Old Town Tonight, I. E. Clark, 1987.
(With Randy L. Adams) *Wyoming: Courage in a Lonesome Land,* edited by Don Lynch, illustrated by Keith Fay, Grace Dangberg Foundation, 1990.

MYSTERIES

Tea and Arsenic, Heuer, 1976.
Mummy Sea, Mummy Do, Heuer, 1976.
Search Me, Performance Publishing, 1977.
Be Our Guest, Performance Publishing, 1979.

PLAYS

No Chance for Error (radio), broadcast by American Radio Theatre, 1980.
A Hostile Action, Heuer, 1981.
Sir Gawain and the Green Knight, Contemporary Drama, 1983.

Ghost of a Chance, Plays, 1983.
Brides and the Lumberjacks, Plays, 1983.
Cradle Camp, Heuer, 1983.
End of the Road, Baker's Place, 1983.
Belle of the Bowery, produced by Iron Springs Chateau in Colorado Springs, CO, 1983.
Americalore, Contemporary Drama, 1985.
Ingenue of the Sierras, Plays, 1985.
Phantom of the Soap Opera, Eldridge, 1987.
Second Hand Kid, Dramatic Publishing, 1992.
Dirty Dealings in Dixie, Eldridge, 1992.

Also author of *The Cracked Pot, Chutluh Calls,* 1974, *Forlorn at the Fort,* 1980, *A Corner Table in Paradise, Happy Anniversary,* and *Every Babysitter's Nightmare,* Eldridge.

OTHER

Also author of coloring books *Ft. Laramie,* 1982, and *Wyoming, the Story of Our State,* 1985.

WORK IN PROGRESS: Several screenplays; *Voices,* a play about high school violence; a juvenile novel.

SIDELIGHTS: Craig Sodaro once told *CA:* "I work mainly in the theatre as a teacher, a playwright, and at times, an actor. While the publication of one's prose work is indeed exciting, nothing quite matches the satisfaction of immediate response from an audience that's achieved through being involved in any aspect of a staged play. This is especially true when one writes (or is a part of) a mystery play or a comedy, because the screams or the laughs, or a combination of the two, means immediate success and gives one good cause to get back to the typewriter!

"During the summers I have my own production company, and we produce melodramas. I usually play the villain. While this isn't typecasting, it keeps me in touch with the actor's problems as well as the playwright's."

*   *   *

SOLZHENITSYN, Aleksandr I(sayevich) 1918-

PERSONAL: Surname is pronounced "sohl-zhe-*neet*-sin"; born December 11, 1918, in Kislovodsk, Russia; immigrated to the United States, 1976; father was an artillery officer in World War I; mother was a typist and stenographer; married Natalya Reshetovskaya (a professor and research chemist), April 27, 1940 (divorced), remarried, 1956 (divorced, 1972); married Natalya Svetlova (a mathematics teacher), April, 1973; children: (third marriage) Yermoli, Ignat, Stepan (sons); stepchildren: one son. *Education:* Moscow Institute of History, Philosophy, and Literature, correspondence course in philology, 1939-41; University of Rostov, degree in mathematics and physics,

1941. *Avocational interests:* Photography, bicycling, hiking, gardening.

ADDRESSES: Home—Cavendish, Vermont. *Office*—c/o Farrar, Straus, & Giroux, 19 Union Square West, New York, NY 10003.

CAREER: Writer. First Secondary School, Morozovka, Rostov, U.S.S.R., physics teacher, 1941; arrested 1945, while serving as commander in Soviet Army; sent to Greater Lubyanka Prison, Moscow, U.S.S.R., 1945; convicted of anti-Soviet actions and sentenced to eight years in prison; sent to Butyrki Prison, Moscow, to work in construction, 1946; transferred to Marfino Prison to work as mathematician in radio and telephone communications research, 1947-50; sent to Ekibastuz labor camp, Kazakhstan, U.S.S.R., to work as bricklayer and carpenter, 1950-53; released from prison and exiled to Kok-Terek, Kazakhstan, to work as mathematics teacher, 1953-56; released from exile, 1956; teacher of mathematics and physics in Riazan, U.S.S.R., until early 1960s; banned from teaching and exiled from Moscow; arrested, 1974; sent to Lefortovo Prison and charged with treason, 1974; exiled from U.S.S.R., 1974. Lecturer. *Military service:* Soviet Army, 1941-45; became captain of artillery unit; decorated twice (stripped of rank and decorations when arrested).

MEMBER: American Academy of Arts and Sciences, Hoover Institute on War, Revolution, and Peace (honorary).

AWARDS, HONORS: Nominated for Lenin Prize, 1964; Prix du Meilleur Livre Etranger (France), 1969, for *The First Circle* and *Cancer Ward;* Nobel Prize for Literature, 1970; Freedoms Foundation Award from Stanford University, 1976; prize for "progress in religion" from Templeton Foundation. Honorary degrees from various institutions, including Harvard University, 1978, and Holy Cross, 1984.

WRITINGS:

Odin den'Ivana Denisovicha (novella), first published in *Novy Mir,* 1962, Flegon Press (London), 1962, translation by Ralph Parker published as *One Day in the Life of Ivan Denisovich,* Dutton, 1963.

Dlya polzy'dela (novella), first published in *Novy Mir,* 1963, Russian Language Specialties, 1963, translation by David Floyd and Max Hayward published as *For the Good of the Cause,* Praeger, 1964.

Sluchay na stantsii Krechetovka [i] Matrenin dvor (two short novels; titles mean "An Incident at Krechetovka Station" and "Matryona's House"), first published in *Novy Mir,* 1963, Flegon Press, 1963, translation by Paul W. Blackstock published as *We Never Make Mistakes,* University of South Carolina Press, 1963.

"Ztiudy i Krokhotnye Rasskazy" (short story), first published in *Grani* (Frankfurt), 1964, published as *Krokhotnye Rasskazy,* Librarie des Cinq Continents (Paris), 1970.

Sochininiia (selected works), [Frankfurt], 1966.

V kruge pervom (novel), Harper, 1968, translation by Thomas P. Whitney published as *The First Circle,* Harper, 1968.

Rakovyl korpus (novel), Bodley Head, 1968, translation by Nicholas Bethell and David Burg published as *Cancer Ward* (two volumes), Bodley Head, 1968-69, published as *The Cancer Ward,* Farrar, Straus, 1969.

Olen'i shalashovka (play), Flegon Press, 1968, translation by Bethell and Burg published as *The Love Girl and the Innocent* (also see below), Farrar, Straus, 1969.

Svecha na vetru (play), Flegon Press, 1968, published in *Grani,* 1969, translation by Keith Armes and Arthur Hudgins published as *Candle in the Wind,* University of Minnesota Press, 1973.

Les Droits de l'ecrivain (title means "The Rights of the Writer"), Editions du Seuil, 1969.

Krasnoe koleso (multi-volume novel), translation published as *The Red Wheel;* Volume 1: *Avgust chetyrnadtsatogo,* Flegon Press (London), 1971, translation by Michael Glenny published as *August 1914,* Farrar, Straus, 1972, translation by Harry Willetts, 1989; Volume 2: *Oktyabr' shestnadtsatogo,* YMCA Press, 1984, translation by Willetts published as *October 1916,* Farrar, Straus, in press.

Stories and Prose Poems by Aleksandr Solzhenitsyn, translated by Glenny, Farrar, Straus, 1971.

Six Etudes by Aleksandr Solzhenitsyn, translated by James G. Walker, College City Press, 1971.

Nobelevskara lektsira po literature, YMCA Press, 1972, translation by F. D. Reeve published as *Nobel Lecture by Aleksandr Solzhenitsyn,* Farrar, Straus, 1972.

A Lenten Letter to Pimen, Patriarch of All Russia, translated by Theofanis G. Staurou, Burgess, 1972.

Arkhipelag Gulag, 1918-1956: Op 'bit khudozhestvennopo issledovaniia, YMCA Press, 1973, translation published as *The Gulag Archipelago, 1918-1956: An Experiment in Literary Investigation,* Harper, Volume 1, translated by Thomas P. Whitney, 1974, Volume 2, translated by Whitney, 1976, Volume 3, translated by Willetts, 1979.

Mir i nasilie (title means "Peace and Violence"), [Frankfurt], 1974.

Prusskie nochi: pozma napisappaja v lagere v 1950 (title means "Prussian Nights: Epic Poems Written at the Forced Labor Camp, 1950"), YMCA Press, 1974.

Pis'mo vozhdram Sovetskogo Soruza, YMCA Press, 1974, translation by Hilary Sternberg published as *Letter to the Soviet Leaders,* Harper, 1974.

(And photographer with others) *Solzhenitsyn: A Pictorial Autobiography,* Farrar, Straus, 1974.

Bodalsra telenok s dubom, YMCA Press, 1975, translation published as *The Oak and the Calf,* Association Press, 1975, translation by Willetts published as *The Oak and the Calf: Sketches of Literary Life in the Soviet Union,* Harper, 1980.

Lenin v Tsiurikhe, YMCA Press, 1975, translation by Willetts published as *Lenin in Zurich,* Farrar, Straus, 1976.

Amerikanskie rechi (title means "American Speeches"), YMCA Press, 1975.

(With others) *From under the Rubble,* English translation by Michael Scammell, Little, Brown, 1975, published as *From under the Ruins,* Association Press, 1975.

(With others) *Detente: Prospects for Democracy and Dictatorship,* Transaction Books, 1975.

Warning to the West, Farrar, Straus, 1976.

A World Split Apart (commencement address), Harper, 1979.

The Mortal Danger, Harper, 1981.

Victory Celebrations: A Comedy in Four Acts [and] *Prisoners: A Tragedy* (plays), translated by Helen Rapp and Nancy Thomas, Bodley Head, 1983.

Also author of unpublished works, including "The Right Hand" (story); "The Light That Is in You" (play); "The Tanks Know the Truth" (screenplay); "Feast of the Victors" (play). Contributor to periodicals, including *New Leader.*

ADAPTATIONS: The Love Girl and the Innocent was adapted for the stage by Paul Avila Mayer, 1970.

WORK IN PROGRESS: The final volumes of *The Red Wheel,* to be published in translation as *March 1917* and *April 1917.*

SIDELIGHTS: Very rarely does an author burst so dramatically upon the world as Aleksandr Solzhenitsyn, who became famous seemingly overnight with the publication of his novella *One Day in the Life of Ivan Denisovich.* The first published Soviet work of its kind, the novella centers on the concentration camps in which millions died under dictator Joseph Stalin. *Ivan Denisovich,* which initially seemed to signal the beginning of relaxed Soviet censorship, instead contributed to the political demise of Premier Nikita Khrushchev, who supported de-Stalinization before being deposed in 1964. There followed a decade of creativity and conflict for Solzhenitsyn. Ultimately, this was to the chagrin of Soviet authorities, who deported him in 1974.

An appraisal of Solzhenitsyn's life and work must address irresolvable paradoxes—he has acquired fame as a protest writer, but at heart he is an aesthete. His moral and spiritual authority comes from the way he has borne witness to twentieth-century totalitarianism, but his dislike of publicity and his reclusiveness makes him an anachronism. Solzhenitsyn's work needs to be discussed in relation to the tradition from which it comes, for he responds to Socialist Realism, which was proclaimed in 1932 as the only acceptable form of art in the Soviet Union. Socialist Realism literature resembles many Western best-sellers in its accessible style, positive heroes, and happy endings, and thus it cut off Russian literature from its rich heritage of the nineteenth and early twentieth centuries.

In his own way, Solzhenitsyn is engaged in an ongoing attempt to restore wholeness to Russian society by reconnecting the pre- and post-revolutionary periods. He writes to make sense of the evolution of twentieth-century Russia in terms of the lives and works of the nineteenth-century Russian classics. Accordingly, he knows intimately the works of Russian masters such as Aleksandr Pushkin, Nikolay Gogol, Yury Lermontov, Ivan Turgenev, Leo Tolstoy, Fyodor Dostoyevsky, and Anton Chekhov.

The paradoxes of Solzhenitsyn's life began very early. He never knew his father, who died in a hunting accident before Solzhenitsyn was born, and his mother, daughter of a wealthy landowner, was denied sufficient employment by the Soviet government, thus mother and son lived in relative squalor from 1924 to 1936. Young Solzhenitsyn was a child of his era: the parades and speeches of the Pioneers, the Soviet equivalent of the Boy Scouts, had an effect on him, and he later joined the Communist Youth League. In *Solzhenitsyn: A Biography,* Michael Scammell quotes him as saying of this period: "Inside me I bore this social tension—on one hand, they used to tell me everything at home, and on the other, they used to work on our minds at school. And so this collision between two worlds gave birth to such social tensions within me that it somehow defined the path I was to follow for the rest of my life."

Perhaps it was such conflict that prompted Solzhenitsyn to begin writing in his youth. He had some sense of his literary ambition by the age of nine, and before he was eighteen he resolved to write a major novel about the Revolution. But he regrets that his literary education was haphazard and that he read little Western literature. Yet his aestheticism breaks out even in the most adverse conditions. After he was arrested in 1945 and sent to Moscow's notorious Lubyanka prison, which had a relatively good library, he read otherwise unobtainable works by such authors as Yevgeny Zamyatin, the great Soviet prose writer of the 1920s, and American novelist John Dos Passos, whose expressionist style later influenced Solzhenitsyn's own writing.

Solzhenitsyn turned to poetry in the years 1946 to 1950, when he was interred just outside of Moscow at a *sharashka,* or special prison. This was a unique creation of Stalinism—a high-level research institute in which all the scientists and technicians were prisoners. Because everything he wrote was subject to constant inspection, Solzhenitsyn composed poetry in his head and kept his memory precise by repeating certain portions of his verse each day. He continued to compose what was essentially oral poetry during the years 1950-1953, which he spent in a Central Asian concentration camp in Ekibastuz, Kazakhstan.

In March of 1953 Solzhenitsyn was released from the concentration camp and sent into exile in Kok-Terek in Central Asia, where he taught mathematics and physics in a secondary school. In Kok-Terek, he had pen and paper and wrote down both a long poem and some plays. He also began making notes for a novel. Freed from exile in April of 1956, he returned to central Russia, and, in September of 1957, he took a position as a teacher of physics and astronomy in the city of Ryazan.

During this time Solzhenitsyn had been reading aloud carefully selected excerpts from his works to acquaintances in Ryazan and Moscow. Encouraged by the progress of de-Stalinization, they urged him to submit something to poet and editor Aleksandr Tvardovsky's *Novy Mir.* Solzhenitsyn initially resisted, believing that nothing of his would be published while he was alive. Nevertheless, he allowed himself to be persuaded that "Shch-854," a short prose work which he wrote in 1959, might pass censorship. Though skeptical, he eventually sent the story—which became *Ivan Denisovich*—to *Novy Mir,* where it made its way from sub-editors to Tvardovsky and then to Khrushchev himself.

Ivan Denisovich presents a day in the life of a simple prisoner who wants only to serve out his sentence with a certain integrity. Solzhenitsyn's strategy was to reverse the usual procedure of Socialist Realism, which imposed thoughts and feelings on its readers, and thus he rendered his tale in an ironic, understated, elliptical manner. His purpose with this sparse style was to elicit feelings, rather than impose them, as the official propaganda had done for so long.

With *Ivan Denisovich* Solzhenitsyn realized considerable success. The issue of *Novy Mir* in which the story appeared sold out immediately, and editor Tvardovsky kept asking Solzhenitsyn for new works. In 1963, Solzhenitsyn published three more stories in *Novy Mir:* "Matryona's House," a story about the quiet dignity of an elderly woman who had been his landlady; "Incident at Koche-tovka Station," about an over-zealous young officer who turns an innocent man over to the secret police; and "For the Good of the Cause," which involves the abuse of power by local party officials.

Solzhenitsyn's principal fiction achievements of the 1960s, however, were his novels *The First Circle* and *Cancer Ward.* In *The First Circle* he drew on his experiences in the *sharashka,* or special prison, in the late 1940s, and in *Cancer Ward,* he drew on his stay in a Tashkent hospital where he was treated for cancer in the 1950s. Both works are set in institutions cut off from society, and both feature characters with diverse backgrounds and philosophies debating the issues of the day.

The First Circle begins outside the prison with Innokenty Volodin, an idealistic young diplomat who makes a telephone call to the American embassy, a call that eventually results in his arrest and imprisonment in a *sharashka.* The principal prisoners are Lev Rubin, a Jew and a dedicated Communist; Dmitry Sologdin, an engineer and idiosyncratic spiritual teacher; and Gleb Nerzhin, a scientist and aspiring writer. At the end of the novel, Nerzhin is taken away to a far more difficult camp, Sologdin is about to gain a pardon, and Rubin is kept behind. With *The First Circle* Solzhenitsyn countered stifling Socialist Realism by relating his work to both Russian classics and Western culture. The three principal prisoners, for example, each correspond to the siblings of Dostoyevsky's *Brothers Karamazov,* while the *sharashka*—and the title itself—recall the first circle of hell in Dante's *Inferno.*

Like *The First Circle, Cancer Ward* presents an isolated environment. The latter work, drawing a parallel between the hospital and Soviet society, thus constitutes another meditation on the human condition. The work's principal protagonists present two extremes, yet their illness makes them draw back into themselves instead of widening their sympathies and understanding. Pavel Rusanov, a bureaucrat with connections to the secret police, expects special treatment and deference, while Oleg Kostoglotov, a former camp inmate, tolerates no elitism. Both benefit from their treatment, but each leaves the hospital with unchanged attitudes.

Solzhenitsyn's most important work of nonfiction is *The Gulag Archipelago,* a detailed account of Stalinist repression. *Gulag* is predicated on the fact that arrest and torture were everyday practices in the Soviet Union. Solzhenitsyn proceeds as a scientist might, creating a taxonomy of arrests and tortures. In one passage, he even invites readers to participate with him in deciding which forms of torture belong in which categories. Solzhenitsyn makes his narrative vivid and direct. Again and again, he speaks of his own experiences, such as his arrest and confinement in different prisons and concentration camps. He also includes many personal narratives, replete with horrifying detail from other victims of arbitrary violence.

In *Gulag* Solzhenitsyn finds all Russians—including himself—accountable for the horrors of Stalinism. "We didn't love freedom enough," he writes. "We purely and simply deserved everything that happened afterward." He also observes that "the line dividing good and evil cuts through the heart of every human being." A lesson of *Gulag,* then, is that to divide the world into good and evil is itself a fallacy and evil.

Solzhenitsyn wrote *Gulag* between 1964 and 1968. Through intermediaries, he sent the manuscript to Paris, where it was published on December 28, 1973. A few months later he was expelled from the Soviet Union.

In 1970 Solzhenitsyn received the Nobel Prize for literature, but he had only just begun what he thought of as his life's work—a multi-volume novel to be known as *The Red Wheel.* Much of *August 1914,* the first volume in the series, centers on the battle of Tannenberg, which is filtered through the eyes of two of the novel's central characters: Colonel Georgy Vorotyntsev, a graduate of the Russian equivalent of West Point, and Arseny Blagodaryov, an enlisted man whom Vorotyntsev befriends. Vorotyntsev and Blagodaryov see various kinds of action, ultimately serving with a group of Russian soldiers who are surrounded by advancing German troops and who succeed in breaking through enemy lines.

Like Solzhenitsyn's other major works, *August 1914* is polyphonic in its technique. This remarkably diverse novel consists of fifty-eight fictional chapters, two newspaper sections, five film segments (passages written in a cryptic style designed to have a cinematic quality), four historical surveys of troop movements, one interpretive historical essay, and six collections of contemporary documents. Both the film segments and the selections of newspaper clippings from the time show the continuing influence of Dos Passos.

The second volume of *The Red Wheel, October 1916,* is approximately twice as long as *August 1914* and contains proportionately more characters, thereby creating a society in all its intriguing variety. If *August 1914* is a war novel, then *October 1916* is a peace novel. It presents very little military action but emphasizes the effect of the war on the home front. Among the various storylines is one involving Vorotyntsev, who is married but nonetheless falls in love with a woman professor at Petrograd University.

The Russian-language publication of *March 1917* in 1986 and 1987 marked another major change in the emphasis of *The Red Wheel.* In this extraordinarily long volume—it occupies four books and runs to well over two thousand pages—the fictional characters all but disappear. There are a few isolated chapters on Vorotyntsev in Moscow, but virtually all the action takes place in revolutionary Petrograd, and virtually all the characters are historical ones. Politicians such as Pavel Milyukov and Vasily Maklakov connive and deal; generals consult each other; and members of the imperial family convey their uncertainty and anxiety. There are scenes of public confusion and domestic tranquility. Solzhenitsyn minutely details various episodes, describing weather and clothing as well as actions and emotions. He therefore allows his readers to experience what happens when a society slowly but inexorably falls apart.

Throughout his canon, from *One Day in the Life of Ivan Denisovich* through *The Red Wheel,* Solzhenitsyn's great theme is not the effect of the revolution—for no revolution or reformation in the Marxist-Leninist sense actually occurred in Russia—but both the dissolution of an anachronistic, deeply divided society under the stress of great events and the response of individuals to that dissolution. His achievement, like his ambition, is admirable.

BIOGRAPHICAL/CRITICAL SOURCES:

BOOKS

Allaback, Steven, *Alexander Solzhenitsyn,* Taplinger, 1978.

Barker, Francis, *Solzhenitsyn: Politics and Form,* Barnes & Noble, 1977.

Carter, Stephen, *The Politics of Solzhenitsyn,* Macmillan, 1977.

Contemporary Literary Criticism, Gale, Volume 1, 1973, Volume 2, 1974, Volume 4, 1975, Volume 7, 1977, Volume 9, 1978, Volume 10, 1979, Volume 18, 1981, Volume 26, 1983, Volume 34, 1985.

Curtis, James M., *Solzhenitsyn's Traditional Imagination,* University of Georgia Press, 1984.

Dunlop, John B., and others, editors, *Solzhenitsyn in Exile: Critical Essays and Documentary Materials,* Hoover Institution Press, 1985.

Dunlop, John B., Richard Haugh, and Alexis Klimoff, editors, *Aleksandr Solzhenitsyn: Critical Essays and Documentary Materials,* Nordland, 1973.

Feuer, Kathryn, editor, *Solzhenitsyn: A Collection of Critical Essays,* Prentice-Hall, 1976.

Labedz, Leopold, *Solzhenitsyn: A Documentary Record,* Indiana University Press, 1973.

Medvedev, Zhores, *Ten Years After "Ivan Denisovich,"* Knopf, 1973.

Rothberg, Abraham, *Alexander Solzhenitsyn: The Major Novels,* Cornell University Press, 1971.

Scammell, Michael, *Solzhenitsyn: A Biography,* Norton, 1984.

Solzhenitsyn, Aleksandr I., *The Gulag Archipelago, 1918-1956: An Experiment in Literary Investigation,* Harper, 1974-1979.

PERIODICALS

Nation, October 7, 1968.
National Review, October 15, 1976.
New Republic, May 11, 1963.
New Yorker, August 14, 1971.
New York Review of Books, December 19, 1968.
New York Times Book Review, September 15, 1968; September 10, 1972; March 3, 1974.
Saturday Review, August 23, 1975.*

—*Sidelights by James Malcolm Curtis*

*   *   *

SPEER, Albert   1905-1981

PERSONAL: Surname pronounced "shpair"; born March 19, 1905, in Mannheim, Germany; died September 1, 1981, of a cerebral hemorrhage, in London, England; son of Albert (an architect) and Wilhelmina Speer; married Margaret Weber, August 28, 1928; children: Albert, Hilde, Friedrich, Margaret, Arnold, Ernst. *Education:* Attended technical universities in Karlsruhe and Munich, Germany; Technical University of Berlin, diploma in engineering, 1927. *Politics:* "Skeptical of technocratic overdevelopment." *Religion:* Protestant.

CAREER: Technical University of Berlin, Berlin, Germany, assistant professor of architecture, 1927-31; freelance architect in Mannheim, Germany, 1931-33; served as architect-in-chief to Adolf Hitler, 1933-42; German Minister of Armaments and War Production, 1942-45; member of German Reichstag (parliament) and colonel in the SS, during the Second World War; convicted of war crimes, including the use of slave labor, by Nuremberg Tribunal and sentenced to 20 years in prison, 1946, released, 1966.

WRITINGS:

Erinnerungen, Propylaen (Berlin), 1969, translation by Richard Winston and Clara Winston published as *Inside the Third Reich: Memoirs* (Literary Guild selection and Book-of-the-Month Club alternate selection), Macmillan, 1970.
Spandauer Tagebuecher, Propylaen, 1975, translation by R. Winston and C. Winston published as *Spandau: The Secret Diaries,* Macmillan, 1976.
Architektur: Arbeiten, 1933-1942, Propylaen, 1978.
Technik und Macht, Bechtle, 1979.
Die Sklavenstaat: meine Auseinandersetzungen mit der SS, Deutsche Verlags-Anstalt, 1981, translation by Joachim Neugroschel published as *Infiltration: The SS and German Armament,* Macmillan, 1981, (published in England as *The Slave State: Heinrich Himmler's Masterplan for SS Supremacy,* Weidenfeld & Nicolson, 1981.)

SIDELIGHTS: Albert Speer was a leading member of the National Socialist government of Germany, commonly called the Nazis. In his role as architect-in-chief to Nazi leader Adolf Hitler, Speer designed the outdoor arena at Nuremberg, Germany, in which the Nazis held their immense annual rallies. He also designed the Nazi Party headquarters in Munich and the chancellery building in Berlin. Once the Second World War began, Speer was named Minister of Armaments and War Production. Some eighty percent of Germany's wartime industry was under his administration. For three years Speer kept German industrial output at record levels in spite of constant aerial bombardment by the Allied forces. Writing in the *Washington Post,* J. Y. Smith called Speer an "administrative genius." At war's end, Speer was one of 24 Nazis put on trial for war crimes. He admitted having used slave labor, mostly prisoners of war and civilians of occupied countries, in German factories during the war. For this crime, he was sentenced to twenty years in prison.

Speer began his career as an architect, following in his father's and grandfather's footsteps. At a Nazi rally in 1931 he met Adolf Hitler, who impressed Speer with his plans for rebuilding Berlin once the Nazi Party had seized power. Hitler called for a three-mile-long street in downtown Berlin, lined with magnificent government buildings and leading to a domed hall capable of holding 150,000 people at a time. He told Speer of his plans to build a triumphal arch 50 times larger than the Arc de Triomphe in Paris, a stadium for 300,000 spectators, and many other projects. The young Speer was dazzled. When the Nazi Party took power in 1933, he was named Hitler's architect-in-chief.

The most impressive architectural achievement of Speer's early work was undoubtedly the massive stadium he designed at Nuremberg. This stadium was the site for an annual rally at which the Nazis remembered their abortive 1923 revolution and celebrated their accomplishments as Germany's new leaders. Speer stage-managed the proceedings, including the innovative night rallies where 130 giant antiaircraft searchlights, aimed skyward, surrounded the audience to create a dynamic "Cathedral of Light" effect. Together with the martial music, flags and banners, and the mesmerizing speeches of Hitler himself, the rallies had an overwhelmingly powerful effect upon the audience. The Nuremberg rallies are still considered among the most effective, albeit sinister, examples of mass propaganda in modern times.

Following the death of the Minister of Armaments and War Production in a 1942 plane crash, Speer was appointed to take his place. In this role, he was responsible for Germany's industrial production of arms for the war effort. Despite constant bombardment by Allied bombers, Speer managed to increase industrial output to record levels. When the war began in 1939, for example, the German air force had only 700 fighter planes. Under Speer's direction, over 40,000 fighter planes were built and delivered in 1944 alone. Some of this remarkable achievement can be attributed to Speer's own innate abilities. As the London *Times* noted, Speer "was a gifted administrator who was able to organize the—admittedly colossal—resources of manpower at his disposal to accomplish . . . targets of production which must still be a source of wonder." Some of the increase in industrial production can be attributed to Speer's use of slave labor in the arms factories. Prisoners of war, civilians, and political prisoners were forced to work long hours in the plants turning out war materiel. Some of them were worked to death. Others faced the threat of execution if they failed to work hard. In some plants, an average worker's life expectancy was under four months.

This use of slave labor led to Speer's arrest at war's end. At the subsequent Nuremberg trials, the Allies charged leading Nazis—including Speer—with having violated international law. Such activities as the building of concentration camps, use of slave labor, and execution of prisoners of war were deemed to be "crimes against humanity." Of the Nazis convicted at Nuremberg, only Speer admitted any degree of responsibility for his crimes, although he too entered a plea of "not guilty." While some Nazis were executed, Speer received a prison sentence of twenty years.

Following his release from Spandau Prison in 1966, Speer devoted his time to writing his memoirs, a process he had begun while still in prison. Prevented from having writing implements of any kind, he nonetheless scribbled notes for his book on toilet paper and smuggled them out with the help of a friendly guard. In 1969, he published his memoirs in Germany. The following year they were published in English translation as *Inside the Third Reich: Memoirs.*

Inside the Third Reich was an immediate bestseller in the United States, selling over one million copies. Critical reaction was enthusiastic. Kurt P. Tauber in the *Virginia Quarterly Review* called the book "the most important memoirs that have so far come from the former leadership of the Third Reich," while Keith R. Johnson of *Time* described *Inside the Third Reich* as "the last, best first-person story of what took place at the power center as Hitler moved from political triumph to military disaster."

Christopher Lehmann-Haupt explained why the book was so important. "Imagine," he wrote in the *New York Times,* "the most significant and dramatic episode in a century of history. Then imagine that episode's most representative figure stepping out of the past and presenting us with his version of the episode. And then imagine the book containing that version fulfilling its every premise—describing with the coolest objectivity all that one might hope it would describe, yet revealing between its lines what made its author so representative. Imagine all that and you will begin to understand the importance of Albert Speer's 'Memoirs' and the impact of reading them."

Other critics called attention to Speer's honesty in recounting his past. According to Franklin H. Littell in *Christian Century,* "the first thing that strikes the reader is that this is an honest book." Also writing in *Christian Century,* Markus Barth stated: "Speer's is a self-searching, intimately personal book that reveals the humanity of its author and also his temporal loss of humanity. As such, it makes the reader examine his own values and intentions, and brings him face to face with human shortcomings."

In his book, Speer recalls a friend telling him of a concentration camp in Silesia he had just visited, a camp the friend nervously advised Speer never to visit. "I did not investigate," Speer wrote, "for I did not want to know what was happening there." The camp was Auschwitz. "Because I failed at that time," Speer related, "I still feel responsible for Auschwitz in a wholly personal sense." Tauber noted that "it is a measure of [Speer's] palpable candor, modesty, and moral rectitude that the reader looks back with no trace of bitterness, but only with sadness, upon the young architect whose vanity, vaulting ambition, and technocratic ruthlessness destroyed not only his own life but in the process also the lives of millions of others."

Speer's portrait of Nazi leader Adolf Hitler was also praised. "If Adolf Hitler had ever had a friend," Speer wrote, "I would have been that friend." The two men were on close terms for some twelve years, with Speer even buying a house near Hitler's Berchtesgaden residence. Speer remembered conversations with Hitler in which the fuehrer displayed a more personal side. He recalled that Hitler made fun of gestapo chief Herman Goering's love of hunting, "today, when anybody with a fat belly can safely shoot the animal down from a distance." Speer also discussed Hitler's obsession, even as he planned war, with building a hall of fame to the fallen soldiers to come, complete with sarcophagi of the victorious military commanders. As Lincoln Kirstein wrote in the *Nation,* "Speer's Hitler is human as well as diabolical. . . . No other witness has drawn Hitler as man rather than maniac."

In 1976, Speer followed *Inside the Third Reich* with *Spandau: The Secret Diaries,* detailing his life in prison and his attempts to come to terms with his war years. The book was selected from some 20,000 pages of notes that Speer secretly compiled while serving his prison sentence. "Because Speer did not think of later publication while jotting down his notes," F. E. Hirsch observed in *Library Journal,* "this volume may surpass his first book as a genuine historical source and human document."

Spandau: The Secret Diaries presents a vivid look at the daily life of a prisoner. Writing in the *National Review,* R. W. Merry noted: "The trouble with this prison memoir is that it is so engrossing a prison memoir. That is to say, Speer's narrative of the droning, numbing Spandau years is graced with such piquancy and simple humanity that it would be easy to miss the book's essential significance. In his unadorned yet vivid style, the author effectively captures all the mundanities of prison life."

Neal Ascherson, writing in the *New York Review of Books,* found that Speer's diaries had inadvertently said more than Speer had intended to say. Ascherson claimed that Speer "was more profoundly a fascist than we knew—or than he knows. It is true that he never led a march on Rome, screamed about geopolitical determination from a platform, or took notice of racist theory and practice. But the reader of these diaries will find . . . that the idea of Albert Speer as the unpolitical technocrat who simply followed his specialty and ignored wider responsibilities is not adequate. He was the essential Janus figures of twentieth-century fascism, one face staring back into the glories and certainties of the past, the other—its eyes half-closed—turned forward as the legs stride ahead into an industrialized future." Speaking of *Inside the Third Reich* and *Spandau: The Secret Diaries,* Smith claimed that they were "two of the most remarkable books ever published about the Nazi era. . . . Through his personality, his career, and—most importantly, perhaps—through his books, Albert Speer provided insights of enormous value into the how and why of Hitler and his movement."

In an interview with the *Washington Post* in 1976, Speer asked that history remember him as "one of the closest collaborators of Hitler. What I said at Nuremberg, that I was responsible for everything that happened to me, will stick with me, rightly. It will be my stamp. I hope it will also be remembered that I was capable of three other things: to be an architect, manager and writer." In an interview with *Playboy* in 1971, Speer was asked about his work as Minister of Armaments and War Production: "Intellectually, I have accepted that it is wrong to be proud of such things, but emotionally, I still feel a surge of pride when I think of the obstacles I overcame and the goals we achieved. I would be dishonest if I said otherwise."

BIOGRAPHICAL/CRITICAL SOURCES:

BOOKS

Fishman, Jack, *The Seven Men of Spandau,* Rinehart, 1954.
Speer, Albert, *Erinnerungen,* Propylaen, 1969, translation by Richard Winston and Clara Winston published as *Inside the Third Reich: Memoirs,* Macmillan, 1970.
Speer, Albert, *Spandauer Tagebuecher,* Propylaen, 1975, translation by R. Winston and C. Winston published as *Spandau: The Secret Diaries,* Macmillan, 1976.

PERIODICALS

Atlantic, January, 1971.
Christian Century, December 23, 1970.
Commentary, November, 1970, pp. 85-90.
Library Journal, March 15, 1976.
Los Angeles Times Book Review, August 30, 1981, p. 10.
Nation, September 14, 1970, p. 216; March 24, 1971, pp. 376-378.
National Review, May 28, 1976.
Newsweek, August 31, 1970.
New York Review of Books, March 18, 1976.
New York Times, August 24, 1970; May 13, 1971.
New York Times Book Review, October 4, 1981, p. 14.
Observer, October 18, 1970.
Playboy, June, 1971.
Time, September 7, 1970, pp. 58-59.
Virginia Quarterly Review, winter, 1971, pp. 145-148.
Washington Post Book World, August 16, 1981, p. 14.

OBITUARIES:

PERIODICALS

New York Times, September 2, 1981.
Times (London), September 3, 1981.
Washington Post, September 2, 1981.*

*   *   *

STAHL, Hilda 1938-

PERSONAL: Born September 13, 1938, in Chadron, NE; daughter of Jay (a ranch hand) and Zelma (a housekeeper; maiden name, Fehrenholz) Clements; married Norman August Stahl (an artist), August 1, 1959; children: Jeffery, Laurie, Bradley, Mark, Sonya, Evangelynn, Joshua. *Education:* Wayne State Teachers College (now Wayne State College), Wayne, NE, Normal Degree, 1956.

ADDRESSES: Home—5891 Wood School Rd., Freeport, MI 49325.

CAREER: Rural school teacher in Winnebago, NE, 1956-57; writer, 1968—; Happy Time Nursery Pre-School, Hastings, MI, teacher, 1971-72.

MEMBER: Society of Children's Book Writers.

WRITINGS:

Gently Touch Sheela Jenkins, Bethel Publishing, 1989.
Blossoming Love, Bethel Publishing, 1991.

"AMBER AINSLIE" DETECTIVE SERIES

Deadline, Bethel Publishing, 1990.
Abducted, Bethel Publishing, 1990.
Undercover, Bethel Publishing, 1991.
Blackmail, Bethel Publishing, 1991.

"THE WHITE PINE CHRONICLES" SERIES

The Covenant, Thomas Nelson, 1991.
The Inheritance, Thomas Nelson, 1992.
The Dream, Thomas Nelson, 1992.

YOUNG ADULT NOVELS

Melody of Love, Moody, 1975.
Surprise at the Big Key, Tyndale, 1985.
The Swamp Monster, Tyndale, 1985.

"TINA" SERIES

Tina's First Love, Moody, 1972.
Tina's Dangerous Secret, Tyndale, 1980.
Tina's Elusive Enemy, Tyndale, 1981.
Tina's Reluctant Friend, Tyndale, 1981.
Tina's Unwelcome Intruder, Tyndale, 1982.
Tina's Secret Rival, Tyndale, 1982.
Tina's Eighteenth Summer, Tyndale, 1983.
Tina's Surprise Romance, Tyndale, 1983.

"ELIZABETH GAIL" SERIES

Elizabeth Gail and the Mystery at the Johnson Farm, Tyndale, 1979.
Elizabeth Gail and the Secret Box, Tyndale, 1979.
Elizabeth Gail and the Teddy Bear Mystery, Tyndale, 1979.
Elizabeth Gail and the Dangerous Double, Tyndale, 1980.
Elizabeth Gail and the Trouble at Sandhill Ranch, Tyndale, 1980.
Elizabeth Gail and the Strange Birthday Party, Tyndale, 1980.
Elizabeth Gail and the Terrifying News, Tyndale, 1980.
Elizabeth Gail and the Frightened Runaways, Tyndale, 1981.
Elizabeth Gail and Trouble from the Past, Tyndale, 1981.
Elizabeth Gail and the Silent Piano, Tyndale, 1981.
Elizabeth Gail and Double Trouble, Tyndale, 1982.
Elizabeth Gail and the Holiday Mystery, Tyndale, 1982.
Elizabeth Gail and the Missing Love Letters, Tyndale, 1982.
Elizabeth Gail and the Music Camp Romance, Tyndale, 1983.

Elizabeth Gail and the Handsome Stranger, Tyndale, 1983.
Elizabeth Gail and the Secret Love, Tyndale, 1983.
Elizabeth Gail and the Summer for Weddings, Tyndale, 1984.
Elizabeth Gail and the Time for Love, Tyndale, 1984.
Elizabeth Gail and the Great Canoe Conspiracy, Tyndale, 1991.
Elizabeth Gail and the Hidden Key Mystery, Tyndale, 1992.
Elizabeth Gail and the Secret of the Gold Charm, Tyndale, 1992.

Also author of video cassette adaptation of *Elizabeth Gail and the Mystery at the Johnson Farm.*

"TEDDY JO" SERIES

Teddy Jo and the Terrible Secret, Tyndale, 1982.
Teddy Jo and the Yellow Room Mystery, Tyndale, 1983.
Teddy Jo and the Stolen Ring, Tyndale, 1983.
Teddy Jo and the Strangers in the Pink House, Tyndale, 1983.
Teddy Jo and the Strange Medallion, Tyndale, 1983.
Teddy Jo and the Wild Dog, Tyndale, 1984.
Teddy Jo and the Abandoned House, Tyndale, 1984.
Teddy Jo and the Ragged Beggars, Tyndale, 1984.
Teddy Jo and the Kidnapped Heir, Tyndale, 1984.
Teddy Jo and the Great Dive, Tyndale, 1985.
Teddy Jo and the Magic Quill, Tyndale, 1985.
Teddy Jo and the Missing Portrait, Tyndale, 1985.
Teddy Jo and the Mystery of the Broken Locket, Tyndale, 1985.
Teddy Jo and the Missing Family, Tyndale, 1986.

"TYLER TWINS" SERIES

Tyler Twins and the Surprise at the Big Key Ranch, Tyndale, 1986.
Tyler Twins and the Swamp Monster, Tyndale, 1987.
Tyler Twins and the Pet Show Adventure, Tyndale, 1988.
Tyler Twins and the Tree House Hideaway, Tyndale, 1988.
Tyler Twins and the Latchkey Kids, Tyndale, 1989.
Tyler Twins and the Mystery of the Missing Grandfather, Tyndale, 1989.

"SADIE ROSE" ADVENTURE SERIES

Sadie Rose and the Daring Escape, Crossway, 1989.
Sadie Rose and the Cottonwood Creek Orphan, Crossway, 1989.
Sadie Rose and the Outlaw Rustlers, Crossway, 1990.
Sadie Rose and the Double Secret, Crossway, 1990.
Sadie Rose and the Mad Fortune Hunters, Crossway, 1991.
Sadie Rose and the Phantom Warrior, Crossway, 1991.
Sadie Rose and the Champion Sharpshooter, Crossway, 1991.

Sadie Rose and the Secret Romance, Crossway, 1992.
Sadie Rose and the Impossible Birthday Wish, Crossway, 1992.

"KAYLA O'BRIEN" ADVENTURE SERIES

Kayla O'Brien and the Dangerous Journey, Crossway, 1990.
Kayla O'Brien and the Trouble at Bitter Creek Ranch, Crossway, 1990.
Kayla O'Brien and the Runaway Orphans, Crossway, 1991.

"SENDI LEE MASON" ADVENTURE SERIES

Sendi Lee Mason and the Milk Carton Kids, Crossway, 1990.
Sendi Lee Mason and the Stray Striped Cat, Crossway, 1990.
Sendi Lee Mason and the Big Mistake, Crossway, 1991.
Sendi Lee Mason and the Great Crusade, Crossway, 1991.

"DAISY PUNKIN" SERIES

Daisy Punkin, Crossway, 1991.
Daisy Punkin and the Bratty Brother, Crossway, 1992.

"WREN HOUSE" MYSTERY SERIES

The Mystery at the Wheeler Place, David Cook, 1992.
Disappearance of Amos Pike, David Cook, 1992.
Tim Avery's Secret, David Cook, 1992.
The Missing Newspaper Caper, David Cook, 1992.
The Case of the Missing Money, David Cook, 1992.

"BEST FRIENDS" SERIES

Chelsea and the Outrageous Phone Bill, Crossway, 1992.
Trouble for Roxie, Crossway, 1992.
Kathy and the Babysitting Hassle, Crossway, 1992.
Hannah and the Special 4th of July, Crossway, 1992.
Roxie and the Red Rose Mystery, Crossway, 1992.
Kathy's New Brother, Crossway, 1992.
Made-Over Chelsea, Crossway, 1992.
No Friends for Hannah, Crossway, 1992.

OTHER

Also author of book on audio cassette, *The Great Adventures of Super J*A*M,* produced by Studio 7 Productions. Contributor of more than four hundred stories to religious and educational journals.

WORK IN PROGRESS: An adult mystery; books for young people; and a new children's series.

SIDELIGHTS: "I was born and raised in the Nebraska Sandhills with sand between my toes and wind in my hair," commented Hilda Stahl. "My five sisters and three brothers enjoyed listening to me tell stories that I'd read or that I'd made up. I was a good reader and enjoyed losing myself in books. I walked the prairie, enjoying the vastness and the solitude, and never once thought about writing or being a writer. I wanted to be a rancher and raise horses and cattle. But I became a country school teacher, and later I married Norman and moved to Michigan. I yearned to do something great, something that others would know about even long after I was dead. But I didn't know what to do.

"After three of my children were born and a fourth was on the way, it hit me that if I wanted to watch my kids grow up I couldn't get a job outside the home. There was no way to become 'great.' So, I decided to find a way just to make a little money by myself at home. One day I saw a magazine ad for a correspondence course in writing. I sent for the test, passed it, and worked on the lessons at home in between changing diapers, doing dishes, feeding babies, and being laughed at for thinking that I could be a writer. I grabbed time to write when the babies were in bed and when the kids were in school. I wrote when rejection slips piled high around me. I wrote when I was too tired to see. I wrote and I wrote, and then I began to sell almost everything that I wrote.

"My books are full of mystery and romance and adventure because I know that children enjoy reading that kind of book. I write about sensitive subjects because children want to know how to handle situations in their lives, and I show them that God is always there to help them. I enjoy speaking at schools and organizations on writing. It's a pleasure to teach others how to write. I know that if I could learn and be a success at writing that anyone can with hard work and perseverance."

Stahl once described her writing technique to *CA:* "I have learned to write an outline of my story and from that to write the book. I very seldom rewrite—except in my head. I try to write so that the reader can't put down the book until he or she has finished it. From all over the world I receive fan mail from girls, a few boys, and adults who love my books. They always beg for more and, of course, it keeps me going.

"In my writing I want to entertain as I teach, and I always have a happy ending. I want the reader to *know* that my books will leave them feeling good, and feeling that life is beautiful even if there are negative situations that must be faced. . . .

"Reading is important to me. I read several books a week, usually in the genre in which I'm writing. Reading what other authors write helps me to improve my skills, I think, and I love to read, but mostly I love to write." She added: "All seven of my children are out of school now, giving me more time to write; six are married and I have seven grandchildren. A shy country girl with sand between her toes and wind in her hair made it as a writer."

STEAD, Christina (Ellen) 1902-1983

PERSONAL: Born July 17, 1902, in Rockdale, Sydney, New South Wales, Australia; died March 31, 1983, in Sydney, Australia; daughter of David George (a naturalist) and Ellen (Butters) Stead; married William James Blake, 1952 (an author; surname originally Blech; died, 1968). *Education:* Attended Teachers' College, Sydney University, received teacher's certification.

CAREER: Novelist, short story writer, editor, and translator. Worked as a public school teacher, a teacher of abnormal children, and a demonstrator in the psychology laboratory of Sydney University, all in Australia; grain company clerk, London, England, 1928-29; bank clerk in Paris, France, 1930-35; senior writer for Metro-Goldwyn-Mayer, 1943; instructor in Workshop in the Novel, New York University, 1943-44; Australian National University, Canberra, fellow in creative arts, 1969.

AWARDS, HONORS: Aga Khan Prize, *Paris Review,* 1966; Arts Council of Great Britain grant, 1967; first recipient of Patrick White Award, 1974; honorary member, American Academy and Institute of Arts and Letters, 1982; Victorian Fellowship, Australian Writers Awards, 1986, for *An Ocean of Story;* Premiere's Award for Literature, Premiere of New South Wales, Australia; several times nominated for the Nobel Prize.

WRITINGS:

NOVELS

Seven Poor Men of Sydney, Appleton, 1935.
The Beauties and Furies, Appleton, 1936.
House of All Nations, Simon & Schuster, 1938, reprinted, Holt, 1972.
The Man Who Loved Children, Simon & Schuster, 1940, reprinted with introduction by Randall Jarrell, Holt, 1965.
For Love Alone, Harcourt, 1944.
Letty Fox: Her Luck, Harcourt, 1946.
A Little Tea, a Little Chat, Harcourt, 1948.
The People with the Dogs, Little, Brown, 1952.
Dark Places of the Heart, Holt, 1966 (published in England as *Cotters' England,* Secker & Warburg, 1966).
The Little Hotel, Angus & Robertson, 1973, Holt, 1975.
Miss Herbert (the Suburban Wife), Random House, 1976.
I'm Dying Laughing: The Humorist, Holt, 1987.

STORIES

The Salzburg Tales, Appleton, 1934.
The Puzzleheaded Girl (four novellas), Holt, 1967.
An Ocean of Story (uncollected stories), edited by R. G. Geering, Viking, 1986.

OTHER

(Contributor) *The Fairies Return,* P. Davies, 1934.
(Editor with husband, William J. Blake) *Modern Women in Love,* Dryden Press, 1946.
(Editor) *South Sea Stories,* Muller, 1955.
(Translator) Fernand Gigon, *Colour of Asia,* Muller, 1955.
(Translator) Jean Giltene, *The Candid Killer,* Muller, 1956.
(Translator) August Piccard, *In Balloon and Bathyscape,* Cassell, 1956.
A Christina Stead Reader, selected by Jean B. Read, Random House, 1978.

Contributor of short stories to *Southerly, Kenyon Review,* and *Saturday Evening Post,* and of reviews to various papers. Stead's novels have been translated into foreign languages.

SIDELIGHTS: Australian-born novelist and short story author Christina Stead—whose work went unregarded for a large part of her life—is considered by many critics to be one of the most gifted writers of the twentieth century. "To open a book, any book, by Christina Stead and read a few pages," Angela Carter wrote in the *London Review of Books,* "is to be at once aware that one is in the presence of greatness." Stead's novel *The Man Who Loved Children,* which depicts a boisterous, often cruel family led by an idealist father, is generally regarded as her masterpiece.

Stead was born in 1902, the daughter of a prominent naturalist. Her mother passed away when Stead was two years old. At the age of 26, Stead left Australia for England, working as a clerk until her health failed her the following year. With her companion William J. Blake (the couple was married in 1952), she then traveled over Europe, living in such cities as Brussels, Antwerp, and Basel. During World War II she and Blake lived in the United States, where Stead worked for a time—unhappily—as a screenwriter for Metro-Goldwyn-Mayer. The couple returned to Europe at war's end.

In 1934 Stead published her first book, a collection of short stories entitled *The Salzburg Tales.* Based on Stead's idea that every fairy tale has a modern equivalent, *The Salzburg Tales* display a matter of fact Gothic quality which Stead would later employ in her realistic novels of modern family life. These early stories are, Carter stated, "glittering, grotesque short fictions, parables and allegories. . . . contrived with a lush, jewelled exquisiteness of technique." Writing in *Southerly,* Michael Wilding found the same collection to be "running riot" with "adolescent-like fantasy and whimsy."

During the 1930s Stead published several novels set in her native Australia, including *Seven Poor Men of Sydney,* a tale of an impoverished fishing community. Her biggest critical and financial success, however, came with the publication of *House of All Nations,* an 800-page epic novel tracing the decline and final collapse of a Swiss banking house. The novel's myriad characters, its behind-the-scenes look at currency manipulations, and the glamorous lifestyles it depicted guaranteed the story a wide and appreciative audience. R. G. Geering, writing in *Christina Stead,* found *House of All Nations* to be "Stead's greatest intellectual achievement—its knowledge of the workings of international finance and its revelation of the fraud, the ruthlessness, the energy, the sheer luck, and the genius that go into money-making, are by any standards remarkable." Writing in *New Statesman,* Elaine Feinstein claimed that *House of All Nations,* "for all its flaws, marks out an extraordinary terrain of avarice with as much passion as other novelists have given to the violence of sexual love."

Stead followed *House of All Nations* with a quite different novel, *The Man Who Loved Children,* the story of a self-centered man, his suffering wife, and their young daughter. Writing in her study *Christina Stead,* Joan Lidoff found that "at the heart of Christina Stead's fiction echoes the persistent moral issue: egotism. She sees everyone striving by subtle or overt manipulations to subordinate others to his or her own needs and desires, trying to take as much while giving as little as possible. In her 1940 masterpiece, *The Man Who Loved Children,* Stead criticizes this ongoing struggle between competing egoisms, not only in her characterization and analysis, but in the very form of her fiction. This novel takes as protagonist no single hero, but an entire family." In contrast, Dorothy Green claimed in *The Australian Experience: Critical Essays on Australian Novels:* "Stead has created what is extremely rare in modern literature: three archetypal characters who have a life of their own, independent of their author."

When first published in 1940 *The Man Who Loved Children* was both a critical and popular failure. For years, it led an underground existence, read and admired by only a few. But in 1965, Randall Jarrell arranged a reprint of the novel which brought it to the attention of the reading public. In his introduction to the reprint Jarrell proclaimed: "[*The Man Who Loved Children*] seems to me as plainly good as *Crime and Punishment* and *Remembrance of Things Past* and *War and Peace* are plainly great. I call it a good book, but it is a better book, I think, than most of the novels people call great; perhaps it would be fairer to call it great. It has one quality that, ordinarily, only a great book has: it makes you a part of one family's immediate existence as no other book quite does. One reads the book, with an almost ecstatic pleasure of recognition. You get used to saying, 'Yes, that's the way it is'; and you say many times, but can never get used to saying, 'I didn't

know *anybody* knew that. Henny, Sam, Louie, and the children are entirely real to the reader, and reality is rare in novels."

Some critics compared Stead's approach in *The Man Who Loved Children* to that used by certain writers of the nineteenth century. Christopher Ricks wrote: "In its sense of growth and of generations, in its generality and specificity, above all in the central place which it accords to feelings of indignation and embarrassment, *The Man Who Loved Children* is in the best tradition of the nineteenth-century novel. . . . Like George Meredith at his best, [Stead] is fascinated by the way we speak to ourselves in the privacy of our skulls, and she is able to remind us of what we would rather forget—that we are all continually employing, to ourselves and to others, a false rhetoric, overblown, indiscriminately theatrical, and yet indisputably ours."

The novel's grimly domestic focus caught the attention of other critics. Carter noted that the book's "single-minded intensity of its evocation of domestic terror gives it a greater artistic cohesion than Stead's subsequent work, which tends towards the random picaresque. And Stead permits herself a genuinely tragic resolution." Similarly, Green stated that *The Man Who Loved Children* "presents the observer with the spectacle of a struggle for survival in a habitat which is too small and too impoverished for the 'fighting fish' it contains." Eleanor Perry remarked that the novel is "not a slice of life. It is life," while Jose Yglesias of the *Nation* proclaimed *The Man Who Loved Children* "a funny, painful, absorbing masterpiece, obviously the work of a major writer."

Speaking of Stead's career as a novelist and short story writer, Jarrell wrote: "There is a bewitching rapidity and lack of self-consciousness about Christina Stead's writing; she has much knowledge, extraordinary abilities, but is too engrossed in what she is doing ever to seem conscious of them, so that they do not cut her off from the world but join her to it." Although best known for her achievements in *The Man Who Loved Children,* "in all her work, Stead displays a similar originality of concept, a brilliant, almost obsessive hold on subject and character and a headlong rush of language, more like a force of nature than a literary process, which is her unique signature," Helen Yglesias commented in the *Los Angeles Times Book Review.* A writer for the London *Times* stated that "in the end [Stead] did achieve a fame almost commensurate with her towering and always human achievement. She was one of the great originals, by whom it was almost impossible to be influenced." Yglesias called her "a master novelist of our time, for whom a resting place in the literature of the English language is assured."

BIOGRAPHICAL/CRITICAL SOURCES:

BOOKS

Contemporary Literary Criticism, Gale, Volume 2, 1975, Volume 5, 1976, Volume 8, 1978, Volume 32, 1985.
Geering, R. G., *Christina Stead,* Twayne, 1969.
Jarrell, Randall, *The Third Book of Criticism,* Farrar, Straus, 1969.
Lidoff, Joan, *Christina Stead,* Ungar, 1982.
Ransome, W. S., editor, *The Australian Experience: Critical Essays on Australian Novels,* Australian National University, 1974, pp. 174-208.

PERIODICALS

Atlantic, March, 1965; June, 1965; August, 1976.
Books, August, 1966.
Book Week, April 18, 1965.
Book World, September 10, 1967.
Chicago Tribune Book World, December 24, 1978, Section 7, p. 1.
Christian Science Monitor, December 28, 1967.
Journal of Commonwealth Literature, August, 1980, pp. 107-113.
London Magazine, November, 1967, pp. 98-100; June, 1968, pp. 112-113.
London Review of Books, September 16, 1982, pp. 11-13.
Los Angeles Times, May 19, 1986.
Los Angeles Times Book Review, October 4, 1987, p. 12; November 8, 1987, p. 11.
Nation, April 5, 1965; October 24, 1966; April 26, 1975, pp. 501-503.
New Leader, September 29, 1975, pp. 21-22.
New Republic, September 9, 1967, pp. 30-31; February 24, 1979, pp. 36-37.
New Statesman, June 14, 1974, p. 856; August 21, 1981, pp. 21-22.
New Yorker, August 18, 1975; August 9, 1976.
New York Review of Books, June 17, 1965; December 15, 1966; September 28, 1967; June 26, 1975.
New York Times Book Review, December 10, 1967; May 11, 1975; February 4, 1979, p. 9; March 15, 1981, p. 35; May 25, 1986, p. 7; August 23, 1987, p. 28; September 20, 1987, p. 26.
Observer, July 25, 1982, p. 31.
Punch, May 31, 1967; April 10, 1968.
Saturday Review, April 10, 1965; May 31, 1975.
Southerly (Sydney), 1962; Volume 27, number 1, 1967, pp. 20-33.
Stand, Volume 10, number 1, 1968, pp. 30-37.
Times (London), January 12, 1985; April 24, 1986.
Times Literary Supplement, September 25, 1981, p. 1110; May 16, 1986, p. 535; April 24, 1987, p. 435.
Tribune Books (Chicago), October 4, 1987, p. 3.
Virginia Quarterly Review, winter, 1968.
Washington Post Book World, June 1, 1975, pp. 1-2; May 25, 1986, p. 6; August 2, 1987, p. 12; December 20, 1987, p. 9.

OBITUARIES:

PERIODICALS

New York Times, April 13, 1983.
Times (London), April 7, 1983.*

*   *   *

STEINHARDT, Herschel S. 1910-

PERSONAL: Born May 21, 1910, in Zambrow, Poland; emigrated to the United States in 1920; son of Abraham (a rabbi and teacher) and Zelda (Shafran) Steinhardt; wife deceased; children: Dr. Joyce Steinhardt Garber, Judie Steinhardt Goldstein. *Education:* Attended Wayne State University, 1930-31; New School for Social Research, 1938-40; Hunter College, 1946-47. *Religion:* Jewish.

ADDRESSES: Home—18216 Maryland, Southfield, MI 48075.

CAREER: Writer. Worked variously as a newsboy and theater usher in Detroit, MI, and as a cook on a dredging boat in Florida. Federal Theater Project, New York City, writer in playwriting dept., 1938-40. Displaced Persons Program, New York City, press representative, 1944-52.

MEMBER: Dramatist Guild.

WRITINGS:

PLAYS

No One Walks Alone (originally produced on radio), American Jewish Committee, 1946.
Sons of Men (three-act; originally produced as "Precinct," *Robert Montgomery Presents,* NBC, c. 1958), Bookman Associates, 1959.
A Star in Heaven (three-act; originally produced at Concept East, Detroit, MI, 1963), New Voices, 1967.
I Never Went to Pittsburgh, Aran Press, 1990.
The Wind and the Rain (first produced at Wayne State University, Detroit, 1955) Aran Press, 1990.

Also author of numerous other plays, including *Children of Flesh, The Big Dollar, A Little Sunshine, The Red Ball, The Power of the Dog, Before the Morning, The Artistic Street Cleaner,* "A Man's Household Are His Enemy," *The Hand of the Potter* (two-act), *The Third Hour of the Night,* "Our Daily Bread," *Men Without Names,* and "A Jealous God," all published by Aran Press. Works have been published in periodicals, including *Young Israel Viewpoint,* 1948-49, and *Impresario,* 1961.

Author's unpublished plays include *Six Men Seated on a Subway* (one-act), first produced at Henry Street Settlement Playhouse, New York City; *God's In His Heaven,* first produced at Wayne State University, Detroit, MI, 1962; *The Voice of the Bell,* recorded and distributed by Citizens Committee for Displaced Person, 1946. Author of several other unproduced full-length plays and a number of one-act plays.

OTHER

A Playwright's Life (autobiography), Aran Press, 1990.

SIDELIGHTS: Performances of Herschel Steinhardt's stage drama, *No One Walks Alone,* have been broadcast on radio in Switzerland, West Germany, the Netherlands, and Jerusalem.

*   *   *

STERN, Richard Martin 1915-

PERSONAL: Born March 17, 1915, in Fresno, CA; son of Charles Frank (a banker) and True (Aiken) Stern; married Dorothy Atherton, December 20, 1937; children: (adopted) Mary Elisabeth Emery (Mrs. Robert Michael Vinton). *Education:* Attended Harvard College (now Harvard University), 1933-36.

ADDRESSES: *Home*—Rte. 7, Box 55, Santa Fe, NM 87501. *Agent*—Brandt & Brandt, 1501 Broadway, New York, NY 10036.

CAREER: Hearst Corp., New York City, trainee, 1936-37; worked at Exhibitors Art and Design, San Francisco, CA, 1938, and Boothe Fruit Co., Modesto, CA, 1938-39; Lockheed Aircraft Corp., Burbank, CA, manufacturing engineer, 1940-45; free-lance writer, 1945—.

MEMBER: Authors Guild, Authors League of America, Mystery Writers of America (director, 1961-63, 1965-66, 1969-70; vice-president, 1962-63; president, 1971), Crime Writers Association, Press Club (London), Quien Sabe Club.

AWARDS, HONORS: Edgar Award for best first mystery novel, Mystery Writers of America, 1958, for *The Bright Road to Fear.*

WRITINGS:

The Bright Road to Fear, Ballantine, 1958.
The Search for Tabatha Carr, Scribner, 1960.
These Unlucky Deeds, Scribner, 1961.
High Hazard, Scribner, 1962.
Cry Havoc, Scribner, 1963.
Right Hand Opposite, Scribner, 1964.
I Hide, We Seek, Scribner, 1965.
The Kessler Legacy, Scribner, 1967.

Merry Go Round, Scribner, 1969.
Brood of Eagles, World Publishing, 1969.
Manuscript for Murder, Scribner, 1970.
Murder in the Walls, Scribner, 1971.
You Don't Need an Enemy, Scribner, 1972.
Stanfield Harvest, World Publishing, 1972.
Death in the Snow, Scribner, 1973.
The Tower, McKay, 1973.
Power, McKay, 1974.
The Will, Doubleday, 1976.
Snowbound Six, Doubleday, 1977.
Flood, Doubleday, 1979.
The Big Bridge, Doubleday, 1982.
Wildfire, Norton, 1986.
Tsunami, Norton, 1988.
Tangled Murders, Pocket Books, 1989.
(Contributor) *The Rigby File,* Hodder & Stoughton, 1989.
Missing Man, Pocket Books, 1990.
Interloper, Pocket Books, 1990.

Contributor of short stories to periodicals, including *Saturday Evening Post, Cosmopolitan, Argosy, Good Housekeeping,* and *McCall's.* Member of editorial board, *Writer,* 1976—.

ADAPTATIONS: *The Tower* was filmed in 1974 by Twentieth Century-Fox Film Corp. as *The Towering Inferno.*

SIDELIGHTS: Richard Martin Stern once told *CA:* "To paraphrase John D. MacDonald, when you spend your life doing what you would rather do than anything else—write stories—and you are paid for it, that is a license to steal."

BIOGRAPHICAL/CRITICAL SOURCES:

PERIODICALS

Armchair Detective, spring, 1990, p. 251.
Books and Bookmen, June, 1975.
New York Times, October 19, 1973.
New York Times Book Review, May 16, 1971; July 4, 1976.
Observer, February 8, 1970.
Publishers Weekly, December 15, 1989, p. 61.
Times Literary Supplement, March 5, 1970.
Washington Post Book World, May 20, 1973.

*   *   *

STITH, John E(dward) 1947-

PERSONAL: Born July 30, 1947, in Boulder, CO; son of George Allen (an electronics engineer) and Virginia (a piano teacher; maiden name, Kenway) Stith; married Nancy West, June 8, 1969 (divorced, 1979); married Annette Chamness (a bookstore owner), May 24, 1981. *Education:* University of Minnesota—Twin Cities, B.A., 1969.

ADDRESSES: Home—1242 Amsterdam Dr., Colorado Springs, CO 80907-4004. *Agent*—Russell Galen, Scott Meredith Literary Agency, Inc., 845 Third Ave., New York, N.Y. 10022-6687.

CAREER: System Development Corp., Colorado Springs, CO, programmer and analyst, 1973-75; Wyle Laboratories, Colorado Springs, manager of software department, 1976-79; Kaman Sciences Corp., Colorado Springs, manager, 1979-91. *Military service:* U.S. Air Force, space systems analyst and space object identification analyst, 1969-72; became first lieutenant.

MEMBER: Science-Fiction and Fantasy Writers of America, Mystery Writers of America (Rocky Mountain regional vice-president, 1984-86).

AWARDS, HONORS: Nebula Award nomination, 1990, for *Redshift Rendezvous.*

WRITINGS:

SCIENCE FICTION

Scapescope, Berkley Publishing/Ace Books, 1984.
Memory Blank, Berkley Publishing/Ace Books, 1985.
Death Tolls, Berkley Publishing/Ace Books, 1987.
Deep Quarry, Berkley Publishing/Ace Books, 1989.
Redshift Rendezvous (a Science Fiction Book Club selection), Berkley Publishing/Ace Books, 1990.
Manhattan Transfer, Tor Books, 1993.

OTHER

Also author of screenplay with Alexandra Tana, *This Family Notion,* 1993.

WORK IN PROGRESS: Reunion on Neverend, a science fiction novel for Tor Books, expected in 1994.

SIDELIGHTS: John E. Stith told *CA:* "My interests lie primarily in the mystery and science fiction fields. Therefore, my novels contain elements of both genres. If I am lucky, the books will attract readers from both genres.

"I think that centuries from now men and women will feel most of the same motivations that exist now. They will, though, be subjected to new and different pressures and be called upon to function in altered and strange situations. I enjoy imagining how we might respond to those new pressures and picturing new directions in which we might grow. That's also partly why the mystery-suspense field appeals to me; it, too, looks at how people respond under pressures to which they are unaccustomed, to overcome challenges with which they may not be properly prepared to cope.

"My characters tend to see the humor, even in tense situations. They are people who do their best to avoid merely being swept along with the flow, to impose their own wills

on conditions they want changed. Not all the problems they face are problems that don't exist now; my characters so far have had to cope with obstacles such as unfeeling governments, strained relationships, bigotry, and misused communication media. My works reflect my optimism about our ability to solve old and new problems. It has always been more interesting to me to figure out how a person can find an inventive way to overcome an obstacle rather than explore ways that people can be beaten into submission."

*   *   *

STONE, I(sidor) F(einstein)   1907-1989

PERSONAL: Name originally Isidor Feinstein; legally changed, 1938; born December 24, 1907, in Philadelphia, PA; died of a heart condition, June 19, 1989, in Washington, DC; son of Bernard (a dry goods merchant) and Katherine (Novak) Feinstein; married Esther M. Roisman, July 7, 1929; children: Celia, Jeremy J., Christopher D. *Education:* Attended University of Pennsylvania, 1924-27.

ADDRESSES: Home—4420 29th St. N.W., Washington, DC 20008.

CAREER: Haddonfield Press, Haddonfield, NJ, reporter, 1923-24; *Courier Post,* Camden, NJ, reporter, 1924-25, reporter and editor, 1927-33; *Philadelphia Inquirer,* Philadelphia, PA, copy editor, 1925-27; *Philadelphia Record,* Philadelphia, editorial writer, 1933; *New York Post,* New York City, editorial writer, 1933-39; *The Nation,* New York City, associate editor, 1938-40, Washington editor, 1940-46; *PM, New York Star, New York Post,* and *New York Daily Compass,* all New York City, editorial writer and columnist, 1942-52; *I. F. Stone's Weekly,* Washington, DC, publisher and editor, 1953-67; *I. F. Stone's Bi-Weekly,* Washington, publisher and editor, 1967-71. Contributing editor of *New York Review of Books,* 1971-89; distinguished scholar in residence, American University, 1974.

AWARDS, HONORS: George Polk Memorial Award, Long Island University, 1970; journalism award, Columbia University, 1971; A. J. Liebling Award, 1972; Eleanor Roosevelt Peace Award, National Committee for a Sane Nuclear Policy, 1975. Earned honorary degrees from numerous educational institutions, including Amherst College, 1970, Brown University, 1971, Reed College, 1976, New School for Social Research and American University, both 1978, University of Southern California, 1981, and Colby College, 1982. Awarded A.B. degree from University of Pennsylvania and made official member of class of 1928, 1978.

WRITINGS:

The Court Disposes, Covici-Friede, 1937.

Business as Usual: The First Year of Defense, Modern Age, 1941.

Underground to Palestine, Boni & Gaer, 1946, reprinted with an additional segment, "Reflections and Meditations Thirty Years After," Pantheon, 1979.

This Is Israel, photographs by Robert Capa and others, Boni & Gaer, 1948.

The Hidden History of the Korean War (also see below), Monthly Review Press, 1952.

The Truman Era (collected articles; also see below), Monthly Review Press, 1953, new edition, Random House, 1972.

The Haunted Fifties (collected articles; also see below), Random House, 1963.

In a Time of Torment (collected articles; also see below), Random House, 1967.

Polemics and Prophecies, 1967-70 (also see below), Random House, 1970.

The Killings at Kent State: How Murder Went Unpunished, Vintage Books, 1971.

The I. F. Stone's Weekly Reader, Random House, 1973.

The Trial of Socrates, Little, Brown, 1988.

A Non-Conformist History of Our Times, Little, Brown, includes *The Hidden History of the Korean War, 1950-51,* 1988, *The Truman Era, 1945-1952,* 1988, *The War Years, 1939-1945* (collected articles), 1988, *The Haunted Fifties, 1953-1963,* 1989, *Polemics and Prophecies, 1967-1970,* 1989, and *In a Time of Torment,* 1989.

Also author of *The Best of I.F. Stone's Weekly.* Contributor of articles and reviews to numerous periodicals, including *New York Review of Books.*

ADAPTATIONS: A television special on I. F. Stone's life and work appeared on the National Educational Television Network in 1971; a one-hour movie, *I. F. Stone's Weekly,* was made by Gerry Brock, Jr.

WORK IN PROGRESS: Studies in "freedom of thought and expression in human society."

SIDELIGHTS: The late I. F. Stone spent an entire career debunking the claims of establishment politics. As an independent journalist and publisher of *I. F. Stone's Weekly,* Stone investigated the real truths behind the public statements issued from Washington's corridors of power. Throughout his long life, Stone enjoyed describing himself as an anarchist, a rebel, and a nonconformist. Reviewers often compared his weekly statements to the essays of the leading American muckrakers and the greatest of the Enlightenment pamphleteers, including Tom Paine, Alexis de Tocqueville, and Edmund Burke. *New York Times* contributor Peter B. Flint called the author "a tireless exam-

iner of public records, a hectoring critic of public officials, a persistent attacker of Government distortions and evasions and a pugnacious advocate of civil liberties, peace and truth."

Stone was born Isidor Feinstein in Philadelphia in 1907. While he was still young his parents moved to nearby Haddonfield, New Jersey, where they opened a dry goods store. As a youth Stone was a voracious reader who chafed at the restricting atmosphere of public schooling. At the age of fourteen he began a journalistic career with a friend when they published their own newspaper. Called *The Progressive,* Stone's little publication carried advertising, poetry, and editorials praising the likes of Woodrow Wilson, Gandhi, and the League of Nations. The venture lasted only a few months and was suspended because it interfered with Stone's schoolwork. The youthful foray into journalism, the highlight of Stone's otherwise lackluster school career, paved the way for other reporting jobs.

While still in high school Stone began working for the *Haddonfield Press.* Stone then majored in philosophy at the University of Pennsylvania, but he also managed to hold part-time positions with the Camden, New Jersey *Courier Post* and the *Philadelphia Inquirer.* By his junior year he had decided that the life of an academic was not particularly appealing, so he dropped out of college and returned to the *Courier Post* as a full-fledged reporter. In a little more than a decade, Stone moved from the paper in Camden to a succession of positions on left-wing dailies in New York City, especially the New York *Post.* He added the surname Stone and adopted the initials in his early thirties, making his pen name his legal name in 1938.

Early in his career Stone joined the Socialist party. He abandoned partisan politics, however, because he wanted to be unbiased in his investigative reporting. In 1938 he joined the staff of the *Nation,* a powerful liberal monthly. So popular did his work there prove that in 1940 he was named Washington editor for the magazine. By 1941 Stone had established himself as a relentless critic of the national government. In addition to his *Nation* editorials, he published a full-scale indictment of defense spending entitled *Business as Usual: The First Year of Defense.* Immediately following the Second World War, Stone became known as a spirited advocate of Jewish settlement in Palestine as well as an equally spirited critic of the Cold War politics.

In 1949 Stone joined the staff of the *New York Daily Compass* as a headlining columnist. When the *Daily Compass* folded in 1952, Stone found himself unemployed with no offers forthcoming—his radical views made him nearly untouchable. Stone was one of the few journalists who openly questioned America's involvement in the Korean War. His books *The Hidden History of the Korean War* and *The Truman Era* did not further endear him to establishment journalism, so he had to find an alternate means of support. With his wife's help, an investment of $6500 and the mailing list from two defunct liberal newspapers, he launched *I. F. Stone's Weekly,* his very own "little fleabit publication."

To quote Flint, issues of *I. F. Stone's Weekly* were "essentially one-man, four-page pamphlets that charged official Washington, particularly the Pentagon, with misleading the press and the people." Skeptical of government mouthpieces and their press conferences, Stone poured through official documents instead, unearthing a wealth of inconsistencies, contradictions, and evasions. These he exposed in his weekly, "hoisting the government on its own petard," as a *Washington Post Book World* writer put it. *New York Times* contributor David E. Rosenbaum wrote: "The newsletter was devoted to deflating the political establishment, and it led a generation of journalists, once young and now middle-aged, to hold [Stone] in awe." Long before it was fashionable to do so, Stone challenged McCarthyism, segregation, the nuclear arms race, and the Vietnam War, all of which he perceived as blots on democracy.

During the 1950s Stone was ostracized by the mainstream press and even attacked as a disloyal, un-American radical. Times changed, however, and the intrepid journalist's fortunes changed with them. *Washington Post* correspondent Jim Naughton wrote: "In the '60s Stone reaped the benefits of seeds sown many years earlier. The New Left adopted him as a hero and the circulation of the Weekly soared to 36,000. His integrity and enthusiasm had made him a cult figure. Many of today's most celebrated investigative reporters cite Stone as their inspiration." In fact Stone's influence was even greater than his paper's circulation might suggest, because many subscribers were political activists, academics, and other journalists. "Izzy" Stone found that he had lived long enough to become a national celebrity. "Those are the rewards of old age," he told the *Washington Post.* "When you are younger you get blamed for crimes you never committed and when you're older you begin to get credit for virtues you never possessed. It evens itself out."

Having set out on a shoestring budget with only his wife as an assistant, Stone eventually achieved not only notoriety but financial security as well. Circulation of *I. F. Stone's Weekly* hit 70,000 in the late 1960s when, to quote Peter Osnos in the *New York Times,* Stone "was at the height of his powers, as a writer, as a speaker, as an inspirer of the antiwar and civil rights movement." Unfortunately, ill health curtailed Stone's activities as the 1970s began. He had always suffered from deafness and poor eyesight, but he also developed heart trouble. For a time he published his paper on a bi-weekly basis, but in 1971

he reluctantly stepped down. He was not idle long, however. Despite his failing eyesight he embarked on an ambitious project to chart the history of freedom of thought and expression in society, and this led him to the study of ancient Greece, particularly Athens. He taught himself the ancient Greek language so he could read the primary sources, and he did his writing on a specially-adapted computer with very large type.

As he read about the democracy in Athens, Stone became more and more perplexed by that city's execution of Socrates, its most famous philosopher. Stone began working on a book that would present Socrates not from the perspective of his adoring pupil Plato, but rather from the point of view of Athenian citizens who perceived him as a threat to their government. *The Trial of Socrates* was published in 1988 and—to Stone's amazement—found its way onto the *New York Times* bestseller list. *New York Times* reviewer Christopher Lehmann-Haupt noted that in *The Trial of Socrates,* "Western Civilization's first great philosopher stands accused of snobbery, class prejudice, conceit, arrogance, negativism and coldness to his wife. Behind the famous irony lay an insulting sneer of contempt, or so Mr. Stone argues." Stone's ultimate point— that Socrates actually held democracy in contempt— excited a great deal of critical debate when the book was published. In the *New York Review of Books,* M. F. Burnyeat concluded that, questionable though Stone's assertions may be, "the attack on Socrates does not spring from intemperance, but from Stone's devotion to ancient Athens, cradle of freedom, democracy, and the love of justice and truth. These are the values for which Stone has fought, on behalf of us all, in the contemporary world."

Much of Stone's work is still in print, including his book about Israel, *Underground to Palestine.* Stone died of heart trouble in 1989, and journalists across the country lamented his loss. A *Washington Post* editorial writer claimed that the author "spent his life with his face pressed against the window. He was not wistful about it, and certainly not self-pitying. The wonder of his life and his work was that he showed so many people that outside was the place to be if you really want to know what is happening on the inside." Also in the *Washington Post,* Eric Alterman maintained that Stone's "complete lack of pretension and fiercely independent intellectual ethic were contagious. His inability to countenance conventional wisdom inspired a similar skepticism in those who spent time with him." Alterman concluded: "[Stone's] patriotism was not the flag-waving kind. It was based on a determination to hold his government to the same standards of honesty and fairness he had been taught when he was growing up outside Philadelphia."

Reflecting on his career late in life, Stone told the *Chicago Tribune:* "Some people become radical out of hatred. Others become radical out of love and sympathy. I come out of the second class. I have hated very few people." He told the *Village Voice* that his strong views were the by-product of an essential optimism. "I have faith," he said, "despite the imperfections of the human race, that a better society, a better world, a more just world, a kindlier world can come into being."

BIOGRAPHICAL/CRITICAL SOURCES:

BOOKS

Paterson, Thomas G., editor, *Cold War Critics: Alternatives to American Foreign Policy in the Truman Years,* Quadrangle, 1971.
Patner, Andrew, *I. F. Stone: A Portrait,* Pantheon, 1988.

PERIODICALS

Chicago Tribune, January 6, 1988.
Chicago Tribune Books, February 14, 1988.
Christian Science Monitor, November 30, 1967.
Commonweal, January 26, 1968.
Globe & Mail (Toronto), April 30, 1988.
Life, January 21, 1972.
Listener, October 24, 1968; October 31, 1968.
Los Angeles Times Book Review, February 14, 1988; February 26, 1989.
Mother Jones, June, 1988.
Nation, April 14, 1979.
New Republic, January 27, 1979.
Newsday, January 20, 1968.
Newsweek, December 20, 1971.
New York Review of Books, December 5, 1968; March 31, 1988.
New York Times, November 19, 1968, December 24, 1987, January 18, 1988.
New York Times Book Review, February 7, 1988.
People, April 18, 1988.
Ramparts, February, 1968.
Rolling Stone, April 21, 1988.
Time, February 8, 1971.
Village Voice, December 23, 1971.
Wall Street Journal, July 14, 1970.
Washington Post, June 3, 1970; December 7, 1971; July 9, 1979; March 21, 1983; March 10, 1988; June 20, 1989.
Washington Post Book World, February 25, 1979; February 14, 1988; April 30, 1989.

OBITUARIES:

PERIODICALS

Chicago Tribune, June 21, 1989.
Detroit News, June 19, 1989.
Globe & Mail (Toronto), June 24, 1989.
New York Times, June 19, 1989; June 20, 1989.

Washington Post, July 18, 1989; July 19, 1989.*

—*Sketch by Anne Janette Johnson*

*   *   *

STONE, Ronald H. 1939-

PERSONAL: Born March 26, 1939, in Humboldt, IA; son of Hubert Henry (a contractor) and Bernice (a teacher; maiden name, Tilton) Stone; married Joann Loftus (divorced); married Bebb Wheeler Roberts, 1984; children: (first marriage) Randall Warren, Patricia Bernice. *Education:* Morningside College, B.A., 1960; Union Theological Seminary, New York, NY, B.D., 1963; Columbia University, Ph.D., 1968. *Politics:* Democrat. *Religion:* Presbyterian.

ADDRESSES: Home—6052 Grafton St., Pittsburgh, PA 15206. *Office*—Pittsburgh Theological Seminary, 616 N. Highland Ave., Pittsburgh, PA 15206.

CAREER: United Church of Christ, New York City, assistant to secretary of international relations, 1961-63; Morningside College, Sioux City, IA, instructor, summers, 1964, 1965; Union Theological Seminary, New York City, instructor in social ethics, 1967-68; Columbia University, New York City, assistant professor of religion, 1968-69; Pittsburgh Theological Seminary, Pittsburgh, PA, associate professor of ethics, 1970-72, professor of social ethics, 1972—. Vassar College, visiting instructor in ethics, 1967; Union Theological Seminary, lecturer, 1968-69; University of Pittsburgh, adjunct professor and coordinator of doctoral program in religious studies, 1974-77.

MEMBER: American Society of Christian Ethics, American Academy of Religion, American Theological Society, Society for Values in Higher Education.

AWARDS, HONORS: Reinhold Niebuhr: Prophet to Politician was named a noteworthy title by the *New York Times Book Review,* 1972; Association of Theological Schools fellowships, 1972, 1975, 1985, 1990.

WRITINGS:

(Editor and author of introduction) *Reinhold Niebuhr, Faith and Politics: Essays on Religion, Social and Political Thought in a Technological Age,* Braziller, 1968.
Reinhold Niebuhr: Prophet to Politician, Abingdon, 1972.
Realism and Hope (essays), University Press of America, 1977.
(Editor and author of introduction) Gustavo Gutierrez and Richard M. Shaull, *Liberation and Change,* John Knox, 1977.
Paul Tillich's Radical Social Thought, John Knox, 1980.

(Editor and author of introduction) *Reformed Faith and Politics,* University Press of America, 1983.
Christian Realism and Peacemaking, Abingdon, 1988.
Reformed Urban Ethics: Case Study of Pittsburgh, Mellen Research University Press, 1991.

Contributor to periodicals, including *Commonweal, Religion in Life, Christianity and Crisis,* and *Worldview.* Editor of *Social Action,* 1968.

SIDELIGHTS: Professor of social ethics at Pittsburgh Theological Seminary, Ronald H. Stone is committed "to tuning the Christian message to the secularizing culture," observes Julian N. Hartt in the *New York Times Book Review.* In his book *Paul Tillich's Radical Social Thought,* Stone postulates that the German philosopher and theologian advocated a socialistic form of government that was non-Communist and thus not hindered by the theological shortcomings of Marxist thought. Hartt further describes Stone as "particularly helpful in discussing Tillich's relations with the Frankfurt school of social analysis (including such thinkers as Theodor Adorno and Herbert Marcuse), but not so helpful in relating Tillich's views to American political realities."

BIOGRAPHICAL/CRITICAL SOURCES:

PERIODICALS

Best Sellers, February 15, 1972.
Commonweal, May 5, 1972.
New York Times Book Review, October 6, 1968; March 5, 1972; April 19, 1981.

*   *   *

STONE, Scott C(linton) S(tuart)   1932-

PERSONAL: Born August 4, 1932, in Polk County, TN; son of Randall and Stella (Beaver) Stone; married Barbara Miyashiro, August 8, 1953 (divorced, 1974); married Walelu Lehua, September 30, 1983; children: (first marriage) Alison Tauhere Stone Beddow, Erik Stuart. *Education:* East Tennessee State University, B.S., 1957. *Politics:* Independent. *Religion:* Roman Catholic.

ADDRESSES: Home—P.O. Box 1119, Volcano, HI 96785. *Agent*—Oscar Collier, 2000 Flat Run Rd., Seaman, OH 45679.

CAREER: Began writing as a stringer for the *Chattanooga Times* at age fourteen; reporter on paper on Johnson City, TN, 1955-57; *Dayton Daily News,* Dayton, OH, reporter, 1957-58; *Honolulu Advertiser,* Honolulu, HI, military editor, 1958-63, assistant city editor, 1963-68. Correspondent in Hawaii and Asia for Reuters, 1961-71, and for *National Observer,* 1963-68. Delegate to Smithsonian Institution's

Writers Dialogue on Communications in connection with the National Museum of the American Indian, 1991. *Military service:* Enlisted correspondent in Korea, U.S. Navy and Marine Corps, 1951-54. U.S. Army Reserve, 1960-62; became captain. U.S. Navy Reserve, 1962-87, became commander; served three periods of active duty in Vietnam.

MEMBER: Naval Reserve Association, Reserve Officers Association, Niadh Nask (ancient Gaelic fraternity), Foreign Correspondents Club (Hong Kong).

AWARDS, HONORS: Two Honolulu Press Club awards for reporting from Asia; Edgar Allan Poe Award, Mystery Writers of America, 1970, for *The Dragon's Eye;* first place award for best travel film in America, Discover America Travel Organization, 1973, for *The Possible Dream;* also received various military decorations.

WRITINGS:

The Coasts of War (novel), Pyramid Books, 1966.
A Share of Honor (novel), Lippincott, 1969.
The Dragon's Eye (novel), Fawcett, 1969.
Pearl Harbor: The Way It Was, December 7, 1941, Island Heritage, 1976.
Volcano!!, Island Heritage, 1978.
Spies (novel), St. Martin's, 1980.
(With John E. McGowan) *Wrapped in the Wind's Shawl: Southeast Asia Refugees and the Western World,* Presidio Press, 1980.
Honolulu: Heart of Hawaii, Continental Heritage, 1983.
Land of Fire and Snow, Island Heritage, 1983.
Song of the Wolf (novel), Arbor House, 1985.
Scimitar (novel), Worldwide Library, 1989.
The Dragon Legacy (novel), Taiwan Press, 1989.
The Story of C. Brewer, Island Heritage, 1991.
Infamy and Aftermath, Island Heritage, 1991.
He Mele O Hawaii (title means "A Song of Hawaii"), Copperfield, 1992.

Also author of travel film *The Possible Dream,* 1973. *The Coasts of War* has been published in several countries, including Spain, Sweden, and Denmark; *The Dragon's Eye* has been published in Germany and Sweden.

ADAPTATIONS: Motion Pictures International purchased the film rights to *The Coasts of War.*

WORK IN PROGRESS: Terra Nova; Pavanne, a novel.

SIDELIGHTS: Scott C. S. Stone told *CA:* "I've been the luckiest of men in that my job required me to travel, and travel provided background for most of the books . . . almost all of my books have Asia/Pacific settings. My motivation in writing now is the same as it was then—to try to bring alive this fascinating part of the world, to simply tell a good story. My ancestry is European, my outlook

Pacific, and I think this dual nature will become more common as Americans look to the East in the future as much as they looked to the West in the past. Happily, a few of my books have had foreign publishers, and this ability to reach readers beyond the U.S. is important to me."

BIOGRAPHICAL/CRITICAL SOURCES:

PERIODICALS

Asia Week, April 3, 1981.
Baltimore Daily Record, July 30, 1985.
Boston Globe, June 26, 1969.
Honolulu Advertiser, February 27, 1966; October 19, 1969; May 3, 1972; October 23, 1977; January 18, 1978.
Honolulu Star-Bulletin, May 13, 1970.
New York Times Book Review, May 11, 1969; October 12, 1980.
Public Affairs Quarterly, fall, 1981.
Washington Post, July 15, 1985.

*   *   *

STOTT, John R. W. 1921-

PERSONAL: Born April 27, 1921, in London, England; son of Arnold and Emily Caroline (Holland) Stott. *Education:* Trinity College, Cambridge, B.A., 1943, M.A., 1947; attended Ridley Hall, Cambridge, 1944-45. *Avocational interests:* Bird watching, bird photography.

ADDRESSES: Home and office—12 Weymouth St., London W1, England.

CAREER: Ordained minister, Church of England, 1945; All Souls Church, London, England, assistant curate, 1945-50, rector, 1950-75, rector emeritus, 1975—; London Institute for Contemporary Christianity, London, director, 1982-86, president, 1986—. Appointed chaplain to Her Majesty, Elizabeth II, 1959-91, and served as extra chaplain, 1991. Has conducted periodical university missions in Canada, the United States, Australia, New Zealand, Africa, Southeast Asia, and Great Britain, 1952-77. Honorary general secretary of Evangelical Fellowship in Anglican Communion, 1960-81; president, Universities and Colleges Christian Fellowship, 1961-62, 1971-72, 1977-78, and 1981-82, British Scripture Union, 1974, British Evangelical Alliance, 1973-74, and TEAR Fund (honorary), 1983—. Chairman, Church of England Evangelical Council, 1967-84, National Evangelical Literature Trust, 1971—, and council of management of Care and Counsel (Christian service organization), 1975-81; vice-president for Europe, United Bible Societies, 1982-85. Executive, Lausanne Continuation Committee, 1974-81.

AWARDS, HONORS: D.D., Lambeth, Cambridge University, 1983.

WRITINGS:

Men with a Message, Longmans, Green, 1954, published as *Basic Introduction to the New Testament,* Eerdmans, 1964.
Fundamentalism and Evangelism, Crusade, 1956, Eerdmans, 1959.
Basic Christianity, Inter-Varsity Press (London), 1958, Eerdmans, 1959, revised edition, Inter-Varsity Press (London), 1971.
What Christ Thinks of the Church, Lutterworth, 1958, Eerdmans, 1959, revised edition published as *Word,* Harold Shaw, 1990.
Your Confirmation, Hodder & Stoughton, 1958, revised edition, 1991.
The Preacher's Portrait, Eerdmans, 1961.
The Epistles of John, Eerdmans, 1964.
Confess Your Sins, Hodder & Stoughton, 1964, Westminster, 1965.
Men Made New, Inter-Varsity Press (London), 1966, Inter-Varsity Press (Chicago), 1967.
The Canticles and Selected Psalms, Hodder & Stoughton, 1966.
Our Guilty Silence, Hodder & Stoughton, 1967, Eerdmans, 1969.
Only One Way, Inter-Varsity Press (Chicago), 1968.
One People, Falcon, 1969, Inter-Varsity Press (Chicago), 1970, revised edition, Fleming Revell, 1982.
Christ the Controversialist, Tyndale, 1970, Inter-Varsity Press (Chicago), 1972.
Understanding the Bible, Scripture Union, 1972.
Your Mind Matters, Inter-Varsity Press (Chicago), 1972.
Guard the Gospel, Inter-Varsity Press (London), 1973.
The Lausanne Covenant, World Wide Publications, 1975, published as *Explaining the Lausanne Covenant,* Scripture Union, 1975.
Balanced Christianity, Inter-Varsity Press (Chicago), 1975.
Christian Mission in the Modern World, Inter-Varsity Press (Chicago), 1975.
Baptism and Fullness, Inter-Varsity Press (Chicago), 1975.
Christian Counter-Culture, Inter-Varsity Press (Chicago), 1978.
God's New Society, Inter-Varsity Press (Chicago), 1979.
Focus on Christ, Collins, 1979.
The Bible Book for Today, Inter-Varsity Press (Chicago), 1982, published as *You Can Trust the Bible,* Discovery House, 1990.
I Believe in Preaching, Eerdmans, 1982, published as *Between Two Worlds,* 1982.
Issues Facing Christians Today, Marshalls, 1984, Revell, 1985, revised edition published as *Decisive Issues Facing Christians Today,* Revell, 1990.
The Authentic Jesus, Inter-Varsity Press (Chicago), 1985.

The Cross of Christ, Inter-Varsity Press (Chicago), 1986.
(With David L. Edwards) *Essentials,* Hodder & Stoughton, 1988.

"BIBLE SPEAKS TODAY" SERIES

The Message of Galatians: Only One Way, Inter-Varsity Press (Chicago), 1968.

The Message of 2 Timothy: Guard the Gospel, Inter-Varsity Press, 1973.

The Message of the Sermon on the Mount: Christian Counter-Culture, Inter-Varsity Press (Chicago), 1978.

The Message of Ephesians: God's New Society, Inter-Varsity Press (Chicago), 1979.

The Message of Acts: To the Ends of the Earth, Inter-Varsity Press (Chicago), 1990.

The Message of Thessalonians: Preparing for the Coming King, Inter-Varsity Press (Chicago), 1991.

*   *   *

STRAND, Mark 1934-

PERSONAL: Born April 11, 1934, in Summerside, Prince Edward Island, Canada; son of Robert Joseph (a salesman) and Sonia (Apter) Strand; married Antonia Ratensky, September 14, 1961 (divorced, 1974); married Julia Garretson, March 15, 1976; children: (first marriage) Jessica. *Education:* Antioch College, B.A., 1957; Yale University, B.F.A., 1959; State University of Iowa, M.A., 1962.

ADDRESSES: Home—475 3rd Ave., Salt Lake City, UT 84103. *Office*—Department of English, University of Utah, Salt Lake City, UT 84102.

CAREER: University of Iowa, Iowa City, instructor in English, 1962-65; University of Brazil, Rio de Janeiro, Fulbright lecturer, 1965-66; Mount Holyoke College, South Hardley, MA, assistant professor, 1967; Brooklyn College of the City University of New York, New York City, associate professor, 1970-72; Princeton University, Princeton, NJ, Bain-Swiggett Lecturer, 1973—; University of Utah, Salt Lake City, professor of English, 1981—. Visiting professor at University of Washington, 1968, 1970, Columbia University, 1969, 1980, Yale University, 1969-70, University of Virginia, 1977, and Harvard University, 1980. Columbia University, adjunct associate professor, 1969-72.

AWARDS, HONORS: Fulbright scholarship for study in Italy, 1960-61; Ingram Merrill Foundation grant, 1966; National Endowment for the Arts grant, 1967-68, 1978-79, and 1986-87; Rockefeller Foundation grant, 1968-69; Edgar Allan Poe award, Academy of American Poets, 1974, for *The Story of Our Lives;* National Institute

of Arts and Letters and American Academy awards in Literature, both 1975; Guggenheim fellowship, 1975-76; Fellowship of the Academy of American Poets, 1979; *Selected Poems* was named one of the American Library Association's Notable Books for 1980; MacArthur Foundation fellowship, 1987; U.S. Poet Laureate, Library of Congress, 1990.

WRITINGS:

POETRY

Sleeping with One Eye Open, Stone Wall Press, 1964.
Reasons for Moving, Atheneum, 1968.
Darker, Atheneum, 1970.
The Story of Our Lives, Atheneum, 1973.
The Sargeantville Notebook, Burning Deck, 1974.
Elegy for My Father, Windhover, 1978.
The Late Hour, Atheneum, 1978.
Selected Poems, Atheneum, 1980.
The Continuous Life, Knopf, 1990.

CHILDREN'S BOOKS

The Planet of Lost Things, illustrated by William Pene du Bois, C. N. Potter, 1982.
The Night Book, illustrated by Pene du Bois, C. N. Potter, 1983.
Rembrandt Takes a Walk, illustrated by Red Grooms, C. N. Potter, 1986.

OTHER

(Editor) *The Contemporary American Poets,* New American Library, 1968.
(Editor) *New Poetry of Mexico,* Dutton, 1970.
(Editor and translator) *18 Poems from the Quechua,* Halty Ferguson, 1971.
(Editor and translator) Rafael Alberti, *The Owl's Insomnia,* Atheneum, 1973.
(Editor with Charles Simic) *Another Republic: Seventeen European and South American Writers,* Ecco, 1976.
(Translator) Carlos Drummond de Andrade, *Souvenir of the Ancient World,* Antaeus Editions, 1976.
The Monument (prose), Ecco, 1978.
(Contributor) *Claims for Poetry,* edited by Donald Hall, University of Michigan Press, 1982.
(Editor) *The Art of the Real* (art criticism), C. N. Potter, 1983.
Mr. and Mrs. Baby and Other Stories (short stories), Knopf, 1985.
(Editor with Thomas Colchie; translator with Elizabeth Bishop, Colchie, and Gregory Rabassa) Carlos Drummond de Andrade, *Traveling in the Family,* Random House, 1987.
William Bailey (art criticism), Abrams, 1987.

Contributor of articles, reviews and essays to numerous periodicals, including the *New York Times Book Review* and *Quarterly West*.

WORK IN PROGRESS: More poems; short stories, essays and a novel.

SIDELIGHTS: Recognized as one of the premier contemporary American poets as well as an accomplished editor, translator and prose writer, Mark Strand's hallmarks are precise language, surreal imagery, and the recurring theme of absence and negation. Named the U.S. Poet Laureate in 1990, Strand has spent the past three decades crafting poetry that has won numerous accolades from critics as well as found a loyal following among readers.

Born on Prince Edward Island, Canada, Strand grew up in various cities across the United States due to the frequent relocation of his father, a salesman. As a youngster, Strand expressed an interest in painting and hoped to become an artist. His interest waned, however, and by the age of twenty, he decided to become a poet instead. "I was never much good with language as a child," Strand recalled during an interview with Bill Thomas for the *Los Angeles Times Magazine*. "Believe me, the idea that I would someday become a poet would have come as a complete shock to everyone in my family." Perhaps even more shocking to Strand himself is the level of popularity and critical acclaim he has achieved with his verse. His 1990 collection of poems, *The Continuous Life*, went into a second printing within a year of publication; his poetry readings are usually standing-room-only. "I think of my readers as being my friends, but I sell more books than I have friends, so I must have readers somewhere," he told Thomas.

Following college graduation, Strand began teaching at various colleges and universities, including Yale, Princeton, and Harvard. Although his primary concern was writing poetry, Strand found teaching essential to paying his bills. "The most money I've ever made from a poem?" he mused for Thomas. "Well, it would have to be something I sold in the 1970s to the *New Yorker*. They paid me $1,100. Big money in those days. It's big money today. They ran that one for two full pages. But $1,100 poems, I can assure you, are few and far between." Despite the lack of financial rewards in writing poetry, Strand admitted there were some benefits to being a poet during the turbulent 1960s. "Groupies were a big part of the scene," he told Thomas. "Poets were underground pop stars, and when we made the campus circuit, girls would flock around. It wasn't bad. I rather liked the uncertainties of my life then."

Strand paved the way to fame in 1964 with his first book, *Sleeping with One Eye Open*. It was here that Strand debuted his distinctive approach to poetry. "The restlessness

of his personae—as evidenced by the title poem—and the general sense of apprehension and foreboding form the dark backdrop for all Strand's writing," wrote Thomas McClanahan in the *Dictionary of Literary Biography*. In the first stanza of the frequently anthologized poem "Keeping Things Whole," Strand sets the tone and presents the themes which continue to dominate his later work: "In a field/ I am the absence/ of field./ This is/ always the case./ Wherever I am/ I am what is missing." "These lines distill [Strand's] metaphysics, a kind of reversed Cartesianism wherein to be is not to be and thinking throws existing into question," observed Sven Birkerts in the *New Republic*.

The speakers in Strand's early poetry are characterized by an intense concern with self and identity. David Kirby remarked in *Mark Strand and the Poet's Place in Contemporary Culture:* "Many poems in Strand's first book show an uneasy preoccupation with self, and the vehicle used to express that preoccupation is often a dream state in which the speaker is divided between two worlds and can locate himself comfortably in neither." The identity theme that permeates the poems collected in *Sleeping with One Eye Open* is woven through Strand's later work, as well. "The basic themes are treated in the poems with a growing unease that the reader feels more intensely than before—as his skill increases, so does the poet's power to disturb," Kirby explained. Strand related his view of the self in poetry in a 1971 interview excerpted by McClanahan: "The sense of self I have is coordinated and related in ways that depend on a high degree of selection. It is a chosen self. The way memory is chosen. But the raw self is me, too, just as I am also much more than I choose to remember at any given time. . . . the true self may reside in the unremembered, unorganized, unthought of." McClanahan views the comment as an "instructive perspective from which to view [Strand's] poetry."

Strand's reputation as a dark, brooding poet haunted by death was built upon his early collections of poetry but Strand himself does not call them "especially dark," he told Thomas. "I find them evenly lit," he continued. 1970's *Darker* convinced critics of Strand's affirmation of life despite his concern with its limitations. "We have seen in [Strand's] first two books both the expression of certain morbid concerns and the dawning of possible remedies to them. It would make sense to expect a lessening of the morbidity and a corresponding increase in self-awareness in this next book, but poetry doesn't necessarily work that way," Kirby theorized. "The New Poetry Handbook," included in the beginning of *Darker*, bespeaks Strand's slight shift in perspective. While many of the poems that follow it express a concern with the apparent meaninglessness of life, "The New Poetry Handbook" offers a solution: poetry. Strand seriously considers the place of poetry in the universe, concluding that when "a man finishes a poem/ he shall bathe in the blank wake of his passion/ and be kissed by white paper." Kirby viewed the poem as an answer to the problem of self. "Strand is now saying that poetry can be curative as well as expressive, and from this point on in his work poetry will figure not only as a medium but also as a subject," he concluded.

While Strand's focus had grown to include an affirmation of the positive, he remained "a poet of mood, of integrated fragments, of twilit landscape, and of longing," wrote Henri Cole in *Poetry*. In 1980's *Selected Poems*, Strand relies on an "ethereal, cumulative effect" to express the idea that "the two fixed points of a man's life are the self and God; both are darknesses, one leading to another," Cole continued. In the prose poem "Two Letters," Strand further expounds his philosophy: "With death always imminent, do we not keep hoping to be reborn? This is the human condition. We are citizens of one world only when we apply to the next; we are perpetual exiles, living on the outside of what is possible." In the *New York Review of Books*, Irvin Ehrenpreis found a weakness in the recurring theme of elusiveness of self in *Selected Poems:* "For all his mastery of rhythm and music, Strand does not open the lyric to the world but makes it a self-sustaining enterprise." Ehrenpreis criticized this concern with self because it moves toward solipsism—the belief that the self is the only existent thing. "If I recommend the short lyric of self-definition as the proper modern poem, it is not because the character of a poet is the most important focus of a literary work," he continued. "It is because through this frame the poet can describe human nature and the world." Strand, Ehrenpreis concluded, does not achieve this purpose.

In 1982, Strand made a foray into the children's literature market with *The Planet of Lost Things*. As with his poetry, Strand focused on questions of loss, using the story to address the common childhood worry about where things go when they are lost. "Strand's book is ambitious in the very fact of its taking on such a many-layered riddle, but confused and divided about the terms of the story's resolution," observed Leonard S. Marcus in the *Washington Post Book World*. The story centers around a boy who dreams his rocketship lands on a planet where he finds all the missing items of everyday life, from lost pets to misplaced change. He soon meets the inhabitants of the planet, a man and a woman named Unknown Soldier and Missing Person. They take the boy on a sightseeing tour of their planet, pointing out such highlights as a region of extinct animals, the place "where everything goes that magicians make disappear," and even a collection of all the helium balloons that ever escaped human hands. Although his tour guides' aimless wandering causes him to forget where he has left his rocket, the boy eventually chances upon it and quickly returns home, only to awaken in his bed with

a just a vague memory of his strange dream. Marcus finds that *The Planet of Lost Things*' "beguiling, rarefied atmosphere is the aura of the uncanny. In such an atmosphere, so aptly fitted to the open-ended, unself-conscious questioning of children, the final resort to stage magicians' vanished properties is a diminishment, a sentimental reduction of the story's sense of the magical; the boy's 'perfect' takeoff as he heads home seems emblematic of a sleek technical exercise at the end of which [the book] remains largely unexplored."

Strand's second children's story, *The Night Book*, was written for an audience aged three to six and is appropriately simple. The story, about a girl who is so frightened of the dark that she has her dog keep watch for monsters by the window, is "a cheerful, brief story with the luxurious paintings of Pene du Bois," wrote Kristina Gregory in the *Los Angeles Times Book Review*. In *Rembrandt Takes a Walk*, Strand ventures back into the fantastic, this time telling the story of a young boy who finds himself in the company of Rembrandt when the fifteenth century painter miraculously steps out of a self-portrait the boy's rich uncle keeps in his world-class collection. Young Tom's adventures with the old master and his eventual success in convincing him to return to his painting will likely charm adults more than children, opined J. Hoberman in the *New York Times Book Review*. "The premise is as precious as the art historical references are arcane," Hoberman continued. "Mr. Strand's tone wavers between the patronizing and the bland. Even if the reader is amused by the notion of Rembrandt rearranging a Cezanne to suit himself, he is unlikely to find Rembrandt's pet explicatives—'Holy Hollandaise!' and 'Great Gouda'—anything more than feeble."

A frequent contributor of short stories to periodicals, Strand decided to publish a collection of prose narratives in 1985. The resulting volume, entitled *Mr. and Mrs. Baby*, featured as its title story the tale of Bob and Babe Baby, a stereotypical California couple who are completely absorbed in their trivial lives. Strand's recurrent concern with the superficiality of life is clearly apparent in this satirical tale, which Alan Cheuse of the *Los Angeles Times Book Review* described as "a mixture of irony and affection." Other stories in the collection include one about a man who confesses to his wife that he used to be a collie and another about a man convinced his deceased father has been reincarnated in the form of a fly. "These prose inventions," Cheuse continued, "give us the privilege of watching a first-rate artist try out his genius in another mode."

Strand "brings to prose fiction many of the special attributes of his poems. One might expect in Strand's stories the immaculately refined and spare language and sensibility of his poems . . . and the collection fulfills that expectation exactly," wrote Catherine Petroski in the *Chicago Tribune.* Describing the stories as "odd, surrealistic sketches of alienation and rootlessness," *New York Times* critic Michiko Kakutani found them "so slight, so tentative, that they evaporate into the air." Strand's characters, Kakutani criticized, are like Strand himself—"so obsessed with death and the shadow that death casts over our existence . . . that they haven't time to savor everyday joys and pains." The collection elicited praise from Ellen Lesser of the *Village Voice,* who wrote: "By far the greatest pleasures of *Mr and Mrs. Baby* are not to be found in its mysteries, comic vision, or even its hapless picture of the contemporary male, but rather in the writing. On practically every page, one can be dazzled by Strand's language. When it comes to turning a shimmering phrase, he has the touch of a poet."

While Strand devoted time over the next decade to editing and translating the works of others, in 1990 he published another collection of poems entitled *The Continuous Life.* In the *New York Times Book Review,* Alfred Corn commented that the book "doesn't strike me so much as a capstone of Mr. Strand's career as one more turning in his development." Corn pointed to changes in meter, diction and point of view. "This is a poetry written, as it were, in the shadow of high mountains, and touched with their grandeur," he concluded. Michael Dirda of the *Washington Post Book World* maintained that the book showed Strand "writing at his absolute peak." Dirda praised the collection's diverse range of poetic styles and structures, adding that Strand "writes with mastery in any style he chooses." Strand's appointment as U.S. Poet Laureate brought the book even more attention. Dirda declared, "These are terrific poems. Mark Strand's not the poet laureate for nothing."

In his role as poet laureate, Strand found ample opportunity to display his "open comic flair," a quality that has turned him into "the Steve Martin or Woody Allen of modern verse," according to Larry Kart of Chicago *Tribune Books.* Strand lamented the lack of a job description for the poet laureate, a year-long post awarded by the Library of Congress, in an interview for the *Los Angeles Times Magazine.* "That's probably because there isn't much popular interest in poetry, or good literature," he admitted to Thomas. "The junk people read is appalling. . . . Unfortunately, even with the title of poet laureate, there's not much I can do about it." Strand conceded that poetry may not be for everyone. "In a way, I suppose, poetry *is* elitist," he observed. "You have to read well to read poetry, and the sad fact is that most people don't have the patience or the talent to do that." Jane Candia Coleman summarized Strand's role as contemporary American poet in *Western American Literature:* "Mark Strand is not a poet for Everyone. His is not work that will be set

to music or sung on the streets. The cursory reader will be bewildered, lost. But the reader who delves, who meets the poet halfway, will be rewarded by glimpses of a different world, that changeable one of dreams and the elusive beauty that haunts us all."

BIOGRAPHICAL/CRITICAL SOURCES:

BOOKS

Contemporary Literary Criticism, Gale, Volume 41, 1987, pp. 431-441, Volume 71, 1992, pp. 277-291.
Dictionary of Literary Biography, Volume 5: *American Poets since World War II,* edited by Donald J. Greiner, Gale, 1980, pp. 308-309.
Kirby, David, *Mark Strand and the Poet's Place in Contemporary Culture,* University of Missouri Press, 1990.
Strand, Mark, *Darker,* Atheneum, 1970.
Strand, *The Planet of Lost Things,* C. N. Potter, 1982.
Strand, *Selected Poems,* Atheneum, 1980.
Strand, *Sleeping with One Eye Open,* Stone Wall Press, 1964.

PERIODICALS

Chicago Tribune, March 24, 1985.
Los Angeles Times Book Review, June 2, 1985, p. 1; May 18, 1986, p. 13.
Los Angeles Times Magazine, January 13, 1991, p. 14.
New Republic, December 17, 1990, pp. 36-38.
New York Review of Books, October 8, 1981, pp. 45-47.
New York Times, March 13, 1985.
New York Times Book Review, November 9, 1986, p. 54; March 24, 1991, p. 26; September 15, 1991, pp. 36-37.
Poetry, April, 1991, pp. 54-57.
Tribune Books (Chicago), December 23, 1990, p. 4.
Village Voice, April 30, 1985, p. 47.
Washington Post Book World, November 7, 1982, p. 17; March 3, 1991, p. 6.
Western American Literature, summer, 1991, pp. 178-179.

—*Sketch by Cornelia A. Pernik*

*　　*　　*

SYDNEY, Cynthia
   See TRALINS, S(andor) Robert

*　　*　　*

SZOEVERFFY, Joseph 1920-

PERSONAL: Born June 19, 1920, in Clausenbourgh, Transylvania (now part of Romania); came to the United States in 1962, naturalized U.S. citizen; son of Louis (a businessman) and Anna Ilona (von Simkovith) de Szoeverffy. *Education:* St. Emeric College, Budapest, Hungary, B.A., 1939; Budapest University, Ph.D., 1943; State Teachers College, Budapest, staatsexamen, 1944; University of Fribourg, Dr.Phil.Habil., 1950. *Religion:* Armenian Catholic. *Avocational interests:* Higher education reform in the United States, photography, journalism and public opinion, public lecturing on East-Central European affairs, folklore, mythology, modern culture.

ADDRESSES: Home—374 Canton St., Randolph, MA 02368.

CAREER: Budapest University, Budapest, Hungary, assistant professor of German philology, 1943-48; Hungarian General Credit Bank, Budapest, assistant to the vice-president, 1944-48; Glenstal College, County Limerick, Ireland, professor of modern languages, 1950-52; Irish Folklore Commission, University College, Dublin, Ireland, archivist and special research librarian, 1952-57; University of Ottawa, Ottawa, Ontario, lecturer in classics, 1957-58, assistant professor of classical and medieval Latin literature, 1958-59; University of Alberta, Edmonton, assistant professor, 1959-61, associate professor of Germanic philology and German literature, 1961-62; Yale University, New Haven, CT, associate professor of medieval German literature and philology and fellow of Calhoun College, 1962-65; Boston College, Chestnut Hill, MA, professor of German and medieval studies, 1965-70; State University of New York at Albany, professor of comparative and world literature and of German, 1970-77, chairman of department, 1972-75.

University of Fribourg, Fribourg, Switzerland, visiting lecturer in medieval studies, 1949-50; visiting professor, University of Poitiers, 1961, and University of Vienna, 1984-88; Harvard University, James C. Loeb memorial lecturer, 1967, visiting professor, 1968, honorary research associate, 1975—; Dumbarton Oaks Center for Byzantine Studies, Washington, DC, visiting professor of Byzantine studies, 1977-78; Freie University, Berlin, Richard Merton Visiting Professor of Medieval Studies, 1980-83. Fellow, Center of Medieval and Renaissance Studies, 1973—, and Institute for Advanced Study, Berlin, 1982-83. State University of New York, lifetime faculty exchange scholar, 1974—. Dumbarton Oaks Center for Byzantine Studies, project director, 1984-87. Foederatio Emericana in Budapest, secretary-general, 1943-46; Institute for Early Christian Iberian Studies, member of board of directors. Public speaker.

MEMBER: International Platform Association, Internationale Vereinigung der Germanisten, Comparative Literature Association, Modern Language Association of America, Mediaeval Academy of America, American Folklore Society, American Association of University Professors, American Association of Teachers of German, Canadian Linguistic Association, Northeast Modern Language Association (chairman of Renaissance and Baroque section, 1972-74), Connecticut Academy of Arts and Sciences.

AWARDS, HONORS: Folklore prize, University of Chicago, 1954; Canada Council lecture grant, 1960-61; American Council of Learned Societies grants, 1960-61, 1964, 1967; Guggenheim fellowships, 1961, 1969-70, grants, 1963, 1965, 1970, 1975; American Philosophical Society fellowships, 1964-65, 1973; Ella Lyman Cabot grant, 1965; Federal Republic of Germany grant, 1969; Government of Portugal grant, 1969; State University of New York Research Foundation fellowships, 1971, 1972; University of Copenhagen research fellowship in Middle Danish studies, 1983.

WRITINGS:

Der heilige Christophorus und sein Kult (title means "St. Christopher and His Cult"), Budapest University Press, 1943.

Irisches Erzaehlgut in Abendland (title means "Irish Literary Tradition in the Western World"), Erich Schmidt Verlag, 1957.

An Ungair (title means "Hungary"), FAS (Dublin), 1958.

Annalen der lateinischen Hymnendichtung (title means "Annals of Medieval Latin Hymnody"), Erich Schmidt Verlag, Volume 1, 1965, Volume 2, 1965.

A Mirror of Medieval Culture: Saint Peter Hymns of the Middle Ages, Connecticut Academy of Arts and Sciences, 1965.

Weltliche Dichtungen des lateinischen Mittelalters (title means "Secular Latin Lyrics of the Middle Ages"), Volume 1, Erich Schmidt Verlag, 1970.

Iberian Hymnody: Survey and Problems, Classical Folia Editions, 1971.

(Author of Volume 1 and of notes to text in Volume 2) Peter Abelard, *Hymnarius Paraclitensis,* E. J. Brill, 1975.

A Guide to Byzantine Hymnography, E. J. Brill, Volume 1, 1979, Volume 2, 1980.

Repertorium Novum Hymnorum Medii Aevi (four volumes), E. J. Brill, 1983.

Religious Lyrics of the Middle Ages, E. J. Brill, 1983.

A Concise History of Medieval Latin Hymnody, E. J. Brill, 1985.

Marianische Motive der Hymen, E. J. Brill, 1985.

Zum Standort der europaeischen Literatur (title means "Intellectual Rank of Medieval European Literature"), E. J. Brill, 1986.

Marienhymnen in Oesterreich (title means "Marian Hymns in Austria"), E. J. Brill, 1987.

Typology of Latin Hymns, Brepols, 1988.

Across the Centuries: Latin Poetry, Irish Legends and Hymnody—Harvard Lectures, E. J. Brill, 1988.

Sequences in Oesterreich (title means "Sequences in Austria"), Classical Folia Edition, 1990.

Contributor to *New Catholic Encyclopedia,* McGraw, 1967; co-editor, *Mittellateinisches Jahrbuch,* 1970—. Editor of series "Medieval Classics: Text and Studies" and "Baroque, Romanticism and the Modern Mind". Contributor of articles and reviews to sixty international scholarly journals. Member of editorial board, *Mediaevalia.*

WORK IN PROGRESS: Researching German folklore, the lyric poetry of the Middle Ages, literature and politics, language minorities abroad, and the cultural history of Transylvania.

SIDELIGHTS: Joseph Szoeverffy has traveled in thirty-four countries abroad and has acquaintance with fourteen languages.

T

TEMPLE, Robert (Kyle Grenville) 1945-

PERSONAL: Born January 25, 1945; married Olivia Moyra Nockolds (an artist), December 30, 1972. *Education:* University of Pennsylvania, B.A., 1965, graduate study, 1965-67.

ADDRESSES: Agent—David Higham Associates Ltd., 5-8 Lower John St., Golden Sq., London W1R 4HA, England.

CAREER: Writer, independent television producer, and industrial consultant. Director, Robert Temple Productions Ltd. Originator of *Romanian Roulette* for Channel Four, 1990; producer and co-director of British material for series *Frontiers of the Unknown* (with Producers Group of Toronto) for Discovery Channel, 1990; producer of pilot films of *The Thoughts of Charles,* 1991; co-producer and presenter of television series *The Genius of China* (series postponed indefinitely after Tiananmen Square massacre); originator and associate producer of *Blind to Science* for British Broadcasting Corporation (BBC-TV); producer of vocational training films. Senior research fellow, New Horizons Research Foundation, 1985-86. Consultant to British Aerospace, 1991.

MEMBER: British Interplanetary Society (fellow), British School at Rome, Royal United Services Institute for Defence Studies, Royal Astronomical Society (fellow), Royal Institution of Great Britain, American Association for the Advancement of Science, PEN, Egypt Exploration Society, Society for the Promotion of Hellenic Studies, Institute of Historical Research, Foreign Press Association of London, English-Speaking Union (and Club).

WRITINGS:

The Sirius Mystery, Sidgwick & Jackson, 1976.
Goetter, Orakel und Visionen, Umschau Verlag, 1982.
Strange Things, Sphere, 1983.
(Author of introduction) *The Dream of Scipio,* Aquarian, 1983.
Conversations with Eternity, Hutchinson, 1984.
China: Land of Discovery and Invention, Patrick Stephens, 1986, published as *The Genius of China,* Simon & Schuster, 1991.
Open to Suggestion: The Uses and Abuses of Hypnosis, Aquarian, 1989.
He Who Saw Everything: A Verse Translation of the Epic of Gilgamesh, Rider, 1991.

Also author of play, "The Ideas of February," produced in Edinburgh, 1973, and of video promotional films. Co-producer, author, and narrator of pilot film "Joseph Needham in China," 1987, and author of stage version of *He Who Saw Everything: The Epic of Gilgamesh* for National Theatre Studio, London, 1992-93. Contributor to *Biographical Dictionary of British Radicals in the Seventeenth Century,* 1982-84, and *Dictionary of National Biography,* 1991. Contributor to periodicals, including *Times* (London), *Guardian, Illustrated London News, Books and Bookmen, Sydney Morning Herald, Sunday Times, Sunday Telegraph, Mail on Sunday, Sunday Express, Independent, Harper's, New Scientist, Economist, Spectator, Life, Discover, People, Orgyn, Helix,* and *Nature.*

WORK IN PROGRESS: Screenplay adaptation of Daphne du Maurier's *No Motive;* translation from the German of Rainer Maria Rilke's *Sonnets to Orpheus,* with Stefan Zweig's memorial address at Rilke's memorial service; an article suggesting that the dialogue *Menexenos* attributed to Plato was actually written by Aristotle; a drama about England's King Henry III.

BIOGRAPHICAL/CRITICAL SOURCES:

PERIODICALS

Daily Telegraph, February 26, 1976.

Guardian, February 27, 1976.
Observer, March 7, 1976.
Sunday Express, January 25, 1976; December 18, 1983.
Sunday Telegraph, August 12, 1984.
Sunday Times (London), February 12, 1984.
Times (London), February 26, 1976; February 27, 1976;
   February 29, 1976.*

*   *   *

TePASKE, John J(ay) 1929-

PERSONAL: Born December 8, 1929, in Grand Rapids,
MI; son of Leo Henry (an engineer) and Leone Kloote (a
housewife) TePaske; married Neomi Lynn Gray, August
18, 1951; children: two. *Education:* Michigan State College (now Michigan State University), B.A., 1951; Duke
University, M.A., 1953, Ph.D., 1959.

ADDRESSES: Office—Department of History, Duke
University, 226 Carr Bldg., Durham, NC 27708.

CAREER: Memphis State University, Memphis, TN, assistant professor of history, 1958-59; Ohio State University, Columbus, instructor, 1959-60, assistant professor,
1960-64, associate professor of history, 1964-67; Duke
University, Durham, NC, associate professor, 1967-69,
professor of history, 1969—.

MEMBER: American Historical Association (vice president, 1986-89), Social Science History Association, Conference on Latin American History (chairman, 1981),
Latin American Studies Association, Society for Spanish
and Portuguese Studies.

AWARDS, HONORS: Fellow of Tinker Foundation,
1975-77, National Endowment for the Humanities, 1977,
and American Philosophical Society, 1981; fellowships
from Committee on the International Exchange of Scholars, 1983, Social Science Research Council, 1985-86, Bank
of Spain, 1986-87, and National Humanities Center,
1989-90.

WRITINGS:

The Governorship of Spanish Florida, 1700-1763, Duke
   University Press, 1963.
Three American Empires, Harper, 1967.
(Contributor) Bernardo Garcia Martinez, editor, *Historia
   y Sociedad en el Mundo de Habla Espanola* (title
   means "History and Society in the Spanish-speaking
   World"), Colegio de Mexico, 1971.
(Contributor) Val Lorwin and Jacob Price, editors, *Di-
   mensions of the Past,* Yale University Press, 1972.
(Editor) *Discourse and Political Reflections on the King-
   doms of Peru,* University of Oklahoma Press, 1978.
*Research Guide to Andean History: Bolivia, Chile, Ecua-
   dor, and Peru,* Duke University Press, 1982.

(With Herbert Sanford Klein) *The Royal Treasuries of the
   Spanish Empire in America,* Duke University Press,
   Volume 1: *Peru,* 1982, Volume 2: *Upper Peru (Bo-
   livia),* 1982, Volume 3: *Chile and Rio de la Plata,*
   1982, Volume 4: *Mexico,* 1982, Volume 5: (with Al-
   varo Jara) *Eighteenth-Century Ecuador,* 1990.
(Editor) John Tate Lanning, *The Royal Protomedicato,*
   Duke University Press, 1985.

Contributor to both history and Latin American studies
journals.

WORK IN PROGRESS: A book on the fiscal structure of
the Spanish Empire, 1580-1820, with Herbert Sanford
Klein; a book on early eighteenth century Peru.

SIDELIGHTS: John J. TePaske told *CA:* "History is difficult to write because historical explanation is so difficult.
My interest in quantitative history and the royal accounts
of the Spanish empire stems from the deep-seated desire
to explain historical change more accurately and more
precisely, to fuse more traditional kinds of historical analysis and historical evidence with statistical data to give the
past more clarity."

*   *   *

THOMAS, Gordon 1933-

PERSONAL: Born February 21, 1933, in Carmarthen,
South Wales; son of Gwynfor and Helena (Griffiths)
Thomas; married Anne Nightengale (a television presenter and disc jockey with the British Broadcasting Corporation), June 17, 1962; married Edith Maria Kraner (an
accountant); children: Alexander, Lucy, Nicholas,
Natasha. *Education:* Attended schools in Egypt and South
Africa, completing education in England at Bedford Modern School and Huntingdon Grammar School.

ADDRESSES: Home—The Old Rectory, Ashford,
County Wicklow, Ireland. *Agent*—(literary) Russell
Galen, Scott Meredith Literary Agency, 845 Third Ave.,
New York, NY 10022; (film) Ronald B. Leif, Contempo-
rary Artists Ltd., 1427 Third St. Promenade, Suite 205,
Santa Monica, CA 90401; and Steve Kenis, William Mor-
ris Agency, 31/32 Soho Square, London W1B 5DG, En-
gland.

CAREER: The Hunts Post, Cambridge, England, reporter
and feature writer, 1951-53; *The People,* London, England, investigative reporter, 1953-54; *Daily Express,* London, England, foreign correspondent, 1954-59; *Today,*
London, England, literary editor, 1959-62; BBC-TV, London, writer, director, and producer, 1963-69; *Sunday Express,* contributing foreign correspondent, 1970-75; *Toronto Globe and Mail,* contributing foreign correspondent,

1976-84; *Toronto Sunday Star,* contributing foreign correspondent, 1984-86; The Press Association, London, contributing foreign correspondent, 1986-90.

MEMBER: Screenwriters Guild, Institute of Journalists.

AWARDS, HONORS: Critics' and Jurys' Prize, Monte Carlo Film Festival, 1969, for film *A Bit of an Experience;* Edgar Allan Poe Award, 1974, for *Shipwreck;* Mark Twain Society Awards, 1977, for *Enola Gay,* and 1979, for *The Day the Bubble Burst.*

WRITINGS:

(With Scotty Young) *Descent into Danger,* Wingate, 1954.
Physician Extraordinary, Wingate, 1955.
(With Michael Blondini) *Bed of Nails: The Story of the Amazing Blondini,* Wingate, 1956.
Heroes of the RAF, Hale, 1957.
They Got Back, Hale, 1958.
Miracle of Surgery, Hamilton, 1958, Panther, 1959.
The Camp on Blood Island, Panther Books, 1958.
The National Health Service and You, Panther Books, 1959.
Thames Number One, Wingate, 1960.
Midnight Traders, Harrap, 1961.
The Jack Spot Story, Wingate, 1962.
(With Ian Donald Hudson and Vincent Pippet) *The Parents Home Doctor,* Panther Books, 1966, revised edition, Auerbach Books, 1969, revised edition, Mayflower Books, 1973.
(With Ronald Hutchinson) *Turn by the Window: The Trial and Imprisonment in Japan of Signalman Graham Nicholls,* Cassell, 1968, Panther Books, 1969.
(With Max Morgan-Witts) *The Day the World Ended* (Literary Guild selection), Stein & Day, 1969.
(With Hudson) *What to Do until the Doctor Comes,* Auerbach, 1970.
Torpedo Run, Panther Books, 1971.
(With Morgan-Witts) *The San Francisco Earthquake* (Book-of-the-Month Club selection), Stein & Day, 1971, published in England as *Earthquake: The Destruction of San Francisco,* Souvenir Press, 1971.
Issels: The Biography of a Doctor, Hodder & Stoughton, 1972, published in the United States as *Dr. Issels and His Revolutionary Cancer Treatment,* P. H. Wyden, 1973.
(With Morgan-Witts) *Shipwreck: The Strange Fate of the Morro Castle,* Stein & Day, 1972.
(With Morgan-Witts) *Voyage of the Damned* (Literary Guild selection), Stein & Day, 1974.
(With Morgan-Witts) *Guernica: The Crucible of World War II,* Stein & Day, 1975, published in England as *The Day Guernica Died,* Hodder & Stoughton, 1975.
(With Morgan-Witts) *Enola Gay* (Book-of-the-Month Club selection), Stein & Day, 1977, published in England as *Ruin from the Air: The Atomic Mission to Hiroshima,* Hamish Hamilton, 1977.
(With Morgan-Witts) *The Day the Bubble Burst: A Social History of the Wall Street Crash of 1929,* Doubleday, 1979.
(With Morgan-Witts) *Trauma: The Search for the Cause of Legionnaires' Disease,* Hamish Hamilton, 1981, published in the United States as *Anatomy of an Epidemic,* Doubleday, 1982.
(With Morgan-Witts) *Pontiff* (Book-of-the-Month Club alternate selection), Doubleday, 1983.
(With Morgan-Witts) *Averting Armageddon,* Doubleday, 1984, published in England as *The Year of Armageddon: The Pope and the Bomb,* Granada Publishing, 1984.
The Operation: The Dramatic True Story of a Woman's Brain Surgery, Doubleday, 1985.
Desire and Denial: Celibacy and the Church, Little, Brown, 1986.
The Trial: The Life and Inevitable Crucifixion of Jesus, Bantam, 1987.
Journey into Madness: Medical Torture and the Mind Controllers, Bantam, 1988.
Enslaved, Bantam, 1990, Pharos Books, 1991.
Chaos under Heaven, Birch Lane Press, 1991.
Deadly Perfume, Chapmans, 1991, HarperCollins, 1992.
Godless Icon, Chapmans, 1992.
Voices in the Silence, Chapmans, 1993.

Also author of film scripts, including *The Rotherham Candidate, Two Weeks in a New Town, The Third Bed,* and *Two Bob Short.*

ADAPTATIONS: The Day the World Ended was adapted for film by Warner Brothers; *Voyage of the Damned* was adapted for film by Embassy; *Enola Gay* was adapted for television by the National Broadcasting Company (NBC-TV); *The Day the Bubble Burst* was adapted for television by Fox/NBC-TV; *Miracle of Surgery* was adapted for television by the British Broadcasting Corporation; screen rights to *Desire and Denial* have been sold to Hatherford Films; screen rights to *Deadly Perfume, Godless Icon,* and the next four novels featuring the central character of David Morton have been sold to Paragraph Productions.

SIDELIGHTS: Gordon Thomas's books have sold more than forty million copies in some three dozen countries worldwide. An author or co-author of far-reaching social histories, Thomas has investigated the bombing of Hiroshima by the crew of the *Enola Gay,* the Wall Street Crash of 1929, and the destruction of the town of Guernica during the Spanish Civil War. Thomas is perhaps best known for his works on the Catholic church. His books such as *Pontiff* and *Averting Armageddon* probe Vatican politics in the age of nuclear war.

Chicago Tribune reporter Bill Neikirk calls the writing team of Thomas and Max Morgan-Witts "an institution," with lucrative film deals for their books and a veritable army of accountants, lawyers, and researchers. Thomas and Morgan-Witts have been known to spend as much as $600,000 in research fees before they even begin writing a book. The investments have not been in vain—most of the authors' titles have been book club selections and have sold well in both hard cover and paperback. *Washington Post* correspondent Joseph McLellan notes: "Gordon Thomas and Max Morgan-Witts have established a substantial reputation for reporting that is as solid as it is vivid. Their efforts have enjoyed a Hollywood success that is rare for nonfiction—undoubtedly because they clothe their facts in the kind of small, concrete detail that is one of the virtues of good fiction; because they take the reader into the minds and feelings of the real people they write about as though these characters were their own creations."

Thomas was born in Wales, but his parents travelled widely. He was educated in Cairo, Egypt and in South Africa before returning to England for secondary studies. The author told *CA* that his mother "taught me to read and write, she helped me to practice shorthand and corrected my typing exercises. The only books she has in her parlour are mine. To those who ask why, she says, with a pride in her voice which brings a lump to my throat, that her eldest boy has written all she needs to read. Hardly, but it would be a cruel son who would take away from such a touching sentiment."

As a youngster Thomas became fascinated by writing. He sold his first essay to the *Boys' Own Paper* in Great Britain when he was only nine. After that, he spent much of every evening scribbling in journals, working under the sheets with a flashlight in the wee hours. "Just after my seventeenth birthday, I had completed my first full-length book, *Descent into Danger*," he told *CA*. " . . . With nervous hope I sent the book to Allan Wingate, a publisher whose list I had long admired. . . . Wingate took the book, advanced me one hundred pounds, sold it to the [London Daily] *Express* for one thousand pounds as a four part serialisation, placed my share on deposit in a bank, and signed me for a second book. I began to give interviews and appear on BBC radio programmes, and *Boys' Own Paper* ran a story on how they had discovered me all those years before."

Thomas joined the staff of the *Express* at the age of twenty-one and became a foreign correspondent. His assignments took him into a number of dangerous situations, from the Suez crisis and South African treason trials to the Algerian war and the civil war on Cyprus. "I have been arrested three times, deported twice and shot at once in the course of doing my job," he told *CA*.

Eventually Thomas joined the British Broadcasting Corporation as a script writer. There he met his sometimes writing partner, Max Morgan-Witts. As an author, Thomas was influenced by the works of Lillian Ross and Cornelius Ryan—both nonfiction writers who were able to enliven their books with the techniques of fiction. Thomas told *CA:* "I, too, wanted to produce a piece of journalism that would read like a novel, but have the credibility of fact; it would both be true and have the freedom of imagination that fiction allowed."

Thomas used his experiences as a reporter and researcher to gather information on such diverse topics as brain surgery, the San Francisco earthquake of 1906, and the pope's use of briefings by the Central Intelligence Agency. Several of his books, including *The Day the World Ended, Voyage of the Damned,* and *Enola Gay* have been bestsellers that were subsequently made into films. McLellan commends Thomas for the way he handles "highly dramatic material . . . with clarity and impact." The critic concludes that in many of his books Thomas has "assembled an enormous mass of complex material in a readable, credible form."

In 1990, Thomas gave up his career as a foreign correspondent to become a full-time thriller and suspense writer. He was encouraged to make this career change by his new publishers, Ian and Marjory Chapman, whose long and distinguished track record includes the discoveries of Alastair MacLean, Gerald Seymour, and other notable thriller writers. They contracted Thomas to write a series of six novels that all revolve around the central character of intelligence officer David Morton, who has been described as "the James Bond of the '90s."

BIOGRAPHICAL/CRITICAL SOURCES:

PERIODICALS

Chicago Tribune, March 17, 1980.

Globe and Mail (Toronto), September 8, 1984; February 6, 1988.

New York Times, April 15, 1969.

New York Times Book Review, February 15, 1976; August 14, 1977; October 14, 1979.

Spectator, January 24, 1976.

Times Literary Supplement, July 24, 1969; January 23, 1976; November 2, 1984.

Washington Post, June 21, 1983.

Washington Post Book World, August 17, 1986.

—*Sketch by Anne Janette Johnson*

TINER, John Hudson 1944-

PERSONAL: Born October 8, 1944, in Pocahontas, AR; son of John A. (a pipeline construction inspector) and Martha (a clerk; maiden name, Hudson) Tiner; married Delma Jeanene Watson (an elementary school teacher), May 5, 1962; children: John Watson, Lambda Jeanene. *Education:* Harding College (now Harding University), B.S., 1965; Duke University, M.A.T., 1968; also attended Arkansas State University, 1965-68. *Politics:* Independent. *Religion:* Church of Christ.

ADDRESSES: Home—6440 Kathy Ln., High Ridge, MO 63049. *Office*—P.O Box 38, House Springs, MO 63051.

CAREER: Pipeline construction worker, 1960-62; high school teacher of mathematics and science in Harrisburg, AR, 1965-68, head of mathematics department, 1968; junior high school mathematics teacher in High Ridge, MO, 1968-72; high school teacher of physics, astronomy, and science in House Springs, MO, 1972-77; Defense Mapping Agency, Aerospace Center, St. Louis, MO, photogrammetric cartographer, 1977-80, mathematician, 1980-83, supervisory mathematician, 1983-85, supervisory computer specialist, 1986-91, supervisory geodesist, 1991—. Jefferson College, Hillsboro, MO, instructor, 1972-77. *Harrisburg Modern News,* photographer, 1966-68.

MEMBER: Mystery Writers of America, Missouri Writers Guild.

AWARDS, HONORS: Plaque from Missouri Writers Guild, 1977, for *Johannes Kepler: Giant of Faith and Science;* National Science Foundation grants.

WRITINGS:

When Science Fails, Baker Book, 1974.
Isaac Newton (juvenile), Mott Media, 1976.
Johannes Kepler: Giant of Faith and Science (juvenile), Mott Media, 1977.
How to Earn Extra Income as a Free-Lance Writer, Pamphlet Publications, 1977.
Evolution versus Creation, Pamphlet Publications, 1978.
Space Colonies, Pamphlet Publications, 1978.
College Physical Science, Accelerated Christian Education, 1980.
Seven Day Mystery, Baker Book, 1981.
Word Search: Favorite Bible Stories from Genesis, Quality Publications, 1981.
Extra-Terrestrials, Pamphlet Publications, 1982.
Evolution and Creation on Trial, Pamphlet Publications, 1982.
Word Search: They Followed Jesus, Standard Publishing, 1982.
Science Bulletin Boards, Quality Publications, 1983.
The Ghost Lake (juvenile; biography of Louis Agassiz), Baker Book, 1983.

Bible Word Search Puzzles, Broadman, 1983.
College Algebra I, Accelerated Christian Education, 1983.
Word Search: Favorite Bible Stories from Acts, Standard Publishing, 1986.
Jesus the Teacher Word Search, Standard Publishing, 1986.
Samuel F. B. Morse, Mott Media, 1987.
Physics, Accelerated Christian Education, 1987.
Build Your Bible Knowledge: Acts, Quality Publications, 1987.
Robert Boyle, Mott Media, 1989.
Louis Pasteur, Mott Media, 1990.

Contributor of more than five hundred articles, stories, and poems for children and adults to religion periodicals. Editor and publisher, *Bible Truth,* 1978-83.

WORK IN PROGRESS: Breakthroughs in Medicine, for *Nature Friend Magazine; The Client with the Lackluster Diamonds,* an adult mystery.

SIDELIGHTS: John Hudson Tiner's writings cover a wide variety of subjects and styles. He has written mysteries and science fiction, scientific papers, and articles on such subjects as coin collecting, photography, and astronomy. His religion writings have been published by most Christian denominations. Tiner once told *CA:* "I like to write, especially biographies of historical characters. After the research is finished and the outline complete, a magic moment occurs when the story takes over and the characters come alive. No longer am I a writer, but a time traveler who stands unobserved in the shadows and reports the events as they occur. The time traveling goes forward in time as well as backward. What is committed to paper today will speak to readers who are not yet born.

"Writing gives a person leverage. The relatively simple action of putting words on paper has the potential to produce far-reaching and longlasting results. Because of this potential I believe a writer should feel strongly about his subject and express himself clearly and forcefully. And the writer has the responsibility to state the truth as he understands it.

"My backgrounds in science and strong Christian faith have attracted me to write about the interaction of science and religion. In a sense the two activities, science and religion, are closely related because both scientists and Christians have a relentless dedication to truth.

"Young readers of today deserve to experience the thrill and wonder of learning about science. They delight in learning new facts, especially if the facts are presented in an exciting way. Recently, I have begun to write straight science books—*Breakthroughs in Medicine,* for example—from a Christian point of view."

TOMB, David A(lan) 1944-

PERSONAL: Born January 27, 1944, in Pittsburgh, PA; son of Alva H. (an engineer) and Mary (Woodring) Tomb; married Jane McGarr (a medical researcher), June 10, 1967; children: Collin (daughter), Ian. *Education:* College of Wooster, B.A., 1965; attended University of Virginia, 1966-68; Pennsylvania State University, M.D., 1972.

ADDRESSES: Home—Salt Lake City, UT. *Office*—School of Medicine, University of Utah, Salt Lake City, UT 84132. *Agent*—Sallie Gouvenier, 220 East 85th St., New York, NY 10028.

CAREER: University of Utah, School of Medicine, Salt Lake City, resident in psychiatry and fellow in child psychiatry, 1972-78, assistant professor, 1978-85, associate professor of psychiatry, 1985—.

MEMBER: American Medical Association, Association for Academic Psychiatry.

WRITINGS:

Psychiatry for the House Officer, Williams & Wilkins, 1981, 3rd edition, 1988.
Child Psychiatry and Behavioral Pediatric Case Studies, Medical Examination Publishing, 1983.
Growing Old, Viking, 1984.
(With Dan C. Christensen) *Psychiatry Case Studies for the House Officer,* Williams & Wilkins, 1987.
Psychiatry, Williams & Wilkins, 1992.
Post Traumatic Stress Disorders, Saunders, in press.

SIDELIGHTS: David A. Tomb told *CA:* "My goal in writing as I do is to try to make the (at times) arcane fields of psychiatry and psychology better understood and to help the uninitiated see them as both scientific and relevant. I am committed to providing information in place of misinformation, although I fully realize that as humans we have a need to provide explanations for our own psychology that are partly illusory. And yet, the real explanations are often as fantastic as those we wish were true."

*   *   *

TOOLE, Rex
   See TRALINS, S(andor) Robert

*   *   *

TORRANCE, E. Paul 1915-

PERSONAL: Born October 6, 1915, in Milledgeville, GA; son of Ellis Watson and Jimmie Pearl (Ennis) Torrance; married J. Pansy Nigh, 1959. *Education:* Georgia Military College, associate in arts, 1936; Mercer University, B.A. (summa cum laude), 1940; University of Minnesota, M.A., 1944; University of Michigan, Ph.D., 1951. *Religion:* Baptist. *Avocational interests:* Photography.

ADDRESSES: Home and office—183 Cherokee Ave., Athens, GA 30606.

CAREER: Midway Vocational High School, Milledgeville, GA, teacher, 1936-37; Georgia Military College, Milledgeville, teacher, counselor, and principal, 1937-44; Kansas State College of Agriculture and Applied Science (now Kansas State University), Manhattan, counselor, 1946-48, director of Counseling Bureau, 1949-51; U.S. Air Force, Survival Research Field Unit, Stead Air Force Base, NV, director, 1951-57; University of Minnesota, Minneapolis, professor of educational psychology, 1958-66; University of Georgia, Athens, professor of educational psychology, 1966-73, Alumni Distinguished Professor, 1973-84, Alumni Foundation Distinguished Professor Emeritus, 1985—, chairman of department, 1966-78. Visiting scholar, Japan Society for the Promotion of Science; fellow, National Academy of Physical Education. Member of board of trustees, Creative Education Foundation, 1975-79.

MEMBER: American Educational Research Association, American Psychological Association, National Association for Gifted Children, American Sociological Society, Phi Delta Kappa, Psi Chi.

AWARDS, HONORS: Award of American Personnel and Guidance Association for *Guiding Creative Talent; Booklist* award for outstanding education book of the year, 1970-71, for *Creative Learning and Teaching;* distinguished alumnus award, Georgia Military College, 1972; Association for the Gifted award for distinguished contribution to the understanding and education of gifted children, 1975; Kappa Delta Pi award for excellence as a teacher educator, 1975; National Association for Gifted Children award for outstanding pioneering work in identifying and developing creative talent; Psi Chi award for outstanding contribution to psychology; Educational Press Association of America distinguished achievement award for excellence in educational journalism; Georgia College distinguished service award; Sertoma Clubs of Hawaii Service to Mankind Award; Phoenix Medal, University of Hiroshima, Japan; Founders Medal, Creative Education Foundation; Viktor Lowenfeld Medal in Art Education; Distinguished Scholar Award, National Association for Gifted Children; Arthur Lipper Award, Olympics of the Mind; Award of the National Future Problem Solving Program as the founder and continued supporter; named to the Hall of Fame, National Association for Creative Children and Adults.

WRITINGS:

(Editor) *Education and Talent,* University of Minnesota Press, 1960.

Guiding Creative Talent, Prentice-Hall, 1962.

Education and the Creative Potential, University of Minnesota Press, 1963. *Constructive Behavior: Stress, Personality, and Mental Health,* Wadsworth Publishing, 1965.

Gifted Children in the Classroom, Macmillan, 1965.

Rewarding Creative Behavior: Experiments in Classroom Creativity, Prentice-Hall, 1965.

(With Cunnington) *Sounds and Images,* Ginn, 1965.

(With Myers) *Invitations to Thinking and Doing,* Ginn, 1965.

Invitations to Speaking and Writing Creatively, Ginn, 1965.

(Editor with R. D. Strom) *Mental Health and Achievement,* Wiley, 1965.

(With Myers) *Can You Imagine?,* Ginn, 1965.

Torrance Tests of Creative Thinking, Personnel Press, 1966.

Dimensions of Early Learning: Creativity, Adapt Press, 1969.

(With Myers) *Creative Learning and Teaching,* Harper, 1970.

(With W. F. White) *Issues and Advances in Educational Psychology,* F. E. Peacock, 1970, revised edition, 1975.

Encouraging Creativity in the Classroom, National Education Association, 1970.

(With J. C. Gowan and Joe Khatena) *Educating the Ablest,* F. E. Peacock, 1971, revised edition, 1979.

(With wife, J. Pansy Torrance) *Is Creativity Teachable?,* Phi Delta Kappa, 1973.

(With Khatena) *Thinking Creatively with Sounds and Words,* Ginn, 1973.

What Research Says to the Teacher: Creativity in the Classroom, National Education Association, 1977.

(With Khatena) *Khatena-Torrance Creative Perception Inventory,* Charles Stoelting, 1977.

Discovery and Nurturance of Giftedness in the Culturally Different, Council for Exceptional Children, 1977.

Search for Creativity, Creative Education Foundation, 1979.

Children Soar, Japan Britannica, 1979.

Sociodrama and the Creative Process, Geigy Pharmaceuticals, 1979.

The Search for Satori and Creativity, Creative Education Foundation, 1979.

Thinking Creatively in Action and Movement, Scholastic Testing Service, 1981.

(With O. E. Ball) *The Torrance Tests of Creative Thinking Streamlined Manual, Forms A and B,* Scholastic Testing Service, 1984.

Mentor Relationships, Bearly Limited, 1984.

(With W. Taggart and B. Taggart) *The Human information Processing Survey,* Scholastic Testing Service, 1984.

(With W. Taggart) *Human Information Processing Survey Administrator's Manual,* Scholastic Testing Service, 1984.

(With D. Weiner, J. Presbury, and M. Henderson) *Save Tomorrow for the Children,* Bearly Limited, 1987.

Survey of the Uses of the Torrance Tests of Creative Thinking, Scholastic Testing Service, 1987.

Guidelines for Administration and Scoring: Comments on Using the Torrance Tests of Creative Thinking, Scholastic Testing Service, 1987.

Using the Torrance Tests of Creative Thinking to Guide the Teaching of Creative Behavior, Scholastic Testing Service, 1987.

Style of Learning and Thinking: Administrator's Manual, Scholastic Testing Service, 1988.

(With H. T. Safter) *The Incubation Model of Teaching: Getting Beyond the Aha!,* Bearly Limited, 1990.

Also author of "Imagi/Craft" series, Ginn, 1965; author of *Thinking Creatively in Action and Movement* and *Your Style of Learning and Thinking,* both 1979.

CONTRIBUTOR

A. P. Hare, E. F. Borgatta, and R. F. Bales, *Small Groups,* Knopf, 1955.

J. L. Moreno, *Sociometry and the Science of Man,* Beacon House, 1956.

A. H. Rubinstein and C. J. Haberstroh, *Some Theories of Organization,* Dorsey, 1960.

L. Petrullo and B. M. Bass, *Leadership and Interpersonal Behavior,* Holt, 1961.

S. J. Parnes and H. F. Harding, *A Source Book for Creative Thinking,* Scribner, 1962.

G. Z. F. Bereday and J. A. Lauwreys, *The Gifted Child,* Harcourt, 1962.

L. D. Crow and Alice Crow, editors, *Readings in Human Learning,* McKay, 1963.

L. D. Crow and A. Crow, *Mental Hygiene for Teachers,* Macmillan, 1963.

W. W. Charters, Jr. and N. L. Gage, editors, *Readings in the Social Psychology of Education,* Allyn & Bacon, 1963.

J. M. Seidman, *Educating for Mental Health,* Crowell, 1963.

C. W. Taylor and F. Barron, *Scientific Creativity: Its Recognition and Development,* Wiley, 1963.

Taylor, *Creativity: Progress and Potential,* McGraw, 1964.

Taylor, *Widening Horizons in Creativity,* Wiley, 1964.

J. S. Roucek, *The Difficult Child,* Philosophical Library, 1964.

R. D. Strom, *Inner-City Teacher,* Merrill, 1966.

Taylor and F. E. Williams, *Instructional Media and Creativity,* Wiley, 1966.
Roucek, *Programmed Instruction,* Philosophical Library, 1966.
J. C. Gowan and G. D. Demos, *The Disadvantaged and Potential Dropout,* C. C. Thomas, 1966.
F. J. Sternberg, *The Nature of Creativity,* Cambridge University Press, 1988.
R. R. Schmeck, *Learning Strategies and Learning Styles,* Plenum Publishing Corp., 1988.
D. Ratcliff, *Handbook of Preschool Religious Education,* Religious Education Press, 1988.
C. J. Maker and S. W. Schiever, *Critical Issues in Gifted Education: Defensible Programs for Cultural and Ethnic Minorities,* Pro-ed, Inc., 1989.
Taylor, *Expanding Awareness of Creative Potentials Worldwide,* Brain Talent-Powers Press, 1990.
C. R. Reynolds and R. W. Kamphaus, *Handbook of Psychological and Educational Assessment of Children,* Guilford Press, 1990.

Contributor to professional journals.

WORK IN PROGRESS: Predicting Creative Behavior; Images of the Future of Gifted Children; Uses of Tests in Understanding and Predicting Creative Behavior; Longitudinal Studies of Creative Achievement; The Blazing Drive: The Creative Person; Learning to Fly; Creativity: The Fire Within; Sociodrama and a Creative Problem Solving Process; Mentors for Disadvantaged Children; Mentoring from Cross-Cultural Perspective; Creative Giftedness and Learning Disabilities; The Beyonders.

SIDELIGHTS: Torrance Tests of Creative Thinking has been translated into over forty languages; *Guiding Creative Talent* has been published in Japanese and Spanish; *Creative Learning and Teaching* has been published in Spanish and Portuguese; *Gifted Children in the Classroom* has been published in Japanese and Spanish; *Is Creativity Teachable?* has been published in Portuguese; *Encouraging Creativity in the Classroom, The Search for Satori and Creativity,* and *Children Soar* have been translated into Japanese.

*   *   *

TRACY, Leland
   See TRALINS, S(andor) Robert

*   *   *

TRAINOR, Richard
   See TRALINS, S(andor) Robert

TRALINS, Bob
   See TRALINS, S(andor) Robert

*   *   *

TRALINS, Robert S.
   See TRALINS, S(andor) Robert

*   *   *

TRALINS, S(andor) Robert   1926-
   (Bob Tralins, Robert S. Tralins; pseudonyms: Ray Z. Bixby, Norman A. King, Alfred D. Laurance, Keith Miles, Sean O'Shea, Rex O'Toole, Cynthia Sydney, Rex Toole, Leland Tracy, Richard Trainor, Ruy Traube, Dorothy Verdon)

PERSONAL: Born April 28, 1926, in Baltimore, MD; son of Emanuel (a shipbuilder) and Rose (Miller) Tralins; married Sonya Lee Mandel (died, 1988); children: Myles J., Alan H. *Education:* Attended Eastern College (now University of Baltimore), 1946-48.

ADDRESSES: Home—Sonya Lee (a sailboat moored in Clearwater, FL). *Office*—309 Pinellas Street, Suite 2, Clearwater, FL 34616. *Agent*—The Adele Leone Agency, 26 Nantucket Place, Scarsdale, NY 10583.

CAREER: Writer. Scriptwriter for *The Arthur Godfrey Show,* 1976. *Military service:* U.S. Marine Corps Reserve, 1943-45.

WRITINGS:

How to Be a Power Closer in Selling, Prentice-Hall, 1960.
Dynamic Selling, Prentice-Hall, 1961.
Torrid Island, Novel Books, 1961.
Pleasure Was My Business (autobiography of Madame Sherry [pseudonym of Ruth Barnes] as told to Tralins), Lyle Stuart, 1961.
Caesar's Bench, Tuxedo Books, 1961.
Law of Lust, Tuxedo Books, 1961.
Congo Lust, Tuxedo Books, 1961.
Naked Hills, Tuxedo Books, 1961.
Hillbilly Nymph, Tuxedo Books, 1962.
Freak Woman, Novel Books, 1962.
Nymphokick, Merit Books, 1962.
Four Queens, Novel Books, 1962.
Seductress, Novel Books, 1962.
Female Rapist, Novel Books, 1962.
Love Goddess, Novel Books, 1962.
Primitive Orgy, Novel Books, 1962.
Passion Potion, Novel Books, 1962.
Hired Nymph, Novel Books, 1962.
Office Girl, Novel Books, 1962.

Four Wild Dames, Novel Books, 1962.
Seduction Salon, Novel Books, 1962.
International Girl, Novel Books, 1962.
Barechested Beauty, Novel Books, 1962.
Smuggler's Mistress, Novel Books, 1962.
Jazzman in Nudetown, Bedside Books, 1963.
Orgy of Terror, Novel Books, 1963.
Freak Lover, Novel Books, 1963.
Colossal Carnality, Novel Books, 1963.
Love Experiment, Novel Books, 1963.
The Ultimate Passion, Novel Books, 1964.
Experiment in Desire, Novel Books, 1964.
Love Worshiper, Novel Books, 1964.
Erotic Play, Novel Books, 1964.
Goddess of Raw Passion, Novel Books, 1964.
Donna Is Different, Novel Books, 1964.
The One and Only Jean, Novel Books, 1964.
Rites of the Half-Women, Novel Books, 1965.
Squaresville Jag, Belmont Books, 1965.
(With Dr. Michael M. Gilbert) *Twenty-One Abnormal Sex Cases,* Paperback Library, 1965.
They Make Her Beg, Novel Books, 1965.
Beyond Human Understanding: Strange Events, Ace Books, 1966.
The Miss from S.I.S., Belmont Books, 1966.
The Chic Chick Spy, Belmont Books, 1966.
The Cosmozoids, Belmont Books, 1966.
The Ring-a-Ding UFO's, Belmont Books, 1966.
Strange Events beyond Human Knowledge, Avon Books, 1967.
(Under pseudonym Ray Z. Bixby) *The Rites of Lust,* Softcover Library, 1967.
(Under pseudonym Rex Toole) *Soft Sell,* Bee-Line Books, 1967.
(Under pseudonym Rex Toole) *Nymphet Syndrome,* Award Books, 1967.
Cairo Madam, Paperback Library, 1968.
Clairvoyant Strangers, Popular Library, 1968.
Weird People of the Unknown, Popular Library, 1969.
Children of the Supernatural, Lancer, 1969.
Fetishism, Paperback Library, 1969.
Runaway Slave, Lancer, 1969.
Slave's Revenge, Lancer, 1969.
Panther John, Lancer, 1969.
Supernatural Strangers, Popular Library, 1970.
The Hidden Spectre, Avon, 1970.
ESP Forewarnings, Popular Library, 1970.
Clairvoyant Women, Popular Library, 1970.
Clairvoyance in Women, Lancer, 1971.
Supernatural Warnings, Popular Library, 1972.
Ghoul Lover, Popular Library, 1973.
(Under pseudonym Keith Miles) *Dragon's Teeth,* Popular Library, 1973.
Android Armageddon, Pinnacle Books, 1974.

Buried Alive, Merit Publications, 1977.
Chains, New English Library, 1981.

"JACK LUND" SERIES

Flight Signals, Pinnacle Books, 1990.
Signal: Intruder, Pinnacle Books, 1991.
Signal: Blackbird, Pinnacle Books, 1992.

UNDER PSEUDONYM NORMAN A. KING

French Leave, Midwood, 1967.
Turn Your House into a Money Factory, Morrow/Quill, 1982.

Also author of *So Cold, So Cruel,* 1966, *Hide and Seek,* 1966, and *The Flyers,* 1967.

UNDER PSEUDONYM SEAN O'SHEA

Whisper, Softcover Library, 1965.
What a Way to Go, Belmont Books, 1966.
Sex Variations in Voyeurism, Award Books, 1967.
Psychokick, Lancer Books, 1967.
Operation Boudoir, Belmont Books, 1967.
Win with Sin, Belmont Books, 1967.
The Nymph Island Affair, Belmont Books, 1967.
The Invasion of the Nymphs, Belmont Books, 1967.
Topless Kitties, Belmont Books, 1968.

UNDER PSEUDONYM REX O'TOOLE

Cheating and Infidelity in America, Belmont Books, 1968.

Also author of *Remember to Die,* 1967, *Variations in Exhibitionism,* 1967, *Confessions of an Exhibitionist,* 1968, and *Gigolos,* 1969.

UNDER PSEUDONYM CYNTHIA SYDNEY

Lure of Luxury, Midwood Books, 1966.
Trick or Treat, Midwood Books, 1966.
Sin Point, Midwood Books, 1966.
Hideaway Lane, Midwood Books, 1966.
Ripe and Ready, Midwood Books, 1966.
Lost and Found, Midwood Books, 1966.
Executive Wife, Midwood Books, 1967.
Take Me Out in Trade, Midwood Books, 1967.

Also author of *Stay until Morning,* 1966, *The Higher the Price,* 1966, *The Love Business,* 1966, *Office Swinger,* 1966, and *Give and Take,* 1967.

UNDER PSEUDONYM RUY TRAUBE

The Seduction Art, Belmont Books, 1967.
Uninhibited, Belmont Books, 1968.
Memoirs of a Beach Boy Lover, Lancer, 1969.

OTHER

Also author of *Death before Dishonor,* 1962, *Captain O'Six,* 1962, *Artist Swinger,* 1963, *Devil's Hook,* 1963, *The*

Smugglers, 1964, *The Pirates,* 1964, *Gunrunner,* 1964, *Slave King,* 1965, *Sexual Fetish,* 1966, *Gomer Pyle, USMC,* 1966, *Dragnet '67,* 1966, *Remember to Die,* 1966, (under pseudonym Dorothy Verdon) *First Try,* 1966, (under pseudonym Leland Tracy) *Song of Africa,* 1968, (under pseudonym Richard Trainor) *Yum-Yum Girl,* 1968, *Black Brute,* 1969, *The Mind Code,* 1969, *ESP Forewarnings,* 1969, *Black Pirate,* 1970, *The Hidden Spectre,* 1970, (under pseudonym Alfred D. Laurance) *Homer Pickle the Greatest,* 1971, *Illegal Tender* (screenplay), 1975, and *The Star of India* (screenplay). Author of the introduction to *Psychic Women,* 3rd edition, Merit Publications, 1977. Contributor to several magazines and trade journals, sometimes under pseudonyms.

WORK IN PROGRESS: A novel about the events leading up to the Holocaust.

SIDELIGHTS: "Talking to author [S.] Robert Tralins is like stepping into the pages of one of his novels," describes Christine R. Vaughn in *Bee Publications.* "His conversation is peppered with stories of the rich and the famous, the powerful and the fallen. And there's adventure and intrigue to go with every character. Pick a topic, any topic, and he's either studied it or written a book about it. Or both." Author of over two-hundred novels, Tralins lives aboard the sailboat named for his late wife, the *Sonya Lee,* writing wherever he may be (including Clearwater Beach, Florida, which he considers home, and the Caribbean). With such a prolific output, Tralins has covered a wide range of topics over the course of his career, including everything from adventure and science fiction to psychology and the occult. In explaining his writing technique to Laura Griffin in the *St. Petersburg Times,* he says, "When you're writing, you have to create a character and think as that character thinks. . . . You sort of become that character for a while." "To make it today," asserts Tralins to Vaughn, " 'a writer has to leave out the philosophy and write to entertain.' But Tralins also admitted he writes to 'make the world a better place, hoping to enrich it with his contribution.' "

BIOGRAPHICAL/CRITICAL SOURCES:

PERIODICALS

Bee Publications, January 9, 1992.
Los Angeles Times Book Review, November 11, 1982.
St. Petersburg Times, January 12, 1992.

*　　*　　*

TRAUBE, Ruy
　See TRALINS, S(andor) Robert

TREPP, Leo 1913-

PERSONAL: Born March 4, 1913, in Mainz, Germany; son of Maier (a businessman) and Selma (Hirschberger) Trepp; married Miriam de Haas (a public school teacher), April 26, 1938; children: Susan. *Education:* Attended University of Frankfurt, University of Berlin, and Frankfurt Rabbinical School; University of Wuerzburg, Ph.D. (magna cum laude), 1935; Berlin Rabbinical Seminary, Rabbi, 1936; additional study in London, England, 1938-39, and at Harvard University and University of California, Berkeley, 1944-51. *Politics:* Democrat. *Avocational interests:* Music (especially opera), good conversation, hiking, swimming, and travel.

ADDRESSES: Home—295 Montecito Blvd., Napa, CA 94558. *Office*—Department of Humanities and Philosophy, Napa College, Napa, CA 94558.

CAREER: Landesrabbiner in Oldenburg, Germany, 1936-38; rabbi of congregations in Greenfield, MA, Somerville, MA, Tacoma, WA, Berkeley, CA, 1940-51, Santa Rosa, CA, 1951-61, and of Congregation Beth El, Eureka, CA, 1961—; Napa College, Napa, CA, 1951—, currently professor emeritus of philosophy and humanities, director of study travel, 1954-69, chairman of Liberal Arts Division, 1974-82. Member of department of humanities, Santa Rosa Junior College, Santa Rosa, 1956-74. Visiting professor of religion, University of Hamburg, 1971, 1979, 1981, University of Oldenburg, 1972, and University of Mainz, 1983, 1985, 1986; visiting lecturer, University of Heidelberg, 1985; honorary Professor of Jewish Studies, University of Mainz, 1988. Jewish chaplain, Veterans Home of California, 1954—. Chairman, Napa Citizens Library Committee, 1962-63; member, Napa City Planning Commission, 1964-69.

MEMBER: Central Conference of American Rabbis, Rabbinical Assembly, American Philosophical Association.

AWARDS, HONORS: Great Seal Award, City of Oldenburg, West Germany (now Germany), 1971; George Washington Honor Medal, Freedom Foundation at Valley Forge, 1979; Doctor of Divinity, honoris causa, Hebrew Union College—Jewish Institute of Religion, 1985; Ph.D., honoris causa, University of Wuerzburg, 1985, University of Oldenburg, 1989; named honorary citizen of City of Oldenburg, 1990.

WRITINGS:

Taine, Montaigne, Richeome: Ihre Auffassungen von Religion und Kirche: Ein Beitrag zur Franzoesischen Wesenskunde, Pfund, 1935.
Eternal Faith, Eternal People: A Journey into Judaism, Prentice-Hall, 1962.

Die Landesgemeinde der Juden in Oldenburg, State of Nie-
dersachsen and City of Oldenburg, 1965.
Judaism: Development and Life, Dickenson, 1966, 3rd re-
vised edition, Wadsworth, 1982.
Das Judentum Geschichte und lebendige Gegenwart, Ro-
wohlt, 1966, revised edition, 1992.
Die Oldenburger Judenschaft, Holzberg, 1973.
A History of the Jewish Experience, Behrman, 1973.
The Complete Book of Jewish Observance, Summit Books,
1980.
Una Historia de la Experiencia Judia (based on *A History
of the Jewish Experience* and adapted for a South
American audience), [Buenos Aires], 1980.
Juedische Ethik, Kohlhammer (Stuttgart), 1984.
Die Amerikanischen Juden: Profil einer Gemeinschaft, Ko-
hlhammer, 1991.
Der Juedische Hofferdienst: Gestalt und Entwicklung, Ko-
hlhammer, 1992.

Contributor of Jewish biographical and historical articles,
essays, education and philosophical articles, and short stories to magazines and professional journals. Contributing
editor, *Reconstructionist,* 1943-52.

*   *   *

TROYNA, Barry 1951-

PERSONAL: Born September 6, 1951, in London, England; son of Sam (a shopkeeper) and Sylvia (Park)
Troyna. *Education:* Nottingham College of Education,
B.Ed., 1974; University of Leicester, M.Phil., 1978; University of Nottingham, Ph.D., 1991.

ADDRESSES: Office—Department of Education, University of Warwick, Coventry CV4 7AL, England.

CAREER: Leicester University, Leicester, England, research officer at Center for Mass Communication Research, 1978-80; University of Aston, Birmingham, England, fellow at Research Unit in Ethnic Relations,
1981-84; University of Warwick, Coventry, England, senior research fellow at Center for Research in Ethnic Relations, 1984-85; Sunderland Polytechnic, Sunderland,
England, reader in education, 1986-87; University of Warwick, senior lecturer in education, 1988—.

WRITINGS:

*Public Awareness and the Media: A Study of Reporting on
Race,* Commission for Racial Equality, 1981.
(With Ernest Ellis Cashmore) *Black Youth in Crisis,* Allen
& Unwin, 1982.
(With Cashmore) *Introduction to Race Relations,* Rout-
ledge & Kegan Paul, 1983. 2nd edition, Falmer Press,
1990.

(With D. I. Smith) *Racism, School, and the Labour Mar-
ket,* National Youth Bureau, 1983.
(With Jenny Williams) *Racism, Education, and the State,*
Croom Helm, 1985.
Racial Inequality in Education, Routledge & Kegan Paul,
1987.
(With B. Carrington) *Children and Controversial Issues,*
Falmer Press, 1988.
(With R. Hatcher) *Racism in Children's Lives,* Routledge
& Kegan Paul, 1992.
Racism and Education: Research Perspectives, Open Uni-
versity Press, 1993.
Researching Educational Reforms, Falmer Press, 1993.

SIDELIGHTS: Barry Troyna once told *CA:* "As a former
teacher and someone involved with antiracist politics for
over ten years, I wanted to fuse my professional and political commitments—hence my focus on racism in education. My particular interest is in exploring the trend toward antiracist education in local contexts and the impact
of local commitments on the routine practices, organization, and administration of schools in the United Kingdom. This impact is inhibited by central government's determination to restrict expenditure in education and by its
refusal to endorse a commitment to antiracist orthodoxies.
The prospect for the legitimization and institutionaliza-
tion of antiracist education is, therefore, bleak."

*   *   *

TUCKER, Ruth A(nne) 1945-

PERSONAL: Born July 17, 1945, in Spooner, WI; daughter of Percy W. (a farmer) and Jennie (a nurse's aide;
maiden name, Carlton) Stellrecht; married Lyman Rand
Tucker, Jr. (an editor), August 10, 1968; children: Carlton
Rand. *Education:* LeTourneau College, B.A., 1967; Baylor University, M.A., 1969; Northern Illinois University,
Ph.D., 1979. *Politics:* Independent. *Religion:* Reformed
Church of America. *Avocational interests:* Tennis, bicycling.

ADDRESSES: Home—927 Giddings Ave. S.E., Grand
Rapids, MI 49506. *Office*—Trinity Evangelical Divinity
School, 2065 Half Day Rd., Deerfield, IL 60015.

CAREER: Grand Rapids School of the Bible and Music,
Grand Rapids, MI, instructor, 1978-87; visiting professor
at Trinity Evangelical Divinity School, Deerfield, IL,
1982—, and at Moffat College of Bible, Kijabe, Kenya,
East Africa, 1985-89; adjunct interim professor at Calvin
College, 1987—, and at Fuller Theological Seminary,
1990. Guest speaker for various organizations, including
the 700 Club, Moody Bible Institute, and Lutheran School
of Theology in Chicago.

MEMBER: American Historical Association, American Society of Church History, American Society of Missiology, Evangelical Theological Society.

AWARDS, HONORS: Gold Medallion Awards, Christian Publishers Association, 1984, for *From Jerusalem to Irian Jaya: A Biographical History of Christian Missions,* and 1989, for *First Ladies of the Parish: Historical Portraits of Pastors' Wives.*

WRITINGS:

How to Set Up Your Own Neighborhood Preschool, Arlington House, 1979.

From Jerusalem to Irian Jaya: A Biographical History of Christian Missions, Zondervan, 1983.

Women and the Church: A History of Changing Perspectives, Zondervan, 1986.

(With Walter Liefeld) *Daughters of the Church: A History of Women and Ministry from New Testament Times to the Present,* Zondervan, 1987.

First Ladies of the Parish: Historical Portraits of Pastors' Wives, Zondervan, 1988.

Guardians of the Great Commission: The Story of Women in Modern Missions, Zondervan, 1988.

Christian Speakers Treasury, Harper, 1989.

Another Gospel: Alternative Religions and the New Age Movement, Zondervan, 1989.

Sacred Stories: Daily Devotions from the Family of God, Zondervan, 1989, published as *Stories of Faith,* 1990.

Women in the Maze: Questions and Answers on Biblical Equality, InterVarsity, 1992.

Multiple Choices: Making Wise Decisions in a Complicated World—A Women's Guide, Zondervan, 1992.

Contributor to magazines, including *Missiology, Christianity Today, Christian History, Evangelical Missions Quarterly,* and *Church Herald.* Associate editor of *Missiology,* 1988—; member of editorial advisory board for *Christian History,* 1990-92.

WORK IN PROGRESS: Slain in the Spirit: Charismata and the Quest for Holiness, for Zondervan.

*   *   *

TUROW, Scott 1949-

PERSONAL: Born April 12, 1949, in Chicago, IL; son of David D. (a physician) and Rita (a writer; maiden name, Pastron) Turow; married Annette Weisberg (an artist), April 4, 1971; children: Rachel, Gabriel, Eve. *Education:* Amherst College, B.A., 1970; Stanford University, M.A., 1974; Harvard University, J.D., 1978. *Religion:* Jewish.

ADDRESSES: Office—Sonnenschein Carlin Nath & Rosenthal, Sears Tower, Suite 8000, Chicago, IL 60606.

CAREER: Stanford University, Stanford, CA, E. H. Jones Lecturer in Creative Writing, 1972-75; United States Court of Appeals (7th District), Chicago, IL, assistant United States attorney, 1978-86; Sonnenschein Carlin Nath & Rosenthal, Chicago, IL, partner, 1986—. Writer, 1972—.

AWARDS, HONORS: Writing award, College English Association and Book-of-the-Month Club, 1970; Edith Mirrielees fellow, 1972; Silver Dagger Award, Crime Writers Association, 1988, for *Presumed Innocent.*

WRITINGS:

One L: An Inside Account of Life in the First Year at Harvard Law School (nonfiction), Putnam, 1977.

Presumed Innocent (novel; Book-of-the-Month club selection), Farrar, Straus, 1987.

The Burden of Proof (novel), Farrar, Straus, 1990.

Work anthologized in *Best American Short Stories,* 1971, 1972. Contributor of stories, articles, and reviews to literary journals, including *Transatlantic Review, Ploughshares, Harvard, New England,* and *Place,* and to newspapers.

ADAPTATIONS: Presumed Innocent, a film based on Turow's novel of the same name, was released by Warner Brothers in 1990.

SIDELIGHTS: Scott Turow uses his insider's knowledge of the American legal system to form the basis for bestselling suspense novels. A practicing attorney who has also studied creative writing, Turow is the author of *Presumed Innocent* and *The Burden of Proof,* both of which explore the murky terrain of urban justice through highly-plotted fiction. "No one on the contemporary scene writes better mystery-suspense novels than Chicago attorney Scott Turow," notes Bill Blum in the *Los Angeles Times Book Review.* "In a genre overcrowded with transparent plots and one-dimensional super-sleuths, Turow's first novel, 'Presumed Innocent,' was a work of serious fiction as well as a gripping tale of murder and courtroom drama." *New York Times Magazine* correspondent Jeff Shear praises Turow for the "brash, backroom sensibility that informs his work as a novelist."

It is a rare writer indeed who collects millions from a first novel. Even more rare is the author who crafts a novel while holding a full-time, high-profile job. Turow did both, writing drafts of *Presumed Innocent* in his spare moments on the commuter train while working as an assistant United States attorney in Chicago. *Washington Post* contributor Steve Coll claims that through his determination to write fiction without sacrificing his profession, Turow "has fulfilled every literate working stiff's fantasy."

For his part, Turow maintains that his background in the legal system has provided him with subject matter for fiction as well as practical experience in crafting a narrative. He told *Publishers Weekly:* "As a lawyer, I never decided I didn't want to be a writer. I decided it would have to be a private passion, rather than something I could use. . . . My idea was to stay *alive* as a writer, just to continue to nurture that part of my soul." Turow not only "stayed alive" as a writer, he prospered. His novels have topped the bestseller lists and have found favor with many of the nation's book critics. *Time* magazine reviewer Paul Gray contends that the author's works "revolve around a nexus of old-fashioned values: honesty, loyalty, trust. When those values are violated—sometimes salaciously, always entertainingly—lawyers and the legal system rush in to try to set things right again. But the central quest in Turow's fiction is not for favorable verdicts but for the redemption of souls, the healing of society. Bestsellers seldom get more serious than that."

Turow was born and raised in the Chicago area, the son of an obstetrician. In his early years, the family lived in the city. Later they moved to an affluent suburb, Winnetka, Illinois, where Turow attended New Trier High School. Turow told the *Washington Post* that he inherited his own driving ambition from his father, who was "out delivering babies at all hours of the day and night and wasn't around very much." The author added: "I suppose that's the embedded mental image of the hard-working male that I have become." Both of Turow's parents helped to nurture that spirit of hard work—they wanted their son to become a physician too. Turow had other ideas. Even though he flunked freshman English at New Trier High, he grew to love writing, eventually becoming the editor of the school newspaper. He decided he wanted to be a writer, and he enrolled in Amherst College in Massachusetts as an English major. "I didn't want my father's life," he told the *Washington Post.*

At Amherst Turow began to write short stories and novels. A few of his short pieces were printed in literary magazines such as the *Transatlantic Review,* a rare feat for an undergraduate. After earning his bachelor's degree in 1970, Turow won a fellowship to the Stanford University creative writing program. There he taught while working on a novel about Chicago called *The Way Things Are.* He began to question the direction of his career when he received twenty-five rejections for *The Way Things Are.* Only one publisher, Farrar, Straus & Giroux, offered even the slightest encouragement. Turow told the *New York Times Magazine* that the cool reception his novel earned "made me realize that I wasn't one-tenth the writer I hoped to be. . . . I could not sustain the vision of myself as a writer only." In a *Los Angeles Times* interview he said: "I became convinced that one could not make a living in

the U.S. writing serious fiction. I was never terribly bitter about that. I didn't see why the world had an obligation to support novelists."

Even while writing *The Way Things Are* Turow realized that he was becoming very interested in the law. In 1975 he entered Harvard Law School. Even then he put his writing talents to work. His literary agent was able to secure him a contract for a personal, nonfiction account of the first year in the fabled law school. He took notes during his hectic class schedule and finished the book during the summer recess. In 1977, Putnam published Turow's *One L: An Inside Account of Life in the First Year at Harvard Law School.* The work sold modestly at first, but it has since become "required reading for anyone contemplating a career in law," to quote Justin Blewitt in *Best Sellers. New York Times* correspondent P. M. Stern calls *One L* "a compelling and important book. It is compelling in its vivid portrayal of the high-tension competitiveness of Harvard Law School and of the group madness it seems to induce in the student body. It is important because it offers an inside look at what law students do and don't learn and who they are and are not equipped to represent when they graduate."

After receiving his law degree in 1978, Turow returned to Chicago to work with the United States Attorney's office. As a prosecutor, he was assigned to the infamous "Operation Greylord," a series of trials that exposed judicial corruption in the city's courts. Turow was a member of the team that prosecuted Circuit Court Judge Reginald Holzer and former Illinois Attorney General William J. Scott. Little by little, the intrigues of corruption and legal wrangling began to work their way into the notebooks Turow kept for his fiction. He set aside a novel he was drafting and began to tinker with a story about an attorney. "I was learning a lot about bribery and I wanted to write about that," he told the *Washington Post.*

For several years Turow did his writing in the little spare time left him after meeting the demands of Operation Greylord and his growing family in the suburbs. He edited chapters of his new novel during his commute to and from work on the train, and he rose early in the morning to work on the fiction before he left for the office. Finally his wife convinced him to quit his job and finish the novel. He accepted a partnership at the downtown Chicago firm of Sonnenschein Carlin Nath & Rosenthal and then took a three-month hiatus from the law in order to write. His finished manuscript was mailed to a New York agent just two weeks before he was due to start his new job.

Turow was confident that his novel would be published, but he was astonished by the level of interest shown by New York's biggest publishing houses. A bidding war ensued over the rights to publish the work, and the sums soon exceeded $200,000. Ultimately Turow did not choose the high bidder but instead took an offer from Farrar, Straus because of its literary reputation—and because of the encouragement he had received from its editors during his student days. The $200,000 payment Farrar, Straus offered Turow was the largest sum that company had ever paid for a first novel.

Presumed Innocent tells the story of a troubled deputy prosecutor in a big city who is assigned to investigate the murder of a female colleague. As the nightmare case unfolds, the prosecutor—Rusty Sabich—finds himself on trial for murdering the woman, with whom he had an adulterous affair. Gray writes that in *Presumed Innocent* Turow "uses [a] grotesque death as a means of exposing the trail of municipal corruption that has spread through [fictitious] Kindle County. The issue is not merely whether a murderer will be brought to justice but whether public institutions and their guardians are any longer capable of finding the truth." Turow told *Publishers Weekly* that his book is "a comment on the different kinds of truth we recognize. If the criminal-justice system is supposed to be a truth-finding device, it's an awkward one at best. There are all kinds of playing around in the book that illuminate that, and yet by the same token, the results in the end are just. And that's not accidental. . . . Absolutely everybody in the novel is guilty of something. That's a truth of life that I learned as a prosecutor. We all do things we wish we hadn't done and that we're not necessarily proud of."

Fellow attorney-turned-author George V. Higgins notes in the *Chicago Tribune* that *Presumed Innocent* is a "beautifully crafted tale. . . . Packed with data, rich in incident, painstakingly imagined, it snags both of your lapels and presses you down in your chair until you've finished it." Likewise, Toronto *Globe & Mail* correspondent H. J. Kirchhoff contends that the novel is "surprisingly assured," adding: "The prose is crisp and polished, every character is distinct and fully realized, and the dialogue is authentic. Turow has blended his experience in the rough-and-tumble of the criminal courts with a sympathetic eye for the vagaries of the human condition and an intimate understanding of the dark side of the human soul." Jeff Shear concludes that the criminal-justice system *Presumed Innocent* portrays, "without tears or pretense, has seldom appeared in literature quite like this."

"*Presumed Innocent* won the literary lottery," observes Mei-Mei Chan in *USA Weekend*. The novel spent more than forty-three weeks on the bestseller lists, went through sixteen hard cover printings, and sold four million paperback copies. Turow reaped three million dollars for the paperback rights and another million for the movie rights. A film adaptation of the work, released in 1990, was one of the ten top-grossing movies of that year. When Turow published his second novel—almost simultaneously with the debut of the movie version of *Presumed Innocent*—he joined the ranks of Ernest Hemingway, J. D. Salinger, and Alex Haley by becoming the 92nd writer to appear on the cover of *Time* magazine.

By the time *The Burden of Proof* appeared in the summer of 1990, Turow had established a routine that included several hours a day for his writing. He still practices law, but he spends his mornings at home, in contact with the downtown firm by telephone and fax machine. His schedule is still daunting, however, as his celebrity status has made him a sought-after interview subject in the various media. Turow told *New York Times Magazine* that he does his best work under such pressure. "I run on a combination of fear, anxiety, and compulsion," he said. "I have to control my habit to work all the time."

The Burden of Proof takes its hero from among the characters in *Presumed Innocent*. Sandy Stern is a middle-aged defense attorney who returns home from a business trip to find his wife dead, a suicide. As he confronts the loss—and the circumstances behind it—he becomes enmeshed in a web of family intrigues, insider stock trading schemes, and unanswered questions about his wife's private life. Toronto *Globe & Mail* reviewer Margaret Cannon maintains that in *The Burden of Proof* Turow "has let his imagination loose and, while courtroom derring-do is still a hefty part of the plot, it doesn't subsume the tragic story about some very damaged people." In the *Washington Post Book World*, Jonathan Yardley writes: "Scott Turow's second novel proves beyond any reasonable doubt that his hugely successful first was no fluke. . . . It's that rare book, a popular novel that is also serious, if not 'literary' fiction. *The Burden of Proof* means to entertain, and does so with immense skill, so if all you want is intelligent amusement it will serve you handily: but it is also a complex, multi-layered meditation on 'the heartsore arithmetic of human events,' and as such rises far above the norm of what is generally categorized as 'commercial' fiction."

Turow has said repeatedly that he does not intend to retire from his law practice, even though the profits from his writing career give him that option. The author told the *Chicago Tribune* that he spent many years defining himself as a writer before he became a lawyer. "I really didn't have any sense of identity as a lawyer. I really felt I was faking it," he said. "Somewhere along the way that changed; somewhere along the line I went through this kind of shift of identity. People ask me what I do. I certainly answer I am a lawyer. I don't say I'm a writer. I find that kind of a grandiose claim for somebody who spends 60 hours a week doing something else." Turow told *Publishers Weekly* that he is grateful for the level of success he has achieved with his books, but that his perspective on writing has not changed. "Making money was not my intention," he said. "I wrote out of the same impulse that everyone else writes out of—I wrote because there were parts of my experience that I could best deal with that way." He concluded: "Obviously it was enormously fulfilling."

BIOGRAPHICAL/CRITICAL SOURCES:

BOOKS

Bestsellers 90, Issue 3, Gale, 1991.

PERIODICALS

Best Sellers, November, 1977.

Chicago Tribune, June 7, 1987; June 10, 1987; February 16, 1990.

Detroit News, May 1, 1988; June 1, 1990.

Globe & Mail (Toronto), July 11, 1987; August 8, 1987; June 16, 1990.

Los Angeles Times, July 24, 1987; October 12, 1989; June 3, 1990; June 11, 1990; July 27, 1990; September 9, 1990.

Los Angeles Times Book Review, June 3, 1990.

Newsweek, October 17, 1977; June 29, 1987; June 4, 1990.

New York Times, September 15, 1977; February 8, 1987; June 15, 1987; August 6, 1987; December 1, 1987; April 19, 1988; May 31, 1990.

New York Times Book Review, September 25, 1977; June 3, 1990.

New York Times Magazine, June 7, 1987.

Publishers Weekly, July 10, 1987; September 15, 1989.

Time, July 20, 1987; June 11, 1990.

Times (London), October 8, 1987; October 22, 1987.

USA Weekend, June 1-3, 1990.

Washington Post, October 2, 1977; August 30, 1987; June 9, 1990; June 12, 1990; July 27, 1990.

Washington Post Book World, June 3, 1990; December 2, 1990.*

—Sketch by Anne Janette Johnson

U

ULLENDORFF, Edward 1920-

PERSONAL: Born January 25, 1920; son of Frederic and Cilli Ullendorff; married Dina Noack, 1943. *Education:* Hebrew University, Jerusalem, M.A., 1942; Oxford University, D.Phil., 1952. *Avocational interests:* Music, traveling in Scotland.

ADDRESSES: Home—4 Bladon Close, Oxford, England.

CAREER: British Military Government, Eritrea, Ethiopia, chief examiner for censorship, 1942-43; British Ministry of Information, Eritrea, editor of African publications, 1943-45; British Military Administration, Eritrea, assistant political secretary, 1945-46; British Mandatory Government of Palestine, Jerusalem, Palestine, assistant secretary, 1947-48; Oxford University, Institute of Colonial Studies, Oxford, England, research officer and librarian, 1948-49; University of St. Andrews, St. Andrews, Scotland, lecturer, 1950-56, reader in Semitic languages, 1956-59; University of Manchester, Manchester, England, professor of Semitic languages and literatures, 1959-64; University of London, School of Oriental and African Studies, London, England, professor of Ethiopian studies, 1964-79, professor of Semitic languages, 1979-82, professor emeritus, 1982—. Schweich Lecturer, British Academy, 1967. Joint organizer, Second International Congress of Ethiopian Studies, 1963. Catalogued Ethiopian manuscripts in Royal Library, Windsor Castle. Member of advisory board, British Library, 1975-83.

MEMBER: Society for Old Testament Study (president, 1971), Association of British Orientalists (chairman, 1963-64), Anglo-Ethiopian Society (chairman, 1965-68; vice-president, 1969-77), Royal Asiatic Society (fellow; vice-president, 1975-79), British Academy (fellow; vice-president, 1980-82).

AWARDS, HONORS: Carnegie traveling fellow, Ethiopia, 1958; Imperial Ethiopian Gold Medallion, 1960; M.A., University of Manchester, 1962; D.Litt., University of St. Andrews, 1972; Haile Selassie International Prize, 1972, for Ethiopian studies; D.Phil., Hamburg University.

WRITINGS:

The Definite Article in the Semitic Languages, Tarbiz, 1941.

Exploration and Study of Abyssinia, Lunedi dell'Eritrea, 1945.

Catalogue of Ethiopian Manuscripts in the Bodleian Library, Clarendon Press, 1951.

The Semitic Languages of Ethiopia, Taylor's Foreign Press, 1955.

The Ethiopians, Oxford University Press, 1959, 3rd edition, 1973.

(With Stephen Wright) *Catalogue of Ethiopian Manuscripts in Cambridge University Library,* Cambridge University Press, 1961.

(Contributor) *Studi Semitici,* [Rome], 1961.

(Co-editor) *Studies in Honour of G. R. Driver,* Manchester University Press, 1962.

(Contributor) H. H. Rowley, *Companion to the Bible,* T. & T. Clark, 1963.

(With S. Moscati and others) *An Introduction to the Comparative Grammar of the Semitic Languages,* Harrassowitz, 1964.

(Co-editor) *Ethiopian Studies,* Manchester University Press, 1964.

The Challenge of Amharic, Oxford University Press, 1965.

An Amharic Chrestomathy, Oxford University Press, 1965, 2nd edition, 1978.

Ethiopia and the Bible, Oxford University Press, 1968.

(Translator and author of notes) Haile Selassie, *My Life and Ethiopia's Progress, 1892-1937: The Autobiogra-*

445

phy of Emperor Haile Selassie I, Oxford University Press, 1976.

Is Biblical Hebrew a Language?, Harrassowitz, 1977.

(With M. A. Knibb) *Book of Enoch,* Oxford University Press, 1978.

The Bawdy Bible, School of Oriental and African Studies, University of London, 1979.

(Co-editor) *The Amharic Letters of Emperor Theodore of Ethiopia to Queen Victoria,* Oxford University Press, 1979.

(With C. F. Beckingham) *The Hebrew Letters of Prester John,* Oxford University Press, 1982.

A Tigrinya Chrestomathy, Steiner Verlag, 1985.

Studia Aethiopica et Semitica, Steiner Verlag, 1987.

The Two Zions, Oxford University Press, 1988.

From the Bible to Enrico Cerulli, Steiner Verlag, 1990.

H. J. Polotsky, 1905-1991, Steiner Verlag, 1992.

Contributor to *Encyclopaedia Britannica* and *Encyclopaedia of Islam.* Contributor of articles and reviews to professional journals. Joint editor, *Journal of Semitic Studies,* 1961-64; chairman of editorial board, *Bulletin of the School of Oriental and African Studies,* 1968-78.

BIOGRAPHICAL/CRITICAL SOURCES:

PERIODICALS

Journal of Semitic Studies, January, 1990.

*   *   *

UNGER, Barbara   1932-

PERSONAL: Born October 2, 1932, in New York City; daughter of David (a businessman) and Florence (a pianist; maiden name, Schuchalter) Frankel; married Bernard Unger (divorced, 1976); married Dr. Theodore Kiichiro Sakano, 1987; children: (first marriage) Deborah, Suzanne. *Education:* City College (now City College of the City University of New York), B.A., 1954, M.A., 1957; further graduate study at New York University. *Avocational interests:* Collecting antique post cards.

ADDRESSES: Home—101 Parkside Dr., Suffern, NY 10901. *Office*—Rockland Community College, 145 College Rd., Suffern, NY 10901.

CAREER: Bucks Rock Work Camp, New Milford, CT, creative writing counselor, 1958-65; educational reporter for *Rockland Country Citizen,* 1961-63; English teacher in Nyack, NY, 1963-67; high school counselor in Ardsley, NY, 1967-69; Rockland Community College, Suffern, NY, professor of English, 1969—, currently head of creative writing and fiction program, and co-director, Visiting Writers' Series. Resident writer, Squaw Valley Community of Writers, 1980, Edna St. Vincent Millay Colony

for the Arts fellow, 1984, Ragdale Foundation fellow, 1985, 1986, and 1989, Writer-in-Residence, Rockland Center for the Arts, 1986, Hambidge Center for the Creative Arts & Sciences, Dorset Colony, 1989, Kalani Honua Conference Center and Retreat, HI, 1990, and Djerassi Foundation, Woodside, CA, 1991; Breadloaf Scholar, 1978; judge and guest writer, Wildwood Writers Conference, Harrisburg Area Community College, 1992.

AWARDS, HONORS: Fellowships from National Endowment for the Arts and National Endowment for the Humanities, both 1975, and New York State Council on the Arts, 1986; West Virginia Poetry Prize, *Laurel Review,* 1981; Chester H. Jones National Poetry Foundation award, 1982; Pushcart Press Prize nomination, 1987; Goodman Award, Thorntree Press, 1988; Anna Davidson Rosenberg Award for Poems on the Jewish Experience, Judah L. Magnes Museum, 1989; *New Letters* Literary Award finalist, 1990, for story "Grandma Rose"; Faculty Resource Scholar, New York University, 1991; H. G. Roberts Writing Award, 1991, for poem "The Audition"; poetry award, John Williams Narrative Poetry Competition, 1992, for poem "Letter to the Co-eds."

WRITINGS:

POETRY

Basement, Isthmus Press, 1975.

The Man Who Burned Money, Bellevue Press, 1980.

Inside the Wind, Linwood Publishers, 1986.

Learning to Foxtrot, Bellevue Press, 1989.

Blue Depression Glass, Thorntree Press, 1991.

Contributor of poems to about fifty periodicals, including *Negative Capability, Denver Quarterly, Massachusetts Review, Midstream, Southern Humanities Review, Beloit Poetry Journal,* and *South Coast Poetry Review.*

FICTION

Dying for Uncle Ray and Other Stories, Kendall/Hunt Publishing Co., 1990.

OTHER

Stories anthologized in *True to Life Adventure Stories,* Crossing Press, 1981, *American Fiction: The Best Short Stories by Emerging Writers,* Birch Lane/Carol, 1990, and other anthologies. Contributor of stories to *Midstream, Beloit Fiction Journal, Reconstructionist, Jewish Currents, Paragraph, Crazyquilt, Savvy Woman, Cache Review,* and other periodicals. Also contributor of reviews to *Contact/II* and *South Florida Review.*

WORK IN PROGRESS: A novel; short fiction; poetry; co-editing an anthology about Bronx authors.

SIDELIGHTS: Barbara Unger told *CA:* "I prefer to work on the points of contact between realism and fantasy;

mainstream and experimental fiction. Most of my poems are free-verse lyrics with a strong narrative thread. My short fiction is ethnic, experimental, fantasy, feminist, autobiographical and humorous. The dialogue of poetry and prose is important to my work, and becoming increasingly important with time.''

The same themes and characters reappear throughout her poems, she wrote. For example, the story "The Gambler's Daughter" draws from poems in her two most recent collections of poetry, *Learning to Foxtrot* and *Blue Depression Glass.* Unger added, "Perhaps the critic Pat Wilcox has put it best when she writes of 'discrete details that may live on their own in . . . . sketch or study, yet build, piece by piece, to peaks of full-dress performance.'

"Feminist concerns are inescapable for me living through these times. I am pleased to have my work included in women's anthologies from Crossing Press, Papier-Mache Press, Milkweed Editions, Herbooks, and other publishers of work by women, as well as in general anthologies such as *80 on the '80s: A Decade's History in Verse, Disenchantments: An Anthology of Modern Fairy Tale Poetry, American Yearbook of Magazine Verse and Poetry* and *Life in the Line: Selections on Words and Healing,* as well as many others.

"William Heyen has said of *Inside the Wind* that it 'moves . . . through a Depression childhood in incisive and sharp-edged poems.' Alicia Ostriker has said of my work that it contains 'poignance of past, raw necessity of future, city, suburb, clarity throughout, packed not only with personal history but the changes a generation has experienced.' John Allman has said that my poems 'are distinguished to us of a process by which love and art cleanse the ego. They are defiant where politeness would be compromise. Honest and true, they are rich in the aesthetics of survival.' Maurice Kenny calls mine 'a voice to be reckoned with.' A reviewer for *Ms.* magazine has characterized my fiction as 'endowed with a healing humor,' one of a group of 'bold, powerful, often raunchy voices.' Patti Tana has said that my poems 'say something important about knowing and naming her self, about the dance and the struggle between women and men, about the magic of flesh and the reality of dreams.' Judith Johnson (Sherwin) has said of my work that 'it brings the ordinary and the surreal together to make a bridge to what is deeply felt in our inner lives.' Patricia Wilcox says, ' . . . she moves one by precision of witness and craft.' Reviewer Virginia Scott writes, 'Finally, it is craft, the construction of apt metaphor, the language itself—that compels me to place Barbara Unger's poems within the context of the work of the major poets of her generation.' "

URDANG, Laurence 1927-

PERSONAL: Born March 21, 1927, in New York, NY; son of Harry (a teacher) and Annabel (a teacher; maiden name, Schafran) Urdang; married Irena Ehrlich vel Sluszny (an antiques dealer), May 23, 1952 (divorced); children: Nicole Severyna, Alexandra Stefanie. *Education:* Columbia University, B.S., 1954.

ADDRESSES: Home—Essex, CT.

CAREER: Funk & Wagnalls Co., New York, NY, editor, 1955-57; Random House, Inc., New York City, reference editor, 1957-61, director of reference department, 1962-69; Laurence Urdang, Inc. (preparer of reference books), Essex, CT, president, beginning 1969. Lecturer, New York University, 1956-61. Head of Laurence Urdang Associates Ltd., Aylesbury, England, 1970-85. *Military service:* U.S. Naval Reserve, active duty, 1944-45.

MEMBER: Dictionary Society of North America, American Dialectic Society, American Name Society, Association for Computing Machinery, Association for Literary and Linguistic Computing, American Association for Applied Linguistics, American Society of Indexes, Name Society (England), British Association for Applied Linguistics, European Association for Lexicography, New York Academy of Sciences, Society of Authors (London), Naval Club (London), Athenaeum (London), Century Association (New York).

WRITINGS:

EDITOR

The Random House Vest Pocket Dictionary of Synonyms and Antonyms, Random House, 1960.
The Random House Dictionary of the English Language, college edition, Random House, 1968.
The Random House College Dictionary, Random House, 1968.
The New York Times Everyday Reader's Dictionary of Misunderstood, Misused, Mispronounced Words, Quadrangle, 1972, revised edition published as *New York Times Dictionary of Misunderstood, Misused, and Mispronounced Words,* Dutton, 1987.
Dictionary of Advertising Terms, Tatham-Laird & Kudner, 1977.
Verbatim, Verbatim, *Volumes I and II,* 1978, *Volumes III and IV,* 1981, *Volumes V and VI,* 1981, and *Index: Volumes I-VI,* 1981.
Roget's Thesaurus, Dale Books, 1978.
Webster's Dictionary, Dale Books, 1978 (published in England as *Nelson's New Compact Webster's Dictionary,* Thomas Nelson, 1978).
The Basic Book of Synonyms and Antonyms, New American Library, 1978, revised edition published as *The Random House Basic Dictionary: Synonyms and Ant-*

onyms, Ballantine Books, 1991 (published in England as *A Basic Dictionary of Synonyms and Antonyms,* Pan Books, 1979, revised edition, 1991).

Synonym Finder, Rodale Press, 1978, revised edition, Warner Books, 1986.

Nelson's Children's Encyclopedia, Thomas Nelson, 1978.

Word for Word, Verbatim, 1979.

Twentieth Century American Nicknames, H. W. Wilson, 1979.

British English: A to Zed, Verbatim, 1979.

Dictionary of Allusions, Gale, 1980, 2nd edition published as *Allusions—Cultural, Literary, Biblical and Historical: A Thematic Dictionary,* 1986.

Dictionary of Suffixes in English, Gale, 1980.

Treasury of Picturesque Expressions, Gale, 1980.

Timetables of American History, Simon & Schuster, 1981.

World Almanac Dictionary of Dates, World Almanac, 1982.

Modifiers, Gale, 1982.

Literary, Rhetorical, and Linguistics Terms Index, Gale, 1983.

Loanwords Index, Gale, 1983.

Mosby's Medical and Nursing Dictionary, Mosby, 1983.

Fine and Applied Arts Terms Index, Gale, 1983.

Idioms and Phrases Index, Gale, 1983.

Prefixes and Other Word-Initial Elements of English, Gale, 1984.

Slogans, Gale, 1984.

(Editorial director) *Holiday and Anniversaries of the World,* Gale, 1985.

The Facts on File Dictionary of Numerical Allusions, Facts on File, 1986.

(With Frank Abate and Ceila D. Robbins) *Mottoes,* Gale, 1986.

(With Abate) *Loanwords Dictionary,* Gale, 1987.

Names and Nicknames of Places and Things, G. K. Hall, 1987.

Children's Illustrated Dictionary, Book Sales, 1987.

Dictionary of Confusable Words, Facts on File, 1988 (published in England as *Dictionary of Differences,* Bloomsbury, 1988).

The Whole Ball of Wax and Other Colloquial Phrases, Putnam, 1988.

Oxford Thesaurus, Oxford University Press, 1991.

Dictionary of Borrowed Words, Gleneida, 1991.

Dictionary of Uncommon Words, Gleneida, 1991.

A Fine Kettle of Fish and Other Figurative Phrases, Gale, 1991.

OTHER

Editor and publisher of *Verbatim: The Language Quarterly,* 1974—.

URIS, Leon (Marcus) 1924-

PERSONAL: Born August 3, 1924, in Baltimore, MD; son of Wolf William (a shopkeeper) and Anna (Blumberg) Uris; married Betty Katherine Beck, 1945 (divorced January, 1968); married Margery Edwards, September 8, 1968 (died February 20, 1969); married Jill Peabody (a photographer), February 15, 1970; children: (first marriage) Karen Lynn, Mark Jay, Michael Cady; (third marriage) Rachael Jackson, one other child. *Education:* Attended public schools in Baltimore, MD. *Avocational interests:* Skiing, bowling, trail-biking, and tennis.

ADDRESSES: Home—Aspen, CO. *Office*—c/o Doubleday & Co. Inc., 666 Fifth Ave., New York, NY 10103.

CAREER: Writer. Worked previously as a circulation district manager for the *San Francisco Call-Bulletin. Military service:* U.S. Marine Corps, 1942-45; served in the Pacific at Guadalcanal and Tarawa.

MEMBER: Writers League, Screenwriters Guild.

AWARDS, HONORS: Daroff Memorial Award, 1959; National Institute of Arts and Letters grant, 1959; California Literature Silver Medal award, 1962, for *Mila 18,* and Gold Medal award, 1965, for *Armageddon;* honorary doctorates, University of Colorado, 1976, Santa Clara University, 1977, Wittenberg University, 1980, and Lincoln College, 1985; John F. Kennedy Medal, Irish/American Society of New York, 1977; gold medal, Eire Society of Boston, 1978; Jobotinsky Medal, State of Israel, 1980; Hall Fellowship (with wife, Jill Uris), Concord Academy, 1980; Scopus Award, Hebrew University of Jerusalem, 1981; Books for the Teen Age designation, New York Public Library, 1980-82, for *Exodus.*

WRITINGS:

NOVELS

Battle Cry (also see below), Putnam, 1953.

The Angry Hills, Random House, 1955.

Exodus (also see below) Doubleday, 1957.

Mila 18, Doubleday, 1960.

Armageddon: A Novel of Berlin, Doubleday, 1964.

Topaz, McGraw, 1967.

QB VII, Doubleday, 1970.

Trinity, Doubleday, 1976.

The Haj, Doubleday, 1984.

Mitla Pass (Literary Guild main selection), Doubleday, 1988.

SCREENPLAYS

Battle Cry, Warner Brothers, 1954.

Gunfight at the O.K. Corral (also see below), Paramount, 1957.

OTHER

(Author of commentary) *Exodus Revisited,* photographs by Dimitrios Harissiadis, Doubleday, 1959, published in England as *In the Steps of Exodus,* Heinemann, 1962.

The Third Temple (essay), bound with William Stevenson's *Strike Zion,* Bantam, 1967.

Ari (book and lyrics based on his novel, *Exodus;* also known as *Exodus, the Musical*), music by Walt Smith, produced on Broadway, 1971.

(Author of commentary) *Ireland: A Terrible Beauty: The Story of Ireland Today,* photographs by wife, Jill Uris, Doubleday, 1975.

(With J. Uris) *Jerusalem, Song of Songs,* photographs by J. Uris, Doubleday, 1981.

Contributor to several anthologies, including *Fabulous Yesterdays,* Harper, 1961; *American Men at Arms,* compiled by F. Van Wyck Mason, Little, Brown, 1965; *A Treasury of Jewish Sea Stories,* edited by Samuel Sobel, Jonathan David, 1965; and *Great Spy Stories from Fiction,* by Allan Dulles, Harper, 1969. Also contributor to periodicals, including *Esquire, Coronet, Ladies' Home Journal,* and *TWA Ambassador.* Author's work has been translated into other languages, including Spanish, Italian, and Portuguese.

ADAPTATIONS: Gunfight at the O.K. Corral was novelized by Nelson C. Nye, Norden Publications, 1956. *The Angry Hills* was adapted for film and released by Metro-Goldwyn-Mayer, 1959; *Exodus* was adapted for a film directed by Otto Preminger, United Artists (UA), 1960; *Topaz* was adapted for a film directed by Alfred Hitchcock, UA, 1969; *QB VII* was adapted into a television movie, ABC-TV, 1974.

SIDELIGHTS: American writer Leon Uris is the author of several bestselling novels based upon details and events drawn from contemporary history. He received acclaim early in his career as the author of such popular books as *Exodus,* a landmark novelization of the history of the Jewish settlement of modern Israel, and the espionage thriller *Topaz.* Uris's later works include *QB VII,* a semi-autobiographical account of the trial of an author charged with libel by a German physician and former Nazi, and *Trinity,* a novel set amid Ireland's political and religious turmoil. Panoramic historical fiction that has proved to be commercially successful, Uris's fast-paced novels have earned him a dedicated readership. Yet, throughout his career critical opinion on his work has been mixed. While critics praise his storytelling abilities—the appeal of his novels has been sometimes described as cinematic in nature—Uris is sometimes cited for problems with grammatic technique, for his occasionally cardboard characters and stiff dialogue, and for taking liberties with historical

facts. Sharon D. Downey and Richard A. Kallan, noting both Uris's immense popular appeal and what they perceive as flaws in regards to traditional literary standards, assert in *Communications Monographs,* "in short, Uris remains a reader's writer and a critic's nightmare."

Uris began writing in the early 1950s, inspired by his four-year tour of duty with the U.S. Marine Corps during World War II. His first novel, *Battle Cry,* was published by G. P. Putnam in 1953 after making the rounds of several publishing houses. "There were those who thought I was crazy, others who gave me encouragement," Uris told Bernard Kalb in *Saturday Review.* "My guiding thought throughout was that the real Marine story had not been told. We were a different breed of men who looked at war in a different way." The book was praised by reviewers for its realistic depiction of the dedicated men who risked their lives in the front lines of battle. Commenting on the unique approach to the subject of war in *Battle Cry,* critic Merle Miller notes in the *Saturday Review* that the novel "may have started a whole new and healthy trend in war literature." The book proved to be as popular with readers as it was with critics, and Uris went on to write the screenplay for the film version of his novel, which was released by Warner Brothers in 1954.

The success of *Battle Cry* encouraged Uris to continue writing and he was soon at work on his second novel, *The Angry Hills.* Loosely based on the diary of an uncle who had fought in Greece with a Jewish unit of the British armed forces, the work was published in 1955. Although the response from critics was that as an adventure story, the book was too fast-paced, *The Angry Hills* is significant in that it focused Uris's interest in the Middle East, the Palestinian issue, and the history of Israel, home to many of his relatives. Although his preoccupation with these subjects would stay out of his major work for the next few years—after publication of his second novel, Uris was soon at work on a screenplay for the classic western drama, *Gunfight at the O.K. Corral*—it would figure prominently in several of his later novels, most notably *Exodus,* which would become one of the largest-selling books in publishing history.

Exodus is the history of European Jews and their efforts to establish the state of Israel as a Jewish homeland. Although faulting Uris for what they perceive to be a tendency towards lengthy and partisan passages, critics have hailed *Exodus* as a gripping human drama and a novel of heroic proportions. A descriptive account of the Warsaw Ghetto included in this novel provided the seed for Uris's next book, *Mila 18,* which continued his fascination with the predicament of Jews in the twentieth century. From there, he worked with noted Greek photographer Dimitrios Harissiadis on the photo-essay *Exodus Revisited,* a complement to the research he did for *Mila 18.* The author's lifelong passion for the Jewish people and for Israel would be the motivation behind several other books, including *The Haj,* an account of the birth of Israel told from the point of view of a Palestinian Arab, and *Mitla Pass,* a novel about an Israeli soldier during the Sinai War that was published in 1988 to mixed reviews but immediate bestseller status.

Some critics have viewed flaws of a technical nature as an acceptable tradeoff for a well-wrought story when reviewing Uris's novels. Pete Hamill writes in the *New York Times Book Review:* "Leon Uris is a storyteller, in a direct line from those men who sat around fires in the days before history and made the tribe more human. The subject is man, not words; story is all, the form it takes is secondary." Although not unaware of the problematic aspects of the novel genre, Hamill states: "It is a simple thing to point out that Uris often writes crudely, that his dialogue can be wooden, that his structure occasionally groans under the excess baggage of exposition and information. Simple, but irrelevant. None of that matters as you are swept along in the narrative." Critic Dan Wakefield agrees, noting in a review of *Exodus* for the *Nation:* "The plot is so exciting that the characters become exciting too; not because of their individuality or depth, but because of the historic drama they are involved in." Wakefield goes on to add, "The real achievement . . . lies not so much in its virtues as a novel as in its skillful rendering of the furiously complex history of modern Israel in a palatable, popular form that is usually faithful to the spirit of the complicated realities."

In order to write *Exodus,* Uris read almost three hundred books, traveled twelve thousand miles within Israel's boundaries, and interviewed more than twelve hundred individuals. Similar efforts went into his other books, including *Trinity,* which arose out of the people and places Uris and his third wife, photographer Jill Peabody Uris, encountered on a trip to document modern Ireland. The wealth of historical background in his novels has caused Uris's books to be alternately called "non-fiction" novels, "propaganda" novels, or just plain "journalism" by critics. A reviewer for the *Christian Science Monitor* addresses the danger in mixing fact and fiction: "Few readers are expert enough to be 100 percent certain where Mr. Uris's imagination has taken over the record." Nevertheless, as Maxwell Geismar points out in the *Saturday Review:* "If Mr. Uris sometimes lacks tone as a novelist, if his central figures are social types rather than individual portraits, there is also a kind of 'underground power' in his writing. No other novel I have read recently has had the same capacity [as *Exodus*] to refresh our memory, inform our intelligence, and to stir the heart." In the same vein, Hamill writes of *Trinity:* "The novel sprawls, occasionally bores, meanders like a river. . . . But when the story is finished

the reader has been to places where he or she has never been before. The news items . . . will never seem quite the same again."

Webster Scott offers his assessment of the author's work in the *Washington Post Book World.* Novelists with mass audience appeal such as Uris, in which group Scott includes noted authors James A. Michener and James Clavell, "may tell us relatively little about our inner weather, but they report on storms and setting suns outside. They read the environment we must function in. Occasionally they replicate our social structures. They sift the history that brought us to the present. They give us the briefing papers necessary to convert news stories into human stories. All of which serve our emotional need to make order out of confusion" concludes Scott, "to explain the inexplicable."

BIOGRAPHICAL/CRITICAL SOURCES:

BOOKS

Authors in the News, Gale, Volume 1, 1976, Volume 2, 1976.
Bestsellers 89, Issue 2, Gale, 1989.
Contemporary Literary Criticism, Gale, Volume 7, 1977, Volume 32, 1985.
Contemporary Novelists, 4th edition, St. James Press/St. Martin's, 1986.

PERIODICALS

Atlantic, July, 1964.
Chicago Tribune, November 24, 1988.
Chicago Tribune Book World, April 29, 1984, p. 33.
Christian Science Monitor, December 4, 1958; November 16, 1967.
Commentary, October, 1961.
Communication Monographs, September, 1982.
Globe and Mail (Toronto), January 7, 1989.
Inside Books, November, 1988, pp. 25-26.
Los Angeles Times Book Review, September 27, 1984, p. 8; October 30, 1988, p. 12.
Nation, April 11, 1959.
Newsweek, May 21, 1984, p. 84.
New York Herald Tribune Book Review, September 28, 1958.
New York Review of Books, April 16, 1964.
New York Times, October 12, 1958; April 27, 1984.
New York Times Book Review, June 4, 1961; June 28, 1964; October 15, 1967; March 14, 1976, p. 5; April 22, 1984, p. 7; January 1, 1989, p. 14.
Philadelphia Bulletin, March 31, 1976.
Publishers Weekly, March 29, 1976, pp. 6-7; September 23, 1988, p. 59.
Saturday Review, April 25, 1953, pp. 16-17; September 27, 1958.

Time, December 8, 1958; June 2, 1961.
Times Literary Supplement, October 27, 1961.
Washington Post Book World, April 1, 1984, pp. 1-2; October 30, 1988.*

V

VALLANCE, Elizabeth (Mary) 1945-

PERSONAL: Born April 8, 1945, in Glasgow, Scotland; daughter of William Henderson (an engineer) and Jean (Kirkwood) McGonnigill; married Iain David Thomas Vallance (a finance director), August 5, 1967; children: Rachel Emma, Edmund William Thomas. *Education:* University of St. Andrews, M.A. (with first class honors), 1967; London School of Economics and Political Science, London, M.Sc. (with distinction), 1968; Queen Mary College, London, Ph.D., 1978.

ADDRESSES: Office—Department of Political Studies, Queen Mary and Westfield Colleges, University of London, Mile End Rd., London E1 4NS, England.

CAREER: University of London, Queen Mary and Westfield Colleges, College, London, England, assistant lecturer in politics, 1968-70, lecturer in government and political studies, 1971-79, senior lecturer in government and political studies, 1980-85, reader in politics, 1985—, visiting professor in politics, 1990—, head of Department of Political Studies, 1985, governor, 1985-88. HMV Group, Ltd., director, 1990—. Governor of London Grammar School. Member of National Committee for Electoral Reform.

MEMBER: Political Studies Association of the United Kingdom, Association of University Teachers.

AWARDS, HONORS: Leverhulme fellowship, 1977-78; European Economic Community fellowship, 1983-84; Sloan fellowship, London Business School, 1989; Royal Society of Arts fellowship, 1990.

WRITINGS:

(Contributor) R. J. Benewick and T. A. Smith, editors, *Direct Action and Democratic Politics,* Allen & Unwin, 1972.

(Editor and contributor) *The State, Society, and Self-Destruction,* Allen & Unwin, 1975.

Women in the House: A Study of Women Members of Parliament, Humanities, 1979.

(Editor) *Europa Biographical Dictionary of British Women,* Europa, 1984.

Women of Europe: Women Members of the European Parliament and Equality Policy, Cambridge University Press, 1986.

(With Lisanne Radice and Virginia Willis) *Member of Parliament,* Macmillan, 1988, 2nd edition, 1990.

(Editor and contributor) *Business Ethics in a New Europe,* Kluwer Academic Press, 1992.

Contributor of numerous articles and many reviews to academic journals and newspapers.

WORK IN PROGRESS: A book on business ethics for Cambridge University Press.

SIDELIGHTS: Elizabeth Vallance once wrote: "Although much of my writing has been professionally inspired, I enjoy writing in an *ad hominem* way as much as in a formal style. My forays into journalism are therefore in many ways as indicative of my style and interests as the more extended works."

BIOGRAPHICAL/CRITICAL SOURCES:

PERIODICALS

Glasgow Herald, November 6, 1979.
Scotsman, August 13, 1979.
Times Literary Supplement, April 6, 1984, p. 380; June 24, 1988, p. 711.

VANCIL, Richard F(ranklin) 1931-

PERSONAL: Born September 17, 1931, in St. Louis, MO; son of George K. and Pearl (Cochran) Vancil; married Emily C. Robinson, June 17, 1955; children: Richard C., Robinson C., Virginia C. *Education:* Northwestern University, B.S., 1953; Harvard University, M.B.A., 1955, D.B.A., 1960.

ADDRESSES: Home—12 Lambert Rd., Belmont, MA 02178.

CAREER: Harvard University, Harvard Business School, Boston, MA, instructor in control, 1958-60, assistant professor, 1960-64, associate professor of business administration, 1964—, Lovett Learned Professor, 1977—. Certified public accountant, Illinois and Massachusetts. Chairman of the board, Management Analysis Center, Inc., Cambridge, MA; director, CIGNA Corporation; management consultant to various businesses. Joslin Diabetes Foundation, Boston, MA, trustee, 1965—. *Military service:* U.S. Army, Finance Corps, 1955-58; became first lieutenant.

MEMBER: American Institute of Certified Public Accountants, American Accounting Association, Financial Executives Institute, Institute of Management Sciences, Beta Gamma Sigma, Beta Alpha Psi.

WRITINGS:

(With J. L. Treynor) *Machine Tool Leasing,* Management Analysis Center, 1956.
(With Neil E. Harlan) *Cases in Accounting Policy,* Prentice-Hall, 1961.
(With Harlan and Charles Christenson) *Managerial Economics: Text and Cases,* Irwin, 1962.
(With Robert F. Vandell) *Cases in Capital Budgeting,* Irwin, 1962.
Leasing of Industrial Equipment, McGraw, 1963.
(With Robert D. Buzzell and Walter J. Salmon) *Product Profitability and Merchandising Decisions,* Harvard Business School, 1965.
(With Robert N. Anthony and John Dearden) *Management Control Systems: Cases and Readings,* Irwin, 1965, revised edition, 1972.
(With John Desmond Glover) *Management of Transformation: A Report to Top Management of the Telephone Industry,* International Business Machines Corporation, 1968.
Workshop for Planning Executives, 3rd edition, Harvard Business School, 1970.
Financial Executive's Handbook, Irwin, 1970.
(With Roman L. Weil) *Replacement Cost Accounting: Readings on Concepts, Uses, and Methods,* Thomas Horton, 1976.

(With William J. Bruns) *A Primer on Replacement Cost Accounting,* Thomas Horton, 1976.
(With Peter Lorange) *What Kind of Strategic Planning System Do You Need?,* Alfred P. Sloan School of Management, Massachusetts Institute of Technology, 1976.
Accounting for Inflation, Thomas Horton, 1976.
(Editor with Lorange) *Strategic Planning Systems,* Prentice-Hall, 1977.
Decentralization: Managerial Ambiguity by Design, Dow Jones-Irwin, 1979.
The CFO's Handbook, Dow Jones-Irwin, 1986.
Passing the Baton: Managing the Process of C.E.O. Succession, Fitzhenry & Whiteside, 1987.

Contributor of articles to professional journals. Editor, *Formal Planning Systems.*

BIOGRAPHICAL/CRITICAL SOURCES:

PERIODICALS

Globe and Mail (Toronto), December 19, 1987.*

*   *   *

Van STEENWYK, Elizabeth (Ann) 1928-

PERSONAL: Born July 1, 1928, in Galesburg, IL; daughter of Wilson Andrew and Edith Viola Harler; married Donald H. Van Steenwyk (an executive), June 12, 1949; children: Kedrin (daughter), Matthew, Brett, Gretchen. *Education:* Knox College, B.A., 1950. *Politics:* Republican. *Religion:* Methodist. *Avocational interests:* Hiking and watching sunsets at family walnut ranch, reading.

ADDRESSES: Home and office—885 Chester Ave., San Marino, CA 91108; and 5785 Adelaida Rd., Paso Robles, CA 93446.

CAREER: WGIL-Radio, Galesburg, IL, producer, 1948-51; KTSM-TV, El Paso, TX, producer, 1951-52; writer. Member of board of directors of family business; president of Cardiac League, Guild of Huntington Memorial Hospital. Lecturer and speaker to schools and writers' groups.

MEMBER: International PEN, Society of Children's Book Writers, Phi Beta.

AWARDS, HONORS: Silver medal, International Film and Television Festival, 1979, for film adaptation of her book *The Best Horse;* Patriotic Feature of the Year Award, *Highlights for Children* magazine, 1987, for short story "Secrets of the State House"; selection as one of 300 Best Books for Teenagers in 1988, New York Public Library, for *Dwight David Eisenhower, President;* nomination for Bluebonnet Award (Texas), 1989, and Rebecca

Caudill Young Readers' Book Award (Illinois), 1991, both for *Three Dog Winter;* Helen Keating Ott Award, Church and Synagogue Library Association, 1990, for outstanding contribution to children's literature.

WRITINGS:

JUVENILES

Dorothy Hamill: Olympic Champion, Harvey House, 1976.
Women in Sports: Figure Skating, Harvey House, 1976.
The Best Horse, Scholastic Book Services, 1977.
Larry Mahan, Grosset, 1977.
Barrel Horse Racer, Walker & Co., 1977.
Women in Sports: Rodeo, Harvey House, 1978.
Mystery at Beach Bay, Bowmar, 1978.
Ride to Win, Bowmar, 1978.
Cameo of a Champion, McGraw, 1978.
Fly Like an Eagle, and Other Stories, Walker & Co., 1978.
Rivals on Ice, Albert Whitman, 1978.
Illustrated Skating Dictionary for Young People, Harvey House, 1979.
God, Why Did He Die?, Concordia, 1979.
Presidents at Home, Messner, 1980.
Tracy Austin, Childrens Press, 1980.
Quarter Horse Winner, Albert Whitman, 1980.
Stars on Ice, Dodd, 1980.
Illustrated Riding Dictionary for Young People, Harvey House, 1980.
Bucky, Economy Co., 1981.
The Ghost of Pilgrim Creek, Economy Co., 1981.
Triangle of Fear, Economy Co., 1981.
Three Dog Afternoon, Economy Co., 1981.
Dance with a Stranger, Tempo, 1982.
Southpaw from Sonora Mystery, Childrens Press, 1983.
Ghost in the Gym, Childrens Press, 1983.
Terror on the Rebound, Childrens Press, 1983.
Secrets of the Painted Horse, Childrens Press, 1983.
Lonely Rider, Tempo, 1983.
The Witness Tree, Tempo, 1983.
Behind the Scenes at the Amusement Park, Albert Whitman, 1983.
The Face of Love, Dutton, 1983.
Harness Racing, Crestwood, 1983.
Will You Love My Horse Forever, Dutton, 1984.
Rachel Has a Secret, Willowisp Press, 1987.
Sarah's Great Idea, Willowisp Press, 1987.
Dwight David Eisenhower, President, Walker & Co., 1987.
Three Dog Winter, Walker & Co., 1987.
Lorie for President, Willowisp Press, 1988.
Levi Strauss: The Blue Jeans Man, Walker & Co., 1988.
Can You Keep a Secret?, Willowisp Press, 1990.
The California Gold Rush: West with the Forty-Niners, F. Watts, 1991.
Ida B. Wells-Barnett: Woman of Courage, F. Watts, 1992.

OTHER

Also author of *The Witch Switch, New Girl in Town,* and *Friends Are Like That,* all Willowisp Press. Contributor of more than one hundred fifty articles and stories to periodicals. Developer of a primary reading kit, "TOYS," for Educational Insights.

ADAPTATIONS: The Best Horse was made into a motion picture by Learning Corp. of America, 1979; *Three Dog Winter* has been optioned by PBS for a ninety-minute television movie.

WORK IN PROGRESS: Ely S. Parker: Citizen of Two Worlds, "a biography of a Native American who moved easily between two cultures and achieved much, ignoring discrimination he received in the white world"; *Will the Real Me Please Stand Up?; California Missions; Frederic Remington: Wild West Artist.*

SIDELIGHTS: Elizabeth Van Steenwyk once told *CA:* "Why do I write for children? I can sum it up in the words of a child who wrote to me after reading one of my books. She said, 'Happiness must be writing children's books.' I wonder how she knew? Simply, I write for young readers because there are so many more possibilities than limitations."

*   *   *

VENISON, Alfred
    See POUND, Ezra (Weston Loomis)

*   *   *

VERDON, Dorothy
    See TRALINS, S(andor) Robert

*   *   *

VERNON, Raymond 1913-

PERSONAL: Born September 1, 1913, in New York, NY; married Josephine Stone, 1935; children: Heide Vernon Wortzel, Susan Patricia Vernon Gerstenfeld. *Education:* City College (now City College of the City University of New York), A.B., 1933; Columbia University, Ph.D., 1941.

ADDRESSES: Home—1 Dunstable Rd., Cambridge, MA 02138. *Office*—John F. Kennedy School of Government, Harvard University, Cambridge, MA 02138.

CAREER: Affiliated with Securities and Exchange Commission, 1935-46; U.S. Department of State, Washington,

D.C., held various positions, 1946-51, deputy and acting director, Office of Economic Defense and Trade Policy, 1951-54; U.S. Government, President's Committee for Economic Policy, Washington, D.C., member of staff, 1954; planning and control director, Hawley & Hoops, Inc., 1954-56; New York Metropolitan Region Study, New York, NY, director, 1956-59; Harvard University, Cambridge, MA, professor of international trade and investment, 1959-69, Herbert F. Johnson Professor of International Business Management, 1969-79, Clarence Dillon Professor of International Affairs, 1978-84, Clarence Dillon Professor of International Affairs Emeritus, 1984—, director of Development Advisory Service, 1962-66, director of Center for International Affairs, 1973-78. Consultant to U.S. Department of State, U.S Department of the Treasury, and various United Nations agencies.

MEMBER: Academy of International Business (fellow), American Economic Association, Council on Foreign Relations (fellow), American Academy of Arts and Sciences, Association of Public Policy Analysis and Management, Phi Beta Kappa.

AWARDS, HONORS: Meritorious Service Award, U.S. Department of State; M.A., Harvard University, 1959; Order of the Rising Sun (Japan), 1985.

WRITINGS:

The Regulation of Stock Exchange Members, Columbia University Press, 1941.

The Changing Economic Function of the Central City, Committee for Economic Development, 1959.

(With Edgar M. Hoover) *Anatomy of a Metropolis,* Harvard University Press, 1959.

Metropolis, 1985, Harvard University Press, 1960.

The Dilemma of Mexico's Development, Harvard University Press, 1963.

(Editor) *Public Policy and Private Enterprise in Mexico,* Harvard University Press, 1964.

The Myth and Reality of Our Urban Problems, Harvard University Press, 1966.

(Editor and contributor) *How Latin America Views the United States Investor,* Praeger, 1966.

Manager in the International Economy, Prentice-Hall, 1968, 6th edition, 1989.

(Editor, and contributor with William H. Gruber) *The Technology Factor in International Trade,* Columbia University Press, 1970.

Sovereignty at Bay: The Multinational Spread of U.S. Enterprise, Basic Books, 1971.

The Economic and Political Consequences of Multinational Enterprise: An Anthology, Division of Research, Harvard Business School, 1972.

(With Louis T. Wells, Jr.) *The Economic Environment of International Business,* Prentice-Hall, 1972, 5th edition, 1989.

(Editor) *Big Business and the State: Changing Relations in Western Europe,* Harvard University Press, 1974.

(Editor) *The Oil Crisis,* Norton, 1976.

Storm over the Multinationals: The Real Issues, Harvard University Press, 1977.

(Editor with Yair Aharoni, and author of introduction) *State-Owned Enterprises in the Western Economies,* Croom Helm, 1980.

Two Hungry Giants: The United States and Japan in the Quest for Oil and Ores, Harvard University Press, 1983.

Exploring the Global Economy: Emerging Issues in Trade and Investment, University Press of America, 1985.

(Editor) *The Promise of Privatization,* Council on Foreign Relations, 1988.

(With Debora Spar) *Beyond Globalism: Remaking American Foreign Economic Policy,* Free Press, 1989.

(With Spar and Glenn Tobin) *Iron Triangles and Revolving Doors: Cases in U.S. Foreign Economic Policymaking,* Praeger, 1991.

(Editor with Ethan Kapstein) *The Search for Security in a Global Economy,* Daedalus, 1991.

(Editor with Ravi Ramamurti) *Privatization and Control of State-Owned Enterprises,* World Bank, 1991.

(Editor with Armand Clesse) *The European Community after 1991: A Role in World Politics?,* Nomos Verlagsgesellschaft, 1991.

(Editor with Kapstein) *Defense and Dependance in a Global Economy,* Congressional Quarterly Press, 1992.

Contributor to over forty-five books, including *Essays in International Finance,* Princeton University Press, 1954; *Public Policy, 1964-65,* Harvard University Press, 1966; *Business Problems of the Seventies,* edited by Jules Backman, New York University Press, 1974; *Revitalizing American Industry,* edited by Milton S. Hochmuth and William H. Davidson, Ballinger, 1985; *The Global Economy,* edited by William Brock and Robert Hormats, Norton, 1990; and *Corporate and Industry Strategies for Europe,* Elsevier, 1991. Contributor to *Enciclopedia del Novecento,* Instituto dell'Enciclopedia Italiana, 1979.

Also author of government reports. Contributor to *Proceedings* of American Society of International Law, 1960, and other proceedings and to *Conference on the Politics of National Statistics,* Social Science Research Council, 1983. Contributor of numerous articles to economic and international affairs journals, including *American Economic Review, Business in the Contemporary World, Challenge, CTC Reporter, Etudes Internationales, Foreign Trade Review, Foreign Policy, French-American Commerce, Har-*

vard *International Review,* and *Journal of Finance.* Editor of *Journal of Policy Analysis and Management,* 1980-84.

WORK IN PROGRESS: Contributing to *Foreign Direct Investment.*

SIDELIGHTS: Raymond Vernon's *Sovereignty at Bay: The Multinational Spread of U.S. Enterprises* has been translated into Swedish, Korean, Spanish, French, and Portuguese; *Storm over the Multinationals: The Real Issues* has been translated into Japanese, Italian, Spanish, and Russian; and *The Economic and Political Consequences of Multinational Enterprises: An Anthology* has been translated into French.

* * *

VOIGT, Cynthia   1942-

PERSONAL: Born February 25, 1942, in Boston, MA; daughter of Frederick C. (a corporate executive) and Elise (Keeney) Irving; married September, 1964 (divorced, 1972); married Walter Voigt (a teacher), August 30, 1974; children: Jessica, Peter. *Education:* Smith College, B.A., 1963. *Politics:* Independent.

ADDRESSES: Home—Deer Isle, ME.

CAREER: Glen Burnie, MD, high school English teacher, 1965-67; The Key School, Annapolis, MD, English teacher, 1968-69, department chairman, 1971-79, part-time teacher and department chairman, 1981-88.

AWARDS, HONORS: Newbery Medal, 1983, for *Dicey's Song,* and runner-up citation, 1984, for *A Solitary Blue;* Edgar Award (juvenile mystery), 1984, for *The Callender Papers;* Silver Pencil Award (Dutch), 1988, Deutscher Jugend Literator Preis, 1989, and ALAN Award, 1989, all for *The Runner;* California Young Reader's Award, 1990, for *Izzy—Willy, Nilly.*

WRITINGS:

YOUNG ADULT FICTION

Homecoming, Atheneum, 1981.
Tell Me If the Lovers Are Losers, Atheneum, 1982.
Dicey's Song, Atheneum, 1982.
The Callender Papers, Atheneum, 1983.
A Solitary Blue, Atheneum, 1983.
Building Blocks, Atheneum, 1984.
The Runner, Atheneum, 1985.
Jackeroo, Atheneum, 1985.
Izzy—Willy, Nilly, Atheneum, 1986.
Come a Stranger, Atheneum, 1986.
Sons from Afar, Macmillan, 1987.
Tree by Leaf, Macmillan, 1988.
Seventeen Against the Dealer, Macmillan, 1989.
On Fortune's Wheel, Macmillan, 1990.

David and Jonathan, Scholastic, 1992.
Orfe, Macmillan, 1992.

JUVENILE

Stories About Rosie, Macmillan, 1986.

ADULT FICTION

Glass Mountain, Harcourt, 1991.

Also author of *The Vandemark Mummy,* 1991.

SIDELIGHTS: Since her first young-adult novel, *Homecoming,* appeared in 1981, Cynthia Voigt has had more than a dozen books published and has received the prestigious Newbery Medal for *Homecoming*'s sequel, *Dicey's Song.* In a Voigt novel, notes *Washington Post Book World* contributing critic Alice Digilio, the author "never takes sides in the war of generations. Instead she promotes understanding between adults and children, and she values the efforts of children, as well as those of adults, to appreciate the other's point of view."

Homecoming begins the saga of the Tillermans, four fatherless children aged six through thirteen who are abandoned in a shopping mall parking lot by their mentally ill mother. Dicey, the eldest, takes it upon herself to care for all four, and they eventually move to their grandmother's home in distant Maryland. Despite "the alarmingly hostile characterization of most [adult characters]," says Kathleen Leverich in a *New York Times Book Review* article, *Homecoming* is "a glowing book. Its disturbing undercurrent of hostility and cynicism is counterbalanced by the four's obvious love and loyalty to one another." *Dicey's Song* continues the Tillerman's story, concentrating on young Dicey's emerging understanding of her new life and her relationships with her siblings and grandmother. This novel, according to Marilyn Kaye in another *New York Times Book Review* piece, "is a series of movements and contrasts. But under it all there's a goal of harmony that's eventually realized as Dicey learns what to reach out for and what to give up."

Among Voigt's other novels, two are set in the past: *The Callender Papers* and *Tell Me If the Lovers Are Losers.* In the latter book, three distinctly different teenage girls become roommates at a women's college in the Northeast. All three join the school's volleyball squad, where "we see the clash of values and the broadening of perspective as compromises are worked out and a team is forged," remarks Leverich. And while the critic feels that exaggerated characterizations and "the sacrifice of the theme to improbable theatrics" mar the book, she concludes that Voigt "is a wonderful writer with powerfully moving things to say. . . . When she dispenses with contrivances and sensationalism, her characters and scenes come alive in their own unique and exciting way."

BIOGRAPHICAL/CRITICAL SOURCES:

PERIODICALS

Horn Book, August, 1983.
New York Times Book Review, May 10, 1981; May 16, 1982; March 6, 1983; November 27, 1983.
Times Literary Supplement, August 30, 1985.
Washington Post Book World, May 8, 1983; November 6, 1983; June 10, 1984.*

W

WALLACE-HADRILL, Andrew (Frederic) 1951-

PERSONAL: Born July 29, 1951, in Oxford, England; son of John Michael (a medieval historian) and Anne (a lexicographer; maiden name, Wakefield) Wallace-Hadrill; married Josephine Claire Braddock (a teacher of classics), July 31, 1976; children: Sophie, Michael. *Education:* Corpus Christi College, Oxford, B.A., 1973, M.A., 1975, D.Phil., 1980.

ADDRESSES: Office—Department of Classics, University of Reading, Whiteknights, Reading R96 2AA, England.

CAREER: Magdalene College, Cambridge, England, fellow and director of studies in classics, 1976-83; University of Leicester, Leicester, England, lecturer in ancient history, 1983-87; University of Reading, Reading, England, professor of classics, 1987—, chairman, Department of Classics, 1987—. Editor, *Journal of Roman Studies,* 1991—.

WRITINGS:

Suetonius: The Scholar and His Caesars, Yale University Press, 1983.

(Author of introduction and notes) *Ammianus Marcellinus: The Roman Empire,* translated by W. Hamilton, Penguin, 1986.

(Editor) *Patronage in Ancient Society,* Routledge, 1989.

(Editor with John Rich) *City and Country in the Ancient World,* Routledge, 1991.

The Roman Social Habitat: Studies of Housing at Pompeii and Herculaneum, Princeton University Press, 1993.

Augustan Rome, Bristol Classical Press, in press.

WORK IN PROGRESS: A study of the cultural transformation of Rome in the late Republic and early Empire.

SIDELIGHTS: Andrew Wallace-Hadrill told *CA:* "My interest in the Ancient World stems from traditional British classical education; I first turned towards Roman imperial history by reading English historian Edward Gibbon. I chose the topic of Suetonius to research as a bridge between the study of Latin literature and Roman social history and used my book, *Suetonius: The Scholar and His Caesars,* to explore how an author's approach to his topic can illuminate his own society and culture. More recently, my focus has been on issues of social and cultural history that involve archaeology and art history."

*   *   *

WALTON, Douglas N(eil) 1942-

PERSONAL: Born June 2, 1942, in Hamilton, Ontario, Canada; son of Charles Mitchell (a real estate agent) and Olive (a housewife; maiden name, Mercer) Walton; married Karen G. Jacklyn (a fitness instructor), May 25, 1968. *Education:* University of Waterloo, B.A., 1964; University of Toronto, Ph.D., 1972. *Politics:* Conservative. *Religion:* Protestant.

ADDRESSES: Home—760 Campbell St., Winnipeg, Manitoba, Canada R3N 1C6. *Office*—Department of Philosophy, University of Winnipeg, Winnipeg, Manitoba, Canada R3B 2E9.

CAREER: University of Winnipeg, Winnipeg, Manitoba, lecturer, 1969-71, assistant professor, 1971-75, associate professor, 1976-81, professor of philosophy, 1982—. Adjunct professor at University of Manitoba, 1977-78; member of Hastings Center.

MEMBER: Canadian Philosophical Association, American Philosophical Association, American Society of Political and Legal Philosophy, American Psychological Association.

AWARDS, HONORS: Canada Council fellow at Victoria University of Wellington, 1975-76; Social Science and Humanities Research Council of Canada, grants, 1977, 1989-91; fellowship at University of Auckland, 1980-81; *American Philosophical Quarterly* essay prize, 1985; Killiam Research Fellowship, 1987-89; Erica and Arnold Rogers Award for excellence in research and scholarship, 1988; fellowship-in-residence at Netherlands Institute for Advanced Study in the Humanities and Social Sciences, 1989-90; International Society for the Study of Argumentation prize, 1991.

WRITINGS:

On Defining Death, McGill-Queen's University Press, 1979.
Brain Death: Ethical Considerations, Purdue University Press, 1980.
Topical Relevance in Argumentation, John Benjamins, 1982.
(With John Woods) *Argument: The Logic of the Fallacies,* McGraw, 1982.
The Ethics of Withdrawal of Life-Support Systems: Case Studies of Decision-Making in Intensive Care, Greenwood Press, 1983.
Arguer's Position, Greenwood Press, 1985.
Physician-Patient: Decision-Making, Greenwood Press, 1985.
Courage: A Philosophical Investigation, University of California Press, 1985.
Analyzing the Informal Fallacies, John Benjamins, 1986.
Informal Logic: A Handbook for Critical Argumentation, Cambridge University Press, 1989.
Question-Reply Argumentation, Greenwood Press, 1989.
Practical Reasoning: Goal-Driven, Knowledge-Based, Action-Guiding Argumentation, Rowman & Littlefield, 1990.
Begging the Question: Circular Reasoning As a Tactic of Argumentation, Greenwood Press, 1991.
Slippery Slope Arguments, Oxford University Press, 1992.
Plausible Argument in Everyday Conversation, State University of New York Press, 1992.

Contributor to philosophy journals. Member of editorial board, *Argumentation, Informal Logic, Philosophy, and Rhetoric* and *American Philosophical Quarterly.*

SIDELIGHTS: Douglas N. Walton once told *CA:* "It's always hard to know one's true motivations as a philosopher. I have always found my work comes back to an admiration for, and a need to understand, the value of the practical. Perhaps that is why, going against the tug of philosophy towards the theoretical, I have found myself drawn, again and again, back to practical logic and medi-

cal ethics, where the problems are often of a practical nature. I have always admired practical people who have done the best they can in difficult and unfavorable situations. Why then devote my life to philosophy, a theoretical subject? Is that a contradiction? Yes, it is, to some extent, and it is the struggle with deep contradictions that is perhaps the mainspring of philosophy for many of us who have found our way into the field. It could be that my deepest motivation is to understand and find value for the practical way of life by seeking out the timeless and general aspects of particular activities, skills, and problems."

*   *   *

WARNER, Philip   1914-

PERSONAL: Born May 19, 1914, in England; son of William T. and Maude A. Warner; widowed; children: three. *Education:* Cambridge University, B.A., M.A., 1939.

ADDRESSES: Agent—Jim Reynolds Associates, Westbury Mill, Westbury, Near Brackley, Northamptonshire NN13 5JS, England.

CAREER: Writer and lecturer. *Military service:* British Army, 1939-45.

WRITINGS:

Sieges of the Middle Ages, Bell, 1969.
The Medieval Castle, Arthur Barker, 1971.
Special Air Service, 1941-71, Kimber, 1971.
The Japanese Army of World War II, Osprey, 1972.
The Crimean War: A Reappraisal, Taplinger, 1973.
Dervish: The Rise and Fall of an African Empire, Taplinger, 1974.
The Soldier: His Daily Life through the Ages, Taplinger, 1975.
Guide to Castles in Britain: Where to Find them and What to Look For, New English Library, 1976.
The Best of British Pluck: "Boys Own Paper" Revised, Macdonald & Jane's, 1976.
The Battle of Loos, Kimber, 1976.
Panzer, Weidenfeld & Nicolson, 1977.
Zeebrugge Raid, Kimber, 1978.
(Editor) Richard Temple Godman, *Fields of War,* J. Murray, 1978.
Famous Welsh Battles, Fontana, 1978.
(Editor) *Best of "Chums,"* Cassell, 1978.
Invasion Road, Cassell, 1980.
The D-Day Landings, Kimber, 1980.
Auchinleck, Buchan & Enright, 1981.
Horrocks, Hamish Hamilton, 1984.
The British Cavalry, Dent, 1984.
Kitchener, Hamish Hamilton, 1985, Atheneum, 1986.
Passchendaele, Sidgwich & Jackson, 1987.
Firepower, Grafton, 1988.

World War II, Bodley Head, 1988.
The Vital Link, Leo Cooper, 1989.
The Battles of France, Simon & Schuster, 1990.
Field Marshall Earl Haig, Bodley Head, 1991.
The Harlequins, Bredon, 1992.
The Great British Soldier, David & Charles, 1992.

Contributor of articles and reviews to magazines and newspapers including *Daily Telegraph, Spectator,* and *Times Literary Supplement.*

WORK IN PROGRESS: A history of the First World War.

BIOGRAPHICAL/CRITICAL SOURCES:

PERIODICALS

Times (London), August 29, 1985.
Times Literary Supplement, December 13, 1985.

*   *   *

WEBSTER, Elizabeth 1918-

PERSONAL: Born July 13, 1918, in Congleton, England; daughter of Lancelot (a civil engineer) and Marjorie (a classical singer; maiden name, Rennie) Heygate; children: Andrew, Joss Webster Pearson, Godfrey. *Education:* Attended Bussage House, 1931-34; Amy James Piano School, L.R.A.M. (piano and composition), 1936; Royal Academy of Music, L.R.A.M. (speech and drama), 1961.

ADDRESSES: Home—Gloucestershire, England. *Agent*—Maggie Noach, 21 Redan St., London W14 0AB, England.

CAREER: Residential and Day Nursery for Problem Children, Wateringbury, Kent, England, founder and principal, 1948-55; teacher of music and drama at school in Tonbridge, England, 1955-61; teacher of music, drama, and creative English at junior school in Cheltenham, England, 1962-69; Young Arts Centre, Cheltenham, founder and director, 1967—. Member of British Council Tours Department, 1938-39.

WRITINGS:

ADULT BOOKS

Gregory and the Angels (mini-opera; produced in Cheltenham, England, at Shaftesbury Hall, 1964), Lengnik, 1965.
Child of Fire, Piatkus Books, 1983.
Johnnie Alone, Piatkus Books, 1984.
A Boy Called Bracken, Piatkus Books, 1984, published in the United States as *Bracken,* St. Martin's, 1985.
To Fly a Kite, Piatkus Books, 1985.
Chico, the Small One, Piatkus Books, 1986.
The Flight of the Swan, St. Martin's, 1990.

Shadow into Sunlight, St. Martin's, 1991.
Dolphin Sunrise, Souvenir Press, 1992.

Contributor to magazines and newspapers. Music critic for *Musical Opinion, Music and Musicians,* and *Musical Times,* 1958—, and for *Gloucestershire Echo,* 1958-84.

WORK IN PROGRESS: Home Street Home, a book about the homeless youth of London.

SIDELIGHTS: Elizabeth Webster once told *CA:* "*Child of Fire,* written during the United Nations' Year of the Child, describes the plight of the Vietnamese boat children, innocently caught up in adult wars. *Johnnie Alone,* written in the United Nations' Year of the Disabled, is about a partially deaf and battered child. *Bracken* is concerned with facing up to terminal illness and the reassurance of the natural world around us, a theme that touches us all. *To Fly a Kite* deals with the difficulties of an institutionalized girl as she emerges into the everyday world.

"Most fiction (especially for women) deals with trivia. I think that is an insult to intelligence. I prefer to deal with major issues, to try to tell my stories simply and directly without intellectual claptrap, for ordinary people. I feel that children have their own highly intelligent thoughts and feelings, which are misrepresented and/or ignored because the adult world mostly fails to understand. And since children are the next citizens of the world, they deserve our full attention.

"My themes are always big, serious, adult ones—and children come into them as the victims of adult mistakes and incomprehension. Thus, *Child of Fire* is about war and its effect on the innocent children who are its victims. *Johnnie Alone* is about a battered, partially deaf child and his struggle to grow up as a normal human being in an unhelpful adult world. It is also about communication and the crippling isolation of deafness. *Bracken* is about an adult dying of leukemia and how the straightforward, uncluttered views of a boy change his outlook on death.

"*To Fly a Kite* examines the efforts of a young adult girl emerging into our kind of materialistic world from the sheltered existence of institutional life, and a man trying to come to terms with a stroke and its disabilities. *Chico, the Small One* looks at world poverty, badly planned agriculture, water supplies, and the greed of rich communities at the expense of the poor ones."

In her novels *The Flight of the Swan, Shadow into Sunlight,* and *Dolphin Sunrise,* Webster tackles environmental and women's issues. "*The Flight of the Swan* is about a battered young wife who leaves her violent husband to make a new life with her two frightened children," Webster recently added. "*Shadow into Sunlight* is about the plight of the 'carer' in society—a young woman who devotes her life to looking after her mother, and then is left alone to build a new, independent future. *Dolphin Sunrise* is about the plight of the dolphins in the oceans of the world linked with the life of a lonely boy orphaned by a fire and trying to find himself some roots.

"All these themes set out my belief that we worry too much about trivialities instead of tackling the big problems that really need our attention," Webster once commented. "It is no good worrying about the mortgage or a new car if someone on the other side of the world is worrying about one grain of rice or two for their next meal, or whether they will be alive tomorrow at all."

* * *

WEINBERGER, Eliot 1949-

PERSONAL: Born February 6, 1949, in New York, NY.

ADDRESSES: Home—202 West 10th St., New York, NY 10014.

CAREER: Writer and translator.

AWARDS, HONORS: Award for Younger Writers, General Electric Foundation, 1986; first recipient of P.E.N./ Gregory Kolovakos Award for promotion of Latin American literature in the U.S., 1992.

WRITINGS:

Works on Paper (essays), New Directions Publishing, 1986.
(With Octavio Paz) *Nineteen Ways of Looking at Wang Wei* (criticism), Moyer-Bell, 1987.
Outside Stories (essays), New Directions Publishing, 1992.
(Editor) *Una antologia de la poesia norteamericana desde 1950,* Ediciones del Equilibrista (Mexico), 1992.
(Editor) *American Poetry since 1950: Avant-Gardists, Innovators and Outsiders,* Marsilio Publishing, 1993.

EDITOR AND TRANSLATOR

Paz, *Eagle or Sun?,* October House, 1970, new edition, New Directions Publishing, 1976.
Paz, *A Draft of Shadows,* New Directions Publishing, 1980.
Homero Aridjis, *Exaltation of Light,* Boa Editions, 1981.
Paz, *Selected Poems,* New Directions Publishing, 1984.
Jorge Luis Borges, *Seven Nights,* New Directions Publishing, 1984.
Paz, *The Collected Poems 1957-1987,* New Directions Publishing, 1987, revised edition, 1991.
Vicente Huidobro, *Altazor,* Graywolf, 1988.
Paz, *A Tree Within,* New Directions Publishing, 1988.
Paz, *Sunstone,* New Directions Publishing, 1991.
Cecilia Vicuna, *Unravelling Words and the Weaving of Water,* Graywolf, 1992.

Xavier Villaurrutia, *Nostalgia for Death,* Copper Canyon Press, 1993.

OTHER

Work is represented in anthologies, including five editions of *Pushcart Prize: The Best of the Small Press.* Contributor to more than eighty periodicals. Editor, *Montemora,* 1975-82; contributing editor, *Stony Brook Poetics Journal,* 1968-1969, *Contemporary Buddhist Thought,* 1979-1980, *Sulfur,* 1981—, *Destinations,* 1982-83, and *Artes de Mexico,* 1991—; New York correspondent for *Vuelta* (Mexico City), 1989—.

Some of Weinberger's essays have been translated into Spanish, French, Catalan, Russian, Polish, and Portuguese.

* * *

WEISMAN, John 1942-

PERSONAL: Born August 1, 1942, in New York, NY; son of Abner I. Weisman and Syde (Lubowe) Kremer; married Susan Lee Povenmire, February 12, 1983. *Education:* Bard College, A.B., 1964; graduate study at University of California, Los Angeles, 1965-67. *Religion:* Jewish.

ADDRESSES: Home—5522 Trent St., Chevy Chase, MD 20815. *Office*—Annenberg Washington Program, 1455 Pennsylvania Ave. NW, Suite 230, Washington, DC 20006. *Agent*—Lucy Kroll Agency, 390 West End Ave., New York, NY 10024.

CAREER: Stage manager for repertory companies, including New York Shakespeare Festival, 1964-69; *Coast* (magazine), Los Angeles, CA, managing editor, 1969-70; *Rolling Stone* (magazine), San Francisco, CA, film critic and staff writer, 1971; *Detroit Free Press,* Detroit, MI, assistant to the entertainment editor, 1971-73; *TV Guide,* Radnor, PA, associate editor, 1973-77, chief of Washington Bureau, 1977-89; Northwestern University, Washington, DC, Annenberg Washington program, senior fellow, 1989—. Member of board of directors, *Writing* magazine.

MEMBER: National Press Club, Washington Press Club, Federal City Club, Players (New York City), White House Correspondents Association, Bard College Alumni Association (member of board of governors, 1975-81; president, 1981-83), Army and Navy Club (Washington).

WRITINGS:

Guerrilla Theater: Scenarios for Revolution (nonfiction), Doubleday, 1973.
(With Brian Boyer) *Heroin Triple Cross,* Pinnacle Books, 1974.
Evidence (novel), Viking, 1980.
Watchdogs (novel), Viking, 1983.

Blood Cries (novel), Viking, 1987.

(With Felix I. Rodriguez) *Shadow Warrior* (nonfiction), Simon & Schuster, 1989.

SIDELIGHTS: John Weisman is perhaps best known as a journalist, working for several news agencies throughout his career, including *Rolling Stone, Detroit Free Press,* and *TV Guide.* An interest in the entertainment field and in politics, plus the experience he has in dealing with both, have contributed to his success as an author. A talented writer, Weisman has extended his range to include both novels and nonfiction works. From the direct effects of street theater on society to espionage and mystery, Weisman reveals his versatility and varied interests.

Guerrilla Theater: Scenarios for Revolution, Weisman's first book, is a work of nonfiction that focuses on the correlation between popular street theater and social change. Guerrilla theater includes sketches and improvisations that have a political agenda, a direction, a message that people must hear. Theater reaches everyone in a way the printed word cannot, and can serve as inspiration to such groups as minorities. In California, theater groups like El Teatro Campesino played a role in organizing the migrant farmworkers through their ability to reach and teach large numbers. Written mostly in an open letter format with eleven plays included, *Guerrilla Theater* is Weisman's account of his involvement with El Teatro Campesino, and his view of the meaning and purpose of street theater. Curt Davis, writing in *Library Journal,* praised the effort and depth of topic coverage, but criticized the presentation, noting that Weisman "overtly emphasizes the importance of what he's saying," rather than letting readers figure it out on their own. A reviewer in *Publishers Weekly* also lauded *Guerrilla Theater,* calling it "an enlightening essay" full of "direct advice."

Weisman jumps the gap between nonfiction and fiction with his first novel, *Evidence.* Using his own background as a journalist, Weisman takes a close look at the life of a reporter, his relationships, and his motivation to be the first to write the story. Robert Mandel is the protagonist, a tough, driven reporter who lives by his own rules and works for a large Detroit daily. When his friend, Jack Fowler, is killed while doing a story on the homosexual underworld, Mandel takes over the story and uncovers almost more than he can deal with—starting with Fowler's secret life. Mandel struggles with his feelings of friendship and betrayal, and his need to write the truth. "The novel is graphic," wrote a reviewer in *Publishers Weekly.* "But after Weisman sets his stage, little comes as a surprise." Newgate Callendar, writing in the *New York Times Book Review,* also commented on the graphic scenes in the novel, calling the sexual "stuff . . . perhaps unnecessarily gamy," and concluded: "Yet, even with a few flaws, *Evidence* is a brilliant book, one that probes the mind of a

dedicated newspaperman and psychological cripple, written in a realistic prose, with characters sharply delineated."

From newspapermen, Weisman turns his focus to the Secret Service in *Watchdogs,* another novel of intrigue and personal dilemma. William Chapman, the aged chief of the Presidential Protective Detail of the Secret Service, becomes aware of a plot to kill the first Jewish President initiated by a fanatical South Korean Christian cult. The problem is that the cult's agent has been a member of the group surrounding the President for many years, and Chapman has no idea who the killer may be—perhaps a reporter, or someone on the Presidential staff, even the members of his own Secret Service staff are suspect. Nancy Smith, in *Voice of Youth Advocates,* commented that guessing the killer's identity "will keep the interest of the readers." Several critics issued mixed reviews, commenting on the lack of an original and suspense-filled plot. A reviewer in *Publishers Weekly* noted that Weisman's detailed portrayal of Washington society was "plush but dull." Elisabeth Jakab, writing in the *New York Times Book Review,* described *Watchdogs* as "one of those glossy dramas that touches all the right bases but without much inspiration or originality," and added that "too many of the punches in this book have been telegraphed." *Library Journal* contributor Richard R. Ring also reported the plot as "perfunctory," and remarked that *Watchdogs* might appeal to readers who love conspiracies, while "for others the thrill of the feats may not be enough."

One of Weisman's latest books, *Blood Cries,* is more than just an action-adventure novel. It is filled with moral and political dilemmas, personal choices, romance, and assassination. The protagonist, Jared Paul Gordon, is an American Jew in Israel working as a bureau chief of *World Week* magazine. After witnessing the assassination of a powerful Arab and his family by an Israeli army unit, Gordon writes a story containing both the truth and his outrage. When the Israeli government censors it and his girlfriend supports the government, he must reconcile his idealized version of Israel with the reality he sees around him. He must decide between being a good journalist or a good Jew, because he is unable to be both. As faith in Israel becomes commitment to its cause, Gordon undergoes a spiritual journey that strips away his idealism. James Kaufmann in the *Los Angeles Times Book Review* commented that Weisman spends a great portion of the book pondering the necessity of Israel's violent actions, and concluded, "Weisman writes well enough, and his narrative's framework is strong enough to support the kind of Machiavellian musing that must take place in any honest and realistic novel about Israel today, which *Blood Cries* is, indisputably." Stewart Kellerman, writing in the *New York Times Book Review,* had a similar opinion: "Mr.

Weisman has a tendency to overwrite . . . but *Blood Cries* is an engaging, provocative and troubling book."

BIOGRAPHICAL/CRITICAL SOURCES:

PERIODICALS

Library Journal, April 15, 1973, p. 1305; January 15, 1983, p. 147.
Los Angeles Times, July 15, 1973.
Los Angeles Times Book Review, July 19, 1987, p. 11.
New York Times Book Review, May 4, 1980, p. 24; May 22, 1983, p. 43; July 19, 1987, p. 20.
Publishers Weekly, March 12, 1973, p. 66; February 1, 1980, p. 103; January 14, 1983, pp. 69-70.
Voice of Youth Advocates, October, 1983, p. 209.

—*Sketch by Terrie M. Rooney*

*　　*　　*

WHEELER, Thomas H(utchin) 1947-
(Tom Wheeler)

PERSONAL: Born December 15, 1947, in West Point, NY; son of Lester Lewes (a career army officer) and Dorothy (Hutchin) Wheeler; married Anne Lowe, January 8, 1983; children: Daniel Lowe, Matthew Lowe, Joseph Lowe. *Education:* University of California, Los Angeles, B.A., 1969; Loyola School of Law, Juris Doctor, 1975. *Politics:* Democrat. *Avocational interests:* Photography, backpacking, working on educational films, playing guitar, "trying to read the books I should have read in college."

ADDRESSES: Office—School of Journalism, University of Oregon, Eugene, OR 97403.

CAREER: Worked as musician and guitar instructor in Los Angeles, CA, 1971-76; GPI Publications, Cupertino, CA, assistant editor of *Guitar Player,* 1977-79, associate editor and managing editor, 1979-81, editor, 1981-91; Miller Freeman Publishers, San Francisco, CA, consulting editor, 1991—; University of Oregon, Eugene, associate professor of journalism, 1991—.

MEMBER: National Association of Music Merchants.

WRITINGS:

UNDER NAME TOM WHEELER

The Guitar Book (foreword by B. B. King), Harper, 1974, revised edition (with photographs by Wheeler), 1978.
American Guitars, Harper, 1982, revised edition, 1992.

Author of column in *Crawdaddy,* 1977. Contributor to periodicals, including *Loyola Law Review, Rolling Stone,* and *Player* (Japan).

WORK IN PROGRESS: The Environmental Impact of Print Media: Processes and Practices.

SIDELIGHTS: Thomas H. Wheeler told *CA:* "I began to teach myself—slowly and inefficiently—to play guitar at age thirteen when I lived in Alaska. I had been enchanted with Chuck Berry, and I adopted his style as best I could. I discovered soul music in Atlanta during my high school years, and at the same time was swept up in the British musical invasion. In college my delusions of being Chuck Berry matured into delusions of being Eric Clapton. I embraced electric blues and performed in various bands, one of which lucked into a job following Duke Ellington every night. I majored in political science at UCLA for no particular reason, and attended Loyola School of Law in Los Angeles on a teaching fellowship, with a vague notion of doing one of the 'so many things you can do with a law degree.' After nine months of monastic research, an article of mine, 'Drug Lyrics, the FCC, and the First Amendment,' appeared in the *Loyola Law Review.* The first draft, which had taken six months, was hacked to ribbons by editors and cite-checkers, and (while contemplating nonlegal careers) I learned good lessons about writing and research.

"In the early 1970's I played guitar, wrote songs, and recorded elaborate demo tapes as part of some nebulous scheme to become a record producer. Before graduating from law school and while teaching music in a West Los Angeles studio, I began to write a brief guitar method book. It was to have a four-page appendix. I began work on the appendix, found that I loved to write prose, couldn't stop, and eventually wound up with an encyclopedia on guitars.

"*The Guitar Book*'s topics include history, resonance and acoustics, types of guitars, guitar construction, parts and adjustments, mechanical and electronic accessories, amplifiers, speakers, special effects, guitar synthesizers, systems and methods of tuning, dealers, trade-ins, retailing, collector's items, photo tours through several factories, plus a general attempt throughout to make sense of American guitar, a phenomenon shot through with fable and rumor."

The Guitar Book has been translated into Japanese and Dutch.

*　　*　　*

WHEELER, Tom
See WHEELER, Thomas H(utchin)

WHITE, Melvin R(obert) 1911-

PERSONAL: Born January 7, 1911, in Chugwater, WY; son of Robert Reid (a building contractor) and Cecelia Rebecca (Danielson) White. *Education:* University of Iowa, B.A., 1932, M.A., 1933; University of Wisconsin, Ph.D., 1948; postdoctoral study at Columbia University and Television Workshop, 1949, and Institute for Advanced Study in Theatre Arts, 1959-60. *Politics:* Republican. *Religion:* Congregationalist.

ADDRESSES: Home—583 Boulevard Way, Piedmont, CA 94610.

CAREER: High school principal in Andrew, IA, 1933-34; high school teacher in Galesburg, IL, 1934-38; Washington State University, Pullman, instructor in radio, 1938-40; Indiana University, Bloomington, assistant professor of speech, 1941-42; University of Wyoming, Laramie, assistant professor of speech and chairman of department, 1946-47; University of Hawaii, Honolulu, associate professor of speech, 1948-51; Brooklyn College of the City University of New York, Brooklyn, NY, associate professor of speech and theater, 1952-68, deputy chairman of department, 1965-68; California State College at Hayward (now California State University, Hayward), associate professor of speech and drama, 1968-71; Chaminade College of Honolulu, Honolulu, HI, professor of speech, 1971; University of Hawaii—Hilo College, Hilo, director of theatre, 1972-73; University of Arizona, Tucson, professor of speech communication, 1974; California Polytechnic State University, San Luis Obispo, lecturer in speech, 1974-75, 1978, 1981. Visiting summer professor at University of Oklahoma, 1949, University of Wisconsin, 1950, University of Arkansas, 1964; exchange professor, University of Hawaii, 1962-63; adjunct professor of speech, Brooklyn College of the City University of New York, summers, 1973, 1974. Director of Bay Area Drama Quartet, 1970-91; workshop director of readers theater productions, and lecturer throughout United States, and in El Salvador, Guatemala, Japan, Korea, and Canada. Consultant to Texas Fine Arts Commission; consultant on little theater program, McGraw-Hill Book Co. *Military service:* U.S. Naval Reserve, active duty, 1942-45.

MEMBER: International Theatre Institute of UNESCO, American Educational Theatre Association (executive secretary-treasurer, 1965-66), American National Theatre and Academy (member of board of directors), Speech Association of America, American Community Theatre Association (executive secretary-treasurer, 1965-66), Children's Theatre Conference (executive secretary-treasurer, 1965-66), United States Institute for Theatre Technology (member of board of directors), Army Theatre Arts Association (president, 1982-84), Mended Hearts, Inc. (vice-president of chapter 84, 1982-83), California Retired Teachers Association (vice-president of East Bay chapter, 1982-87; director of scholarship foundation, 1984-92), California Speech Arts Association (consultant, 1987-92).

AWARDS, HONORS: American Educational Theatre Association Award, 1962, for outstanding service; silver trophy presented by Adjutant General, U.S. Army, 1967, for contribution to Army theater project; Gold Masque award, U.S. Army Southern Command, 1967; College of Fellows of the American Theatre fellow, 1979; commendation, Army Theatre Arts Association, 1981.

WRITINGS:

Radio and Assembly Plays, Northwestern Press, 1941.
Highlights of History, Northwestern Press, 1942.
Children's Programs for Radio Broadcast, Northwestern Press, 1948.
(With Jean Hinton Bennion) *Mr. Geography,* Northwestern Press, 1948.
Radio Materials for Practice and Broadcast, Northwestern Press, 1950.
Beginning Radio Production, Northwestern Press, 1950.
Microphone Technique for Radio Actors, Northwestern Press, 1950.
Beginning Television Production, Burgess Publishing, 1953.
(With Leslie Irene Coger) *Studies in Readers Theatre,* S & F Press, 1963.
The Mikado for Readers' Theatre and Stage, S & F Press, 1964.
From the Printed Page, S & F Press, 1965.
(With Coger) *Readers Theatre Handbook: A Dramatic Approach to Literature,* Scott, Foresman, 1967, revised edition, 1973, 4th edition, Meriwether Publishing, in press.
(With Frank Whiting) *Playreaders Repertory: Anthology for an Introduction to Theatre,* Scott, Foresman, 1970.
(With James Carlsen) *Literature on Stage: Readers Theater Anthology,* Samuel French, 1980.

SCRIPTS AND SCRIPT COLLECTIONS

Readers Theatre Starter Packet #1, Contemporary Drama Service, 1975.
The Mikado (based on the operetta by William Schwenck Gilbert and Arthur Sullivan), Contemporary Drama Service, 1976.
As You Like It (based on the play by William Shakespeare), Contemporary Drama Service, 1976.
Christmas Comes but Once a Year, Contemporary Drama Service, 1976.
Lyrics for Living (based on the work of Alfred G. Walton), Contemporary Drama Service, 1977.
The Tell-Tale Heart (based on the short story by Edgar Allen Poe), Contemporary Drama Service, 1977.

Readers Theatre Starter Packet #2, Contemporary Drama Service, 1978.
Children's Stories for Readers Theatre, Contemporary Drama Service, Volume 1, 1979, Volume 2, 1981, Volume 3, 1991.
Let Us Give Thanks, Contemporary Drama Service, 1979.
While Shepherds Watched Their Flocks, Contemporary Drama Service, 1979.
The Wizard of Oz (based on the book by L. Frank Baum), Contemporary Drama Service, 1979.
Readers Theatre Starter Packet #3, Contemporary Drama Service, 1980.
Toad the Terror (adapted from *The Wind in the Willows* by Kenneth Grahame), Contemporary Drama Service, 1982.
Adam and Eve, Ltd., Contemporary Drama Service, 1983.
Readers Theatre Starter Packet #4, Contemporary Drama Service, 1985.
Now Christmas Has Come, Contemporary Drama Service, 1985.
Readers Theatre Sample Packet #5 (includes *The Love Potion of Ikey Schoenstein, The Necklace, An Encounter with an Interviewer,* and *Sire de Maletroit's Door*), Contemporary Drama Service, 1987.
Readers Theatre Sample Packet #6 (includes *The Same Old Wonderful Stuff, The Wonderful World of Dorothy Foree, The Legacy, Truth in Flying* and *Little Runt*), Contemporary Drama Service, 1989.
Readers Theatre Sample Packet #7 (includes *The Visitor, Christmas by Injunction, George Washington, The Wind in the Willows,* and *Departure Time Is None of Your Business*), Contemporary Drama Service, 1991.
Melvin White's Readers Theatre Anthology, Meriwether Publishing, 1992.

OTHER

Contributor to books, including *Your Speech and Mine,* Lyons & Carnahan, 1945; and *Christmas on Stage,* edited by Theodore O. Zapel, Meriwether Publishing, 1990. Editor, *Directory of the American Educational Theatre Association,* 1965. Contributor of more than fifty articles and about twenty reviews to speech and theater journals. *Players,* editor of radio section, 1947-49, associate editor of magazine, 1950-51, editor of makeup department, 1957-61; *Educational Theatre Journal,* special editor of Thomas Wood Stevens Memorial Issue, December, 1951, managing editor and business editor, 1958-61, 1965-67.

SIDELIGHTS: Melvin R. White told *CA:* "I do less work on materials for performance now, but manage to teach Readers Theatre at an occasional *Elderhostel,* and supply those senior citizens, usually but not always younger than I am, with scripts to challenge their acting/reading skills. To make available the nondramatic writings of others for dramatic use is my main joy."

WHYTE, William Foote 1914-

PERSONAL: Born June 27, 1914, in Springfield, MA; son of John and Isabel (Van Sickle) Whyte; married Kathleen King (a commercial artist), 1938; children: Joyce, Martin, Lucy, John. *Education:* Swarthmore College, A.B., 1936; attended Harvard University, 1936-40; University of Chicago, Ph.D., 1943. *Politics:* Democrat. *Religion:* Presbyterian.

ADDRESSES: Home—1 Sundowns Rd., Ithaca, NY 14850. *Office*—New York State School of Industrial and Labor Relations, Cornell University, P.O. Box 1000, Ithaca, NY 14853.

CAREER: University of Oklahoma, Norman, assistant professor, 1942-43; University of Chicago, Chicago, IL, 1944-48, began as assistant professor, became associate professor of sociology; Cornell University, New York State School of Industrial and Labor Relations, Ithaca, NY, professor, 1948-79, professor emeritus, 1979—, director of Social Science Research Center, 1956-61.

MEMBER: Society for Applied Anthropology (president, 1964), American Sociological Association (fellow; president, 1981), Industrial Relations Research Association (president, 1963, 1980), American Academy of Arts and Sciences, Phi Beta Kappa.

AWARDS, HONORS: Career research award, National Institute of Mental Health, 1964-79; Doctor of Humane Letters, Swarthmore College, 1984; Career Achievement Award, Society of Applied Anthropology, 1992.

WRITINGS:

Street Corner Society, University of Chicago Press, 1943, 3rd edition, 1981.
Human Relations in the Restaurant Industry, McGraw, 1948.
Pattern for Industrial Peace, Harper, 1951.
Money and Motivation, Harper, 1955.
Man and Organization, Irwin, 1959.
Men at Work, Irwin, 1961.
Action Research for Management, Irwin, 1965.
Organizational Behavior, Irwin, 1969.
Organizing for Agricultural Development, Transaction Books, 1975.
Power, Politics, and Progress, Elsevier Science, 1977.
Worker Participation and Ownership, ILR Press, 1983.
Higher Yielding Human Systems for Agriculture, Cornell University Press, 1984.
Learning from the Field, Sage Publications, 1984.
Making Mondragon: The Growth and Dynamics of the Worker Cooperative Complex, ILR Press, 1988.
(Editor) *Participatory Action Research,* Sage Publications, 1990.

Social Theory for Action: How Individuals and Organizations Learn to Change, Sage Publications, 1991.

Also co-author of *Dominacion y cambios en el Peru rural,* 1969. Co-editor of "Sociology and Anthropology" series, Dorsey, 1959-63, and "Behavioral Science in Business" series, Irwin, 1960-63. Contributor of articles to professional journals. Editor of *Industry and Society,* 1946, and *Human Organization* (journal of the Society of Applied Anthropology), 1956-61, 1962-63.

WORK IN PROGRESS: Research on worker participation in management, employee ownership, and worker cooperatives in the U.S. and Spain; an autobiography.

SIDELIGHTS: William Foote Whyte once told *CA:* "My best known book is *Street Corner Society,* which more than forty years after its initial publication is still widely used in college sociology courses. In dropping out of active teaching, . . . I expect to push ahead with articles and books on the topics noted above, and I have also written drafts of the first part of an autobiography."

Whyte has been involved in Latin American research since 1954, principally in Venezuela and Peru, but also in Mexico, Guatemala, and Costa Rica.

*   *   *

WIESEL, Elie(zer) 1928-

PERSONAL: Born September 30, 1928, in Sighet, Romania; came to the United States, 1956, naturalized U.S. citizen, 1963; son of Shlomo (a grocer) and Sarah (Feig) Wiesel; married Marion Erster Rose, 1969; children: Shlomo Elisha. *Education:* Attended Sorbonne, University of Paris, 1948-51. *Religion:* Jewish.

ADDRESSES: Office—University Professors, Boston University, 745 Commonwealth Ave., Boston, MA 02215. *Agent*—Georges Borchardt, 136 East 57th St., New York, NY 10022.

CAREER: Foreign correspondent at various times for *Yedioth Ahronoth,* Tel Aviv, Israel, *L'Arche,* Paris, France, and *Jewish Daily Forward,* New York City, 1949—; City College of the City University of New York, New York City, distinguished professor, 1972-76; Boston University, Boston, MA, Andrew Mellon professor in the humanities, 1976—; Whitney Humanities Center, Yale University, New Haven, CT, Henry Luce visiting scholar in Humanities and Social Thought, 1982-83; Florida International University, Miami, distinguished visiting professor of literature and philosophy, 1982. Chairman, United States President's Commission on the Holocaust, 1979-80, U.S. Holocaust Memorial Council, 1980-86.

MEMBER: Amnesty International, PEN, Authors League, Foreign Press Association (honorary lifetime member), Writers and Artists for Peace in the Middle East, Royal Norwegian Society of Sciences and Letters, Phi Beta Kappa.

AWARDS, HONORS: Prix Rivarol, 1963; Remembrance Award, 1965, for *The Town beyond the Wall* and all other writings; William and Janice Epstein Fiction Award, Jewish Book Council, 1965, for *The Town beyond the Wall;* Jewish Heritage Award, 1966, for excellence in literature; Prix Medicis, 1969, for *Le Mendiant de Jerusalem;* Prix Bordin, French Academy, 1972; Eleanor Roosevelt Memorial Award, 1972; American Liberties Medallion, American Jewish Committee, 1972; Frank and Ethel S. Cohen Award, Jewish Book Council, 1973, for *Souls on Fire;* Martin Luther King, Jr., Award, City College of the City University of New York, 1973; Faculty Distinguished Scholar Award, Hofstra University, 1973-74; Joseph Prize for Human Rights, Anti-Defamation League of B'nai B'rith, 1978; Zalman Shazar Award, State of Israel, 1979; Jabotinsky Medal, State of Israel, 1980; Prix Livre-International, 1980, and Prix des Bibliothecaires, 1981, both for *Le Testament d'un poete juif assassine;* Anatoly Scharansky Humanitarian Award, 1983; Congressional Gold Medal, 1984; humanitarian award, International League for Human Rights, 1985; Freedom Cup award, Women's League of Israel, 1986; Nobel Peace Prize, 1986; Special Christopher Book Award, 1987; achievement award, Artists and Writers for Peace in the Middle East, 1987; Profiles of Courage award, B'nai B'rith, 1987; Human Rights Law Award, International Human Rights Law Group, 1988; S. Y. Agnon Gold Medal.

Litt.D., Jewish Theological Seminary, 1967, Marquette University, 1975, Simmons College, 1976, Anna Maria College, 1980, Yale University, 1981, Wake Forest University, 1985, Haverford College, 1985, Capital University, 1986, Long Island University, 1986; D.H.L., Hebrew Union College, 1968, Manhattanville College, 1972, Yeshiva University, 1973, Boston University, 1974, Wesleyan University, 1979, Notre Dame University, 1980, Brandeis University, 1980, and Kenyon College, 1982; Doctor of Hebrew Letters, Spertus College of Judaica, 1973; Ph.D., Bar-Ilan University, 1973, and University of Haifa, 1986; LL.D., Hofstra University, 1975, Talmudic University, 1979, and La Salle University, 1988; L.H.D., St. Scholastica College, 1978, Hobart and William Smith Colleges, 1982, Emory University, 1983, Florida International University, 1983, Siena Heights College, 1983, Fairfield University, 1983, Dropsie College, 1983, Moravian College, 1983, Colgate University, 1984, State University of New York, Binghamton, 1985, Lehigh University, 1985, College of New Rochelle, 1986, Tufts University, 1986, Georgetown University, 1986, Hamilton College,

1986, Rockford College, 1986, Villanova University, 1987, College of St. Thomas, 1987, University of Denver, 1987, Walsh College, 1987, Loyola College, 1987, Sorbonne, 1987, and Ohio University, 1988; H.H.D., University of Hartford, 1985, Lycoming College, 1987, and University of Miami, 1988.

Awards established in Wiesel's name include the Elie Wiesel Award for Holocaust Research, University of Haifa, the Elie Wiesel Chair in Holocaust Studies, Bar-Ilan University, the Elie Wiesel Endowment Fund for Jewish Culture, University of Denver, 1987, and the Elie Wiesel Distinguished Service Award, University of Florida, 1988.

WRITINGS:

Un Di Velt Hot Geshvign (title means "And the World Has Remained Silent"), [Buenos Aires], 1956, abridged French translation published as *La Nuit* (also see below), foreword by Francois Mauriac, Editions de Minuit, 1958, translation by Stella Rodway published as *Night* (also see below), Hill & Wang, 1960.

L'Aube (also see below), Editions du Seuil, 1961, translation by Frances Frenaye published as *Dawn* (also see below), Hill & Wang, 1961.

Le Jour (also see below), Editions du Seuil, 1961, translation by Anne Borchardt published as *The Accident* (also see below), Hill & Wang, 1962.

La Ville de la chance, Editions du Seuil, 1962, translation by Stephen Becker published as *The Town beyond the Wall,* Atheneum, 1964, new edition, Holt, 1967.

Les Portes de la foret, Editions du Seuil, 1964, translation by Frenaye published as *The Gates of the Forest,* Holt, 1966.

Le Chant des morts, Editions de Seuil, 1966, translation published as *Legends of Our Time,* Holt, 1968.

The Jews of Silence: A Personal Report on Soviet Jewry (originally published in Hebrew as a series of articles for newspaper *Yedioth Ahronoth*), translation and afterword by Neal Kozodoy, Holt, 1966, 2nd edition, Vallentine, Mitchell, 1973.

Zalmen; ou, La Folie de Dieu (play), 1966, translation by Lily and Nathan Edelman published as *Zalmen; or, The Madness of God,* Holt, 1968.

Le Mendiant de Jerusalem, 1968, translation by the author and L. Edelman published as *A Beggar in Jerusalem,* Random House, 1970.

La Nuit, L'Aube, [and] *Le Jour,* Editions du Seuil, 1969, translation published as *Night, Dawn,* [and] *The Accident: Three Tales,* Hill & Wang, 1972, reprinted as *The Night Trilogy: Night, Dawn, The Accident,* Farrar, Straus, 1987, translation by Rodway published as *Night, Dawn, Day,* Aronson, 1985.

Entre deux soleils, Editions du Seuil, 1970, translation by the author and L. Edelman published as *One Generation After,* Random House, 1970.

Celebration Hassidique: Portraits et legendes, Editions du Seuil, 1972, translation by wife, Marion Wiesel, published as *Souls on Fire: Portraits and Legends of Hasidic Masters,* Random House, 1972.

Le Serment de Kolvillag, Editions du Seuil, 1973, translation by M. Wiesel published as *The Oath,* Random House, 1973.

Ani maamin: A Song Lost and Found Again (cantata), music composed by Darius Milhaud, Random House, 1974.

Celebration Biblique: Portraits et legendes, Editions du Seuil, 1975, translation by M. Wiesel published as *Messengers of God: Biblical Portraits and Legends,* Random House, 1976.

Un Juif aujourd'hui: Recits, essais, dialogues, Editions du Seuil, 1977, translation by M. Wiesel published as *A Jew Today,* Random House, 1978.

(With others) *Dimensions of the Holocaust,* Indiana University Press, 1977.

Four Hasidic Masters and Their Struggle against Melancholy, University of Notre Dame Press, 1978.

Le Proces de Shamgorod tel qu'il se deroula le 25 fevrier 1649: Piece en trois actes, Editions du Seuil, 1979, translation by M. Wiesel published as *The Trial of God (as It Was Held on February 25, 1649, in Shamgorod): A Play in Three Acts,* Random House, 1979.

Images from the Bible, illustrated with paintings by Shalom of Safed, Overlook Press, 1980.

Le Testament d'un poete juif assassine, Edition du Seuil, 1980, translation by M. Wiesel published as *The Testament,* Simon & Schuster, 1981.

Five Biblical Portraits, University of Notre Dame Press, 1981.

Somewhere a Master, Simon & Schuster, 1982, reprinted as *Somewhere a Master: Further Tales of the Hasidic Masters,* Summit Books, 1984.

Paroles d'etranger, Editions du Seuil, 1982.

The Golem: The Story of a Legend as Told by Elie Wiesel (fiction), illustrated by Mark Podwal, Summit Books, 1983.

Le Cinquieme Fils, Grasset (Paris), 1983, translation by M. Wiesel published as *The Fifth Son,* Summit Books, 1985.

Against Silence: The Voice and Vision of Elie Wiesel, three volumes, edited by Irving Abrahamson, Holocaust Library, 1985.

Signes d'exode, Grasset & Fasquelle (Paris), 1985.

Job ou Dieu dans la tempete, Grasset & Fasquelle, 1986.

Le Crepuscule au loin, Grasset & Fasquelle, 1987, translation by M. Wiesel published as *Twilight,* Summit Books, 1988.

(With Albert H. Friedlander) *The Six Days of Destruction,* Paulist Press, 1989.

L'Oublie: Roman, Seuil, 1989.

(With Philippe-Michael de Saint-Cheron) *Evil and Exile,* translated by Jon Rothschild, University of Notre Dame Press, 1990.

The Forgotten (novel), translated by Stephen Becker, Summit, 1992.

Also author of *A Song for Hope,* 1987, *The Nobel Speech,* 1987, and *From the Kingdom of Memory* (essays), 1990. Contributor to numerous periodicals.

SIDELIGHTS: In the spring of 1944, the Nazis entered the Transylvanian village of Sighet, Romania, until then a relatively safe and peaceful enclave in the middle of a war-torn continent. Arriving with orders to exterminate an estimated 600,000 Jews in six weeks or less, Adolf Eichmann, chief of the Gestapo's Jewish section, began making arrangements for a mass deportation program. Among those forced to leave their homes was fifteen-year-old Elie Wiesel, the only son of a grocer and his wife. A serious and devoted student of the Talmud and the mystical teachings of Hasidism and the Cabala, the young man had always assumed he would spend his entire life in Sighet, quietly contemplating the religious texts and helping out in the family's store from time to time. Instead, along with his father, mother, and three sisters, Wiesel was herded onto a train bound for Birkenau, the reception center for the infamous death camp Auschwitz.

For reasons he still finds impossible to comprehend, Wiesel survived Birkenau and later Auschwitz and Buna and Buchenwald; his father, mother, and youngest sister did not (he did not learn until after the war that his older sisters also survived). With nothing and no one in Sighet for him to go back to, Wiesel boarded a train for Belgium with four hundred other orphans who, like him, had no reason or desire to return to their former homes. On orders of General Charles de Gaulle, head of the French provisional government after World War II, the train was diverted to France, where border officials asked the children to raise their hands if they wanted to become French citizens. As Wiesel (who at that time neither spoke nor understood French) recalls in the *Washington Post,* "A lot of them did. They thought they were going to get bread or something; they would reach out for anything. I didn't, so I remained stateless."

Wiesel chose to stay in France for a while, settling first in Normandy and later in Paris, doing whatever he could to earn a living: tutoring, directing a choir, translating. Eventually he began working as a reporter for various French and Jewish publications. But he could not quite bring himself to write about what he had seen and felt at Auschwitz and Buchenwald. Doubtful of his—or of anyone's—ability to convey the horrible truth without diminishing it, Wiesel vowed never to make the attempt.

The young journalist's self-imposed silence came to an end in the mid-1950s, however, after he met and interviewed the Nobel Prize-winning novelist Francois Mauriac. Deeply moved upon learning of Wiesel's tragic youth, Mauriac urged him to speak out and tell the world of his experiences, to "bear witness" for the millions of men, women, and children whom death, and not despair, had silenced. The result was *Night,* the story of a teen-age boy plagued with guilt for having survived the camps and devastated by the realization that the God he had once worshipped so devoutly allowed his people to be destroyed. For the most part autobiographical, it was, says Richard M. Elman in the *New Republic,* "a document as well as a work of literature—journalism which emerged, coincidentally, as a work of art."

Described by the *Nation*'s Daniel Stern as "undoubtedly the single most powerful literary relic of the holocaust," *Night* is the first in a series of nonfiction books and autobiographical novels this "lyricist of lamentation" has written that deal, either directly or indirectly, with the Holocaust. "He sees the present always refracted through the prism of these earlier days," comments James Finn in the *New Republic.* The *New York Times*'s Thomas Lask agrees, stating: "For [more than] twenty-five years, Elie Wiesel has been in one form or another a witness to the range, bestiality and completeness of the destruction of European Jewry by the Germans. . . . Auschwitz informs everything he writes—novels, legends, dialogues. He is not belligerent about it, only unyielding. Nothing he can say measures up to the enormity of what he saw, what others endured. The implications these experiences have for mankind terrify him. . . . He is part conscience, part quivering needle of response and part warning signal. His writing is singular in the disparate elements it has unified, in the peculiar effect of remoteness and immediacy it conveys. He is his own mold."

Other novels by Wiesel about the Jewish experience during and after the Holocaust include *Dawn* and *The Accident,* which were later published together with *Night* in *The Night Trilogy: Night, Dawn, The Accident.* Like *Night,* the other two books in the trilogy have concentration camp survivors as their central characters. *Dawn* concerns the experiences of one survivor just after World War II who joins the Jewish underground efforts to form an independent Israeli state; and *The Accident* is about a man who discovers that his collision with an automobile was actually caused by his subconscious, guilt-ridden desire to commit suicide. In two of Wiesel's later novels, *The Testament* and *The Fifth Son,* the author also explores the effects of the Holocaust on the next generation of Jews. Some critics such as *Globe and Mail* contributor Bronwyn Drainie have questioned the validity of the author's belief that children of Holocaust survivors would be "as morally galvanized by the Nazi nightmare as the survivors themselves." But, asserts Richard F. Shepard in the New York Times, even if the feelings of these children cannot be generalized, "the author does make all of us 'children' of that generation, all of us who were not there, in the sense that he outlines for us the burdens of guilt, of revenge, of despair."

Indeed, the Holocaust and the Jewish religious and philosophical tradition involve experiences and beliefs shared by a great many people, including other writers. But as Kenneth Turan declares in the Washington Post Book World, Elie Wiesel has become "much more than just a writer. He is a symbol, a banner, and a beacon, perhaps the survivor of the Holocaust. . . . He seems to own the horror of the death camps, or, rather, the horror owns him." But it is a moral and spiritual, not a physical, horror that obsesses Wiesel and obliges him to compose what Dan Isaac of the Nation calls "an angry message to God, filled with both insane rage and stoical acceptance; calculated to stir God's wrath, but careful not to trigger an apocalypse." Explains Isaac's Nation colleague Laurence Goldstein: "For Elie Wiesel memory is an instrument of revelation. Each word he uses to document the past transforms both the work and the memory into an act of faith. The writings of Elie Wiesel are a journey into the past blackened by the Nazi death camps where the charred souls of its victims possess the sum of guilt and endurance that mark the progress of man. It is a compulsive, fevered, single-minded search among the ashes for a spark that can be thrust before the silent eyes of God himself."

Unlike those who dwell primarily on the physical horror, then, Wiesel writes from the perspective of a passionately religious man whose faith has been profoundly shaken by what he has witnessed. As Goldstein remarks, "He must rediscover himself. . . . Although he has not lost God, he must create out of the pain and numbness a new experience that will keep his God from vanishing among the unforgettable faces of the thousands whose bodies he saw." According to Maurice Friedman of Commonweal, Wiesel is, in fact, "the most moving embodiment of the Modern Job": a man who questions—in books that "form one unified outcry, one sustained protest, one sobbing and singing prayer"—why the just must suffer while the wicked flourish. This debate with God is one of the central themes of what a Newsweek critic refers to as Wiesel's "God-tormented, God-intoxicated" fiction.

In addition to his intense preoccupation with ancient Jewish philosophy, mythology, and history, Wiesel displays a certain affinity with modern French existentialists, an affinity Josephine Knopp believes is a direct consequence of the Holocaust. Writes Knopp in Contemporary Literature: "To the young Wiesel the notion of an 'absurd' universe would have been a completely alien one. . . . The traditional Jewish view holds that life's structure and meaning are fully explained and indeed derive from the divinely granted Torah. . . . Against this background the reality of Auschwitz confronts the Jew with a dilemma, an 'absurdity' which cannot be dismissed easily and which stubbornly refuses to dissipate of its own accord. . . . The only possible response that remains within the framework of Judaism is denunciation of God and a demand that He fulfill His contractual obligation [to protect those who worship Him]. This is the religious and moral context within which Wiesel attempts to apprehend and assimilate the events of the Holocaust. [He seeks] to reconcile Auschwitz with Judaism, to confront and perhaps wring meaning from the absurd." In a more recent novel, Twilight, Wiesel explores this absurdity—in this case, he goes so far as to call it madness—of the universe. Again, the protagonist is a Jew, who begins to wonder, as New York Times reviewer John Gross explains, whether "it is mad to go on believing in God. Or perhaps . . . it is God who is mad: who else but a mad God could have created such a world?"

The strong emphasis on Jewish tradition and Jewish suffering in Wiesel's works does not mean that he speaks only to and for Jews. In fact, maintains Robert McAfee Brown in Christian Century, "writing out of the particularity of his own Jewishness . . . is how [Wiesel] touches universal chords. He does not write about 'the human condition,' but about 'the Jewish condition.' Correction: in writing about the Jewish condition, he thereby writes about the human condition. For the human condition is not generalized existence; it is a huge, crazy-quilt sum of particularized existences all woven together."

To Stern, this time commenting in the Washington Post Book World, it seems that "Wiesel has taken the Jew as his metaphor—and his reality—in order to unite a moral and aesthetic vision in terms of all men." Manes Sperber of the New York Times Book Review expresses a similar view, stating that "Wiesel is one of the few writers who, without any plaintiveness, has succeeded in revealing in the Jewish tragedy those features by which it has become again and again a paradigm of the human condition."

According to Michael J. Bandler in the Christian Science Monitor, Wiesel conveys his angry message to God "with a force and stylistic drive that leaves the reader stunned." Concise and uncluttered, yet infused with a highly emotional biblical mysticism, the author's prose "gleams again and again with the metaphor of the poet," writes Clifford A. Ridley in the National Observer. Though it "never abandons its tender intimacy," reports Sperber, "[Wiesel's] voice comes from far away in space and time. It is the voice of the Talmudic teachers of Jerusalem and Babylon; of medieval mystics; of Rabbi Nachman of Bratzlav whose tales have inspired generations of Hasidim and so many writers." As Lask observes, "[Wiesel] has made the form of the telling his own. The surreal and the supernatural combine abrasively with the harsh fact; the parable, the rabbinic tale support and sometimes substitute for narrative. The written law and oral tradition support, explain and expand the twentieth-century event." Goldstein, noting the author's "remarkably compassionate tone," declares that "he writes with that possessive reverence for language that celebrates, as much as describes, experience. The written word becomes a powerful assertion, the triumph of life over death and indifference. . . . Words carved on gravestones, legend torn from the pit where millions of broken bodies lie. This is the inheritance which Elie Wiesel brings to us. His voice claims us with its urgency. His vision lights the mystery of human endurance."

Several critics, however, feel Wiesel's prose does not quite live up to the demands of his subject. Commenting in the *New York Times Book Review,* for example, Jeffrey Burke states that the author occasionally "slips into triteness or purple prose or redundancy," and a reviewer for the *New Yorker* finds that Wiesel becomes "nearly delirious" in his intensity. *Newsweek*'s Geoffrey Wolff believes that Wiesel's work at times "suffers from unnecessary confusions, linguistic cliches, dense and purple thickets, and false mystifications. Ideas tend to hobble about . . . on stilts. . . . The language, seeking to transport us to another world, collapses beneath the weight of its burden much too often." Concludes Burke: "No one can or would deny the seriousness and necessity of Elie Wiesel's role as witness. . . . It is natural that such a mission would remain uppermost in the writer's mind, but that the requirements of art should proportionately diminish in significance is not an acceptable corollary. [Wiesel tends] to sacrifice the demands of craft to those of conscience."

In defense of Wiesel, Turan states that "his is a deliberate, elegant style, consciously elevated and poetic, and if he occasionally tries to pack too much into a sentence, to jam it too full of significance and meaning, it is an error easy to forgive." Elman, this time writing in the *New York Times Book Review,* also finds that "some of Wiesel's existentialist parables are deeply flawed by an opacity of language and construction, which may confirm that 'the event was so heavy with horror . . . that words could not really contain it.' But Wiesel's work is not diminished by his failure to make his shattering theme—God's betrayal of man—consistently explicit." Thus, according to Jonathan Brent in the *Chicago Tribune Book World,* Wiesel is "the type of writer distinguished by his subject rather than his handling of it. . . . Such writers must be read not for themselves but for the knowledge they transmit of events, personalities, and social conditions outside their fiction itself. They do not master their material esthetically, but re-

main faithful to it; and this constitutes the principle value of their work."

Few agree with these assessments of Wiesel's stylistic abilities, but many support Brent's conclusion that the author is almost compulsively faithful to his subject. As Lawrence L. Langer observes in the *Washington Post Book World:* "Although Elie Wiesel has announced many times in recent years that he is finished with the Holocaust as a subject for public discourse, it is clear . . . that the Holocaust has not yet finished with him. Almost from his first volume to his last, his writing has been an act of homage, a ritual of remembrance in response to a dreadful challenge 'to unite the language of man with the silence of the dead.' . . . If Elie Wiesel returns compulsively to the ruins of the Holocaust world, it is not because he has nothing new to say. . . . [It is simply that] the man he did not become besieges his imagination and compels him to confirm his appointments with the past that holds him prisoner."

Wiesel expresses what *Commonweal*'s Irving Halpern calls "the anguish of a survivor who is unable to exorcise the past or to live with lucidity and grace in the present" in the book *Night,* his first attempt to bear witness for the dead. Wiesel writes: "Never shall I forget that night, the first night in camp, which has turned my life into one long night, seven times cursed and seven times sealed. Never shall I forget that smoke. Never shall I forget the little faces of the children, whose bodies I saw turned into wreaths of smoke beneath a silent blue sky. Never shall I forget those flames which consumed my Faith forever. Never shall I forget that nocturnal silence which deprived me, for all eternity, of the desire to live. Never shall I forget those moments which murdered my God and my soul and turned my dreams to dust. Never shall I forget these things, even if I am condemned to live as long as God Himself. Never."

Concern that the truths of the Holocaust, and memories in general, might in time be forgotten has often fueled Wiesel's writing. In comparing his many works, Wiesel remarked to *Publishers Weekly* interviewer Elizabeth Devereaux, "What do they have in common? Their commitment to memory. What is the opposite of memory? Alzheimer's disease. I began to research this topic and I discovered that this is the worst disease, that every intellectual is afraid of this disease, not just because it is incurable, which is true of other diseases, too. But here the identity is being abolished." From this realization Wiesel created *The Forgotten,* a novel in which a Holocaust survivor fears he is losing his memories to an unnamed ailment. He beseeches his son to listen and remember as he recounts the events of his life.

Many years after *Night,* Wiesel is still torn between words and silence. "You must speak," he told a *People* magazine interviewer, "but how can you, when the full story is beyond language?" Furthermore, he once remarked in the *Washington Post,* "there is the fear of not being believed, . . . the fear that the experience will be reduced, made into something acceptable, perhaps forgotten." But as he went on to explain in *People:* "We [survivors] believe that if we survived, we must do something with our lives. The first task is to tell the tale." In short, concluded Wiesel, "The only way to stop the next holocaust—the nuclear holocaust—is to remember the last one. If the Jews were singled out then, in the next one we are all victims." For his enduring efforts to keep the memory of the Holocaust alive so that such a tragedy would not repeat itself ever again, Wiesel was awarded the Nobel Peace Prize in 1986. In a *New York Times* article on the event, James M. Markham quotes Egil Aarvik, chairman of the Norwegian Nobel Committee: "Wiesel is a messenger to mankind. . . . His message is one of peace, atonement and human dignity. His belief that the forces fighting evil in the world can be victorious is a hard-won belief . . . repeated and deepened through the works of a great author."

BIOGRAPHICAL/CRITICAL SOURCES:

BOOKS

Authors in the News, Volume 1, Gale, 1976.
Cohen, Myriam B., *Elie Wiesel: Variations sur le Silence,* Rumeur des ages, 1988.
Contemporary Authors Autobiography Series, Volume 4, Gale, 1986.
Contemporary Issues Criticism, Volume 1, Gale, 1982.
Contemporary Literary Criticism, Gale, Volume 3, 1975, Volume 5, 1976, Volume 11, 1979, Volume 37, 1986.
Dictionary of Literary Biography, Volume 83: *French Novelists since 1960,* Gale, 1989.
Dictionary of Literary Biography Yearbook: 1987, Gale, 1988.
Rosenfeld, Alvin, *Confronting the Holocaust,* Indiana University Press, 1978.
Wiesel, Elie, *Night,* translated by Stella Rodway, Hill & Wang, 1960.

PERIODICALS

America, November 19, 1988, pp. 397-401.
Atlantic, November, 1968.
Best Sellers, March 15, 1970; May, 1981.
Book Week, May 29, 1966.
Chicago Tribune Book World, October 29, 1978; March 29, 1981.
Christian Century, January 18, 1961; June 17, 1970; June 3, 1981.

Christian Science Monitor, November 21, 1968; February 19, 1970; November 22, 1978.
Commonweal, December 9, 1960; January 6, 1961; March 13, 1964; October 14, 1966.
Contemporary Literature, spring, 1974.
Detroit Free Press, April 12, 1992, p. 9P.
Detroit News, April 4, 1992, pp. 1C, 4C.
Globe and Mail (Toronto), April 20, 1985; August 6, 1988.
London Times, September 3, 1981.
Los Angeles Times Book Review, June 19, 1988.
Nation, October 17, 1966; February 24, 1969; March 16, 1970; January 5, 1974.
National Observer, February 2, 1970.
National Review, June 12, 1981.
New Leader, December 30, 1968; June 15, 1981.
New Republic, July 5, 1964; December 14, 1968.
Newsweek, May 25, 1964; February 9, 1970.
New Yorker, March 18, 1961; January 9, 1965; August 20, 1966; July 6, 1970; July 12, 1976.
New York Herald Tribune Lively Arts, January 1, 1961; April 30, 1961.
New York Review of Books, July 28, 1966; January 2, 1969; May 7, 1970.
New York Times, December 15, 1970; March 10, 1972; April 3, 1981; April 16, 1984; March 21, 1985; October 15, 1986; June 10, 1988.
New York Times Book Review, July 16, 1961; April 15, 1962; July 5, 1964; January 21, 1979; April 12, 1981; August 15, 1982; April 30, 1989.
People, October 22, 1979.
Publishers Weekly, April 6, 1992, pp. 39-40.
Saturday Review, December 17, 1960; July 8, 1961; July 25, 1964; May 28, 1966; October 19, 1968; January 31, 1970; November 21, 1970.
Time, March 16, 1970; May 8, 1972; July 12, 1976; December 25, 1978; April 20, 1981.
Times Literary Supplement, August 19, 1960; November 20, 1981; June 6, 1986.
TV Guide, February 15, 1969.
Washington Post, October 26, 1968; February 6, 1970; November 15, 1986; November 4, 1989.
Washington Post Book World, October 20, 1968; January 18, 1970; August 8, 1976; October 29, 1978; April 12, 1981; May 29, 1988.*

* * *

WILDE, Larry 1928-

PERSONAL: Surname originally Wildman; born February 6, 1928, in Jersey City, NJ; son of Selig and Gertrude (Schwartzwald) Wildman; married Maryruth Poulos, June 2, 1974. *Education:* University of Miami, B.A., 1952. *Politics:* Liberal. *Religion:* Jewish. *Avocational interests:*

Golf, skiing, cooking (with salads as the specialty of the house).

ADDRESSES: Home—116 Birkdale Rd., Half Moon Bay, CA 94019. *Agent*—Jane Jordan Browne, 410 South Michigan Ave., Chicago, IL 60605.

CAREER: Comedian, performing in night clubs, on stage, and in television. Made professional appearances while attending the University of Miami, has since performed in more than nine hundred cities in forty-nine states, as well as Australia, Canada, the Caribbean, and Europe, sharing the bill with such stars as Vikki Carr, Jack Jones, Diahann Carroll, Ann-Margaret, Debbie Reynolds, Pat Boone, and Andy Williams; night club engagements include the Copacabana in New York, Harrah's at Lake Tahoe, Desert Inn in Las Vegas, and Latin Casino in Philadelphia. Has appeared on stage in the revue, *One Damn Thing after Another,* a comedy play, *Send Me No Flowers,* the musical, *Of Thee I Sing,* and the musical drama, *Candide.* Has appeared on television programs, including *The Tonight Show, The Today Show, The Merv Griffin Show,* and on situation comedies such as *The Mary Tyler Moore Show* and *Sanford and Son.* Has also done commercials for State Farm Insurance, Exxon, Chevrolet, Wrigley gum, and others. Lecturer on comedy at universities, including University of Southern California, University of California, University of Miami, and New York University. Conducts humor workshops for corporate executives and public speakers. Founder of National Humor Month. *Military service:* U.S. Marine Corps, Special Services, 1946-48; mainly writer, director, and actor in service musicals and variety shows.

MEMBER: PEN (president, Los Angeles Center, 1981-83), Screen Actors Guild, American Federation of Television and Radio Artists.

WRITINGS:

The Great Comedians Talk about Comedy (compendium of taped interviews), Citadel, 1968, revised edition published as *The Great Comedians,* 1973.
How the Great Comedy Writers Create Laughter, Nelson-Hall, 1976.
The Complete Book of Ethnic Humor, Corwin, 1978.
The Larry Wilde Book of Limericks, Bantam, 1982.
The Larry Wilde Library of Laughter, Jester Press, 1988.
The Larry Wilde Treasury of Laughter, Jester Press, 1992.

"OFFICIAL" JOKE BOOKS

The Official Polish/Italian Joke Book, Pinnacle Books, 1973.
The Official Jewish/Irish Joke Book, Pinnacle Books, 1974.
The Official Virgins/Sex Maniacs Joke Book, Pinnacle Books, 1975.

The Official Black Folks/White Folks Joke Book, Pinnacle Books, 1975.
More of the Official Polish/Italian Joke Book, Pinnacle Books, 1975.
The Official Democrat/Republican Joke Book, Pinnacle Books, 1976.
The Official Religious/Not So Religious Joke Book, Pinnacle Books, 1976.
The Official Ethnic Calendar for 1977, Pinnacle Books, 1977.
The Official Smart Kids/Dumb Parents Joke Book, Pinnacle Books, 1977.
The Official Golfers Joke Book, Pinnacle Books, 1977.
The Last Official Polish Joke Book, Pinnacle Books, 1977.
The Official Dirty Joke Book, Pinnacle Books, 1977.
The Official Cat Lovers/Dog Lovers Joke Book, Pinnacle Books, 1978.
The Last Official Italian Joke Book, Pinnacle Books, 1978.
More of the Official Jewish/Irish Joke Book, Pinnacle Books, 1979.
The Official Book of Sick Jokes, Pinnacle Books, 1979.
More of the Official Smart Kids/Dumb Parents Joke Book, Pinnacle Books, 1979.
More of the Official Democratic/Republican Joke Book, Pinnacle Books, 1979.
The Official Bedroom/Bathroom Joke Book, Pinnacle Books, 1980.
The Last Official Jewish Joke Book, Bantam, 1980.
More of the Official Sex Maniacs Joke Book, Bantam, 1981.
The Official Doctors Joke Book, Bantam, 1981.
The Official Lawyers Joke Book, Bantam, 1982.
The Last Official Sex Maniacs Joke Book, Bantam, 1982.
The Last Official Irish Joke Book, Bantam, 1983.
The Absolutely Last Official Polish Joke Book, Bantam, 1983.
The Last Official Smart Kids Joke Book, Bantam, 1983.
The Official Rednecks Joke Book, Bantam, 1984.
The Official Politicians Joke Book, Bantam, 1984.
The Official Book of John Jokes, Bantam, 1985.
The Official Sports Maniacs Joke Book, Bantam, 1985.
The Absolutely Last Official Sex Maniacs Joke Book, Bantam, 1985.
The Official Executives Joke Book, Bantam, 1986.
More of the Official Doctors Joke Book, Bantam, 1986.
The Official All-American Joke Book, Bantam, 1988.
The Official W.A.S.P. Joke Book, Bantam, 1988.
(With Steve Wozniak) *The Official Computer Freaks Joke Book,* Bantam, 1989.
The Official Locker Room Joke Book, Bantam, 1991.
The Official Merriest Christmas Humor Joke Book, Bantam, 1991.
The Official Golf Lovers Joke Book, Bantam, 1992.

"ULTIMATE" JOKE BOOKS

The Ultimate Jewish Joke Book, Bantam, 1986.
The Ultimate Lawyers Joke Book, Bantam, 1987.
The Ultimate Sex Maniacs Joke Book, Bantam, 1989.
The Ultimate Ethnic Humor Joke Book, Bantam, 1989.
The Ultimate Pet Lovers Joke Book, Bantam, 1990.

OTHER

Has recorded albums, including *The Joker Is Wild,* Dot Records, and *The Official Polish/Italian Comedy Album,* Samada Records. Contributor to *Equity* and other trade periodicals; contributor of articles to *Coronet, Gallery, Genesis,* and *Penthouse.*

WORK IN PROGRESS: A novel; more comedy books.

SIDELIGHTS: "You can hardly walk into a bookstore these days without coming upon a new collection of jokes by Larry Wilde," writes Clarence Peterson in the *Chicago Tribune.* Wilde's books have sold over eleven million copies and are available in fifty-three countries. In a *Publishers Weekly* article, Wilde explains his popularity: "Really offensive ethnic jokes may not be exactly tasteful, but from time immemorial this sort of comedy has met a primal need, whether it be for the pure fun of it or because it releases some basic tension and fear in man. The ethnic joke has become America's most popular form of wisecracking." While ethnic humor often comes under attack, Wilde feels it will survive. "Ethnic humor will stay with us in spite of those who think of it as being 'sick, mean-spirited and sacreligious,' " he adds. "We are a nation of many peoples from many lands, and if we have learned anything about the human spirit it is that in order to survive we must laugh at ourselves."

Wilde once told *CA:* "I love comedy. Making people laugh has been a significant part of my life for over thirty years. I like hearing that a hospital patient enjoyed one of my joke books or that someone needing a lift got big giggles from some of my gags. When I learn that an aspiring comedian or comedy writer was motivated or influenced by having read one of my serious works on humor it makes me proud. I feel I've made some small contribution to the potential of future professionals."

Wilde's *The Great Comedians Talk about Comedy* has been serialized in *TV Guide* and in newspapers; his National Humor Month commences each April to "spotlight the importance of laughter in our lives."

BIOGRAPHICAL/CRITICAL SOURCES:

PERIODICALS

Chicago Tribune, July 7, 1987.
Publishers Weekly, November 25, 1983.

WILDER, Thornton (Niven) 1897-1975

PERSONAL: Born April 17, 1897, in Madison, WI; died of a heart attack, December 7, 1975, in Hamden, CT; son of Amos Parker (a newspaper editor and U.S. Consul to China) and Isabella Thornton (Niven) Wilder. *Education:* Attended Oberlin College, 1915-17; Yale University, A.B., 1920; attended American Academy in Rome, 1920-21; Princeton University, A.M., 1926. *Politics:* Democrat. *Religion:* Congregationalist.

ADDRESSES: Home—Hamden, CT.

CAREER: Dramatist, novelist, essayist, and scriptwriter. French teacher and assistant master of Davis House, Lawrenceville School, Lawrenceville, NJ, 1921-25; tutor and writer in the United States and abroad, 1925-27; master, Davis House, Lawrenceville School, 1927-28. Lecturer in comparative literature, University of Chicago, Chicago, IL, 1930-36; visiting professor, University of Hawaii, Honolulu, 1935; American delegate to Institut de Cooperation Intellectuelle, Paris, France, 1937; goodwill representative to Latin America for U.S. Department of State, 1941; International PEN Club Congress delegate with John Dos Passos, 1941; Charles Eliot Norton Professor of Poetry, Harvard University, 1950-51; chief of U.S. delegation to UNESCO Conference of Arts, Venice, 1952. Actor in *Our Town,* New York City and summer stock, beginning 1939, and in *The Skin of Our Teeth,* stock and summer theaters. *Military service:* United States Coast Artillery Corps, 1918-19; became corporal; U.S. Army, 1942-45; commissioned captain, advancing to lieutenant colonel; received Legion of Merit and Bronze Star.

MEMBER: American Academy of Arts and Letters, Modern Language Association of America (honorary member), Authors Guild, Authors League of America, Actors Equity Association, Hispanic Society of America, Bayerische Akademie (corresponding member), Akademie der Wissenschaften und der Literatur (Mainz, West Germany), Bavarian Academy of Fine Arts (honorary member), Century Association (New York), Players (honorary member), Graduate Club, Elizabethan Club, Alpha Delta Phi.

AWARDS, HONORS: Pulitzer Prize, 1928, for *The Bridge of San Luis Rey,* 1938, for *Our Town,* and 1943, for *The Skin of Our Teeth;* Chevalier, Legion of Honor, 1951; Gold Medal for Fiction, American Academy of Arts and Letters, 1952; Friedenspreis des Deutschen Buchhandels, 1957; Sonderpreis des Oesterreichischen Staatspreises, 1959; Goethe-Plakette, 1959; Brandeis University Creative Arts Award, 1959-60, for theater and film; Edward MacDowell Medal (first time presented), 1960; Century Association Art Medal; Medal of the Order of Merit (Peru); Order Pour le Merite (Bonn, West Germany); invited by President Kennedy's cabinet to present reading,

1962; Presidential Medal of Freedom, 1963; National Book Committee's National Medal for Literature (first time presented), 1965; National Book Award, 1968, for *The Eighth Day;* honorary member of the Order of the British Empire; honorary degrees from New York University, Yale University, Kenyon College, College of Wooster, Harvard University, Northeastern University, Oberlin College, University of New Hampshire, Goethe University, and University of Zurich.

WRITINGS:

NOVELS

The Cabala (excerpt first published in *Double Dealer,* September, 1922; also see below), Boni, 1926.

The Bridge of San Luis Rey (also see below), Boni, 1927, published with new introduction by Kay Boyle, Time, Inc., 1963, limited edition with illustrations by William Kaughan, Franklin Library, 1976.

The Woman of Andros (based on *Andria* by Terentius Afer, Publius; also see below), Boni, 1930.

Heaven's My Destination (Book-of-the-Month Club selection), Longmans, Green, 1934.

The Ides of March (Book-of-the-Month Club selection), Harper, 1948.

The Eighth Day, Harper, 1967.

Theophilus North, Harper, 1973.

PLAYS

The Trumpet Shall Sound (first published in *Yale Literary Magazine,* 1919-20), produced at American Laboratory Theater, 1926.

Love and How to Cure It (one-act play; produced in New Haven, CT, 1931; also see below), Samuel French, 1932.

The Long Christmas Dinner (produced in New Haven, CT, 1931; also see below), Samuel French, 1933, revised edition, 1960.

The Happy Journey to Trenton and Camden (also see below), produced in New Haven, CT, 1931, produced with *The Respectful Prostitute* by Jean-Paul Sartre, on Broadway, 1948.

The Queens of France (one-act play; produced in Chicago, 1932; also see below), Samuel French, 1931.

(Adaptor and translator) *Lucrece* (based on *The Rape of Lucrece* by Andre Obey; produced on Broadway, 1932), Houghton, 1933.

(Adaptor and translator) Henrik Ibsen, *A Doll's House,* first produced in New York City, 1937, produced on Broadway, 1938.

Our Town (three-act play; first produced in Princeton, NJ, 1937; produced on Broadway, 1938; also see below), Coward, 1938, acting edition, Coward, 1965, limited edition with introduction by Brooks Atkinson and illustrations by Robert J. Lee, Limited Editions Club, 1974.

The Merchant of Yonkers: A Farce in Four Acts (based on *Einen Jux will er sich Machen* by Johann Nestroy; produced on Broadway, 1938), Harper, 1939, revised version published as *The Matchmaker* (first produced in Edinburgh, Scotland at the Edinburgh Festival, 1954; produced on Broadway, 1955; also see below), Samuel French, 1957.

The Skin of Our Teeth (three-act play; first produced in New Haven, CT, 1942; produced on Broadway, 1942; also see below), Harper, 1942.

Our Century (three-scene burlesque; produced in New York City, 1947), Century Association, 1947.

(Translator) Jean-Paul Sartre, *The Victors,* produced Off-Broadway, 1949.

The Alcestiad (based on Euripides' *Alcestis;* also see below), produced as *A Life in the Sun* in Edinburgh, Scotland, 1955.

The Wreck of the 5:25, produced in West Berlin, Germany at Congresshalle Theater, 1957.

Bernice, produced at Congresshalle Theater, 1957.

The Drunken Sisters (first published in centennial issue of *Atlantic Monthly,* 1957; first produced as fourth act of *Die Alkestiade* [also see below]; produced in Brooklyn Heights, NY, 1970; also see below), Samuel French, 1957.

Childhood (one-act play; first published in *Atlantic Monthly,* November, 1960; also see below), Samuel French, 1960.

(Author of libretto) Paul Hindemith, translator, *Das Lange Weihnachtsmal* (opera; adapted from play, *The Long Christmas Dinner;* first produced in Mannheim, Germany, 1961), music by Hindemith, Schott Music, 1961.

Infancy, A Comedy in One Act (also see below), Samuel French, 1961.

Plays for Bleecker Street (three volumes; contains *Childhood, Infancy, A Comedy in One Act,* and *Someone from Assisi;* produced Off-Broadway, 1962), Samuel French, 1960-61.

(Author of libretto) *Die Alkestiade* (opera; adaptation of *A Life in the Sun*), music by Louise Talma, first produced in Frankfurt, West Germany, 1962.

Pullman Car Hiawatha (also see below), produced Off-Broadway, 1964.

Thornton Wilder's Triple Bill (contains *The Long Christmas Dinner, The Queens of France,* and *The Happy Journey to Trenton and Camden*), produced Off-Broadway, 1966.

Adaptor, with Jerome Kilty, of stage version of *The Ides of March.*

OMNIBUS VOLUMES

The Angel That Troubled the Waters and Other Plays (contains *Nascunter Poetae, Proserpina and the Devil, Fanny Otcott, Brother Fire, The Penny That Beauty Spent, The Angel on the Ship, The Message and Jehanne, Childe Roland to the Dark Tower Came, Centaurs, Leviathan, And the Sea Shall Give Up Its Dead, Now the Servant's Name Was Malchus, Mozart and the Gray Steward, Hast Thou Considered My Servant Job?, The Flight into Egypt,* and *The Angel That Troubled the Waters*), Coward, 1928.

The Long Christmas Dinner and Other Plays in One Act (contains *The Long Christmas Dinner, Pullman Car Hiawatha, Such Things Only Happen in Books, The Happy Journey to Trenton and Camden, Love and How to Cure It,* and *The Queens of France*), Yale University Press, 1931.

The Stories of Thornton Wilder: The Bridge of San Luis Rey, The Cabala, The Woman of Andros, Longmans, Green, 1934.

(And author of preface) *Three Plays: Our Town, The Skin of Our Teeth, The Matchmaker,* Harper, 1938, revised edition with critical notes by Travis Bogard, 1962, published as *Our Town; The Skin of Our Teeth; The Matchmaker,* Penguin Books, 1962, limited edition with illustrations by Dick Brown, Franklin Library, 1979.

A Thornton Wilder Trio: The Cabala, The Bridge of San Luis Rey, The Woman of Andros, introduction by Malcolm Cowley, Criterion, 1956.

The Cabala and The Woman of Andros, Harper, 1968.

The Alcestiad: or, A Life in the Sun: A Play in Three Acts, with a Satyr Play, the Drunken Sisters, Harper, 1977, limited edition published as *The Alcestiad: or, A Life in the Sun; The Drunken Sisters,* illustrations by Daniel Maffia, Franklin Library, 1977.

OTHER

(Author of preface) Gertrude Stein, *Narration,* University of Chicago Press, 1935.

We Live Again (screenplay; based on *Resurrection* by Leo Tolstoy), Metro-Goldwyn-Mayer, 1936.

(Author of preface) *The Geographical History of America,* Random House, 1936.

(Contributor) Augusto Centeno, editor, *The Intent of the Artist,* Princeton University Press, 1941.

(Author of preface) *Four in America,* Yale University Press, 1947.

An Evening with Thornton Wilder, April thirtieth, 1962, Washington, D.C. (consists of third act of *Our Town*), Harper, 1962.

American Characteristics and Other Essays, edited by Donald Gallup, foreword by Isabel Wilder, Harper, 1979.

The Journals of Thornton Wilder: With Two Scenes of an Uncompleted Play, "The Emporium," edited by Donald Gallup, Yale University Press, 1985.

Author of screenplays, *Our Town,* released by United Artists, 1940, and *Shadow of a Doubt,* Universal, 1943. Contributor to periodicals, including *Harper's, Hudson Review, Poetry, Atlantic Monthly,* and *Yale Review.* Theater reviewer, *Theatre Arts Monthly,* 1925.

The autograph of *The Bridge of San Luis Rey* is housed in the American Literature Collection of the Beinecke Rare Book and Manuscript Library, Yale University.

ADAPTATIONS: The Bridge of San Luis Rey was adapted for film three times, initially in 1929; also adapted for film were *Our Town,* 1940, and *The Matchmaker,* 1958. *The Matchmaker* was also adapted by Michael Stewart into a musical, *Hello, Dolly!,* with words and music by Jerry Herman, and opened in 1964, with an initial run of almost 3,000 performances; in 1964, *Hello Dolly!* became the longest running musical on Broadway; *Hello, Dolly!* subsequently became a popular film. *Our Town* was adapted into the musical *Grover's Corners,* by Harvey Schmidt and Tom Jones, in 1987. *Theophilus North* was made into the movie *Mr. North* by John Huston, starring Danny Huston, Anjelica Huston, and Robert Mitchum. There have also been radio and television adaptations of many of Wilder's works.

WORK IN PROGRESS: Two cycles of plays, *The Seven Ages of Man* and *The Seven Deadly Sins.*

SIDELIGHTS: Because of the popularity of such plays as *Our Town,* Thornton Wilder is best known as a dramatist. His first and last major works, however, were novels, *The Cabala* and *Theophilus North.* During his forty-seven-year career he wrote seven novels, many short plays, six long plays, and a collection of essays on such diverse figures as American poet Emily Dickinson, British dramatist George Bernard Shaw, and Irish novelist James Joyce. Wilder even acted occasionally in his plays, assisted with their production, and wrote screenplays in Hollywood. In addition, he distinguished himself as a professor at both the University of Chicago and Harvard University. In short, Wilder was a major figure in the literary and cultural life of twentieth-century America.

Wilder's creativity was rewarded with critical acclaim and mass popularity throughout his career. He was awarded the Pulitzer Prize on three separate occasions; for his novel *The Bridge of San Luis Rey* and for the plays *Our Town* and *The Skin of Our Teeth.* Wilder was also honored with the National Book Award for his novel *The Eighth Day. The Bridge of San Luis Rey* sold more than three hundred thousand copies in its first two years; in its first year Wilder's fourth novel, *Heaven's My Destination,* sold ninety thousand copies in the United States, two-hundred-fifty-thousand in England, and five-hundred-thousand in Germany; *Theophilus North* held a prominent position on the *New York Times* best-seller list for twenty-one weeks.

One reason for Wilder's general recognition as a dramatist rather than as a novelist is that his novels were less experimental than his plays. Even within the pages of his books, however, Wilder was searching for forms most conducive to his chosen themes. He worked with the genres of parable, allegory, mystery, and epic, as well as with the bildungsroman, or life story; the picaresque tale, which relates the adventures of a wanderer; and the epistolary novel, composed entirely of letters. Yet in his drama, he was emphatically the innovator. Travis Bogard in *Modern Drama: Essays in Criticism* labels Wilder as "a man who, along with Eugene O'Neill, freed the American theater from its traditional forms through his experiments in *Our Town* and *The Skin of Our Teeth.* "

In *Our Town,* although Wilder applied lessons from such sources as Greek tragedy, Chinese drama, and Japanese Noh drama, the outcome proved both uniquely American and universal. The minimalistic setting and action, the use of pantomime, and the creation of the Stage Manager as a character in the play who simultaneously directs it contributed to an effort that represents a major step in the development of American theater. In *The Skin of Our Teeth,* Wilder brought to stage a family who encapsulates the history of mankind with action spanning five thousand years. As Donald Haberman notes in *The Plays of Thornton Wilder,* Wilder conceived the plays's action, dialogue, and themes in response to James Joyce's novel *Finnegans Wake.*

Despite critical recognition of his innovation and despite his popular successes and many awards, Wilder was criticized for failing to address the problems at the fore of the modern social consciousness. As Martin Gardner observes in *University of Kansas City Review,* Wilder's work paints no pictures of slaughter houses, tenements, or oppressed minorities, often the material of modern realism. This avoidance of life's most painful realities associates Wilder with the nineteenth-century Genteel Tradition of correctness and conventionality and with the humanitarian standards, moral values, spirituality, optimism, and interest in the past associated with the philosophical movement called the New Humanism. In addition, a hint of didacticism runs throughout his dramas and novels, thus further emphasizing his moralistic and spiritual tone. Wilder's approach to the world made him popular with the American middle-class public but controversial for literary critics. Critics practicing their art on Wilder's realistic contemporaries Theodore Dreiser, Sinclair Lewis, Upton Sinclair, John Dos Passos, F. Scott Fitzgerald, and Ernest Hemingway found his novels somewhat strange and unsatisfactory.

Although Wilder's optimism and moral approach certainly appealed to middle-class readers around the world—his message was extremely popular, for example, in post-World War II Europe, especially in Germany—his writing also contains darker nuances. Although the works do not specifically detail life's unpleasantries, they actually ignore few of its problems. *The Cabala* touches upon sexual obsession, incest, infidelity, the grubbiness of American intellectual and moral materialism, suicide, and the failure of Puritanism. *The Bridge of San Luis Rey* deals directly with death and religion, while *The Woman of Andros* is populated by the disfigured, the crass moneymaker, and the morally and spiritually corrupt. *The Skin of Our Teeth* stages man's cyclic struggle to survive his own mistakes. As these examples show, Wilder's subject matter places him closer to the realistic novelists than some critics have assumed.

Wilder's themes also clearly mark him as a twentieth-century American writer. Just as he did not totally neglect social issues, he did not ignore other themes prevalent in modern literature—despair, nihilism, isolation, and the failure of love and tradition. He also had a definite perspective on the literary tradition within which he worked and contributed to this tradition significantly. For example, in *The Cabala* Wilder weaves the themes of American Puritan innocence and mature European decadence into a novel of Olympian individualism, thus evoking the American novelistic tradition of Nathaniel Hawthorne and Henry James. In *The Skin of Our Teeth* he reworks Joyce's *Finnegans Wake,* and in *The Eighth Day* his characters squat in South American villages and, echoing Hemingway, speak of life's *nada,* or nothingness.

However, Wilder is distinguished from more realistic twentieth-century writers by his preoccupation with the mythic nature of life and his belief that life will continue to renew itself. Wilder provided an insight into this philosophy in "Goethe and World Literature," an essay collected in *American Characteristics and Other Essays.* There he identified himself with authors who shared a "planetary consciousness": a consciousness "of the multiplicity of souls," of "the deep abyss of time," of the idea that "every man and woman born is . . . in a new relation to the whole," and of "the unity of the human spirit." He further defined this sense of planetary consciousness in the preface to *Three Plays: Our Town, The Skin of Our Teeth, The Matchmaker:* "Every action which has ever taken place—every thought, every emotion—has taken place only once, at one moment in time and place. 'I love you,' 'I rejoice,' 'I suffer,' have been said and felt billions of times, and never twice the same. Every person who has ever lived has lived an unbroken succession of unique occasions. Yet the more one is aware of this individuality in experience (innumerable! innumerable!) the more one becomes attentive to what these disparate moments have in common, to repetitive patterns." From these remarks, a clearer picture of Wilder's method begins to emerge. Although he was interested in the action of Americans in society, his main concern was with how these acts establish one's place within the unity of all humanity.

Wilder's idea of a world literature shares features with mythic literature and myth criticism. The function of myth, according to David Bidney in *Myth and Literature,* is "to promote social solidarity as well as solidarity with nature as a whole in a time of social crisis. Mythical thought is especially concerned to deny and negate the fact of death and to affirm the unbroken unity and continuity of life." John Frey in *Journal of English and Germanic Philology* marks this "predilection for the metaphysical" as one of the characteristics that separates Wilder's novels from other American novels. Warren French, in the introduction to *A Vast Landscape: Time in the Novels of Thornton Wilder,* places even more importance on recognizing Wilder's metaphysical qualities: "The only way we are ever going to respond adequately to Wilder's work is to accept his vision as mystical and to attempt to share it; yet the mystical qualities of his vision have rarely been acknowledged and often deliberately avoided."

Another reason for Wilder's mixed critical reception was that his mythic themes were characterized by a pervasive religious feeling. Wilder attempted to provide a religious rhetoric that could renew the spiritual energy of his readers. He felt that theological doctrine was largely a system of words designed to persuade; in the foreword to *The Angel That Troubled the Waters and Other Plays,* he stated that "the revival of religion is almost a matter of rhetoric." He regarded literature, not doctrinal tracts, as the proper vehicle for this revival. In the same foreword, Wilder clarified his purpose: "I hope, through many mistakes, to discover the spirit that is not unequal to the elevation of the great religious themes, yet which does not fall to a repellent religious didacticism." He knew that this purpose would not be universally well-received: "There has seldom been an age in literature when such a vein was less welcome and understood." Nevertheless, Wilder insisted, someone must make the effort because "all that is fairest in the Christian tradition [has been] made repugnant to the new generations by reason of the diction in which it is expressed. The intermittent sincerity of generations of clergymen and teachers has rendered embarrassing and even ridiculous all the terms of spiritual life." Wilder spent his entire career searching for a diction that would revitalize the various myths underlying Christianity.

Wilder's spiritual and literary purpose stemmed from his response to a world in which traditional religious forms and beliefs were under constant attack. As Wilder declared in the foreword to *The Angel That Troubled the Waters and Other Plays,* in this world the individual felt himself "shrinking to nullity in the immensity of the universe as revealed by science, in which the individual's very existence is threatened by means of destruction he himself has created." Wilder's literature thus focuses on one of twentieth-century man's central concerns: the problem of maintaining spiritual identity in a hostile or unfeeling universe.

The form which Wilder's metaphysical predilection assumed also distinguishes his realism from that of many other twentieth-century writers. Aligning himself with authors like T. S. Eliot, Ezra Pound, and Joyce, Wilder viewed the individual's life as a miniature version of the universal, leading him toward more abstract forms of art. He wrote in *The Intent of the Artist* that "the myth, the parable, the fable are the fountainhead" of all literature and contended that imaginative narration seeking the repetitive universal symbol in the commonplace "inevitably reaches the point where exposition passes into illustration, into parable, metaphor, allegory and myth." Therein lies a paradox in Wilder's work: He consistently focused on events from the physical and spiritual life of twentieth-century America but translated and transformed them into metaphysical symbols of the universal.

In short, Wilder, through a combination of allegory and myth, sought in his writing to provide a nonsectarian religious rhetoric that would restore the mystic power of his readers' faith in their harmony with the universe. Wilder turned to literature to provide a solution to modern problems because he believed in the power of literature to restore man's spiritual view of the world, to make the ordinary sacred. He thus affirmed that every experience can be transformed into a sacred mythic experience. Through their journeys toward faith, Wilder's protagonists undergo mythic transformations, becoming his versions of modern religious beings; or, as Louis Macneice writes in *Varieties of Parables,* "he imitates the gods, the culture's heroes, or the mythical ancestors." Ironically, Wilder's work most likely would have received a more positive critical reception had it made its appearance in the later decades of the twentieth century, for its mythopoetic qualities are akin to those in the works of such successful contemporary American authors as Joyce Carol Oates, Walker Percy, and Carson McCullers. Like the literature of these writers, Wilder's canon reflects the many disparate paths in life and the mythic qualities that unite them.

BIOGRAPHICAL/CRITICAL SOURCES:

BOOKS

Allen, Walter, *The Modern Novel,* Anchor, 1965.
Authors in the News, Volume 2, Gale, 1976.

Bogard, Travis, and William I. Oliver, editors, *Modern Drama: Essays in Criticism,* Oxford University Press, 1965.

Broussard, Louis, *American Drama,* University of Oklahoma Press, 1962.

Burbank, Rex, *Thornton Wilder,* Twayne, 1961, 2nd edition, 1978.

Centeno, Augusto, editor, *The Intent of the Artist,* Princeton University Press, 1941.

Cohn, Ruby, *Dialogue in American Drama,* Indiana University Press, 1971, pp. 170-225.

Cole, Toby, editor, *Playwrights on Playwriting,* Hill & Wang, 1961.

Contemporary Literary Criticism, Gale, Volume 1, 1973, pp. 364-367, Volume 5, 1976, pp. 493-496, Volume 6, 1976, pp. 571-578, Volume 10, 1979, pp. 531-537, Volume 15, 1980, pp. 569-576, Volume 35, 1985, pp. 435-447.

Cowley, Malcolm, editor, *Writers at Work: The Paris Review Interviews,* Viking, 1957, pp. 99-118.

Cowley, Malcolm, *After the Genteel Tradition: American Writers, 1910-1930,* Southern Illinois University Press, 1964.

Dictionary of Literary Biography, Gale, Volume 4: *American Writers in Paris, 1920-1939,* 1980, pp. 414-415, Volume 7: *Twentieth-Century American Dramatists,* 1981, pp. 304-319, Volume 9: *American Novelists, 1910-1945,* 1981, pp. 146-153.

Edelstein, J. M., compiler, *A Bibliographical Checklist of the Writings of Thornton Wilder,* Yale University Press, 1959.

Fergusson, Francis, *The Human Image in Dramatic Literature,* Doubleday, 1957.

French, Warren, *A Vast Landscape: Time in the Novels of Thornton Wilder,* edited by Mary Ellen Williams, Idaho State University Press, 1979.

Goldstein, Malcolm, *The Art of Thornton Wilder,* University of Nebraska Press, 1965.

Goldstone, Richard H., *Thornton Wilder: An Intimate Portrait,* Dutton, 1975.

Grebanier, Bernard, *Thornton Wilder,* University of Minnesota Press, 1964.

Haberman, Donald, *The Plays of Thornton Wilder,* Wesleyan University Press, 1967.

Harrison, Gilbert A., *The Enthusiast: A Life of Thornton Wilder,* Ticknor and Fields, 1983.

Kuner, M. C., *Thornton Wilder: The Bright and the Dark,* Crowell, 1972.

Macneice, Louis, *Varieties of Parables,* Cambridge University Press, 1965.

Papajewski, Helmut, *Thornton Wilder,* translated by John Conway, Unger, 1969.

Scanlan, Tom, *Family, Drama, and American Dreams,* Greenwood Press, 1978, pp. 180-217.

Simon, Linda, *Thorton Wilder: His World,* Doubleday, 1979.

Stresau, Herman, *Thornton Wilder,* translated by Frieda Schultze, Unger, 1971.

Vickery, John, editor, *Myth and Literature,* University of Nebraska Press, 1966.

Wagenknecht, Edward, *Cavalcade of the English Novel,* Holt, 1943.

Wescot, Glenway, *Images of Truth,* Harper, 1962.

Wilder, Amos Niven, *Spiritual Aspects of the New Poetry,* Harper, 1940.

Wilder, Amos Niven, *Thorton Wilder and His Public,* Fortress, 1980.

Wilder, Thorton, *The Angel That Troubled the Waters and Other Plays,* Coward, 1928.

Wilder, Thorton, *Three Plays: Our Town, The Skin of Our Teeth, The Matchmaker,* Harper, 1938.

Wilder, Thorton, *American Characteristics and Other Essays,* edited by Donald Gallup, foreword by Isabel Wilder, Harper, 1979.

Wilson, Edmund, *A Literary Chronicle: 1920-1950,* Anchor Books, 1956.

PERIODICALS

AB Bookman's Weekly, January 5, 1976.

Chicago Tribune, February 14, 1986.

Chicago Tribune Book World, October 14, 1979, p. 21.

Commentary, March, 1970, pp. 20, 22, 24.

Commonweal, February 7, 1958, pp. 486-488.

Educational Theatre Journal, Volume 13, 1961, pp. 167-731.

English Journal, May, 1956, pp. 243-249.

Intercollegiate Review, summer, 1974, pp. 149-158.

Journal of English and Germanic Philology, Volume LIV, 1955, p. 193.

Modern Drama, February, 1959, pp. 258-264; September, 1972.

Nation, September 3, 1955.

New Republic, August 8, 1928, pp. 303-305; August 2, 1975, pp. 31-32; January 5-12, 1980, pp. 32-34.

New Yorker, December 6, 1969, p. 166.

New York Times, November 24, 1986; December 20, 1987; December 5, 1988; December 11, 1988, pp. 7, 37.

New York Times Book Review, December 30, 1979, pp. 8-9, 18; September 13, 1987, p. 58.

Philadelphia Inquirer, December 14, 1975.

Renascence, spring, 1974, pp. 123-138.

Saturday Review, October 6, 1956, pp. 13-14, 50-52.

Saturday Review of Literature, June 11, 1938, pp. 10-11; August 6, 1949, pp. 33-34.

Sewanee Review, Volume LXIV, 1956, pp. 544-573.

Texas Quarterly, autumn, 1976, pp. 76-79.

University of Kansas City Review, Volume VII, 1940, pp. 83-91.

Washington Post, May 29, 1987, pp. B1, B4.
Washington Post Book World, June 29, 1986, p. 12.

OBITUARIES:

PERIODICALS

Detroit Free Press, December 8, 1975, pp. 1A, 7A.
Detroit News, December 8, 1975, p. 20A.
Newsweek, December 22, 1975, p. 67.
New York Times, December 8, 1975, pp. 1, 40.
Publishers Weekly, December 15, 1975.
Washington Post, December 8, 1975, p. B10.*

—*Sidelights by Michael J. Vivion*

*   *   *

WILLEY, Margaret 1950-

PERSONAL: Born November 5, 1950, in Chicago, IL; daughter of Foster L. (an artist) and Barbara (an artist; maiden name, Pistorius) Willey; married Richard Joanisse (a professor), March 15, 1980; children: Chloe. *Education:* Grand Valley State College, B.Ph., B.A., 1975; Bowling Green State University, M.F.A., 1979.

ADDRESSES: Home—431 Grant, Grand Haven, MI 49417.

CAREER: Writer.

MEMBER: Authors Guild, Children's Reading Round Table.

AWARDS, HONORS: Creative Artist Grant, Michigan Council of the Arts, 1984-85; American Library Association citation as one of year's best books for young adults, 1983, for *The Bigger Book of Lydia,* 1986, for *Finding David Dolores,* 1988, for *If Not for You,* and 1990, for *Saving Lenny.*

WRITINGS:

YOUNG ADULT NOVELS

The Bigger Book of Lydia, Harper, 1983.
Finding David Dolores, Harper, 1986.
If Not for You, Harper, 1988.
Saving Lenny, Bantam, 1990.
The Melinda Zone, Bantam, 1993.

OTHER

Contributor to periodicals, including *Redbook, Quarry West, Sou'wester, Heresies,* and *Good Housekeeping.*

WORK IN PROGRESS: The Thanksgiving Uncles, a children's picture book illustrated by Lloyd Bloom, for HarperCollins.

SIDELIGHTS: Margaret Willey once told *CA:* "I have always been concerned with the transformation from child-hood to adulthood, especially for women. I love writing for and about teenagers. My books have touched on such adolescent concerns as anorexia nervosa, the death of a parent, aversion to school, depression, sexism in school, the need for creative outlets, and mother-daughter dynamics."

*   *   *

WILLIAMS, Patrick J.
See BUTTERWORTH, W(illiam) E(dmund III)

*   *   *

WILLMOTT, Phyllis

PERSONAL: Born in London, England; daughter of Alec George (a builder) and Harriet (Mann) Noble; married Peter Willmott (a sociologist), July 31, 1948; children: Lewis, Michael. *Education:* Attended grammar school in Greenwich, London, England. *Religion:* None.

ADDRESSES: Home—27 Kingsley Place, Highgate, London N6 5EA, England.

CAREER: Hackney Hospital, London, England, hospital social worker, 1947-49; homemaker, 1949-55; London School of Economics and Political Science, London, research assistant, 1955-56; Institute of Community Studies, London, social research officer, 1956-67, senior research officer, 1972-82; Croydon College, London, part-time lecturer in social administration, 1967-72; writer, 1982—. Chairman of grants committee, Family Welfare Association. *Military service:* Women's Auxiliary Air Force (WAAF), 1943-46.

MEMBER: British Association of Social Workers, Society of Authors.

WRITINGS:

Consumer's Guide to the British Social Services, Penguin, 1967, 4th edition, 1978.
(Editor) *Public Social Services,* National Council of Social Service, 1973.
Growing Up in a London Village: Family Life Between the Wars (autobiography), Peter Owen, 1979.
(With Susan Mayne) *Families at the Centre,* Bedford Square Press, 1983.
(With husband, Peter Willmott, and Robert Mitton) *Unemployment, Poverty, and Social Policy in Europe,* Bedford Square Press, 1983.
A Green Girl (autobiography), Peter Owen, 1983.
Under One Roof: Manor Gardens Centre, 1913-1988, Manor Gardens Centre, 1988.
Coming of Age in Wartime (autobiography), Peter Owen, 1988.

A Singular Woman; The Life of Geraldine Aves, 1898-1986, Whiting & Birch, 1992.

Contributor of articles and reviews to literary and social service journals.

WORK IN PROGRESS: Walter Noble, 1862-1946, a biographical portrait of the author's grandfather; *Bethnal Green Journal, 1954-55,* a social history.

SIDELIGHTS: Social worker and author Phyllis Willmott told *CA:* "I trained for a career in social work after the end of World War II because I wanted to do something worthwhile. I was ideologically committed to the creation of the Welfare State. In time I became aware of defects that marred its effectiveness, in particular its complexity. It was this that prompted me to write my first book, *Consumer's Guide to the British Social Services.* Much of my later writing focused on ways and means of improving services. Unfortunately, at the present time in Britain, economizing on services has the greatest priority and threatens deterioration rather than improvement."

A Singular Woman: The Life of Geraldine Aves was also a book that grew out of Willmott's longstanding interest in the formation of the modern British Welfare State. Providing a vivid portrait of one of the main figures active in shaping the British social service system during the 1920s and '30s, the biography of Dame Geraldine Aves is based on both research and personal knowledge. The book was compiled after many conversations with Dame Aves, a personal friend of Willmott's until her death in 1986, as well as interviews with friends and associates in the social welfare field. Willmott's friendship with her subject allowed her the opportunity to spend long hours going through vast quantities of personal papers and other documents to gain the information necessary to complete her biography of Aves, a woman who dedicated her life to helping the poor, who had the courage to attain a position in the male-dominated Ministry of Health through which she could battle dysfunctional Poor-Law institutions, and who, through such efforts, came to be considered one of the most outstanding social workers in Britain. *A Singular Woman* was praised by critic Paul Barker in the *Independent* as "an enlightening slice of social history."

"Writing for me began with an ink-blotted journal scribbled in an old school exercise book," noted Willmott. "I was sixteen. I have continued to keep a journal on and off—mostly on—ever since. My autobiographical books, *Growing Up in a London Village, A Green Girl,* and *Coming of Age in Wartime,* developed out of this compulsion to try to encapsulate the present and subsequently to recreate the past."

BIOGRAPHICAL/CRITICAL SOURCES:

BOOKS

Wheeler-Bennett, Joan, *Women at the Top: Achievement and Family Life,* Peter Owen, 1977.

PERIODICALS

Independent, November 12, 1992, p. 29.

*   *   *

WILSON, Clyde N(orman, Jr.)   1941-

PERSONAL: Born June 11, 1941, in Greensboro, NC; son of Clyde Norman (a fire fighter) and Ruby (a bookkeeper; maiden name, Smith) Wilson; married Diane Carter, September 20, 1964 (divorced, 1987); children: Anne, Lee (daughter). *Education:* University of North Carolina, Chapel Hill, A.B., 1963, M.A., 1964, Ph.D., 1971.

ADDRESSES: Home—467 Pittsdowne Rd., Dutch Fork, SC 29210. *Office*—Department of History, University of South Carolina, Columbia, SC 29208.

CAREER: Richmond News Leader, Richmond, VA, reporter, 1964-65; *Charlotte News,* Charlotte, NC, reporter, 1965-66; University of North Carolina, Chapel Hill, manuscript librarian, 1967-71; University of South Carolina, Columbia, assistant professor, 1971-76, associate professor, 1976-83, professor of history, 1983—.

MEMBER: Southern Texts Society, St. George Tucker Society.

WRITINGS:

(With Susan B. Blosser) *The Southern Historical Collection: A Guide to Manuscripts,* University of North Carolina Library, 1970.
(Author of introduction) Hermann E. von Holst, *John C. Calhoun,* Chelsea House, 1980.
Carolina Cavalier: The Life and Mind of James Johnston Pettigrew, University of Georgia Press, 1990.
John C. Calhoun: A Bibliography, Meckler, 1990.
(Author of introduction) Margaret L. Coit, *John C. Calhoun: American Portrait,* University of South Carolina Press, 1991.
(Author of introduction) Thomas Nelson Page, *In Ole Virginia,* J. S. Sanders, 1991.

EDITOR

(And author of introduction and notes) *The Papers of John C. Calhoun,* University of South Carolina Press, Volume 10, 1977, Volume 11, 1978, Volume 12, 1979, Volume 13, 1980, Volume 14, 1981, Volume 15, 1983,

Volume 16, 1985, Volume 17, 1986, Volume 18, 1989, Volume 19, 1990, Volume 20, 1991.

(And author of introduction and notes) James H. Hammond, *Selections from the Letters and Speeches of the Hon. James H. Hammond, of South Carolina*, Reprint Co., 1978.

(And contributor) *Dictionary of Literary Biography*, Gale, Volume 17: *Twentieth-Century American Historians*, 1978, Volume 30: *American Historians, 1607-1865*, 1984, Volume 47: *American Historians, 1866-1912*, 1986.

(And contributor) *Why the South Will Survive*, University of Georgia Press, 1981.

(With David R. Chesnutt) *The Meaning of South Carolina History*, University of South Carolina Press, 1991.

The Essential Calhoun: With Selections from Writings, Speeches, and Letters, Transaction Books, 1992.

OTHER

Contributor to books, including *The New Right Papers*, edited by Robert W. Whitaker, St. Martin's, 1982. Contributor to periodicals, including *Civil War Times Illustrated, Intercollegiate Review, Continuity*, and *Modern Age*. Contributing editor, *Chronicles: A Magazine of American Culture*.

WORK IN PROGRESS: A book-length study of John C. Calhoun's political thought, for Kansas University Press, "designed to reach a more profound and currently relevant description than the standard interpretations."

SIDELIGHTS: Clyde N. Wilson once told *CA:* "My academic career has been that of a scholar in American history, specializing in the Jacksonian era and in American historiography. I have written scholarly articles and reviews, but my main effort has been the comprehensive edition of *The Papers of John C. Calhoun*. I inherited this project in time to produce the tenth volume in 1977 and in 1991 published the twentieth volume.

"I have also been working toward a new interpretive work, updating the relevance of Calhoun's political thought. John C. Calhoun's reputation has had its ups and downs. He was a very controversial character. Yet, certainly he was one of the handful of major figures during the critical middle period of American history, and he was also a political thinker of permanent interest. Not only are a number of important American scholars looking seriously at Calhoun again, but so are scholars in other countries, such as Italy and Japan. The edition will be useful, I believe, for many generations and countries, and my interpretations in the introduction of each volume will help to advance the thinking of American historians about the period. I have also in recent years produced a comprehensive Calhoun bibliography and *The Essential Calhoun*. *The Essential Calhoun* is a one-volume collection of Calhoun's best thought, which I believe shows him in a light not seen before.

"Another part of my scholarly publishing effort has grown out of my interest in American historiography. This involves the editing of three volumes of the *Dictionary of Literary Biography* devoted to American historical writers. In these volumes I have somewhat surprised the academic historians by treating all kinds of historical writers, popular as well as academic, and also be treating historians as literary men—authors with literary careers.

"Historians are at present accustomed to thinking of themselves largely as academics and as social scientists rather than as writers. For this reason, the editing of these volumes has been a splendid opportunity to focus attention once more on the literary aspect of history. I happen to believe—and this is by no means original or unique to me—that the historical profession took a wrong turn in the late nineteenth century toward considering itself a 'scientific' discipline. It is past time that the pendulum swings back toward history as art rather than history as science. As a scholar I think I have already done a few things that will be left behind as evidence of a more than generally useful labor.

"In another part of my career, my writing has been not hard scholarship but deliberate polemics. Although I like to think that I have been scholarly and literate, in a wide variety of books and journals of opinion I have commented rather freely on politics, literature, and society from what can be fairly described as a conservative and Southern point of view, consciously in the tradition of the Southern agrarian writers.

"My most important contribution in this field was the gathering and editing of the essays that were published by the University of Georgia Press as *Why the South Will Survive*, by fifteen Southerners. The book's theme is a celebration of the continued distinctiveness and the positive virtues of the American South, and it affirms that this distinctiveness is a national asset that ought to be preserved rather than attacked."

Wilson adds: "*Why the South Will Survive* was supplemented with a symposium I edited called 'Recovering Southern History' which was published as an entire issue of the historical journal *Continuity*. In recent years I have been active as a contributing editor of *Chronicles: A Magazine of American Culture*, regularly producing articles, reviews, and editorials on history, literature, and current events, which have occasionally been reprinted around the country or commented on in nationally syndicated columns."

WISEMAN, T(imothy) P(eter) 1940-

PERSONAL: Born February 3, 1940, in Bridlington, England; son of Stephen (an educational psychologist) and Winifred A. (Rigby) Wiseman; married Anne Williams (a teacher), September 15, 1962. *Education:* Balliol College, Oxford, B.A., 1961, M.A., 1964, D.Phil., 1967.

ADDRESSES: Home—22 Hillcrest Park, Exeter, England. *Office*—Classics Department, University of Exeter, Exeter EX4 4QH, England.

CAREER: University of Leicester, Leicester, England, lecturer in classics, 1963-73, reader in Roman history, 1973-76; University of Exeter, Exeter, England, professor of classics, 1977—.

AWARDS, HONORS: Fellow, British Academy, 1986; honorary D.Litt., University of Durham, 1988.

WRITINGS:

Catullan Questions, Humanities, 1969.
New Men in the Roman Senate 139 B.C.-A.D. 14, Oxford University Press, 1971.
Cinna the Poet and Other Roman Essays, Humanities, 1974.
Clio's Cosmetics, Rowman & Littlefield, 1979.
(With wife, Anne Wiseman) *Julius Caesar: The Battle for Gaul,* David Godine, 1980.
Roman Political Life 90 B.C.-A.D. 69, University of Exeter Press, 1985.
Catullus and His World, Cambridge University Press, 1985.
Roman Studies: Literary and Historical, Francis Cairns, 1987.
Death of an Emperor, University of Exeter Press, 1991.
Talking to Virgil, University of Exeter Press, 1992.
(With Christopher Gill) *Lies and Fiction in the Ancient World,* University of Texas Press, 1992.

Contributor to classical studies journals, including *Journal of Roman Studies, Classical Quarterly,* and *Classical Review.*

WORK IN PROGRESS: Remus and the Other Rome, for Cambridge University Press; research in Roman history, literature, and topography.

SIDELIGHTS: T. P. Wiseman told *CA:* "All we have is evidence and argument. Evidence is what survives from the past, in particular the remains of artefacts, including texts; argument is what we have to apply to make the evidence *mean* something. I am not at all hostile to critical theory if its effect is to improve the quality of the argument, to define more precisely the limits of our knowledge and the propriety of our hypotheses. What leaves me cold is self-reflexive theory, by writers who don't share the aim of trying to understand the experience and idiom of other cultures. Yes, all propositions about the past are by their nature unverifiable. That is true, but trivial: it doesn't mean they are all equally valid, or equally pointless. We are never going to know for certain what happened, what it was like, what the author intended—but we *can* use what evidence survives to make inferences which are more or less convincing.

"Sir Ronald Syme, the most important single influence on my work, summed up the point in a pithy phrase: 'There is work to be done.' There is always more evidence to be discovered, there are always more questions demanding more argument. So why waste time on what you find unhelpful?"

BIOGRAPHICAL/CRITICAL SOURCES:

PERIODICALS

Times (London), June 27, 1985.
Times Higher Education Supplement, January 18, 1980.
Times Literary Supplement, May 2, 1975; February 8, 1980; November 1, 1985; July 10, 1992.

*   *   *

WOLFE, Bertram D(avid) 1896-1977

PERSONAL: Born January 19, 1896, in Brooklyn, NY; died February 21, 1977, in San Jose, CA; son of William D. and Rachel (Samter) Wolfe; married Ella Goldberg (a teacher of Spanish), April 18, 1917. *Education:* City College of New York (now City College of the City University of New York), B.A. (cum laude), 1916; University of Mexico, M.A., 1925; Columbia University, M.A., 1932.

CAREER: Writer. Boys High School, Brooklyn, NY, teacher of English, 1916-17; Miguel Lerdo High School, Mexico City, Mexico, teacher of English and head of foreign language department, 1922-25; Workers School, New York City, director, 1925-29; Stanford University, Hoover Library, Stanford, CA, senior fellow in Slavic studies, 1949-50; Stanford University, Stanford, visiting instructor in Hispanic culture, 1950; organizer and director of U.S. State Department's ideological advisory staff, 1951-54; Columbia University, Russian Institute, New York City, fellow, 1951, research fellow with Russian History Project, 1956-57, research assistant with Project on the History of the Communist Party of the Soviet Union, 1957; Distinguished Visiting Professor of Russian History, University of California, 1961-62; Hoover Library, Stanford University, Stanford, senior fellow in Slavic studies, 1965-68; Hoover Institution on War, Revolution and Peace, Stanford, CA, senior research fellow, 1966-77; University of Miami, Miami, FL, adjunct professor of foreign affairs, beginning 1976.

MEMBER: Authors Guild, Authors League of America, PEN, American Historical Association, American Association for the Advancement of Slavic Studies, Phi Beta Kappa.

AWARDS, HONORS: Guggenheim fellowships, 1949, 1950, and 1954; Relm Foundation fellow, 1960, 1963, and 1964; LL.D., University of California, 1962; Townshend Harris Medal, City University of New York, 1964; Award for Distinguished Contributions to Slavic Studies, American Association for the Advancement of Slavic Studies, 1972.

WRITINGS:

El Romance Tradicional en Mexico, [Madrid], 1925.
(With Diego Rivera) *Portrait of America,* Covici, 1934.
(With Rivera) *Portrait of Mexico,* Covici, 1937.
Civil War in Spain, Workers Age Publishers, 1937.
(With Norman M. Thomas) *Keep America Out of War,* Stokes, 1939.
Diego Rivera: His Life and Times, Knopf, 1939.
Diego Rivera, Pan American Union, 1947.
Three Who Made a Revolution: Lenin, Trotsky, Stalin, Dial, 1948, 4th revised edition published as *Three Who Made a Revolution: A Biographical History,* 1964.
Khrushchev and Stalin's Ghost, Praeger, 1956.
Six Keys to the Soviet System, Beacon, 1956.
(Editor) John Reed, *Ten Days That Shook the World,* Random House, 1960.
Communist Totalitarianism, Beacon, 1961.
Roas Luxemburg and the Russian Revolution, University of Michigan Press, 1961.
The Fabulous Life of Diego Rivera, Stein & Day, 1963.
Marxism: One Hundred Years in the Life of a Doctrine, Dial, 1964.
Strange Communists I Have Known, Stein & Day, 1965.
Lenin and the Origins of Totalitarianism, Hoover Institution and Harper, 1966.
The Bridge and the Abyss: The Troubled Friendship of Maxim Gorky and V. I. Lenin, Praeger, 1967.
(Author of introduction) Leon Trotsky, *Stalin: An Appraisal of the Man and His Influence,* Stein & Day, 1967.
An Ideology in Power: Reflections on the Russian Revolution, Stein & Day, 1969.
Lenin, Stein & Day, 1978.
A Life in Two Centuries, Stein & Day, 1979.
Revolution and Reality: Essays on the Origin of the Soviet System, University of North Carolina Press, 1981.

TELEVISION SCRIPTS

(With Walter Cronkite) *The Russian Revolution,* Columbia Broadcasting System (CBS), 1957.
Nikita Khrushchev: A Profile, CBS, 1959.

The Fall of Nikita Khrushchev, British Broadcasting Corporation (BBC), 1964.

OTHER

Contributor to symposia and to periodicals, including *Foreign Affairs, Russian Review, Slavic and East European Review, U.S. News and World Report, Commentary, Life, Reader's Digest, New York Times, New York Herald Tribune, Annals of the Academy of Political Science,* and *Harper's.* Editor of *Communist,* late 1920s.

SIDELIGHTS: One of the founders of the American Communist Party in 1919, Bertram D. Wolfe left the party once it became obvious to him that Soviet leader Joseph Stalin was creating a personality cult around himself. He spent the rest of his life writing scholarly works on modern communism, exposing the totalitarian nature of the ideology.

Wolfe was first attracted to the communist movement because of its apparently pacifist orientation. As he once explained to *CA:* "In 1917, at 21, I was stirred by the fact that the United States entered the First World War and Russia left the war the same year. My interest in Russia began at that moment, with one of my few successful prophecies. When the February, 1917, Revolution destroyed the old apparatus of command, and obedience, I predicted that no one could keep Russia in the war and an attempt to do so would lead to a second revolution within the year. I opened up too large a credit to the second revolution, believing that it was intended to abolish war, an evil which I had been taught was no longer possible in the 'civilized 20th Century.'"

The Bolshevik Revolution of 1917 inspired Wolfe to join with other young people to found an American version of the Bolshevik Party, the name for the Russian communist movement at the time. In 1919, they founded the Workers Communist Party. Wolfe spent much of the 1920s working on behalf of the party. At first he pursued postgraduate work at the University of Mexico and taught at a high school in Mexico City. In 1925, however, the Mexican government forced him to leave the country for his promotion of communist ideas among the railroad workers. Upon his return from Mexico, Wolfe began working as director of the Workers School in New York City. The school taught budding communists the rudiments of Marxist thought, how to organize strikes, and the intricacies of spreading the communist message. He became a frequent speaker at communist rallies, edited the party organ, *Communist,* and ran for Congress in 1928.

In 1929, Wolfe was an American delegate and a member of the executive committee to the Third Communist International (COMINTERN) in Moscow. He met such Soviet revolutionaries as Trotsky, Bukharin, and Stalin. At that time, Stalin had not yet established himself as sole dictator of the Soviet Union; some debate over policy was still possible. Wolfe and Jay Lovestone, the head of the American communists, argued with Stalin over the direction the party was taking. Both Americans were worried that Stalin was grabbing too much power for himself. Because of these arguments, the men were detained in Moscow for two months, then thrown out of the communist movement. Writing in the *New Leader,* Lewis S. Feuer reported that "the secret police followed [Wolfe's] every move, and Wolfe signed cables to fellow City College alumni in the American Communist leadership 'I. M. Shmendrick'—which succeeded in completely bewildering the Soviet agents." After Wolfe and Lovestone returned home, an ideological battle split the Workers Communist Party into three factions. Fistfights and arguments broke out at party meetings. Wolfe associated himself with an anti-Stalin faction of the party.

Speaking of this period, Wolfe explained to *CA:* "A close up view of the new regime in Russia in 1929 and a prolonged argument with Joseph Stalin, who had not yet perfected his technique for cutting short discussion, caused me to write off the spiritual investment of a decade as a total loss. Russia was too painful a topic for me ever to think of again."

During the 1930s, although still active in socialist and union causes, Wolfe devoted most of his time to producing books with his friend Diego Rivera, the Mexican muralist. They had become friends when Wolfe was teaching in Mexico City in the 1920s. Together the pair published *Portrait of America* and *Portrait of Mexico,* both of which featured Rivera's paintings and Wolfe's commentary on them.

In 1939, Wolfe returned to writing about politics. He explained to *CA:* "When Stalin and Hitler signed a pact in 1939, I signed a contract to write a history of the Russian Revolution. Nine years in the writing, it taught me the unreliability of witnesses and even documents, the need to master the Russian tongue and thought and culture, to search for the truths of the defeated, check them against the truths of the victorious, the available documentary records, and the inherent probabilities in the evaluation of each person and event. The result of the nine years' work was my *Three Who Made a Revolution* (1948)." The book, described by Wolfgang Saxon in the *New York Times* as "a classic study of Lenin, Trotsky and Stalin" and by Feuer as "an enduring work of history," has been translated into 28 languages.

In the following years Wolfe continued to write about Soviet history and society. In *Marxism: One Hundred Years in the Life of a Doctrine* Wolfe examined Marx's thought as it evolved over the course of his life and described the relationship between Marx's ideas and the ideas of later Marxists. In *The Bridge and the Abyss* he wrote of the stormy relationship between Russian writer Maxim Gorky and Soviet leader Lenin. *An Ideology in Power: Reflections on the Russian Revolution* gathered together a number of Wolfe's essays on the Soviet system, including his much-reprinted "The Durability of Despotism in the Soviet System."

Wolfe's position as a Soviet expert was formidable. Robert H. Johnston in *Library Journal* called Wolfe "one of the most perceptive observers on the Soviet scene," while Saxon described Wolfe as "one of the country's foremost experts on the Soviet Union." Speaking of Wolfe's career as a writer, Alexander Dallin in the *Saturday Review* claimed that the author "wields the facile pen of a seasoned and skillful polemicist, readily produces colorful similes and memorable quotes, and elegantly launches poison arrows at antagonists as he mercilessly exposes wishful thinking or naive *non sequiturs.*"

A Life in Two Centuries, Wolfe's posthumously published autobiography, details his long career as a political activist and writer. In this memoir, he tells of organizing the Communist Party with fellow radical John Reed, how he and Reed rejected democracy in favor of the "dictatorship of the proletariat," the rise of the Communist International and its control of communist parties throughout the world, and his eventual disillusionment with Stalin's dictatorial regime. Wolfe's memoir was meant as a testimony to the mistakes he and the communist movement had made. Writing in the *New York Times Book Review,* John Patrick Diggins called *A Life in Two Centuries* "a key intellectual document in the history of the American left."

BIOGRAPHICAL/CRITICAL SOURCES:

BOOKS

Wolfe, Bertram D., *A Life in Two Centuries,* Stein & Day, 1979.

PERIODICALS

American Spectator, December, 1981, p. 14.
Commentary, September, 1981, p. 80.
Human Events, June 7, 1980, p. 12.
Listener, May 23, 1968.
National Review, August 10, 1965, p. 696; November 4, 1969, p. 1122; May 16, 1980, p. 606.
New Leader, October 13, 1969, pp. 16-19.
New Republic, December 6, 1980, p. 35.
Newsweek, August 11, 1969.
New York Times Book Review, March 22, 1981, p. 1.
Observer, March 31, 1968.
Saturday Review, September 27, 1969.
Stanford Campus Report, March 23, 1972.
Times Literary Supplement, April 27, 1967.

Washington Post Book World, November 5, 1967.

OBITUARIES:

PERIODICALS

New York Times, February 22, 1977.*

*　　　*　　　*

WOLITZER, Hilma　1930-

PERSONAL: Born January 25, 1930, in Brooklyn, NY; daughter of Abraham V. and Rose (Goldberg) Liebman; married Morton Wolitzer (a psychologist), September 7, 1952; children: Nancy, Margaret. *Education:* Attended Brooklyn Museum Art School, Brooklyn College of the City University of New York, and New School for Social Research.

ADDRESSES: *Home*—500 East 85th St., Apt. 18H, New York, NY 10028. *Agent*—Amanda Urban, ICM, 40 West 57th St., New York, NY 10019.

CAREER: Writer and teacher of writing workshops. Has also worked as nursery school teacher and portrait artist at a resort. Bread Loaf Writers Conference, staff assistant, 1975 and 1976, staff member, 1977-78 and 1980-92. Visiting lecturer in writing at University of Iowa, 1978-79 and 1983, Columbia University, 1979-80, New York University, 1984, and Swarthmore College, 1985.

MEMBER: International PEN, Authors Guild (executive board member), Authors League of America, Writers Guild of America East.

AWARDS, HONORS: Bread Loaf Writers Conference scholarship, 1970; fellowships from Bread Loaf Writers Conference, 1974, Guggenheim Foundation, 1976-77, and National Endowment for the Arts, 1978; Great Lakes College Association award, 1974-75, for *Ending;* New York State English Council Excellence in Letters Award, 1980; American Academy and Institute of Arts and Letters Award (literature), 1981; Janet Heidinger Kafka Prize (honorable mention), University of Rochester, 1981, for *Hearts.*

WRITINGS:

NOVELS

Ending, Morrow, 1974.
In the Flesh, Morrow, 1977.
Hearts, Farrar, Straus, 1980.
In the Palomar Arms, Farrar, Straus, 1983.
Silver, Farrar, Straus, 1988.

JUVENILE

Introducing Shirley Braverman, Farrar, Straus, 1975.
Out of Love, Farrar, Straus, 1976.

Toby Lived Here, Farrar, Straus, 1978.
Wish You Were Here, Farrar, Straus, 1985.

CONTRIBUTOR TO ANTHOLOGIES

From Pop to Culture, Holt, 1970.
Gordon Lish, editor, *The Secret Life of Our Times,* Doubleday, 1973.
Pat Rotter, editor, *Bitches and Sad Ladies,* Harper Magazine Press, 1975.
Robert Pack and Jay Parini, editors, *The Bread Loaf Anthology of Contemporary Short Stories,* Bread Loaf, 1987.
R. Pack and J. Parini, editors, *The Bread Loaf Anthology of Contemporary American Essays,* Bread Loaf, 1989.
John Mukand, M.D., editor, *Vital Lines,* St. Martin's Press, 1990.

Also contributor to *All Our Secrets Are the Same,* edited by G. Lish, Norton.

OTHER

Also author of screenplay adaptations for her novels *In the Flesh* and *Ending,* an episode from the series *Family,* ABC-TV, three shows for PBS-TV, and *Single Women, Married Men* (teleplay), CBS-TV.

Contributor of stories and reviews to *Saturday Evening Post, Esquire, New American Review, Ms., Ploughshares, Newsday, New York Times,* and *Washington Post.*

ADAPTATIONS: *Ending, In the Flesh,* and *Hearts* have been optioned for motion picture production.

WORK IN PROGRESS: A sequel to the novel *Hearts.*

SIDELIGHTS: Hilma Wolitzer was a housewife in the suburbs of New York City until, at the age of 35, she began to write fiction. "It looked for a while," she told Wayne Warga in the *Los Angeles Times,* "as though [our family was] not going to miss one cliche. I would never have expected that at 40 I'd be attending Bread Loaf as a scholar." Since beginning her new career, Wolitzer has become a successful novelist. Her fiction is set in the middle-class households she knows best, although she hasn't experienced the problems around which her stories are built. Also central to her novels are well-developed, realistic characters. Martha Saxton in *Ms.* comments on the flavor of Wolitzer's work, calling her "a poet of domestic detail."

Most of Wolitzer's novels concern typical domestic situations that are familiar to many modern readers. For example, in *Ending,* a young wife must face her husband's struggle with terminal cancer; *In the Flesh* features a woman who learns to grow after her husband leaves her; in *Hearts,* a widow tries to deal with her late husband's stepdaughter; and *In the Palomar Arms* chronicles a young college student's affair with a married man. Jonathan Yardley in the *Washington Post Book World* feels that Wolitzer's use of a familiar story fails in *In the Palomar Arms*. He notes that "for all the abundant skills Wolitzer brings to [the novel] she merely retells a twice-told tale; it's a great pleasure to read *In the Palomar Arms*, but at the end what you know more than anything else is that you've been there before."

However, many critics believe that Wolitzer handles her time-honored plots with enough expertise to make the stories seem fresh. R. Z. Sheppard indicates in *Time* that *Ending* "could easily have been a dreadful book," because of its familiar storyline. "Instead, it is an extraordinarily good one." Elizabeth Pochoda in *Ms.* comments that the domestic characters and plot of *Hearts* "would be forbidding stuff for nearly anyone except Wolitzer." In the *Chicago Tribune Book World*, reviewer L. M. Rosenberg points out that *Hearts* "is a small masterpiece—not a big book, not a philosophically sophisticated book, but perfect and true in its own ineffable way." *Newsweek* contributor Raymond Sokolov praises Wolitzer's use of a typical suburban setting in *In the Flesh*, indicating that she implies "a world of pain and aspiration underneath the studied and malign banality. [The novel] is an utterly poised and fine achievement, as good in its unostentatious way as anything in recent fiction." Anne Tyler in the *Detroit News*, writing of *In the Palomar Arms*, suggests that Wolitzer's "unerring eye for the detail that sums up a world" makes the novel come alive.

Wolitzer's stories present ordinary characters realistically, but she has been accused by some reviewers of making her characters so ordinary that they are bland. Lis Harris comments in the *New Yorker* on *In the Flesh*, indicating that "it is impossible to dislike any of the characters" in the novel. But she feels that it "is equally impossible . . . to generate much enthusiasm for them, because they're cut from such predictable molds . . . [Wolitzer] makes them so easily identifiable and innocuous that she robs them of any emotional force." Joyce Carol Oates in the *New York Times Book Review* remarks similarly of *In the Palomar Arms*, pointing out that the novel's "primary weakness . . . is a certain blandness of characterization; Daphne and Kenny and Axel and Nora all sound exactly alike, musing to themselves in precisely the same idioms and speech rhythms."

Doris Grumbach expresses a different viewpoint in the *Washington Post Book World*, stating that Wolitzer's typical characters are true to life and accurately portrayed. She indicates that *Hearts* is a "novel so rich in well-realized characters . . . that it raises ordinary people and everyday occurrences to a new height." Grumbach praises the development of the protagonist, noting that "the reader has the extraordinary feeling she exists in real life

and that he is encountering a perfectly ordinary young woman of little character or distinction." "Wolitzer is able to suggest," continues Grumbach, "as few modern writers can, the true ambivalence of human character, the duality of feeling that lives in us all. The expected stereotype falls away before her subtleties." Yardley also commends Wolitzer's writing, remarking that she "adamantly refuses to sentimentalize her characters or to allow them easy answers to life's difficulties."

Wolitzer has built a substantial following for her novels, earning a "mini-cult of fiction fans," states Dan Wakefield in *Nation*. Commenting to Warga on her choice of subject, Wolitzer says: "I think domestic life is very interesting. I believe what happens in the kitchen and bedroom is as important as what goes on in the Pentagon. You can [reveal] a whole society simply by describing the intimate life of one family."

BIOGRAPHICAL/CRITICAL SOURCES:

BOOKS

Contemporary Literary Criticism, Volume 17, Gale, 1981.

PERIODICALS

Chicago Tribune Book World, November 23, 1980.
Detroit News, June 19, 1983.
Los Angeles Times, November 17, 1980; January 16, 1981.
Ms., October, 1977; December, 1980.
Nation, November 8, 1980.
New Republic, November 15, 1980.
Newsweek, September 19, 1977; December 15, 1980.
New Yorker, December 26, 1977.
New York Times, October 7, 1977; November 27, 1980; May 14, 1983.
New York Times Book Review, September 11, 1977; November 9, 1980; June 5, 1983.
Publishers Weekly, July 17, 1978.
Time, August 26, 1974.
Times Literary Supplement, July 23, 1982; May 25, 1984.
Washington Post Book World, July 28, 1974; October 26, 1980; May 22, 1983.

*　　*　　*

WOOD, A(rthur) Skevington 1916-

PERSONAL: Born April 21, 1916, in Ashbourne, Derbyshire, England; son of William Arthur (a school headmaster) and May (Cooper) Wood; married Mary Fearnley, January 1, 1943. *Education:* Attended Wesley Theological College, Leeds, 1936-40; University of London, B.A., 1939; New College, Edinburgh, Ph.D., 1951.

ADDRESSES: Home—17 Dalewood Rd., Sheffield S8 0EB, England.

CAREER: Methodist circuit minister, 1940-62; Movement for World Evangelization, West Croydon, Surrey, England, lecturer, 1962-70; Cliff College, Derbyshire, England, senior tutor in theology, 1970-77, principal, 1977-83. Vice-president, National Young Life Campaign.

MEMBER: Royal Historical Society (fellow), British Christian Endeavour Union (president, 1959-60), Society for Ecclesiastical History (founding member), Church Historical Society, Evangelical Alliance, Evangelization Society, Wesley Historical Society (life member), Victory Tract Club.

WRITINGS:

Thomas Haweis, 1734-1820, S.P.C.K., for Church Historical Society, 1957.

And with Fire: Messages on Revival, Pickering & Inglis, 1958.

Luther's Principles of Biblical Interpretation, Tyndale Press, 1960.

The Inextinguishable Blaze: Spiritual Renewal and Advance in the Eighteenth Century, Eerdmans, 1960.

The Bible Is History, Bible Testimony Fellowship, 1960.

Life by the Spirit, Zondervan, 1963 (published in England as *Paul's Pentecost: Studies in the Life of the Spirit from Romans 8,* Paternoster Press, 1963).

Designed by Love: Short Studies in the Plan of Salvation, Christian Endeavour Union, 1963.

Prophecy in the Space Age: Studies in Prophetic Themes, Zondervan, 1963.

William Grimshaw of Haworth, Evangelical Library, 1963.

Heralds of the Gospel: Message, Method, and Motive in Preaching, Marshall, Morgan & Scott, 1963, published as *The Art of Preaching: Message, Method, and Motive in Preaching,* Zondervan, 1964.

Evangelism: Its Theology and Practice, Zondervan, 1966.

The Principles of Biblical Interpretation as Enunciated by Irenaeus, Origen, Augustine, Luther, and Calvin, Zondervan, 1967.

The Burning Heart: John Wesley, Evangelist, Paternoster Press, 1967, Eerdmans, 1968.

Captive to the Word: Martin Luther, Doctor of Sacred Scripture, Eerdmans, 1969.

Signs of the Times: Biblical Prophecy and Current Events, Lakeland Paperbacks, 1970, Baker Book, 1971.

The Evangelical Understanding of the Gospel, CEIM, 1974.

The Nature of Man, Scripture Union, 1978.

For All Seasons: Sermons for the Christian Year, Hodder & Stoughton, 1979.

What the Bible Teaches about God, Kingsway, 1980.

Studying Theology: An Introduction, CEIM, 1981.

The Call of God: Studies in Prophetic Vocation, OMF Books, 1984.

Let Us Go On: One Hundred Years of the Southport Convention, Moorley's, 1985.

The Gift of Love: Daily Readings with John Wesley, Templegate, 1987.

The Kindled Fame: The Witness of the Methodist Revival Fellowship, Headway, 1987.

Third Wave or Second Coming?: The Relevance of Biblical Prophecy, Flame Trust, 1992.

Brothers in Arms: John Wesley's Early Clerical Associates, Wesley Historical Society, 1992.

Revelation and Reason: Wesleyan Responses to Eighteen-Century Rationalism, Wesley Fellowship, 1992.

Contributor to over ten books, including *Crusade in Scotland,* edited by Tom Allan, Pickering & Inglis, 1955; *Grace Unlimited,* edited by Clark H. Pinnock, Bethany Fellowship, 1975; *A Guide to the Spiritual Life,* edited by Peter Toon, Marshall Pickering, 1988; and *John Wesley: Contemporary Perspectives,* edited by John Stacey, Epworth Press, 1988.

Also contributor to *International Standard Bible Encyclopedia, Baker's Dictionary of Theology, New Bible Dictionary, Zondervan Pictorial Encyclopedia of the Bible, Baker's Dictionary of Christian Ethics, Expositor's Bible Commentary,* and *New Dictionary of Theology.* Contributor to *Evangelical Quarterly, Christian Update, Epworth Review,* and *Christianity Today.* Contributor to *Proceedings of the Wesley Historical Society.*

WORK IN PROGRESS: Research on the rise of Anglican evangelicalism in the London area; entries for *A Dictionary of Evangelical Biography, 1730-1860,* edited by Donald M. Lewis.

SIDELIGHTS: A. Skevington Wood told *CA:* "As a historian I regard writing as an opportunity to share the results of research and submit them for criticism. As a minister in the Methodist church I see such contributions as an extension of my calling. In addition to the output of technical material, I recognize the need to write for a more general readership in order to present the fruits of scholarship in a popular form. I like to think that this is an area where some measure of success has been achieved; publishers and reviewers seem to agree.

"The urge to write seized me at an early age for as a boy I edited and largely composed a manuscript magazine which circulated amongst friends of my educationist parents, some of whom were actually prepared to confess that they read it. My launching-pad into publication took the form of articles both for learned and rather less learned journals, and my first book developed from a doctoral thesis. Time for writing has had to be carved out of a busy vocational career and has involved late nights and (what I prefer) early mornings. There is no short cut to productivity.

"I frankly admit that at the start of a project the task appears to be daunting and indeed unlikely ever to be accomplished. The first few chapters in draft are often hard going. But the secret is to press on, however dissatisfied one is, and leave the revision until later. Although the end product is never all that a writer might wish it to be, it is thankfully much better than he initially thought it could be. Toil, sweat, and even an experience close to tears are inescapable ingredients of a worthwhile book. That, anyway, is how I find it."

BIOGRAPHICAL/CRITICAL SOURCES:

PERIODICALS

Encounter, autumn, 1968.

*　　*　　*

WUORIO, Eva-Lis 1918-

PERSONAL: Name is pronounced "A-va-lees *Worry-oh*"; born in 1918, in Viipuri, Finland; immigrated to Canada about 1929. *Education:* Attended schools in Finland and Canada.

ADDRESSES: Home—Finland. *Agent*—c/o Delacorte Press, 1 Dag Hammarskjold Plaza, 245 East 47th St., New York, NY 10017.

CAREER: Employed by *Toronto Evening Telegram* and *Toronto Globe and Mail;* became assistant editor for *Maclean's Magazine;* author.

AWARDS, HONORS: The Island of Fish in the Trees, illustrated by Edward Ardizzone, was awarded a Best Illustrated Children's Books of the Year citation by the *New York Times,* 1962.

WRITINGS:

Return of the Viking, illustrations by William Winter, Clarke, Irwin, 1955.
The Canadian Twins, illustrations by Balant S. Biro, J. Cape, 1956.
The Island of Fish in the Trees, illustrations by Edward Ardizzone, World Publishing, 1962.
The Woman with the Portuguese Basket, Dobson, 1963, Holt, 1964.
The Land of Right Up and Down, illustrations by Ardizzone, World Publishing, 1964.
Tal and the Magic Barruget, illustrations by Bettina Bauer Ehrlich, World Publishing, 1965.
Z for Zaborra, Dobson, 1965, Holt, 1966.
Midsummer Lokki, Holt, 1966.
October Treasure, illustrations by Carolyn Cather, Holt, 1966.
Forbidden Adventure, illustrations by Bernadette Watts, Whiting & Wheaton, 1967.

Kali and the Golden Mirror, illustrations by Ardizzone, World Publishing, 1967.
Venture at Midsummer, Holt, 1967.
Save Alice!, Holt, 1968.
The Happiness Flower, illustrations by Don Bolognese, World Publishing, 1969.
The Singing Canoe, illustrations by Irving Boker, World Publishing, 1969.
Code: Polonaise, Holt, 1971.
To Fight in Silence, Holt, 1973.
Escape If You Can: Thirteen Tales of the Preternatural, Viking, 1977.
Detour to Danger: A Novel, Delacorte, 1987.

SIDELIGHTS: Though Eva-Lis Wuorio left Finland for Canada at the age of eleven, she carried with pride her vivid images of that Scandinavian country. The author often relies on her first-hand knowledge of the Finnish culture and history in setting up the background for her stories. In *Midsummer Lokki* she weaves a tale of international intrigue involving a young Canadian of Finnish heritage. "Along with good mystery and action is a complete, enticing travelog of Finland," says a critic for *Publishers Weekly.* However, a reviewer for the *New York Times Book Review* observes: "[Wuorio] doesn't handle her male protagonist convincingly . . . and she applies a serious treatment to a light and foolish plot of international malefaction. What keeps one reading is a great deal of Finnish local color, culture, and history."

The author spent several months on the island of Skyros in the Aegean Sea and incorporated its atmosphere into her book, *Kali and the Golden Mirror.* The plot deals with a young girl on an archaeological dig, but as in Wuorio's previous books, it is the story's descriptive location that attracts the critic's eye. "Wuorio has brought the physical beauty of her milieu into sharp focus and has sustained the spirit of the islanders," notes Shulamith Oppenheim in a review for the *New York Times.*

Wuorio continued to capture the mood and characterizations of a particular environment in her book, *To Fight in Silence.* In this suspenseful story the author focuses on the countries of Norway and Denmark during World War II. A reviewer for the *Bulletin of the Center for Children's Books* writes, "The pace is fast and exciting, the characters well-defined, the setting vividly evoked."

BIOGRAPHICAL/CRITICAL SOURCES:

PERIODICALS

Bulletin of the Center for Children's Books, November, 1973.
New York Times Book Review, August 14, 1966; May 14, 1967; June 18, 1967.
Publishers Weekly, January 30, 1967.

Saturday Review, November 10, 1962.*

* * *

WYATT, Woodrow Lyle 1918-

PERSONAL: Born July 4, 1918; son of Robert Harvey Lyle and Ethel (Morgan) Wyatt; married Lady Moorea Hastings, 1957 (marriage ended, 1966); married Veronica Banszky, 1966; children: (first marriage) one son; (second marriage) one daughter. *Education:* Worcester College, Oxford, M.A.

ADDRESSES: Home—19 Cavendish Ave., London NW8, England. *Office*—House of Lords, SW1A 0PW, England.

CAREER: Parliament, London, England, Labour member of Parliament for Aston Division of Birmingham, 1945-55, personal assistant to Sir Stafford Gibbs Cabinet Mission to India, 1946, under-secretary of state at War Office, 1951; British Broadcasting Corp. (BBC-TV), England, co-creator of *Panorama,* 1955-59; Parliament, Labour member of Parliament for Bosworth Division of Leicester, 1959-70. Chairman of Horserace Totalisator Board, 1976—. *Military service:* British Army, 1939-45; became major; mentioned in dispatches.

MEMBER: Zoological Society of London (member of council, 1968-71, 1973-77).

AWARDS, HONORS: Knighted, 1983; created Life Peer, Lord Wyatt of Weeford, Staffordshire, 1987.

WRITINGS:

NONFICTION

Southwards from China: A Survey of Southeast Asia since 1945, Hodder & Stoughton, 1952.
Into the Dangerous World, Weidenfeld & Nicolson, 1952.
The Peril in Our Midst, Phoenix House, 1956.
Distinguished for Talent: Some Men of Influence and Enterprise, Hutchinson, 1958.
Turn Again, Westminster, Deutsch, 1973.
What's Left of the Labour Party?, Sidgwick & Jackson, 1977.
To the Point, Weidenfeld & Nicolson, 1981.
Confessions of an Optimist, Collins, 1985.

Also author of *The Jews at Home,* 1950.

FICTION

(Editor) *The Way We Lived Then,* Collins, 1989.

FOR CHILDREN

The Exploits of Mr. Saucy Squirrel, Allen & Unwin, 1976.
The Further Exploits of Mr. Saucy Squirrel, Allen & Unwin, 1977.

OTHER

High Profiles (play), Samuel French, 1991.

Author of weekly columns in *Reynolds News,* 1949-61, *Daily Mirror,* 1965-73, *Sunday Mirror,* 1973-83, and *News of the World,* 1983—. Author of fortnightly column, London *Times,* 1983—. Founder and editor of *English Story,* 1940-50; member of editorial staff of *New Statesman and Nation,* 1947-48.

* * *

WYNKOOP, Mildred Bangs 1905-

PERSONAL: Surname is pronounced "*wine*-coop"; born September 9, 1905, in Seattle, WA; daughter of Carl Oliver (a builder) and Mery (Dupertius) Bangs; married Ralph Carl Wynkoop (a clergyman), December 27, 1928. *Education:* Pasadena Nazarene College, A.B., 1931; Western Evangelical Seminary, M.Div., 1948; University of Oregon, M.S., 1952; Northern Baptist Theological Seminary, Th.D., 1955. *Religion:* Protestant. *Avocational interests:* Photography, stamp collecting, history, hiking.

ADDRESSES: Home—Nashville, TN. *Office*—Nazarene Theological Seminary, 1700 East Meyer Blvd., Kansas City, MO 64131.

CAREER: Ordained minister in Church of the Nazarene, 1934; minister of churches in Los Angeles, CA, 1930-34, Coos Bay, OR, 1934-38, and Portland, OR, 1944-60; Western Theological Seminary, Portland, OR, professor of theology, 1955-60, chairman of religion department, 1955-60; Western Evangelical Seminary, Portland, OR, dean and professor, 1960-62; Japan Nazarene Seminary, Chiba, Japan, president, 1962-66; Trevecca Nazarene College, Nashville, TN, professor of religion and philosophy, 1966-67, chairman of department of religion and philosophy, 1967-70, chairman of department of missiology and human services, 1970-76; Nazarene Theological Seminary, Kansas City, MO, distinguished professor, 1976—.

MEMBER: International Society for Mission Studies, American Society of Missiology, Society of Biblical Literature, American Society of Church History, American Catholic Historical Society, Wesley Theological Society (president, 1972-74), Wesley Historical Society (England).

AWARDS, HONORS: Denominational citation of merit, Trevecca College, 1976.

WRITINGS:

John Wesley: Christian Revolutionary, Beacon Hill Press, 1967.
Foundations of Wesleyan-Arminianism, Beacon Hill Press, 1968.

Theology of Love: The Dynamic of Wesleyanism, Beacon
    Hill Press, 1972.
The Trevecca Story: Seventy-Five Year History of a College,
    Trevecca Nazarene College, 1976.
The Mirror Image, Beacon Hill Press, 1976.
The Occult and the Supernatural, Beacon Hill Press, 1976.

Also contributor to *Journal of the Wesley Theological Society* and *Asbury Theological Seminary Journal.*

SIDELIGHTS: Mildred Wynkoop has lived in Europe
and in the Orient, and speaks French, German, Greek,
Hebrew, and Spanish. Her books have been translated into
Spanish and Japanese.*

Y

YALOM, Marilyn K. 1932-

PERSONAL: Born March 10, 1932, in Chicago, IL; daughter of Samuel (in business) and Celia (a housewife; maiden name, Katz) Koenick; married Irvin Yalom (a psychiatrist), June 26, 1954; children: four. *Education:* Wellesley College, B.A., 1954; Harvard University, M.A.T., 1956; Johns Hopkins University, Ph.D., 1963.

ADDRESSES: Home—951 Matadero, Palo Alto, CA 94306. *Office*—Institute for Research on Women and Gender, Stanford University, Stanford, CA 94305.

CAREER: University of Hawaii at Manoa, Honolulu, lecturer in French, 1961-62; California State University, Hayward, assistant professor, 1963-67, associate professor, 1967-71, professor of French, 1971-76; Stanford University, Stanford, CA, Institute for Research on Women and Gender, deputy director, 1976-87, senior scholar, 1987—.

WRITINGS:

(Editor with Hellerstein, Hume, Offen, and others) *Victorian Women,* Stanford University Press, 1981.
(Editor with Barrie Thorne) *Rethinking the Family,* Longman, 1982, 2nd edition, Northeastern University Press, 1992.
(Editor) *Women Writers of the West Coast: Speaking of Their Lives and Careers,* Capra, 1983.
(Editor with Diane Middlebrook) *Coming to Light: American Women Poets in the Twentieth Century,* University of Michigan Press, 1985.
Maternity, Mortality, and the Literature of Madness, Pennsylvania State University Press, 1985.
(Editor with Susan Groag Bell) *Revealing Lines: Autobiography, Biography, and Gender,* State University of New York Press, 1991.

Blood Sisters: The French Revolution in Women's Memory, Basic Books, 1993.

SIDELIGHTS: Marilyn K. Yalom once told *CA:* "My move from a traditional career as a French professor of the broader arena of feminist scholarship was motivated by the women's movement in the mid-seventies. My book *Maternity, Mortality, and the Literature of Madness* focuses on ways in which the option or experience of motherhood plugs into mental illness, as communicated by women writers."

She adds, "My new book is a study of women's memoirs of the French Revolution, following on the heels of one written in French on the same subject for the bicentennial of the Revolution (*Le Temps des orages,* Maren Sell (Paris), 1989)."

*   *   *

YANCEY, Philip D(avid) 1949-

PERSONAL: Born November 4, 1949, in Atlanta, GA; son of Marshall Watts and Mildred (a teacher; maiden name, Diem) Yancey; married Janet Norwood (a social work director), June 2, 1970. *Education:* Columbia Bible College, Columbia, SC, B.A., 1970; Wheaton College, Wheaton, IL, M.A., 1972; University of Chicago, Chicago, IL, M.A., 1990. *Religion:* Protestant.

ADDRESSES: Home—657 W. Wellington Ave., Chicago, IL 60657.

CAREER: Campus Life, Wheaton, IL, editor, 1971-77, publisher, 1978-79; free-lance writer, 1980—.

AWARDS, HONORS: Golden Medallion Award from Evangelical Christian Publishers Association, 1978, for *Where Is God When It Hurts?,* 1980, for *Fearfully and*

Wonderfully Made, 1985, for *In His Image,* 1989, for *The Student Bible,* and 1990, for *Disappointment with God.*

WRITINGS:

After the Wedding, Word, Inc., 1976.
Where Is God When It Hurts?, Zondervan, 1977.
(With Tim Stafford) *Unhappy Secrets of the Christian Life,* Zondervan, 1979.
(With Paul Brand) *Fearfully and Wonderfully Made,* Zondervan, 1980.
Open Windows, Thomas Nelson, 1982.
(With Brand) *In His Image,* Zondervan, 1984.
The Student's Guide to the Bible, Zondervan, 1988.
Disappointment with God: Questions Nobody Asks Aloud, Zondervan, 1989.
A Guided Tour of the Bible: Six Months of Daily Readings, Zondervan, 1990.
I Was Just Wondering, Eerdmans, 1990.
Reality and the Vision, Word Books, 1990.

Praying with the KGB, 1992. Contributor of about 800 articles to magazines, including *Reader's Digest, Saturday Evening Post,* and *Christianity Today.*

SIDELIGHTS: Philip D. Yancey's books are "fast becoming classics of the evangelical literature," according to a *Publishers Weekly* article by Miriam Berkley. Yancey was raised in an atmosphere of strict Christian fundamentalism, where "anything you could think of that was fun was wrong." He remarked to Berkley: "You cannot imagine, unless you've been in a background like that, how narrow it is." He eventually rejected the fundamentalist tradition, in part because of exposure to Orwellian literature, which he says "shattered my airtight framework of what the world was like. That's probably one of the main reasons why I'm a writer today: because there are millions of people in a [closed] world like [the one in which I was raised]. Literature for me . . . opened the cage door that let me fly out."

Despite his renunciation of strict fundamentalism, Yancey remained religiously active and, after college, he began writing for the Christian magazine *Campus Life.* He told Berkley that many of his assignments were " 'drama in real life' articles, where people have been involved in tragedy, and as a Christian I was puzzled by this problem of pain. Why would God allow it? Why does he let us suffer?" His musings on these questions eventually formed the basis for his book, *Where Is God When It Hurts?,* an award-winning volume that has currently sold over 500,000 copies.

BIOGRAPHICAL/CRITICAL SOURCES:

PERIODICALS

Publishers Weekly, March 9, 1984.

YOUNG, Gary 1951-

PERSONAL: Born September 8, 1951, in Santa Monica, CA; son of Claude Young and Jeanne Ewing. *Education:* University of California, Santa Cruz, B.A., 1973; University of California, Irvine, M.F.A., 1975.

ADDRESSES: *Home*—3965 Bonny Doon Rd., Santa Cruz, CA 95060.

CAREER: University of California, Santa Cruz, lecturer in English, 1972; Greenhouse Review Press, Santa Cruz, editor, 1975—. Writing residency, Ucross Foundation, 1985; writer-in-residence, Writers Community of the Writer's Voice at West Side Center for the Arts, New York City, 1990. Host of *The Poetry Show,* a weekly program on KUSP-FM Radio. Associate editor, Brandenburg Press. Vice-President, AE Foundation.

AWARDS, HONORS: National Endowment for the Arts grant, 1981, fellowship, 1986; James D. Phelan Award in Literature, San Francisco Foundation, 1983, for *The Dream of a Moral Life;* John Ciardi Fellowship in Poetry, 1990; Young Artists Recognition Award in Literature, Dewar's, 1990; Ludwig Vogelstein Grant in Poetry, 1991; Pushcart Prize, 1992.

WRITINGS:

POETRY

Hands, Jazz, 1979.
Six Prayers, Greenhouse Review Press, 1984.
In the Durable World, Bieler, 1985.
The Dream of a Moral Life, Copper Beech Press, 1990.
A Single Day, Good Book Press, 1991.
Nine Days: New York, Greenhouse Review Press, 1991.
Wherever I Looked, Robin Price, 1993.

OTHER

Contributor to periodicals, including *Poetry, Antaeus, Nation, Kenyon Review, American Poetry Review, New England Review,* and *Missouri Review.*

WORK IN PROGRESS: *Braver Deeds,* poems.

SIDELIGHTS: Gary Young once told *CA:* "The poems come slower and with more difficulty, in part because of the demands made upon my time as a printer, book designer, and print-maker, but also because I write less from the necessity to write per se than from the necessity to write a certain poem. As I do for all of my art, I hope that my poems will allow a small step closer to the world, to myself, and to God."

Contemporary Authors®
NEW REVISION SERIES

Contemporary Authors
was named an
"Outstanding
Reference Source" *by*
the American Library
Association Reference
and Adult Services
Division after its 1962
inception.
In 1985 it was listed by
the same organization
as one of the
twenty-five most
distinguished reference
titles published in the
past twenty-five years.